Employment Law

ASPEN CASEBOOK SERIES

Employment Law

Private Ordering and Its Limitations

Second Edition

Timothy P. Glynn
Professor of Law
Seton Hall Law School

Rachel S. Arnow-Richman
Associate Professor of Law
University of Denver Sturm College of Law

Charles A. Sullivan
Professor of Law
Seton Hall Law School

Wolters Kluwer
Law & Business

AUSTIN   BOSTON   CHICAGO   NEW YORK   THE NETHERLANDS

Aspen Publishers
Attn: Permissions Department
76 Ninth Avenue, 7th Floor
New York, NY 10011-5201

To contact Customer Care, e-mail customer.service@aspenpublishers.com, call 1-800-234-1660, fax 1-800-901-9075, or mail correspondence to:

Aspen Publishers
Attn: Order Department
PO Box 990
Frederick, MD 21705

Printed in the United States of America.

1 2 3 4 5 6 7 8 9 0

ISBN 978-0-7355-9791-4

Library of Congress Cataloging-in-Publication Data

Glynn, Timothy P., 1967-
  Employment law : private ordering and its limitations / Timothy P. Glynn,
Rachel S. Arnow-Richman, Charles A. Sullivan. — 2nd ed.
    p. cm. — (Aspen casebook series)
  Includes index.

  ISBN-13: 978-0-7355-9791-4
  ISBN-10: 0-7355-9791-X
  I. Arnow-Richman, Rachel, 1970- II. Sullivan, Charles A. III. Title.

KF3455.G59 2011
344.7301 — dc22

                                                                    2010052085

About Wolters Kluwer Law & Business

Wolters Kluwer Law & Business is a leading provider of research information and workflow solutions in key specialty areas. The strengths of the individual brands of Aspen Publishers, CCH, Kluwer Law International and Loislaw are aligned within Wolters Kluwer Law & Business to provide comprehensive, in-depth solutions and expert-authored content for the legal, professional and education markets.

CCH was founded in 1913 and has served more than four generations of business professionals and their clients. The CCH products in the Wolters Kluwer Law & Business group are highly regarded electronic and print resources for legal, securities, antitrust and trade regulation, government contracting, banking, pension, payroll, employment and labor, and healthcare reimbursement and compliance professionals.

Aspen Publishers is a leading information provider for attorneys, business professionals and law students. Written by preeminent authorities, Aspen products offer analytical and practical information in a range of specialty practice areas from securities law and intellectual property to mergers and acquisitions and pension/ benefits. Aspen's trusted legal education resources provide professors and students with high-quality, up-to-date and effective resources for successful instruction and study in all areas of the law.

Kluwer Law International supplies the global business community with comprehensive English-language international legal information. Legal practitioners, corporate counsel and business executives around the world rely on the Kluwer Law International journals, loose-leafs, books and electronic products for authoritative information in many areas of international legal practice.

Loislaw is a premier provider of digitized legal content to small law firm practitioners of various specializations. Loislaw provides attorneys with the ability to quickly and efficiently find the necessary legal information they need, when and where they need it, by facilitating access to primary law as well as state-specific law, records, forms and treatises.

Wolters Kluwer Law & Business, a unit of Wolters Kluwer, is headquartered in New York and Riverwoods, Illinois. Wolters Kluwer is a leading multinational publisher and information services company.

For My Parents
T.P.G.

For My Students, Past, Present & Future
R.S.A.R.

For the Usual Suspects
C.A.S.

Summary of Contents

Contents

PART TWO PRIVATE ORDERING AND DEFAULT TERMS 59

Preface

Few institutions receive greater attention in Americans' private lives and in public policy debates than employment. Employment is everywhere: it is the means by which most Americans make their living; it is, for many, where they spend the majority of their waking hours and develop most of their interpersonal relationships; and it provides the primary economic input ("human capital") firms and government agencies rely on to produce their goods and services.

Because of its pervasiveness and importance, employment-related issues, such as outsourcing to foreign countries or whether to raise the minimum wage, receive significant public attention. More profoundly, many of the fundamental policy disputes of the day — immigration, health care, civil rights, environmental regulation, information privacy, globalization, social security, and tax policy — are either inherently entangled with employment or heavily influenced by employment-related considerations.

Thus, the institution of employment is paramount not just for individual workers and employing firms and government agencies, but also for society as a whole. Correspondingly, then, the legal rules governing the employment relationship have profound implications beyond the two parties to that relationship. This book will introduce you to the core aspects of this body of law and its implications.

As you work your way through the book, you will discover that the structure of employment law is complex and varied. It derives from multiple sources, including contract, tort, agency law, state and federal statutes, and, at least for government workers, federal and state constitutions. In addition, its application varies greatly depending upon a number of factors, including type of worker (e.g., employee v. non-employee, unionized v. nonunionized, white collar v. blue collar, disabled v. nondisabled); type of employer (large v. small, public v. private); type of industry; and jurisdiction (state v. state). Moreover, because American employment law leaves fundamental aspects of the relationship largely for the parties to determine, the "law" governing the American workplace is subject to immense individual variation. Indeed, for many workers, the most important terms of their relationship — including wage levels, benefits, hours, job security, and privacy considerations — are far more likely to be determined by market forces than by externally imposed legal mandates. Finally, like the structure of the workplace itself, the law of employment is ever changing.

Given its intricate and dynamic nature, employment law is challenging to understand and apply. This is what makes your study of it so critical. Workers and firms must rely heavily on counsel for advice on how to (1) structure working relationships to protect their interests and minimize their risks and (2) advocate on behalf of these interests when disputes arise. Similarly, employment policy makers need a solid understanding of the legal doctrines that govern employment, their implications and limitations, and how the varied aspects of the law interact with one another. This need for employment law expertise extends well beyond those engaged in employment-related work since employment and its legal rules have implications for a wide range of other areas and disciplines.

This text provides an accessible and comprehensive introduction into the study of employment law. Following the Introduction, the book contains seven parts with thirteen chapters exploring various employment law topics. You will be introduced immediately to our unifying theme of private ordering and its limitations — that is, the core tension in the law between the terms the parties themselves establish and publicly imposed mandates. In pursuing this theme through the various subtopics that make up our discipline, not only will you master (sometimes abstruse) doctrine but you will also be asked repeatedly to consider the law from transactional, counseling, litigation, and policy-making perspectives.

We have included standard cases to provide you with a solid background in each topic area. These are supplemented with more recent decisions addressing cutting-edge issues in the twenty-first century, including the growth of outsourcing and contingent (semi- or non-permanent) work arrangements, the role of new whistleblower protections such as those in the Sarbanes-Oxley and Dodd-Frank laws, privacy in the workplace, the enforcement of noncompetition agreements, new issues in antidiscrimination law, the law's role in facilitating the work/family balance, and the growth in various risk-management techniques by employers. We also provide extensive notes and commentary that offer further background and probe deeper into the compelling and difficult employment developments of the day. Finally, each chapter contains problems designed to expose you to the real-world challenges employment counsel face as both planners and litigators. If you want to sample even more recent developments in employment law, visit the casebook's website at http://law. shu.edu/private_ordering.

We believe this text offers a cohesive, thorough, and fascinating first look at employment-law theory and practice. We hope you enjoy it.

A Note on Editing

In cases and law review excerpts, all omissions are indicated by ellipses or brackets, except for footnotes and citations, many of which have been deleted or shortened to enhance readability. The footnotes that remain retain their original numbers.

Timothy P. Glynn
Rachel S. Arnow-Richman
Charles A. Sullivan

December 2010

Acknowledgments

Like all casebooks, EMPLOYMENT LAW: PRIVATE ORDERING AND ITS LIMITATIONS builds on the experiences of its authors in wrestling with the problems of employment law with their law students at Seton Hall and the University of Denver. At each of these law schools, colleagues provided important insights in the formation of our pedagogic approaches. In a more focused way, we are indebted to Mike Zimmer of Loyola Chicago (emeritus at Seton Hall) and Rebecca Hanner White, Dean of Georgia, for their generosity in allowing us to abridge portions of CASES AND MATERIALS ON EMPLOYMENT DISCRIMINATION (Aspen, 7th ed. 2008) and to Mike Zimmer and to Deborah Calloway of the University of Connecticut for permitting us to draw on a precursor to the present book, CASES AND MATERIALS ON EMPLOYMENT LAW (Aspen, 1993). Despite these deep intellectual debts, PRIVATE ORDERING is a radical departure from earlier efforts, offering a new understanding of employment law as both a scholarly discipline and a vibrant field of practice.

This casebook would not have been possible without the support of Aspen's Barbara Roth, Carol McGeehan, Richard Mixter, Troy Froebe, Kathy Langone, and Sylvia Rebert. Moreover, we all want to thank Mike Zimmer and Judd Sneirson who were brave enough to teach out of the first edition as it was being written and provided us with invaluable feedback. Professor Arnow-Richman particularly acknowledges the support of Melissa Hart, Martin Katz, Nantiya Ruan, and Catherine Smith. We are also grateful to the unidentified professors who Aspen retained to review chapters as they emerged from the three authors. While we do not know who these reviewers are, they will see our responses to their critiques throughout this work.

Then there are the individuals who helped us turn this project into reality. They include Silvia Cardoso, Beth Krauzlis, and Latisha Porter, Professors Sullivan's and Glynn's administrative assistants at Seton Hall, and the following Seton Hall research assistants for both Professors Sullivan and Glynn: Michael Amalfe, Kelly Bradshaw, Mark Heftler, Temenouga R. Kolarova, Renee Levine, Steven Morris, and Caitlin Petry, class of 2012; Alison Andolena, class of 2011; Michele Austin, Christina Bae, Joseph Fanning, Robert Flanagan, Angela Kopolovich, Gregory Reid, and Allison Scaduto, class of '08; Lauren DeWitt, Rawan Hmoud, and Mohamed Shiliwala, class of '07; Julie Yoo, class of '06; and Monica Perrette, Shulamit Shvartsman, and Lauren Walter, class of '05. Professor Arnow-Richman would like to thank Melissa Brand, Lindsay Burleson, Keenan Jones, Crystal Littrell-Miller, Lindsay Noyce, Marlys Hartley Roehm, and

Cristel Shepherd from the University of Denver; James Boyer and Ralph Powell from Temple Law School; and her fall 2005 Law of the Workplace students.

As the copious citations to scholarship indicate, we have benefited greatly from the many scholars who have focused their research on employment issues. We have collected the citations in a Table of Selected Secondary Authorities at page 983, but we acknowledge more directly the following for permission to reprint parts of their work:

David Barstow & Lowell Bergman, *Dangerous Business: A Workplace in Turmoil: At a Texas Foundry, An Indifference to Life*, New York Times (Jan. 8, 2003). Copyright 2003. The New York Times Company. Reprinted with permission.

David Barstow & Lowell Bergman, *Dangerous Business: Failures of Regulation: Deaths on the Job, Slaps on the Wrist*, New York Times, (Jan. 10, 2003). Copyright 2003. The New York Times Company. Reprinted with permission.

Price Fishback & Shawn Kantor, *The Adoption of Worker's Compensation in the United States, 1900–30*, 41 J.L. & Econ. 305, 315-19 (1998). Reprinted with permission.

Ethan Lipsig et al., Planning and Implementing Reductions in Force, C922 ALI-ABA 1165, 1231-36 (1994). Reprinted with permission.

Orly Lobel, *Interlocking Regulatory and Industrial Relations: The Governance of Workplace Safety*, published in Administrative Law Review, Volume 57, No. 4, Fall 2005. ©2005 by the American Bar Association. Reprinted with permission.

Introduction

Private Ordering and Its Limitations

For most of its history, employment law in the United States has been a constant struggle between private ordering and government mandates. The term "private ordering" refers to the rules the parties themselves establish to govern their relationship. Such ordering may occur by the parties' express agreement, such as in a collective bargaining agreement or an individual employment contract. Absent formal agreement, such terms may be implied from the circumstances. In addition, private ordering may occur in absence of any express or implied agreement through a "default rule" establishing terms unless the parties "opt out" by an agreement to the contrary. As you will explore in later chapters, the most prominent default rule in American employment law is the notion that the relationship is "at will" — that is, that it may be terminated by either party at any time for any reason.

In contrast to a pure private-ordering regime, public mandates are government-imposed limitations that directly set terms and conditions of employment or affect such terms and conditions indirectly. Mandates range from flat commands — such as the requirement that employers pay a minimum wage, grant leave for certain family and medical needs, or provide compensation for workplace injuries — to rules creating procedural mechanisms to govern the workplace. Unionization and collective bargaining are the prime examples of the latter. Mandates are often negative: Employers must not discriminate on the basis of race, sex, or religion. But sometimes they are positive: Employers must reasonably accommodate disabilities if doing so would not cause an undue hardship. Mandates are often distinctive to employment law — such as the requirement that mass layoffs be conducted only with sufficient advance warning. However, they also come from more general sources of law; for instance, the U.S. Constitution provides federal and state government workers some protections that their private sector counterparts lack. A critical aspect of true mandates is the inability of workers to waive the substantive rights provided.

From the 30,000-foot level, the law governing the employment relationship has moved away from purely private ordering and toward greater government regulation. During much of the nineteenth century, laissez faire and "freedom of contract" prevailed in employment — with the striking exception of the law being largely constitutive of the subordination of African Americans and women (indeed, often removing both groups from "employment").

Thus, in the post–Civil War era, the law tended to view employers and employees as equals, whose participation in "market transactions" would result in employment contracts — often "at will" — that the courts would then neutrally enforce. The reality of this view was always dubious. Many scholars have pointed out that cases such as *Bradwell v. Illinois*, 83 U.S. 130 (1873) (upholding a state statute barring women from the practice of law), and the use of antitrust laws to repress unions showed that the law was far from a neutral arbiter and often placed a heavy thumb on the side of the scale favoring employers and the interests of capital. Nevertheless, the prevailing ideology during the nineteenth century and well into the twentieth was one of the supremacy of private ordering, reflected most dramatically by "*Lochner* Era" court decisions that struck down public mandates regulating work in the name of freedom of contract. *See, e.g., Lochner v. New York*, 198 U.S. 45 (1905) (regulation of bakers' working hours); *Coppage v. Kansas*, 235 U.S. 1 (1915) (prohibition on agreements barring employees from joining unions); *Adkins v. Children's Hospital*, 261 U.S. 525 (1923) (minimum wage mandate for female workers).

Even as *Lochner* was decided, however, change was in the air. In the next two decades, workers' compensation regimes would supplant the minimal protections tort law accorded to workers injured on the job. Perhaps critically, however, this statutory inroad for workers involved a trade-off of more certain liability for lower recoveries and therefore was also in the interests of employers who avoided the risks of a developing tort regime. In any event, as the twentieth century proceeded, workers' rights became increasingly recognized in the law. The Great Depression brought the New Deal, and the New Deal brought, among other initiatives, the National Labor Relations Act ("NLRA"), 29 U.S.C. §§ 151-69 (2006), protecting the right to unionize and bargain collectively, and the Fair Labor Standards Act ("FLSA"), 29 U.S.C. §§ 201-19 (2006), establishing a federal minimum wage and regulating overtime and child labor practices. The demise of *Lochner* in the wake of President Roosevelt's court-packing proposal, *see West Coast Hotel Co. v. Parrish*, 300 U.S. 379 (1937), signaled for many the beginning of the end of private ordering.

Fast-forward 30 years, private ordering suffered another assault, beginning with a legislative response to the Civil Rights movement. Title VII of the Civil Rights Act of 1964, 42 U.S.C. § 2000e-2000e-17 (2006), ushered in, for the first time on a national level, federal regulation effectively limiting employers' ability to hire and fire at will, by prohibiting discrimination on the basis of race, sex, national origin, and religion. That statute was followed within three years by the Age Discrimination in Employment Act ("ADEA"), 29 U.S.C. §§ 621-634 (2006), and, after two more decades, by the Americans with Disabilities Act ("ADA") of 1990, 42 U.S.C.A. §§ 12101-12213 (2010). As a result of these three laws, most employers no longer have free rein in their hiring and firing decisions, and states, even in what had been the Deep South, added their own legislation prohibiting discriminatory employment practices to reach many employers too small to be covered by the federal antidiscrimination laws.

The 1970s saw two further federal inroads on private ordering in employment, the Employee Retirement Income Security Act ("ERISA"), 29 U.S.C. §§ 1001-1381 (2006), and the Occupational Safety and Health Act ("OSHA"), 29 U.S.C. §§ 651-78 (2006). ERISA was a response to horror stories of employers firing workers to avoid paying their pensions or otherwise reneging on promises of long-term benefits. The statute was designed to provide both carrots and sticks to ensure an equitable private retirement system.

OSHA, more directly command-and-control, was intended to be proactive in protecting worker safety. While the workers' compensation regimes enacted decades earlier ensured payment for injuries suffered, OSHA was designed to prevent injuries in the first place through a series of explicit administrative regulations and corresponding agency enforcement.

On top of these statutory assaults on private ordering, state courts were busy cutting back on what they viewed as the excesses of the at-will rule. This movement produced two major strands — one contractual, the other tort-based. First, drawing on general contract principles, the courts in most states expanded protections for job security beyond formal, written employment contracts to include oral agreements and terms implied from the circumstances. They also began to enforce job security provisions in personnel manuals and read individual agreements or circumstances to provide something more than at-will status. Second, drawing in part on the statutes that proscribe certain reasons as illegitimate bases for employment decisions, the courts began to formulate a tort-based "public policy" exception to the at-will doctrine. That is, while employers remained generally free to fire an employee for most reasons, there were certain reasons that the courts declared to be impermissible. Unlike earlier efforts in this direction that condemned specific reasons for termination (e.g., antiunion animus, race), the newer decisions were more open-ended. An actionable termination was one which offended "public policy," a term whose meaning depends upon judicial interpretation. While employers still did not need a good reason to fire someone, they could not act from bad reasons, and the list of bad reasons was no longer confined to statutory prohibitions like the antidiscrimination laws.

Thus, by the mid-1980s, public mandates appeared to be winning the day, and private ordering correspondingly seemed in eclipse. But this view was accurate, if at all, only at the 30,000-foot level. Closer to the ground, the picture was significantly different. The NLRA, for example, legalized unions and put the power of the federal government behind collective bargaining. But statutory amendments and court and National Labor Relations Board decisions limited the economic power of unions. In part as a result of these subsequent legal developments, union representation of the private-sector workforce has experienced a steady decline over the past half century. Similarly, the FLSA provides for a minimum wage and overtime protection, but it has always contained significant exemptions, and the failure of Congress to increase minimum wage levels to keep pace with inflation means that the federal floor provides very limited, and arguably inadequate, protection. In the antidiscrimination arena, legislative expansion has been countered by judicial contraction, with judicially crafted doctrines and proof problems blunting the thrust of the antidiscrimination laws. This was particularly true of the ADA whose definition of "disability" was subject to such narrow interpretations by the Supreme Court that Congress reacted with the Americans with Disabilities Act Amendments Act of 2008 ("ADAAA"), Pub. L. 110-325, 122 Stat. 3553, to try to provide rights to workers with a broader range of physical and mental impairments. Finally, both OSHA and ERISA have been harshly criticized as ineffective. Indeed, ERISA has come to be seen as a barrier to workers' rights. An example is the 2006 decision striking down a Maryland law requiring very large employers, such as Wal-Mart, to provide health insurance for their workers. The court held that the law was preempted by ERISA, which regulates, but does not require, employers to provide any benefits to its workforce. *Retail Indus. Leaders Ass'n v. Fielder*, 435 F. Supp. 2d 481 (D. Md. 2006), *aff'd*, 475 F.3d 180 (4th Cir. 2007). In reality then, despite substantial federal regulation, the many aspects of the most important terms of the employment relationship — job security, wages, and benefits — are left to private ordering between employers and employees.

In addition, in recent decades there has been a retreat from mandates and a corresponding increased commitment to private ordering at the state level. While the public policy tort for wrongful discharge has survived, its reach has been narrowed in many states. Further, progressive state contract-law decisions on employee handbooks have been largely negated by judicial approval of employer-drafted disclaimers of contractual liability. In the privacy area, state common-law protections that had emerged in the 1970s have largely disappeared as a practical matter, except where embodied in a few state statutes. Meaningful federal protections are scarce as well, contained only in a few discrete statutes like the Employee Polygraph Protection Act, 29 U.S.C. §§ 2001-2009 (2006), and the newly enacted Genetic Information Nondiscrimination Act of 2008 ("GINA"), Pub. L. 110-233, 122 Stat. 881 (May 21, 2008) (codified in various sections of 26, 29, and 42 U.S.C.).

Other recent developments in employment-law mandates have been mixed as well. For example, in enacting the Family and Medical Leave Act ("FMLA") in 1993, 29 U.S.C. §§ 2601-54 (2006), Congress finally responded to the calls for protection for employees who want to balance work and family demands. Yet the protection provided is limited both in substance (eligible workers receive only unpaid leave) and scope (only larger employers are covered). Similarly, there has been a substantial growth in statutory whistleblower protections at the state and federal levels, the most prominent examples being the Sarbanes-Oxley Act of 2002 ("SOX"), Pub. L. No. 107-204, 116 Stat. 745, the health care reform law, Pub. L. 111-148, 124 Stat. 119, and the Dodd-Frank financial reform statute, Pub. L. 111-203, 124 Stat. 1376. All of these statutes provide whistleblower protections for employees who report behavior by their employers that violates the substantive provisions of those laws. But these protections, too, tend to be fairly narrowly drawn, leaving workers with perhaps less protection in reality than they might think.

Finally, employers are becoming increasingly creative in augmenting their baseline rights through contract. This can be seen in the widespread reliance on noncompetition clauses and other restrictive covenants. In addition, employers are developing new forms of private ordering, including various liability and forum management provisions (e.g., arbitration clauses, severance agreements, and forum-selection provisions) that, despite meaningful limitations, fundamentally alter the law's control over private ordering, leaving employers freer to protect their interests and minimize their liability risks.

In short, employment law is a story of private ordering and its limitations. But today, more than ever, it is a complex story, and one in which neither private ordering nor mandates has achieved unqualified primacy. Importantly, the tension between these competing conceptions generally plays out not at the 30,000-foot level but on the ground in particular employment law practices and disputes. Because the practice of law is largely done from a close-up perspective, it is important to understand what is left to private ordering and what is not and, to recognize that today's sphere of free enterprise may be tomorrow's field of government regulation (or vice versa).

The Importance and Elusiveness of Employment Law

This struggle between private ordering and public mandates within American employment law occurs in the context of a universally important relationship. Almost every adult in the United States is or has been an employee. The employment relationship is not only the vehicle though which most Americans make their living but the workplace is also the place where they spend most of their waking hours and develop a large number of their interpersonal relationships. For many, personal identity is bound up not only with what they do but with where they do it. Professor Paul Weiler summarized this reality:

> The job rather than the state has become the source of most of the social safety net on which people must rely when they are not employed — that is, when they are sick, disabled, or retired. And the plants and offices in which we work are the places where we spend much of our adult lives, where we develop important aspects of our personalities and our relationships, and where we may be exposed to a variety of physical and psychological traumas.

PAUL WEILER, GOVERNING THE WORKPLACE: THE FUTURE OF LABOR AND EMPLOYMENT LAW 3 (1990). The stakes today are perhaps even higher. The development of technology has tended to push the "workplace" further into what was previously personal time and space, and aspects of the employment safety net have eroded, making access to "quality" employment (in terms of stability, flexibility, accommodations, wages, benefits, and prospects for intra- or inter-firm mobility, etc.) even more important to workers.

From the employer's perspective, the employment relationship is the means by which firms produce most of their value and government agencies provide most of their services. Indeed, in the modern economy, employers' success often depends more on the quality of their workers — their creativity, cooperation, adaptability, and productivity — than on other assets: "However rich its natural resources, however costly and sophisticated the capital technology, a firm or an economy which does not have a skilled or committed work force will not be able to transform those physical assets into efficient and productive enterprises." *Id.*

Thus, the institution of employment matters a great deal to individual workers, employing firms, government agencies, and society as a whole. Naturally then, the legal rules that govern this relationship have profound, wide-ranging implications.

Yet despite the overview laid out above, employment law is not easy to define or summarize. Even the threshold question of what constitutes "employment" — as opposed to one of several different kinds of relationships in which human beings work with and for others — is uncertain. Unlike other disciplines such as constitutional law, the law of employment does not flow from a single source, nor does it derive from a single doctrinal regime like contracts or torts. Rather, because employment law governs a relationship that is both pervasive and variable, it draws from many sources, for example, contract, tort, agency law, constitutional law, and federal and state statutes.

Just as the sources of employment law vary, so too do its rules. Different legal doctrines apply depending on the state in which an employee works, whether the workplace is unionized, and whether the employer is a public or private entity. Even federal statutes do not provide complete uniformity, but rather govern some employment relationships and not others. This is due to limitations on coverage (small employers are typically exempted, with "small" being defined differently in different statutes) and various codified exemptions (certain "professional" employees, for instance, are excluded from the maximum hours provisions of the FLSA and many agricultural and transportation workers are excluded from coverage completely). The governing law therefore depends on factors such as the type of occupation and the size of the employer. In application, it may also depend on more nebulous factors such as the autonomy and economic vulnerability of the worker, key considerations in determining whether a worker is an employee protected by federal employment statutes.

In addition, as suggested above, many of the terms governing a particular relationship may be established by, and therefore are unique to, the parties in that relationship. The "law" in the American workplace, as it is currently constituted, leaves ample — some would say, too much — room for individual variation in its most important terms, including wage levels, benefits, hours, job security, and privacy protections. All of these critical terms and conditions of employment are far more likely to be determined by the parties' reactions to market forces than by legal constraints. Again, for example, the federally mandated minimum wage is too low to have a direct effect on most workers' negotiating for compensation because both employers and workers start compensation discussions at a point far in excess of that wage. In light of its patchwork nature, understanding when and how the law constrains or promotes these terms, either directly or indirectly, is a formidable challenge.

Finally, the law of employment is dynamic because the workplace is ever-evolving: Tomorrow's workplace will be different than today's, and so will tomorrow's law — a law you will help shape after you graduate. At best, then, we can say that employment law embodies the legal rules and standards that govern the employment relationship, but those legal rules and standards vary enormously in kind, substance, and application.

The breadth and variability of employment law poses significant challenges to workers and firms trying to understand their rights and obligations. There is in fact much misunderstanding regarding both, especially among workers. One particularly important example is that most workers believe that the law provides them with greater job security than it actually does, as you will explore in Chapter 2. This misperception can affect worker behavior, for instance, lulling them into thinking they need not seek greater protections, whether through unions, individual contracts, or otherwise. In addition, uncertainty in the law can inflict real costs on employers, not only ex post (litigation expenses and unexpected liabilities) but also ex ante (in terms of risk aversion and investments in planning and compliance).

The maze of employment-law doctrines also creates enormous difficulties for counsel seeking to advise parties on how to comply with the law, protect their interests, and avoid liability and other risks attendant to employment relationships. Given the increasing importance of human capital in our information- and technology-driven economy, a basic understanding of the law of the workplace and its implications is essential even for lawyers practicing in other areas. For example, a grasp of employment law should be standard fare for attorneys in the corporate and intellectual property fields. Indeed, surveys of corporate general counsel often show that, of the legal risks faced by their firms, labor and employment litigation ranks at or near the top. *See e.g.,* Adele Nicholas, *GCs Reveal Their Litigation Fears and Headaches,* CORP. LEGAL TIMES 72 (October 2004) (indicating that 62 percent of survey respondents ranked labor and employment litigation as their number one potential exposure). This concern is especially legitimate in tough economic times, like the Great Recession, when employers are more likely to layoff workers and terminated workers are less able to find replacement employment. The year 2010 saw the largest number of filings on record at the EEOC — nearly 100,000 — although a variety of other factors besides the economy may explain this surge. *See* Bureau of National Affairs, *EEOC's New Charges Reach High, But Agency Slows Growth of Case Backlog,* 24 LABOR RELATIONS WEEK 1972 (2010); Nathan Koppel, *Claims Alleging Job Bias Rise With Layoffs,* WALL STREET JOURNAL, Sept. 24, 2010, at A6.

The nature and scope of employment law mean that a single course cannot even attempt to cover every legal issue and doctrine that may govern or affect the workplace. Largely for this reason, most law schools offer other courses addressing areas of employment law, including courses in Employment Discrimination, Labor Law, Workers' Compensation, Employee Benefits, and even more particularized disciplines, such as Disability Discrimination and Labor and Employment Arbitration. In addition, some of these areas, most notably Labor Law (which governs unionization and collective bargaining), are sufficiently distinct doctrinally that they are best left to separate study, except to the extent they provide context for broader inquiries.

Private Ordering and Its Limitations as a Framework

So how should one approach beginning to learn employment law? Despite employment law's disparate sources and wide variability, there is, as we suggested at the outset, a theme common to the law of the workplace. Employment law is, at its core, a course about *private ordering and its limitations*. This description not only captures the core historical conflict over employment regulation but also provides a framework for analyzing the key pressure points in the various aspects of what we call "employment law" today. It is the lens through which we can not only begin to discuss what the law is and what it ought to be in a multitude of contexts but also explore various legal risks and incentives of the parties and the extent to which these may be altered by planning.

This tension between public ordering and private mandates is scarcely unique to employment law. Yet, because the employment relationship is consensual, pervasive, and of profound importance to individual stakeholders and society, this relationship is one of the primary contexts — both qualitatively and quantitatively — in which the law seeks to balance contractual freedoms and market forces with countervailing social interests. Indeed, this tension runs through each doctrinal area in employment, from formation (i.e., whether worker and firm have an "employment" relationship or some other kind of legal status or relationship defined purely by contract) to job security to issues of worker autonomy (e.g., privacy) to discrimination to accommodations for workers' personal needs to employment compensation to how and where employment disputes are resolved.

How to resolve this conflict is therefore a paramount issue in employment law. Unsurprisingly, it is the source of ongoing political, judicial, and scholarly controversy. Whether or not you have seen the term "private ordering" before, you undoubtedly have seen or heard of the conflict between private ordering and its limitations playing out in public policy debates. It is a central theme in the cyclical debates over whether to increase the minimum wage. It also appears frequently in discussions of the "hot" employment issues of the day, including whether to mandate certain types of employer health care coverage, whether to require employers to provide paid parental leave, the extent to which employees ought to be protected from intrusive employer monitoring or oversight, whether to expand whistleblower and other related protections for employees, and whether employers should be able to compel private arbitration of employment disputes.

Many scholars have argued that the various terms of employment should be almost exclusively the product of private ordering. They claim that leaving the terms of employment to individual bargaining ultimately will produce socially optimal arrangements, and that various market forces (such as workers' supposed ability to freely reject or abandon employment) will generally prevent abuse. Indeed, perhaps most famously (or infamously, depending on one's perspective), Professor Richard Epstein has urged that we ought to abandon antidiscrimination laws because market forces ultimately will do a better job of correcting the effects of status-based discrimination. *See generally* RICHARD A. EPSTEIN, FORBIDDEN GROUNDS: THE CASE AGAINST EMPLOYMENT DISCRIMINATION LAWS (1992).

Of course, the scholarly responses to these types of arguments have been legion. Private ordering raises two different sets of concerns. First, scholars have identified a number of "market failures" in labor markets, which they argue justify greater mandated protections for workers. Many have pointed out that individual workers, often due to economic and social vulnerabilities, lack the power and resources to bargain effectively on their own behalf. Other scholars have contended that, even when workers are not economically powerless to protect themselves, they may suffer from informational disadvantages and cognitive constraints in assessing proposed terms of employment. Still others argue for public mandates because, in their view, employer preferences often are based on factors or biases that are not rational in an economic sense, leading to inefficient, discriminatory, or otherwise problematic decisions about who to hire, retain, or promote, and under what terms and conditions. Some of these critiques of private ordering have marshaled empirical evidence to support their claims.

In addition, there is the question of the extent to which private ordering must be constrained because of the negative impact the parties' actions may have on third parties or society as a whole. Few would question whether the public has an interest in protecting itself from employee/employer conduct that inflicts direct and substantial social harm. Indeed, the NLRA was in large part a response to the economic (and sometimes physical) warfare between unions and management that impeded the flow of goods and services to the public. The current debate centers on when such harm exists, when it is sufficient to justify public intervention, how the law ought to intervene, and which decision makers ought to resolve these issues. Indeed, as you work your way through this book, you will see the potential tensions between the interests of worker, firm, and the public, as well as the differing views on when and how to address these competing interests, play out again and again.

This casebook will help you identify the role of private ordering and its limitations in each area and demonstrate how the law currently strikes a balance between them. You will be challenged to think critically about that balance and its effects on workplace incentives and risks from a policy perspective. At the same time, the focus on private ordering means that this casebook is designed to assist you in learning how to be an employment-law practitioner — someone whose decisions help create and structure, that is "order," work relationships. Of course, the lawyer's role includes understanding how to develop persuasive legal arguments in litigation and other employment disputes on behalf of both employees and employers. But, at least as importantly, it also includes assessing and managing risk. The defining aspect of private ordering is the ability of employees and employers to structure their work relationships to protect their interests and reduce legal risks — transactional skills that are becoming more and more dominant in the practice of employment law.

Employment Law at the Beginning of the Twenty-first Century

Now that you have been introduced to the challenges of learning and practicing employment law and the core tension that binds aspects of this discipline together, it is worth taking a moment to appreciate where the law is today. What we now think of as "employment law" in the United States reflects a relatively new development having its roots in the Industrial Revolution. Before that, "employment" in this country took a variety of forms, including indentured servitude, slavery, self-employment, personal service, and family work (primarily on farms). Employment as we know it, was not the primary means of earning a living.

After the Civil War, the United States rapidly industrialized and agriculture became increasingly less important. The population of employees grew, including for the first time large numbers of women working outside the home/farm and domestic service. By the dawn of the twentieth century, industry became the rule rather than the exception, and employment typically became not merely another option but the only choice. As a result, workers become increasingly dependent on their ability to obtain and retain positions working for others in order to survive. While ''contract'' theoretically ordered the relationship between these workers and their employers, the increasing economic dependency of employees severely diminished their bargaining power, thus tending to erode their rights.

Although some workers obtained greater protection by virtue of individual employment contracts specifying the terms and conditions of their work, most employers refused to enter into such arrangements with most workers. Employers preferred to be free to hire and fire as they wished, and the common law accommodated this desire by characterizing employment relationships as ''at will'' unless the parties were especially specific in providing otherwise.

While facially neutral, the at-will rule generally favored employers since they could easily replace an employee who quit; in contrast, a fired employee's options in a period of limited geographic mobility were typically very limited and often very unpalatable. The unrestrained power of employers sometimes manifested itself in starvation wages, unsanitary and dangerous working conditions, long hours, child labor, and little or no job security for many employees.

As sketched above, these conditions led to attempts to deal with the problem of unrestricted industrial power in sweeping ways. In addition to federal approaches to curbing abuse of industrial power, such as antitrust laws, state legislatures made some early attempts to deal directly with the exercise of such power as it affected employment, such as laws regulating maximum hours of work. Again, prior to the New Deal, *Lochner* Era courts repeatedly found such regulation unconstitutional. Still, there were some early reform successes, most notably the widespread creation and adoption of workers' compensation regimes during the Progressive Era.

Also during this period, the American union movement began to make some headway in securing rights for employees despite organized employer resistance and government hostility. The rallying cry of unions was the plight of the workers who were subjected to the unbridled power of employers. The ''union solution'' was to create countervailing power through the aggregation of workers in the hope that the resultant conflict would produce a balance in the interests of both workers and employers. *See generally* John Kenneth Galbraith, American Capitalism: The Concept of Countervailing Power (1952).

Unions were concerned with compensation, hours, job safety, and job security. Job security served unions not only by protecting individual members but also as a means to other ends (e.g., eliminating competition between union members to avoid weakening unity and protecting against employer retaliation). As a result, unions typically tried to negotiate contracts with employers limiting the power to discharge individual workers to situations involving ''just cause'' and specifying how employees should be treated in economic reductions in force, typically by requiring that workers be selected for layoff in reverse order of seniority.

Other initiatives also worked to strengthen job security, albeit among particular subgroups of workers. One was the civil service movement in government employment, which preserved employment ''during good behavior'' for those who qualified. While civil service protections originated in the nineteenth century, the growth of government during the twentieth century resulted in these systems covering significantly more employees. In addition, advocates of academic tenure (and the job security it provides) were also likewise successful not only for the college and university professors for whom tenure was originally devised, but also for teachers in public elementary and secondary schools. From an economic perspective, both civil service and academic tenure were originally viewed as a tradeoff between lower compensation, on the one hand, and less pressure combined with greater job security on the other.

The Great Depression ushered in leaders more interested in expanding government power and addressing the plight of the common worker. The revised view of government power brought on by the Depression enabled federal and state legislation according employees' basic rights to survive constitutional attack. New Deal legislation was in two forms: first, statutes protecting and supporting employees' efforts to bargain collectively with their employers, and, second, legislation providing the first effective national regulation of some terms and conditions of employment.

Regarding the first category, the NLRA granted workers the right to engage in "concerted action" by protecting such action from employer retaliation. The statute also established a structure for the recognition of unions as "exclusive bargaining representatives" for workers and imposed on employers a duty to bargain with them. This federal labor legislation (and subsequent state efforts aimed at the public sector) did not impose any particular terms and conditions on employers. Rather, it dealt with workplace problems indirectly by establishing a procedure whereby such problems could be resolved by bargaining between the parties. Where unions were strongest, the result was collective bargaining agreements that provided detailed regulation not only of wages and hours, but of many other aspects of employment, including job safety and job security. In its most developed form, this regulation is implemented by a quasi-judicial system of arbitration of disputes between labor and management.

In the short run, unionization became a dominant mode of regulating the employment relationship. Prior to the NLRA, the unionized percentage of the American workforce was less than 15 percent. By the mid 1950s, the number had increased to nearly 40 percent. But, over the next several decades, especially in the 1980s, the union movement faltered. Unions now represent a smaller percentage of American workers—11.9 percent overall and less than 7 percent in the private sector—than before the NLRA was passed. The causes of the decline of the union movement are contested, although, as described previously, less favorable statutory, judicial, and agency treatment has certainly played a role. The merits of unions and collective bargaining remain disputed, but the decline in unionization is undeniable. Thus, for better or worse, although most employees enjoy protections for concerted actions under the NLRA, the vast majority are not employed under or governed by a collective bargaining regime.

The second form of regulation that emerged during the New Deal and thereafter directly regulated the terms and conditions of private employment. The FLSA, setting a minimum hourly wage, is one example. During this period, the federal government also regulated the terms and conditions of "unemployment" by fostering unemployment compensation.

Perhaps in part due to the notion that collective bargaining would address most problems, there was little new direct regulation of terms and conditions of employment for almost 40 years. The 1970s saw Congress enact both OSHA and ERISA: again, despite their differences—OSHA was designed to protect worker safety through a traditional New Deal–style command-and-control approach while ERISA embodied a carrot-and-stick approach to promoting and then protecting employee benefit plans — both regimes remain the subject of significant controversy and criticism. It is worth noting that ERISA was primarily intended to ensure pension benefits for workers, but it also addresses welfare benefits including employer-provided health insurance. It has been expanded over the years by some important amendments, and it now guarantees continuation of health coverage in most terminations of employment — assuming the employee had health benefits to begin with and assuming she is able to bear the group-rate costs of the insurance. However, as discussed previously, this has come at a price since ERISA's preemptive effect has served as a barrier to state-level benefits reforms, most notably in the health care context.

None of these statutory regimes deals primarily or directly with job security; rather, they regulate various aspects of employment. Nevertheless, job security is implicated in most of these laws, at least to the extent that they contain provisions barring employers from retaliating against employees who exercise their statutory rights. A different approach to regulating employer abuses emerged most dramatically in the 1960s — beginning with Title VII and thereafter supplemented by the ADEA, the ADA, and other statutes. The centerpiece of these laws was not direct regulation of terms and conditions of employment; rather, they ruled out certain reasons for employer actions (race, sex, age, disability). Employers, at least in theory, remained free to hire and fire and structure their workplaces for any reason — good or bad — so long as these defined reasons did not influence their decisions. The states were also active during this period, enacting antidiscrimination laws that sometimes went beyond the protections provided by the federal government. One notable example is the numerous state laws prohibiting discrimination based on sexual orientation, which is not yet explicitly prohibited under Title VII or any other federal statute.

In sum, by the 1970s, a variety of different legal regimes addressed different aspects of the employment relationship. With respect to job security, individual employees with sufficient bargaining power could negotiate contractual protection. In addition, there were statutes encouraging "procedural" solutions for all workers (such as regulating unionism and the collective bargaining process) and statutes directly providing job security for civil servants and academics. Finally, there were statutes providing some degree of job security by prohibiting certain reasons for firing employees. With respect to terms and conditions of employment, workers were protected by the same set of laws, supplemented by additional statutes directly regulating certain matters (e.g., minimum wages, maximum hours) for private and public, unionized and nonunionized employees.

Although some may have thought this collection of protections adequate, others perceived more exceptions than rules. Certainly, the average worker (employed by a nonunionized, private, nonacademic employer) had relatively narrow protections. Such a person was unlikely to have a personal employment contract and thus was an "at will" employee. Beyond the floor protections provided by minimum wage laws, workers' compensation, OSHA, and prohibitions on status discrimination, a worker would have very little in the way of legal protections.

This reality triggered state common-law efforts to limit employer power and expand employee rights by carving away at the at-will principle through a more expansive view of contract protections and through the public policy tort. While some of these decisions have become a permanent part of the employment landscape, there has also been significant judicial retrenchment in these areas. Similarly, while new state statutory whistleblower and related protections have codified and even expanded the common law developments of the 1970s and 1980s, major new legislation seemed stalled until, in response to examples of corporate misfeasance, SOX provided employee protections, although admittedly not as an end in themselves but rather as a means to ensure an honest securities market. In the wake of the Great Recession, there has been a new spate of whistleblower protections on the federal level as part of the stimulus package and the comprehensive legislation dealing with health care and financial institution regulation. Like SOX, the goals of these provisions are not designed to protect employees per se but to encourage employees to report violations of the laws' substantive provisions.

Compounding the ferment in the law was a radical restructuring of the economy. As the twentieth century was coming to a close, changes in the nature of the American economy, the workforce, and the structure of the workplace brought new issues to the fore and, correspondingly, presaged new legal developments. For example, consistent with the growing number of households in which all employable adults work, there has been a growing awareness of the need for accommodation of workers' familial and personal needs. Legislative reforms along these lines have been modest, but they include the FMLA, which provides limited protections for employees' life needs in the form of mandated unpaid leave due to a personal medical condition or that of a family member. A few states provide paid leave or more generous unpaid leave. Similarly, the ADA requires "reasonable accommodation" of disabled individuals in many circumstances and the enactment of the ADAAA promises to revive the significance of this requirement.

Moreover, as discussed previously, as the American economy has transformed into one dominated by services, information, and technology, the value of certain employees has increased. In significant sectors, firms are becoming more dependent on employee creativity, information, and innovation, resulting in a heightened concern among *employers* about protecting themselves. Some find it more than a little telling that a pure at-will regime is now being challenged not merely by advocates of employee interests but also by employers who find themselves increasingly at risk. There has been a rise in litigated conflicts between employers and (often former) employees in such areas as trade secrets, copyrights, and ownership of employee inventions, and claims to business good will, customer lists, and various types of confidential information. Because the default protections for employer interests — employee fiduciary duties and employer intellectual property and trade secrets protections — are limited and often difficult to enforce, there has been dramatic growth in the use of restrictive covenants in recent years. These covenants — including noncompetition, nondisclosure, nonsolicitation, and holdover agreements — are becoming more common, as are questions about the limits the law ought to place on them. Because the stakes on both sides are higher than in past decades, the validity and extent of such agreements are much more frequently litigated.

The governing employment law regime itself, market forces, and other factors have also fostered dramatic changes in the structure of the American workplace. Among the most important is the growth in the outsourcing — both domestic and foreign — of various aspects of production to independent firms or suppliers of labor and the rise of nontraditional working relationships, including growth in independent contracting and part-time work. Undoubtedly, firms take advantage of such nontraditional work structures to avoid some of the legal requirements of "employment" and reduce risks associated with having "employees." By avoiding "employment" relationships and opting instead for independent contractors or other work structures, firms can avoid most statutory protections — which apply only to "employees" and "employers" — along with other legal consequences of an employment relationship, including such things as respondeat superior liability and obligations under immigration laws. The corresponding rise in what some have called the "contingent workforce" may have significant social consequences because these workers, on average, are more likely to be both on the economic margins and less likely — for both legal and practical reasons — to be able to enforce whatever work-related rights they may have.

Yet another change in the workplace is the shift from a fairly hierarchical structure to less formal, more team-oriented workplaces. While hierarchy remains alive and well in many settings, the past decades have seen a flattening of hierarchies as tiers of management are replaced with more collaborative working arrangements. The result is, in one sense, fewer bosses and, in another, more bosses. Such structural changes pose a variety of challenges for the law, especially in areas like sexual harassment.

All of these trends are being affected, in one way or another, by the Great Recession the country is currently experiencing. While the recession has been declared officially over as of this writing, unemployment remains stubbornly near the 10 percent level and many predict a long period before substantial improvement in the labor markets. There is even talk of the "new normal," a scenario in which long-term high unemployment rates dominate. Although it is still too early to say precisely how economic conditions will affect employment going forward, one does not need a crystal ball to predict that a large number of qualified unemployed workers hanging over the market would have dramatic effects on employment practices.

In short, the law continues to struggle to address these fundamental changes, both as a matter of doctrine and of on-the-ground enforcement. Despite the growth of regulation, the law leaves many decisions regulated only in skeletal ways. Nevertheless, the intersection of various legislative regimes and common-law doctrines means that few employment-related decisions are entirely immune from legal challenge. This reality has produced one final, burgeoning area of employment law, counseling, and litigation. Recent years have seen the rise of "second-level" risk management techniques, usually used by employers, to control or minimize the risks of downstream employment-related conflicts or liabilities. These techniques include internal compliance practices such as the implementation of sexual harassment policies and internal investigations, mandatory pre-dispute arbitration agreements, a rise in substantial severance pay in exchange for releases of claims upon termination, and the inclusion of choice-of-law and choice-of-forum clauses in employment contracts. The substantive law governing these various approaches to risk management differs, as does their success in shifting risk from employers to employees. However, as long as the law of the employment relationship remains uncertain, risk management techniques and the legal rules that constrain them will continue to play a central role in the life of the employment lawyer.

As you can see from this short tour of employment law, the American legal approach to employment in the twenty-first century is a crazy quilt of regulation and laissez faire. For many employees and employers, this means market forces remain far more important than "law" in determining the most important terms of their relationship, including whether "employment" exists at all and how long such a relationship lasts. But there are some significant legal constraints that frame the parties' choices. Understanding this patchwork of laws governing workplace relationships — a combination of contract-law principles operating against a backdrop of tort law rules and general and employment-specific statutes and regulations — presents serious challenges for workers, firms, policy makers, legal counsel, and, of course, law students.

The Organization of This Book

This casebook is organized in seven parts containing 13 chapters. Part I addresses issues of formation of an employment relationship, that is, whether there is an "employment" relationship at all — as opposed to some other type of relationship — and the consequences that flow from that determination. The two chapters in Part II then address how employment terms are set or limited by contract, particularly terms related to job security. They explore the contours of the at-will rule and its exceptions and the interpretation and enforcement of express agreements that vary from this rule and set other important terms of employment, such as compensation.

Part III then turns to tort-based protections for employees: Chapter 4 explores the public policy exception, state statutory antiretaliation and whistleblower provisions modeled on the public policy decisions, and federal approaches, focusing on Sarbanes-Oxley. Chapter 5 covers traditional workplace torts, including intentional interference with the employment relationship, defamation, intentional infliction of emotional distress, and fraud. The two chapters in Part IV then shift the focus to worker autonomy interests, that is, privacy and speech. In both of these contexts, the disparate sources of potential protection are considered (in both the public and the private employer settings) as well as the balance the law strikes between legitimate employer interests and the autonomy interests of workers.

Part V turns to workplace property rights and related interests of employers. Chapter 8 explores various legal safeguards for these interests, including those flowing from fiduciary duty, trade secrets, and intellectual property protections. It also addresses employers' attempts to supplement these legal protections through contract — for example, restrictive covenants such as noncompetition, nonsolicitation, and holdover agreements — and the limits the law places on the scope and enforcement of such provisions.

Part VI contains four chapters addressing the principal statutory regimes that govern directly or indirectly various terms and conditions of employment: Chapter 9 explores antidiscrimination mandates; Chapter 10 examines required accommodations for aspects of workers lives, including workers' disabilities, health, pregnancy, and family caregiving needs. Chapter 11 discusses regulation of employee wages and benefits; and Chapter 12 reviews legal regimes addressing workplace safety and health. These chapters cover not only the primary federal statutes addressing these matters — such as, Title VII, the ADEA, the ADA, the FMLA, the FLSA, ERISA, and OSHA — but also state workers' compensation regimes (Chapter 12) and state efforts to supplement federal antidiscrimination, accommodation, wage, and benefit protections and enforcement.

Finally, Part VII offers a fitting conclusion to the study of employment law by exploring various methods of managing the risks and costs of potential liabilities of employment — liabilities arising from the contractual, common-law, and statutory aspects of employment law you will have explored in earlier chapters. In other words, Chapter 13 addresses the second-level private ordering techniques that employers commonly utilize to control the risks and costs of employment disputes by minimizing liability exposure or choosing the forum within which such disputes are resolved. They include policies for preventing and correcting discriminatory harassment, internal investigations of misconduct, release and severance agreements, arbitration agreements, liquidated damages provisions, liability insurance, and bankruptcy protection. Of course, this survey discusses not only the content of these practices and contractual provisions but also the limitations the law imposes them.

Part One

THE BENEFITS AND BURDENS OF EMPLOYMENT

1

The Stakes of "Employment"

A useful starting point in the study of employment law is this fundamental question: Why does the existence of an "employment" relationship matter? Organizations, both governmental and private, structure their activities in a wide variety of ways, and the individuals who perform work or provide services for these institutions may have various kinds of legal relationships with them and with one another. For example, a person who works on a firm's behalf may be its sole proprietor, a partner, an employee, or an independent contractor. In addition, firms engage other firms to perform some of their productive activities, leaving to the second firm the task of engaging workers to perform these tasks. For instance, growing attention has focused on outsourcing various services across international borders and utilizing "contingent" — that is, temporary or nonpermanent — workers.

Distinguishing between employment and other types of relationships is important because each offers its own mix of risks and benefits, both legal and nonlegal — what we call the stakes of employment. For example, many of the best-known legal protections for workers apply only to "employees." Firms owe duties to employees that they do not owe to other workers, although they may also benefit from employer status in various ways. The nature of the work relationship also has important consequences for third parties, who are far more likely to be able to hold firms or government entities liable for injuries caused by their employees than by independent contractors.

To understand the stakes of employment, you must have a basic grasp of the potential rights and obligations arising from the employment relationship and how they differ from those arising from other relationships. Thus, in this chapter we explore not only the definitions of "employee" and "employer" and the distinctions between employment and other types of legal relationships but also the consequences of employment for employees, employers, and third parties. Workers may prefer to be employees for some reasons and in some circumstances but not others; similarly, firms and government agencies may seek to avoid being employers for certain purposes but may benefit from employer status in other ways. And third

3

parties and the public may have an independent interest in treating some workers as employees but not others.

As you work your way through these preferences and interests, think about the role private ordering should play — that is, the extent to which worker and firm ought to be able to define the nature of their relationship though contract. Should such agreements be enforceable and dispositive, or should the law limit parties' ability to decide whether theirs is an "employment" relationship?

Before reading the cases and notes in this chapter, take a moment to consider the following problem:

PROBLEM

1-1. A Blossoming Business. Urban Tropical Flowers, Inc. ("UTF") is a small nursery specializing in growing tropical flowers and other exotic plants, and designing and tending live tropical flower arrangements for offices and other indoor commercial spaces. Fern and Charlie Davidson founded UTF several years ago and remain the firm's only owners. Fern is the CEO and Charlie is the CFO, although they both are involved in all aspects of the business. Until very recently, UTF's operation had been small enough that Fern and Charlie could operate the business almost entirely on their own, needing only a part-time administrative assistant/receptionist and occasional assistance while transporting and installing larger flower arrangements.

However, as a result of the attention surrounding their award-winning entry in a regional tropical and exotic flower show, UTF has now entered into agreements for long-term installations with four new customers, all of which dwarf UTF's current projects in terms of size, design, and maintenance complexity. Moreover, Fern and Charlie are in discussions with a dozen other potential customers, some of whom are interested in installations in facilities 50 to 100 miles away from the nursery.

After consulting with a business advisor, Fern and Charlie have created a strategic plan that calls for (1) dramatically expanding the nursery; (2) improving UTF's information management systems; (3) upgrading the firm's Web site, marketing plan, and informational materials; and (4) standardizing its transportation, installation, and maintenance processes. To implement this plan, Fern and Charlie will continue to manage the entire operation, but they will need to hire the following people within the next six months:

- Four gardeners, who will maintain UTF's plants both in the nursery and at the various sites
- One or two floral designers, who will begin by assisting Fern and Charlie in designing arrangements and ultimately take responsibility for much of the firm's creative work
- A software engineer and/or information technology expert who will design and, if necessary, maintain an information management system to keep track of the installations and nursery inventory, and provide detailed maintenance schedules (including watering, fertilizing, soil composition, pruning, plant rotation, etc.)

- A salesperson who will engage in customer relations and eventually take responsibility for most of UTF's marketing and sales
- Additional workers to transport plants and heavy installation equipment and assist in manual tasks during peak planting or installation periods

Consider this hypothetical from the following perspectives. First, why might UTF decide to treat these workers as employees or independent contractors, or, alternatively, to hire an independent firm to supply the labor or perform particular tasks? Second, why might some of the workers prefer employment with UTF while others may prefer a different relationship? Finally, might the public or third parties have a preference, and, if so, when should their interests override the interests of the parties? And, relatedly, to what extent should UTF's or a worker's expectations, or an agreement between UTF and a worker, determine the nature of the relationship? Continue to consider these questions as you read the material in this chapter.

A. DISTINGUISHING "EMPLOYEE" FROM "INDEPENDENT CONTRACTOR"

By far the most commonly litigated issue in defining the employment relationship is whether a worker is an employee or an independent contractor. This is true for three reasons. First, as explored below, a host of legal consequences that flow from the workers' status often make this issue worth litigating. Second, most workers — that is, participants in the production of firm goods and services — are either employees or independent contractors (as opposed to, inter alia, sole proprietors, corporate directors, or partners or some other type of co-owner). Finally, distinguishing between employees and independent contractors is often both difficult and highly fact-intensive.

Somewhat surprisingly, most statutes regulating employment do not attempt to define the term, other than by borrowing the definition of "employee" from the common law. Thus, the test that courts apply for determining whether a worker is an independent contractor or an employee typically derives from the definition of employee or "servant" found in the common law of agency. As summarized in the Restatement (Second) of Agency, a "master" or employer is "a principal who employs an agent to perform service in his affairs and who controls or has the right to control the physical conduct of the other in the performance of the service." RESTATEMENT (SECOND) OF AGENCY, §2(1) (1958). Correspondingly, a servant or employee is "an agent employed by a master to perform service in his affairs whose physical conduct in the performance of the service is controlled or is subject to the right to control by the master." *Id.* §2(2). In contrast, an independent contractor is one "who contracts with another to do something for him but who is not controlled by the other nor subject to the other's right to control with respect to his physical conduct in the performance of the undertaking." *Id.* §2(3). The Restatement goes on to provide a more detailed definition of "servant," a term that has since been displaced by "employee," containing a nonexclusive list of factors for determining servant/employee status:

§ 220. Definition of Servant

(1) A servant is a person employed to perform services in the affairs of another and who with respect to the physical conduct in the performance of the services is subject to the other's control or right to control.

(2) In determining whether one acting for another is a servant or an independent contractor, the following matters of fact, among others, are considered:

(a) the extent of control which, by the agreement, the master may exercise over the details of the work;

(b) whether or not the one employed is engaged in a distinct occupation or business;

(c) the kind of occupation, with reference to whether, in the locality, the work is usually done under the direction of the employer or by a specialist without supervision;

(d) the skill required in the particular occupation;

(e) whether the employer or the workman supplies the instrumentalities, tools, and the place of work for the person doing the work;

(f) the length of time for which the person is employed;

(g) the method of payment, whether by the time or by the job;

(h) whether or not the work is a part of the regular business of the employer;

(i) whether or not the parties believe they are creating the relation of master and servant; and

(j) whether the principal is or is not in business.

The Restatement (Third) of Agency contains a similar definition, although the wording varies slightly, including abandonment of "servant" in favor of "employee." *See* RESTATEMENT (THIRD) OF AGENCY § 7.07 (3)(a) (2006) ("an employee is an agent whose principal controls or has the right to control the manner and means of the agent's performance of work").

In contrast, the most recent draft of the new Restatement of Employment Law frames the inquiry somewhat differently. It provides that an employment relationship exists whenever a worker acts, at least in part, to serve the interests of the employer; the employer consents to receive the services of the worker; and the worker is not rendering services as an independent business, which means that the worker does not exercise entrepreneurial control over the manner and means of the work. *See* RESTATEMENT (THIRD) OF EMPLOYMENT LAW (Tentative Draft No. 2, April 3, 2009) § 1.01. Although control over the manner and means of the work remains central in this formulation, the test is framed in the negative, namely, that a worker is an employee *unless he or she exerts entrepreneurial control.* The section goes on to define entrepreneurial control as "control over important business decisions, including whether to hire and where to assign assistants, whether to purchase and where to deploy equipment, and whether and when to service other customers." *Id.*

Keep in mind that the ultimate impact of this new Restatement will remain unknown for some time because it has yet to receive final approval from the American

Law Institute ("ALI"), and no jurisdiction has yet to adopt it. Moreover, the very notion of such a Restatement of Employment Law has been criticized as being misconceived, in large part because the field is still evolving and many feel that it is too early to try to "freeze" the law into its present pattern. *See, e.g.*, Kenneth G. Dau-Schmidt, *A Conference on the American Law Institute's Proposed Restatement of Employment Law*, 13 EMP. RTS. & EMP. POL'Y J. 1 (2009); Michael J. Zimmer, *The Restatement of Employment Law Is the Wrong Project*, 13 EMP. RTS. & EMP. POL'Y J. 205 (2009). Nevertheless, as you read this chapter, consider whether such a formulation might change the outcome in any of the cases and, if so, whether it is better or worse than existing approaches.

═══
═══ ## *McCary v. Wade*
═══ *861 So. 2d 358 (Miss. Ct. App. 2003)*

LEE, J.

. . . On August 2, 1999, appellants Jettie McCary and Lillie Fulwiley were riding in a van on their way home from work and were traveling north on Highway 25. The van was being driven by John Isonhood who was employed by Choctaw Maid Farms, the appellants' employer, to transport the workers from the facility to their homes. As Isonhood approached the intersection of Highway 25 and County Road, Grace Mills pulled out from County Road onto Highway 25 traveling south. However, Mills pulled out in front of another driver, Dexter Myrick, who was driving a logging truck. Myrick was forced to hit his breaks [sic] to avoid a collision with Mills, and this forced him into the opposite lane of traffic where he collided with the appellants' northbound van.

McCary incurred approximately $110,000 in related medical expenses and approximately $45,000 in past and future lost wages as a result of her injuries from the collision. She is totally disabled and has significant disfigurement to her lower body. Fulwiley incurred approximately $20,000 in related medical expenses, an estimated $20,000 in future medical expenses and approximately $100,000 in past and future lost wages.

McCary and Fulwiley filed suit against Myrick, Georgia Pacific Corporation, . . . Mills, John Isonhood, Choctaw Maid Farms, Inc., which provided the van transportation, Chris Wade who had contracted with Georgia Pacific for sale of timber, and Wade Land Management which was Chris Wade's company.

A question arose concerning whether or not Myrick was acting as an employee of Wade at the time of the accident and, if so, whether Wade could be held vicariously liable for Myrick's actions. Details of the employment relationship are addressed in more depth in the following discussion.

Discussion . . .

In their motion for summary judgment, Chris Wade and Wade Land Management ("WLM") argued that Myrick was an independent hauler for WLM and, therefore, WLM was not liable to the plaintiffs/appellants via *respondeat superior* for Myrick's negligence in causing the accident.

The general rule is that the employer of an independent contractor has no vicarious liability for the torts of the independent contractor or for the torts of the independent contractor's employees in the performance of the contract. In determining whether a[n] employer-employee or independent contractor relationship existed, especially where third parties are affected, courts are not confined to the terms of the contract, but may look as well to the conduct of the parties. In addition to the general rule . . . we have recognized many "tests" or aspects of a relationship to examine in determining whether a person is an employee or an independent contractor:

> [W]hether the principal master has the power to terminate the contract at will; whether he has the power to fix the price in payment for the work, or vitally controls the manner and time of payment; whether he furnishes the means and appliances for the work; whether he has control of the premises; whether he furnishes the materials upon which the work is done and receives the output thereof, the contractor dealing with no other person in respect to the output; whether he has the right to prescribe and furnish the details of the kind and character of work to be done; whether he has the right to supervise and inspect the working during the course of the employment; whether he has the right to direct the details of the manner in which the work is to be done; whether he has the right to employ and discharge the sub employees and to fix their compensation; and whether he is obliged to pay the wages of said employees.

Miller v. Shell Oil Co., 783 So. 2d 724 (¶11) (Miss. Ct. App. 2000). We look to the facts of this case *de novo* . . . to determine whether Myrick was an independent contractor or an employee of WLM, such that summary judgment was or was not proper in this case.

WLM purchases timber and sells it to wood yards. In 1996, WLM contracted with Georgia Pacific to provide timber, and WLM in turn hired haulers to move the timber, one of whom was Myrick. Myrick and WLM entered into a contract in 1996 whereby Myrick would cut and haul lumber to Georgia Pacific for WLM. Myrick was not subject to any quotas set by WLM concerning delivery amounts, and Georgia Pacific would accept any amount of the specified lumber that Myrick chose to deliver.

In his deposition, which is included in the record, Chris Wade explained that Myrick bought his own timber, cut it, and hauled it all himself, and Wade never knew where or when Myrick was producing any wood until Myrick called him alerting that he had a load of logs to sell. Wade affirmed that "he didn't have to pay a cent" for Myrick's cutting operation and that he only used independent contractors because otherwise he would have to pay for the haulers' trucks and operation costs. Wade explained that to his knowledge Myrick had other contracts with companies to deliver wood, just the same as he had a contract with WLM.

Myrick testified in his deposition that he decided his own work hours, which days he would work, and where he would work. He exclusively made decisions concerning harvest, sorting, loading and transportation of the timber. Myrick stated that he owned all of the equipment needed for his operation, including his two-ton truck which he and his brother exclusively purchased, repaired and maintained, and he had never gotten a loan for his logging business. Myrick testified that on the day of the accident he had left Georgia Pacific and was en route to his home at the time of the collision. Under the previously described test for determining independent contractor status, we find Myrick's relationship with WLM to be that of an independent contractor and not employee/employer. Having so found, we next direct our attention to *Richardson v. APAC-Mississippi, Inc.*, 631 So. 2d 143 (Miss. 1994), which the appellants cite in support of their argument. . . . The appellants direct our attention to *Richardson's* addition of a public policy test to determine liability. The supreme court defined this new test as follows:

> . . . When a contract is made between two parties that as between themselves creates an independent contractor relationship and involves employment generally performed under a simple master/servant or employer/employee relationship, it will be upheld as between the parties. When, however, third parties are adversely affected, this Court will carefully scrutinize the contract to see if public policy should permit the transformation of an ordinarily employer/employee relationship into that of an independent contractor. A necessary condition precedent for the application of this factor, however, is that the party challenging the claimed relationship will be adversely affected, and denied an adequate legal remedy. In the absence of this, the right of parties to contract as they please is a constitutionally-protected right. Conversely, neither of the parties should be permitted to dispute a contractually-created independent contractor relationship between them when to do so adversely affects an injured third party.

Id. (citations omitted). . . . In the present case, Myrick was shown to be bankrupt and without insurance coverage. Thus, the appellants claim that since Myrick was not insured and had no money to compensate them for their injuries, WLM should be made to pay in the interests of public policy.

The Fifth Circuit addressed the *Richardson* case in *McKee v. Brimmer*, 39 F.3d 94 (5th Cir. 1994), . . . and surmised the following:

> The public policy factor from *Richardson* becomes an issue when the relationship between the alleged employer and the alleged employee would "ordinarily" be characterized as that of an employer/employee, but they have a contract which defines their relationship as that of independent contractors. In that case, the court will scrutinize the contract to see if the parties should be allowed to transform an employer/employee relationship into that of an independent contractor. In essence, an employer will not be allowed to escape liability by drafting a contract which labels its employee an independent contractor, but retains employer-like control over him.

Id. (citations omitted). . . . [S]ince the evidence presented shows Myrick was an independent contractor and there is no evidence of any attempt by WLM to control Myrick through written contracts or otherwise, the appellants' public policy argument fails.

In the present case, the *Richardson* public policy test is not applicable because Myrick undeniably was an independent contractor in his work with WLM. . . . We find no confusion as to Myrick's role as working independently of WLM as employer. . . .

≡
≡ ## *Fitzgerald v. Mobil Oil Corporation*
≡ *827 F. Supp. 1301 (E.D. Mich. 1993)*

FEIKENS, District Judge.

Plaintiff [Fitzgerald], a tractor-trailer driver, was injured on the job when he fell from the top of the tanker trailer he used to deliver oil. The trailer was owned by defendant Montgomery Tank Lines, Inc., and leased to Mobil Oil. The tractor was owned by a third party, Jerry Rieger, and also leased to Mobil Oil. Plaintiff was hired to deliver loads of oil from Mobil Oil's Woodhaven Lube Plant and Terminal in Woodhaven, Michigan to various Mobil Oil customers. Plaintiff's Complaint alleges that both defendants negligently provided plaintiff with an unsafe and defective tanker, and that the tanker was not equipped with adequate safety devices.

Mobil Oil's defense is based on the "exclusive remedy provision" of Michigan's Worker's Disability Compensation Act. M.S.A. § 17.237(131). It provides that "[t]he right to the recovery of benefits as provided in this act shall be the employee's exclusive remedy against the employer." Consequently, Mobil Oil's motion turns on whether or not it can be considered plaintiff's employer. Plaintiff denies that Mobil Oil was his employer. . . . Although plaintiff's employment situation was complex and confusing,[1] the facts, when interpreted in light of Michigan precedent, are susceptible of only one inference — Mobil Oil was plaintiff's employer.

Plaintiff was initially hired by Jerry Rieger, the owner and lessor of the tractor plaintiff used to haul loads. But before Rieger would agree to hire him, plaintiff had to pass a road test administered by Mobil Oil at a Mobil Oil facility in Pennsylvania. At the time, plaintiff knew that he was being considered for work involving Mobil Oil, and that if he failed the road test he would not have a job.

Plaintiff telephoned a Mobil dispatcher at least once a day for work assignments. The dispatcher told him where to deliver oil and how much to deliver. Plaintiff also contacted Jerry Rieger on a daily basis; and submitted his paperwork — travel logs, unloading records, fuel and other expense receipts — to Rieger on a weekly basis. Determination of his wages depended on these records. But plaintiff's paycheck was issued by yet another company, TLI, Inc. TLI had a contract with Mobil Oil to provide tractor-trailer drivers for Mobil Oil's use. Mobil reimbursed the company for driver wages and other expenses, including worker's compensation insurance premiums. However, the contract specifically disclaims the existence of an employer/employee relationship between Mobil Oil and TLI-supplied drivers. After his injury, plaintiff received worker's compensation benefits from TLI.

Mobil Oil argues that both TLI and Mobil Oil were plaintiff's employers for purposes of the worker's compensation laws. *Renfroe v. Higgins Rack Coating & Manufacturing Co.*, 169 N.W.2d 326 (Mich. Ct. App. 1969), recognized the "triangular relationship" that exists between a worker, a supplier of temporary workers (or labor broker) and a user of those workers. *Renfroe* concluded that both the labor broker and the end-user are employers of the worker, and therefore protected by the exclusive remedy provision. Plaintiff's situation involves a fourth player, Jerry Rieger. However, Rieger and TLI, in combination, fill the labor broker role. . . .

The relationship between TLI and Mobil Oil does not match this description in all respects. Plaintiff was on long-term assignment to Mobil Oil, and, because of the nature of his job, was not closely supervised by Mobil Oil personnel. As a truck driver, plaintiff was unlikely to be subjected to the same close supervision often associated with factory and office work. This fact arguably decreases the closeness of the relationship between plaintiff and Mobil Oil. On the other hand, the fact that plaintiff was on long-term assignment to Mobil Oil strengthens their relationship. On balance the differences are not enough to alter the outcome.

---

1. In his deposition plaintiff states: "I was totally confused the whole time I was there about who I was working for or who I was getting paid by."

Economic Realities Test

Michigan courts rely on the economic realities test to establish the existence of an employer/employee relationship. . . . The language of a written agreement, such as the one between TLI and Mobil Oil, is not controlling. Furthermore, the same test is used whether asserted by the plaintiff as a sword or by the defendant as a shield.

The economic realities test includes four elements: "(1) control of a worker's duties, (2) the payment of wages, (3) the right to hire and fire and the right to discipline, and (4) the performance of the duties as an integral part of the employer's business towards the accomplishment of a common goal." *Askew v. Macomber*, 247 N.W.2d 288 (Mich. 1976). No single element is controlling; the totality of the circumstances must be considered.

Control. Plaintiff's deposition indicates that he contacted a Mobil Oil dispatcher by phone on a daily basis to obtain work assignments. Those assignments involved hauling oil from Mobil Oil's Woodhaven processing plant and delivering it to Mobil Oil customers. The oil was generally loaded into plaintiff's tanker by Mobil Oil employees and unloaded by plaintiff. Plaintiff kept his truck at Mobil Oil's Woodhaven facility when it was not in use, and hauled exclusively for Mobil Oil. Plaintiff also contacted Mobil Oil when the tanker needed to be washed, to complain about the tanker, and to complain about other Mobil Oil employees.

On the other hand, plaintiff was trained by an individual who appeared to be an employee of Jerry Rieger. He invariably telephoned Rieger after receiving an assignment from Mobil Oil to obtain Rieger's approval. And on at least one occasion plaintiff refused an assignment after Rieger told him not to accept it. Plaintiff delivered his travel logs and other paperwork to Rieger. He contacted Rieger when his tractor needed servicing, and Rieger arranged for repairs.

These facts indicate that plaintiff's job duties were controlled, at least in significant part, by Mobil Oil. . . .

Payment of Wages. Mobil Oil clearly satisfies this element of the economic realities test. [The lease agreement between TLI and Mobil Oil provided that Mobil Oil was liable to TLI for reimbursement of various driver expenses, all wages and benefit payments that TLI made to drivers for services rendered, and Mobil Oil's share of the Social Security taxes, workers' compensation, and federal and state unemployment and liability premiums.] Payment of wages in this indirect fashion was enough to establish the wages element in several Michigan cases.

Right to Hire, Fire, and Discipline. Under the terms of Mobil Oil's contract with TLI it had the right to refuse plaintiff's services. Plaintiff argues that TLI had other customers, and that if Mobil Oil refused his services, he could have worked for another customer. According to plaintiff, only TLI or Jerry Rieger had the power to completely take away his livelihood.

However, the fact remains that plaintiff was hired for a specific job. If Mobil Oil had terminated his services he would have been without an assignment, at least temporarily. The power to stop plaintiff from engaging in the daily tasks he relied on for wages is enough to satisfy the test.

Moreover, approval by Mobil Oil was a condition precedent to plaintiff's hiring. Plaintiff was required to pass a road test administered by Mobil at a Mobil Oil facility in

Pennsylvania before Rieger agreed to hire him. Without Mobil's approval plaintiff would have never been employed by Rieger or TLI.

Performance of Duties as an Integral Part of Employer's Business. As a deliverer of Mobil Oil's product, plaintiff's work constituted an integral part of the company's business. Delivery is an ongoing and necessary function, not a short term or irregular project. Furthermore, although truck drivers are often independent contractors, this is not necessarily the usual or normal arrangement. Mobil Oil satisfies this element of the test as well.

In conclusion, the economic realities of the situation are that Mobil Oil was plaintiff's employer. All of the relevant factors lean heavily in Mobil Oil's favor. Taken as a whole, there can be no doubt that Mobil Oil satisfies the test. As a consequence, Mobil Oil is protected from suit by the exclusive remedy provision of the Worker's Disability Compensation Act. . . .

Plaintiff argues with some force that Mobil Oil has effectively insulated itself from all responsibility for workers. By using a labor broker, Mobil Oil is relieved of direct responsibility for worker's compensation insurance premiums and payment of benefits. Presumably, Mobil Oil obtains other advantages from denying the existence of an employer/employee relationship as well. On the other hand, Mobil Oil escapes the potential tort liability non-employers normally face. Justice Ryan of the Michigan Supreme Court recognized this imbalance of rights in his dissenting opinion in *Farrell v. Dearborn Manufacturing Co.*, 330 N.W.2d 397:

> My colleague's approach suggests that if two companies can divide the attributes of employment equally enough, *both* will be entitled to the "exclusive remedy" bar of the statute, even though only one set of workers' compensation insurance premiums must be paid. In short, my colleague's opinion advertises "two bars for the price of one."

Moreover, from a purely policy perspective, the Court's decision enables a company to insulate itself from the economic consequences of an unsafe workplace. It seems clear that the Legislature contemplated that either total liability or higher workers' compensation insurance rates would provide an economic incentive for every company to care about worker safety. It now appears that the labor broker scheme may be an expedient method of avoiding either type of liability.

However, this was not the prevailing opinion. As a federal judge, I am not in a position to change the law, especially state law. Only the Michigan Legislature can address this inequity. [The court therefore granted Mobil Oil's motion for summary judgment, dismissing it from the case.]

NOTES

1. *Tests for Determining Employee/Independent Contractor Status.* Each court articulates a test for determining whether the worker at issue was an employee or independent contractor. How much do these tests differ from one another? What are the elements of each? Is there a particular element or consideration that appears predominant in both? Which case more closely tracks the common-law approach as reflected in the Restatement of Agency? Why might that be? *Hint:* Consider *why* the common-law test distinguishes between employees and independent contractors and

what is at stake in each case. Now briefly consider whether application of the test set forth in the draft Restatement of Employment Law might alter the outcome in one or both of these cases. If so, would that be a better result in either case?

2. *Disparate Stakes and Outcomes.* In each of these cases, the worker was a truck driver, a firm for whom the worker was performing services was sued as the result of an accident relating to the operation of the vehicle, and the underlying issue the court had to resolve was whether the worker was an employee or an independent contractor of the defendant firm. Yet one employer — WLM — argued that its driver was an independent contractor while the other — Mobil Oil — contended its driver was an employee. Why? In answering this question, consider a key factual difference: The plaintiff in *McCary* was a third party while the plaintiff in *Fitzgerald* was a worker. Interestingly, *both* defendants prevailed, despite both courts' acknowledging counter-vailing public policy concerns. Based on the facts and public policy, did the two courts reach the right results? Would you reach the same conclusion if the facts were identical but the claims were reversed? That is, suppose Myrick had sued WLM in tort for injuries he suffered in the accident and a third-party tort victim had sued Mobil Oil for Fitzgerald's negligence in operating the truck. What would WLM and Mobil Oil have argued in these lawsuits regarding the status of the two workers?

3. *The Role of Private Ordering.* The *Fitzgerald* court found that Fitzgerald was an employee of Mobil Oil although Mobil's contract with TLI specifically disclaimed the existence of an employer/employee relationship between it and TLI-supplied drivers. What role should express contract terms play in determining whether the worker is an employee? In some circumstances, the intent or expectations of the firm and worker are different than the terms stated in the governing contract. If so, which should control? Does it matter who is relying on or disavowing the agreement (i.e., the firm, worker, or third party)? Ironically, the *Fitzgerald* court's willingness to look beyond the contract provision facilitated Mobil's victory in this case, but one might question whether this result really serves the firm's larger interests. Presumably, Mobil structured its arrangements as it did for good reasons, and the economic realities approach in *Fitzgerald* that resulted in the court finding Mobil to be an employer in this case could backfire when Mobil's status arises in another context.

4. *Respondeat Superior.* The doctrine of respondeat superior at issue in *McCary* may be the most important risk allocation doctrine in tort law. It provides that an employer is vicariously (hence strictly) liable for torts committed by its employees within the scope of their employment. *See, e.g.,* RESTATEMENT (SECOND) OF AGENCY § 219(1). As suggested in *McCary*, the doctrine is premised on protecting third parties and the public by extending accountability for workers' tortuous acts to those who exercise significant control over their conduct. By contrast, the tortious conduct of independent contractors generally does not give rise to vicarious liability for the principal. There are some important exceptions to the general rule that principals are not liable for the torts of their independent contractors, such as where the principal intended the violations, the principal was under a special duty to protect others from harm, or the principal's duty was, for one of various reasons, nondelegable to third parties. *See, e.g., id.* § 212, § 214, and § 219(2); *see also American Telephone & Telegraph Company v. Winback & Conserve Program,* 42 F.3d 1421, 1435 (3d Cir. 1994) (stating a principal is liable if she authorized or directed the agent's injurious act or intended the result); *Wiggs v. City of Phoenix,* 10 P.3d 625, 628 (Ariz. 2000) (finding a principal cannot avoid liability by delegating performance of a "special duty" to an independent contractor). Nevertheless, because employees generate

tort liability risks under the doctrine of respondeat superior while independent contractors usually do not, the doctrine provides a strong incentive for businesses to outsource to independent firms or individuals, particularly those activities that pose a high risk to the public. *See, e.g.*, Eric W. Orts, *Shirking and Sharking: A Legal Theory of the Firm*, 16 YALE L. & POL'Y REV. 265, 305 (1998); Deanne M. Mosley & William C. Walter, *The Significance of the Classification of Employment Relationships in Determining Exposure to Liability*, 67 MISS. L. J. 613, 613-15 (1998). *But cf.* Richard R.W. Brooks, *Liability and Organizational Choice*, 45 J.L. & ECON. 91 (2002) (arguing that keeping some risky activities within the firm may be economically advantageous).

5. *Workers' Compensation.* Unlike respondeat superior liability, workers' compensation law creates potentially conflicting incentives for firms with regard to employee/independent contractor status. As discussed in Chapter 5, workers' compensation regimes are premised on the trade-off of greater coverage but lower benefits: Employers pay premiums into a disability fund or insurance program from which employees injured on the job — regardless of fault — receive a defined amount of compensation for medical expenses and for lost wages while they are disabled and unable to work; in exchange, the workers' compensation program is the employees' exclusive remedial scheme for workplace injuries, thereby shielding the employer from more costly tort liability. ARTHUR A. LARSON & LEX K. LARSON, WORKERS' COMPENSATION LAW §§ 1.01, 100.01 (Matthew Bender & Co., Inc., 2010). Thus, when a worker is injured on the job, firms generally have an incentive to claim that the worker is an employee to preclude the possibility of tort liability. On the other hand, because workers' compensation coverage is no-fault and otherwise broader than tort liability, firms occasionally claim that a worker is an independent contractor and not entitled to coverage, particularly when the employee would have a weak tort claim against the firm. *See, e.g.*, *Chouteau v. Netco Const.*, 132 S.W.3d 328 (Mo. Ct. App. 2004); *Roads West, Inc. v. Austin*, 91 P.3d 81 (Okla. Civ. App. 2003); Dean J. Haas, *Falling Down on the Job: Workers' Compensation Shifts from a No-Fault to a Worker-Fault Paradigm*, 79 N.D. L. REV. 203, 234 (2003). In addition, by classifying workers as independent contractors, the firm may avoid paying compensation insurance premiums for those individuals during their employment. How does this information shed light on Mobil's intentions in setting up its relationship with Fitzgerald?

6. *Legal Advantages of Common-Law "Employee" Status for Workers.* Fitzgerald provides one example of a worker's status as an employee under a statutory regime — workers' compensation — harming the worker's interests. Yet, in many other circumstances, workers have significant legal incentives to be classified as employees rather than independent contractors. For example, most of the federal statutory protections for workers studied in this course cover only "employees." These include federal labor, wage, hour, and benefit protections; *see, e.g.*, Labor Management Relations Act of 1947, 29 U.S.C. §152(2)-(3) (2006); National Labor Relations Act, 29 U.S.C. §158(b)(4)(i) (2006); Employee Retirement and Income Security Act, 29 U.S.C. §1002 (5)-(6) (2006) ("ERISA"); Fair Labor Standards Act of 1938, 29 U.S.C. §201(2) (2006); Family Medical Leave Act of 1993, 29 U.S.C. §2611(3) (2006), as well as most federal prohibitions on status discrimination, *see, e.g.*, Age Discrimination in Employment Act of 1967, 29 U.S.C. §630(f) (2006); Civil Rights Act of 1964, Title VII, 42 U.S.C. §2000e(f) (2006); Americans with Disabilities Act of 1990, 42 U.S.C. §12111(4) (2006). One notable exception is 42 U.S.C. §1981, which prohibits race and alienage discrimination in most contractual relations. *See Runyon v. McCrary*, 427 U.S. 160 (1976).

7. *Defining "Employee" for Statutory Purposes.* In virtually all of the foregoing statutes, however, Congress failed to define meaningfully "employee" or "employer," offering only the unhelpful and circular statement that an "employee" is "an individual employed by an employer." Thus, in determining the meaning of "employee" and "employer" in these regimes, the Supreme Court has often held that Congress intended to describe the master-servant relationship as understood by common-law agency doctrine. *See, e.g., Nationwide Mut. Ins. Co. v. Darden,* 503 U.S. 318, 322-23 (1992) (ERISA); *Cmty. for Creative Non-Violence v. Reid,* 490 U.S. 730, 739-40 (1989) (Copyright Act). Regulatory definitions of "employee" from other areas, such as tax law, likewise offer variations on the common law definition.

Some courts seeking to determine worker status for purposes of social welfare legislation such as the Fair Labor Standards Act ("FLSA")—which provides wage and hour protections by specifying a minimum wage and requirements for overtime pay—and some state workers' compensation laws, have taken a somewhat more inclusive approach. These courts suggest that the definition of employee and employer serve the broad remedial purposes of the statute and therefore expand the common-law definition by, among other things, focusing on worker dependence. This inquiry is sometimes referred to as the "economic realities test"—the term used by the *Fitzgerald* court. *See, e.g., Bartels v. Birmingham,* 332 U.S. 126, 130 (1947); *Robincheaux v. Radcliff Material, Inc.,* 697 F.2d 662 (5th Cir. 1983); *Real v. Driscoll Strawberry Assoc., Inc.,* 603 F.2d 748 (9th Cir. 1979). Of course, *Fitzgerald* is somewhat ironic, since the court utilizes this expanded test designed to benefit workers to deny Fitzgerald's claim. However, the multifactored tests that the courts adopt, including those that seek to determine status based on so-called "economic reality," tend to use factors that, like the common law, emphasize employer control along with other considerations. *See Bartels,* 332 U.S. at 130 ("[P]ermanency of the relation, the skill required, the investment in the facilities for work and opportunities for profit or loss from the activities were also factors that should enter into judicial determination as to the coverage of the Social Security Act."); *Secretary of Labor v. Lauritzen,* 835 F.2d 1529, 1534 (7th Cir. 1987); RESTATEMENT (THIRD) OF EMPLOYMENT LAW (Tentative Draft No. 2, April 3, 2009) § 1.01 cmt. a (suggesting that courts that have relied on the common-law and economic realities approaches have tended to utilize the same factors and reach the same results); *see also Oestman v. National Farmers Union Ins. Co.,* 958 F.2d 303, 305 (10th Cir. 1992) (suggesting a "hybrid" approach that considers both control and dependence). Indeed, some courts deny any substantive difference between the tests. *See, e.g., Murray v. Principal Fin. Group, Inc.,* 613 F.3d 943, 945 (9th Cir. 2010) (clarifying that "there is no functional difference" between the tests of common-law control, economic realities, and a so-called hybrid of the two).

In sum, the common-law approach and related multifactored inquiries to distinguish employees from other types of workers continue to dominate. This is true despite the significant growth in employment statutes over the last half century. Thus, in most circumstances, to enjoy statutory labor and employment protections, workers must be common-law "employees."

8. *Legal Advantages of Employment Relationships for Firms.* The doctrine of respondeat superior and the legal protections for employees discussed in Note 6 may provide strong incentives for firms to contract with third parties for services and avoid direct employment relationships. As *Fitzgerald* suggests, workers' compensation laws may offer a countervailing incentive to hire workers as employees rather than independent contractors, at least in some circumstances.

In addition, firms may prefer employment over other statuses because employees may owe the firm more demanding fiduciary duties. As will be discussed in Chapter 8, the reach and content of such duties are controversial. Nevertheless, they may be particularly important from the firm's perspective when it is vulnerable to worker attempts to usurp its opportunities or good will or otherwise compete with it for business.

For example, in *Midwest Ink Co. v. Graphic Ink Systems*, No. 98 C 7822 2003 WL 360089 (N.D. Ill. Feb. 18, 2003), Midwest Ink brought a breach of fiduciary duty claim against one of its former salesmen, Dave Scott, and Scott's new firm, Graphic Ink Systems. Midwest Ink argued that, during his tenure at Midwest, Scott was an employee, and as such, owed fiduciary duties to the firm. Among these duties is the duty of loyalty, which includes the duty not to compete with the employer or usurp the employer's business opportunities while employed. Midwest Ink submitted evidence that, during Scott's tenure on its sales force, he had formed Graphic Ink Systems with his wife and had solicited and ultimately lured away Midwest Ink customers. Scott denied that he had been an employee and, hence, had owed such duties.

The court held that whether Scott was an employee or independent contractor was dispositive on the issue of whether he owed Midwest Ink a duty not to compete with the firm. Despite the different stakes, the court applied a common-law test similar to the rules announced in *McCary* and *Fitzgerald*. In *Midwest Ink*, however, the court found circumstances strongly suggesting both independent contractor and employee status. For example, the facts suggesting Scott was an independent contractor included the following:

- His control of his daily sales activity
- His independence in terms of hours worked and vacation time taken
- His lack of formal training
- His responsibility for paying his own expenses from sales calls
- Midwest Ink's withholding no taxes from his paychecks and providing him with a 1099 form (normally used for independent contractors)
- His pay being based exclusively on sales commissions

Other factors suggested employee status, including the following:

- Midwest Ink's providing Scott an office, office equipment, and car
- Its control of the prices he charged
- Its withholding Federal Insurance Contributions Act ("FICA") tax from his pay and providing health insurance to him
- The integral part that Scott's sales activities played in the business
- The fact that Scott worked exclusively for Midwest Ink for the first three years of his tenure and listed himself as an employee on tax returns

In light of the conflicting evidence, the court denied Midwest Ink's motion for summary judgment, finding disputed issues of fact with regard to Scott's status. *See Midwest Ink Co.* at *4-6. Imagine you were the factfinder. How would you rule? Would Scott's conduct and Midwest Ink's vulnerability affect your decision? Should it?

Given the facts and lack of a clear resolution of the issue of Scott's status, one wonders whether either Midwest Ink or Scott could have done a better job structuring the relationship to increase the probability of a favorable outcome or, in the alternative, could have taken other steps to protect their interests. With that in mind, turn to the following case. As you read, consider how a firm with a strong incentive to have workers treated as employees for certain purposes might protect its interests even without assurance of a judicial finding of an employment relationship. Similarly, consider the circumstances in which workers may prefer to be independent contractors rather than employees, and whether — and how — if they still may be found to be employees, they might achieve at least some of the benefits of independent contractor status.

Natkin v. Winfrey
111 F. Supp. 2d 1003 (N.D. Ill. 2000)

CASTILLO, District Judge.

This case is about eleven photographs of Oprah Winfrey taken by Plaintiffs Paul Natkin and Stephen Green on the set of her (rather) well-known television show. The photographs were subsequently published in Winfrey's book *Make the Connection*, co-authored with Bob Greene and published in 1996 by Buena Vista Books under the name Hyperion, without [Natkin's or Green's] permission. That publication resulted in this copyright infringement action and various other causes of action under the Lanham Act and Illinois state law. The defendants counterclaim seeking a declaration of rights.

. . . At base, we must decide whether either side has definitively established ownership of the copyrights to the photographs: To succeed on their motion, Natkin and Green must show that they own the copyrights to the exclusion of the defendants. . . . For the reasons that follow, we conclude that there is no genuine issue that the defendants authored the photographs, either solely or jointly, but that a triable issue exists as to whether the defendants used the pictures pursuant to a valid license. . . .

Background

Natkin and Green are both professional "live event" photographers. Natkin owns (and owned during the relevant times) a private photography studio, Photo Reserve, Inc., and throughout the relevant time period he photographed concerts, live television broadcasts, movie sets, rock video productions, and album/CD covers. Green, since 1982, has been employed by the Chicago Cubs baseball organization, but also engages in freelance photography for others, such as the organizers of the World Series and NBA playoff games.

Natkin photographed *The Oprah Winfrey Show* between 1986 and 1993; Green worked on the show from 1989 to 1996. The photos at issue here were taken between 1988 and 1995. Natkin and Green primarily shot pictures of the show while it was being taped live in the Chicago studio. On occasion, however, when the show was broadcast from another location, they traveled with the show to take pictures. Additionally, Natkin and Green took posed photographs of Winfrey, usually with her more famous guests, either at the show's studio or their own studios. Both men used their own camera equipment and lenses, brought additional equipment (such as lights and backdrops) when taking posed shots, chose the appropriate film, and usually processed the film themselves. The record contains conflicting evidence about who arranged to process the film when Natkin and Green did not perform that task, which company processed the film, and in all cases who stored the negatives.

When photographing the live show, Natkin and Green had no control over the position or appearance of their subjects (i.e., Winfrey and her guests, the audience, etc.), the layout and design of the sets, or even the lighting of the set — Harpo [Winfrey's production firm and one of the defendants in the case] prohibited Natkin and Green from using flash bulbs or any other light source not provided by the studio. Additionally, during live taping of the show, Natkin and Green were restricted to certain locations — they were allowed to move freely about the set only during commercial breaks. But, as to creating the photographs, Natkin and Green had complete discretion over the technical aspects of the shoot: They chose which cameras, lenses, and film to use; the appropriate shutter speed, aperture settings, and timing for the shots; and how to frame the images.

During the relevant times, neither Natkin nor Green worked pursuant to a written agreement. Both men billed Harpo Productions a flat fee for each show they photographed and for any related expenses, including such items as parking and film. Harpo never withheld federal income taxes, FICA, or state income taxes from their payments to Natkin and Green and reported those payments to the IRS on 1099 forms (rather than W-2 forms) as "nonemployee compensation." Additionally, Harpo did not provide health or life insurance, pension benefits, or paid vacation to either Natkin or Green, and both men purchased the insurance for their equipment. Neither photographer was ever given a copy of the Harpo employee manual, but both received paid parking, access to the company cafeteria, Harpo security, and invitations to Harpo staff functions. Additionally, both were referred to, and referred to themselves as, staff photographers for the show. When Natkin or Green was unable to photograph a show due to other commitments, they hired the substitute photographer and billed Harpo.

Green's invoices each contained the following provision: "*Terms/Conditions:* One time, non exclusive reproduction rights to the photographs listed above, solely for the uses and specifications indicated. . . . Acceptance of this submission constitutes acceptance of these terms." . . . Natkin's invoices explicitly reserved his copyright to the invoiced photos: "All photos remain the property of, and copyrights remain with, Photo Reserve Inc." Natkin and Green contend that they were freelance photographers that were hired by Harpo and Winfrey as independent contractors to take pictures for publicity purposes only. They claim they are the sole authors of the photographs and, having never transferred their copyrights, are the sole owners of the rights to the pictures. Additionally, Natkin and Green maintain that the only possible license Harpo or Winfrey could have obtained was an oral, non-exclusive license to use the photos for publicity purposes. Thus, according to Natkin and Green, publication of the photos in *Make the Connection* infringed their copyrights.

The defendants, on the other hand, contend that Harpo and Winfrey are the authors of the pictures and thus own the copyrights to them. The defendants assert that Natkin and Green were employees of Harpo and that the pictures were taken within the scope of their employment. Alternatively, they argue that Harpo and Winfrey are joint authors of the photographs because they controlled the vast majority of the picture elements. Finally, as to the infringement claim, the defendants allege that their publication of the pictures in the book was pursuant to a valid license. . . .

I. Copyright Infringement Claims

To establish copyright infringement, Natkin and Green must demonstrate that they own the copyrights to the photographs. Under the Copyright Act, ownership of a copyright "vests initially in the author or authors of the work." Usually, the author of a work is "the person who translates an idea into a fixed, tangible expression entitled to copyright protection." *Community for Creative Non-Violence v. Reid*, 490 U.S. 730, 737 (1989). Under normal circumstances, a photographer is the author of his or her photographs. But, as with any general rule, exceptions exist. Two specific exceptions are relevant to this case: the "work made for hire" and "joint work" exceptions.

A. *Works Made for Hire*

Works made for hire are "authored" by the hiring party, and the "initial owner of the copyright is not the creator of the work but the employer or the party that commissioned the work." A work made for hire is "(1) a work prepared by an employee within the scope of his or her employment; or (2) a work specially ordered or commissioned . . . if the parties expressly agree in a written instrument signed by them that the work shall be considered a work made for hire." 17 U.S.C. §101. The defendants concede that they do not have a written "work made for hire" agreement with either Natkin or Green covering the eleven photographs. Instead, they argue that Natkin and Green were Harpo employees, as opposed to independent contractors, when they took the pictures.

The Supreme Court has set forth a nonexhaustive, thirteen-factor test for determining whether a creator is an employee within the meaning of the Copyright Act's work made for hire provision. The *Reid* factors are

> the hiring party's right to control the manner and means by which the product is accomplished[;] . . . the skill required; the source of the instrumentalities and tools; the location of the work; the duration of the relationship between the parties; whether the hiring party has the right to assign additional projects to the hired party; the extent of the hired party's discretion over when and how long to work; the method of payments; the hired party's role in hiring and paying assistants; whether the work is part of the regular business of the hiring party; whether the hiring party is in business; the provision of employee benefits; and the tax treatment of the hired party.

Additionally, *Reid* instructs courts to use general common law agency principles to analyze whether the author of a work for hire is an independent contractor or an employee.

Applying the *Reid* factors to our circumstances demonstrates that Natkin and Green were not Harpo employees. Both men were highly skilled professionals specializing in live-action photography; both used (and insured) their own equipment; and both exercised discretion in hiring substitute photographers when they themselves were unavailable and paid those substitutes. Most importantly, neither photographer was ever treated like an employee in terms of compensation, benefits, and taxes: Natkin and Green, via their companies, billed Harpo for their services and expenses, they did not receive regular paychecks or salary; they received none of the employee benefits traditionally associated with employee status, such as health insurance, life insurance, and paid vacation;[5] and Harpo never withheld any payroll taxes on behalf of the photographers.

Further, Harpo's IRS reports describe the payments to Green and Natkin as "nonemployee compensation." We believe this factor alone would outweigh those few factors, discussed below, that favor the defendants' position. Harpo may not obtain the benefits associated with hiring an independent contractor and, at the same time, enjoy the advantages of treating that person as an employee; it must choose. Here, as to Natkin and Green, Harpo chose the independent contractor route and cannot now change its position to reap a different benefit it probably had not considered when making its choice (i.e., ownership of the photographs).

The only factors clearly favoring the defendants are that the defendants are engaged in business and the duration of the parties' relationship. That Harpo is a business and that Green and Natkin worked for Harpo over an extended period of time (seven years each) doesn't come close to overriding the impact of the factors favoring the photographers' status as independent contractors. Moreover, that Natkin and Green were referred to as "staff photographers" carries very little weight.

The remaining factors are either inconclusive or add insignificant weight in favor of either party's position. For example, all of the parties exercised control over the manner and means of production to some extent: Harpo controlled the appearance of Winfrey and her guests, the sets, and the lighting, while Natkin and Green controlled the technical aspects of taking the photographs (i.e., lenses, film speed, etc.) and, ultimately, the image on the photographs. However, because the task was to create photographs, this factor weighs slightly in favor of independent contractor status. In any event, Harpo's control of the product here resembles the defendants' control over the statue at issue in *Reid*, where the Supreme Court concluded the artist was an independent contractor. . . .

Finally, the parties vigorously contest whether "the work is part of [Harpo's] regular business." Natkin and Green contend that the defendants are in the business of producing a television show, not taking pictures of the show, whereas the defendants maintain that they are in the business of promoting Oprah Winfrey, which includes taking photographs of her on the show. Even assuming this factor weighs in favor of the defendants' position, Harpo's treatment of Natkin and Green as independent contractors in terms of pay, taxes, and benefits; the photographers' use of their own equipment, judgment, and expertise; and that the relationship was technically between Harpo and the photographers' companies definitively establishes that Natkin and Green were independent contractors.

On the basis of the record before us, we conclude there is no genuine issue that Natkin and Green were ever Harpo employees. They were not. Harpo hired Natkin and Green as independent contractors, and they continued in that capacity during their tenures with the show. Thus, Harpo must produce a written work made for hire agreement signed by both sides to successfully claim exclusive ownership of the copyrights to these photographs. Harpo does not have such a document. Consequently, we grant Natkin and Green's motion for partial summary judgment on the work made for hire issue.

---

5. The defendants' argument that staff parking, security on the set, and invitations to Harpo staff functions are employee benefits provided to Natkin and Green that weigh in favor of their employee status is unavailing, particularly in the face of the utter lack of any employee benefit normally associated with one's status as an employee.

[The court went on to grant summary judgment denying defendants' claim that the photographs were a "joint work" of them and Natkin and Green, but denied summary judgment on defendants' claim that they had a license to publish the photographs.]

NOTES

1. *Conflicting Legal Incentives and Trying to Have It Both Ways.* You will learn more about the growing implications of employment on intellectual property rights (including copyrights) and other workplace intangibles in Chapter 8. Nevertheless, by now you have seen some of the considerations that influence a firm's decision to hire employees versus independent contractors, as well as the benefits and disadvantages of these two relationships for workers. These incentives may conflict depending on the context, and such a conflict is apparent in *Fitzgerald, Natkin,* and *Midwest Ink.* Of course, decisions about the structure of a relationship are typically made at the point of hire, before the circumstances that might give rise to a dispute are known. Does this give firms a reason to be intentionally vague about the status of their workforce? *Natkin* suggests that one must take the bitter with the sweet: "Harpo may not obtain the benefits associated with hiring an independent contractor and, at the same time, enjoy the advantages of treating that person as an employee; it must choose." On the other hand, the *Fitzgerald* court was willing to look beyond Mobil Oil's express disclaimer of an employer/employee relationship.

And at least some workers have similarly conflicting incentives. For example, Scott, the worker in *Midwest Ink*, bargained for several terms consistent with an employment relationship, including health care benefits, an office, and a car, and he even listed himself as an "employee" on his tax returns. He then argued during litigation that he was an independent contractor. Should he be allowed to have it both ways?

In a famous case litigated in the 1990s, workers originally hired by Microsoft Corporation to perform various technical services — including editing, proofreading, and testing — claimed that they were employees entitled to take advantage (retroactively) of the firm's lucrative profit sharing plans, even though they had signed agreements expressly stating that they were "independent contractors" not entitled to participate. *See Vizcaino v. Microsoft Corporation*, 120 F.3d 1006 (9th Cir. 1997) (en banc). Of course, Microsoft had various incentives to classify the workers originally as independent contractors, including avoiding a number of tax obligations. But the workers also arguably benefited from this arrangement since they did not have taxes and other amounts withheld from their paychecks. Indeed, the workers did not complain about their status or their exclusion from the plans until after the Internal Revenue Service ("IRS") determined, applying its own variation of the common-law test in a separate dispute with Microsoft, that they were employees for tax purposes. After a long series of twists and turns, the workers achieved a partial victory, and Microsoft agreed to pay the class $97 million. *See Employee Benefits — Contingent Workforce: Microsoft to Pay $97 Million to Settle Temporary Workers' Class Action Lawsuits*, 69 U.S.L.W. 2363 (Dec. 19, 2000).

As in *Midwest Ink*, the parties in *Microsoft* wanted to have it both ways: Microsoft wanted to exercise fairly exacting control over workers, but wanted them treated as independent contractors for various reasons; the workers seemingly benefited in some ways from this arrangement, but later wanted to be treated as employees for other purposes. The difference is that the relationship in *Microsoft* had not been left ambiguous since the parties had expressly agreed up front that the workers were independent contractors. Should the workers have been held to the terms to which they initially agreed, just as Harpo Productions was in *Natkin*? What might justify the different outcome? Note that, whether the terms to which the parties had initially agreed were enforced or not, the prevailing party in *Microsoft* was going to have succeeded in having it both ways, at least to some extent.

2. *Contracting to Have It Both Ways.* The last question addresses again the core issue of what role contract or party intent or expectations should play in defining the nature of the relationship between worker and firm. Now take this inquiry one step further. Suppose that, rather than leaving aspects of the relationship vague, an agreement provides unambiguously that a worker is an employee for purposes of workers' compensation and intellectual property laws, but an independent contractor for all other purposes. Should a court enforce the agreement, or are there reasons the law ought not to permit the parties to define their relationship in this way? To what extent do the stakes — that is, what and whose interest(s) the underlying legal doctrine is designed to protect — matter, if at all?

3. *Protecting Interests Despite Employee/Independent Contractor Status.* Although there are limits on firms' ability to disclaim employment status, parties can contract in some circumstances to avoid the default consequences of that relationship. For example, assuming the workers in *Natkin* and *Midwest Ink* were independent contractors, how might the firms have still protected their interests? If Harpo Productions could have protected its rights in the photographs and Midwest Ink could have protected itself against Scott's competitive conduct regardless of employee/independent contractor status, then are these cases simply examples of poor planning?

In fact, not all consequences of relationship status may be altered or eliminated by contract. For example, an independent contractor cannot bargain for protection under federal antidiscrimination laws. The worker may bargain for some similar protections, for example, a just-cause term that explicitly or implicitly prohibits termination based on age, race, or sex, but that would not enable her to sue under the federal statutes. Likewise, once a firm is found to be a covered employer, it cannot bargain its way out of federal prohibitions on status discrimination. See Chapters 9 and 10. Nor can employers or employees waive the wage and hour requirements of the FLSA, via contract or otherwise. See Chapter 11. And, obviously, many third parties (including tort victims) will have no opportunity to contract around the legal implications of a worker's employment status. Thus, although private ordering can virtually eliminate the legal consequences of employment status in some contexts and ameliorate them in others, the status of the relationship still has enormous implications.

4. *Worker Status and Socioeconomic Considerations.* Distinctions that reflect the socioeconomic class of workers — skilled and unskilled, managerial and nonmanagerial, white collar and blue collar, permanent and temporary — pervade employment law and policy discussions. Consider the differences between the workers in *McCary* and *Fitzgerald* as compared to *Natkin* and *Midwest Ink*, and how the benefits and costs of employment status align with the workers' socioeconomic status in those cases. On balance, most workers, and particularly lower-skilled workers, probably would choose employee status over being an independent contractor or a worker hired through an independent supplier of labor. This is not simply because of the legal protections described above but also because regular employees tend to have greater job, hour, and wage stability, and better benefits. On the other hand, workers with skills or knowledge in high demand may benefit (personally, professionally, and economically) from the greater control and flexibility independent contractor status may afford. Indeed, workers with creative skills like the photographers in *Natkin* and those with established customer relationships like the salesperson in *Midwest Ink* may have incentives to retain as much independence as possible. The workers in *Microsoft* might fall somewhere in the middle, since they have technical skills but not highly valuable talents or customer connections.

Given the differing market value, bargaining power, and vulnerabilities of such workers, should the role of contract in determining worker status also vary by workers' socioeconomic class? In which circumstances would a firm's "having it both ways" be more troublesome? Do the courts agree?

5. *Other Costs of Employment for Potential Employers.* As we have seen, a firm often has strong employment-law-related reasons to avoid hiring "employees." Yet other regulatory regimes create further incentives to hire independent contractors or outsource labor to independent subcontracting firms. As the *Microsoft* case suggests, one is the avoidance of employment-related tax withholding and payment requirements, including income, FICA, and unemployment taxes. Indeed, firm avoidance of such obligations through "misclassification" of workers as independent contractors costs federal and state governments billions of dollars in tax revenue each year, and recently has led to enhanced enforcement efforts as well as some high-profile disputes. *See, e.g.,* LINDA H. DONAHUE ET AL., THE COST OF WORKER MISCLASSIFICATION IN NEW YORK STATE (Feb. 2007), *available at* http://digitalcommons.ilr.cornell.edu/cgi/viewcontent.cgi?article=1009&context=reports (finding that misclassification of workers as independent contractors in New York has a significant adverse impact on state and federal tax revenues); Steven Greenhouse, *U.S. Cracks Down on "Contractors" as a Tax Dodge,* N.Y. TIMES, Feb. 17, 2010, at A1; Greg Morcroft, *IRS Orders FedEx to Pay $319 Mln,* MARKETWATCH (December 22, 2007), *available at* http://www.marketwatch.com/news/story/irs-orders-fedex-pay319/story.aspx?guid=%7B4270B177-25A2-4939-8535-A3C3749F7AEB%7D.

Another such regime is the Immigration Reform and Control Act of 1986 ("IRCA"), 8 U.S.C. §§ 1324a et seq. (2006). The Act prohibits employers from knowingly hiring or retaining workers who are "unauthorized aliens." It also requires employers to examine specific documents that establish worker identity and authorization to work in the United States. Hired workers, in turn, must provide the documentation required and also attest in writing (on Form I-9) that they are a U.S. citizen, an alien lawfully admitted to permanent residence, or an alien otherwise authorized to work. The employer must retain the Form I-9 and make it available for inspection by the Immigration and Naturalization Service.

By outsourcing to a labor contractor, a firm can reduce the risk of violating IRCA (it remains liable only if it knows a worker is unauthorized), avoid compliance costs, and, often at the same time, reduce labor costs. Unlike the legal protections for employees described above, at least some workers — those that are in the country illegally or at least not authorized to work here — have strong incentives to participate in this arrangement when, as is often the case in certain industries, the subcontracting firm is less likely to demand or scrutinize documentation. *See, e.g.,* John A. Pearce II, *The Dangerous Intersection of Independent Contractor Law and the Immigration Reform and Control Act: The Impact of the Wal-Mart Settlement,* 10 LEWIS & CLARK L. REV. 597 (2006); Steven Greenhouse, *Wal-Mart Raids by U.S. Aimed at Illegal Aliens,* N.Y. TIMES,

Oct. 24, 2003, at A1. As discussed below, however, the downside for these workers is that such subcontracting firms may also be less likely to comply with other legal mandates, including wage and hour laws, and, as undocumented workers, they may be functionally unable to vindicate these rights. *See* Steven Greenhouse, *Among Janitors, Labor Violations Go with the Job*, N.Y. TIMES, July 13, 2005, at A1.

6. *Why Are There Still So Many Employees?* Despite the many forgoing disincentives, firms and government agencies may have nonlegal incentives to hire workers as employees. Among these are worker preferences for employment, which matter in competitive markets for labor; economies of scale and other efficiencies; the productivity-enhancing or synergistic effects of intra-firm interaction; greater retention of sensitive or valuable information or techniques; and worker morale and a heightened sense of ownership over firm objectives.

But perhaps the most important overarching reason for choosing to employ workers rather than outsource or contract with independents is to exercise greater control over worker activities. Control over the enterprise — over the various aspects of the creation, production, marketing, sale, and/or distribution of the goods, services, and information the firm or agency provides — has enormous value. When control over work details or daily affairs is less valuable, for example, where work activities require few skills or no particularized training or where sufficient quality can be maintained without close supervision, outsourcing to independent workers or firms may be an attractive option (particularly when such outsourcing reduces costs). Yet when the exercise of more exacting control is perceived as necessary to maintain quality or content, preserve confidentiality, retain good will, ensure coordination between components of the enterprise, or reduce business or legal risks, hiring workers as employees may be preferable.

7. *Control and the Limits of Planning.* The centrality of control in the stakes of employment should now be apparent. Recall the cases we have seen so far: Although each articulates a slightly different test or standard for determining whether one is an employee or independent contractor, *all focus on the level of firm control over the activities of the worker.* Each test includes one or more factors that mention control explicitly, and most other factors address aspects of control, including supervisory authority, the power to terminate, and dominion over tools, tasks, the workspace, etc. This means that party expectations regarding the nature of the relationship, whether embodied in an agreement or not, often will not be dispositive in the face of countervailing facts about who exercises control over the worker's performance. Again, the *Microsoft* case provides an example. Microsoft and the workers expressly agreed that the workers were independent contractors, yet, in practice, Microsoft treated them much like its ordinary employees — that is, it integrated them into its regular workforce and exercised significant control over their work. This resulted in the IRS's determination and Microsoft's later concession in the litigation with the workers that they were in fact "employees" for legal purposes. *See Vizcaino*, 120 F.3d, at 1008-10. Thus, although there are strong legal incentives for firms to avoid employer status, the need for control is a key incentive for employing workers rather than outsourcing. As the cases suggest, this tension between firm incentives to exercise control and incentives to avoid the legal consequences of employment creates difficult planning challenges. It also accounts for many of the thousands of cases addressing independent contractor/employee status.

8. *The Common-Law Approach Critiqued.* The common-law approach to determining employment status across areas of employment regulation is problematic for a number of reasons. First, as the cases above illustrate, the test and its derivatives are highly fact-intensive and therefore often create uncertainties regarding the relationship. These uncertainties may impose real costs on both workers and firms: They increase ex ante planning and risk management costs and ex post costs, including the costs of litigation. Indeed, this lack of predictability may be particularly problematic for workers who have legitimate expectations — e.g., of workers' compensation coverage for workplace injuries — which ultimately are defeated ex post.

However, one should consider the counterargument: While bright-line rules offer greater predictability, there may be no bright line to draw, and thus, any such rule may suffer from over- or underinclusiveness. Having reviewed the material, isn't it clear that there is no phenomenon we can label "employment," but rather that the law pastes the term on situations in which it wants particular results to follow (or denies that label in situations in which other results are more desirable)? In addition, unless it is well calibrated to serve the remedial or other purposes of the underlying employment doctrine, a clearer but less fact-intensive rule may defeat these purposes; for example, if employment status were determined by the parties' agreement or firm-worker intent alone, firms often would be able to avoid altogether the strictures of wage and hour, and antidiscrimination laws.

A second, frequent criticism of the common-law test is that it was originally intended to draw a distinction between employees and independent contractors only for determining whether the worker's principal is liable under the doctrine of respondeat superior to a third party harmed by the workers' tortious conduct. Indeed, this is why the level of control is so central in the analysis: Tort and agency law seek to link legal accountability with control. Yet other forms of employment regulation serve different ends. Because the regimes discussed in this book — e.g., wage and hour protections, antidiscrimination laws, and whistleblower protections — advance social policies separate and distinct from the ends that respondeat superior was designed to serve, the common-law definition is ill-suited to determine who is subject to such regulation. *See, e.g.,* Steven F. Befort, *Revisiting the Black Hole of Workplace Regulation: A Historical and Comparative Perspective of Contingent Work,* 24 BERKELEY J. EMP. & LAB. L. 153, 168 (2003); Dennis R. Nolan et al., *Working Group on Chapter 1 of the Proposed Restatement of Employment Law: Existence of Employment Relationship,* 13 EMP. RTS. & EMP. POL'Y 43 (2009); Lewis L. Maltby & David C. Yamada, *Beyond "Economic Realities": The Case for Amending Federal Employment Discrimination Laws to Include Independent Contractors,* 38 B.C. L. REV. 239, 241 (1997).

In his concurrence in a case in which the Seventh Circuit held that migrant agriculture workers hired to pick cucumbers are "employees" under the FLSA and, hence, entitled to minimum wage protection, Judge Easterbrook offers such a critique:

> [The independent contractor doctrine] is a branch of tort law, designed to identify who is answerable for a wrong (and therefore, indirectly, to determine who must take care to prevent injuries). To say "X is an independent contractor" is to say that the chain of vicarious liability runs from X's employees to X but stops there. . . . All the details of the common law independent contractor doctrine having to do with the right to control the work are addressed to identifying the best monitor and precaution-taker. . . . The reasons for blocking vicarious liability at a particular point have nothing to do with the functions of the FLSA.

Secretary of Labor v. Lauritzen, 835 F.2d 1529, 1544-45 (7th Cir. 1987) (Easterbrook, J., concurring). What then should be the test for employee status under the FLSA? Judge Easterbrook suggests that the inquiry ought to reflect the purposes of the

FLSA and that, thus, the statute should cover all workers (common-law "employees" or not) with few or no skills — those "who possess *only* dedication, honesty, and good health." *Id.* at 145. Is this approach more appropriate than the common law or related economic reality approach? Are there other problems to his approach? And, should the definition of employee and employer under the FLSA be different from other federal employee protections?

All of this leads to a further question: When, if ever, should the statutory purpose trump the Supreme Court's repeated insistence that Congress's use of "employee" without meaningful gloss effectively incorporates the common law by reference? Consider, for example, whether the court correctly determined in *Lerohl v. Friends of Minnesota Sinfonia*, 322 F.3d 486 (8th Cir. 2003), that two female musicians were independent contractors of the symphony for which they performed regularly (until they were terminated) and therefore were unable to claim sex and disability discrimination under Title VII and the ADA. In analyzing the workers' status, the court purported to apply the factors set forth in §220(2) of the RESTATEMENT (SECOND) OF AGENCY. In so doing, it recognized that the symphony's conductor exercised significant, almost exclusive, control over the work itself, namely, the production of music in rehearsals and concerts. Yet because the musicians were highly skilled professionals, required no on-the-job training, retained the discretion to play for others, could reject playing in particular performances (upon adequate notice), and were not treated as employees for tax and benefit purposes, the court found that they were not employees as a matter of law. *See also Alberty-Velez v. Corporacion de P.R. para la Difusion Publica*, 361 F.3d 1 (1st Cir. 2004) (holding that the host and producer of a local television show host was an independent contractor and thus could not sue the station for discrimination under Title VII). *But see Jackson v. Gaylord Entertainment Co*, 2007 U.S. Dist. LEXIS 92514 (M.D. Tenn. Dec. 14, 2007) (finding sufficient facts to support the contention that a performer at the Grand Old Opry was an employee for statutory purposes and distinguishing *Lerohl* because of the terms of the written agreement in this case suggesting employment).

Whether the outcome in *Lerohl* was correct even under the common-law approach is debatable. *See* Jeff Clement, Lerohl v. Friends of Minnesota Sinfonia: *An Out of Tune Definition of "Employee" Keeps Freelance Musicians from Being Covered by Title VII*, 3 DEPAUL BUS. & COM. L.J. 489 (2005). Nevertheless, in the status discrimination context, it is not readily apparent why protection ought to hinge on such a balance of control and worker independence. *See generally* Lewis L. Maltby & David C. Yamada, *Beyond Economic Realities: The Case for Amending Federal Employment Discrimination Laws to Include Independent Contractors*, 38 B.C. L. Rev. 239, 241-42 (1997). Should workers who are somewhat less controlled by those for whom they work or are less economically dependent because of their skills be unprotected from, say, sex discrimination? Or should these protections not hinge on such distinctions? Is there a more appropriate way to determine who ought to be free from discrimination in paid work?

PROBLEM

1-2. Suppose you have been retained as employment counsel by Microsoft. The firm plans to launch a number of new software products over the next several years. As in earlier years, it will need a large number of code and text reviewers—proofreaders, testers, and editors—to assist in final stages of production. If possible, the firm would prefer to hire these workers as independent contractors for various reasons, including flexibility in an uncertain, post-recession economy; the fact that the workers' services will be needed only for discrete projects; its belief that many skilled reviewers might prefer such an arrangement; and the avoidance of various legal obligations to them. The firm does not know how long it might retain these workers—that will depend on how well the software products perform and how robust sales are. It concedes that it will need to maintain quality control, which will require monitoring and reviewing the workers' performance, although it does not need to oversee their work on a daily basis.

Microsoft asks you to offer your advice as to how to structure the relationships to reduce the probability that the workers might be found to be its "employees" for one or more regulatory purposes. Obviously, the firm's earlier problems with the IRS and the benefits litigation that followed loom large, and the firm wants to avoid any similar problems in the future. With that in mind, here are some additional facts—"hints"—from that case. The Ninth Circuit described the circumstances regarding the workers' tenure at Microsoft as follows:

> At various times before 1990, Microsoft hired the Workers to perform services for it. They did perform those services over a continuous period, often exceeding two years. They were hired to work on specific projects and performed a number of different functions, such as production editing, proofreading, formatting, indexing, and testing. "Microsoft fully integrated [the Workers] into its workforce: They often worked on teams along with regular employees, sharing the same supervisors, performing identical functions, and working the same core hours. Because Microsoft required that they work on site, they received admittance card keys, office equipment and supplies from the company."
>
> Microsoft did not withhold income or Federal Insurance Contribution Act taxes from the Workers' wages, and did not pay the employer's share of the FICA taxes. Moreover, Microsoft did not allow the Workers to participate in the [firm's profit sharing benefit plans]. The Workers did not complain about those arrangements at that time.

Vizcaino v. Microsoft Corporation, 120 F.3d 1006, 1008 (9th Cir. 1997) (en banc). However, the workers were treated differently in other ways:

> They had different color employee badges, different e-mail addresses, and were not invited to company parties and functions. Instead of receiving a regular paycheck from Microsoft's Payroll department (like Microsoft's regular employees), [these workers] submitted invoices for their services to the Accounts Payable department.

Id. at 1019 (O'Scannlain, concurring in part and dissenting in part). In addition, the workers signed contracts that provided, among other things, the following terms:

> CONTRACTOR is an independent contractor for [Microsoft]. Nothing in this Agreement shall be construed as creating an employer-employee relationship, or as a guarantee of a future offer of employment. CONTRACTOR further agrees to be responsible for all federal and state taxes, withholding, social security, insurance and other benefits. . . .

> [A]s an Independent Contractor to Microsoft, you are self-employed and are responsible to pay all your own insurance and benefits.

Id.

What would you recommend the firm do if, in fact, it is serious about hiring "real" independent contractors to do software editing and testing? Specifically, what language and provisions should it include in its contracts with the workers, and how should it structure its interactions (e.g., pay, training, oversight, allocation of risk, and provision of office space and resources) with the workers? How confident would you be in your advice — that is, in your ability to ensure that the firm avoids its earlier fate?

Note on the Rise of the "Contingent Worker"

The term "contingent worker" encompasses a range of workers in different industries who have, for one reason or another, a less permanent relationship with the firm or government agency for which they work than the typical employee. This is merely a descriptive term, having no uniform definition, and one's status as a contingent worker has no independent legal significance. These workers may be short-term employees or independent contractors of the primary firm, or may work (again, as employees or independent contractors) for another firm — a temporary help agency, labor subcontractor, or some other kind of intermediary — that performs services for the primary firm. Indeed, each of the workers at issue in the three cases in the last section (Myrick, Fitzgerald, Natkin, and Green) could be viewed as a "contingent worker."

Yet the growth and plight of contingent workers as a class has been the subject of intense scholarly interest. *See, e.g.*, Steven F. Befort, *Revisiting the Black Hole of Workplace Regulation: A Historical and Comparative Perspective of Contingent Work*, 1 Berkeley J. Emp. & Lab. L. 153 (2003); Richard S. Belous, *The Rise of the Contingent Work Force: The Key Challenges and Opportunities*, 52 Wash. & Lee L. Rev. 863, 876-78 (1995); Kenneth G. Dau-Schmidt, *The Labor Market Transformed: Adapting Labor and Employment Law to the Rise of the Contingent Work Force*, 52 Wash & Lee L. Rev. 879 (1995); *see also* Matthew Bidwell, *Do Peripheral Workers Do Peripheral Work?: Comparing the Use of Highly Skilled Contractors and Regular Employees*, 62 Indus. & Lab. Rel. Rev. 200 (2009). Although its parameters are far from clear, the contingent workforce continues to grow faster than the overall workforce, and it now accounts for tens of millions — perhaps 30 percent — of American workers. *See, e.g.*, Gideon Kunda et al., *Why Do Contractors Contract? The Experience of Highly Skilled Technical Professionals in a Contingent Labor Market*, 55 Indus. & Lab. Rel. Rev. 234, 235 (2002) (discussing various studies and trends that suggest dramatic growth in the contingent labor force in the late twentieth century). Moreover, the economic uncertainty prevailing since the economic downturn of 2008 may have further accelerated the trend toward contingent work relationships. *See, e.g.*, Michael Luo, *Recession Adds to Appeal of Short-Term Jobs*, N.Y. Times, Apr. 19, 2010, at A14.

For the same reasons that firms may prefer contingent workers, many workers' interests may be harmed by such relationships. For example, on average, contingent workers receive lower wages and fewer benefits — vacation, disability insurance, medical coverage, etc. — than ordinary employees, and have less wage stability than their counterparts in more traditional employment relationships. *See, e.g.*, Eileen Silverstein & Peter Goselin, *Intentionally Impermanent Employment and the Paradox of Productivity*, 26 STETSON L. REV. 1, 5-10 (1996). Given all of this and the fact that members of this group tend to have lower skills, they are more likely to be on the economic margins. They are also disproportionately female and African American. *See, e.g.*, Befort, *supra*, at 164; *see also* Michelle A. Travis, *Telecommuting: The Escher Stairway of Work/Family Conflict*, 55 ME. L. REV. 261 (2003) (discussing how one form of contingent work — telecommuting — is producing greater gender inequalities).

While the law does not treat these workers as either a single or distinct group, recent litigation in a few areas of employment law addresses issues facing many contingent working relationships. One involves the wage and overtime protections of the Fair Labor Standards Act — *Ansoumana v. Gristede's Operating Corp.*, 255 F. Supp. 2d 184 (S.D.N.Y. 2003), reproduced below, is a good example. But the vexing question is whether and how employment law ought to be reformed to confront more holistically the policy issues raised by the tremendous growth of these kinds of work arrangements. *See, e.g.*, Katherine V.W. Stone, *The New Psychological Contract: Implications of the Changing Workplace for Labor and Employment Law*, 48 U.C.L.A. L. REV. 519, 572-76 (2001) (discussing some of the implications of the changing nature of the workforce for existing workplace regulation).

B. THE FLIP SIDE: WHO IS AN "EMPLOYER"?

The prior section introduced you to the realities of the modern business enterprise. For example, fewer and fewer workers and firms are engaged in what was traditionally thought of as the standard employment relationship — that is, a (long-term) relationship in which the managers of a single firm exert exclusive control over their workers' day-to-day activities in the production of the firm's goods or services. These changes have created challenges for parties, regulators, and courts as more and more workers and entities fit less neatly into the traditional categories of independent contractor, employee, and employer. Indeed, whether they were correctly decided or not, none of the principal cases in the last section (*McCary*, *Fitzgerald*, and *Natkin*) involved what an observer from the middle of the last century would view as a typical employee-employer relationship.

While that section focused primarily on the distinction between employees and independent contractors, this section explores the obviously related questions of who is an "employer" and how to distinguish employers both from nonemployer firms and from "employees." Given the structure of the modern business enterprises, two commonly litigated issues surrounding the definition of employer are (1) to whom to extend employer status and (2) the status of firm owners — manager-owners and parent corporations.

1. "Employer" Status and Accountability for Violations in Disaggregated Enterprises

Business enterprises are now frequently splintered into smaller, independent parts. The arrangements in *McCary* and *Fitzgerald* are examples of this phenomenon—in each case, a large, end-user firm had contracted with smaller, independent firms to perform certain tasks within the enterprise, and these smaller firms then retained workers (employees or independent contractors) to provide labor. Although there are other reasons for end-user firms to outsource services and production, as you are now aware, limitations on liability for work-law violations invite these arrangements. Once limited to the margins, these kinds of structures now are present in most large enterprises, capturing many millions of workers.

Such disaggregation may create significant enforcement obstacles for workers' vindicating their work-related rights, particularly at the low end of the labor market. Smaller operations are less visible, so detection of violations by regulators and others who might offer assistance to vulnerable workers is more difficult. Moreover, workers may be left to seek remedies against an undercapitalized labor supplier, which is likely to lead to unpaid judgments, heavily discounted settlements, or unprosecuted claims. Outsourcing therefore may do more than shift legal responsibility from one firm to others: It may allow end-user firms to avoid noncompliance risks while benefitting from labor at a price discounted by the low probability of enforcement of employment-law mandates.

A frequently litigated question then is whether and when "employer" status—that is, legal responsibility for employment law violations—can be extended beyond the third-party labor supplier that retained the workers. As foreshadowed in the note about contingent workers, this issue now often arises in FLSA litigation (as well as suits under state wage and hour laws).

The FLSA is a Depression-era statute that requires employers to pay employees a minimum wage, as well as overtime pay for hours worked beyond a 40-hour work week. *See* 29 U.S.C.A. §§ 206(a)-(b), 207(a)(1) (2010). It also bans sex discrimination in pay for equal work, *see id.* § 206(d), and child labor, *see id.* § 212(c). Most of the planning, litigation, and public policy issues relate to the wage and hour requirements. The FLSA requires nonexempt "employees" to be paid a minimum hourly wage and receive overtime compensation at one and one half their "regular rate of pay" for hours worked in excess of 40 hours per week. The minimum wage, set by Congress, currently is $7.25 per hour, although, as discussed in Chapter 11, some states and municipalities have their own laws that set a higher minimum wage.

In most circumstances, the substantive requirements of the FLSA are straightforward; in other words, when they apply, the FLSA's wage and hour requirements are mandatory and fairly simple. Thus, FLSA litigation often focuses on the statute's coverage, including whether workers are employees or independent contractors in the first instance—as discussed in the last section—and whether employees are exempt or nonexempt, which is taken up in Chapter 11. The next case addresses who—that is, *which* firms and firm managers—are potentially accountable as "employers" or "joint employers" for unpaid wages.

═══
Ansoumana v. Gristede's Operating Corp.
255 F. Supp. 2d 184 (S.D.N.Y. 2003)

HELLERSTEIN, District Judge.

Plaintiffs Faty Ansoumana et al., and the class they represent, were delivery workers for supermarkets and drugstore chains, including stores owned and operated by Duane Reade, Inc., a defendant. The delivery workers were hired by the Hudson/

Chelsea group of defendants[1] and assigned to Duane Reade stores to make deliveries to customers and to provide general in-store services, as directed by the store supervisors. I am asked to decide, on these cross-motions for summary judgment, whether, as to the Hudson/Chelsea defendants, the plaintiffs were independent contractors or employees entitled to be paid a minimum wage and time-and-a-half for overtime and, if plaintiffs were employees, whether Duane Reade was a "joint employer," jointly obligated with the Hudson/Chelsea defendants to pay minimum wages and overtime. I will be applying, in determining the issues put to me, the Fair Labor Standards Act ("FLSA"), 29 U.S.C. §§ 201-219 (2002), and the New York Minimum Wage Act, N.Y. Lab. Law §§ 650-665 (2002).

The defendant, Duane Reade, Inc. is a large retail drugstore chain in the New York metropolitan area. Duane Reade outsourced its requirements for delivery workers by engaging the Hudson/Chelsea defendants to provide delivery workers to the Duane Reade stores, at the rate of $250 to $300 per week, per worker. The Hudson/Chelsea defendants, in turn, paid the delivery workers whom they assigned $20-$30 per day, characterizing them as independent contractors in order to avoid the minimum wage and overtime provisions of federal and New York law.

I hold in this decision that those delivery workers who were assigned to work in Duane Reade stores and made deliveries on foot were not independent contractors, that the Hudson/Chelsea defendants are liable to them for violations of the FLSA and the New York Labor law, and that Duane Reade and the Hudson/Chelsea defendants were joint employers within the meaning of those laws and were jointly and severally obligated to pay minimum wages and overtime to the delivery workers. . . .

I. Background

Plaintiffs filed this action on January 13, 2000 against three large chains of New York supermarkets and drugstores, and several companies and individuals who hired employees to work as deliverymen in such chains. Plaintiffs alleged that the defendants were operating in violation of the FLSA and the New York Minimum Wage Law. They claimed that the defendants, who had hired the delivery workers, and the chains to which they were assigned and in which they worked were jointly and severally liable to them. In May 2001, I certified a class of delivery workers and dispatchers who had worked for defendants between January 13, 1994 and May 24, 2001 and who had not been paid the minimum wage or overtime required under New York law. More than 500 delivery workers have filed consents and are participating in this lawsuit pursuant to the collective action provisions of the FLSA.

The delivery workers involved in the motion before me were hired by the Hudson/Chelsea defendants and were assigned to and worked for Duane Reade stores in Manhattan. The workers are mainly unskilled immigrants, mostly from West Africa. They provided services in the stores and made deliveries from the stores, and, despite working eight to eleven hours a day, six days a week, were paid a flat rate of between $20-$30 per day, well below minimum wage requirements.

---

1. The group is made up of Scott Weinstein, Steven Pilavin, Hudson Delivery Service, Inc., and Chelsea Trucking, Inc. Hudson Delivery Service, Inc. is owned and operated by Weinstein, and Chelsea Trucking, Inc. is owned and operated by Pilavin, Weinstein's brother-in-law. The opinion will refer to these defendants as "the Hudson/Chelsea defendants."

The record developed in discovery shows that the Hudson/Chelsea defendants hired the delivery workers for 45 to 60 of the 200 Duane Reade stores located in Manhattan and the boroughs. By oral agreement between Duane Reade and the Hudson/Chelsea defendants, Duane Reade has depended on the Hudson/Chelsea defendants exclusively, since 1994, to supply its stores with delivery workers and has been paying the Hudson/Chelsea defendants a flat weekly rate of $250-$300 per worker. The Hudson/Chelsea defendants hired their workers essentially without advertising, from recommendations by one worker to another, and provided them with uniforms and delivery carts. Since 1989, the Hudson/Chelsea defendants have regarded their delivery workers as independent contractors, not employees, and have required some of the workers to sign statements so acknowledging. The Hudson/Chelsea defendants have not withheld federal, state, or local taxes, nor made FICA or other statutory required withholdings from the payments to the workers, and have given them IRS Forms 1099 rather than W-2s to reflect their compensation. The Hudson/Chelsea defendants did not maintain a system for tracking the delivery workers' hours or pay and did not keep records of any tips the delivery workers received.

In March 2000, the Hudson/Chelsea defendants entered into a collective bargaining agreement with those of its delivery workers who had joined Local 338, Retail, Wholesale and Department Store Workers Union, AFL-CIO. That agreement required that all employees hired by the Hudson/Chelsea defendants earn at least $5.15 an hour and time and a half for overtime. Employees assigned to drug stores are allowed $1.65 of the wage to be credited as tip allowance. Since the agreement was signed, the Hudson/Chelsea defendants have been issuing IRS Forms W-2 to their delivery workers.

The delivery workers assigned to Duane Reade stores reported to the Duane Reade store to which they had been assigned and received directions from Duane Reade personnel in that store. Generally, they were assigned to the pharmacy departments and made deliveries of pharmaceutical items to customers. Duane Reade personnel provided the pharmaceutical stickers, issued the delivery instructions and, if payment was to be collected, instructed the delivery workers how much money to bring back from the customer. The Duane Reade stores maintained logs at the stores, and the delivery workers signed in and out of the logs upon each delivery, recording deliveries and receipts. In their spare time, the delivery workers were often asked to help customers with heavy items, provided bagging services at check-out registers, helped with security, stocked shelves, and moved products from one Duane Reade store to another. If a delivery worker was unsatisfactory, the Duane Reade manager asked Hudson/Chelsea to reassign the worker and provide another to replace him. Thus, the delivery worker, although not hired or paid by Duane Reade, was directed by Duane Reade managers and supervisors and provided services essentially similar to other Duane Reade employees.

II. Legal Framework

A. *The Fair Labor Standards Act*

The Fair Labor Standards Act mandates that "employees" receive a minimum wage and overtime pay of time and a half of the workers' regular hourly rate for each hour worked in excess of forty hours per workweek.[2] 29 U.S.C. §§ 206(a)(1), 207(a)(1) (2002). The FLSA defines an "employee," with certain exceptions not relevant here, as "any individual employed by an employer." *Id.* § 203(e)(1). The statute in turn defines "employ" as "to suffer or permit to work," *id.* § 203(g), and "employer" to include "any person acting directly or indirectly in the interest of an employer." *Id.* § 203(d). The terms are to be expansively defined, with "striking breadth," in such a way as to "stretch . . . the meaning of 'employee' to cover some parties who might not qualify as such under a strict application of traditional agency law principles." *Nationwide Mut. Ins. Co. v. Darden*, 503 U.S. 318, 326 (1992). As the Second Circuit has ruled, the FLSA, in accordance with its remedial purpose, has been written in the "broadest possible terms," *Carter v. Dutchess Cmty. Coll.*, 735 F.2d 8, 12 (2d Cir. 1984), and is to be construed broadly, for it would run "counter to the breadth of the statute and to the Congressional intent to impose a qualification which permits an employer who exercises substantial control over a worker . . . to escape compliance with the Act."

The regulations implementing the FLSA contemplate that an employee may have more than one employer. 29 C.F.R. § 791.2(a) ("a single individual may stand in the relation of an employee to two or more employers at the same time" under the FLSA). Such "joint employment" arises when the employee "performs work which simultaneously benefits two or more employers" and "one employer is acting directly or indirectly in the interest of the other employer (or employers) in relation to the employee." 29 C.F.R. § 791.2(b). This question of joint employment of plaintiffs, by Duane Reade and by the Hudson/Chelsea defendants, is a central issue in these cross motions.

[The New York Minimum Wage Act largely tracks the FLSA, although at times it has required a higher wage than did the federal statute.]

III. Plaintiffs Are Employees of the Hudson/Chelsea Defendants

There is no dispute that the plaintiffs were hired by one or the other of Scott Weinstein, Hudson Delivery Service, Inc., Steven Pilavin, and Chelsea Trucking, Inc. (also known as Hudson York) — the defendants to whom I have been referring as "the Hudson/Chelsea defendants." These defendants also do not dispute that they may be treated interchangeably. Thus, if one corporate entity is held liable, that finding may extend to the others. There is also no dispute that the Hudson/Chelsea defendants regarded the plaintiffs as independent contractors, not employees, and until the collective bargaining agreement with Local 338, which became effective March 26, 2000, the Hudson/Chelsea defendants did not keep the records mandated for employees by the FLSA and the New York Minimum Wage Act, did not pay minimum wages or overtime, did not withhold taxes or FICA from payroll, and issued IRS Forms 1099, rather than W-2s.

An employer's characterization of an employee is not controlling, however, for otherwise there could be no enforcement of any minimum wage or overtime law.

---

2. During the class period, January 13, 1994 to May 24, 2001, the minimum wage was $4.25 until September 30, 1996, $4.75 between October 1, 1996 and August 31, 1997, and $5.15 thereafter.

There would be nothing to prevent old-fashioned labor contractors from rounding up workers willing to sell their labor cheaply, and assigning them to perform outsourced work, without complying with minimum wage requirements. Thus, not the characterization of a hiring hall, but the test of "economic reality," governs how a relationship of employment is to be characterized in relation to the FLSA.

In *Brock v. Superior Care, Inc.*, 840 F.2d 1054, 1059 (2d Cir. 1988), the Court set out an "economic reality" test to distinguish between employees and independent contractors. The test considers five factors: (1) the degree of control exercised by the employer over the workers; (2) the workers' opportunity for profit or loss and their investment in the business; (3) the degree of skill and independent initiative required to perform the work; (4) the permanence or duration of the working relationship; and (5) the extent to which the work is an integral part of the employer's business. *Brock*; *United States v. Silk*, 331 U.S. 704 (1947). No one factor is dispositive; the "ultimate concern" is "whether, as a matter of economic reality, the workers depend upon someone else's business for the opportunity to render service or are in business for themselves." *Brock*.

Normally, the existence and degree of each factor is a question of fact, and the legal conclusion to be drawn from those facts is a question of law. *Id*. Here, however, as the discussion below makes clear, there is no genuine issue of material fact as to plaintiffs' proper status as employees.

The Hudson/Chelsea defendants argue that they merely "placed" workers with the Duane Reade stores, and it was the store managers and supervisors, not the Hudson/Chelsea defendants, who exercised control. However, the Hudson/Chelsea defendants were more than a placement agency. Hudson/Chelsea, not Duane Reade, paid the delivery workers, and controlled their hiring, firing, transfer and pay. If a worker assigned to a Duane Reade store met with disfavor, the store manager asked the Hudson/Chelsea defendants to transfer him out and assign someone else. Moreover, the Hudson/Chelsea defendants never offered proof of any license as an employment agency, and did not function, vis-à-vis Duane Reade, in the manner of an employment agency, receiving a commission based on several weeks or months of earnings.

The Hudson/Chelsea defendants' relationship with plaintiffs satisfies the first of the *Brock* considerations, showing a substantial degree of control over the workers. As *Brock* made clear, "[a]n employer does not need to look over his workers' shoulders every day in order to exercise control." . . . The fact that the Hudson/Chelsea defendants hired, fired, transferred and paid the delivery workers weighs substantially in favor of finding an employment relationship between the Hudson/Chelsea defendants and plaintiffs.

The second consideration of *Brock*—opportunity for investment, and profit or loss—also weighs heavily in favor of an employment relationship. As defendants conceded, plaintiffs' investment in the business was negligible. Plaintiffs are not asked to invest in Duane Reade, Hudson/Chelsea, or their own jobs. Hudson/Chelsea provided the delivery workers with delivery carts that they could rent and uniforms that they could purchase; the workers did not have to make an up-front investment in such things in order to be hired or assigned to a Duane Reade store.

Hudson/Chelsea argues that delivery services require plaintiffs to exercise "skill and independent initiative," the third consideration of *Brock*, but clearly this is not so in any objective sense. The Duane Reade stores are located throughout Manhattan and the boroughs, and customers typically reside within a neighborhood of a few blocks.

Little "skill" or "initiative" is needed to find one's way from a Duane Reade store to a customer's residence.

The fourth consideration, the permanence and duration of the plaintiffs' working relationship with the Hudson/Chelsea defendants, is disputed. Plaintiffs claim that most delivery workers have been working for the Hudson/Chelsea defendants for years, but offer testimony of only four deliverymen, of approximately 500 delivery workers who opted into the lawsuit, to support their claim, and even these four had only a three-year working relationship with the Hudson/Chelsea defendants. Nevertheless, the transience of the work force here says less about the status of the worker than about the nature of the job. Many delivery workers do not endure for long periods of time in this line of work due to the long hours, the low pay, the dangers of the streets, and the vagaries of the weather inherent in delivery work. Any transience of the work force therefore reflects "the nature of [the] profession and not [the workers'] success in marketing their skills independently." *Brock.*

The fifth consideration looks at the extent to which the work is integral to the business, and it also weighs heavily in favor of an employment relationship. The Hudson/Chelsea defendants concede that they are engaged primarily in the business of providing delivery services to retail establishments and that plaintiffs perform the actual delivery work. Thus, plaintiffs' services constitute an integral part of the Hudson/Chelsea defendants' business.

It is clear, from the "economic reality" and the totality of circumstances, that the delivery workers depend upon the Hudson/Chelsea defendants for the opportunity to sell their labor and are not in any real sense in business for themselves. . . . The delivery workers, as a matter of law, are employees, not independent contractors, and are entitled to summary judgment against the Hudson/Chelsea defendants. . . .

IV. Defendants Weinstein and Pilavin Are Individually Liable as Employers

Plaintiffs argue that, along with their companies Hudson Delivery Service, Inc. and Chelsea Trucking, Inc., Scott Weinstein and Steven Pilavin are "employers," and are therefore individually liable under the FLSA for underpayments of minimum wages and overtime. Plaintiffs are correct.

Officers and owners of corporations may be deemed employers under the FLSA where "the individual has overall operational control of the corporation, possesses an ownership interest in it, controls significant functions of the business, or determines the employees' salaries and makes hiring decisions." *Lopez v. Silverman*, 14 F. Supp. 2d 405, 412 (S.D.N.Y. 1998). In *Herman v. RSR Security Services, Ltd.*, 172 F.3d 132 (2d Cir. 1999), the Second Circuit found that a shareholder and member of the board was an "employer" under the FLSA where he had the authority to hire managerial staff, occasionally supervised and controlled employee work schedules, and had the authority to sign payroll checks. The Court emphasized that "the overarching concern is whether the alleged employer possessed the power to control the workers in question," and looked at the "totality of the circumstances" in determining whether defendant had "operational control." Thus, it did not matter that the putative employer did not directly hire workers, but only managerial staff, and that he did not have direct control over the workers in question; instead, the Court looked at whether he had "operational control" over the business.

Weinstein and Pilavin argue that they should not be held individually liable for underpayments because they did not directly control the delivery workers. Clearly, however, Weinstein and Pilavin exercised operational management of Hudson Delivery and Chelsea Trucking, and that is sufficient under the law to satisfy the broad statutory definition of "employer." *See* 29 U.S.C. § 203(d). Weinstein and Pilavin are the founders, owners, and sole shareholders of Hudson Delivery Service and Chelsea Trucking, and together they personally oversee and operate the companies and their agents on a daily basis. Thus, under *Herman*, each is an "employer" under the FLSA, and can be held individually liable for failure to pay minimum wages to their employees.

Weinstein and Pilavin argue that they could not be said to exercise control over the delivery workers if Duane Reade exercised such control. This argument misses the point; as I discuss below, the FLSA recognizes joint employment, meaning that more than one employer can be responsible for FLSA obligations. Because Weinstein and Pilavin had operational control over Hudson Delivery Service and Chelsea Trucking, they are individually liable under the FLSA for any underpayments in plaintiffs' salaries. Thus, plaintiffs are entitled to summary judgment against Weinstein and Pilavin, as well as against Hudson Delivery Services, Inc. and Chelsea Trucking, Inc.

V. Duane Reade Is a Joint Employer

The FLSA contemplates that more than one employer may be responsible for underpayments of minimum wages and overtime. 29 C.F.R. § 791.2(a)-(b). Duane Reade may be liable to plaintiffs for such underpayments, jointly and severally with the Hudson/Chelsea defendants, if Duane Reade was also their "employer" under the FLSA. The issue is determined by an "economic reality" test, which takes into account the real economic relationship between the employer who uses and benefits from the services of workers and the party that hires or assigns the workers to that employer.

In *Rutherford Food Corporation v. McComb*, 331 U.S. 722 (1947), meat boners who worked on the premises of a slaughterhouse were hired by another employer under contract with the slaughterhouse, much as the delivery workers for Duane Reade were hired to work there by the Hudson/Chelsea defendants. The issue in *Rutherford* was whether the slaughterhouse should be considered the employer of the meat boners when there already was an employer, the head boner who had hired the workers, and also managed and paid them.

The Supreme Court held that the slaughterhouse was a joint employer with the head meat boner for the purpose of minimum wage obligations under the FLSA. The Supreme Court considered that the boners' work was "part of the integrated unit of production," and that the workers did a "specialty" job on the production line, integral to the entire operation of the line. It was the boners themselves, not their company, functioning like piece-workers on a production line, who used the premises and equipment of the slaughterhouse to do their work, rather than shifting from one slaughterhouse to another as "an enterprise that actually depended for success upon the initiative, judgment or foresight of the typical independent contractor."

In *Carter v. Dutchess Community College*, 735 F.2d 8, 12 (2d Cir. 1984), the Second Circuit considered a work-release program of the New York State Department of Correctional Services ("DOCS"), which assigned inmates to work at sites of private employers. The plaintiff was a prison inmate and, under a DOCS program for college graduates, was assigned to work as a teaching assistant at Dutchess County Community College ("DCC"). DOCS paid plaintiff a stipulated allotment, less than the minimum wage, and plaintiff sued under the FLSA for back wages, punitive damages, and an injunction requiring defendants to pay all tutors, including inmate tutors, the same compensation.

The Second Circuit set out a four-part set of criteria to help determine whether DOCS, or DCC, or both, were "employers" required to pay minimum wages, examining who hired and fired the workers; who supervised and controlled their work schedules and conditions of employment; who determined the rate and method of payment; and who was to maintain employment records. Applying the criteria, the Court of Appeals found that it was DCC that had initially proposed to employ prisoners and suggested the wage to pay them; that DCC had established the standards to decide who would be eligible to be a teaching assistant and had identified several inmates whom it proposed to accept; that DCC reserved the right to refuse those inmates whom it did not want; and that DCC had decided for how many sessions and for how long an inmate would be permitted to tutor. On this record, the Court of Appeals held that there were questions of fact whether DCC had exercised sufficient control over the prison inmates to make DCC an "employer" required to pay minimum wages and overtime under the FLSA. Nevertheless, even taking into account the plaintiff's status as a prisoner, the Court did not rule out the possibility that he had FLSA claims against DCC as an employer, stating that the record, while not perhaps reflecting "the full panoply of an employer's prerogatives," may be sufficient to warrant FLSA coverage.

In *Torres-Lopez v. May*, 111 F.3d 633, 642-44 (9th Cir. 1997), farm laborers were procured through a labor agent, who hired them and assigned them to a farm. The Ninth Circuit Court of Appeals found that because these laborers constituted an integral part of the farm's business and because the farm exercised indirect control over them by supervising them and controlling the harvest schedule and the number of workers it needed for harvesting, the farm was a joint employer, along with the labor agent who hired them.

Like the meat boners in *Rutherford*, [and] the farm workers in *Torres-Lopez* . . . , the delivery workers assigned to Duane Reade performed an integral service for the stores in which they worked, enabling Duane Reade to compete more effectively with mail order fulfillment companies and other drug stores by offering drug deliveries to its customers. The delivery workers worked from the premises of the Duane Reade stores, and assisted other workers in those stores with bagging items at check-out counters, stocking shelves, providing security, and making inter-store deliveries.

Duane Reade offers an analogy to Federal Express, United Parcel, and other delivery services, but the analogy is misplaced. Duane Reade's delivery workers worked out of the Duane Reade stores, and not from a central depot; deliveries were made directly from the pharmacy counters to customers' homes, and not via a central facility; and control was exercised throughout by Duane Reade, and not by some independent service. Duane Reade used the delivery workers to extend its shelves and counters to the homes of customers, allowing them the convenience of shopping from home instead of having to come physically into a store. Duane Reade managers and supervisors directed the delivery workers in their tasks, instructing them what to pick up, where to make deliveries, how to log their deliveries, and how much to receive in payment. The delivery workers worked as individuals, and not as a group shifting from store to store according to seasonal and hourly needs. Indeed, it was not until they were organized by Local 338, in March 2000, that they even had a bargaining representative to negotiate for them as a collective. Clearly, the economic reality of the relationship between Duane Reade and the delivery workers reveals that Duane Reade was an employer of the delivery workers, responsible for assuring that they were paid the wages required by the FLSA and the New York Minimum Wage Act as a condition of their employment.

Additionally, the relationship between Duane Reade and the Hudson/Chelsea defendants establishes joint employment. That relationship was "so extensive and regular as to approach exclusive agency." The Hudson/Chelsea defendants acted directly in the interest of Duane Reade in relation to the delivery workers, 29 C.F.R. § 791.2, and Duane Reade used the Hudson/Chelsea defendants' services almost exclusively, for a lengthy period of years, since 1994, showing consistent dependence on them for delivery services.

I therefore hold, looking at the "circumstances of the whole activity," that plaintiffs were economically dependent on both the Hudson/Chelsea defendants and Duane Reade, and that both were their "employers" under the FLSA and the New York Minimum Wage Act. . . .

VII. Conclusion

Duane Reade had the right to "outsource" its requirement for delivery services to an independent contractor, here the Hudson/Chelsea defendants, and seek, by such outsourcing, an extra measure of efficiency and economy in providing an important and competitive service. But it did not have the right to use the practice as a way to evade its obligations under the FLSA and the New York Minimum Wage Act. Both Duane Reade and the Hudson/Chelsea defendants were the "employers" of the plaintiffs under these laws, jointly and severally obligated for underpayments of minimum wage and overtime during the period between January 13, 1994 and March 26, 2000. . . .

NOTES

1. *The FLSA and Contingent Workers.* Duane Reade's use of independent suppliers of laborers reflects the common practice of contracting out low-skilled work by large corporations and other end-user firms. *See, e.g.*, Cynthia Estlund, *Who Mops the Floors at the Fortune 500? Corporate Self-Regulation and the Low-Wage Workplace*, 12 Lewis & Clark L. Rev. 671, 685 (2008). Avoidance of the FLSA's requirements (and corresponding liability risks) is among the most cited and controversial reasons for outsourcing. *See, e.g.*, Stephen F. Befort, *Labor and Employment Law at the Millennium: A Historical Review and Critical Assessment*, 43 B.C. L. Rev. 351, 367-71 (2002); Richard R. Carlson, *Why the Law Still Can't Tell an Employee When It Sees One and How It Ought to Stop Trying*, 22 Berkeley J. Emp. & Lab. L. 295, 360 (2001); Katherine V.W. Stone, *Legal Protections for Atypical Employees: Employment Law for Workers Without Workplaces and Employees Without Employers*, 27 Berkeley J. Emp. & Lab. L. 251 (2006); Alan Hyde, *Who Speaks for the Working Poor?: A Preliminary Look at the Emerging Tetralogy of Representation of Low-Wage Service Workers*, 13 Cornell J. L. & Pub. Pol'y 599 (2004).

Although many violations go unchallenged, this phenomenon has resulted in a significant number of FLSA and state-law wage and hour suits. As exemplified by *Ansoumana*, these disputes implicate the employee/independent contractor distinction, the definition of employer and joint employer, or both. Most of these challenges have arisen in areas commonly known to be rife with wage and other employment-law violations, including delivery services, garment work, light manufacturing, janitorial services, light construction, and landscaping. Some have led to high-profile wage and hour litigation, including the claims by janitorial workers against Wal-Mart, *see e.g., Zavala v. Wal-Mart Stores, Inc.*, 393 F. Supp. 2d 295 (D.N.J. 2005), and the numerous suits by drivers against FedEx, *see, e.g., In re FedEx Ground Package Sys., Inc. Employment Practices Litig.*, 2010 U.S. Dist. LEXIS 53733 (N.D. Ind. May 28, 2010) (holding that FedEx misclassified plaintiff driver as an independent contractor instead of an employee and noting that there were over 60 pending wage-related lawsuits pending against FedEx in other jurisdictions); Todd D. Saveland, *FedEx's New "Employees": Their Disgruntled Independent Contractors*, 36 Transp. L. J. 95 (2009). Note, however, that wage and hour claims also have emerged in unexpected contexts, such as the recent rash of claims brought by exotic dancers against the clubs that use their services. *See, e.g., Chaves v. King Arthur's Lounge, Inc.*, 2009 Mass. Super. LEXIS 298 (Mass. Super. Ct. July 30, 2009); Paul Schwartzman, *Exotic Dancer Uses Labor Law to Sue D.C. Club over Wages*, The Washington Post, Mar. 15, 2010.

2. *Individual Liability.* The *Ansoumana* court found that Defendants Weinstein and Pilavin were "employers" under the FLSA, along with the entities they owned, because they had direct managerial control over the firms. There are a few other contexts in which individual owners and supervisors may be held individually liable for employment-law violations. Employees may have personal liability to a discrimination victim under § 1981. *See, e.g., Jemmott v. Coughlin*, 85 F.3d 61 (2d Cir. 1996); *Gierlinger v. New York State Police*, 15 F.3d 32 (2d Cir. 1994). Likewise, those who engage or assist in violations of the FMLA may be subject to aiding and abetting liability or FLSA-like supervisory liability. *See* Chapter 10; *see also* 29 C.F.R. § 825.104(d) ("As under the FLSA, individuals such as corporate officers 'acting in the interest of an employer' are individually liable for any violations of the requirements of FMLA."). Individual officers and directors also are potentially liable for violations of Sarbanes-Oxley's whistleblower protections (discussed in Chapter 4). *See* 18 U.S.C. § 1514A(a) (2006). Moreover, individual employees may be liable as tortfeasors for the commonly litigated workplace torts not involving personal injury — intentional interference with contract/business advantage, defamation, intentional infliction of emotional distress, and fraud (discussed in Chapter 5). Finally, a small number of states have enacted narrow "veil piercing" statutes providing that certain shareholders can be held personally liable for unpaid wages. *See* N.Y. Bus. Corp. Law § 103 (McKinney 2003); Wis. Stat. Ann. § 180.0622 (West 2002).

However, under most common-law and statutory schemes, only the entity (whether a partnership, limited liability company, corporation, or government agency) is the "employer." Thus, manager-owners, supervisors, and other employees within the entity generally are not subject to liability. For example, federal circuit courts are in agreement that supervisory or controlling persons are not subject to liability as employers under Title VII, the ADEA, or the ADA. *See, e.g., Butler v. City of Prairie Village*, 172 F.3d 736 (10th Cir. 1999) (ADA); *Miller v. Maxwell's Int'l, Inc.*, 991 F.2d 583 (9th Cir. 1993) (Title VII and ADEA); *see also Indest v. Freeman Decorating*,

Inc., 164 F.3d 258, 267 (5th Cir. 1999); *Hiller v. Brown*, 177 F.3d 542, 545-46 (6th Cir. 1999); *Gastineau v. Fleet Mortgage Corp.*, 137 F.3d 490, 494 (7th Cir. 1998).

What purposes does individual liability serve in circumstances like *Ansoumana*? Are such purposes unique to the FLSA and small number of other regimes that provide for individual liability? Or are there similar reasons to hold firm managers and controlling personnel liable for other firm torts and statutory violations? Consider how the risk of individual liability might alter firm incentives and affect choices regarding how to structure firm activities and manage liability risk. *See generally* Timothy P. Glynn, *Beyond "Unlimiting" Shareholder Liability: Vicarious Tort Liability for Corporate Officers*, 57 VAND. L. REV. 329 (2004).

3. *"Joint Employer" Liability.* The court also held that Duane Reade is subject to FLSA liability as a "joint employer" because of Duane Reade's direct supervision of the plaintiffs, plaintiffs' economic dependence on it, and Duane Reade's relationship with the Hudson/Chelsea defendants. The joint employer doctrine occasionally is recognized in other contexts as well. *See, e.g.*, EEOC COMPLIANCE MANUAL, Section 2: Threshold Issues, No. 915.003, section 2-III.B.1.a.iii.b (discussing application of the joint employer doctrine under antidiscrimination laws); *see also* RESTATEMENT (THIRD) OF EMPLOYMENT LAW (Tentative Draft No. 2, April 3, 2009) § 1.04 (recognizing that workers can be employees of two more employers at the same time).

Is the joint employer doctrine socially beneficial, and, if so, how far should it extend? On the positive side, how might it enhance compliance? On the other hand, might this kind of enterprise liability also create incentives for firms to change their operations in ways that actually harm the interests of at least some kinds of contingent workers? Relatedly, how might contracting firms such as Duane Reade seek to avoid "joint employer" status?

4. *Beyond "Employer" and "Joint Employer" Liability.* Despite the significant amount of litigation discussed in Note 1 and the FLSA's reach in terms of potentially accountable "employers" and "joint employers," enforcement of wage and hour laws at the low end of the labor market remains rare and is, according to many commentators and employee rights advocates, inadequate. There are many reasons for this, including the socioeconomic vulnerability of low-wage workers; regulatory agencies' limited enforcement resources; often insufficient economic incentives for plaintiffs' attorneys to bring suit; and, as suggested above, the fact that down-enterprise labor suppliers often operate below the radar and are judgment-proof. *See generally* Cynthia Estlund, *Rebuilding the Law of the Workplace in an Era of Self-Regulation*, 105 COLUM. L. REV. 319 (2005); Craig Becker & Paul Strauss, *Representing Low-Wage Workers in the Absence of a Class: The Peculiar Case of Section 16 of the Fair Labor Standards Act and the Underenforcement of Minimum Labor Standards*, 92 MINN. L. REV. 1317 (2006); Nanitya Ruan, *Bringing Sense to Incentives: An Examination of Incentive Payments to Named Plaintiffs in Employment Discrimination Class*, 10 EMP. RTS. & EMP. POL'Y J. 101 (2006); Noah Zatz, *Working Beyond the Reach or Grasp of Employment Law*, in THE GLOVES-OFF ECONOMY: WORKPLACE STANDARDS AT THE BOTTOM OF AMERICA'S LABOR MARKET 31 (Annette Bernhardt et al. eds., Cornell University Press 2008). But another reason is that the reach of employer and joint employer liability, although arguably more expansive under the FLSA than elsewhere, remains limited to firms exercising fairly detailed control over the work.

While these concerns have resulted in various calls for regulatory and doctrinal reform, one potentially promising approach involves expanding liability beyond controlling persons and firms — that is, beyond those who exercise sufficient control to be deemed "employers" or "joint employers." The central idea is to counteract the powerful incentives for end-user (or top-of-the-enterprise) firms to undercut the market by purchasing labor services over which they need not exercise exacting control from labor suppliers that maintain low prices by violating wage laws. Although such reform has not emerged at the federal level, a number of states have enacted provisions that extend liability for wage violations beyond its traditional limits. *See* CAL. LAB. CODE § 2810(a) (Deering 2010) (holding firms in certain low-skill industries responsible for labor violations committed by subcontractors where such violations were reasonably foreseeable from the terms of the contract); 820 ILL. COMP. STATS. § 175(85) (2010) (extending responsibility for staffing agency violations in certain industries to firms purchasing such agencies' services). In addition, commentators have proposed extending liability beyond firms and persons with direct control over workers. *See generally* Zatz, *supra*, at 31-32, 50-56 (offering a number of proposals to expand responsibility beyond employers); Brishen Rogers, *Toward Third-Party Liability for Wage Theft*, 11 BERKELEY J. EMPL. & LAB. L. 1 (2010) (proposing a third-party negligence regime under which firms would be held to a duty of reasonable care to prevent wage and hour violations within their domestic supply chains).

5. *Immigration, Wages, and Wage Protections.* As the court noted, many of the plaintiffs in *Ansoumana* were immigrants. Although the plaintiffs' immigrant status was not central to this case, immigration and wage protection issues often are closely linked. For example, a recurring issue in the contemporary immigration reform debate is the effect of both documented and undocumented immigration on wages, given that immigration has provided a steady supply of low-skilled workers, and whether that effect (combined with other benefits and costs of immigration) is good or bad for the country. *See, e.g.*, Harry J. Holzer, *Economic Impacts of Immigration, Testimony of Harry J. Holzer to the Committee on Education and the Workforce, U.S. House of Representatives*, Nov. 16, 2006, *available at* http://www.urban.org/url.cfm?ID=900908 (indicating that immigration depresses wages modestly, but also considering other benefits and costs of immigration); Arian Campo-Flores, *Why Americans Think (Wrongly) That Illegal Immigrants Hurt the Economy*, NEWSWEEK, May 14, 2010, at A1 (arguing that the negative effects such as straining public services and moderately depressing wages are outweighed by other positive economic and social effects).

Another concern is the plight of immigrant workers, since undocumented workers in particular are highly vulnerable to work and wage abuses. As a group, immigrants (both documented and undocumented) constitute a significant portion of the workforce at compensation levels at or near the minimum wage. *See id.* at 2-3; Randolph Capps et al., *A Profile of the Low-Wage Immigrant Workforce*, *in* "Immigrant Families and Workers: Facts and Perspectives": Brief No. 4, Oct. 27, 2003, *available at* http://www.urban.org/url.cfm?ID=310880 (discussing that although immigrants represent only 11 percent of all U.S. residents, they constitute 20 percent of low-wage workers). Thus, in *Ansoumana* and many similar FLSA minimum wage cases — and particularly those also involving the outsourcing of low-skilled work to subcontracting firms (which is also motivated by the IRCA, *see* page 23) — the plaintiff workers are immigrants. *See, e.g.*, Scott L. Cummings, *Hemmed In: Legal Mobilization in the Los Angeles Anti-Sweatshop Movement*, 30 BERKELEY J. EMP. & LAB. L. 1 (2009); Shirley Lung, *Exploiting the Joint Employer Doctrine: Providing a Break for Sweatshop Garment Workers*, 34 LOY. U. CHI. L.J. 291 (2003).

Whether and when undocumented workers may take advantage of federal labor and employment protections remains unresolved. For example, in *Hoffman Plastic*

Compounds, Inc. v. NLRB, 535 U.S. 137 (2002), the Court held that federal immigration policy, as expressed by Congress in the Immigration Reform and Control Act of 1986, foreclosed the National Labor Relations Board from awarding back pay to an undocumented alien after the employer terminated the worker for engaging in union organizing activities. However, *Hoffman* and its reasoning may not extend to other contexts. Most notably, recent decisions have generally held that undocumented workers are entitled to full FLSA protections. *See, e.g., Zavala v. Wal-Mart Stores, Inc.*, 393 F. Supp. 2d 295 (D.N.J. 2005) (holding that undocumented immigrants employed through maintenance contractors who performed janitorial services for Wal-Mart Stores were not precluded from seeking relief under FLSA on unpaid minimum wage and overtime claims). Yet even though such workers have wage protections in theory, they often cannot take advantage of them. Immigrants present or working in the country illegally face various risks, including deportation, if they seek enforcement of these protections. *See, e.g.*, Tyche Hendricks, *Worker Wins Her Rights But Loses Hope: Someone Told Feds She's Here Illegally*, S.F. CHRON., May 11, 2006. As a practical matter then, these workers often have little recourse against employer abuses.

Although there may be other reasons for hiring undocumented workers, avoiding wage and hour mandates is one obvious and problematic incentive. *See, e.g.*, Holzer, *supra*, at 3; Hendricks, *supra*. This moral hazard raises important policy and enforcement questions in both the employment and immigration areas. For further discussion of the intersection between employment law and immigration law, *see, e.g.*, Robert I. Correales, *Did* Hoffman Plastic Compounds, Inc., *Produce Disposable Workers?*, 14 LA RAZA L.J. 103 (2003); Lori A. Nessel, *Undocumented Immigrants in the Workplace: The Fallacy of Labor Protection and the Need for Reform*, 36 HARV. C.R.-C.L. L. REV. 345 (2001); Leticia M. Saucedo, *A New "U": Organizing Victims and Protecting Immigrant Workers*, 42 U. RICH. L. REV. 891 (2008); Rebecca Smith & Catherine Ruckelshaus, *Solutions, Not Scapegoats: Abating Sweatshop Conditions for All Low-Wage Workers as a Centerpiece of Immigration Reform*, 10 N.Y.U. J. LEGIS. & PUB. POL'Y 555 (2007); Note, *Developments in the Law — Jobs and Borders: Legal Protections for Illegal Workers*, 118 HARV. L. REV. 2224 (2005).

6. *FLSA Enforcement and the Role of Unions.* The workers in *Ansoumana* got exceedingly lucky. First, although it is not mentioned in the opinion, they had the support of the National Employment Law Project and state authorities. The local retail union also successfully organized these workers into a union before the resolution of the case, although, according to one commentator, the union was unhelpful in the litigation. *See* Hyde, *supra*, at 607-08. Nevertheless, in the future, union representation might help these workers obtain and maintain greater protections.

Unionization of such workers is rare since there are practical and statutory impediments to organizing contingent workers (which you will study if you take Labor Law). And without such unionization and the rights and resources that result, this segment of the workforce has little protection at all — no statutory regulation, no access to the courts, and no collective bargaining.

7. *"Professional" Workers as Contingent Laborers.* The discussion in this section has focused primarily on low-skilled workers. Recall, however, that higher-skilled workers — such as the photographers in *Natkin* and the technical workers in *Microsoft* — also can be described as contingent laborers. There are obvious differences between such workers and those at issue in *Ansoumana* as well as differences between what was at stake in the underlying cases. Such high-skilled workers may benefit from their contingent status. Indeed, in his dissent in the *Microsoft* case, Judge O'Scannlain speculated that the plaintiffs may have enjoyed higher wages as independent contractors than they would have if they had been hired as standard employees. *See Vizcaino*, 120 F.3d at 1021. Moreover, these workers may not fit within the category of "involuntary, impermanent" contingent workers for whom commentators express the most concern.

On the other hand, just because a worker is skilled does not ensure that he or she will be treated fairly or will have the power or sophistication to bargain for alternative protections. What is to prevent an employer who saves money by hiring contract workers or through temporary staffing agencies from pocketing the difference rather than passing along a portion of that benefit to its workers in the form of higher pay? Moreover, as discussed previously, many firms have responded to hard economic times by converting employee positions to independent contractor positions, often with loss of benefits. Should differences in the professional status of workers matter in determining who is an employee or how far to extend accountability of employment-law violations?

8. *Is Enterprise Disaggregation and Contingent Work Too Socially Costly?* In light of what you have learned thus far in this chapter, consider some of the bigger questions arising from increasing enterprise disaggregation and the growth of contingent work arrangements. These phenomena are likely to have various social effects—perhaps both good and bad. Think about possible effects both within and outside the firm. Might increased reliance on contingent or third-party supplied labor harm firms' long-term productivity? Consider the court's observation in *Microsoft* that the benefits associated with employment status "guarantee a competent and happy workforce." As for the interests of the public, we have already discussed how worker misclassification may reduce tax revenues and how disaggregation may lead to greater noncompliance with employment law standards in certain sectors. Does a firm's ability to externalize certain costs by outsourcing or engaging independent contractors harm society in other ways? Consider, for instance, how our society manages the costs of a nonnegligent personal injury sustained on the job by a worker not covered by workers' compensation or the company health plan. While we might expect firms to strike the optimal balance on contingent/permanent labor with respect to their productivity and morale, they have little incentive to take account of costs borne by society, as in the personal injury example. Do such costs justify legal reform? If so, what kind?

2. Determining the Status of Firm Owners

As *Ansoumana* demonstrates, high-ranking supervisory personnel, including owner-managers, may be liable as "employers" under the FLSA and in a few other contexts, and independently chartered firms exercising sufficient control over workers employed by another entity, may be liable as "joint employers." Elsewhere, however, firm owners rarely are considered "employers" for liability purposes.

Nevertheless, unresolved questions regarding the status of firm owners remain. The most frequently litigated issue relates to individual owners: Since they usually are not employers for liability purposes, when, if ever, are owner-managers considered "employees"? The next two cases address this issue. A note at the end of this section addresses a second question: When, if ever, may an employee of a subsidiary "pierce the corporate veil" to hold a parent corporation liable as an "employer" for the subsidiary's employment law violations?

As originally conceived, the common-law test was designed to distinguish employees from independent contractors. It does not purport to distinguish employees from others who perform services for a firm but are more akin to firm owners than employees (e.g., partners, stakeholders in professional corporations, members of limited liability companies, and shareholders in closely held corporations). Determining the status of such workers has been the subject of intense litigation in the federal employment discrimination area. Whether owners are treated as employees rather than employers (or vice versa) matters for two reasons. First, the number of statutory employees often determines whether a particular firm meets the threshold for coverage under the various employment statutes that might be invoked in a suit by an employee. Workers who are deemed to be employers are not counted for these purposes. Second, if the worker is considered an employer, rather than employee, then, like independent contractors, he or she will not be protected by applicable employment statutes.

≡ *Clackamas Gastroenterology Associates v. Wells*
538 U.S. 440 (2003)

STEVENS, J.

The Americans with Disabilities Act of 1990 ("ADA" or "Act"), 42 U.S.C. §12101 *et seq.*, like other federal antidiscrimination legislation,[1] is inapplicable to very small businesses. Under the ADA an "employer" is not covered unless its workforce includes "15 or more employees for each working day in each of 20 or more calendar weeks in the current or preceding calendar year." §12111(5). The question in this case is whether four physicians actively engaged in medical practice as shareholders and directors of a professional corporation should be counted as "employees."

I

Petitioner, Clackamas Gastroenterology Associates, P.C., is a medical clinic in Oregon. It employed respondent, Deborah Anne Wells, as a bookkeeper from 1986 until 1997. After her termination, she brought this action against the clinic alleging unlawful discrimination on the basis of disability under Title I of the ADA. Petitioner denied that it was covered by the Act and moved for summary judgment, asserting that it did not have 15 or more employees for the 20 weeks required by the statute. It is undisputed that the accuracy of that assertion depends on whether the four physician-shareholders who own the professional corporation and constitute its board of directors are counted as employees.

[The district court relied on an economic realities test and concluded that the four doctors were "more analogous to partners in a partnership than to shareholders in a general corporation" and therefore were "not employees for purposes of the federal antidiscrimination laws." The Ninth Circuit reversed. It saw "no reason to permit a professional corporation to secure the 'best of both possible worlds' by allowing it both to assert its corporate status in order to reap the tax and civil liability advantages

---

1. *See, e.g.*, 29 U.S.C. §630(b) (setting forth a 20-employee threshold for coverage under the Age Discrimination in Employment Act of 1967 (ADEA)); 42 U.S.C. §2000e(b) (establishing a 15-employee threshold for coverage under Title VII of the Civil Rights Act of 1964).

and to argue that it is like a partnership in order to avoid liability for unlawful employment discrimination."]

II

"We have often been asked to construe the meaning of 'employee' where the statute containing the term does not helpfully define it." *Nationwide Mut. Ins. Co. v. Darden*, 503 U.S. 318, 322 (1992). The definition of the term in the ADA simply states that an "employee" is "an individual employed by an employer." 42 U.S.C. § 12111(4). That surely qualifies as a mere "nominal definition" that is "completely circular and explains nothing." *Darden*. As we explained in *Darden*, our cases construing similar language give us guidance on how best to fill the gap in the statutory text.

In *Darden* we were faced with the question whether an insurance salesman was an independent contractor or an "employee" covered by the Employee Retirement Income Security Act of 1974 (ERISA). Because ERISA's definition of "employee" was "completely circular," we followed the same general approach that we had previously used in deciding whether a sculptor was an "employee" within the meaning of the Copyright Act of 1976, see *Community for Creative Non-Violence v. Reid*, 490 U.S. 730 (1989), and we adopted a common-law test for determining who qualifies as an "employee" under ERISA. Quoting *Reid*, we explained that "when Congress has used the term 'employee' without defining it, we have concluded that Congress intended to describe the conventional master-servant relationship as understood by common law agency doctrine."

Rather than looking to the common law, petitioner argues that courts should determine whether a shareholder-director of a professional corporation is an "employee" by asking whether the shareholder-director is, in reality, a "partner." The question whether a shareholder-director is an employee, however, cannot be answered by asking whether the shareholder-director appears to be the functional equivalent of a partner. Today there are partnerships that include hundreds of members, some of whom may well qualify as "employees" because control is concentrated in a small number of managing partners. Thus, asking whether shareholder-directors are partners — rather than asking whether they are employees — simply begs the question.

Nor does the approach adopted by the Court of Appeals in this case fare any better. The majority's approach, which paid particular attention to "the broad purpose of the ADA," is consistent with the statutory purpose of ridding the Nation of the evil of discrimination. *See* 42 U.S.C. § 12101(b).[6] Nevertheless, two countervailing considerations must be weighed in the balance. First, . . . the congressional decision to limit the coverage of the legislation to firms with 15 or more employees has its own

---

6. The meaning of the term "employee" comes into play when determining whether an individual is an "employee" who may invoke the ADA's protections against discrimination in "hiring, advancement, or discharge," 42 U.S.C. § 12112(a), as well as when determining whether an individual is an "employee" for purposes of the 15-employee threshold. See § 12111(5)(A). Consequently, a broad reading of the term "employee" would — consistent with the statutory purpose of ridding the Nation of discrimination — tend to expand the coverage of the ADA by enlarging the number of employees entitled to protection and by reducing the number of firms entitled to exemption.

justification that must be respected—namely, easing entry into the market and preserving the competitive position of smaller firms. Second, as *Darden* reminds us, congressional silence often reflects an expectation that courts will look to the common law to fill gaps in statutory text, particularly when an undefined term has a settled meaning at common law. . . .

Perhaps the Court of Appeals' and the parties' failure to look to the common law for guidance in this case stems from the fact that we are dealing with a new type of business entity that has no exact precedent in the common law. State statutes now permit incorporation for the purpose of practicing a profession, but in the past "the so-called learned professions were not permitted to organize as corporate entities." 1A W. Fletcher, Cyclopedia of the Law of Private Corporations § 112.10 (rev. ed. 1997-2002). Thus, professional corporations are relatively young participants in the market, and their features vary from State to State.

Nonetheless, the common law's definition of the master-servant relationship does provide helpful guidance. At common law the relevant factors defining the master-servant relationship focus on the master's control over the servant. The general definition of the term "servant" in the RESTATEMENT (SECOND) OF AGENCY § 2(2) (1958), for example, refers to a person whose work is "controlled or is subject to the right to control by the master." See also *id.* § 220(1). In addition, the Restatement's more specific definition of the term "servant" lists factors to be considered when distinguishing between servants and independent contractors, the first of which is "the extent of control" that one may exercise over the details of the work of the other. *Id.* § 220(2)(a). We think that the common-law element of control is the principal guidepost that should be followed in this case.

This is the position that is advocated by the Equal Employment Opportunity Commission (EEOC), the agency that has special enforcement responsibilities under the ADA and other federal statutes containing similar threshold issues for determining coverage. It argues that a court should examine "whether shareholder-directors operate independently and manage the business or instead are subject to the firm's control." . . .

We are persuaded by the EEOC's focus on the common law touchstone of control . . . and specifically by its submission that each of the following six factors is relevant to the inquiry whether a shareholder-director is an employee:

> Whether the organization can hire or fire the individual or set the rules and regulations of the individual's work
> Whether and, if so, to what extent the organization supervises the individual's work
> Whether the individual reports to someone higher in the organization
> Whether and, if so, to what extent the individual is able to influence the organization
> Whether the parties intended that the individual be an employee, as expressed in written agreements or contracts
> Whether the individual shares in the profits, losses, and liabilities of the organization.[7]

As the EEOC's standard reflects, an employer is the person, or group of persons, who owns and manages the enterprise. The employer can hire and fire employees, can

---

7. The EEOC asserts that these six factors need not necessarily be treated as "exhaustive." We agree. . . .

assign tasks to employees and supervise their performance, and can decide how the profits and losses of the business are to be distributed. The mere fact that a person has a particular title — such as partner, director, or vice president — should not necessarily be used to determine whether he or she is an employee or a proprietor. See *ibid.* ("An individual's title . . . does not determine whether the individual is a partner, officer, member of a board of directors, or major shareholder, as opposed to an employee"). Nor should the mere existence of a document styled "employment agreement" lead inexorably to the conclusion that either party is an employee. See *ibid.* (looking to whether "the parties intended that the individual be an employee, as expressed in written agreements or contracts"). Rather, as was true in applying common law rules to the independent-contractor-versus-employee issue confronted in *Darden*, the answer to whether a shareholder-director is an employee depends on "'all of the incidents of the relationship . . . with no one factor being decisive.'"

III

Some of the District Court's findings — when considered in light of the EEOC's standard — appear to weigh in favor of a conclusion that the four director-shareholder physicians in this case are not employees of the clinic. For example, they apparently control the operation of their clinic, they share the profits, and they are personally liable for malpractice claims. There may, however, be evidence in the record that would contradict those findings or support a contrary conclusion under the EEOC's standard that we endorse today. Accordingly, as we did in *Darden*, we reverse the judgment of the Court of Appeals and remand the case to that court for further proceedings consistent with this opinion. . . .

GINSBURG, J., with whom BREYER, J. joins, dissenting.

"There is nothing inherently inconsistent between the coexistence of a proprietary and an employment relationship." *Goldberg v. Whitaker House Cooperative, Inc.*, 366 U.S. 28, 32 (1961). As doctors performing the everyday work of petitioner Clackamas Gastroenterology Associates, P.C., the physician-shareholders function in several respects as common-law employees, a designation they embrace for various purposes under federal and state law. Classifying as employees all doctors daily engaged as caregivers on Clackamas' premises, moreover, serves the animating purpose of the [ADA]. Seeing no cause to shelter Clackamas from the governance of the ADA, I would affirm the judgment of the Court of Appeals.

An "employee," the ADA provides, is "an individual employed by an employer." 42 U.S.C. §12111(4). Where, as here, a federal statute uses the word "employee" without explaining the term's intended scope, we ordinarily presume "Congress intended to describe the conventional master-servant relationship as understood by common-law agency doctrine." *Nationwide Mut. Ins. Co. v. Darden.* The Court today selects one of the common-law indicia of a master-servant relationship — control over the work of others engaged in the business of the enterprise — and accords that factor overriding significance. I would not so shrink the inquiry.

Are the physician-shareholders "servants" of Clackamas for the purpose relevant here? The Restatement defines "servant" to mean "an agent employed by a master to perform service in his affairs whose physical conduct in the performance of the service is controlled or is subject to the right to control by the master." RESTATEMENT (SECOND)

OF AGENCY § 2(2) (1958) (hereinafter Restatement). When acting as clinic doctors, the physician-shareholders appear to fit the Restatement definition. The doctors provide services on behalf of the corporation, in whose name the practice is conducted. . . . The doctors have employment contracts with Clackamas, under which they receive salaries and yearly bonuses, and they work at facilities owned or leased by the corporation. In performing their duties, the doctors must "compl[y] with . . . standards [the organization has] established."

The physician-shareholders, it bears emphasis, invite the designation "employee" for various purposes under federal and state law. The Employee Retirement Income Security Act of 1974 (ERISA), much like the ADA, defines "employee" as "any individual employed by an employer." 29 U.S.C. § 1002(6). Clackamas readily acknowledges that the physician-shareholders are "employees" for ERISA purposes. Indeed, gaining qualification as "employees" under ERISA was the prime reason the physician-shareholders chose the corporate form instead of a partnership. Further, Clackamas agrees, the physician-shareholders are covered by Oregon's workers' compensation law. . . . Finally, by electing to organize their practice as a corporation, the physician-shareholders created an entity separate and distinct from themselves, one that would afford them limited liability for the debts of the enterprise. I see no reason to allow the doctors to escape from their choice of corporate form when the question becomes whether they are employees for purposes of federal antidiscrimination statutes.

Nothing in or about the ADA counsels otherwise. As the Court observes, the reason for exempting businesses with fewer than 15 employees from the Act, was "to spare very small firms from the potentially crushing expense of mastering the intricacies of the antidiscrimination laws, establishing procedures to assure compliance, and defending against suits when efforts at compliance fail." The inquiry the Court endorses to determine the physician-shareholders' qualification as employees asks whether they "ac[t] independently and participat[e] in managing the organization, or . . . [are] subject to the organization's control." Under the Court's approach, a firm's coverage by the ADA might sometimes turn on variations in ownership structure unrelated to the magnitude of the company's business or its capacity for complying with federal prescriptions.

This case is illustrative. In 1996, Clackamas had 4 physician-shareholders and at least 14 other employees for 28 full weeks; in 1997, it had 4 physician-shareholders and at least 14 other employees for 37 full weeks. Beyond question, the corporation would have been covered by the ADA had one of the physician-shareholders sold his stake in the business and become a "mere" employee. Yet such a change in ownership arrangements would not alter the magnitude of Clackamas' operation: In both circumstances, the corporation would have had at least 18 people on site doing the everyday work of the clinic for the requisite number of weeks.

The Equal Employment Opportunity Commission's approach, which the Court endorses, it is true, "excludes from protection those who are most able to control the firm's practices and who, as a consequence, are least vulnerable to the discriminatory treatment prohibited by the Act." As this dispute demonstrates, however, the determination whether the physician-shareholders are employees of Clackamas affects not only whether they may sue under the ADA, but also — and of far greater practical import — whether employees like bookkeeper Deborah Anne Wells are covered by the Act. Because the character of the relationship between Clackamas and the doctors supplies no justification for withholding from clerical worker Wells federal protection against discrimination in the workplace, I would affirm the judgment of the Court of Appeals.

NOTES

1. *Employer vs. Employee Muddle?* The issue in *Clackamas* is *not* the plaintiff's employment status, but that of her bosses. Only if the physicians are counted as employees can the defendant be a covered employer meeting the 15-employee threshold. Given this very different question, why is the common-law test — originally fashioned to distinguish employees from independent contractors for purposes of respondeat superior liability — given such prominence in the *Clackamas* analysis? The dissent argues that, given the remedial purposes of the ADA, its coverage should be interpreted broadly in terms of who is an employee and, therefore, who is a covered employer.

Should "employee" mean different things even within the same statute depending on what issue the court is seeking to address? For example, should "employee" mean one thing when, as here, the issue is whether the firm is large enough to be covered, but something else when the issue is whether the alleged victim(s) of unlawful discrimination are employees, as would be the case had one of the four doctors sued? A well-known case in which "owners" alleged unlawful discrimination against the firm is *EEOC v. Sidley Austin Brown & Wood*, 315 F.3d 696 (7th Cir. 2002). The underlying claim in *Sidley* was that a law firm mandatory retirement policy resulting in the demotion of 32 partners violated the ADEA. The parties disputed whether the partners affected by the policy were "employees" in light of the firm's management and control structure. The court did not resolve the issue, and the case ultimately settled, with the firm's agreeing to pay $27.5 million to the partners. Judge Posner's majority opinion and Judge Easterbrook's concurrence provide a useful survey of the difficult issues raised in this context and the considerable differences — within and between courts prior to *Clackamas* — in analyzing the proper status given to workers with ownership interests. *See also* Leonard Bierman & Rafael Gely, *So, You Want to Be a Partner at Sidley & Austin?*, 40 Hous. L. Rev. 969, 990 (2003); Tiffani N. Darden, *The Law Firm Caste System: Constructing a Bridge Between Workplace Equity Theory and the Institutional Analyses of Bias in Corporate Law Firms*, 30 Berkeley J. Emp. & Lab. L. 85 (2009); Donald J. Labriola, *But I'm Denny Crane! Age Discrimination in the Legal Profession After* Sidley, 72 Alb. L. Rev. 367, 368 (2009); Ann C. McGinley, *Functionality or Formalism? Partners and Shareholders as "Employees" Under the Anti-Discrimination Laws*, 57 S.M.U. L. Rev. 3 (2004).

2. *Significance of the Corporate Form.* The majority in *Clackamas* downplayed the significance of the physicians' choice to organize their practice as a professional corporation, indicating that it would look beyond mere formalities and titles and focus instead on the substantive question of whether the physicians exercised employer-like control over the enterprise. The Court did so in part because it seemed to assume that individuals who are "employers" or, at least, exercise employer-like control, cannot also be "employees." Is this a correct assumption? Aren't firm owners also frequently employed by the corporations, LLCs, and partnerships for which they work? *See generally* Frank Menetrez, *Employee Status and the Concept of Control in Federal Employment Discrimination Law*, 63 SMU L. Rev. 137 (2010) (arguing that applying the common law control test should often, perhaps usually, result in owners of the enterprise also being employees).

Indeed, why did the physicians organize their practice as a corporation in the first place? Recall that the physicians had classified themselves as shareholders, directors, *and* supervisory employees. As the dissent mentioned, it seems that the physicians incorporated in order to gain employee status for ERISA and workers' compensation purposes. It also appears likely that the corporate form was used to take advantage of the legal fiction that the corporation itself, and not its physician-owners, is the principal-employer. That would limit individual exposure of each physician to malpractice (and other third-party liability) for the acts of the other physicians. Indeed, it seems ironic that the majority suggested that the physicians may be akin to employers under the common-law test, given that the original purpose of that test was to determine when a controlling party is liable under the doctrine of respondeat superior, and the physicians incorporated their practice to *avoid* such liability (and other forms of liability) by shifting employer-principal status to the corporation. Undoubtedly, if the practice had been slightly larger — 15 undisputed employees — and plaintiff's discrimination claim therefore had been viable, the physicians would have argued that, despite their control of the enterprise, the corporation is the only "employer" subject to potential liability in this case. And, as discussed in Note 1 following *Ansoumana*, page 38, *supra*, they almost certainly would have won this argument.

3. *Different Inquiry, Same Problems and Policy Issues?* Recall some of the recurring themes in the previous cases in the chapter: (1) private ordering's role in determining employment status, (2) whether a firm or worker "can have it both ways" in terms of such status, (3) the importance of the case's posture and the underlying interests at stake, and (4) the central role that control plays when determining if an employment relationship exists. How do these themes play out in *Clackamas?* Should the questions raised be answered differently when the court is not assessing the status of the plaintiff herself but rather the status of others on whom her right to relief depends?

In addition, how successful is the opinion in avoiding or addressing the other two concerns discussed throughout this chapter, namely, the costs of uncertainty and the disconnect between the test for determining employee/employer status and the aims of the underlying employment doctrine? In thinking about this question, put yourself in the shoes of corporate counsel. In light of the Court's analysis, how might you structure a small business to minimize the likelihood of being subject to the ADA's obligations? How confident are you that such structuring would achieve its purposes?

4. *"Covered Employers."* Like the ADA, many other federal employment statutes limit the definition of employer based on the number of employees. Title VII, for example, has a 15-employee floor, *see* 42 U.S.C. § 2000e(b) (2006), and the ADEA applies only to employers with twenty or more employees, *see* 29 U.S.C. § 630(b) (2006). The Family and Medical Leave Act ("FMLA") applies only to employers with 50 or more employees, and only to employees employed at a worksite where the employer employs at least 50 employees within a 75-mile radius. *See* 29 U.S.C. § 2611(2)(B)(ii), (4)(A)(i) (2006). Federal employment statutes also contain other exceptions to employer status; for example, religious entities are exempted from Title VII's prohibition of discrimination on the basis of religion. *See* 42 U.S.C. § 2000e-1(a). Thus, the issue presented in *Clackamas* will be relevant anytime a small business is sued by an employee raising claims under any number of employment protection statutes.

Whether an employer is public or private also affects statutory coverage or remedies. Some federal labor statutes, including the Labor Management Relations Act and National Labor Relations Act, do not apply to public employers, *see* 29 U.S.C. § 152(2) (2006), although the federal government has its own regime for federal employees and states frequently have their own statutes governing state and local public sector labor relations. On the other hand, federal constitutional protections — including constitutional rights to speech, association, religious freedom, and due process — apply only in public workplaces. Moreover, federal, state, and local government employees often enjoy substantive protections pursuant to civil service codes that are unavailable in the private sector.

5. *"Covered Employees."* Not all employees fall within the coverage of every employment regulation. Limitations on the "protected class" in certain antidiscrimination statutes provide an obvious example. *See, e.g.*, ADEA, 29 U.S.C. § 631(a) (2006) (defining "age" to include only those 40 years of age or older); ADA, 42 U.S.C.A. § 12112(b)(5) (2010) (stating that the duty to reasonably accommodate under the ADA is owed to one who is a "qualified individual with a disability"). In addition, the FMLA excludes new employees and part-time workers, see Chapter 10, and the FLSA exempts many professional employees from its minimum wage and overtime protections, see Chapter 11.

Yates v. Hendon
541 U.S. 1 (2004)

GINSBURG, J.

This case presents a question on which federal courts have divided: Does the working owner of a business (here, the sole shareholder and president of a professional corporation) qualify as a "participant" in a pension plan covered by the Employee Retirement Income Security Act of 1974 (ERISA or Act), 29 U.S.C. § 1001 *et seq.* The answer, we hold, is yes: If the plan covers one or more employees other than the business owner and his or her spouse, the working owner may participate on equal terms with other plan participants. Such a working owner, in common with other employees, qualifies for the protections ERISA affords plan participants and is governed by the rights and remedies ERISA specifies. In so ruling, we reject the position, taken by the lower courts in this case, that a business owner may rank only as an "employer" and not also as an "employee" for purposes of ERISA-sheltered plan participation.

I

A

[ERISA's four titles regulate covered employee pension plans in a variety of ways. One of the benefits of an ERISA plan is favorable tax treatment.]

B

Dr. Raymond B. Yates was the sole shareholder and president of Raymond B. Yates, M.D., P.C., a professional corporation. The corporation maintained the Raymond B. Yates, M.D., P.C. Profit Sharing Plan (Profit Sharing Plan or Plan), for which Yates was the administrator and trustee. From the Profit Sharing Plan's inception, at least one person other than Yates or his wife was a participant. The Profit Sharing Plan qualified for favorable tax treatment under § 401 of the Internal Revenue Code (IRC). As required by both the IRC and Title I of ERISA, the Plan contained an anti-alienation provision. That provision, entitled "Spendthrift Clause," stated in relevant part: "Except for . . . loans to Participants as [expressly provided for in the Plan], no benefit or interest available hereunder will be subject to assignment or alienation, either voluntarily or involuntarily."

In December 1989, Yates borrowed $20,000 at 11 percent interest from the Raymond B. Yates, M.D., P.C. Money Purchase Pension Plan (Money Purchase Pension Plan), which later merged into the Profit Sharing Plan. The terms of the loan agreement required Yates to make monthly payments of $433.85 over the five-year period of the loan. Yates failed to make any monthly payment. In June 1992, coinciding with the Money Purchase Pension Plan-Profit Sharing Plan merger, Yates renewed the loan for five years. Again, he made no monthly payments. In fact, Yates repaid nothing until November 1996. That month, he used the proceeds from the sale of his house to make two payments totaling $50,467.46, which paid off in full the principal and interest due on the loan. Yates maintained that, after the repayment, his interest in the Profit Sharing Plan amounted to about $87,000.

[Three weeks after Yates repaid the loan to the Profit Sharing Plan, Yates's personal creditors filed an involuntary petition against him under Chapter 7 of the Bankruptcy Code. The Bankruptcy Trustee (overseeing the bankruptcy estate for the benefit of Yates' creditors) asked the Bankruptcy Court to avoid the $50,467.46 payments to the Profit Sharing Plan and to order Yates to pay over that amount plus interest to them. The Bankruptcy Court ruled in favor of the Trustee. In its ruling, the court found that the Profit Sharing Plan and Yates could not rely on the Plan's anti-alienation provision — which protects the Plan's assets from transfer or attachment — to prevent the Bankruptcy Trustee from recovering the loan repayment because, as "a self-employed owner of the professional corporation that sponsor[ed] the pension plan," Yates could not "participate as an employee under ERISA." Since Yates could not participate in the Plan as an employee, he could not rely on ERISA's provisions to avoid transferring the payments to the Trustee.

The District Court agreed. Since Dr. Yates was not qualified to participate in an ERISA-protected plan, none of his contributions to the Plan as an "employee" were protected, including the $50,467.46 he returned to the Plan." The Sixth Circuit affirmed.]

We granted certiorari in view of the division of opinion among the Circuits on the question whether a working owner may qualify as a participant in an employee benefit plan covered by ERISA.

II

A

ERISA's definitions of "employee," and, in turn, "participant," are uninformative.[*] We therefore look to other provisions of the Act for instruction. ERISA's text contains multiple indications that Congress intended working owners to qualify as

---

*[ERISA defines the term "participant" as "any employee or former employee of an employer" who is eligible to receive benefits under an employee pension plan. *See* 29 U.S.C. § 1002(7). "Employee," means "any individual employed by an employer," *id.* § 1002(6), and "employer" includes "any person acting directly as an employer, or indirectly in the interest of an employer, in relation to an employee benefit plan," *id.* § 1002(5). — Eds.]

plan participants. Because these indications combine to provide "specific guidance," there is no cause in this case to resort to common law.[3]

Congress enacted ERISA against a backdrop of IRC provisions that permitted corporate shareholders, partners, and sole proprietors to participate in tax-qualified pension plans. Working shareholders have been eligible to participate in such plans since 1942. Two decades later, still prior to ERISA's adoption, Congress permitted partners and sole proprietors to establish tax-favored pension plans, commonly known as "H. R. 10" or "Keogh" plans. Thus, by 1962, working owners of all kinds could contribute to tax-qualified retirement plans.

ERISA's enactment in 1974 did not change that situation. Rather, Congress' objective was to harmonize ERISA with longstanding tax provisions. Title I of ERISA and related IRC provisions expressly contemplate the participation of working owners in covered benefit plans. Most notably, several Title I provisions partially exempt certain plans in which working owners likely participate from otherwise mandatory ERISA provisions. Exemptions of this order would be unnecessary if working owners could not qualify as participants in ERISA-protected plans in the first place.

To illustrate, Title I frees the following plans from the Act's fiduciary responsibility requirements:

> (1) a plan which is unfunded and is maintained by an employer primarily for the purpose of providing deferred compensation for a select group of management or highly compensated employees; or
> (2) any agreement described in section 736 of [the IRC], which provides payments to a retired partner or deceased partner or a deceased partner's successor in interest.

The IRC defines the term "highly compensated employee" to include "any employee who . . . was a 5-percent owner at any time during the year or the preceding year." A "5-percent owner," the IRC further specifies, is "any person who owns . . . more than 5 percent of the outstanding stock of the corporation or stock possessing more than 5 percent of the total combined voting power of all stock of the corporation" if the employer is a corporation, or "any person who owns more than 5 percent of the capital or profits interest in the employer" if the employer is not a corporation. Under these definitions, some working owners would fit the description "highly compensated employees." Similarly, agreements that make payments to retired partners, or to deceased partners' successors in interest, surely involve plans in which working partners participate. . . .

Particularly instructive, Title IV and the IRC, as amended by Title II, clarify a key point missed by several lower courts: Under ERISA, a working owner may have dual status, *i.e.*, he can be an employee entitled to participate in a plan and, at the same time, the employer (or owner or member of the employer) who established the plan. Both Title IV and the IRC describe the "employer" of a sole proprietor or partner. *See* 29 U.S.C. § 1301(b)(1) ("An individual who owns the entire interest in an unincorporated trade or business is treated as his own employer, and a partnership is treated as the employer of each partner who is an employee within the meaning of

---

3. *Cf. Nationwide Mut. Ins. Co. v. Darden*, 503 U.S. 318 (1992), and *Clackamas Gastroenterology Assocs., P.C. v. Wells*, [reproduced at page 44], (finding textual clues absent, Court looked to common law for guidance).

section 401(c)(1) of [the IRC]."); 26 U.S.C. §401(c)(4) ("An individual who owns the entire interest in an unincorporated trade or business shall be treated as his own employer. A partnership shall be treated as the employer of each partner who is an employee within the meaning of [§401(c)(1)]."). These descriptions expressly anticipate that a working owner can wear two hats, as an employer and employee. *Cf. Clackamas Gastroenterology Assocs., P.C. v. Wells* (Ginsburg, J., dissenting) ("Clackamas readily acknowledges that the physician-shareholders are 'employees' for ERISA purposes.").

In sum, because the statute's text is adequately informative, we need not look outside ERISA itself to conclude with security that Congress intended working owners to qualify as plan participants.

Congress' aim is advanced by our reading of the text. The working employer's opportunity personally to participate and gain ERISA coverage serves as an incentive to the creation of plans that will benefit employer and nonowner employees alike. Treating working owners as participants not only furthers ERISA's purpose to promote and facilitate employee benefit plans. Recognizing the working owner as an ERISA-sheltered plan participant also avoids the anomaly that the same plan will be controlled by discrete regimes: federal-law governance for the nonowner employees; state-law governance for the working owner. ERISA's goal, this Court has emphasized, is "uniform national treatment of pension benefits." *Patterson v. Shumate*, 504 U.S. 753, 765 (1992). Excepting working owners from the federal Act's coverage would generate administrative difficulties and is hardly consistent with a national uniformity goal. . . .

NOTES

1. *A Different Approach. Yates* offers an initial taste of how technical — perhaps painfully technical — ERISA interpretation and litigation is, something you can explore in detail in an Employee Benefits class. More pertinent for our purposes here, however, is the stark contrast between the Court's analytic approach in this case and that in *Clackamas*. The *Yates* majority explicitly avoided analyzing Yates' employment status under the common-law framework that dominated the *Clackamas* decision, opting instead to focus only on the language of ERISA and its predecessors, and the purposes behind the statutory scheme. It was also far more willing, in this case, to take into account formalistic distinctions relating to a working owner's status and role. Why are the approaches in these two decisions, which the Court handed down in successive terms, so different? Does the answer lie in the differences between the statutory schemes at issue, or is there a more fundamental difference?

2. *The Bitter with the Sweet. Yates* seems to resolve definitively the question raised in *Clackamas* whether an owner can "have it both ways" in terms of employment status, at least for ERISA purposes. This makes sense, doesn't it? After all, it would frustrate the purposes of Statute *A* if someone it was designed to protect was denied those protections simply because she was not covered by Statute *B*. But does this make you reconsider the conclusions you reached in connection, for example, with *Natkin*, reproduced at page 17? On this point, however, recall Justice Ginsberg's opinion in *Clackamas*, which suggested that one needs to take the bitter with the sweet: "Finally, by electing to organize their practice as a corporation, the physician-shareholders created an entity separate and distinct from themselves, one that would afford them limited liability for the debts of the enterprise. I see no reason to allow the doctors to escape from their choice of corporate form when the question becomes whether they are employees for purposes of federal antidiscrimination statutes." What reason does she see in *Yates* to allow the doctor there to escape from his choice of the corporate form?

Note on Parent Corporation Liability for Employment-law Violations

Clackamas and *Yates* introduced you to the role of the corporate form — limiting owners' liability for the debts and other obligations of the enterprise. Indeed, limited liability is the *primary reason* why business owners incorporate or charter an alternative limited liability entity, such as an LLC or limited partnership. Keep in mind, however, that business entities also are owners (e.g., shareholders) of other entities — that is, their subsidiaries. Although there are a number of reasons why firm managers might separately assign aspects of their enterprise's operations into parent and subsidiary firms, avoiding liability exposure for the larger enterprise (from the obligations of one or more of its subdivisions) is central among them. Akin to the rise of outsourcing, the splintering of enterprises into separately chartered entities has proliferated in recent years.

Such formal intra-enterprise distinctions may matter a great deal in the employment context. As an initial matter, at least in some circumstances, corporate formalities themselves may define the limits of employment-related protections. For example, until the Dodd-Frank Wall Street Reform and Financial Protection Act extended coverage, *see* 111 Pub. L. 203, §922, 124 Stat. 1376, §922, amending 18 U.S.C.A. §1514A (2010), employees of privately held subsidiaries of publicly traded firms who reported possible securities violations were found to be outside of the scope of the Sarbanes-Oxley's whistleblower protections, *see* Richard E. Moberly, *Unfulfilled Expectations: An Empirical Analysis of Why Sarbanes-Oxley Whistleblowers Rarely Win*, 49 Wm. & Mary L. Rev. 65, 71, 109, 134 (2007).

More broadly, where this kind of structure exists, a question of growing importance in the employment context is whether and when an employee of a subsidiary entity can hold the parent liable for employment-law violations. Given what you already have learned, you can deduce what might be at stake. It may be that, like the fly-by-night labor contractors discussed in the FLSA context, a subsidiary lacks the capital or insurance to cover its employment-related legal obligations or liabilities. Or it may be that, similar to the circumstances in *Clackamas*, a subsidiary alone has too few employees to be a covered employer under various statutory protections, even though it is part of a large enterprise. In addition, the ability of the plaintiff to reach the parent may affect other matters, such as the extent to which evidence of practices and violations elsewhere in the enterprise might be relevant and discoverable.

If the subsidiary's corporate veil could never be pierced to hold the parent accountable for the subsidiary's employment-law violations, one can imagine the compliance-avoidance techniques that firms might implement. While parent corporations do not enjoy such absolute protection, the law on when parents are accountable for subsidiaries' employment-law violations is far from clear. This is not surprising, since the more generalized "veil piercing" and "enterprise-entity liability" doctrines governing the liability of corporate parents in other contexts are in conceptual disarray. *See generally* Timothy P. Glynn, *Beyond "Unlimiting" Shareholder Liability: Vicarious*

Tort Liability for Corporate Officers, 57 VAND. L. REV. 329 (2004); Stephen M. Bainbridge, *Abolishing Veil Piercing*, 43 CORP. PRAC. COMMENTATOR 517 (2001). Under these theories, a plaintiff typically must show, at the very least, significant control by the parent over the subsidiary's activities and some failure to maintain formal distinctions between the two entities, but application varies wildly. *See* Glynn, *supra*, at 353-56. This kind of traditional veil-piercing analysis may also apply to employment-law claims brought against parent corporations. *See, e.g., Corrigan v. U.S. Steel Corp.*, 478 F.3d 718 (6th Cir. 2007) (applying a traditional piercing framework and granting summary judgment on state-law claims brought against a parent by a subsidiary's employees because plaintiffs failed to show that the parent exercised "complete control" over the subsidiary such that the firms were fundamentally indistinguishable).

Although there is no broadly applicable statutory treatment of this question under federal or state employment laws, in a 1984 amendment to the ADEA and the 1991 Civil Rights Act (abrogating *EEOC v. Arabian American Oil Co.*, 499 U.S. 244 (1991)), Congress addressed a related issue when it extended the reach of antidiscrimination laws to American employees working in foreign countries for U.S. employers or their subsidiaries. *See* 29 U.S.C. § 623(h) (2006) (ADEA); 42 U.S.C. § 2000e-1(c) (2006) (Title VII); 42 U.S.C. § 12112(c)(2) (2006) (ADA). Title VII and the ADA now provide that if "an employer controls a corporation whose place of incorporation is a foreign country, any [violation] . . . engaged in by such corporation shall be presumed to be engaged in by such employer." The determination of whether an employer controls a corporation is based on the following factors:

- The interrelation of operations
- The common management
- The centralized control of labor relations
- The common ownership or financial control of the employer and the corporation

See 42 U.S.C. § 2000e-1(c) (2006); 42 U.S.C. § 12112(c)(2)(2006).

Outside the context of application abroad, increasing numbers of lower courts appear to be confronting the issue of holding parents accountable for employment-law violations by subsidiaries, and a number of circuit courts have now addressed the question in the antidiscrimination context. There are similarities in the courts' approaches; for example, each of the circuit courts and the EEOC has adopted a framework focused on the level of parent-corporation control and operational entanglement that is similar to or mirroring the four-factor test Congress adopted in the foreign entity context. *See Sandoval v. American Bldg. Maintenance Indus., Inc.*, 578 F.3d 787 (8th Cir. 2009); *Frank v. U.S. West, Inc.*, 3 F.3d 1357 (10th Cir. 1993); *Johnson v. Flowers Indus., Inc.*, 814 F.2d 978 (4th Cir. 1987); EEOC COMPLIANCE MANUAL, Section 2: Threshold Issues, No. 915.003, section 2-III.B.1.a.iii.a (addressing "integrated enterprises" in the context of determining whether a employer has a sufficient number of employees to be subject to antidiscrimination laws).

But there are also important differences. Contrary to Congress's approach to the treatment of foreign entities, most of the circuit courts have stated that, in light of the doctrine of limited liability, there is a "strong presumption" against finding a parent corporation liable to subsidiary's employees. *See Johnson*, 814 F.2d at 980-81; *Frank*, 3 F.3d at 1362 (suggesting that such an extension of accountability beyond the employing subsidiary should occur only in extraordinary circumstances). However, the Eighth

Circuit recently adopted — consistent with EEOC guidance — an approach less hostile to finding that a parent and subsidiary form an integrated enterprise. *Sandaval,* 578 F.3d at 792-96 EEOC Compliance Manual, *supra* (focusing on control and articulating no presumption against a finding of sufficient integration).

Like the common-law and related approaches to determining "employee" status, as well as the "joint employer" doctrine and the test adopted in *Clackamas,* such a fact-specific, multifactored test focused on control is destined to produce variations in outcomes over time, unless a "strong presumption" against extension of liability to the parent corporation sets the bar prohibitively high. It also raises the kinds of planning, litigation, and policy challenges we have discussed throughout the chapter. How should we balance the benefits (and, arguably, legislative preference) for shareholder limited liability against the moral hazard — the incentive to utilize corporate formalities to slice up the enterprise into undercapitalized or otherwise unaccountable subparts — that may result from adhering to strictly the formal distinctions between parents and subsidiaries? How might a rule be crafted to reflect this balance?

PROBLEM

1-3. A Second Look at "A Blossoming Business." Building on what you have learned in this chapter, return again to the Blossoming Business hypothetical on page 2.

Assume first that you represent UTF. In light of what you have now learned about the stakes of employment and the scope of the employment relationship, what legal advice would you give regarding how UTF ought to structure its relationships with the various types of workers? What arrangements — contract provisions, management structures, corporate formalities, use of third-party labor suppliers, provision of resources (tools, equipment, vehicles) — might assist in achieving the desired outcome? And think about the types of additional information you would need or want from Fern and Charlie before offering such advice. For example, with regard to the drivers and additional workers, how might the need for specialized training and detailed oversight matter? How might your advice to the engineer be affected by the fact that the software to be developed would be so firm-specific that it likely would be of limited use to others in the industry? With regard to the designers and salesperson, would it make a difference if there were significant barriers to entry into the local tropic flower arrangement market, such as high start-up costs, special equipment needs, and a limited number of potential clients? Would your advice with regard to one or more categories of workers depend on how close to having 15 workers the firm is (or will become)? Finally, how confident are you that, once you are satisfied that you have all of the client information you need, your advice will produce optimal results for your client?

Now assume you represent each of the workers. What expectations do you believe each worker may have regarding his or her employment status? How likely is it that each worker will be able to bargain for protections that meet these expectations? If a worker is in a position to bargain, what kind of relationship and additional protections should he or she seek? What kinds of contractual provisions are most likely to achieve these ends? How confident are you that the result of the bargaining would be accepted by a court?

Finally, consider whether and when the public has an interest in determining the type of relationship that exists between UTF and each of its workers. When, if ever, should the public interest or the interests of third parties trump the interests of the firm and worker? And, relatedly, when and to what extent should UTF's or a worker's intent, or an agreement between the two, determine the nature of the relationship?

Part Two

PRIVATE ORDERING AND DEFAULT TERMS

2

The "At-Will" Default Rule and Its Limits

What rights does an employee have to job security under our legal system? In contrast to most European countries, employment in the United States is "at will," meaning that both the employer and the employee may terminate the relationship at any time and for any reason in the absence of a special exception. The rule is considered a "default" rule because it may be varied by the parties. The employer and employee may agree, for instance, that their relationship will endure for a certain number of years, or until the employer has just cause to terminate the worker. Barring such a contract, however, the law deems the relationship to be terminable at will.

Most employees implicitly understand part of this equation. They know that they can quit their job any time they want without providing an explanation. Indeed, popular culture is replete with images of workers who, fed up with the daily grind, spontaneously decide to walk off the job, usually following a final snide remark to the boss.

What many employees do not appreciate is that at will is a two-way street. The default rules of the workplace allow employers to terminate workers at any time, with or without reason. If asked the right question, employees may acknowledge that they are at will. But with surprising illogic, empirical studies of employee perceptions of workplace law reveal that most workers simultaneously, and mistakenly, believe that they can be fired only for cause, and they believe, again wrongly, that they are entitled to advance notice of termination.

What accounts for this disconnect? It may be due in part to the fact that employer practices tend to be in accord more with employee expectations of how employers should act than with what the law allows employers to do. Most employers do not terminate employees unless there is a business-related reason, such as poor performance or economic necessity. After all, employers benefit from a consistent, high-quality workforce. They also benefit from good workforce morale, which job security occasions. That said, most employers do not promise their employees job security. That is, they rarely contractually bind themselves to terminate only for cause, except in the instances of agreements with individual high-level employees or collectively bargained agreements. They prefer to give more than the law requires without changing the rules of the game. Indeed, employers go to great lengths to try to ensure that the at-will rule remains the default position for their employees.

This raises several questions. What is the function of the at-will default rule in the modern employment regime in light of basic managerial practices? How does this legal principle intersect with nonlegal (or, at least, "unlawyered") aspects of the employment relationship? Should the expectations of employees or the implicit commitments they make to their jobs have any bearing on their legal entitlements? Should the actions of the employer — its past practices, its procedures for discipline and termination, and its promises to its workers — affect at-will status? In short, when, if ever, should courts imply job security absent an explicit negotiated agreement between the parties? And what type of job protection, if any, should apply?

This chapter explores such questions. It begins with a description of employment at will and the historical approach to deviations from the default principle. It then considers the erosion of the traditional at-will approach through contract and related common law doctrines which courts have adopted in responding to inequitable terminations.

A. JOB SECURITY AND THE PRINCIPLE OF AT-WILL EMPLOYMENT

≡ *Hanson v. Central Show Printing Co., Inc.*
≡ *130 N.W.2d 654 (Iowa 1964)*

THOMPSON, J.

. . . The case as made by the plaintiff's evidence is that he was a skilled pressman, and had been in the employ of the defendant corporation at Mason City for many years prior to 1959. In the autumn of that year he had an opportunity to obtain a steady job with the Stoyles Printing Company, also of Mason City. He knew that the defendant's business was often slack in the winter, and contacted G. C. Venz, the president of defendant, to learn whether he would have steady work with it. This resulted, after some negotiations, in an arrangement expressed in a letter from Venz to the plaintiff, which is set out:

Oct. 21, 1959
Mr. Harry Hanson,

Starting today Oct. 21, I will guarantee you 40 hours work per week thru out the entire year each year until you retire of your own choosing.

/s/ G. C. Venz, Pres.

The plaintiff thereupon elected to remain in the employ of the defendant, and did so until October 21, 1961, when he was discharged, without cause. His hourly rate of pay was $2.77 1/2. He asks "damages in the past and in the future at the rate of

$2.77 1/2 per hour for 40 hours per week throughout the entire year for each year and until he retires, all according to the terms of the employment contract," and for costs. At the close of his evidence the trial court granted the defendant's motion for a directed verdict. . . .

The question before us is essentially a simple one, and has been before the courts of the various jurisdictions many times. The rule which has been generally followed is thus set forth:

> [I]n the absence of additional express or implied stipulation as to the duration of the employment or of a good consideration additional to the services contracted to be rendered, a contract for permanent employment, for life employment, for as long as the employee chooses, or for other terms purporting permanent employment, is no more than an indefinite general hiring terminable at the will of either party.

This rule fits the situation before us, where the employment was to be "until you retire of your own choosing." . . .

The defendant urges here lack of mutuality; that is, it contends the plaintiff was not bound to any specific or enforceable term of employment. This is true; but lack of mutuality is not always proof of want of consideration. We have said: "If the lack of mutuality amounts to a lack of consideration, then the contract is invalid. But mere lack of mutuality in and of itself does not render a contract invalid. Though consideration is essential to the validity of a contract, it is not essential that such consideration consist of a mutual promise." *Standard Oil Co. v. Veland*, 224 N.W. 467, 469 [(Iowa 1929)].

So the lack of mutuality in itself is not fatal to plaintiff's case, if there is other consideration. He contends that he gave up the opportunity to take other employment; that this was a detriment to him, and so furnished consideration for the agreement. But it has been repeatedly held that this is not sufficient in contracts for permanent employment, or, as the plaintiff contends here, until he should "retire of your own choosing."

. . . The question was extensively considered in *Skagerberg v. Blandin Paper Co.*, 266 N.W. 872 (Minn. 1936). The plaintiff's case showed that he was a consulting engineer, specializing in the field of heating, ventilating, and air conditioning. While he was employed by the defendant, he received an offer from Purdue University for employment at a yearly salary, which would leave him free for three months to continue his practice; and while performing his duties at the university he would be permitted to carry on his private work so far as time permitted. He communicated this offer to the defendant, which promised, if he would refuse the Purdue offer, it would give him permanent employment. . . .

With reference to plaintiff's contention that consideration passed from him to the defendant, the court said: [The plaintiff] "merely abandoned other activities and interests to enter into the service of defendant — a thing almost every desirable servant does upon entering a new service, but which, of course, cannot be regarded as constituting any additional consideration to the master."

. . . In *Faulkner v. Des Moines Drug Co.*, 90 N.W. 585 (Iowa 1902), . . . the plaintiff claimed a contract for employment "until mutually agreed void." Much of [this Court's] discussion pertained to the indefiniteness of the contract, as to amount of prospective earnings, and the length of time the damages should be computed.

We said: . . . "if it be said that the profits earned before the breach of the contract furnish a basis for estimating future returns, then for what length of time shall they be computed? Shall it be for one month, one year, ten years, or for the entire period of the plaintiff's expectancy of life? Who can place any reasonable estimate upon the period which would probably elapse before the parties 'mutually agree' that the contract between them shall be considered 'void'?" If we substitute for the "mutually agree" the words "until you retire of your own choosing," an equally uncertain happening, we have the identical case. . . . How would the trier of the facts have any guide as to how many years it might be "until he chose to retire"; or how much his loss might be mitigated by other employment which he might secure? . . .

There is a class of cases in which sufficient consideration to uphold a contract for permanent, or life, employment, or employment so long as the employee chooses, has been found. These are cases in which the servant has been found to have paid something for the promise of the employment, in addition to his agreement to render services. A majority of them are cases in which the employer, faced with a claim for damages, agreed to give the claimant permanent employment in consideration of the release of his claim. A case involving a different but also valid consideration is *Carning v. Carr*, 46 N.E. 117 (Mass. 1897), [in which the] plaintiff had been engaged in a competing business with the defendant, and had accepted permanent employment which involved the abandonment of his own enterprise. The defendant thereby received the benefit of removal of competition. . . .

We think the real basis for the majority rule is that there is in fact no binding contract for life employment when the employee has not agreed to it; that is, when he is free to abandon it at any time. So in the instant case, the plaintiff was bound only so long as he chose to work. It does not help to say that a contract for life employment, or permanent employment, may be binding if it is fully agreed upon, even though the only consideration furnished by the employee is his agreement to serve. The fact is he has not agreed to serve for life, or permanently; but only so long as he does not elect to "retire of his own choosing." What the rule might be if he had bound himself to work for life, or so long as he was able, we have no occasion to determine. These observations go to the lack of mutuality and would not be important if there was other consideration. Many difficulties would arise even if such a contract had been made and upheld, in the way of determining the damages because of uncertainty of type of employment, or rate of pay, or how much his loss might be mitigated, in the event of wrongful discharge, by other employment which he might find. But we have no occasion to go further into those questions here. . . .

NOTES

1. *The "Additional Consideration" Requirement.* The *Hanson* court articulates the traditional rule that, absent an express term of employment or "additional" consideration to the employer, a contract of employment is deemed terminable at will. What does the court mean by "additional" consideration? Additional to what?

2. *The Express Term Exception.* Is the additional consideration requirement even relevant here? The court says that additional consideration is necessary where the parties do not agree to a fixed term of employment. Look at the employer's letter. It promises Hanson 40 hours per week each week of every year until his retirement. Isn't that an express provision as to the duration of employment? As a general rule, courts treat indefinite time periods like this — as well as promises of "lifetime employment," "permanent employment," or "long-term employment" — as expressing nothing more than an ordinary at-will relationship. *See, e.g., Turner v. Newsom,* 3 So. 3d 913, 915 (Ala. App. 2008); *Henkel v. Educ. Research Council,* 344 N.E.2d 118, 121-22 (Ohio 1976); *Forrer v. Sears, Roebuck & Co.,* 153 N.W.2d 587, 589-90 (Wis. 1967). Why? Don't these phrases suggest intent to provide job security, albeit for an indefinite term?

3. *Proof of Additional Consideration.* What would Hanson have had to prove in order to show additional consideration? Why isn't it sufficient that Hanson turned down a "steady job" at another printing company? In *Skagerberg v. Blandin Paper Co.,* 266 N.W. 872 (Minn. 1936), described in *Hanson,* the Minnesota Supreme Court rejected the plaintiff's argument that he had supplied sufficient additional consideration upon accepting the defendant's offer of "permanent" employment by foregoing a faculty position at Purdue University. Compare these facts (and the facts in *Hanson* itself) to the two precedents cited in the opinion in which the courts found proof of additional consideration. Those cases involved the settlement of a claim against the employer and the surrender of a competitive business. Do you see the distinction between these cases and *Hanson?* Can you think of other factual scenarios in which a plaintiff might be able to establish additional consideration as understood by these courts? *See, e.g, Kabe's Rest. v. Kinter,* 538 N.W.2d 281, 284 (Iowa 1995) (finding fact that employee personally invested in employer's business and was a motivating force in its creation to be evidence of additional consideration sufficient to submit breach of contract claim to a jury). Are there any circumstances under which simply rejecting alternative employment should constitute additional consideration? Does it matter whether the plaintiff is a new employee choosing between competing offers (as in *Skagerberg*) or an existing employee who is contemplating leaving (as in *Hanson*)?

4. *The Uncertain Damages Rationale.* The court talks about the difficulty of calculating damages where the duration of employment is uncertain. Do you find this a convincing rationale for the additional consideration requirement? Consider that courts routinely calculate lost earnings as damages in commercial cases involving a going concern in which it is uncertain how long the business would have endured. They also calculate lost wages in cases involving breach of a fixed-term contract (as where the employer promises continued employment for a set number of years), although the employee could have departed before the expiration of the term. Suppose that Hanson is 50 years old at the time of the letter agreement. Can you think of a fair way to calculate his damages had the court found an enforceable contract for job security? What proof would you expect each side to submit on this issue?

5. *A Historical View of At Will.* The wide adoption of the at-will presumption by American jurisdictions is generally attributed to an 1877 treatise on "master and servant" law by attorney Horace Gray Wood. In it, Wood famously stated that, unlike the British system,

> [w]ith us the rule is inflexible, that a general or indefinite hiring is *prima facie* a hiring at will, and if the servant seeks to make it out a yearly hiring, the burden is upon him to establish it by proof. . . . [I]t is an indefinite hiring and is determinable at the will of either party.

Horace G. Wood, Master and Servant § 134 (1877).

Some modern scholars have cast doubt on the accuracy of Wood's statement as a reflection of the law of his time. *See, e.g.,* Jay Feinman, *The Development of the*

Employment At Will Rule, 20 Am. J. Legal Hist. 118, 126-27 (1976) (noting that the cases cited by Wood did not support his conclusion and that he incorrectly stated that no American court had adopted the British rule that an indefinite hiring is presumed to endure one year). Nonetheless, "Wood's rule" has not only become black letter doctrine, it is arguably the centerpiece of all of American employment law.

What accounts for the vast appeal of the at-will presumption? Professor Feinman has suggested that the rule reflected the development of American capitalism in the late nineteenth century. He explains:

> [T]hrough the first half of the nineteenth century owners and managers of smaller businesses comprised the bulk of the commercial middle class. Enterprises were not usually impersonal; the managers were frequently the owners of the businesses. . . . As the century progressed and the scale of production increased, however, enterprises became larger and more impersonal and many workers became farther removed from ownership. . . . Salaried employees with little control of their employment situation became a larger proportion of the work force and an important segment of the economy. Thus the many suits brought [by mid-level managers] to establish interests in their jobs were an attempt by a newly-important group in the economy to apply a traditional doctrine to their new situation, but the courts rejected the attempt and instead announced the new principle of employment at will. The reasons for this lie in the class division fundamental to the capitalist system: the distinction between owners and non-owners of capital. . . .
>
> Employment at will is the ultimate guarantee of the capitalist's authority over the worker. The rule transformed long-term and semi-permanent relationships into non-binding terminable at will. If employees could be dismissed on a moment's notice, obviously they could not claim a voice in the determination of the conditions of work or the use of the product of their labor. Indeed, such a fleeting relationship is hardly a contract at all. . . .

Id. at 132.

6. *Other Bases for the At-Will Rule?* If you are not convinced by the rationales put forth by the *Hanson* court in support of the historical presumption of at-will employment, can you think of other justifications for the rule? Consider the arguments put forth in the next case, decided some 20 years later.

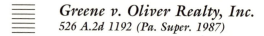

Greene v. Oliver Realty, Inc.
526 A.2d 1192 (Pa. Super. 1987)

Cirillo, President Judge.

. . . Appellant, William Greene[,] began working for Grant Building, Inc. in 1959. Greene allegedly agreed to work at a pay rate below union scale in exchange for a promise that Grant would employ him "for life." In 1975, appellee Oliver Realty, Inc. took over management of Grant Building but Oliver's president assured former Grant employees that existing employment contracts would be honored. During that same year Greene explained the terms of his agreement to an Oliver Realty supervisor. The supervisor stated that he would look into the matter but never got back to Greene. . . . In 1983, Greene was laid off and he brought this action for breach of contract. The trial court ruled that under Pennsylvania law a contract "for life" is a contract at will. The court also held that a contract at will may become a contract for a reasonable time if it is supported by sufficient additional consideration other than the employee's services. The court stated that there was no such consideration in this case. . . . [T]he court granted Oliver's motion for summary judgment. . . .

Contemporary contract law generally provides that a contract is enforceable when the parties reach mutual agreement, exchange consideration and have outlined the terms of their bargain with sufficient clarity. An agreement is sufficiently definite if the parties intended to make a contract and there is a reasonably certain basis upon which a court can provide an appropriate remedy. . . .

However, there is one area of contract law which is strikingly idiosyncratic. That is the law of employment contracts. It has developed contrary to all of the standard, modern contract principles discussed above. If the parties to an employment contract do not specify the duration of the contract, a court will not imply a reasonable duration. The contract is considered terminable at will. If the parties contract for "lifetime" employment, many courts will refuse to enforce their bargain even if their intentions are clear. Even if the agreement is oral, courts refuse to consider the surrounding circumstances. Though mutuality of obligation is a discredited notion, it is often required in the employment context, even when the employment agreement is a unilateral contract. Also, courts routinely refuse to enforce employment contracts if they entail a single promise made in exchange for several promises. In reaching these results, courts rely on anachronistic theories which they would never apply in other fields of contract law. The strong resistance of employment law to modern contract doctrine is a testament to the influence of a uniquely American legal tradition: the at-will presumption. . . .

[T]here are five policies underlying the presumption: (1) The policy of freedom of contract; (2) the need for mutuality of obligation; (3) common experience that it usually effectuates the intent of the parties; (4) as a procedural protection against meritless but vexatious lawsuits; and (5) fairness and equity. . . .

[F]reedom of contract implies that the parties are free to determine the terms of their relationship. The at-will presumption was supposedly based upon this principle. Yet, courts [have] formalistically enforced the rule, allowing it to become a substantive limitation upon the parties' freedom to contract. . . . If two parties desire to contract "for life," courts should be encouraged to enforce their agreement. Of course, the at-will presumption may still be a sound legal rule. It is only when it is allowed to conclusively foreclose proof of the parties['] intent that it becomes an obstacle to freedom of contract. . . .

One rationale for the rule which is illogical and undeserving of perpetuation is that of mutuality of obligation. Courts have often held that mutuality of obligation is lacking in the employment context, particularly in regard to contracts for permanent employment. . . .

However, consideration may be any bargained for benefit or detriment. An employer is free to promise lifetime employment to someone in exchange for that person coming to work for the employer. Once that person accepts and starts work, the employer has received exactly what he bargained for. The employee has performed the desired act. That act is the consideration for the employer's promise and their agreement is a unilateral contract. It is irrelevant that the employee's services are also consideration for his salary. Modern contract law recognizes that consideration may be a single act exchanged for several promises. *See* RESTATEMENT CONTRACTS (SECOND) § 79. Therefore, an employee is free to sell his services in exchange for wages *and* a promise of lifetime employment.

Once the employee begins work, the employer may be the only party obligated, but that is standard in situations involving a unilateral contract. The promisor has requested a performance as the price of his promise. Once he receives that performance, it would defy all notions of equity to allow him to avoid his obligation by claiming that the promisee is no longer obligated. He is no longer obligated because he has already performed the agreed upon acts. . . .

The at-will presumption, like most other legal presumptions, is also based upon common experience. In the vast majority of employer-employee relationships, both sides are silent about the expected duration of the employment agreement. The employee usually feels free to leave and take another job if it presents a more desirable opportunity. Similarly, the employer generally feels free to discharge the employee if he no longer wants his services. The at-will presumption is simply a legal recognition of the parties' normal expectations. . . . It is a waste of time and resources to require parties to re-prove time and again that which experience shows is normally true. It is much more efficient . . . [to] require the parties to demonstrate if exceptional circumstances are present. . . .

The at-will presumption also provides another important procedural protection. If there were no such rule, any dismissed employee could file suit based on an alleged oral contract. The ensuing lawsuit would then hinge solely on credibility. We note that a jury is much more likely to be composed of employees as opposed to employers. We hope that it does not exhibit too cynical a view of humanity for us to be concerned that this might affect more than an occasional verdict. The law is replete with procedural rules designed to guard against the danger of prejudicial jury verdicts. The at-will presumption . . . can be rebutted by clear evidence that the parties intended a contrary result. This is a sufficient safeguard. It balances the need to protect against prejudicial verdicts with the legal system's obligation to enforce the individual parties['] expectations. . . . A contract for life is a heavy burden to impose upon an employer. Courts should be careful that when such a burden is imposed it is because that is what was contracted for. . . . The parties may have used the words "permanently" or "for life" in an off-hand manner. These words are much too ambiguous to provide the sole basis for a jury's imposition of such a tremendous obligation. Courts must look to the surrounding circumstances to determine the parties['] intent. . . .

Another policy supporting continued recognition of the at-will presumption is that of simple fairness. . . .

[W]here the employer and employee both agree that the employment relation is to last for a definite period[, b]oth parties are then bound for that period. If the employer fires the employee, he can sue his former boss and recover damages. However, if the employee quits before the agreed upon period of time has expired, what recourse is available to the employer? If he sues the employee, he will have difficulty proving damages. He will need to show that the loss of this one employee caused his business to lose money. Even if the employer wins a judgment he would then have to enforce it. The old adage that you cannot get blood from a stone is particularly apt in this situation. Most individuals do not have the resources to satisfy anything but the most meager judgment. Therefore, an aggrieved employee will probably have a legal remedy, but an aggrieved employer will not. . . .

The at-will presumption is a partial response to this quandary. . . . The presumption may make it slightly more difficult for the employee to recover if he brings an action. But this merely serves as a partial redress of the unfair situation which would otherwise occur. . . .

Therefore, our review of the applicable policies demonstrates that the at-will presumption remains a sound legal rule. It provides a sensible balance of the relevant concerns. . . . But, courts must remain flexible and not allow the presumption to foreclose proof of the parties' intent. . . .

[I]n cases involving lifetime employment contracts, many courts ignore the parties' desires. In some jurisdictions, lifetime employment contracts are terminable at will unless the[r]e is proof of "sufficient additional consideration." . . . In these jurisdictions, the presumption will not be rebutted even by strong, independent evidence that the parties intended the contract to last for life. . . .

However, other courts utilize a more flexible approach. These courts view the presence of such consideration as proof that the parties intended the employment relation to be more binding than the standard terminable at will agreement. These courts view additional consideration as a factor to consider in determining the parties intent but not as a rigid requirement. . . .

If the parties exchanged "extra" consideration, it is logical that they expected their relationship to be more lasting than the usual employment agreement. However, it is very possible that the parties so intended but did not exchange additional consideration. The surrounding circumstances and the parties' own expressions may still provide clear evidence of that intent. . . .

We agree with [this] reasoning. The at-will presumption may only be rebutted by clear evidence that the parties contracted for a definite period. . . . A promise of permanent or lifetime employment may be nothing more than a casual aside. Or, it may be purely aspirational. The employer may be expressing his hope that a valued employee will stay with him forever. However, he may not have intended to create a binding agreement. These dangers are sufficiently real that courts must look to the circumstances surrounding the parties' agreement. . . . The presence of additional consideration is only a single factor, albeit an important one, which a court must consider to ascertain that intent. When the court is certain of the parties' intent, it must enforce that intent, irrespective of whether additional consideration is present. . . .

In the instant case, Oliver Realty impliedly adopted Grant Building's promise to Greene of lifetime employment. In exchange for that promise, Greene alleges that he worked for twenty-four years at a pay rate below union scale. . . . The [trial] court concluded that Greene worked at sub-union rates in exchange for a promise that he would not be laid off and not in exchange for a lifetime contract. This is an inappropriate conclusion. . . . Greene's belief that he had been promised lifetime employment was sufficiently strong that he explained his position to a supervisor after Oliver took over Grant Building. The court must allow the jury to consider Greene's alleged "additional consideration" as well as all the circumstances surrounding the agreement. A jury might reasonably . . . conclude that Greene has clearly rebutted the at-will presumption. . . .

NOTES

1. *Policy Support for At Will? Greene* provides a more considered analysis of the validity of the at-will presumption than *Hanson*. The court rejects the doctrinal arguments grounded in notions of mutuality and criticizes precedents invoking the additional consideration requirement. Yet the court ultimately comes out in favor of the at-will presumption based largely on pragmatic concerns. Articulate these concerns and the policy arguments the court advances in favor of the at-will rule. Are they convincing?

2. *Employer and Employee Expectations.* The *Greene* court suggests that treating at will as a presumption is administratively efficient because it accords with what most parties want. If at will is in fact a "legal recognition of the parties' normal expectations," then using the presumption reduces costs that litigating this issue would entail. Do you agree with the premise of this argument? Do most "parties" desire an at-will relationship? Some commentators say yes, citing the prevalence of at-will relationships. Given that parties can contract out of at will, the fact that they generally do not, attests to their preference for at-will relationships. *See, e.g.,* Richard A. Epstein, *In Defense of the Contract at Will*, 51 U. CHI. L. REV. 947, 951-52 (1984); J. Hoult Verkerke, *An Empirical Perspective on Indefinite Term Employment Contracts: Resolving the Just Cause Debate*, 1995 WIS. L. REV. 837. Other commentators see the predominance of at-will relationships as a reflection of employee vulnerability and suggest that a rule favoring continued employment more closely approximates employee expectations and preferences. *See, e.g.,* Lawrence E. Blades, *Employment at Will vs. Individual Freedom: On Limiting the Abusive Exercise of Employer Power*, 67 COLUM. L. REV. 1404, 1404-05 (1967); Clyde W. Summers, *The Contract of Employment and the Rights of Individual Employees: Fair Representation and Employment At Will*, 52 FORDHAM L. REV. 1082, 1105-06 (1984). Which position do you find more persuasive?

Do employees even think in terms of negotiating for job security? In her studies of workers' perceptions of employment rights, Professor Pauline Kim found that a majority of respondents erroneously believed that the law protected them from certain types of arbitrary discharge. *See* Pauline T. Kim, *Bargaining with Imperfect Information: A Study of Worker Perceptions of Legal Protection in an At-Will World*, 83 CORNELL L. REV. 105, 133-36 (1997). If most employees do not fully understand the at-will regime, is it possible to draw conclusions about their contractual preferences? If not, which "party" does the at-will presumption protect? Does the prevalence of misinformation and the risk of employer overreaching suggest a need to rethink at will as a default rule? *See* Cynthia Estlund, *How Wrong Are Employees About Their Rights?*, 77 N.Y.U. L. REV. 21-27 (2002) (suggesting that erroneous beliefs held by employers that they are overly vulnerable to litigation and those of employees — that they can only be fired for just cause — justify a need for a law requiring an explicit waiver of just cause protection). For additional scholarship supporting employment at will reform on various grounds, see Jeffrey M. Hirsch, *The Law of Termination: Doing More with Less*, 68 MD. L. REV. 89 (2008); Ann C. McGinley, *Rethinking Civil Rights and Employment at Will: Toward a Coherent National Discharge Policy*, 57 OHIO ST. L. J. 1443 (1996); Cornelius J. Peck, *Unjust Discharges from Employment*, 40 OHIO ST. L. J. 1 (1979); Nicole B. Porter, *The Perfect Compromise: Bridging the Gap Between At-Will Employment and Just Cause*, 87 NEB. L. REV. 62, 84 (2008); Theodore J. St. Antoine, *A Seed Germinates: Unjust Discharge Reform Heads Toward Full Flower*, 67 NEB. L. REV. 56 (1988).

3. *Who Is the Employer?* What does it mean to talk about the interests of the "employer"? Since the employer is usually an entity, not a person, actions or decisions of its individual representatives — its managers, supervisors, and executives — may not be consistent. Note that in *Greene* the employer that made the alleged lifetime employment commitment was Grant Building; the defendant in the case was Oliver Realty, a successor company. Unionized employees generally have provisions in their collective bargaining agreement dealing with the possibility of a change of control, but unrepresented workers without written contracts may be at the mercy of the new employer. Similar problems can arise in the context of ordinary managerial turnover. What one supervisor tells a subordinate may not be acceptable to his or her replacement in subsequent years, or even to that supervisor's own immediate supervisor who may be unaware of the assurances being made. Does the risk of managerial turnover or changes in corporate philosophy suggest the need for greater job security for the workers? Or does it underscore the need for the flexibility that the at-will presumption protects?

4. *The Role of the Jury.* What do you make of the court's concern about jury sympathies? Does this reflect an elitist view of the intellectual capabilities and emotional susceptibility of ordinary people? Or do you think there are legitimate reasons to distrust juries in employment cases? Is this situation any different from other cases involving a single individual suing a business or commercial entity?

5. *Mutuality of Obligation.* Both *Hanson* and *Greene* allude to "mutuality of obligation," a notion historically invoked by courts as a justification for the additional consideration requirement. Mutuality is the idea that, where there is an exchange of promises, both parties must be bound for the court to recognize a contract. Mutuality does not, however, require equivalency of obligation. So viewed, it is just another term for consideration. *See Avion Syst. v. Thompson*, 666 S.E.2d 464, (Ga. App. 2008) ("[Where] the employer offers employment and agrees to pay definite compensation, this consideration is adequate to sustain the contract, and '[t]he fact that the employee agrees to further restrictions and warranties not placed upon the employer does not divest the contract of mutuality.' "); *Worley v. Wyoming Bottling Co.*, 1 P.3d 615, 623 (Wyo. 2000) ("The demand for mutuality of obligation, although appealing in its symmetry, is simply a species of the forbidden inquiry into the adequacy of consideration."). The *Hanson* court seems to acknowledge this, noting that "lack of mutuality in itself is not fatal to the plaintiff's case" if consideration has passed. But the court ultimately finds against the plaintiff, concluding "that there is in fact no binding contract for life employment when the employee has not agreed to it; that is, when he is free to abandon it at any time." Similarly, although *Greene* disclaims the relevance of mutuality of obligation, it expresses concern that the employer and employee do not have equal ability to enforce their contractual rights. That is, in a situation where the employer and employee both agree to be bound for a set period of time, it can be difficult for the employer to obtain relief if the employee breaches the agreement. Don't such statements cast doubt on the courts' assertions that mutuality, in the sense of equivalency of obligation, is a dead letter? Are the concerns raised by *Greene*, with respect to remedies, relevant in a case where no one is alleging a fixed commitment by the employee? Or is the court just bringing mutuality of obligation in through the back door?

6. *Employment and Unilateral Contract Theory.* A further criticism of the mutuality rationale draws on the distinction between unilateral and bilateral contracts. Recall your first-year contracts class. Bilateral contracts involve two promises, made in exchange for each other, which each party is obligated to perform. The presence of a promise on each side creates mutuality. Unilateral contracts involve a single promise made in exchange for a performance, which obligates the promisor only if the offeree renders the requested performance. *See generally Cook v. Johnson*, 221 P.2d 525, 527 (Wash. 1950). In a unilateral contract there is no mutuality, nor is mutuality required, because the contract is formed following performance, at which point only the promisor is bound. Historically, employment has been viewed as unilateral: The employer promises to pay wages if the employee performs the job. However, the employee is not obligated to work; he or she may quit at any point. Do you agree with this characterization of the relationship? Does the employee make any return promises to the employer? If so, do they make the relationship bilateral? If the relationship is unilateral, as courts suggest, mutuality should not pose an obstacle to claims for job security. On the other hand, there may be reasons why treating the relationship as bilateral can benefit employees, for instance, in cases involving implied contracts for job security based on employer policies, which will be discussed later in this chapter.

   7. *Understanding the Significance of a Presumption.* What is the status of the at-will presumption in Pennsylvania following *Greene*? What factors are relevant in determining whether a contract for job security exists? Does *Greene*'s refinement of the additional consideration requirement alter the traditional at-will presumption articulated in Wood's treatise? Or does it represent a return to the true meaning of presumption as a vehicle for determining intent? Consider Professor Clyde Summers' view of the additional consideration requirement as traditionally applied by courts:

> [One] spurious contractual doctrine, sometimes used [by courts] . . . was that to overcome the presumption that employment for an indefinite term was employment at will the employee must give some additional consideration. . . . An employee must give something more. Why something more than faithful service was required was never clearly explained. There seems to be an assumption that because wages for work performed had been paid, the work could not be consideration for a promise of continued employment. As any first semester law student knows, however, one performance can be consideration to support two or even twenty promises. The work performed could be consideration for both the wages paid and the promise of future employment. The requirement of additional consideration was but a device for converting [the at-will] presumption into a substantive rule so that even an express promise of permanent employment would not bind the employer.

Clyde W. Summers, *The Contract of Employment and the Rights of Individual Employees: Fair Representation and Employment At Will*, 52 FORDHAM L. REV. 1082, 1098 (1984).
   Compare the following defense of the historical rule:

> The Wood formulation has been characterized as unduly rigid, in that it "force[s]" courts to ignore facts and circumstances indicative of the intention of the parties. But there is nothing "rigid" or inflexible about Wood's formulation. Wood does not suggest that it should be impermissible or even difficult for a plaintiff to prove that the parties intended that the employment relationship would last for a certain length of time. All it says is that plaintiff has the burden of proving that a contract of employment with no express duration was nevertheless intended by the parties to continue for a fixed duration. Nothing in the rule forecloses a jury from considering all the facts and circumstances from which inferences might be drawn concerning what the contract had been. Of course, that is the role of a presumption: to decide issues where facts are skimpy or absent; presumptions are not supposed to keep facts from being introduced into evidence, nor are they supposed to decide what "surrounding circumstances" may count as a fact.

Mayer G. Freed & Daniel D. Polsby, *The Doubtful Provenance of "Wood's Rule" Revisited*, 22 ARIZ. ST. L.J. 551, 553 (1990).

8. *A Phoenix from the Ashes?* In *Scott v. Extracorporeal*, 545 A.2d 334 (Pa. Super. Ct. 1988), decided by the same court one year after *Greene*, the plaintiff alleged breach of a contract for job security on the basis of a combination of circumstances, including her manager's promise of "permanent" employment, references to permanent employment status and to "for cause" bases for discipline and termination in the employer's personnel manual, and the employee's execution of an agreement assigning any inventions derived during employment to the employer. The court disregarded the references to "permanent" employment as "too broad to be enforced" and found nothing in the personnel manual suggesting that discharge could only be for cause. *Id.* at 337. The court also held that the assignment of inventions agreement did not constitute additional consideration. It explained:

> [T]here is no indication that appellant brought any abilities to the job, aside from the services for which she was compensated, which were beneficial to her employer or that she sacrificed anything tangible pursuant to the agreement beyond that for which she was paid. The at-will presumption is not overcome every time a worker sacrifices theoretical rights and privileges. . . . We have no indication that she did conceive anything of value during her employment, or that at the time she was hired it was reasonably likely she would. The privileges and rights which appellant sacrificed were so minimal that in no sense can we say the agreement rose to the level of "additional consideration" as our courts have defined it.
>
> . . . We do not read Greene [v. Oliver Realty] to stand for the proposition that any time a discharged employee talismanically recites that he was promised "permanent" employment, the case must automatically proceed to trial.

Id. at 339-40. Does this excerpt change your understanding of the significance of *Greene*? While the strength of the employment at will presumption may vary in particular cases, it is important to bear in mind that some modern courts continue to hold fast to the historical version of the rule set out in *Hanson*. *See, e.g., Turner v. Newsome*, 3 So. 3d 913, 922 (Ala. App. 2008) (written promise to employ plaintiff "until the retirement of the President" was an indefinite contract and employee accepting additional responsibilities and work hours, putting educational opportunities on hold, and not revealing employer's "immoral conduct" were not sufficient consideration to support an "extraordinary" contract for lifetime employment).

9. *Just Cause and Legislative Reform.* One U.S. jurisdiction has statutorily rejected the employment at will presumption. The Montana Wrongful Discharge from Employment Act of 1987 ("WDEA") alters the at-will presumption by creating a statutory cause of action for employees terminated without "good cause" subsequent to their completion of the employer's designated probationary period. *See* MONT. CODE ANN. § 39-2-904(2) (2005). Similarly, under the proposed Model Employment Termination Act of 1991 ("META"), an employer may not terminate without good cause unless the parties mutually agree to waive the good cause requirement in a written agreement. *See* META §§ 3(a), 4(c). These approaches essentially reverse the at-will presumption, making job security the default rule. In exchange for this benefit, they place certain limits on damages that protect employers. *See, e.g.,* MONT. CODE ANN. § 39-2-905 (2005) (capping damages at four years of wages and disallowing other forms of compensatory damages). Although comparable legislation has been introduced in other jurisdictions, to date no state has adopted META or followed Montana's lead. Why do you think that is?

History suggests a possible answer. The movement to adopt unjust dismissal legislation came about in the 1980s following the issuance of several pro-plaintiff decisions, several of which you will read in the subsequent sections. Many perceived these decisions as heralding judicial adoption of a broad rule requiring just cause for termination. In such an environment, employers were willing to support unjust dismissal legislation that offered increased predictability over common law expansion of employee rights and created an opportunity for employer interest groups to exact some pro-business concessions in the legislative drafting process. Indeed, both the WDEA and META were widely viewed as compromise proposals, and employers played a significant role in securing adoption of the Montana law. *See* Alan B. Krueger, *The Evolution of Unjust-Dismissal Legislation in the United States*, 44 INDUS. & LAB. REL. REV. 644 (1990-91); Daniel J. Libenson, *Leasing Human Capital: Toward A New Foundation for Employment Termination Law*, 27 BERKELEY J. EMP. & LAB. L. 111 (2006); Theodore J. St. Antoine, *The Making of the Model Employment Termination Act*, 69 WASH. L. REV. 361 (1994).

As the previous note suggests, however, fears of a full-scale retreat from employment at will proved unfounded. In fact, contemporary developments have led some to speculate that the law is moving in the opposite direction, toward a refortified presumption of employment at will. *See e.g.,* Rachel Arnow-Richman, *Employment as Transaction*, 39 SETON HALL L. REV. 447 (2009); Jonathan Fineman, *The Inevitable Demise of the Implied Employment Contract*, 29 BERKELEY J. EMP. & LAB. L. 345 (2008); *cf.* Matthew Finkin, *Shoring Up the Citadel (At-Will Employment)*, 24 HOFSTRA LAB. & EMP. L.J. 1, 27 (2006) (arguing that the draft Restatement of Employment Law chapter on termination "manhandles doctrine to achieve a specific end — to permit employers to free themselves of what they might conceive in hindsight to be an undesirable commitment to job security"). If such assertions are true, it is perhaps unsurprising that employer support for legal reform (and consequently the ability to pass unjust dismissal legislation) ultimately dwindled.

PROBLEM

2-1. Suppose that William Greene hires you to serve as his trial attorney on remand following the Superior Court's decision. What litigation strategy would you pursue? Would you try to demonstrate additional consideration? Can you? What other evidence, if any, can Greene use to establish the parties' intention to create a lifetime employment contract? Who would you rather have as a client given the rules articulated by the Superior Court — Greene or Hanson?

B. ORAL AND IMPLIED CONTRACT RIGHTS TO JOB SECURITY

As you can see from *Greene*, despite the entrenched idea of employment at-will, modern courts have questioned the justifications for the rule and the inflexible manner in which it has traditionally been applied. Indeed, in the last several decades, courts have recognized a variety of exceptions grounded in contract and related common-law principles that have significantly weakened the at-will presumption. No one reason explains this trend. Depending on the case and the court, judicial resistance to the at-will presumption may reflect disenchantment with the rule on policy grounds, doctrinal objections to its application as a presumption, sympathy for individual plaintiffs in particular cases, or a desire to make the law conform more closely to the real expectations of parties in a complex relationship.

As you read, keep these possible explanations in mind. In each case, consider whether courts are correctly applying contract doctrine, whether the result they reach is fair under the particular facts, and what policy implications flow from the decision, both in terms of how the result will influence employers in running their businesses and the ultimate social consequences to employees. Is it fair to say that the contract rules surrounding at-will employment are in disarray, as some commentators have suggested, or can you see any unifying themes in the exceptions?

1. Reliance on Offers of Employment

The ability to terminate employment at will can have harsh effects on neophyte employees who may quit an existing job, relocate, or turn down other job offers in order to accept a new position. Should the law provide any recourse for at-will employees terminated shortly after accepting work?

Goff-Hamel v. Obstetricians & Gynecologists
588 N.W.2d 798 (Neb. 1999)

WRIGHT, J.

[Julie] Goff-Hamel worked for Hastings Family Planning for 11 years. Prior to leaving Hastings Family Planning, Goff-Hamel was earning $24,000 plus [benefits].

In July 1993, Goff-Hamel met with representatives of Obstetricians regarding the possibility of employment. Present at the meeting were [Dr. George Adam, a part owner of Obstetricians] and Larry Draper, a consultant of Obstetricians involved in personnel decisions. Adam had approached Goff-Hamel in June 1993 about working for him as a patient relations and outreach coordinator. [She initially declined the offer.] Adam spoke to her one month later, asking her to reconsider and whether she was ready to "jump ship and come work for him." Goff-Hamel told Adam she would be interested in hearing some details, and an interview was set for July 27 at Adam's office.

At the meeting, Adam represented to Goff-Hamel that the position would be full time and would start at a salary of $10 per hour and that she would be provided 2 weeks' paid vacation, three or four paid holidays, uniforms, and an educational stipend. A retirement plan would start after the end of the second year, retroactive to the end of the first year. The job would not provide health insurance.

Goff-Hamel was offered a job with Obstetricians during the July 27, 1993, meeting, and she accepted the job offer at that time. . . . [I]t was agreed that she would start her employment on October 4. Goff-Hamel gave notice to Hastings Family Planning in August. . . .

Subsequently, Goff-Hamel was provided with uniforms for her job. She was given a copy of her schedule for the first week of work. . . .

On October 3, 1993, Goff-Hamel was told by Draper that she should not report to work the next morning as had been planned. Draper told her that Janel Foote, the wife of a part owner of Obstetricians, Dr. Terry Foote, opposed the hiring of Goff-Hamel.

. . . Goff-Hamel sought replacement employment, but was unable to obtain employment until April 1995, when she was employed part time at the rate of $11 per hour.

The trial court concluded that since Goff-Hamel was to be employed at will, her employment could be terminated at any time, including before she began working. The court concluded that under either contract law or promissory estoppel, Obstetricians was entitled to a judgment as a matter of law. . . .

We have consistently held that when employment is not for a definite term and there are no contractual, statutory, or constitutional restrictions upon the right of discharge, an employer may lawfully discharge an employee whenever and for whatever cause it chooses. Therefore, the trial court correctly determined as a matter of law that Goff-Hamel could not bring a claim for breach of an employment contract.

Goff-Hamel's second cause of action was based upon promissory estoppel. "'[T]he development of the law of promissory estoppel "is an attempt by the courts to keep remedies abreast of increased moral consciousness of honesty and fair representations in all business dealings."" ' *Rosnick v. Dinsmore*, 457 N.W.2d 793, 801 (Neb. 1990).

Promissory estoppel provides for damages as justice requires and does not attempt to provide the plaintiff damages based upon the benefit of the bargain. It requires only that reliance be reasonable and foreseeable. It does not impose the requirement that the promise giving rise to the cause of action must be so comprehensive in scope as to meet the requirements of an offer that would ripen into a contract if accepted by the promisee.

We have not specifically addressed whether promissory estoppel may be asserted as the basis for a cause of action for detrimental reliance upon a promise of at-will employment. . . .

Other jurisdictions which have addressed the question of whether a cause of action for promissory estoppel can be stated in the context of a prospective at-will employee are split on the issue. Some have held that an employee can recover damages incurred as a result of resigning from the former at-will employment in reliance on a promise of other at-will employment. They have determined that when a prospective employer knows or should know that a promise of employment will induce an employee to leave his or her current job, such employer shall be liable for the reliant's damages. Recognizing that both the prospective new employer and the prior employer could have fired the employee without cause at any time, they have concluded that the employee would have continued to work in his or her prior employment if it were not for the offer by the prospective employer. Although damages have not been allowed for wages lost from the prospective at-will employment, damages have been allowed based upon wages from the prior employment and other damages incurred in reliance on the job offer.

In contrast, other jurisdictions have held as a matter of law that a prospective employee cannot recover damages incurred in reliance on an unfulfilled promise of at-will employment, concluding that reliance on a promise consisting solely of at-will employment is unreasonable as a matter of law because the employee should know that the promised employment could be terminated by the employer at any time for any reason without liability. These courts have stated that an anomalous result occurs when recovery is allowed for an employee who has not begun work, when the same employee's job could be terminated without liability 1 day after beginning work. . . .

In *Grouse v. Group Health Plan, Inc.*, 306 N.W.2d 114 (Minn. 1981), a pharmacist working at a drugstore desired employment with a hospital or clinic. He accepted employment with a clinic and gave 2 weeks' notice to the drugstore. During this period, he declined a job with a hospital because he had accepted employment with the clinic. Upon reporting to work, he was told that someone else had been hired because the pharmacist did not satisfy certain hiring requirements of the clinic. He had difficulty obtaining other full-time employment and suffered wage loss as a result.

. . . The court stated:

> [A]ppellant had a right to assume he would be given a good faith opportunity to perform his duties to the satisfaction of respondent once he was on the job. He was not only denied that opportunity but resigned the position he already held in reliance on the firm offer which respondent tendered him.

Id. at 116.

The court also recognized that under appropriate circumstances, promissory estoppel could apply even if the employee was fired after he had commenced employment, thus concluding that its ruling would not necessarily create an anomalous result.

[The court went on to summarize additional cases from other jurisdictions.]

Having reviewed and considered decisions from other jurisdictions, we conclude under the facts of this case that promissory estoppel can be asserted in connection with the offer for at-will employment and that the trial court erred in granting Obstetricians summary judgment. A cause of action for promissory estoppel is based upon a promise which the promisor should reasonably expect to induce action or forbearance on the part of the promisee which does in fact induce such an action or forbearance. Here, promissory estoppel is appropriate where Goff-Hamel acted to her detriment in order to avail herself of the promised employment. . . .

Stephan, J., dissenting.

I respectfully dissent. In my opinion, the district court correctly determined as a matter of law that Goff-Hamel could not proceed under either a breach of contract or a promissory estoppel theory of recovery. I cannot reconcile the result reached by the majority or its rationale with our firmly established legal principles governing at-will employment. As succinctly and, in my view, correctly stated by the district court: "Since plaintiff could have been terminated after one day's employment without the defendant incurring liability, logic dictates she could also be terminated before the employment started."

The majority relies in part on *Grouse v. Group Health Plan, Inc.*, which concluded that the principles of promissory estoppel set forth in the Restatement of Contracts § 90 (1932) could apply to a termination of at-will employment which occurred before the employee actually started working because "under appropriate circumstances we believe [Restatement of Contracts] section 90 would apply even after employment has begun." However, we held in *Merrick v. Thomas*, 522 N.W.2d 402 (Neb. 1994), that an at-will employee who was discharged a short time after she began working could not, as a matter of law, assert a promissory estoppel claim for damages resulting from resignation of her previous employment. Thus, this essential premise of the holding in *Grouse* is directly contrary to our law. Another basis for the decision in *Grouse*, as quoted in the majority opinion, is that one who is offered employment has "a right to assume he would be given a good faith opportunity to perform his duties to the satisfaction" of the employer. This concept is foreign to our law and entirely inconsistent with the established principle, acknowledged by the majority, that in the absence of contractual, statutory, or constitutional restrictions, an employer may discharge an at-will employee "whenever and for whatever cause it chooses." *Myers v. Nebraska Equal Opp. Comm.*, 582 N.W.2d 362 (Neb. 1998). Thus, whether an at-will employee performs in a satisfactory manner is immaterial to the employer's right to discharge, and there is no basis under our law for an assumption that satisfactory performance by such an employee would create an entitlement to continued employment. . . .

The conflict between the court's decision today and the law of at-will employment is further demonstrated by the manner in which the majority addresses the issue of damages. Goff-Hamel's damage claim is based entirely upon her allegation that after learning on October 3, 1993, that appellee had withdrawn its offer of employment, she was unable to find "comparable" full-time employment until May 15, 1995. The majority acknowledges that under the theory of recovery which it recognizes in this case, damages cannot be "based upon the wages the employee would have earned in the prospective employment because the employment was terminable at will." Following the same logic, damages based upon wage loss during any *interval* between withdrawal of a promise of at-will employment and the securing of "comparable" employment would not be recoverable, because the promised employment could have been terminated by either party at any time after it had begun. Thus, the record reflects no factual basis upon which damages claimed by Goff-Hamel could be awarded under the remedy which the majority recognizes.

I would follow what I consider to be the better reasoned view, that promissory estoppel may not be utilized to remedy an unfulfilled promise of at-will employment. I acknowledge that this reasoning would produce a seemingly harsh result from the perspective of Goff-Hamel under the facts of this case, but to some degree, this is inherent in the concept of at-will employment. For example, in *Hamersky v. Nicholson Supply Co.*, 517 N.W.2d 382, 385 (Neb. 1994), a 22-year employee was discharged "without any notification, cause or reason," and although this action may seem harsh, we held that it was permissible where there was no contractual provision for employment of specific duration. Similarly, an employer which has made a significant expenditure in training an at-will employee may feel harshly treated if, upon completing the training, the employee immediately utilizes his or her newly acquired skills to secure more remunerative employment with a competitor. If the law of at-will employment were regularly bent to circumvent what some may consider a harsh result in a particular case, its path would soon become hopelessly circuitous and impossible to follow.

Employment for a specific duration imposes certain benefits and burdens upon each party to the relationship. Under our established law, parties wishing to create such a relationship must do so by contract. Where, as in this case, the parties have not chosen to impose contractual obligations upon themselves, it is my view that a court should not utilize the principle of promissory estoppel to impose the subjective expectations of either party upon the other. I agree with the view that in the context of an employment relationship, promissory estoppel "should be construed 'in such a way that it compl[e]ments, rather than undermines, traditional contract principles.' "

NOTES

1. *Promissory Estoppel, Employment At Will, and Newly Hired Employees.* In recognizing the plaintiff's promissory estoppel claim, *Goff-Hamel* cites *Grouse v. Group Health Plan* for the proposition that an employee is entitled to a good faith opportunity to perform to the employer's satisfaction. The dissent criticizes this premise as "directly contrary" to employment at will. Which opinion do you find more convincing? In practice, many employers designate starting employees as "probationary," reinforcing the idea that the employee has no job security during the first few months of employment. Does this point to a logical flaw in the courts' analyses in *Goff-Hamel* and *Grouse*? Or is it still possible to reconcile promissory estoppel protection with the at-will presumption?

2. *The One-Day Worker.* A Minnesota court directly addressed the scenario of the one-day-hired, one-day-fired employee described in *Goff-Hamel* and *Grouse*. In *Gorham v. Benson Optical*, 539 N.W.2d 798 (Minn. Ct. App. 1995), Gorham accepted a job offer as a regional manager with the defendant. After confirming the position he gave notice to his current employer, who tried to entice him to stay by offering him a raise, which he declined. Prior to starting his new job, however, the company officer who had hired Gorham left, and Gorham was terminated on his first day at work. In addressing his subsequent promissory estoppel claim, the court opined:

> We see no relevant difference between Gorham, who reported to the national sales meeting on his first day of employment, and Grouse, who was denied even one day on the job. Both men relied to their detriment on the promise of a new job, only to discover that the opportunity had disintegrated before they ever actually started working. Neither man had a "good faith opportunity to perform his duties."

Id. at 801. Gorham was fired the very day he showed up for work. How much more time would have constituted a "good faith opportunity" to perform his duties? Two weeks? A month? More?

3. *Reasonableness of Reliance.* Courts rejecting the applicability of promissory estoppel often do so on the grounds that, while the worker does in fact rely, the reliance is not reasonable if the offer is for at-will employment. *See, e.g., White v. Roche Biomedical Labs., Inc.*, 807 F. Supp. 1212, 1219-20 (D.S.C. 1992) (concluding that "reliance on a promise consisting solely of at-will employment is unreasonable as a matter of law since such a promise creates no enforceable rights in favor of the employee other than the right to collect wages accrued for work performed"); *cf. Petitte v. DSL*, 925 A.2d 457, 463 (2007) (noting in rejecting plaintiff's breach of contract claim based on revoked offer of employment that "this clarification of the law serves to put employees on notice of the risk they take when leaving existing employment for another one."). Pushed to its logical conclusion, this argument would seem to foreclose promissory estoppel liability entirely since, by definition, there is no promise of continued employment and any reliance to the contrary would be ipso facto unreasonable.

Do you agree? Can it be reasonable (as a practical matter) for an employee to rely on a job offer even if there is no legal commitment to continued employment? If you said yes, does your answer change if the employer is more explicit about the plaintiff's at-will status? In *Petitte, supra*, the plaintiff accepted an oral offer of employment and resigned his current employment. Subsequently, he signed a written offer letter stating that he was not guaranteed employment for any length of time and could be terminated without reason. On what was to be the first day of his new job, the employer told him that there was a problem with some of his references and rescinded its offer. The court rejected plaintiff's subsequent breach of contract claim, asserting that there was no way to distinguish the at-will nature of the job from the at-will nature of the offer. You will soon see that written language disclaiming job security, like that in *Petitte*, has become common in a variety of employment documents. Its legal significance, both in the context of rescinded offers and other types of termination disputes, is an unsettled question to which we will frequently return.

4. *Remedy.* The majority in *Goff-Hamel* is careful to point out the limited nature of the promissory estoppel remedy. Understand the difference between the amount of damages permitted under these opinions and what would have been available had the plaintiffs been able to establish breach of a contract for job security. Suppose, for instance, that Goff-Hamel earned $1500 per month in her old job and was promised $1600 per month by the defendant. After being terminated, she searches unsuccessfully for alternate employment for two months before accepting a position at $1400 per month. How should the court calculate her damages, assuming she prevails on remand? Now suppose instead that following her termination Goff-Hamel's former employer happily takes her back at the same salary she had earned prior to giving notice. Is she entitled to anything?

As a general rule, damages in promissory estoppel cases are calculated based on the plaintiff's *prior* employment. But what if that position was itself at will? Should that limit recovery? After all, there is no guarantee that the plaintiff would have remained in the prior job. The employer in *Toscano v. Greene Music*, 21 Cal. Rptr. 3d 732 (Ct. App. 2004), a case involving the retraction of a sales management position, made such an argument in seeking to limit the plaintiff's damages to wages lost between resigning his prior employment and the anticipated start date of the promised job. The court rejected the limitation, holding that lost future wages with a prior employer are recoverable under a promissory estoppel theory, provided they are not "speculative, remote, contingent or merely possible." *Id.* at 738. It went on, however, to hold that the trial court's award of lost wages until plaintiff's retirement was improper under this standard because it was based solely on the fact that Toscano had a history of remaining with his current employer until offered new employment.

Do results like this diminish the significance to employees of courts' recognition of the promissory estoppel cause of action? Or do such limitations strike an appropriate balance in light of the presumption of employment at will? Given the result in *Toscano*, how would you go about helping a future plaintiff overcome such hurdles to establishing damages? *Cf. Helmer v. Bingham Toyota Isuzu*, 29 Cal. Rptr. 3d 136 (Ct. App. 2005) (affirming award of damages of lost future wages with prior employer from time of resignation through retirement on plaintiff's promissory fraud claim where prior supervisor testified that plaintiff was a reliable employee and would have been rehired but for a strict no-rehire policy).

5. *Proof of Reliance.* What constitutes detrimental reliance for purposes of promissory estoppel? The most convincing cases are those involving employees who relocate or incur significant expense in preparing for their new job. *See e.g., Sheppard v. Morgan Keegan & Co.*, 266 Cal. Rptr. 784, 787 (Ct. App. 1990) ("[A]n employer cannot expect a new employee to sever his former employment and move across the country only to be terminated before the ink dries on his new lease[.]"). *Goff-Hamel* suggests giving up one's current job alone is sufficient to state a promissory estoppel claim.

In *Grouse*, the employee gave up his job and turned down a second offer. What if the employee simply refrains from applying to other jobs based on the assurances of his or her current employer? *See Hanly v. Riverside Methodist Hosps.*, 603 N.E.2d 1126, 1131 (Ohio Ct. App. 1991) (no promissory estoppel claim where plaintiff neither looked for nor turned down other employment nor was expressly dissuaded by employer from seeking outside opportunities). If an employee truly refrains from seeking alternative work because of a promise of job security, isn't that still reliance? In such a situation, what evidence could there be other than the employee's "bare assertion" of foregoing a job search? Perhaps the issue is not whether the employee actually relied on the promise in not looking for work, but rather, whether that reliance was detrimental. *See Fregara v. Jet Aviation Business Jets*, 764 F. Supp. 940, 949 (D.N.J. 1991) (no promissory estoppel claim where plaintiff was unemployed at time of job offer and therefore did not forego anything of value in accepting position). If so, would it be enough to show that more lucrative alternative positions were available?

6. *Other Issues of Fact.* Difficulties in proving reliance are not the only potential pitfall for plaintiffs pursuing a promissory estoppel claim. As you read the next case, consider the other elements of a promissory estoppel cause of action, and whether employees will likely be able to establish them.

Schoff v. Combined Insurance Company of America
604 N.W.2d 43 (Iowa 1999)

TERNUS, Justice.

. . . Viewed in a light most favorable to the plaintiff, the record shows the following facts. Prior to his employment by the defendant, Schoff was a sixteen-year employee of MidAmerican Energy Corporation. On February 28, 1996, Schoff interviewed with Michael Hageman, a district manager for [defendant Combined Insurance Co.]. At the time of his interview, Schoff completed a written application for employment. The application stated that bonding by Combined's bonding company was a condition of employment. It also asked about Schoff's criminal history. In response to the question, "Have you ever been convicted of a felony?" Schoff answered, "No." Schoff had, however, been convicted of two serious misdemeanors, and he voluntarily disclosed this fact to Hageman during the interview. Hageman understood that Schoff revealed this information to be sure that Schoff's criminal record would not cause a problem with his potential employment by Combined.

Hageman questioned Schoff about the incident resulting in the convictions, and Schoff answered all of Hageman's questions. Hageman never asked, however, whether Schoff had ever been *charged* with a felony, and Schoff did not volunteer the fact that the original charges resulting in his misdemeanor convictions were felony charges. At the time Hageman interviewed Schoff, Hageman understood that only felony convictions, as opposed to charges, were pertinent to bonding. Therefore, he believed that Schoff's criminal record, which he understood involved only misdemeanor convictions, would not adversely affect Schoff's employment with Combined. When Schoff asked Hageman whether this incident would cause any problem with Schoff's potential employment by Combined, Hageman assured Schoff that "as long as [you] have no felony convictions, [your] criminal record [will] be no problem."

Hageman subsequently offered Schoff a position as a sales representative for Combined. Prior to accepting this offer, Schoff specifically asked Hageman whether his criminal record would have any impact on his employment with Combined. Hageman again assured Schoff that it would not. Hageman also stated that only felony convictions were relevant to employment and bonding decisions. Schoff accepted the position offered by Hageman and terminated his employment with MidAmerican.

Upon acceptance of the job offered by Combined, Schoff was required to apply for fidelity bond coverage. Hageman completed an enrollment form for Schoff, in Schoff's presence, asking Schoff specific questions when the need arose. Hageman did not answer the question, "Have you ever been convicted, sentenced or imprisoned?" He told Schoff that only felony convictions were relevant and, therefore, Hageman simply wrote "N/A" after the question. Schoff signed the form and it was forwarded to the bonding company.

Schoff then entered a training period of several weeks. At the end of this period, he signed an employment contract with Combined. This agreement was on a standard form and explicitly stated that the employment contract was "terminable at will by either party."

Schoff began selling insurance for Combined and proved to be an excellent employee. After only three months on the job, however, he was taken out of the field because his application for a fidelity bond had been denied. Schoff was told that the bonding company refused to issue a bond for him due to his criminal record. Combined asserted that the bonding company denied coverage because Schoff had been charged with two felonies and had failed to disclose the information about his conviction history on the enrollment form. Schoff was subsequently officially terminated from his employment with Combined.

[The district court granted Combined's motion for summary judgment on Schoff's claim that Combined was "estopped from terminating him on the basis of the criminal charges he had disclosed," but it first rejected the employer's argument that the at-will relationship barred recovery under a theory of promissory estoppel, and then turned to the defendant's alternative argument that, as a matter of law, the plaintiff cannot prove the elements of promissory estoppel.]

A. Undisputed Facts

As the facts reviewed above demonstrate, it is undisputed that Schoff was fired because the bonding company refused to issue a bond. In addition, it is uncontroverted in the record that the bonding company refused to issue a bond because Schoff had two felony charges on his record and/or because he did not reveal his criminal record on his bond application. Thus, in order to estop Combined from firing him for these reasons, Schoff must establish a clear and definite promise by Combined that he would not be fired if he failed to qualify for a bond, or that he would be bonded despite his felony charges and/or failure to reveal his criminal record.

It is helpful at this juncture to compare the reasons for Schoff's discharge with the alleged promises made by Combined. Although there are some minor discrepancies between Hageman's and Schoff's recollections of their conversations, the facts viewed most favorably to the plaintiff would support a finding that Hageman told Schoff that Schoff's criminal record would not affect his employment with Combined. In addition, the record would support a finding that Hageman told Schoff that only felony convictions were relevant to employment and bonding decisions. We turn now to whether these statements provide a basis to estop Combined from firing Schoff because he did not qualify for a fidelity bond.

B.   Meaning of Terms

We start our analysis with a discussion of the meaning of the requirement that the plaintiff prove a clear and definite promise. A "promise" is "[a] declaration . . . to do or forbear a certain specific act." *Black's Law Dictionary* 1213 (6th ed. 1990). A promise is "clear" when it is easily understood and is not ambiguous. *See Webster's Third New International Dictionary* 419 (unab. ed. 1993). A promise is "definite" when the assertion is explicit and without any doubt or tentativeness. *See id.* at 592.

C.   Proof of a Promise

Initially, we conclude that any statements made by Hageman that only felony convictions were important do not constitute an assertion that Combined would forbear a certain specific act, namely, discharging Schoff because of his felony charges and/or his failure to be bonded. These statements by Hageman more clearly fall within the common definition of a representation: "a statement . . . made to convey a particular view or impression of something with the intention of influencing opinion or action." Statements that only felony convictions are relevant to employment and bonding decisions are not the equivalent of a declaration that Combined would not fire Schoff because of his felony record. Hageman's statements merely conveyed his *impression* or *understanding* of a certain fact — that only felony convictions were relevant; as a matter of law, these statements do not constitute a promise.

Although this distinction may appear to be a technical one, it is of utmost importance. . . . [W]e will not imply a promise from representations made by an employer, but will require strict proof that the defendant promised to do or not to do a specific act, and did not simply state the employer's view or impression of something.

That brings us to the other statement made by Hageman — that Schoff's criminal record would not be a problem. Although we have serious reservations whether this statement constitutes a promise, we need not resolve that issue because any such "promise" was not clear and definite, as we now discuss.

D.   Proof That the Promise Was
Clear and Definite

Schoff does not claim that he and Hageman ever discussed the felony charges that were filed against Schoff. Indeed, the record is undisputed that Schoff never disclosed this aspect of his criminal record to Hageman. Consequently, any statement that Schoff's "criminal record" would not affect his employment is subject to some ambiguity in that the parties did not have the same knowledge with respect to the nature and extent of Schoff's criminal record. This ambiguity is crucial because Schoff was not fired because of his criminal record in general; he was fired because he could not be bonded. Similarly, he was not denied a bond due to his criminal record in general; rather he was not bonded because he had been charged with felonies and/or had not revealed his criminal record on his bond application. As a matter of law, any "promises" that Schoff's criminal record would not be a problem simply do not clearly and definitely encompass a promise that Schoff's felony charges would not be a problem or that his failure to be bonded would not be a problem. Therefore, the statement upon which the plaintiff bases his claim does not meet the strict standard required for a clear and definite promise.

NOTES

1. *Promises, Offers, and Representations.* According to the court, "in order to estop Combined from firing him, [Schoff had to be able to] establish a clear and definite promise by Combined that he would not be fired if he failed to qualify for a bond, or that he would be bonded despite his felony charges and/or failure to reveal his criminal record." The court then goes to some length to distinguish between the "representations" made by Hageman and the type of definitive promise required for promissory estoppel. Do you understand the distinction the court is drawing? Do you agree with its characterization of the issue? Consider that in promissory estoppel claims outside of the employment context courts have held that the plaintiff need not demonstrate a definite offer to contract in order to show the defendant made a promise justifying reliance. *See, e.g., Hoffman v. Red Owl Stores, Inc.*, 133 N.W.2d 267, 276 (Wis. 1965) (noting in suit over promise to provide a franchise that §90 "does not impose the requirement that the promise . . . be so comprehensive in scope as to meet the requirements of an offer that would ripen into a contract if accepted"). Yet the court in *Schoff*, as well as courts in other employment cases, often construe the elements of a promissory estoppel claim more strictly. *See, e.g, Dumas v. Infinity Broadcasting Corp*, 416 F.3d 671, 677 (7th Cir. 2005) (suggesting that disc jockey who gave up previous job based on negotiations for employment that failed to come to fruition could not sustain a claim for promissory estoppel unless capable of establishing all of the elements of a valid contract other than consideration); *Ruud v. Great Plains Supply, Inc.*, 526 N.W.2d 369, 372 (Minn. 1995) (finding statements that "good employees would be taken care of" and plaintiff would be offered a "similar" position if things did not work out after he accepted relocation to management position at unprofitable store insufficiently definite to give rise to promissory estoppel claim). Does the employment context require a different interpretation of the doctrine than in other failed contract scenarios? Or is it something particular about Schoff's situation that motivates the result in this case?

2. *Protection for Workers with Criminal Histories.* Although Iowa does not, several states have statutes prohibiting employers from considering an applicant's criminal and/or arrest records absent job-relatedness. *See, e.g.,* MASS. GEN. LAWS ANN. ch. 151B, §4(9) (2006) (prohibiting employer or its agent from requesting information regarding, inter alia, "an arrest . . . in which no conviction resulted" or any conviction of a misdemeanor which occurred five years prior to date of employee's application); N.Y. CORRECT. LAW §752 (McKinney) (2005) (prohibiting denial of employment based on previous conviction of applicant unless there is "a direct relationship" between the offenses and the specific license or position or where accepting

the applicant would involve "an unreasonable risk" to property or public safety); *see also* Chapter 6 (discussing these and other state statutes designed to protect employee privacy). Would such a law have helped Schoff?

Laws prohibiting discrimination based on criminal history serve important social goals, ensuring not only fairness to the individual worker but also helping to facilitate ex-convicts' reentry into the mainstream economy, an important factor in preventing recidivism. For their part, employers often legitimately fear damage or loss to their property or business as well as possible tort liability to other employees or third parties in the event that the worker commits another offense. For instance, where an employer knows (or should know) of a worker's criminal history and that individual subsequently injures or assaults a co-worker, the employer may be found to have engaged in a negligent hiring. Do the statutory examples provided above offer a way of striking a balance between employers' risk-management concerns and other societal interests? Could an employer faced with a negligent hiring claim use such a statute as a defense to liability? We will return to the issue of negligent hiring in Chapter 5.

3. *Promissory Estoppel in the Real World.* As *Schoff* suggests, although many courts have recognized the availability of promissory estoppel claims in at-will relationships, they often establish high thresholds for proving the elements of the claim, making it difficult for employees to prevail. In a study of all reported promissory estoppel cases decided on the merits during a two-year period in the mid-1990s, Professor Robert Hillman found that employees were successful only 4.23 percent of the time. *See* Robert A. Hillman, *The Unfulfilled Promise of Promissory Estoppel in the Employment Setting*, 31 RUTGERS L. J. 1, 2 (1999). In contrast, the general win rate among promissory estoppel plaintiffs in nonemployment contexts was more than three times greater. *Id.* Professor Hillman speculates that the low success rate among employees can be partially explained by the litigation strategy of "tacking on" a relatively weak promissory estoppel claim to a larger lawsuit. He suggests, however, that the most significant obstacles employees face are judicial preference for written agreements and the longstanding veneration of the at-will rule. *Id.* at 24-26.

4. *Reliance by Mid-Term Employees.* The cases considered in this section involve newly hired employees, some of whom had not even begun working. To what extent are long-term employees protected when relying on promises of continued employment? Does promissory estoppel provide an appropriate avenue for relief to an employee who turns down an outside employment opportunity at his or her current employer's bidding? What about other types of assurances given by employers to their workers, such as promises about salary, promotions, or benefits?

In *Peters v. Gilead*, 533 F.3d 594 (7th Cir. 2008), the worker underwent corrective surgery for a shoulder injury and sought, and was initially granted, leave under the Family/Medical Leave Act ("FMLA"). The employer's handbook recited that all employees who met specified hour requirements would be eligible for FMLA leave, and the employer sent letters to the plaintiff confirming this. In fact, the plaintiff was not eligible for leave because the site at which he was employed did not meet the statutory requirements for coverage. The Seventh Circuit, applying Indiana law, determined that, while it was unclear whether a binding contract had been established, the worker had brought a valid promissory esptoppel claim based on the employer's representations that he was entitled to leave. It remanded for consideration of both forms of liability. As we will see, the use of handbooks and other policies as a basis for contractual or reliance liability is common in claims brought by mid-term employees. What other legal theories might apply on such facts? Consider the next series of cases.

2. Assurances of Continued Employment

≣ *Shebar v. Sanyo Business Systems Corp.*
544 A.2d 377 (N.J. 1988)

GARIBALDI, J.

I

In viewing the record on the [defendant's] motion for summary judgment we give the plaintiff the benefit of all reasonable inferences that may be drawn in his favor. . . .

Defendant, Sanyo Business Systems Corp., a Delaware corporation, hired plaintiff, Arthur Shebar, as National Sales Manager for its Computer Division on December 14, 1981. Sanyo's parent is a Japanese firm. . . .

When defendant initially hired plaintiff, the parties did not execute an employment contract. The terms of plaintiff's employment were outlined in a Sanyo memo to him that stated his annual salary was to be $35,000, with an additional amount of $10,000 as a bonus. Plaintiff continued to work for Sanyo for several years.

The parties disagree over plaintiff's job performance in the years following his employment. Plaintiff asserts that his performance was good and that he received regular salary increases. He claims Sanyo repeatedly commended him for his efforts and accomplishments. Plaintiff states that in June 1984, Dr. Nakahara, defendant's Director of Factory Operations in Guma, Japan, congratulated him for a large sale of Sanyo products to the Internal Revenue Service. Further, plaintiff asserts that on numerous occasions, Mr. Yamazaki, Sanyo's President, and Mr. Yamashita, Sanyo's Executive Vice President, congratulated him on his division's sales record. . . .

Defendant on the other hand asserts that plaintiff's performance was unsatisfactory during 1982, 1983, and 1984. According to Sanyo, plaintiff's superiors informed him on several occasions by memoranda of his unsatisfactory performance in repeatedly failing to meet sales and profit quotas established by himself and by defendant. According to plaintiff, his Sanyo superiors insisted the critical memos he received were not meant to chastise him but rather were intended to push him and the division he headed to their "utmost." Shebar claims that he was told by his superiors that the "Japanese" procedure was to establish sales forecasts and objectives "which were not only extraordinarily high but, frankly, incapable of fulfillment." . . .

Plaintiff concluded by September 1984 that Sanyo's business practices were not sound practices for use in this country. . . . Plaintiff also felt that Sanyo primarily promoted Japanese nationals to its senior management positions and thus the company would by-pass him in filling senior positions in its American operations in the future. At around this same time, plaintiff communicated with an executive search firm to discuss other job opportunities. The firm arranged an interview for plaintiff at the Sony Corporation. . . .

[Subsequently] Sony offered plaintiff a position as national sales manager with an express assurance that he would become a vice president within a reasonable period of time.

The critical events allegedly occurred on October 1, 1984, when plaintiff accepted the Sony offer and tendered his written resignation to Sanyo. According to Shebar's certification, Sanyo's president, Mr. Yamazaki, called him into his office after he received plaintiff's letter of resignation. When plaintiff went into Mr. Yamazaki's office, Mr. Yamashita, executive vice president of Sanyo, was also present. According to plaintiff, Mr. Yamashita told him that he was personally insulted by his resignation, that his performance was exceptionally good, that plaintiff should have brought any problems or dissatisfaction to his attention, and that the company did not want plaintiff to resign, but rather wanted to eliminate any problems that existed. Yamazaki apparently agreed with Yamashita. Yamazaki held the resignation letter, ripped it to shreds, and said "I will not accept your resignation. We will solve your problems."

Plaintiff claims that Yamazaki and Yamashita expressly stated to him that Sanyo does not fire its managers. They told him, plaintiff contends, that he had a job for the rest of his life, and that Sanyo had never fired, and never intended to fire, a corporate employee whose rank was manager or above. Plaintiff acknowledges that they did not discuss money at this meeting, but maintains that they assured him that he would receive a substantial raise in March 1985.

As a result of this meeting and in reliance on the assurances made to him there, plaintiff revoked his acceptance of Sony's offer. Thereafter, he informed Mr. Yamashita that he had rejected the Sony offer. According to plaintiff, Yamashita congratulated him on a wise decision, and again assured him that he was "married" to Sanyo and no divorce was allowed.

A few days later, plaintiff communicated with the executive search firm that had arranged the Sony interview and explained why he rejected Sony's offer. Plaintiff's contact at the firm, Mr. Stephen Mersand, was very surprised by plaintiff's account of the assurances that had been made to him by his Sanyo superiors. Mersand stated he was aware that Sanyo was actively seeking to replace him.

Subsequently, plaintiff confronted Yamashita with the information he received from Mersand. Yamashita, according to plaintiff, responded that Mersand was lying, that Sanyo was not seeking to replace him, and that Mersand just wanted to earn his fee by placing Shebar with another firm.

Some four months later, on February 5, 1985, as Shebar was preparing to leave for Minneapolis on business, Mr. Tomochika, Sanyo's new president, called Shebar into his office and fired him. He said "you will leave the company. You are fired. Clean out your desk. Leave now." . . .

II

The primary issue in this appeal is plaintiff's breach of contract claim. The trial court construed Sanyo's oral promises of lifetime employment as unenforceable "friendly assurances." The court, relying on *Savarese v. Pyrene Manufacturing Co.*, 89 A.2d 237 [N.J. 1952], found that in the absence of an enforceable promise to terminate plaintiff's employment only for cause, he remained an at-will employee, whose employment could be terminated without cause. . . .

III . . .

In *Savarese v. Pyrene Manufacturing Co*, this Court set forth the generally prevailing rule on at-will employment:

> [I]n the absence of additional express or implied stipulations as to duration, a contract for permanent employment, for life employment or for other terms purporting permanent employment, where the employee furnishes no consideration additional to the services incident to the employment, amounts to an indefinite general hiring terminable at the will of either party, and therefore, a discharge without cause does not constitute a breach of such contract justifying recovery of money damages therefore.

In *Savarese*, an employee's supervisors induced him to play on the company softball team. Plaintiff-employee hesitated insisting that he was too old to play on the team. His superior reportedly answered, " 'If you get hurt I will take care of you. You will have a foreman's job the rest of your life.' " Plaintiff alleges that the supervisor specified the job as " 'the one I had, the one I earned.' " This agreement was never reduced to writing. While playing baseball, the plaintiff sustained leg injuries.

Despite his injury, Savarese returned to the company and continued to work there for twenty-one years, at which point the company terminated his employment. Afterwards, Savarese sued, contending that the company breached his contract of lifetime employment and that he was entitled to money damages.

In *Savarese*, we specifically observed that because of the unusual nature of a contract for lifetime employment, "[t]he responsibilities assumed and the obligations imposed will be neither created nor spelled out by mere inference when they are not clearly and unequivocally expressed in the contract itself." The plaintiff in *Savarese* could not demonstrate the requisite elements of an enforceable lifetime contract. The only possible foundation for a contract was the vice president's statement that "You will have a foreman's job for the rest of your life." These words, according to the Court, were "vague and uncertain" and did not "comply with the precision and clarity required by the law. . . . They partake more of the nature of a 'friendly assurance of employment.' " Thus, we held that there was no enforceable contract of lifetime employment between the parties. . . .

The reason *Savarese* required that a contract for lifetime employment be demonstrated by unmistakably clear signs of the employer's intent was that at the time such contracts were deemed "to be at variance with general usage and sound policy." This is still so today, given the unlikelihood of an employer promising to protect an employee from any termination of employment, and the difficulty of determining the terms and enforcing such an agreement. Indeed, [this court has] recognized that such contracts for lifetime employment were extraordinary, and would be enforced only in the face of clear and convincing proof of a precise agreement setting forth all of the terms of the employment relationship, including the duties and responsibilities of both the employer and the employee. *Woolley v. Hoffmann-LaRoche, Inc.*, 491 A.2d 1257 (N.J. 1985). However, a lifetime contract that protects an employee from any termination is distinguishable from a promise to discharge only for cause. The latter protects the employee only from arbitrary termination.

To determine the type of contract the parties intended, a court must closely examine the terms of the contract and the surrounding circumstances. . . .

IV

We find that plaintiff has presented a material issue of fact concerning whether his employer orally promised to discharge him only for cause. Plaintiff's superiors specifically represented to him that he would have continued employment at the company. Those representations were obviously intended to induce plaintiff to remain with Sanyo as Sanyo's computer sales manager and revoke his acceptance of Sony's employment offer. Plaintiff acted in reliance on the alleged promise by forgoing the job opportunity he had secured at Sony. Having made such representations, on which plaintiff relied, Sanyo may not escape the possibility that its representations transformed plaintiff's at-will employment into employment with termination for cause only.

Furthermore, we hold that a factfinder could conclude that plaintiff gave valuable consideration for Sanyo's promise of continued employment with termination only for cause. The essential requirement of consideration is a bargained-for exchange of promises or performance that may consist of an act, a forbearance, or the creation, modification, or destruction of a legal relation. . . .

Taking plaintiff's allegations as true, he agreed to relinquish his new position at Sony in exchange for job security at Sanyo. Sanyo, in turn, agreed to relinquish its right to terminate plaintiff's employment at will in exchange for the retention of a valued employee. Such bargained-for and exchanged promises furnish ample consideration for an enforceable contract. Here, the factfinder could infer that Shebar gave additional consideration for continued employment by Sanyo. We hold that in this case a jury could find that plaintiff gave valuable additional consideration by forgoing his employment at Sony. We caution that not every relinquishment of a prior job or job offer constitutes additional consideration to support the modification of an at-will employment into employment with termination for cause only. The enforceability of each contract will depend on the intent of the parties as established under ordinary principles of contract law.

Additionally, in order to be enforceable the terms of such a contract must be sufficiently clear and capable of judicial interpretation. We find that as a matter of law, the purported contract at issue is not so vague and indefinite that it cannot be enforced. The circumstances surrounding the statements made to plaintiff were such that a factfinder could infer the terms and conditions of an employment contract from plaintiff's existing employment, namely, that Shebar would be employed in the same position at the same salary. Furthermore, the factfinder could infer that Sanyo's promise not to terminate plaintiff's employment existed for a reasonable period of time, and such employment was terminable only for cause.

We do not suggest that any such inferences are required, but merely that the finder of fact could reasonably infer such factual conclusions on this record. Accordingly, since plaintiff has presented a material issue of fact in respect of the existence of such an oral promise and his reliance thereon, the granting of summary judgment was improper. . . .

NOTES

1. *Contract or Reliance?* What legal theory is the court applying in permitting Shebar's claim to go forward? Review the opinion and note the various places where the court (1) invokes concepts of consideration and exchange, and (2) discusses

Shebar's reliance on defendant's promise. As you now know from the previous subsection, the difference between contract and promissory estoppel is significant in terms of the remedy. Which is it here, and why the confusion?

2. *The Nature of the Promise.* Note the court's treatment of *Savarese v. Pyrene Manufacturing Co.*, 89 A.2d 237 (N.J. 1952), which articulates the traditional rule that "permanent" employment is considered at will absent additional consideration. In declining to follow that precedent, the court appears to distinguish between promises of "lifetime" employment and promises to terminate only for cause, characterizing Sanyo's promise as the latter. Do you see a meaningful factual difference between the promises in the two cases? If not, what is the critical distinction between *Shebar* and *Savarese*? Most employees and supervisors do not consider the legal significance of the language they use when discussing job security, and yet the scope of the promise can be critical to determining the existence of a contract. Does that make inquiries like this spurious? Should the court simply have overruled *Savarese*?

3. *Oral Promises and the Statute of Frauds.* In cases based on oral promises of job security, employees frequently face challenges based on the statute of frauds, a rule of contract law that requires particular classes of contracts to be evidenced by a written instrument. In most jurisdictions, the requirements of the statute of frauds apply to contracts "not capable of performance within a year from the time of their formation." RESTATEMENT (SECOND) OF CONTRACTS §178(1) (1981). This rule may provide employers with a valid defense, at least in cases involving oral promises guaranteeing a fixed term of employment, such as employment for three years. Employers sometimes argue that "lifetime" or "permanent" employment contracts similarly cannot be completed within a year and therefore must be established through written evidence. A majority of courts have rejected this argument, however, noting that such contracts *could* be fully performed within one year, for example, where the employee dies or quits or the employer has cause to terminate the employee within a year of his or her hiring. *See, e.g., Foley v. Interactive Data Corp.*, 765 P.2d 373 (Cal. 1988). While some judges have criticized such legal gymnastics, the rejection of the statute-of-frauds defense in cases involving oral employment contracts is consistent with the general contract law trend limiting the application of the statute of frauds to situations where completion within one year is truly foreclosed.

4. *Proof on Remand.* One historical justification for the statute of frauds was that evidence of oral contracts is likely to be factually unreliable, yet highly persuasive to juries. An interested plaintiff has a strong incentive to testify untruthfully about past promises or, absent bad faith, to misremember the defendant's precise statements. Is this a good reason to insist on a writing in cases like *Shebar*? How will Shebar prove his claim on remand? Is it just his word against the company's? Or are there other facts that might help a jury assess the credibility of his allegations?

5. *Cultural Differences at Work.* The facts suggest that some of Shebar's dissatisfaction with his employment reflected cultural differences between him and his Japanese employer. Shebar feared that Japanese nationals were favored in the company hierarchy and believed the " 'Japanese' procedure" of setting unreachable performance objectives was unsound. Shebar did not allege that he had been selected for termination based on his race or nationality; such conduct would have constituted actionable discrimination, a topic that will be discussed in Chapter 9. Yet cultural differences are likely to be relevant in the resolution of his case. If Shebar is successful in establishing his oral contract for job security, the inquiry will turn to whether the defendant had just cause to terminate him. At that point, it will be important for the factfinder to understand Sanyo management's perspective on goal-setting and attainment in order to assess whether Shebar was legitimately terminated for failure to meet sale and profit targets. What evidence should Shebar's attorney look for to help demonstrate a practice of setting aspirational performance standards?

6. *"Married" to the Company.* Assuming Shebar's rendition of his employer's statements is true, long-term employment among high-level employees was the norm at Sanyo. As anyone who has worked more than one job knows, organizations differ widely in their treatment and expectations of their workers. These differences may result from a combination of factors, including the employer's corporate philosophy, the management styles of key personnel, the nature of the work itself, industry standards, and the personality of the company's clientele and workforce. The organizational culture of a particular workplace can create shared understandings about the way work relationships will progress and under what circumstances they may be terminated. Thus, employees may feel deeply wronged when denied regular raises and promotions, long-term employment absent poor performance, and other benefits and rewards commonly bestowed within the organization. Such shared understandings are sometimes referred to as "psychological" or "implicit" contracts of employment. *See, e.g.*, Katherine V.W. Stone, *The New Psychological Contract: Implications of the Changing Workplace for Labor and Employment Law*, 48 UCLA L. Rev. 519, 549-50 (2001). To what extent should employer practices, worker expectations, and organizational culture affect the existence of legally recognized job security rights? Consider the case that follows.

Pugh v. See's Candies, Inc.
171 Cal. Rptr. 917 (Cal. App. 1981)

GRODIN, J.

After 32 years of employment with See's Candies, Inc., in which he worked his way up the corporate ladder from dishwasher to vice president in charge of production and member of the board of directors, Wayne Pugh was fired. [Asserting that he had been fired in breach of contract, he sued his former employer for wrongful termination. The trial court granted defendants' motions for nonsuit, and this appeal followed.]

Pugh began working for See's at its Bay Area plant (then in San Francisco) in January 1941 washing pots and pans. From there he was promoted to candy maker, and held that position until the early part of 1942, when he entered the Air Corps. Upon his discharge in 1946 he returned to See's and his former position. After a year he was promoted to the position of production manager in charge of personnel, ordering raw materials, and supervising the production of candy. When, in 1950, See's moved into a larger plant in San Francisco, Pugh had responsibility for laying out the design of the plant, taking bids, and assisting in the construction. While working at this plant, Pugh sought to increase his value to the company by taking three years of night classes in plant layout, economics, and business law. When See's moved its San Francisco plant to its present location in South San Francisco in 1957, Pugh was given responsibilities for the new location similar to those which he undertook in 1950. By this time See's business and its number of production employees had increased substantially, and a new position of assistant production manager was created under Pugh's supervision.

In 1971 Pugh was again promoted, this time as vice president in charge of production and was placed upon the board of directors of See's northern California subsidiary, "in recognition of his accomplishments." In 1972 he received a gold watch from See's "in appreciation of 31 years of loyal service."

In May 1973 Pugh traveled with Charles Huggins, then president of See's, and their respective families to Europe on a business trip to visit candy manufacturers and to inspect new equipment. Mr. Huggins returned in early June to attend a board of director's meeting while Pugh and his family remained in Europe on a planned vacation.

Upon Pugh's return from Europe on Sunday, June 25, 1973, he received a message directing him to fly to Los Angeles the next day and meet with Mr. Huggins.

Pugh went to Los Angeles expecting to be told of another promotion. The preceding Christmas season had been the most successful in See's history, the Valentine's Day holiday of 1973 set a new sales record for See's, and the March 1973 edition of See's Newsletter, containing two pictures of Pugh, carried congratulations on the increased production.

Instead, upon Pugh's arrival at Mr. Huggins' office, the latter said, "Wayne, come in and sit down. We might as well get right to the point. I have decided your services are no longer required by See's Candies. Read this and sign it." Huggins handed him a letter confirming his termination and directing him to remove that day "only personal papers and possessions from your office," but "absolutely no records, formulas or other material"; and to turn in and account for "all keys, credit cards, et cetera." The letter advised that Pugh would receive unpaid salary, bonuses and accrued vacation through that date, and the full amount of his profit sharing account, but "No severance pay will be granted." Finally, Pugh was directed "not to visit or contact Production Department employees while they are on the job."

The letter contained no reason for Pugh's termination. When Pugh asked Huggins for a reason, he was told only that he should "look deep within [him]self" to find the answer, that "Things were said by people in the trade that have come back to us." Pugh's termination was subsequently announced to the industry in a letter which, again, stated no reasons.

When Pugh first went to work for See's, Ed Peck, then president and general manager, frequently told him: "if you are loyal to [See's] and do a good job, your future is secure." Laurance See, who became president of the company in 1951 and served in that capacity until his death in 1969, had a practice of not terminating administrative personnel except for good cause, and this practice was carried on by his brother, Charles B. See, who succeeded Laurance as president.

During the entire period of his employment, there had been no formal or written criticism of Pugh's work.[1] No complaints were ever raised at the annual meetings which preceded each holiday season, and he was never denied a raise or bonus. He received no notice that there was a problem which needed correction, nor any warning that any disciplinary action was being contemplated.

---

1. Huggins testified that in 1953 there was some personality conflict between Pugh and Huggins' assistant, a Mr. Forrest, on account of which Huggins recommended to Laurance See that Pugh be terminated, but See declined. Huggins again recommended Pugh's termination in 1968, under circumstances to be described in this opinion, and again See declined. It does not appear that Huggins' actions in this regard, or the criticism of Pugh which they implied, were made known to Pugh.

Pugh's theory as to why he was terminated relates to a contract which See's at that time had with the defendant union. . . .

In 1968 [See's supplemental union contract] contained a new rate classification which permitted See's to pay its seasonal employees at a lower rate. At a company meeting prior to the 1968 negotiations, Pugh had objected to the proposed new seasonal classification on the grounds that it might make it more difficult to recruit seasonal workers, and create unrest among See's regular seasonal workers who had worked previously for other manufacturers at higher rates. Huggins overruled Pugh's objection and (unknown to Pugh) recommended his termination for "lack of cooperation" as to which Pugh's objection formed "part of the reason." His recommendation was not accepted. . . .

In April of that year, Huggins asked Pugh to be part of the negotiating team for the new union contract. Pugh responded that he would like to, but he was bothered by the possibility that See's had a "sweetheart contract" with the union. In response, someone banged on the table and said, "You don't know what the hell you are talking about." Pugh said, "Well, I think I know what I am talking about. I don't know whether you have a sweetheart contract, but I am telling you if you do, I don't want to be involved because they are immoral, illegal and not in the best interests of my employees." At the trial, Pugh explained that to him a "sweetheart contract" was "a contract whereby one employer would get an unfair competitive advantage over a competitor by getting a lower wage rate, would be one version of it." He also felt, he testified, that "if they in fact had a sweetheart contract that it wouldn't be fair to my female employees to be getting less money than someone would get working in the same industry under the same manager." . . .

The presumption that an employment contract is intended to be terminable at will is subject, like any presumption, to contrary evidence. This may take the form of an agreement, express or implied, that the relationship will continue for some fixed period of time. Or, and of greater relevance here, it may take the form of an agreement that the employment relationship will continue indefinitely, pending the occurrence of some event such as the employer's dissatisfaction with the employee's services or the existence of some "cause" for termination. Sometimes this latter type of agreement is characterized as a contract for "permanent" employment, but that characterization may be misleading. In one of the earliest California cases on this subject, the Supreme Court interpreted a contract for permanent employment as meaning "that plaintiffs' employment . . . was to continue indefinitely, and until one or the other of the parties wish, *for some good reason*, to sever the relation."

A contract which limits the power of the employer with respect to the reasons for termination is no less enforceable because it places no equivalent limits upon the power of the employee to quit his employment. "If the requirement of consideration is met, there is no additional requirement of . . . equivalence in the values exchanged, or 'mutuality of obligation.' " Rest. 2d Contracts § 81.

Moreover, while it has sometimes been said that a promise for continued employment subject to limitation upon the employer's power of termination must be supported by some "independent consideration," i.e., consideration other than the services to be rendered, such a rule is contrary to the general contract principle that courts should not inquire into the adequacy of consideration. "A single and undivided consideration may be bargained for and given as the agreed equivalent of one promise or of two promises or of many promises." 1 Corbin on Contracts § 125 (1963).

Thus there is no analytical reason why an employee's promise to render services, or his actual rendition of services over time, may not support an employer's promise both to pay a particular wage (for example) and to refrain from arbitrary dismissal.

The most likely explanation for the "independent consideration" requirement is that it serves an evidentiary function: it is more probable that the parties intended a continuing relationship, with limitations upon the employer's dismissal authority, when the employee has provided some benefit to the employer, or suffers some detriment, beyond the usual rendition of service. . . .

In determining whether there exists an implied-in-fact promise for some form of continued employment courts have considered a variety of factors in addition to the existence of independent consideration. These have included, for example, the personnel policies or practices of the employer, the employee's longevity of service, actions or communications by the employer reflecting assurances of continued employment, and the practices of the industry in which the employee is engaged. . . .

[In this case] there were facts in evidence from which the jury could determine the existence of such an implied promise: the duration of appellant's employment, the commendations and promotions he received, the apparent lack of any direct criticism of his work, the assurances he was given, and the employer's acknowledged policies. While oblique language will not, standing alone, be sufficient to establish agreement, it is appropriate to consider the totality of the parties' relationship: Agreement may be " 'shown by the acts and conduct of the parties, interpreted in the light of the subject matter and of the surrounding circumstances.' " We therefore conclude that it was error to grant respondents' motions for nonsuit as to See's.

Since this litigation may proceed toward yet uncharted waters, we consider it appropriate to provide some guidance as to the questions which the trial court may confront on remand. We have held that appellant has demonstrated a prima facie case of wrongful termination in violation of his contract of employment. The burden of coming forward with evidence as to the reason for appellant's termination now shifts to the employer. Appellant may attack the employer's offered explanation either on the ground that it is pretextual (and that the real reason is one prohibited by contract or public policy), or on the ground that it is insufficient to meet the employer's obligations under contract or applicable legal principles. Appellant bears, however, the ultimate burden of proving that he was terminated wrongfully. *Cf. McDonnell Douglas Corp. v. Green* (1973) 411 U.S. 792.

By what standard that burden is to be measured will depend, in part, upon what conclusions the jury draws as to the nature of the contract between the parties. The terms "just cause" and "good cause," "as used in a variety of contexts . . . have been found to be difficult to define with precision and to be largely relative in their connotation, depending upon the particular circumstances of each case." Essentially, they connote "a fair and honest cause or reason, regulated by good faith on the part of the party exercising the power." Care must be taken, however, not to interfere with the legitimate exercise of managerial discretion. "Good cause" in this context is quite different from the standard applicable in determining the propriety of an employee's termination under a contract for a specified term. And where, as here, the employee occupies a sensitive managerial or confidential position, the employer must of necessity be allowed substantial scope for the exercise of subjective judgment. . . .

NOTES

1. *Cause on Remand.* At the end of the opinion, the court sets out the procedural steps for determining whether See's had cause to terminate Pugh's employment. When employees allege implied contracts for job security, demonstrating the existence of such a contract is only half the battle; the plaintiff must then show that the employer is in breach. As *Pugh* cautions, in determining whether a termination was justified, courts must not interfere with subjective managerial decision making. The burden of proof, coupled with this deference to management, can make it difficult for an employee to ultimately prevail. Indeed, Pugh himself did not succeed. On retrial, the jury returned a verdict for the defendant, crediting Huggins's testimony that Pugh was "rude, argumentative, belligerent, and uncooperative" on their trip to Europe and testimony of other See's employees that Pugh was "disrespectful to his superiors and subordinates, disloyal to the company, and uncooperative with other administrative staff." *See Pugh v. See's Candies, Inc.* (*Pugh II*), 250 Cal. Rptr. 195, 214 (Ct. App. 1988) (affirming judgment for defendant).

2. *Terminations That Offend Public Policy.* Pugh believed he was terminated for objecting to corruption in his employer's negotiations with union representatives. In an omitted portion of the opinion, he alleged that he had been tortiously discharged in violation of public policy, in addition to claiming breach of an implied contract. Pugh's tort argument was rejected. In Chapter 4, you will take up public policy torts. When you do, try to figure out why Pugh lost on this count.

3. *Additional Consideration Revisited.* Both *Pugh* and *Shebar* invoke the traditional rule that additional consideration is required to support a promise of job security. How does their treatment of this doctrine compare to the *Hanson* and *Greene* decisions you read earlier? What does the court in *Pugh* mean by the "evidentiary function" of additional consideration?

4. *Implied-in-Fact Theory.* In answering the last question, consider the contractual theory that the court espouses. An implied-in-fact contract is one in which an agreement to be legally bound is implied from the circumstances, albeit without any clear oral or written communication between the parties. A classic example of an implied-in-fact contract is riding a bus: When you step aboard, you agree to pay the fare and the driver agrees to take you to your stop, although none of this is stated. How does this theory of liability compare to the others you have seen so far — oral contract and promissory estoppel? Does the idea of an implied-in-fact contract better reflect the realities of workplace relationships? Or does it seem a contrived way of doing justice under the circumstances?

5. *Hard Facts?* There is an adage that hard facts make bad law. *Pugh* is a rags-to-riches tale in which the employer seemingly takes advantage of the industry and dedication of a long-term employee. From the first sentence of the opinion it is clear which way the court will hold. Was the court unduly influenced by sympathy for the employee, or is there a broader justification for the decision?

Dean Stewart Schwab suggests there is. Under the "efficiency-wage" theory of long-term employment relationships, employers set wages to rise steadily over the course of employment in order to motivate employees throughout the relationship. *See* Stewart J. Schwab, *Life-Cycle Justice: Accommodating Just Cause and Employment At Will*, 92 MICH. L. REV. 8, 39 (1993). As a result, new employees may be underpaid relative to the value they produce while senior employees may actually earn more than their marginal work product (because wages continue to rise when productivity reaches its zenith). *Id*. at 16-17. While the difference balances out if the employment relationship is allowed to run its full course, senior employees may be at risk of opportunistic firings, at which point the employer has already reaped the benefits of the arrangement. As Dean Schwab explains:

> [E]mployees invest heavily as they pursue a career with a single employer. First, they obtain training that is more useful for their own employer than it would be elsewhere — what economists term job-specific human capital. Second, they join the company's career path [which] ties pay, promotions, and benefits to seniority and generally forbids lateral entry. A major cost of pursuing a career with one firm is that one forgoes other ladders and must start over at the bottom if one leaves the firm. Additionally, as they plan for a lifetime with an employer, workers put down roots, establish networks of friends in the workplace and the community, buy homes within commuting distance of the job, and build emotional ties to the community. . . .
>
> [T]hese investments, roots, and ties are sunk costs that trap the worker in his current firm, inhibiting him from departing voluntarily. Even if the career does not proceed as anticipated, the employee is reluctant to quit because the job remains preferable to alternative jobs. Such trapped workers are vulnerable to opportunism. The employer might pay them less than the implicit contract requires or work them harder, knowing they cannot easily quit. . . .
>
> Court scrutiny of opportunistic firings may offer [one] method of policing long-term contracts. . . . The danger, of course, is that court intervention will diminish the employer's flexibility in firing [shirkers]. The question is whether court intervention can be limited to opportunistic firings, rather than to a broader supervision against unfair firings in general.

Id. at 24-28. As the excerpt suggests, while judicial intervention may be appropriate in some instances, the risk of opportunistic firings does not necessarily justify a general rule requiring just cause for all terminations. Can courts craft an administrable rule that will identify only opportunistic firings? Does the multi-factored test articulated in *Pugh* succeed?

Guz v. Bechtel National, Inc.
8 P.3d 1089 (Cal. 2000)

BAXTER, J.

This case presents questions about the law governing claims of wrongful discharge from employment as it applies to an employer's motion for summary judgment. Plaintiff John Guz, a longtime employee of Bechtel National, Inc. (BNI), was released [when his work unit was eliminated and its tasks transferred to another office]. Guz sued BNI and its parent [(collectively Bechtel) alleging] breach of an implied contract to be terminated only for good cause and breach of the implied covenant of good faith and fair dealing. The trial court granted Bechtel's motion for summary judgment. [T]he Court of Appeal reversed. . . .

In 1971, Bechtel hired Guz as an administrative assistant at a salary of $750 per month. Throughout his Bechtel career, Guz worked in "management information," performing, at various times, duties on both the "awarded" and "overhead" sides of this specialty. He received steady raises and promotions. His performance reviews were generally favorable. . . .

BNI, a division of Bechtel Corporation, is an engineering, construction, and environmental remediation company that focuses on federal government programs, principally for the Departments of Energy and Defense. . . .

Guz had worked for BNI-MI, [BNI's six staff member Management Information Group] since 1986. In 1992, at age 49, he was employed as a financial reports supervisor. . . .

During this time, Bechtel maintained Personnel Policy 1101, dated June 1991, on the subject of termination of employment (Policy 1101). Policy 1101 stated that "Bechtel employees have no employment agreements guaranteeing continuous service and may resign at their option or be terminated at the option of Bechtel."

Policy 1101 also described several "Categories of Termination," including "Layoff" and "Unsatisfactory Performance." With respect to Unsatisfactory Performance, the policy stated that "[e]mployees who fail to perform their jobs in a satisfactory manner may be terminated, provided the employees have been advised of the specific shortcomings and given an opportunity to improve their performance." A layoff was defined as "a Bechtel-initiated termination [ ] of employees caused by a reduction in workload, reorganizations, changes in job requirements, or other circumstances. . . ." Under the Layoff policy, employees subject to termination for this reason "may be placed on 'holding status' if there is a possible Bechtel assignment within the following 3-month period." Guz understood that Policy 1101 applied to him.

[In 1992, Robert Johnstone became president of BNI and soon became unhappy with the size, cost, and performance of BNI-MI. In April 1992, he advised BNI's manager of government services, Edward Dewey, Guz's manager, Ronald Goldstein, and Guz that BNI-MI's work could be done by three people.] . . .

On December 9, 1992, Goldstein informed Guz that BNI-MI was being disbanded, that its work would be done by another unit of Bechtel, SFRO-MI (San Francisco Regional Office Management Information Group), and that Guz was being laid off. Goldstein told Guz the reason he had been selected for layoff was to reduce costs. . . .

[Two members of BNI-MI, were transferred to SFRO-MI, while all the remaining BNI-MI employees, like Guz, were laid off. During early 1993, while Guz was on holding status, three other positions became available in SFRO-MI, partly because of that unit's expanded responsibilities for BNI-MI. Two of these positions were filled by SFRO-MI employees and one was filled by a newcomer.]

Guz sought to furnish evidence that the cost reduction and workload downturn reasons given him for the elimination of BNI-MI, and his own consequent layoff, were arbitrary, false, and pretextual. To rebut the implication that a general business slowdown required BNI to lay off workers, Guz submitted an excerpt from Bechtel Corporation's 1992 Annual Report. There, Bechtel Corporation's president stated that the "Bechtel team had an exceptional year," and that the company as a whole had achieved healthy gains in both revenue from current projects and new work booked. In his own declaration, Goldstein stated that BNI-MI's 1992 and projected 1993 workload was high, . . . [and that] the net savings from elimination of BNI-MI were only a small fraction of its budget.

Guz also submitted . . . Bechtel's 1989 Reduction-in-Force Guidelines (RIF Guidelines) and Bechtel's Personnel Policy 302 (Policy 302).

Policy 302 described a system of employee ranking . . . based on the fair, objective, and consistent evaluation of employees' comparative job-relevant skills and performance. . . .

The RIF Guidelines specified that when choosing among employees to be retained and released during a reduction in force, the formal ranking system set forth in Policy 302 was to be employed. . . .

The RIF Guidelines also explained the term "holding status" and its benefits [which included] "[t]ransfer and [p]lacement [a]ssistance." . . . In his deposition, BNI president Johnstone agreed that Bechtel's practice was to place an employee on holding status prior to termination, to attempt to reassign the employee during this period, and to "continue to look for positions even after the employee has been laid off."

In their declarations, Goldstein and Guz insisted Guz was qualified for each of the several vacant positions in SFRO-MI, as well as for several other positions that became available within Bechtel. . . .

The trial court granted summary judgment. The court reasoned that "[Guz] was an at-will employee and has not introduced any evidence that he was ever told at any time that he had permanent employment or that he would be retained as long as he was doing a good job. [The Court of Appeal reversed, reasoning that, under *Foley v. Interactive Data*, 765 P.2d 373 (Cal. 1988)], Guz's longevity, promotions, raises, and favorable performance reviews, together with Bechtel's written progressive discipline policy and Bechtel officials' statements of company practices, raised a triable issue that Guz had an implied-in-fact contract to be dismissed only for good cause. There was evidence that Bechtel breached this term by eliminating BNI-MI, on the false ground that workload was declining, as a pretext to weed out poor performers without applying the company's progressive discipline procedures.

II. *Implied contract claim . . .*

While the statutory presumption of at-will employment is strong, it is subject to several limitations. . . .

One example of a contractual departure from at-will status is an agreement that the employee will be terminated only for "good cause." . . .

The contractual understanding need not be express, but may be implied in fact, arising from the parties' conduct evidencing their actual mutual intent to create such enforceable limitations. In *Foley* we identified several factors, apart from express terms, that may bear upon "the existence and content of an . . . [implied-in-fact] agreement" placing limits on the employer's right to discharge an employee. These factors might include "'the personnel policies or practices of the employer, the employee's longevity of service, actions or communications by the employer reflecting assurances of continued employment, and the practices of the industry in which the employee is engaged.'" *Id.* (quoting *Pugh* . . .).

Foley asserted that "the totality of the circumstances" must be examined to determine whether the parties' conduct, considered in the context of surrounding circumstances, gave rise to an implied-in-fact contract limiting the employer's termination rights. We did not suggest, however, that every vague combination of *Foley* factors, shaken together in a bag, necessarily allows a finding that the employee had a right to be discharged only for good cause, as determined in court.

On the contrary, "courts seek to enforce the actual understanding" of the parties to an employment agreement. Whether that understanding arises from express mutual words of agreement, or from the parties' conduct evidencing a similar meeting of minds, the exact terms to which the parties have assented deserve equally precise scrutiny. . . .

Every case thus turns on its own facts. Where there is no express agreement, the issue is whether other evidence of the parties' conduct has a "tendency in reason" to demonstrate the existence of an actual mutual understanding on particular terms and conditions of employment. . . .

Guz alleges he had an agreement with Bechtel that he would be employed so long as he was performing satisfactorily and would be discharged only for good cause. Guz claims no express understanding to this effect. However, he asserts that such an agreement can be inferred by combining evidence of several *Foley* factors, including (1) his long service; (2) assurances of continued employment in the form of raises, promotions, and good performance reviews; (3) Bechtel's written personnel policies, which suggested that termination for poor performance would be preceded by progressive discipline, that layoffs during a work force reduction would be based on objective criteria, including formal ranking, and that persons laid off would receive placement and reassignment assistance; and (4) testimony by a Bechtel executive that company practice was to terminate employees for a good reason and to reassign, if possible, a laid-off employee who was performing satisfactorily.

Guz further urges there is evidence his termination was without good cause in two respects. First, he insists, the evidence suggests Bechtel had no good cause to eliminate BNI-MI, because the cost reduction and workload downturn reasons Bechtel gave for that decision (1) were not justified by the facts, and (2) were a pretext to terminate him and other individual BNI-MI employees for poor performance without following the company's progressive discipline rules. Second, Guz asserts, even if there was good cause to eliminate his work unit, his termination nonetheless lacked good cause because Bechtel failed to accord him fair layoff rights set forth in its written personnel rules, including (1) use of objective force ranking to determine which unit members deserved retention, and (2) fair consideration for other available positions while he was in holding status.

As we shall explain, we find triable evidence that Bechtel's written personnel documents set forth implied contractual limits on the circumstances under which Guz, and other Bechtel workers, would be terminated. On the other hand, we see no triable evidence of an implied agreement between Guz and Bechtel on additional, different, or broader terms of employment security. . . .

At the outset, Bechtel insists that the existence of implied contractual limitations on its termination rights is negated because Bechtel expressly disclaimed all such agreements. Bechtel suggests the at-will presumption was conclusively reinforced by language Bechtel inserted in Policy 1101, which specified that the company's employees "have no . . . agreements guaranteeing continuous service and may be terminated at [Bechtel's] option." . . .

[N]either the disclaimer nor the statutory presumption necessarily foreclosed Guz from proving the existence and breach of [an agreement limiting Bechtel's termination rights]. Cases in California and elsewhere have held that at-will provisions in personnel handbooks, manuals, or memoranda do not bar, or necessarily overcome, other evidence of the employer's contrary intent. [But even if a handbook disclaimer is not controlling, such language must be taken into account, along with all other pertinent evidence, in ascertaining the terms on which a worker was employed.]

At the outset, it is undisputed that Guz received no individual promises or representations that Bechtel would retain him except for good cause, or upon other specified circumstances. Nor does Guz seriously claim that the practice in Bechtel's industry was to provide secure employment. Indeed, the undisputed evidence suggested that because Bechtel, like other members of its industry, operated by competitive bidding from project to project, its work force fluctuated widely and, in terms of raw numbers, was in general decline.

However, Guz insists his own undisputed long and successful service at Bechtel constitutes strong evidence of an implied contract for permanent employment except upon good cause. . . .

A number of post-*Foley* California decisions have suggested that long duration of service, regular promotions, favorable performance reviews, praise from supervisors, and salary increases do not, without more, imply an employer's contractual intent to relinquish its at-will rights. These decisions reason that such events are but natural consequences of a well-functioning employment relationship. . . .

We agree that an employee's mere passage of time in the employer's service, even where marked with tangible indicia that the employer approves the employee's work, cannot alone form an implied-in-fact contract that the employee is no longer at will. Absent other evidence of the employer's intent, longevity, raises and promotions are their own rewards for the employee's continuing valued service.. . . .

On the other hand, long and successful service is not necessarily irrelevant to the existence of such a contract. Over the period of an employee's tenure, the employer can certainly communicate, by its written and unwritten policies and practices, or by informal assurances, that seniority and longevity do create rights against termination at will. The issue is whether the employer's words or conduct, on which an employee reasonably relied, gave rise to that specific understanding. . . .

Insofar as *Foley* applied the long service factor to its own facts, it did so consistent with the principles of implied-in-fact contracts. In *Foley*, the employer claimed the employee's six years and nine months of service was too short a period to evidence an implied agreement not to discharge at will. We answered that "[l]ength of employment [was] a relevant consideration" and the plaintiff's length of service was "sufficient time for conduct to occur on which a trier of fact could find the existence of an implied contract." Prominent among the conduct alleged by the *Foley* plaintiff was "repeated oral assurances of job security."

. . . Guz claims no particular " 'actions or communications by [Bechtel]' " and no industry customs, practices, or policies which suggest that by virtue of his successful longevity in Bechtel's employ, he had earned a contractual right against future termination at will.

If anything, Bechtel had communicated otherwise. The company's Policy 1101 stated that Bechtel employees had no contracts guaranteeing their continuous employment and could be terminated at Bechtel's option. Nothing in this language suggested any exception for senior workers, or for those who had received regular raises and promotions. While occasional references to seniority appear in other sections of Bechtel's personnel documents, the narrow context of these references undermines an inference that Bechtel additionally intended, or employees had reason to expect, special immunities from termination based on their extended or successful service.

Finally, Guz asserts there is evidence that, industry custom and written company personnel policies aside, Bechtel had an unwritten "polic[y] or practice[ ]" to release its employees only for cause. As the sole evidence of this policy, Guz points to the deposition testimony of Johnstone, BNI's president, who stated his understanding that Bechtel terminated workers only with "good reason" or for "lack of [available] work."

But there is no evidence that Bechtel employees were aware of such an unwritten policy, and it flies in the face of Bechtel's general disclaimer. This brief and vague statement, by a single Bechtel official, that Bechtel sought to avoid arbitrary firings is insufficient as a matter of law to permit a finding that the company, by an unwritten practice or policy on which employees reasonably relied, had contracted away its right to discharge Guz at will.

In sum, if there is any significant evidence that Guz had an implied contract against termination at will, that evidence flows exclusively from Bechtel's written personnel documents. . . .

The parties do not dispute that certain of these provisions, expressly denominated "Policies" . . . were disseminated to employees and were intended by Bechtel to inform workers of rules applicable to their employment. There seems little doubt, and we conclude, a triable issue exists that the specific provisions of these Policies did become an implicit part of the employment contracts of the Bechtel employees they covered, including Guz.

As Bechtel stresses, Policy 1101 itself purported to disclaim any employment security rights. However, Bechtel had inserted other language, not only in Policy 1101 itself, but in other written personnel documents, which described detailed rules and procedures for the termination of employees under particular circumstances. Moreover, the specific language of Bechtel's disclaimer, stating that employees had no contracts "guaranteeing . . . continuous service" (italics added) and were terminable at Bechtel's "option," did not foreclose an understanding between Bechtel and all its workers that Bechtel would make its termination decisions within the limits of its written personnel rules. Given these ambiguities, a fact finder could rationally determine that despite its general disclaimer, Bechtel had bound itself to the specific provisions of these documents. . . .

The Court of Appeal did not address Guz's second theory, i.e., that Bechtel also breached its implied contract by failing, during and after the reorganization, to provide him personally with the fair layoff protections, including force ranking and reassignment help, which are set forth in its Policies and RIF Guidelines. This theory raises difficult questions, including what the proper remedy, if any, should be if Guz ultimately shows that Bechtel breached a contractual obligation to follow certain procedural policies in the termination process. . . . On remand, the Court of Appeal should confront this issue and should determine whether Guz has raised a triable issue on this theory.

III. *Implied covenant claim . . .*

Guz urges that even if his contract was for employment at will, the implied covenant of good faith and fair dealing precluded Bechtel from "unfairly" denying him the contract's benefits by failing to follow its own termination policies.

Thus, Guz argues, in effect, that the implied covenant can impose substantive terms and conditions beyond those to which the contract parties actually agreed. [However, the] covenant of good faith and fair dealing, implied by law in every contract, exists merely to prevent one contracting party from unfairly frustrating the other party's right to receive the benefits of the agreement actually made. . . . It cannot impose substantive duties or limits on the contracting parties beyond those incorporated in the specific terms of their agreement.

[The presumption is] that an employer may terminate its employees at will, for any or no reason. A fortiori, the employer may act peremptorily, arbitrarily, or inconsistently, without providing specific protections such as prior warning, fair procedures, objective evaluation, or preferential reassignment. Because the employment relationship is "fundamentally contractual," limitations on these employer prerogatives are a matter of the parties' specific agreement, express or implied in fact. The mere existence of an employment relationship affords no expectation, protectible by law, that employment will continue, or will end only on certain conditions, unless the parties have actually adopted such terms. Thus if the employer's termination decisions, however arbitrary, do not breach such a substantive contract provision, they are not precluded by the covenant.

This logic led us to emphasize in *Foley* that "breach of the implied covenant cannot logically be based on a claim that [the] discharge [of an at-will employee] was made without good cause." As we noted [in *Foley*], "[b]ecause the implied covenant protects only the parties' right to receive the benefit of their agreement, and, in an at-will relationship there is no agreement to terminate only for good cause, the implied covenant standing alone cannot be read to impose such a duty."

The same reasoning applies to any case where an employee argues that even if his employment was at will, his arbitrary dismissal frustrated his contract benefits and thus violated the implied covenant of good faith and fair dealing. Precisely because employment at will allows the employer freedom to terminate the relationship as it chooses, the employer does not frustrate the employee's contractual rights merely by doing so. . . .

Similarly at odds with *Foley* are suggestions that independent recovery for breach of the implied covenant may be available if the employer terminated the employee in "bad faith" or "without probable cause," i.e., without determining "honestly and in good faith that good cause for discharge existed." Where the employment contract itself allows the employer to terminate at will, its motive and lack of care in doing so are, in most cases at least, irrelevant.

Of course, as we have indicated above, the employer's personnel policies and practices may become implied-in-fact terms of the contract between employer and employee. If that has occurred, the employer's failure to follow such policies when terminating an employee is a breach of the contract itself.

A breach of the contract may also constitute a breach of the implied covenant of good faith and fair dealing. But insofar as the employer's acts are directly actionable as a breach of an implied-in-fact contract term, a claim that merely realleges that breach as a violation of the covenant is superfluous. This is because, as we explained at length in *Foley*, the remedy for breach of an employment agreement, including the covenant of good faith and fair dealing implied by law therein, is solely contractual. In the employment context, an implied covenant theory affords no separate measure of recovery, such as tort damages. Allegations that the breach was wrongful, in bad faith, arbitrary, and unfair are unavailing; there is no tort of "bad faith breach" of an employment contract.

We adhere to these principles here. To the extent Guz's implied covenant cause of action seeks to impose limits on Bechtel's termination rights beyond those to which the parties actually agreed, the claim is invalid. To the extent the implied covenant claim seeks simply to invoke terms to which the parties did agree, it is superfluous. Guz's remedy, if any, for Bechtel's alleged violation of its personnel policies depends on proof that they were contract terms to which the parties actually agreed. The trial court thus properly dismissed the implied covenant cause of action.

NOTES

1. Pugh *Claims Post*-Pugh. What does *Guz* suggest about the significance of *Pugh* in the twenty-first century? Seven years after *Pugh*, the California Supreme Court reaffirmed its holding in *Foley v. Interactive Data Corp.*, 765 P.2d 373 (Cal. 1988), discussed at length in *Guz*. Foley worked for six years as a product manager, during which time he received steady salary increases, promotions, bonuses and positive performance evaluations, before being terminated, allegedly for reporting that his supervisor was under FBI investigation for embezzlement. Like Pugh, Foley alleged he received repeated assurances that his job was secure so long as his performance remained adequate. In allowing the claim to go forward, the court declined the defendant's invitation to distinguish *Pugh* based on the fact that Foley had worked for the defendant only six years. *See id.* at 387-88. It also explicitly disagreed that employment security agreements are "inherently harmful or unfair to employers," finding that "[o]n the contrary, employers may benefit from the increased loyalty and productivity that such agreements may inspire." *Id.* at 387.

However, the California Supreme Court's subsequent decision in *Guz* offers a much narrower view of the kinds of employer conduct that will give rise to an implied in fact promise. In light of *Guz*, can you articulate the type of evidence that would create a prima facie case of breach of an implied contract in California? Can you identify the type of evidence that might preclude such a claim? How concerned do contemporary employers need to be about the costs associated with implied-in-fact rights? Professor Jonathan Fineman argues that companies have little to fear as long as they keep their house in order. *See The Inevitable Demise of the Implied Employment Contract*, 29 BERKELEY J. EMP. & LAB. L. 345 (2008). He explains:

> [Following judicial recognition of implied-in-fact contract claims, e]mployers began restructuring their employment documents, policies and practices to avoid liability [and] eventually were able to find a way to immunize themselves against implied contract claims. With careful drafting of personnel documents, employers today have little fear of implied contract lawsuits. As a result, many employees are arguably now worse off than they were in the 1970s.
>
> [T]his failure of implied contract doctrine law to provide enduring job protections was inevitable. Although courts seeking to enforce implied employment contracts have some flexibility to interpret contract principles to reach a "fair" result, [w]hen faced with a clear expression of employer intent that the employment relationship be at-will, there is only so much a court can do. In this respect, the implied contract remedy is fundamentally different from other "exceptions" to the at-will rule. Unlike antidiscrimination statutes that impose upon the parties certain unavoidable obligations based on public policy, implied contract doctrine does not import external values into the employment relationship.
>
> Conceptualizing the employment relationship as one of private contract, the terms of which as a practical matter are established by employers, means that we will always end up with employment contracts that benefit employers. As long as individual employers are able to define the scope of their own obligations, efforts to instill more structured, effective and binding workplace norms through the doctrine of implied contracts will be unsuccessful.

Id. at 349-50. Do you agree with this critique, or is Professor Fineman overly pessimistic about the viability of employee claims? If you represented an employer, would you feel confident that with careful planning you could fully eliminate the risk of a successful employee claim in a situation where your client did not intend to provide job security?

2. The Decline of Long-Term Employment. *Pugh* and *Guz* together suggest that longevity and consistent advancement may be necessary although not sufficient facts from which a court can discern an implied-in-fact contract. How typical is it for workers to have 20- to 30-year employment records like the plaintiffs in those cases? In the contemporary economy, long-term employment with a single company is in decline, as are clear promotional hierarchies within individual firms. Instead, many employees have what Professor Katherine Stone describes as "boundaryless careers." She explains:

> A boundaryless career is a career that does not depend upon traditional notions of advancement within a single hierarchical organization. It includes an employee who moves frequently across the borders of different employers, such as a Silicon Valley technician, or one whose career draws its validation and marketability from sources outside the present employer, such as professional and extraorganizational networks. It also refers to changes within organizations, in which individuals are expected to move laterally, without constraint from traditional hierarchical career lattices. . . .
>
> The concept of a boundaryless career, like that of the new psychological contract, reflects the shift in job structures away from [early twentieth century] internal labor markets. Instead of job ladders along which employees advance within stable, long-term employment settings, there are possibilities for lateral mobility between and within firms, with no set path, no established expectations, and no tacit promises of job security. As [writer Peter] Drucker says, "there is no such thing as 'lifetime employment' anymore. . . ."

Katherine V.W. Stone, *The New Psychological Contract: Implications of the Changing Workplace for Labor and Employment Law*, 48 U.C.L.A. L. Rev. 519, 554-55 (2001). As a result, Professor Stone suggests that parties no longer share an implicit expectation of long-term employment. Rather, employers reward loyal work by enhancing their employees' marketability, by providing skills training, networking opportunities, and externally competitive pay. *Id.* at 568-72. Does this trend suggest that the utility of implied-in-fact contract theory is diminishing? Or might implied-in-fact theory be adapted to redress other types of opportunistic employer behavior that violate what Professor Stone calls the "new psychological contract" of employment?

Professor Arnow-Richman has suggested as much. She argues that rather than implying job security rights, the law should enforce the contemporary psychological contract by imposing an obligation on employers to provide advance notice (or its equivalent in pay) to terminated workers. *Just Notice: Re-Reforming Employment At-Will*, 58 UCLA L. Rev. 1 (2010). She explains:

> [T]he distinguishing feature of the new social contract of employment is the increased expectation of possible job loss. If employers no longer implicitly offer workers long-term job security, and employees no longer expect to remain in the same job for their lifetime, the guiding theory of worker protection should focus on enabling continued labor market participation rather than on preserving particular jobs.
>
> [This] could take the form of a legislative "pay-or-play" obligation upon termination. Under such a system, employers would be obligated to provide workers advance notice of termination or, at the employer's election, continued pay and benefits for the duration of the notice period. This system would allow employees a degree of income continuity,

enabling them to search for new employment or, in the event the employer elects sever-ance pay, to invest in training.

Just cause reform, with its focus on the reason for termination and its goal of job preservation, would do [little to help workers in the contemporary economy]. In contrast, pay-or-play reform would advance an entirely different set of goals and expectations. [W]hereas just cause would foster job retention, pay-or-play would ease employment transitions, . . . giving legal force to employers' implicit promise of long-term employ*ability*. . . . Whereas just cause protection would oblige employers to justify ter-mination, in effect to defend their deviation from the norm of continued employment, a pay-or-play system would translate the implicit promise of marketability into a legal obligation to directly underwrite the costs of re-employment.

Id. at 38-41. Recall the discussion in Note 9, page 73 of the history of unjust dismissal in Montana or elsewhere. How viable is Professor Arnow-Richman's alternative reform strategy? Would "pay or play" reform be appealing only to employees or might employers support it as well? What are the limitations of such an approach? Does a system that allows employers the right to terminate arbitrarily (for the right price) overlook workers' dignity (if not their property) interest in their jobs?

3. *Policies as Contracts. Pugh* identified the "policies and practices" of the employer as an important factor to consider in determining the existence of an implied contract. It involved an employer that allegedly made a *practice* of retaining workers long term. In contrast, *Guz* involves employer *policies*, written materials that set forth the formal rules and procedures of the company. Such documents are increasingly common in large companies, and, as *Guz* describes, they offer advantages to both employers and employees. A frequent source of employer policies is the company's personnel manual or handbook, a collection of materials usually provided to employ-ees upon hire. Courts can treat polices and handbooks in at least two ways: as evidence of an implied-in-fact contract or as a contract in and of themselves (generally analyzed as a unilateral contract). How does *Guz* use Bechtel's policies in determining the plaintiff's rights? Does the existence of the policies help Guz's case? Hurt it? Both? The role of personnel manuals, and in particular language in such documents that disclaim employee rights, will be explored in greater detail in the next section.

4. *The Implied Duty of Good Faith.* In addition to his implied contract claim, Guz proceeded under the theory that the employer had breached an implied duty of good faith. As you may recall from your first year, every contract contains an implicit promise that the parties will do nothing to interfere with the other's ability to reap the fruits of the agreement. *See* RESTATEMENT (SECOND) OF CONTRACTS § 205. An important limi-tation on the implied duty, however, is that it may not be used to alter other terms of the parties' agreement. For this reason, at-will employees have generally fared poorly in using the good faith duty to challenge the reason for their termination. *See, e.g., Murphy v. American Home Prod. Corp.* 448 N.Ed.2d 86 (N.Y. 1983) (rejecting breach of implied duty of good faith claim by at-will accountant, allegedly terminated for revealing internal financial irregularities, noting that "parties may by express agree-ment limit or restrict the employ's right of discharge, but to imply such a limitation from the existence of an unrestricted right would be internally inconsistent"). There are two exceptions, however. Some early cases allowed breach of the implied duty of good faith claims in situations where the plaintiff's termination violated public policy principles. In *Monge v. Beebe Rubber Co.*, 316 A.2d 549, 552 (N.H. 1974), for instance, the court sanctioned the good faith claim of a woman who was terminated for refusing to date her foreman. Today such cases would be pursued on statutory grounds (for instance, as sex discrimination) or as claims of wrongful discharge violating public policy, topics that will be explored in later chapters. The other situation in which plaintiffs have succeeded is where the termination resulted in the plaintiff losing vested compensation or benefits. *See, e.g., Fortune v. National Cash Register*, 364 N.E.2d 1251 (Mass. 1977) (recognizing limited cause of action for lost commission where plaintiff was terminated after consummation of large sale but prior to merchandise delivery date upon which final installment of earned commissions were to be paid). We will pick up this theory in Chapter 3 when we turn to compensation.

PROBLEMS

2-2. James Pert worked for 15 years at Thistletown Race Track, a family run horse track in Ohio. He started his employment as a stable boy and worked his way up to being a track manager and judge. Pert had no written contract of employment. Throughout his employment he received positive evaluations and consistent salary increases. At one point during Pert's tenure, the track fell on hard times and Pert asked the president of the race track, Edward DeBart, if he should consider looking for other work. DeBart responded, "There's no need. You have been one of our best employees. Whatever happens, your future is secure."

Recently, Pert's wife received a desirable job offer in Florida. The couple had always wanted to live in a warmer climate, but they knew they could not afford to move without Pert's salary. The national market for track judges tends to be tight because there are relatively few jobs and limited turnover in the position. Pert met with DeBart and asked him if it would be possible for him to keep his job working part-time from Florida and flying back to Ohio at his own expense for the four races per year that the track sponsored. DeBart agreed to this proposal. "We are more than willing to accommodate you," he said, "and if things don't work out in Florida, your job is always open here."

Pert and DeBart shook hands to seal the long-distance arrangement, but they did not draft any written document. Pert and his wife sold their house, bought a house in Florida, and moved their belongings. One year later, Ed DeBart passed away and his daughter, Donna York, assumed responsibility for the track. Several months later, DeBart received a notice of termination from York, stating that the company had decided to eliminate the "part-time manager position." Pert subsequently learned that he had been replaced by a full-time manager on location in Ohio.

Suppose that you are hired to represent Pert in an action against Thistletown. Do you think Pert can establish an implied-in-fact contract? Are any other theories of recovery that you have studied in this chapter relevant to his situation? What further information would you need to know to answer these questions? *See generally Pertz v. Edward J. DeBartoloo Corp.*, No. 98-3895, 1999 WL 644339 (6th Cir. Aug. 18, 1999).

2-3. Christine Montell had been working as a student loan account representative for the Huntington Corporation for ten years, when she received a competing offer for a position with the Student Loan Fund ("SLF"). SLF offered her an annual salary of $50,000, a 5 percent increase above her current salary with Huntington, an annual three to 6 percent bonus based on performance, and moving expenses. Montell needed the extra cash, but was reluctant to leave her current employment because she had a good relationship with her boss, Keith Berner, had always received good feedback and training, and was reluctant to relocate. Before responding to the offer, she e-mailed Berner and asked whether Huntington would be able to match SLS's offer.

    (a)   Suppose that prior to answering Montell's e-mail, Berner contacts his own boss, Janis Goodman, who has the foresight to contact you, the company's legal counsel. Goodman would like to do everything possible to retain Montell, including matching SLF's salary and offering Montell a promotion, but does not want to put the company at risk of long-term liability. What do you recommend she do? Is there anything in particular that Goodman or Berner should avoid saying or doing in responding to Montell's e-mail?

    (b)   Suppose instead that Montell does not send an e-mail, but rather meets with Berner over lunch to discuss her competing offer. Upon hearing the offer, Berner immediately promises to meet SLF's salary. Berner also tells Montell, "You are a valuable member of our team, and the only one with the technical expertise to run student loans. Losing you would really hurt the company. If you stay, I promise Huntington will take care of you for the long run." As in-house counsel, you learn about this exchange only after you come across the paperwork altering Montell's title and pay, and contact Berner to inquire about it. What concerns might you have at this point about the statements Berner made to Montell? Is there anything you recommend doing now that could reduce the risk of any long-term obligation on the part of the company?

---

3. Written Employment Manuals and Employee Contract Rights

As you saw in *Guz*, the written documents prepared by an employer and distributed in the workplace can in some cases be a source of employee rights. Depending on what the documents say, they can also be a means by which employers constrict rights or reinforce the idea that employment is at will. Thus, from the lawyer's perspective, reviewing employment documents is a critical component of assessing the viability of an employee claim or, on the employer's side, in preventing claims and avoiding liability. This section looks at two recurring situations in which a plaintiff's success in challenging termination turns on the documentation provided by the employer — situations in which employer documentation seeks to disclaim the existence of contractual rights and situations in which employers try to alter existing employment policies.

In both situations, the analysis begins with what today is a relatively uncontroversial principle — that employment manuals and other written policies can be contractually binding. That idea was first established in two influential 1980s decisions, *Woolley v. Hoffmann-LaRoche, Inc.* 491 A.2d 1257 (N.J. 1985), and *Toussaint v. Blue Cross & Blue Shield*, 292 N.W.2d 880 (Mich. 1980). In *Woolley*, the employer distributed a "Personnel Policy Manual" to all its employees, including the plaintiff, who received it shortly after he began employment. The self-described purpose of the manual was to offer "a practical operating tool in the equitable and efficient administration of our employee relations program." The New Jersey Supreme Court summarized the provisions related to termination:

> [The manual] defines "the types of termination" as "layoff," "discharge due to performance," "discharge, disciplinary," "retirement" and "resignation." As one might expect, layoff is a termination caused by lack of work, retirement a termination caused by age, resignation a termination on the initiative of the employee, and discharge due to performance and discharge, disciplinary, are both terminations for cause. There is no category set forth for discharge without cause. The termination section includes "Guidelines for discharge due to performance," consisting of a fairly detailed procedure to be used before an employee may be fired for cause. Preceding these definitions of the five categories of termination is a section on "Policy," the first sentence of which provides: "It is the policy of Hoffmann-La Roche to retain to the extent consistent with company requirements, the services of all employees who perform their duties efficiently and effectively."

491 A.2d at 1258. Rejecting the defendant's contention that the manual was "simply an expression of the company's 'philosophy,'" the court found a jury question as to whether the manual contained an enforceable implied promise that termination would occur only for cause. The court concluded first that the manual could constitute a contractual offer:

> In determining the manual's meaning and effect, we must consider the probable context in which it was disseminated and the environment surrounding its continued existence. The manual, though apparently not distributed to all employees, [covers all of them. It] represents the most reliable statement of the terms of their employment. At oral argument counsel conceded that it is rare for any employee [to have an individual contract]. Having been employed, like hundreds of his co-employees, without any individual employment contract, by an employer whose good reputation made it so attractive, the employee is given this one document that purports to set forth the terms and conditions of his employment, a document obviously carefully prepared by the company with all of the appearances of corporate legitimacy that one could imagine. If there were any doubt about it (and there would be none in the mind of most employees), the name of the manual dispels it, for it is nothing short of the official policy of the company, it is the Personnel Policy Manual. As every employee knows, when superiors tell you "it's company policy," they mean business.
>
> The [Manual's] changeability—the uncontroverted ability of management to change its terms—is argued as supporting its non-binding quality, but one might as easily conclude that, given its importance, the employer wanted to keep it up to date, especially to make certain, given this employer's good reputation in labor relations, that the benefits conferred were sufficiently competitive with those available from other employers, including benefits found in collective bargaining agreements. The record suggests that the changes actually made almost always favored the employees.
>
> Given that background, then, unless the language contained in the manual were such that no one could reasonably have thought it was intended to create legally binding obligations, the termination provisions of the policy manual would have to be regarded as an obligation undertaken by the employer. It will not do now for the company to say it

did not mean the things it said in its manual to be binding . . . no matter how sincere its belief that they are not enforceable.

Job security is the assurance that one's livelihood, one's family's future, will not be destroyed arbitrarily; it can be cut off only "for good cause," fairly determined. Hoffmann-La Roche's commitment here was to what working men and women regard as their most basic advance. It was a commitment that gave workers protection against arbitrary termination.

Many of these workers undoubtedly know little about contracts, and many probably would be unable to analyze the language and terms of the manual. Whatever Hoffmann-La Roche may have intended, that which was read by its employees was a promise not to fire them except for cause.

Id. at 1265-66.

The court went on to consider whether this offer had been accepted by Hoffmann-La Roche's employees:

In most of the cases involving an employer's personnel policy manual, the document is prepared without any negotiations and is voluntarily distributed to the workforce by the employer. It seeks no return promise from the employees. It is reasonable to interpret it as seeking continued work from the employees, who, in most cases, are free to quit since they are almost always employees at will, not simply in the sense that the employer can fire them without cause, but in the sense that they can quit without breaching any obligation. Thus analyzed, the manual is an offer that seeks the formation of a unilateral contract—the employees' bargained-for action needed to make the offer binding being their continued work when they have no obligation to continue.

Id. at 1267. The court noted that its analysis was "perfectly adequate for that employee who was aware of the manual and who continued to work intending that continuation to be the action in exchange for the employer's promise; it is even more helpful in support of that conclusion if, but for the employer's policy manual, the employee would have quit." *Id.* Absent such evidence, however, the court suggested that reliance on the manual should be presumed. It drew on *Toussaint*, in which the Michigan court analyzed the legal effect of a personnel manual containing similar statements. In discussing workers' reliance on the manual, *Toussaint* noted:

While an employer need not establish personnel policies or practices, where an employer chooses to establish such policies and practices and makes them known to its employees, the employment relationship is presumably enhanced. The employer secures an orderly, cooperative and loyal work force, and the employee the peace of mind associated with job security and the conviction that he will be treated fairly. No pre-employment negotiations need take place and the parties' minds need not meet on the subject; nor does it matter that the employee knows nothing of the particulars of the employer's policies and practices or that the employer may change them unilaterally. It is enough that the employer chooses, presumably in its own interest, to create an environment in which the employee believes that, whatever, the personnel policies and practices, they are established and official at any given time, purport to be fair, and are applied consistently and uniformly to each employee. The employer has then created a situation "instinct with an obligation."

Toussaint, 292 N.W.2d at 892.

Woolley went on the address possible concerns of employers. Seemingly undermining its plaintiff-friendly holding, the final paragraphs of the decision offer employers a way to avoid contractual liability for the promises made in their manuals:

> Our opinion need not make employers reluctant to prepare and distribute company policy manuals. Such manuals can be very helpful tools in labor relations, helpful both to employer and employees, and we would regret it if the consequence of this decision were that the constructive aspects of these manuals were in any way diminished. We do not believe that they will, or at least we certainly do not believe that that constructive aspect should be diminished as a result of this opinion.
>
> All that this opinion requires of an employer is that it be fair. It would be unfair to allow an employer to distribute a policy manual that makes the workforce believe that certain promises have been made and then to allow the employer to renege on those promises. What is sought here is basic honesty: If the employer, for whatever reason, does not want the manual to be capable of being construed by the court as a binding contract, there are simple ways to attain that goal. All that need be done is the inclusion in a very prominent position of an appropriate statement that there is no promise of any kind by the employer contained in the manual; that regardless of what the manual says or provides, the employer promises nothing and remains free to change wages and all other working conditions without having to consult anyone and without anyone's agreement; and that the employer continues to have the absolute power to fire anyone with or without good cause.

491 A.2d at 1271.

Woolley is important for several reasons. Like *Pugh* and *Guz*, it stands for the proposition that in the workplace contractual rights are determined by an examination of factual circumstances, including the reasonable expectations of employees inculcated by management policy and practice. This line of decisions is distinguishable from traditional contracts jurisprudence, which tends to draw a clearer line between what are sometimes called "relational" norms and enforceable obligations. *See generally* Melvin A. Eisenberg, *Why There is No Law of Relational Contracts*, 94 Nw. U. L. Rev. 805 (2000) (distinguishing classical contract doctrine and relational contract theory).

Woolley is also notable for its use of unilateral contract principles in assessing the legal enforceability of Hoffmann-La Roche's manual. For better or worse, this approach has been espoused by most courts dealing with disputes over manuals and written policies. How convincing do you find *Woolley*'s analysis of offer and acceptance? Consider one commentator's view:

> [U]nilateral contract analysis fits uneasily into the handbook context. Except for the communication prerequisite, all of [the] unilateral contract elements are implied by the court rather than intended by the parties. [M]ost employers have no intention of extending a contractual offer when issuing an employee handbook. Similarly, the court infers the employee's acceptance and consideration from conduct that, in reality, could occur regardless of the handbook's existence.
>
> The notion of a bargained-for exchange in this setting is a fiction, but the fiction is convenient and understandable. These advantages have induced courts to stretch unilateral contract theory in order to achieve a desirable policy result: the enforcement of handbook promises that benefit employers by creating legitimate expectations among the work force.

Stephen F. Befort, *Employee Handbooks and the Legal Effect of Disclaimers*, 13 Indus. Rel. L. J. 326, 342-43 (1991/1992). In the cases that follow, consider whether unilateral contract theory offers an accurate description of the parties' relationship. Consider also the degree to which this theory allows courts to achieve particular policy goals.

Finally, *Woolley* is important because of its particular facts and its concluding dicta, which together create uncertainty about the extent to which any particular manual will be held enforceable. An critical fact in the case is the strength of the assurances in the company's manual. Does it surprise you that Hoffmann-La Roche was willing to make such an explicit commitment to job security? How common is it for modern employers to make such statements, let alone in writing? *Cf. Green v. Vermont Country Store*, 191 F. Supp. 2d 476, 481 (D. Vt. 2002) ("value statement" in employer handbook espousing equal treatment contained only general statements of policy and did not constitute a definitive promise for a specific course of treatment). An even more important limitation is the final paragraph permitting employers to disclaim the contractual significance of their handbooks. What drafting techniques would you expect management attorneys to adopt in light of the court's opinion? As you will see, this final paragraph is the source of a great deal of case law limiting the enforceability of written manuals and polices in the contemporary workplace.

Conner v. City of Forest Acres
560 S.E.2d 606 (S.C. 2002)

WALLER, Justice.

. . . Respondent Evelyn Conner worked for the City of Forest Acres ("the City") as a police dispatcher. She was hired in July 1984 and was terminated in October 1993. At the time of her termination, J.C. Rowe was the Chief of Police, and Corporal Lewis Langley was her immediate supervisor. Beginning in November 1992, Conner received numerous reprimands for such things as violating the dress code, tardiness, performing poor work, leaving work without permission, and using abusive language. In July 1993, Conner was evaluated as unsatisfactory and placed on a 90-day probation. She was reprimanded twice in August 1993, and her October 1993 evaluation showed only slight improvement; therefore, the City terminated her on October 7, 1993.

Conner filed a grievance, and at the hearing before the grievance committee, she disputed many of the reprimands. The grievance committee voted 2-1 to reinstate Conner. The City Council, however, rejected the grievance committee's decision and voted to uphold Conner's termination.

During her employment, Conner received two employee handbooks. After receiving each one, Conner signed an acknowledgment form. The 1993 acknowledgment stated as follows:

> I acknowledge that I have received a copy of the City of Forest Acres Personnel Policy and Procedures Manual (Adopted July 1, 1993). I understand that I am responsible for reading, understanding, and abiding by the contents of these policies and procedures. I further understand that all the policies contained herein are subject to change as the need arises. I further understand that nothing in these policies and procedures creates a contract of employment for any term, that I am an employee at-will and nothing herein limits the City of Forest Acres's rights for dismissal.

On page 1 of the handbook, entitled INTRODUCTION, there is the following language:

Important Notice

MANY OF THE POLICIES CONTAINED IN THIS HANDBOOK ARE BASED ON LEGAL PROVISIONS, INTERPRETATIONS OF LAW, AND EMPLOYEE RELATIONS PRINCIPLES, ALL OF WHICH ARE SUBJECT TO CHANGE. FOR THIS REASON, THIS HANDBOOK IS CONSIDERED TO BE A GUIDELINE AND IS SUBJECT TO CHANGE WITH LITTLE NOTICE. THE HANDBOOK DOES NOT CONSTITUTE A CONTRACT OF EMPLOYMENT FOR ANY TERM. NOTHING IN THIS HANDBOOK SHALL BE CONSTRUED TO CONSTITUTE A CONTRACT. THE CITY HAS THE RIGHT, AT ITS DISCRETION, TO MODIFY THIS HANDBOOK AT ANY TIME. NOTHING HEREIN LIMITS THE CITY'S RIGHTS TO TERMINATE EMPLOYMENT. ALL EMPLOYEES OF THE CITY ARE AT-WILL EMPLOYEES. NO ONE EXCEPT THE CITY ADMINISTRATOR HAS THE AUTHORITY TO WAIVE ANY OF THE PROVISIONS OF THIS HANDBOOK, OR MAKE REPRESENTATIONS CONTRARY TO THE PROVISIONS OF THIS HANDBOOK.

This same language appears on the last page of the handbook.

The handbook contained a section entitled "Code of Conduct." In this section, the handbook states that conduct "reflecting unfavorably upon the reputation of the City, the Department, or the employee will not be tolerated." Furthermore, this section advises that:

This code of conduct is designed to guide all employees in their relationship with the City.

The following is a non-exclusive list of acts which are considered a violation of the Code of Conduct expected of a City employee, and such conduct will be disciplined in accords with its seriousness, recurrence, and circumstances. Degrees of discipline are given under the section entitled "Discipline" in this manual.

The list enumerates 23 different acts.

The Disciplinary Procedures section of the handbook states that it is the "duty of all employees to comply with, and to assist in carrying into effect [t]he provisions of the personnel policy and procedures." Additionally, the handbook states the following:

Ordinarily, discipline shall be of an increasingly progressive nature, the step of progression being (1) oral or written reprimand, (2) suspension, and (3) dismissal. Discipline should correspond to the offense and therefore NO REQUIREMENT EXISTS FOR DISCIPLINE TO BE PROGRESSIVE. FIRST VIOLATIONS CAN RESULT IN IMMEDIATE DISMISSAL WITHOUT REPRIMAND OR SUSPENSION.

Furthermore, this section states that violations of the code of conduct "*are declared*" to be grounds for discipline and that discipline "*will be used* to enforce the City's Code of Conduct." (Emphasis added.) Finally, the grievance procedure is outlined in detail. In this section, the handbook states "[i]t is the policy of the City of Forest Acres that all employees shall be treated fairly and consistently in all matters related to their employment."

[Conner brought suit against the City alleging breach of contract. The trial court granted the defendants' motions for summary judgment, but the Court of Appeals reversed.]

The City argues there was no contract created by the handbook because: (1) the procedures in the employee handbook did not alter Conner's at-will status, (2) the disclaimers in the handbook were conspicuous and therefore effective, and (3) Conner signed acknowledgments of her at-will status. Additionally, the City contends that even if the handbook did create a contract, it did not breach the contract because it followed the prescribed procedures.

The general rule is that termination of an at-will employee normally does not give rise to a cause of action for breach of contract. However, where the at-will status of the employee is altered by the terms of an employee handbook, an employer's discharge of an employee may give rise to a cause of action for wrongful discharge. Because an employee handbook may create a contract, the issue of the existence of an employment contract is proper for a jury when its existence is questioned and the evidence is either conflicting or admits of more than one inference.

The Court in *Small* [*v. Springs*, 357 S.E.2d 452, 455 (S.C. 1987)] stated that "[i]t is patently unjust to allow an employer to couch a handbook, bulletin, or other similar material in mandatory terms and then allow him to ignore these very policies as 'a gratuitous, nonbinding statement of general policy' whenever it works to his disadvantage." The *Small* Court instructed that if an employer wishes to issue written policies, but intends to continue at-will employment, the employer must insert a conspicuous disclaimer into the handbook. However, in *Fleming v. Borden*, 450 S.E.2d 589 (S.C. 1994), the Court indicated that whether the disclaimer is conspicuous is generally a question for the jury. Specifically, the *Fleming* Court stated that "[i]n most instances, summary judgment is inappropriate when the handbook contains both a disclaimer and promises."

Relying primarily on *Fleming*, the Court of Appeals in the instant case found that summary judgment was inappropriate. We agree. While the City argues that its handbook contained disclaimers which were effective as a matter of law and that Conner signed acknowledgments of her at will status, the fact remains that the handbook outlines numerous procedures concerning progressive discipline, discharge, and subsequent grievance. The language in the handbook is mandatory in nature[4] and therefore a genuine issue of material fact exists as to whether Conner's at-will status was modified by the policies in the handbook.

The City also argues that if a contract exists, then as a matter of law, it did not breach the contract because it followed the procedures outlined in the handbook. The Court of Appeals found that because "Conner disputes the City's version of the events resulting in her reprimands and subsequent termination," summary judgment was not proper "on the issue of whether Conner was fired for cause."

Although this is a closer question, we agree with the Court of Appeals that there is a genuine issue of material fact as to whether Conner was wrongfully terminated. The appropriate test on the issue of breach is as follows: "If the fact finder finds a contract to terminate only for cause, he must determine whether the employer had *a reasonable*

---

4. For example, the handbook states that: (1) violations of the Code of Conduct *will be* disciplined," (2) "discipline *shall be* of an increasingly progressive nature," and (3) "all employees *shall be* treated fairly and consistently in all matters related to their employment." (Emphasis added.)

good faith belief that sufficient cause existed for termination."[5] We note that the fact finder must not focus on whether the employee actually committed misconduct; instead, the focus must be on whether the employer reasonably determined it had cause to terminate.

Conner's basic argument is there was no just cause for her termination. Although it appears that the City followed its handbook procedures in effectuating Conner's termination, the grievance committee voted to reinstate Conner; i.e., the committee found no just cause for Conner's firing. Subsequently, the City Council overturned the committee's decision. While the committee and City Council both could have reached their respective conclusions reasonably and in good faith, it nonetheless appears that reasonable minds can differ as to whether just cause existed to support Conner's termination. Thus, there remains the ultimate question of whether the City had a reasonable good faith belief that sufficient cause existed for termination. This is a question that generally should not be resolved on summary judgment, and therefore, the Court of Appeals correctly reversed the trial court's grant of summary judgment in favor of the City. . . .

NOTES

1. *Putting* Woolley *and* Conner *Together.* Why did the city of Forest Acres lose this case? Didn't its manual contain the requisite *Woolley* disclaimers in abundance? What exactly is the outstanding factual issue on the enforceability of the manual that requires a remand?

2. *Clarity and Conspicuousness.* One reason that plaintiffs sometimes prevail despite the presence of at-will language in a handbook or other document is because the clause is not clear or conspicuous. *See Evenson v. Colorado Farm Bureau Mut. Ins. Co.*, 879 P.2d 402, 409 (Colo. Ct. App. 1993) (jury question presented on whether handbook formed contract where language disclaiming contractual significance was clear, but not "emphasized"); *Nicosia v. Wakefern Food Corp.*, 643 A.2d 554, 560 (N.J. 1994) (disclaimer ineffective under *Woolley* because it contained "legalese" such as "not contractual," "consideration," and "subject to . . . interpretation"); *Sanchez v. Life Care Ctrs. of Amer., Inc.*, 855 P.2d 1256, 1259 (Wyo. 1993) (reversing summary judgment for employer where disclaimer language was "not bold lettered," was "buried in introductory paragraphs," was "not designed to attract attention," and was "stated in language that does not tell the employee what he needs to know"); *see generally* Michael A. Chagares, *Utilization of the Disclaimer as an Effective Means to Define the Employment Relationship*, 17 Hofstra L. Rev. 365, 381-86 (1989). From what you can tell, was the disclaimer in *Conner* prominently placed? Was the text emphasized in any way? Assuming it was noted and read, was it understandable to an employee?

3. *Judicial Deference to Employer Disclaimer Language. Connor* represents one extreme in judicial treatment of employer disclaimers. Not all courts parse so closely the language of the manual or recognize possible inconsistencies of the type that led to

---

5. The Court in *Small* noted that where the jury found that a handbook created an employment contract, it was for the jury to decide whether the employer "reasonably could have determined that Small's actions" warranted immediate discharge as a "serious offense." Therefore, it is generally a jury question as to whether the employer acted reasonably pursuant to the employment contract.

a plaintiff victory in *Connor*. Recall *Guz*, for instance, in which the California Supreme Court rejected the employee's claim, based in part on the at-will provision of the employer's manual, notwithstanding other provisions and policies that made promises about the method by which workers would be selected for termination. In contrast to *Connor*, many courts treat disclaimer language as dispositive of employee contract rights, routinely awarding summary judgment to employers in such cases. *See, e.g., Grossman v. Computer Curriculum Corp.*, 131 F. Supp. 2d 299, 305-06 (D. Conn. 2000); *Rowe v. Montgomery Ward & Co.*, 473 N.W.2d 268, 271 (Mich. 1991); *Finch v. Farmers Co-op Oil Co. of Sheridan*, 109 P.3d 537, 541-42 (Wyo. 2005). Some scholars have speculated that judicial tendency to "rubberstamp" employer disclaimer language may be on the rise. *See* Arnow-Richman, *Employment as Transaction, supra*, at 468-71 (linking judicial treatment of disclaimers to larger trend of increasing deference to private ordering in employment relationships); Fineman, *The Inevitable Demise, supra*, at 365-77 (tracing increasing judicial deference to disclaimer language in California as employers refined their drafting techniques to avoid liability).

4. *Disclaimers and Oral Assurances.* The effectiveness of written disclaimers is a recurring theme in all types of employment contract disputes, not just those centered on manuals. In part as a result of cases like *Woolley*, employers frequently place recitals of at-will status in a variety of personnel materials, including employment applications, offer letters, and reimbursement forms. Often these are standardized documents that are distributed as a matter of course to all personnel. The effect of these statements in the face of other evidence suggesting a contract for job security is unclear. Depending on the facts and the court, the contrary evidence may be treated as inadmissible parol statements, evidence of a modification, or simply additional evidence to be submitted to a fact finder who will determine the contractual status of the employee under the circumstances. Not surprisingly, the outcomes of such cases tend to be highly fact-dependent, and it is not uncommon for courts to reach disparate results. *Compare Worley v. Wyoming Bottling Co.*, 1 P.3d 615 (Wyo. 2000) (plaintiff may proceed with breach of contract and promissory estoppel claims based on express assurances of job security by supervisor despite at-will disclaimers contained in job application, non-compete and employee handbook) *with Dore v. Arnold Worldwide, Inc.*, 139 P.3d 56 (Cal. 2006) (no triable issue of fact on plaintiff's breach of contract claims where statement in offer letter that employment was terminable at any time was unambiguous and precluded introduction of evidence of prior oral assurances that employment would be long term).

5. *Turnabout Is Fair Play.* Most cases turning on the significance of disclaimer language involve suits by employees who, like Connor, claim their employer breached a promise of job security. However, employers occasionally have found themselves in the uncomfortable position of having to circumvent their own language in trying to enforce promises made by employees. Such cases can arise in situations where the employer has placed an arbitration policy or a prohibition on post-employment competition in its handbook. When an employee subsequently engages in prohibited behavior — for instance, filing suit against the employer in court — the company is at pains to explain why the employee's commitment should be enforced when the handbook in which it was found expressly disclaims its contractual significance. *See, e.g., Heurtebise v. Reliable Bus. Computers*, 452 N.W.2d 243, 247 (Mich. 1996) (policy in handbook did not constitute enforceable arbitration agreement where handbook's opening statement disclaiming contractual significance of manual "demonstrate[d] that employer did not intend to be bound to any provision [it] contained"); *Gibson v. Neighborhood Health Clinics, Inc.*, 121 F.3d 1126, 1132-33 (7th Cir. 1997) (Cucahy, J., concurring) ("[W]hatever 'promise' is contained in the Associate Policy Manual is illusory because it is subject to the sweeping disclaimer language contained in the opening two paragraphs of the Manual."). Unfortunately, for employees, such victories are short-lived. Employers are able to correct the problem easily by removing such commitments from the general personnel handbook and placing them in formal contract documents separately signed by the employee. *See, e.g., Currier, McCabe & Assocs. v. Maher*, 906 N.Y.S.2d 129, 131 (N.Y. App. 2010) (defendant-employee bound by handbook's tuition repayment policy despite disclaimer where employee's separately executed employment agreement provided the he had "read the EMPLOYEE HANDBOOK and agrees to [its] terms and conditions"). If you find yourself representing management, you would do well to remember these examples.

PROBLEM

2-4. Imagine that, following *Woolley*, the Human Resources director at Hoffmann-La Roche contacts you about revising the company's personnel manual. The HR director feels that the manual is good for employee morale and would like to continue using it, but hopes to alter the language so as to protect the company from future contractual liability. Look at footnote 2 of *Woolley*, which contains the key language that gave rise to Woolley's claim. How would you redraft this? What might you add? Will the revision you create satisfy the company's goals?

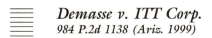

Demasse v. ITT Corp.
984 P.2d 1138 (Ariz. 1999)

FELDMAN, Justice.

The United States Court of Appeals for the Ninth Circuit certified to us [the following question] of Arizona law. . . .

1. Once a policy that an employee will not be laid off ahead of less senior employees becomes part of the employment contract . . . as a result of the employee's legitimate expectations and reliance on the employer's handbook, may the employer thereafter unilaterally change the handbook policy so as to permit the employer to layoff employees without regard to seniority? . . .

ITT hired Roger Demasse, Maria A. Garcia, Billy W. Jones, Viola Munguia, Greg Palmer, and Socorro Soza (collectively "Demasse employees") as hourly workers at various times between 1960 and 1979. Although it is unclear when ITT first issued an employee handbook, evidently there have been five editions, the most recent in 1989. . . .

The issues presented focus on the 1989 handbook, which included two new provisions. First, a disclaimer added to the first page "Welcome" statement provided that "nothing contained herein shall be construed as a guarantee of continued employment. . . . ITT Cannon does not guarantee continued employment to employees and retains the right to terminate or layoff employees." Second, this Welcome statement included a new modification provision, which read:

> Within the limits allowed by law, ITT Cannon reserves the right to amend, modify or cancel this handbook, as well as any or all of the various policies, rules, procedures and programs outlined in it. Any amendment or modification will be communicated to affected employees, and while the handbook provisions are in effect, will be consistently applied.

. . . When the 1989 handbook was distributed, ITT employees signed an acknowledgment that they had received, understood, and would comply with the revised handbook.

Four years passed before ITT notified its hourly employees that effective April 19, 1993, its layoff guidelines for hourly employees would not be based on seniority but on each employee's "abilities and documentation of performance." Demasse, Soza, and Palmer were laid off ten days after the new policy went into effect, Munguia five days later, and Jones and Garcia almost nine months later. All were laid off before less senior employees but in accordance with the 1993 policy modification.

The Demasse employees brought an action in federal district court alleging they were laid off in breach of an implied-in-fact contract created by the pre-1989 handbook provisions requiring that ITT lay off its employees according to seniority. [The court granted summary judgment for the employer finding that the employer had validly modified its layoff policy in the 1993 handbook.]

A. The Implied-in-Fact Contract . . .

At-will employment contracts are unilateral and typically start with an employer's offer of a wage in exchange for work performed; subsequent performance by the employee provides consideration to create the contract. Thus, before performance is rendered, the offer can be modified by the employer's unilateral withdrawal of the old offer and substitution of a new one: The employer makes a new offer with different terms and the employee again accepts the new offer by performance (such as continued employment). Thus a new unilateral contract is formed — a day's work for a day's wages. . . .

While employment contracts without express terms are presumptively at will, an employee can overcome this presumption by establishing a contract term that is either expressed or inferred from the words or conduct of the parties. . . .

When employment circumstances offer a term of job security to an employee who might otherwise be dischargeable at will and the employee acts in response to that promise, the employment relationship is *no longer at will* but is instead governed by the terms of the contract. . . .

This, of course, does not mean that all handbook terms create contractual promises. A statement is contractual only if it discloses "a promissory intent or [is] one that the employee could reasonably conclude constituted a commitment by the employer. If the statement is merely a description of the employer's present policies . . . it is neither a promise nor a statement that could reasonably be relied upon as a commitment." *Soderlun v. Public Serv. Co.*, 944 P.2d 616, 620 (Colo. App. 1997). An implied-in-fact contract term is formed when "a reasonable person could conclude that both parties intended that the employer's (or the employee's) right to terminate the employment relationship at-will had been limited." *Metcalf v. Intermountain Gas Co.*, 778 P.2d 744, 746 (Idaho 1989).

When an employer chooses to include a handbook statement "that the employer should reasonably have expected the employee to consider as a commitment from the employer," that term becomes an offer to form an implied-in-fact contract and is accepted by the employee's acceptance of employment. . . .

B. Modification

ITT argues that it had the legal power to unilaterally modify the contract by simply publishing a new handbook. But as with other contracts, an implied-in-fact contract term cannot be modified unilaterally. . . . [3]

[T]o effectively modify a contract, whether implied-in-fact or express, there must be: (1) an offer to modify the contract, (2) assent to or acceptance of that offer, and (3) consideration.

The 1989 handbook, published with terms that purportedly modified or permitted modification of pre-existing contractual provisions, was therefore no more than an offer to modify the existing contract. Even if the 1989 handbook constituted a valid offer, questions remain whether the Demasse employees accepted that offer and whether there was consideration for the changes ITT sought to effect.

1. Continued Employment Alone Does Not Constitute Consideration for Modification

. . . Consideration will be found when an employer and its employees have made a "bargained for exchange to support [the employees'] . . . relinquishment of the protections they are entitled to under the existing contract."

The cases ITT cites hold that continued work alone both manifested the Demasse employees' assent to the modification and constituted consideration for it. We disagree with both contentions and the cases that support them. Separate consideration, beyond continued employment, is necessary to effect a modification.

. . . Any other result brings us to an absurdity: The employer's threat to breach its promise of job security provides consideration for its rescission of that promise.

2. Acceptance

Continued employment after issuance of a new handbook does not constitute acceptance, otherwise the "illusion (and the irony) is apparent: To preserve their right

---

3. In the unilateral or at-will context, once the offer is accepted by commencement of performance, the terms cannot be changed. RESTATEMENT (SECOND) OF CONTRACTS § 45. Thus, if an employer offers a day's pay for a day's work, the employer cannot, after employee performance, reduce the offer of pay that induced the performance.

under the [existing contract] . . . plaintiffs would be forced to quit." *Doyle* [*v. Holy Cross*, 708 N.E.2d 1140 (Ill. 1999)]. It is "too much to require an employee to preserve his or her rights under the original employment contract by quitting working." *Brodie* [*v. General Chem. Corp.*, 934 P.2d 1263, 1268 (Wyo. 1997)]. Thus, the employee does not manifest consent to an offer modifying an existing contract without taking affirmative steps, beyond continued performance, to accept. . . . If passive silence constituted acceptance, the employee "could not remain silent and continue to work. Instead [he] would have to give specific notice of rejection to the employer to avoid having his actions construed as acceptance. Requiring an offeree to take affirmative steps to reject an offer . . . is inconsistent with general contract law." The burden is on the employer to show that the employee assented with knowledge of the attempted modification and understanding of its impact on the underlying contract.

To manifest consent, the employee must first have legally adequate notice of the modification. Legally adequate notice is more than the employee's awareness of or receipt of the newest handbook. An employee must be informed of any new term, aware of its impact on the pre-existing contract, and affirmatively consent to it to accept the offered modification.

When ITT distributed the 1989 handbook containing the provisions permitting unilateral modification or cancellation, it did not bargain with those pre-1989 employees who had seniority rights under the old handbooks, did not ask for or obtain their assent, and did not provide consideration other than continued employment. The employees signed a receipt for the "1989 handbook stating that they had received the handbook[,] understood that it was their responsibility to read it, comply with its contents, and contact Personnel if they had any questions concerning the contents." The Demasse employees were not informed that continued employment—showing up for work the next day—would manifest assent, constitute consideration, and permit cancellation of any employment rights to which they were contractually entitled. Thus, even if we were to agree that continued employment could provide consideration for rescission of the job security term, that consideration would not have been bargained for and would not support modification. . . .

C . . .

If a contractual job security provision can be eliminated by unilateral modification, an employer can essentially terminate the employee at any time, thus abrogating any protection provided the employee. For example, an employer could terminate an employee who has a job security provision simply by saying, "I revoke that term and, as of today, you're dismissed"—no different from the full at-will scenario in which the employer only need say, "You're fired." This, of course, makes the original promise illusory. . . .

To those who believe our conclusion will destroy an employer's ability to update and modernize its handbook, we can only reply that the great majority of handbook terms are certainly non-contractual and can be revised, that the existence of contractual terms can be disclaimed in the handbook in effect at the time of hiring and, if not, permission to modify can always be obtained by mutual agreement and for consideration. In all other instances, the contract rule is and has always been that one should keep one's promises.

JONES, Vice Chief Judge, concurring in part and dissenting in part:

I respectfully dissent. . . . The [majority's] response undermines legitimate employer expectations in a remarkable departure from traditional at-will employment principles. It transforms the conventional employer-employee contract from one that is *unilateral* (performance of an act in exchange for a promise to pay) to one that is *bilateral* (a promise for a promise). The decision is unsupported by Arizona precedent and unwarranted as a matter of law.

The majority exacts from the certified question the premise that the employment relationship between the Demasse plaintiffs and ITT is "no longer at-will." I disagree. A single contract term in a policy manual may, while it exists, become an enforceable condition of employment, but it does not alter the essential character of the relationship. In my view, ITT, as the party unilaterally responsible for inserting it into the manual may, on reasonable notice, exercise an equal right to remove it.

For purposes of this discussion, it is assumed the reverse-seniority layoff provision became part of the "employment contract" years earlier when ITT initially placed it into the policy manual and that it remained a part of the "contract" as long as it remained a part of the manual. The simple question put to us is whether ITT may unilaterally bring about its removal and thereafter be free of any prospective reverse-seniority obligation in the event of a layoff. That question does not catapult the case beyond the reach of at-will employment principles.

. . . ITT added a contract disclaimer to its 1989 handbook: "[N]othing contained herein shall be construed as a guarantee of continued employment." In the same handbook, ITT expressly reserved "the right to amend, modify, or cancel this handbook, as well as any or all of the various policies, rules, procedures, and programs outlined within it." Each of the Demasse plaintiffs signed a certification acknowledging that the new policy had been received and reviewed.

The "at-will" status of the Demasse-ITT contract both before and after the 1989 amendments is confirmed by at least two factors: (1) the contract was always one of indefinite duration, and (2) the Demasse employees had the absolute right to quit at any time. . . .

The right to quit in opposition to changed policies, despite the majority's view, is properly characterized as a right. It is an inherent feature of at-will employment. . . .

When ITT modified its policy manual in 1989 by adding the contract disclaimer and the power to amend, and offered continuing employment to employees having received notice and having signed the acknowledgment, the employees effectively gave their acceptance to the amendment by continuing to work. Moreover, in 1993, when ITT revised its layoff policy, the employees had known for four years that such change could occur.

The majority overlooks another point. Just as at-will employees are unilaterally free to quit at any time, employers may be unilaterally forced by economic circumstance to curtail or shut down an operation, something employers have the absolute right to do. When the employer chooses in good faith, in pursuit of legitimate business objectives, to eliminate an employee policy as an alternative to curtailment or total shutdown, there has been forbearance by the employer. Such forbearance constitutes a benefit to the employee in the form of an offer of continuing employment. The employer who provides continuing employment, albeit under newly modified contract terms, also provides consideration to support the amended policy manual. . . .

The majority imposes a bilateral principle on the at-will relationship by holding that in order for ITT to eliminate the reverse-seniority layoff policy, some form of new consideration, in addition to an offer of continuing employment, is necessary to support each individual employee's assent to the amended manual. The majority's approach effectively mandates that ITT, in order to free itself of future reverse-seniority obligations, would be required to give a wage increase, a one-time bonus, or some other new benefit to the employees with the explicit understanding that such benefit was given in exchange for the amendment to the policy manual. This becomes artificial because it is foreign to the unilateral at-will relationship and, as a practical matter, it leaves the employer unable, at least in part, to manage its business. I disagree with the proposition that "new" consideration is necessary.

The majority further asserts that ITT's exercise of the unilateral right to amend the handbook renders the employer's original reverse-seniority promise illusory. Once again, I disagree. An illusory promise is one which by its own terms makes performance optional with the promisor whatever may happen, or whatever course of conduct he may pursue. The reverse-seniority promise was not illusory because it was not optional with ITT as long as it remained a part of ITT's handbook policy. During the years of its existence, it was fully enforceable. . . .

The majority opinion produces the net result that the reverse-seniority layoff policy, as a permanent term of the "employment contract" with respect to any employee who at any time worked under it, gains parity with a negotiated collective bargaining agreement having a definite term, usually three years. In fact, the ITT policy would have force and effect even greater than a collective agreement because its existence, as to the Demasse plaintiffs and others similarly situated, becomes perpetual. This result grants preferential treatment to every employee who worked under the policy but denies such treatment to employees hired after its removal. A collective bargaining agreement is bilateral, and to impose a bilateral relationship on simple at-will employment is, in my view, an attempt to place a square peg in a round hole. Inevitably, this will impair essential managerial flexibility in the workplace. It will also cause undue deterioration of traditional at-will principles. . . .

Principles of equity and pragmatic reason have also governed the employer's unilateral right to change an implied-in-fact term in a handbook. The federal district court, applying Arizona law in *Bedow* [*v. Valley National Bank*, 5 BNA IER CAS 1678 (D. Ariz. 1988)], correctly asserted that the last-distributed handbook controls employment conditions and trumps prior inconsistent handbook terms:

> *Any other conclusion would create chaos for employers who would have different contracts of employment for different employees depending upon the particular personnel manual in force when the employee was hired.* Such a result would effectively discourage employers from either issuing employment manuals or subsequently upgrading or modifying personnel policies.

. . . The majority's answer to the certified question will frustrate the legitimate expectations of both employers and employees. The notion that one term in an employee handbook — a reverse-seniority layoff term — can be perpetually binding as to some but not all employees will effectively undermine [cases] on which employers have relied for years. The opinion unduly punishes ITT and other employers similarly situated. We said [previously] that employers should place contract disclaimer language in their handbooks to preserve the at-will relationship. ITT responded by inserting such language. We should leave it at that.

NOTES

1. *"Separate" Consideration.* The majority rejects the idea that continued employment can be consideration for the change in ITT's layoff policy, insisting on "separate" consideration for the modification. What is "separate" consideration? Is it any different from the discredited notion of "additional" consideration used by courts to defeat plaintiffs' claims to "permanent" or "lifetime" employment? Recall from your first-year contracts class the general common law rule that contract modifications require consideration to be binding. A corollary to this rule is that a "pre-existing legal duty" does not constitute consideration. *See* RESTATEMENT (SECOND) OF CONTRACTS § 370 (1981). Does the pre-existing legal duty concept help you distinguish between the "permanent" employment and handbook modification scenarios? Or is *Demasse* simply co-opting the additional consideration doctrine in order to turn the tables on employers?

2. *The Fiction of Assent.* The majority suggests that even if continued employment constituted consideration it could not suffice as an acceptance because it was not given knowingly. If tacit acceptance worked in *Woolley* to establish contractual rights based on a handbook, why doesn't it work here? Are *Demasse* and *Woolley* inconsistent? Which court's treatment of assent is more in keeping with basic contract law? Must parties actually negotiate terms in order to be contractually bound? Must they at least know what the terms are? Know they are contracting?

3. *Advising the Employer.* The law of personnel manual modification is currently evolving; not every jurisdiction has addressed the issue, nor has there been agreement among those that have. *Compare Torosyan v. Boehringer Ingelheim Pharmaceuticals, Inc.*, 662 A.2d 89, 98-99 (Conn. 1995) (employee continuing work does not constitute acceptance of a modified handbook that "substantially interferes with [the] employee's legitimate expectations") *with Asmus v. Pac. Bell*, 999 P.2d 71, 78 (Cal. 2000) (unilaterally conferred contract rights may be reduced or eliminated unilaterally); *see generally Fleming v. Borden, Inc.*, 450 S.E.2d 589, 594-95 (S.C. 1994) (summarizing various court approaches to enforceability of employer's unilateral modification of handbook to include disclaimer). This uncertainty can pose difficulties for employers. Assuming the law in your jurisdiction is undecided, how would you advise an employer seeking to modify the terms of a pre-existing handbook? Would you recommend trying to comply with the majority opinion in *Demasse*? If yes, by what means would you recommend obtaining employee assent? Would it be enough to amend the signature receipts to include an explanation of the modifications? Now consider what you might provide as "separate" consideration. Would a one-time bonus of $1000 suffice? How about a one-time bonus of $10? Does the employer have to provide something that is distinct from the usual adjustments made regularly to employee salaries? For instance, what about making the modification coincident with an annual cost-of-living adjustment? Might these examples offer ways to avoid the "chaos" envisioned by the dissent of different manuals applying to different employees depending on their date of hire?

4. *Square Peg in a Round Hole?* Consider the various objections raised by the dissent. Chief among them is a disagreement with the majority's premise that, upon the employer's adoption of the original personnel manual, the parties' relationship changed from a unilateral at-will relationship to a bilateral relationship with job security. Who is right? In commercial settings, it is not uncommon for parties to have long-term sales or service contracts that are terminable at will but which bind both parties to a variety of terms during the life of the agreement. Generally such contracts provide that a designated amount of notice must be given prior to termination. Does the commercial context offer a viable analogy for handbook modifications?

The draft Restatement of Employment Law adopts a comparable approach. It rejects efforts to apply contract principles to employer handbooks as "analytically unsatisfying" and permits the employer to "modify or revoke an obligation established pursuant to a unilateral statement" by providing "reasonable notice" of the change. *See* RESTATEMENT (THIRD) OF EMPLOYMENT (Tentative Draft No. 2) § 3.05 (April 3, 2009). If notice is the touchstone for enforceable unilateral modifications, how much time is reasonable? In *Demasse*, four years passed between ITT's change in policy and the lay-offs in question. Would four months suffice? Four days? *See, e.g., Asmus v. Pac. Bell*, 999 P.2d at 78 (sanctioning unilateral modification made two years after notice to employees that job security program might be eliminated); *Bankey v. Storer Broad. Co.*, 443 N.W.2d 112, 117-20 (Mich. 1989) (denying breach of contract claim by employee discharged two months after unilateral modification of employer's policy digest in recognition of employer's need for managerial flexibility). What is the point of notice — to allow employees who are unhappy to seek another job? If so, does that help determine the proper length of notice?

PROBLEM

2-5.   During the mid-1990s, Pacific Telecom was facing competitive pressure from the burgeoning technology industry in California and lost several key employees to start up ventures offering stock option deals. In response, the company disseminated a new "Management Employment Security Policy" to all management personnel. The document provided, "It will be our policy to offer all management employees who continue to meet our changing business expectations employment security through reassignment to and retraining for other management positions, even if their present jobs are eliminated."

Five years later, following a crash in the tech sector, Pacific Bell realized it could not afford to maintain its employment security policy and needed to institute a reduction in force. It announced to all management personnel that the Employment Security Policy had been terminated and was being replaced with a new Management Force Reduction Program under which designated employees would be offered enhanced pension and severance benefits in exchange for their voluntary resignations. Craig Astor was a technical manager at Pacific Telecom who received both documents. He declined to resign under Pacific's Reduction Program. Six months later he was involuntarily terminated.

(a)   Suppose Astor sues for breach of an implied contract for job security under the original Security Policy. Is he likely to succeed? Are there any other legal theories he might be able to pursue?

(b)   How would it affect your analysis if Pacific Telecom had sent a notice to all managers one year prior to announcing its Management Force Reduction Program, alerting them to the fact that it would shortly be altering its Security Policy?

(c)   What if the original Security Policy contained the following additional sentence: "This Policy will remain in effect unless and until changing market conditions necessitate its revocation"?

3

Written Contracts and Expressly Negotiated Terms of Employment

As discussed in the previous chapter, the at-will presumption is merely a default rule; the words, actions, and practices of the employer can confer greater contractual rights to job security. This chapter continues our discussion of how parties alter the default rules of their relationship. While Chapter 2 dealt primarily with oral and implied promises, this chapter looks at situations where the employer and an individual employee explicitly discussed particular terms of employment — issues such as job duration, bases for termination, and methods of compensation — and then took the time to reduce those terms to writing, sometimes with the help of a lawyer.

Employers and employees who opt for a written contract do so for the same reasons that parties choose written contracts in other contexts. They hope to memorialize their understanding in a fixed form so that it will not be forgotten or challenged by competing understandings in the future. For employers, written contracts might also be desirable given the uncertainty of implied contract theory. An employer may use a writing to make clear that the employment relationship is at will in order to avoid subsequent claims to job security based on oral assurances or workplace practices like those explored in the last chapter. In contrast, employees will desire written contracts mostly to lock in employment and its benefits.

However, written employment agreements are relatively rare. Drafting such an agreement requires time, advanced planning, and, where a lawyer is involved, expense. From the perspective of the employer, the party who generally controls whether a written contract will be executed, the default rule already adequately protects its interest in being able to terminate at will. As a result, written employment contracts are found primarily in those situations in which the employee has sufficient bargaining power to insist that the employer commit to more generous terms. These include the collective bargaining context where unionized employees (through their union representatives) negotiate a written "collective bargaining agreement," a process generally studied in a separate course on Labor Law. These "CBAs" govern all workers in the relevant "bargaining unit" and are often very detailed, covering various terms and conditions of employment including job security. Individual written contracts, by contrast, are used most frequently with high-level employees, such as executives and upper-level managers, who command significant pay and hold critical positions

125

that enable them to insist on generous terms and justify a written instrument. Individual written contracts are also used with some regularity among sales employees and other workers whose compensation fluctuates based on performance. In those instances, the writing likely does not reflect the worker's bargaining power so much as the employer's practical need to document a complex commission or bonus structure.

While written contracts will resolve some uncertainties, they can create others. Planning and drafting are imperfect processes that can result in a document that is ambiguous, vague, or simply incomplete. Although such difficulties plague all types of contracts, they are especially likely in the employment context where the parties' expectations change, sometimes dramatically, over the course of the relationship. Think how hard it would be to capture every obligation of the employer and employee in a particular work relationship in a single written document. Even if you could do it, circumstances and expectations are almost certain to change over time, especially in the high-powered situations where such contracts are typically used. As a result, when employment disputes arise, parties often find that their written contracts are silent as to a particular issue or even inconsistent with the way the relationship has developed.

This chapter deals with how to understand written contracts in the context of a dynamic employment relationship. Section A begins by looking at situations where the written contract is ambiguous as to job security, either because of the language itself or the circumstances surrounding the agreement. Section B turns to how written provisions conferring job security apply in the context of termination, as where an employee's performance is substandard or an employer fails to comply with specific obligations. Finally, Section C tackles problems related to special compensation arrangements such as commissions and profit sharing. Note throughout how context and other circumstances extraneous to the written instrument affect both the parties' perception of their obligations to one another and the court's interpretation of their contract. Consider whether and how parties might have avoided litigation by drafting their agreement differently and what the resulting decisions say about the value and efficacy of written employment contracts.

A. JOB SECURITY TERMS

1. Identifying and Interpreting Job Security Provisions

≡ ***Tropicana Hotel Corporation v. Speer***
≡ *692 P.2d 499 (Nev. 1985)*

GUNDERSON, Justice.

This appeal arises out of the brief association of Donald Speer with Tropicana Hotel. In July 1975 Mitzi Stauffer Briggs acquired a controlling interest in the Tropicana Hotel Corporation ... [and] looked for a competent general manager who could restore the hotel to its former prosperity. She offered the position to Donald Speer, general manager at the Desert Inn.

Speer indicated that he would accept the position only if, in addition to a generous salary, he could have equity in the Tropicana Hotel Corporation. After some preliminary discussions, Briggs invited Speer, his counsel and her counsel to her home in Atherton, California, in the hope of concluding an agreement. It is undisputed that agreement was reached on the terms of the employment contract; the parties could not agree, however, on how the stock should be transferred.

After Speer returned to Las Vegas, he left his position at the Desert Inn and began working as general manager at the Tropicana Hotel. Two months later Briggs signed an employment agreement prepared by her attorneys according to drafts of the Atherton discussions, and forwarded it to Speer. Speer never signed the agreement. He testified at trial that his counsel advised him not to sign it until a satisfactory stock option agreement was prepared and signed by Briggs.

In March 1976 a culinary strike forced the hotel to close. Disagreements over hotel management developed between Speer and Briggs, and after two of Speer's trusted subordinates were fired by the executive committee, Speer left the hotel. The parties disagreed at trial over whether Speer had resigned or whether he had been terminated. Speer filed suit [alleging breach of an oral employment contract reached at Atherton by his termination without cause and] breach of an oral stock option agreement. The district court, sitting without a jury, found that binding oral agreements existed, and that Tropicana had breached the employment contract. . . . [H]owever, it found that the statute of frauds rendered the stock option agreement unenforceable.

We turn first to the stock option transfer. . . . We need not decide here whether [the statute of frauds] applies to stock option agreements executed in connection with employment contracts, because our examination of the record compels us to conclude that no agreement on the transfer of stock was ever reached.

The record shows that at Atherton the parties merely agreed that Speer would receive $100,000 worth of points, or approximately 3.2% of Briggs's holding. The parties could not agree on the precise form of the transfer, because Speer wished to be left with $100,000 after the payment of his capital gains tax, and counsel could not work out the tax consequences to their satisfaction. Even after the meeting at Atherton, numerous drafts of proposed agreements circulated between counsel but were never satisfactory to both parties. When important terms remain unresolved, a binding agreement cannot exist.

We next turn to Speer['s claim of] breach of his oral employment contract. . . .

The record shows that during their negotiations the parties contemplated that any agreement concerning Speer's employment would become effective only when reduced to writing and signed by the parties.[3] At trial Speer as well as Briggs admitted that the terms of the proposed written agreement corresponded to the terms agreed on at Atherton. Nevertheless, on advice of counsel Speer decided not to sign the draft

---

3. This is shown by the testimony of Speer himself.

Counsel for Tropicana: Mr. Speer, when you left the Atherton meeting, was it your understanding that a written contract embodying the terms of your employment contract as well as the points would be drawn up and signed by the parties?

Speer: I did.

Counsel for Tropicana: Mr. Speer, it was always your intention, was it not, both preAtherton, at Atherton and postAtherton that you would have a written contract or that you would be protected as far as your position as general manager at the Tropicana Hotel; is that true?

Speer: That's true.

until Briggs signed a satisfactory stock option agreement. Clearly, Speer withheld his signature to pressure Briggs to consummate the stock option transfer, and his conduct is inconsistent with his assertion that the oral agreement reached at Atherton was intended to be immediately binding. Had the proposed written agreement been merely a memorialization of a binding oral contract, Speer's signature would not have been of sufficient legal significance to exert any influence on Briggs. We have previously stated that since some measure of agreement must usually be reached before a written draft is prepared, the evidence that the parties intended to be presently bound must be convincing and subject to no other reasonable interpretation. . . .

A similar situation confronted us in *Loma Linda Univ. v. Eckenweiler*, 469 P.2d 54 (Nev. 1970). Negotiations regarding plaintiff's employment contract continued during his employment by the University. A written agreement was prepared but rejected by the plaintiff. Neither party signed the agreement. After plaintiff's employment was terminated, he attempted to enforce an alleged oral agreement regarding severance pay. We held that even accepting the district court's view that the parties had reached a meeting of the minds on the issue of severance pay, judgment for plaintiff had to be reversed. The proposed written agreement was an offer by the University which plaintiff had declined to accept. Important terms remained unresolved and the oral agreement was incomplete; moreover, the parties had contemplated consummation by written agreement and plaintiff himself had rejected the written contract. Similarly, since Speer refused to sign the written draft and clearly demonstrated his intent not to be immediately bound, no contract arose between the parties.

Speer contends that the fact that he commenced his employment at the Tropicana Hotel before a written contract was even prepared shows that he regarded the oral employment agreement as binding. Generally, performance by a party after agreement has been reached but before a writing has been prepared is regarded as some evidence that the writing was only a memorial of a binding agreement. However, where the evidence clearly shows that the party performing did not consider the agreement to be binding, the fact that he began performance does not compel a contrary conclusion.

Moreover, even assuming *arguendo* that a binding agreement existed, Speer has not demonstrated that it was breached. The district court determined that the termination of two of Speer's trusted associates by Briggs and the executive committee so undermined Speer's ability to perform his duties that it amounted to a constructive discharge. We do not find this theory persuasive. In spite of protracted negotiations, the continued employment of members of Speer's "team" was never suggested as a term of any proposed agreement. In the absence of such an understanding, the termination of the two men over Speer's objections cannot be regarded as an invasion of Speer's authority sufficient to amount to a constructive discharge. . . .

We affirm [the denial of damages] for breach of an alleged stock option agreement . . . [and] reverse judgment for Speer on the alleged employment agreement. . . .

NOTES

1. *Significance of an Unsigned Writing.* Understand the difference between drafting a written contract and memorializing an oral one. When parties draft a written document, they generally expect their execution of that document (i.e., their signatures on the page) to consummate the deal. Their discussions, including oral commitments, that led up to that point are viewed as part of the negotiation process. It is this assumption that undergirds core contracts principles, such as the parol evidence rule, which (you may be disappointed to learn) we will be revisiting shortly.

However, *Speer* suggests that it is possible in some instances that parties will intend to reach an agreement orally and use a subsequent writing merely to capture after the fact what they have already committed to. In those situations, there is the intent to be bound requisite to contract enforcement from the moment of the oral agreement. Which of these two scenarios describes what happened in *Speer*? How does the court know?

2. *Intent of the Parties.* Consider the role of party intent in your response to the preceding note. Based in part on the testimony set out in footnote 3, the court concludes that Speer and Tropicana "contemplated that any agreement concerning Speer's employment would become effective only when reduced to writing and signed by the parties." Does it necessarily follow that there was no binding contract? Even if, at that point in time, no contract existed, Speer started working and continued in his position for roughly a year, so he had to be subject to some employment agreement. Might the parties have impliedly agreed to those terms by their conduct? What does the court think the terms of the parties' oral or implied contract were if not those agreed to in the writing? *Cf. Hendricks v. Smartvideo Techs. Inc.*, 511 F. Supp. 2d 1219, 1228 (M.D. Fla. 2007) (finding question of fact as to whether parties entered into contract notwithstanding plaintiff's failure to sign written agreement where "Hendricks reported for work and remained employed for several months [and] Smartvideo also partially performed, paying Hendricks a salary pursuant to the alleged agreement").

3. *The Stock Option Agreement.* It appears that the only written term on which the parties could not agree was the stock option provision. Would it have been a better litigation strategy for Speer to concede he had no stock rights and seek to enforce only the other terms of employment? The court suggests that Speer withheld his signature from the final written document in order to pressure Tropicana into conceding to his stock demands. If so, the court arguably should not allow Speer to have his cake and eat it too — that is, to have the benefit of terms he deliberately chose to reject in order to secure a bargaining advantage. If that is what happened, perhaps Speer got his just deserts. On the other hand, is this view of the facts consistent with Speer accepting employment absent an executed agreement? What bargaining advantage could he gain at that point by refusing the written document? The opinion does not indicate how Speer was compensated during his one year of employment. Suppose, however, that he was being paid the exact salary that the parties had agreed to in the unsigned contract. How would this affect your understanding of what happened?

4. *Restitution.* Another way to conceptualize this arrangement is as a failed contract — the parties never agreed to final terms of employment but began performance nonetheless. If so, should Speer be entitled to the reasonable value of his services under a restitution theory? *See generally* RESTATEMENT (SECOND) OF CONTRACTS § 370 (1981). The employer would be credited for whatever wages it paid Speer, but that does not necessarily compensate him for the reasonable value of his services. Since the parties contemplated additional compensation in the form of stock options, restitution seems to offer an alternative approach to compensating Speer.

5. *Constructive Discharge.* Understand the significance of the penultimate paragraph in the opinion. Speer does not contend that Tropicana actually terminated him, but rather that it "constructively discharged" him by breaching its contractual obligations. The concept of constructive discharge is important in many areas of employment law. In its absence, employers would be able to avoid liability for unlawful termination by creating working conditions so intolerable as to force the employee to resign. In the context of status discrimination, constructive discharge analysis can be used, for example, to hold employers liable for damages that result when an employee reasonably quits in response to workplace harassment based on a protected characteristic such as race or gender. See Chapter 9. The challenge with any allegation of constructive discharge is figuring out whether the employer's conduct was sufficiently severe to justify the employee's resignation. Otherwise, the law deems the employee's departure a voluntary separation.

Under discrimination law, adverse employment actions amounting to a constructive discharge include "a humiliating demotion, extreme cut in pay, or transfer to a position [involving] unbearable working conditions." *Pa. State Police v. Suders*, 542 U.S. 129, 134 (2004). Claims of constructive discharge in cases involving a contract for job security have had mixed success. *Compare Guiliano v. Cleo, Inc.*, 995 S.W.2d 88 (Tenn. 1999) (finding constructive discharge where vice president of marketing was stripped of responsibilities, reassigned to his home, and told to await future assignments, which never came), *with Rubin v. Household Comm. Fin. Servs., Inc.*, 746 N.E.2d 1018, 1028 (Mass. App. Ct. 2001) (no constructive discharge of plaintiff-CEO where temporary management team brought in to turn around company circumvented plaintiff on some financial issues but plaintiff retained title and position and management team continued to rely on plaintiff's expertise on customers and production). Often the determination turns on whether the employer's behavior was itself in breach of the parties' employment agreement. In what way does Speer claim Tropicana breached its contract? How critical is the fact that there were no specific terms in the proposed written agreement dealing with Speer's staff?

≡ *Cave Hill Corporation v. Hiers*
≡ *570 S.E.2d 790 (Va. 2002)*

COMPTON, Senior Justice.

. . . The central question is whether the trial court erred in refusing to rule that the [employment] contract was clear and unambiguous, and in submitting to a jury the interpretation of the agreement.

To set the stage, relevant facts, mostly undisputed, that furnish the background and details of this controversy must be reviewed. In 1993, plaintiff Phillip T. "Chuck" Hiers commenced work as a sales person for defendant Cave Hill Corporation in its division, Atlantic Fabritech, located in Rockingham County. The defendant manufactures above ground storage tanks, primarily for use in the oil and lubrication industry.

On September 9, 1998, the plaintiff and defendant, through its president and sole shareholder, Walter M. Hopkins, executed the one-page contract that is the subject of this dispute. The agreement was "composed" by plaintiff and Hopkins, and was typewritten on a page of Atlantic Fabritech stationery.

The contract is labeled:

EMPLOYMENT AGREEMENT
EMPLOYEE: PHILLIP T. 'CHUCK' HIERS
TITLE: SALES MANAGER
EFFECTIVE DATES: August 14, 1998-August 1, 2003

In a preamble, the writing stated: "This work agreement established on August 14, 1998 between Cave Hill Corporation, d/b/a Atlantic Fabritech and Phillip T. Hiers is based on the following conditions."

Paragraph 1 provided for a $25,000 annual salary plus a cost-of-living increase.

Paragraph 2 provided, in part, for a two per cent commission to be paid plaintiff "on Atlantic Fabritech tank sales quoted, processed, generated and sold by Chuck."

Paragraphs 3 and 4 provided for use of a company vehicle and for an expense allowance.

Paragraph 5 provided: "Thirty (30) days' notice will be given by both the employee and the employer in the case of leave or dismissal."

Paragraphs 6 and 7 provided for a vacation period, and for medical and dental insurance.

The agreement concluded with an unnumbered paragraph delineating plaintiff's job responsibilities.

During the negotiations for the contract, Hopkins told the plaintiff that one Stacey Sinnett, a former Cave Hill employee, would be reemployed. The plaintiff understood that Sinnett was to work for him in sales and in product development. However, the plaintiff learned the day after the contract was signed that Sinnett was to be the general manager of Atlantic Fabritech and that the plaintiff would have "to report to" Sinnett.

Thereafter, disagreement between plaintiff and Hopkins developed over job duties, commissions on sales, and plaintiff's overall performance of his assigned work. Specifically, plaintiff contended that, under the employment agreement, he was entitled to commissions on all sales, that is, not only on sales that he made but also on sales that Sinnett made. Hopkins took the position that the plaintiff was not entitled to a commission on Sinnett's sales.

During the period from September 1998 to May 6, 1999, the disagreement continued, with Sinnett issuing "warnings" to plaintiff about the performance of his duties. Finally, Sinnett recommended to Hopkins that plaintiff's employment be terminated because of "the way he handled several volume accounts . . . not making as many sales calls . . . as he should, not traveling as much as we needed . . . [and] not having his office organized." Hopkins had observed that plaintiff "repeatedly" was late for work and that he was "working on other projects," including "selling guns and cars . . . during company business time." Additionally, according to Hopkins, plaintiff was unable "to get along with" Sinnett, would not conform to new policies established by Sinnett, and "fell out with some of the customers."

Eventually, plaintiff was discharged. In a May 6 letter to the plaintiff, Sinnett wrote: "We find it necessary to terminate your employment with Cave Hill Corporation as the Sales Manager for the Atlantic Fabritech Division effective this date. You will receive your salary for the month of May, which we will give you today."

Subsequently, plaintiff filed the present action seeking damages for breach of the employment contract. . . .

During an August 2001 jury trial, the trial court permitted the plaintiff to testify extensively, over defendant's objection, to his "understanding" of many of the terms of the employment contract. For example, plaintiff said his "understanding" was that he "would be paid 2% commission on . . . all tank sales" not "just 2% of what [he] personally sold to a customer." Also, plaintiff testified about "the intent of the parties" as set forth in the final paragraph of the agreement relating to job responsibilities.

The trial court, over defendant's objection, permitted the jury to interpret the contract, ruling that the agreement was unclear and ambiguous. The court instructed the jury that it "must determine whether the contract is for a definite term of employment or whether it is a contract for employment that is terminable at will." The court also told the jury that just cause was required for an employer to terminate a fixed-term employment contract prior to the end of the term.

The jury found in favor of the plaintiff on his claim. . . .

Although the parties dwell upon the admissibility of parol evidence with regard to those portions of the contract dealing with commissions and job responsibilities, the core of these appeals is the question whether the trial court erred in refusing to rule, as urged by defendant, that the contract was clear and unambiguous in establishing an employment that was terminable at will. Stated differently, the crux of the controversy upon review is whether the trial court erred in determining that a jury issue was created regarding the nature of the contract.

Settled principles are applicable here. "In Virginia, an employment relationship is presumed to be at-will, which means that the employment term extends for an indefinite period and may be terminated by the employer or employee for any reason upon reasonable notice." *County of Giles v. Wines*, 546 S.E.2d 721, 723 (Va. 2001). However, when the employment is for a definite period, the presumption of at-will employment is rebutted and an employee may be terminated only for just cause. And, when there is a conflict in the evidence concerning the terms of an employment contract, the question whether the employment is at will or for a definite term becomes one of fact to be resolved by the jury.

In the present case, the trial court submitted the interpretation of the contract to the jury because the court ruled that its terms were ambiguous. "An ambiguity exists when language admits of being understood in more than one way or refers to two or more things at the same time." *Renner Plumbing, Heating & Air Conditioning, Inc. v. Renner*, 303 S.E.2d 894, 898 (Va. 1983). However, "[c]ontracts are not rendered ambiguous merely because the parties or their attorneys disagree upon the meaning of the language employed to express the agreement." *Doswell Ltd. P'ship v. Virginia Elec. and Power Co.*, 468 S.E.2d 84, 88 (Va. 1996). And, "[e]ven though an agreement may have been drawn unartfully, the court must construe the language as written if its parts can be read together without conflict." *Id.* at 88.

On appeal, the plaintiff contends the trial court did not err in permitting the jury to interpret the agreement. He argues there was a conflict over the contract's terms and their meaning. In particular, he maintains he "presented evidence and argument that the Contract was for a definite term of five years ('Effective Dates: August 14, 1998-August 1, 2003' . . .) and that, therefore, the Contract was terminable only upon just cause and with termination effective only following thirty days notice." We do not agree.

We hold that the contract was clear and unambiguous. In plain terms, the contract was effective for a designated period of time. Nevertheless, the agreement specifically was subject to certain "conditions," as mentioned in the preamble. The significant condition relevant here is that either party could terminate the contract upon 30 days notice, according to the clear terms of paragraph 5. This notice provision trumped the effect of the designated time period.

Nowhere in this writing is there any reference to a "just cause" requirement for job termination by the employer. In order to find such a requirement, one would have to insert words into the writing contrary to the elementary rule that the function of the court is to construe the contract made by the parties, not to make a contract for them.

Consequently, we hold that the trial court committed reversible error in refusing to decide as a matter of law that the contract was one terminable at will and in permitting the jury to interpret the agreement. Because plaintiff was an at-will employee, the defendant properly terminated him upon giving 30 days notice, and the defendant's conduct in this regard is not actionable.

In view of the foregoing ruling, the parol evidence question becomes a subsidiary issue. It necessarily follows from what we already have said that the trial court also erred in admitting extrinsic evidence of the plaintiff's "understanding" to explain the terms of the agreement relating to commissions. "Parol evidence of prior or contemporaneous oral negotiations are generally inadmissible to alter, contradict, or explain the terms of a written instrument provided the document is complete, unambiguous, and unconditional."

We address the parol evidence issue only because the plaintiff did have an employment contract, albeit one that was terminable at will. Thus, he had a potential claim for failure of defendant to pay commissions due under the contract. However, we hold that paragraph 2 plainly provides for commissions on "tank sales quoted, processed, generated and sold by Chuck," and not upon such sales sold by Sinnett.

Consequently, the judgment in favor of the plaintiff will be reversed. . . .

NOTES

1. *Termination of Fixed-Term Contracts.* Hiers did not claim that the contract by its terms prevented the employer from firing him in the absence of just cause. Indeed, the contract contains no language to that effect. Rather, Hiers claimed that his contract established a fixed term of employment: from August 1998 to August 2003. Yet both the trial court and the Supreme Court assumed that such a contract could be terminated for "just cause." This is the generally accepted understanding of fixed-term employment contracts, *see, e.g., Sarvis v. Vermont State Colleges,* 772 A.2d 494, 497 (Vt. 2001), and it is consistent with the contract principle of material breach: If an individual performs so poorly that he is in material breach of his or her duties as an employee, then the employer is excused from performing its end of the bargain and may terminate the agreement. In the next section, we will take up the question what constitutes "just cause" or poor performance sufficient to create material breach. For now, it is important to know that even a fixed-term contract is not an absolute guarantee of employment. Even it if were perfectly clear that Hiers had such a contract, Cave Hill would still have been permitted to argue that its decision to terminate him had been justified.

2. *Notice Provisions.* The court describes this as an at-will relationship, but it is quite different from that of an employee without any written contract — Hiers had a right to 30 days' notice of termination, which makes his relationship with his employer more like a month-to-month agreement than a purely at-will arrangement. Contracts with notice provisions are generally treated as definite-term agreements for the duration of the notice period as of the date notice is given. The remedy for an employer's failure to give notice is damages equal to the compensation that would have been paid during the notice period. *See, e.g., Shivers v. John H. Harland Co.*, 423 S.E.2d 105, 107 (S.C. 1992).

3. *Ambiguous Language and the At-Will Presumption.* The court holds that it was error for the trial court to allow the plaintiff to testify as to his understanding of the agreement. As a general rule, courts will treat a final written document as exclusive evidence of the contracting parties' agreement. A major exception to this rule, however, is contract ambiguity. Where express language is unclear, courts will admit extrinsic evidence to explain what the parties understood the contract to mean, including parol evidence. In *Baum v. Helget Gas Products, Inc.*, 440 F.3d 1019 (8th Cir. 2006), the contract consisted of handwritten notes signed by both parties. The notes contained three columns, dated 2002 through 2004, with job responsibilities, salary, and bonus calculations listed for each year and the statement that the employer would buy out Baum's car lease in the event of a " 'discharge before contract expires.' " Baum was fired nine months later. In his suit for breach of contract, he argued that the agreement promised a fixed term of employment for the period 2002-2004, while the employer argued that the columns merely reflected the terms and conditions of employment during those years should the relationship continue. On appeal from an award of summary judgment to the employer, the Eighth Circuit found the agreement was reasonably susceptible to both parties' interpretations and reversed for a factual determination of the issue. What distinguishes *Baum* from *Hiers*? Did *Hiers* apply a different standard of "ambiguity" or do the facts in that case more easily lend themselves to a determination as a matter of law?

Articulate the best possible argument that Hiers' agreement falls within this ambiguity exception to the parol evidence rule. Why wasn't that argument successful? Is it fair to call Hiers' employment contract "clear and unambiguous"? Perhaps it would be more accurate to say the contract was silent as to the permissible reasons for termination. If so, is the court's consideration of the at-will presumption consistent with its own rule? In other words, isn't the court considering "additional evidence" as to the contract's meaning while reversing the trial court for allowing the jury to do the same? Or is the court applying a rule of law, not a factual presumption?

4. *The Parol Evidence Rule.* On the secondary issue of commissions, the court holds that any testimony about receiving proceeds on sales other than the plaintiff's is precluded by the parol evidence rule. Recall what you learned about parol evidence from your first year Contracts class. One of the subtler aspects of parol evidence is that courts must determine whether a written agreement is fully or partially "integrated" (that is, final) before deciding what, if any, parol evidence can be admitted. If an agreement is "completely integrated," no parol evidence may be admitted; but if the agreement is only "partially integrated," evidence may be admitted to supplement the agreement. In no case, however, may parol evidence be used to contradict the written terms. *See generally* RESTATEMENT (SECOND) OF CONTRACTS §213 (1981). You will review these principles in greater detail in the next case, but was the written instrument complete with respect to all terms of Hiers' employment? Is it even complete on the issue of job security? Why does the court think it is?

5. *Plaintiff's Parol Evidence.* What is the plaintiff's parol evidence anyway? In other words, what extra-contractual information does Hiers want the court to consider? Does it matter? The answer depends on the jurisdiction. *Hiers* determined that, because the plaintiff's contract was complete on its face, extrinsic evidence, regardless of its nature, was inadmissible. In many jurisdictions, as you will see in the next case, the court examines the parol evidence itself in making the initial determination whether an agreement is complete. Consider the following facts related to the commission dispute, which were alleged by the plaintiff and recounted in the appellate court decision:

> In July of 1998, Hopkins and Defendant Stacey Sinnett agreed that the company would hire Sinnett. Also in July 1998, Hopkins assured Hiers that he would supervise Sinnett and that all of Sinnett's negotiations and contracts would be approved and processed by Hiers. Sinnett was ultimately hired in September 1998 and in October was given the position of General Manager of Atlantic Fabritech. After obtaining this position, Sinnett began to set up sales networks separate from those established and used by Hiers and began to negotiate and approve sales contracts without Hiers' approval. Due to Sinnett's actions, Hiers was denied payment of commissions because he did not process and approve the sales. When Hiers complained to Hopkins, Hopkins told him "I am the boss. I do not care about the contract."

Hiers v. Cave Hill Corp., No. CL99-117788, 2000 WL 145359, at *1 (Va. Cir. Ct. Jan. 6, 2000). Do these allegations influence your view of whether the written contract was complete and whether the court was correct in its decision? Are the allegations relevant to the resolution of the commission issue? Or to the job security issue?

6. *Rate-of-Pay Recitals.* A recurring question is whether the inclusion of a compensation period, such as an annual salary term, in an offer letter or other document indicates an intention that employment will endure for at least the length of the pay period. According to the traditional British rule, a hiring at a stated price per week, month, or year is presumed to be a hiring for the named time period. Under the modern American rule, however, a stated term of compensation does not in itself defeat the presumption that employment is at will. *See, e.g., Thomas v. Ballou-Latimer Drug Co.*, 442 P.2d 747, 751 (Idaho 1968) (adopting "the American rule . . . that [a rate of pay] a term, standing by itself, fixes the rate of compensation and not the period of employment"). *But see* GA. CODE ANN. § 34-7-1 (2006) ("If a contract of employment provides that wages are payable at a stipulated period, the presumption shall arise that the hiring is for such period"). Of course, that presumption, like the at-will presumption itself, can always be rebutted. *See, e.g., Carriker v. Am. Postal Workers Union*, No. 13900, 1993 WL 385807 (Ohio Ct. App. Sept. 30, 1993) (finding that, while contract containing annual pay rate is presumed to be at will, such a term coupled with a provision providing for periodic pay increases over three years created sufficient ambiguity as to duration of contract to justify admission of additional evidence regarding parties' intent).

═══ **Esbensen v. Userware International, Inc.**
14 Cal. Rptr. 2d 93 (Ct. App. 1992)

WIENER, Acting P.J.

. . .

Factual and Procedural Background

Userware is a company which provides computer-related services for small businesses and individuals. In 1977 Userware hired Esbensen as a computer programmer pursuant to an oral contract between Esbensen and Richard Rhodes, an officer and one of the founders of Userware. At Esbensen's insistence, the contract was later reduced to writing and beginning in May 1979, a series of three virtually identical one-year contracts was signed. In addition to a monthly salary, Esbensen was entitled to a 10 percent "commission" on sales of software products he developed.

Several provisions of the final three-page contract executed in 1981 bear on the issues presented by this case. In the first paragraph, the contract specifies that Esbensen "will receive a regular weekly salary of $675.00 which amount will be reviewed on an annual basis." Paragraph IV is titled "Term of Agreement" and provides: "This agreement is effective June 1, 1981, for a period of one year; however, this agreement may be terminated earlier as hereinafter provided." Paragraph V, titled "Termination," goes on to state: "This agreement may be terminated by either party by giving two weeks written notice of termination to the other party. Upon termination for any reason, all salary shall cease on the effective date of termination. [Userware] will continue to pay commission as outlined in section II for a period of 180 days after the effective date of termination."

In January 1982, Esbensen was terminated by Userware allegedly, among other reasons, because he failed to timely report for work following a vacation. Esbensen responded by filing suit for breach of contract, asserting he had been told by Rhodes that the series of one-year contracts would be renewed perpetually as long as he was doing his job. In effect, according to Esbensen, his contract included an implied term that he could not be terminated except for good cause.

Userware filed a motion *in limine* to exclude evidence of any oral understanding between Esbensen and Rhodes concerning an implied "good cause" requirement for termination. [The trial court agreed with Userware, permitting Esbensen to proceed only on the basis of breach of the contract provision providing him six months of continued commissions upon termination.]

Discussion

Userware makes a three-pronged argument in support of the trial court's ruling excluding Esbensen's proffered evidence of an oral agreement that he would not be terminated except for good cause. According to Userware, paragraph V of the contract, which provides for termination before the expiration of the one-year term, allows for termination at any time for any reason. Thus, Esbensen's testimony is assertedly inadmissible as inconsistent with this portion of the written contract. . . .

1. *Is the Employment Relationship Terminable At Will?*

We agree with Esbensen that paragraph V does not make the contract terminable at will. Userware relies on several cases in which the employment contracts specified that the employee could be terminated "at any time" and "for any reason."

Here, in contrast, the "for any reason" language relied on by Userware does not refer to the grounds for termination but rather explains that Userware is not obliged to pay salary but is obliged to continue paying Esbensen's commission regardless of the reason for the termination. The written contract, as we read it, is silent on the acceptable grounds for termination.

2. Was the Written Contract Fully Integrated?

Even if the employment contract is not terminable at will, Userware argues the written agreement is fully integrated, precluding the admission of extrinsic evidence to add additional terms. In contract law, "integration" means the extent to which a writing constitutes the parties' final expression of their agreement. To the extent a contract is integrated, the parole [sic] evidence rule precludes the admission of evidence of the parties' prior or contemporaneous oral statements to contradict the terms of the writing, although parol evidence is always admissible to interpret the written agreement. . . .

If a writing is intended by the parties as a "complete and exclusive statement of the terms of the agreement" the contract is "fully" or "completely" integrated and parol evidence is inadmissible even to add terms not inconsistent with the writing. Obviously, such a determination must be based on proof of the parties' intent and a critical element in that proof is the nature of the alleged consistent oral understanding. *Masterson v. Sine*, 436 P.2d 561 (Cal. 1968). [T]he court must convince itself at a minimum that such an understanding would not "naturally" have been excluded from the writing.

[W]e conclude the written employment contract represents only a partial integration. Here as in *Masterson,* the written contract "does not explicitly provide that it contains the complete agreement. . . ." Moreover, as we explained earlier, the contract is silent as to the grounds for termination. It is hardly unnatural to think that small business entrepreneurs and a computer programmer, unsophisticated in legal matters and unadvised by lawyers, might have discussed those uncertainties and resolved them orally.[5] Because it is only by implication that we can determine what the parties intended with regard to the proper bases for termination, that reasoning process ought to be informed by whatever relevant extrinsic evidence exists which casts light on the parties' intent.

3. Was the Parol Evidence Offered to Prove a Consistent Collateral Agreement?

Despite the parties' focus on the question of integration, our conclusion that the agreement was only partially integrated does not fully resolve the case. Assuming partial integration, parol evidence is admissible only to prove an oral term of the contract not inconsistent with the written memorialization. Parol evidence may not be offered to contradict the terms of even a partially integrated writing.

---

5. The evidence indicated that oral agreements were standard at Userware. Esbensen testified that he was the only Userware employee to have a written contract.

Esbensen sought to introduce evidence of his conversations with Rhodes to the effect that Userware had promised to renew the annual contracts so long as Esbensen performed competently. Userware argues that such an agreement would be flatly inconsistent with the written contract which provides, on one hand, for a term of one year and then creates a separate termination procedure which under some unspecified set of circumstances allows for dismissal before the expiration of the contract term. Even if it could not fire Esbensen for any reason at any time, at a minimum, Userware asserts, the fact that the contract was for a term of one year gives it the right to terminate Esbensen at the *end of the year* for any reason.

We agree with Userware that the one-year term provision of the contract must have some meaning. We disagree, however, that the only possible reason for including this provision was to allow for Esbensen's termination at the end of the year for any reason. As Esbensen points out, the contract specifically provided that his salary would be reviewed on an annual basis. If the written contract was supplemented by an oral understanding that the one-year agreements would be renewed absent good cause not to do so, it might be that the one-year contract term merely reflected the interval between salary reviews. Under such circumstances, "good cause" for nonrenewal would necessarily include the parties' failure to agree on the terms for renewal. In effect, the parties would be obligated to negotiate in good faith at the end of each year toward the goal of renewal on mutually acceptable terms.

. . . It could be argued that the failure to specify grounds [for termination] necessarily implies that *any* reason was acceptable. As we have explained, however, the fact that something is presumed or implied in the absence of an express statement to the contrary does not preclude a party to an incomplete written contract from attempting to demonstrate an express oral agreement contrary to the term which would otherwise be presumed or implied.

We wish to emphasize that our conclusion parol evidence should have been admitted is but a small step on Esbensen's path to ultimate success. A jury must yet determine that the oral representations alleged by Esbensen were in fact made. Assuming they were, the jury must further determine the exact nature of the oral agreement between Rhodes and Esbensen. Assuming this is found to be an understanding that the contract would be perpetually renewed unless there was good cause not to do so, the jury must finally decide whether Userware had "good cause" to terminate Esbensen.

NOTES

1. *The "Naturally Excluded" Test.* In determining the evidentiary question in this case, the court asks whether the oral understanding sought to be admitted might "naturally" have been excluded from the written contract. This approach, sometimes referred to as the "modern" or "California" approach to parol evidence, tends to favor the admission of extrinsic evidence that stricter approaches (like that followed in *Hiers*) would exclude. What facts suggest that the permissible reasons for termination and nonrenewal of Esbensen's contract might naturally have been excluded from the written contract? Given the informal nature of most workplaces, won't parties to a written employment contract typically have oral discussions and understandings that fall outside the written document? Perhaps the real question here is not whether such oral understandings might naturally occur, but rather, whether they are intended to have the same legal significance as the parties' written terms. Does the court consider the latter issue? Will the jury?

2. *Comparing* Hiers *and* Esbensen. What accounts for the different results in these two cases? Are the courts simply following two different sets of rules on ambiguity and parol evidence or are there important factual differences between the cases as well? How would *Hiers* have come out had the court adopted the "naturally excluded" test?

3. *Of Language and Bargaining Power.* What should Userware have done differently in contracting with Esbensen in order to avoid this result? Would it have been enough to change "[u]pon termination for any reason . . ." to "[u]pon termination, *which may be* for any reason . . ."? What about adding a merger clause to the effect that the written document supersedes all other understandings? Would Esbensen have accepted those changes? In *Gerdlund v. Electronic Dispensers International*, 235 Cal. Rptr. 279 (Ct. App. 1987), the plaintiffs were employed for ten years as sales representatives for the defendant, during which time they developed a customer base and dramatically increased defendant's sales. In the eighth year of the relationship they entered into a six-page written contract that provided for termination "for any reason" and recited that "there are no oral or collateral agreements of any kind." In the plaintiffs' subsequent suit for breach of contract, the court allowed the jury to consider the employer's repeated oral assurances, both before and after the execution of the written contract, that the plaintiffs were not in jeopardy of losing their jobs and that a sales territory would be theirs. The appellate court reversed. Noting the merger clause and reference to termination for any reason, the court held "there is no room for a separate collateral agreement regarding reasons for termination; the precise subject is already covered in the writing." *Id.* at 272. In addition, the court noted that one "[plaintiff] actually helped draft the entire agreement, including the termination clause, while employed . . . in a management position; thus he cannot claim it to be a contract of adhesion." *Id.* Neither *Hiers* nor *Esbensen* mentions who drafted the agreement or the bargaining positions of the parties. Do you think either of these plaintiffs had the power to refuse or insist on specific contract terms? Is that relevant?

4. *Extrinsic Evidence and Disclaimers.* As discussed in Chapter 2, employers often place disclaimers of contractual rights or recitals of employees' at will status in the various personnel documents they distribute in the workplace. How should courts interpret these documents in the face of prior oral assurances about job security or other terms of employment? In *Dore v. Arnold Worldwide*, 139 P.3d 56 (Cal. 2006), the plaintiff orally agreed to relocate for a position with the defendant on the assurance that his employment would be long term. He subsequently received an offer letter, which he signed and returned, that stated his employment was "at will" and that the employer "has the right to terminate your employment at anytime." On Dore's subsequent breach of contract claim, the California Supreme Court held that the language of the offer letter unambiguously indicated that the employer could terminate without cause, precluding any consideration of extrinsic evidence that Dore had an oral or implied agreement for greater job security. Does the later California Supreme Court decision in *Dore* call into question the precedential value of the appellate court decision in *Esbensen*? Is it surprising that the court took a stricter view of the admissibility of extrinsic evidence in *Dore*, which involved an offer letter, than in *Esbensen*, which involved an actual written contract? After all, an offer letter generally does not purport to be the parties' entire agreement. Or is there a way to reconcile these two cases?

The legal significance and preclusive effect of subsequent writings and disclaimers remains an open question, and results will vary depending on the jurisdiction, the precise written language, and the nature of the extrinsic evidence. In contrast to *Dore*, consider *Nattah v. Bush*, 605 F.3d 1052 (D.C. Cir. 2010). There an Arabic interpreter, proceeding pro se, sued his former employer, a government contractor, for alleged breach of an oral contract agreed to at a career fair. Nattah claimed that he was promised certain fringe benefits, job security, and assignment to Kuwait. He later signed an "offer letter," which described the parties' relationship as "voluntary" and stated that "nothing in this offer of employment constitutes an express or implied contract." Ultimately, Nattah was sent to Iraq, and he did not receive the living conditions allegedly promised. On appeal from the district court's dismissal of the complaint, the court rejected the employer's argument that the signed writing precluded Nattah's oral contract claim and reversed the district court's dismissal of the complaint. Noting that the offer letter was "silent" as to the benefits allegedly promised, the court concluded that "even assuming Nattah was an at-will employee, [the employer] might nonetheless be obligated to provide promised benefit." Can you identify the factual differences that distinguish this case from *Dore*? Do you see where the *Nattah* employer went wrong in drafting its "offer letter"?

5. *Prior or Contemporaneous Evidence.* An important limitation on the parol evidence rule is that it bars evidence only of agreements or actions prior to or contemporaneous with the execution of the written contract. It has no application to subsequent agreements, which are admissible either for interpretative purposes or to show the parties modified their written agreement. Consider the description of *Gerdlund* in Note 3. Do you see where the court might have erred? Although subsequent statements are not barred by the parol evidence rule, employees face a separate set of obstacles when trying to prove that such a statement modified a written contract. For instance, contract formation rules generally require that modifications be supported by consideration, and the statue of frauds may apply to modified agreements not capable of being performed within one year.

6. *Value of an Imperfect Writing.* Why do you think the parties' agreement in *Esbensen* did not specify the reasons for termination? Sometimes gaps in a contract result from failure to anticipate issues or carelessness in drafting. Other times, particularly in heavily negotiated contracts, gaps mean that the parties were unable to come to agreement on those points. Contract drafters sometimes "punt" on hard issues, using indefinite terms to paper over their disagreement. Which is more likely the case in *Esbensen*? Should it matter? Note that Esbensen pushed for a written contract in contrast to the employer's usual practices. All told, was this a good choice on his part? Where would he have been had he tried to argue the existence of the same oral understanding in the absence of a written contract?

7. *Significance of the Default Rule, Revisited.* Compared to *Hiers*, how important is the at-will presumption in *Esbensen*? Does the court even consider the default rule? In the last part of the opinion, the court explains how Esbensen's oral understanding about termination and renewal can be read as consistent with the parties' written document. This is a critical step in parol evidence analysis because, even where a contract is deemed less than complete, oral understandings that contradict written terms must always be excluded. If at will is really a presumption, is it fair to describe an oral understanding on job security as consistent with the parties' contract? How would the *Hiers* court respond to this question? How would it have decided Esbensen's case?

8. *Esbensen's Chances of Success.* Now that the court has ruled in Esbensen's favor on the evidentiary dispute, what are the parties' next steps? Look at the last paragraph of the opinion. Why does the court take the time to emphasize the hurdles Esbensen will face on remand? Is this a hollow victory for Esbensen? Or is it likely that the defendant, faced with a jury trial, will make a substantial settlement offer?

9. *Existence of Cause.* Given the court's ruling, the presence or absence of cause to terminate will become an issue should this case be tried. The opinion provides only limited factual information, but consider the employer's alleged basis for terminating Esbensen. Do you have an instinctive reaction to the employer's charge that Esbensen failed to timely report to work following vacation? How is this claim likely to play before a jury? If Userware felt confident that it had cause to terminate, why did it bother spending so much time and money opposing admission of Esbensen's oral testimony on evidentiary grounds? Can you think of some advantages to this litigation strategy? Is it one you would recommend in counseling an employer?

PROBLEMS

3-1. Paula Adams, a travel agent, is employed by Evan's Vacation, Inc. under a written contract which sets out Adams's salary and benefits and contains a noncompete agreement. The contract includes the following language:

5. **Term.** The "Term of Employment," as used herein, shall mean a period commencing January 1, 2010 and ending on the third anniversary of such date (the "Ending Date"); provided, however, that the occurrence of any of the following prior to the Ending Date shall result in the immediate termination of the Term of Employment, but shall not result in the termination of this Agreement:

    i. the termination by the Employer of the Term of Employment for any reason, including, but not limited to, the commission by the Employee of any act constituting a dishonest or other act of material breach or a fraudulent act or a felony under the laws of any state or of the United States to which the Employer or Employee is subject; or

    ii. the death of the Employee; or

    iii. the failure of the Employee to perform her duties hereunder.

Suppose that in January 2012 Evan's Vacation decides to reduce its staff due to a downturn in business and selects Adams for layoff. Prior to informing Adams, the company consults you. What would you advise the company about its legal obligations under this agreement? Can you make a plausible argument that would support the employer's decision if it goes through with the termination? Would it matter if the contract contained the following additional language?

Employee shall be on a probationary employment period ("Probationary Period") of ninety (90) days under which Employer has the sole right to terminate Employee without cause.

What would your ultimate recommendation be with respect to whether the employer should terminate Adams under each of these scenarios? Is there any other information you would like to know before deciding? Regardless of your ultimate conclusion, can you think of a better way for the company to draft this agreement in the future? *See generally Evan's World Travel, Inc. v. Adams*, 978 S.W.2d 225 (Tex. App. 1998).

3-2.   Irving Sliff was hired as general counsel of Condec Corp. At the time, Sliff was 55 years old and had been employed for 20 years as general counsel at Shell Corp. where he was fully vested in his employer's pension plan. During his negotiations with the president of Condec, Sliff made clear that he was not interested in the new position unless he was guaranteed employment until such time as he would fully vest in Condec's pension plan, which would require a minimum employment term of ten years. The president orally assured him that this would be the case, and Sliff accepted the position. Several years later, as a result of changes in the management, Sliff became concerned that he had nothing in writing to confirm his oral understanding with the company. He prepared the following memo for execution by the president:

> This will confirm our discussions, both prior and subsequent to my employment, relating to my completion of sufficient years of service during my employment as General Counsel of Condec Corporation to qualify for 100% vesting in each of the employee benefit plans currently offered, as they now exist or may be modified or amended in the future, and any such plans which may hereafter be adopted. It is agreed that I shall be employed by Condec Corporation at a competitive and adequate compensation for at least such period of years as is required to accomplish 100% vesting in the employee benefit plans referred to above, unless discharged for due cause, i.e., dishonesty, or criminal conduct injurious to Condec.

Suppose that the president refuses to sign the memo asserting that it is "too specific." One year later, Sliff is terminated for unsatisfactory performance. When asked for an explanation, he is told by the president that he "hasn't grown with the job."

Does Sliff have a viable claim for breach of contract? Of what significance, if any, is the unsigned memo? If Sliff has a contract for a fixed term equaling the number of years until he is 100% vested in the company pension plans, can he be fired prior to that time nonetheless? On what grounds? *See generally Slifkin v. Condec Corp.*, 538 A.2d 231 (Conn. App. Ct. 1988).

2.   Defining "Just Cause" to Terminate

In assessing whether a terminated worker has a legitimate breach of contract claim, analyzing whether the contract contemplates a fixed term of employment or contains some other type of job security term is just the beginning of the inquiry. Assuming a contractual right to job security exists, either based on clear language in the contract or through the resolution of ambiguous circumstances in favor of the employee, the court must then determine whether the employee's right has been violated. In other words, did the employer breach the job security provision of the contract in terminating the employee?

This question raises a number of related legal issues. Typically, a breach depends on whether the employer had "just cause" to terminate the employee. Some employment contracts expressly define that term, some do not. If the contract defines cause, the question becomes one of interpretation: Does the conduct at issue meet the definition the parties adopted in their agreement? But what happens if the employee commits misconduct that does not fall within the contractual definition? Is the employer still liable to the employee, or can it argue that the employee materially breached his or her duties to the employer? On the other hand, what happens if the contract fails to define cause? As a practical matter, this is frequently the case even in expressly negotiated written instruments. What standard should be used to determine if the termination was justified in such a case? And who gets to decide whether that standard was satisfied — the judge or the jury?

A variety of factual issues also are implicated in breach of contract inquiries. For obvious reasons, employees generally do not admit engaging in misconduct. Suppose the employer argues that it terminated an employee for embezzling funds from the company. The employee will no doubt deny the charge, creating a factual issue as to whether the embezzlement occurred. Who bears the burden of proof on this issue, the employer or the employee? Is it necessary even to establish that the misconduct occurred, or is it enough that the employer believed it occurred? If the latter, must that belief be objectively reasonable, reached in good faith, or both? Finally, regardless of whether the misconduct actually occurred, to what extent should courts inquire into the honesty of the employer's asserted reason for termination? It is entirely possible for an employer to fire an employee for a reason prohibited under the contract, but justify its decision based on a reason permitted under the contract. How should breach of contract be resolved where the employer's motive is in doubt?

These questions have yet to be fully resolved by courts. Indeed, most breach of employment contract cases will raise only a small subset of these issues, and it is not always clear which ones are implicated or what standards courts are using to address them.

Benson v. AJR, Inc.
599 S.E.2d 747 (W. Va. 2004)

Per Curiam:

Danny L. Benson appeals from [a grant of summary judgment to AJR, Inc. in connection with his claim of breach of employment contract]. [W]e determine that there is a genuine issue of material fact concerning the basis for [defendant's] decision to terminate Mr. Benson's employment with AJR. Accordingly, the grant of summary judgment was improper. . . .

I. Factual and Procedural Background

AJR is a small heavy manufacturing business engaged in the manufacture and welding of truck beds. At the time when Appellant was first employed by AJR as a general welder in 1990, the company was owned by three individuals: Jackie L. Benson; Robert W. Benson; and Patricia Benson. Appellant is the son of Jackie Benson. On May 1, 1997, Appellant was promoted to supervisor and was assigned primary responsibility over three aspects of the company's operations, one of which was safety. In his supervisory position, Appellant was charged with the responsibility for directing and leading the company's safety programs and ensuring that AJR's safety rules were both observed and enforced.

During the summer of 1997, the three AJR shareholders decided to sell the company to an employee, Appellee John M. Rhodes. As part of the sales transaction, Mr. Rhodes agreed to enter into an employment agreement with Appellant whereby Mr. Benson would be guaranteed employment for a period of eight years beginning on August 29, 1997.[2] While AJR had the right to terminate appellant with only one day's written notice under this agreement, it was required to continue paying Mr. Benson his salary for the balance of the eight-year term of employment in the absence of three specified conditions. Those conditions were: (a) dishonesty; (b) conviction of a felony; and (c) voluntary termination of the agreement by Appellant.[3]

Within less than a month after the execution of the employment agreement, Appellant acknowledged in writing his receipt of an employee manual which specified certain acts that were grounds for termination. Those grounds included the sale, possession, or use of controlled substances while on the job, during working hours, or while on company business. At the end of September 1997, concurrent with his receipt of the employee manual, Appellant signed a consent form permitting his employer to conduct random controlled substance tests.

On March 2, 1998, a drug test was administered to the employees of AJR. The results of the drug testing revealed that Appellant had more than three times the limit utilized by the United States Department of Transportation ("DOT") to establish drug use and impairment. Between the time when the drug test was administered and the results were made available, Mr. Rhodes conducted meetings with various AJR personnel during which he inquired of those in attendance whether anyone was aware of an employee who was using illegal drugs or who was arriving at work with illegal drugs or alcohol in their system. Appellant attended one of those meetings and admits that he did not respond to this question despite personal knowledge that his drug test would come back positive.

Along with eleven other employees who also tested positive for drug use, Appellant was terminated from the employ of AJR on March 6, 1998. AJR prepared two different termination forms in connection with Appellant's dismissal from the company. The first of the two forms indicated that Mr. Benson had resigned from

---

2. In explanation of why this agreement was entered into, the document states that "it is in the best interests of the Company that key management employees, including the Employee [Mr. Benson], continue to be employed by the Company upon" the sale of AJR.

3. This Court *sua sponte* recognized an issue regarding the contract's interpretation based on the words chosen to draft the agreement. Because the contract was written in terms of permitting AJR to terminate Appellant "without cause," and because the subsequent salary payment obligations arise in reference to a termination "without cause," we initially questioned whether the payment obligations would be invoked in a case, such as this, where the employee was undeniably dismissed for cause. We determine, however, that the contract should be read in the fashion undertaken by the parties and the court below predominantly because the three contractual conditions that excuse AJR's requirement to pay Appellant his salary (two of which are clearly "for cause" type of dismissals) would be rendered meaningless if the payment provisions could only be invoked in a non-cause dismissal situation.

his employment.[7] The second of the two termination forms lists a different reason for termination — "controlled substance testing" and "tested positive for cocaine." . . .

Discussion

A. *Breach of Employment Contract*

At the center of this dispute is whether AJR is required to comply with the salary payment obligation contained in the employment agreement. Under the terms of the agreement, in the event AJR decided to terminate Mr. Benson, the company was required to pay Appellant the salary that was in effect on August 29, 1997, absent a dismissal that was based on dishonesty, conviction of a felony, or if Mr. Benson voluntarily terminated the employment agreement. Appellant contends that the lower court erred in its determination that the basis for AJR's termination of Mr. Benson was dishonesty. . . .

To resolve the critical question of whether Appellant's positive drug test fell within the parameters of "dishonest" conduct, the trial court defined the term "dishonesty" by referring to entries in Webster's Dictionary and Black's Law Dictionary.[9] Relying on these generalized definitions, the lower court concluded that Appellant's "actions in failing a drug test and arriving at work with drugs in his system demonstrates a lack of integrity, probity, or adherence to a code of moral values." Rather than limiting its analysis to just the definition of "dishonesty," however, the circuit court included a listing of various definitions of "integrity" and found that "[a]ctions which lack integrity are, by definition, dishonest." After weighing these two definitions in essentially *pari materia,* the trial court ruled that "[p]laintiff's positive drug test, in light of all the facts and circumstances of the case, demonstrates dishonesty and a lack of integrity."[10]

In marked contrast to the trial court's willingness to define the term "dishonesty" within the meaning of the employment contract at issue, we recognize the futility of attempting to fashion a "one size fits all" definition for such term. Dishonesty, like any term that has significance in a given contract, must be defined based on the subject matter of the contract and the intent of the document's drafters. We note, however, that it has been observed that "[d]ishonesty, unlike embezzlement or larceny, is not a term of art." More often than not, the issue of whether conduct qualifies as dishonest is determined to be a question best resolved by a jury.

In this case, the record evidences Mr. Benson's admission that he was dishonest in connection with his failure to truthfully answer the question posed by Mr. Rhodes with regard to his awareness of drug use by any AJR employees. Given Appellant's clear

---

7. While Appellant was given the opportunity to resign from AJR, he did not choose to resign his employment.

9. The trial court cited a definition in Webster's, which described dishonesty as "a lack of honesty or integrity; a disposition to defraud or deceive." As defined by the legal dictionary, dishonesty included a "[d]isposition to lie, cheat, deceive, or defraud; untrustworthiness; lack of integrity."

10. One of the circumstances relied upon by the trial court was Mr. Benson's admission that he had been dishonest in failing to answer Mr. Rhodes' question regarding knowledge of drug use in the work place when he "knew to an absolute certainty that he had used illegal drugs and had them in his system when asked the question." Additional evidence cited by the trial court to support its conclusion regarding Appellant's dishonesty was the fact that "[p]laintiff admitted that he used cocaine and does not challenge the drug test."

admission of dishonesty, we proceed to determine what impact, if any, this admission of dishonesty has on the case at hand.

The lower court appears to have assumed that upon finding conduct that qualified as dishonest, this case could be resolved solely on legal grounds without requiring the assistance of a jury. The trial court reasoned that "[n]o reasonable jury could find that Plaintiff's failing of the drug test, under all the circumstances present herein, was not dishonest behavior." Critically, however, a factual issue that must be determined for purposes of ascertaining whether AJR was required under the terms of the contract to pay Appellant his salary for the remainder of the eight-year contractual period is the *reason* upon which AJR relied in terminating Mr. Benson's employment. Under the employment contract at issue, the determining factor that controls the issue of continued salary payment is whether the basis for the termination was "dishonesty" or "conviction of a felony," or, alternatively, whether there was a "voluntary termination of . . . [the] agreement."

The record in this case is unclear as to whether AJR dismissed Mr. Benson from its employ for drug use or for dishonesty. As Appellant emphasizes in his argument, nowhere on either of the two termination forms that were introduced below is there any indication that he was dismissed for dishonesty. We are unwilling to make the leap that the trial court did to broadly encompass testing positive for drug use within the meaning of the term "dishonesty." Consequently, we conclude that Appellant is entitled to have a jury determine the basis for AJR's decision to terminate Mr. Benson from its employ. If the jury determines that drug use, rather than dishonesty, was the basis for the dismissal, then the provisions of the employment contract with regard to continued payment of Appellant's salary for the duration of the contractual term are applicable. If, however, the jury determines that Mr. Benson was in fact terminated for being dishonest, then AJR is not required to pay his salary under the terms of the employment contract. . . .

MAYNARD, C.J., concurring, in part, and dissenting, in part.

What a terrible message this case sends to small West Virginia employers and businesses! This Court tells this company that it should not have fired an employee who:

1. admitted that he used cocaine;
2. reported to work with cocaine in his system;
3. failed a drug test in which he tested positive for cocaine;
4. misrepresented his drug use by failing to truthfully answer management's inquiries about drug use;
5. worked in a plant where steel fabrication involving constant welding occurs;
6. continually worked around large quantities of explosives and highly volatile gases and liquids including acetylene, oxygen tanks, thinner paint, and other explosive substances; and, here is the icing on the cake;
7. was the SAFETY DIRECTOR of the company!! Appalling!

This Court now says that AJR was wrong to fire a deceitful, coke-head safety director in a plant where tanks of acetylene, oxygen, and other explosives are everywhere! The irony is that if there had been some explosion or other accident which killed or seriously injured another employee, the victim of that accident could have successfully sued under our workers' compensation deliberate intent statute and obtained a large verdict. This Court doubtless would have upheld the large verdict based on the fact that the company allowed a cocaine user to be its safety director.

In distinguishing between dishonesty and drug use under the specific facts of this case, the majority opinion does one of the finest jobs of legalistic hairsplitting in the history of American jurisprudence. The undisputed facts show that if Appellant was terminated for dishonesty, AJR was not obligated to pay Appellant his salary for the balance of the employment agreement. Appellant was responsible for safety at AJR's facility including enforcing AJR's drug-free workplace policy. Appellant received a copy of AJR's employee manual which states, in part, that employees may be terminated for the sale, possession, or use of controlled substances while on the job, during work hours, or while on company business. After Appellant failed a drug test, he admitted that he used cocaine the Saturday immediately prior to the Monday drug test. Finally, he also admitted that he was dishonest with management when he failed to answer management's questions regarding possible drug use in the workplace because he knew to an absolute certainty that he had used illegal drugs and had them in his system when asked the question.

Given these facts, I must disagree with the majority that a jury could determine that drug use rather than dishonesty was the basis for Appellant's dismissal. This is a distinction without a difference. Appellant's drug use, established by the positive drug test, demonstrates dishonesty. Specifically, Appellant, who was responsible for enforcing a drug-free workplace, knowingly violated his employer's drug-free workplace policy by coming to work with cocaine in his system. This is dishonest conduct. Actually testing positive for the drug use is evidence of this dishonest conduct. Therefore, it is irrelevant whether the official reason for Appellant's dismissal was dishonesty or drug use.

Finally, troubling also is the majority opinion's failure to address AJR's argument that Appellant's decision to appear for work under the influence of cocaine was tantamount to a willful quit; substantial public policy against rewarding a person for his or her dishonesty; and the impact of Appellant's admission of dishonesty. The plain fact is that any of these matters would have been sufficient for this Court to affirm the summary judgment on behalf of AJR. . . .

STARCHER, J., concurring.

I write separately to emphasize what the majority's opinion really says, and what it does not say.

This case is all about the power of a contract. The defendant-employer, AJR, Inc., entered into a written contract in 1997 with plaintiff-employee Danny L. Benson that guaranteed Mr. Benson employment until August 2005. Nobody disputes the clarity of this part of the agreement.

However, nowhere does the contract say that Mr. Benson cannot be fired. The contract did allow the defendant-employer to show Mr. Benson the door with pink slip in hand any time it chose to do so. But the contract also contained a clear, black-and-white penalty clause which said that if the defendant-employer let Mr. Benson go, then the defendant-employer would still be required to pay Mr. Benson his remaining wages through August 2005. Again, none of the parties disputes the clarity of this penalty clause built into the agreement.

The fuzzy area in this case is a loophole for the defendant-employer that was built into the contract which allowed the defendant-employer to escape the penalty clause if Mr. Benson was fired because of "dishonesty." The contract does not define "dishonesty." So, when Mr. Benson's drug use was discovered, and the defendant-employer fired him, the question was raised whether Mr. Benson's firing was motivated by Mr. Benson's dishonesty, or for some other reason.

The defendant-employer vigorously asserts that it fired Mr. Benson because the owner of the company conducted meetings with company employees that included Mr. Benson, at which time the owner asked if anyone was aware of an employee who was using illegal drugs or was arriving for work with illegal drugs in his or her system; Mr. Benson said nothing when asked the question. The defendant-employer now asserts that Mr. Benson was fired when the cocaine test results were returned because his dishonesty — in the form of not responding to the question — was revealed. The defendant-employer therefore asserts that it does not have to pay Mr. Benson his remaining wages in compliance with the penalty clause.

The problem with the employer's argument is the written documentation surrounding Mr. Benson's firing. When Mr. Benson was fired, the employer completed a form indicating he was fired in accordance with the employees' manual (which mandated automatic termination for drug usage) for "controlled substance testing" and "tested positive for cocaine." This position was reiterated in writing several times by the company's owner and the company's counsel. The contractual "dishonesty" loophole was not raised by the employer until sometime later, when Mr. Benson asserted his contractual right to his remaining years of wages.

The competing positions taken by the employer raise, beyond a doubt, is a question of fact for jury resolution as to the true motivating factor behind Mr. Benson's termination. The circuit court was wrong to substitute its judgment on this factual question for that of the jury. A jury should hear the witnesses to Mr. Benson's firing testify, should review the documentation surrounding that firing, and should decide for themselves if Mr. Benson's firing was motivated by (a) dishonesty or (b) drug use. If the jury's answer is the former, Mr. Benson gets nothing; if the jury's answer is the latter, the defendant-employer must comply with the written employment contract and pay Mr. Benson his wages under the contract's penalty clause.

That said, let's get straight what this case is *not* about. This case is not — as my dissenting colleague suggests — a case that says a small employer cannot fire an employee who uses drugs. The employer in this case was fully within its rights to fire Mr. Benson — but it had to be willing to pay the price if that firing breached the employment contract. A contract is a promise, and a breach of that promise carries consequences. I disagree with my dissenting colleague's implicit suggestion that because of bad facts, this Court should make bad law, throw hundreds of years of contract law to the wind, and find that because Mr. Benson's actions are less-than-palatable, the contract should be ignored.

If anything, this case says that small employers should not give their employees open-ended contracts guaranteeing them employment. The defendant-employer in this case could have easily put in the contract a clause allowing Mr. Benson to be fired, without penalty to the defendant-employer, for using illicit substances on the job. Luckily, the majority opinion makes clear that the defendant-employer might still be able to hang its hat on the vague term "dishonesty," and prevail before a jury by showing that a lack of veracity on Mr. Benson's part was the motivating factor behind his termination.

NOTES

1. *Clarifying the Issue.* The various opinions in this case express very different views about what is at stake. What is the majority trying to accomplish by remanding, given that Benson has admitted to both drug use and dishonesty? Do you see, as the majority does, a meaningful distinction between the possible grounds for termination under these facts? Or, to use the dissent's term, is this just "legalistic hairsplitting"? If you do see a difference, do you think it will ultimately affect the outcome? In other words, how do you think the jury will receive Benson's argument? (Stay tuned for the answer to this question.)

2. *The Meaning of Dishonesty. Benson* takes the lower court to task for using a dictionary definition of "honesty" rather than attempting to elucidate what the parties meant by this term. Consider why this might have mattered had the issue not been moot as a result of Benson's admission. Benson's purported "dishonesty" consists of the failure to own up to his drug use and his appearance at work with drugs in his system. Does this seem like dishonesty to you? If you answered no, or if you are unsure, then perhaps Benson made a tactical error in conceding this point. Certainly the employer appears to have made an error in carving out a "dishonesty" exception without defining that term. Or might there be a reason why it chose to leave "dishonesty" vague?

3. *Pretext Analysis.* As the majority suggests, the key factual issue that must be determined in this case is the employer's motive for terminating Benson. How does a party prove motive, and who bears the burden of proof on this issue? Motive issues arise with great frequency in the context of status discrimination where the employee alleges that the employer based its decision to terminate on a protected characteristic such as gender or race. The employer typically responds by asserting a legitimate personnel-based reason for its decision. In discrimination cases, the plaintiff bears the ultimate burden of proving that discrimination was at least a motivating factor in the employer's decision. See Chapter 9. By contrast, in the typical express contract case, once the employee has established a contractual right to job security, the employer typically has the burden of proving that cause to terminate existed (e.g., was the employee late, insubordinate, a poor performer). . . . As we will see in *Uintah Basin Med. Ctr. v. Hardy, infra,* courts apply several different standards in determining the first issue. But this is a different inquiry from that in *Benson,* where factual cause has already been established. It is unclear how the burden of proof should be allocated on the remaining question, whether a particular cause actually motivated the decision to terminate. Given the doctrine laid out above, what arguments might each party make with respect to the proper allocation of proof on remand in *Benson?* Are there any policy arguments that can be made in support of allocation to one party over the other? Is the allocation of proof likely to have an impact on the outcome in this case?

4. *Contractual Definitions of Cause. Benson* makes clear that the meaning of cause depends on the terms of the agreement. For this reason, attention to drafting is extremely important when hiring an employee whose termination rights will turn on the presence or absence of cause. Recall the maxim of contract interpretation "construe a contract against its drafter." *Benson* is just one example of cases where employers lost due to the narrowness of their own clauses. A dramatic example of this is a case in which a panel of arbitrators found that the CEO of Massachusetts Mutual Life Insurance was not properly fired for cause despite the fact that he had affairs with two female employees, made millions in profits by trading using the previous day's closing price, and misused the company's aircraft. None of this conduct, the panel concluded, constituted "willful gross misconduct" resulting in "material harm" to the company, as required under the executive's contract. Julie Creswell, *Firing Chief Was Wrong, Panel Says*, N.Y. TIMES, Oct. 21, 2006, at C1. In response to this problem, drafters have taken different approaches, some insisting on significant detail and formality and others opting for more general language. Compare, for instance, the handwritten "Termination Agreement" of the plaintiff-vice president in *Chard v. Iowa Machinery & Supply Co.*, 446 N.W.2d 81, 83 (Iowa Ct. App. 1989), which defined cause as "no performance, violation of company policy, insubordination, etc.," to the following language in the contract of an executive assistant in *Ten Cate Enbi, Inc. v. Metz*, 802 N.E.2d 977, 979 (Ind. Ct. App. 2004):

> Cause shall mean (i) a reasonable certainty exists establishing that [Metz] has engaged in embezzlement, theft, misappropriation or conversion of any assets of [Enbi]; (ii) a material breach by [Metz] of a provision of this agreement or the Basic Business Regulations unless cured by [Metz] within ten days after [Enbi] gives [Metz] written notice thereof excepting that no notice need be given by [Enbi] in the event of a second material breach by [Metz] of the same provision, and (iii) [Metz's] failure or refusal to follow standard policies of [Enbi] or the reasonable directions of and guidelines established by the Board of Directors unless cured by [Metz] within ten days after [Enbi] gives [Metz] written notice thereof excepting that no notice need be given by [Enbi] in the event of a second material failure or refusal by [Metz] of the same policy, direction or guideline.

Which contract provision would you prefer as an employer? If you were the employee?

5. *Managing Risk upon Termination.* Another lesson from *Benson* is that employers should carefully review an employee's contract before making a personnel decision. Note the critical piece of evidence that, according to the concurrence, allows Benson to survive summary judgment: The reason for termination contained in his separation notice (drug use) differed from the reason the employer advanced in the litigation (dishonesty). A similar inconsistency resulted in a jury verdict for the employee in *Ainsworth v. Franklin County Cheese Corp.*, 592 A.2d 871 (Vt. 1991). There the plaintiff was a plant manager whose contract provided for severance upon termination without cause. In August 1986, the employer requested the plaintiff's resignation, providing no explanation for its decision. The plaintiff acquiesced and went about training a replacement and winding down his work. At one point he inquired when his severance benefits would commence, to which the company president responded that he "hadn't gotten that far yet." One month later, the plaintiff received a letter stating that he had been terminated for cause for "failure to follow [the president's] directions . . . and the Company Operations Manual" and that he was not entitled to severance. The employee prevailed before a jury on his breach of contract claim, and the Vermont Supreme Court affirmed. It held that, even assuming cause for termination existed, the jury could reasonably have concluded that the employer terminated the plaintiff pursuant to the no cause provision of his contract and was therefore obligated to pay severance. From the employer's perspective, both *Ainsworth* and *Benson* illustrate the risks of poorly planned terminations. Had the employers examined the contracts at issue and consulted with counsel before acting, liability might have been avoided. The employee likewise can benefit from a better understanding of his or her agreement. In *Benson*, wouldn't it have been better for the plaintiff to have admitted his drug use when asked since the contract permitted discharge for dishonesty, but not for drug use? Of course, there are obvious downsides to admitting addictions, and perhaps he was not in a condition to make such decisions.

6. *Forms of Job Security in Written Contracts.* We have now studied several cases in which employees allege rights based on a fixed-term contract. As you can see, a fixed term is not a guarantee of employment so much as a guarantee of pay. Of course, either party to any contract can decide that it is in its best interest to breach the agreement and pay damages rather than perform. Since an employee cannot be ordered to specifically perform, it would be a rare case in which an employer were required, as a matter of contract law, to either reinstate the employee or pay damages in excess of the agreed compensation. In the employment context, many agreements providing job security are expressly structured to ensure this result, using entitlement to severance pay as a means of discouraging arbitrary or opportunistic firings while at the same time limiting employer liability to the compensation specified. A typical executive employee contract, for instance, will provide for both termination for cause and termination without cause, granting the employee different rights depending on which provision of the agreement the employer invokes. Under the "for cause" provision, the terminated executive will get little or no compensation or benefits, compared to what is generally a very lucrative payout under the "no cause" provision. *See generally* Stewart Schwab & Randall Thomas, *An Empirical Analysis of CEO Employment Contracts: What Do Top Executives Bargain For?* 63 WASH. & LEE L. REV. 231 (2006).

That said, the universe of possible job security provisions is unlimited, and for important positions, contracts may be extremely complex and highly idiosyncratic. Consider the following provision in the 2005 "offer letter" provided by Microsoft to its Chief Operating Officer, Kevin Turner:

> **Replacement of Forfeited Compensation.** [W]e recognize you are forfeiting a very significant amount of accumulated equity compensation when you leave your current employer. Accordingly, as a replacement for that compensation, we offer the following on-hire cash payment and Stock Award grant.
>
> An on-hire payment of $7,000,000 will be made to you within 14 days after our receipt of your signed [contract.] This amount represents our genuine interest in your joining Microsoft. . . . In the unlikely event that you leave the company of your own volition or due to termination for cause by the company prior to completing 12 months of employment, 100% of the $7,000,000 must be returned to Microsoft. [If you leave after completing between 12 and 24 months of employment, $4,700,000 of the signing bonus must be returned. If you leave after completing between 24 and 36 months of employment, $2,300,000 of the signing bonus must be returned.] For purposes of this letter, "for cause" means a good faith determination by the company that: (a) you have engaged in material dishonesty, fraud, or theft in connection with the business of the company or its affiliates; (b) you have engaged in conduct in violation of policies of the company designed to prevent violations of law, such as, without limitation, policies pertaining to compliance with the laws prohibiting unlawful discrimination, harassment, or insider trading; (c) you have been convicted of, or pled nolo contendere to, a felony; (d) you have materially breached the terms of your Employee Agreement; (e) your employment with the company violates any obligation to any third party not to engage in such employment; or (f) you fail to perform your material duties as an employee. . . .

You will be granted a Stock Award of 320,000 shares in Microsoft Corporation under the Microsoft Corporation 2001 Stock Plan. Subject to continued employment through each vesting date, this award will vest as follows:

- 25% — September 1, 2008
- 25% — September 1, 2010
- 50% — Upon retirement from the company at age sixty or older. . . .

Termination of Employment by Microsoft. If Microsoft terminates your employment for any reason other than "for cause" as defined above, the payback provisions of the $7,000,000 on-hire payment will become void (i.e., no payback of any portion of the on-hire payment will be required). . . .

In contrast to *Benson*, the Microsoft offer calls for a return of money to the company in the event of a "for cause" termination or voluntary departure, rather than a payout in the event of a termination without cause. Why might parties prefer this arrangement instead of a structure based on severance? Does the prospect of the employee paying the company, rather than the reverse, change parties' incentives? Are there other interests in play here besides concerns about permissible bases for an employer-initiated termination?

7. *Severance as Liquidated Damages.* Along these lines, it can be useful to think about severance as a type of liquidated damages clause that specifies an amount to be paid to the employee in the event that the employer terminates the relationship in breach of contract. It is generally difficult to predict whether and to what extent an employee will be injured by an unlawful termination, as damages will depend on various factors outside the parties' control, such as the future market for the employee's services. This makes job security contracts a good candidate for a liquidated damage provision. Note, however, that while liquidated damages clauses are presumptively valid under contract law, they will not be enforced if they provide for damages that are disproportionate to actual or foreseeable loss. *See* RESTATEMENT (SECOND) OF CONTRACTS § 356 (1981). Can an employer avoid its obligation to pay an employee upon termination by arguing that the amount of pay provided for in the contract is excessive? *See Guiliano v. Cleo, Inc.*, 995 S.W.2d 88, 101 (Tenn. 1999) (upholding contractual severance in excess of $90,000 for terminated employee who found immediate reemployment at higher salary because, at the time of contract formation, "[i]t was within the fair contemplation of the parties that [plaintiff] might not be able to find a similar professional position . . . and might suffer damages that would be difficult to prove, including loss of professional status, prestige, and advancement opportunities.").

8. *The Right to Fire?* The concurring justice in *Benson* emphasizes that the court's decision does not constrain the employer's ability to fire at will but merely enforces the continuation of the salary provision the parties adopted in their agreement. The dissent, in contrast, believes the court's decision saddles the employer with an irresponsible and potentially dangerous worker who is effectively immune from termination. Which justice gets it right? Consider that Benson's contract ran from 1997 to 2005. Isn't there some truth to the assertion that a small, family-run business like the defendant is unlikely to be able to shoulder the expense of paying a terminated employee for that length of time while employing someone else to do his job? Does this observation incline you toward the dissent's conclusion? Or does it just mean, as the concurrence points out, that small employers should be more prudent in entering

into job security agreements with their workers? Which approach is ultimately better for future employees, most of whom are unlikely to engage in similarly egregious behavior?

9. *Choosing Between Cause and No Cause.* In *Benson*, AJR could have fired Benson for any reason and paid his salary, or fired him for an enumerated reason (dishonesty) and avoided further liability. While it may seem like an obvious choice, employers often elect to fire high-level employees under no cause provisions despite the financial disincentives to doing so. Sometimes this choice simply reflects a desire to avoid conflict or publicity. It may also reflect an unwillingness to risk legal exposure. In cases involving more obscure or less serious performance deficiencies than *Benson*, it can be difficult for the employer to establish poor performance or that the employee's behavior constituted cause within the contractual definition of the term. Perhaps most critically, terminating without cause allows the executive and the company to part amicably, preserving key relationships in the small world of big business.

Yet there are disadvantages to the strategy as well. By making sizeable and seemingly unwarranted payouts to departing executives, firm directors may put themselves at risk of shareholder derivative suits and, in some circumstances, intense public criticism that may be even more damaging than legal action. In a recent and highly publicized example, shareholders of the Walt Disney Company sued the company's board of directors for breach of fiduciary duty based on its 1996 decision to terminate former CEO, Michael Ovitz, without cause. Ovitz left his position with Disney after a turbulent 14 months of employment, with a severance package estimated at $140 million. Employers' decisions as to whether and on what grounds to terminate an executive are usually insulated by the business judgment rule, and the Disney plaintiffs ultimately lost on the merits following a bench trial. *Brehm v. Eisner*, 906 A.2d 27 (Del. 2006). The fact that the class was successful in getting to trial, however, was widely seen as a cautionary tale in the business community about the growing reluctance of the public (and the judiciary) to give companies free rein on rewarding their own. *See Brehm v. Eisner*, 746 A.2d 244, 249 (Del. 2000) (noting that "the sheer size of the payout to Ovitz . . . pushes the envelope of judicial respect for the business judgment of directors in making compensation decisions").

10. *Material Breach Analysis.* An employer's argument that it had "just cause" to terminate is sometimes framed in terms of the employee committing a "material breach" of the employment agreement that relieves the employer of its contractual obligations. In *Prozinski v. Northeast Real Estate Services, Inc.*, 797 N.E.2d 415 (Mass. App. 2003), the employee was the chief operating and financial officer of a newly formed firm. His contract provided: " 'During the first 24 months of employment if your employment is terminated by the Company then the Company will pay you the equivalent of 1 full year's pay including benefits.' " It said nothing about just cause and contained no termination clause. Less than a year later, the firm terminated Prozinski for misconduct and withheld severance. In Prozinski's subsequent suit for breach of contract the court agreed that the agreement constituted a 24-month, fixed-term contract, but held that genuine issues of fact precluded an award of summary judgment in favor of the employee. Specifically, the court held that the alleged behavior giving rise to Prozinski's termination — financial misconduct and sexual harassment — might have excused the employer's duty to pay. It explained:

> The record in this case reflects a genuine issue of material fact on the question whether Prozinski's conduct amounted to a material breach of his contract with Northeast and not

simply . . . "boorish conduct" and "sloppy record keeping." As COO-CFO, Prozinski owed Northeast the duties of loyalty, utmost good faith, and of protecting Northeast's interests.

. . . First, Northeast alleged, with some support, that Prozinski knowingly submitted false expense reports. Second, for his own purposes, Prozinski fostered an environment within the workplace that was hostile to its female employees. . . .

Prozinski's placement of his own interests above those of the company he served could be found by a fact finder to constitute an act of disloyalty. One claim of sexual harassment or discrimination can be sufficient to establish a hostile work environment and subject the company to liability. "Under Massachusetts law, officers and directors owe a fiduciary duty to protect the interests of the corporation they serve" Prozinski's conduct put Northeast at risk of litigation.

A fact finder could also conclude that any such breach of Prozinski's fiduciary duty to Northeast amounted to a material breach of his contract, i.e., a "substantial breach going to the root of the contract." *See generally* RESTATEMENT (SECOND) OF CONTRACTS § 241. Such a conclusion would terminate Northeast's obligation to fulfill the contractual promises it had made, for "it is well established that a material breach by one party excuses the other party from further performance under the contract." *See* RESTATEMENT (SECOND) OF CONTRACTS § 237.

Id. at 423-24. Does this result make sense? If the parties agree that severance will be paid and do not provide for any contingencies in their contract, why shouldn't the courts enforce that provision? *See, e.g., Fields v. Thompson Printing Co.*, 363 F.3d 259, 269 (3d Cir. 2004) (finding in favor of employee denied benefits and pay upon termination for sexual harassment because "[the contract] requires [the employer] to pay certain sums if they terminated Fields, ostensibly for any reason, including improper and offensive conduct. Had [the employer] intended to avoid this result, [it] could have bargained for a limiting provision"). Suppose an employer and an employee drafted an agreement containing the following language: "If Employer terminates employee for any reason, including a material breach of this agreement by Employee, Employer shall pay Employee's salary for the balance of the contract period." Would the *Prozinski* court enforce this clause? Should it?

11. *The Faithless Servant Doctrine.* In *Prozinski* (as in *Benson*) the issue was the employee's entitlement to future compensation in the form of continued salary. In some cases, employers have successfully compelled disgorgement of *past* compensation paid to employees who had committed serious breaches of fiduciary duties. In *Astra USA, Inc. v. Bildman*, 914 N.E.2d 36 (Mass. 2009), the court ordered disgorgement by defendant Bildman, a former chief executive officer who was found to have conducted a pattern of sexual harassment, retaliation, cover-up (including paying off victims from corporate funds), and a variety of financial misdeeds over a period of several years. The court held that, under New York's "faithless servant" doctrine, the employee must "forfeit all of his salary and bonuses from Astra for the period of disloyalty" even if the faithless servant "otherwise performed valuable services for his principal." Does this strike you as an unusually harsh remedy? It is perhaps hard to have much sympathy for Bildman, a highly compensated corporate officer who engaged in egregious breaches of fiduciary duty. But what about ordinary employees engaged in more run-of-the-mill misconduct? In dicta, *Astra* suggested that the disgorgement remedy could apply to lower-level employees as well. When, if ever, is it fair to make an employee *pay back* wages already earned? Does the notion of fiduciary duties help draw a distinction? We will discuss fiduciary duties and employee duties of loyalty in Chapter 8.

12. *Material vs. Immaterial Performance Deficiencies.* In your first-year Contracts course, you probably learned that a material breach is one that goes to the essence of the contract. Engaging in sexual harassment and stealing from the company undoubtedly provide good support for an employer's argument that an employee materially breached his or her employment agreement, but what about less egregious conduct? *See, e.g., Central Alaska Broadcasting, Inc. v. Bracale*, 637 P.2d 711, 712 (Alaska 1981) (finding employee's refusal to obey order of Board of Directors to terminate subordinate a material breach where employee's contract granted him "management authority and right over . . . personnel . . . subject to the supervision and control of the Board"); *Shah v. Cover-It, Inc.*, 859 A.2d 959, 963 (Conn. 2004) (manager materially breached employment contract where he overstayed vacation, did not report to work for weeks upon return, and spent long time periods at work visiting Internet Web sites unrelated to his job).

What about drug use like that at issue in *Benson*? In the ordinary case the answer depends on the severity of the employee's conduct. Off-duty behavior that does not affect on the job performance will rarely if ever constitute a material breach. Thus the analysis would turn on such things as whether Benson actually showed up to work impaired, how often, and whether, if there were only isolated instances of impairment, special circumstances (like access to or use of hazardous materials or equipment) justified a finding of material breach.

If Benson's drug use did rise to this level, the question would be whether the material breach could excuse the employer's payment obligation given the termination provision in the contract. Indeed, this question brought Benson's case back before the West Virginia Supreme Court six years after the remand ordered in the opinion you just read. *See Benson v. AJR*, 698 S.E.2d 638 (W. Va. 2010) (*Benson II*). At trial, AJR argued both that dishonesty (not drug use) motivated its termination decision and that Benson's drug use was a material breach relieving them of contractual liability. The jury returned a general verdict stating that plaintiff had materially breached and, on special interrogatories also submitted to the jury, answered that drug use, not dishonesty, had motivated the employer's decision. The judge awarded Benson his lost wages. AJR appealed, and the West Virginia Supreme Court affirmed:

> Mr. Benson's material breach of the Employment Agreement is not an enumerated reason that would relieve AJR of the duty to pay him his salary under the remainder of the contract period. Thus, while the [jury found] that Mr. Benson had materially breached his employment contract such a judgment did not finally resolve the central issue of whether AJR remained obligated to pay Mr. Benson contractual damages when it terminated his employment. [W]hether Mr. Benson may recover damages from AJR is governed solely by the parties' Employment Agreement. . . . AJR is not relieved of its obligation to pay damages to Mr. Benson thereunder. Given the plain language of the Employment Agreement, the circuit court was bound to enforce its terms.

Id. at *14. In light of this result (and the mixed verdict), do you think AJR's material breach argument helped or hurt its case? Do you think the jury might have reached a different conclusion had it been given only a general verdict asking whether the plaintiff or the defendant had breached the contract?

It would appear from *Benson II* that a contractual definition of cause will in some situations preclude a generic material breach argument. Given the availability of material breach analysis under ordinary contract law, why would an employer ever choose to enumerate causes for termination in an employment agreement? A concurring justice in *Benson II* concluded that the parties' "amazingly narrow" agreement indicated that "[F]rom a business sense, the eight years of employment was . . . factored into the purchase price of AJR." *Id.* at *15. Does this description shed some light on the question?

═══ ## *Uintah Basin Medical Center v. Hardy*
═══ *110 P.3d 168 (Utah Ct. App. 2005)*

JACKSON, Judge.

. . . Background

Dr. Hardy is a board-certified pathologist. On November 29, 1994, he executed an employment agreement [to provide pathology services for Uintah Basin Medical Center. Under the Agreement, which consists of only two pages taken almost verbatim from that of Dr. Hardy's predecessor, UBMC was to refer certain types of laboratory work to Dr. Hardy and pay a $400 monthly laboratory director's fee. In return, Dr. Hardy would work as the director of UBMC's laboratory and provide related services, which included weekly visits to the hospital. The Agreement does not include a fixed termination date; rather, it would "continue to bind parties . . . until terminated after ninety (90) days written notice for just cause of termination by either party or by mutual consent of the parties to a shorter notice period." The Agreement does not define "just cause" or otherwise clarify what grounds would justify termination.

On July 29, 1996, UBMC sent Dr. Hardy notice of termination and later hired Dr. Thomas Allred in his place. [UBMC brought a suit for declaratory judgment to establish that its termination of the Agreement with Dr. Hardy was for "just cause" and Dr. Hardy counterclaimed for breach of contract. The trial court granted UBMC's motion for summary judgment, finding the Agreement unreasonable in duration based on Dr. Hardy's deposition testimony that he understood the agreement to be terminable only upon his death or incapacity, or the hospital's discontinuance of pathology services.]

Analysis

I. *Interpretation of the "Just Cause" Provision*

The key question in this case is what the "just cause" provision in the Agreement means. Once this question is answered, we may gauge . . . whether UBMC had just cause to terminate Dr. Hardy.

To interpret the "just cause" provision, the trial court relied primarily on extrinsic evidence, namely Dr. Hardy's deposition testimony regarding his understanding of the term. . . .

Although both parties here have ascribed different meanings to the "just cause" provision, we cannot conclude that the term is ambiguous. UBMC has taken the position that it has "just cause" to terminate Dr. Hardy's employment when the business exigencies of the hospital and the interests of the patients warrant a change in personnel. In contrast, Dr. Hardy testified in his post-remand affidavit that he understood the "just cause" provision to allow UBMC to terminate the Agreement only under specific circumstances:

> In essence, UBMC would have just cause to terminate my Agreement if I failed to perform or something substantial changed as to the need of UBMC for pathology services (e.g., hospital closure) which may be caused by financial concerns. Those financial concerns, however, could not include merely getting a lower price for the pathology services or histology lab supervision.

Hardy also asserts that he understood "just cause" to imply that

> [i]f UBMC perceived a need for changes in scope or manner of the provided pathology services, I expected them to approach me regarding such a need, and if jointly agreed upon, I would have adjusted accordingly. If I could not accommodate these changes, then UBMC would be free to terminate the Agreement.

Dr. Hardy's interpretation is ultimately untenable for two reasons. First, the evidence on record does not indicate that the parties understood the "just cause" provision to have a unique meaning particular to the Agreement, much less the detailed meaning understood by Dr. Hardy. The parties have stipulated that the Agreement is, for all practical purposes, identical to that of Dr. Hardy's predecessor, Dr. Joseph Sannella. The "just cause" termination provision was copied from the Sannella contract and included in the Agreement without any substantial negotiation. The parties did not incorporate other documents, such as the UBMC bylaws, to define when either party would have cause to terminate the Agreement. Thus, we must conclude that any particular meaning of "just cause" as understood or intended by Dr. Hardy is unique to himself and is, as he concedes in his brief, irrelevant to its interpretation.

Second, Dr. Hardy's interpretation of "just cause" is at odds with the ordinary meaning of the term. Unlike an at-will employment agreement, which allows an employer to discharge an employee for any, or no, reason, termination for just cause is widely understood to permit discharge only for "a fair and honest cause or reason, regulated by good faith . . . as opposed to one that is trivial, capricious, unrelated to business needs or goals, or pretextual." *Guz v. Bechtel Nat'l, Inc.*, 8 P.3d 1089, 1100 (Cal. 2000) This broad definition of just cause allows an employer to discharge an employee not only for misconduct or poor performance but also for other legitimate economic reasons.[4] Courts have recognized that " '[i]n deciding whether [just] cause exists, there must be a balance between the employer's interest in operating its business efficiently and profitably and the employee's interest in continued

---

4. *See also Zoerb v. Chugach Elec. Ass'n*, 798 P.2d 1258, 1262-1263 (Alaska 1990) ("A reduction in work force compelled by legitimate and sufficient business reasons may constitute 'good cause' to terminate an employee."); *Havill v. Woodstock Soapstone Co.*, 783 A.2d 423, 428 (Vt. 2001) ("Economic circumstances that necessitate employer layoffs constitute good cause for termination." (quotations, citation, and alteration omitted)).

employment. . . . Care must be exercised so as not to interfere with the employer's legitimate exercise of managerial discretion.'" *Cotran v. Rollins Hudig Hall Int'l, Inc.*, 948 P.2d 412, 417 (Cal. 1998).

In sum, absent evidence that the parties intended a meaning of "just cause" unique to this particular agreement, we must conclude that the parties intended the term to have its ordinary meaning. Accordingly, we hold that the "just cause" provision is unambiguous and is ordinarily understood to provide employers with power to terminate an employee for legitimate business reasons and in the interest of improving client services as long as the justification is not a mere pretext for a capricious, bad faith, or illegal termination. . . .

III. UBMC's Just Cause to Terminate

The only remaining issue is whether the Board discharged Dr. Hardy for just cause. Because the trial court did not reach this issue in its summary judgment ruling, we remand for the trial court to determine whether the Board terminated Dr. Hardy for legitimate business reasons or whether the termination was capricious, in bad faith, or illegal.

However, we address here the question of what an employer must show to prove it terminated an employee for just cause, a matter of first impression for Utah courts. There appear to be three different approaches to this question. Some courts seem to give deference to the justifications stated by the employer. *See e.g., Gaudio v. Griffin Health Servs. Corp.*, 733 A.2d 197, 208 (Conn. 1999) ("[A]n employer who wishes to terminate an employee for cause must do nothing more rigorous than 'proffer a proper reason for dismissal.'"). A few other courts have taken the opposite approach and required the employer to prove that the conditions necessitating termination actually existed. *See, e.g., Toussaint v. Blue Cross & Blue Shield of Mich.*, 292 N.W.2d 880, 895 (Mich. 1980) ("[W]here an employer has agreed to discharge an employee for cause only, its declaration that the employee was discharged for unsatisfactory work is subject to judicial review. The jury as trier of fact decides whether the employee was, in fact, discharged for unsatisfactory work.").

A far greater number of states have adopted a more balanced approach that requires an employer to justify termination with an objective good faith reason supported by facts reasonably believed to be true by the employer. *See, e.g., Towson Univ. v. Conte*, 862 A.2d 941, 950-51, 954 (Md. App. 2004) ("[I]n the just cause employment context, a jury's role is to determine the objective reasonableness of the employer's decision to discharge, which means that the employer act in objective good faith and base its decision on a reasoned conclusion and facts reasonably believed to be true by the employer.") These courts recognize that an employer's justification for discharging an employee should not be taken at face value but also recognize that a judge or jury should not be called upon to second-guess an employer's business decisions.

We agree with the majority of courts and adopt the objective reasonableness approach. Accordingly, in order to establish just cause on remand, UBMC need not prove that the Board's assumptions in terminating Dr. Hardy were true or that the benefits it expected were actually realized. Rather, UBMC need only show that the Board acted in good faith by adequately considering the facts it reasonably believed to be true at the time it made the decision.

NOTES

1. *Cause in the Absence of a Contractual Definition. UBMC* deals with the problem of determining whether termination of a contractually protected employee was based on "cause" where the parties' agreement fails to define the term. In answering that question, a court has essentially two choices: Either it can apply a general definition or standard of cause, or it can try to ascertain the parties' intended definition of cause in the particular agreement. In *UBMC*, the court opts for the former approach, concluding that "cause" is an unambiguous term subject to a generally understood meaning.

The choice of approach, however, will vary depending on the court, the contract, and the circumstances. In *Joy v. Hay Group, Inc.*, 403 F.3d 875 (7th Cir. 2005), a case arising under Illinois law, Joy was hired as an executive compensation consultant under a contract providing for one year's salary in the event of termination "for reasons other than cause." She was subsequently fired for failing to meet her billing quota and denied severance. In her suit for breach of contract, Joy argued that upon receiving the contract she asked what cause meant and was told it meant "serious wrongdoing." The employer asserted that cause unambiguously meant unsatisfactory performance in the opinion of the employer. In an opinion by Judge Posner, the court reversed summary judgment for the employer, permitting Joy to present her understanding of the agreement to a jury:

> [T]here may be a difference between "cause" for discharge and "cause" for denial of severance pay. Business firms almost always reserve the right to fire an employee . . . if the firm decides that the employee's performance is unsatisfactory. But it is precisely because of the insecurity of such employment — the determination that Joy's performance was unsatisfactory was based on a criterion selected by the firm after she went to work for it, rather than being specified in her employment contract — that employment contracts often provide for severance pay. Joy was leaving a good job to go to work for HGI and in doing so may have been taking a risk . . . especially since she was going to be working in what was a new line of business for HGI. If she lost her job she would need money to tide her over while she looked for a new job. Hence the severance-pay provision in her employment contract with HGI.

Id. at 877. Do you agree with Posner's distinction between severance and termination? Does it help explain the approach taken by the court in *UBMC*? Are there other factual differences that might justify the decision to treat "cause" as having a generally understood meaning in *UBMC* but permit the plaintiff to demonstrate a unique meaning in *Joy*?

2. *Cause Not Attributable to Performance.* If there is a generally understood definition of cause, as *UBMC* suggests, what does it encompass? In *UBMC*, the employer offered an economic reason for its decision to terminate Dr. Hardy: By hiring a replacement, it could obtain pathology services more cost-effectively. In finding in favor of the employer, the court asserts that a business reason of this sort fits within the "widely understood" meaning of cause, despite the fact that it is unrelated to the employee's performance. Does this statement of the legal definition of cause surprise you? Is it consistent with your own understanding of what constitutes just cause for termination?

Collective bargaining agreements almost always distinguish between terminations (which can only be for just cause related to performance) and "layoffs," which can be for economic reasons and are usually done on the basis of seniority—last in, first out. *See* Roger I. Abrams & Dennis R. Nolan, *Toward a Theory of "Just Cause" in Employee Discipline Cases*, 1985 DUKE L. J. 594-95 ("Virtually every collective bargaining agreement contains [limitations on employer's power to discipline or discharge workers] by far the most common of which is the requirement that there be 'just cause' for discipline. This requirement is so well accepted that often it is found to be implicit in the collective agreement, even when there is no stated limitation on the employer's power to discipline."). A similar distinction exists in both academic tenure and civil service. In the latter situation, the source of just cause protection is frequently statutory rather than contractual, but the focus is on the conduct of the particular employee, and economic concerns are addressed under a different rubric. *See, e.g., Yoder v. Town of Middleton*, 876 A.2d 216, 218 (N.H. 2005) (cause for removal of police chief pursuant to state statute requires demonstration of unfitness or incapacity to perform job duties).

In cases like those we have been studying involving individual private sector employment contracts, whether economic bases for termination constitute cause is a question that often turns on the form and context of the parties' agreement. Consistent with *UMBC*, courts generally interpret cause as encompassing legitimate, non-performance-based reasons for termination in indefinite just cause contracts like Dr. Hardy's, that is, contracts promising protection against arbitrary dismissal but guaranteeing no particular term of employment. The same is true of the just cause definition adopted by statute in Montana, the only state to have legislatively superseded the common-law employment at will rule, and the unadopted but influential Model Employment Termination Act ("META"). *See* MONT. CODE ANN. § 39-2-903(5) ("'Good cause' means reasonable job-related grounds for dismissal based on a failure to satisfactorily perform, . . . disruption of the employer's operation, or other legitimate business reason"); META § 1(4) (including in definition of "good cause" the employer's "exercise of business judgment, including its setting of economic or institutional goals, . . . reorganizing operations, . . . and changing standards of performance"). On the other hand, under a contract providing for a fixed term of employment, courts usually treat cause as meaning a reason for termination related to the employee's conduct or performance. *See* RESTATEMENT (THIRD) OF EMPLOYMENT, Tentative Draft No. 2 § 2.03 cmt. g (April 3, 2009).

3. *Termination Based on Poor Results.* Once it is clear that an employee's contract requires a performance-based reason for termination (either by its express terms or as interpreted by a court), the question remains how serious the employee's performance problems must be to constitute cause. Must the employee engage in intentional misconduct, or is there sufficient cause when an employee performs in good faith but achieves poor results? The answer often turns on the specific facts of the case, including the circumstances of hire, performance expectations of the parties, and, of course, the terms of the contract. *See, e.g., Chard v. Iowa Machinery & Supply Co.*, 446 N.W.2d 81 (Iowa Ct. App. 1989) (finding vice president entitled to severance under "no cause" provision of contract where plaintiff was hired to turn around lagging division over the long term and was fired after only two months on the job, during which time state legislature was debating economic recovery legislation that had chilling effect on sales market); *Cole v. Valley Ice Garden, L.L.C.*, 113 P.3d 275, 280 (Mont. 2005) (firing ice hockey coach based on team's poor win-loss record constituted termination for cause despite his good faith efforts and the fact that contract did not contain performance goals).

4. *Actual Cause vs. Reasonable Decision Making.* A related factual question is whether the grounds asserted by the employer in support of termination are true. What happens, for instance, if an employer terminates a worker for embezzlement — something that everyone would agree constitutes cause — but the employer was mistaken about the employee's culpability? For both procedural and strategic reasons, the parties in many reported appellate decisions concerning breach of employment contract have either stipulated or assumed for the purpose of argument that particular facts led to the employee's discharge. At trial, however, most employees vigorously contest the truth of the employer's proffered reason, particularly where employee misconduct is alleged. As previously discussed, courts generally agree that the employer bears the burden of proof where cause is disputed, at least with respect to express contracts, but they disagree about what exactly the employer needs to prove. The last part of *UMBC* describes a number of approaches that courts take, ranging from significant deference to the employer's proffered reason to requiring the employer to establish that cause in fact existed. Which approach discussed in *UBMC* makes the most sense as a policy matter? Consider the following rationale for applying a reasonable good faith test like that adopted in *UBMC*:

> The decision to terminate an employee for misconduct is one that not uncommonly implicates organizational judgment and may turn on intractable factual uncertainties, even where the grounds for dismissal are fact specific. If an employer is required to have in hand a signed confession or an eyewitness account of the alleged misconduct before it can act, the workplace will be transformed into an adjudicatory arena and effective decisionmaking will be thwarted. Although these features do not justify a rule permitting employees to be dismissed arbitrarily, they do mean that asking a civil jury to reexamine in all its factual detail the triggering cause of the decision to dismiss — including the retrospective accuracy of the employer's comprehension of that event — months or even years later, in a context distant from the imperatives of the workplace, is at odds with an axiom underlying the jurisprudence of wrongful termination. That axiom . . . is the need for a sensible latitude for managerial decisionmaking and its corollary, an optimum balance point between the employer's interest in organizational efficiency and the employee's interest in continuing employment.

Cotran v. Rollins Hudig Hall Int'l, Inc., 948 P.2d 412, 421 (Cal. 1998). From a management perspective, this is certainly understandable, but doesn't it amount to allowing some employers to get away with breach? After all, if there really was no cause, there was no contractually legitimate basis for the termination. In contrast, consider a typical commercial contract involving a sale of goods. Clearly a buyer could not reject a shipment under contract merely because he or she in good faith, but mistakenly, thought the goods were defective. Is there a reason why a lower standard should govern employment?

One consideration may be the type of contract involved. *Cotran* was based on an implied just cause agreement rather than a written job security contract. Should the source of protection, express versus implied agreement, matter at all? *See Townson Univ. v. Conte*, 862 A.2d 941 (Md. App. 2004) (no difference); *Khajavi v. Feather River Anesthesia Med. Group*, 100 Cal. Rptr. 2d 627 (Ct. App. 2000) (holding that, unlike wrongful discharge based on an implied contract, employment for a specified term may not be terminated prior to the term's expiration based upon employer's honest but mistaken belief of misconduct).

5. *Procedural Aspects of Just Cause.* In *UBMC*, Dr. Hardy argued not only that there was no cause for termination but also that the employer should have consulted with him first about its desire to reduce costs. Some courts incorporate a procedural component in the obligation to dismiss only for cause. *See Nadeau v. Imtec, Inc.,* 670 A.2d 841, 844 (Vt. 1995) ("To be upheld, a discharge for just cause must meet two criteria: first, that the employee's conduct was egregious enough that the discharge was reasonable, and second, that the employee had fair notice, express or implied, that such conduct could result in discharge."); *Cotran,* 948 P.2d at 422 (good cause means "fair and honest reasons . . . supported by substantial evidence gathered through an adequate investigation that includes notice of the claimed misconduct and a chance for the employee to respond."). *But see New England Stone v. Conte,* 962 A.2d 30, 33 (R.I. 2009) (declining to impose any "due-process mandates" on the employer where a contract enumerated grounds for cause and provided "that cause 'shall be determined by the [c]ompany in good faith' "). Why should procedure matter, at least if the employer can ultimately prove cause? If a procedural component exists and is breached, what should the remedy be? What could a court award Dr. Hardy if his contract required the hospital to consult with him about costs?

6. *Satisfaction Contracts.* A variant on the contract conferring just cause protection is a contract that promises employment so long as the employee performs to the employer's "satisfaction." Courts vary in their interpretation of such agreements, but they are generally understood to provide less job security than a just cause agreement. *See, e.g., Silvestri v. Optus Software, Inc.,* 814 A.2d 602, 607-08 (N.J. 2003) (subjective assessment of employer satisfaction applies where contract preserved right to terminate). As with all employment contracts, however, interpretation ultimately hinges on the language of the agreement. *See, e.g., McKnight v. Simpson's Beauty Supply, Inc.,* 358 S.E.2d 107 (N.C. Ct. App. 1987) (contract requiring plaintiff to perform "to the reasonable satisfaction of employer" did not mean plaintiff was subject to dismissal for failing to satisfy unreasonable or capricious demands, but only for not carrying out his duties in a reasonably diligent and effective manner).

7. *It Isn't Over 'Til It's Over.* Dr. Hardy lost this round of the litigation but subsequently defeated UBMC's motion for summary judgment on the issue of cause. On remand, UBMC filed for summary judgment arguing that there was no material factual issue in dispute as to the reason for termination, asserting various business-related reasons for replacing Dr. Hardy with Dr. Allred. The trial court granted the motion, but the Utah Supreme Court reversed, finding that the facts, read in the light most favorable to Dr. Hardy, could support the conclusion that the reasons proffered by UBMC were pretextual. *See UBMC v. Hardy (UBMC II),* 179 P.3d 786 (Utah 2008). It explained:

> First, UBMC did not give Dr. Hardy any contemporaneous reason for the termination of his Agreement. UBMC simply thanked Dr. Hardy for his service and told him that he had been replaced. And UBMC's administrator, Brad LeBaron, admitted in his deposition that he told Dr. Hardy after the termination that he would need to look and see what kind of potential issues could be raised to defend UBMC's decision. In addition, even though UBMC now relies on its desire for an on-site pathologist as a justification for the termination decision, this desire was never expressed to Dr. Hardy before his Agreement was terminated, and Dr. Hardy was given no opportunity to cure or address any demonstrated need or desire of UBMC for an on-site pathologist. Indeed, UBMC undertook no investigation into the actual need or the financial impact of hiring an on-site

pathologist before it terminated Dr. Hardy's Agreement. This lack of investigation before the termination suggests that UBMC's stated need for an on-site pathologist was merely pretextual. The facts also establish that UBMC failed to conduct a comprehensive investigation of Dr. Allred prior to hiring him. . . . Finally, UBMC did not terminate Dr. Hardy for poor performance, misconduct, breach of the Agreement, or failure to fulfill his obligations.

Id. at 790-91. Does this victory for the employee surprise you given the very deferential standard adopted by the court in *UBMC I*? Does it give you insight into the advantages of the litigation strategies that parties often pursue in termination cases? The result perhaps explains why employers often vehemently dispute the existence of contractual job security protection even when they have a plausible reason for terminating.

PROBLEM

3-3.   Bonnie Blackwell was hired by the board of directors of a television merchandising company for the position of general manager. During Blackwell's employment there was significant conflict on the board of directors, involving accusations by the chair of the board and company president that two other board members were improperly documenting withdrawals of company funds. The Chair on several occasions asked Blackwell informally to look into this problem. Blackwell, reluctant to get involved in an internal matter between board members, repeatedly resisted this request explaining that it was outside her authority. One year into her employment, Blackwell submitted a request for a two-week unpaid leave of absence for health reasons, a benefit available to all employees per company policy. Upon receiving the request, the president called Blackwell to his office and informed her that it was "a very bad time to plan a vacation." He cited the recent loss of a cable affiliate and an upcoming meeting with a possible new affiliate and stated that it was a "critical time" for the company. Blackwell responded that her request was not for vacation and that the meeting could be handled by her subordinates. Blackwell did not appear at work for the next two weeks, although she conferenced into the meeting with the potential affiliate by telephone. When she returned to work, she was terminated, effective immediately, and given no severance pay. During her one year of employment, Blackwell received only one performance evaluation, which was positive, and the company met all of its sales and budgetary goals under her leadership.

Assess whether Blackwell has any claim against the company under each of the following scenarios:

A.   Blackwell's contract provides: "This agreement shall run for two years from the date of hire unless terminated earlier on the basis of just cause. Just cause means gross misconduct, dishonesty, commission of a crime, or other conduct that seriously jeopardizes the company."

B.   Blackwell's contract provides: "This agreement shall run for two years from the date of hire. In the event that the company terminates Blackwell prior to that date, Blackwell shall receive her full salary for the remainder of the contract term."

C. Blackwell's contract provides: "This agreement can only be terminated on the basis of just cause and upon one month's notice."

See generally Video Catalog Channel v. Blackwelder, No. 03A01-9705-CH-00155, 1997 Ten. App. LEXIS 636 (Tenn. Ct. App. Sept. 19, 1997).

B. COMPENSATION TERMS

Job security and cause for discharge are not the only contractual issues fueling litigation in sophisticated employment relationships. The main reason job security is important to workers, after all, is that it ensures a steady flow of income. For high-level employees, that can mean much more than base wages. You have already seen that written contracts frequently promise exit pay or other separation benefits upon termination. High-level employees are often paid during the course of their relationship pursuant to complex compensation schemes that include incentive pay.

"Incentive pay" generally refers to compensation that is tied to performance, such as bonuses, stock options, profit sharing or other arrangements under which the amount of compensation varies depending on the success of the employee or the company as a whole. Where compensation structures are properly aligned with performance indicators and the health and success of the firm, they can be extremely beneficial to both parties. From the perspective of the employer, such arrangements not only encourage superior performance, they help retain good workers who might otherwise defect to competitors (the so-called "golden handcuffs" effect). For employees, incentive pay arrangements offer a degree of control over their earning capacity and create the potential for high payoffs. Indeed, for some employees, incentive pay greatly exceeds their base salary.

However, many believe that this is not the way incentive compensation works in practice. A wide body of literature has criticized the current system for rewarding executives for moderate or even poor firm performance. *See generally* Lucian Arye Bebchuk et al., *Managerial Power and Rent Extraction in the Design of Executive Compensation*, 69 U. CHI. L. REV. 751, 761-83 (2002) (describing and critiquing the "optimal contract approach" to executive compensation). It suggests that outsize pay packages result not from legitimate market forces but rather from cozy relationships between corporate managers and directors, and arrangements that encourage executives to place short-term management interests ahead of larger corporate goals. Professors Lucien Bebchuk and Jesse Fried explain some of these concerns:

> According to the "official" view of executive compensation, corporate boards setting pay arrangements are guided solely by shareholder interests and operate at arm's-length from the executives whose pay they set. [This] view serves as the practical basis for legal rules and public policy. . . .
>
> The official arm's-length story is neat, tractable, and reassuring. But it fails to account for the realities of executive compensation. . . .

Directors have had and continue to have various economic incentives to support, or at least go along with, arrangements that favor the company's top executives. A variety of social and psychological factors — collegiality, team spirit, a natural desire to avoid conflict within the board, friendship and loyalty, and cognitive dissonance — exert additional pull in that direction. Although many directors own some stock in their companies, their ownership positions are too small to give them a financial incentive to take the personally costly, or at the very least unpleasant, route of resisting compensation arrangements sought by executives. In addition, limitations on time and resources have made it difficult for even well-intentioned directors to do their pay-setting job properly. Finally, the market constraints within which directors operate are far from tight and do not prevent deviations from arm's-length contracting outcomes in favor of executives. . . .

The same factors that limit the usefulness of the arm's-length model in explaining executive compensation suggest that executives have had substantial influence over their own pay. Compensation arrangements have often deviated from arm's-length contracting because directors have been influenced by management, insufficiently motivated to insist on shareholder-serving compensation, or simply ineffectual. Executives' influence over directors has enabled them to obtain "rents," benefits greater than those obtainable under true arm's-length contracting.

Pay Without Performance: Overview of the Issues, 30 J. CORP. L. 647, 653-59 (2005); *see also* Sanjai Bhagat & Roberta Romano, *Reforming Executive Compensation: Focusing and Committing to the Long-Term,* 26 YALE J. REG. 359 (2009) (calling out the "perverse incentives" of executives "to emphasize short-term stock prices over long-term value"). Such issues have gained increased public attention in the wake of the economic crisis of 2008. *See* Heather Landy, *Growing Sense of Outrage Over Executive Pay,* WASH. POST, November 15, 2008, at A8.

It is important to remember, however, that not all recipients of incentive compensation are high-level executives able to secure lucrative pay packages and other favorable terms of employment. Many sales workers, for instance, are compensated primarily through commissions, a structure that can create hardships for workers struggling to generate revenue in difficult economic times. In addition, incentive compensation is often deferred, meaning that under the employer's policy a worker may not realize payment until a future date, possibly after the entitlement has "accrued." We have seen that high-level employees generally negotiate contractual protection against termination. For mainstream workers, however, the employer's unfettered ability to terminate can jeopardize the realization of incentive compensation. Thus the interplay between employment at will and contractual bonus and commission schemes is important in evaluating employee compensation rights.

For all of these reasons, alleged failures to pay earned compensation are a common source of employment litigation. These disputes raise issues similar to those that arise with respect to job security or any other contractual term of employment, such as whether the employer's promise is binding and whether it has been breached. The following section begins with the first question, namely, when does an employee have a contractual right to incentive pay? We then turn to issues of drafting and interpreting terms of compensation, including what happens to workers' rights to deferred compensation upon termination of employment.

1. Contractual Rights to Incentive Pay

A threshold issue in any dispute over incentive pay is whether the employee has a legal entitlement as opposed to a contingent right or a mere expectation of compensation based on employer practices. Consider the common practice of providing "bonuses" to employees who meet certain performance targets or develop business for the employer. Where a bonus system gives the employer discretion in determining whether to compensate and how much, courts generally treat the bonuses as gratuities. *See, e.g., Jensen v. International Business Machines Corp.*, 454 F.3d 382, 388 (4th Cir. 2006); *Arby's, Inc. v. Cooper,* 454 S.E.2d 488 (Ga. 1995); *Namad v. Salomon Inc.*, 537 N.Y.S.2d 807 (N.Y. App. Div. 1989). However, the distinction between contractual and discretionary compensation is a fine one, as the next case demonstrates

≡≡≡ ### *Uphoff v. Wachovia Securities*
≡≡≡ *30 IER Cases 138 (S.D. Fla. 2009)*

MARRA, District Judge.

This cause is before the Court upon Defendants' Motion to Dismiss Plaintiff's Complaint. . . .

According to the allegations of the Complaint, Defendants [Wachovia Securities, Wachovia Securities Financial Network, and Wells Fargo] breached an oral promise to pay retention bonuses to their approximately 14,600 financial advisors and brokers in order to retain their services and client base in the wake of a October 2008 announcement by Wachovia Securities, LLC and Wachovia Securities Financial Network, LLC that they would be purchased by Wells Fargo & Company. It is a standard practice in the brokerage/securities business to pay retention bonuses to current brokers and financial advisors when institutional sales and mergers are announced in order to reduce the attrition of established brokers and financial advisors who would otherwise be lured by bonus and compensation promises of competitors. . . .

In October 2008, [the Wachovia Defendants, using their employee telephonic communication system, communicated] to all their brokers and financial advisors the following: (a) "it was probable that the Wachovia securities business would be sold to Wells Fargo & Company as part of Wells Fargo's overall purchase of Wachovia Corporation; (b) each and every broker and financial advisor who stayed with the Wachovia entities after the sale would receive a meaningful 'retention bonus' and (c) this retention bonus would be paid to the brokers and financial advisors in January 2009."

Retention bonuses are generally calculated as a percentage of the individual broker/financial advisor's previous twelve months of earned commissions and fees from clients. These percentages range from a high of 100% or more, for an institution's "top producers," down to approximately 50%, of the earned commissions and fees for the previous twelve month period. Specifically, Plaintiff and the class of brokers/financial advisors each anticipated a minimum of $100,000.00 retention bonus based on industry practice and norms. At the time of the promise [of] the retention bonus in October 2008, these brokers/financial advisors were worth significantly more to competitors because of the state of the financial markets in October 2008 as compared to the date of the filing of the Complaint. In the Fall of 2008, Plaintiff and the class of brokers/financial advisors were approached by competitors who sought to employ them in order to obtain access to Wachovia's client base. Plaintiff, and those similarly situated, chose to rely on Defendants' promise to pay retention bonuses and remained within the Wachovia entities and forewent lucrative potential bonuses from competitors.

In January 2009, the retention bonuses were not paid, however, the Wachovia Defendants promised the brokers/financial advisors that they retention bonuses would be paid in the near future. On February 20, 2009, the Wachovia Defendants announced . . . that no retention bonuses would be paid to any of their brokers/financial advisors. . . .

Defendants move to dismiss and argue that Plaintiff has failed to allege the existence of a valid contract [or] state a claim for promissory estoppel or unjust enrichment. . . .

When considering a motion to dismiss, the Court must accept all of the plaintiff's allegations as true. . . .

A. Breach of Contract Claim

The United States Court of Appeals for the Eleventh Circuit recently discussed the requirements of Florida law with respect to prevailing on a breach of contract claim. In *Vega v. T-Mobile USA, Inc.*, the Court stated:

> For a breach of contract claim, Florida law requires the plaintiff to plead and establish: (1) the existence of a contract; (2) a material breach of that contract; and (3) damages resulting from the breach To prove the existence of a contract, a plaintiff must plead: (1) offer; (2) acceptance; (3) consideration; and (4) sufficient specification of the essential terms.

564 F.3d 1256, 1272 (11th Cir. 2009). Furthermore, to state a cause of action for breach of an oral contract, a plaintiff must allege that the "parties mutually assented to 'a certain and definite proposition' and left no essential terms open." An example of an essential term is price, or in this case, the amount of the bonus for which Plaintiff has brought suit.

Here, the Complaint does not allege a definite amount that Plaintiff, or the other financial advisors, were owed. Instead, Plaintiff merely alleges that [the Wachovia Defendants] promised them a "meaningful 'retention bonus.'" Significantly, the Complaint does not provide a specifically agreed upon amount nor does it provide a method for calculating an amount of the bonus. Instead, the Complaint states that Plaintiff and the class anticipated a minimum of $100,000.00 "based on industry practice and norms." Custom in a particular industry, however, cannot change the requirement of contract law that the parties mutually agree on the essential term of price. . . .

In response, Plaintiff points to *Community Design Corp. v. Antonell*, 459 So.2d 343 (Fla. Dist.Ct. App. 1984). There, the plaintiff sued the defendant corporation for failing to pay him his bonus or paid vacation. The defendant argued that the contract was too indefinite based on, among other factors, the uncertainty regarding the amount of the bonus. The court found that "[w]hile the exact amount of the bonus and the degree of completion required were disputed, there was sufficient evidence for the jury to find an oral contract between the parties." The court did, however, note that "the parties acknowledged [with respect to the amount of the bonus] that a particular amount was offered, which distinguishes this case from those in which the amount is indefinite or left for future agreement." In fact, the court stated that the amount of the bonus was between $20,000 and $35,000. The

Court notes that the facts of *Antonell* differ significantly from the facts of the instant case. Most significantly, the Complaint does not allege that the parties arrived at an exact amount for the retention bonus. In *Antonell*, there is no dispute that a particular sum was reached by the parties. For that reason, it appears that *Antonell* court minimized the disputed issue of fact regarding the $15,000 disparity in the amount of the bonus. . . .

For the foregoing reasons, the Court finds that the breach of contract must be dismissed.

B. Promissory Estoppel Claim

To state a cause of action for promissory estoppel, it is necessary to show that (1) a plaintiff detrimentally relied on a promise made by a defendant, 2) that a defendant reasonably should have expected the promise to induce reliance in the form of action or forbearance on the part of a plaintiff or a third person, and 3) that injustice can be avoided only by enforcement of the promise against a defendant. "[P]romissory estoppel does not turn on mutual assent to be bound in the same way as a contract claim. Rather, the essence of promissory estoppel is detrimental reliance." Significantly, "[t]he doctrine of promissory estoppel comes into play where the requisites of contract are not met, yet the promise should be enforced to avoid injustice."

Here, the Wachovia Defendants promised Plaintiff and the class members retention bonuses in exchange for Plaintiff remaining with Wachovia and rejecting offers to move to competitors. Defendants promised to pay these bonuses in January of 2009. In the end, Plaintiff was left with no retention bonus. Furthermore, Plaintiff and the class members rejected employment offers from competitors.

In moving to dismiss, Defendants argue that Plaintiff has failed to allege a definite promise sufficient to state a claim for promissory estoppel. In support, Defendants rely upon *W.R. Grace* [*v. Geodata Services, Inc.*, 547 So.2d 919, 924 (Fla.1989)]. In that case, a plaintiff's contractor claimed that after the execution of a written contract of mining work, the defendant's employees advised the plaintiff that they would provide the plaintiff additional work beyond the time frame set forth in the contract if the plaintiff would purchase additional equipment. For example, a statement was made to the president of the plaintiff's company who was told that "they *thought* I would be down in Manatee area *probably* three to five years drilling options." (emphasis in original). Here, the statement made was significantly more clear with respect to time, term and reasonableness than the statements made in *W.R. Grace*. For example, Plaintiff was promised a bonus in January as long as he stayed with the company after the sale of Wachovia to Wells Fargo.

Defendants also argue that it was not reasonable for Plaintiff to rely upon the promise of a bonus in foregoing a competitor's offer. The question of whether Plaintiff's reliance was reasonable is a factual issue that cannot be resolved at the motion to dismiss stage.

Lastly, the Court finds that the Complaint adequately alleges injustice. The Complaint alleges that the Wachovia Defendants should have reasonably expected that the promise of the retention bonuses would induce Plaintiff and the class members into remaining with the Wachovia entities and that Plaintiff and the class members relied on that promised to their detriment and suffered the injustice of not receiving the retention bonus.

Accordingly, Defendant's motion to dismiss the promissory estoppel claim is denied.

NOTES

1. *Promissory Estoppel and Incentive Pay.* Why did the court reject the brokers' contract claim but permit their promissory estoppel claim to proceed? Is the court implicitly applying a lower standard to the promissory estoppel claim? Consider the elements that the brokers will need to prove at trial. How will the need to proceed under promissory estoppel affect the brokers' likelihood of success and the remedy they can obtain?

2. *Contract Claims and Employer Discretion.* In contrast to *Uphoff,* consider *Guggenheimer v. Bernstein Litowitz & Grossman, L.L.P.,* 810 N.Y.S.2d 880 (Sup. Ct. 2006), in which the plaintiff was an associate at a law firm specializing in class action litigation. She was told upon hire that she would be eligible for bonuses for bringing successful cases to the firm. There was no written bonus policy, but it was commonly understood that the associate could receive up to 10 percent of the legal fees awarded to the firm.

The plaintiff subsequently brought in and developed several high-profile cases. While they were pending, she wrote a memo to a supervising partner detailing her work and was orally assured that she would receive her bonus. The partner later circulated an e-mail message, titled "Special Bonuses for Business Referrals," stating that fees awarded to associates would be capped at $250,000. Following this message, the partner e-mailed Guggenheimer that the cap would not apply to cases referred to the firm prior to the institution of the new policy.

Ultimately the firm received fees of $1.35 million and $900,000 in two of her cases. The firm offered the plaintiff a bonus of $25,000 for each case and determined that she did not qualify for a bonus on other matters she had initiated. In her subsequent suit, the firm argued that it retained discretion not to award bonus compensation. The court denied its motion to dismiss:

> Whether unpaid "incentive compensation" under a defendant's bonus plan constitutes a discretionary "bonus" or "earned wages" not subject to forfeiture, is an issue of fact. Thus, employees . . . may enforce an agreement to pay an annual bonus made at the onset of the employment relationship, where such bonus constitutes "an integral part of plaintiff's compensation package." . . .
>
> Defendant's assertion that the law firm's policy made payment of a bonus totally discretionary, contradicts plaintiff's conflicting contention that the company entered into an explicit oral employment agreement, reaffirmed by the statements of two of its partners that plaintiff was assured of receiving a bonus as part of her compensation. Thus, although the bonus plan, as conceived by the firm, may have been discretionary, there is a question of fact as to whether there was an oral contract agreeing to exercise that discretion in plaintiff's favor. . . .
>
> The fact that the precise amount of the bonus to be awarded was not specified does not make the contract unenforceable. Employment contracts that contain open additional compensation clauses are nonetheless binding contracts. . . . A determination of whether there exist sufficiently definite guidelines to enable a court to supply a bonus figure is a factual issue and survives a motion to dismiss. . . .

Id. at 885-86. Was the bonus policy in *Guggenheimer* more or less discretionary than the policy in *Uphoff*? What was the source of the alleged contract in *Guggenheimer*? The statements made to the plaintiff upon hire? The firm's past practices? The e-mails the plaintiff exchanged with a partner? All of the above? Neither the firm in *Guggenheimer* nor Wachovia had a written bonus policy. Why? Would reducing the policy to writing necessarily have curtailed the employer's discretion? Can you think of ways of drafting a written policy on behalf of an employer that would have reduced the risk of liability? *See, e.g., Moore v. Illinois Bell Tel. Co.*, 508 N.E.2d 519, 521 (Ill. App. Ct. 1987) (account executives had no contractual right to compensation under written "Incentive Plan" on which they had relied in setting performance goals where document stated it was not a contract and could be modified by employer at any time).

3. *How Much?* A plaintiff's entitlement to incentive pay and the amount owed by the employer are two different issues. Once a court determines that a contractual right exists, it must figure out how to translate that right into dollars. How will the court determine what to award should Guggenheimer prevail? What about in *Uphoff* where the employer promised a "meaningful" bonus? The difficulty of fixing an amount under the *Uphoff* facts may explain in part the court's rejection of the brokers' contract claim. One advantage of promissory estoppel under these facts is that it sidesteps the problem of quantifying the bonus, giving the plaintiff her reliance interest rather than her expectation interest. However, proving reliance might require the *Uphoff* plaintiffs to demonstrate that they would have accepted offers of employment from other firms but for their reliance on the undefined retention bonus. It might also require a court to demonstrate how much better off the plaintiffs would have been if they had left and for how long. Thus, promissory estoppel might simply replace one set of difficult questions with another.

For the same reasons, it is somewhat surprising that the court permitted the case to go forward as a class action. Presumably a court could determine on a classwide basis whether the bonus announcement constituted a sufficiently definite promise to justify reliance. All of the plaintiffs received the same voice mail message. However, the remaining questions—whether the plaintiffs relied on the announcement, how much they would have received had their bonuses been paid, and how much they lost by foregoing other opportunities—all seem to depend on the particular circumstances of each individual.

4. *Bonuses and Public Outrage.* Because the case addresses a motion to dismiss, the only facts recounted in *Uphoff* are those alleged in the plaintiffs' complaint. The opinion does not explain why Wachovia retracted the bonuses, but recent history tells us: The decision came in the midst of the economic crisis of 2008 and shortly after billions of dollars in federal bailout funds were handed over to private financial firms through the Troubled Asset Relief Program (TARP). Public controversy over the federal bailout program grew to a fever pitch in 2009 when several TARP recipients announced millions of dollars in bonuses to employees. Wells Fargo, which bought Wachovia, was a TARP fund recipient. Noting that "the world [had] changed," a Wachovia spokesperson described the decision to forgo bonuses as a response to the public's attitude toward pay in the industry. *See* Tomoeh Murakami Tse, *Wall Street Defends Broker Pay Packages*, WASH. POST, Feb. 28, 2009. How do these additional facts influence your view of which party is in the "right" in *Uphoff*? To what extent will such facts be relevant in the legal analysis of the *Uphoff* claims?

In contrast to Wachovia, insurance giant AIG, which received $170 billion in bailout funds, went forward with paying $165 million in promised bonuses one month after Wachovia's decision to forego them. The company was skewered by Congress and the media for the payments. *See* Liam Pleven et al., *AIG Faces Growing Wrath Over Payouts,* WALL ST. J., March 19, 2009, at A1. AIG defended its decision to pay out, stating that their lawyers had concluded that the bonuses were " 'legal, binding obligations' " of the company. *See id.* Examine the text of the AIG bonus program *available at* http://www.scribd.com/doc/13395005/AIGs-Employee -Retention-Plan. It is certainly more detailed than the promise in *Uphoff*. If it was legally binding, might AIG have invoked any standard contract defenses to abrogate the agreement? *See* Lawrence Cunningham, *A.I.G.'s Bonus Blackmail,* N.Y. TIMES, March 18, 2009, at 27. Raising them might at least have helped AIG's public image.

   5. *The Purpose of Retention Pay.* The "bonuses" at issue in *Uphoff* were designed to encourage workers to remain with Wachovia during its sale to Wells Fargo. This type of "retention" payment differs from performance-based bonuses like that in *Guggenheimer,* which was tied to the associates' success in generating firm business. The 2009 AIG payments were also retention bonuses designed to retain key workers during the economic crisis and the winding down of AIG's financial products division. Confusion between the two doubtlessly fueled public outrage over the payments. AIG's credit default swap strategy generated over $40 billion in losses in 2008 and was widely viewed as one of the perpetrators of the subsequent economic collapse. Thus, many saw the payments as a taxpayer-funded reward to the very company whose risk-taking had thrust the country into crisis. AIG, on the other hand, painted a picture of dedicated employees struggling to clean up the mess left behind by a few bad actors. Even so, some questioned whether the payments were necessary; given the massive blow to Wall Street, there were probably very few opportunities for reemployment to be found by even the best workers. Whichever view you find more persuasive, consider the position of the AIG employees who had been promised the pay. Some of them received death threats upon the announcement of the bonuses; some voluntarily paid their bonuses back. *See* Randall Smith, *Some Will Pay Back AIG Bonuses,* WALL ST. J., March 19, 2009, at A1.

   6. *Reforming Executive Pay.* Calls to end outlandish pay for corporate executives are nothing new, but the recession of 2008 heightened interest in reform. Whereas past calls had focused on the need to protect shareholders, the events of 2008 and 2009 exposed how poorly structured compensation could incent unduly risky behavior with detrimental consequences to the economy as a whole. As a condition of receiving federal bailout funds, firms were obligated to comply with Treasury Department "guidelines" that set limits on executive compensation. The guidelines capped base salaries for top earners at $500,000 annually and severance at one year's compensation. *See* http://www.ustreas.gov/press/releases/tg15.htm. They also prohibited the vesting of awards of restricted stock prior to the repayment of government funds. *See id.* The guidelines, however, do not directly address bonuses, the source of much of the debate over executive compensation. Even so, the threat of oversight proved a strong incentive for companies, several of whom sought to pay back TARP funds early to avoid any pay restrictions. *See* Eric Dash, *10 Large Banks Allowed to Exit U.S. Aid Program,* N.Y. TIMES, June 10, 2009, at A1. Subsequently, Congress imposed executive pay requirements on all publicly traded companies in its financial overhaul legislation, the Dodd-Frank Wall Street Reform and Consumer Protection Act of 2010. While the law does not put any substantive limits on the amounts companies may pay, it requires that pay packages, including "golden parachute" compensation, be put to a shareholder vote, and that executive compensation committee members, as well as their advisors, be independent decision makers. *See* 15 U.S.C.A. §§ 78n-1, 78j-3 (2010). In addition, the law creates new disclosure rules and requires companies to develop a mechanism for recovering erroneously awarded compensation. *See* 15 U.S.C.A. § 78j-4 (2010); 17 C.F.R. 229.402 (2010).

2. Compensation and Contract Ambiguity

Both *Uhoff* and *Guggenheimer* dealt with whether the employer's bonus promise was sufficiently definite to constitute an enforceable contract. Assuming sufficient definiteness such that the employee has a contractual right to a bonus, there may still be questions about how much is actually owed. As with any contract, the answer turns on the language of the policy or individual contract in question, and when that language is unclear, disputes arise.

One common type of dispute concerns the application of the particular formula used to calculate the worker's pay. Such formulas can be very sophisticated and often draw on various indicators of the company's and the worker's performance, all of which change over time. In such situations, parties may disagree over the base amount from which the bonus is determined, the percentage or other mechanism by which the bonus is calculated, the period over which the calculation is made, or any combination of the above. *See, e.g., Bukuras v. Mueller Group*, 592 F.3d 255 (1st Cir. 2010) (policy granting employee upon separation 150 percent of "the bonus" paid the prior fiscal year referred only to bonuses based on annual bonus pool and employer properly excluded one-time "transaction bonus" in calculating award).

A second type of dispute concerns the effect of termination on the award of deferred compensation. Certain types of bonus payments, such as the retention bonuses at issue in *Uphoff*, are specifically premised on the worker remaining with the company. Similarly, courts generally assume that an employee who voluntarily terminates employment forfeits any unpaid annual or holiday bonuses, such as those awarded at the end of the year based on company profits. *See, e.g., Pick v. Norfolk Anesthesia*, 755 N.W.2d 382, 387-88 (Neb. 2008) (distinguishing between retention bonuses and those designed to improve productivity in holding that nurses who left employment prior to the end of December were not entitled to profit-based bonus awarded annually at firm holiday party). A different issue presents, however, where the termination is involuntary and the forfeited pay includes commissions or other compensation that in some sense has been, earned. In that situation, an employee stands to lose pay for which he or she has already performed as the next case indicates.

≡≡≡ *Arbeeny v. Kennedy Exec. Search, Inc.*
893 N.Y.S.2d 39 (App. Div. 2010)

Acosta, J.

On or about January 5, 2006, plaintiff and defendant Kennedy Executive Search (KES), an executive recruitment firm, entered into an agreement whereby KES employed plaintiff as a senior executive search consultant. The agreement, drafted by KES's lawyers and governed by New York law, states that employment may be terminated by plaintiff or KES at any time, with or without cause or prior notice.

The agreement set plaintiff's salary at $125,000 per year and provided that "[s]uch salary shall be reviewed by Management from time to time, and any adjustment to such Salary shall be in the sole discretion of Management." In addition to salary, section 5.1 of the agreement provided that plaintiff was eligible "to earn commission compensation in respect of placements *arranged by* Employee on behalf of KES" as set out in article 5 (emphasis added). Section 5.2 of the agreement set forth a formula by which commissions were to be calculated. Sections 5.3 and 5.7 provided that the commission amount would be paid to plaintiff in the calendar month following the month in which payment in full of the net fee income was received by KES from the client, provided KES had recovered plaintiff's salary and other costs. Section 5.6 (a), the portion at issue in this case, provides that "[n]o commission shall be due" in the event plaintiff "is not in the employ of KES at the date the commission payment would otherwise be made."

KES unilaterally reduced plaintiff's salary to $100,000 a year in October 2006, and terminated him on March 28, 2007 because he refused to accept KES's demand that he accept a reduction in his commissions. According to KES, it received a fee in March for a placement plaintiff had handled. Pursuant to section 5.3, payment to plaintiff would have been due in April if plaintiff were still employed. To avoid unnecessary disputes, however, KES paid plaintiff $35,000 "without prejudice." KES received other fees originated by plaintiff after March 2007, but no further commissions were paid to plaintiff.

In April 2007, plaintiff brought the instant action against KES. . . . He alleged that he was owed $12,500 in unpaid salary for six months, $223,970 in unpaid commissions, and another unspecified amount for placements that he was working on when he was terminated. . . .

[KES moved to dismiss.] In granting the motion, the court noted that "the employment agreement expressly deprives plaintiff of post-termination commissions," and there was "no allegation that [KES] failed to pay to [plaintiff] commissions for placements he finalized and for which fees were received prior to his termination." . . .

Plaintiff's claim for $12,500 in unpaid salary for the reduction in pay from $125,000 to $100,000 is unavailing inasmuch as the agreement clearly stated that "any adjustment to such Salary shall be in the sole discretion of Management."

Plaintiff, however, has sufficiently stated a breach of contract claim for unpaid earned commissions that he "arranged" prior to his termination. Although generally an at-will employee is not entitled to post-termination commissions, the parties are certainly free to provide otherwise in a written agreement. For example, in *Yudell v Israel & Assoc.* (248 AD2d 189 [1998]), the employee earned commissions based on a percentage of all fees actually received that were "originated by" her. She brought an action to recover commissions for her role in securing two placements that were completed post-termination. The employer contended that as a matter of law, the employee could not recover commissions for placements that were finalized after she left. In denying summary judgment, this Court held that the words "placements . . . originated by you" did not alone specify when or how the placement must be completed in order to entitle the employee to a commission. Had the employer meant to foreclose the possibility of the employee earning a post-termination commission on a placement unquestionably originated by her, it could have said so explicitly, such as "placements . . . originated and completed by you" or "placements . . . originated by you which occur during your employment here." . . .

Here, as in *Yudell*, plaintiff seeks commissions for placements "arranged" by him during his tenure at KES. Had KES "meant to foreclose the possibility that plaintiff might earn a post-termination commission on a placement" arranged by plaintiff, it "could have said so explicitly." Under the doctrine of contra proferentem, an employment agreement should be construed against the drafter. Instead, section 5.1 states simply that plaintiff was entitled to commissions arranged by him. Sections 5.2, 5.3 and 5.7 merely provide the formula for determining the amount of the commission and the date when it vests, as well as the month when payment was to be made. They do not, however, otherwise modify the term arranged set forth in section 5.1. Being employed, after plaintiff fully performed by arranging a placement, has no bearing on the various calculations specified in sections 5.2 and 5.7.

Section 5.6 (a), which states that "[n]o commission shall be *due*" in the event plaintiff "is not in the employ of KES at the date the commission payment would otherwise be made," is thus enforceable only to the extent it seeks to foreclose the right to prospective commissions for the indefinite future. . . . Indeed, the provision does not explicitly express an intent that earned commissions will be retroactively lost upon termination. Rather, the employment agreement provides for an increase in the commission percentage based on annual revenue targets. It also provides that the first year's commissions, i.e. 2006, were based specifically on that year's numbers, and subsequent commissions would be based on the "Employee's salary for the then current calendar year" (section 5.7). Finally, the agreement provides, in section 5.2, that in calculating commissions based on revenues, "there will be no carry-over to the next calendar year or look-back to the preceding year in determining commissions earned." These references support an interpretation that section 5.6 was intended not to cut off retroactive commissions earned during a calendar year, but rather to prevent prospective commissions in later years. Enforcing it in the manner argued by defendants would deprive plaintiff of earned commissions, and thus would be inconsistent with section 5.1 of the agreement as well as the public policy against forfeiting commissions.

> Aside from the wording of the contract, inasmuch as an employee is entitled to the fruits of his or her labor, the at-will doctrine should not preclude plaintiff from raising a breach of contract claim for earned commissions. The implied covenant of good faith does not give rise to a contract action for the wrongful discharge of an at-will employee (*Murphy v American Home Prods. Corp.*, 58 N.Y.2d 293, 304-05 [1983]). While an at-will employee cannot recover for termination per se, an employee's "contract for payment of commissions creates rights distinct from the employment relation, and . . . obligations derived from the covenant of good faith implicit in the commission contract may survive the termination of the employment relationship. A covenant of good faith should not be implied as a modification of an employer's right to terminate an at-will employee because even a whimsical termination does not deprive the employee of benefits expected in return for the employee's performance. This is so because performance and the distribution of benefits occur simultaneously, and neither party is left high and dry by the termination. Where, however, a covenant of good faith is necessary to enable one party to receive the benefits promised for performance, it is implied by the law as necessary to effectuate the intent of the parties."

Wakefield v. Northern Telecom, Inc., 769 F.2d 109, 112 ([2d Cir.] 1985).

Although an at-will employee such as plaintiff would not be able to sue for wrongful termination of the contract, he should nonetheless be able to state a claim that the employer's termination action was specifically designed to cut off commissions that were coming due to the employee. A contract "cannot be read to enable the defendant to terminate an employee for the purpose of avoiding the payment of commissions which are otherwise owed. Such an interpretation would make the performance by one party the cause of the other party's non-performance." *Wakefield*. . . .

NOTES

1. *Ambiguous Language?* Section 4.6(a) of Arbeeny's contract stated that "no commission shall be due" if the plaintiff "is not in the employ of KES at the date the commission payment would otherwise be made." Doesn't this language clearly preclude Arbeeny's claim? Yet the court concludes that this language refers only to prospective commissions, as opposed to those earned but unpaid. How would you respond to this decision if you were a management lawyer? Can you redraft the employment agreement in a way that better reflects the defendant's intent? What is defendant's intent, anyway? Suppose the contract language clearly stated, as the defendant contends, that its policy was to withhold commissions earned prior to termination. Would a $120,000 employee like Arbeeny have accepted such a term? Do the circumstances surrounding Arbeeny's separation from the firm help you answer these questions?

2. *The Duty of Good Faith, Take Two.* Was it necessary for the court to construe the contract language as it did in finding for Arbeeny? In the final two paragraphs, the court suggests that an employee is entitled to receive the fruits of his labor, including payment of earned commissions, under the implied duty of good faith. Recall the discussion of the implied duty in *Guz v. Bechtel* in Chapter 2. There the court rejected the employee's claim that by terminating him unfairly the employer breached the duty of good faith, concluding that such an interpretation ran counter to employment at will, which specifically allows arbitrary and unfair terminations. However, plaintiffs have often been successful in using the implied duty to challenge refusals to pay earned wages or benefits as opposed to challenging the termination itself. A classic example is *Fortune v. National Cash Register*, 364 N.E.2d 1251 (Mass. 1977). The employer's policy provided that employees would receive commissions on sales in their territories in two stages: a portion upon placement of the customer's order and a portion on delivery and installation provided the territory was assigned to the employee as of that date. Fortune was terminated a few days after closing on a record-breaking sale and prior to delivery on that order. He consequently received only the first installment of the commission. On his suit for the remainder, the Supreme Court of Massachusetts held that, while there was no breach under the express terms of the contract, it was reasonable for the jury to find bad faith in breach of the implied duty. It explained:

> Fortune argues that, in spite of the literal wording of the contract, he is entitled to a jury determination on NCR's motives in terminating his services under the contract and in finally discharging him. We agree. . . .
>
> We do not question the general principles that an employer is entitled to be motivated by and to serve its own legitimate business interests; that an employer must have

wide latitude in deciding whom it will employ in the face of the uncertainties of the business world. . . . However, we believe that where, as here, commissions are to be paid for work performed by the employee, the employer's decision to terminate its at will employee should be made in good faith. . . .

In so holding we are merely recognizing the general requirement in this Commonwealth that parties to contracts and commercial transactions must act in good faith toward one another. Good faith and fair dealing between parties are pervasive requirements in our law; it can be said fairly, that parties to contracts or commercial transactions are bound by this standard.

. . . Where the principal seeks to deprive the agent of all compensation by terminating the contractual relationship when the agent is on the brink of successfully completing the sale, the principal has acted in bad faith and the ensuing transaction between the principal and the buyer is to be regarded as having been accomplished by the agent. The same result obtains where the principal attempts to deprive the agent of any portion of a commission due the agent. . . .

NCR argues that there was no evidence of bad faith in this case; therefore, the trial judge was required to direct a verdict in any event. We think that the evidence and the reasonable inferences to be drawn there from support a jury verdict that the termination of Fortune's twenty-five years of employment as a salesman with NCR the next business day after NCR obtained a $5,000,000 order from First National was motivated by a desire to pay Fortune as little of the bonus credit as it could.

Id. at 1256-58. Is this result (and the dicta in *Arbeeny*) consistent with the court's rejection of the implied duty claim in *Guz*? How do these decisions affect how you would draft a commissions policy if you were representing an employer?

3. *Proving Bad Faith.* Suppose the court rejected Arbeeny's contract interpretation theory and his ability to recover his bonus rested on his good faith claim. Would he have succeeded? According to the court, an employee states a claim where "the employer's termination action was specifically designed to cut off commissions that were coming due to the employee." How does a plaintiff convince the factfinder that his or her employer had the requisite negative intent? Not surprisingly, employers are unlikely to admit to such intent, and the employee often must rely on circumstantial evidence, such as the timing of the termination relative to the anticipated payment and the length and history of the employment relationship. *See Maddaloni v. Western Mass. Bus Lines, Inc.*, 438 N.E.2d 351, 354-55 (Mass. 1982). At least one case has seemingly loosened the intent requirement, finding it sufficient that a termination without cause deprived an employee of anticipated commissions. In *Gram v. Liberty Mutual Insurance Co.*, 429 N.E.2d 21 (Mass. 1981), an insurance salesman, who was the most productive seller in his office, was terminated after a disagreement over a letter sent to clients. As a result, he lost out on potential commissions from policy renewals. The court determined that the termination was without cause, but that the evidence did not support a finding that the employer had considered Gram's accrual of commissions in making its decision. In nonetheless allowed Gram's claim of breach of an implied duty of good faith, explaining:

> The question . . . is whether we should allow recovery for breach of a contract of employment at will where an employee is discharged without cause by an employer who had no improper motive for discharging the employee, unless one regards the absence of good cause itself or the mistaken belief that there is good cause as conclusively demonstrative of bad faith. . . . We decline at this time to adopt a general rule that the discharge of an

at-will employee without cause is alone a violation of an employer's obligation of good faith and fair dealing. We are aware of no case that has gone this far. . . .

There is in this case, however, an element of Gram's compensation that requires special consideration. Although there is no evidence warranting an inference that Liberty discharged Gram for the purpose of appropriating his renewal commissions, the fact remains that Gram lost reasonably ascertainable future compensation based on his past services. Gram had a reasonable expectancy of some renewal commissions. . . . We think that the obligation of good faith and fair dealing imposed on an employer requires that the employer be liable for the loss of compensation that is so clearly related to an employee's past service, when the employee is discharged without good cause.

Id. at 28-29. Does the court do a convincing job of balancing an expanded good faith claim with the principle of employment at will? The dissent accused the court of "restructur[ing] an at-will employment agreement to reflect an imposed condition never heretofore recognized by this court and one of doubtful legitimacy." *Id.* at 30.

4. *Vested Benefits versus Anticipated Earnings Under the Implied Duty of Good Faith.* In both *Arbeeny* and *Fortune*, the parties limited their damages claim to the value of the lost commissions and salary that had vested or accrued prior to termination. In some cases, the tie between the employee's past performance and the benefits sought is less certain. In *Gram*, described above, the court permitted the plaintiff to seek recovery for commissions that would have accrued upon renewal of policies he serviced. *Gram*, 429 N.E.2d at 29. The dissent called this "ordering the trier of fact to engage in extravagant speculation." *Id.* at 30; *see also Coll v. PB Diagnostic Sys. Inc.*, 50 F.3d 1115, 1125 (1st Cir. 1995) (rejecting CEO's claim for loss of incentive payments as a result of termination due to corporate restructuring where at least two of the four specified performance goals on which payment contingent could not have been met). Although courts differ on the degree of certainty required to permit recovery for anticipated benefits under a good faith theory, it is generally agreed that plaintiffs cannot recover future wages, as would be available under breach of an implied or express contract for job security. Nor are punitive damages available, despite the cause of action's close relationship to tort. *See Foley v. Interactive Data Corp.*, 765 P.2d 373 (Cal. 1988). These restrictions place a critical limitation on the cause of action as a vehicle for challenging at-will terminations.

5. *Unjust Enrichment.* Courts sometimes explain the good faith claim in terms of redressing unjust enrichment. *See, e.g., Gram v. Liberty Mut. Ins. Co.*, 461 N.E.2d 796, 798 (Mass. 1984) ("*Gram II*") ("Our goal is and has been simply to deny . . . any readily definable, financial windfall resulting from the denial . . . of compensation for past services."). If an employer incentivizes successful performance through a bonus or commission plan, then terminates an employee before payments become due, the employer arguable reaps the benefit of its program without incurring the associated costs. Does this theory apply in *Arbeeny*? In contrast, consider what happened in *Fortune*, described above, where the commissions that the plaintiff had earned were paid to another sales person. If the employer does not gain a "windfall" from the termination, should that constitute a defense to a good faith claim?

6. *Wage Payment Laws.* In seeking to recover unpaid bonuses or commissions, plaintiffs sometimes bring claims under state wage payment laws. In an omitted part of the opinion, the *Arbeeny* court held that the plaintiff qualified for protection under a provision of New York law, which prohibits the willful failure to pay earned wages. However, the viability of such claims rests on the plaintiff's ability to show that the bonus is in fact an earned wage. As a result, such statutes serve principally to enhance damages for workers who can demonstrate the existence of a vested benefit and would consequently have succeeded under common law. *See, e.g.*, N.Y. Lab. Law § 198(1-a) (McKinney 2009) (providing for 25 percent penalty on wages wrongfully withheld and attorney's fees). They generally are unavailing for plaintiffs alleging entitlement to discretionary or non-performance-based bonuses, such as those based on retention or firm performance. *See, e.g., Ziotas v. Reardon Law Firm*, 997 A.2d 453 (Conn. 2010) (rejecting law firm associate's claim to double damages under Connecticut Wage Act where bonus was to be determined annually by board of directors based on assessment of multiple subjective factors including productivity, performance quality, and firm loyalty).

7. *Doing the Numbers.* So now that we know Arbeeny is entitled to his bonus, how much does he get? Read Section 5.2 of the agreement. Suppose that as a result of placements arranged by Arbeeny prior to his departure, the firm received $1.5 million in "Net Fee Income." Assume for simplicity that this amount is above the "annual threshold" referred to in the contract. How much should the court award?

PROBLEMS

3-4. Roseland Property Company, a real estate development firm, entered into an agreement with Carol Naderny to serve as the main developer in its new Boston office. The relevant parts of her contract provided:

4. Your title will be that of "Partner," although your relationship to Roseland, and your interests in projects, will be established and governed by the provisions of this agreement. . . .

8. You will be entitled to a participation interest in all new projects which originate out of Roseland's Boston office during the period of your employment. Your participation interest in each applicable project will be equal to 15 percent of the cash distributed to the Roseland Entity after the Roseland Entity has received cash distributions equal to the Roseland Entity's capital contributions plus an 8 percent return on such contributions for such project. Your interest in such new projects will vest at the same time that the Roseland Entity's interests vest. Your participation percentage is subject to review each year.

14. Roseland will have and retain sole ownership and control of all new business developed by you while at Roseland and all Roseland business will remain with Roseland following termination of our relationship for any reason.

15. The relationship between you and Roseland is and at all times will be strictly an "at will" relationship, and either you or Roseland may terminate your employment and this relationship at any time with or without cause, for any reason or no reason, and with or without notice.

Three years later, Roseland and Naderny amicably parted ways as a result of differences in their business philosophy. During her employment, Naderny had initiated four projects but none had closed or begun construction as of the date of her departure. As a result, Roseland did not pay her a "participation interest." One year later, however, Roseland succeeded in closing on one of Naderny's projects and received a sizeable sum. Naderny has since sent Roseland a demand letter requesting my "15 percent interest now that the project has vested."

(a) Suppose you represent Roseland. How would you respond to Naderny's letter?

(b) Suppose you had represented Roseland during the negotiation of Naderny's contract. How would you have drafted it to prevent future liabilities to terminated employees?

(c) Suppose you represented Naderny during the negotiation of her contract. How would you have drafted it to ensure that she received her cut on all projects she initiated?

(d) Returning to part (a), suppose that as a result of your efforts on behalf of Roseland, the parties reach a settlement, resolve their differences, and decide they want to work together again. In order to avoid any possible future disputes, they would like to enter into a revised contract that clarifies any points of ambiguity. Consider the competing versions of the contract you have created in response to parts (b) and (c). Can you think of ways in which the parties might compromise their positions to achieve an agreement? What would it look like in writing?

3-5. Don Broadbent was employed by Westport Inc. as a Senior Vice President in charge of operations. He was hired under a five-year written contract containing the following provisions related to termination:

Termination without cause. If the Executive is involuntarily terminated without cause, the Executive will receive severance equaling two years' salary and 25,000 shares of common stock.

Termination for cause. If the Executive is involuntarily terminated for cause, the Executive forfeits rights to further payment and all obligations of the Company under this contract will cease.

Termination following a change in control. If the Executive is involuntarily terminated within six months of a sale of substantially all of the Company's assets, or a merger in which the Company is not the surviving entity, the Executive will receive severance equal to one year's salary and 25,000 shares of the common stock of the purchasing or surviving entity.

Three years after hiring Broadbent, Westport experiences legitimate and sustained financial difficulties. It begins discussions with Motoport Co., a successful competitor, about the possibility of Motoport buying the company. In order to make itself more marketable, Westport undertakes a corporate restructuring and lays off a significant percentage of its workforce, including Broadbent, who is paid pursuant to the "termination without cause" provision of his contract. Five months later, Motoport purchases Westport, and Motoport's stock rises significantly as a result of the acquisition.

Broadbent subsequently reads about Motoport's purchase and stock rise in the newspaper. He pulls out a copy of his contract, does the math, and realizes that, due to the dramatic increase in stock price, he would have come out with a lot more money had he been terminated under the "change in control" provision of his contract despite the lesser amount of severance he would have received. Might he have a viable breach of contract claim?

Part Three

TORT-BASED PROTECTIONS FOR WORKERS

4

The Public Policy Exception to the At-Will Rule

When is the firing of an employee tortious under the common law? Prior to the 1970s, the conventional answer to this question would have been never. Actions taken *in connection with* a discharge could be tortious, even if the discharge itself were not. For example, an employee who was coercively interrogated in connection with employer investigation of a theft might have a cause of action for false imprisonment, or one who was publicly slandered in connection with his discharge could have sued in defamation. While such torts continue to constrain employer conduct, see Chapter 5, it was not until the late 1970s that some discharges themselves became tortious and employees were no longer limited to claims based on contract or statutory law.

Currently, many jurisdictions recognize the termination of an employee as actionable in tort in a number of circumstances. This new law encompasses several theories; some are expansive of older theories and others are true innovations. Perhaps the most developed approach is frequently denominated "the public policy exception" to the at-will rule. Often this is referred to as "wrongful discharge," although that term also embraces other theories. Although some courts have viewed the doctrine as partially contractual, the more widely held view is that discharging an employee for a reason that offends public policy constitutes a tort. It is this tort that will be the subject of section A of this chapter.

A natural outgrowth of the common-law public policy exception was legislation codifying protection for employees who engage in conduct required or permitted by public policy. Thus, a number of statutes provide protection that may be viewed as ancillary to the main thrust of the law itself. For example, Title VII of the Civil Rights Act of 1964 bars discrimination on account of race, sex, religion, and national origin, but also bars retaliation for employees who file charges of discrimination or otherwise oppose unlawful employment practices under the statute. See Chapter 9. As this example indicates, a wide range of federal and state laws have statute-specific provisions aimed at protecting employees from reprisal for engaging in particular activities. But increasingly there are also more general statutes, often described as "whistleblower" laws, which create protection for employees who engage in a wide, but not unlimited, range of activities furthering public policy. This topic is the subject of Section B.

A. THE COMMON-LAW PUBLIC POLICY EXCEPTION

The emergence of a public policy exception to the at-will rule has been one of the most important developments in employment law. Not only has it provided employees with an important new source of rights but it has also led employers to reconsider their entire approach to termination. While relatively few discharges may, in the final analysis, implicate public policy, employers are well advised to ensure that all terminations are reviewed carefully. Research shows that even public *allegations* of corporate financial misdeeds can have significant adverse effects on a firm. Robert M. Bowen, Andrew C. Call, & Shivaram Rajgopal, *Whistle-Blowing: Target Firm Characteristics and Economic Consequences*, 85 ACCOUNTING REV. 1239 (2010) (finding, inter alia, that "whistle-blowing announcements were associated with a negative 2.8% market-adjusted five day stock price reaction, and this reaction was especially negative for allegations involving earnings management (7.3%)").

The paradigm public policy case arises when an employee claims that she has been discharged for engaging in conduct that has been mandated, or at least encouraged, by some public policy not directly connected with employment. For example, an employee may claim that she has been fired because she testified truthfully before a legislative body or court. When such testimony adversely affects the employer, it is easy to see the motivation for discharge. Originally, the common law recognized no legal bar to discharging an at-will employee in these circumstances, however reprehensible it might seem and however perverse from a societal perspective. But courts have moved away from that position. An early case recognizing a cause of action in such circumstances was *Petermann v. International Brotherhood of Teamsters*, 344 P.2d 25 (Cal. App. 1959), which held that an employee had a cause of action when he was fired for refusing to perjure himself before the California legislature. This tort was at first very limited — *Petermann* stressed that the employee had been fired for refusing to commit a felonious act — but it gradually expanded. By 1975, for example, a court recognized that discharge of an employee for serving on a jury was actionable, even though at the time there was no state statute according protection against adverse employment actions on that ground. *See Nees v. Hocks*, 536 P.2d 512 (Or. 1975).

As cases accumulated where courts encountered actions by employers that tended to frustrate matters of public concern, the downside of pure private ordering became apparent. Whether it was appropriate to leave to an agreement of the employer and employee questions that affected them alone, a different set of considerations developed when the relationship between the two affected third parties — such as legislative investigation in *Petermann* or the availability of qualified jurors in *Nees*. Thus, there gradually developed what came to be called the wrongful discharge or public policy tort: Where public policy is sufficiently implicated, a discharge in contravention of that policy is actionable as a tort. Understanding this tort requires considering a number of related questions. The initial one — whether the courts (as opposed to the legislature) recognize such a cause of action — has been generally resolved in favor of court action although some jurisdictions have rejected the tort entirely. *See Murphy v. Am. Home Prods. Corp.*, 448 N.E.2d 86, 89 (N.Y. 1983) ("Plaintiff would have this court adopt this emerging view. We decline his invitation, being of the opinion that such a significant change in our law is best left to the Legislature.").

Others have applied the tort sparingly as a kind of gap filler where the state had announced a policy in a statute but did not legislate directly with respect to the employment setting. For example, some state legislation creating workers' compensation schemes failed to explicitly provide a cause of action for employees discharged for filing a claim. In such instances, it was common for states to vindicate the public policy underlying workers' compensation by protecting those who filed claims. *See, e.g., Freas v. Archer Servs., Inc.*, 716 A.2d 998 (D.C. 1998) (recognizing public policy tort for discharge for seeking unemployment compensation). The notion that the public policy tort is a kind of gap filler is further indicated by those courts that have refused to apply the tort when predicate legislation provides its own remedial scheme. For example, most courts have been unwilling to find a public policy tort based on sex discrimination. While there is obviously a strong public policy against such conduct, it is expressed in statutes that provide their own enforcement schemes, and these courts have held that there is therefore no need to recognize a separate tort. *See, e.g., Makovi v. Sherwin-Williams Co.*, 561 A.2d 179 (Md. 1989) (sex discrimination); *Sands Regent v. Valgardson*, 777 P.2d 898 (Nev. 1989) (age discrimination); *Cormier v. Littlefield*, 13 F. Supp. 2d 127 (D. Mass. 1998) (disability); *see also Baron v. Arizona*, 270 F. App'x 706 (9th Cir. 2008) (because the Arizona Civil Rights Act provided a remedy for sex discrimination, plaintiff could not sue under the state's whistleblower law). *But see Hill v. Ky. Lottery Corp.*, 2010 Ky. LEXIS 82 (Ky. Apr. 22, 2010) ("Because the statutes that declare the unlawful act of perjury are not the same statutes that declare and remedy civil rights violations, the Hills' claims under KRS Chapter 344 does not preempt the Hills' common law claims for wrongful discharge based on the public policy against perjured testimony."). *See generally* Jarod Spencer González, *State Anti-Discrimination Statutes and Implied Preemption of Common Law Torts: Valuing the Common Law*, 59 S. CAR. L. REV. 115 (2007).

Assuming that a court accepts the premise of the public policy tort, what should count as "public policy"? In its narrowest formulation, the tort might bar employers only from discharging employees for doing what the law requires or for not doing what the law forbids. For instance, in *Petermann*, a state statute required truthful testimony in response to a subpoena, and permitting an employer to discharge someone for providing such testimony would discourage this conduct. At the other extreme, the public policy tort could bar employers from terminating workers for activities that the judiciary views as "socially useful." For instance, education is generally viewed as a social good, but is it appropriate to bar employers from terminating someone for enrolling in law school? *See Scroghan v. Kraftco Corp.*, 551 S.W.2d 811 (Ky. App. 1977) (no). As might be expected, the cases are strung along this spectrum, with conflicting views of the scope of the tort competing for attention.

One recent attempt to bring coherence to the cases is the American Law Institute's ("ALI") proposed Restatement (Third) of Employment Law. Tentative Draft No. 2 (April 3, 2009) provides:

§ 4.02 Employer Discipline in Violation of Public Policy: Protected Activities

An employer is subject to liability in tort under § 4.01 for disciplining an employee who acting in an [sic] reasonable manner

(a) refuses to commit an act that the employee reasonably and in good faith believes violates a law or established principle of a code of professional conduct or an occupational code protective of the public interest;

(b) performs a public duty or obligation that the employee reasonably and in good faith believes is imposed by law;

(c) files a charge or claims a benefit in good faith under the procedures of an employment statute or law (irrespective of whether the charge or claim is meritorious);

(d) refuses to waive a nonnegotiable or nonwaivable right or agree to a condition of employment whose enforcement would violate public policy;

(e) reports or inquires about employer conduct that the employee reasonably and in good faith believes violates a law or an established principle of professional conduct or an occupational code protective of the public interest; or

(f) engages in other activity directly furthering a substantial public policy.

Although there have been serious critiques of this formulation, Restatement §4.02 was tentatively approved by the ALI membership. As you work through this chapter, consider whether this proposal is an accurate "restatement" of the law as it has evolved or as it should be formulated in the future.

But before you begin this study, note what is *not* protected by the public policy tort: an employee's conscientious performance of his duties to his employer. The seminal case for this proposition is *Foley v. Interactive Data Corp.*, 765 P.2d 373, 380 (Cal. 1988), where plaintiff claimed he had been discharged for reporting internally that a supervisor was being investigated for embezzlement from another company. The court rejected the public policy tort:

> Whether or not there is a statutory duty requiring an employee to report [to his own employer] information relevant to his employer's interest, we do not find a substantial public policy prohibiting an employer from discharging an employee for performing that duty. Past decisions recognizing a tort action for discharge in violation of public policy seek to protect the public, by protecting the employee who refuses to commit a crime . . . or who discloses other illegal, unethical, or unsafe practices. . . . No equivalent public interest bars the discharge of the present plaintiff. When the duty of an employee to disclose information to his employer serves only the private interest of the employer, the rationale underlying the [public policy] cause of action is not implicated.

Id. This limitation is consistent with the idea that a public policy must concern the public interest, not just a private matter between a worker and employer. In an extreme example of this, one court rejected a public policy claim when a female employee was fired because of an incident in which she was the victim of an assault and rape. *Green v. Bryant*, 887 F. Supp. 798 (E.D. Pa. 1995). *See also Lloyd v. Drake Univ.*, 686 N.W.2d 225 (Iowa 2004) (security guard had no claim even if he was fired for reasonably trying to save a female student from assault). As a commentator summarized, the public policy tort "may be limited to those situations where the public's health and safety are affected; it may not apply if only the internal affairs of the employer are involved." Clyde W. Summers, *Employment At Will in the United States: The Divine Right of Employers*, 3 U. PA. J. LAB. & EMP. L. 65, 74 (2000).

While some legal commentators and many would-be plaintiffs are not happy with the result, it reflects the law's line-drawing between private ordering and its limitations. The employer is free to structure its internal operations and reward (or punish) those who serve its private interests. When, however, actions taken against employees have effects on third parties, it is appropriate to constrain the employer's freedom of action.

Fitzgerald v. Salsbury Chemical, Inc.
613 N.W.2d 275 (Iowa 2000)

CADY, Justice.

Tom Fitzgerald was employed by Salsbury Chemical, Inc. at its production plant in Charles City. Salsbury manufactures chemicals and pharmaceutical bulk actives. Fitzgerald was employed as a production foreman at the plant.

Fitzgerald was terminated from his employment with Salsbury on September 19, 1995. The termination followed an incident on August 30, 1995, involving a production worker named Richard Koresh. Koresh failed to properly monitor the temperature and pressure of a tank used to mix a chemical compound. His conduct created a potentially dangerous condition.

Koresh was suspended from his employment on September 4, 1995, after Salsbury conducted a preliminary investigation into the incident. He was ultimately terminated on September 19, 1995, a few hours prior to the time Fitzgerald was terminated. Fitzgerald was responsible for supervising Koresh on the date of the incident.

Salsbury asserted Fitzgerald was terminated for failing to properly supervise Koresh and to prevent the potentially dangerous incident. Fitzgerald, however, believed he was discharged because he did not support Salsbury's decision to discharge Koresh and Salsbury officials feared he would provide testimony in support of Koresh in the course of threatened legal action by Koresh.

The events supporting this claim extend back to August 15, 1995, when Koresh gave deposition testimony in a wrongful discharge action against Salsbury by a former employee named John Kelly. Kelly was terminated several years earlier, one day prior to his scheduled deposition in a wrongful death action against Salsbury by the estate of a former employee. The former employee died after a chemical compound he was mixing at the plant overheated and exploded. Salsbury claimed Kelly was terminated because his unsafe conduct caused the explosion. Kelly claimed he was terminated by Salsbury in an effort to cover up its culpability in the incident. During the deposition on August 15, 1995, Koresh contradicted earlier deposition testimony by two Salsbury management officials concerning the internal investigation of the work practices of Kelly. Koresh also testified he believed Kelly was a safe operator. Following the deposition, Koresh felt shunned by Salsbury management. He was also told by a foreman the company was going to find a way to fire him. After Koresh was suspended on September 4, 1995, he told a Salsbury official that he had hired an attorney and was "not going to be another John Kelly."

Fitzgerald engaged in a conversation with the plant operations manager on September 19, 1995, a few hours prior to the time he was told of his termination. The manager asked Fitzgerald what discipline he believed should result to Koresh because of the incident on August 30. Fitzgerald responded he did not believe it was fair to fire Koresh over a single mistake. Fitzgerald also indicated he did not believe Koresh should be fired in light of his long years of service to the company. The manager then informed Fitzgerald he needed to begin to think like a foreman if he was going to be one, and he needed to find out which side he was on. Fitzgerald was also informed the matter may result in a lawsuit. Fitzgerald does not claim he responded to the statements.

Fitzgerald instituted this wrongful discharge action against Salsbury. He alleged his termination violated a public policy of this state to protect workers who oppose the unlawful termination of a co-worker. Additionally, he claimed he was terminated because he intended to provide testimony in Koresh's future wrongful termination lawsuit that would be unfavorable to Salsbury and the company wanted to discredit his potential testimony as a disgruntled former employee. Fitzgerald claims Salsbury's motivation to terminate him violated the public policy of this state to provide truthful testimony in court proceedings.

The trial court dismissed the action following a hearing on the motion for summary judgment. It found no public policy of this state was implicated by the two factual claims urged by Fitzgerald. Although the trial court found the criminal statutes against committing and suborning perjury established a public policy prohibiting such conduct, it found no facts to show the criminal statutes had been violated by Salsbury. . . .

III.   The Employer-Employee Relationship . . .

B.   *The Public Policy Exception*

We have identified the elements of an action to recover damages for discharge in violation of public policy to require the employee to establish (1) engagement in a protected activity; (2) discharge; and (3) a causal connection between the conduct and the discharge. *Teachout v. Forest City Community Sch. Dist.*, 584 N.W.2d 296 (Iowa 1998). These elements properly identify the tort of wrongful discharge when a protected activity has been recognized through the existence of an underlying public policy which is undermined when an employee is discharged from employment for engaging in the activity. However, when we have not previously identified a particular public policy to support an action, the employee must first identify a clear public policy which would be adversely impacted if dismissal resulted from the conduct engaged in by the employee.[2] *See Yockey v. State*, 540 N.W.2d 418 (Iowa 1995) (the public policy in favor of permitting employees to seek workers' compensation benefits not jeopardized by termination from employment for missing work following injury); *Borschel v. City of Perry*, 512 N.W.2d 565 (Iowa 1994) (no public policy in favor of presumption of innocence in work place to give rise to an action for wrongful discharge for conduct which resulted in criminal charges).

---

2. Some courts are beginning to articulate the elements of a cause of action for wrongful discharge as:

1. The existence of a clear public policy (the clarity element).
2. Dismissal of employee under circumstances alleged in the case would jeopardize public policy (the jeopardy element).
3. The plaintiff engaged in public policy conduct and this conduct was the reason for the dismissal (the causation element).
4. Employer lacked an overriding business justification for the dismissal (the absence of justification element).

Gardner v. Loomis Armored, Inc., 913 P.2d 377 (Wash. 1996); *Collins v. Rizkana*, 652 N.E.2d 653 (Ohio 1995).

This approach is derived from the methodology proposed by Dean and Law Professor Henry H. Perritt, Jr. *See generally* Henry H. Perritt, Jr., *The Future of Wrongful Dismissal Claims: Where Does Employer Self-Interest Lie?*, 58 U. Cin. L. Rev. 397 (1989). This four part structure of proof is now detailed in Professor Perrit's multi-volume treatise on the subject. EMPLOYEE DISMISSAL LAW AND PRACTICE [now in its 5th edition, 2006]. . . .

1. Determining Public Policy

In first recognizing the public policy exception to the at-will employment doctrine, we were careful to limit the tort action for wrongful discharge to cases involving only a well-recognized and clear public policy. This requirement has been incorporated in our subsequent cases. This important element sets the foundation for the tort and it is necessary to overcome the employer's interest in operating its business in the manner it sees fit. It also helps ensure that employers have notice that their dismissal decisions will give rise to liability.

In determining whether a clear, well-recognized public policy exists for purposes of a cause of action, we have primarily looked to our statutes but have also indicated our Constitution to be an additional source. We have not been asked to extend our sources of public policy beyond our statutes and Constitution, but recognize other states have used additional sources such as judicial decisions and administrative rules.

Some statutes articulate public policy by specifically prohibiting employers from discharging employees for engaging in certain conduct or other circumstances.[3] Yet, we do not limit the public policy exception to specific statutes which mandate protection for employees. *Teachout.* Instead, we look to other statutes which not only define clear public policy but imply a prohibition against termination from employment to avoid undermining that policy. *See Borschel.*

Our insistence on using only clear and well-recognized public policy to serve as the basis for the wrongful discharge tort emphasizes our continuing general adherence to the at-will employment doctrine and the need to carefully balance the competing interests of the employee, employer, and society. An employer's right to terminate an employee at any time only gives way under the wrongful discharge tort when the reason for the discharge offends clear public policy.

The need for clarity in public policy is similarly recognized in our reluctance to search too far beyond our legislative pronouncements and constitution to find public policy to support an action. Thus, we must proceed cautiously when asked to declare public policy to support an exception to the at-will doctrine, and only utilize those policies that are well recognized and clearly defined. Any effort to evaluate the public policy exception with generalized concepts of fairness and justice will result in an elimination of the at-will doctrine itself. Moreover, it could unwittingly transform the public policy exception into a "good faith and fair dealing" exception, a standard we have repeatedly rejected.

2. Determining Jeopardy to Public Policy

Once a clear public policy is identified, the employee must further show the dismissal for engaging in the conduct jeopardizes or undermines the public policy.

---

3. *See* Iowa Code §§ 29A.43 (2005) (absences for membership in military reserves protected); 49.109-.110 (absence for voting protected); 70A.2 (employee may take medical leave of absence upon recommendation of physician without retaliation); 70A.28 (no retaliation for whistleblower reporting of mismanagement of funds); 85.18 (workers' compensation rights protected); . . . (actions for wage and hour disputes are protected); 598.22 (employee cannot be terminated based upon child support withholdings) . . . 607A.45 (absence for jury duty is protected); 642.21 (garnishments for consumer credit transactions); 730.2-.4 (employee may not be blacklisted for terminating relationship, employer may not mislead former employee's potential employer with false statement, nor require successful polygraph test); 731.2 (employment may not be denied to employee based upon membership in labor union).

Thus, this element requires the employee to show the conduct engaged in not only furthered the public policy, but dismissal would have a chilling effect on the public policy by discouraging the conduct. In *Lara* [*v. Thomas*, 512 N.W.2d 777 (Iowa 1994)], we said

> Employers cannot be permitted to intimidate employees into foregoing the benefits to which they are entitled in order to keep their jobs. To hold otherwise in this context would create a chilling effect by permitting an employer to indirectly force an employee to give up certain statutory rights.

Thus, when the conduct of the employee furthers public policy or the threat of dismissal discourages the conduct, public policy is implicated. On the other hand, if a public policy exists, but is not jeopardized by the discharge, the cause of action must fail. *See Yockey, French* [*v. Foods, Inc.*, 495 N.W.2d 768 (Iowa 1993)] (public policy against suborning perjury not implicated if employer terminates the employee after using coercive and high-handed tactics to obtain confession). This element guarantees an employer's personnel management decisions will not be challenged unless the public policy is genuinely threatened.

3. Claim of Public Policy to Oppose Wrongful Termination of Co-Employee

Fitzgerald first claims there is a public policy in this state which protects an employee from discharge by an employer for opposing the wrongful termination of a co-employee. He claims this public policy in favor of opposing the unlawful termination of a co-employee is derived from [state and federal antidiscrimination statutes]. While those laws prohibit retaliation only where the employee is opposing a discriminatory practice as defined by the legislation, plaintiff argues that such statutes "reveal a broad public policy for employees to oppose all unlawful employment practices including the termination of a co-employee which is contrary to public policy."[4] Fitzgerald claims the termination of Koresh was contrary to public policy of this state to provide truthful testimony and he should be afforded the same protection as the law provides Koresh.

We are reluctant to infer a broad public policy from a statute which is limited in its scope to specific discriminatory practices. Instead, we continue to adhere to our guiding principle to only declare public policy which is clearly articulated by a statute or other appropriate source. The statutes identified by Fitzgerald clearly do not expressly protect his conduct. . . .

We also observe Fitzgerald has failed to show how any public policy in favor of opposing the claimed unlawful termination of a co-employee would be jeopardized by his dismissal. Fitzgerald offered no evidence that he expressed

---

4. It is not necessary for us to specifically decide if the public policy to support the tort of wrongful discharge in Iowa can be derived from a federal statute. There is a split of authority among the states. *See, e.g., Faulkner v. United Techs. Corp.*, 693 A.2d 293, 297-98 (Conn. 1997) (a federal law can be a source of public policy); *Griffin v. Mullinix*, 947 P.2d 177 (Okla. 1997) (federal statute cannot serve as a basis for state public policy); *see also* Perritt § 7.13, at 31-32. The issue gives rise to a host of considerations, including potential federal preemption issues. *See* 1 Henry H. Perritt, Jr., Employee Dismissal Law and Practice §§ 2.39-.46, at 168-91 (4th ed. 1998).

opposition to the discharge of a co-worker because it was unlawful. Instead, Fitzgerald admits the only objection he voiced to his employer over the termination of Koresh was the length of his employment service and the lack of prior infractions. He offered no evidence he objected to the termination of Koresh for providing truthful deposition testimony. The conduct of Fitzgerald, therefore, did not promote the claimed public policy, and his actions were not necessary to enforce any public policy. Fitzgerald failed to tie his conduct with his claim of public policy.

4. Claim of Public Policy to Provide Truthful Testimony in a Legal Proceeding

We next address the claim by Fitzgerald that he was terminated because he intended to provide truthful testimony, adverse to his employer, in a threatened future lawsuit of a co-employee against Salsbury. Our first task is to decide whether a public policy exists in this state against discharge of an employee for giving or intending to give truthful testimony in a legal proceeding.

Before considering our statutes, we observe other jurisdictions have recognized a public policy against firing an employee for giving testimony in court proceedings. [Here the court cited *Petermann*, an early case that first recognized a cause of action for wrongful discharge when an employee was terminated for refusing to perjure himself at his employer's request.]

This same reasoning has appealed to other courts when faced with actions by employees who were discharged either for refusing to perjure themselves or for testifying truthfully against their employers. Similarly, we find ample statutory support for a public policy in Iowa in favor of refusing to commit perjury. Our statutes make it a crime to commit perjury, suborn perjury, or tamper with a witness. Moreover, this public policy is not simply confined to the refusal to commit perjury but clearly embraces a broader public policy to provide truthful testimony in legal proceedings. *Page v. Columbia Natural Resources, Inc.*, 480 S.E.2d 817 (W. Va. 1996). A policy in favor of refusing to commit perjury necessarily implies an inverse corresponding public policy to provide truthful testimony. Additionally, the integrity of the judicial system, its fundamental ability to dispense justice, depends upon truthful testimony. This principle forms the basis for our perjury and related statutes. Furthermore, a reasonable employer should be aware that attempts to interfere with the process of obtaining truthful testimony, whether through intimidation or retaliation, is a violation of this public policy. Thus, we conclude the public policy derived from our statutes against perjury and suborning perjury also supports a public policy to provide truthful testimony. We next consider whether this public policy is undermined when an employee is discharged from employment for engaging in the conduct claimed by Fitzgerald.

[Defendant argued that this public policy was inapplicable because "Fitzgerald never testified in a legal proceeding, was never requested to testify in a legal proceeding, and never expressed an intent to testify."]

We agree a dismissed employee must engage in conduct related to public policy before the discharge can undermine that public policy. However, we view the good faith intent to engage in a protected activity the same as performing the protected activity. This is because employees would be discouraged from engaging in the public policy if they were discharged for their intent to engage in the public policy the same as if they actually engaged in the conduct. Thus, Fitzgerald must only show he had a good faith intent to truthfully testify.

An essential element of proof to establish the discharge undermines or jeopardizes the public policy necessarily involves a showing the dismissed employee engaged in conduct covered by the public policy. Although proof the employee engaged in the conduct is also a part of the causation element of the tort, we must review Fitzgerald's conduct in this case to determine if it sufficiently matched the public policy of providing truthful testimony.[5]

Fitzgerald did not directly express an intention to testify truthfully in the lawsuit threatened by Koresh. Furthermore, he never told any company officials he possessed any particular damaging information about the threatened lawsuit. These facts suggest Fitzgerald did not contemplate testifying in a threatened lawsuit by Koresh prior to his discharge. Thus, we must review the summary judgment record to determine if a reasonable inference can be drawn that Fitzgerald maintained a good faith intent to testify truthfully in a lawsuit action prior to the discharge. . . .

The conduct engaged in by Fitzgerald prior to his discharge amounted to internal opposition to the termination of a co-employee. Generally, mere internal opposition by an employee to the employer's decision to discharge a co-employee would not suggest an inference the employee intended to give truthful testimony in future litigation brought by the discharged co-employee. The internal expression of support for a co-employee under these circumstances is far removed from the external concepts of perjury and truthful testimony in court proceedings. However, there are additional facts which must be considered in our analysis at this stage of the proceedings.

This case is not simply about Fitzgerald expressing support for Koresh. Salsbury not only admonished Fitzgerald for failing to support his employer, but warned him that the matter could result in litigation and he must decide which side he would support. Thus, Salsbury placed Fitzgerald's support for Koresh in the context of litigation and transformed the conversation into choosing sides in a lawsuit. There was no evidence to suggest Fitzgerald backed down from his support for Koresh after the conversation turned to litigation. These facts permit a reasonable inference to be drawn that Fitzgerald, prior to his discharge, developed an intent to testify in threatened future litigation against his employer.

There are, of course, other inferences that could be drawn from the evidence. However, at this stage we are required to draw those reasonable inferences in favor of Fitzgerald as the nonmoving party to the summary judgment proceedings. In light of these inferences, we conclude that there is evidence to support the claim Fitzgerald engaged in policy-based conduct.

Nevertheless, Salsbury argues the jeopardy element of the tort cannot be satisfied as a matter of law because it never requested Fitzgerald to testify inconsistent with the public policy. . . .

---

5. No jeopardy can be shown if the plaintiff fails to match the conduct with the public policy. Causation, however, also involves proof of conduct. With this element, the plaintiff must show the dismissal resulted from the protected conduct, and not for some other reason.

Some jurisdictions require the employer to actually make a request to the employee to commit perjury before finding the public policy against perjury is implicated. *Bushko v. Miller Brewing Co.*, 396 N.W.2d 167 (Wis. 1986). Thus, a discharge based on an employer's concern that the employee will testify truthfully if asked to testify or that the employee intends to testify contrary to the interests of the employer is insufficient to support a cause of action under the public policy exception. *See Daniel v. Carolina Sunrock Corp.*, 436 S.E.2d 835 (N.C. 1993) (statement by employer reminding employee for whom she worked and to say as little as possible prior to providing testimony was insufficient to implicate the public policy against the perjury).

We believe the dismissal of an employee can jeopardize public policy when the employee has engaged in conduct consistent with public policy without a request by the employer to violate public policy just as it can when the employee refuses to engage in conduct which is inconsistent with public policy when requested by the employer. The focus is on the adverse actions of the employer in response to the protected actions of the employee, not the actions of the employer which may give rise to the protected actions of the employee. Furthermore, in considering whether the dismissal undermines public policy, we not only look to the impact of the discharge on the dismissed employee, but the impact of the dismissal on other employees as well. Public policy applies to all employees. If the dismissal of one employee for engaging in public policy conduct will discourage other employees from engaging in the public policy conduct, public policy is undermined.

In this case, if Salsbury was motivated to dismiss Fitzgerald because he intended to testify truthfully in a future lawsuit, a dismissal would have a chilling effect on other employees by discouraging them from engaging in similar conduct. Thus, it makes no difference that a dismissal in this particular case may give the employee an enhanced incentive to testify after a dismissal. The action by the employer could inhibit other employees from truthfully testifying in the future out of fear of dismissal.

Salsbury further argues that interpreting the tort to include conduct alleged by Fitzgerald will open the flood gates to litigation for wrongful discharge on public policy grounds whenever an employee internally expresses reservations over the termination of a co-employee and then is later dismissed for some valid reason unrelated to the prior termination of the co-employee. This argument, however, can be made to practically every public policy claim which serves as the basis for a wrongful discharge action. We simply recognize a tort for discharge in violation of a public policy to provide truthful testimony, and leave it to the jury to determine if the facts support the claim. The action in this case is based in part upon an internal complaint by the employee, but is enough to withstand summary judgment because the context of the internal complaint justifies an inference of an intent to testify against the employer which may have caused the employer to dismiss the employee.

5. Causation Element

We next consider if the evidence is sufficient to support a casual connection between the conduct engaged in by Fitzgerald and the discharge. The protected conduct must be the determinative factor in the decision to terminate the employee. Of course, if the employer has no knowledge the employee engaged in the protected activity, causation cannot be established. Similarly, the existence of other legal reasons or motives for the termination are relevant in considering causation.

The causation standard is high, and requires us to determine if a reasonable fact finder would conclude Fitzgerald's intent to testify truthfully was the determinative factor in the decision to discharge him. Generally, causation presents a question of fact. Thus, if there is a dispute over the conduct or the reasonable inferences to be drawn from the conduct, the jury must resolve the dispute. Additionally, any dispute over the employer's knowledge of the conduct is generally for the jury, as well as the existence of other justifiable reasons for the termination. . . .

In this case, the different inferences to be drawn from the evidence precludes [sic] summary judgment. After a recommendation was made to Salsbury to terminate Koresh, Salsbury wanted to know if Fitzgerald supported Koresh. Moreover, Salsbury gathered this information in the context of a potential lawsuit threatened by Koresh. In light of these inferences, summary judgment was improper. . . .

NOTES

1. *Recognition of the Public Policy Tort.* As reflected in the *Fitzgerald* decision, Iowa is one of the vast majority of jurisdictions that recognize some version of what is now generally called the public policy tort. There are, however, states where the tort is still not recognized. For example, New York has continued to adhere to a strict version of the at-will rule: No matter the degree to which public policy may be implicated, a firing is not actionable unless there is a statute expressly according such a right to an employee. *See Murphy v. Am. Home Prods. Corp.*, 448 N.E.2d 86, 87 (N.Y. 1983). In that case, plaintiff asserted that he was fired in retaliation for reporting to his employer's officers and directors that "he had uncovered at least $50 million in illegal account manipulations of secret pension reserves which improperly inflated the company's growth in income and allowed high-ranking officers to reap unwarranted bonuses from a management incentive plan." Although this conduct might currently be actionable for a publicly traded company under the Sarbanes-Oxley Act, see page 225, there was no New York or federal statute providing a cause of action for an employee at that time.

For the New York Court of Appeals, this was a sufficient basis to deny plaintiff's claim since "such a significant change in our law is best left to the Legislature," which was better equipped to answer not only the fundamental question of whether such liability should be recognized but also to craft the appropriate solution:

> The Legislature has infinitely greater resources and procedural means to discern the public will, to examine the variety of pertinent considerations, to elicit the views of the various segments of the community that would be directly affected and in any event critically interested, and to investigate and anticipate the impact of imposition of such liability. Standards should doubtless be established applicable to the multifarious types of employment and the various circumstances of discharge. If the rule of nonliability for termination of at-will employment is to be tempered, it should be accomplished through a principled statutory scheme, adopted after opportunity for public ventilation, rather than in consequence of judicial resolution of the partisan arguments of individual adversarial litigants.

Id. at 79-80. Does this make sense to you, given that the at-will rule is a judicial innovation to begin with? Or is the point less separation of powers than institutional competence? In other words, that common law development over a wide variety of settings may be seen as an inefficient method of furthering the public interest.

Most states follow some version of Iowa's approach, not New York's. *See generally* RESTATEMENT (THIRD) OF EMPLOYMENT LAW § 4.01 cmt. a Tentative Draft No. 2 (April 3, 2009) (listing seven states rejecting the public policy tort). This is true even in states with statutes providing protection in varying situations. Such focused legislative interventions have not generally been viewed as a reason for the courts to refuse to recognize the broader tort. Indeed, Iowa seems to have a grab bag of statutes that protect employees in a variety of settings, but *Fitzgerald* did not view that as a reason to stay the judicial hand. Nevertheless, the diversity of rules emerging in the jurisdictions adopting the tort suggests that there is something to be said for a statutory solution. Indeed, we will see that several states have enacted comprehensive laws, sometimes called whistleblowing statutes, to address the problem. In New York itself, there has been an outpouring of special-purpose statutes focusing on what *Murphy* called "the various circumstances of discharge." Nevertheless, New York remains largely true to *Murphy*, 448 N.E.2d 86. *See Horn v. New York Times*, 790 N.E.2d 753 (N.Y. 2003) (refusing to recognize a public policy tort for a physician who claimed that her employer directed her to provide other departments with employee confidential medical records and to misinform employees about whether their injuries were work related to reduce workers' compensation claims). *But see Wieder v. Skala*, 609 N.E.2d 105 (N.Y. 1992), discussed in Note 9.

2. *Retreating from* Fitzgerald? *Ballalatak v. All Iowa Agric. Ass'n*, 781 N.W.2d 272, 276 (Iowa 2010), involved a dispute plaintiff had with his supervisor about whether two co-workers would receive workers' compensation in the wake of an accident. While the court recognized that retaliation for seeking workers' compensation for oneself would be illegal and assumed that an employee's threat to retain an attorney to represent himself would be protected (the two rights in question), it held plaintiff unprotected for attempting "to ensure his employer did not violate the statutory rights of other employees." But wasn't that also the case in *Fitzgerald*? Indeed, Ballalatak claimed that he was accused of lying when he reminded his supervisor that he had assured the co-workers they would be compensated. Couldn't this be viewed as expressing an intent to testify in a later compensation hearing?

3. *Specificity of the Public Policy.* Some courts have been hesitant to limit employer freedom when the predicate public policy is too generalized. *Fitzgerald* is obviously not one of those cases since it allows a very generic policy (truthful testimony) to be the predicate for the tort. Can you imagine public policies that are so diffuse as to not justify a restriction on the employer's right to discharge a worker? *See Turner v. Mem'l Med. Ctr.*, 911 N.E.2d 369 (Ill. 2009) (discharge for a respiratory therapist reporting his hospital's deviation from an electronic patient-charting accreditation standard not actionable; although providing good medical care is in the public interest, the court required a more focused public policy). *See also* RESTATEMENT § 4.03 cmt. d ("Broad, vague, and highly abstract language in judicial decisions, however, do [sic] not provide a sufficiently defined source of public policy upon which the wrongful discharge tort may be based."). Tentative Draft No. 2 (April 3, 2009).

4. *The Jeopardy Element.* The principal case notes that an employee must not only identify a clear public policy but "must further show the dismissal for engaging in the conduct jeopardizes or undermines the public policy," which requires "the employee to show the conduct engaged in not only furthered the public policy, but dismissal would have a chilling effect on the public policy by discouraging the conduct." The Washington Supreme Court addressed the jeopardy question in *Danny v. Laidlaw Transit Servs., Inc.*, 193 P.3d 128, 138 (Wash. 2008). In that case, the employer fired the plaintiff for absenteeism related to an incident in which she was the victim of domestic violence. The court had little problem with finding a state policy "to prevent domestic violence by encouraging domestic violence victims to escape violent situations, protect children from abuse, report domestic violence to law enforcement, and assist efforts to hold their abusers accountable." But it was considerably more hesitant as to whether the employer's actions jeopardized this policy:

> In this case, for example, in order for Danny to show that her conduct satisfies the "jeopardy" element, she will have to show that the time that she took off work was the *only available adequate means* to prevent domestic violence against herself or her children or to hold her abuser accountable. This inquiry will turn on the nature of the danger, the particular actions that Danny took, and the details of her work schedule. For example, if she wished to get a protection order, but the court was open only during her scheduled work hours, time off may have been necessary. The amount of time off would turn on her distance from the court and other relevant factual circumstances.

Id. It might seem unlikely that plaintiff will be able to satisfy this showing, but does the court's analysis suggest that employers in Washington State need to ask questions about why workers are absent, rather than merely terminate for absenteeism?

5. *The Predicate Policy Must Protect the "Public." Fitzgerald* suggests that opposition to unwise or unfair employment decisions or policies (as opposed to illegal ones) is not a basis for tort protection. As we have seen, this is consistent with allowing private ordering full rein except when the conduct in question affects the public interest. Recall *Foley v. Interactive Data Corp.*, 765 P.2d 373 (Cal. 1988), where plaintiff claimed that he was discharged after he informed management that his new supervisor was under criminal investigation for embezzlement. California had previously recognized a public policy tort, but the court cautioned:

> [W]e must still inquire whether the discharge is against public policy and affects a duty which inures to the benefit of the public at large rather than to a particular employer or employee. For example, many statutes simply regulate conduct between private individuals, or impose requirements whose fulfillment does not implicate fundamental public policy concerns. . . . Whether or not there is a statutory duty requiring an employee to report information relevant to his employer's interest, we do not find a substantial public policy prohibiting an employer from discharging an employee for performing that duty.

Id. at 379-80. Justice Mosk's dissent in *Foley* stressed the intolerable choice facing the plaintiff: remaining silent, and abandoning his duty to his employer or speaking up and risking discharge. But isn't that the essence of the at-will rule — good reason, bad reason, or no reason?

Many courts agree with the *Foley* point, that the thrust of the tort is to protect third parties and society as a whole, *see* RESTATEMENT §4.01, cmt. a Tentative Draft No. 2 (April 3, 2009), but the distinction between public and private has shifted over time. Recall *Murphy*, in which the plaintiff claimed that his employer fired him for opposing its accounting improprieties. The New York court rejected limiting the at-will rule, essentially because it viewed the matter as affecting only the rights of employer and employee. Where only two parties are concerned, private ordering is normally appropriate. But were the facts of *Murphy* to arise today, the dispute would be viewed very differently: After the enactment of Sarbanes-Oxley ("SOX"), which is discussed in more detail at page 225, this scenario might be seen as implicating a public interest precisely because "third parties" — shareholders and the securities market generally — would now be seen as affected. American Home Products was publicly traded, and *Murphy* raised serious questions about financial mismanagement or worse. Of course, since *Murphy* rejects a public policy tort entirely, a New York employee's only resort might be SOX itself. But could you imagine other states taking a broader view of conduct harming third parties in the wake of SOX and the Great Recession, whose causes included much conduct that years ago would have been viewed as purely private? In any event, the critical point is that courts must see some adverse consequences on some person *outside* the employment relationship in order for the public policy tort to have traction. Thus, even today, after SOX, *Foley* itself would still be within the private sphere because the plaintiff was questioning the wisdom of employing an embezzler, not claiming that he was embezzling. And, of course, even a claim of embezzlement from the employer would not trigger federal protection if the employer were a closely held, rather than a publicly traded, company. In short, the public/private distinction remains operative, even if the borders are in flux.

6. *Wrongful Discipline?* The public policy tort arose in the context of discharges, and most cases have considered employees who are challenging terminations. As with employment discrimination, however, the public policy tort has been applied to constructive discharge cases, *e.g.*, *Colores v. Bd. of Trustees*, 130 Cal. Rptr. 2d 347 (App. 2003), and even adverse employment actions that fall short of either actual or constructive discharge. *See, e.g.*, *Trosper v. Bag 'N Save*, 734 N.W.2d 704 (Neb. 2007) (recognizing cause of action for retaliatory demotion); *Brigham v. Dillon Cos.*, 935 P.2d 1054 (Kan. 1997) (wrongful demotion). *Accord* RESTATEMENT OF EMPLOYMENT LAW §4.01. *But see Mintz v. Bell Atl. Leasing Sys. Int'l*, 909 P.2d 559 (Ariz. App. 1995) (no cause of action for wrongful failure to promote).

7. *Judge and Jury Functions.* Who decides what is public policy? In an omitted portion of its opinion, the *Fitzgerald* court wrote: "It is generally recognized that the existence of a public policy, as well as the issue whether that policy is undermined by a discharge from employment, presents questions of law for the court to resolve. . . . On the other hand, the elements of causation and motive are factual in nature and generally more suitable for resolution by the finder of fact." 613 N.W.2d at 282. This is the general approach. *See, e.g.*, *Turner v. Mem'l Med. Ctr.*, 911 N.E.2d 369 (Ill. 2009). If the question is protecting the public interest, shouldn't the jury be allowed to decide whether a public policy qualifies for the tort?

8. *Tort or Contract?* *Fitzgerald* takes the majority view that the public policy cause of action sounds only in tort, but a few jurisdictions define it as contract-based and not tortious, generally looking to the implied duty of good faith. *See, e.g.*, *Knight v. Am. Guard & Alert, Inc.*, 714 P.2d 788 (Alaska 1986); *Brockmeyer v. Dun & Bradstreet*, 335 N.W.2d 834 (Wis. 1983). Viewing the cause of action as contractual limits plaintiff's recovery to economic damages, while tort law permits recovery for mental distress, *see, e.g.*, *Wendeln v. Beatrice Manor, Inc.*, 712 N.W.2d 226 (Neb. 2006), and only in torts where punitive damages may be awarded. However, statutes of limitations are typically longer for contracts than torts, so a time-barred tort suit might be "cured" by a timely contract action.

9. *Reasonable or Right?* Should protection depend on the employee being correct or just reasonable in the perception that he or she is acting in the public interest? Suppose the employee believes, for example, that the company's actions violate the law? Would an employee be protected if she "blew the whistle" to state agencies even if her charges were incorrect, as long as she reasonably and/or in good faith believed the company was violating a criminal statute? Revisit § 4.02 of the draft Restatement on page 185. Several of the categories of protection require the employee to act "reasonably and in good faith," which seems to require both subjective and objective reasonableness. But other categories in § 4.02 require only good faith or have no intent requirement. Do you see why? In any event, the notion that the employee has to be reasonable generally reflects what the courts are doing with the public policy tort and parallels the general rule with respect to retaliation for opposing discrimination. See Chapter 9, page 648. That means that, no matter how clear the public policy, the plaintiff may not recover unless he is reasonable in believing that the employer is contravening it. *See Fine v. Ryan Int'l Airlines*, 305 F.3d 746 (7th Cir. 2002) (in determining whether employer is acting unlawfully, a reasonable employee might rely on what she learns from co-workers).

10. *Advising the Employee.* Suppose an employee comes to you for advice in Mr. Fitzgerald's situation. That is, she has previously been in hot water for backing another employee suit, and she now believes that her supervisor is sending signals that she had better "cooperate" with respect to the discharge of another worker. *Fitzgerald* states the law, but isn't the real problem proof? Do you advise your client to elicit less ambiguous orders that she commit perjury? Do you advise her to secretly tape record any conversations in order to have proof later? How would she do this and what are the risks?

Of course, before you consider the latter course, you should ascertain whether secret taping is criminal in the jurisdiction. In most jurisdictions, the secret taping of a conversation by one of the parties (as opposed to a third party) is not criminal. A few states declare such conduct criminal; for example, California criminalizes taping a "confidential" conversation without the consent of all parties. Cal. Penal Code § 632 (2010). There is also a private cause of action for any person injured as a result of such a taping. *See Friddle v. Epstein*, 21 Cal. Rptr. 2d 85 (App. 1993). Even absent criminal repercussions, there have been ethical concerns for attorneys when tape recording or advising clients to tape record conversations, although those concerns seem less now in light of the American Bar Association's Formal Opinion 01-422, which concludes that undisclosed taping is not necessarily prohibited. If it is not unethical for you to tape or advise your client to tape, are there still reasons to be wary of it?

11. *Advising the Employer.* Suppose you represent an employer in a public policy-saturated setting — say, a pharmaceutical company whose manufacturing is subject to detailed regulation by the Food and Drug Administration. Maybe virtually everything you do has public policy implications. Management is ready to fire a compliance officer because, although he is very good at his job, he is a perfectionist whose demands make it impossible to work with the team. What advice do you have for your client?

Note on Attorneys and the Public Policy Tort

In footnote 2, the *Fitzgerald* court suggested that an element for a public policy case is that "[e]mployer lacked an overriding business justification for the dismissal (the absence of justification element)." Since it is hard to imagine a justification for perjury, *Fitzgerald* itself never pursued that element. But justifications for some dismissals implicating public policy are possible, typically those in which there is a countervailing public policy. One such scenario is when an attorney blows the whistle on his client. Client confidentiality requirements generally bar such disclosure, although there are situations in which it is permitted or even required. *See* MODEL RULES OF PROF'L CONDUCT R. 1.6 (2003). Isn't it clear that a law firm can discharge an attorney who reports a client's violation to public authorities, at least where the reporting violates state ethics rules? In that case, one public policy (confidentiality) cancels out the other. *See* Alex Long, *Whistleblowing Attorneys and Ethical Infrastructures*, 68 MD. L. REV. 786 (2009); Alex Long, *Retaliatory Discharge and the Ethical Rules Governing Attorneys*, 79 U. COLO. L. REV. 1043 (2008).

Suppose instead that the attorney is discharged for refusing to perform an illegal act. Is the public policy tort available now? Even New York, which is generally hostile to the public policy tort, has recognized something akin to a public policy tort in this situation. *Wieder v. Skala*, 609 N.E.2d 105 (N.Y. 1992), involved an associate in a law firm who claimed to have been discharged because he insisted that the firm report another associate's misconduct to the Disciplinary Committee, as required by the state's Code of Professional Responsibility. While reaffirming that New York did not recognize a general public policy tort, the Court of Appeals found the attorney had stated a cause of action in contract. Wieder's role in providing legal services to the firm's clients as a member of the Bar "was at the very core and, indeed, the only purpose of his association" with the law firm and his "responsibilities as a lawyer and as an associate of the firm" are "incapable of separation." *Id.* at 635. Further, the ethical rule at issue was indispensable to attorney self-regulation, and Wieder's failure to comply with it put him at risk of serious discipline. The unique characteristics of the legal profession made the relation of an associate to a law firm employer "intrinsically different" from such relationships as financial manager to corporate employers as in *Murphy*. The court also stressed that both Wieder and the firm were bound to follow the ethical rule in question. MODEL CODE OF PROF'L RESPONSIBILITY DR 1-103 (A). Is this a fair distinction, or was the *Wieder* court just trying to protect one of its own? Or perhaps the court felt it had a greater responsibility in the regulation of attorney conduct than in employment generally, which is best left to the legislature.

Other courts have found that the special role that lawyers play in our society makes the public policy tort inappropriate precisely because lawyers are governed by the rules of ethics. For example, in *Herbster v. North American Co. for Life & Health Ins.*, 501 N.E.2d 343 (Ill. App. 1986), the court held that an in-house attorney who was discharged for refusing to destroy information sought in discovery had no cause of action. The court stressed the right of a client to end the relationship at will. *See also Balla v. Gambro Inc.*, 584 N.E.2d 104 (Ill. 1991) (no cause of action because attorneys already have a duty to abide by rules of professional ethics); *Tartaglia v. UBS PaineWebber, Inc.*, 961 A.2d 1167 (N.J. 2008) (holding that in order to prevail on a common law public policy tort claim, plaintiff must "demonstrate that the employer's behavior about which she complained actually violated [the Rules of Professional Conduct]. Any lesser standard of proof . . . would inappropriately intrude on the role of our disciplinary authorities."). This is true even when there is a state whistleblower law that does not contain an explicit exception. *See Kidwell v. Sybaritic*, Inc., 784 N.W.2d 220 (Minn. 2010) (the court found no general exception for disclosures related to job duties under the state whistleblower law; rather, the question is whether the employee, in this case an in-house counsel, is acting to expose illegal conduct rather than simply seeking to bring his client into compliance).

≡ **Rackley v. Fairview Care Centers, Inc.**
≡ *23 P.3d 1022 (Utah 2001)*

HOWE, J. . . .

[In] 1993, plaintiff Cathleen L. Rackley began working as an at-will employee for defendant Fairview Care Centers, Inc., as the administrator of a nursing home known as Fairview West.

Sometime in February 1994, Karleen Merkley, the manager responsible for resident funds at Fairview West, informed most of the members of the staff that a check for $720 from the Veteran's Administration was expected to arrive for resident Ms. Mellen, and that Ms. Mellen was not to be notified when it came. Plaintiff was not informed of that prohibition. Sharon Mellen, Ms. Mellen's daughter-in-law who had been aiding Ms. Mellen in managing her financial affairs for many years, had requested that Ms. Mellen not be told about the money because she feared Ms. Mellen would try to use it to move out of Fairview West and attempt to live on her own. Sharon wanted to inform Ms. Mellen of the check's arrival personally and to convince her to use the money to purchase a new wheelchair.

In the latter part of February, upon notification that the check had arrived, Sharon went to Fairview West, signed an authorization form in the presence of a witness, and took the check and deposited it in Ms. Mellen's personal bank account. Soon thereafter, plaintiff became aware that the check had arrived and had been picked up by Sharon. She notified Ms. Mellen of that fact. Ms. Mellen was upset that she had not been informed of the check's arrival or subsequent deposit and consequently requested that plaintiff contact Sharon on her behalf.

There is some dispute about the content of the phone call to Sharon. Plaintiff contends that she simply told Sharon she had notified Ms. Mellen of the arrival of the check and expressed concern about the impropriety of keeping the information from Ms. Mellen. Plaintiff asserts that Sharon "screamed" at her for telling Ms. Mellen about the money because "she was promised that nobody would find out about the money, that Karleen had talked to her and nobody should find out about it." Sharon contends that plaintiff called her at her place of work, yelled at her over the phone, and accused her of dishonesty and improper conduct. She stated, "all she did was kept telling me, you're stealing Ms. Mellen's money, you can't do that, you need to turn it — return the money to Fairview West. . . . She was very unprofessional. She had me in tears." Plaintiff did not then notify Joseph Peterson, owner and general manager of Fairview, of what had transpired or request investigation by any outside authority.

[However, Sharon later contacted Peterson and told him her version of what had happened. Peterson ultimately reprimanded Merkley, and Sallie Maroney, the manager of Fairview East, for failing to tell Ms. Mellen about the check. A new policy was promulgated requiring that residents be informed of their incoming funds. Plaintiff, however, was reprimanded for calling Sharon at work and later terminated.]

The parties dispute the precise issue before us. Fairview contends that the key issue is whether notification to care center residents of the arrival of their personal funds is a clear and substantial public policy. . . . We agree with plaintiff that if we were to require the law to be so specifically tailored, the public policy exception would be meaningless. Thus, we hold that the proper issue before us is whether a care facility resident's right to manage her own funds constitutes a clear and substantial public policy.

[To succeed on a public policy wrongful discharge claim], plaintiff must satisfy a four-pronged test. Plaintiff must prove that (1) her employment was terminated; (2) a clear and substantial public policy existed; (3) the plaintiff's conduct implicated that clear and substantial public policy; and (4) the termination and conduct in furtherance of the public policy are causally connected. Because Fairview concedes for purposes of this case that plaintiff was terminated, we move directly to the second prong.

I. Clear and Substantial Public Policy

The public policy exception to the employment at-will presumption is much narrower than traditional notions of public policy. Only "clear and substantial public policies will support a claim of wrongful discharge in violation of public policy." . . .

We have stated that a public policy is "clear" if it is plainly defined by one of three sources: (1) legislative enactments; (2) constitutional standards; or (3) judicial decisions. *See Dixon v. Pro Image Inc.*, 987 P.2d 48 (Utah 1999). For example, we have held that the enforcement of a state's criminal code that reflects Utah policy constitutes a clear and substantial public policy. *See Peterson* [*v. Browning*, 832 P.2d 1280 (Utah 1992)] (holding that employer who fired employee for refusing to feloniously provide false information on tax forms could be held liable for wrongful termination).

We have also held that a public policy is "substantial" if it is of "overreaching importance to the public, as opposed to the parties only." *Ryan* [*v. Dan's Food Stores, Inc.*, 972 P.2d 395 (Utah 1998)]. "We must . . . inquire whether the discharge is against public policy and affects a duty which inures to the benefit of the public at large rather than to a particular employer or employee." *Foley v. Interactive Data Corp.*, 765 P.2d 373 (Cal. 1988); *see, e.g., Fox* [*v. MCI Commun. Corp.*, 931 P.2d 857 (Utah 1997)] (holding that retaliatory termination for reporting possible criminal conduct of co-workers to employer does not give rise to a violation of substantial public policy). Statutes that simply regulate conduct between private individuals or impose requirements whose fulfillment does not implicate fundamental public policy concerns are not sufficient to require an exception to the at-will presumption. . . .

[The court stressed that "not every employment termination that has the effect of violating some public policy is actionable." Rather, the scope of the public policy exception must be kept narrow "to avoid unreasonably eliminating employer discretion in discharging employees."]

Plaintiff first asserts that two provisions in the Utah Constitution form the basis of a clear public policy. Article I, section 1 of the Utah Constitution provides in pertinent part that "all men have the inherent and inalienable right to . . . acquire, possess and protect property. . . ." Article I, section 27 provides that "frequent recurrence to fundamental principles is essential to the security of individual rights and the perpetuity of free government." While these two provisions do protect the right to acquire, possess, and protect property, they do not enunciate the narrow type of policy envisioned by our case law creating the public policy exception. The right of a care facility resident to manage her own funds is not "plainly defined by . . . [these] constitutional standards." . . .

Next, plaintiff contends that 42 U.S.C. §§ 3058g(a)(3) and (5), and sections 62A-3-201 to 208 of the Utah Code also plainly define such a public policy.[5] Plaintiff specifically points to subsections (a)(3) and (a)(5) in support of her position. However, subsections (a)(3) and (a)(5) are devoid of any language relating to a resident's right to manage her funds. While these provisions broadly discuss the duty of the ombudsman to monitor and protect the rights of care facility residents, they in no way state a narrow and clear public policy necessary for an exception to the at-will rule. This statute governs the duties and functions of the office of the ombudsman and its representatives and entities, and in no way enunciates rights of care facility residents.

Similarly, we find sections 62A-3-201 and -202 of the Utah Code unavailing. The stated purpose of these provisions "is to establish within the division [of Aging and Adult Services] the [Utah] long-term care ombudsman program for the aging . . . and identify duties and responsibilities of that program . . . in order to address problems relating to long-term care." In pertinent part, the ombudsman is to address the difficulties of the aging citizens of the state by assisting in asserting their civil and human rights as residents of care facilities through legal means. We similarly find this language too broad to constitute a clear and substantial specific public policy. . . .

[As for 42 U.S.C. § 1396r(c)(6),] which governs the requirements care facilities must meet to obtain grants for medical assistance programs, provides that "the nursing facility . . . may not require residents to deposit their personal funds with the facility." Subsection (c)(6) includes guidelines for how care facilities are to manage resident funds when management of such funds has been authorized by the resident. Although not clearly stated, this section could imply that care facility residents have the right to manage their own financial affairs. In the past we have held that we may look beyond the provision in question to determine whether the motivating policy behind it constitutes a clear and substantial public policy. However, we conclude that a mere hint to such an underlying policy, as is the case here, is insufficient to constitute the type of clear and substantial policy necessary to establish an exception to the employment-at-will doctrine. Thus, we hold that 42 U.S.C. § 1396r(c)(6) does not rise to the level of a clear public policy.

Rule 432-150-4.400 of the Utah Administrative Code provides that "the resident has the right to maintain his financial affairs and the facility may not require a resident to deposit his personal funds with the facility." Both of these sections plainly state that care facility residents have the right to manage their own finances.

Additionally, 42 C.F.R. § 483.10, governing resident rights that must be recognized by long-term care facilities, provides the most detailed and applicable provision. It states:

> The resident has a right to a dignified existence, self-determination, and communication with and access to persons and services inside and outside the facility. A facility must protect and promote the rights of each resident, including . . . the right to manage his or her financial affairs, and the facility may not require residents to deposit their personal funds with the facility.

5. In general, 42 U.S.C. § 3058g provides that in order to receive federal funding for state long-term care ombudsman programs, states must meet certain requirements, including appointing an ombudsman and establishing an official office of the ombudsman. *See* 42 U.S.C. § 3058g(a)(1), (2).

This regulation explicitly states that care facility residents have the right to manage their own funds.

However, we have earlier pointed out that a clear public policy must be found in our statutes or constitutions, or judicial decisions. The provision in 42 C.F.R. § 483.10 is an executive agency regulation that governs practice and procedure before federal administrative agencies. Similarly, R432-150-4.400 is a provision in the Utah Administrative Code.

Administrative regulations by their very nature are not "substantial" under our case law. The character of the public policy exception is that it furthers policies that "protect the public or promote public interest." Agency regulations are created by the agencies themselves and are tailored to govern specific agency needs. The public policy exception must be "narrow enough in its scope and application to be no threat to employers who operate within the mandates of the law and clearly established public policy as set out in the duly adopted laws." Thus, we hold that while 42 C.F.R. § 483.10 and R432-150-4.400 of the Utah Administrative Code expressly state that care facility residents have the right to manage their own funds, our case law does not allow for administrative regulations alone to constitute expressions of clear public policy.[8]

In so holding, we recognize that care facility residents are often at the mercy of the facilities in which they reside. Residents face many challenges as their mobility decreases and their ability to take care of themselves physically, mentally, and emotionally deteriorates. However, while we agree with plaintiff that "the rights of nursing home residents, especially with the increasing longevity of Utah residents and the growth of Utah's population, are a matter of most significant public concern," we also recognize the reality that many residents, while remaining in control of their funds, voluntarily seek the assistance of family members or friends with their banking and spending decisions. That appears to have been the situation in the instant case. Such efforts by honest and helpful advisors should be encouraged and not discouraged by rigid, government-imposed requirements. . . .

DURHAM, Justice, dissenting:

I respectfully dissent. There is, I believe, abundant support for the proposition that a long-term care facility resident's right to manage her own funds is a matter of clear and substantial public policy. We are dealing here with one of our system's most fundamental and well-understood rights: the right of a legally competent person to control her property and manage her financial affairs. . . .

This court is now faced with the question of whether to recognize a public policy exception protecting the right of a legally competent long-term care facility resident to manage her own financial affairs. I believe that the majority's view of the legitimacy of the public policy in question is mistaken. We can, and should, recognize administrative regulations as a valid source of Utah public policy for exceptions to the at-will employment doctrine; the regulatory process occurs through legislative delegation and under legislative oversight. It is undertaken by persons and entities with considerable expertise and knowledge regarding legislative intent. Furthermore, there is clear and substantial public policy supporting a long-term care facility resident's right to manage

---

8. We do not hold that an administrative regulation may not provide support to a legislatively or judicially created public policy.

her funds in related federal regulations identical to those adopted by this state, in the Utah Probate and Criminal Code, in Utah case law, and in the Utah Constitution. . . .

[The dissent, in reviewing other sources of public policy, cited *In re Guardianship of Valentine*, 294 P.2d 696 (Utah 1956), a case involving the appointment of a guardian for the property of an alleged incompetent; *Valentine* held that "the right of every individual to handle his own affairs even at the expense of dissipating his fortune is a right jealous[l]y guarded and one which will not be taken away except in extreme cases." It interpreted Sharon Mellen's request to Ms. Merkeley, the Fairview employee in charge of residents' funds, not to inform Ms. Mellen of the arrival of a check as an effort to manage Ms. Mellen's affairs for her. As stated in *Valentine*] the right of every individual to manage his or her own financial affairs is jealously guarded. It is impossible for one to manage one's financial affairs if one is purposefully deprived of the knowledge of relevant information, such as the arrival or deposit of a personal check. . . .

It is important to note that Ms. Merkeley and Ms. Maroney received written reprimands from Fairview for failing to tell Ms. Mellen about her check. In fact, a new policy was instituted by Fairview after this incident requiring that residents be informed of all their incoming funds, regardless of who assists them with their financial affairs. This change was, I submit, an acknowledgment by Fairview of what the laws and public policy of Utah require. . . .

NOTES

1. *Sources of Public Policy.* In states recognizing the public policy tort, the first question is what policies count, that is, what sources may a court look to? *Fitzgerald* and *Rackley* both deal with the sources of public policy that will support a tort suit. *Fitzgerald* writes that the state constitution and state statutes will suffice, but it does not decide whether administrative regulations will do so. What about *Rackley*? Is the court too grudging in its analysis of applicable public policies? Even assuming that the Utah constitutional provisions relating to owning property are too generalized, don't the federal and state laws requiring an ombudsmen to protect residents of nursing homes nevertheless indicate a strong public interest in maintaining the integrity and autonomy of such persons? If there is any doubt about this, isn't it resolved by the federal and state laws related to safeguarding the property of nursing home residents?

Other states have recognized judicially created public policies, *see Feliciano v. 7-Eleven, Inc.* 559 S.E.2d 713 (W. Va. 2001) (judicially recognized policy favoring self-defense could trump the at-will rule where store employee violated company policy to disarm a robber). Perhaps the most far-reaching decision in terms of sources of public policy is *Pierce v. Ortho Pharm. Corp.*, 417 A.2d 505 (N.J. 1980), which holds that even a professional code of ethics might be a source of public policy. The draft Restatement adopts this view. §4.02(e). *See also* Note on Attorneys and the Public Policy Tort, page 198. Under this view, might Ms. Rackley have prevailed? Where would you look for codes of conduct that bear on her situation?

2. *Administrative Regulations.* The *Rackley* court recognizes that administrative regulations directly address a patient's right to manage her own financial affairs. But it refuses to accord "public policy" status to such regulations. Are you persuaded by the court's analysis? Isn't it true, at least on the federal level, that courts view (valid) administrative regulations as an exercise of congressional law-making authority delegated to the agency? *See Chevron U.S.A. Inc. v. Nat. Resources Def. Council, Inc.,*

467 U.S. 837 (1984); *United States v. Mead Corp.*, 533 U.S. 218 (2001). Why should such laws be insufficient predicates for the public policy tort? Is it because regulations may be too detailed and technical? Even so, aren't regulated industries expected to obey governing regulations? Why should they be free to fire employees whose actions further the regulatory regime? The dissent in *Rackley* stressed that other states recognized regulations as an appropriate source of public policy. *See Saffels v. Rice*, 40 F.3d 1546, 1550 (8th Cir. 1994); *Green v. Ralee Engr. Co.*, 960 P.2d 1046 (Cal. 1998).

In one sense, *Rackley* may seem divorced from much of employment law because it involves a set of statutes and administrative regulations focused on one particular setting — the nursing home. But it is common in our highly regulated society for particular segments of the economy to be subject to detailed administrative controls. *Rackley* involved only one aspect of the highly regulated health care industry where public policy concerns are pervasive. Other highly regulated industries include transportation and energy. An attorney advising employees or employers in these settings must be alert to the potential of the public policy tort limiting the employer's discretion to terminate, a matter that would otherwise be left to private ordering.

Notice the Catch-22* that *Rackley* creates for employees. Constitutional and statutory provisions are likely to be too general to address a particular question. Precisely for that reason, Congress and state legislatures authorize agencies to provide more specific rules through regulations. However, the very regulations that are specific enough to satisfy the court in this respect are not of sufficient authority to state public policy. Reread footnote 8. Is the court suggesting that in some cases regulations may make general policy statements sufficiently concrete to support the tort? If so, why was this not true in *Rackley* itself?

3. *Federal Law Supporting State Public Policy Torts.* In a system with an enormous amount of federal regulation, the relationship between the state public policy tort and federal law is critical. In a footnote, *Fitzgerald* avoided deciding whether federal law could have provided the underlying public policy for a tort action in Iowa. Other cases have looked to federal law as a source of state public policy. As *Fitzgerald*'s footnote 4 indicates, this has raised the question whether the federal statute preempts even consistent state law, perhaps by occupying the field. While a few decisions have found preemption by particular federal law, *see, e.g., Fasano v. FRB*, 457 F.3d 274 (3d Cir. 2006) (federal reserve banks not subject to state employment laws); *Chrisman v. Philips Indus., Inc.*, 751 P.2d 140 (Kan. 1988) (state tort action for discharge for refusing to approve defective nuclear products preempted by federal energy law), most have not. *See, e.g., Sargent v. Cent. Natl. Bank & Trust Co.*, 809 P.2d 1298 (Okla. 1991) (no National Bank Act preemption); *Fragassi v. Neiburger*, 646 N.E.2d 315 (Ill. App. 1995) (no OSHA preemption). *See generally* Nancy Modesitt, *Wrongful Discharge: The Use of Federal Law as a Source of Public Policy*, 8 U. PA. J. LAB. & EMP. L. 623 (2006)

4. *Plaintiff's Conduct.* Suppose the dissent had prevailed as to the requisite public policies. Did plaintiff's call to Sharon further those policies? Even if it did, would Fairview have been within its rights to discharge Ms. Rackley for the *manner*

---

* "There was only one catch and that was Catch-22, which specified that a concern for one's own safety in the face of dangers that there were real and immediate was the process of a rational mind. Orr was crazy and could be grounded. All he had to do was ask; and as soon as he did, he would no longer be crazy and would have to fly more missions. . . . If he flew them he was crazy and didn't have to; but if he didn't want to he was sane and had to. . . ."

JOSEPH HELLER, CATCH-22, 46 (1961).

in which she made the call—calling Sharon at work and screaming at her? Of course, plaintiff denied she screamed, but would that matter if Fairview thought (reasonably?) that she had? *See Curlee v. Kootenai County Fire & Rescue*, 224 P.3d 458 (Idaho 2008) (an employee terminated for documenting her co-workers' time-wasting activities had a triable claim under the Idaho whistleblowing statute, which protects one who "communicates in good faith the existence of any waste of public funds, property or manpower").

Reviewing the Public Policy Exception

We saw earlier that §4.02 of the proposed Restatement (Third) of Employment Law identifies six categories under the public policy exception. There is considerable debate both as to whether these categories are too restrictive and whether the formulation of the categories accurately captures the decisions in the area, but understanding the various possible headings for the tort is important.

Refusing to Commit an Illegal Act. Perhaps the most obviously justifiable instance of protection is where the employee is discharged for refusing to perform an illegal act, or violate a code of professional conduct or other occupational code. The employee must only reasonably and in good faith believe the conduct to be illegal or a violation. *See McGarrity v. Berlin Metals Inc.*, 774 N.E.2d 71 (Ind. App. 2002) (refusal to be a party to an illegal tax underreporting scheme for the purpose of defrauding the state and creditors). The principle has been applied to protect employees who testified against their employer's wishes in legal proceedings. *Reust v. Alaska Petroleum Contrs., Inc.*, 127 P.3d 807 (Alaska 2005) (retaliation against employees who testify in legal proceedings actionable, in part because the tort "reduces the temptation for employees, fearing adverse responses from their employers, to provide false testimony or disobey a subpoena"); *Ludwick v. This Minute of Carolina*, 337 S.E.2d 213 (S.C. 1985) (finding protected an employee's appearing at workers' compensation hearing in response to a subpoena). *But see Harney v. Meadowbrook Nursing Ctr.*, 784 S.W.2d 921 (Tenn. 1990) (termination of nurse who testified at a co-worker's compensation hearing did not implicate public policy tort if the employer had a good faith belief that her testimony was perjured).

Whistleblowing. The proposed Restatement also protects an employee who "reports or inquires about employer conduct that the employee reasonably and in good faith believes violates a law or established principle of professional conduct or an occupational code protective of the public interest." §4.02(e). Many believe that, after protecting employees for refusing to violate the law, the next most compelling case for protection is when the employee reports a serious violation of law. Unlike instances where employees testify under court process, citizens generally do not have any affirmative duty to make such reports. It, therefore, cannot be said that the employer who discharges a worker for reporting a violation forces her to choose between retaining her job and violating the law; an employee who did not volunteer information would be acting perfectly legally. *See* WAYNE R. LaFAVE, CRIMINAL LAW, §13.6(c) (4th ed. 2003). Nevertheless, it is certainly in the public interest for individuals to report violations; indeed, the federal False Claims Act, *see* note on page 239, essentially offers bounties for pursuing fraud where federal funds are involved.

And, as *Fitzgerald* indicated, all states bar interference with witnesses. Accordingly, a great number of cases have recognized a public policy suit where the employee alleges that she was discharged for reporting violations to appropriate public authorities. *See, e.g., Schriner v. Meginnis Ford Co.*, 421 N.W.2d 755 (Neb. 1988) (reporting odometer falsification to state attorney general); *Prince v. Rescorp Realty*, 940 F.2d 1104 (7th Cir. 1991) (reporting faulty fire safety equipment to town).

However, some courts limit this principle. A number of cases distinguish between reports to public authorities and internal reports. The former are protected but the latter are not, presumably because of the absence of effects beyond the two parties to the employment relationship. *See, e.g., Bielser v. Prof'l Sys. Corp.*, 177 F. App'x 655 (9th Cir. 2006). Note that whether external reporting is required is distinct from whether the public interest is implicated: The plaintiff in *Bielser* claimed that her employer was defrauding a customer. That clearly violated public policy, and, had she reported it to the authorities, she would have been protected. While an external reporting requirement limits the tort in terms of what conduct is protected, isn't it a perverse rule even from an employer's perspective insofar as it tends to require employees to wash their company's dirty laundry in public rather than seek to remedy problems internally? *See* John A. Gray, *The Scope of Whistleblower Protection in the State of Maryland: A Comprehensive Statute Is Needed*, 33 U. BALT. L. REV. 225 (2004).

Performing a Public Duty. As framed by the proposed Restatement, employees are also protected when "perform[ing] a public duty or obligation that the employee reasonably and in good faith believes is imposed by law." The cases dealing with refusals to commit perjury could be so described. The other major "public duty" category is jury service. *Nees v. Hock*, 536 P.2d 512 (Or. 1975). There have been relatively few decisions on this point, perhaps because the matter frequently is addressed explicitly by statutes. Indeed, when the Alabama Supreme Court refused to protect jury service from employer retaliation, the legislature promptly responded by providing statutory protection. *See* ALA. CODE § 12-16-8.1 (2010); *Meeks v. Opp Cotton Mills, Inc.*, 459 So. 2d 814 (Ala. 1984). The draft Restatement views this as a very narrow category: The obligation must be a public one, "not merely a personal, familial, or moral obligation." § 4.02, cmt. c.

But the line between the two is not always so bright. Illustrations 9 and 10 of § 4.02 would protect an employee who is late to work because the police "require" him to fill out a witness report about an accident he observed, but they would not protect an employee who is late to work because his own child requires medical attention. Suppose the employee is late because the police *request* him to comfort an injured family member until the EMTs arrive? *See Gaspar v. Peshastin Hi-Up Growers*, 128 P.3d 627 (Wash. Ct. App. 2006) (recognizing a public policy encouraging cooperation with police and prosecutors in criminal investigations). *But see Brennan v. Cephalon, Inc.*, 298 F. App'x 147 (3d Cir. 2008) (a "statutorily imposed duty" claim failed because the statutes in question did not impose an affirmative duty on the employee to report his audit findings to the Food and Drug Administration; while the employer was required to disclose certain "compliance indicators," it was not required to conduct an audit or report the findings of any audit it conducted).

Claiming a Benefit. Still another category of protection under the draft Restatement is "fil[ing] a charge or claim[ing] a benefit in good faith" under "an employment statute or law (irrespective of whether the charge or claim is meritorious)." §4.02(c). This is sometimes called "the exercise of a public right." The prototype cases in this classification are decisions recognizing a cause of action for filing a workers' compensation claim. *See, e.g., Springer v. Weeks & Leo Co.*, 429 N.W.2d 558 (Iowa 1988); *Hansen v. Harrah's*, 675 P.2d 394 (Nev. 1984). Similarly, decisions finding a cause of action for a discharge for refusing to take a polygraph examination can be placed in this group. *See, e.g., Ambroz v. Cornhusker Square Ltd.*, 416 N.W.2d 510 (Neb. 1987). Other cases can also be traced to statutes enacted, at least in part, for the protection of employees. *See, e.g., Cloutier v. Great A. & P. Tea Co.*, 436 A.2d 1140 (N.H. 1981) (policy in favor of employee safety implicated where store required manager to travel to bank to deposit daily receipts in a "very dangerous area").

Several courts take a broader view of "public right," *see Bowman v. State Bank of Keysville*, 331 S.E.2d 797 (Va. 1985) (holding that a shareholder-employee could not be fired in order to influence his voting), although it is not always clear what makes a right "public." For example, a number of cases rejected claims by employees who were fired for doing what, in normal speech, we would say they had a right to do. *See, e.g., Beam v. IPCO*, 838 F.2d 242 (7th Cir. 1988) (hiring an attorney not protected); *Scroghan v. Kraftco Corp.*, 551 S.W.2d 811 (Ky. Ct. App. 1977) (discharge of an employee for attending law school permitted); *Miller v. SEVAMP, Inc.*, 362 S.E.2d 915 (Va. 1987) (testifying at grievance hearing not protected by public policy). The Restatement's solution is to limit protection to instances where the right is accorded by "an employment statute or law." Is this a sensible choice? The draft would, however, partially counterbalance this by protecting workers who act in "good faith," thus avoiding any objective reasonableness requirement. Is this a good compromise?

Waiving a Nonwaivable Right. The most recent draft of the Restatement also recognizes a public policy tort for an employee's refusal to waive a nonwaivable right. Section 4.02 provides: "An employer is subject to liability in tort under §4.01 for disciplining an employee who acting in an reasonable manner . . . (d) refuses to waive a nonnegotiable or nonwaivable right or agree to a condition of employment whose enforcement would violate public policy." Tentative Draft No. 2 (April 3, 2009). It relies on *Edwards v. Arthur Andersen LLP*, 189 P.3d 285, 289 (Cal. 2008), where the court recognized that firing an employee for refusing to waive his statutory rights to compete with, and to be indemnified by, his employer would be actionable. That court, however, tempered the decision by reading the indemnity waiver not to violate this principle. The waiver was framed in terms of "any and all" claims, including "claims that in any way arise from or out of, are based upon or relate to Employee's employment by, association with or compensation from" the employer. Nevertheless, the court found this not specific enough to include the nonwaivable right of indemnification.

The Catchall? Although hotly debated, the Restatement retains a catchall category, inserted because of concerns that limiting the public policy tort to the other categories would tend to freeze the law and not permit appropriate judicial responses to situations that might arise in the future. Accordingly, §4.02(f) protects an employee from discipline for "engag[ing] in other activity directly furthering a substantial public policy." Illustration 20 involves an armored car driver who, in violation of company policy, left his vehicle to rescue a hostage during a bank robbery. Is *Danny v. Laidlaw Transit Services, Inc.*, 193 P.3d 128, 138 (Wash. 2008), a real-life example? There, the court recognized "a clear public policy of protecting domestic violence survivors and their children and holding domestic violence perpetrators accountable." The result would be to preclude the employer from firing the plaintiff for absences due to her dealing with domestic violence, at least if such absences were unavoidable.

The public policy exception necessarily means that the right of an employee to blow the whistle trumps any employer expectation that the employee's duty of loyalty forbids such disclosure. See Chapter 8. *See generally* Orly Lobel, *Lawyering Loyalties: Speech Rights and Duties Within Twenty-First Century New Governance*, 77 FORDHAM L. REV. 1245 (2010). But the relationship between the two conflicting obligations is ill defined, and the debate over the extent of the duty of loyalty at the American Law Institute may require revisiting the scope of protection. The core example is the employee who is approached by the FBI investigating the employer—say, in a False Claims Act case. See page 239. The employee doesn't believe the employer has done anything wrong, so she doesn't fit within § 4.02(e). The law does not require her to cooperate with the FBI, so it's not a "public duty or obligation," which raises questions about § 4.02(b) (although maybe she would "reasonably believe" that the law required her to respond). There might be a "public right" to cooperate with a criminal government investigation, but the Restatement is limited to rights connected to employment. Is the catchall provision the solution? Cooperating with the government has to be protected, doesn't it? And it can't violate the duty of loyalty, can it?

Note on Free Speech and the Public Policy Tort

Many of the public policies we have examined implicate speech rights, but the First Amendment articulates a policy against *state* repression of speech. Under that view, public policy concerns do not reach beyond state action. *See Grinzi v. San Diego Hospice Corp.*, 14 Cal. Rptr. 3d 893 (Ct. App. 2004) (First Amendment free speech not a basis for a public policy claim against a private employer); *Edmondson v. Shearer Lumber Products*, 75 P.3d 733 (Idaho 2003) (free speech is not a sufficiently strong public policy to sustain a wrongful discharge cause of action). A few courts, however, have found private coercion of political activity to be actionable even if restrictions on free speech, as such, are not. *See Chavez v. Manville Products. Corp.*, 777 P.2d 371 (N.M. 1989) (dismissal for refusal to participate in company's lobbying efforts actionable). Even in the public sector, which is treated in more detail in Chapter 7, much employee speech is unprotected: (1) The matter must be one of "public concern," (2) the matter must not be part of the employee's official duties, and (3) the employee's speech must not be too disruptive. *See Garcetti v. Ceballos*, 547 U.S. 410 (2006), reproduced at page 377.

One state generally protects speech against private interference. Connecticut's Free Speech Act, CONN. GEN. STAT. § 31-51q (2006), bars adverse action against an employee "on account of the exercise of rights under the first amendment of the United States Constitution" or under the corollary provisions of the Connecticut constitution. This prohibition is subject to the condition that the employee's "activity does not substantially or materially interfere with the employee's bona fide performance or the working relationship between the employee and the employer. . . ." A few other states have limited laws prohibiting discrimination on the basis of political affiliation or have statutes guaranteeing the right to run for office or to vote. See CAL. LABOR L. §1101 (2009).

Would a public employee who spoke out as Fitzgerald or Rackley did be protected from discharge by the First Amendment? Did either of them speak on matters of public concern? What about under the Connecticut statute?

PROBLEMS

4-1. Lauren Lopez was a fifth-year associate at one of the top defense firms in Gotham. In the course of representing Dr. Sidley in a medical malpractice case, Lopez became suspicious that her client used cocaine. Sidley was a surgeon, and the case involved a claim by a woman who was left paralyzed after back surgery. The basis for Lopez's suspicions of Sidley's drug use included a constantly irritated nose, occasional "high" states, and extreme mood swings during the course of the two-year representation. As the case neared trial, Lopez became increasingly convinced that Sidley had a drug addiction problem. She received what she believed to be confirmation of this when she interviewed one of the prospective witnesses, an operating room nurse, who told her, "off the record," that Sidley "had had a cocaine problem, but was really working on it."

Lopez took her concerns to the partner supervising her section, L.L. Cohen. He downplayed her worries, telling her she was no expert on symptoms of drug abuse, and she shouldn't believe the nurse's "hearsay." He concluded, "Just forget about it." She was still worried about the matter a week later when Cohen called her into his office on another case and, as she was leaving, said, "Oh, by the way, we've settled that claim against Sidley." Lopez was surprised, since she would normally have been involved in the settlement negotiations. When she asked what the settlement was, Cohen named a figure that was several hundred thousand dollars higher than what Cohen had previously said Sidley's malpractice carrier would be willing to pay.

Rather than lay her concerns to rest, this settlement actually increased Lopez's distress. After wrestling with her conscience, Lopez decided that she had to report her concerns to the state licensing authorities. She wrote a letter to them, copying both Sidley and Cohen and setting forth the bases for her concern.

A day after the letter was sent, Cohen came into Lopez's office and said, "I got your letter. You know I don't agree with you, but I guess we all have to do what we all have to do." He never mentioned the matter again.

You are managing partner of the firm. Both Cohen and Lopez separately speak with you about these events. Lopez is scheduled to be considered for partnership next year. The general sentiment before this episode was that she was unlikely to make partner, although no formal action has been taken. What, if anything, should you do?

4-2. Now imagine you represent Lopez, who is concerned about these events and her consideration for partnership. What advice would you give her? Would it be a good idea to contact the firm before the partnership decision? If so, what would you say or write? If you decide to do nothing, and she is turned down for partnership, what course of action would you advise?

B. STATUTES CREATING PUBLIC POLICY CAUSES OF ACTION

The early public policy cases looked to preexisting statutes for the public policy they discerned. But as the courts began to expand the public policy tort, some legislatures responded by enacting laws designed to protect employees. Such statutes create their own causes of action. The materials that follow explore these statutes and their relationship to the public policy tort created by the courts.

Even before more general law, some statutes contained public policy protections basically framed in terms of barring employers from retaliating against employees for initiating or participating in enforcement proceedings. For example, the Fair Labor Standards Act bars retaliation for seeking enforcement of that statute's minimum wage and maximum hour provisions. 29 U.S.C.S. §215(a)(3) (2010). Less directly related to employment are whistleblowing provisions in federal statutes regulating such areas as nuclear energy, *see* Energy Reorganization Act of 1974, 42 U.S.C. §5851(a) (2006); transportation, *see* Surface Transport Assistance Act, 49 U.S.C. §2305(a) (2006); and heath care, *see* Patient Protection and Affordable Care Act, Pub. L. No. 111-148, 124 Stat. 119, §1150B(d) (2010) (penalizing long-term care facilities for retaliation against an employee who engaged in lawful acts).

While these and similar state laws could be viewed as whistleblowing statutes, that term is often reserved for more open-ended enactments that create civil remedies for employees who are discharged or otherwise adversely treated by their employees because they disclose violations of the law or engage in other conduct in which there is a legitimate public concern. Limited steps in this direction are state statutes, such as New York's Civil Service Law §75-b (McKinney 1989) and, on the federal level, the Civil Service Reform Act, 5 U.S.C. §§2301, 2302(b)(8) (1978), which provide public employees with protection. *See Bush v. Lucas*, 462 U.S. 367 (1983) (federal civil service protections were sole source of remedy for claimed discharge in violation of the First Amendment).

Prior to 1980, however, there were no general statutes, at either the state or federal level, that broadly protected private whistleblowers. Indeed, it was the absence of such statutes that led a number of courts to recognize a public policy suit for discharges of employees who reported violations of the law to relevant authorities. In the wake of such decisions, however, several states enacted whistleblower statutes — that is, laws providing a measure of protection to employees, whether in the public or private sector, for conduct the legislature deemed to be worthy of protection. For a listing of state laws against whistleblowing, both comprehensive statutes and more limited enactment, *see* Whistleblower Statutes Laws — Information on the Law About Whistleblower Statutes, http://law.jrank.org/pages/11824/Whistleblower-Statutes.html (last visited July 7, 2010). At the federal level, there is still no comprehensive statute, but a new wave of protection has taken hold this century, starting with the Sarbanes-Oxley Act, 107-204, 116 Stat. 745, which, *inter alia*, grants federal protection to employees of publicly traded companies in certain situations where the employee reports possible financial misreporting. The Obama administration's signature legislative initiatives in 2009 and 2010, including the stimulus package, health care reform, and financial reform, incorporated this approach, expanding federal public policy protection broadly. Although each was very controversial, there was little opposition in Congress to the whistleblower aspects of the various bills.

1. State Approaches

State statutes have varying substantive provisions, but an appreciation of the problems faced in drafting and applying these laws may be gained by comparing two state statutes in detail.

≡
≡ *Conscientious Employee Protection Act ("CEPA")*
≡ *N.J. Stat. Ann. § 34:19-1 (2010)*

§ 34:19-3. Retaliatory action prohibited

An employer shall not take any retaliatory action against an employee because the employee does any of the following:

a. Discloses, or threatens to disclose to a supervisor or to a public body an activity, policy or practice of the employer, or another employer, with whom there is a business relationship, that the employee reasonably believes:

(1) is in violation of a law, or a rule or regulation promulgated pursuant to law, including any violation involving deception of, or misrepresentation to any shareholder, investor, client, patient, customer, employer, former employee, retiree or pensioner of the employer or any governmental entity, or, in the case of an employee who is a licensed or certified health care professional, reasonably believes constitutes improper quality of patient care; or

(2) is fraudulent or criminal, including any activity, policy or practice of deception or misrepresentation which the employee reasonably believes may defraud any shareholder, investor, client, patient, customer, employee, former employee, retiree or pensioner of the employer or any governmental entity;

b. Provides information to, or testifies before, any public body conducting an investigation, hearing or inquiry into any violation of law, or a rule or regulation promulgated pursuant to law by the employer, or another employer, with whom there is a business relationship, including any violation involving deception of, or misrepresentation to, any shareholder, investor, client, patient, customer, employee, former employee, retiree or pensioner of the employer or any governmental entity, or, in the case of an employee who is a licensed or certified health care professional, provides information to, or testifies before, any public body conducting an investigation, hearing or inquiry into the quality of patient care; or

c. Objects to, or refuses to participate in any activity, policy or practice which the employee reasonably believes:

(1) is in violation of a law, or a rule or regulation promulgated pursuant to law, including any violation involving deception of, or misrepresentation to, any shareholder, investor, client, patient, customer, employee, former employee, retiree or pensioner of the employer or any governmental entity, or, if the employee is a licensed or certified health care professional, constitutes improper quality of patient care;

(2) is fraudulent or criminal, including any activity, policy or practice of deception or misrepresentation which the employee reasonably believes may defraud any shareholder, investor, client, patient, customer, employee, former employee, retiree or pensioner of the employer or any governmental entity; or

(3) is incompatible with a clear mandate of public policy concerning the public health, safety or welfare or protection of the environment.

CEPA goes on to provide for a one-year statute of limitations and a jury trial. § 34:19-5. Remedies include legal or equitable relief, including punitive damages, attorneys' fees, and a civil fine. In an unusual provision, § 34:19-6 allows the reasonable attorneys' fees and court costs to the *employer* "if the court determines that an action brought by an employee under this act was without basis in law or in fact."

Minn. Stat. § 181.932 (2009)

Disclosure of Information by Employees

1. Prohibited action.

An employer shall not discharge, discipline, threaten, otherwise discriminate against, or penalize an employee regarding the employee's compensation, terms, conditions, location, or privileges of employment because:

(1) the employee, or a person acting on behalf of an employee, in good faith, reports a violation or suspected violation of any federal or state law or rule adopted pursuant to law to an employer or to any governmental body or law enforcement official;

(2) the employee is requested by a public body or office to participate in an investigation, hearing, inquiry;

(3) the employee refuses an employer's order to perform an action that the employee has an objective basis in fact to believe violates any state or federal law or rule or regulation adopted pursuant to law, and the employee informs the employer that the order is being refused for that reason;

(4) the employee, in good faith, reports a situation in which the quality of health care services provided by a health care facility, organization, or health care provider violates a standard established by federal or state law or a professionally recognized national clinical or ethical standard and potentially places the public at risk of harm; or

(5) a public employee communicates the findings of a scientific or technical study that the employee, in good faith, believes to be truthful and accurate, including reports to a governmental body or law enforcement official.

The disclosures protected pursuant to this section do not authorize the disclosure of data otherwise protected by law.

NOTES

1. *Applying the Statutes.* Suppose CEPA had been in effect in Utah. Would Rackley have fared better? Section 3 protects disclosures, inter alia, to "supervisors" of "an activity, policy or practice of the employer that the employee reasonably believes is in violation of a law. . . ." Did Rackley satisfy this standard? What about Iowa — would it have affected Fitzgerald's suit? Fitzgerald won under the Iowa common law.

Would he have won under CEPA? Read § 3 carefully. Now apply the Minnesota analysis to the facts of the two cases. Rackley's conduct might or might not be protected, depending in part on whether it relates to the quality of health care the home provided.

2. "*Exhaustion*." CEPA's § 4 requires the employee to have brought the problem "to the attention of [her] supervisor . . . *by written notice*" (emphasis added) before the employee makes disclosure to a public body. This departs from the common-law cases, which have not generally imposed any duty of "exhaustion of internal remedies," much less required a writing. Indeed, to the extent that many states do not extend public policy tort protection to internal complaints, it is a radical departure. The Minnesota statute requires notice (and does not require it be in writing) in only one circumstance, when the employee "refuses an employer's order to perform an action that the employee has an objective basis in fact to believe violates any state or federal law or rule or regulation adopted pursuant to law." In such cases, protection depends on the employee's informing the employer that the order is being refused for that reason. § 181.932(1)(c). If your jurisdiction were considering a statute along the lines of the CEPA or the Minnesota law, would you recommend any requirement of resort to internal remedies? If so, when?

3. *Reasonable Belief.* How certain must an employee be that his employer is violating public policy in order to receive statutory protection? Neither state requires the employee to be correct. CEPA speaks in terms of the employee's "reasonable belief," but the Minnesota statute is even more protective. It protects "good faith" reports of violations, § 181.932(1)(c) — although, when the employee refuses to perform what he views as an illegal act, he must have an "objective basis in fact" for believing that the performance would violate the law. § 181.932(1)(c). An "objective basis in fact" appears to be something akin to a "reasonable belief." Why do you suppose the Minnesota legislature decided to include different standards in subparts (a) and (c)?

In contrast to the expansive approaches of Minnesota and New Jersey, a few other states take an "at the employee's peril" approach. *Pooler v. Maine Coal Products*, 532 A.2d 1026 (Me. 1987), applied that state's narrow law protecting employees who refuse to follow an employer order that violates a law and would put anyone's health and safety at risk. It held that an employee who refused to drive an allegedly unsafe truck must prove an actual safety violation. Which of these three approaches is preferable?

4. *Complaint Box or 1-800 Number?* Section 7 of CEPA requires an employer to designate "the persons . . . to receive written notifications pursuant to section 4 of this act." Would you consider retaining individuals who are required to keep the name of the notifying employee confidential from others within the company? Such an approach, if effective, would tend to immunize complainers from retaliation and thereby tend to protect you from suit. How could you make the confidentiality provision credible? Name an ombudsman? Choose an outside professional such as an attorney? Ironically, in *Estate of Roach v. TRW, Inc.*, 754 A.2d 544 (N.J. 2000), the employer set up a hotline staffed by its attorneys, but the plaintiff's call "fell through the cracks."

5. *Scope of Public Policy.* CEPA and the Minnesota statute seem to be both broader and narrower than the common law. For example, neither protects an employee from reprisal for "claiming a benefit arising from employment." On the other hand, CEPA's catch-all language — protecting an employee who refuses to participate in an activity she reasonably believes to be "incompatible with a clear mandate of public policy concerning the public health, safety, or welfare or protection of the environment," 3(c)(3) — seems to go far beyond a refusal to participate in activities that are "illegal." And Minnesota has the provision protecting communicating "the findings of a scientific or technical study," whose origins and meaning are somewhat obscure but nevertheless does not require any nexus to public policy. Again, imagine you are drafting a statute for your jurisdiction. How would you frame the substantive protections in terms of the scope of public policy?

6. *Limitations on Whistleblowing. Fitzgerald* recognized the possibility that an employer's retaliation might be justified if the employee's whistleblowing were somehow inappropriate, and we saw in the Note on Attorneys and the Public Policy Tort on page 198 that professional ethics might bar disclosure of client confidences and therefore, justify actions against an attorney who violated those confidences. CEPA contains no explicit exceptions to its protection, but the Minnesota statute expressly excludes from its general protection (1) most disclosures of "the identity of any employee making a report to a governmental body or law enforcement official"; (2) false disclosures — that is, "statements or disclosures [made by an employee] knowing that they are false or that they are in reckless disregard of the truth"; and (3) and disclosure of "confidential information" — that is, "disclosures that would violate federal or state law or diminish or impair the rights of any person to the continued protection of confidentiality of communications provided by common law." § 181.932 (2), (3), (5). If you were drafting a statute, would you include any exceptions? If so, do the Minnesota ones make sense? Do you understand what the last one is driving at?

7. *Electing Remedies.* CEPA explicitly allows a choice between the state's common-law public policy tort, first recognized in *Pierce v. Ortho Pharm. Corp.,* 417 A.2d 505 (N.J. 1980), and the statutory cause of action. But it does require an election between the two in § 34:19-8, which provides that while the act does not diminish other employee rights, "the institution of an action in accordance with this act shall be deemed a waiver of the rights and remedies available under any other contract, collective bargaining agreement, State law, rule or regulation or under the common law." What are the advantages of suit under CEPA as opposed to claiming a common-law tort? Attorneys' fees are one obvious plus, although there is also a countervailing risk to the losing plaintiff because a fee can be awarded against her in certain circumstances. § 34:19-6. The statute of limitations under the statute is only one year; in New Jersey, tort suits are normally subject to a two-year limitation, *see McGrogan v. Till,* 771 A.2d 1187 (N.J. 2001).

8. *A Job Duties Exception?* When we reach Chapter 7, we will discover that First Amendment protection does not extend to public employees whose actions fall within their job duties. Does such an exception operate under the New Jersey or Minnesota laws? Should it? In *Kidwell v. Sybaritic, Inc.,* 784 N.W.2d 220 (Minn. 2010), Minnesota rejected recognizing such an exception under that state's statute, largely because it was inconsistent with the broad statutory language. However, "we do not go so far as to hold that an employee's job duties are irrelevant in determining whether an employee has engaged in protected conduct." The court was concerned that a protected employee be motivated by a desire to "expos[e] an illegality," and when action was within an employee's job duties, it might not have been taken for this purpose. In the case before it, *Kidwell* found that the plaintiff, in-house general counsel for the defendant, had not adduced sufficient evidence to allow a jury to find that his opinion concerning the legality of his client's withholding discovery was offered in order to expose illegality. *See generally* Nancy Modesitt, *The* Garcetti *Virus* (forthcoming).

PROBLEMS

4-3. Review Problem 4-1. How would you resolve it under the New Jersey and Minnesota statutes?

4-4. Review Problem 4-2. How would you resolve it under the New Jersey and Minnesota statutes?

Maimone v. City of Atlantic City
903 A.2d 1055 (N.J. 2006)

SKILLMAN, J.

This appeal involves a claim under the [CEPA] by a police officer who alleges he was transferred from detective to patrolman in retaliation for his objections to the Chief of Police's decision to terminate enforcement of provisions of the Code of Criminal Justice prohibiting promotion of prostitution and restricting the location of sexually-oriented businesses.

I.

Plaintiff Angelo Maimone has been a member of the Atlantic City Police Department since 1988. He was transferred in 1991 from a patrolman position to detective in the Special Investigations Unit. As a result, plaintiff became contractually entitled after one year to receive an additional 3% of his base salary. Beginning in 1993, plaintiff was assigned to conduct investigations of prostitution and other sexually-related offenses, which he continued to do until early 2001.

In May 2000, defendant Arthur C. Snellbaker was appointed Chief of the Atlantic City Police Department. According to plaintiff, around eight months after Snellbaker's appointment, Captain William Glass told him at a staff meeting that he could not initiate any new promotion of prostitution investigations unless they "directly impacted the citizens of Atlantic City." Shortly thereafter, plaintiff's immediate supervisor, Sergeant Glenn Abrams, directed him to terminate all pending investigations into the promotion of prostitution and to conduct only narcotics investigations. Plaintiff alleges that Abrams told him that "they," referring to prostitution investigations, "don't exist." Plaintiff, who at that point was the only detective still actively involved in promotion of prostitution investigations, understood this directive to apply not only to him but also to all other officers in the Special Investigations Unit.

Around the same time Abrams gave plaintiff this directive, the files plaintiff had maintained regarding persons involved in the promotion of prostitution were removed from a filing cabinet under his control, and thereafter, plaintiff's access to those files was restricted. When plaintiff complained to Abrams about his loss of access to these files, Abrams allegedly told him: "You're never going to see the files again."

[In April 2001, plaintiff sent a memorandum to Sergeant Abrams complaining about his inability to access those files. It noted that he routinely updated files "on Escort and Massage services working in Atlantic City," and referred to "at least seven new services operating this month alone." The memorandum complained about the absence of file space for new files and the absence of any means of cross-referencing these files against current files. It asked for Chief Snellbaker's response.]

According to plaintiff, after Abrams read this memorandum, he shook his head and said to plaintiff: "You're asking for it."

In 2001, Maimone also complained about Atlantic City's failure to enforce *N.J.S.A.* 2C:34-7, which makes it a fourth-degree offense for a sexually-oriented business to operate within 1,000 feet of a church or school. After the county prosecutor decided that *N.J.S.A.* 2C:34-7 should be enforced by the revocation of the mercantile licenses of offenders rather than by criminal prosecution, plaintiff wrote letters to the municipal solicitor requesting the initiation of proceedings to revoke the licenses of sexually-oriented businesses that were operating in violation of this prohibition. When the city solicitor failed to take any action, plaintiff sent a memorandum to Abrams, dated May 26, 2001, which stated in part:

> I am respectfully asking, that this Office request that the mercantile license of AC News and Video be revoked, due to the fact that this location is clearly in violation of 2C:34-7. This location is clearly a detriment to the neighborhood. There is a Covenant House for juveniles on the same block as well as an elementary school and Synagogue being nearby. As you are aware, it has been and continues to be the practice of the Atlantic County Prosecutor's Office, not to prosecute this statute. It is their contention that civil remedies (IE: Removal of Mercantile license) would be sufficient and thus relieving the Prosecutors Office from utilizing their limited resources in prosecution.
>
> If the city chooses not to enforce this statute in this matter, all future prosecutions will be jeopardized.

Within days after he sent this memorandum, Captain Glass said to plaintiff: "You're out of here, you're going to patrol." Effective June 10, 2001, plaintiff was transferred from his detective position in the Special Investigations Unit to patrol officer. Plaintiff was told that the reason for his transfer was an April 17, 2001 newspaper story that disclosed he had attended the wedding of a daughter of a suspected organized crime figure.

II.

[The trial court granted summary judgment to the defendants because plaintiff could not create a genuine issue of material fact that he reasonably believed Atlantic City's decision to cease enforcing the provisions of the Code relating to promotion of prostitution and restricting the location of sexually oriented businesses "violat[ed] . . . a clear mandate of public policy." The Appellate Division reversed, and Supreme Court granted defendants' petition for certification.]

III.

Plaintiff's CEPA claim is based on *N.J.S.A.* 34:19-3c, which provides:

An employer shall not take any retaliatory action against an employee because the employee does any of the following. . . .

    c. Objects to, or refuses to participate in any activity, policy or practice which the employee reasonably believes:

        (1) is in violation of a law, or a rule or regulation promulgated pursuant to law . . . ;

        (2) is fraudulent or criminal; or

        (3) is incompatible with a clear mandate of public policy concerning the public health, safety or welfare or protection of the environment.

[T]he Court held in *Dzwonar* [*v. McDevitt,* 828 A.2d 893 (N.J. 2003)] that a plaintiff who brings an action under this section must demonstrate that:

(1) he or she reasonably believed that his or her employer's conduct was violating either a law, rule, or regulation promulgated pursuant to law, or a clear mandate of public policy; (2) he or she performed a "whistle-blowing" activity described in *N.J.S.A.* 34:19-3c; (3) an adverse employment action was taken against him or her; and (4) a causal connection exists between the whistle-blowing activity and the adverse employment action.

These requirements must be liberally construed to effectuate CEPA's important social goals.

    Defendants do not dispute that plaintiffs' objections to Atlantic City's alleged policy decision to cease enforcement of the provisions of the Code that prohibit promotion of prostitution and restrict the location of sexually-oriented businesses constituted a "whistle-blowing" activity, thus satisfying the second requirement of a claim under *N.J.S.A.* 34:19-3c identified in *Dzwonar*. However, defendants argue that the evidence plaintiff presented in opposition to their motion for summary judgment was insufficient to establish the other three requirements of a claim under this section. We address those requirements in the order set forth in *Dzwonar*.

A.

    Plaintiff rests his claim solely on subsection (3) of *N.J.S.A.* 34:19-3c. At the outset, it is appropriate to compare the elements of a claim under this subsection with a claim under c(1). While an employee who proceeds under c(1) must show that he or she reasonably believed that the employer's activity, policy or practice "violat[ed]" a law, rule, or regulation, an employee who proceeds under c(3) is only required to show that the employer's activity, policy, or practice is "incompatible" with a clear mandate of public policy. To "violate" a law, a person must commit "[a]n infraction or breach of the law," BLACK'S LAW DICTIONARY 1564 (7th ed.1999), but a person's conduct may be found "incompatible" with a law based solely on a showing that the conduct is "irreconcilable" with that law, *id.* at 768. Moreover, since the recognized sources of public policy within the intent of c(3) include state laws, rules and regulations, *Mehlman v. Mobil Oil Corp.*, 707 A.2d 1000 (N.J. 1998), a plaintiff who pursues a CEPA claim under this subsection may rely upon the same laws, rules and regulations that may be the subject of a claim under c(1).). Consequently, it is easier for an employee who proceeds under c(3) to prove that he or she reasonably believed the employer's conduct was "incompatible" with a clear mandate of public policy expressed in a law, rule or regulation than to show, as required by c(1), a reasonable belief that the employer's conduct "violated" a law, rule or regulation.

However, an employee who proceeds under c(3) must establish an additional element that is not required to prove a claim under c(1). Although an employee may pursue an action under c(1) based on objections to employer conduct that he or she reasonably believes violated any law, rule or regulation, an employee who proceeds under c(3) must make the additional showing that the "clear mandate of public policy" he or she reasonably believes the employer's policy to be incompatible with is one that "concern[s] the public health, safety or welfare or protection of the environment." *See Estate of Roach v. TRW, Inc.*, 754 A.2d 544 (N.J. 2000). This requirement is "unique" to c(3). *Id.*

The significance of this additional element of a claim under c(3) is illustrated by *Maw v. Advanced Clinical Commc'ns*, 846 A.2d 604 (N.J. 2004), in which an employee brought a CEPA claim challenging her termination for refusing to execute an employment agreement containing what the employee believed to be an overly expansive do-not-compete clause. This Court concluded that case law which allows a no-compete provision only if it is reasonable does not constitute "a clear mandate of public policy" within the intent of c(3) because an employer's attempt to impose an unreasonable no-competition agreement impacts solely upon the individual employee and does not "implicate the public interest." *Maw.*

Unlike in *Maw* the provisions of the Code of Criminal Justice that prohibit promotion of prostitution and restrict the location of sexually-oriented businesses constitute "a clear mandate of public policy concerning the public health, safety or welfare[.]" The Code makes promotion of prostitution either a third or fourth-degree offense, depending on the circumstances, *see N.J.S.A.* 2C:34-1b(2) and *N.J.S.A.* 2C:34-1c(3), and it makes the operation of a sexually-oriented business within 1,000 feet of a school or church a fourth-degree offense, *N.J.S.A.* 2C:34-7. These provisions reflect a legislative recognition that the promotion of prostitution and other commercial sexual activities are a source of "venereal disease, . . . profit and power for criminal groups who commonly combine it with illicit trade in drugs and liquor, illegal gambling and even robbery and extortion[,] . . . [and] corrupt influence on government and law enforcement machinery." II *The New Jersey Penal Code, Final Report of the N.J. Criminal Law Revision Commission*, 301-2-cmt. 1 on NJSA § 2C:34-2 (1971).

To prevail on a CEPA claim under c(3), plaintiff is not required to show that defendants' alleged policy decision to cease enforcement of the provisions of the Code prohibiting the promotion of prostitution and restricting the location of sexually-oriented businesses actually violated or was incompatible with a statute, rule or other clear mandate of public policy. *See Dzwonar.* Plaintiff only has to show that he had an "objectively reasonable belief" in the existence of such a violation or incompatibility. Plaintiff may carry this burden by demonstrating that "there is a substantial nexus between the complained-of conduct" — the cessation of investigations of promotion of prostitution and failure to enforce laws relating to the location of sexually-oriented businesses — and "[the] law or public policy identified by . . . plaintiff" — in this case the provisions of the Code proscribing such criminal conduct.

We conclude that plaintiff's proofs met this burden. Viewing the evidence in the light most favorable to plaintiff, as required on a motion for summary judgment, it could support a finding that he had an objectively reasonable belief that defendants made a policy decision to cease all investigation and enforcement of the Code provisions prohibiting the promotion of prostitution and restricting the location of sexually-oriented businesses. Plaintiff testified that Captain Glass told him at a staff meeting in January 2001 not to initiate any new prostitution investigations unless they directly impacted the citizens of Atlantic City, and shortly thereafter, Sergeant Abrams issued a directive to terminate all pending promotion of prostitution investigations. Around the same time Sergeant Abrams issued this directive, the files plaintiff had maintained regarding persons involved in the promotion of prostitution were removed from a filing cabinet under his control, and thereafter, his access to those files was severely restricted. Since plaintiff was the only detective still actively involved in promotion of prostitution investigations at that time, he could reasonably have believed that the intent of Sergeant Abrams' directive and the removal of his investigation files was to terminate all such investigations in Atlantic City.

In addition, when plaintiff sent a memorandum requesting his superiors' assistance in persuading the municipal solicitor to initiate proceedings to revoke the mercantile licenses of sexually-oriented businesses operating in violation of *N.J.S.A.* 2C:34-7, the only response he received was Captain Glass' comment: "You're out of here, you're going to patrol." Plaintiff further testified that the City never took any action to revoke the licenses of sexually-oriented businesses that were operating in violation of *N.J.S.A.* 2C:34-7. Therefore, a trier of fact could find that plaintiff had an objectively reasonable belief that Atlantic City had made a policy decision not to enforce this statutory prohibition.

[Unlike an earlier case in which plaintiff had alleged that his employer had failed to follow his recommendations regarding two petitions of exclusion from casinos, Maimone's] claim is not simply that defendants decided to assign a "lower degree of priority" to investigations of violations of the Code provisions prohibiting promotion of prostitution and restricting the location of sexually-oriented businesses, but rather that they made a policy decision to terminate all enforcement of these criminal laws. Plaintiff was not told, and had no other reason to believe, that this alleged policy decision was due to budgetary constraints or an administrative determination that there was a need to assign additional officers to the investigation of more serious crimes. Therefore, a trier of fact could find that plaintiff had an objectively reasonable belief that defendants made a policy decision that was incompatible with a clear mandate of public policy concerning the public health, safety and welfare.

B.

We next consider defendants' argument that plaintiff failed to present sufficient evidence to support a jury finding that "an adverse employment action" was taken against him.

CEPA prohibits an employer from taking "retaliatory action" against an employee for protected conduct. *N.J.S.A.* 34:19-3. "Retaliatory action" is defined by CEPA to mean "the discharge, suspension or demotion of an employee, or *other adverse employment action* taken against an employee *in the terms and conditions of employment*." *N.J.S.A.* 34:19-2(e) (emphasis added). Under this definition, any reduction in an employee's compensation is considered to be an "adverse . . . action . . . in the terms and conditions of employment." Moreover, even without any reduction in compensation, a withdrawal of benefits formerly provided to an employee may be found in some circumstances to constitute an adverse employment action.

Plaintiff presented sufficient evidence that his transfer from a detective position to patrol duty resulted in both a reduction in his compensation and a loss of other benefits to satisfy this element of a cause of action under *N.J.S.A.* 34:19-3. Although plaintiff's transfer to patrol duty was not considered a demotion in rank, it resulted in a 3% reduction in his compensation. . . . In addition, plaintiff testified that detectives have an opportunity to earn substantially more overtime than officers assigned to patrol duty, that the 3% salary differential is reflected in the calculation of a retiring police officer's pension, and that detectives are assigned unmarked police cars that they can use to commute back and forth to work. We conclude that this alleged reduction in compensation and loss of other benefits as a result of plaintiff's transfer from his detective position to patrol duty could support a finding that he suffered an "adverse employment action."

C.

The requirement that an employee who brings a CEPA claim under *N.J.S.A.* 34:19-3 must show "a causal connection exists between the whistle-blowing activity and the adverse employment action[,]" *Dzwonar*, can be satisfied by inferences that the trier of fact may reasonably draw based on circumstances surrounding the employment action, *Roach v. TRW, Inc.* The temporal proximity of employee conduct protected by CEPA and an adverse employment action is one circumstance that may support an inference of a causal connection. . . .

Furthermore, there is evidence that would support a finding that the reason defendants gave for plaintiff's transfer to patrol was pretextual. On April 17, 2001, during the period plaintiff was complaining to Sergeant Abrams about the City's alleged non-enforcement of the laws relating to the promotion of prostitution, Chief Snellbaker requested the Internal Affairs Bureau to conduct an investigation into plaintiff's attendance at the 1998 wedding of the daughter of a suspected organized crime figure. On May 25, 2001, the Internal Affairs Bureau issued a report that concluded plaintiff's superiors had authorized his attendance at the wedding for the purpose of "gathering intelligence information," and that plaintiff had submitted an intelligence report after the wedding describing what he had observed and heard. Consequently, the Internal Affairs Bureau concluded plaintiff's attendance at the wedding was "justified, legal and proper." Although the Internal Affairs Bureau exonerated plaintiff of any wrongdoing in connection with his attendance at the wedding, plaintiff was told that this was the reason for his transfer to patrol duty. The implausibility of this explanation for plaintiff's transfer is an additional circumstance that could support a finding that the real reason for this adverse employment action was plaintiff's complaints about defendants' alleged failure to enforce the laws relating to promotion of prostitution and the location of sexually-oriented businesses. . . .

IV.

The dissent charges that our opinion "appears to graft a new limitation on the discretionary governance prerogatives of an employer[.]" However, there is nothing novel in the proposition that a statute — in this instance the Code of Criminal Justice — constitutes a "clear mandate of public policy" within the intent of CEPA. Plaintiff does not seek, as the dissent asserts, "to determine law enforcement policy for [the] entire [Atlantic City Police Department]." He only seeks to avail himself of the judicial remedies provided by CEPA for the adverse employment action taken against him for objecting to the police department's alleged policy decision to cease enforcement of the Code provisions prohibiting promotion of prostitution and restricting the location of sexually-oriented businesses. Plaintiff's claim does not rest simply on his personal disagreement with this policy decision, but on an objectively reasonable belief that it "is incompatible with a clear mandate of public policy concerning the public health, safety or welfare[.]" *N.J.S.A.* 34:19-3c(3). Therefore, our recognition of plaintiff's right to pursue this claim before a jury is mandated by the State legislative policy expressed in CEPA to protect employee whistle-blowing activity. . . .

RIVERA-SOTO, Justice, dissenting. . . .

I.

In this case, a police officer alleges that his reassignment was precipitated by his complaints that the Atlantic City Police Department was not enforcing the laws against prostitution and related offenses to a degree that was personally satisfactory to that police officer. . . . Highlighting the patent absurdity that results from allowing a rank-and-file police officer to determine law enforcement policy for an entire department, the trial court narrowed the inquiry to the decision-making discretion vested in the police officer on patrol and made the common sense observation that "[i]t is self-evident that no police officer can, without prioritizing, effectively prosecute every violation of the law that comes to his or her attention." The trial court further noted that "[o]ne may reasonably conclude that a police officer should have the discretion to determine that there are legitimate priorities that would preclude the investment of the same level of resources in the enforcement of every provision of law."

[The trial court's decision was correct in viewing plaintiff's claim as "an unsupportable extension" of CEPA "to afford to every police officer the ability, under the authority of a CEPA claim, to hold his or her department accountable to the officer for any discretionary determinations of resource allocation and law enforcement priorities solely because those determinations differed from the officer's views." Further, "[i]t would be manifestly inappropriate to substitute, for the City's judgment, [plaintiff's] view or that of a court or jury with regard to the appropriate priorities for applying the law enforcement resources available to the City."]

II.

There is a further notion in the majority's reasoning that is particularly troublesome. . . .

Under the majority's view, a municipality now must be governed by its lowest common denominator or risk the imposition of liability. Stripped to its essence, the majority rules that plaintiff's claim survives summary judgment not because of any wrongful municipal action, but because "[p]laintiff was not told, and had no other reason to believe, that this alleged policy decision [to limit the resources assigned to combat the promotion of prostitution or sexually oriented businesses] was due to budgetary constraints or an administrative determination that there was a need to assign additional officers to the investigation of more serious crimes." That turns the basis of the employer/employee relationship on its head, requiring that, in order to avoid a potential CEPA lawsuit, an employer must explain every discretionary decision to the satisfaction of every line employee. That was never CEPA's purpose or intendment. . . .

NOTES

1. "*Whistleblowing Activity.*" One of the elements of a CEPA violation is what the *Maimone* court describes as a "whistle-blowing activity." Under paragraph (c), that reaches not only refusal to participate in the defined conduct but also "objecting to" such conduct. The plaintiff did not, even metaphorically, blow a whistle — he just stood up to his bosses, but that was apparently enough to count as "objecting." The Supreme Court has similarly construed Title VII's antiretaliation provision, which in part protects individuals who "oppose" unlawful employment practices. *Crawford v. Metropolitan Government of Nashville & Davidson County*, 129 S. Ct. 846, 851 (2009), ("[W]e would naturally use ['oppose'] to speak of someone who has taken no action at all to advance a position beyond disclosing it. Countless people were known to 'oppose' slavery before Emancipation, or are said to 'oppose' capital punishment today, without writing public letters, taking to the streets, or resisting the government.").

Whatever the reach of paragraph (c), paragraphs (a) and (b) describe yet additional kinds of protected conduct, some of which are more intuitively whistleblowing. But *Maimone* quickly determines that (a) does not apply — to be protected under that prong, the employee must reasonably believe that the "activity, policy, or practice" being disclosed "is in violation of a law." Accordingly to the court, there was no way a police officer could reasonably believe a shift in law enforcement priorities was illegal. What if plaintiff believed that the new policy was the result of a payoff to Snellbaker? That would be in violation of law, but, absent more information, would Maimore have had a basis to "reasonably believe" (as opposed to suspect) that that was the explanation?

Thus, as interpreted by the court, (c) is broader than (a). The employee must, again, reasonably believe that what he·objects to occurs, but the policy or practice does not have to violate any law or regulation. *See also Estate of Frank L. Roach v. TRW, Inc.*, 754 A.2d. 544, 551 (N.J. 2000) (Paragraph (c)(3) "evidences a legislative recognition that certain forms of conduct might be harmful to the public although technically not a violation of a specific statute or regulation."). Doesn't the structure of (3) clearly justify this conclusion? After all, if an employee objects to what she reasonably believes is a violation of law, she is already protected by paragraph (c)(1). But the result is a sweeping statute that cuts the statutory protection loose from any particular statute. Can you identify why, exactly, the court felt Maimone's conduct was protected?

2. *Patent Absurdity?* The dissent speaks of the majority "allowing a rank-and-file police officer to determine law enforcement policy for an entire department." Surely, that's an overstatement. The question isn't whether the department must follow Maimone's views of proper enforcement priorities; rather, it's whether the department can retaliate against Maimone for objecting to the new priorities. But note that paragraph (c)(1) protects employees not only for objecting to activities but also for "refusing to participate" in them. Might the dissent have been concerned that, had Maimone continued to pursue sex-based violations, he couldn't have been demoted for insubordination?

3. *Reasonable Belief.* The *Maimone* decision stresses that plaintiff need not be correct about the activity in question violating a law or a clear mandate of public policy; he or she need only be reasonable. This is a consistent theme in the New Jersey cases. *See Mehlman v. Mobil Oil Corp,* 707 A.2d 1000, 1015-16 (N.J. 1998) ("The object of CEPA is not to make lawyers out of conscientious employees but rather to prevent retaliation against those employees who object to . . . conduct that they reasonably believe to be unlawful or indisputably dangerous to the public health, safety or welfare."). But the court has suggested some limitations. In *Estate of Roach v. TRW, Inc.,* 754 A.2d 544, 552 (N.J. 2000), for example, plaintiff claimed to have been terminated because he reported two of his co-workers for conflicts of interest and for false expense reports and time cards. It wrote:

> Although the term "reasonably believes" in sections 3c.(1) and 3c.(2) provides ample justification to sustain the jury's verdict in the present case, we caution that in future cases that language may prove fatal to an employee's claim. For instance, if an employee were to complain about a co-employee who takes an extended lunch break or makes a personal telephone call to a spouse or friend, we would be hard pressed to conclude that the complaining employee could have "reasonably believed" that such minor infractions represented unlawful conduct as contemplated by CEPA. CEPA is intended to protect those employees whose disclosures fall sensibly within the statute; it is not intended to spawn litigation concerning the most trivial or benign employee complaints.

4. *Adverse Employment Action.* In most of the cases we have seen so far, the claim is for "wrongful dismissal," but plaintiff in *Maimone* wasn't discharged—he was demoted with relatively minor economic consequences. The court, nevertheless, found that the requisite adversity for a violation of CEPA. This is an important point of distinction between statutory claims and common-law claims. While some courts have applied the common-law tort to less severe actions than dismissal, whistleblower statutes tend to be framed to reach at least any actions with economic consequences. This is generally true even under the more restrictive federal decisions requiring an "adverse employment action" in the discrimination context. See Chapter 9.

5. *Notifying the Employer.* CEPA protects employees for actions directed at their employer. Thus, paragraph (a) reaches disclosures to a supervisor and paragraph (c) protects the kind of objection Maimone made. But CEPA also protects disclosure to a public body, paragraph (a), as well as participating in a public hearing or investigation. Paragraph (b). However, in the latter case, CEPA requires the employee to bring the matter "to the attention of a supervisor of the employee by written notice." § 34:19-4. Had Maimone later taken his concerns to the state attorney general, his memorandum presumably would have satisfied this requirement. The written notice requirement is not applicable where the employee "is reasonably certain that the activity, policy, or practice is known to one or more supervisors." *Id.* Isn't this likely to almost always be true? The notice requirement is also inapplicable "where the employee reasonably fears physical harm as a result of the disclosure." *Id.*

6. *Relationship of CEPA to the Public Policy Tort and Other Causes of Action.* The question of the relationship of a whistleblower statute to whatever other claims might exist is an important one. Section 34:19-8 preserves an employee's rights under other laws, including any "federal or State law or regulation or under any collective bargaining agreement or employment contract," but simultaneously provides that the institution of a CEPA action "shall be deemed a waiver of the rights and remedies available under any other contract, collective bargaining agreement, state law, rule or regulation, or under the common law." This is evidently intended to preserve claims of employment discrimination as well as breach of just cause provisions in individual contracts and collective bargaining agreements. But it also seems to require the employee to elect between pursuing CEPA claims and the other causes of action. *Young v. Schering Corp.*, 660 A.2d 1153 (N.J. 1995), held that this provision does not require dismissal of tort and contract claims because they are sufficiently distinct from the CEPA claim. Rejecting a literal reading, the court wrote, "we are thoroughly convinced the Legislature did not intend to penalize former employees by forcing them to choose between a CEPA claim and other legitimate claims that are substantially, if not totally, independent of the retaliatory discharge claim." *Id.* at 25. Prior to CEPA, however, New Jersey had recognized a common-law public policy tort. Presumably, such tort claims would not be "independent of the retaliatory discharge claim" and an employee would have to elect between them and the statute.

Other states have also addressed the relationship of their whistleblower acts to the public policy tort. For example, Montana recognizes a cause of action for "retaliation for the employee's . . . reporting a violation of public policy." Mont. Code Ann., §39-2-901; §2-904(1) (2010). In turn, §2-903(7) of the Montana statute defines public policy as "a policy in effect at the time of the discharge concerning the public health, safety, or welfare established by constitutional provision, statute or administrative rule." Section 2-913 expressly preempts common law remedies. *But see McCool v. Hillhaven Corp.*, 777 P.2d 1013 (Or. App. 1989) (whistleblowing statute was not exclusive remedy for plaintiff, who was still permitted to bring tort suit).

2. Federal Whistleblower Protection

While statutory protection is increasingly common in the states, the federal government has long had statutes providing protection for specific disclosures. Generally speaking, however, these were intended to bulwark particular regulatory regimes, such as nuclear energy or transportation or the antidiscrimination laws. As a result of Enron and other corporate meltdowns, Congress enacted the most sweeping federal statute providing whistleblower protections in the form of the Sarbanes-Oxley Act ("SOX") of 2002, Pub. L. 107-204, 116 Stat. 745. While SOX is not a true general whistleblower statute, in the sense that it does not provide protection for conduct furthering a range of public policies, it is the first federal enactment that broadly reaches the private sector. Further, it is only one of a number of more aggressive uses of whistleblower protections in federal legislation. As we will see, the Obama adminstration's stimulus package, health care reform legislation, and financial reform law all have whistleblowing provisions. These, however, are not only too new to generate any interpretive law but also tend to be variations on the SOX theme, which is explored below.

Professor Miriam Cherry summarized the origins of SOX:

As the accounting scandals surrounding Enron and WorldCom dominated the headlines and business ethics became increasingly suspect, two whistleblowers became symbols of integrity to the American public. Indeed, Sherron Watkins and Cynthia Cooper were among "The Whistleblowers" named as Time magazine's "Persons of the Year" for 2002. At significant risk to their careers, financial well-being, and mental health, Cooper and Watkins alerted high-level executives at their respective companies to accounting fraud. Unfortunately, most whistleblowers take all these risks when they report illegal activities occurring within their organizations. The magnitude of these recent frauds is startling and, unfortunately, appears to be indicative of a widespread problem. . . .
In response to the corporate scandals of 2002, Congress enacted the Sarbanes-Oxley Act (the Act) to prevent future corporate corruption and securities fraud. The Act contains a provision, § 806, that aims to protect whistleblowers such as Cooper and Watkins who report accounting fraud. [The Act covers] all workers at publicly traded companies who "blow the whistle" on suspect accounting practices, whether that whistleblowing is done within the organization, to government agencies, or as part of a shareholder lawsuit. . . .

Miriam A. Cherry, *Whistling in the Dark? Corporate Fraud, Whistleblowers, and the Implications of the Sarbanes-Oxley Act for Employment Law*, 79 WASH. L. REV. 1029, 1031-33, 1063-64 (2004). *See also* Elizabeth C. Tippett, *The Promise of Compelled Whistleblowing: What the Corporate Governance Provisions of Sarbanes-Oxley Mean for Employment Law*, 11 EMPL. RTS. & EMPLOY. POL'Y J. 1 (2007).

Collins v. Beazer Homes USA, Inc.
334 F. Supp. 2d 1365 (N.D. Ga. 2004)

STORY, District Judge. . . .

Background

This case arises out of Plaintiff Judy Collins' employment with and termination from Defendant Beazer Homes Corp. [a wholly owned subsidiary of Beazer Homes Holding Corp., which is a wholly owned subsidiary of Beazer Homes USA, Inc., which is a publicly traded company. Beazer Homes Corp.] offered Collins a position as Director of Marketing for its Jacksonville, Florida division. According to the offer, Collins would be subject to a ninety day assessment review period during which "either you or the Company may decide to terminate employment without giving a reason." Collins accepted the offer and began work around June 10, 2002.

Soon after starting with the company, Collins began having conflicts with her manager, Division President Bill Mazar, and her coworker, Director of Sales Mary Ann Hashem. [The conflicts regarded the use of the Montello Advertising Agency. Collins contracted with a new advertising agency but "believed that Mazar and Hashem continued to use Montello's services behind her back even after she had terminated the agency." She raised her concerns with Marilyn Gardner, Vice President of Sales and Marketing for Beazer Homes USA, Inc., including her concern that marketing costs were not being properly categorized in the company accounting records. Gardner informed her these were "serious allegations" and "something very important." Gardner then arranged for Collins to meet with Jennifer Jones, Vice President of Human Resources for Beazer USA.]

On August 5, 2002, Collins met with Jones for about an hour and a half. Collins tape recorded the meeting but the tape ran out before the end of the meeting. During her meeting with Jones, Collins raised numerous concerns. Jones described four main concerns that Collins expressed, including concerns that (1) the division was putting product on the land that she did not think were reasonable; (2) they were paying Montello for bills that should not be paid and were being forced to use the agency by the President of the Jacksonville division Marty Shaffer; (3) she did not particularly care for the management style of Mazar; and (4) sales agents were discontented with Hashem and the length of time it took to complete a home. Based on Collins' statements to Jones, Jones began to investigate Collins' claims and spoke with various company officials. Jones sought to determine whether the issues that Collins had raised were merely business issues or whether something criminal, against the law or against company policy was taking place.

Regarding Collins' concerns about the types of homes being built, Jones spoke with Michael Furlow, Executive Vice President and Chief Operating Officer of Beazer USA. Furlow informed Jones that this was a strategic business decision and not a human resources issue. Furlow reached the same conclusion about Collins' complaint about Mazar's management style. Regarding the payments to Montello, Jones spoke with Ian McCarthy, Chief Executive Officer of Beazer USA. McCarthy directed Jones to speak directly with Shaffer. Shaffer informed Jones that the president of Montello had called him about a past due invoice that Collins had refused to pay. Shaffer told Mazar to review the invoice, and to pay it if Beazer owed the agency money, and if not, to discuss it with Montello. Mazar reviewed the invoices from Montello and paid them. Collins states that Mazar spoke with Shaffer and then told her that Shaffer wanted her to pay Montello regardless of the amount because Shaffer and Montello's president were friends. Jones also investigated the concerns surrounding the sales agents. Jones' investigation surrounding the sales agent problems ultimately resulted in Hashem's reprimand and termination.

On August 11, 2002, Collins sent an email letter to the Chief Executive Officer of Beazer USA, Ian McCarthy. In her letter, she alluded to her meetings with Jones and Gardner and asserted that a "cover-up/corruption" existed. She did not indicate, however, any specifics. McCarthy discussed the letter with Jones and asked her to continue her investigation and report her findings to him. McCarthy responded to Collins by email through his assistant and stated that the matter would be investigated and she should plan to attend the previously scheduled meeting with Shaffer scheduled for August 19, 2002.

On August 14, 2002, Collins emailed Gardner. In the four page email, Collins again expressed her frustration with the investigation and complained about Montello. She alleged that Mazar told her to pay Montello regardless of the amount, that she suspected kickbacks in lumber purchases, and that marketing costs were not being properly broken-down in order to hide information. Prior to the August 19, 2002 meeting with Collins, Shaffer discussed Collins' complaints with Jones. Jones informed Shaffer that Collins had made a series of complaints including allegations of a break in company policy. Shaffer and Jones also discussed whether they should continue Collins' employment. Shaffer questioned Jones about the circumstances under which he could terminate Collins.

On August 19, 2002, Collins met with Shaffer. Shaffer understood that one of the purposes of the meeting was for him to discuss with Collins possible violations of company policy. She also tape recorded this conversation. At that meeting Collins expressed numerous complaints including: her lack of input with sales agents, that Hashem did not want her in the Jacksonville office, that she could not get the information she needed to do her job, and that she was having conflicts with Mazar and Hashem over the Montello agency. Collins did not specifically tell Shaffer that illegal activity was taking place in the company. At the end of the meeting, Shaffer told Collins that "I don't see that this situation is going to work out between [you, Mazar and Hashem]." Shaffer noted that Mazar and Hashem had been with the company for some time, and since it did not appear that the conflict with Collins was going to end, he would have to let her go.

Although Shaffer consulted with Jones regarding Collins' termination, he states that he was the sole person responsible for terminating her. Shaffer stated that he terminated Collins for several reasons including Mazar's dissatisfaction with her job performance, a presentation he viewed by Collins that was "way off the mark," but primarily because she could not get along with any of her fellow employees.

[Collins filed a complaint with the Department of Labor Occupational Safety and Health Administration in October 2002; in May 2003, she filed suit under Sarbanes-Oxley and Florida's Whistleblower's Act, Fla. Stat. § 448.102. OSHA issued findings and preliminary order on May 22, 2003.]

Discussion . . .

II. Motion for Summary Judgment . . .

Plaintiff asserts that Defendants retaliated against her in violation of Sarbanes-Oxley and Florida's Whistleblower's Act for reporting violations of Defendants' internal accounting controls in violation of Securities laws. Plaintiff contends that fourteen days after she first met with the Vice President of Human Resources to report the violations and eight days after emailing the CEO of the company, she was terminated. Defendants move for summary judgment and assert that Plaintiff did not engage in protected activity. Moreover, Defendants contend that Plaintiff was terminated during her initial ninety day probationary period because of personality conflicts with her coworkers and her inability to get along with them and not for any protected activity.

III. The Sarbanes-Oxley Act of 2002

Plaintiff's claims arose almost in tandem with the enactment of Sarbanes-Oxley and come before the Court as a matter of first impression. The Sarbanes-Oxley Act of 2002 was enacted on July 30, 2002. *See* Procedures for Handling of Discrimination Complaints Under Section 806 of the Corporate and Criminal Fraud Accountability Act of 2002, Title VIII of the Sarbanes-Oxley Act of 2002, 29 C.F.R. § 1980 (2003) (hereinafter "Sarbanes-Oxley Regulations" or "the Regulations"). Title VIII of Sarbanes-Oxley is designated as the Corporate and Criminal Fraud Accountability Act of 2002. Section 806, codified at 18 U.S.C. § 1514A, is the provision that provides "whistleblower" protection to employees of publicly traded companies.[4] Pursuant to section 806, an employer may not discriminate against any employee in the terms and conditions of employment because of any lawful act done by the employee

> (1) to provide information, cause information to be provided, or otherwise assist in an investigation regarding any conduct which the employee reasonably believes constitutes a violation of section 1341, 1343, 1344, or 1348, any rule or regulation of the Securities and Exchange Commission, or any provision of Federal law relating to fraud against shareholders, when the information or assistance is provided to or the investigation is conducted by —
>   (A) a Federal regulatory or law enforcement agency;
>   (B) any Member of Congress or any committee of Congress; or
>   (C) a person with supervisory authority over the employee (or such other person working for the employer who has the authority to investigate, discover, or terminate misconduct). . . .

18 U.S.C. § 1514A(a)(1). . . .

B. Legal Burdens of Proof

Given the scarcity of case law on Sarbanes-Oxley, the Court must look to decisional law applying provisions of other federal whistleblower statutes for guidance. [These include the Wendell H. Ford Aviation Investment Reform Act for the 21st Century ("AIR 21"), 29 C.F.R. § 1979; the Surface Transportation Assistance Act ("STAA"), 29 C.F.R. § 1978; and the Energy Reorganization Act ("ERA"), 29 C.F.R. 24.] Moreover, the legal burdens of proof in Sarbanes-Oxley are taken from AIR 21, 49 U.S.C. § 42121.

When a plaintiff files suit in federal court under Sarbanes-Oxley, the court conducts a de novo review of the plaintiff's claim. 18 U.S.C. § 1514A(b)(1)(B). The evidentiary framework for a claim under Sarbanes-Oxley is specifically set forth in the statute. *Id.* § 1514A(b)(2)(C). An action brought under Sarbanes-Oxley "shall be governed by the legal burdens of proof set forth in section 42121(b) of title 49, United States Code." *Id.*[12]

Under the statutory framework, a plaintiff in federal court must show by a preponderance of the evidence that the plaintiff's protected activity was a contributing factor in the unfavorable personnel action alleged in the complaint. 49 U.S.C. § 42121(b)(2)(B)(iii).[13] That is, the plaintiff must show by a preponderance of the

---

4. Publicly traded companies include any "company with a class of securities registered under section 12 of the Securities Exchange Act of 1934 (15 U.S.C. 78l), or that is required to file reports under section 15(d) of the Securities Exchange Act of 1934 (15 U.S.C. 78o(d)), or any officer, employee, contractor, subcontractor, or agent of such company." 18 U.S.C. § 1514A(a).

12. Section 806 refers to the evidentiary framework in 49 U.S.C. § 42121(b) as governing both the administrative procedure before OSHA and the filing of a complaint in federal court. . . .

13. 49 U.S.C. § 42121(b)(2)(B)(iii) states in pertinent part that a determination that a violation occurred may be made only if "the complainant demonstrates that any [protected] behavior . . . was a contributing factor in the unfavorable personnel action alleged in the complaint." In *Dysert v. Sec. of Lab.*, 105 F.3d 607 (11th Cir. 1997), the Eleventh Circuit Court of Appeals examined the proper application of the statutory burdens of proof in the whistleblower protection provisions of the ERA, 42 U.S.C. § 5851(b)(3). Notably, like the legal burden of proof in this case under 49 U.S.C. § 42121(b)(2)(B)(iii),

evidence that (1) she engaged in protected activity; (2) the employer knew of the protected activity; (3) she suffered an unfavorable personnel action; and (4) circumstances exist to suggest that the protected activity was a contributing factor to the unfavorable action. *See Stone & Webster [Engr. Corp. v. Herman,* 115 F.3d 1568 (11th Cir. 1997)] (analyzing these factors under provisions of ERA); *Bechtel Constr. Co. v. Sec. of Lab.,* 50 F.3d 926, 933-34 (11th Cir. 1995) (same). Proximity in time is sufficient to raise an inference of causation. *Bechtel.* The defendant employer may avoid liability if it can demonstrate by clear and convincing evidence that it "would have taken the same unfavorable personnel action in the absence of [protected] behavior." 49 U.S.C. §42121(b)(2)(B)(iv).

1. Whether Plaintiff Engaged in Protected Activity

Sarbanes-Oxley protects employees who provide information which the employee "reasonably believes constitutes a violation of section 1341, 1343, 1344, or 1348, any rule or regulation of the Securities and Exchange Commission, or any provision of Federal law relating to fraud against shareholders." 18 U.S.C. §1514A(a)(1). Therefore, a plaintiff is not required to show an actual violation of the law, but only that she "reasonably believed" that there was a violation of one of the enumerated laws or regulations. *Id.* The legislative history of Sarbanes-Oxley states that the reasonableness test "is intended to impose the normal reasonable person standard used and interpreted in a wide variety of legal contexts." Legislative History of Title VIII of HR 2673: The Sarbanes-Oxley Act of 2002, Cong. Rec. S7418, S7420 (daily ed. July 26, 2002), *available at* 2002 WL 32054527 (hereinafter "Legislative history"). "The threshold is intended to include all good faith and reasonable reporting of fraud, and there should be no presumption that reporting is otherwise, absent specific evidence." *Id.*

Defendants assert that Plaintiff did not engage in protected activity because she never specifically alleged securities or accounting fraud and because her complaints were too vague to constitute protected activity. Defendants contrast the type of disclosures made by Sherron Watkins, the former Enron Vice President, to the disclosures made by Plaintiff. Defendants point out that Watkins was an accountant whose job it was to review Enron's securities, that she outlined specific accounting procedures and transactions about which she was concerned, and that she expressed concerns that specific securities laws were being violated. By contrast, Defendants contend, Plaintiff was the Director of Marketing who expressed only vague concerns that amounted to nothing more than personality conflicts and differences in marketing strategies.

Plaintiff points to four specific disclosures which she made that she alleges are within the coverage of Sarbanes-Oxley. Plaintiff states that (1) she alleged that the division was knowingly overpaying invoices to Montello; (2) the division was using Montello because of a personal relationship between management and Montello; (3) Hashem was violating the division's commissions scheme by overpaying sales

---

the language in the ERA stated that a finding that a violation occurred was proper only if "the complainant has demonstrated" certain behavior. In *Dysert* the Eleventh Circuit found that the term "demonstrated" was ambiguous, and therefore, left room for an administrative interpretation. The court noted that the Secretary had interpreted "demonstrated" to mean "proved by a preponderance of the evidence." . . . The Eleventh Circuit held that to be a reasonable interpretation which was entitled to deference.

agents who were her personal friends; and (4) there were kickbacks involving the purchase of lumber. Plaintiff contends that these disclosures are protected because they allege attempts to circumvent the company's system of internal accounting controls and therefore state a violation of Section 13 of the Exchange Act.[15]

The Court finds that Defendants cannot establish as a matter of law that Plaintiff did not engage in protected activity under Sarbanes-Oxley. Though this is a close case, considering the posture of the case, the lack of guidance in the caselaw and the broad remedial purpose behind Sarbanes-Oxley, the Court finds that there is a genuine issue of material fact whether Plaintiff engaged in protected activity.[16] It is evident that Plaintiff's complaints do not rise to the level of complaints that were raised by Sherron Watkins at Enron. However, the mere fact that the severity or specificity of her complaints does not rise to the level of action that would spur Congress to draft legislation does not mean that the legislation it did draft was not meant to protect her. In short, if Congress had intended to limit the protection of Sarbanes-Oxley to accountants, or to have required complainants to specifically identify the code section that they believe was being violated, it could have done so. It did not. Congress instead protected "employees" and adopted the "reasonable belief" standard for those who "blow the whistle on fraud and protect investors." Legislative history at S7420; *see* 18 U.S.C. § 1514A(a).

Additionally, though Defendants contend that Plaintiff's complaints were too vague to constitute protected activity, the individuals to whom they were addressed understood the serious nature of Plaintiff's allegations. For instance, after her initial conversation with Plaintiff, Gardner understood Plaintiff's complaints regarding the payment of invoices and miscategorization of invoices as a "serious allegation" that raised questions about improper accounting. After Jones met with Plaintiff on August 5, 2002, she began to investigate Plaintiff's claims in order to determine whether there was something that may be criminal, against the law or against company policy, including violations of the company's Standards of Corporate Conduct.[17] The Court agrees with Defendants that the connection of Plaintiff's complaints to the substantive law protected in Sarbanes-Oxley is less than direct. However, Plaintiff's allegations detailed violations of the company's internal accounting controls in favor of preferential treatment based on personal relationships.

After an investigation, Defendants ultimately determined that some of Plaintiff's allegations lacked merit. However, this does not change the fact that they understood the nature and type of allegations that she made and that those allegations were within the zone of protection afforded by Sarbanes-Oxley. *See* Legislative history at S7420

---

15. Section 13 of the Securities Exchange Act of 1934 requires companies to "devise and maintain a system of internal accounting controls." 15 U.S.C. § 78m(b)(2)(B). Section 13 further states that "No person shall knowingly circumvent or knowingly fail to implement a system of internal accounting controls." *Id*. at 78m(b)(3)(B)(5).

16. Defendants insist that OSHA found that "the preponderance of *credible evidence* did not support [Plaintiff's] contention that she provided information alleging a violation of any federal law regarding [Defendants'] conduct." (OSHA findings at 3.) (emphasis added). First of all, this Court is charged with conducting a de novo review and is not required to give deference to the agency's findings. Furthermore, it is not for this Court on a motion for summary judgment to determine the credibility of the evidence, but only whether there exists a genuine issue of material fact. The Court finds that such an issue does exist.

17. Jones was involved in the development of the company's Standards of Corporate Conduct. They are used to "guide the company [in] the use of the assets of the company, for the benefit of the shareholders of the company." She also recognized that the Standards of Corporate Conduct were part of the company's internal controls, meant to make sure that the company's assets are being used for the benefit of the company and the shareholders.

("Certainly, although not exclusively, any type of corporate or agency action taken based on the information, or the information constituting admissible evidence at any later proceeding would be strong indicia that it could support such a reasonable belief.").[19] Because reasonable jurors could find by a preponderance of the evidence that Plaintiff engaged in protected activity, Defendants are not entitled to judgment as a matter of law.

2. Whether Defendants Knew of Plaintiff's Protected Activity

Sarbanes-Oxley protects employees who provide information to any "person with supervisory authority over the employee (or such other person working for the employer who has the authority to investigate, discover, or terminate misconduct)." 18 U.S.C. § 1514A(a)(1)(C). Plaintiff made numerous complaints to her supervisors, including complaints to Gardner, a meeting with Jones, an email to Gardner, an email to McCarthy and her final meeting with Shaffer. Defendants do not contest that they were aware of Plaintiff's complaints. Defendants, however, assert that Shaffer was the sole decision maker in Plaintiff's termination and that he did not know of Plaintiff's letters to Gardner and McCarthy. Shaffer did, however, discuss Plaintiff with Jones including Plaintiff's series of complaints, discussion of payment of the Montello invoices, and the circumstances in which it would be acceptable for him to terminate her. To permit an employer to simply bring in a manager to be the "sole decision-maker" for the purpose of terminating a complainant would eviscerate the protection afforded to employees by Sarbanes-Oxley. The Court finds that Defendants were aware of Plaintiff's protected activity. . . .

4. Whether Circumstances Exist to Suggest That the Protected Activity Was a Contributing Factor to the Unfavorable Action

Under the evidentiary framework, Plaintiff must also establish that there are circumstances which suggest that the protected activity was a contributing factor to the unfavorable action. 49 U.S.C. § 42121(b)(2)(B)(iii). Defendants contend that Plaintiff cannot establish the causal connection because the person responsible for firing her, Shaffer, was not aware of Plaintiff's letters to McCarthy and Gardner and because she did not bring any illegal activities to Shaffer's attention.[20] Defendants further state that temporal proximity is not sufficient to create circumstances to suggest causation. . . .

The Court finds that the temporal proximity between the time when Plaintiff made her complaints and the time she was terminated is sufficient to establish circumstances which suggest that protected activity was a contributing factor to the unfavorable personnel action. *See* 29 C.F.R. § 1984.104(b)(2); *Bechtel* (stating that under

---

19. Jones' investigation into Plaintiff's complaint regarding the Director of Sales, Mary Ann Hashem, ultimately resulted in Hashem being reprimanded and terminated.

20. Plaintiff states that she did not bring illegal activity to Shaffer's attention because she believed that he was involved in the wrongdoing.

whistleblower provisions of ERA, proximity in time is sufficient to raise an inference of discrimination).

Although Defendants cite *Wascura v. City of South Miami,* 257 F.3d 1238, 1248 (11th Cir. 2001), for the proposition that temporal proximity alone is not sufficient to establish causation in the Eleventh Circuit, the holding in that case is not as broad as Defendants suggest. In that case, the Eleventh Circuit upheld the district court's grant of summary judgment on the plaintiff's claim for interference with rights under the Family Medical and Leave Act. The plaintiff claimed that she was terminated because she stated that she may need time off from work to care for her son's medical needs. The court held that in light of conflicting evidence before the court, "the three and one-half month temporal proximity is insufficient to create a jury issue on causation." Here, Plaintiff first complained to Jones on August 5, 2002 and was terminated fourteen days later on August 19, 2002. Therefore, the proximity in time provides the circumstances to suggest that the protected activity was a contributing factor to the unfavorable personnel action. Moreover, it is clear that Shaffer had discussed Plaintiff's complaints with Jones and was aware that she had complained about violations of company policy when he terminated her.

Reasonable jurors could find that Plaintiff has established by a preponderance of the evidence that she engaged in protected activity, that Defendants knew of her protected activity, that she suffered an unfavorable personnel action and that circumstances exist which create an inference that the protected activity was a contributing factor to the unfavorable personnel action. . . .

5. Whether Defendants Can Show That They Would Have Taken the Same Unfavorable Personnel Action in the Absence of Plaintiff's Protected Activity

Only if Defendants can establish by clear and convincing evidence that they would have fired Plaintiff absent her participation in protected activity, would Defendants be entitled to summary judgment. Defendants argue that Shaffer was the sole decision maker with regard to Plaintiff's termination and that she was terminated for three reasons: (1) personality conflicts with her co-worker and manager; (2) Mazar's dissatisfaction with her; and (3) Shaffer's belief that Plaintiff had made a presentation that was "way off the mark."

The Court finds that Defendants have not established by clear and convincing evidence as a matter of law that they would have terminated Plaintiff even absent her protected activity. First of all, Defendants contend that Shaffer fired Plaintiff based on her personality conflicts with Hashem and Mazar and based on Mazar's dissatisfaction with her performance. While Plaintiff does admit that there was a conflict among the three of them, Mazar stated that he did not believe he had a personality conflict with Plaintiff. Mazar stated that he had discussed some concerns about Plaintiff's job performance with Shaffer, but he had not yet made the decision to terminate her and was planning to meet with her to discuss the problems. Moreover, Mazar may have expressed some concerns to Shaffer, but he was not involved in the decision to terminate Plaintiff and did not learn of her termination until after the fact. It appears that none of her supervisors ever met with Plaintiff to discuss her job performance or the personality conflicts prior to her termination. Finally, the only discussion where Defendants discussed the potential termination of Plaintiff took place between

Jones and Shaffer and did not involve Mazar, who was Plaintiff's direct supervisor and one of the individuals with whom Defendants stated that she had the personality conflict.

Defendants in their representations to OSHA indicated that reasons for Plaintiff's termination were her "discontent with her job" and her "extreme unhappiness" with the company. It is evident that Plaintiff made numerous complaints to her supervisors, many of which would not constitute protected activity under Sarbanes-Oxley. To allow Defendants to obtain summary judgment by singling out these complaints and insisting that only unprotected complaints were the basis for their action against Plaintiff would thwart the purpose of Sarbanes-Oxley. *See Stone & Webster* [*Engr. Corp. v. Herman*, 115 F.3d 1568 (11th Cir. 1997)]. Again, whether Defendants would have terminated Plaintiff absent her protected activity presents a close question. It appears that she got off on the wrong foot with some of her co-workers from the very beginning, and that her supervisors had some concerns about her ability to adapt to the home building industry. It also appears that Mazar thought she did a good job with respect to Internet marketing and the hiring of the new marketing firm, an area of purported dispute. Though Defendants emphasize that Plaintiff was in her ninety day assessment period, the short history of Plaintiff's employment only makes it more difficult to discern whether the problems that Plaintiff had would have ultimately resulted in her termination absent participation in protected activity or whether they would have simply been addressed and resolved. Because there is a genuine issue of material fact whether Defendants have established by clear and convincing evidence that they would have fired Plaintiff absent her protected activity, Defendants are not entitled to judgment as a matter of law.

NOTES

1. *Protected Conduct Under SOX.* As *Collins* suggests, the conduct at issue must be of a certain nature to come within SOX protection. The statute bars a publicly traded company from taking an adverse employment action "because of any lawful act done by the employee . . . to provide information, cause information to be provided, or otherwise assist in an investigation regarding any conduct which the employee reasonably believes" constitutes a violation of six identified federal statutes. These include mail fraud, 18 U.S.C. § 1341, wire fraud, § 1343, bank fraud, § 1344, or securities fraud, § 1348, or "any [SEC] rule or regulation . . . or any provision of Federal law relating to fraud against shareholders, when the information or assistance is provided to . . . a person with supervisory authority over the employee . . ." 18 U.S.C. § 1514A(a)(1). As might be expected, the cases raise issues of the scope of the securities laws. *See, e.g., Flake v. United States DOL*, 248 F. App'x 287 (2007) (alternative holding that ARB decision not clearly erroneous in finding that SOX did not apply when there were fewer than 300 holders of the employer's securities, and the employer therefore had no duty to file certain reports). Similarly, plaintiffs have lost SOX claims because they could not identify a predicate law or establish a nexus between that law and the alleged protected conduct, *see Platone v. United States DOL*, 548 F.3d 322 (4th Cir. 2008) (employee had to alert management to more than the fact that the company's near-term profits were affected by billing discrepancies in order to meet the standard of definitively and specifically alleging mail or wire fraud), or because the employee could not reasonably believe a violation of that law

occurred. *Livingston v. Wyeth, Inc.*, 520 F.3d 344, 355 (4th Cir. 2008) ("even if Wyeth had made the false statements to compliance auditors and the FDA that Livingston supposed could be made, none would amount to a material statement as necessary to violate § 10(b) of the Securities Exchange Act and Rule 10b-5.").

2. *Objectively and Subjectively Reasonable.* Closely connected with the question of identifying a predicate law is establishing the employee's belief that that law was violated. *See, e.g., Gale v. United States Dep't of Labor*, 2010 U.S. App. LEXIS 13104 (11th Cir. June 25, 2010) (upholding agency determination that plaintiff, although uncomfortable with the ethics of certain company practices, did not himself believe they were illegal, much less have a reasonable belief to that effect); *Day v. Staples, Inc.*, 555 F.3d 42 (2009) (inefficient business practices, even if they might lead to a short-term reduction in profits, could not support an objectively reasonable belief that they were "shareholder fraud"); *Allen v. Admin. Review Bd.*, 514 F.3d 468, 482 (5th Cir. 2008) ("[a] reasonable person could conclude that Stewart did not violate a rule or regulation of the SEC because Waldon knew that Stewart's internal financial documents did not need to be SAB-101 compliant").

With respect to an employee's belief, the circuit courts have interpreted SOX to impose both a subjective and objective standard. *See, e.g., Harp v. Charter Communs., Inc.*, 558 F.3d 722, 723 (7th Cir. 2009) (plaintiff "must actually have possessed that belief, and that belief must be objectively reasonable"). However, the plaintiff need not know precisely what federal law is being violated. *Harp*, 558 F.3d at 725 ("If the specific conduct reported was violative of federal law, the report would be sufficient to trigger Sarbanes-Oxley protection even if the employee did not identify the appropriate federal law by name."). *But see Getman v. Admin. Review Bd.*, 265 F. App'x. 317 (5th Cir. 2008) (no protection when analyst was discharged after telling review committee that she could not award "strong buy" rating to client's stock where she was not asked to change her recommendation and she never informed committee why she believed that upgrade would violate securities laws). Does this seem odd to you? Collins would have to be reasonable in believing conduct was "wrong" even though she would not need to know what made it wrong. Does *Harp* help?

3. *Proof of a Contributing Factor.* Since the judge was deciding only whether a jury trial was necessary, Ms. Collins has not yet won. And it is not clear that she will prevail at trial — there seem to be a number of legitimate reasons that could explain her discharge. But SOX requires only that a complaining party prove that her protected conduct was a "contributing factor" to the challenged employment action. 49 U.S.C. § 42121 (2006) (incorporated by reference in 18 U.S.C. § 1514A). If plaintiff does so, it is the employer's burden to prove that it would have made the same decision in any event. *See Taylor v. Admin. Review Bd.*, 288 F. App'x 929 (5th Cir. 2008) (upholding an agency finding that defendant's clear and convincing evidence of plaintiff's insubordinate conduct, which included belligerence and even screaming at her supervisor, would have caused her dismissal regardless of whether SOX-protected conduct was a motivating factor). *Cf. Roadway Express, Inc. v. United States DOL*, 612 F.3d 660 (7th Cir. 2010) (upholding agency decision that employer would not have fired driver under the Surface Transportation Assistance Act but for his protected conduct). This burden of persuasion should be very helpful to Collins, at least if the judge and jury can figure out what a "contributing factor" is. In approaching this question, it is helpful to remember that "standard" causation analysis in the law requires at a minimum "but for" causation, that is showing that the event in question would not have occurred but for the act (e.g., negligence) in question. Notions of "proximate cause" in torts sometimes require more than but-for causation, but they do not normally require less. SOX is an exception.

While the issue is explored in more detail in Chapter 9, antidiscrimination law originally used but-for causation, requiring a showing that discriminatory intent was a "determinative factor" for the decision in question. That standard still operates under the Age Discrimination in Employment Act, *Gross v. FBL Fin. Servs.*, 129 S. Ct. 2343 (2009), and means that the plaintiff can prevail only if he can show that, but for the intent to discriminate, the adverse employment action would not have occurred. However, a lower standard applies under Title VII the 1991 Amendments reduced the level of causation required to "motivating factor." As a result, discriminatory intent can be a "motivating factor" and therefore violate Title VII, even if the trier of fact ultimately concludes that the employer would have made the "same decision" even had it not been motivated by the prohibited consideration. *See generally* Martin J. Katz, *The Fundamental Incoherence of Title VII: Making Sense of Causation in Disparate Treatment Law*, 94 GEO. L. J. 489 (2006).

"Motivating factor" as used in Title VII is scarcely self-explanatory in the confused world of causation. Further, Congress's use of "contributing factor" in Sarbanes-Oxley suggests the same or perhaps even a lower level of causation. Presumably, it is the slightest degree that can still be said to "play a role" in the termination decision. *Collins* cites legislative history to this effect. Further, SOX makes clear that a plaintiff does not have to prove but-for causation: she can establish that a factor "contributed" to the decision even though defendant can still prevail by proving that it would have made the same decision even had plaintiff not engaged in protected conduct. This necessarily means that plaintiff's proof can be less than but-for causation since the defendant's affirmative defense of "same decision anyway" amounts to establishing the absence of "but for" causation. While the plaintiff's proof of "contributing factor" must be something less than "but for," how much less is not clear. Note also that the field is not level. The plaintiff must prove a "contributing factor" only by a preponderance of the evidence, while defendant must establish that it "would have taken the same unfavorable personnel action in the absence of [the protected] behavior" by "clear and convincing evidence."

This proof structure makes the question of what suffices for proof of a contributing factor critical. *Collins* finds a two-week "temporal proximity" enough to avoid summary judgment on contributing factor, despite other reasons why defendant might have wanted to discharge the plaintiff. A jury, therefore, could find that her protected conduct played a role in the decision to discharge her. If it so concludes by a preponderance of the evidence, she will prevail — unless the jury also concludes that the defendant established by clear and convincing evidence that she would have been fired in any event. Will such a short period always suffice to create a triable issue? Recall that Ms. Collins's 90-day "assessment period" would have ended around September 10. Had the defendant waited to discharge her at that point, would there still be sufficient "temporal proximity"? What kind of evidence would suffice to prove contributing factor other than closeness in time? Presumably, SOX courts will borrow from the more developed law under the antidiscrimination statutes in answering such questions.

4. *Administrative Prerequisites to SOX Suits.* Sarbanes-Oxley requires resort to the Department of Labor's Occupational Safety and Health Administration ("OSHA"). The statute of limitations for filing was originally 90 days, *see Rzepiennik v. Archstone-Smith, Inc.*, 331 F. App'x 584 (10th Cir. 2009), but has been expanded to 180 days by the Dodd-Frank Financial Reform Act, 18 U.S.C.A. § 1514A(b)(2)(D). OSHA, in turn, processes the complaint in a quasi-judicial setting, which involves a hearing before an administrative law judge, an administrative appeal, and judicial review in the appropriate circuit court. How then was Collins in front of a district court? To guard against agency delay, the statute provides, "if the Secretary has not issued a final decision within 180 days of the filing of the complaint and there is no showing that such delay is due to the bad faith of the claimant," the claimant may bring suit in federal district court. 18 U.S.C.A. § 1514A(b). However, the regulations also provide that a plaintiff must file a notice of her intent to file a complaint in federal court 15 days in advance of doing so. 29 C.F.R. § 1980.114(b). Filing this notice of intent to sue presumably gives the agency a last chance to complete its proceedings, which would then deprive the employee of de novo court review.

In an omitted portion of the decision, the court permitted Ms. Collins to seek a judicial remedy due to the agency's delay. *See also Stone v. Instrumentation Lab. Co.,* 591 F.3d 239 (4th Cir. 2009). Note that two days after the court complaint was filed, OSHA did issue its order, holding against her. Why wasn't this preclusive? The statute authorizes plaintiff to bring "an action at law or equity for de novo review in the appropriate district court of the United States, which shall have jurisdiction over such an action without regard to the amount in controversy." The term "de novo" suggests that the agency decision is not in any way preclusive, although it is possible that such a decision may be introduced in evidence in the civil suit. *See Chandler v. Roudebush,* 425 U.S. 840, 864 (1976) ("Prior administrative findings made with respect to an employment discrimination claim may, of course, be admitted as evidence at a federal-sector trial de novo. *See* Fed. Rule Evid. 803(8)(c)."). The use of "law or equity" seems to authorize damages and, therefore, a jury trial.

When the claim is pursued through the administrative process, there is a right to review in the appropriate federal circuit court. However, the standard of review is deferential. *Getman v. Admin. Review Bd.,* 265 F. App'x. 317 (5th Cir. 2008) (agency decision will be upheld unless it is arbitrary or capricious, although agency conclusions of law are reviewed de novo). The effectiveness of the administrative process has been questioned. Richard Moberly, *Unfulfilled Expectations: An Empirical Analysis of Why Sarbanes-Oxley Whistleblowers Rarely Win,* 49 Wm. & Mary L. Rev. 65 (2007) (during its first three years, only 3.6 percent of SOX whistleblowers won relief through the initial administrative process that adjudicates such claims, and only 6.5 percent of whistleblowers won appeals through the process). *See also* Terry Morehead Dworkin, *SOX and Whistleblowing,* 105 Mich. L. Rev. 1757 (2007). *But see* Richard E. Moberly, *Sarbanes-Oxley's Structural Model to Encourage Corporate Whistleblowers,* 2006 BYU. L. Rev. 1107, 1109 (arguing that SOX's structural model is an improvement over prior efforts in providing a structure that encourages whistleblowers).

5. *State Claims.* In another portion of the opinion not reproduced, the *Collins* court also denied defendant summary judgment on plaintiff's claims under the Florida Whistleblower's Act ("FWA"), Fla. Stat. § 448.102. Suppose that this case arose in New Jersey or Minnesota. Would Ms. Collins have a cause of action under those state statutes? If so, would such an action arise only because of the public policy evinced in SOX itself, or would the claim have been actionable even before that federal statute was passed as a means of vindicating the federal policy in favor of accurate disclosures of financial information by publicly traded companies? Recall that in *Murphy v. American Home Prods. Corp.,* 448 N.E.2d 86 (N.Y. 1983), New York rejected the public policy tort in a setting much more extreme than anything at issue in *Collins.*

If you conclude that the discharge would have been actionable under either or both state laws only because SOX created a right to be free of reprisal for engaging in this conduct, do you think there is any problem with the states creating a cause of action that duplicates the federal one? Would the federal claim be prejudiced by the state cause of action? Before you answer no too quickly, wouldn't a state claim allow an employee to end-run the requirement of filing with OSHA? Sarbanes-Oxley provides that "[n]othing in this section shall be deemed to diminish the rights, privileges, or remedies of any employee under any Federal or State law, or under any collective bargaining agreement." 18 U.S.C. § 1514A. But if a state were to predicate a public policy tort on SOX itself, would this language apply?

6. *Employer Reaction.* There is considerable irony that *Collins* relies in part on the defendant's reaction to the plaintiff's allegations to conclude that her conduct is protected — Gardner's description of plaintiff's complaints as a "serious allegation," and the recognition of the possibility that "there was something that may be criminal, against the law or against company policy, including violations of the company's Standards of Corporate Conduct." If Gardner or Jones called you after their meetings with plaintiff, how would you advise them to proceed? Remember that the validity of the allegations is a separate question from whether they are protected as reasonable under the statute. And what about Hashem? Footnote 19 recounts that she was fired as a result of Jones's investigation of Collins's claims. As Beazer's counsel, would you have recommended this action while Ms. Collins could potentially bring a SOX suit? Does her discharge lend weight to plaintiff's claims? Even if so, would a failure to discharge or discipline Hashem be problematic on other grounds?

7. *The Meaning of Investigation.* Why didn't the judge pay more attention to the language of the statute? It protects employees who "provide information, cause information to be provided, or otherwise assist in an investigation." Does this language suggest the statute does *not* protect employees who merely bring a complaint to management absent an actual investigation?

8. *Remedies.* SOX provides for "all relief necessary to make the employee whole, including "reinstatement with the same seniority status" and "back pay, with interest," 18 U.S.C. § 1514A. Punitive damages are not available but "compensation for any special damages sustained as a result of the discrimination, including litigation costs, expert witness fees, and reasonable attorney fees" is to be awarded. *Id.* Although it was unclear whether SOX as originally passed accorded a right to jury trial, *see generally* Jarod Spencer Gonzalez, *SOX, Statutory Interpretation, and the Seventh Amendment: Sarbanes-Oxley Act Whistleblower Claims and Jury Trials*, 9 U. PA. J. LAB. & EMPL. L. 25 (2006). The Dodd-Frank Wall Street Reform and Financial Protection Act amended SOX to so provide. 18 U.S.C.A. § 1514A(b)(2)(e).

9. *No Mandatory Arbitration of SOX Claims.* Consistent with the general rule for arbitration agreements, see Chapter 13, the courts interpreted SOX, as originally enacted, to permit an arbitration agreement to trump both administrative and judicial avenues of relief, *e.g., Guyden v. Aetna, Inc.*, 544 F.3d 376 (2nd Cir. 2008) (requiring arbitration of SOX suit). However, Dodd-Frank amended SOX to bar such arbitration (while also barring mandatory arbitration of the new whistleblower protection it established). 18 U.S.C.A. § 1514(e). The parties can still agree to arbitrate, but only after a dispute has arisen.

10. *A New Wave of Federal Protection.* SOX appears to have been just the first in a new wave of federal laws containing antiretaliation provisions that may help workers. The American Recovery and Reinvestment Act of 2009, 111 P.L. 5, 123 Stat. 115, better known as the stimulus package, adopted new whistleblower protections for employees of private employers or of state and local governments who make certain disclosures. The protected disclosures must be related to "covered funds" and include "gross mismanagement" and "gross waste" as well as other violations of law or regulation. Similarly, the Patient Protection and Affordable Care Act of 2010, 111 P.L. 148, 124 Stat. 119, better known as the health care reform act, added a number of protections, including safeguarding employees who provide information to their employer or to the government regarding violations of employer health insurance mandates. § 1558.

Finally, the Dodd-Frank Wall Street Reform and Consumer Protection Act, better know as financial reform act, Pub. L. 111-203, § 922, 124 Stat. 2129, created three new whistleblower protections related to the Commodities Futures Trading Commission ("CFTC"), Securities and Exchange Commission ("SEC"), and newly established Consumer Financial Protection Bureau ("CFPB"). With respect to both the CFTC and SEC, the statute creates both a bounty system and an antiretaliation provision. This antiretaliation protection is enforced through court suit, not an administrative procedure, and double back-pay is one of the remedies provided. As for protection of disclosures related to the new CFPB, the coverage reaches a broad array of entities dealing with financial products. This protection, however, is enforced through an administrative filing although, like SOX, de novo suit may be brought if the Department of Labor does not act quickly enough. Like SOX, the burden-shifting provisions are plaintiff-friendly. All three provisions generally bar predispute arbitration agreements or other waivers of rights and remedies.

Note on the False Claims Act

The False Claims Act ("FCA"), 31 U.S.C. § 3730(b) (2006), is not merely a "whistleblower" act, but rather, it functions as a very powerful source of employee rights in a wide range of situations. Its general thrust is to empower any citizen to bring a claim, often referred to as a qui tam suit, in the name of the United States against any entity that submits "a false or fraudulent claim for payment" to the federal government. Because of the federal government's huge expenditures on Medicare and Medicaid reimbursement, much FCA litigation has centered on the health care industry, *see* Joan H. Krause, *"Promises to Keep": Health Care Providers and the Civil False Claims Act*, 23 Cardozo L. Rev. 1363 (2002), but claims may arise with any corporation that does business with the government. Although the FCA traces its origins back to the Civil War, a series of recent amendments designed to make it more effective show Congress's continued commitment to using a bounty system to protect the federal fisc. *See generally* Daniel C. Lumm, Comment, *The 2009 "Clarifications" to the False Claims Act of 1863: The All-Purpose Antifraud Statute with the Fun Qui Tam Twist*, 45 Wake Forest L. Rev. 527 (2010). *See also* Jarod González, *A Pot of Gold at the End of the Rainbow: An Economic Incentives-Based Approach to OSHA Whistleblowing*, 14 Empl. Rts & Empl. Pol'y J. *** (forthcoming 2010) (recommending a similar bounty approach for OSHA violations). Thus, the statute now prohibits retaliation for "lawful acts done by an employee . . . in furtherance of an action under this section or other efforts to stop" FCA violations. Further, Dodd-Frank expanded the FCA's coverage to reach "any subsidiary or affiliate whose financial information is included in the consolidated financial statements" of a covered company. 18 U.S.C.A. § 1514A.

False Claims actions are often very attractive from the plaintiff's perspective since the statute authorizes award of from 15 to 30 percent of any recovery to the private plaintiff. 31 U.S.C. § 3730(d). *See generally* Marsha J. Ferziger & Daniel G. Currell, *Snitching for Dollars: The Economics and Public Policy of Federal Civil Bounty Programs*, 1999 U. ILL. L. REV. 1141 (1999). Health care fraud is big business, and the government typically recovers a billion dollars a year. *See* HHS & DOJ, Health Care Fraud and Abuse Control Program Annual Report for FY 2009 (May 2010), *available at* http://www.justice.gov/dag/pubdoc/hcfacreport2009.pdf (reporting that Pfizer agreed to pay a $2.3 billion settlement, the largest health care fraud settlement in the history of the DOJ). For a listing of the largest federal recovery of FCA damages to date, *see* TAF- Top 20 False Claims Act Cases, http://www.taf.org/top20.htm (last visited July 8, 2010). While only a portion of this amount is recovered under the FCA, there have been significant recoveries by private plaintiffs (referred to as "relators" in these claims). *See* Daniel C. Vock, *Qui Tam Suit Spurs Payout of $76 Million*, CHICAGO DAILY L. BULL., June 26, 2002 (two whistleblowers will receive $14.4 million under the settlement agreement). Beyond the health care industry, both military procurement and disaster relief offer large opportunities for employees who believe their employer is seeking compensation from the federal government to which it is not entitled.

Since employees are typically in the best position to know when a company may be submitting false claims for reimbursement, the FCA is often invoked in what otherwise seems a garden-variety dispute about employment. *See ex rel. Mikes v. Straus*, 274 F.3d 687 (2d Cir. 2001) (plaintiff doctor sued her former employer not only for damages caused by wrongful discharge but also sought the bounty provided by recovery on a qui tam basis for false Medicare reimbursement claims). In addition, the statute has a section explicitly providing any employee "discharged, demoted, suspended, threatened, harassed, or in any other manner discriminated against in the terms and conditions of employment" for furthering of False Claim Act actions is "entitled to all relief necessary to make the employee whole," including "2 times the amount of back pay" due. 31 U.S.C. § 3730(h). As a result, when an employee can plausibly claim that her discharge was due to a dispute about incorrectly billing the government, the potential recoveries include not only normal remedies but also double back pay and the statutory bounty.

The False Claims Act has somewhat unusual procedures. As described by Ferziger & Currell:

> [A] private citizen may also initiate a qui tam action on the government's behalf. An FCA informant — termed a relator due to his involvement in the litigation — files his "complaint and written disclosure of substantially all material evidence" in the case with the government. The government holds the complaint under seal for up to sixty days for review before unsealing it and serving it on the defendant. The government may choose to pursue the litigation, in which case the relator has the right to either continue as a party to the case or remain on the sidelines. If the Attorney General chooses not to pursue the case, the citizen-prosecutor may litigate on the government's behalf. In any scenario, a person initiating successful FCA litigation will receive some percentage of the government's take — more if he pursues the case himself (up to thirty percent) and less if the government pursues the case on its own or with his help (between fifteen percent and twenty-five percent).

1999 U. ILL. L. REV. at 1206.

However, merely reporting a possible violation to the government is not sufficient to earn a bounty under the statute. The plaintiff must actually file suit as a relator.

In such a suit, the plaintiff must establish that the defendant submitted a false claim within the meaning of the statute. However, the FCA contains what the Supreme Court has described as "three categories of jurisdiction-stripping disclosures," although they seem to be more properly viewed as exceptions to the statute provision that they bar actions based on "public disclosure" in (1) criminal, civil, or administrative hearings; (2) a congressional, or administrative report or investigation; or (3) the news media, "unless . . . the person bringing the action is an original source of the information." § 3730(e)(4)(A). *See Graham County Soil & Water Conservation Dist. v. United States ex rel. Wilson*, 130 S. Ct. 1396 (U.S. 2010) (holding that state or local government reports satisfied the public disclosure bar).

Because the FCA offers the possibility of recoveries far in excess of the damages suffered by the plaintiff from an adverse employment action (and can in fact be brought by present employees), such claims are very attractive to potential plaintiffs. Given the stakes, employers are well advised to be proactive in avoiding and resolving such claims, even if the employer sees relatively little likelihood of losing on the merits.

5

Traditional Torts in the Employment Relationship

The history of tort law's approach to the employment relationship starts with the struggle during the latter part of the nineteenth century about injuries sustained in the workplace. At the time, tort law theoretically offered redress for workplace injuries. In fact, however, employees seeking compensation for negligence were often frustrated by three doctrines — contributory negligence, assumption of risk, and the fellow servant rule — that together rendered it difficult or impossible for employees to recover from their employers. In large measure, then, tort law left workplace safety to private ordering. Rather than abolishing these restrictive doctrines, populist reformers advanced workers' compensation laws as the means of reform. The system, which won universal acceptance, was a compromise between full compensation for employees and the hit-or-miss cause of action for negligence. Workers' compensation laws replaced the common-law tort of negligence with an administrative system of strict liability for work-related injuries and diseases, providing more certain recovery but restricting the amounts recovered. *See generally* ARTHUR A. LARSON & LEX K. LARSON, LARSON'S WORKERS' COMPENSATION LAW (Matthew Bender, Rev. ed. 2008); Price Fishback & Shawn Everett Kantor, *The Adoption of Workers' Compensation in the United States*, 1900-1930, 41 J. L. & ECON. 305 (1998). The trade-off of lower amounts for more certain recovery required that workers' compensation be the exclusive remedy against the employer for physical injuries to employees in accidents arising out of their employment. Thus, tort law as a means to redress employee injuries largely disappeared during the twentieth century.

We will explore the parameters of workers' compensation exclusivity and the system as a whole at the end of this chapter. For now it is enough to know that workers' compensation systems typically left intentional torts actionable. Employee suits for intentional torts against their employers or individual supervisors or co-workers are therefore possible, but they remain problematic and more the exception than the rule in employment law. A few torts play an occasional role. For example, employees sometimes claim assault and battery for physical altercations, *Kelly v. County of Monmouth*, 883 A.2d 411 (N.J. App. Div. 2005) (suit against co-worker who grabbed plaintiff's genitals when hand-shaking contest escalated into a "testosterone type thing"), and occasionally allege false imprisonment, most often in the context of

243

too-enthusiastic interrogation during employer investigations of employee dishonesty. *See Chellen v. John Pickle Co.*, 446 F. Supp. 2d 1247 (D. Okla. 2006) (false imprisonment claims by foreign workers upheld when employer confiscated their travel documents, posted guards outside their dormitory, and threatened them with arrest if they left); *Foley v. Polaroid Corp.*, 413 N.E.2d 711 (Mass. 1987) (jury question as to whether employee was physically restrained, but the threat of discharge if employee left the office during interrogation could not constitute imprisonment for tort purposes). *Cf. Smith v. Kwik Fuel Ctr.*, 2006 Tenn. App. LEXIS 206 (Tenn. Ct. App. Mar. 27, 2006) (malicious prosecution tort did not lie where employer merely reported employee to police and did not control his subsequent prosecution). These kinds of intentional torts are also commonly deployed as ancillary causes of action to other claims. For example, in the sexual harassment context, the tort of assault may allow suit against the individual harasser, who might otherwise not be personally liable since discrimination statutes typically apply only to the corporate employer. See Chapter 9. Even here, however, some courts have found tort suits for sexual assault to be barred by workers' compensation exclusivity. See page 281.

Of somewhat more general application are four other intentional torts that are treated in this chapter, and privacy torts, which are treated in Chapter 6. Of these, only one — intentional interference with contract or prospective advantage — is primarily used to seek compensation for lost employment per se. For that reason intentional interference is treated first in Section A. The other three torts focus more on terms and conditions of employment than with job security and are only incidentally concerned with discharge. They are treated here in declining order of their importance in the employment law landscape. Defamation, taken up in Section B, and intentional infliction of emotional distress, treated in Section C, both focus on the employee's right to be treated with dignity. Although both may be implicated in terminations, that is not their primary focus, and both offer relatively weak protection in this context. Finally, fraud or misrepresentation is typically raised in the context of inducement to enter employment or with respect to compensation or other benefits, but it may also be raised in connection with termination. Discussed in Section D, it is a very powerful tool when applicable, but is so narrowly confined as to be rarely useful for employees.

This chapter concludes with Section E, which considers two important limitations on the use of tort doctrines. First, there is some question as to the extent to which the exclusivity provisions of state workers' compensation laws we have noted bar tort suit. Second, the increased recognition of tort actions for employee termination under state law has led to questions about whether such state causes of action are preempted by federal labor and employment law.

A. INTENTIONAL INTERFERENCE WITH THE EMPLOYMENT RELATIONSHIP

Tort law has long protected parties to a contract from third parties intentionally interfering with their relationship. In the employment field, this tort has traditionally been asserted by employers seeking to prevent other employers from "pirating" their workers or seeking compensation for the loss of key employees. See Chapter 8. But employees can use this tort too. The employment relationship between company and worker may be viewed as the contract (or at least the "prospective advantage") interfered with, and, if so, the question becomes whether a third party has unjustifiably interfered with that relationship. *See generally* Alex Long, *Tortious Interference with Business Relations: "The Other White Meat" of Employment Law*, 84 MINN. L. REV. 863 (2000).

The draft RESTATEMENT (THIRD) OF EMPLOYMENT LAW states the general rule:

> An employer may be subject to liability for reasonably foreseeable pecuniary loss suffered by an employee or former employee because the employer intentionally and without a legitimate business justification causes another employer not to enter into or to discontinue an employment relationship with the employee or former employer.

§ 6.03(a) (Preliminary Draft No. 6, May 21, 2009). *See, e.g., Reeves v. Hanlon*, 95 P.3d 513 (Cal. 2004) (immigration law firm could recover damages for intentional interference against former employees who had persuaded other employees to quit and join their newly established firm); *In re IBP Confidential Business Documents Litigation*, 797 F.2d 632 (8th Cir. 1986) (en banc) (upholding a verdict against plaintiff's former employer when his present employer discharged him six days after he had testified adversely to the former employer before a congressional committee).

A threshold question is whether the tort applies to at-will employment. While there is clearly a cause of action when there is the requisite interference with a contract for a specified term, the tenuous nature of at-will employment has generated questions about the applicability of the tort to this relationship. Nevertheless, as the Restatement reflects, most courts have found at-will contracts still to be contracts and so within the tort, and, in any event, the intentional interference tort reaches not only contracts but also interference with "prospective advantage." *See, e.g., Reeves v. Hanlon, supra; Hensen v. Truman Med. Ctr., Inc.*, 62 S.W.3d 549, 553 (Mo. Ct. App. 2001); *Sterner v. Marathon Oil Co.*, 767 S.W.2d 686 (Tex. 1989). There is, however, some contrary authority. *See, e.g., Stanton v. Tulane Univ.*, 777 So. 2d 1242 (La. Ct. App. 2001) (at-will employee could not assert the tort); *McManus v. MCI Comm. Corp.*, 748 A.2d 949 (D.C. 2000) (same); *see generally* Frank J. Cavico, *Tortious Interference with Contract in the At-Will Employment Context*, 79 U. DET. MERCY L. REV. 503 (2002); Alex Long, *The Disconnect Between At-Will Employment and Tortious Interference with Business Relations: Rethinking Tortious Interference Claims in the Employment Context*, 33 ARIZ. ST. L. J. 491 (2001). However, the scope of the privilege to interfere is broader when the employment is at will. *See CRST Van Expedited, Inc. v. Werner Enters.*, 479 F.3d 1099, 1106-07 (9th Cir. 2007) ("If CRST's employment contract provided for 'at-will' employment of Spencer and Chatman when Werner allegedly induced them to leave their posts, there would be an additional requirement that CRST allege an *independently wrongful act* by Werner.") (emphasis in original).

A more difficult problem arises when the interference is by someone who is, in some sense, the employer itself. The draft RESTATEMENT speaks in terms of liability when an employer "causes *another employer* not to enter into or to discontinue an employment relationship" (emphasis added). This means that the employer cannot be liable for the tort when it terminates its own employee. The RESTATEMENT OF TORTS likewise imposes liability only for interference "with the performance of a contract . . . between another and a third person by inducing or otherwise causing the third person not to perform the contract." §766. In *Cambio Health Solutions, L.L.C. v. Reardon*, 234 F. App'x. 331 (6th Cir. 2007), the question was whether three corporations with majority ownership in the employer could be sued for interference. The court found the defendants liable for intentional interference with plaintiff's employment contract after concluding that a company with less than one hundred percent interest in a subsidiary did not enjoy a qualified privilege to interfere with the contractual relations of the subsidiary.

Can an officer or director of an employer be liable for causing the employer to fire someone? How about a co-worker? Jurisdictions have taken inconsistent approaches to whether a defendant is a third party with respect to the plaintiff's contract or business relationship with the employer. One view is that a supervisor is not a "third party" since the supervisor has an absolute privilege to interfere with the employment relationship. *See, e.g., Halvorsen v. Aramark Unif. Servs., Inc.*, 77 Cal. Rptr. 2d 383, 390 (Ct. App. 1998). Under this approach, a co-worker may be liable since his interference will not normally be within the scope of his employment, but a supervisor will not be.

In most jurisdictions, the answer turns on whether the defendant is acting within the scope of his or her employment. *E.g., Trail v. Boys & Girls Clubs of Northwest Ind.*, 845 N.E.2d 130, 138 (Ind. 2006) ("[W]hen officers or directors act in their official capacity as agents of the corporation, they act not as individuals but as the corporation itself. In doing so, they are not acting as a third party, but rather as a party to the contract and cannot be personally liable for tortious interference with the contract."); *Porter v. Oba, Inc.*, 42 P.3d 931, 935 (Or. Ct. App. 2002) ("A corporate agent who induces a corporation to breach a contract with another party cannot be liable for intentional interference with that contract if the agent acted in the scope of the agent's employment. In that situation, the agent is the corporation."); *Eggleston v. Phillips*, 838 S.W.2d 80, 83 (Mo. App. 1992) (a supervisor is legally justified in interfering with an employee's at-will relationship because the corporate employer vested the supervisor with its authority to terminate). *Cf. Ramsey v. Greenwald*, 414 N.E.2d 1266, 1273 (Ill. App. Ct. 1980) (employee supervisor with no power to discharge the petitioner was a third party liable for intentional interference).

However, according to §228 of the Restatement (Second) of Agency (1957), acting within the scope of employment requires that the supervisor be motivated, at least in part, by a desire to serve the principal. Thus, a supervisor will be liable only when his actions are intended to further only "some individual or private purpose not related to the interests of the employer." *Huff v. Swartz*, 606 N.W.2d 461, 467 (Neb. 2000). As one court framed it, "While a party to a contract may breach it, it is logically impossible for a party to interfere tortiously with its own contract. However, if the agent's sole purpose is one that is *not* for the benefit of the corporation, the agent is not acting within the scope of employment and may be liable." *Kaelon v. USF Reddaway, Inc.*, 42 P.3d 344 (Ore. Ct. App. 2002); *Reed v. Michigan Metro Girl Scout Council*, 506 N.W.2d 231, 233 (Mich. Ct. App. 1993) ("[i]t is now settled law that corporate agents are not liable for tortious interference with the corporation's contracts unless they acted solely for their own benefit with no benefit to the corporation").

Think about the desirability of these various approaches as you consider the next case.

Kumpf v. Steinhaus
779 F.2d 1323 (7th Cir. 1985)

EASTERBROOK, Circuit Judge.

From 1973 until August 1983 William A. Kumpf was the president and chief executive officer of Lincoln National Sales Corp. of Wisconsin (Lincoln Wisconsin). He owned 20% of Lincoln Wisconsin's stock. Lincoln National Sales Corp. (Lincoln Sales) owned the other 80% of the stock, and two of the three members of Lincoln Wisconsin's board of directors were employees of Lincoln Sales. Lincoln Sales is in turn a subsidiary of Lincoln National Life Insurance Co. (Lincoln Life). Lincoln Sales is the marketing arm of Lincoln Life; Lincoln Wisconsin was the Wisconsin agency of Lincoln Sales.

In April 1981 Orin A. Steinhaus became an executive vice-president of Lincoln Life, leaving a post as head of Lincoln's sales agency in Columbus, Ohio. The president of Lincoln Life gave Steinhaus and other employees the task of revising the firm's sales structure, which was losing money. Lincoln Life closed 25 sales agencies and decided to consolidate others. In August 1983 Steinhaus decided to consolidate five Midwestern sales agencies into a single agency. (Doubtless other officers of Lincoln Life concurred in these decisions, but for simplicity we write as if Steinhaus made all decisions himself.) He instructed Lincoln Sales's directors on the board of Lincoln Wisconsin to approve a merger of Lincoln Wisconsin into Lincoln Chicago Corp. (Lincoln Chicago); Lincoln Wisconsin's board approved the merger by a vote of two to one, over Kumpf's dissent. Lincoln Wisconsin disappeared, and so did Kumpf's job. This litigation is the residue.

The district court dismissed most of Kumpf's claims for relief but sent to the jury a claim that Steinhaus and the Lincoln corporations tortiously interfered with the employment contract between Kumpf and Lincoln Wisconsin. Kumpf was an employee at will, but even at-will employment is contractual and therefore potentially the basis of a tort action. *Mendelson v. Blatz Brewing Co.*, 101 N.W.2d 805 (Wis. 1960). Kumpf was fired by Lincoln Wisconsin, and Lincoln Wisconsin cannot "interfere" with its own employment relations. But because Lincoln Sales owned only 80% of Lincoln Wisconsin's stock, Kumpf argued that other participants in the Lincoln family of firms could not intervene.

The defendants maintain that their interference with Kumpf's contract was privileged because it took place in the course of business. Kumpf replied that it was not privileged because it was done with an improper motive. After the reorganization, Steinhaus became president of Lincoln Chicago. In the insurance business the head of an agency receives a percentage of the agency's revenue. Income that used to go to Kumpf now went to Steinhaus, and the reorganization increased Steinhaus's total income. Kumpf argued that Steinhaus engineered the reorganization to advance his personal interests, and that this defeats the claim of privilege.

Kumpf asked the judge to instruct the jury that if the defendants' acts were "based—even in part—upon personal considerations, malice or ill will" then their acts were not privileged. Kumpf later proposed an instruction that would make privilege turn on "predominant" motivation. The district court, however, told the jury that "if you find that the actions of the defendants were motivated solely by a desire for revenge, ill will or malice, or in the case of the defendant Orin Steinhaus, solely by personal considerations, then you may find their actions improper." The jury returned a verdict for the defendants, and Kumpf attacks the "sole motive" instruction. . . .

Malice, ill will, and the like mean, in Wisconsin, an intent to act without justification. *Mendelson.* So the initial question is whether Kumpf has identified an unsupportable consideration that led to his dismissal. The only one Kumpf presses on us is Steinhaus's self-interest (Kumpf calls it "greed"). . . .

The basis of the privilege in question is the economic relations among the Lincoln family of corporations. The managers of the firm at the apex of the structure have an obligation to manage the whole structure in the interests of investors. Kumpf and Lincoln Wisconsin knew that when they started — when Kumpf took the risks associated with owning 20% of the stock, and holding one of three seats on the board, in a subsidiary of Lincoln Life. The superior managers in such a structure try to serve the interests of investors and other participants as a whole, and these interests will not always be congruent with the interests of managers of subsidiaries. Corporate reorganizations may reduce the costs of operation and put the structure in the hands of better managers, though this may be costly to existing managers.

If Kumpf had directly challenged the wisdom of a business decision of the managers of Lincoln Life, he would have been rebuffed with a reference to the business judgment doctrine — a rule of law that insulates business decisions from most forms of review. Courts recognize that managers have both better information and better incentives than they. The press of market forces — managers at Lincoln Life must continually attract new employees and capital, which they cannot do if they exploit existing participants or perform poorly — will more effectively serve the interests of all participants than will an error-prone judicial process. *See* Daniel R. Fischel, *The Business Judgment Rule and the Trans-Union Case*, 40 Bus. Law. 1437, 1439-43 (1985).

The privilege to manage corporate affairs is reinforced by the rationale of employment at will. Kumpf had no tenure of office. The lack of job security gave him a keen motive to do well. Security of position may diminish that incentive. *See* Richard A. Epstein, *In Defense of the Contract at Will*, 51 U. Chi. L. Rev. 947 (1984). Employment at will, like the business judgment doctrine, also keeps debates about business matters out of the hands of courts. People who enter a contract without a fixed term know there is some prospect that their business partners may try to take advantage of them or simply make a blunder in deciding whether to continue the relationship. Yet people's concern for their reputation and their ability to make other advantageous contracts in the future leads them to try to avoid both mistakes and opportunistic conduct. Contracting parties may sensibly decide that it is better to tolerate the risk of error — to leave correction to private arrangements — than to create a contractual right to stay in office in the absence of a "good" reason. The reason for a business decision may be hard to prove, and the costs of proof plus the risk of mistaken findings of breach may reduce the productivity of the employment relation.

Many people have concluded otherwise; contracts terminable only for cause are common. But in Wisconsin, courts enforce whichever solution the parties select. A contract at will may be terminated for any reason (including bad faith) or no reason, without judicial review; the only exception is a termination that violates "a fundamental and well-defined public policy as evidenced by existing law." *Brockmeyer v. Dun & Bradstreet*, 335 N.W.2d 834 (Wis. 1983). Greed — the motive Kumpf attributes to Steinhaus — does not violate a "fundamental and well-defined public policy" of Wisconsin. Greed is the foundation of much economic activity, and Adam Smith told us that each person's pursuit of his own interests drives the economic system to produce more and better goods and services for all. "It is not from the benevolence of the butcher, the brewer, or the baker, that we expect our dinner, but from their regard to their own interest. We address ourselves, not to their humanity but to their self-love, and never talk to them of our own necessities but of their advantages." *The Wealth of Nations* 14 (1776; Modern Library ed.).

The reasons that led Wisconsin to hold in *Brockmeyer* that it is "unnecessary and unwarranted for the courts to become arbiters of any termination that may have a tinge of bad faith attached" also establish that greed is not the sort of prohibited motive that will support Kumpf's tort action. In *Mendelson* the court stated that majority shareholders possess a privilege "to take whatever action they deem[ ] advisable to further the interests of the corporation." The court then quoted with approval from a text stating that a person enjoys no privilege "if his object is to put pressure upon the plaintiff and coerce him into complying with the defendant's wishes in some collateral matter."

If Steinhaus got rid of Kumpf because Kumpf would not marry Steinhaus's daughter, that would have been pressure in a "collateral matter." It is quite another thing to say that a jury must determine whether Steinhaus installed himself as head of Lincoln Chicago "predominantly" because he thought that would be good for Lincoln Life or "predominantly" because Steinhaus would enjoy the extra income. The decision to consolidate agencies and change managers is not "collateral" to the business of Lincoln Life, and the rationale of the business judgment rule interdicts any attempt to look behind the decision to determine whether Steinhaus is an astute manager.

Often corporations choose to align the interests of investors and managers by giving the managers a share of the firm's revenue or profits. Commissions, the ownership of stock or options, and bonuses all make managers and investors do well or poorly together. Lincoln Life chose to give managers a financial stake in each agency's revenues. Steinhaus was privileged to act with that incentive in mind. Suppose a major auto manufacturer decides to pay its chief executive officer $1 per year plus a percentage of the firm's profit. The officer then closes an unprofitable subsidiary (owned 80% by the firm), discharging its employees. Under Kumpf's theory any of the employees would be entitled to recover from the executive if the jury should estimate that in the executive's mind making money for himself predominated over making money for the firm. Yet since the two are the same thing, that would be a bootless investigation, and one with great potential to stifle the executive's vigorous pursuit of the firm's best interests. We do not think this is the law in Wisconsin or anywhere else.

Kumpf presents one last argument. He asked the judge to charge the jury that it should consider "recognized ethical codes or standards for a particular area of business activity" and "concepts of fair play" in deciding whether the defendants' acts were privileged. This "business ethics" instruction, Kumpf contends, would have allowed the jury to supplement the rules of tort and contract with "the rules of the game" in business. Although language of this sort appears in the Restatement (Second) of Torts §767 comment j (1979), it was not designed to be given to a jury. It would leave the jury at sea, free to impose a brand of ethics for which people may not have bargained. No case in Wisconsin has required an instruction even remotely like this one.

The "rules of the game" are important in deciding what sorts of acts are privileged. If Lincoln Life had assured Kumpf that his agency would not be obliterated without his being given an opportunity to take a new job within the firm, that might cast a different light on his claim for interference with contract. But Kumpf does not say that he received such assurance or that any other understood "rule" has been breached. He therefore had to be content with the rules reflected in the definition of privileged acts.

The contention that businesses should be more considerate of their officers should be addressed to the businesses and to legislatures. Some firms will develop reputations for kind treatment of executives, some will be ruthless. Some will seek to treat executives well but find that the exigencies of competition frustrate their plans. The rule of this game is that Kumpf was an employee at will and had no right to stay on if his board wanted him gone. His board was dominated by people who answered to Lincoln Sales, which answered to Lincoln Life. Kumpf did not bargain for legal rights against Lincoln Life, and the judge properly declined to allow the jury to convert moral and ethical claims into legal duties.

NOTES

1. *Proper and Improper Motives.* In the movie *Wall Street*, Gordon Gekko, played by Michael Douglas, celebrates the virtues of greed:

> The point is, ladies and gentlemen, that greed, for lack of a better word, is good; greed is right; greed works; greed clarifies, cuts through and captures the essence of the evolutionary spirit; greed in all its forms: greed for life, for money, for love, knowledge, has marked the upward surge of mankind, and greed—you mark my words—will not only save Teldar Paper but that other malfunctioning corporation called the U.S.A.

(20th Century Fox 1987). *See also* M. Todd Henderson & James C. Spindler, *Corporate Heroin: A Defense of Perks, Executive Loans, and Conspicuous Consumption*, 93 Geo. L. J. 1835 (2005). *But see* Eric A. Posner, *The Jurisprudence of Greed*, 151 U. Pa. L. Rev. 1097 (2003). Is this the point of Judge Easterbrook's defense of Steinhaus's conduct? Because *Kumpf* finds that greed is not an improper motive, it need not address whether liability would be appropriate if the termination decision was based only in part on that motive. Had greed counted as an improper motive, how should the mixed-motive question have been decided? We encountered this question in Chapter 4 in connection with Sarbanes-Oxley liability for whistleblowers and we will meet it again in Chapter 9 in connection with the antidiscrimination laws, but it is not clear that these statutory questions will influence the common law on issues such as intentional interference.

2. *A Detour into Judgecraft.* Judge Easterbrook is associated with the Chicago School of economic analysis of the law. One of the chief thrusts of the Chicago School is that "economic efficiency" ought to inform legal rules, frequently displacing (or at least modifying) notions of ethics and morals, and Easterbrook gives short shrift to the plaintiff's "business ethics" argument. Further, as Easterbrook's citation indicates, Professor Epstein is a strong defender of the economic efficiency of the at-will rule. As a federal judge deciding a diversity case like *Kumpf*, Easterbrook is supposed to be applying Wisconsin law, not the theories of the Chicago School. *See Erie R.R. v. Tompkins*, 304 U.S. 64 (1938). Do you think that he is faithful to *Erie*?

3. *More on Motives.* Kumpf argued that pursuit of self-interest by Steinhaus, as distinct from pursuit of corporate interests, suffices to make the interference actionable. What's wrong with that argument, aside from the mixed-motive question? Judge Easterbrook appeals to the business-judgment analogy, which ordinarily insulates corporate directors from liability for their decisions. But business-judgment protection may be lost if one or more directors are interested in the transaction. *See* R. CLARK, CORPORATE LAW § 3.4 (1987).

In addition, reading Easterbrook's opinion, one might forget that the business judgment rule applies to protect decisions of *directors* of a corporation, acting in their capacity as board members, not all of its "managers." Indeed, Easterbrook's language elides this distinction and effectively extends the business judgment rule to "managers" without benefit of any citation: "Courts recognize that managers have both better information and better incentives than they. The press of market forces — managers at Lincoln Life must continually attract new employees and capital, which they cannot do if they exploit existing participants or perform poorly — will more effectively serve the interests of all participants than will an error-prone judicial process." But is he right on what the law should be? Does Easterbrook's auto manufacturer hypothetical help you? He may be right that the CEO should not be subject to suit by ex-employees if he closes an unprofitable subsidiary. But suppose the CEO's only motive was to increase his personal profits, regardless of whether his corporation lost or made money. Should this be actionable under the intentional interference tort?

One way to avoid this entire problem would be doctrinal — holding that Steinhaus is absolutely privileged to take the actions he did. While some states take this approach, Wisconsin is not one of those jurisdictions, leaving Judge Easterbrook to struggle with the question of what motives taint a decision. If greed does not count as an improper motive in Wisconsin, what motives will? Easterbrook suggests that Kumpf would have had a good claim if Steinhaus had persuaded his firm to fire Kumpf because Kumpf refused to marry Steinhaus's daughter. But in a subsequent Seventh Circuit case, Judge Posner rejected an interference claim based on the defendant having fired him to advance his lover:

> But unless courts are to be overwhelmed by suits by disgruntled former employees against corporate officers, more is required than that a discharge be tainted by some private motive, such as greed, personal dislike, or, in this case perhaps, a personal attachment to a competing employee. Few are the employees whose actions are motivated solely by a selfless devotion to the employer's interests. The plaintiff must prove both that the employer did not benefit from the defendant's act and that the act was independently tortious, for example as fraud or defamation.

Preston v. Wis. Health Fund, 397 F.3d 539, 543-44 (7th Cir. 2005). This goes further than Easterbrook because it would appear to take the court out of the business of deciding motives at all and leave only "independent" torts as actionable and even then, only if there was no benefit at all to the employer.

4. *Personal Enough?* In *Kaelon v. USF Reddaway, Inc.*, 42 P.3d 344 (Ore. Ct. App. 2002), plaintiff claimed that an executive had "openly carried on a romantic affair with another female employee and gave preferential employment treatment to this employee," and that he believed (incorrectly) that plaintiff had gossiped about the affair. She claimed that, in retaliation, he had denied her promotion and belittled and humiliated her to force her to leave her employment. Contrary to *Preston*, the court found such conduct would be actionable:

> [A] reasonable juror could find that defendant, in humiliating plaintiff in the workplace, in denying her promotions, and in causing her to leave her employment, was retaliating against plaintiff for complaining about his romantic relationship with Hiepler. Under

several of our prior cases, such a finding by the jury would support the further finding that defendant acted solely for his own benefit, and not at all for the benefit of Reddaway.

Id. at 348. While the defendant would not be liable unless the jury found that his actions were taken purely out of personal motives, summary judgment could not be granted against defendant where plaintiff produced sufficient evidence to establish the personal motive. In short, the dispute would be whether the defendant acted solely from that motive or instead (or also) from a desire to advance his employer's interests. *See also Stanek v. Greco*, 323 F.3d 476 (6th Cir. 2003) (discharge by president because plaintiff had reported his misuse of funds actionable); *Sides v. Duke Hospital*, 328 S.E.2d 818 (N.C. App. 1985) (doctors who induced a hospital to discharge plaintiff, a nurse, because her deposition in a malpractice suit was damaging to them were acting for improper or strictly personal motives).

5. *Terminology.* The threshold question of whether the defendant is a "third party" tends to merge with the question of justification for his conduct or privilege, although note that the defendant need only be motivated "partially" by an intent to serve the employer. Thus, some courts recognize that the supervisor is not the employer but nevertheless is privileged to cause the employer to breach its contract. As we have seen, some jurisdictions see the privilege as absolute, *Halvorsen v. Aramark Unif. Servs., Inc.*, 77 Cal. Rptr. 2d 383 (Ct. App. 1998) (recognizing an absolute "manager's privilege" to interfere), but most courts view it as qualified. *See, e.g., Luketich v. Goedecke*, 835 S.W.2d 504, 508 (Mo. Ct. App. 1992) ("defendant-employer was justified in attempting to enforce its rights under the non-compete agreement with its former employee as long as the former employer had a reasonable, good faith belief in the validity of the agreement"); *Nordling v. N. States Power Co.*, 478 N.W.2d 498, 506 (Minn. 1991) ("A company officer, agent or employee is privileged to interfere with or cause a breach of another employee's employment contract with the company, if that person acts in good faith, whether competently or not, believing that his actions are in furtherance of the company's business. This privilege may be lost, however, if malice and bad faith predominantly motivate the defendant's actions, that is, by personal ill-will, spite, hostility, or a deliberate intent to harm the plaintiff employee.").

6. *Reputational Constraints.* The court in *Steinhaus* suggests that the law need not provide a remedy to deter harms like the one inflicted on the plaintiff because the market is generally self-correcting: "[P]eople's concern for their reputation and their ability to make other advantageous contracts in the future leads them to try to avoid both mistakes and opportunistic conduct." Obviously, such a "remedy" provides little solace for individual plaintiffs, but are you convinced that reputational consequences sufficiently reduce mistakes and opportunism? Summarizing the literature, Professor Sam Estreicher describes reputation as "a late-appearing deus ex machina explaining why opportunistic behavior by employers . . . is likely to be relatively unimportant," and questions whether it is likely to have this effect in employment markets. *Employer Reputation at Work*, 27 HOFSTRA LAB. & EMP. L. J. 1 (2009). *See also* Seth D. Harris, *Re-Thinking the Economics of Discrimination:* U.S. Airways v. Barnett, *the ADA, and the Application of Internal Labor Market Theory*, 89 IOWA L. REV. 123 (2003) (questioning the significance of reputational effects for ADA accommodation); Gillian Lester, *Restrictive Covenants, Employee Training, and the Limits of Transaction-Cost Analysis*, 76 IND. L. J. 49, 64 (2001) (explaining why there is ample room for opportunism with respect to restrictive covenants despite potential reputational consequences).

PROBLEM

5-1.   Marco Ramirez, the President of Free Market Enterprises, Inc., called Ashley Appleton into his office at salary review time near the end of the year. He congratulated her on a superlative job that year and told her that she would receive a 15 percent raise. Appleton was very happy until, at the end of the meeting, Ramirez told her that he was sure she would "show her gratitude with a small gift, say of 5 percent of her salary, in cash — small bills only, please."

Appleton comes to you for help. She had heard rumors from co-workers of required kickbacks, but this is the first time that she has been asked for money. Free Market Enterprises is a publicly held company, although your client believes that Ramirez, its founder, holds about 20 percent of the stock and is generally thought to have a controlling interest. Next, suppose Appleton does not make a gift and the following year, Ramirez selects her for termination in a company-wide layoff. Advise her.

B.   DEFAMATION

Defamation originated as a common-law tort designed to protect an individual's reputation against false and harmful words. A cause of action for defamation arises when statements made in writing (libel) or orally (slander) "harm the reputation of another so as to lower him in the estimation of the community or to deter third persons from association or dealing with him." RESTATEMENT (SECOND) OF TORTS § 558 (1977). The Restatement establishes four elements of the tort: "(a) a false and defamatory statement concerning another; (b) an unprivileged publication to a third party; (c) fault amounting at least to negligence on the part of the publisher; and (d) either actionability of the statement irrespective of special harm or the existence of special harm caused by the publication." *See generally* RESTATEMENT (THIRD) OF EMPLOYMENT LAW § 6.01 (Preliminary Draft No. 6, May 21, 2009) ("[a]n employer may be subject to liability for reasonably foreseeable pecuniary loss suffered by an employee or a former employee of the employer because the employer intentionally, recklessly, or negligently caused the publication of a statement concerning the employee or former employee that the employer knew or should have known was false and defamatory").

When judges enforce the law of defamation, however, they impose restrictions on speech, restrictions that may interfere with the constitutional free speech interests of defamation defendants. Much of the modern law of defamation, therefore, focuses on balancing the conflicting interests of reputation and freedom of speech inherent in every defamation case. The weight accorded to speech interests varies, however, with the identity of the parties to the suit. When public officials or public figures sue the media for defamation, the media's free speech interests predominate and constitutional standards play a large role in the case. *New York Times v. Sullivan*, 376 U.S. 254 (1964). At the other extreme, when a private individual sues a nonmedia defendant, the individual's interest in reputation predominates and the constitution plays a far lesser role in limiting the common law of defamation. *Dun and Bradstreet v. Greenmoss Builders*, 472 U.S. 749 (1985). Because defamation in the context of employment almost always involves the latter situation, this section will concentrate on traditional common-law issues that dominate employment-related defamation law, including the meaning of "publication," when a statement can be characterized as defamatory, and when defamation is privileged. We will also consider the fault element of defamation in the employment context.

Government Micro Resources, Inc. v. Jackson
624 S.E.2d 63 (Va. 2006)

Lacy, J.

Alan W. Jackson sued his former employer Government Micro Resources, Inc. (GMR) and its Chairman of the Board, Humberto Pujals, Jr., for breach of contract and defamation. The jury returned a verdict in favor of Jackson awarding him $200,500 in compensatory damages on his breach of contract claim and $5,000,000 and $1,000,000 as compensatory and punitive damages, respectively, on his defamation claim. The trial court granted the defendants' post-trial motion for remittitur, reducing the breach of contract award to $112,500, the defamation compensatory damages to $1,000,000, and the punitive damages to the statutory maximum of $350,000. . . .

[W]e conclude that Jackson's defamation claim was not opinion, was timely and properly pled and proven; that actual malice was shown by clear and convincing evidence; and that in holding that the compensatory damage award was excessive, the trial court did not consider factors in evidence relevant to that damage award.

Facts

The following facts are relevant to both appeals and we recite them in the light most favorable to Jackson, the party prevailing in the trial court.

In 2001, GMR, a technology resale and services company, sought to increase its services business. To accomplish this goal, GMR recruited Jackson [with prior service in the military and at the National Security Agency] to serve as president and chief executive officer because of his connections with the federal government, his top secret security clearances, and his extensive experience with technology services in both the public and private sectors.

Jackson began work at GMR on July 9, 2001. Within a short period, Jackson realized the company's financial situation differed significantly from what he was led to believe when he accepted the position. For example, GMR's line of credit was significantly reduced because Pujals caused a transfer of properties from the company to himself by using the company's line of credit to satisfy the mortgages on the properties. Jackson also learned of a $1.1 million loss GMR sustained in the first six months of 2001, a $400,000 accounting error reported by the chief financial officer in August, and a $1.4 million discrepancy between the company's listed inventory and that which it actually held.

In October 2001, as part of its effort to increase its services business, GMR began discussions with Seisint, Inc. (Seisint), a technology company with a super computer it wished to market to the federal government. Seisint did not have contacts with the federal government, but GMR could provide those contacts through Jackson. The Seisint executives, Henry E. Asher and Daniel W. Latham, worked directly with Jackson. Eventually, GMR and Seisint executed a memorandum of understanding detailing GMR and Seisint's agreement to jointly market Seisint's super computer to the federal government.

The remainder of 2001 and the early months of 2002 did not bring a significant change in GMR's financial status. On March 5, 2002, GMR terminated Jackson's employment for cause. The termination letter accused Jackson of "gross mismanagement" of GMR's finances. Pujals admitted, however, that when he wrote the letter he did not have "a specific amount of money in mind" as a basis for that statement.

According to Asher, Pujals called Asher either the day Jackson was terminated, or the next day, and told Asher that Jackson "mismanaged the company and cost him a tremendous amount of money." Latham testified that at a meeting in April 2002 between GMR and Seisint executives Pujals initiated the subject of Jackson's firing and said that "Jackson had been removed from his job because he lost $3 million." Pujals testified that at the April meeting he had responded to Asher's question regarding the details of Jackson's termination by saying the company, and not Jackson, lost $3 million, which resulted in Pujals having to let Jackson go. Pujals admitted that Jackson did not lose $3 million for GMR and that "it would be false if someone said that."

Following his termination, Jackson entered employment discussions with Seisint. Because of the information Asher received from Pujals, Seisint, at Asher's direction did not hire Jackson for a management position but rather engaged him as a sales representative and consultant from March 6, 2002 until December 31, 2002. On January 1, 2003, Seisint hired Jackson as senior vice-president of government programs, which Jackson did not consider a management position.

Pujals was upset when he heard that Jackson was working for Seisint because Jackson would not have known about Seisint if not for GMR. Particularly, Pujals said: "And to find out—and to find out that after we fired him for cause, that he's already employed immediately after and he has already a relationship right after was very, very—a very, very mean thing for him to do."

I. The Defamatory Statements

The jury was instructed to return a verdict in favor of Jackson if it found that Jackson proved either of the following two statements:

> Mr. Pujals called Hank Asher within a few days of terminating Mr. Jackson (March 5, 2002). Mr. Pujals told Mr. Asher that Mr. Jackson had mismanaged GMR, had lost what Mr. Asher perceived or recalled as an exorbitant amount of money, and that Mr. Pujals had to let him go as a result; or
> In April 2002, Mr. Pujals told Daniel Latham, President of Homeland Defense [and] Seisint, Inc., and/or Mr. Asher, founder and CEO of Seisint, Inc., that he fired Al Jackson because Mr. Jackson lost $3 million.

GMR contends that the first statement was not contained in Jackson's pleadings and was not timely asserted, that both statements were opinion and therefore could not be the subject of a defamation claim, and that Jackson did not prove that GMR uttered either statement in haec verba or with malice. . . .

B. Opinion

GMR next argues that the statements at issue were matters of opinion and thus could not be the basis of a defamation claim. According to GMR, the terms "exorbitant" and "mismanaged" contained in the allegedly defamatory statements submitted to the jury represented Pujals' subjective judgments and were expressions of opinion only.

Statements that express only the speaker's opinion and not matters of fact are not actionable as defamation because such statements cannot be shown to be false. *Fuste v. Riverside Healthcare Ass'n, Inc.*, 575 S.E.2d 858, 861 (Va. 2003). "Statements that are relative in nature and depend largely upon the speaker's viewpoint are expressions of opinion." Whether a statement is a statement of fact or opinion is a matter of law and is reviewed de novo on appeal.

In *American Communications Network, Inc. v. Williams*, 568 S.E.2d 683, 686 (Va. 2002), we held that in considering whether a statement was one of fact or opinion, we do not isolate parts of an alleged defamatory statement. Rather, the alleged defamatory statement must be considered as a whole to determine whether it states a fact or non-actionable opinion.

The alleged defamation in this case is that Jackson's mismanagement caused GMR to lose money in 2001 which, in turn, was the basis for Jackson's termination. Whether a company's financial loss is the result of mismanagement is a fact that can be proven. Indeed, in this case, the parties introduced substantial evidence regarding the cause or causes of GMR's financial losses. The evidence also established that government contracting was a very competitive business and success was often based on contacts with "the appropriate people." The trial court observed that the evidence showed that Pujals' statements were made as a matter of fact "with the intent to defame Mr. Jackson so that he would not be able to go to Seisint and get employment with them and cut GMR out of the picture."

Accordingly, we conclude that the trial court did not err in ruling that the alleged defamatory statements were not opinion.

C. Proof of Defamation

. . . GMR contends that because neither Asher nor Latham could recall the exact words of the first or second statement, respectively, Jackson failed to carry his burden of proof and the trial court should have struck the defamation claim. However, Asher and Latham were not the only persons who testified as to the content of the defamatory statements.

Jackson testified, "in the telephone call with Dan Latham, he told me that . . . Mr. Pujals said I had lost $3 million for GMR, and that's why I had been fired." Jackson also testified that Asher told Jackson that he understood Jackson "lost $3 million for GMR" and that is why Jackson was fired. Pujals testified that he told

Asher and Latham that the company lost $3 million dollars and "we had to let Jackson go."

Latham testified that Asher was present when Pujals told Latham that Jackson was fired because Jackson had "lost $3 million," and that $3 million "was a large sum of money for a company the size [of] GMR." Asher testified that he had one and possibly two conversations with Pujals in which Pujals told Asher that Jackson had "mismanaged the company" and cost the company "tremendous" amounts of money.

This evidence is sufficient to satisfy the standard that the defamatory words "must be substantially proven as alleged." . . .

II. Proof of Actual Malice

GMR also assigns error to the trial court's failure to strike Jackson's claim for punitive damages asserting Jackson failed to provide clear and convincing proof of actual malice [which would also satisfy the fault element for the tort itself since Virginia requires only negligence for actionable defamation against a private person]. GMR contends that the test we have established for such proof requires "much more than mere falsity" to sustain a finding of actual malice. Citing *Jordan* [*v. Kollman* 612 S.E. 2d 203 (Va. 2005) and *The Gazette, Inc. v. Harris*, 325 S.E. 2d 713, 746 (Va. 1985)], GMR asserts that this Court has determined that to establish actual malice, a plaintiff must produce clear and convincing proof that there were reasons for a defendant to doubt the veracity of the defamatory statement or that all judgment and reason were abandoned and no objective basis existed for the defamatory charge. GMR misstates the law and misapplies these cases.

To recover punitive damages in a defamation case, the plaintiff must prove actual malice by "clear and convincing evidence that [the defendant] *either* knew the statements he made were false at the time he made them, or that he made them with a reckless disregard for their truth." *Ingles v. Dively*, 435 S.E. 2d 641, 646 ([Va.] 1993) (emphasis added). A plaintiff seeking punitive damages can prevail by establishing either circumstance by clear and convincing evidence.

In both cases cited by GMR, the second circumstance — reckless disregard for the truth — was relied upon to show actual malice. In *Jordan*, the defendant claimed that he did not know that the statements at issue were false; rather, he believed the statements to be true. Similarly in *The Gazette*, the Court assumed without deciding that the plaintiff failed to prove that the defendant knew the defamatory statements were false. These cases are not relevant to the instant case because Jackson predicates his case of actual malice on Pujals' knowledge that his defamatory statements were false.

In considering GMR's assertion that Jackson did not provide clear and convincing evidence of actual malice, we independently review the record, *The Gazette*, and we review the facts in the light most favorable to the party prevailing below. *Jordan*. The record in this case contains clear and convincing evidence that at the time Pujals made the statements ascribing GMR's loss of large amounts of money in 2001 to Jackson, he knew those statements were false.

Pujals himself testified that he knew Jackson did not lose $3 million for GMR and that "it would be false if someone said that." According to Asher, Pujals called Asher either the day of or the day after Jackson's termination and told Asher that Jackson had mismanaged GMR and lost a tremendous or exorbitant amount of money. Latham testified that at a meeting in April, Pujals also initiated the conversation regarding

Jackson stating that "Jackson had been removed from his job because he lost $3 million." In neither of these conversations did Pujals mention that the company's financial situation had been affected by a reduced line of credit, the $1.1 million loss in the first half of 2001, the $400,000 accounting error, or the $1.4 million drop-ship inventory problem, none of which could be attributed to Jackson.

In summary, Pujals knew his statements were false. He initiated both conversations in which he defamed Jackson. Our independent review of the record, considering the evidence in the light most favorable to Jackson, shows clear and convincing proof of actual malice; thus, the trial court did not err in refusing to strike Jackson's punitive damage claim.

III. Qualified Privilege

The principle of qualified privilege protects a communication from allegations of defamation if made in good faith, to and by persons who have corresponding duties or interests in the subject of the communication. *Smalls v. Wright*, 399 S.E.2d 805, 807 ([Va.] 1991). A plaintiff can overcome the privilege by providing evidence that the statements were made with malice. *Fuste.* In this case, the trial court concluded that the privilege did not exist and declined to instruct the jury on the issue. GMR asserts this holding was error.

We need not resolve whether qualified privilege applied to the alleged defamation in this case because, even if it did, the trial court's failure to instruct the jury was harmless error. . . .

In this case, even if the alleged defamation was entitled to a qualified privilege, the privilege would have been lost if the jury found Pujals uttered the statements with actual malice. As discussed above, the jury was required to and did find that the statements were made with actual malice when it awarded punitive damages. Because we have already concluded that the record supports the award of punitive damages, we hold that any failure to instruct the jury on qualified privilege was harmless error because the privilege would have been lost upon the jury's finding of actual malice.

IV. Remittitur

[The court found abuse of discretion in concluding the $5 million jury verdict was excessive. In so determining, "the trial court did not address the injuries presumed in defamation per se or the evidence regarding the impact of the defamation on Jackson's emotional state, reputation, and employment opportunities, all of which the jury was entitled to consider." The court also "declined to compare verdicts as a means to measure a verdict's excessiveness, but instead analyze, as we have today, whether the jury was influenced by passion, corruption, or prejudice, or misunderstood the facts or law."]

NOTES

1. *The Meaning of "Defamatory."* Pujal's statements were highly critical of plaintiff. Is that enough for defamation? Statements accusing the plaintiff of a crime are obviously defamatory, *see Forster v. W. Dakota Veterinary Clinic, Inc.*, 689 N.W.2d 366 (N.D. 2004), but much less damning comments may also be actionable. The statements in *Jackson* seem to merely describe him as incompetent. Apparently, that was enough for the court.

Even vaguer statements challenging an employee's competence have been found to be defamatory. In *Falls v. Sporting News Publishing Co.*, 834 F.2d 611, 613-15 (6th Cir. 1987), plaintiff was a columnist for a newspaper. He successfully established defamation based on his editor's comment, made in response to a reader's inquiry about the discontinuance of plaintiff's column: "I know Joe brightened a lot of hearts with his column through the years but we felt it was time to make a change, with more energetic columnists who attend more events and are closer to today's sports scene." Similarly defamatory was a statement by another Sporting News official, "Those who seem to have reached maturity and are on the downswing are giving way to up-and-coming young writers who we think deserve a chance."

The test of whether a statement is defamatory, according to section 559A of the RESTATEMENT (SECOND) OF TORTS, is whether it "tends so to harm the reputation of another as to lower him in the estimation of the community or to deter third persons from associating or dealing with him." The "community" includes any "substantial and respectable minority of members of the community." It is not enough, however, if the statement "offends some individual or individuals with views sufficiently peculiar to regard as derogatory what the vast majority of persons regard as innocent." § 559 cmt. e. Who was the "community" in *Jackson*? In *Falls*? In the employment context, would not any statement explaining a former employee's deficiencies in the job risk being sufficiently defamatory to be actionable?

2. *Fact versus Opinion.* As *Jackson* indicates, whether the statement is "fact" or "opinion" will determine whether a defamatory statement is actionable. The *Jackson* court had little difficulty with that issue. Are you convinced that "mismanagement" is a fact? Perhaps more surprisingly, the *Falls* court found both at-issue statements actionable:

> [Looking at the phrase "reached maturity and on the downswing,"] whether "a person has 'reached maturity' may be a statement of fact, and insofar as plaintiff is concerned [57 years old], it could not be false." It also might be viewed as a derogatory opinion, a mild form of ridicule, but it reasonably could not be regarded as defamatory. *See* RESTATEMENT (SECOND) OF TORTS § 559 (1977). However, the statement that plaintiff was "on the downswing" is capable of bearing a defamatory meaning since a jury could reasonably find that it implied that Waters knew undisclosed facts that would justify such an opinion — for example, that plaintiff's writing and reasoning abilities had deteriorated, or that the quality of his work had declined to the point that others had to rewrite or cover for him. . . .
>
> Similarly, Barnidge's [the editor] letter can be construed, by negative implication, as an expression of opinion that plaintiff was inferior to his replacements because he was less energetic than other columnists, attended fewer events, and was not as close as they to the current sports scene. This comment creates a reasonable inference that it is justified by the existence of undisclosed facts, such as, for example, that plaintiff did not work hard or he was prevented by his physical condition from exerting himself; that he did not frequently attend sports events to obtain first-hand knowledge of the events reported in his sports columns; and that he was out-of-touch with current sports personalities, an outsider who lacked good "sources." Obviously, these kinds of undisclosed facts could be defamatory. In the alternative, the letter can be viewed as expressing a derogatory opinion of

plaintiff — that he was inferior to his replacements — based on Barnidge's own statement as fact that the new writers were more energetic, attended more events, and were closer to the sports scene. If these stated facts were found to be false and defamatory, Barnidge would be subject to liability for the factual statements but not for the expression of opinion.

834 F.2d at 616. Courts have had great difficulty formulating standards for distinguishing fact from opinion. Are you satisfied with the *Falls* resolution? And what about First Amendment concerns? *See Milkovich v. Lorain J. Co.*, 497 U.S. 1 (1990) (finding no absolute constitutional protection for opinions). *See generally* John Bruce Lewis & Gregory V. Mersol, *Opinion and Rhetorical Hyperbole in Workplace Defamation Actions: The Continuing Quest for Meaningful Standards*, 52 DEPAUL L. REV. 19 (2002).

3. *Truth as a Defense.* Defamation is sometimes confused with falsehood. A statement can be both defamatory and true, although truth is an absolute defense to liability for defamation. A plaintiff was traditionally not required to prove that a defamatory statement was false, but merely to allege falsity, in order to make out a prima facie case of defamation. The burden was on the defendant to establish the truth of the statement. While many states continue to allocate the burden on truth in this fashion, Supreme Court decisions raise questions about the constitutionality of this approach. The First Amendment may require, as a prerequisite to liability, proof that the defendant is at fault with respect to the falsity of a communication. *See Philadelphia Newspapers, Inc. v. Hepps*, 475 U.S. 767, 776 (1986); *BE&K Construction Co. v. NLRB*, 536 U.S. 516 (2002). *See generally* RESTATEMENT (SECOND) OF TORTS § 581A cmts. a, b (1977). The proposed Restatement of Employment Law speaks in terms of actionable statements "being false and defamatory."

4. *Publication and Self-Publication.* "Publication" is a term of art in defamation. It consists merely of "communication [of defamatory matter] intentionally or by a negligent act to one other than the person defamed." RESTATEMENT (SECOND) OF TORTS § 577 (1977). In *Jackson* there was no dispute about publication: Pujals made his comments to the plaintiff's prospective employer. In *Falls*, some of the defamation was published in the more intuitive meaning of the word: It had been printed in a newspaper.

Suppose, however, that Pujals had made similar statements about Jackson's performance to another Government Micro Resources employee, perhaps the Director of Human Resources. Comment i of Restatement § 577 states that "[t]he communication within the scope of his employment by one agent to another agent of the same principal" is a publication. Thus, intracorporate communications will constitute publication under the Restatement. *See also* RESTATEMENT (THIRD) OF EMPLOYMENT LAW § 6.01(3) (Preliminary Draft No. 6, May 21, 2009) ("An employer may cause the publication of a false and defamatory statement concerning an employee or former employee by another employee of the employer by intentionally, recklessly, or negligently causing the publication of the statement to a third employee of the same employer."); *Trail v. Boys & Girls Clubs of Northwest Ind.*, 845 N.E.2d 130, 136 (Ind. 2006) (employee evaluations communicated intracompany to management personnel are published for purposes of defamation); *Taggart v. Drake Univ.*, 549 N.W.2d 796 (Iowa 1996) (communications between corporate supervisors concerning a corporate employee may be subject to a qualified privilege, but they are published). *But see Halsell v. Kimberly-Clark Corp.*, 683 F.2d 285, 288-89 (8th Cir.

1982) ("Until the defamatory statement is communicated outside the corporate sphere or internal organization, it has not been published."). A few courts have even found the defendant responsible when the plaintiff himself republishes the defamation under the "compulsory self-publication" doctrine. *See, e.g., Lewis v. Equitable Life Assurance Soc'y*, 389 N.W.2d 876 (Minn. 1986). *But see Emery v. Northeast Ill. Reg'l Commuter R.R. Corp.*, 880 N.E.2d 1002, 1011-12 (Ill. App. Ct. 2007) (rejecting the compulsory self-publication doctrine as a minority rule in only four states). Where this doctrine exists, an employee's revealing the reasons for his former employer's adverse action against him in order, say, to obtain a new position will satisfy the publication requirement. *See generally* Markita D. Cooper, *Between a Rock and a Hard Case: Time for a New Doctrine of Compelled Self-Publication*, 72 NOTRE DAME L. REV. 373 (1997). There is currently a debate within the American Law Institute as to whether the doctrine should be recognized in the proposed Restatement of Employment Law.

5. *Actions as Statements.* A number of cases have considered whether actions can be treated as statements for defamation purposes, which is especially important in the employment context. For example, *Krolikowski v. University of Massachusetts Memorial Medical Center*, 2002 U.S. Dist. LEXIS 8984 (D. Mass. May 16, 2002), upheld a cause of action by a doctor who claimed she was defamed when the Chair of the Radiology Department barred her from reading mammograms; she argued that this sent a signal to her colleagues that she had serious performance problems. While there was a fact question as to whether a "supervisory privilege" was exceeded, the defendant's conduct was actionable. Similarly, in *Tyler v. Macks Stores of N.C. Inc.*, 272 S.E.2d 633 (S.C. 1980), an employee was required to take a polygraph and soon afterward was discharged. He argued that this led other employees and others to believe that his discharge was based on some wrongful activity and that "this insinuation and inference of wrongdoing can amount to the publication of defamatory matter." The court agreed. Defamation may be "by actions or conduct as well as by word" and "need not be accomplished in a direct manner. To render the defamatory statement actionable, it is not necessary that the false charge be made in a direct, open and positive manner. A mere insinuation is as actionable as a positive assertion if it is false and malicious and the meaning is plain." *Id.* at 634. However, mere silence has been held not actionable even when it was alleged that the natural inference was defamatory. *See Trail v. Boys & Girls Clubs of Northwest Ind.*, 845 N.E.2d 130, 137 (Ind. 2006) (where an allegation refers only to a speculative effect of "non-actionable silence" on plaintiff's reputation, "[i]t would be an odd use of the defamation doctrine to hold that silence constitutes actionable speech.").

If defamation may be accomplished through actions as well as through words, is the act of sending security guards to escort a fired employee from the building defamatory? Does it matter whether this was standard practice in cases of suspension or discharge? *See Phelan v. May Dep't Stores Co.* 819 N.E.2d 550 (Mass. 2004) (employer's conduct during investigation of potential theft too ambiguous to be actionable by employee).

6. *Counseling the Employer.* What can an employer do to protect against defamation actions? Obviously, care should be taken to ensure that discharges are based on proven violations. Truth will avoid liability. Even after careful investigation, however, erroneous judgments will sometimes be made. Would you advise an employer not to tell employees the reason they are being discharged? Informing only the employee would not be actionable because of the publication requirement — but recall the compelled self-publication doctrine. One commentator recommends regularly scheduled, objective evaluations, accessible only by those with a need to see them, and

investigation of possible employee misconduct, preferably by a designated person to ensure consistency. When discharge is necessary:

> Handle terminations sensitively. Make sure termination is done only after a proper and thorough investigation. Release information about the discharged employee to only those in the organization who need to know. Take action to prevent and/or stop false rumors that might begin circulating. . . . To the extent possible, assist the employee in locating new employment. Remember that lawsuits of this nature are brought by disgruntled employees who believe they were not treated fairly by the employer. . . . Consider asking for a signed release from the employee which authorizes you to release information to prospective employers who may inquire.
>
> Respond carefully to reference inquiries. Direct inquiries to a centralized office such as personnel or human resources offices. Verify the identity of the person seeking the information to confirm that they have a legitimate need for the information. Insist that inquiries be made in writing. Disclose only dates of employment, positions held, and wage/salary information, or keep discussions with prospective employers limited to other verifiable and objective facts. Avoid giving subjective or emotional evaluations.
>
> Correct mistakes. Take prompt action to correct any inaccuracies in information provided about the employee.
>
> Train supervisory personnel in the proper methods of employee evaluation, investigation and termination. . . .

Thomas A. Jacobson, *Avoiding Claims of Defamation in the Workplace*, 72 N. Dak. L. Rev. 247, 264-65 (1996). What do you think of this advice? How will implementing the suggested practices help employers avoid defamation liability? Might adopting these practices create other legal risks or costs for the employer?

7. *Mishandling Matters.* For a good example of how *not* to handle a reference request, consider *Matthews v. Wis. Energy Corp.*, 534 F.3d 547, 553-54 (7th Cir. 2008), which is all the more striking because a lawyer caused the problem. The case arose from settlement of a discrimination suit. The employer's in-house attorney, English, recited the terms regarding references in open court, which required the company to follow its policy of limited disclosure, "what you call name, rank, and serial number." That is, the company would "confirm people worked there, the dates of employment, and their position or at least their last position." Later, Matthews hired Schwartz to help find employment, and Schwartz ended up talking to English on the phone. In that conversation, she discussed far more than name, rank, and serial number, and, according to Schwartz, displayed an "obvious sense of distrust" of Matthews. The Seventh Circuit found the attorney's comments actionable:

> As represented by Wisconsin Energy, its policy entailed verifying only the dates of employment, final salary, and the title of the last position held. Neither participant in the conversation denies that English told Schwartz of Matthews's litigation history. This information went well beyond the objective information concerning Matthews's dates of employment, final salary, and final position held. A jury could believe Schwartz's version of the conversation, which included what would be unfavorable information regarding Matthews. And it could likewise conclude that the parties agreed that Wisconsin Energy would provide only the objective information set out in its "policy." If so, this would show that Wisconsin Energy breached the settlement agreement.

Note that this is not defamation per se, but rather breach of a settlement agreement. Note also that for the same reason, the plaintiff would be limited to contract damages rather than the lucrative damages available under tort law.

8. *Overly Positive Recommendations.* Another reason for an employer to adopt a policy limiting the information that will be provided about present or former employees is to limit liability to third parties when an employment reference is too favorable. This can arise when an employer provides a reference while withholding negative information about a former employee from a prospective employer, perhaps for fear of a defamation suit, and the employee subsequently engages in misconduct or causes injury upon being hired by the new employer. While liability in such situations is rare, it is not unknown and is most common in cases involving affirmative misrepresentations, rather than mere nondisclosure. *See, e.g., Kadlec Med. Ctr. v. Lakeview Anesthesia Assocs.,* 527 F.3d 412 (5th Cir. 2008) (no duty for a hospital to disclose doctor's narcotic addiction to another hospital when its letter merely confirmed dates of work; however, glowing letters from a practice group to second hospital were actionable because they were misleading); *Randi W. v. Muroc Joint Unified School Dist.,* 929 P.2d 582 (Cal. 1997) (although "ordinarily a recommending employer should not be held accountable to third persons for failing to disclose negative information regarding a former employee, nonetheless liability may be imposed" if the recommendation letter amounts to an affirmative misrepresentation presenting a foreseeable and substantial risk of physical harm to a third person). *See also Thomas v. Dep't of Hous. & Urban Dev.,* 124 F.3d 1439, 1442 (Fed. Cir. 1997) (criticizing settlement agreement "requiring the whitewashing of an employee's disciplinary record," which results in "some agency officials [being] willing to palm off their problems on others, including sister agencies," and suggesting that perhaps "as a matter of sound governmental administration such agency agreements should be prohibited."). *See generally* Deborah A. Ballam, *Employment References — Speak No Evil, Hear No Evil: A Proposal for Meaningful Reform,* 39 Am. Bus. L. J. 445 (2002).

9. *Libel and Slander.* To this point, we have spoken of "defamation" without distinguishing the old common-law categories of libel and slander. For most purposes, these categories are no longer important, but in some jurisdictions they retain some vitality. Libel is a defamation embodied in a permanent form such as a letter or a newspaper article, or on the Internet. According to the Restatement (Second) of Torts § 568A, libel in the modern world also includes "[b]roadcasting of defamatory matter by means of radio or television . . . whether or not it is read from a manuscript." The "downswing" statement in *Falls* was libel. Slander is characterized by impermanence and includes, therefore, unrecorded spoken words as well as gestures. The statements in *Jackson* were slander.

The significance of the distinction lies in whether the plaintiff must prove "special damages" in order to sustain an action. "Special damages" (as opposed to "general damages") refers to actual provable damages such as loss of employment. *See* Restatement (Second) of Torts § 75 cmt. b (1977). Libel, because its permanence rendered it more dangerous, was traditionally actionable without proof of "special damages." An action for slander, however, could be maintained only if there were such proof, with several defined exceptions: where the slander concerned a loathsome disease, criminal conduct, unchastity, or where it slandered a person's trade or profession. *See Wilcox v. Newark Val. Cent. School Dist.,* 904 N.Y.S.2d 523, 527 (3d Dep't 2010) (teacher had actionable claim for slander per se, based on principal's statement to other school officials that she should take leave of absence "for safety" of students; in the context of the highly publicized scandal involving the alleged rape by her significant other of a student, "a reasonable listener could interpret the statement as implying plaintiff's possible participation in or awareness of the crimes against the students, or as linking her to immoral and reprehensible conduct"). These were the so-called slander "per se" categories, for which there was no need to make any further showing of damages in order to recover. In the employment context, loss of employment or inability to secure employment is a form of special damages. However, special damages need not be proven in order to maintain an action for slander of a person's trade or profession. As a result, the distinction between libel and slander will not often be significant in defamation cases in the employment setting, even if it retains some significance in other contexts in a particular jurisdiction.

10. *Reconsidering Perverse Incentives.* Potential liability for defamation discourages providing references to prospective employers. As the extract in Note 7 suggests, many employers have adopted policies regarding employment references, under which supervisors and Human Resources officers are told to provide minimal information. For example, such policies often limit the information to be given to confirming the fact of employment, the position, and the dates. In some cases, the policy allows confirming last salary. Adherence to such policies will, obviously, limit defamation exposure and the possibility of liability for overly positive recommendations. Of course, it also limits the extent to which any potential employer can be sure about the work history and habits of an applicant. In extreme cases, the failure to provide information may result in the hiring of a sexual predator or a thief. For that reason, there have been repeated calls for statutory immunity for employment references. As of 2009, thirty-nine states have enacted job reference immunity statutes, *see* MATTHEW FINKIN, PRIVACY IN EMPLOYMENT LAW 911-38 (3d ed. 2009), but the provisions vary widely, and scholars do not believe that such laws have meaningfully changed employer unwillingness to provide references. *See generally* Matthew W. Finkin & Kenneth G. Dau-Schmidt, *Solving the Employee Reference Problem: Lessons from the German Experience*, 57 AM. J. COMP. L. 387 (2009); Markita D. Cooper, *Job Reference Immunity Statutes: Prevalent But Irrelevant*, 11 CORNELL J.L. & PUB. POL'Y 1 (2001); *cf.* J. Hoult Verkerke, *Legal Regulation of Employment Reference Practices*, 65 U. CHI. L. REV. 115, 199 (1998) (finding that the "existing combination of defamation liability for falsely negative references and the conditional common interest privilege applicable to supplying reference information strikes an appropriate balance between quantity and quality concerns," but recommending modest reforms such as "adopting targeted reporting and disclosure systems for certain high-risk occupations."). Reconsider the need for such statutes after you have read the next principal case, which explores the concept of privilege.

Shannon v. Taylor AMC/Jeep, Inc.
425 N.W.2d 165 (Mich. Ct. App. 1988)

McDONALD, J.

. . . Plaintiff worked for Taylor for approximately twelve years, the last eight years as parts manager. Plaintiff's employment was terminated in June, 1982, for his alleged involvement with stolen parts.

During his employment as parts manager, one of the employees under plaintiff's supervision was Laurie Cherup. Around the beginning of 1982, plaintiff had to discipline Cherup and eventually fire her. Rick Howard, the AMC branch manager responsible for Taylor AMC, reinstated Cherup and told plaintiff to leave her alone. Howard and Cherup were involved in a physical relationship in late 1981 or early

1982. Following plaintiff's termination, Cherup became the new parts manager. Cherup was overheard on several occasions telling customers over the phone that plaintiff was no longer parts manager because plaintiff had "gotten caught stealing," and that plaintiff was fired "for being involved in theft of parts."

Plaintiff testified that he was not involved with stolen parts for profit or personal gain, but was working with Taylor Police Officer James Black in an attempt to set up persons attempting to sell stolen parts to Taylor. On June 15, 1982, plaintiff was contacted on the phone and asked if he wanted to buy a Jeep hardtop. The phone call made plaintiff suspicious that the hardtop was stolen, so plaintiff called Black, a personal friend, for advice. Black advised plaintiff that the police would need "hard evidence" such as names and driver's license numbers of the suspects. Plaintiff purchased two hardtops which he suspected to be stolen, and placed them in the back of the parts department. When another Taylor employee indicated that a customer was interested in purchasing one of the hardtops, plaintiff responded that they were not for sale as he had reason to believe the hardtops were stolen. Plaintiff was fired the same day Black was allegedly going to write up a report on the stolen goods. . . .

[This appeal questions the propriety of the verdict of no cause of action on the slander claim. The court held that the trial judge erred in instructing the jury on qualified privilege and actual malice.]

A communication is defamatory if it tends to lower an individual's reputation in the community or deter third persons from associating or dealing with him. *Swenson-Davis v. Martel*, 354 N.W.2d 288 (Mich. App. 1984). Slander per se is found where the words spoken are false and malicious and are injurious to a person in his or her profession or employment. *Swenson-Davis.*

Here, the trial court found that Cherup's statements about plaintiff to defendant's customers were protected from action by a qualified privilege. The initial determination of whether a privilege exists is one of law for the court. *Lawrence v. Fox*, 97 N.W.2d 719 (Mich. 1959). In general, a qualified privilege extends to "all communications made bona fide upon any subject matter in which the party communicating has an interest, or in reference to which he has a duty, to a person having a corresponding interest or duty. . . ."

Thus, in order to have a qualified privilege, the communication must be: (1) bona fide; (2) made by a party who has an interest, or a duty to communicate the subject matter; and (3) made to a party who has a corresponding interest or duty.

Although in the instant case neither party addresses the first prerequisite, the "bona fide" nature of the communication, we question whether Cherup's statements were bona fide. Not only had plaintiff previously fired Cherup, but there was testimony indicating that another employee overheard a conversation between Cherup, Howard and two others regarding possible ways in which to "get rid of" plaintiff, and wherein Howard allegedly suggested that they "link" plaintiff with some stolen parts.

Nonetheless, even if the statements were bona fide, we find that they do not meet the remaining two requirements. The problem with determining if a qualified privilege applies is that privilege varies with the situation; it is not a constant. Defendant Taylor contends that the particular facts of this situation call for the application of qualified privilege, arguing that it had a duty to inform customers that the parts manager (plaintiff) had been fired for purchasing stolen parts. Taylor asserts that if the customers were not presently told and found out years later that stolen parts were purchased from Taylor, they would cease to do business with the dealership. In Taylor's opinion, the potential detrimental effect on customer relations justifies the application of qualified privilege to the statements. We disagree.

For defendant's argument to have merit, and before defendant could acquire an interest in telling customers why plaintiff was fired, a determination should have been made as to whether stolen goods were actually sold to customers. Taylor knew that plaintiff had possession of the Jeep hardtops. There was no reason to believe that any stolen goods ended up in customers' hands. Therefore, there was no qualified privilege to tell customers that plaintiff was fired because he dealt with stolen parts. Thus, absent evidence that stolen parts had been passed along to customers, plaintiff's good name should have been protected by not allowing an employee to tell customers why plaintiff was fired. When dealing with a duty/interest privilege, the Michigan Supreme Court has said "the occasion determines the question of privilege." *Bacon v. The Michigan C.R. Co.*, 33 N.W. 181 (Mich. 1887). The instant occasion did not give the employer a qualified privilege to defame plaintiff.

Furthermore, we find no corresponding interest or duty to hear the communication on the part of the customers. In *Merritt v. Detroit Memorial Hospital*, 265 N.W.2d 124 (Mich. App. 1978), this Court stated that an employer has a qualified privilege to tell those of its employees responsible for hiring and firing of accusations of employee misconduct. However, an employer cannot tell all employees why someone was fired in order to quiet rumors or restore morale. *Sias v. General Motors Corp.*, 127 N.W.2d 357 (Mich. 1964). In the instant case Taylor does not allege or offer proof that any customer received stolen goods purchased from plaintiff. If Taylor had a good faith belief that stolen auto parts had been sold to a particular customer, the customer may have had an interest, but that is not the situation in the instant case. Here, the customer's interest is like the employees' interest in *Sias*: just a general interest or curiosity in finding out why a former employee was fired.

The trial court erred in instructing the jury that a qualified privilege existed. Absent the existence of a qualified privilege, plaintiff would not have been required to prove actual malice. We cannot say that the instructional error was harmless beyond a reasonable doubt and therefore reverse for a new trial.

NOTES

1. *Underpinnings of the Privilege*. As *Shannon* indicates, defamatory information communicated in the ordinary course of the employment relationship frequently will be subject to a qualified privilege. The law recognizes a public policy interest in frank and open communication when the speaker has a duty to speak or an interest in speaking. In the employment context, this includes employment references and communications between employers and employees, employees complaining to supervisors, supervisors evaluating and reviewing employees' work product, and employers informing employees of the reason for disciplinary action. It may also include customers of the business. *See* RESTATEMENT (SECOND) OF TORTS §§ 594-96 (1977).

In *Shannon*, the court found that no privilege existed to inform customers: The customers had no interest in the matter because there was no claim plaintiff had been selling stolen goods to them. In contrast, *Grice v. FedEx Ground Package Sys.*, 925 So. 2d 907, 912 (Miss. Ct. App. 2006), dealt with statements to co-workers and contractors that plaintiff had tuberculosis. These were qualifiedly privileged because the individuals informed "had a genuine interest in knowing whether a co-worker with whom they were in frequent contact had a highly contagious disease." Even if there were no privilege to tell customers, in *Shannon*, there may have been a privilege as to internal communications. This suggests the highly contextual nature of conditional privileges.

2. *Qualified vs. Absolute Privileges.* Privileges may be absolute or qualified. An absolute privilege confers immunity from liability regardless of motive. For example, while communication of a reason for discharge to courts or agencies, such as an unemployment compensation board, clearly constitutes publication, that communication serves the needs of a judicial or quasi-judicial process and therefore is absolutely privileged. In *Fulghum v. United Parcel Service, Inc.*, 378 N.W.2d 472 (Mich. 1985), the court held that accusations of dishonesty made during the course of the grievance procedure under a collective bargaining agreement are accorded an absolute privilege. According to the court, actions for defamation based on statements made about an employee during a proceeding about the discharge of that employee would "directly and severely impair the functioning of the agreed-upon grievance procedure. . . ." *See also Rosenberg v. Metlife, Inc.*, 866 N.E.2d 439 (N.Y. 2007) (statements made in brokerage's U-5 filing with NASD were absolutely privileged). *But see Galarneau v. Merrill Lynch, Pierce, Fenner & Smith Inc.*, 504 F.3d 189 (1st Cir. 2007) (U-5 filings were only conditionally privileged).

Most privileges, however, are not absolute, but rather are qualified in that false statements made with actual malice are not privileged even if made in what ordinarily would be a privileged context. A qualified privilege obviously reflects a lower public interest in free communication. The burden lies with the defendant to establish that the defamation is subject to a qualified privilege, but such a privilege may be lost (i.e., exceeded) in a variety of ways. For example, §6.01 of the proposed RESTATEMENT OF EMPLOYMENT LAW provides:

> An employer has a privilege in the reasonable course of business to publish facts or opinions concerning its employee or former employee to agents of the employer and to other employers unless the publication was
>
> (a) made to harm the employer or former employee and not in furtherance of a legitimate interest of the publishing employer or another employer, or
> (b) made with knowledge of falsity or disregard of its truth or falsity

What does the draft Restatement mean by a publication "in the reasonable course of business"? One common way in which an employer may exceed the privilege is by communicating defamatory information beyond those with "a need to know" within the organization. Is this captured by "reasonable course of business language"? Were the statements made in *Falls*, the case about the newspaper columnist, subject to a qualified privilege?

3. *Malice and the Privilege.* As the draft Restatement suggests, the second way in which a qualified privilege can be lost is if the employer made the defamatory statements with knowledge of their falsity or without regard to whether they are true. This is sometimes referred to as "actual malice." Recall that, ordinarily, in most states defamation may be established by demonstrating mere negligence. Actual malice requires something more: The court must find that the defendant knew the statement

to be false or made the statement recklessly without regard to its truth or falsity. Some courts also find malice when the speaker was actuated by improper motives, regardless of whether she believed her statements to be true. Is that what the *Shannon* court had in mind when it questioned whether Cherup's statements were "bona fide"? What else could it have meant? *See Gambardella v. Apple Health Care, Inc.*, 969 A.2d 736 (Conn. 2009) (any qualified privilege was lost for two reasons: " 'actual malice,' namely, the publication of a false statement with actual knowledge of its falsity or reckless disregard for its truth, [and] 'malice in fact,' namely, the publication of a false statement with bad faith or improper motive"). In general, the privilege seeks to balance the defendant's legitimate need to speak and the listener's legitimate need to hear against the possible damage to the plaintiff's reputation. These competing interests are reconciled by permitting the defendant to speak if she honestly and reasonably believes the information is true, but not if she knows the information is false or is reckless as to the possibility that it is false.

In *Soto-Lebron v. Fed. Express Corp.*, 538 F.3d 45, 64 (1st Cir. 2008), the court found that circulation of written statements within the corporation to the effect that plaintiff had shipped cocaine were actionable. The statements were published, although only circulated internally, and the conditional privilege was properly found to have been exceeded: "once FedEx was on notice that the drug allegations were questionable, it was obligated to either stop repeating them or adequately investigate them. It did neither. As a result, the jury was entitled to conclude that FedEx had 'improper motives' and thereby lost the benefit of the conditional privilege because it acted with reckless disregard for the truth."). *Cf. Dugan v. Mittal Steel USA, Inc.*, 929 N.E.2d 184, 189 (Ind. 2010) (the common interest qualified privilege for intracompany communications about theft of company property does not apply only for statements made on personal knowledge; reporting information received from others may be privileged).

4. *Damages.* Prevailing plaintiffs in defamation actions are entitled to compensatory damages, damages for emotional distress, and potentially punitive damages. The latter forms of damages are important because it may be difficult for an at-will employee to prove compensatory damages. In both *Falls* and *Sannon*, for example, the loss of the plaintiffs' jobs was separate from the defamation—and therefore lost salary and benefits were not caused by the defamation. In *Soto-Lebron*, the court affirmed a finding of liability but vacated the damages award because the jury might have been improperly influenced by plaintiff's testimony as to his emotional distress and his inability to get other jobs. There was no showing that either was linked to the libelous statements, as opposed to the fact that he was terminated. 538 F.3d at 67.

As for punitive damages, we saw in *Jackson* that they are available when "the defendants' conduct is shown to be motivated by evil motive or intent, or when it involves reckless or callous indifference to the federally protected rights of others." Some courts will not award punitive damages unless there have been actual damages as well, while others require a showing of actual malice as a prerequisite to recovery in defamation actions. See SPEISER, KRAUSE & GANS, THE AMERICAN LAW OF TORTS § 29.124–29.131 (Clark, Boardman & Callaghan 1991 & Supp. 2010). In some states, tort reform has affected punitive awards. An extreme example is Massachusetts, which denies plaintiffs any such recovery in defamation actions. *See* MASS. GEN. LAWS ch. 231, §93 (2010) ("In no action of slander or libel shall exemplary or punitive damages be allowed, whether because of actual malice or want of good faith or for any other reason.").

PROBLEMS

5-2. Tina Kim is a carpenter. Until recently, she worked for Cozy Cabinets, a small company producing custom-built furniture. Tina was responsible for completing the finish work on some of the more elaborate designs. Last week, Mr. Gregory, the Vice President in charge of production at Cozy Cabinets, discharged Tina. Gregory told Tina that she was fired. His explanation was that Jim Mineta, Tina's supervisor, had evaluated her finish work as "just not up to Cozy's standards." Tina has come to you for advice. She is afraid to apply for any carpentry jobs because she doesn't know what Cozy will say about her discharge, and she is certain that she won't get another job if she explains why Cozy let her go. She tells you that she thinks Mineta "had it in for her" because a few weeks ago, she complained to Gregory that Mineta had failed to provide her with adequate supplies to complete a job on time. Tina worked for Cozy for two years and all of her previous evaluations were good. She is an at-will employee. Tina is terribly upset because she is afraid that she will never get another carpentry job. She wants to know if there is any way to get her job back or if she has any other remedies.

5-3. Suppose you represent Cozy Cabinets. Gregory received a voice mail from an old friend in the industry who is considering hiring Kim but wants to know "the scoop" on her. Gregory would like to be honest because the two exchange favors all the time. Should he return the call? If so, what should he say?

C. INTENTIONAL INFLICTION OF EMOTIONAL DISTRESS

Subbe-Hirt v. Baccigalupi
94 F.3d 111 (3d Cir. 1996)

NYGAARD, Circuit Judge.

. . . [Elaine Subbe-Hirt was a salesperson for Prudential Insurance Company, and brought suit against Prudential, her former employer] and Robert Baccigalupi, her former supervisor at Prudential, presenting several claims arising out of her employment with Prudential. The district court granted summary judgment in favor of the defendants on Subbe-Hirt's claim for intentional infliction of emotional distress. It held alternatively that her claim was barred by the exclusive remedy provided by the New Jersey Worker's Compensation Act and that, in any event, the claim would fail on its merits because defendants' conduct was not sufficiently outrageous under New Jersey law. Subbe-Hirt appeals from that ruling. [Subbe-Hirt did *not* appeal from the adverse resolution of her other claims, including discrimination claims under New Jersey law. The appeals court first reversed the district court finding that workers' compensation exclusivity barred plaintiff's tort suit and then turned to the tort claim.]

III

Subbe-Hirt contends that the district court also committed legal error by basing its summary judgment on a conclusion that defendants' conduct was not sufficiently outrageous to support a claim for intentional infliction of emotional distress. On this allegation of error we have but two issues to decide: 1) whether Robert Baccigalupi intended to inflict emotional distress upon Elaine Subbe-Hirt; and 2) whether the evidence supports appellant's contention that Baccigalupi succeeded in inflicting that distress. We answer both questions in the affirmative and hold that the record in this case exceeds a threshold showing of outrageous behavior sufficient to preclude summary judgment.

A

The present record, when viewed in the light most favorable to Subbe-Hirt, shows that Robert Baccigalupi unquestionably intended to inflict emotional distress upon Elaine Subbe-Hirt. According to sales manager Mark Parisi, Baccigalupi "would berate [Subbe-Hirt] or talk about getting her." Indeed, Baccigalupi stated, "I'm going to get her."

Moreover, according to the deposition testimony of Parisi and sales manager Robert LaNicca, Baccigalupi stated, in the presence of other managers and on more than one occasion, that he "was going to trim her bush";[1] a blatantly sexist metaphor to brag of how Baccigalupi would handle females in general and Subbe-Hirt in particular. According to sales manager David Meyer, "when it was brought to R. Baccigalupi's attention that [Subbe-Hirt] was soon going to be returning from disability, R. Baccigalupi quickly remarked, 'Well, don't worry about her. I'm going to trim her bush.' " When asked by counsel to explain what he understood Baccigalupi's remark to mean, Meyer testified, "I understood it that he was going to lay into her quite hard and put her in her place." LaNicca said that on another occasion Baccigalupi stated, "Let's bring Elaine in here on Friday and we'll trim her bush." Parisi understood that phrase to mean:

> That he was going to come down on her, whatever his particular style was, forcing her to either go out on disability or leave the company or to cease the union activity. . . . [This] is, unfortunately with Prudential, is an avenue that agents take when they can't take the — you know, when management pressure goes up, and that's what [Baccigalupi] might use that for.

Likewise, Robert King, a district agent, said:

> There came a point in time where it was almost embarrassing for many of us to watch a woman being— . . . it was pretty much obvious that Elaine wouldn't and couldn't bear up under the general atmosphere . . . —her time was expiring. . . . We talked amongst ourselves that, you know, this was a critical stage. . . . There was a persecution going of myself and Elaine, and Elaine in particular. . . . [Baccigalupi said] more or less than [sic] she was history and that if I intended to continue that I would — I should leave things go as they are going.

---

1. i.e., pubic hair. Sales manager David Meyer testified, "Well, he wasn't going to go out and trim her azalea bush at home. It was a sexist remark."

Baccigalupi's intent to inflict emotional distress can be further seen in his total lack of any vestige of compassion for any woman in the office. On one occasion Meyer told Baccigalupi that he "couldn't continue performing 'root canal'[2] on women agents on his staff because they broke down in tears." At that point, Baccigalupi simply selected a woman agent to abuse as a demonstration, saying "Well, don't worry. I'll show you how to handle it." Appellant describes this contrived encounter as follows:

> He then called one of the women agents in for a review, and started the "root canal" and the intimidation on her until she broke down and started crying. R. Baccigalupi kept tearing and pressing into her and when it was over and she had left the office, he was holding out his suspender straps as if to say, "this is how you handle it; don't let their emotions get in your way."

Indeed, Baccigalupi admitted his intent when he said to Subbe-Hirt, "do you know who Joan of Arc is, read between the lines, do you know why I'm looking at your work so closely, do you think I do this to everyone?"

We have no difficulty in concluding that a reasonable jury could find from this evidence that Baccigalupi intended that his conduct subject Elaine Subbe-Hirt to emotional distress, and will turn next to whether Baccigalupi's conduct had its intended effect, and whether that effect was sufficient as a matter of law to state a claim of intentional infliction.

B

1

The district court erred when it held that Subbe-Hirt did not allege, nor did the record on summary judgment show, conduct sufficiently outrageous to state a claim that Baccigalupi had intentionally inflicted emotional distress upon her. In *Buckley v. Trenton Sav. Fund Soc'y*, 544 A.2d 857 (N.J. 1988) the New Jersey Supreme Court applied the view of the Restatement (Second) of Torts § 46 to the tort of intentional infliction. The district court was therefore correct that, under New Jersey law, intentional infliction of emotional distress comprehends conduct "so outrageous in character, and so extreme in degree, as to go beyond all possible bounds of decency, and to be regarded as atrocious, and utterly intolerable in a civilized community." RESTATEMENT (SECOND) OF TORTS § 46 comment d. We disagree, however, with the district court's conclusion that Baccigalupi's conduct was not sufficiently outrageous, and are led inexorably to the conclusion that summary judgment should have been denied.

2 . . .

Baccigalupi created a predatory tactic he descriptively termed "root canal," which he used to control older agents such as Subbe-Hirt. Baccigalupi instructed his sales

2. "Root canal" is a term coined by Baccigalupi to describe intense and emotionally painful sessions in which he would berate and demean disfavored agents with the purpose of forcing them out of the company.

managers how to perform this verbal attack "operation." According to sales manager Meyer, Baccigalupi "came up with the concept of root canal as a way to intimidate and basically destroy these people to the point of submission or of just getting the hell out of the business." Meyer related at his deposition that Baccigalupi picked the term "root canal" specifically because it was made to be a very uncomfortable, pain-producing, anxiety-producing procedure that you would keep going deeper and deeper until you struck a nerve, which would either end up in the agent submitting, or reaching the point of anxiety where they just couldn't stand any job any longer.

According to Meyer, at Thursday management meetings, sales managers would role play with each other how to deal with "problem agents:"

> . . . Bob LaNicca had brought up that he was having problems dealing with [Subbe-Hirt]. And then [Baccigalupi] would role play with Bob LaNicca how to perform root canal on Elaine to harass, intimidate her into submitting to management's requests.

LaNicca's deposition indicates that Subbe-Hirt was "brought in more often than others for performance reviews," which was Baccigalupi's opportunity for using his root canal procedure on her. According to Subbe-Hirt, Baccigalupi "held [her] in the office twice as long as anyone else."

Baccigalupi was relentless in his contumely against Subbe-Hirt. To begin with, according to Meyer and Parisi, Baccigalupi replaced females' given names, and other polite nouns such as "lady" and "woman," with the term "cunt," to depersonalize and deride the women in the office. He would also taunt Subbe-Hirt by asking if she "knew the word heretic" and threaten her "by asking if she knew who Joan of Arc was." Moreover, he would ask Subbe-Hirt for her resignation almost every time she was in the office. Baccigalupi even went so far as to have an unsigned resignation on his desk; we would then ask Subbe-Hirt "why don't you sign it; if you don't want to sign it, go on disability."

In his meetings with Subbe-Hirt, Baccigalupi would "grill" her on work she submitted, asking "why did you do this, what did you do here, what was said here?" If he was not "satisfied" with her answer, he would call Subbe-Hirt's clients in front of her and say "Elaine says this; what do you say?"

Baccigalupi's conduct had a devastating consequence. After one meeting with Baccigalupi, Subbe-Hirt "literally blacked out behind the wheel and hit a tractor trailer just from stress and emotion[,]" suffering severe injuries that required eight days of hospitalization. This incident forced Subbe-Hirt to take temporary disability leave; indeed, her treating psychiatrist has opined that she remains totally disabled with post traumatic stress disorder triggered by Baccigalupi's badgering and intimidation.

Baccigalupi was on notice that such an incident was a distinct possibility. Before the collision, Subbe-Hirt had consulted with her family doctor because of stress. The doctor wrote a letter which Subbe-Hirt showed to Baccigalupi before the incident, asking that it be placed in her personnel file. It stated:

> Elaine Subbe[-Hirt] is currently under my care for tension syndrome. It is my opinion, that she is capable of working a regular forty hour week at her present position. However, she should not be subject [sic] to any undue stress or work load at this time.

When Subbe-Hirt requested that the letter be placed in her personnel file, Baccigalupi refused, his exact words being: "I'll decide what goes in your personnel file."

According to the evidence, "Mr. Baccigalupi handed it back to [her] and said he didn't see that letter, and he never wanted to see it again and he wouldn't put it in [her] file." From this evidence, a jury could well conclude that, in his attempt to drive Subbe-Hirt out of Prudential, Baccigalupi targeted her now-documented weakness, of which he was fully cognizant. Such specific targeting of an individual's weak point is itself a classic form of "outrageous" conduct under Restatement § 46, comment f, which provides:

> The extreme and outrageous character of the conduct may arise from the actor's knowledge that the other is peculiarly susceptible to emotional distress, by reason of some physical and mental condition or peculiarity. The conduct may be heartless, flagrant, and outrageous when the actor proceeds in the face of such knowledge, where it would not be so if he did not know.

We conclude that the record is sufficient to support a finding that Baccigalupi essentially set out to put Subbe-Hirt under unnecessary stress to force her out of the company, all the while knowing that her physician had stated specifically that her condition required her to avoid such stress. We hold that the evidence described above is more than sufficient to withstand defendants' motion for summary judgment. . . .

COWEN, Circuit Judge, dissenting.

[The dissent thought that the district court should be upheld both on grounds of workers' compensation exclusivity and because] the facts of the case as alleged by the plaintiff fall short of the New Jersey cause of action of intentional infliction of emotional distress. The New Jersey Supreme Court has defined this tort as requiring conduct "so outrageous in character and so extreme in degree as to go beyond all possible bounds of decency, and to be regarded as atrocious and utterly intolerable in a civilized community." *Buckley.* The conduct of the perpetrator of such a tort must be by its nature "so severe that no reasonable man could be expected to endure it."

Conduct which the New Jersey courts have found to meet this extremely high level of uncivilized conduct are such matters as a doctor knowingly and untruthfully advising parents that their child had cancer, *Hume v. Bayer*, 428 A.2d 966 (Law Div. 1981); a hospital unable to locate the body of a dead baby for three weeks, *Muniz v. United Hospitals Medical Center*, 379 A.2d 57 (App. Div. 1977). [Indeed, the district court in New Jersey frequently] recognized the extreme difficulty of establishing such a claim in a mere employment relationship when the conduct alleged does not exceed the employer/employee relationship.

The New Jersey Supreme Court has made it abundantly clear in *Buckley*, that when a claim is made for intentional infliction of emotional distress, the trial court must clearly exercise a gatekeeping rule: "the court decides whether as a matter of law such emotional distress can be found" and the jury decides whether it has in fact been proved. It is the obligation of the trial court to determine in the first instance whether the plaintiff has set forth conduct which is sufficiently extreme such that a jury could reasonably conclude that outrageous conduct permits it to award damages. . . .

The district court correctly performed its function by determining that under New Jersey law the facts alleged as a matter of law failed to reach the elevated and high standard required for the cause of action of intentional infliction of emotional distress. The district court recognized that Baccigalupi's statements, if credited, were "inexcusable" and "offensive," but did not rise to the level of outrageous and unacceptable in a civilized society. Plaintiff's claims boil down to an assertion that her supervisor's choice of words required her to put up with "more than the normal pressure of a job." Being subject to "more than normal pressure" at work is a long distance from conduct that is "so outrageous in character and so extreme in degree as to go beyond all possible bounds of decency, and to be regarded as atrocious, and utterly intolerable in a civilized community." Even plaintiff had a difficult time labeling Baccigalupi's actions as anything beyond harmless threats, intimidation, and ridicule. Admittedly, the words allegedly spoken by Baccigalupi were strong and even harsh at times, but they were merely words. There is no proof, nor even an allegation, that Baccigalupi even touched her or that he set in motion any physical or other instrumentality to bring about an injury or illness.

III

The majority is to be lauded in its desire to upgrade the repartee of the workplace and to be offended by language which it deems inappropriate. But the workplace is not the dance of a minuet and employers are not nursemaids. As judges we will rue the day we sat in judgment of the propriety of speech which should transpire in the workplace between an employer and his employee. I respectfully dissent.

NOTES

1. *Outrageous or Merely Offensive.* The majority and dissent seem to basically agree on the legal standard for an intentional infliction of emotional distress claim—also known as the tort of "outrage." Their agreement is not surprising since New Jersey, like most jurisdictions, looks to the Restatement's definition of the elements of the tort. Section 46(1) of the RESTATEMENT (SECOND) OF TORTS provides that "One who by extreme and outrageous conduct intentionally or recklessly causes severe emotional distress to another is subject to liability for such emotional distress. . . ." To limit the tort from reaching garden-variety emotional harms, "[l]iability has been found only where the conduct has been so outrageous in character, and so extreme in degree, as to go beyond all possible bounds of decency, and to be regarded as atrocious, and utterly intolerable in a civilized community." § 46 cmt. d. An important factor in judging outrageousness is whether the defendant is abusing a position of power over the plaintiff. *Id.* at cmt. e. But, as a counterbalance, the "actor is never liable . . . where he has done no more than to insist upon his legal rights in a permissible way, even though he is well aware that such insistence is certain to cause emotional distress." *Id.* at cmt. g.

The problem, of course, is that the tort turns on whether the conduct challenged is "outrageous." This is less a standard than an epithet, and it is not surprising that some, like the majority, will be outraged and others, like the dissent, merely offended. But the dissent would uphold the district court judgment because reasonable minds could *not* differ over whether this was too extreme. Is that possible? You might be surprised to learn that the dissent is more typical of intentional infliction cases than is the majority. Indeed, the situations in which courts have found egregious conduct not sufficiently outrageous to be actionable are legion. *See, e.g., Island v. Buena Vista Resort*, 103 S.W.3d 671, 681 (Ark. 2003) (an employer's sexual advances not sufficiently outrageous because "[w]hile it is clear that the allegations of [the employer's] behavior are egregious, it appears that appellant has failed to offer proof that she suffered damages or emotional distress so severe that no reasonable person could be expected to endure it" since she endured the advancements for several years without protesting); *Crowley v. North Am. Telecomms. Ass'n*, 691 A.2d 1169, 1172 (D.C. 1997) ("Crowley alleges only that he was subjected to contempt, scorn and other indignities in the workplace by his supervisor and an unwarranted evaluation and discharge. While offensive and unfair, such conduct is not in itself of the type actionable on this tort theory.").

Baccigalupi, however, indicates that the theory may sometimes be fruitful, and there are some other successful claims in the employment setting. *See, e.g., Craig v. M&O Agencies, Inc.*, 496 F.3d 1047 (9th Cir. 2007) (individual supervisor liable: "Despite society's 'rough edges,' Craig should not be required to become 'hardened to' her supervisor repeatedly propositioning inside and outside of the office, following her into the bathroom, standing outside the toilet stall and then grabbing her and sticking his tongue in her mouth. While this conduct is deplorable in any setting, a reasonable observer or trier of fact could find it to be 'outrageous' and 'extreme,' particularly in an employment context."); *Archer v. Farmer Bros. Co.*, 70 P.3d 495 (Colo. App. 2002) (worker fired by his supervisors who came to his home to do so while he was in bed recovering from a heart attack); *Dean v. Ford Motor Credit Co.*, 885 F.2d 300 (5th Cir. 1989) (worker was framed by a supervisor who placed checks in her purse to make it appear that she was a thief).

2. *How Is the Workplace Different?* One might take the view that employees are particularly vulnerable to abuse and therefore entitled to heightened protection against infliction of emotional distress. The paucity of successful claims, however, suggests to the contrary that most judges believe the demands of many workplaces require managerial practices that would be unacceptable in other settings. Judge Cowen's dissent stresses "the extreme difficulty of establishing such a claim in a mere employment relationship when the conduct alleged does not exceed the employer/ employee relationship." The argument is essentially that employers are justified in pressuring and disciplining employees in ways that are perhaps inappropriate elsewhere. Further, victims can always quit if they want to avoid further abuse. Look at the last paragraph of the dissent. Is Judge Cowen asserting a free speech claim or privilege for verbal abuse? Is his position equivalent to saying that emotional abuse is "standard operating procedure," at least in some workplaces?

3. *That's Life.* Several years before Judge Cowen wrote his opinion, Professor Regina Austin critiqued such an approach:

> It is generally assumed that employers and employees alike agree that some amount of such abuse is a perfectly natural, necessary, and defensible prerogative of superior rank. It assures obedience to command. Bosses do occasionally overstep the bounds of what is considered reasonable supervision, but, apart from contractually based understandings and statutory entitlements to protection from harassment, there are few objective standards of "civility" by which to judge a superior's treatment of a subordinate. Workers for their part are expected to respond to psychologically painful supervision with passivity, not insubordination and resistance. They must and do develop stamina and resilience. If the supervision is intolerable, they should quit and move on to another job.
>
> In sum, there is little reason for workers to take undue umbrage at the treatment they receive at work. The pain, insults, and indignities they suffer at the hands of employers and supervisors should be met with acquiescence and endurance. That's life. Who believes this?

Regina Austin, *Employer Abuse, Worker Resistance, and the Tort of Intentional Infliction of Emotional Distress*, 41 STAN. L. REV. 1 (1988). *See also* Dennis P. Duffy, *Intentional Infliction of Emotional Distress and Employment at Will: The Case Against
"Tortification" of Labor and Employment Law*, 74 B.U. L. REV. 382 (1994).

4. *Workplace Bullying.* The limitations of the intentional infliction tort have
led some commentators to conclude that it is ineffective in dealing with the phenomenon of workplace bullying, and they have urged legislation to deal with serious emotional and psychological abuse of workers that may, nevertheless, not be sufficiently
"outrageous" to be actionable under current tort law. *See, e.g.*, David C. Yamada,
Crafting a Legislative Response to Workplace Bullying, 8 EMPL. RTS. & EMPLOY.
POL'Y J. 475 (2004); David C. Yamada, *The Phenomenon of "Workplace Bullying"
and the Need for Status-Blind Hostile Work Environment Protection*, 88 GEO. L. J.
475 (2000).

5. *Other Claims.* Because the plaintiff in *Baccigalupi* did not or was unable to
raise her other claims on appeal, the Third Circuit did not consider them. One that
jumps out is sex discrimination, particularly sexual or gender harassment. This topic is
discussed in Chapter 9. *See generally* Kerri Lynn Stone, *From Queen Bees and Wan-
nabes to Worker Bees: Why Gender Considerations Should Inform the Emerging Law of
Workplace Bullying*, 65 N.Y.U. ANN. SURV. AM. L. 35 (2009). Is it clear that Baccigalupi was discriminating against plaintiff because she was a woman? In other words,
might he have been an "equal opportunity harasser" who abused both men and
women alike? The "root canal" strategy was not gender-specific, and a male co-worker,
Robert King, also claimed to be a target of such abuse. However, Baccigalupi's crude
anatomical references certainly suggest a discrimination claim, and the opinion seems
to imply he was targeting plaintiff for especially severe abuse because she was a woman.
Claims of racial or ethnic slurs have also been held actionable under the outrage tort,
see, e.g., Woods v. Graphic Communs., 925 F.2d 1195 (9th Cir. 1991), either as the sole
cause of action or as supplementary to a racial discrimination claim. *See also Pollard v.
E.I. DuPont de Nemours, Inc.*, 412 F.3d 657, 664-65 (6th Cir. 2005) (applying
Tennessee law as the sole cause of action); *Wal-Mart, Inc. v. Stewart*, 990 P.2d
626, 634-36 (Alaska 1999) (race discrimination).

While Title VII expressly allows for supplementary tort claims, 42 U.S.C. § 2000e-
7 (2006), state civil rights statutes vary widely in both their express terms and their
judicial construction, with some preempting tort claims and others permitting overlap.
The outrage tort may function as a "gap filler" or "reinforcement" to civil rights
protection where not preempted. For example, some courts hold that intentional
infliction of emotional distress cannot be brought where "the gravemen of the complaint is really another tort." *Hoffman-La Roche, Inc. v. Zeltwanger*, 144 S.W.3d 438,
447-48 (Tex. 2004). *See also Haubry v. Snow*, 31 P.3d 1186, 1193 (Wash. Ct. App.
2001) ("employee may recover damages of emotional distress . . . but only if the factual basis for the claim is distinct from the factual basis for the discrimination claim").
See also RESTATEMENT (SECOND) OF TORTS § 47 cmt. a (1965) (outrage tort inapplicable
when actor "intends to invade some other legally protected interest"). *See generally*
Martha Chamallas, *Discrimination and Outrage: The Migration from Civil Rights to
Tort Law*, 48 WM. & MARY L. REV. 2115 (2007). Even where a discrimination claim is
viable, a tort cause of action may be helpful in fixing liability on the individual tort-
feasor or in end-running statutory caps on discrimination remedies. See Chapter 9 at
pages 693-94.

PROBLEM

5-4. Wilma is a vegan who had no on-the-job problems with her dietary practices until a new manager was hired. Once he learned that Wilma was a vegan, he continually made negative comments about her eating. They have occurred two or three times a week for the past year, usually when she is leaving for lunch. During the past few weeks, the comments have gotten more extreme. At two recent company social events, the manager sat down next to Wilma, ordered a hamburger ("extra rare, I want to see the blood"), and offered Wilma a bite. Wilma believes that this pattern of abuse is undercutting her ability to interact with co-workers, who are beginning to avoid her. The manager has taken to calling Wilma "Veg." She has experienced stress, nervousness, and difficulty sleeping as a result of the name calling and other comments. The supervisor also "picks on" other co-workers for a variety of personal traits. Wilma does not view her veganism as "religious." Does she have a case under tort law?

D. FRAUD AND OTHER MISREPRESENTATION

In the law, "fraud" is often used broadly to encompass intentional misrepresentation, negligent misrepresentation, and even failure to disclose when there is a duty to do so. It is easiest to establish when used as a shield — that is, when used to avoid a contract. For example, an employee under a contract for a term of years might seek to escape liability for breach by arguing misrepresentation or failure to disclosure material facts. To void a contract, a misrepresentation must be either "fraudulent" or "material." RESTATEMENT (SECOND) OF CONTRACTS § 164 (1981). Voiding a contract for nondisclosure is more difficult but is possible in a variety of circumstances that may arise in entering an employment relation. *Id.* at § 161.

As a sword, however — that is, as a tort cause of action for damages suffered in reliance on false statements — fraud is most often used when an employee is discharged after being recently hired and typically after being recruited from another position and/or relocating to the new job. The employee then claims that, although she was admittedly employed at-will, statements made in the hiring process were false and led her to accept the position. A variation on this scenario occurs when an employer makes false statements in order to retain an employee who is considering a competing offer. What if the employer promises job security to the employee but has no intent to provide such security? An employee who is a victim of such misrepresentation and who subsequently is discharged may have a remedy in tort.

Section 525 of the RESTATEMENT (SECOND) OF TORTS sets forth the elements of the cause of action:

One who [1] fraudulently makes [2] a misrepresentation of fact, opinion, intention or law [3] for the purpose of inducing another to act or to refrain from action in reliance upon it, is subject to liability to the other in deceit for pecuniary loss caused to him by his [4] justifiable reliance upon the misrepresentation.

See also RESTATEMENT (THIRD) OF EMPLOYMENT LAW § 6.05 (Preliminary Draft No. 6, May 21, 2009) ("An employer may be subject to liability for reasonably foreseeable pecuniary loss suffered by an employee or prospective employee, through fraudulent misrepresentation of fact, opinion, current intention, or law, to enter into or to maintain or to refrain from entering into or maintaining an employment relationship with the employer or with another employer.").

In the employment setting, the following case is a classic application of the doctrine.

═══ ### *Shebar v. Sanyo Business Systems*
526 A.2d 1144 (App. Div. 1987), aff'd, 544 A.2d 377 (N.J. 1988)

[The facts of this case, as reflected in the New Jersey Supreme Court's subsequent opinion, are reproduced in Chapter 2, at page 86. In the portion of the opinion there, the Supreme Court dealt with the contract claims; but another part of the opinion affirmed the Appellate Division's decision with regard to the plaintiff's claim of fraud on the basis of the opinion below.]

PRESSLER, J.

[The fraud count] rested upon Shebar's factual assertion that at the time he submitted his resignation and told his Sanyo superiors that he had accepted the Sony offer, Sanyo induced him to stay and to forgo the Sony opportunity with the then intention of replacing him in the near future. He thus asserts that Sanyo made the false promises and representations on which he relied to his detriment, knowing them to be false, intending him to rely upon them, and understanding that if he did rely he would be damaged, as he ultimately was, both by giving up the Sony employment and by losing his Sanyo employment. We are persuaded that this factual thesis not only is supported by permissible inferences which can be drawn from the summary judgment record but also that, if proved, it would support [a fraud cause of action in tort].

As to the fraud allegation, it is well settled that the constituent elements of that cause of action are the defendant's false representation, his knowledge of or belief in its falsity, his intention that plaintiff rely, plaintiff's reasonable reliance, and plaintiff's consequent damage. *See, e.g., Bilotti v. Accurate Forming Corp.*, 188 A.2d 24 (N.J. 1963); *Louis Schlesinger Co. v. Wilson*, 127 A.2d 13 (N.J. 1956). Genuine factual issues as to all these elements have been raised. Insofar as we are able to determine, the trial judge dismissed the fraud count because he did not read the motion papers as supporting the allegation that when Yamashita and Yamazaki made their promises to Shebar and induced him to forego the Sony employment, they then had the intention of firing him in the near future. We disagree with this perception. In our view, the events and their chronology as recited by Shebar, including the information he received from Mersand which his Sanyo superiors expressly denied when he confronted them with it, clearly permitted the inference that they intended, at the time they induced him to revoke his Sony acceptance, to terminate his employment. We do not intend to suggest that any such inference is required to be drawn. The point is simply that such an inference is entirely legitimate, and it is hence for the finder of fact to draw it or not.

NOTES

1. *Fraud versus Contract.* In Chapter 2, we saw that Sanyo's alleged promises stated a cause of action in contract. In this extract, we see that the same promise was also the basis for a fraud claim, but there was, of course, a twist. A mere failure to perform a promise can be actionable in contract but not in tort. For such a failure to be tortious, the defendant must have intended at the time it made the promise not to perform. The theory behind this requirement is that a promisor who makes a promise by that very act implicitly represents that he intends to perform that promise when the time for performance arrives. If the promisor lacks that intent, he has made a misrepresentation of fact (his state of mind), which satisfies one element of fraud. *See, e.g., Clement-Rowe v. Michigan Health Care Corp.*, 538 N.W.2d 20, 23 (Mich. Ct. App. 1995) (evidence suggests that the employer knew that the statement about funding for the position "was untrue or made it without any knowledge of its truth" in order to "allay plaintiff's hesitancy to accept the job because of concern about the financial health of the company"); *Neco, Inc. v. Larry Price & Assocs., Inc.*, 597 N.W.2d 602, 607 (Neb. 1999) (while "fraud cannot be based on predictions or expressions of mere possibilities in reference to future events . . . , fraud may be predicated on the representation that an event, which is in control of the maker, will or will not take place in the future, if the representation as to the future event is known to be false when made or is made in reckless disregard as to its truthfulness or falsity and the other elements of fraud are present."); *Boivin v. Jones & Vining Inc.*, 578 A.2d 187 (Me. 1990) (employee enticed to return to work by promise that he could remain employed until age 65 had fraud cause of action when he was fired as soon as he completed the assignment he was asked to return to do). *See generally* RESTATEMENT (SECOND) OF TORTS § 536 (1977); Frank J. Cavico, *Fraudulent, Negligent, and Innocent Misrepresentation in the Employment Context: The Deceitful, Careless, and Thoughtless Employer*, 20 CAMPBELL L. REV. 1 (2007); Richard P. Perna, *Deceitful Employers: Intentional Misrepresentation in Hiring and the Employment-at-Will Doctrine*, 54 KAN. L. REV. 587 (2006).

Shebar would be merely a breach of contract case but for the evidence that, at the time Sanyo promised to continue plaintiff's employment, it did not intend to perform. The court thought that a jury could find that to be true in the very extreme circumstances at bar — the executive recruiter who had arranged the Sony offer informed plaintiff that Sanyo was searching for his replacement. Further, when Shebar confronted his supervisor with this information, he denied it. Since Sanyo was in fact seeking a replacement after just having promised plaintiff lifetime employment, and lied about whether it was doing so, a jury could find that the promise of lifetime employment was itself fraudulent when made in that Sanyo did not intend to perform it at that time. Proving fraudulent misrepresentation, however, is often difficult. If plaintiff did not have evidence of intent to breach at the time the promise was made, plaintiff would have had only a breach of contract claim.

2. *A Different View.* Not every court allows claims such as Shebar's. *Smalley v. Dreyfus Corp.*, 882 N.E.2d 882, 884-85 (N.Y. 2008), rejected this approach entirely in the at-will context. Several employees had accepted positions with defendant in reliance on its promise that there were no merger talks that would eliminate those positions. Although the Court of Appeals did not seem to question that the elements of fraud were alleged, the court found any misrepresentation not actionable precisely because it occurred in the context of at-will employment:

> The core of plaintiffs' claim is that they reasonably relied on no-merger promises in accepting and continuing employment with Dreyfus, and in eschewing other job opportunities. Thus, . . . plaintiffs alleged no injury separate and distinct from termination of their at-will employment. In that the length of employment is not a material term of at-will employment, a party cannot be injured merely by the termination of the contract—neither party can be said to have reasonably relied upon the other's promise not to terminate the contract. Absent injury independent of termination, plaintiffs cannot recover damages for what is at bottom an alleged breach of contract in the guise of a tort.

Presumably, *Smalley* would have rejected Shebar's claim because he was an at-will employee.

3. *Negligent Misrepresentation.* Some jurisdictions recognize a tort of negligent misrepresentation, in which case it is, of course, unnecessary to prove intent to deceive. In *D'Ulisse-Cupo v. Board of Directors of Notre Dame H.S.*, 520 A.2d 217 (Conn. 1987), for instance, the court held that statements made by the high school principal assuring her that "there would be no problem" with plaintiff teaching the following year and that "everything looked fine for rehire" may have negligently led her to reasonably believe she would be employed for the next year. *See also Berger v. Security Pac. Info. Sys.*, 795 P.2d 1380 (Colo. Ct. App. 1990) (statements about the company's glowing prospects to a prospective employee created a duty to disclose serious problems). *See generally* RESTATEMENT (SECOND) OF TORTS § 552 (1977).

4. *Reliance.* In addition to a misrepresentation and the requisite fault, a plaintiff claiming fraud must show detrimental reliance. *See Coffel v. Stryker Corp.*, 284 F.3d 625, 637 (5th Cir. 2002) (jury could find that plaintiff, in giving up his rights under a prior bonus plan, relied on Stryker's representations that a new bonus plan would adequately compensate him and that this reliance was justified because of Stryker's past practice and assurances). This element may be hard to establish, especially in cases involving current employees who were hired before the allegedly fraudulent statement and who likely cannot show that they abandoned other opportunities because of it. Further, any reliance that the employee can establish must also be reasonable. *See Shelby v. Zayre Corp.*, 474 So. 2d 1069 (Ala. 1985) (reliance on promise of permanent employment unreasonable in face of signed application form that employment was at will).

5. *The Specificity of the Representation.* Some employees have tried to predicate tort claims on more amorphous employer statements than the ones we have seen to this point. In Chapter 2 we considered when an employer's failure to follow its policies might be actionable as a breach of contract under some version of the employee handbook doctrine. But occasionally an employee also asserts a tort claim in that situation. For example, *Daley v. Aetna Life & Casualty Company*, 734 A.2d 112 (Conn. 1999), involved a plaintiff who was repeatedly denied requested accommodations when she became a mother. When she was finally discharged, she claimed, among other things, negligent misrepresentation by Aetna because of numerous statements it had made indicating that it was family-friendly. The court upheld a jury verdict against her:

> In its instructions, the trial court explained the nature of Daley's claim to be that "Aetna negligently represented to [her] that it was committed to helping its employees balance

the demands of work and family and that it would support its employees in balancing their commitments by means of work and family programs including work-at-home options, part-time hours and flextime." In connection with its instructions on the burden of demonstrating that these representations were false, the trial court stated: "In other words, [Daley bears] the burden of establishing that Aetna was *not* committed to help its employees balance the demands of work and family and that it would *not* support its employees in balancing their commitment by means of work and family programs, including work-at-home options, part-time options, and flextime." (Emphasis added.)

Daley contends that the trial court's charge imposed an impossible burden of proof by making it appear that she could not prevail if the jury found that Aetna had any commitment whatsoever to its work and family programs. According to Daley, because Aetna likely had *some* level of commitment to its programs, the charge prevented the jury from determining whether Aetna had been negligent in representing those programs. Daley argues that, in accordance with its proposed instructions, the trial court should have charged the jury that she could prevail upon a showing that Aetna was " 'not as committed' " to helping its employees " 'to the extent [that] it represented.' " Aetna, on the other hand, argues that the trial court's instructions adequately presented the case to the jury because, notwithstanding its flexible scheduling options, Aetna never represented to Daley that a work-at-home arrangement was an entitlement, nor that an employee who relentlessly pursued such an arrangement would not be discharged. In addition, Aetna argues that Daley's proposed instructions would have misled the jury to find Aetna liable without proving an actual misrepresentation. We agree with Aetna. . . .

Id. at 127-28. Thus, *Daley* strongly suggests that general policies will rarely support a claim for negligent misrepresentation and, of course, it would be even harder to pitch an intentional misrepresentation claim on such policies. We will revisit the accommodation issue in Chapter 10, but you might note that the court also upheld a directed verdict for Aetna on Daley's public policy tort claim: There was no "important public policy that requires employers to provide flexible work schedules for working parents, and that prohibits employers from discriminating against individuals who pursue such arrangements." *Id.* at 130.

E.   LIMITATIONS ON TORT ACTIONS

There are two potentially important limitations on tort suits against employers. Although we have previously touched on both workers' compensation and preemption, a more detailed consideration of both follows.

1.   Workers' Compensation

As described earlier in the chapter, workers' compensation statutes embody a fairly explicit trade-off: Employers are strictly liable for on-the-job injuries, but the amount of recovery for employees is much more limited than under traditional tort law. "A predicate of workers' compensation laws is that the compensation system is the exclusive remedy" for covered injuries. For example, the New Jersey statute provides, "If an injury or death is compensable under this article, a person shall not be liable to anyone at common law or otherwise on account of such injury or death for any act or omission occurring while such person was in the same employ as the person injured or killed, except for intentional wrong." N.J. STAT. ANN. § 34:15-8 (West 2000). This clearly precludes tort suits in what was the paradigmatic situation for which workers' compensation was designed: negligently caused personal injury on the job. Ironically, employees originally preferred to be within workers' compensation regimes because of the hostility of the tort system. But, a century later, employees often seek higher damages by claiming that their injuries are not covered by workers' compensation. Concomitantly, employers now frequently seek to defeat tort suits by arguing workers' compensation exclusivity.

The dispute typically centers on the meaning of "except for intentional wrong" or similar language in other states' workers' compensation laws. This may not be as obvious an exclusion as one might think. Recall that in *Subbe-Hirt v. Baccigalupi*, page 269, the majority and dissent disagreed not only on whether the conduct was sufficiently outrageous to be actionable but also as to whether plaintiff's tort claim was barred by the New Jersey workers' compensation exclusivity provisions. There was no doubt that plaintiff had pled an "intentional tort" but some question as to what that meant. Although that portion of the opinions is not reproduced, the majority reasoned that the conduct was actionable if "a plaintiff show[s] *deliberate intention* to avoid the exclusive remedy provided by the Compensation Act," *Baccigalupi*, 94 F.3d at 112-13 (emphasis in original), while the dissent read state workers compensation law as making such conduct actionable in tort only if it was substantially certain to cause the harm plead. *Id.* at 116.

Another example of the uncertain line separating torts that are actionable and those that are preempted by workers' compensation is *Ford v. Revlon, Inc.*, 734 P.2d 580 (Ariz. 1987), in which an employee charged that her supervisor, Karl Braun, sexually harassed her. His conduct included demanding sex from her, threatening reprisals when she rejected him, and physical molestation. Ford tried to get Revlon management to address her complaints for an extended period of time without success. During this period, Braun continued to threaten her and Ford developed "high blood pressure, a nervous tic in her left eye, chest pains, rapid breathing, and other symptoms of emotional stress." Ultimately, she attempted suicide. The suit charged both Braun and Revlon with assault and battery and intentional infliction of emotional distress. One of Revlon's defenses was the exclusivity of Arizona's workers' compensation law, which covered employees "injured by accident arising out of and in the course of employment." ARIZ. REV. STAT. ANN. § 23-1021(B). Further, § 23-1043.01(B) specifically provided that "mental injury" was not "a personal injury by accident" unless "unexpected, unusual or extraordinary stress . . . or some physical injury . . . was a substantial contributing cause."

The Arizona Supreme Court stressed that Ford's severe emotional distress was neither caused by an "accident" nor was it "unexpected." Since the injury was not within the workers' compensation scheme, plaintiff's tort suit remained viable. Judge Feldman concurred with the result, but disagreed with the majority's analysis. He argued that under Arizona law, Ford's injuries were the result of "accident because an 'accident' is any work-connected injury between the extremes of a 'purposely self-inflicted' injury and one inflicted by the employer acting 'knowingly and purposely with the direct object of injuring' the employee." *Id.* at 589 (citations omitted). However, he concluded that plaintiff may nevertheless recover in tort because the challenged conduct was "one of those torts outside the purpose and intent of the workers' compensation scheme." *Id.* at 588. The concurrence explained:

> Regardless of the label placed on the action, it is outside the workers' compensation scheme only if the wrong is one not ordinarily resulting from an inherent risk or danger of the employment and if the essence of the tort action ordinarily is non-physical with physical injury only incidental to emotional, mental, or other injury. Among these types of torts and actions, . . . are defamation, invasion of privacy, false imprisonment, sexual, religious or racial discrimination, wrongful termination, constitutional torts, and similar matters.
>
> . . . The essence of the wrong was sexual harassment. Revlon failed to react to Ford's complaints, in reckless disregard of the consequences, thus making itself liable for outrageous conduct. While the form of the action — intentional infliction of emotional distress — is not always outside workers' compensation, the essence of the tort in the case before us involves a violation of rights protected by law and policy. By law, exposure to sexual harassment is not an inherent or necessary risk of employment, even though it may be or may have been endemic. The cost of such conduct ought not to be included in the cost of the product and passed to the consumer. If my employer invades my right to privacy by tapping my telephone, it is my employer who should pay the piper for such a wrong, not his compensation carrier.

Id. at 590-91. *Revlon* poses sharply the central issue, but the split between majority and concurrence dissent illustrates the kind of problems that arise in this area. The question is complicated because statutory and constitutional provisions differ from state to state. Further, the answer could conceivably differ based on the tort alleged or the particular facts.

The *Revlon* majority's distinction between an "accident" and "intent" is a common approach to the problem. This distinction finds support in the language of many workers' compensation statutes, which define compensable injuries in terms of "accidents" and frequently have an express exclusion for "intentional" harm. *See Grover C. Dils Med. Ctr. v. Menditto,* 112 P.3d 1093, 1102 (Nev. 2005) (per curium) (ruling that the claimant could not recover under Nevada's workers' compensation statutes for a work-related car accident because exacerbation of preexisting symptoms did not constitute "sudden or unforeseen injuries"); *Lichtman v. Knouf,* 445 S.E.2d 114 (Va. 1994) (sexual harassment action not barred by workers' compensation because injury was not an "injury by accident" since it was gradually incurred and not the result of an identifiable incident). Nevertheless, the concurrence's alternative approach, which looks to the purposes of the workers' compensation statute, also has support. *See Cole v. Chandler,* 752 A.2d 1189, 1195 (Me. 2000) ("We have refused to carve out an exception [to worker's compensation exclusivity] for intentional torts" since doing so would counteract the purpose of the workers' compensation exclusivity provision and since the legislature would have provided an exception for intentional torts if they had intended to do so.).

Is the argument persuasive that sexual harassment isn't the kind of injury intended to be within the statute? *See Cox v. Chino Mines/Phelps Dodge,* 850 P.2d 1038 (1993) (workers' compensation does not provide an adequate remedy for sexually harassed workers; such claims are better pursued under other causes of action). *Contra Doe v. Purity Supreme,* 664 N.E.2d 815 (Mass. 1996) (exclusivity provision of workers' compensation precludes an action against an employer for intentional infliction of emotional distress arising out of sexual harassment and even for injuries resulting from a rape or other sexual assault). Isn't association with co-workers an inherent risk of being employed? In a "post-industrial" economy, isn't bureaucratic incompetence a more likely cause of injury than "machinery breaking, objects falling, explosives exploding, tractors tipping, fingers getting caught in gears, excavations caving in," *Ford*, 734 P.2d at 590, which the concurrence cited as the original focus of workers' compensation laws? Is Judge Feldman persuasive when he says that sexual harassment, though "endemic," is not an inherent risk because it is illegal? If a worker's injury were caused by a condition that was illegal under a state fire code, could the employee sue in tort? *See generally* Jane Byeff Korn, *The Fungible Woman and Other Myths of Sexual Harassment*, 67 TUL. L. REV. 1363, 1384-89 (1993); Ruth C. Vance, *Workers' Compensation and Sexual Harassment in the Workplace: A Remedy for Employees, or a Shield for Employers?* 11 HOFSTRA LAB. L. J. 141 (1993).

Even if sexual harassment is outside workers' compensation under this view, what about some of the other types of claims we have examined, such as intentional infliction of emotional distress? *See Gantt v. Sec., USA, Inc.*, 356 F.3d 547 (4th Cir. 2004) (intentional infliction claims not actionable under Maryland law, unless the employer had a deliberate intent to injure). *Driscoll v. General Nutrition Corp.*, 752 A.2d 1069, 1076 (Conn. 2000) (although plaintiff limited her tort action to recovery only for emotional distress and emotional injury, the workers' compensation law could not be "unbundled" for pleading purposes simply to escape the exclusivity provision). *Contra Coates v. Wal-Mart Stores, Inc.*, 976 P.2d 999 (N.M. 1999) (outrage claim not barred).

How about an interference case? *Vacanti v. State Comp. Ins. Fund*, 14 P.3d 234, 243-44 (Cal. 2001) (tortious interference claim not barred). What about defamation? *Nassa v. Hook-SupeRx, Inc.*, 790 A.2d 368 (R.I. 2002) ("The prevalent view throughout the nation, however, is that the exclusive-remedy provisions of workers' compensation laws do not bar employment-related defamation claims.").

The leading treatise, ARTHUR A. LARSON & LEX K. LARSON, LARSON'S WORKERS' COMPENSATION LAW (Matthew Bender, Rev. ed. 2008), would limit workers' compensation to physical injuries, and remit nonphysical harm — such as emotional harm or the reputational damage caused by defamation — to the tort system. § 68.30, at 13-40. *See Hart v. Webster*, 894 N.E.2d 1038 (Ind. 2008) (defamation); *Nassa v. Hook Superx, Inc.* 790 A.2d 368 (R.I. 2002) (slander); *Le v. Federated Dept. Stores*, 595 A.2d 1067 (Md. 1991) (false imprisonment and intentional infliction of emotional distress actionable in tort). *But see Shoemaker v. Myers*, 801 P.2d 1054 (Cal. 1990) (disabling injuries, whether physical or mental, stemming from employment termination are subject to workers' compensation exclusivity, except where a particular statutory right, such as a whistleblower law, suggests otherwise). *See generally* John T. Burnett, *The Enigma of Workers' Compensation Immunity: A Call to the Legislature for a Statutorily Defined Intentional Tort Exception*, 28 FLA. ST. U. L. REV. 491 (2001).

2. Federal Preemption

The law we have studied in this chapter is largely state law and, as such, is vulnerable to being overridden by federal enactments. Indeed, the checkered pattern of federal and state regulation of employment has resulted in frequent preemption issues. For example, in *Ingersoll-Rand Co. v. McLendon*, 498 U.S. 133 (1990), the Court held that a Texas decision recognizing a public policy cause of action for discharge to avoid employer contributions to a pension plan was preempted by the Employee Retirement Income Security Act ("ERISA"), a federal statute regulating pensions and other benefit plans, such as health insurance. ERISA is more fully explained in Chapter 11. *See also Aetna Health Inc. v. Davila*, 542 U.S. 200, 209 (2004) ("any state-law cause of action that duplicates, supplements, or supplants the ERISA civil enforcement remedy conflicts with the clear congressional intent to make the ERISA remedy exclusive and is therefore pre-empted" since the ERISA has "extraordinary preemptive power."). On the other hand, *English v. General Elec.*, 496 U.S. 72 (1990), found that the Energy Reorganization Act did not preempt a state-law claim for intentional infliction of distress in retaliation for nuclear-safety complaints. *See also Schweiss v. Chrysler Motors*, 922 F.2d 473 (8th Cir. 1990) (Occupational Safety and Health Administration ["OSHA"] does not preempt public policy tort for worker terminated for reporting alleged employer violations to OSHA); *Parten v. Consolidated Freightways*, 923 F.2d 580 (8th Cir. 1991) (Surface Transportation Act did not preempt state public policy tort); *But see Andrews v. Alaska Operating Engineers-Employers Training Trust Fund*, 871 P.2d 1142, 1147 (Alaska 1994) (claim for wrongful discharge in contravention of Alaska public policy is preempted by ERISA).

Preemption arises in two varieties, conflict preemption and field preemption. Where there is a conflict between federal and state law, the Supremacy Clause dictates that state law must yield. Thus, any potential conflict between federal and state law will raise a preemption issue. In such a case, a court must decide whether the putative conflict is real. A broader approach is "field preemption," which describes situations where it can be claimed that Congress has "occupied" an entire field such that any state law, even one that seems consistent with federal mandates, is preempted. Even with field preemption, courts must mark out the precise field that Congress has occupied. For example, the defendant in *English v. General Electric* claimed that the Energy Reorganization Act preempted the entire field of nuclear safety. It therefore argued that a state tort claim for retaliation for nuclear-safety complaints was barred. The Court, however, defined the field of exclusive federal authority very narrowly — radiological safety — and even there federal law preempted only those state laws that had a "direct and substantial effect" on such safety.

While preemption can arise in a variety of contexts, one of the most important areas for employment law purposes is just-cause discharge under collective bargaining agreements. On its face § 301 of the National Labor Relations Act, codified at 29 U.S.C. § 185(a) (2006), merely provides a cause of action and federal court jurisdiction over suits for violation of collective bargaining agreements. Nevertheless, it has been interpreted to broadly preempt state law. *See, e.g., Local 174, Teamsters, Chauffeurs, Warehousemen & Helpers of Am. v. Lucas Flour Co.*, 369 U.S. 95 (1962). While § 301 and other labor law preemption doctrines do not apply outside the collective bargaining arena, employers have frequently resisted suits by unionized employees on the basis that federal labor law preempts state remedies. While it will not be explored in detail here, § 301 has been the basis for a very elaborate jurisprudence on the respective roles of state and federal law in the employment arena predicated on a few relatively straightforward principles. First, the law to be applied by both state and federal courts is federal law, a common law to be developed setting uniform standards for the entire country. Second, the touchstone for § 301 preemption is whether the state law in question requires interpreting a collective bargaining agreement.

For example, *Allis-Chalmers Corp. v. Lueck*, 471 U.S. 202 (1985), involved a suit by an employee against both his employer and the insurance company for a nonoccupational back injury. Plaintiff claimed that the defendants "intentionally, contemptuously, and repeatedly failed" to make disability payments under a company-provided disability plan, in breach of their duty "to act in good faith and deal fairly with his disability claims." *Id.* at 206. The Supreme Court found his state law claim preempted because the Wisconsin tort action for breach of the duty of good faith was "inextricably intertwined" with the terms of the labor contract. Since any attempt to assess liability would inevitably involve contract interpretation, the Court held that the claim must either be treated as a § 301 claim or dismissed as preempted by federal labor-contract law.

In contrast to *Lueck*, the Court in *Lingle v. Norge Division of Magic Chef, Inc.*, 486 U.S. 399 (1988), found no preemption. Plaintiff had been fired for allegedly filing a false workers' compensation claim. Although she was protected by a union and in fact filed a grievance under the governing collective bargaining agreement, her tort suit alleged she had been discharged in retaliation for exercising her rights under Illinois's workers' compensation laws. A retaliatory discharge claim did not require interpretation of the collective-bargaining agreement, nor did the defense of such a suit turn on the meaning of the agreement. Since the state-law remedy was "independent" of the collective-bargaining agreement, there was no § 301 preemption. *Id.* at 407. *See also Hawaiian Airlines v. Norris*, 512 U.S. 246, 263 (1994) (holding that claims for discharge in violation of public policy and the Hawaii Whistleblower Protection Act are not preempted by the Railway Labor Act).

In short, the Court has held that an application of state law is preempted by § 301 of the Labor Management Relations Act of 1947 only if such application requires the interpretation of a collective-bargaining agreement. However, the question of whether an interpretation is necessary is more complicated than would appear on its face. This is reflected in varying results in the lower courts as to preemption of various state law tort claims. *See generally* William R. Corbett, *The Narrowing of the National Labor Relations Act: Maintaining Workplace Decorum and Avoiding Liability*, 27 Berkeley J. Emp. & Lab. L. 23 (2006); Rebecca Hanner White, *Section 301's Preemption of State Law Claims: A Model for Analysis*, 41 Ala. L. Rev. 377 (1990); Richard A. Bales, *The Discord Between Collective Bargaining and Individual Employment Rights: Theoretical Origins and a Proposed Reconciliation*, 77 B.U. L. Rev. 687 (1997); Jane Byeff Korn, *Collective Rights and Individual Remedies: Rebalancing the Balance After* Lingle v. Norge Div., 41 Hastings L. J. 1149 (1990).

Part Four

PROTECTING WORKER AUTONOMY

6
Workplace Privacy Protections

The protection of privacy in the workplace is but one aspect of a much larger, burgeoning inquiry into the public policy implications of the recognition and protection of privacy interests. *See, e.g.*, DANIEL J. SOLOVE & PAUL M. SCHWARTZ, INFORMATION PRIVACY LAW (3d ed. 2009). Although employers have always used a variety of means to keep tabs on their workers, both at and away from work, employee privacy interests have become increasingly salient due to technological advances in testing, monitoring, data collection, and record keeping, which allow for far more effective control than previously. Indeed, recent studies have found that most major employers in the United States monitor employee communications and activities. Some employers also test some or all employees for drugs. Still others require physical exams or engage in other potentially intrusive activities upon hiring workers.

Privacy law in the employment context involves interests that are strongly contested. Not only is the workplace considerably more public than some protected areas, such as the home, but there are strong countervailing considerations. After all, while at work, employees are not simply pursuing their own goals but are primarily engaged in furthering their employers' ends. Some commentators go so far as to suggest the law should have close to no role in protecting employee privacy in the workplace. For example, Professor Michael Selmi argues that, as a policy matter, we ought to concede that the workplace is the employers' domain, although he advocates that the law limit strictly employer encroachments into workers' lives outside of work. Michael Selmi, *Privacy for the Working Class: Public Work and Private Lives*, 66 LA. L. REV. 1035, 1042-49 (2006). Even among those arguing for greater privacy protections, there is little agreement on the scope of the right.

Ultimately, an employee's interest in privacy must be balanced against the employer's legitimate business and risk-management reasons for intruding. It is therefore not surprising that this area of law is far from settled, offering significant challenges for employees, firms, policy makers, and, of course, counsel. *See, e.g.*, Pauline T. Kim, *Privacy Rights, Public Policy, and the Employment Relationship*, 57 OHIO ST. L. J. 671 (1996) (exploring employee privacy rights in the nongovernmental workplace). For a review of various aspects of the law of workplace privacy, related doctrinal problems, and proposed solutions, see Symposium, *Examining Privacy in the*

289

Workplace, 66 La. L. Rev. 923 (2006) (articles by Anita Bernstein, Matthew Finkin, Steven Willborn, Pauline Kim, Charles Craver, Rafael Gely and Leonard Bierman, and Catherine Fisk).

Privacy issues arise in a variety of circumstances and implicate many different laws and legal theories. However, the vast majority of the cases in this area fall into one of the following, sometimes overlapping, categories:

1. *Physical and Psychological Testing.* Many employers subject job applicants or employees to intrusive tests. Among these, the most commonly litigated is drug and alcohol testing. *National Treasury Employees Union v. Von Raab*, 489 U.S. 656 (1989), reproduced at page 330, and *Borse v. Piece Goods Shop, Inc.*, 963 F.2d 611 (3d Cir. 1992), reproduced at page 309, address such testing disputes, the former involving a public employer and the latter a private one. Recently, however, other kinds of testing, including physical examinations, psychological examinations, "honesty" testing, polygraphs, and genetic testing, have received growing judicial and legislative attention. Although some employers contend such tests provide important information relevant to applicant and employee qualifications and future job performance (including skills, potential safety concerns, health risks, and compatibility), workers often consider these procedures to be highly intrusive, intimidating, and overreaching. Indeed, as discussed below, privacy concerns have resulted in legislation specifically limiting the use of polygraph, physical examinations, and genetic testing by employers. In addition, *Soroka v. Dayton Hudson Corporation*, 1 Cal. Rptr. 2d 77 (Ct. App. 1991), reproduced at page 340, offers an interesting example of a dispute involving written psychological and honesty testing.

2. *Investigatory Interrogations and Searches of Persons and Spaces.* After receiving reports of misconduct in the workplace, employers sometimes interrogate workers and search their possessions and work spaces, with or without what might be called reasonable suspicion. Interrogations, which may include polygraph examinations, sometimes delve into personal details or otherwise implicate worker privacy interests. Investigatory searches frequently include electronic and cyber searches of worker computer files, e-mail, and Internet activities. *O'Connor v. Ortega*, 480 U.S. 709 (1987), a case discussed extensively in the first section below, involves a typical investigatory search and establishes the analytical framework for determining whether the search violated the target employee's right to privacy.

3. *Monitoring and Surveillance.* Employers engage in various forms of monitoring and surveillance to promote productivity, provide security, and prevent, discover, and remedy worker misconduct. Such monitoring historically had been limited to oversight of supervisors and other personnel and standard audits of activity in the workplace, such as the review of employee timesheets and telephone records. However, recent advances in communications and surveillance technology have dramatically increased the opportunities, effectiveness, and sometimes incentives for greater employee monitoring. The use of video and other surveillance technologies in the workplace and the monitoring of employee computer use, electronic communications, and Internet activities have received much attention in recent years. Thus, it is no surprise that there has been significant litigation in this area recently. A prominent example is the first case in this chapter, *City of Ontario v. Quon*, 130 S. Ct. 2619 (2010).

4. *Inquiries into or Prohibitions of Off-site Conduct.* Another sphere of employee activity with privacy implications is an employee's off-site or after-hours conduct and associations. Employees typically view their activities away from work as beyond their

employer's legitimate concern, unless such activity has some kind of direct impact on their workplace performance. Workers may view some of these activities—including the pursuit of personal interests, intimate relationships, and religious and political preferences—as very private matters. Beyond "privacy" in the sense of protection from disclosure of private activities, employees often view other more "public" activities as "private" in the autonomy sense—they are simply none of the employer's business. These include hobbies or recreational activities, religious or political affiliations, participation in Internet chat rooms, and, most recently, blogging. Nevertheless, employers sometimes have legitimate reasons (e.g., protecting good will, avoiding public relations problems, ensuring loyalty, and preserving morale) to inquire into employees' activities away from work and either regulate or take disciplinary action for such conduct. *Rulon-Miller v. International Business Machines Corp.*, 208 Cal. Rptr. 524 (Ct. App. 1984), reproduced at page 323, explores this tension.

5. *Revelations of Private Matters.* A final type of employer conduct implicating employee privacy interests involves challenges to employer-compelled revelations by employees of private matters or employer publication of employee confidential information. The employer may define as a job requirement (or a supervisor may demand that an employee reveal) something the employee considers very personal. Sometimes these obligations involve physical revelations, such as commands that an employee undress or perform some otherwise-revealing physical act. Such demands or requirements have been challenged occasionally, including in *Feminist Women's Health Center v. Superior Court*, 61 Cal. Rptr. 2d 187 (Ct. App. 1997), reproduced at page 357. Other times, employees have challenged required revelations about information, involving intimate thoughts or beliefs, embarrassing facts, or matters of personal history the employee prefers not to share. In still other situations, an employee challenges not the employer's initial mandate to disclose or reveal information to it, but, rather, the employer's publication or sharing of this information with others.

This chapter is structured around three themes that dominate the inquiry regardless of the circumstances—the five situations discussed above—in which employee privacy interests are implicated. These are (1) the search for sources of protection, (2) the balance between worker and employer interests, and (3) private ordering and the limits of employee consent. To begin thinking about these themes and the various issues they raise, consider the following problem.

PROBLEM

6-1. Data Enterprises, Inc. ("DEI") provides each of its office employees with desktop computers that are linked to DEI's network, access to DEI's e-mail system, and access to the Internet. DEI has included in its employee guidelines a "Computer Use and Electronic Communications Policy," which provides as follows:

> Employees may use office computers to engage in electronic communications for authorized purposes only. As a general matter, an authorized purpose includes work-related activities and communications. However, authorized use also includes limited personal use by employees during non-work time *provided* such use

does not interfere with or disrupt DEI's business in any way, involves minimal additional expense, and does not otherwise harm DEI's interests.

To ensure compliance with this policy and to protect DEI from harm and disruption, DEI may at any time audit, inspect, and/or monitor employee's electronic communications and review, audit, and inspect employee computers and information stored therein.

Amy Smith is an at-will employee working in DEI's main office. She frequently accesses the Internet from her desktop computer during her lunch hour, and, among other things, checks messages and sends e-mails to friends through her personal "Gmail" account. One evening after Smith left the office, her supervisor, with whom she has had some personality conflicts, decided to review her computer and Internet activities. He, along with an IT staff member, noticed Smith's frequent visits to her Gmail Internet page and, after guessing her password (her birthday), accessed her account. The two discovered a number of e-mails sent by Smith to friends who are not co-workers in which she criticizes the supervisor and makes derogatory comments about him and several other employees. All of these messages were sent by Smith on days she was at work and from her work computer, but always during her lunch break. When Smith arrived at the office the next morning, the supervisor terminated her.

As you read the materials in this chapter, consider the following. First, think about whether and in what circumstances Smith might have a cognizable privacy-based claim against DEI. Second, if there is any risk of such liability to DEI, consider how DEI, through better planning, might have reduced this risk. Finally, think like a policy maker and consider whether electronic communications like the e-mails at issue in this situation ought to receive additional protection and, if so, to what extent.

A. SOURCES OF PRIVACY PROTECTION

1. Constitutional Protections

City of Ontario v. Quon
130 S. Ct. 2619 (2010)

KENNEDY, Justice, delivered the opinion of the Court.

This case involves the assertion by a government employer of the right, in circumstances to be described, to read text messages sent and received on a pager the employer owned and issued to an employee. The employee contends that the privacy of the messages is protected by the ban on "unreasonable searches and seizures" found in the Fourth Amendment to the United States Constitution, made applicable to the States by the Due Process Clause of the Fourteenth Amendment. *Mapp v. Ohio*, 367 U.S. 643 (1961). Though the case touches issues of far-reaching significance, the Court concludes it can be resolved by settled principles determining when a search is reasonable.

I

A

The City of Ontario (City) is a political subdivision of the State of California. The case arose out of incidents in 2001 and 2002 when respondent Jeff Quon was employed by the Ontario Police Department (OPD). He was a police sergeant and member of OPD's Special Weapons and Tactics (SWAT) Team. The City, OPD, and OPD's Chief, Lloyd Scharf, are petitioners here. In October 2001, the City acquired 20 alphanumeric pagers capable of sending and receiving text messages. Arch Wireless Operating Company provided wireless service for the pagers. Under the City's service contract with Arch Wireless, each pager was allotted a limited number of characters sent or received each month. Usage in excess of that amount would result in an additional fee. The City issued pagers to Quon and other SWAT Team members in order to help the SWAT Team mobilize and respond to emergency situations.

Before acquiring the pagers, the City announced a "Computer Usage, Internet and E-Mail Policy" (Computer Policy) that applied to all employees. Among other provisions, it specified that the City "reserves the right to monitor and log all network activity including e-mail and Internet use, with or without notice. Users should have no expectation of privacy or confidentiality when using these resources." In March 2000, Quon signed a statement acknowledging that he had read and understood the Computer Policy.

The Computer Policy did not apply, on its face, to text messaging. Text messages share similarities with e-mails, but the two differ in an important way. In this case, for instance, an e-mail sent on a City computer was transmitted through the City's own data servers, but a text message sent on one of the City's pagers was transmitted using wireless radio frequencies from an individual pager to a receiving station owned by Arch Wireless. It was routed through Arch Wireless' computer network, where it remained until the recipient's pager or cellular telephone was ready to receive the message, at which point Arch Wireless transmitted the message from the transmitting station nearest to the recipient. After delivery, Arch Wireless retained a copy on its computer servers. The message did not pass through computers owned by the City.

Although the Computer Policy did not cover text messages by its explicit terms, the City made clear to employees, including Quon, that the City would treat text messages the same way as it treated e-mails. At an April 18, 2002, staff meeting at which Quon was present, Lieutenant Steven Duke, the OPD officer responsible for the City's contract with Arch Wireless, told officers that messages sent on the pagers "are considered e-mail messages. This means that [text] messages would fall under the City's policy as public information and [would be] eligible for auditing." Duke's comments were put in writing in a memorandum sent on April 29, 2002, by Chief Scharf to Quon and other City personnel.

Within the first or second billing cycle after the pagers were distributed, Quon exceeded his monthly text message character allotment. Duke told Quon about the overage, and reminded him that messages sent on the pagers were "considered e-mail and could be audited." Duke said, however, that "it was not his intent to audit [an] employee's text messages to see if the overage [was] due to work related transmissions." Duke suggested that Quon could reimburse the City for the overage fee rather than have Duke audit the messages. Quon wrote a check to the City for the overage. Duke offered the same arrangement to other employees who incurred overage fees.

Over the next few months, Quon exceeded his character limit three or four times. Each time he reimbursed the City. Quon and another officer again incurred overage fees for their pager usage in August 2002. At a meeting in October, Duke told Scharf that he had become " 'tired of being a bill collector.' " Scharf decided to determine whether the existing character limit was too low — that is, whether officers such as Quon were having to pay fees for sending work-related messages — or if the overages were for personal messages. Scharf told Duke to request transcripts of text messages sent in August and September by Quon and the other employee who had exceeded the character allowance.

[At Duke's request,] Arch Wireless provided the desired transcripts. Duke reviewed the transcripts and discovered that many of the messages sent and received on Quon's pager were not work related, and some were sexually explicit. Duke reported his findings to Scharf, who, along with Quon's immediate supervisor, reviewed the transcripts himself. After his review, Scharf referred the matter to OPD's internal affairs division for an investigation into whether Quon was violating OPD rules by pursuing personal matters while on duty.

The officer in charge of the internal affairs review was Sergeant Patrick McMahon. Before conducting a review, McMahon used Quon's work schedule to redact the transcripts in order to eliminate any messages Quon sent while off duty. He then reviewed the content of the messages Quon sent during work hours. McMahon's report noted that Quon sent or received 456 messages during work hours in the month of August 2002, of which no more than 57 were work related; he sent as many as 80 messages during a single day at work; and on an average workday, Quon sent or received 28 messages, of which only 3 were related to police business. The report concluded that Quon had violated OPD rules. Quon was allegedly disciplined.

B

[Quon filed suit in federal court claiming that, by obtaining and reviewing the transcript of Quon's pager messages, the City violated his Fourth Amendment rights, the Stored Communications Act (SCA), 18 U.S.C. § 2701 et seq.; and California law. Quon was joined by the recipients of his text messages: Jerilyn Quon, Jeff Quon's then-wife, from whom he was separated; April Florio, an OPD employee with whom Jeff Quon was romantically involved; and Steve Trujillo, another member of the OPD SWAT Team. The complaint also named Arch Wireless as a defendant, alleging it violated the SCA by turning over the transcript to the City.

Both the district court and the Ninth Circuit held that Quon had a reasonable expectation of privacy in the content of his text messages. The district court would have made liability turn on whether the purpose of the audit was to determine whether Quon was wasting time (impermissible) or assessing the appropriateness of the existing character limits (permissible). The Ninth Circuit reversed in part, holding that even though the search was conducted for "a legitimate work-related rationale," it was not reasonable in scope. The court found that there was a "host of simple ways" for the OPD to achieve its legitimate goals that were less intrusive than the audit.] The Court of Appeals further concluded that Arch Wireless had violated the SCA by turning over the transcript to the City. . . .

II

The Fourth Amendment states: "The right of the people to be secure in their persons, houses, papers, and effects, against unreasonable searches and seizures, shall not be violated. . . ." It is well settled that the Fourth Amendment's protection extends beyond the sphere of criminal investigations. . . . The Fourth Amendment applies as well when the Government acts in its capacity as an employer. *Treasury Employees v. Von Raab*, 489 U.S. 656, 665 (1989) [reproduced at page 330].

The Court discussed this principle in [*O'Connor v. Ortega*, 480 U.S. 709 (1987)]. There a physician employed by a state hospital alleged that hospital officials investigating workplace misconduct had violated his Fourth Amendment rights by searching his office and seizing personal items from his desk and filing cabinet. All Members of the Court agreed with the general principle that "[i]ndividuals do not lose Fourth Amendment rights merely because they work for the government instead of a private employer." A majority of the Court further agreed that " 'special needs, beyond the normal need for law enforcement,' " make the warrant and probable-cause requirement impracticable for government employers. *Id*. at 725 (plurality opinion) (quoting *New Jersey v. T. L. O.*, 469 U.S. 325, 351 (1985) (Blackmun, J., concurring)); *O'Connor* (opinion of Scalia, J.) (quoting same).

The *O'Connor* Court did disagree on the proper analytical framework for Fourth Amendment claims against government employers. A four-Justice plurality concluded that the correct analysis has two steps. First, because "some government offices may be so open to fellow employees or the public that no expectation of privacy is reasonable," a court must consider "[t]he operational realities of the workplace" in order to determine whether an employee's Fourth Amendment rights are implicated. On this view, "the question whether an employee has a reasonable expectation of privacy must be addressed on a case-by-case basis." Next, where an employee has a legitimate privacy expectation, an employer's intrusion on that expectation "for non-investigatory, work-related purposes, as well as for investigations of work-related misconduct, should be judged by the standard of reasonableness under all the circumstances."

Justice Scalia, concurring in the judgment, outlined a different approach. His opinion would have dispensed with an inquiry into "operational realities" and would conclude "that the offices of government employees . . . are covered by Fourth Amendment protections as a general matter." But he would also have held "that government searches to retrieve work-related materials or to investigate violations of workplace rules — searches of the sort that are regarded as reasonable and normal in the private-employer context — do not violate the Fourth Amendment."

Later, in the *Von Raab* decision, the Court explained that "operational realities" could diminish an employee's privacy expectations, and that this diminution could be taken into consideration when assessing the reasonableness of a workplace search. In the two decades since *O'Connor*, however, the threshold test for determining the scope of an employee's Fourth Amendment rights has not been clarified further. Here, though they disagree on whether Quon had a reasonable expectation of privacy, both petitioners and respondents start from the premise that the *O'Connor* plurality controls. It is not necessary to resolve whether that premise is correct. The case can be decided by determining that the search was reasonable even assuming Quon had a reasonable expectation of privacy. The two *O'Connor* approaches — the plurality's and Justice Scalia's — therefore lead to the same result here.

III

A

Before turning to the reasonableness of the search, it is instructive to note the parties' disagreement over whether Quon had a reasonable expectation of privacy. The record does establish that OPD, at the outset, made it clear that pager messages were not considered private. The City's Computer Policy stated that "[u]sers should have no expectation of privacy or confidentiality when using" City computers. Chief Scharf's memo and Duke's statements made clear that this official policy extended to text messaging. The disagreement, at least as respondents see the case, is over whether Duke's later statements overrode the official policy. Respondents contend that because Duke told Quon that an audit would be unnecessary if Quon paid for the overage, Quon reasonably could expect that the contents of his messages would remain private.

At this point, were we to assume that inquiry into "operational realities" were called for, it would be necessary to ask whether Duke's statements could be taken as announcing a change in OPD policy, and if so, whether he had, in fact or appearance, the authority to make such a change and to guarantee the privacy of text messaging. It would also be necessary to consider whether a review of messages sent on police pagers, particularly those sent while officers are on duty, might be justified for other reasons, including performance evaluations, litigation concerning the lawfulness of police actions, and perhaps compliance with state open records laws. These matters would all bear on the legitimacy of an employee's privacy expectation.

The Court must proceed with care when considering the whole concept of privacy expectations in communications made on electronic equipment owned by a government employer. The judiciary risks error by elaborating too fully on the Fourth Amendment implications of emerging technology before its role in society has become clear. *See, e.g., Olmstead v. United States,* 277 U.S. 438 (1928), overruled by *Katz v. United States,* 389 U.S. 347, 353 (1967). In *Katz,* the Court relied on its own knowledge and experience to conclude that there is a reasonable expectation of privacy in a telephone booth. It is not so clear that courts at present are on so sure a ground. Prudence counsels caution before the facts in the instant case are used to establish far-reaching premises that define the existence, and extent, of privacy expectations enjoyed by employees when using employer-provided communication devices.

Rapid changes in the dynamics of communication and information transmission are evident not just in the technology itself but in what society accepts as proper behavior. As one *amici* brief notes, many employers expect or at least tolerate personal use of such equipment by employees because it often increases worker efficiency. Another *amicus* points out that the law is beginning to respond to these developments, as some States have recently passed statutes requiring employers to notify employees when monitoring their electronic communications [(citing DEL. CODE ANN., tit. 19, § 705 (2005)); CONN. GEN. STAT. ANN. § 31-48d (West 2003)]. At present, it is uncertain how workplace norms, and the law's treatment of them, will evolve.

Even if the Court were certain that the *O'Connor* plurality's approach were the right one, the Court would have difficulty predicting how employees' privacy expectations will be shaped by those changes or the degree to which society will be prepared to recognize those expectations as reasonable. Cell phone and text message communications are so pervasive that some persons may consider them to be essential means or necessary instruments for self-expression, even self-identification. That might strengthen the case for an expectation of privacy. On the other hand, the ubiquity of those devices has made them generally affordable, so one could counter that employees who need cell phones or similar devices for personal matters can purchase and pay for their own. And employer policies concerning communications will of course shape the reasonable expectations of their employees, especially to the extent that such policies are clearly communicated.

A broad holding concerning employees' privacy expectations vis-á-vis employer-provided technological equipment might have implications for future cases that cannot be predicted. It is preferable to dispose of this case on narrower grounds. For present purposes we assume several propositions *arguendo:* First, Quon had a reasonable expectation of privacy in the text messages sent on the pager provided to him by the City; second, petitioners' review of the transcript constituted a search within the meaning of the Fourth Amendment; and third, the principles applicable to a government employer's search of an employee's physical office apply with at least the same force when the employer intrudes on the employee's privacy in the electronic sphere.

B

Even if Quon had a reasonable expectation of privacy in his text messages, petitioners did not necessarily violate the Fourth Amendment by obtaining and reviewing the transcripts. Although as a general matter, warrantless searches "are *per se* unreasonable under the Fourth Amendment," there are "a few specifically established and well-delineated exceptions" to that general rule. *Katz.* The Court has held that the " 'special needs' " of the workplace justify one such exception. *O'Connor; Von Raab.*

Under the approach of the *O'Connor* plurality, when conducted for a "noninvestigatory, work-related purpos[e]" or for the "investigatio[n] of work-related misconduct," a government employer's warrantless search is reasonable if it is " 'justified at its inception' " and if " 'the measures adopted are reasonably related to the objectives of the search and not excessively intrusive in light of' " the circumstances giving rise to the search. *O'Connor.* The search here satisfied the standard of the *O'Connor* plurality and was reasonable under that approach.

The search was justified at its inception because there were "reasonable grounds for suspecting that the search [was] necessary for a noninvestigatory work-related purpose." As a jury found, Chief Scharf ordered the search in order to determine whether the character limit on the City's contract with Arch Wireless was sufficient to meet the City's needs. This was, as the Ninth Circuit noted, a "legitimate work-related rationale." The City and OPD had a legitimate interest in ensuring that employees were not being forced to pay out of their own pockets for work-related expenses, or on the other hand that the City was not paying for extensive personal communications.

As for the scope of the search, reviewing the transcripts was reasonable because it was an efficient and expedient way to determine whether Quon's overages were the result of work-related messaging or personal use. The review was also not " 'excessively intrusive.' " *O'Connor* (plurality opinion). Although Quon had gone over his monthly allotment a number of times, OPD requested transcripts for only the months of

August and September 2002. While it may have been reasonable as well for OPD to review transcripts of all the months in which Quon exceeded his allowance, it was certainly reasonable for OPD to review messages for just two months in order to obtain a large enough sample to decide whether the character limits were efficacious. And it is worth noting that during his internal affairs investigation, McMahon redacted all messages Quon sent while off duty, a measure which reduced the intrusiveness of any further review of the transcripts.

Furthermore, and again on the assumption that Quon had a reasonable expectation of privacy in the contents of his messages, the extent of an expectation is relevant to assessing whether the search was too intrusive. *See Von Raab.* Even if he could assume some level of privacy would inhere in his messages, it would not have been reasonable for Quon to conclude that his messages were in all circumstances immune from scrutiny. Quon was told that his messages were subject to auditing. As a law enforcement officer, he would or should have known that his actions were likely to come under legal scrutiny, and that this might entail an analysis of his on-the-job communications. Under the circumstances, a reasonable employee would be aware that sound management principles might require the audit of messages to determine whether the pager was being appropriately used. Given that the City issued the pagers to Quon and other SWAT Team members in order to help them more quickly respond to crises—and given that Quon had received no assurances of privacy—Quon could have anticipated that it might be necessary for the City to audit pager messages to assess the SWAT Team's performance in particular emergency situations.

From OPD's perspective, the fact that Quon likely had only a limited privacy expectation, with boundaries that we need not here explore, lessened the risk that the review would intrude on highly private details of Quon's life. OPD's audit of messages on Quon's employer-provided pager was not nearly as intrusive as a search of his personal e-mail account or pager, or a wiretap on his home phone line, would have been. That the search did reveal intimate details of Quon's life does not make it unreasonable, for under the circumstances a reasonable employer would not expect that such a review would intrude on such matters. The search was permissible in its scope.

The Court of Appeals erred in finding the search unreasonable. It pointed to a "host of simple ways to verify the efficacy of the 25,000 character limit . . . without intruding on [respondents'] Fourth Amendment rights." The panel suggested that Scharf "could have warned Quon that for the month of September he was forbidden from using his pager for personal communications, and that the contents of all his messages would be reviewed to ensure the pager was used only for work-related purposes during that time frame. Alternatively, if [OPD] wanted to review past usage, it could have asked Quon to count the characters himself, or asked him to redact personal messages and grant permission to [OPD] to review the redacted transcript."

This approach was inconsistent with controlling precedents. This Court has "repeatedly refused to declare that only the 'least intrusive' search practicable can be reasonable under the Fourth Amendment." That rationale "could raise insuperable barriers to the exercise of virtually all search-and-seizure powers," because "judges engaged in *post hoc* evaluations of government conduct can almost always imagine some alternative means by which the objectives of the government might have been accomplished." The analytic errors of the Court of Appeals in this case illustrate the necessity of this principle. Even assuming there were ways that OPD could have performed the search that would have been less intrusive, it does not follow that the search as conducted was unreasonable.

Respondents argue that the search was *per se* unreasonable in light of the Court of Appeals' conclusion that Arch Wireless violated the SCA by giving the City the transcripts of Quon's text messages. The merits of the SCA claim are not before us. But even if the Court of Appeals was correct to conclude that the SCA forbade Arch Wireless from turning over the transcripts, it does not follow that petitioners' actions were unreasonable. Respondents point to no authority for the proposition that the existence of statutory protection renders a search *per se* unreasonable under the Fourth Amendment. And the precedents counsel otherwise. *See Virginia v. Moore*, 553 U.S. 164, 168 (2008) (search incident to an arrest that was illegal under state law was reasonable); *California v. Greenwood*, 486 U.S. 35, 43 (1988) (rejecting argument that if state law forbade police search of individual's garbage the search would violate the Fourth Amendment). Furthermore, respondents do not maintain that any OPD employee either violated the law him- or herself or knew or should have known that Arch Wireless, by turning over the transcript, would have violated the law. The otherwise reasonable search by OPD is not rendered unreasonable by the assumption that Arch Wireless violated the SCA by turning over the transcripts.

Because the search was motivated by a legitimate work-related purpose, and because it was not excessive in scope, the search was reasonable under the approach of the *O'Connor* plurality. For these same reasons — that the employer had a legitimate reason for the search, and that the search was not excessively intrusive in light of that justification — the Court also concludes that the search would be "regarded as reasonable and normal in the private-employer context" and would satisfy the approach of Justice Scalia's concurrence. The search was reasonable, and the Court of Appeals erred by holding to the contrary. Petitioners did not violate Quon's Fourth Amendment rights.

C

Finally, the Court must consider whether the search violated the Fourth Amendment rights of Jerilyn Quon, Florio, and Trujillo, the respondents who sent text messages to Jeff Quon. Petitioners and respondents disagree whether a sender of a text message can have a reasonable expectation of privacy in a message he knowingly sends to someone's employer-provided pager. It is not necessary to resolve this question in order to dispose of the case, however. Respondents argue that because "the search was unreasonable as to Sergeant Quon, it was also unreasonable as to his correspondents." They make no corollary argument that the search, if reasonable as to Quon, could nonetheless be unreasonable as to Quon's correspondents. In light of this litigating position and the Court's conclusion that the search was reasonable as to Jeff Quon, it necessarily follows that these other respondents cannot prevail.

[Justice Stephens concurred.] . . .

SCALIA, Justice, concurring in part and concurring in the judgment.

I join the Court's opinion except for Part III-A. I continue to believe that the "operational realities" rubric for determining the Fourth Amendment's application to public employees invented by the plurality in *O'Connor v. Ortega* is standardless and unsupported. In this case, the proper threshold inquiry should be not whether the Fourth Amendment applies to messages on *public* employees' employer-issued pagers, but whether it applies *in general* to such messages on employer-issued pagers.

Here, however, there is no need to answer that threshold question. Even accepting at face value Quon's and his co-plaintiffs' claims that the Fourth Amendment applies to their messages, the city's search was reasonable, and thus did not violate the Amendment. Since it is unnecessary to decide whether the Fourth Amendment applies, it is unnecessary to resolve which approach in *O'Connor* controls: the plurality's or mine. That should end the matter.

The Court concedes as much, yet it inexplicably interrupts its analysis with a recitation of the parties' arguments concerning, and an excursus on the complexity and consequences of answering, that admittedly irrelevant threshold question. That discussion is unnecessary. (To whom do we owe an *additional* explanation for declining to decide an issue, once we have explained that it makes no difference?) It also seems to me exaggerated. Applying the Fourth Amendment to new technologies may sometimes be difficult, but when it is necessary to decide a case we have no choice. The Court's implication that where electronic privacy is concerned we should decide less than we otherwise would (that is, less than the principle of law necessary to resolve the case and guide private action) — or that we should hedge our bets by concocting case-specific standards or issuing opaque opinions — is in my view indefensible. The-times-they-are-a-changin' is a feeble excuse for disregard of duty.

Worse still, the digression is self-defeating. Despite the Court's insistence that it is agnostic about the proper test, lower courts will likely read the Court's self-described "instructive" expatiation on how the *O'Connor* plurality's approach would apply here (if it applied) as a heavy-handed hint about how *they* should proceed. Litigants will do likewise, using the threshold question whether the Fourth Amendment is even implicated as a basis for bombarding lower courts with arguments about employer policies, how they were communicated, and whether they were authorized, as well as the latest trends in employees' use of electronic media. In short, in saying why it is not saying more, the Court says much more than it should.

The Court's inadvertent boosting of the *O'Connor* plurality's standard is all the more ironic because, in fleshing out its fears that applying that test to new technologies will be too hard, the Court underscores the unworkability of that standard. Any rule that requires evaluating whether a given gadget is a "necessary instrumen[t] for self-expression, even self-identification," on top of assessing the degree to which "the law's treatment of [workplace norms has] evolve[d]," is (to put it mildly) unlikely to yield objective answers.

I concur in the Court's judgment.

NOTES

1. *The Fourth Amendment and the Basic Framework.* *Quon* is an important decision because the Court applies the Fourth Amendment to electronic communications on employer-provided equipment, a context rife with litigation and controversy. *See, e.g.,* MATTHEW W. FINKIN, PRIVACY IN EMPLOYMENT LAW 353-56 (3d ed. Supp. 2009) (describing employee use of e-mail and other electronic-based communications as among the most vexing areas in workplace privacy law). However, much of the legal doctrine in *Quon* simply reaffirms the analysis set forth in *O'Connor v. Ortega*, 480 U.S. 709 (1987). In that case, which involved the search of a public employee's office space and drawers, the Court initially recognized that, pursuant to its prohibition on unreasonable searches and seizures, government workers enjoy some Fourth

Amendment protection while at work. This recognition alone was significant: There are more than 23 million government (federal, state, and local) employees in the United States, and, at least as a default matter, they have some claim to privacy while at work.

The *Quon* decision goes on to apply the operative framework set forth in *O'Connor* for determining whether there has been a violation of a public employee's Fourth Amendment rights. It provides a two-step inquiry. First, in order to enjoy any Fourth Amendment protection, the employee must have had a "reasonable expectation of privacy" in the area or thing (physical or metaphorical) intruded upon or searched. Second, if the employee had such an expectation, then it must be determined whether the employer's intrusion into this area or thing was "reasonable." In *Quon*, the Court found it unnecessary to resolve the first inquiry, since it determined that the resulting search was reasonable at its inception. Nevertheless, the Court's arguably gratuitous discussion of the subject — as well as Justice Scalia's scolding response in his concurrence — offers some new guidance and plenty of fodder for debate.

2. *The First Prong: Reasonable Expectation of Privacy.* The Court assumes arguendo that Quon had a reasonable expectation of privacy in the content of the pager messages. Thus, it initially states that it need not resolve definitively which approach — the *O'Connor* plurality's "operational realities" standard or Justice Scalia's categorical approach — governs the determination of whether an employee had a reasonable expectation of privacy. Nevertheless, the majority goes on to discuss in some detail why it cannot and should not adopt a "broad holding concerning employees' privacy expectations vis-á-vis employer-provided technological equipment." Is Justice Scalia right that, in so doing, the majority is endorsing an operational realities approach?

To appreciate what is at stake, take a moment to consider the policy and practical implications that are at the heart of the dispute. The *O'Connor* plurality justified its case-by-case approach to determining the reasonableness of an employee's expectation of privacy (regarding physical spaces in the workplace) this way:

> Individuals do not lose Fourth Amendment rights merely because they work for the government instead of a private employer. The operational realities of the workplace, however, may make *some* employees' expectations of privacy unreasonable when an intrusion is by a supervisor rather than a law enforcement official. Public employees' expectations of privacy in their offices, desks, and file cabinets, like similar expectations of employees in the private sector, may be reduced by virtue of actual office practices and procedures, or by legitimate regulation. . . . The employee's expectation of privacy must be assessed in the context of the employment relation. An office is seldom a private enclave free from entry by supervisors, other employees, and business and personal invitees. Instead, in many cases offices are continually entered by fellow employees and other visitors during the workday for conferences, consultations, and other work-related visits. Simply put, it is the nature of government offices that others — such as fellow employees, supervisors, consensual visitors, and the general public — may have frequent access to an individual's office. We agree with Justice Scalia that "[constitutional] protection against *unreasonable* searches by the government does not disappear merely because the government has the right to make reasonable intrusions in its capacity as employer," but some government offices may be so open to fellow employees or the public that no expectation of privacy is reasonable. Given the great variety of work environments in the public sector, the question whether an employee has a reasonable expectation of privacy must be addressed on a case-by-case basis.

O'Connor, 480 U.S. at 718.

Like the *O'Connor* plurality, Justice Scalia concluded in that case that Ortega had a reasonable expectation of privacy in his office spaces, desk, and office drawers. But, in arriving at this conclusion, he criticized the plurality's case-by-case methodology much as he does in *Quon*. As an initial matter, he expressed concern that the plurality's formulation would lead to uncertainty. *See* 480 U.S. at 729-30 (arguing that the plurality's standard is "so devoid of content that it produces rather than eliminates uncertainty").

He went on to argue that a categorical approach to determining whether the employee had a privacy interest in the space or area is also more consistent with existing Fourth Amendment jurisprudence:

> Whatever the plurality's standard means, however, it must be wrong if it leads to the conclusion on the present facts that if Hospital officials had extensive "work-related reasons to enter Dr. Ortega's office" no Fourth Amendment protection existed. It is privacy that is protected by the Fourth Amendment, not solitude. A man enjoys Fourth Amendment protection in his home, for example, even though his wife and children have the run of the place—and indeed, even though his landlord has the right to conduct unannounced inspections at any time. Similarly, in my view, one's personal office is constitutionally protected against warrantless intrusions by the police, even though employer and co-workers are not excluded. . . . Constitutional protection against *unreasonable* searches by the government does not disappear merely because the government has the right to make reasonable intrusions in its capacity as employer. . . .
>
> I would hold, therefore, that the offices of government employees, and *a fortiori* the drawers and files within those offices, are covered by Fourth Amendment protections as a general matter. (The qualifier is necessary to cover such unusual situations as that in which the office is subject to unrestricted public access, so that it is "[exposed] to the public" and therefore "not a subject of Fourth Amendment protection." *Katz v. United States*, 389 U.S. 347, 351 (1967).) . . .

Id. at 730-32.

Which opinion do you find more convincing? Is one approach more likely to provide public employees with meaningful privacy protections than the other? Should that matter?

Turning back to *Quon*, do you see similar arguments and themes in the majority's discussion of the first prong and in Justice Scalia's response? Is your assessment of which side has the better argument affected at all by the nature of the privacy interest at stake—that is, text messages on an employer-provided communications device—rather than physical spaces in employer-provided offices?

Courts addressing employee Fourth Amendment claims after *O'Connor* (but before *Quon*) usually adopted the plurality's contextual approach, although, as a practical matter, the application of this standard has been categorical with regard to certain types of searches or intrusions. For example, for searches and testing involving an employee's person or bodily fluids, including drug testing, the Supreme Court and other courts have virtually always assumed or found some reasonable expectation of privacy. *See, e.g.*, *Nat'l Treasury Employees Union v. Von Raab*, 489 U.S. 656 (1989) (drug testing) (reproduced at page 330); *Skinner v. Railway Labor Executives' Ass'n*, 489 U.S. 602 (1989) (same). In cases involving intrusions into spheres in which employee privacy expectations are less obvious—for example, physical work spaces like those at issue in *Ortega* and, as more commonly litigated today, electronic files and communications like those at issue in *Quon*—the results are mixed, often hinging on the specific areas of alleged privacy involved and workplace practices and policies. Importantly, then, whether an employee enjoys any Fourth Amendment protection at all will depend on both the nature of the intrusion and the particulars of the workplace.

3. *An Invitation to Regulate Privacy out of Existence? Quon* assumes a reasonable expectation of privacy in the underlying communications, but did plaintiff have one? On a purely technical level, one might ask whether the oral assurance overrode the written policy, which might require an inquiry into agency law. Or is a "reasonable expectation" less a question of what documents say than what most employees in the situation might expect?

Those favoring privacy protections for workers might view *Quon* as a partial victory, given that the Ninth Circuit — applying the *O'Connor* plurality's approach — did find that Quon had a reasonable expectation of privacy in the content of his communications on equipment provided by the City, see *Quon v. Arch Wireless Operating Co., Inc.,* 554 F.3d 769, 772 (9th Cir. 2009) (Wardlaw, J. concurring in denial of *en banc* review), and the Supreme Court expressly left open the question. But because particular workplace practices and circumstances will affect whether such an expectation exists (at least under the contextual approach), the partial victory for the plaintiffs in this case likely was more a function of employer missteps than an expansion of employee privacy interests in electronic communications or otherwise. What are the lessons here for employers who want discretion to review the content of employee electronic communications? What mistakes did the Department make and what steps could an employer take to prevent them? In other words, can a public employer effectively regulate away any reasonable expectation of privacy by establishing and abiding by clear policies and procedures regarding employee communications and work spaces?

Courts analyzing constitutional and other kinds of workplace privacy claims often find that employees have no reasonable expectation of privacy in electronic communications or files on employer-provided devices where the employer has in place a sufficiently broad policy that clearly states that employee communications and files may be monitored. *See, e.g., Biby v. Bd. of Regents,* 419 F.3d 845 (8th Cir. 2005); *Muick v. Glenayre Elecs,* 280 F.3d 741 (7th Cir. 2002); *United States v. Angevine,* 281 F.3d 1130 (10th Cir. 2002); *United States v. Simons,* 206 F.3d 392 (4th Cir. 2000); *see also State v. M.A.,* 954 A.2d 503 (N.J. App. Div. 2008) (concluding employee lacked reasonable expectation of privacy in the personal information stored in his employer-provided computer where employee was advised that computers were company property and that the firm and co-workers had access to it).

When employees are able to establish a reasonable expectation of privacy, it tends to be because the employer did not adhere to the policy (as in *Quon*) or the policy was, for one reason or another, insufficiently clear or broad to cover the particular communications or electronic files in question. *See United States v. Ziegler,* 474 F.3d 1184, 1189-90 (9th Cir. 2007) (holding that an employee possessed a reasonable expectation of privacy in a computer in a locked office despite a company policy that computer usage would be monitored); *Pure Power Boot Camp, Inc. v. Warrior Fitness Boot Camp, LLC,* 587 F. Supp. 2d 548, 560 (S.D.N.Y. 2008) (finding that an employee had a reasonable privacy expectation in personal Hotmail account that he accessed on his employer-provided work computer because the company's e-mail policy did not state that e-mails stored on third-party providers and not within the employer's e-mail system could be subject to inspection); *see also Stengart v. Loving Care Agency, Inc.,* 990 A.2d 650 (N.J. 2010) (stating that an employer policy regarding access to employee e-mail could not trump the employee's attorney-client privilege). It might be that the seemingly idiosyncratic *Quon* facts are more typical than they appear. Employers usually have "appropriate use" policies on paper, but there are many reasons why workplace norms could vary significantly from written policies. Even before *Quon*, if an employer really wished to forestall any expectations of privacy, it was advisable to frequently monitor worker communications — and let them know that's being done. But can you see why employers, whatever documents their attorneys draft, might have been reluctant to do so?

Still, if employer monitoring and review of employee electronic communications is or becomes the standard practice, doesn't this cut against the legitimacy of an expectation that such communications are private? Wouldn't these practices help to form the norms and societal expectations to which the majority refers? Would such expectation-reducing actions by employers have the same effect under Justice Scalia's categorical approach? If his view were to prevail, the reasonableness of an employee's expectation of privacy would not hinge on the particulars of given work-place practices or structures. But what is the likely treatment of the category — electronic communications on employer-provided devices — in a world in which employer monitoring and review are standard practice? In light of these lessons, *Quon* might lead many (most?) employers to act in ways that, as a practical matter, reduce the amount of privacy or autonomy employees enjoy at work or while using employer-provided communications devices. Or are there reasons to be more optimistic?

4. *The Second Prong: The Reasonableness of the Search or Intrusion. Quon*'s central holding was on the second prong of the inquiry: After assuming Quon had a reasonable expectation of privacy in the content of the text messages, the Court concluded that the department's review of the text message transcripts was "reasonable." In *O'Connor*, the Court had determined that the need to balance the legitimate interests of the government employer against the privacy interests of its employees justified exempting work-related searches from the usual Fourth Amendment requirement of obtaining a warrant:

> In our view, requiring an employer to obtain a warrant whenever the employer wished to enter an employee's office, desk, or file cabinets for a work-related purpose would seriously disrupt the routine conduct of business and would be unduly burdensome. Imposing unwieldy warrant procedures in such cases upon supervisors, who would otherwise have no reason to be familiar with such procedures, is simply unreasonable. In contrast to other circumstances in which we have required warrants, supervisors in offices such as at the Hospital are hardly in the business of investigating the violation of criminal laws. Rather, work-related searches are merely incident to the primary business of the agency. Under these circumstances, the imposition of a warrant requirement would conflict with "the common-sense realization that government offices could not function if every employment decision became a constitutional matter." *Connick* v. *Myers*, 461 U.S. 138, 143 (1983).

O'Connor, 480 U.S. at 721-22. The Court also rejected a warrantless "probable cause" standard as impracticable:

> The governmental interest justifying work-related intrusions by public employers is the efficient and proper operation of the workplace. Government agencies provide myriad services to the public, and the work of these agencies would suffer if employers were

required to have probable cause before they entered an employee's desk for the purpose of finding a file or piece of office correspondence. Indeed, it is difficult to give the concept of probable cause, rooted as it is in the criminal investigatory context, much meaning when the purpose of a search is to retrieve a file for work-related reasons. Similarly, the concept of probable cause has little meaning for a routine inventory conducted by public employers for the purpose of securing state property. To ensure the efficient and proper operation of the agency, therefore, public employers must be given wide latitude to enter employee offices for work-related, noninvestigatory reasons.

. . . Public employers have an interest in ensuring that their agencies operate in an effective and efficient manner, and the work of these agencies inevitably suffers from the inefficiency, incompetence, mismanagement, or other work-related misfeasance of its employees. Indeed, in many cases, public employees are entrusted with tremendous responsibility, and the consequences of their misconduct or incompetence to both the agency and the public interest can be severe. In contrast to law enforcement officials, therefore, public employers are not enforcers of the criminal law; instead, public employers have a direct and overriding interest in ensuring that the work of the agency is conducted in a proper and efficient manner. In our view, therefore, a probable cause requirement for searches of the type at issue here would impose intolerable burdens on public employers. The delay in correcting the employee misconduct caused by the need for probable cause rather than reasonable suspicion will be translated into tangible and often irreparable damage to the agency's work, and ultimately to the public interest. . . . [Additionally, it] is simply unrealistic to expect supervisors in most government agencies to learn the subtleties of the probable cause standard. . . .

Id. at 723-24.

Instead, the Court adopted a much less searching "reasonableness" standard for determining the validity of the intrusion. This inquiry addresses the reasonableness of both the inception and scope of the intrusion:

Ordinarily, a search of an employee's office by a supervisor will be "justified at its inception" when there are reasonable grounds for suspecting that the search will turn up evidence that the employee is guilty of work-related misconduct, or that the search is necessary for a noninvestigatory work-related purpose such as to retrieve a needed file. . . .

[A] search will be permissible in its scope when "the measures adopted are reasonably related to the objectives of the search and not excessively intrusive in light of . . . the nature of the [misconduct]."

Id. at 726.

Applying this standard, *Quon* held that the department's review of the text messages was justified at its inception by a legitimate, noninvestigatory work-related rationale and found the level of intrusiveness to be reasonable. Perhaps the most significant doctrinal takeaway from the Court's analysis was its rejection of the Ninth Circuit's finding that the search was unreasonable in scope because the department had less intrusive means at its disposal for achieving the same work-related end. Thus, to survive scrutiny with regard to the extensiveness of the intrusion, a government employer need not utilize the "least intrusive" search practicable. Do you agree with the Court's reasoning? It's hard to imagine a "reasonableness" test that doesn't consider alternatives. Is the Court saying that alternatives are irrelevant or only that the employer doesn't have to use the less intrusive one? If the latter, how unnecessarily intrusive can a search be and still be "reasonable"?

5. *Reasonableness, Deference, and Uncertainty.* As you may have noticed already, deference to government employers' interests plays a crucial role in the Fourth Amendment analysis. For example, as Justice Scalia's critique of the *O'Connor* plurality's approach to the first prong suggests, because actual workplace practices and structures are relevant to determining whether an employee's privacy expectation is reasonable, employers' decisions regarding the need to monitor and search the physical and virtual spaces in the workplace may profoundly affect that inquiry. As for the second prong, the need for some deference to government employers' decision making and practical constraints were central to the *O'Connor* Court's adoption of a reasonableness inquiry instead of imposing the traditional warrant and probable cause requirements. The perceived necessity to give employers some leeway also informed *Quon*'s rejection of a more onerous "least intrusive means" requirement.

Moreover, outcomes in individual cases may hinge on the level of deference courts accord government employers' justifications for their intrusions and the means they utilize to serve these ends. If, as Justice Scalia suggests, the *O'Connor* plurality's approach to the "expectation of privacy" inquiry may lead to uncertainty, the same undoubtedly can be said of the second prong's reasonableness standard as articulated in *O'Connor* and *Quon*. This standard is more deferential to the employer than a probable cause or strict scrutiny requirement would be, but how much deference is to be accorded to the government's articulated justification and chosen means remains unclear. For example, is an intrusion valid as long as an employer is able to articulate (truthfully) some workplace productivity, security, or efficiency justification and the intrusive means it chooses does not extend beyond what is needed to serve this end? The extent to which the level of scrutiny varies by circumstance or by the nature of intrusion likewise remains unresolved. The *Quon* majority states that "the extent of an expectation is relevant to assessing whether the search was too intrusive," but how this seemingly sliding scale is to be applied in other cases is unclear.

The critical role of deference is, of course, not unique to this area; indeed, it may be dispositive whenever a court is asked to scrutinize government activities. But the extent of deference may vary with the nature of the governmental activities and the countervailing interests at stake. How much deference should a court give a government employer in scrutinizing its justification for an intrusion into an employee's sphere of potential privacy? What are the social benefits of such deference and the countervailing costs? Does your answer depend on the type of intrusion at issue — for example, drug testing, office searches, locker searches, video surveillance of work spaces, and monitoring of computer and Internet use? Are your views influenced by your own work experiences and expectations, and the extent to which you may value your privacy in various contexts? We will revisit some of these issues at greater length in Section B.

6. *Due Process Protections for Public Sector Employees.* In addition to the protection accorded by the Fourth Amendment, public employees may enjoy other privacy protections. The Fifth and Fourteenth Amendments' due process clauses protect employees' "liberty interests," including privacy interests, and these interests may be enforceable under 42 U.S.C. §1983 or directly against federal officials under *Bivens v. Six Unknown Named Agents*, 403 U.S. 388 (1971). For example, in *Whalen v. Roe*, 429 U.S. 589 (1977), the Supreme Court recognized constitutional privacy interests in "avoiding disclosure of personal matters" and in "independence in making certain kinds of important decisions." *See also Nixon v. Administrator of General Services*, 433 U.S. 425 (1977) ("[P]ublic officials, including the President, are not wholly without constitutionally protected privacy rights in matters of personal life unrelated to any acts done by them in their public capacity."). Although this right to "information privacy" is widely recognized in the circuits, its contours are not well defined. This may change soon, since the Supreme Court has granted certiorari on a Ninth Circuit decision enjoining the National Aeronautics and Space Administration ("NASA") from requiring that employees in nonsensitive or low-risk positions submit to in-depth background investigations and answer questions about private matters including "adverse information" about financial issues, alcohol and drug abuse, and mental and emotional stability. *See Nelson v. NASA*, 512 F.3d 1134, *vacated and superseded on denial of rehearing en banc*, 530 F.3d 865 (9th Cir. 2008), *cert. granted*, 130 S. Ct. 1755 (2010). For a discussion of the right to information privacy and the implications of the *Nelson* case, *see* Posting of Daniel J. Solove to Concurring Opinions, http://www.concurringopinions.com/archives/2010/03/nasa-v-nelson -is-there-a-constitutional-right-to-information-privacy.html (Mar. 9, 2010, 12:16 EST).

With regard to other types of claims based on "substantive due process" rights, protection depends largely on whether the privacy interest at stake has been identified as "fundamental." Where it has not, the government employer's action must simply be rational or nonarbitrary, and employees invariably lose such challenges. Where, however, the interest has been deemed fundamental — for example, involving marriage or other intimate relations, procreation, abortion, child rearing, or perhaps intimate personal information — the alleged infringement of these rights will be subjected to more searching scrutiny, and courts have found violations in various contexts. *See, e.g., Barrett v. Steubenville City Schs.*, 388 F.3d 967, 974 (6th Cir. 2004) (finding an employee stated a claim of violation of constitutional right to rear a child after school district denied her permanent position because she removed her child from the public schools); *Barrow v. Greenville Indep. Sch. Dist.*, 332 F.3d 844 (5th Cir. 2003) (recognizing the same right); *Thorne v. City of El Segundo*, 726 F.2d 459 (9th Cir. 1983) (holding that the rejection of a police officer candidate in part because a polygraph test revealed her sexual relationship with a married police officer violated the candidate's constitutional rights). However, courts have often rejected such claims, finding either no fundamental right and a legitimate employment-related justification for the action, or that the agency's survives strict scrutiny. *See, e.g., Seegmiller v. Laverkin City*, 528 F.3d 762 (10th Cir. 2008) (holding that a police officer did not have fundamental liberty interest to engage in private act of consensual sex, and that the city reasonably reprimanded officer under its code of ethics, precluding a claim under rational basis review); *Sylvester v. Fogley*, 465 F.3d 851 (8th Cir. 2006) (holding that an investigation into whether a police officer had sexual relations with victim of crime he was investigating did not violate officer's right to privacy because the police investigation was narrowly tailored to serve a compelling interest).

7. *State Constitutions.* Many state constitutions also protect privacy rights of government workers. For example, the plaintiffs in *Quon* claimed violations of Article I, Section 1 of the California Constitution, which provides that all people have inalienable rights, including life, liberty, and "privacy." *See also* AK. CONST. art. I, § 22 ("The right of the people to privacy is recognized and shall not be infringed."); WASH. CONST. art. I, § 7 ("No person shall be disturbed in his private affairs, or his home invaded, without authority of law.").

8. *Statutory Protections for Public Sector Employees.* While there is no comprehensive workplace privacy statute or statutory scheme protecting federal workers' privacy, federal employees have some additional protections from intrusions. For example, under the Civil Service Reform Act, 5 U.S.C. § 2302 (2006), civil service workers are protected against termination for conduct that does not adversely affect their employment performance or the performance of others. Also, federal employees may enjoy protection against the government collecting, using, and disclosing some kinds of personal information under the Privacy Act of 1974, 5 U.S.C. § 552a (2006). State protections for public workers vary, but many have civil service regimes akin to the one under federal law. Many other state statutory protections apply to both public and private sectors.

9. *Spillovers Between the Public and Private Workplace.* Although *Quon* involves a public employer, two of plaintiffs' three primary legal theories — the Stored Communications Act, 18 U.S.C. §§ 2702-2711 (2006), discussed in more detail on page 320, and California constitutional claims — could also be available in the private employer context. Indeed, while most state constitutional protections, like their federal counterparts, are limited to government intrusions, California's privacy provision applies to private actors, including private employers. *See Hernandez v. Hillsides, Inc.*, 211 P.3d 1063 (Cal. 2009); *Soroka v. Dayton Hudson Corp.*, 1 Cal. Rptr. 2d 77 (Ct. App. 1991) (reproduced at page 340); *cf. Hennessey v. Coastal Eagle Point Oil Co.*, 609 A.2d 11 (N.J. 1992) (holding that the right to privacy in the New Jersey Constitution does not apply to private actors directly, but can form part of the basis for a clear mandate of public policy supporting a wrongful discharge claim). Nevertheless, since federal constitutional, most state constitutional, and other statutory protections (like those discussed in Note 8) are available only to government workers, the public/private sector distinction is a potentially dispositive one in the privacy context. *See, e.g.*, S. Elizabeth Wilborn, *Revisiting the Public/Private Distinction: Employee Monitoring in the Workplace*, 32 GA. L. REV. 825 (1998).

Still, there are a number of other ways in which privacy claims in public and private workplace converge. First, Justice Scalia's concurrence in *O'Connor* suggests that private sector norms and practices may be relevant to the reasonableness inquiry. *See O'Connor*, 480 U.S. at 732 (Scalia, concurring) (stating that "searches of the sort that are regarded as reasonable and normal in the private-employer context" do not violate the Fourth Amendment). Reliance on private sector norms and practices might seem odd, given that worker expectations about when the government can intrude upon certain spaces and communications may vary greatly (and legitimately) from their views of when private employers may intrude. Indeed, isn't it likely that the background constitutional and statutory constraints themselves shape public sector employees' expectations differently than those in the private sector? Nevertheless, Justice Scalia's view at least suggests the potential relevance of prevailing private sector practices in the constitutional analysis.

On the flip side, Fourth Amendment cases like *O'Connor* have proven highly influential beyond the public workplace as courts analyzing private sector claims borrow heavily from the legal framework developed in the Fourth Amendment cases. As we will see, the analytical framework set forth in *O'Connor* is similar to those adopted by courts addressing privacy claims based on statutory, state constitutional, and tort theories. For example, as the Ninth Circuit's panel decision in *Quon* stated, the analysis under the California Constitution tracks the Fourth Amendment. *See* 529 F.3d 892, 903 (9th Cir. 2008). This suggests that public sector cases addressing frequently litigated workplace privacy matters such as employee electronic communications have broader implications and may be influential in future decisions, particularly in jurisdictions in which some legal theory — tort, public policy, or statutory — akin to

California's constitutional privacy claim can be used to reach private employers. *Cf.* Jonathan D. Glater, *A Company Computer and Questions About E-Mail Privacy*, N.Y. TIMES (June 27, 2008) (mentioning the Ninth Circuit's *Quon* decision in discussing whether a former employee had a privacy claim against his former employer for reading the messages in his private Yahoo! account after he had left the company).

2. Tort-based Protections

Borse v. Piece Goods Shop, Inc.
963 F.2d 611 (3d Cir. 1992)

BECKER, Circuit Judge.

Plaintiff Sarah Borse brought suit against her former employer, Piece Goods Shop, Inc. ("the Shop"), in the district court for the Eastern District of Pennsylvania. She claimed that, by dismissing her when she refused to submit to urinalysis screening and personal property searches (conducted by her employer at the workplace pursuant to its drug and alcohol policy), the Shop violated a public policy that precludes employers from engaging in activities that violate their employees' rights to privacy and to freedom from unreasonable searches. . . . This appeal requires us to decide whether an at-will employee who is discharged for refusing to consent to urinalysis screening for drug use and to searches of her personal property states a claim for wrongful discharge under Pennsylvania law.

Because we predict that, under certain circumstances, discharging a private-sector, at-will employee for refusal to consent to drug testing and to personal property searches may violate the public policy embodied in the Pennsylvania cases recognizing a cause of action for tortious invasion of privacy, and because the allegations of Borse's complaint are not sufficient for us to determine whether the facts of this case support such a claim, we will vacate the district court's [dismissal for failure to state a claim] and remand with directions to grant leave to amend.

I. The Allegations of the Complaint . . .

Borse was employed as a sales clerk by the Piece Goods Shop for almost fifteen years. In January 1990, the Shop adopted a drug and alcohol policy which required its employees to sign a form giving their consent to urinalysis screening for drug use and to searches of their personal property located on the Shop's premises.

Borse refused to sign the consent form. On more than one occasion, she asserted that the drug and alcohol policy violated her right to privacy and her right to be free from unreasonable searches and seizures as guaranteed by the United States Constitution. The Shop continued to insist that she sign the form and threatened to discharge her unless she did. On February 9, 1990, the Shop terminated Borse's employment.

The complaint alleges that Borse was discharged in retaliation for her refusal to sign the consent form and for protesting the Shop's drug and alcohol policy. It asserts that her discharge violated a public policy, embodied in the First and Fourth Amendments to the United States Constitution, which precludes employers from engaging in activities that violate their employees' rights to privacy and to freedom from unreasonable searches of their persons and property. Plaintiff seeks compensatory damages for emotional distress, injury to reputation, loss of earnings, and diminished earning capacity. She also alleges that the discharge was willful and malicious and, accordingly, seeks punitive damages.

II. Overview of the Public Policy Exception to the Employment-at-Will Doctrine in Pennsylvania

[The Court recognized that, as a federal court sitting in diversity, it must apply Pennsylvania tort law in this case. In so doing, it was obliged to predict how the Pennsylvania Supreme Court would resolve the question of whether discharging an at-will employee who refuses to consent to urinalysis and to searches of his or her personal property located on the employer's premises violates public policy. After a detailed discussion of Pennsylvania Supreme Court and Superior Court cases addressing the public policy exception, and Third Circuit cases applying Pennsylvania law on the exception, the court concluded that Pennsylvania law continues to recognize a claim for wrongful discharge when dismissal of an at-will employee violates a clear mandate of public policy.]

III. Sources of Public Policy

In order to evaluate Borse's claim, we must attempt to "discern whether any public policy is threatened" by her discharge. As evidence of a public policy that precludes employers from discharging employees who refuse to consent to the practices at issue, Borse primarily relies upon the First and Fourth Amendments to the United States Constitution and the right to privacy included in the Pennsylvania Constitution. As will be seen, we reject her reliance on these constitutional provisions, concluding instead that, to the extent that her discharge implicates public policy, the source of that policy lies in Pennsylvania common law.

A. Constitutional Provisions

1. The United States Constitution

Although the Supreme Court has made clear that the Constitution proscribes only the *government* from violating the individual's right to privacy, and to freedom from unreasonable searches, *Skinner v. Railway Labor Executives Association*, 489 U.S. 602 (1989) (Fourth Amendment does not apply to searches by private party), Borse argues that our decision in *Novosel v. Nationwide Insurance Co.*, 721 F.2d 894 (3d Cir. 1983), permits us to consider the public policies embodied in the First and Fourth Amendments despite the lack of state action. In *Novosel*, defendant Nationwide instructed its employees to participate in its effort to lobby the Pennsylvania House of Representatives, which was then considering an insurance reform act. Specifically,

Nationwide directed its employees to clip, copy, and obtain signatures on coupons bearing the insignia of the Pennsylvania Committee for No-Fault Reform. Novosel alleged that he was discharged for refusing to participate in the lobbying effort and for privately stating opposition to his employer's political stand.

In response to Novosel's claim, Nationwide argued that a wrongful discharge action depends upon the violation of a *statutorily* recognized public policy. We disagreed. . . . After noting that the public policy exception applies only in the absence of statutory remedies, we reasoned:

> Given that there are no statutory remedies available in the present case and taking into consideration the importance of the political and associational freedoms of the federal and state Constitutions, the absence of a statutory declaration of public policy would appear to be no bar to the existence of a cause of action. Accordingly, a cognizable expression of public policy may be derived in this case from either the First Amendment of the United States Constitution or Article I, Section 7 of the Pennsylvania Constitution.[5]

In deciding not to extend *Novosel* to Borse's claim, the district court remarked upon the Pennsylvania Superior Court's reluctance to rely upon constitutional provisions as sources of public policy. . . .

To the extent that the district court's opinion suggests that a constitutional provision may never serve as a source of public policy in Pennsylvania wrongful discharge actions, we disagree. . . .

Even though the district court may have overestimated the Superior Court's hostility to reliance upon constitutional provisions as sources of public policy, it correctly refused to extend *Novosel* to Borse's claim. As the district court observed, the Superior Court has refused to extend constitutional provisions designed to restrict governmental conduct in the absence of state action. . . .

The Pennsylvania Supreme Court has not considered the propriety of applying constitutional principles to wrongful discharge actions against private employers. Its most recent decisions regarding the cause of action admonish us, however, that the public policy exception applies "only in the most limited of circumstances," *Paul* [*v. Lankenau Hospital*, 569 A.2d 346, 348 Pa. (1990)]. . . .

Novosel's holding (i.e., that using the power of discharge to coerce employees' political activity violates public policy) is not at issue here and thus we need not decide whether the recent Pennsylvania cases constitute such "persuasive evidence of a change in Pennsylvania law" that we are free to disregard it. Instead, we need only decide whether to *extend* the approach taken in *Novosel*. In light of the narrowness of the public policy exception and of the Pennsylvania courts' continuing insistence upon the state action requirement, we predict that if faced with the issue, the Pennsylvania Supreme Court would not look to the First and Fourth Amendments as sources of public policy when there is no state action. Accordingly, we decline to extend the approach taken in *Novosel* to this case.

---

5. Article I, section 7 states in pertinent part:

The free communication of thoughts and opinions is one of the invaluable rights of man, and every citizen may freely speak, write and print on any subject, being responsible for the abuse of that liberty.

2. The Pennsylvania Constitution

[The court predicted that the Pennsylvania Supreme Court would find that the state constitution does not encompass privacy invasions by private actors and would not look to that constitution's right to privacy as a source of public policy in a wrongful discharge action.]

B. *Pennsylvania Common Law*

Although we have rejected Borse's reliance upon constitutional provisions as evidence of a public policy allegedly violated by the Piece Goods Shop's drug and alcohol program, our review of Pennsylvania law reveals other evidence of a public policy that may, under certain circumstances, give rise to a wrongful discharge action related to urinalysis or to personal property searches. Specifically, we refer to the Pennsylvania common law regarding tortious invasion of privacy.

Pennsylvania recognizes a cause of action for tortious "intrusion upon seclusion." *Marks v. Bell Telephone Co.*, 331 A.2d 424, 430 (Pa. 1975). The Restatement defines the tort as follows:

> One who intentionally intrudes, physically or otherwise, upon the solitude or seclusion of another or his private affairs or concerns, is subject to liability to the other for invasion of his privacy, if the intrusion would be highly offensive to a reasonable person.

RESTATEMENT (SECOND) OF TORTS § 652B.[8]

Unlike the other forms of tortious invasion of privacy,[9] an action based on intrusion upon seclusion does not require publication as an element of the tort. *Harris by Harris v. Easton Publishing Co.*, 483 A.2d 1377, 1383 (1984). The tort may occur by (1) physical intrusion into a place where the plaintiff has secluded himself or herself; (2) use of the defendant's senses to oversee or overhear the plaintiff's private affairs; or (3) some other form of investigation or examination into plaintiff's private concerns. Liability attaches only when the intrusion is substantial and would be highly offensive to "the ordinary reasonable person."

We can envision at least two ways in which an employer's urinalysis program might intrude upon an employee's seclusion. First, the particular manner in which the program is conducted might constitute an intrusion upon seclusion as defined by Pennsylvania law. The process of collecting the urine sample to be tested clearly implicates "expectations of privacy that society has long recognized as reasonable,"

---

8. In *Vogel v. W.T. Grant Co.*, 327 A.2d 133 (Pa. 1974), the Pennsylvania Supreme Court adopted the definition of tortious invasion of privacy as stated in a tentative draft of the RESTATEMENT (SECOND) OF TORTS § 652 (Tent Draft Nov. 13, 1967). Although the Pennsylvania Supreme Court has not expressly adopted the final version of section 652, our analysis of Pennsylvania law in *O'Donnell v. United States*, 891 F.2d 1079 (3d Cir. 1989), led us to predict that it would do so if presented with the issue. *See also Vernars v. Young*, 539 F.2d 966 (3d Cir. 1976) (upholding invasion of privacy claim under Pennsylvania law when corporate officer opened and read personal mail addressed to fellow employee).

9. The action for invasion of privacy encompasses four analytically distinct torts. In addition to intrusion upon seclusion, the tort also includes: (1) appropriation of name or likeness; (2) publicity given to private life; and (3) publicity placing a person in a false light. *See Marks.*

Skinner v. Railway Labor Executives Association, 489 U.S. 602, 617 (1989).[10] In addition, many urinalysis programs monitor the collection of the urine specimen to ensure that the employee does not adulterate it or substitute a sample from another person. . . . Monitoring collection of the urine sample appears to fall within the definition of an intrusion upon seclusion because it involves the use of one's senses to oversee the private activities of another. RESTATEMENT (SECOND) OF TORTS §652B, comment b. *See also Harris*. . . .

Second, urinalysis "can reveal a host of private medical facts about an employee, including whether she is epileptic, pregnant, or diabetic." *Skinner*. A reasonable person might well conclude that submitting urine samples to tests designed to ascertain these types of information constitutes a substantial and highly offensive intrusion upon seclusion.

The same principles apply to an employer's search of an employee's personal property. If the search is not conducted in a discreet manner or if it is done in such a way as to reveal personal matters unrelated to the workplace, the search might well constitute a tortious invasion of the employee's privacy. *See, for example, K-Mart Corp. Store No. 7441 v. Trotti*, 677 S.W.2d 632 (Tex. App. 1984) (search of employee's locker). *See also Bodewig v. K-Mart, Inc.*, 635 P.2d 657 (1981) (subjecting cashier accused of stealing to strip search).

The Pennsylvania courts have not had occasion to consider whether a discharge related to an employer's tortious invasion of an employee's privacy violates public policy. . . .

[W]e believe that when an employee alleges that his or her discharge was related to an employer's invasion of his or her privacy, the Pennsylvania Supreme Court would examine the facts and circumstances surrounding the alleged invasion of privacy. If the court determined that the discharge was related to a substantial and highly offensive invasion of the employee's privacy, we believe that it would conclude that the discharge violated public policy.[11] Indeed, the following language in [*Geary v. United States Steel Corp.*, 319 A.2d 174 (Pa. 1974)] might well be considered to presage such an approach:

> It may be granted that there are areas of an employee's life in which his employer has no legitimate interest. An intrusion into one of these areas by virtue of the employer's power of discharge might plausibly give rise to a cause of action, particularly where some recognized facet of public policy is threatened. . . .

Only a handful of other jurisdictions have considered urinalysis programs implemented by private employers.[12] The majority of these decisions balance the employee's

_____

10. [W]e caution against the wholesale application to private employers of the limitations imposed on public employers by the Fourth Amendment. We find the cases involving government employers helpful, however, in defining the individual privacy interest implicated by urinalysis.

11. The Sixth Circuit recently rejected an invasion of privacy claim challenging an employer's urinalysis program. *Baggs v. Eagle-Picher Industries, Inc.*, 957 F.2d 268 (6th Cir. 1992) (applying Michigan law). Michigan law permits an employer to use "intrusive and even objectionable means to obtain employment-related information about an employee." In contrast, Pennsylvania has not exempted employers from the principles ordinarily applied in actions for tortious invasion of privacy.

12. Several of these cases are inapposite because they involve state law that differs significantly from Pennsylvania's. For example, some state constitutions include a right of privacy that applies to private action. Our discussion in the text focuses on selected cases typifying the various approaches taken in the remaining cases. We are unaware of any case considering whether the dismissal of an at-will employee who refuses to consent to personal property searches violates public policy.

privacy interest against the employer's interests in order to determine whether to uphold the programs. *See, for example, Luedtke v. Nabors Alaska Drilling, Inc.,* 768 P.2d 1123 (Alaska 1989). In *Luedtke,* two employees challenged their employer's urinalysis program, alleging violation of their state constitutional right of privacy, common-law invasion of privacy, wrongful discharge, and breach of the covenant of good faith and fair dealing. (Under Alaska law, the public policy exception to the employment-at-will doctrine is "largely encompassed within the implied covenant of good faith and fair dealing.") After determining that the relevant provision of the Alaska constitution did not apply to private action, the Alaska Supreme Court concluded that a public policy protecting an employee's right to withhold private information from his employer exists in Alaska and that violation of that policy "may rise to the level of a breach of the implied covenant of good faith and fair dealing."

As evidence of public policy, the court looked to the state's statutes,[13] Constitution,[14] and common law.[15] The court concluded:

> Thus, the citizens' rights to be protected against unwarranted intrusions into their private lives has been recognized in the law of Alaska. The constitution protects against governmental intrusion, statutes protect against employer intrusion, and the common law protects against intrusions by other private persons. As a result, there is sufficient evidence to support the conclusion that there exists a public policy protecting spheres of employee conduct into which employers may not intrude.

The court then turned to the question "whether employer monitoring of employee drug use outside the work place is such a prohibited intrusion." The Court reasoned that the boundaries of the employee's right of privacy "are determined by balancing [that right] against other public policies, such as 'the health, safety, rights and privileges of others.'" Because the *Luedtke* plaintiffs performed safety-sensitive jobs, the court concluded that the public policy supporting the protection of the health and safety of other workers justified their employer's urinalysis program.

[The West Virginia Supreme Court also applied a balancing test in *Twigg v. Hercules Corp.,* 406 S.E.2d 52 (W. Va. 1990), reasoning that its holding that requiring employees to submit to polygraph examinations violated public policy should be extended to requiring an employee to submit to drug testing. West Virginia, however, recognized two exceptions: when the urinalysis is based on "reasonable good faith objective suspicion" of an employee's drug use or when the employee's job involves public safety or the safety of others. Not all other jurisdictions have applied a balancing test to urinalysis programs, but the balancing test is more consistent with Pennsylvania law.]

---

13. The court observed that a statute prohibiting employers from requiring employees to take polygraph tests as a condition of employment supports "the policy that there are private sectors of employees' lives not subject to direct scrutiny by their employers." The court also noted that a statute prohibiting employment discrimination on the basis of, among other things, marital status, changes in marital status, pregnancy or parenthood, demonstrates "that in Alaska certain subjects are placed outside the consideration of employers in their relations with employees."

14. The court reasoned that although Alaska's constitutional right of privacy does not proscribe private action, the inclusion of a specific clause protecting the right "supports the contention that this right 'strike[s] as the heart of a citizen's social rights.'"

15. The court observed that the action for tortious intrusion upon seclusion evidences the existence of a common-law right of privacy.

. . . Pennsylvania's intermediate appellate courts have recognized a public policy exception to the employment-at-will doctrine on three occasions and have emphasized the need to examine all the circumstances in a wrongful discharge action. . . . More importantly, under Pennsylvania law an employee's consent to a violation of public policy is no defense to a wrongful discharge action when that consent is obtained by the threat of dismissal.[18]

In view of the foregoing analysis, we predict that the Pennsylvania Supreme Court would apply a balancing test to determine whether the Shop's drug and alcohol program (consisting of urinalysis and personal property searches) invaded Borse's privacy. Indeed, determining whether an alleged invasion of privacy is substantial and highly offensive to the reasonable person necessitates the use of a balancing test. The test we believe that Pennsylvania would adopt balances the employee's privacy interest against the employer's interest in maintaining a drug-free workplace in order to determine whether a reasonable person would find the employer's program highly offensive.

We recognize that other jurisdictions have considered individualized suspicion and concern for safety as factors to be considered in striking the balance, see, for example, *Twigg* (allowing urinalysis based on individualized suspicion or when employee's job implicates safety concerns). We do not doubt that, in an appropriate case, Pennsylvania would include these factors in the balance, but we do not believe that the Pennsylvania Supreme Court would require private employers to *limit* urinalysis programs or personal property searches to employees suspected of drug use or to those performing safety-sensitive jobs.

This precautionary note springs from two sources. First, these limitations originated in cases applying constitutional principles to urinalysis programs conducted by government employers. *See Skinner; Von Raab.* We do not believe that the Pennsylvania courts would transfer the jurisprudence of the cases involving government employers to actions against private employers because the standard applied in cases involving government employers differs significantly from that applied in the tortious invasion of privacy cases. In the cases involving government employers, courts have asked whether the urinalysis program is reasonable under Fourth Amendment principles. In contrast, in order for an invasion of privacy to be tortious, it must be both substantial and highly offensive to the reasonable person. Therefore, even though [we reason] that if a private employer's drug and alcohol program tortiously invaded its employees' privacy, the Pennsylvania Supreme Court would hold that discharges related to that program violated public policy, we do not believe that the Pennsylvania Supreme Court would simply transpose Fourth Amendment limitations on public

---

18. In *Leibowitz v. H.A. Winston Co.*, 493 A.2d 111 (Pa. Super. 1985), plaintiff was fired after a polygraph test indicated that he lied about stealing money from his employer. Because plaintiff had signed a release prior to taking the polygraph test, however, his employer argued that he could not maintain a cause of action for wrongful discharge. The court disagreed. It noted that Pennsylvania law prohibits employers from requiring polygraph tests as a condition of employment and that discharging an employee for refusing to submit to a polygraph test violates public policy, *see Perks v. Firestone Tire & Rubber Co.*, 611 F.2d 1363 (3d Cir. 1979) (upholding wrongful discharge action of employee fired for refusing to take polygraph test). The court then reasoned that although "mere economic or financial pressure [usually] does not suffice to invalidate a release," that rule does not apply when an employer requires an employee to sign a release as a condition of continued employment. Under those circumstances, the release is invalid. *Accord Polsky v. Radio Shack*, 666 F.2d 824 (3d Cir. 1981) (applying Pennsylvania law). *See* Stephen M. Fogel, Gerri L. Kornblut & Newton P. Porter, *Survey of the Law on Employee Drug Testing*, 42 U. MIAMI L. REV. 553, 669 (1988) (criticizing contrary result as creating Catch-22 for employee).

employers to urinalysis programs or personal property searches conducted by private employers.

Second, the case law concerning the public policy exception reflects "a pattern of favoring the employer's interest in running its business," and a willingness to define that interest broadly. . . . Given this backdrop, we find it unlikely that Pennsylvania would impose the strict limitations of the Fourth Amendment cases.

In sum, based on our prediction of Pennsylvania law, we hold that dismissing an employee who refused to consent to urinalysis testing and to personal property searches would violate public policy if the testing tortiously invaded the employee's privacy. [Borse should be accorded leave to amend her complaint to specify how her privacy was invaded.]

NOTES

1. *The Search for a Cause of Action.* Why did the plaintiff have to rely on the public policy exception in this case? An obvious answer is that there was no statutory protection on point and, because the employer in this case is a private employer, federal and state constitutional protections do not apply directly. Thus, as is often the case, the plaintiff here was engaged in a search for a source of protection. Yet, this is not a complete explanation; after all, in its analysis of public policy, the court notes that Pennsylvania courts have recognized the tort of intrusion upon seclusion, which gives employees a cause of action against private employers. In answering this question, consider how the claim here (as well as the remedy sought) is distinguishable from a stand-alone intrusion upon seclusion claim.

2. *The Public Policy Exception.* The *Borse* court concludes that Pennsylvania is likely to recognize a cause of action under the public policy doctrine in this case, if the testing tortiously invaded the employee's privacy. To reach this result, the court explicitly rejects reliance on constitutional sources, relying instead on common-law tort. Some courts in other jurisdictions have recognized public policy claims in the employee drug-testing context, based on state constitutional, statutory, or common-law sources of public policy. In addition to the sources cited in *Borse*, *see*, *e.g.*, *Hennessey v. Coastal Eagle Point Oil Co.*, 609 A.2d 11 (N.J. 1992) (finding public policy embodied in constitutional privacy protections). Other courts have been less amenable to recognition of these claims.

Recall for a moment the discussion of the public policy exception in Chapter 4. To what extent is the *Borse* analysis and ultimate decision consistent with the approach to this tort in the other public policy cases you read? Would Borse be correct under the draft Restatement of Employment Law? *See* page 185. If not, is that a criticism of *Borse* or of the Restatement?

3. *Intrusion upon Seclusion.* *Borse* discusses the tort of intrusion upon seclusion, the most widely recognized common-law privacy claim in the employment context. As *Borse* indicates, the tort requires (1) an intentional intrusion (2) into an area of solitude or seclusion (3) that would be highly offensive to the reasonable person. Note the similarity between this articulation and the Fourth Amendment analysis in *O'Connor* and *Quon*. As in a Fourth Amendment case, much hinges on whether the intrusion was into an area (spatial or otherwise) in which the employee has a reasonable expectation of privacy. This is satisfied in the drug and medical testing and other bodily intrusion contexts since courts agree that one has a reasonable expectation of privacy in his or her person. But whether such an expectation exists with regard to employee work spaces or communications is a more difficult issue that depends on the particulars of the job and workplace. *Compare Fischer v. Mt. Olive Lutheran Church*, 207 F. Supp. 2d 914 (W.D. Wis. 2002) (finding that employee had reasonable expectation in the e-mails in his personal Hotmail account); *Hernandez v. Hillsides, Inc.*, 211 P.3d 1063 (Cal. 2009) (concluding that employees had reasonable expectation that office that could be locked would not be secretly videotaped); *with Thygeson v. U.S. Bancorp*, 2004 U.S. Dist. LEXIS 18863 (D. Or. Sept. 15, 2004) (suggesting an employee has no reasonable expectation of privacy in e-mails on employer's e-mail system).

If there is such an intrusion by the employer, the next inquiry is whether it was objectively offensive. Oddly enough, whether the intrusion is offensive is not measured by how subjectively offensive it is to the employee but rather whether it is justified by a legitimate employer interest and appropriately tailored to serving that interest. In short, a reasonable employee should not be offended by a justifiable intrusion. As in the Fourth Amendment context, resolution of this inquiry often depends on the leeway courts are willing to give employers in terms of their articulated ends and means for achieving them. *Compare Speer v. Ohio Dep't of Rehab. and Corr.*, 624 N.E.2d 251 (Ohio Ct. App. 1993) (finding that a supervisor's hiding in the ceiling of a staff rest room to monitor an employee suspected of misconduct was unreasonable) *with Saldana v. Kelsey-Hayes*, 443 N.W.2d 382 (Mich. Ct. App. 1989) (upholding an employer's surveillance of an employee's home because the employer had a legitimate right to investigate whether the employee's claim of workplace injury was true). *See generally* Daniel P. O'Gorman, *Looking Out for Your Employer: Employers' Surreptitious Physical Surveillance of Employees and the Tort of Invasion of Privacy*, 85 NEB. L. REV. 212 (2006).

4. *Other Privacy Torts.* Other privacy torts are litigated occasionally in the workplace context. For example, RESTATEMENT (SECOND) OF TORTS §652D recognizes the tort of public disclosure of private facts, which creates a cause of action when one publicly discloses a private matter that is "highly offensive" to the reasonable person and as to which the public has no legitimate concern. Employers typically have access to private information about employees (e.g., disabilities or more general health information), and thus, their disclosure of such information to the public or third parties without justification may give rise to liability. *See, e.g., Miller v. Motorola, Inc.*, 560 N.E.2d 900 (Ill. App. Ct. 1990). However, the sharing of such information with workplace personnel may not give rise to liability, either because such a sharing is not sufficiently "public" to satisfy the public disclosure element, or because a legitimate business justification may render such disclosure "reasonable." *See, e.g., Bratt v. Int'l Bus. Machines*, 785 F.2d 352 (1st Cir. 1986) (finding no liability for the sharing of information about an employee's psychological condition with other managerial personnel); *see generally* Jonathan B. Mintz, *The Remains of Privacy's Disclosure Tort: An Exploration of the Private Domain*, 55 MD. L. REV. 425 (1996). Another theory that may provide protection in certain workplace contexts is the tort of false light, that is, where the employer discloses a matter about the employee that places the employee in a "false light" that is "highly offensive" to a reasonable person. *See* RESTATEMENT (SECOND) OF TORTS §652C (1977).

Despite the theoretical applicability of these tort causes of action, the statutory protections discussed in the next subsection are more likely to provide meaningful protection for the workplace privacy interests implicated. However, other workplace tort theories that implicate privacy or related dignitary interests are more likely to be pursued, including defamation, discussed in Chapter 4, and intentional infliction of emotional distress, discussed below.

5. *Intentional Infliction of Emotional Distress.* The means by which an employer may seek to monitor employee activities or gain information from an employee may give rise to an intentional infliction of emotional distress claim. As discussed in this chapter, the Restatement (Second) of Torts provides that such a cause of action exists when "one who by extreme and outrageous conduct intentionally or recklessly causes severe emotional distress to another." In most cases, the key inquiry is whether the employers' conduct — in this context, intrusive actions — is sufficiently "extreme and outrageous" to justify liability. Courts occasionally have found that employers' methods reach this level; indeed, *Rulon-Miller v. Int'l Bus. Machines Corp.*, 208 Cal. Rptr. 524 (Ct. App. 1984), reproduced at page 323, is one example. *See also Bodewig v. K-Mart, Inc.*, 635 P.2d 657 (Or. Ct. App. 1981) (recognizing a claim for intentional infliction of emotional distress after the employer required an employee to disrobe in front of a customer who claimed the employee had taken her money).

6. *The Request for Consent "Catch-22."* Numerous courts have found consent (or, at least, fully informed consent) to an alleged privacy intrusion to be a near-absolute defense to common-law privacy claims. *See, e.g., Stewart v. Pantry, Inc.*, 715 F. Supp. 1361 (W.D. Ky. 1988) (holding consent is a complete defense to an intrusion claim involving polygraph tests); *Jennings v. Minco Tech. Labs, Inc.*, 765 S.W.2d 497 (Tex. Ct. App. 1989) (same in drug-testing context); *cf. Baggs v. Eagle-Picher Indus., Inc.*, 750 F. Supp. 264 (W.D. Mich. 1990) (finding no expectation of privacy because employees were on notice of possible drug testing); *TBG Ins. Services Corp. v. Superior Court*, 117 Cal. Rptr. 2d 155 (Cal. App. 2002) (finding, in the context of a discovery dispute, that employee had no reasonable expectation of privacy in files on an employer-provided home computer because he had agreed in writing to employer's policy that computer use would be monitored). Should an employee's agreement to be tested, searched, or monitored, in response to an employer's request (or insistence) be a defense to a public policy claim? Similarly, should such agreement preclude recovery under an intrusion upon seclusion theory, either because consent destroys any reasonable expectation of privacy or because consent makes the intrusion not objectively offensive? On the other hand, if the employee refuses to agree to the intrusion, and no intrusion thereby occurs (i.e., no drug test, no intrusive questioning, no requested search of spaces or communications), some courts have held that that there is no intrusion upon seclusion claim. *See, e.g., Rushing v. Hershey Chocolate-Memphis*, 2000 WL 1597849 (6th Cir. 2000); *Baggs, supra* (holding that those who did not participate in the drug-testing program cannot recover because there was no intrusion); *Luedtke v. Nabors Alaska Drilling, Inc.*, 768 P.2d 1123 (Alaska 1989) ("[N]o cause of action for invasion of privacy arises where the intrusion is prevented from taking place").

And here lies the catch-22: If the employee agrees to the test, search, or other intrusion, she has consented to it; if she refuses (and loses her job as a result), there is no intrusion. Either way, she has no claim. Under this framework then, an employer can shield itself from liability by always asking for the employee's agreement or waiver before any intrusion occurs because any response by the employee will bar the claim. Obviously, not all courts have taken this view, and some, including *Borse* and *Luedtke*, have recognized that a public policy claim arising out of the employee's termination might exist even if an intrusion upon seclusion claim fails. Nevertheless, the potential waiver of rights and remedies when employers seek consent to otherwise actionable intrusions creates a further incentive for employers to make the demand for consent (to monitoring, surveillance, workplace searches, etc.) standard practice, and employees are then in a very difficult position when deciding how to respond.

3. Statutory Protections

a. Federal Law

While there is no comprehensive federal statutory scheme governing privacy rights or claims in the private workplace, there are a number of federal statutory regimes that protect privacy interests of private sector employees. Some protect such interests incidentally or as part of a larger scheme addressing other regulatory objectives. For example, antidiscrimination statutes provide indirect protection from certain forms of invasive employer activity or inquiries. While the Americans with Disabilities Act ("ADA") explicitly prohibits inquiry into its protected category, these laws more generally prohibit employers from altering the terms and conditions of employment based on an employee's protected status, which means that employers may steer clear of inquiries that may implicate such status — such as one's religion, age, or pregnancy status. *See, e.g.*, *Norman-Bloodshaw v. Lawrence Berkeley Lab.*, 135 F.3d 1260 (9th Cir. 1998) (holding that challenges to employer's medical and genetic testing program raised cognizable discrimination claims because they revealed sex- and race-linked traits or conditions). In addition, offensive intrusions into private matters by supervisors or co-workers may contribute to a discriminatory harassment claim if the conduct is linked to the victim's protected status (e.g., sex or religion). Various employment screening procedures — testing, medical screening, questioning, and so forth — also may violate antidiscrimination statutes if they have a disparate impact on a protected class and cannot be justified by business necessity. *See* Chapter 9.

In the past several decades, however, there have been a number of statutory developments that focus directly on privacy interests. A high-profile recent example is the Genetic Information Nondiscrimination Act of 2008 ("GINA"), Pub. L. 110-233, 122 Stat. 881 (May 21, 2008), which is discussed at the end of this subsection. These statutory regimes offer meaningful protections, but, as you will see, they are sometimes qualified or limited in important respects.

Earlier federal enactments tended to focus on intrusive interrogation techniques and employee surveillance and monitoring. For example, the Employee Polygraph Protection Act of 1988 ("EPPA"), 29 U.S.C. §§ 2001-09 (2006), bans the use of a polygraph for preemployment screening and delineates the circumstances in which polygraphs may be used in employer investigations following a theft of property and the procedures for such use. The EPPA applies to most private employees; however, government employees and employees working in various defense and security contexts are exempted.

In addition, the federal wiretapping statute, now embodied in the Electronic Communications Privacy Act of 1986 ("ECPA"), 18 U.S.C. §§ 2510-22 (2006), protects against various kinds of electronic surveillance and interception of communications by public and private actors, including private employers. It declares unlawful the intentional interception of oral wire communications, other oral communications, and electronic communications (all non-oral wire communications). While this act may appear to provide robust protections for electronic communications, including e-mails and Internet activity, three exemptions from its prohibitions limit protection for employee communications: (1) the law does not protect against interceptions by a service provider (often the employer) to protect the rights or property of the provider, (2) the protections do not apply to interception by certain devices of communications made in the "ordinary course of business," and (3) the protections do not apply when one party to the communication consents to the interception. Moreover, courts have construed "interception" narrowly in various contexts. *See, e.g., Konop v. Hawaiian Airlines, Inc.*, 302 F.3d 868 (9th Cir. 2002) (construing "interception" to cover only communications acquired during transmission). On the other hand, the exceptions also have been interpreted narrowly. *See, e.g., Deal v. Spears*, 980 F.2d 1153 (8th Cir. 1992) (ordinary course of business exception). Nevertheless, these carve-outs — particularly the third — significantly limit protections for most workers.

The Stored Communications Act ("SCA"), 18 U.S.C. §§ 2702-11 (2006), provides similar protections against unauthorized access to stored electronic communications, although it too is subject to the limitations of the ECPA. Recall that in *Quon*, the SCA was one of theories underlying the claims brought against Arch Wireless by Quon and his co-workers. It therefore is a potential source of protection for employees against third parties; indeed, Quon's claims against Arch Wireless as a remote computing service for its unauthorized release of the transcripts of the text messages were successful. For a detailed discussion of the SCA claims in *Quon*, see the underlying panel opinion, *Quon v. Arch Wireless Operating Co., Inc.*, 529 F.3d 892 (9th Cir. 2008). In addition, despite the limited protections against employer monitoring of electronic communications in the workplace, the ECPA and SCA are potential sources of protection from unauthorized employer intrusions into employee communications and other electronic activities outside of work. *See, e.g., Pietrylo v. Hillstone Rest. Group*, No. 06-5754 (FSH), 2009 WL 3128420 (D.N.J. Sept. 25, 2009) (upholding a jury verdict finding that employees' managers violated the SCA by knowingly accessing a chat group on MySpace without authorization).

In recent years, Congress has increasingly focused on privacy interests involving health, medical, and personal financial information. For example, the ADA, 42 U.S.C. § 12112 (2006), prohibits employers from inquiring about or asking applicants whether such applicant is an individual with a disability. The ADA permits an employer to make preemployment inquiries into the applicant's ability to perform job-related functions and to require all entering employees to undergo a medical examination *after* an initial offer of employment has been made. But the statute also prohibits employers from requiring current employees to undergo medical examinations unless they are job-related and "consistent with business necessity." *See* § 12112(d)(4) (prohibiting "inquiries of an employee as to whether [an] employee is an individual with a disability or as to the nature or severity of the disability, unless such examination or inquiry is shown to be job-related and consistent with business necessity"); *see also Karraker v. Rent-a-Center, Inc.*, 411 F.3d 831 (7th Cir. 2005) (finding that the administering of a psychological test to job applicants as part of a regime of exams violated the ADA because the test, as administered and applied, could be used to reveal a mental disorder); *Horgan v. Simmons* 704 F. Supp. 2d 814 (N.D. Ill. 2010) (upholding a claim under this section by HIV-positive employee who allegedly was compelled to respond to supervisor inquiries regarding his medical condition).

In addition, the Health Insurance Portability and Accountability Act ("HIPAA"), 42 U.S.C. § 300gg (2006), imposes certain conditions on the release of medical records by health care providers. Thus, an employer's requirement that an applicant release medical information often must conform to these requirements. Although HIPAA's medical records mandates may sound mundane, employers potentially have great access to this kind of employee information since they frequently provide health insurance. Thus, HIPAA's requirements have had a significant impact on medical record keeping and confidentiality practices. For a discussion of the ADA, HIPAA, and medical testing and records, *see* Sharona Hoffman, *Employing E-Health: The Impact of Electronic Health Records on the Workplace,* 19 KAN. J. L. & PUB. POL'Y 409 (2010); Sharona Hoffman, *Preplacement Examinations and Job-Relatedness: How to Enhance Privacy and Diminish Discrimination in the Workplace,* 49 KAN. L. REV. 517 (2001).

Another federal statute that provides procedural protections for personal information regarding employees and employment applicants is the Fair Credit Reporting Act, 15 U.S.C. §§ 1681-1681x (2006). It requires an employer to notify employees or applicants if it intends to obtain a consumer report on the individual prepared by a consumer reporting agency, obtain written authorization to review such a report, and notify the person promptly if information in the report may result in a negative employment decision (e.g., a decision not to hire or promote).

Finally, Congress enacted GINA in 2008, after various versions of the law had been considered for more than a decade. GINA marked the first direct and comprehensive federal response to the discriminatory use of genetic information by insurers and employers.

At first blush, Congress's concern about this issue might seem puzzling, since few employers have actually engaged in this practice, and there have been only a handful of federal cases addressing it. Nevertheless, concerns about such testing had already produced significant regulatory and legislative responses. A majority of states had imposed some kind of restriction on genetic testing by employers, *see* http://www .ncsl.org/programs/health/genetics/ndiscrim.htm, and discrimination in federal employment based on genetic information has been prohibited by Executive Order. *See* Exec. Order No. 13145, 65 Fed. Reg. 6877 (Feb. 8, 2000). Commentators had also expressed grave concerns about the future of such testing, its potential discriminatory effects, and its implications for employee privacy. *See, e.g.,* Pauline T. Kim, *Genetic Discrimination, Genetic Privacy: Rethinking Employee Protections for a Brave New Workplace,* 96 NW. U. L. REV. 1497 (2002); Jennifer Krumm, *Why Congress Must Ban Genetic Testing in the Workplace,* 23 J. LEGAL MED. 491 (2002); Paul M. Schwartz, *Privacy and the Economics of Personal Health Care Information,* 76 TEX. L. REV. 1 (1997).

What is troubling to many about such testing is precisely what makes it potentially appealing to employers; that is, genetic testing could potentially provide them with otherwise hidden, but highly valuable information about employees or applicants — for example, employers and their insurers could discern which employees or applicants are likely to be more costly in terms of potential health problems or other risks. Thus, GINA addresses the widespread concern that genetic testing might be utilized to make preemptive insurance and employment decisions, including screening out those who are genetically predisposed to developing diseases or other medical conditions. It is also designed to ensure that patients are not deterred from genetic testing for medical purposes out of fear that the data might be utilized to their detriment by health insurers and employers. Interestingly, unlike most other kinds of testing addressed in this chapter, legal decision makers have almost uniformly favored the privacy or autonomy interests at stake over employers' interests in gathering useful information.

Title I of the Act addresses genetic discrimination in health insurance. Of particular note is § 101, which amends ERISA to prohibit generally health plans from requesting or requiring an individual or family members of an individual to undergo genetic testing and requesting, requiring, or purchasing genetic information about an individual or family member. *See* 29 U.S.C.A. §§ 1132, 1182, 1191 (2010). It also prohibits use of genetic information to establish eligibility for health coverage. *See* 42 U.S.C.A. § 300gg-52. The term "genetic information" is defined as information about an individual's genetic tests, the genetic tests of family members of such individual, and the manifestation of a disease or disorder in family members of such individual. The term "genetic test" means "an analysis of human DNA, RNA, chromosomes, proteins, or metabolites that detects genotypes, mutations, or chromosomal changes." 26 U.S.C.A. § 9832; 42 U.S.C.A. § 2000ff.

Title II prohibits employment discrimination based on genetic information. Among other things, it provides that it is unlawful to discriminate against an employee (or applicant) in the terms and conditions of employment because of genetic information with respect to the employee or to limit or classify employees in any way that would deprive them of employment opportunities or adversely affect their status because of their genetic information. Employers are also prohibited from requesting, requiring, or purchasing genetic information with respect to an employee or a family member of the employee, except in certain specified circumstances. These include where the collection of such information is necessary to comply with other federal laws; is for certain law enforcement purposes; is pursuant to health or genetic services offered by the employer (with consent and pursuant to confidentiality measures and other limitations); or is to be used for genetic monitoring of the biological effects of toxic substances in the workplace, but only if various notice, disclosure, and other requirements are satisfied. *See* 42 U.S.C.A. § 2000ff.

Title II further requires employers possessing any genetic information about an employee to treat such information as a confidential medical record, and prohibits disclosure of genetic information except to the employee or in other narrowly defined circumstances. *See* 42 U.S.C.A. § 2000ff-5. In large part, the coverage, remedies, and procedures are applicable under Title VII. The statute does, however, expressly state that disparate impact on the basis of genetic information does not establish a cause of action. *See* 42 U.S.C.A. § 2000ff-7. Finally, GINA prohibits retaliation against anyone who has opposed any act or practice made unlawful under the act or because such individual made a charge, testified, assisted, or participated in any manner in an investigation or proceeding under the statute. *See* 42 U.S.C.A. § 2000ff-6.

The near-unanimous support for GINA in Congress is noteworthy in an age of bitter disagreements over the federal government's role in regulating the workplace. It is possible that this support is explained by the near-total absence of evidence of genetic discrimination, which suggests that few constituencies utilized genetic information for employment or insurance purposes. But that explanation does not account for the long delay in passage of the Act, and, more generally, the strong resistance in recent years (in Congress and elsewhere) to enhancing federal employee protections. Why, do you suppose, is there now consensus on the need for a law prohibiting in most circumstances insurers and employers from collecting and using genetic information? Is it for the reasons discussed above, or is there something more intuitive going on?

Of course, strong support for such a prohibition may not translate into successful claims against employers alleged to have utilized genetic information improperly. Indeed, we will not know for years how GINA-based claims will fair in litigation.

For an overview of the implications of GINA as well as some commentary critical of GINA's scope or other limitations, *see generally* Pauline T. Kim, *Regulating the Use of Genetic Information: Perspectives from the U.S. Experience*, 31 COMP. LAB. L. & POL'Y J. 693 (2010); Jessica L. Roberts, *Preempting Discrimination: Lessons from the Genetic Information Nondiscrimination Act*, 63 VAND. L. REV. 439 (2010); Jessica L. Roberts, *Antisubordination and the Genetic Information Nondiscrimination Act*, NOTRE DAME L. REV. (forthcoming 2010), *available at* http://papers.ssrn.com/sol3/papers.cfm ?abstract_id=1597695.

b. State Law

No state has a statutory scheme that generally governs privacy in the workplace, but some states have enacted laws that provide specific protections for workers. These laws and the protections they provide vary greatly. As stated above, prior to the passage of GINA, most states had restricted employers from testing employees or prospective employees for genetic traits. Many states also have their own statutory protections for communications and surveillance, some of which extend beyond federal protections. *See, e.g.*, CONN. GEN. STAT. § 31-48B (2010) (prohibiting use of certain electronic surveillance devices). Some states also impose restrictions on other medical inquiries such as HIV testing, *see, e.g.*, WIS. STAT. § 103.15(2) (2010), and commitments to medical treatment facilities, *see, e.g.*, MASS. GEN. LAWS. ch. 151B § 4(9) (2006 and Supp. 2010), or existing or past medical or psychological conditions, *see, e.g.*, MD. CODE ANN. LAB. & EMPL. § 3-701 (2010). And a number of states have enacted statutes either limiting drug testing or regulating the means by which drug testing is implemented. *See, e.g.*, CONN. GEN. STAT. § 31-51x (requiring a safety-related interest in drug testing); MINN. STAT. § 181.951(4) (2009) (same). Some state statutes also prohibit employers from asking job applicants questions or making inquiries concerning certain other private matters. *See, e.g.*, NEB. REV. STAT. § 81-1932 (2010) (prohibiting inquiries into sexual practices or marital relationships); OR. REV. STAT. § 659A.885 (2010) (as amended by 2010 Or. L. 1st Sp. Sess. § 102 (S.B. 1045)) (prohibiting inquiries into and use of employees' credit history for employment purposes except in narrowly defined circumstances). Finally, state antidiscrimination laws serve the same intrusion-deterrence function as federal antidiscrimination statutes, and thus protect workers against additional forms of discrimination that implicate private matters, such as discrimination based on sexual orientation, political affiliation, marital status, or physical or psychological conditions not covered under the ADA.

4. Contractual Privacy Protections

Rulon-Miller v. International Business Machines Corp.
208 Cal. Rptr. 524 (Ct. App. 1985)

RUSHING, Associate Justice.

International Business Machines (IBM) appeals from the judgment entered against it after a jury awarded $100,000 compensatory and $200,000 punitive damages to respondent (Virginia Rulon-Miller) on claims of wrongful discharge and intentional infliction of emotional distress. Rulon-Miller was a low-level marketing manager at IBM in its office products division in San Francisco. Her termination as a marketing manager at IBM came about as a result of an accusation made by her immediate supervisor, defendant Callahan, of a romantic relationship with the manager of a rival office products firm, QYX.

Factual Background

IBM is an international manufacturer of computers, office equipment and tele-communications systems. As well, it offers broad general services in the data processing field. . . . IBM is an employer traditionally thought to provide great security to its employees as well as an environment of openness and dignity. The company is organized into divisions, and each division is, to an extent, independent of others. The company prides itself on providing career opportunities to its employees, and respondent represents a good example of this. [Rulon-Miller started in 1967 as a receptionist in the Philadelphia Data Center, and was promoted through several levels and worked in several departments and locations before enrolling at the IBM sales school in Dallas.] After graduation, she was assigned to San Francisco.

Her territory was the financial district. She was given a performance plan by her management which set forth the company's expectations of her. She was from time to time thereafter graded against that plan on a scale of one through five with a grade of one being the highest. After her first year on the job, she was given a rating of one and was felt by her manager to be a person who rated at the top of IBM's scale.

A little over a year after she began in San Francisco, IBM reorganized its office products division into two separate functions. . . . Respondent was assigned to office systems; again she was given ratings of one and while there received a series of con-gratulatory letters from her superiors and was promoted to marketing representative. She was one of the most successful sales persons in the office and received a number of prizes and awards for her sales efforts. IBM's system of rewarding salespersons has a formalistic aspect about it that allows for subtle distinctions to be made while putting great emphasis on performance; respondent exercised that reward system to its fullest. She was a very successful seller of typewriters and other office equipment.

She was then put into a program called "Accelerated Career Development Program" which was a way of rewarding certain persons who were seen by their super-iors as having management potential. IBM's prediction of her future came true and in 1978 she was named a marketing manager in the office products branch.

IBM knew about respondent's relationship with Matt Blum well before her appointment as a manager. Respondent met Blum in 1976 when he was an account manager for IBM. That they were dating was widely known within the organization. In 1977 Blum left IBM to join QYX, an IBM competitor, and was transferred to Philadelphia. When Blum returned to San Francisco in the summer of 1978, IBM personnel were aware that he and respondent began dating again. This seemed to present no problems to respondent's superiors, as Callahan confirmed when she was promoted to manager. Respondent testified: "Somewhat in passing, Phil said: I heard the other day you were dating Matt Blum, and I said: Oh. And he said, I don't have any problem with that. You're my number one pick. I just want to assure you that you are my selection." The relationship with Blum was also known to

Regional Manager Gary Nelson who agreed with Callahan. Neither Callahan nor Nelson raised any issue of conflict of interest because of the Blum relationship.

Respondent flourished in her management position, and the company, apparently grateful for her efforts, gave her a $4,000 merit raise in 1979 and told her that she was doing a good job. A week later, [Callahan] left a message that he wanted to see her.

When she walked into Callahan's office he confronted her with the question of whether she was *dating* Matt Blum. She wondered at the relevance of the inquiry and he said the dating constituted a "conflict of interest," and told her to stop dating Blum or lose her job and said she had a "couple of days to a week" to think about it.[2]

The next day Callahan called her in again, told her "he had made up her mind for her," and when she protested, dismissed her.[3] IBM and Callahan claim that he merely "transferred" respondent to another division.

Discussion . . .

The test for the court here is substantial evidence and without any question there was substantial evidence to support the jury verdict that the respondent was wrongfully discharged rather than routinely reassigned.

---

2. Because of the importance of this testimony, we set it out verbatim. Respondent testified: "I walked into Phil's office and he asked me to sit down and he said: Are you dating Matt Blum?

"And I said, What? I was kind of surprised he would ask me and I said: Well, what difference does it make if I'm dating Matt Blum? . . .

"And he said, well, something to the effect: I think we have a conflict of interest, or the appearance of a conflict of interest here.

"And I said: Well, gee, Phil, you've, you've pointed out to me that there are no problems in the office because I am dating Matt Blum, and I don't really understand why that would have any, you know, pertinency to my job. You said I am doing an okay job. I just got a raise.

"And he said: Well, I think we have a conflict of interest. . . .

"He said: No and he said: I'll tell you what. He said: I will give you a couple of days to a week. Think this whole thing over.

"I said: Think what over?

"And he said: You either stop dating Matt Blum or I'm going to take you out of your management job.

"And I was just kind of overwhelmed."

3. Respondent stated the next day she was again summoned to his office where Callahan sat ominously behind a desk cleared of any paperwork, an unusual scenario for any IBM manager.

She further testified: "I walked into Phil's office, and he asked me to shut the door, and he said he was removing me from management effectively immediately. And I said: What?

"And he repeated it. And I was taken aback, I was a little startled, and I think I said: Well, gee, I thought I had a couple of days to a week to think over the situation that we discussed yesterday.

"And he said: I'm making the decision for you.

"And I said: Phil, you've told me that I'm doing a good job. You told me that we are not losing anybody to QYX because I am dating Matt Blum, that we are not losing any equipment to QYX. I just don't understand what bearing dating has to do with my job.

"And he said: We have a conflict of interest. . . .

"I said: Well, what kind of a job would it be?

"And he said: Well, I don't have it, but it will be non-management. You won't be a manager again. "Pardon me? . . .

"And I think I was getting very upset so I think I said something because of that respect for the individual tenet of IBM's that I really believed in I didn't think that he was following what I thought IBM really did believe in. And he just said: You know, you are removed from management effective immediately.

"And I said: I think you are dismissing me.

"And he said: If you feel that way, give me your I.D. card and your key to the office. [¶] I want you to leave the premises immediately.

"And I was just about to burst into tears, and I didn't cry at work, so I basically fled his office.

"I felt he dismissed me."

The initial discussion between Callahan and respondent of her relationship with Blum is important. We must accept the version of the facts most favorable to the respondent herein. When Callahan questioned her relationship with Blum, respondent invoked her right to privacy in her personal life relying on existing IBM policies. A threshold inquiry is thus presented whether respondent could reasonably rely on those policies for job protection. Any conflicting action by the company would be wrongful in that it would constitute a violation of her contract rights. [*See Pugh v. See's Candies, Inc.*, reproduced at page 91.]

Under the common law rule codified in Labor Code section 2922, an employment contract of indefinite duration is, in general, terminable at "the will" of either party. This common law rule has been considerably altered by the recognition of the Supreme Court of California that implicit in any such relationship or contract is an underlying principle that requires the parties to deal openly and fairly with one another. *Seaman's Direct Buying Service, Inc. v. Standard Oil Co.* (Cal. 1984) 686 P.2d 1158. This general requirement of fairness has been identified as the covenant of good faith and fair dealing. *Tameny v. Atlantic Richfield Co.* (Cal. 1980) 610 P.2d 1330. The covenant of good faith and fair dealing embraces a number of rights, obligations, and considerations implicit in contractual relations and certain other relationships. At least two of those considerations are relevant herein. The duty of fair dealing by an employer is, simply stated, a requirement that like cases be treated alike. Implied in this, of course, is that the company, if it has rules and regulations, apply those rules and regulations to its employees as well as affording its employees their protection.

As can be seen from an analysis of other cases, this is not in any substantial way a variation from general contract law in California, for if an employee has the right in an employment contract (as distinct from an implied covenant), the courts have routinely given her the benefit of that contract. Thus, the fair dealing portion of the covenant of good faith and fair dealing is at least the right of an employee to the benefit of rules and regulations adopted for his or her protection.

In this case, there is a close question of whether those rules or regulations permit IBM to inquire into the purely personal life of the employee. If so, an attendant question is whether such a policy was applied consistently, particularly as between men and women. The distinction is important because the right of privacy, a constitutional right in California could be implicated by the IBM inquiry. Much of the testimony below concerned what those policies were. The evidence was conflicting on the meaning of certain IBM policies. We observe ambiguity in the application but not in the intent. The "Watson Memo" (so called because it was signed by a former chairman of IBM) provided as follows:

> TO ALL IBM MANAGERS:
> The line that separates an individual's on-the-job business life from his other life as a private citizen is at times well-defined and at other times indistinct. But the line does exist, and you and I, as managers in IBM, must be able to recognize that line.
> I have seen instances where managers took disciplinary measures against employees for actions or conduct that are not rightfully the company's concern. These managers usually justified their decisions by citing their personal code of ethics and morals or by quoting some fragment of company policy that seemed to support their position. Both arguments proved unjust on close examination. What we need, in every case, is balanced judgment which weighs the needs of the business and the rights of the individual.

Our primary objective as IBM managers is to further the business of this company by leading our people properly and measuring quantity and quality of work and effectiveness on the job against clearly set standards of responsibility and compensation. This is performance — and performance is, in the final analysis, the one thing that the company can insist on from everyone.

We have concern with an employee's off-the-job behavior only when it reduces his ability to perform regular job assignments, interferes with the job performance of other employees, or if his outside behavior affects the reputation of the company in a major way. When on-the-job performance is acceptable, I can think of few situations in which outside activities could result in disciplinary action or dismissal.

When such situations do come to your attention, you should seek the advice and counsel of the next appropriate level of management and the personnel department in determining what action — if any — is called for. Action should be taken only when a legitimate interest of the company is injured or jeopardized. Furthermore the damage must be clear beyond reasonable doubt and not based on hasty decisions about what one person might think is good for the company.

IBM's first basic belief is respect for the individual, and the essence of this belief is a strict regard for his right to personal privacy. This idea should never be compromised easily or quickly.

/s/ Tom Watson, Jr.

It is clear that this company policy insures to the employee both the right of privacy and the right to hold a job even though "off-the-job behavior" might not be approved of by the employee's manager.

IBM had adopted policies governing employee conduct. Some of those policies were collected in a document known as the "Performance and Recognition" (PAR) Manual. IBM relies on the following portion of the PAR Manual:

A conflict of interest can arise when an employee is involved in activity for personal gain, which for any reason is in conflict with IBM's business interests. Generally speaking, 'moonlighting' is defined as working at some activity for personal gain outside of your IBM job. If you do perform outside work, you have a special responsibility to avoid any conflict with IBM's business interests.

Obviously, you cannot solicit or perform in competition with IBM product or service offerings. Outside work cannot be performed on IBM time, including "personal" time off. You cannot use IBM equipment, materials, resources, or 'inside' information for outside work. Nor should you solicit business or clients or perform outside work on IBM premises.

Employees must be free of any significant investment or association of their own or of their immediate family's [sic], in competitors or suppliers, which might interfere or be thought to interfere with the independent exercise of their judgment in the best interests of IBM.

This policy of IBM is entitled "Gifts" and appears to be directed at "moonlighting" and soliciting outside business or clients on IBM premises. It prohibits "significant investment" in competitors or suppliers of IBM. It also prohibits "association" with such persons "which might interfere or be thought to interfere with the independent exercise of their judgment in the best interests of IBM."

Callahan based his action against respondent on a "conflict of interest." But the record shows that IBM did not interpret this policy to prohibit a romantic relationship. Callahan admitted that there was no company rule or policy requiring an employee to terminate friendships with fellow employees who leave and join competitors. Gary Nelson, Callahan's superior, also confirmed that IBM had no policy against employees socializing with competitors.

This issue was hotly contested with respondent claiming that the "conflict of interest" claim was a pretext for her unjust termination. Whether it was presented a fact question for the jury.

Do the policies reflected in this record give IBM a right to terminate an employee for a conflict of interest? The answer must be yes, but whether respondent's conduct constituted such was for the jury. We observe that while respondent was successful, her primary job did not give her access to sensitive information which could have been useful to competitors. She was, after all, a seller of typewriters and office equipment. Respondent's brief makes much of the concession by IBM that there was no evidence whatever that respondent had given any information or help to IBM's competitor QYX. It really is no concession at all; she did not have the information or help to give. Even so, the question is one of substantial evidence. The evidence is abundant that there was no conflict of interest by respondent.

It does seem clear that an overall policy established by IBM chairman Watson was one of no company interest in the outside activities of an employee so long as the activities did not interfere with the work of the employee. Moreover, in the last analysis, it may be simply a question for the jury to decide whether, in the application of these policies, the right was conferred on IBM to inquire into the personal or romantic relationships its managers had with others. This is an important question because IBM, in attempting to reargue the facts to us, casts this argument in other terms, namely: that it had a right to inquire even if there was no evidence that such a relationship interfered with the discharge of the employee's duties *because* it had the effect of diminishing the morale of the employees answering to the manager. This is the "Caesar's wife" argument; it is merely a recast of the principal argument and asks the same question in different terms.[5] The same answer holds in both cases: there being no evidence to support the more direct argument, there is no evidence to support the indirect argument.

Moreover, the record shows that the evidence of rumor was not a basis for any decline in the morale of the employees reporting to respondent. Employees Mary Hrize and Wayne Fyvie, who reported to respondent's manager that she was seen at a tea dance at the Hyatt Regency with Matt Blum and also that she was not living at her residence in Marin, did not believe that those rumors in any way impaired her abilities as a manager. In the initial confrontation between respondent and her superior the assertion of the right to be free of inquiries concerning her personal life was based on substantive direct contract rights she had flowing to her from IBM policies. Further, there is no doubt that the jury could have so found and on this record we must assume that they did so find.

[The court went on to find that the jury instructions were proper and that the evidence supports the jury verdict in favor of the plaintiff.] . . .

---

5. What we mean by that is that if you charge that an employee is passing confidential information to a competitor, the question remains whether the charge is true on the evidence available to the person deciding the issue, in this case, the respondent's managers at IBM. If you recast this argument in the form of the "Caesar's wife" argument attempted by IBM, it will be seen that exactly the same question arises, namely, "is it true?" Indeed, the import of the argument is that the rumor, or an unfounded allegation, could serve as a basis for the termination of the employee.

NOTES

1. *Contractual Privacy Protection.* As with many other terms and conditions of employment, employees may bargain for specific privacy rights. These may come in the form of particular guarantees not to intrude or monitor, accommodations that may implicate privacy interests, or limits on the scope of employment or employer oversight authority that shield certain employee activities or spaces from employer scrutiny. Yet such express terms are rare in individual employment contracts for various reasons, among them limited bargaining power and the failure to foresee privacy-related "problems" at the outset of the relationship. In addition, there is an inevitable tension in a prospective employee demanding greater than normal privacy — the very demand might reveal information the employee would prefer to keep private. Moreover, some of the most common employer requirements that implicate privacy — various forms of testing, disclosures, and intrusive questioning — occur at the application stage, before an employee has a meaningful ability to bargain. And, ironically, some workers who have the incentives and are in a position to bargain for significant freedom from firm intrusions may end up attaining independent contractor rather than employee status. Indeed, as will be discussed below, express terms generally reduce rather than expand privacy protections: It is far more common for employers to demand that employees consent to various kinds of intrusions and monitoring as a condition of employment and for employees to agree to such conditions to secure the job.

Thus, contract-based protections for employees typically come in several other forms. The first is collective bargaining agreements. One high-profile example of addressing privacy interests through collective bargaining involves the limitations on the use of on steroid testing in Major League Baseball: In response to mounting public pressure, the players' union agreed to a strict testing regimen and stiff penalties after years of protecting the players' privacy interest in avoiding testing. *See, e.g.,* Jack Curry, *Baseball Backs Stiffer Penalties for Steroid Use,* N.Y. TIMES (Nov. 16, 2005). These kinds of terms and related procedures are often addressed in the bargaining process and in labor arbitration thereafter. *See generally* Ariana R. Levinson, *Industrial Justice: Privacy Protection for the Employed*: 18 CORNELL J. L. & PUB. POL'Y 609 (2009).

A second kind of contractual protection, albeit a less direct one, flows from the just-cause provisions contained in some employment contracts. Although a just-cause termination provision would not protect against employer intrusions directly, it would provide a remedy for unjustified adverse employment actions resulting from such intrusions. An employer could not, for instance, terminate an employee simply because it does not like the employee's off-site associations or activities. On the other hand, just-cause provisions may create an incentive for an employer to monitor its employees' activities more closely since, to take adverse actions against them, the employer would need evidence showing employee misconduct or some other legitimate business reason for so acting.

A further kind of contractual privacy protection is implied-in-fact, as recognized in *Rulon-Miller*. Indeed, the *Rulon-Miller* court finds a limited but nevertheless enforceable privacy right from various representations of IBM executives and other circumstances. Recall the discussion of implied-in-fact contract terms in Chapter 2. Is the analysis in *Rulon-Miller* consistent with the courts' approach to implied-in-fact terms in other contexts? In what way might the recognition of implied-in-fact right to privacy in the workplace require a different analysis? Do you agree with the court's reasoning and conclusion in this case?

2. *Tort versus Contract.* Would the plaintiff in *Rulon-Miller* have been able to succeed under the theory of intrusion upon seclusion? More specifically, would the circumstances that gave rise to an implied-in-fact right to privacy in this case generate the reasonable expectation of privacy in an area of "solitude or seclusion" necessary to tort liability? Might tort and contract theories differ in other ways? Might they, for example, give rise to different remedies? In a portion of the opinion not reproduced, the court went on to uphold a jury finding of intentional infliction of emotional distress. After it did so, it also affirmed the jury's award of punitive damages.

3. *Employer Incentives and Employer Policies and Practices After* Rulon-Miller. This case was a victory for the particular employee plaintiff, but the long-term effects may be far less favorable for employees generally. If you were counsel for an employer in the wake of this case, what would you advise your client to do to avoid liability? Would your advice be similar to the advice you would give to avoid the types of implied-in-fact contract claims discussed in Chapter 2 at page 95? What other practices would you advocate your clients adopt to avoid liability for implied-in-fact privacy claims? If employers were to follow such advice, would employees be better off? Do you see parallels between such potential unintended consequences and those that might flow from the Supreme Court's discussion of the reasonable expectation of privacy issue in *Quon*?

B. "BALANCING" EMPLOYEE AND EMPLOYER INTERESTS

If there is a potential source of protection — constitutional, statutory, tort, or contractual — available, and the employer has intruded upon or compromised an employee's privacy interest, the analysis usually focuses next on whether the employer's alleged intrusion and resulting actions were justified. Regardless of the theory, courts often describe this inquiry as one of "balancing" the employer's interests with the privacy interests of the employee. How is this concept recognized or applied in the cases discussed above? Now, consider how the courts in the following two cases engage in this inquiry and the similarities in their approach despite the disparate factual and legal underpinnings of the privacy claims at issue.

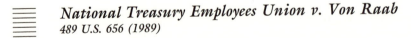

National Treasury Employees Union v. Von Raab
489 U.S. 656 (1989)

KENNEDY, J., with REHNQUIST, C.J. and WHITE, BLACKMUN, and O'CONNOR, JJ. joined.

We granted certiorari to decide whether it violates the Fourth Amendment for the United States Customs Service to require a urinalysis test from employees who seek transfer or promotion to certain positions.

I

A

The United States Customs Service, a bureau of the Department of the Treasury, is the federal agency responsible for processing persons, carriers, cargo, and mail into the United States, collecting revenue from imports, and enforcing customs and related laws. An important responsibility of the Service is the interdiction and seizure of contraband, including illegal drugs. In 1987 alone, Customs agents seized drugs with a retail value of nearly $9 billion. In the routine discharge of their duties, many Customs employees have direct contact with those who traffic in drugs for profit. Drug import operations, often directed by sophisticated criminal syndicates, may be effected by violence or its threat. As a necessary response, many Customs operatives carry and use firearms in connection with their official duties.

In December 1985, respondent, the Commissioner of Customs, established a Drug Screening Task Force to explore the possibility of implementing a drug-screening program within the Service. After extensive research and consultation with experts in the field, the task force concluded that "drug screening through urinalysis is technologically reliable, valid and accurate." Citing this conclusion, the Commissioner announced his intention to require drug tests of employees who applied for, or occupied, certain positions within the Service. The Commissioner stated his belief that "Customs is largely drug-free," but noted also that "unfortunately no segment of society is immune from the threat of illegal drug use." Drug interdiction has become the agency's primary enforcement mission, and the Commissioner stressed that "there is no room in the Customs Service for those who break the laws prohibiting the possession and use of illegal drugs."

In May 1986, the Commissioner announced the implementation of the drug-testing program. Drug tests were made a condition of placement or employment for positions that meet one or more of three criteria. The first is direct involvement in drug interdiction or enforcement of related laws, an activity the Commissioner deemed fraught with obvious dangers to the mission of the agency and the lives of Customs agents. The second criterion is a requirement that the incumbent carry firearms, as the Commissioner concluded that "[p]ublic safety demands that employees who carry deadly arms and are prepared to make instant life or death decisions be drug free." The third criterion is a requirement for the incumbent to handle "classified" material, which the Commissioner determined might fall into the hands of smugglers if accessible to employees who, by reason of their own illegal drug use, are susceptible to bribery or blackmail.

After an employee qualifies for a position covered by the Customs testing program, the Service advises him by letter that his final selection is contingent upon successful completion of drug screening. An independent contractor contacts the employee to fix the time and place for collecting the sample. On reporting for the test, the employee must produce photographic identification and remove any outer garments, such as a coat or a jacket, and personal belongings. The employee may produce the sample behind a partition, or in the privacy of a bathroom stall if he so chooses. To ensure against adulteration of the specimen, or substitution of a sample from another person, a monitor of the same sex as the employee remains close at hand to listen for the normal sounds of urination. Dye is added to the toilet water to prevent the employee from using the water to adulterate the sample.

Upon receiving the specimen, the monitor inspects it to ensure its proper temperature and color, places a tamper-proof custody seal over the container, and affixes an identification label indicating the date and the individual's specimen number. The employee signs a chain-of-custody form, which is initialed by the monitor, and the urine sample is placed in a plastic bag, sealed, and submitted to a laboratory.

The laboratory tests the sample for the presence of marijuana, cocaine, opiates, amphetamines, and phencyclidine. Two tests are used. An initial screening test uses the enzyme-multiplied-immunoassay technique (EMIT). Any specimen that is identified as positive on this initial test must then be confirmed using gas chromatography/mass spectrometry (GC/MS). Confirmed positive results are reported to a "Medical Review Officer," "[a] licensed physician . . . who has knowledge of substance abuse disorders and has appropriate medical training to interpret and evaluate an individual's positive test result together with his or her medical history and any other relevant biomedical information." HHS Reg. §1.2, 53 Fed. Reg. 11980 (1988); HHS Reg. §2.4(g), 53 Fed. Reg. at 11983. After verifying the positive result, the Medical Review Officer transmits it to the agency.

Customs employees who test positive for drugs and who can offer no satisfactory explanation are subject to dismissal from the Service. Test results may not, however, be turned over to any other agency, including criminal prosecutors, without the employee's written consent.

B

[A union of federal employees and a union official filed suit on behalf of current Customs Service employees who sought covered positions claiming that the drug-testing program violated, inter alia, the Fourth Amendment. The District Court agreed and enjoined the drug-testing program. The Fifth Circuit, although holding that requiring an employee to produce a urine sample for chemical testing is a Fourth Amendment search, found the searches at issue to be reasonable under that Amendment. The Supreme Court first affirmed the Fifth Circuit to the extent it upheld the testing of employees directly involved in drug interdiction or required to carry firearms. However, it vacated the judgment to the extent it upheld the testing of applicants for positions requiring the incumbent to handle classified materials, and it remanded for further proceedings.]

II

In *Skinner v. Railway Labor Executives' Assn.*, 489 U.S. 602, decided today, we held that federal regulations requiring employees of private railroads to produce urine samples for chemical testing implicate the Fourth Amendment, as those tests invade reasonable expectations of privacy. Our earlier cases have settled that the Fourth Amendment protects individuals from unreasonable searches conducted by the Government, even when the Government acts as an employer, *O'Connor v. Ortega*, and, in view of our holding in *Railway Labor Executives* that urine tests are searches, it follows that the Customs Service's drug-testing program must meet the reasonableness requirement of the Fourth Amendment.

While we have often emphasized, and reiterate today, that a search must be supported, as a general matter, by a warrant issued upon probable cause, our decision in *Railway Labor Executives* reaffirms the longstanding principle that neither a warrant nor probable cause, nor, indeed, any measure of individualized suspicion, is an indispensable component of reasonableness in every circumstance. As we note in *Railway Labor Executives*, our cases establish that where a Fourth Amendment intrusion serves special governmental needs, beyond the normal need for law enforcement, it is necessary to balance the individual's privacy expectations against the Government's interests to determine whether it is impractical to require a warrant or some level of individualized suspicion in the particular context.

It is clear that the Customs Service's drug-testing program is not designed to serve the ordinary needs of law enforcement. Test results may not be used in a criminal prosecution of the employee without the employee's consent. The purposes of the program are to deter drug use among those eligible for promotion to sensitive positions within the Service and to prevent the promotion of drug users to those positions. These substantial interests, no less than the Government's concern for safe rail transportation at issue in *Railway Labor Executives*, present a special need that may justify departure from the ordinary warrant and probable-cause requirements. . . .

B

Even where it is reasonable to dispense with the warrant requirement in the particular circumstances, a search ordinarily must be based on probable cause. Our cases teach, however, that the probable-cause standard " 'is peculiarly related to criminal investigations.' " In particular, the traditional probable-cause standard may be unhelpful in analyzing the reasonableness of routine administrative functions, especially where the Government seeks to *prevent* the development of hazardous conditions or to detect violations that rarely generate articulable grounds for searching any particular place or person. Our precedents have settled that, in certain limited circumstances, the Government's need to discover such latent or hidden conditions, or to prevent their development, is sufficiently compelling to justify the intrusion on privacy entailed by conducting such searches without any measure of individualized suspicion. We think the Government's need to conduct the suspicionless searches required by the Customs program outweighs the privacy interests of employees engaged directly in drug interdiction, and of those who otherwise are required to carry firearms.

The Customs Service is our Nation's first line of defense against one of the greatest problems affecting the health and welfare of our population. . . .

Many of the Service's employees are often exposed to this criminal element and to the controlled substances it seeks to smuggle into the country. The physical safety of these employees may be threatened, and many may be tempted not only by bribes from the traffickers with whom they deal, but also by their own access to vast sources of valuable contraband seized and controlled by the Service. The Commissioner indicated below that "Customs [o]fficers have been shot, stabbed, run over, dragged by automobiles, and assaulted with blunt objects while performing their duties." At least nine officers have died in the line of duty since 1974. He also noted that Customs officers have been the targets of bribery by drug smugglers on numerous occasions, and several have been removed from the Service for accepting bribes and for other integrity violations.

It is readily apparent that the Government has a compelling interest in ensuring that front-line interdiction personnel are physically fit, and have unimpeachable integrity and judgment. Indeed, the Government's interest here is at least as important as its interest in searching travelers entering the country. . . . This national interest in self-protection could be irreparably damaged if those charged with safeguarding it were, because of their own drug use, unsympathetic to their mission of interdicting narcotics. A drug user's indifference to the Service's basic mission or, even worse, his active complicity with the malefactors, can facilitate importation of sizable drug shipments or block apprehension of dangerous criminals. The public interest demands effective measures to bar drug users from positions directly involving the interdiction of illegal drugs.

The public interest likewise demands effective measures to prevent the promotion of drug users to positions that require the incumbent to carry a firearm, even if the incumbent is not engaged directly in the interdiction of drugs. Customs employees who may use deadly force plainly "discharge duties fraught with such risks of injury to others that even a momentary lapse of attention can have disastrous consequences." We agree with the Government that the public should not bear the risk that employees who may suffer from impaired perception and judgment will be promoted to positions where they may need to employ deadly force. Indeed, ensuring against the creation of this dangerous risk will itself further Fourth Amendment values, as the use of deadly force may violate the Fourth Amendment in certain circumstances.

Against these valid public interests we must weigh the interference with individual liberty that results from requiring these classes of employees to undergo a urine test. The interference with individual privacy that results from the collection of a urine sample for subsequent chemical analysis could be substantial in some circumstances. We have recognized, however, that the "operational realities of the workplace" may render entirely reasonable certain work-related intrusions by supervisors and co-workers that might be viewed as unreasonable in other contexts. See *O'Connor v. Ortega.* While these operational realities will rarely affect an employee's expectations of privacy with respect to searches of his person, or of personal effects that the employee may bring to the workplace, it is plain that certain forms of public employment may diminish privacy expectations even with respect to such personal searches. Employees of the United States Mint, for example, should expect to be subject to certain routine personal searches when they leave the workplace every day. Similarly, those who join our military or intelligence services may not only be required to give what in other contexts might be viewed as extraordinary assurances of trustworthiness and probity, but also may expect intrusive inquiries into their physical fitness for those special positions.

We think Customs employees who are directly involved in the interdiction of illegal drugs or who are required to carry firearms in the line of duty likewise have a diminished expectation of privacy in respect to the intrusions occasioned by a urine test. Unlike most private citizens or government employees in general, employees involved in drug interdiction reasonably should expect effective inquiry into their fitness and probity. Much the same is true of employees who are required to carry firearms. Because successful performance of their duties depends uniquely on their judgment and dexterity, these employees cannot reasonably expect to keep from the Service personal information that bears directly on their fitness. While reasonable tests designed to elicit this information doubtless infringe some privacy expectations, we do not believe these expectations outweigh the Government's compelling interests in safety and in the integrity of our borders.[2]

Without disparaging the importance of the governmental interests that support the suspicionless searches of these employees, petitioners nevertheless contend that the Service's drug-testing program is unreasonable in two particulars. First, petitioners argue that the program is unjustified because it is not based on a belief that testing will reveal any drug use by covered employees. In pressing this argument, petitioners point out that the Service's testing scheme was not implemented in response to any perceived drug problem among Customs employees, and that the program actually has not led to the discovery of a significant number of drug users. Counsel for petitioners informed us at oral argument that no more than 5 employees out of 3,600 have tested positive for drugs. Second, petitioners contend that the Service's scheme is not a "sufficiently productive mechanism to justify [its] intrusion upon Fourth Amendment interests" because illegal drug users can avoid detection with ease by temporary abstinence or by surreptitious adulteration of their urine specimens. These contentions are unpersuasive.

Petitioners' first contention evinces an unduly narrow view of the context in which the Service's testing program was implemented. Petitioners do not dispute, nor can there be doubt, that drug abuse is one of the most serious problems confronting our society today. There is little reason to believe that American workplaces are immune from this pervasive social problem, as is amply illustrated by our decision in *Railway Labor Executives*. Detecting drug impairment on the part of employees can be a difficult task, especially where, as here, it is not feasible to subject employees and their work product to the kind of day-to-day scrutiny that is the norm in more traditional office environments. Indeed, the almost unique mission of the Service gives the Government a compelling interest in ensuring that many of these covered employees do not use drugs even off duty, for such use creates risks of bribery and blackmail against which the Government is entitled to guard. In light of the extraordinary safety and national security hazards that would attend the promotion of drug users to positions that require the carrying of firearms or the interdiction of controlled substances, the Service's policy of deterring drug users from seeking such promotions cannot be deemed unreasonable.

The mere circumstance that all but a few of the employees tested are entirely innocent of wrongdoing does not impugn the program's validity. The same is likely

---

2. The procedures prescribed by the Customs Service for the collection and analysis of the requisite samples do not carry the grave potential for "arbitrary and oppressive interference with the privacy and personal security of individuals," *United States v. Martinez-Fuerte*, 428 U.S. 543, 554 (1976), that the Fourth Amendment was designed to prevent. Indeed, these procedures significantly minimize the program's intrusion on privacy interests. Only employees who have been tentatively accepted for promotion or transfer to one of the three categories of covered positions are tested, and applicants know at the outset that a drug test is a requirement of those positions. Employees are also notified in advance of the scheduled sample collection, thus reducing to a minimum any "unsettling show of authority," *Delaware v. Prouse*, 440 U.S. 648, 657 (1979), that may be associated with unexpected intrusions on privacy. There is no direct observation of the act of urination, as the employee may provide a specimen in the privacy of a stall.

Further, urine samples may be examined only for the specified drugs. The use of samples to test for any other substances is prohibited. *See* HHS Reg. §2.1(c), 53 Fed. Reg. 11980 (1988). And, as the Court of Appeals noted, the combination of EMIT and GC/MS tests required by the Service is highly accurate, assuming proper storage, handling, and measurement techniques. Finally, an employee need not disclose personal medical information to the Government unless his test result is positive, and even then any such information is reported to a licensed physician. Taken together, these procedures significantly minimize the intrusiveness of the Service's drug-screening program.

to be true of householders who are required to submit to suspicionless housing code inspections, *see Camara v. Municipal Court of San Francisco*, 387 U.S. 523 (1967), and of motorists who are stopped at the checkpoints we approved in *United States v. Martinez-Fuerte*, 428 U.S. 543 (1976). The Service's program is designed to prevent the promotion of drug users to sensitive positions as much as it is designed to detect those employees who use drugs. Where, as here, the possible harm against which the Government seeks to guard is substantial, the need to prevent its occurrence furnishes an ample justification for reasonable searches calculated to advance the Government's goal.[3]

We think petitioners' second argument — that the Service's testing program is ineffective because employees may attempt to deceive the test by a brief abstention before the test date, or by adulterating their urine specimens — overstates the case. As the Court of Appeals noted, addicts may be unable to abstain even for a limited period of time, or may be unaware of the "fade-away effect" of certain drugs. More importantly, the avoidance techniques suggested by petitioners are fraught with uncertainty and risks for those employees who venture to attempt them. A particular employee's pattern of elimination for a given drug cannot be predicted with perfect accuracy, and, in any event, this information is not likely to be known or available to the employee. Petitioners' own expert indicated below that the time it takes for particular drugs to become undetectable in urine can vary widely depending on the individual, and may extend for as long as 22 days. Thus, contrary to petitioners' suggestion, no employee reasonably can expect to deceive the test by the simple expedient of abstaining after the test date is assigned. Nor can he expect attempts at adulteration to succeed, in view of the precautions taken by the sample collector to ensure the integrity of the sample. In all the circumstances, we are persuaded that the program bears a close and substantial relation to the Service's goal of deterring drug users from seeking promotion to sensitive positions.[4]

In sum, we believe the Government has demonstrated that its compelling interests in safeguarding our borders and the public safety outweigh the privacy

---

3. The point is well illustrated also by the Federal Government's practice of requiring the search of all passengers seeking to board commercial airliners, as well as the search of their carry-on luggage, without any basis for suspecting any particular passenger of an untoward motive. Applying our precedents dealing with administrative searches, *see, e.g.*, *Camara v. Municipal Court of San Francisco*, 387 U.S. 523 (1967), the lower courts that have considered the question have consistently concluded that such searches are reasonable under the Fourth Amendment. . . . It is true, as counsel for petitioners pointed out at oral argument, that these air piracy precautions were adopted in response to an observable national and international hijacking crisis. Yet we would not suppose that, if the validity of these searches be conceded, the Government would be precluded from conducting them absent a demonstration of danger as to any particular airport or airline. It is sufficient that the Government have a compelling interest in preventing an otherwise pervasive societal problem from spreading to the particular context.

Nor would we think, in view of the obvious deterrent purpose of these searches, that the validity of the Government's airport screening program necessarily turns on whether significant numbers of putative air pirates are actually discovered by the searches conducted under the program. . . . By far the overwhelming majority of those persons who have been searched, like Customs employees who have been tested under the Service's drug-screening scheme, have proved entirely innocent — only 42,000 firearms have been detected during the same period. When the Government's interest lies in deterring highly hazardous conduct, a low incidence of such conduct, far from impugning the validity of the scheme for implementing this interest, is more logically viewed as a hallmark of success.

4. Indeed, petitioners' objection is based on those features of the Service's program — the provision of advance notice and the failure of the sample collector to observe directly the act of urination — that contribute significantly to diminish the program's intrusion on privacy. Thus, under petitioners' view, "the testing program would be more likely to be constitutional if it were more pervasive and more invasive of privacy."

expectations of employees who seek to be promoted to positions that directly involve the interdiction of illegal drugs or that require the incumbent to carry a firearm. We hold that the testing of these employees is reasonable under the Fourth Amendment.

C

We are unable, on the present record, to assess the reasonableness of the Government's testing program insofar as it covers employees who are required "to handle classified material." We readily agree that the Government has a compelling interest in protecting truly sensitive information from those who, "under compulsion of circumstances or for other reasons, . . . might compromise [such] information." We also agree that employees who seek promotions to positions where they would handle sensitive information can be required to submit to a urine test under the Service's screening program, especially if the positions covered under this category require background investigations, medical examinations, or other intrusions that may be expected to diminish their expectations of privacy in respect of a urinalysis test. . . .

It is not clear, however, whether the category defined by the Service's testing directive encompasses only those Customs employees likely to gain access to sensitive information. Employees who are tested under the Service's scheme include those holding such diverse positions as "Accountant," "Accounting Technician," "Animal Caretaker," "Attorney (All)," "Baggage Clerk," "Co-op Student (All)," "Electric Equipment Repairer," "Mail Clerk/Assistant," and "Messenger." We assume these positions were selected for coverage under the Service's testing program by reason of the incumbent's access to "classified" information, as it is not clear that they would fall under either of the two categories we have already considered. Yet it is not evident that those occupying these positions are likely to gain access to sensitive information, and this apparent discrepancy raises in our minds the question whether the Service has defined this category of employees more broadly than is necessary to meet the purposes of the Commissioner's directive.

We cannot resolve this ambiguity on the basis of the record before us, and we think it is appropriate to remand the case. . . . [T]he Court of Appeals should examine the criteria used by the Service in determining what materials are classified and in deciding whom to test under this rubric. [T]he court should also consider pertinent information bearing upon the employees' privacy expectations, as well as the supervision to which these employees are already subject.

Justice SCALIA, with whom Justice STEVENS joins, dissenting.

The issue in this case is not whether Customs Service employees can constitutionally be denied promotion, or even dismissed, for a single instance of unlawful drug use, at home or at work. They assuredly can. The issue here is what steps can constitutionally be taken to *detect* such drug use. The Government asserts it can demand that employees perform "an excretory function traditionally shielded by great privacy," *Skinner v. Railway Labor Executives' Ass'n*, while "a monitor of the same sex . . . remains close at hand to listen for the normal sounds," and that the excretion thus produced be turned over to the Government for chemical analysis. The Court agrees that this constitutes a search for purposes of the Fourth Amendment — and I think it obvious that it is a type of search particularly destructive of privacy and offensive to personal dignity.

Until today this Court had upheld a bodily search separate from arrest and without individualized suspicion of wrongdoing only with respect to prison inmates, relying upon the uniquely dangerous nature of that environment. *See Bell v. Wolfish*, 441 U.S. 520, 558-60 (1979). Today, in *Skinner*, we allow a less intrusive bodily search of railroad employees involved in train accidents. I joined the Court's opinion there because the demonstrated frequency of drug and alcohol use by the targeted class of employees, and the demonstrated connection between such use and grave harm, rendered the search a reasonable means of protecting society. I decline to join the Court's opinion in the present case because neither frequency of use nor connection to harm is demonstrated or even likely. In my view the Customs Service rules are a kind of immolation of privacy and human dignity in symbolic opposition to drug use.

The Court's opinion in the present case . . . will be searched in vain for real evidence of a real problem that will be solved by urine testing of Customs Service employees. Instead, there are assurances that "[t]he Customs Service is our Nation's first line of defense against one of the greatest problems affecting the health and welfare of our population"; that "[m]any of the Service's employees are often exposed to [drug smugglers] and to the controlled substances [they seek] to smuggle into the country"; that "Customs officers have been the targets of bribery by drug smugglers on numerous occasions, and several have been removed from the Service for accepting bribes and other integrity violations"; that "the Government has a compelling interest in ensuring that front-line interdiction personnel are physically fit, and have unimpeachable integrity and judgment"; that the "national interest in self-protection could be irreparably damaged if those charged with safeguarding it were, because of their own drug use, unsympathetic to their mission of interdicting narcotics"; and that "the public should not bear the risk that employees who may suffer from impaired perception and judgment will be promoted to positions where they may need to employ deadly force." To paraphrase Churchill, all this contains much that is obviously true, and much that is relevant; unfortunately, what is obviously true is not relevant, and what is relevant is not obviously true. The only pertinent points, it seems to me, are supported by nothing but speculation, and not very plausible speculation at that. It is not apparent to me that a Customs Service employee who uses drugs is significantly more likely to be bribed by a drug smuggler, any more than a Customs Service employee who wears diamonds is significantly more likely to be bribed by a diamond smuggler—unless, perhaps, the addiction to drugs is so severe, and requires so much money to maintain, that it would be detectable even without benefit of a urine test. Nor is it apparent to me that Customs officers who use drugs will be appreciably less "sympathetic" to their drug-interdiction mission, any more than police officers who exceed the speed limit in their private cars are appreciably less sympathetic to their mission of enforcing the traffic laws. (The only difference is that the Customs officer's individual efforts, if they are irreplaceable, can theoretically affect the availability of his own drug supply—a prospect so remote as to be an absurd basis of motivation.) Nor, finally, is it apparent to me that urine tests will be even marginally more effective in preventing gun-carrying agents from risking "impaired perception and judgment" than is their current knowledge that, if impaired, they may be shot dead in unequal combat with unimpaired smugglers—unless, again, their addiction is so severe that no urine test is needed for detection.

What is absent in the Government's justifications—notably absent, revealingly absent, and as far as I am concerned dispositively absent—is the recitation of *even a single instance* in which any of the speculated horribles actually occurred: an instance, that is, in which the cause of bribe-taking, or of poor aim, or of unsympathetic law enforcement, or of compromise of classified information, was drug use. Although the Court points out that several employees have in the past been removed from the Service for accepting bribes and other integrity violations, and that at least nine officers have died in the line of duty since 1974, there is no indication whatever that these incidents were related to drug use by Service employees. Perhaps concrete evidence of the severity of a problem is unnecessary when it is so well known that courts can almost take judicial notice of it; but that is surely not the case here. The Commissioner of Customs himself has stated that he "believe[s] that Customs is largely drug-free," that "[t]he extent of illegal drug use by Customs employees was not the reason for establishing this program," and that he "hope[s] and expect[s] to receive reports of very few positive findings through drug screening." The test results have fulfilled those hopes and expectations. According to the Service's counsel, out of 3,600 employees tested, no more than 5 tested positive for drugs.

The Court's response to this lack of evidence is that "[t]here is little reason to believe that American workplaces are immune from [the] pervasive social problem" of drug abuse. Perhaps such a generalization would suffice if the workplace at issue could produce such catastrophic social harm that no risk whatever is tolerable — the secured areas of a nuclear power plant, for example, *see Rushton v. Nebraska Pub. Power District*, 844 F.2d 562 (CA8 1988). But if such a generalization suffices to justify demeaning bodily searches, without particularized suspicion, to guard against the bribing or blackmailing of a law enforcement agent, or the careless use of a firearm, then the Fourth Amendment has become frail protection indeed. In *Skinner*, *Bell*, *T.L.O.*, and *Martinez-Fuerte*, we took pains to establish the existence of special need for the search or seizure — a need based not upon the existence of a "pervasive social problem" combined with speculation as to the effect of that problem in the field at issue, but rather upon well-known or well-demonstrated evils *in that field*, with well-known or well-demonstrated consequences. . . .

[I]n extending approval of drug testing to that category consisting of employees who carry firearms, the Court exposes vast numbers of public employees to this needless indignity. Logically, of course, if those who carry guns can be treated in this fashion, so can all others whose work, if performed under the influence of drugs, may endanger others — automobile drivers, operators of other potentially dangerous equipment, construction workers, school crossing guards. A similarly broad scope attaches to the Court's approval of drug testing for those with access to "sensitive information." Since this category is not limited to Service employees with drug interdiction duties, nor to "sensitive information" specifically relating to drug traffic, today's holding apparently approves drug testing for all federal employees with security clearances — or, indeed, for all federal employees with valuable confidential information to impart. Since drug use is not a particular problem in the Customs Service, employees throughout the Government are no less likely to violate the public trust by taking bribes to feed their drug habit, or by yielding to blackmail. Moreover, there is no reason why this super-protection against harms arising from drug use must be limited to public employees; a law requiring similar testing of private citizens who use dangerous instruments such as guns or cars, or who have access to classified information, would also be constitutional.

There is only one apparent basis that sets the testing at issue here apart from all these other situations — but it is not a basis upon which the Court is willing to rely.

I do not believe for a minute that the driving force behind these drug-testing rules was any of the feeble justifications put forward by counsel here and accepted by the Court. The only plausible explanation, in my view, is what the Commissioner himself offered in the concluding sentence of his memorandum to Customs Service employees announcing the program: "Implementation of the drug screening program would set an important example in our country's struggle with this most serious threat to our national health and security." Or as respondent's brief to this Court asserted: "[I]f a law enforcement agency and its employees do not take the law seriously, neither will the public on which the agency's effectiveness depends." What better way to show that the Government is serious about its "war on drugs" than to subject its employees on the front line of that war to this invasion of their privacy and affront to their dignity? To be sure, there is only a slight chance that it will prevent some serious public harm resulting from Service employee drug use, but it will show to the world that the Service is "clean," and — most important of all — will demonstrate the determination of the Government to eliminate this scourge of our society! I think it obvious that this justification is unacceptable; that the impairment of individual liberties cannot be the means of making a point; that symbolism, even symbolism for so worthy a cause as the abolition of unlawful drugs, cannot validate an otherwise unreasonable search. . . .

Soroka v. Dayton Hudson Corp.
1 Cal. Rptr. 2d 77 (Ct. App. 1991)

REARDON, Associate Justice.

Appellants Sibi Soroka, Sue Urry and William d'Arcangelo [hereinafter, collectively "Soroka"] filed a class action challenging respondent Dayton Hudson Corporation's practice of requiring Target Store security officer applicants to pass a psychological screening. The trial court denied Soroka's motion for a preliminary injunction to prohibit the use of this screening pending the outcome of this litigation. . . . We reverse the trial court's order denying a preliminary injunction. . . .

I. FACTS

Respondent Dayton Hudson Corporation owns and operates Target Stores throughout California and the United States. Job applicants for store security officer (SSO) positions must, as a condition of employment, take a psychological test that Target calls the "Psychscreen." An SSO's main function is to observe, apprehend and arrest suspected shoplifters. An SSO is not armed, but carries handcuffs and may use force against a suspect in self-defense. Target views good judgment and emotional stability as important SSO job skills. It intends the Psychscreen to screen out SSO applicants who are emotionally unstable, who may put customers or employees in jeopardy, or who will not take direction and follow Target procedures.

The Psychscreen is a combination of the Minnesota Multiphasic Personality Inventory and the California Psychological Inventory. Both of these tests have been used to screen out emotionally unfit applicants for public safety positions such as police officers, correctional officers, pilots, air traffic controllers and nuclear power plant operators.[4] The test is composed of 704 true-false questions. At Target, the test administrator is told to instruct applicants to answer every question.

The test includes questions about an applicant's religious attitudes, such as: "[¶]67. I feel sure that there is only one true religion. . . . [¶]201. I have no patience with people who believe there is only one true religion. . . . [¶]477. My soul sometimes leaves my body. . . . [¶]483. A minister can cure disease by praying and putting his hand on your head. . . . [¶]486. Everything is turning out just like the prophets of the Bible said it would. . . . [¶]505. I go to church almost every week. [¶]506. I believe in the second coming of Christ. . . . [¶]516. I believe in a life hereafter. . . . [¶]578. I am very religious (more than most people). . . . [¶]580. I believe my sins are unpardonable. . . . [¶]606. I believe there is a God. . . . [¶]688. I believe there is a Devil and a Hell in afterlife."

The test includes questions that might reveal an applicant's sexual orientation, such as: "[¶]137. I wish I were not bothered by thoughts about sex. . . . [¶]290. I have never been in trouble because of my sex behavior. . . . [¶]339. I have been in trouble one or more times because of my sex behavior. . . . [¶]466. My sex life is satisfactory. . . . [¶]492. I am very strongly attracted by members of my own sex. . . . [¶]496. I have often wished I were a girl. (Or if you are a girl) I have never been sorry that I am a girl. . . . [¶]525. I have never indulged in any unusual sex practices. . . . [¶]558. I am worried about sex matters. . . . [¶]592. I like to talk about sex. . . . [¶]640. Many of my dreams are about sex matters."[5]

An SSO's completed test is scored by the consulting psychologist firm of Martin-McAllister. The firm interprets test responses and rates the applicant on five traits: emotional stability, interpersonal style, addiction potential, dependability and reliability, and socialization—i.e., a tendency to follow established rules. Martin-McAllister sends a form to Target rating the applicant on these five traits and recommending whether to hire the applicant. Hiring decisions are made on the basis of these recommendations, although the recommendations may be overridden. Target does not receive any responses to specific questions. It has never conducted a formal validation study of the Psychscreen, but before it implemented the test, Target tested 17 or 18 of its more successful SSO's.

Appellants Sibi Soroka, Susan Urry and William d'Arcangelo were applicants for SSO positions when they took the Psychscreen. [One was hired and two were rejected. Soroka filed a class action alleging discrimination on the basis of race, sex, religion and physical handicap under state discrimination laws, violation of the constitutional right to privacy, and various tort claims.]

In June 1990, Soroka moved for a preliminary injunction to prohibit Target from using the Psychscreen during the pendency of the action. A professional psychologist submitted a declaration opining that use of the test was unjustified and improper, resulting in faulty assessments to the detriment of job applicants. He concluded that its use violated basic professional standards and that it had not been demonstrated to be reliable or valid as an employment evaluation. For example, one of the two tests on which the Psychscreen was based was designed for use only in hospital or clinical settings. Soroka noted that two of Target's experts had previously opined that the

---

4. We view the duties and responsibilities of these public safety personnel to be substantially different from those of store security officers.

5. Soroka challenges many different types of questions on appeal. However, we do not find it necessary to consider questions other than those relating to religious beliefs and sexual orientation.

Minnesota Multiphasic Personality Inventory was virtually useless as a pre-employment screening device. It was also suggested that the Psychscreen resulted in a 61 percent rate of false positives—that is, that more than 6 in 10 qualified applicants for SSO positions were not hired.

Target's experts submitted declarations contesting these conclusions and favoring the use of the Psychscreen as an employment screening device. Some Target officials believed that use of this test has increased the quality and performance of its SSO's. However, others testified that they did not believe that there had been a problem with the reliability of SSO applicants before the Psychscreen was implemented. Target's vice president of loss prevention was unable to link changes in asset protection specifically to use of the Psychscreen. [One of Soroka's rebuttal experts] noted that some of the intrusive, non-job-related questions had been deleted from a revised form of the test because they were offensive, invasive and added little to the test's validity. . . .

The trial court [denied Soroka's motion for preliminary injunction]. The court found that Target demonstrated a legitimate interest in psychologically screening applicants for security positions to minimize the potential danger to its customers and others. It also found that Target's practice of administering this test to SSO applicants was not unreasonable.[6] . . .

II.   Preliminary Injunction . . .

When a trial court decides whether to issue a preliminary injunction, it must consider the likelihood that the plaintiffs will prevail on the merits at trial. . . .

Constitutional Claim

First, Soroka argues that he is likely to prevail at trial on his constitutional right to privacy claim. The parties dispute the standard to be applied to determine whether Target's violation of Soroka's privacy was justified. . . .

1.   The Right to Privacy

The California Constitution explicitly protects our right to privacy. *White v. Davis* 533 P.2d 222 (Cal. 1975); *see* CAL. CONST., art. I, § 1. Article I, section 1 provides: "All people are by nature free and independent and have inalienable rights. Among these are enjoying and defending life and liberty, acquiring, possessing, and protecting property, and pursuing and obtaining safety, happiness, and privacy." "By this provision, California accords privacy the constitutional status of an inalienable right, on a par with defending life and possessing property." [*Luck v. S. Pac. Transp. Co.* (Cal. App. 1990) 267 Cal. Rptr. 618.] Before this constitutional amendment was enacted, California courts had found a state and federal constitutional right to privacy even

---

6. The trial court did find that the test was being administered unnecessarily to some applicants and was thus unreasonable as to those persons. The court issued a partial preliminary injunction prohibiting Target from giving the test to those applicants whom Target had decided did not pass a pretest threshold in the hiring process.

though such a right was not enumerated in either constitution, and had consistently given a broad reading to the right to privacy. Thus, the elevation of the right to privacy to constitutional stature was intended to expand, not contract, privacy rights.

Target concedes that the Psychscreen constitutes an intrusion on the privacy rights of the applicants, although it characterizes this intrusion as a limited one. However, even the constitutional right to privacy does not prohibit *all* incursion into individual privacy. The parties agree that a violation of the right to privacy may be justified, but disagree about the standard to be used to make this determination. At trial, Target persuaded the court to apply a reasonableness standard because Soroka was an applicant, rather than a Target employee. On appeal, Soroka and the ACLU contend that Target must show more than reasonableness — that it must demonstrate a compelling interest — to justify its use of the Psychscreen.

2. Applicants vs. Employees

Soroka and the ACLU contend that job applicants are entitled to the protection of the compelling interest test, just as employees are. The trial court disagreed, employing a reasonableness standard enunciated in a decision of Division Three of this District which distinguished between applicants and employees.

[The court reviewed an older California case indicating that applicants are entitled to less protection than existing employees. Nevertheless, after detailing why the subsequent constitutional amendment was intended to protect applicants as well as employees, and noting prior case law that treated applicants and employees the same, the court found that the law makes no distinction between the right to privacy for applicants and employees.]

In conclusion, we are satisfied that any violation of the right to privacy of job applicants must be justified by a compelling interest. This conclusion is consistent with the voter's expression of intent when they amended article I, section 1 to make privacy an inalienable right and with subsequent decisions of the California Supreme Court.

3. Nexus Requirement

Soroka and the ACLU also argue that Target has not demonstrated that its Psychscreen questions are job-related — i.e., that they provide information relevant to the emotional stability of its SSO applicants. Having considered the religious belief and sexual orientation questions carefully, we find this contention equally persuasive.

Although the state right of privacy is broader than the federal right, California courts construing article I, section 1 have looked to federal precedents for guidance. Under the lower federal standard, employees may not be compelled to submit to a violation of their right to privacy unless a clear, direct nexus exists between the nature of the employee's duty and the nature of the violation. We are satisfied that this nexus requirement applies with even greater force under article I, section 1.

Again, we turn to the voter's interpretation of article I, section 1. The ballot argument — the only legislative history for the privacy amendment — specifically states that one purpose of the constitutional right to privacy is to prevent businesses "from collecting . . . *unnecessary* information about us. . . ." It also asserts that the right to privacy would "preclude the collection of *extraneous* or *frivolous* information." Ballot Pamp., Proposed Amends. to Cal. Const. with arguments to voters, Gen. Elec. (Nov. 7, 1972) p. 28, emphasis added. Thus, the ballot language requires that the information collected be *necessary* to achieve the purpose for which the information has been gathered. This language convinces us that the voters intended that a nexus requirement apply.

The California Supreme Court has also recognized this nexus requirement. When it found that public employees could not be compelled to take a polygraph test, it criticized the questions asked as both highly personal and unrelated to any employment duties. *See Long Beach City Employees Assn. v. City of Long Beach*, 719 P.2d 660 (Cal. 1986). It found that a public employer may require its workers to answer *some* questions, but only those that specifically, directly and narrowly relate to the performance of the employee's official duties. This nexus requirement also finds support in the seminal case from our high court on the right to privacy, which characterizes as one of the principal mischiefs at which article I, section 1 was directed "the *overbroad* collection . . . of unnecessary personal information. . . ." (emphasis added.) If the information Target seeks is not job-related, that collection is overbroad, and the information unnecessary. . . .

4. Application of Law

Target concedes that the Psychscreen intrudes on the privacy interests of its job applicants. . . . Under the legislative history and case law [of article I, section 1], Target's intrusion into the privacy rights of its SSO applicants must be justified by a compelling interest to withstand constitutional scrutiny. Thus, the trial court abused its discretion by committing an error of law — applying the reasonableness test, rather than the compelling interest test.

While Target unquestionably has an interest in employing emotionally stable persons to be SSO's, testing applicants about their religious beliefs and sexual orientation does not further this interest. To justify the invasion of privacy resulting from use of the Psychscreen, Target must demonstrate a compelling interest and must establish that the test serves a job-related purpose. In its opposition to Soroka's motion for preliminary injunction, Target made no showing that a person's religious beliefs or sexual orientation have any bearing on the emotional stability or on the ability to perform an SSO's job responsibilities. It did no more than to make generalized claims about the Psychscreen's relationship to emotional fitness and to assert that it has seen an overall improvement in SSO quality and performance since it implemented the Psychscreen. This is not sufficient to constitute a compelling interest, nor does it satisfy the nexus requirement. Therefore, Target's inquiry into the religious beliefs and sexual orientation of SSO applicants unjustifiably violates the state constitutional right to privacy.[9] Soroka has established that he is likely to prevail on the merits of his constitutional claims.

9. In light of this ruling, we need not address the question of whether the means chosen to achieve a compelling interest must be the least intrusive means.

Statutory Claims

Soroka also contends that he is likely to prevail on the merits of his statutory claims. He makes two statutory claims — one based on the [California] Fair Employment and Housing Act (FEHA) and another based on the [California] Labor Code. . . .

1. Fair Employment and Housing Act

[The FEHA] claims are based on allegations that the questions require applicants to divulge information about their religious beliefs. In its ruling on Soroka's motion for summary adjudication, the trial court found that he did not establish that Target's hiring decisions were based on religious beliefs, nor that the questions asked in the Psychscreen were designed to reveal such beliefs.

In California, an employer may not refuse to hire a person on the basis of his or her religious beliefs. GOV. CODE, § 12940, subd. (a); *see* GOV. CODE, § 12920. Likewise, an employer is prohibited from making any non-job-related inquiry that expresses "directly or indirectly, any limitation, specification, or discrimination as to . . . religious creed. . . ." GOV. CODE, § 12940, subd. (d). FEHA guidelines provide that an employer may make any preemployment inquiry that does not discriminate on a basis enumerated in FEHA. However, inquiries that identify an individual on the basis of religious creed are unlawful unless pursuant to a permissible defense. CAL. CODE REGS., tit. 2, § 7287.3, subd. (b)(1); *see* GOV. CODE, § 12920. Job-relatedness is an affirmative defense. *See* CAL. CODE REGS., tit. 2, § 7286.7, subd. (c). A means of selection that is facially neutral but that has an adverse impact on persons on the basis of religious creed is permissible only on a showing that the selection process is sufficiently related to an essential function of the job in question to warrant its use. *Id.*, § 7287.4, subd. (e); *see* GOV. CODE, § 12920.

The trial court committed an error of law when it found that questions such as "I feel sure that there is only one true religion," "Everything is turning out just like the prophets of the Bible said it would," and "I believe in the second coming of Christ" were not intended to reveal religious beliefs. Clearly, these questions were intended to — and did — inquire about the religious beliefs of Target's SSO applicants. As a matter of law, these questions constitute an inquiry that expresses a "specification [of a] religious creed." GOV. CODE, § 12940, subd. (d).

Once Soroka established a prima facie case of an impermissible inquiry, the burden of proof shifted to Target to demonstrate that the religious beliefs questions were job-related. As we have already determined, Target has not established that the Psychscreen's questions about religious beliefs have any bearing on that applicant's ability to perform an SSO's job responsibilities. Therefore, Soroka has established the likelihood that he will prevail at trial on this statutory claim.[10]

---

10. Soroka also challenges questions relating to physical handicaps or conditions. As we find that use of the Psychscreen violates FEHA regulations against questioning about an applicant's religious beliefs, we need not address these additional claims of error.

2. Labor Code Sections 1101 and 1102

Under California law, employers are precluded from making, adopting or enforcing any policy that tends to control or direct the political activities or affiliations of employees. (LAB. CODE, § 1101, subd. (b).) Employers are also prohibited from coercing, influencing, or attempting to coerce or influence employees to adopt or follow or refrain from adopting or following any particular line of political activity by threatening a loss of employment. These statutes have been held to protect applicants as well as employees. *Gay Law Students Assn. v. Pacific Tel. & Tel. Co.*, 595 P.2d 592 (Cal. 1979).

Labor Code sections 1101 and 1102 protect an employee's fundamental right to engage in political activity without employer interference. [*Id.*] The "struggle of the homosexual community for equal rights, particularly in the field of employment, must be recognized as a political activity." These statutes also prohibit a private employer from discriminating against an employee on the basis of his or her sexual orientation.

The trial court committed an error of law when it determined that Psychscreen questions such as "I am very strongly attracted by members of my own sex" were not intended to reveal an applicant's sexual orientation. On its face, this question directly asks an applicant to reveal his or her sexual orientation. One of the five traits that Target uses the Psychscreen to determine is "socialization," which it defines as "the extent to which an individual subscribes to traditional values and mores and feels an obligation to act in accordance with them." Persons who identify themselves as homosexuals may be stigmatized as "willing to defy or violate" these norms, which may in turn result in an invalid test.

As a matter of law, this practice tends to discriminate against those who express a homosexual orientation. It also constitutes an attempt to coerce an applicant to refrain from expressing a homosexual orientation by threat of loss of employment. Therefore, Soroka has established that he is likely to prevail at trial on this statutory basis, as well.

[The court went on to find that the trial court erred in denying Soroka's motion for preliminary injunction].

NOTES

1. *Sources of Protection.* Since *Von Raab* involves a public employer while *Soroka* a private one, the sources of privacy protection analyzed in each case are different. Indeed, note the various sources upon which the *Soroka* decision relies. If Soroka and the other employees had applied for jobs at Target and had brought the same suit in a state other than California, would they have had any cause of action? Only a small number of states directly restrict employer use of paper and pencil honesty testing, *see, e.g.*, MASS. GEN. LAWS ch. 149, § 19B (2006 and Supp. 2010) and R.I. GEN. LAWS § 28-6.1-1 (2010), but there may be other more indirect forms of protection. For example, referring back to the possible sources of privacy protection already discussed in this chapter, might claimants today have other potential theories of liability against Target in these circumstances? *See, e.g., Karraker v. Rent-a-Center, Inc.*, 411 F.3d 831 (7th Cir. 2005) (finding that the administering of a psychological test to job applicants as part of a regime of exams violated the ADA because the test, as administered and applied, could be used to reveal a mental disorder); *see generally* Scott P. Kramer, *Why Is the Company Asking About My Fear of Spiders? A New Look* *at Evaluating Whether an Employer-Provided Personality Test Constitutes a Medical Examination Under the ADA*, 2007 U. ILL. L. REV. 1279 (2007). David C. Yamada, *The Regulation of Pre-Employment Honesty Testing: Striking a Temporary (?) Balance Between Self-Regulation and Prohibition*, 39 WAYNE L. REV. 1549 (1993). *See also* Susan J. Stabile, *The Use of Personality Tests as a Hiring Tool: Is the Benefit Worth the Cost?*, 4 U. PA. J. LAB. & EMP. L. 279 (2002) (critiquing the use of personality tests as a screening tool).

When there is a recognized cause of action, whether in the private or public sector, the analytical framework for determining liability is often very similar. Indeed, in terms of the overall approach to analyzing whether the employer breached an employee/applicant's right to privacy, isn't *Von Raab* very similar to *Soroka*? And, yet, despite broader similarities, it is often the differences that are dispositive. Are there important differences in the way the two courts approached the question of liability? One might assume (reasonably) that public employees enjoy more robust privacy rights than private employees; does that appear to be the case here?

2. *Comparing* Von Raab *with* O'Connor *and* Quon. The *Von Raab* court relies on *O'Connor* and finds that neither a warrant nor probable cause is needed for the government's drug-testing program. Yet *Von Raab*'s "reasonableness" inquiry may not be consistent with the standards *O'Connor* describes. While *O'Connor* suggested that the employer must merely demonstrate the reasonableness of its privacy intrusion in terms of ends and means, the *Von Raab* court uses language such as "compelling interest" in upholding most aspects of the drug-testing program and suggesting that one portion of the program may be broader than "necessary." The Court's use of such language suggests that some more rigorous level of scrutiny is in play, although the Court never expressly says as much. Isn't this inconsistent with the deferential approach apparent in *Quon*, especially that Court's rejection of the "least intrusive means" inquiry?

One explanation, consistent with at least some of the language in *Quon* (see Note 5, page 306), is that the reasonableness inquiry itself involves a balancing of the interests at stake. In other words, whether the employer's actions are reasonable is determined by using a sliding scale: the more serious the intrusion into an employee's privacy, the more compelling the employer's justification must be. Thus, to be "reasonable," searches involving bodily fluids, including urine testing, must be justified by more substantial governmental interests than other, less serious intrusions. This may also explain why the *Von Raab* majority went out of its way to emphasize that the urine testing in this circumstance was a somewhat less serious intrusion (involving a "diminished" expectation of privacy) than such testing might be in other contexts. Is there a countervailing suggestion in *Quon* that the intrusion at issue there — the review of the text messages — was a less serious one? Would you rather have your bodily fluids tested or have your supervisor rummage through your employer-provided computer?

Of course, Justice Scalia might find all of this particularly ironic, since, in his view, the government failed to demonstrate any pressing need for such a testing program. His objections bring us back yet again to issues of deference; it may matter less what level of scrutiny is articulated than how willing the courts are to accept the government's proffered reasons for acting. In your view, was the *Von Raab* majority correct to accept the interests on which the government relied?

3. *Deference to the Employer's Interest.* What are the interests articulated by the employers in *Von Raab* and *Soroka*? In which case does the employer's interest seem more important to the court? In reality, perceived importance alone may be dispositive. In other words, even though courts may suggest that they are "balancing" the employer interest against the interest of the employee to be free from intrusions into his or her sphere of privacy, if the employer is able to articulate a sufficiently compelling justification, the court is likely to uphold all but the most severe intrusions. For example, drug-testing programs involving employees engaged in inherently dangerous work or work that puts third parties at risk of physical harm are almost always upheld, regardless of whether the policy arises in the public or private context and regardless of the nature of the underlying claim. *See, e.g., Von Raab; Skinner v. Ry. Labor Executives' Ass'n*, 489 U.S. 602 (1989) (upholding drug testing of railroad employees who had been involved in an accident after detailing just how intrusive urinalysis testing is); *Krieg v. Seybold*, 481 F.3d 512 (7th Cir. 2007) (upholding random drug testing of city sanitation worker who operated large vehicles and equipment); *Luedtke v. Nabors Alaska Drilling, Inc.*, 768 P.2d 1123 (Alaska 1989) (upholding drug testing for oil rig workers); *Kramer v. City of Jersey City*, 2010 U.S. Dist. LEXIS 56449 (D.N.J. 2010) (finding no constitutional or other violation for drug-testing regimen for steroid use among police officers); *Robinson v. City of Seattle*, 10 P.3d 452 (Wash. Ct. App. 2000) (holding that a government employer has a compelling interest in drug testing employees in positions that are truly safety sensitive, but no such interest in testing other employees). Similarly, when the employer has well-founded, particularized suspicion that an employee has engaged in unlawful or otherwise harmful conduct, courts almost always uphold resulting searches and the monitoring of work spaces and communications. *See, e.g., United States v. Slanina*, 283 F.3d 670 (5th Cir. 2002) (upholding employer's and law enforcement's searches of employee's computers after employer discovered links to Web sites containing child pornography). And in many settings, the degree of deference the court gives to the employer's assertions regarding the importance of the interests to be served will be dispositive.

When courts perceive the articulated reasons as less compelling, they are more likely to scrutinize closely the employer's methods and show concern for the employee interests. The interest articulated in *Soroka*, and perhaps the one underlying the testing in *Borse*, may be examples of this. Indeed, proffered employer justifications lie along a continuum. Such justifications may include, for example, protecting public health and safety, protecting worker health and safety, addressing known criminal conduct, preventing criminal conduct, protecting employer tangible and intangible property, preventing other types of employee misconduct or shirking, determining who is better qualified for a job or promotion, protecting the employer's public image, and improving workplace morale or efficiency. How would you order the interests in this listing to reflect a continuum from more to less compelling?

4. *Negligent Hiring and Retention.* Another interest employers sometimes advance is the avoidance of civil liability. In a variety of contexts, employers may be liable for failing to prevent employee conduct that causes harm to third parties or other employees. *See, e.g., Doe v. XYC Corp.*, 887 A.2d 1156 (N.J. App. Div. 2005) (holding an employer potentially liable to daughter of employee who posted nude photographs of herself on the Internet after employer was placed on notice that employee was viewing graphic forms of pornography — although not necessarily child pornography — on his workplace computer; there was a triable claim that the employer failed to exercise reasonable care to report and/or take effective action to stop employee's Internet activities). Sometimes avoiding such harm may require greater monitoring of employee conduct or intrusions into private or intimate matters. *See generally*

Niloofar Nejat-Bina, Comment, *Employers as Vigilant Chaperones Armed with Dating Waivers: The Intersection of Unwelcomeness and Employer Liability in Hostile Work Environment Sexual Harassment Law*, 20 BERKELEY J. EMP. & LAB. L. 325 (1999) (discussing potential employer liability for sexual harassment when supervisors become romantically involved with subordinates and employer responses thereto).

Along these lines, in recent years there has been growth in the number of negligent hiring, supervision, and retention claims brought against employers by third parties (including co-workers) injured by the employer's workers. Although the elements of negligence theories vary, most are based on section 213 of the RESTATEMENT (SECOND) OF AGENCY (1957), which provides that an employer is liable if it is negligent or reckless:

> (b) in the employment of improper persons or instrumentalities in work involving risk of harm to others;
> (c) in the supervision of the activity; or
> (d) in permitting, or failing to prevent, negligent or other tortious conduct by persons, whether or not his servants or agents, upon premises or with instrumentalities under his control.

See also RESTATEMENT (SECOND) OF TORTS § 317 (1965) (providing for a negligent supervision claim where the employer fails to exercise reasonable care to prevent an employee from intentionally harming others on the employer's premises or in other circumstances in which the employer can exercise control). Liability under these theories is often difficult to establish. For example, to prevail on a negligent hiring where a third party is harmed by an employee's criminal act, the plaintiff normally must establish not only that the employer failed to exercise ordinary care in selecting the employee — that is, failed to perform an adequate background check — but also that the exercise of such care would have made the type of crime the employee later committed reasonably foreseeable. *See, e.g., Monroe v. Universal Health Servs., Inc.*, 596 S.E.2d 604 (Ga. 2004) (finding that, although the mental health assistant who sexually assaulted plaintiff — a patient of employer — had provided incomplete or inaccurate information during his application process, employer did not breach its duty of care because the application and background investigation process had not revealed a risk of violent or criminal activity); *Saine v. Comcast Cablevision of Arkansas, Inc.*, 126 S.W.3d 339 (Ark. 2003) (finding no cognizable negligent hiring claim because employer had performed an adequate background check before hiring cable repair employee).

Nevertheless, these sources of potential liability create strong incentives for employers to engage in robust background screening and testing of applicants, establish intrusive techniques for monitoring current employees, and conduct very thorough investigations of employees alleged to have engaged in tortious or wrongful conduct. *See, e.g., Saine*, 126 S.W.3d at 343-45 (while adequate background check precluded negligent hiring claim, finding material issues of fact with regard to negligent supervision and retention claims because employer had notice of complaints of inappropriate conduct of employee toward another female cable customer prior to his rape and attempted murder of plaintiff).

5. *The Employee's Interest.* As discussed in each of the cases in this chapter, in order for an employee or applicant to have a cognizable breach of privacy claim (of any kind), he or she must have a legitimate or reasonable expectation of privacy in the sphere upon which the employer intruded. Without such an expectation, there is nothing to "balance" against the employer's interest. As discussed above, establishing the existence of such an expectation may often be the employee's most difficult hurdle.

Assuming the worker can establish such an expectation, however, the value the court places on the interest, and hence, the scrutiny the court will apply, may vary by the perceived intrusiveness of the employer's conduct. *See, e.g., Anchorage Police Dep't Empls. Ass'n v. Municipality of Anchorage*, 24 P.3d 547 (Alaska 2001) (upholding portions of drug-testing program linked to hiring, promotion, and investigating accidents but striking down random drug testing in part because it is more intrusive); *Robinson v. City of Seattle*, 10 P.3d 452 (Wash. Ct. App. 2000) (stating that government intrusions into certain personal information or confidentiality interests receive rational basis scrutiny while infringements of the right to autonomy warrant strict scrutiny). As *Von Raab* suggests, intrusions involving bodily functions or integrity — drug and medical testing, polygraph testing, strip searches, video surveillance of locker rooms or restrooms — may be subjected to the most rigorous scrutiny.

Slightly less intrusive conduct, such as questioning applicants about intimate matters, monitoring personal communications at work, audio surveillance, and searches of personal work spaces and stored data, may receive somewhat less scrutiny. Still less intrusive practices, such as overt video surveillance of less personal work areas, periodically auditing work-related communications (as in *Quon*), and monitoring or searches of less personal spaces and data compilations, often receive the least scrutiny.

Even if there is general agreement about which employer activities are more or less intrusive, and thus, which should receive greater scrutiny, "balancing" such intrusions against employer interests remains elusive. Despite common references to that term, courts and other lawmakers avoid the unwieldy task of attempting to weigh and then balance these competing interests in particular contexts. For example, although genetic and polygraph tests could produce a number of efficiencies for employers, protect employees themselves from various risks, and even benefit the public in some circumstances, legislative enactments addressing these forms of testing often include outright prohibitions across categories of employment, rather than provide for any type of balancing of interests in particular cases.

6. *The "Nexus" Requirement.* Once it is determined that there are both legitimate employer and employee privacy interests at stake, courts — including the *Von Raab* and *Soroka* courts — often focus on the nexus between the articulated interest and the nature of the intrusion. While *Quon* used different terminology, it too acknowledged that reasonableness of the intrusion is measured not just by the work-related purpose of the search, but also by the relationship between that purpose and the means utilized (i.e., the scope of the search). Thus, under the analytical framework provided in each of these cases, intrusions justified for reasons of equal importance may not receive equal treatment by the courts because the means chosen in one context might be more closely tailored to serve the end than in the other context. However, some decisions diverge on how closely the means must be tied to the purpose. Recall that *Quon* rejected arguments that the employer must utilize the least intrusive means, holding that the review of the text messages was reasonable despite the availability of less intrusive alternatives. Contrast that analysis with *Soroka*. Doesn't the *Soroka* opinion suggest that intrusions may be held unlawful not only when they are clearly overbroad, or but also when they are unnecessarily broad — that is, when the same legitimate employer interest may be served as effectively by less intrusive means? Much may depend on the deference courts are willing to give employers when it comes to this nexus; that is, courts may vary in how demanding they may be in requiring narrow tailoring. Ultimately, how much deference should the employer's chosen means be given?

7. *The Limits on Drug Testing.* On the same day the Supreme Court decided *Von Raab*, it decided *Skinner v. Ry. Labor Executives' Ass'n*, 489 U.S. 602 (1989), which upheld as permissible under the Fourth Amendment mandatory blood and urine tests, for alcohol and drugs, of railroad employees who have been involved in railroad accidents. In both cases, the majority focused on the safety sensitive or high-risk nature of the positions. Since these two cases were decided, lower courts have routinely upheld mandatory drug-testing programs (random or otherwise) in safety- or security-sensitive positions in public workplaces and pursuant to regulatory requirements in some private workplaces.

However, in *Chandler v. Miller*, 520 U.S. 305 (1997), the Supreme Court struck down a Georgia law that required candidates for some state offices to take a drug test to qualify for election. In so doing, the Court distinguished *Von Raab* and *Skinner*, noting that Georgia had presented no evidence that the state's elected officials performed the kinds of high-risk or safety-sensitive tasks that the employees in the previous cases performed. The Court then rejected the symbolic value—that is, commitment to the fight against drug abuse—of such a testing program as being sufficiently important to justify the intrusion. Recall Justice Scalia's opinion in *Von Raab*. Courts recognizing breach of privacy claims for drug testing in the private employer context have likewise tended to focus on the nature of the employee's job and, hence, the importance of the testing program. *See, e.g., Lanier v. City of Woodburn*, 518 F.3d 1147 (9th Cir. 2008) (holding that the City violated plaintiff's constitutional rights by rescinding her offer of employment as a library page after she refused to submit to drug testing since it offered no evidence of a drug problem in the targeted population, the link between the drug screening and the interest in protecting children was tenuous, and the applicants were neither involved in drug interdiction nor typically performed safety-sensitive tasks); *AFT-West Virginia. v. Kanawha County Bd. of Educ.*, 592 F. Supp. 2d 883 (S.D. W. Va. 2009) (enjoining suspicionless random drug testing of public school teachers because the need for the testing was symbolic rather than premised on a concrete safety risk); *Robinson*, 10 P.3d at 469 (finding no compelling interest for a municipal drug-testing program except for workers in positions in which public safety is implicated); *Luedtke*, 768 P.2d at 1123; *Hennessey v. Coastal Eagle Point Oil Co.*, 609 A.2d 11 (N.J. 1992).

Occasionally, however, the methods or procedures utilized in drug testing have been invalidated even in safety-sensitive contexts. *See, e.g., Anchorage Police Dep't Empls. Ass'n*, 24 P.3d at 557-60 (striking down only random portion of drug-testing program); *AFGE v. Sullivan*, 744 F. Supp. 294 (D.D.C. 1990) (enjoining testing regulations in part because government articulated insufficient reasons for requiring urine samples be provided under direct visual observation); *see generally* JOHN GILLIOM, SURVEILLANCE, PRIVACY AND THE LAW: EMPLOYEE DRUG TESTING AND THE POLITICS OF SOCIAL CONTROL (1994); Stephen M. Fogel et al., *Survey of the Law on Employee Drug Testing*, 42 U. MIAMI L. REV. 553 (1988); Pauline T. Kim, *Collective and Individual Approaches to Protecting Employee Privacy: The Experience with Workplace Drug Testing*, 66 LA. L. REV. 1009 (2006); Lindsay J. Taylor, *Congressional Attempts to "Strike Out" Steroids: Constitutional Concerns About the Clean Sports Act*, 49 ARIZ. L. REV (2007); John B. Wefing, *Employer Drug Testing: Disparate Judicial and Legislative Responses*, 63 ALB. L. REV. 799 (2000).

In light of this backdrop, and assuming testing procedures themselves are reasonable, what classes of employees are unlikely to prevail in challenges against mandatory drug-testing requirements? Any employee with access to a firearm? Any employee working with hazardous materials or chemicals? Any employee who drives a motor vehicle? Any teacher?

8. *Applicant vs. Employee.* Some statutory and common-law privacy protections draw a distinction between applicants for employment and employees — protecting the latter to a greater extent than the former. *Soroka* recognizes, but ultimately rejects, the possible distinction between employees and applicants. Are there good reasons to protect employees to a greater extent than applicants? Are there ways in which employees are more vulnerable than the applicants? How about vice versa?

Even if breach of privacy claims are equally available to applicants, establishing such a breach may be more difficult for them. An applicant may not have the same expectation of privacy as current employees. Also, it is highly unlikely that an applicant could establish a contract-based privacy claim, since, at the application stage, no express or implied contract will have been formed. Moreover, the "catch-22" described in Note 6 on page 318 is even more pronounced for applicants than employees because applicants must consent even to be considered for the job; yet such consent may bar his or her claims.

Note on Off-site Activities Including Blogging and Internet Use

A broad array of off-site activities or lifestyle choices — from political and religious affiliations, to intimate relationships, to hobbies and leisure activities, to consumption choices (food, alcohol, tobacco, etc.) might conflict with employer preferences and affect their hiring, retention, and promotion decisions. In private, at-will employment, employees historically have enjoyed few protections from employer retaliation for such activities, choices, or associations. *See, e.g., Brunner v. Al Attar*, 786 S.W.2d 784 (Tex. Ct. App. 1990) (dismissing an employee's claim alleging breach of privacy after employer terminated employee for volunteering for the AIDS Foundation). Many such off-site conduct and associational claims are unsuccessful, often because they do not fit neatly within statutory or common-law theories. *See, e.g., Curay-Cramer v. The Ursuline Acad. of Wilmington*, No. 04-4628, 2006 U.S. App. LEXIS 13956 (3d Cir. June 7, 2006) (rejecting employee's Title VII retaliation theory in circumstances in which employee was terminated from her position as a teacher at a Catholic school after allowing her name to be included in a prochoice advertisement in the local newspaper and admitting her association with a prochoice organization); *Edmondson v. Shearer Lumber Prods.*, 75 P.3d 733 (Idaho 2003) (refusing to recognize a public policy claim for a worker terminated for participating in a local government task force).

However, as *Soroka* and *Rulon-Miller* suggest, there is some protection from employer interference with or repercussions from some such activities and choices. When available, such protection often hinges on whether the employer can articulate a sufficient business-related reason for its actions. For example, in both *Soroka* and *Rulon-Miller*, the employer was found to have breached worker privacy rights, at least in part because it inquired into such private matters outside the workplace and acted upon those inquiries without sufficient justification. Also, a growing number of state legislatures have protected workers against adverse employment actions caused by a worker's political and other affiliations, recreational activities, or other kinds of legal off-site conduct where employers do not have a sufficiently compelling reason for taking such action. *See, e.g.,* CAL. LAB. CODE §§ 96(k), 98.6 (2010) (prohibiting adverse employment actions in response to lawful employee conduct occurring during nonworking hours away from the employer's premises); COL. REV. STAT. § 24-34-402.5 (2009) (prohibiting employers from terminating employees for lawful off-site activities absent job relatedness); MINN. STAT. § 181.938 (2009) (prohibiting employers from taking adverse actions against employees or applicants because the applicant or employee uses or enjoys lawful consumable products — including food, alcohol, and tobacco products — if the use or enjoyment takes place off the employer's premises during nonworking hours, unless the employer can demonstrate a bona fide occupational requirement for doing so or to avoid a conflict of interest); N.Y. LAB. LAW § 201-d (2010) (prohibiting employers in most circumstances from taken adverse actions against employees based on employee political affiliations, legal use of consumable products, recreational activities, or union membership). Of course, whether these statutes will provide meaningful protection for employees' offsite activities and associations may depend on judicial interpretation and application. *See, e.g., McCavitt v. Swiss Reins. Am. Corp.* 237 F.3d 166 (2001) (finding "romantic dating" of a co-worker not to be a protected recreational activity under the New York statute). For further discussion of the burgeoning workplace conflicts over such activities and choices, and the range of legal issues raised regarding employer prohibitions or other responses, *see* Terry Morehead Dworkin, *It's My Life — Leave Me Alone: Off the Job Employee Associational Privacy Rights*, 35 AM. BUS. L. J. 47 (1997); Rafael Gely & Leonard Biermanm, *Workplace Blogs and Workers' Privacy*, 66 LA. L. REV. 1079 (2006) (discussing blogging and its privacy implications); James A. Sonne, *Monitoring for Quality Assurance: Employer Regulation of Off-Duty Behavior*, 43 GA. L. REV. 133 (2008); Stephen D. Sugarman, *"Lifestyle" Discrimination in Employment*, 24 BERKELEY J. EMP. & LAB. L. 377 (2003).

One growing area of potential employer-employee conflict is Internet activities. As we have seen, employers may have significant interests in regulating employee Internet use at work or on employer time, networks, or equipment. As the discussion in Note 3 following *Quon* suggested, *see* page 303, employers often prevail in such Internet monitoring and computer search cases. *See also Thygeson v. U.S. Bancorp*, 2004 U.S. Dist. LEXIS 18863 (D. Or. Sept. 15, 2004) (rejecting breach of privacy claims after employer monitored Web site addresses employee accessed and searched e-mail files). *But see Fischer v. Mt. Olive Lutheran Church, Inc.*, 207 F. Supp. 2d 914 (W.D. Wis. 2002) (finding that employee had reasonable expectation of privacy in e-mails in his Web-based e-mail account, which employer searched after guessing employee's password, for intrusion upon seclusion claim). Of course, that does not mean employees like such monitoring; indeed, a number of federal judges themselves became quite irate when they discovered that their Internet activity was to be monitored under a newly enacted Judicial Conference policy. *See* Hardeep Kaur Josan & Sapna K. Shah, Note, *Internet Monitoring of Federal Judges: Striking a Balance Between Independence and Accountability*, 20 HOFSTRA LAB. & EMP. L. J. 153 (2002).

But what about employee Internet activities — including blogging, maintaining personal Web sites, social networking, participation in interactive Web sites or chat rooms, or basic surfing — that occur off-site, during nonwork hours, and without use of employer equipment? Many employers have adopted "blogging" policies, warning workers about potential adverse consequences if employee blogging activities or other Web-based activities harm the employer. And, unsurprisingly, employees are terminated for such activities with growing frequency, particularly when they make online statements critical of their employers. *See, e.g.*, Posting of Jeffrey M. Hirsh to Workplace Prof. Blog, http://lawprofessors.typepad.com/laborprof_blog/2009/08/the -dangers-of-facebook.html (Aug. 11, 2009); Posting of Richard Bales to Workplace Law Blog, http://lawprofessors.typepad.com/laborprof_blog/2009/03/fired-for-faceb .html (Mar. 9, 2009). Case law and legislation on the subject remains sparse, although litigation over such issues appears to be growing. *See, e.g., Pietrylo v. Hillstone Rest. Group,* No. 06-5754 (FSH), 2009 WL 3128420 (D.N.J. Sept. 25, 2009) (upholding a jury verdict finding that employees' managers violated the Stored Communications Act (SCA) by knowingly accessing a chat group on a social networking Web site without authorization); *see also Dible v. City of Chandler,* reproduced at page 395 (upholding summary judgment on police officer's speech, privacy, and other claims arising out of his termination by the City for maintaining sexually explicit Web site featuring him and his wife). The potential employment consequences of Internet activities have received a significant amount of recent attention, particularly in the context of high-profile firings. *See generally* Ian Shapira, *When Young Teachers Go Wild on the Web,* WASH. POST, Apr. 28, 2008, *available at* http://www.washingtonpost.com/wp-dyn/content/ article/2008/04/27/AR2008042702213.html (discussing ramifications of explicit and otherwise inappropriate Facebook postings by teachers). In addition, if workers utilize social networking or other electronic means to discuss work-related conditions with one another, their communications may be protected as "concerted activity" under the National Labor Relations Act. *See* 29 U.S.C. § 157 (2006); *see also* page 413, *infra* (discussing protection for concerted activity). Indeed, in a potentially groundbreaking case, the National Labor Relations Board filed a complaint in October 2010 alleging that an employer engaged in an unfair labor practice by terminating an employee after she criticized her supervisor on her Facebook page. *See, e.g.*, Steven Greenhouse, *Company Accused of Firing Over Facebook Post,* N.Y. TIMES, November 8, 2010, at B1.

At this point, and despite some calls for legislative action by the blogger community and others, the potential sources of protection are limited. As will be discussed in the next chapter, public employee speech on the Internet enjoys qualified First Amendment protection, and may be protected if the topic of that speech is wholly unrelated to employment. *See, e.g., City of San Diego v. Roe,* 543 U.S. 77, 80 (2004); *United States v. Nat'l Treasury Employees,* 513 U.S. 454, 465 (1995). Also, in the private employment context, Internet activities that touch on other protected spheres, such as religious or political affiliations, may receive some protection under federal antidiscrimination law, state associational protections, or, conceivably, the public policy exception.

It is unlikely, however, that most intrusion upon seclusion or other breach of privacy claims relating to Internet activity will succeed since rarely will one have a reasonable expectation of privacy in postings or other activities on the Internet. And, of course, unless protected as "concerted activity," the more closely the content of the Internet activity or speech relates to areas of employer concern—for example, complaints about the employer or co-workers, statements that may embarrass or otherwise harm the employer or co-workers, revelations of confidential or proprietary interests, and so forth—the less likely the conduct is to be protected. *See, e.g., Roe, supra* (finding no constitutional violation where city terminated employee after employee made clear references to his status as a police officer in sexually explicit videos he sold on an online auction site); *see also* Helen Norton, *Constraining Public Employee Speech: Government's Control of Its Workers' Speech to Protect Its Own Expression*, 59 Duke L.J. 1 (2009) (discussing how courts are increasingly concluding that off-duty/off-site conduct by government workers — including Internet activities — affect employer interests).

As a practical matter then, at-will employees and job applicants ought to assume that they have little protection against adverse employment actions resulting from things they say or see on the Internet. Indeed, workers, and job applicants in particular, would be well advised to assume that anything they say or post in publicly accessible areas of the Internet will become known to potential employers since many employers now conduct Internet searches for information on prospective employees. *See, e.g.,* Microsoft Online Reputation Data Study, *Online Reputation in a Connected World* (Jan. 2010) *available at* http://www.microsoft.com/privacy/dpd/research.aspx (finding that 70 percent of employers in the United States have rejected employees because of information discovered online, and that nearly all employers believe it is appropriate to consider prospective employees' online reputation as appropriate); Posting of Daniel Solove to Concurring Opinions, http://www.concurringopinions .com/archives/2009/08/employers-researching-applicants-online.html (Aug. 20, 2009, 6:37 EDT) (discussing the survey findings and their implications). Although anonymous participation may provide greater protections, maintaining such anonymity forever may be both difficult and costly (in the sense that one cannot take credit for his or her postings), and examples of repercussions upon an employer's discovery of the true identity of a blogger or poster now abound. *See, e.g.,* Jonathan Miller, *He Fought the Law. They Both Won*, N.Y. Times, Jan. 22, 2006 (discussing the strange journey of David Lat, who, while serving as an Assistant United States Attorney, led a secret life as "Article III Groupie," a supposedly female blogger who maintained an irreverent, gossipy blog about the federal judiciary called "Underneath Their Robes," until he revealed his true identity and ultimately changed careers).

On the other hand, employers occasionally can get into trouble legally or otherwise for overly aggressive off-site surveillance or investigatory activities to flush out anonymous posters or leakers. One very high-profile example is the scandal surrounding Hewlett-Packard's use of highly aggressive spying techniques and deceptive tactics to discover the identity of a leaker (who turned out to be on its board of directors). The storm of controversy that followed resulted in a number of directors and officers in the company resigning. *See, e.g.,* Damon Darlin, *H.P., Red-Faced but Still Selling*, N.Y. Times, Oct. 1, 2006 at 31. Criminal charges against the chair of Hewlett-Packard's board of directors ultimately were dismissed, although one of its investigators did plead guilty to theft and conspiracy. *See* Matt Richtel, *Charges Dismissed in Hewlett-Packard Spying Case*, N.Y. Times, Mar. 15, 2007, *available at* http://www.nytimes.com/2007/03/15/technology/15dunn.html?_r=1&ref= patricia_c_dun. In addition, Hewlett-Packard ultimately agreed to pay $14.5 million to settle a civil suit brought by the California attorney general. *See* Damon Darlin, *H.P Will Pay $14.5 Million to Settle Suit*, N.Y. Times, Dec. 8, 2006, *available at* http:// www.nytimes.com/2006/12/08/technology/08hewlett.html.

Note on Employee Dress and Appearance

Choices about dress and grooming are often an expression of individual autonomy and dignitary interests. For this reason, disputes over employee appearance in the workplace may be conceptualized as matters of worker privacy. Despite significant scholarly and public attention in recent years, there are few protections for worker preferences with regard to their appearance, and challenges to employer policies and practices in this area rarely succeed. Statutory protections that address dress and grooming choices directly are rare, and, where they exist, they may be subject to significant limitations. *See, e.g.* D.C. Code § 2-1402.11 (2010) (formerly § 1-2512) (prohibiting discrimination based on "personal appearance" but expressly exempting various policies, including those that relate to cleanliness, health or safety, and uniform requirements that apply across a class of employees). In the absence of free speech or free exercise implications, public employees' challenges to dress and grooming policies on substantive due process grounds are unlikely to be successful since they are subject only to rational basis review. *See, e.g., Kelley v. Johnson*, 425 U.S. 238 (1976) (rejecting a challenge to hair-grooming standards for members of a police force).

Perhaps the most important sources of potential protection in this area are those that prohibit status-based discrimination, including antidiscrimination statutes and the First Amendment's Free Exercise Clause. Employees have had some success challenging some such policies as discriminatory. *See, e.g., Frank v. United Airlines*, 216 F.3d 845 (9th Cir. 2000) (striking down the airline's disparate weight standards for male and female flight attendants as facially discriminatory); *FOP Newark Lodge No. 12 v. City of Newark*, 170 F.3d 359 (3d Cir. 1999) (holding the city's refusal to accommodate officers whose religion required them to wear beards violated the free exercise clause); Press Release, EEOC, *UPS Freight to Pay $46,000 to Settle EEOC Religious Discrimination Lawsuit* (Feb. 17, 2010) *available at* http://www.eeoc .gov/eeoc/newsroom/release/2-17-10.cfm (announcing settlement of a religious discrimination lawsuit brought by the EEOC after UPS Freight refused to accommodate the Rastafarian religious beliefs of an employee and fired him for failing to adhere to the firm's grooming policy). However, other such challenges have failed, including claims addressing gender-specific differences in dress and grooming codes, and the disparate effects of such codes on women and religious and other minorities. *See, e.g., Webb v. City of Philadelphia*, 562 F.3d 256 (3d Cir. 2009); *Jespersen v. Harrah's Operating Co.*, 444 F.3d 1104 (9th Cir. 2006) (en banc); *Harper v. Blockbuster Entm't Corp.*, 139 F.3d 1385 (11th Cir. 1998). Courts afford employers substantial deference in making decisions about the appearance of their workers even when the result is to reinforce gender-conformity norms. The limiting principle is that no particular protected group may be singled out or subjected to far greater burdens. There may also be legal restrictions on dress requirements that increase the risk that women will be subjected to sexual harassment from customers or co-workers. *But see* Elizabeth Dwoskin, *Is This Woman Too Hot to Be a Banker?*, Village Voice (June 1, 2010) (discussing a sex-discrimination lawsuit filed by a former Citibank employee alleging that she was terminated because the male bosses found her attractive dress and appearance too distracting). Despite the limits of current law, many commentators have focused attention on the discriminatory effect of such policies and other sources of pressure to conform to "majority" expectations with regard to appearance, habits, and demeanor while at work. *See, e.g.*, Katharine T. Bartlett, *Only Girls Wear Barrettes: Dress and Appearance Standards, Community Norms and Workplace Equality*, 92 Mich. L. Rev. 2541, 2543-46 (1994); Mary Anne C. Case, *Disaggregating Gender from Sex and Sexual Orientation: The Effeminate Man in the Law and Feminist Jurisprudence*, 105 Yale L. J. 1, 68-69 (1995); Catherine L. Fisk, *Privacy, Power, and Humiliation at Work: Re-Examining Appearance Regulation as an Invasion of Privacy*, 66 La. L. Rev. 1111 (2006); Roberto J. Gonzalez, *Cultural Rights and the Immutability Requirement in*

Disparate Impact Doctrine, 55 STAN. L. REV. 2195, 2227 (2003); Tristin K. Green, *Work Culture and Discrimination*, 93 CAL. L. REV. 623 (2005); Karl E. Klare, *Power/Dressing: Regulation of Employee Appearance*, 26 NEW ENG. L. REV. 1395 (1992); Gowri Ramachandran, *Intersectionality as "Catch-22": Why Identity Performance Demands Are Neither Harmless nor Reasonable*, 69 ALB. L. REV. 299 (2005); Camille Gear Rich, *Performing Racial and Ethnic Identity: Discrimination by Proxy and the Future of Title VII*, 79 N.Y.U. L. REV. 1134 (2004); Kenji Yoshino, *Covering*, 111 YALE L. J. 769 (2002); *see generally* Symposium, *Makeup, Identity Performance & Discrimination*, 14 DUKE J. GENDER L. & POL'Y 1 (2007).

C. PRIVATE ORDERING: ARE THERE ANY LIMITS TO CONSENT?

The first part of this chapter discussed contract as a possible source of privacy rights. One might say, from the employee perspective, that the use of contract to create or expand the sphere of employee privacy protection is the "positive" side of private ordering. On the "negative" side is the use of contract, workplace guidelines and practices, and employee consent to eliminate or reduce the legally cognizable sphere of privacy that otherwise might exist.

In light of this, and employers' increasing use of employment "privacy" policies and waiver forms, whether otherwise cognizable privacy rights may be limited or eliminated through such private ordering may be the most important question in this area today. And it raises critical, ultimate questions: Are there and should there be any limitations on employers' ability to extract employee consent to intrusions or, more broadly, eliminate spheres of expected privacy? If so, what kinds? Consider these questions as you read the next case.

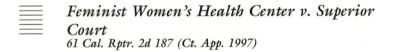

Feminist Women's Health Center v. Superior Court
61 Cal. Rptr. 2d 187 (Ct. App. 1997)

PUGLIA, P.J., with SPARKS, J., and NICHOLSON, J., concurring.

The issue presented by this petition is whether a female health center employee who agrees voluntarily to demonstrate a cervical self-examination to female clients and employees at the health center may sue the health center (and several of its supervisory employees) because the self-examination violates her constitutional right to privacy.

Respondent superior court granted summary adjudication of all of plaintiff Claudia Jenkins's claims except the one alleging she was wrongfully terminated from employment in violation of her right to privacy. The defendants—Feminist Women's Health Center ("Center") and several of its employees—filed the instant petition seeking a writ to compel the superior court to adjudicate this remaining claim in their favor. We shall order the writ to issue. . . . [1]

___

1. Plaintiff's first cause of action alleged a breach of the implied covenant of good faith and fair dealing. The second alleged intentional infliction of emotional distress. In the third cause of action, a violation of the

Plaintiff alleged: She was hired by defendants as a health worker pursuant to an oral contract entered in August 1993; defendants mandated that all female employees disrobe and display their vaginas to the employee defendants and various other employees; those who refused were advised that they either would be fired or would not receive promotions or raises; plaintiff refused to disrobe and was transferred to an intake clerk position before being terminated from employment on January 6, 1994; defendants' policy violated plaintiff's right to privacy and her right freely to maintain and practice religious and cultural beliefs as they pertained to the treatment and care of her body. . . .

Defendant Dido Hasper, executive director of the Center, declared that the Center was founded as a nonprofit corporation in Chico in 1974. The Center was created because unmarried women found it difficult to obtain abortion and midwifery services as well as information regarding birth control, adoption and reproduction. The Center was inspired by the existence of similar centers in Los Angeles and Oakland. The Chico Center began offering services in 1975, including abortion services, pregnancy screening, well-woman gynecology, family planning, and a speakers' bureau on women's health topics. The Center expanded and presently has four clinics, located in Chico, Sacramento, Santa Rosa, and Redding.

Hasper's declaration discussed self-help groups at which cervical self-examination was demonstrated. Hasper defined a self-help group as a gathering of women who want to learn more about their bodies and reproductive health care. She declared: "The goal is to give women the opportunity to talk to each other, share experiences, learn from each other, and learn about their own bodies. A common realization of participants in self-help groups is that women's bodies and their normal reproductive functions have been medicalized and remain a mystery to them. The goal of self-help is to demystify and redefine the normal functions of a woman's body. Our unique and effective, although not strictly necessary tool to accomplish this is for women to visualize their own cervixes and vaginas, which are not usually seen with the naked eye without the use of a vaginal speculum. In many, but not necessarily all, self-help clinic sessions, women are given the opportunity to learn how to use a plastic speculum. . . . The Health Center offers self-help 'clinics' as a community education service to other women's groups, high school and college classes, and makes self-help group facilitators available for any appropriate gathering of interested women. . . . When self-examination occurs in a self-help group, two customs are observed. A woman does self-examination only if and when she feels comfortable doing so, and she looks at her own cervix first before any of the other participants in the self-help group."

Hasper declared that the position of "feminist health worker" (for which plaintiff was hired) was a unique one, requiring, at a minimum, "a great deal of empathy and training, strict absence of judgmentalism, a sophistication to react to a variety of clients' circumstances in a calm, respectful manner, and the ability to think on one's feet and appropriately respond to the needs of Health Center clients."

Hasper further declared that an element of the health worker's training process was an orientation to the self-help educational process. A senior health worker or

---

California Fair Employment and Housing Act was alleged. In the fourth cause of action — which is the only one at issue herein — plaintiff alleged wrongful termination in violation of California public policy (violation of privacy). There also was a supernumerary "fourth cause of action," for a civil conspiracy.

director presides over the orientation, which includes a slide show about the history of the women's self-help movement and self-examination. Self-examination of the cervix thereafter is demonstrated for those attendees who express an interest. A plastic speculum is used to observe the cervix, and attendees are given the opportunity to take one home to examine themselves. Hasper concluded: "It is not the goal of self-help or of the Health Center, nor is it possible, to compel or require any woman to do self-examination of her own cervix. . . . Many senior health workers become facilitators for self-help clinics, although this too is not a job requirement. It has been the Center's experience that those health workers who are genuinely enthusiastic about the concept of self-help, if they possess the other qualities stated above, become outstanding staff members, embracing the goals of their organization. . . . A health worker cannot perform as a woman's advocate during the abortion process at the Health Center's standard if she has a strong aversion to the self-help concept."

Defendant Lisa Williams, the clinic manager for the Center's Sacramento office in August 1993, submitted a declaration detailing the circumstances of plaintiff's employment. Williams declared that plaintiff was hired as a health worker at the Center's Sacramento branch in August 1993. Williams interviewed plaintiff and explained the role of the health worker in the abortion clinic. She gave plaintiff a copy of the health worker job description, which plaintiff read and acknowledged reading. Williams detailed the training program for health workers. She explained the self-help philosophy of the clinic and that health workers, as part of their training, would be oriented to self-help and invited to participate in a self-help clinic. In October 1993, several months after plaintiff had been hired, plaintiff applied for a vacant position of intake clerk. Williams explained to plaintiff that she would have to undergo a new interview process for the intake clerk position, since a different supervisor was involved. Williams declared that plaintiff never expressed dissatisfaction with self-help, even though she had many opportunities to do so at regularly scheduled staff meetings where dissent was encouraged. Williams declared that she did not participate in the decision to hire or fire plaintiff from the intake worker position.

Appended to Williams's declaration is a hiring interview form, signed by plaintiff, which states in part: "I have read and understand the job description for the position I am being hired. [sic] [¶] I have read and understand the Personnel Policies of the Feminist Women's Health Center."

The health worker job description which plaintiff reviewed also was appended. Under "qualifications" for the health worker position, two of the qualifications emphasize self-help:

1. Must attend Orientation and Self-Help demonstration
. . .
3. Must have an interest in women's healthcare and Self-Help

Under the heading "responsibilities and duties" in the health worker job description, participation in self-help clinics and the demonstration of the self-cervical exam at those clinics is explicitly stated:

1. *Attends and conducts self-help clinics as assigned.*
. . .

4. Is a Healthworker for drop-in pregnancy screening and pregnancy screening groups as scheduled:
   a. Facilitates pregnancy screening groups.
   b. *Demonstrates self cervical exam to pregnancy screening groups.*
   c. Counsels clients about pregnancy screening.
   d. Makes appropriate referrals for clients.
   e. Performs UCG pregnancy test or early urine pregnancy tests for clients.
   f. Acts as an advocate during exams by the medical professional as needed.

Defendants argued that their evidence establishes that plaintiff's wrongful termination cause of action lacks merit because plaintiff, as an at-will employee, was subject to reasonable conditions of employment, of which cervical self-examination was one.

In order to rebut defendants' showing that plaintiff understood and expressly agreed to demonstrate cervical self-examination, plaintiff's opposition papers explain the circumstances surrounding self-help and how she was pressured into demonstrating it. Plaintiff declared that during her employment interview "I was not told it was mandatory to disrobe and insert a speculum in my vagina in front of a group of health workers." At a September 1993 self-help session (one month after she was hired), plaintiff was instructed by defendant Eileen Schnitger to disrobe and insert a speculum in her vagina. Plaintiff refused. After further refusals, defendant Lisa Williams instructed plaintiff that she was required to participate in self-help. In October 1993, plaintiff applied for an intake clerk position because it was her understanding that it would not require participation in self-help, although she wasn't sure. Plaintiff became an intake worker on November 1, 1993, at the same rate of pay she had received as a health worker. Tensions were high at this time due to the self-help controversy. Plaintiff and fellow employee Kimya Lambert tried to defuse the problem by suggesting less personally intrusive methods such as using mannequins or privately inserting the speculum and then discussing results in the group sessions. Defendant Eileen Schnitger steadfastly refused these alternatives.

In December 1993, at the insistence of plaintiff and others, volunteer nurse Maggie Gunn wrote [an anonymous letter requesting that the Center "stop pressuring people to do the self-help"]. Gunn and another employee, Shirley Anderson, quit soon thereafter because of the self-help mandate. Plaintiff and Kimya Lambert were fired because of their work performance. Plaintiff's declaration concluded: "I believe and continue to believe 'self-help' in general has no relation to my position as a health worker because as a health worker I did not counsel clients about 'self-help.' I merely assisted in the abortion process. In fact, many of the movies we viewed at 'self-help' meetings featured issues such as how to climax and I know for certain I was not going to discuss this with any abortion client. I had a very difficult time sitting through these movies about climaxing but did so to preserve my job. I had to draw the line, although, at the request to disrobe in front of a group of people."

Shirley Anderson, employed as a nurse and health worker at the Center from May 1993 to January 1994, submitted a declaration in which she declared that she was not informed that she would have to disrobe in front of people as part of self-help. It was only after a few sessions that Eileen Schnitger clarified that self-examination was a job requirement. Lisa Williams told her she would receive no raises or promotions unless she participated in self-examination.

[The trial court granted summary judgment as to all claims except the one for wrongful termination in violation of public policy, and as to that, "limited [it] to the exception with regard to a contention of discharge in invasion of the right of privacy." After the court denied defendants' motion for reconsideration, the instant petition was filed.]

Defendants argue there can be no liability of the Center or its employees for terminating an employee who, having been hired as a health worker whose duties included the demonstration of cervical self-examination before groups of women, objected to and refused to perform that job duty. Defendants argue it was undisputed that the written job description for the health worker position for which plaintiff was hired expressly states that cervical self-examination is a job duty of the health worker. In defendants' view, the trial court ignored this express agreement and also failed to engage in the balancing analysis required in cases involving an alleged violation of the constitutional right to privacy. Defendants posit that the court's denial, pro tanto, of their summary adjudication motion cripples the Center's health education program and threatens the Center's existence by giving every health worker the right to sue for damages for violation of privacy rights.

Plaintiff responds that these arguments are specious as the superior court's order "does not prohibit or eliminate anything nor declare anything illegal." Plaintiff contends that summary adjudication was properly denied based on the existence of a number of disputed issues, namely: whether there was a self-help program in effect during plaintiff's employment; whether such a program included cervical self-examination; whether cervical self-examination was a vital part of the self-help program; whether the cervical self-examination required employees to disrobe in front of other females; whether an employee had the right to refuse to perform cervical self-examination; and whether the Center's interest outweighed plaintiff's right to privacy.

[After reviewing the relevant caselaw, the court concluded that California's constitutional right to privacy forms a sufficient touchstone of public policy to serve as a basis for plaintiff's wrongful termination claim. The defendants did not dispute the existence of such a cause of action, but argued instead that there is no material factual dispute that plaintiff's right to privacy was not violated.]

The principal case discussing the elements of a violation under California's constitutional privacy provision is *Hill v. National Collegiate Athletic Ass'n,* [865 P.2d 633 (Cal. 1994), involving university students' action against the National Collegiate Athletic Association ("NCAA") to enjoin the NCAA's drug testing program for student athletes. The Supreme Court held that] the drug testing program did not violate the California Constitution's right to privacy.

The court summarized the elements of a privacy claim and defenses thereto as follows:

> [W]e hold that a plaintiff alleging an invasion of privacy in violation of the state constitutional right to privacy must establish each of the following: (1) a legally protected privacy interest; (2) a reasonable expectation of privacy in the circumstances; and (3) conduct by defendant constituting a serious invasion of privacy.
>
> Whether a legally recognized privacy interest is present in a given case is a question of law to be decided by the court. Whether plaintiff has a reasonable expectation of privacy in the circumstances and whether defendant's conduct constitutes a serious invasion of privacy are mixed questions of law and fact. If the undisputed material facts show no reasonable expectation of privacy or an insubstantial impact on privacy interests, the question of invasion may be adjudicated as a matter of law.
>
> A defendant may prevail in a state constitutional privacy case by negating any of the three elements just discussed or by pleading and proving, as an affirmative defense, that

the invasion of privacy is justified because it substantially furthers one or more counter-vailing interests. The plaintiff, in turn, may rebut a defendant's assertion of countervailing interests by showing there are feasible and effective alternatives to defendant's conduct which have a lesser impact on privacy interests. Of course, a defendant may also plead and prove other available defenses, e.g., consent, unclean hands, etc., that may be appropriate in view of the nature of the claim and the relief requested.

The existence of a sufficient countervailing interest or an alternative course of conduct present threshold questions of law for the court. The relative strength of countervailing interests and the feasibility of alternatives present mixed questions of law and fact. Again, in cases where material facts are undisputed, adjudication as a matter of law may be appropriate.

In *Hill*, the court accepted as given that the NCAA's policy of observing athletes urinate into vials impinged on a legally protected privacy interest. The court further concluded, though, that student athletes had diminished expectations of privacy by reason of their participation in intercollegiate athletic activities and advance notice of the drug testing. Notwithstanding the diminished expectation of privacy resulting therefrom, the court evaluated the competing interests at stake due to the seriousness of the privacy invasion. The court ultimately concluded that "[t]he NCAA's information-gathering procedure (i.e., drug testing through urinalysis) is a method reasonably calculated to further its interests in enforcing a ban on the ingestion of specified substances in order to secure fair competition and the health and safety of athletes participating in its programs."

Applying the analytical framework of *Hill*, we agree with plaintiff that the observation of the insertion of a speculum into plaintiff's vagina by fellow employees and female clients of the Center infringes a legally protected privacy interest. This invasion is at least as serious as observing urination, and we do not question plaintiff's assertions that it was contrary to her religious and cultural beliefs.

The reasonableness of plaintiff's expectation of privacy is no greater than in the *Hill* case, however. In *Hill*, the student athletes had diminished expectations of privacy by reason of occasional communal undress and the sharing of information regarding physical fitness and bodily condition. Two elements of the NCAA's drug testing program further diminished the student athlete's reasonable expectation of privacy: advance notice and the opportunity to consent to testing. The court acknowledged that participation in athletic contests was conditioned on consent to testing, but that this did not render the consent involuntary, since the students did not have a right to participate in such competitions.

In the present case, the evidence established that plaintiff agreed to demonstrate cervical self-examination as a job requirement. She signed a form which manifested her understanding of and agreement to fulfill certain job duties. Those duties included participating in self-help and demonstrating cervical self-examinations to pregnancy screening groups.

Plaintiff did not dispute that she had agreed to these employment terms. Her dispute, rather, centered on the meaning of the phrase "demonstrates self-cervical exam to pregnancy screening groups." According to plaintiff's declaration, "I was not told it was mandatory to disrobe and insert a speculum in my vagina in front of a group of health workers." Assuming this statement to be true, it still fails to undermine her agreement to demonstrate cervical self-examinations. Disrobing and inserting a speculum in the vagina is a means by which cervical self-examination is demonstrated. Plaintiff's professed ignorance of the particulars of cervical self-examination does not vitiate her agreement to perform it.

The real issue is whether this type of cervical self-examination may reasonably be required of the Center's employees. In other words, the seriousness of the privacy invasion leads us to the third part of the *Hill* test: consideration of the Center's countervailing interests and the feasibility of the alternatives proposed by plaintiff.

Defendant Dido Hasper, the Center's executive director, stated the following reasons for use of cervical self-examination: "The goal is to give women the opportunity to talk to each other, share experiences, learn from each other, and learn about their own bodies. A common realization of participants in self-help groups is that women's bodies and their normal reproductive functions have been medicalized and remain a mystery to them. The goal of self-help is to demystify and redefine the normal functions of a woman's body. Our unique and effective, although not strictly necessary tool to accomplish this is for women to visualize their own cervixes and vaginas, which are not usually seen with the naked eye without the use of a vaginal speculum. In many, but not necessarily all, self-help clinic sessions, women are given the opportunity to learn how to use a plastic speculum."

It is true, as plaintiff notes, that Hasper's declaration reveals that the job requirement of cervical self-examination varies with the circumstances. These variations give rise to an inference that self-help is not an inflexible part of the Center's self-examination orientation sessions or demonstrations to interested groups.

But the declaration also makes clear that cervical self-examination is important in advancing the Center's fundamental goal of educating women about the function and health of their reproductive systems. Other parts of Hasper's declaration also show that the ability to demonstrate self-examination properly and without reservation identified employees who would be outstanding health care workers and potential group leaders. The declaration implied that the identification and retention of such employees was critical to the continued success of the Center. Considering the Center's expansion since its inception some 20 years ago, it was not unreasonable for Hasper to infer that new clients were drawn to the candid knowledge and intimacy imparted by the Center's unique methods, of which cervical self-examination was one.

The Center also could reasonably conclude that the alternative methods of self-examination proposed by plaintiff would have stifled such candor. These alternatives, such as the use of mannequins, or the private use of the speculum followed by discussion, are pale imitations of uninhibited group cervical self-examination.

It goes without saying that certain individuals would have an aversion to cervical self-examination or other aspects of self-help which were used to advance the Center's goal of shared experiences and learning. Plaintiff, for one, acknowledges that her religious and cultural background was not well suited to the practices of the Center.

In balancing these competing interests, we return to plaintiff's consent to demonstrate cervical self-examination as part of her employment agreement with the Center. The Center was not obligated to hire plaintiff, and consent remains a viable defense even in cases of serious privacy invasions. (*Hill.*) Therefore, we believe the facts as disclosed in the trial court give rise to the following inferences only: the requirement that health workers perform cervical self-examinations in front of other females is a reasonable condition of employment and does not violate the health worker's right to privacy where the plaintiff's written employment agreement evidences her knowledge of this condition and agreement to be bound by it. Where the employee thereafter refuses to abide by the agreement, the employee's wrongful termination claim based on a violation of the right to privacy is rendered infirm. Such is the case under the facts presented, and the superior court should have granted summary adjudication of this claim.

As plaintiff's wrongful discharge claims against the individual employees of the Center depend on her claim against the Center, they necessarily fail as well. . . .

NOTES

1. Quon *and* FWHC: *Disparate Facts, Common Themes.* In some ways, the cases that begin and end this chapter — *Quon* and *Feminist Women's Health Center* ("*FWHC*") — are very different. First, the claims involve different types of employers, one public, one private, and therefore derive from different sources of law. In addition, *Quon* involves a fairly typical challenge to employer monitoring of electronic communications. *FWHC* addresses a unique set of circumstances, involving an employee challenge to a highly unusual job requirement — the cervical self-examination demonstration — allegedly tied to the employer's particular mission. Indeed, the controversy underlying *FWHC* and the resulting litigation over privacy rights seem ironic, given that a core component of the employer's mission is to further women's autonomy.

Yet consider what these cases have in common. As we have seen throughout this chapter, although the factual circumstances and articulations of the legal standards may differ, the courts tend to ask the same questions: whether the employee has a legitimate expectation of privacy, whether the employer has articulated a workplace-related interest to justify the alleged intrusion, the strength or importance of this employer interest, the nexus between the employer interest and the intrusion, and the extent to which the employee consented to or was on prior notice of the intrusion(s).

2. *The Role of Consent.* As a formal matter, there are two different ways in which explicit or implicit employee consent to particular intrusions defeat privacy claims. The employer electronic communications and computer use policy cases mentioned above provide an example of the first. These claims frequently fail because the employee's consent to monitoring and oversight eliminates any reasonable expectation of privacy in the underlying communications or files. Now consider why the *FWHC* analysis is different. Ask yourself, does plaintiff in *FWHC* have a reasonable expectation of privacy even though she consented? If yes, then how does consent operate to defeat her claim?

Given these potential effects of consent, and the growing sophistication of employers in crafting employment policies and waivers, the more courts accept private ordering in the workplace, the less privacy protection will exist for workers. The fact that *FWHC* is a California decision may be particularly troubling to workplace privacy advocates since California is one of the few jurisdictions that recognizes a state constitutional right to privacy in the private workplace and is considered among the *most* amenable to employee privacy claims. And recall that employees may fare no better even if they are in a position to challenge ex ante employer demands for consent because of the "Request for Consent Catch-22." Thus, the employer's request for consent itself may effectively preclude many privacy claims. Could plaintiff in *FWHC* have sued if she had been denied a job when she first applied because of the job description?

3. *The Limits of Consent.* Some of the particular statutory protections discussed in this chapter — for example, prohibitions on polygraph, genetic, and forms of medical testing — cannot be waived by employees, even by express consent. Also, in the public employer context, employees cannot be compelled to shed their constitutional rights at the workplace door, *see Pickering v. Board of Educ.*, 391 U.S. 563 (1968), although, as *Quon* and the *O'Connor* plurality's framework suggest, implicit consent to work-place monitoring, surveillance, testing, and other intrusive activities may limit or destroy an employee's legitimate expectation of privacy, and hence, any real hope of establishing a Fourth Amendment or due process violation.

Should there be other limits to the immunizing effect of consent? As we have seen in other contexts, one reason to curtail private ordering between worker and firm is to protect the public or third parties. Is the public interest implicated in the privacy context? If so, when, how, and to what extent? *Cf. Cramer v. Consol. Freightways, Inc.*, 255 F.3d 683 (9th Cir. 2001) (en banc) (holding that even if collective bargaining agreement expressly contemplated employer's video surveillance of employee restrooms, the term would be unenforceable because such surveillance violated a California criminal statute).

Should there be further substantive or procedural limitations? For example, in *Quon* the possibility that the employees had a reasonable expectation of privacy in the text messages despite the employers' fairly clear use policy suggests that inconsistent employer practices or representations can defeat apparent expectation-eliminating language in written policies or waivers. But, assuming no such inconsistency, how clear must a workplace policy or practice be before a court should find that it immunizes the employer from liability? In a case like *FWHC*, how explicit should the disclosure of the job requirement be in order to preclude the employee from later challenging the requirement? Should consent be limited at all by the importance of the employer interest to be served or the "nexus" between that interest and the particular intrusion to which the employee has consented? Should consent obtained at the start of employment be treated differently than consent obtained or notice provided after the employee has started work?

Are there other reasons for discounting even clear and unequivocal forms of express consent to employer intrusions? Although, to date, few courts have addressed this question directly, in *Stengart v. Loving Care Agency, Inc.*, 990 A.2d 650, 664-65 (N.J. 2010), the New Jersey Supreme Court held that communications between an employee and her attorney through the employee's personal e-mail account but on an employer-provided computer were both private and privileged, despite the presence of an electronic communication policy in which the employer reserved the right to monitor and audit such communications. The court reached this conclusion in part because the policy did not address directly the use of personal, Web-based e-mail accounts accessed on company equipment. *See id.* Later in the opinion, however, the court suggested that such communications would have been protected even if the employer's policy had been unambiguous: "Because of the important public policy concerns underlying the attorney-client privilege, even a more clearly written company manual — that is, a policy that banned all personal computer use and provided unambiguous notice that an employer could retrieve and read an employee's attorney-client communications, if accessed on a personal, password-protected e-mail account using the company's computer system — would not be enforceable." *Id.* at 665. For a discussion of the role of consent in the workplace privacy context and various potential limitations on it, *see generally* Steven L. Willborn, *Consenting Employees: Workplace Privacy and the Role of Consent*, 66 La. L. Rev. 975 (2006); *see also* James A. Sonne, *Monitoring for Quality Assurance: Employer Regulation of Off-Duty Behavior*, 43 Ga. L. Rev. 133, 166 (2008).

4. *Is There and Should There Be a Right to Privacy in the Workplace?* If someone were to ask you whether there is a right to privacy in the workplace, how would you respond? You have learned about a number of specific constitutional and statutory protections, various other potential sources of protection, and some common themes — including the role of deference and private ordering. But could you articulate a more general set of guiding principles or limitations? Note that the American Law Insitute intends to include a privacy chapter in the forthcoming Restatement of Employment Law. However, because of the controversy surrounding existing legal approaches and the conceptualization of workplace privacy, there is every indication that this chapter will be the most intensely debated one in the entire project.

Now, in light of what you have learned about existing doctrine, the competing interests at stake, and the potential role of private ordering, consider whether you are satisfied with the law's current approach, and if not, try to identify its shortcomings. If you believe there are circumstances in which the law is too protective of employee privacy interests, how should it be changed to accommodate better the countervailing interests of employers? If, on the contrary, you believe that there are circumstances in which the law does not provide enough protection, how should it be changed to address this problem? Either way, how much should depend on the parties' dealings (expressed in a written agreement or not) and the norms of the particular workplace?

PROBLEM

6-2. Return now to the facts in Problem 6-1 set forth at the outset of this chapter. If DEI is a private sector employer, what potential claims might be available to Smith, the terminated employee? Obviously, given the nature of the intrusion, the Stored Communications Act might provide a starting point, but what limitations discussed above might preclude recovery under this theory? Assuming there is no liability under the Act, what other theories might be available? What barriers might there be to recovery? What other kinds of information would you need to assess the possibilities? Would your answer change if DEI is a public sector employer?

Now turn to counseling the employer. To the extent DEI faces potential liability, what could it have done differently to prevent or reduce the risk of this liability? Again, what additional information would be useful in providing advice? As a general matter, how confident are you in your assessments?

Finally, think about these circumstances from a policy perspective. Should Smith's communications be protected? Why or why not?

7

Workplace Speech and Association Protections

Another area where employee and employer prerogatives and preferences often collide is employee expression, whether in the form of speech or association. The employee interests at stake in this area often differ from the interests underlying privacy claims. Speech rights protect one's ability to express or "share" through words (and sometimes conduct) one's views or beliefs and to associate with those who have common views. Privacy rights, on the other hand, often shield one from having to share; that is, these rights allow the exclusion of others from one's "space" (literal or metaphorical).

Despite their differences, speech and privacy in the workplace have much in common. First, speech and privacy rights both protect aspects of autonomy, and, in fact, some autonomy interests could be characterized as implicating both spheres. For example, one could conceptualize various expressive activities at work—such as dress and grooming—and conduct away from work—including associational, leisure, and Internet activities—as either "speech" or "private" activities. See Chapter 6 at page 352. Accordingly, various protections for worker expressive activities and off-site conduct could be viewed as preserving either speech or privacy rights.

Moreover, because worker speech and privacy protections both involve a clash between worker autonomy and employer prerogatives, the themes dominating the public policy debates and legal inquiry are often similar. For instance, as with privacy, public employees enjoy qualified constitutional protections for speech and association, while employees in the private sector may lack a "source" of such protection. Indeed, in the speech context, the divide between public and private employment is even greater, with public employees enjoying at least limited protection for certain kinds of speech and association and private employees left largely unprotected. In addition, where there is a potential source of protection, the courts often focus on the balance between employee and employer interests, and, as in the privacy cases, the level of deference a court accords the employer's justification for its speech-related restriction or actions is often dispositive. Finally, private ordering may alter the rights and obligations of employee and employer.

Workplace speech cases tend to fall into three broad categories. The first, exemplified by *Connick v. Myers*, 461 U.S. 138 (1983) and *Garcetti v. Ceballos*,

126 S. Ct. 1951 (2006), reproduced at pages 368 and 379, respectively, involves disputes arising out of adverse employment actions resulting from employee speech or expressive activity at, or related to, work. The second concerns employer regulation of, coercion of, or retaliation for an employee's political, religious, or other associational preferences or affiliations. *Edmondson v. Shearer Lumber Products*, 75 P.3d 733 (Idaho 2003), reproduced at page 414, is an example of such litigation in the private employer context. Finally, the third category, addressed in *Dible v. City of Chandler*, 515 F.3d 918 (2008), reproduced at page 395, includes disputes over employer attempts to control employee speech and expression outside of work.

Although these three types of claims raise distinct issues, the public/private employer divide is by far the most important in terms of assessing the potential scope of protection for employee speech or association. This chapter explores potential rights and claims in each of these settings. Most of this chapter is devoted to the public context for a simple reason: While public employees often enjoy less-than-robust protections for their speech and association, protections in the private context are even more limited.

A. THE PUBLIC WORKPLACE

Connick v. Myers
461 U.S. 138 (1983)

WHITE, J.

In *Pickering v. Board of Education*, 391 U.S. 563 (1968), we stated that a public employee does not relinquish First Amendment rights to comment on matters of public interest by virtue of government employment. We also recognized that the State's interests as an employer in regulating the speech of its employees "differ significantly from those it possesses in connection with regulation of the speech of the citizenry in general." The problem, we thought, was arriving "at a balance between the interests of the [employee], as a citizen, in commenting upon matters of public concern and the interest of the State, as an employer, in promoting the efficiency of the public services it performs through its employees." We return to this problem today and consider whether the First and Fourteenth Amendments prevent the discharge of a state employee for circulating a questionnaire concerning internal office affairs.

I

The respondent, Sheila Myers, was employed as an Assistant District Attorney in New Orleans for five and a half years. She served at the pleasure of petitioner Harry Connick, the District Attorney for Orleans Parish. During this period, Myers competently performed her responsibilities of trying criminal cases.

In the early part of October 1980, Myers was informed that she would be transferred to prosecute cases in a different section of the criminal court. Myers was strongly opposed to the proposed transfer[1] and expressed her view to several of her supervisors, including Connick. Despite her objections, on October 6, Myers was notified that she was being transferred. Myers again spoke with Dennis Waldron, one of the First Assistant District Attorneys, expressing her reluctance to accept the transfer. A number of other office matters were discussed and Myers later testified that, in response to Waldron's suggestion that her concerns were not shared by others in the office, she informed him that she would do some research on the matter.

That night Myers prepared a questionnaire soliciting the views of her fellow staff members concerning office transfer policy, office morale, the need for a grievance committee, the level of confidence in supervisors, and whether employees felt pressured to work in political campaigns. Early the following morning, Myers typed and copied the questionnaire. She also met with Connick who urged her to accept the transfer. She said she would "consider" it. Connick then left the office. Myers then distributed the questionnaire to 15 Assistant District Attorneys. Shortly after noon, Dennis Waldron learned that Myers was distributing the survey. He immediately phoned Connick and informed him that Myers was creating a "mini-insurrection" within the office. Connick returned to the office and told Myers that she was being terminated because of her refusal to accept the transfer. She was also told that her distribution of the questionnaire was considered an act of insubordination. Connick particularly objected to the question which inquired whether employees "had confidence in and would rely on the word" of various superiors in the office, and to a question concerning pressure to work in political campaigns which he felt would be damaging if discovered by the press. . . .

II

For at least 15 years, it has been settled that a State cannot condition public employment on a basis that infringes the employee's constitutionally protected interest in freedom of expression. Our task, as we defined it in *Pickering*, is to seek "a balance between the interests of the [employee], as a citizen, in commenting upon matters of public concern and the interest of the State, as an employer, in promoting the efficiency of the public services it performs through its employees." . . .

A

. . . Connick contends at the outset that no balancing of interests is required in this case because Myers' questionnaire concerned only internal office matters and that such speech is not upon a matter of "public concern," as the term was used in *Pickering*. Although we do not agree that Myers' communication in this case was wholly without First Amendment protection, there is much force to Connick's submission. The repeated emphasis in *Pickering* on the right of a public employee "as a citizen, in commenting upon matters of public concern," was not accidental. This language, reiterated in all of *Pickering*'s progeny, reflects both the historical evolvement of

---

1. Myers' opposition was at least partially attributable to her concern that a conflict of interest would have been created by the transfer because of her participation in a counseling program for convicted defendants released on probation in the section of the criminal court to which she was to be assigned.

the rights of public employees, and the common-sense realization that government offices could not function if every employment decision became a constitutional matter.

For most of this century, the unchallenged dogma was that a public employee had no right to object to conditions placed upon the terms of employment — including those which restricted the exercise of constitutional rights. The classic formulation of this position was that of Justice Holmes, who, when sitting on the Supreme Judicial Court of Massachusetts, observed: "[A policeman] may have a constitutional right to talk politics, but he has no constitutional right to be a policeman." *McAuliffe v. Mayor of New Bedford*, 29 N.E. 517, 517 (Mass. 1892). For many years, Holmes' epigram expressed this Court's law.

The Court cast new light on the matter in a series of cases arising from the widespread efforts in the 1950's and early 1960's to require public employees, particularly teachers, to swear oaths of loyalty to the State and reveal the groups with which they associated. In *Wiemann v. Updegraff*, 344 U.S. 183 (1952), the Court held that a State could not require its employees to establish their loyalty by extracting an oath denying past affiliation with Communists. In *Cafeteria Workers v. McElroy*, 367 U.S. 886 (1961), the Court recognized that the government could not deny employment because of previous membership in a particular party. . . .

In all of these cases, the precedents in which *Pickering* is rooted, the invalidated statutes and actions sought to suppress the rights of public employees to participate in public affairs. The issue was whether government employees could be prevented or "chilled" by the fear of discharge from joining political parties and other associations that certain public officials might find "subversive." The explanation for the Constitution's special concern with threats to the right of citizens to participate in political affairs is no mystery. The First Amendment "was fashioned to assure unfettered interchange of ideas for the bringing about of political and social changes desired by the people." *Roth v. United States*, 354 U.S. 476, 484 (1957); *New York Times Co. v. Sullivan*, 376 U.S. 254, 269 (1964). "[Speech] concerning public affairs is more than self-expression; it is the essence of self-government." *Garrison v. Louisiana*, 379 U.S. 64, 74-75 (1964). Accordingly, the Court has frequently reaffirmed that speech on public issues occupies the " 'highest rung of the hierarchy of First Amendment values,' " and is entitled to special protection.

Pickering v. Board of Education followed from this understanding of the First Amendment. In *Pickering*, the Court held impermissible under the First Amendment the dismissal of a high school teacher for openly criticizing the Board of Education on its allocation of school funds between athletics and education and its methods of informing taxpayers about the need for additional revenue. Pickering's subject was "a matter of legitimate public concern" upon which "free and open debate is vital to informed decisionmaking by the electorate."

Our cases following *Pickering* also involved safeguarding speech on matters of public concern. . . . Most recently, in *Givhan v. Western Line Consolidated School District*, 439 U.S. 410 (1979), we held that First Amendment protection applies when a public employee arranges to communicate privately with his employer rather than to express his views publicly. . . .

Pickering, its antecedents, and its progeny lead us to conclude that if Myers' questionnaire cannot be fairly characterized as constituting speech on a matter of public concern, it is unnecessary for us to scrutinize the reasons for her discharge. When employee expression cannot be fairly considered as relating to any matter of political, social, or other concern to the community, government officials should enjoy wide latitude in managing their offices, without intrusive oversight by the judiciary in the name of the First Amendment. Perhaps the government employer's dismissal of the worker may not be fair, but ordinary dismissals from government service which violate no fixed tenure or applicable statute or regulation are not subject to judicial review even if the reasons for the dismissal are alleged to be mistaken or unreasonable. . . .

Whether an employee's speech addresses a matter of public concern must be determined by the content, form, and context of a given statement, as revealed by the whole record.[7] In this case, with but one exception, the questions posed by Myers to her co-workers do not fall under the rubric of matters of "public concern." We view the questions pertaining to the confidence and trust that Myers' co-workers possess in various supervisors, the level of office morale, and the need for a grievance committee as mere extensions of Myers' dispute over her transfer to another section of the criminal court. . . . [W]e do not believe these questions are of public import in evaluating the performance of the District Attorney as an elected official. Myers did not seek to inform the public that the District Attorney's Office was not discharging its governmental responsibilities in the investigation and prosecution of criminal cases. Nor did Myers seek to bring to light actual or potential wrongdoing or breach of public trust on the part of Connick and others. Indeed, the questionnaire, if released to the public, would convey no information at all other than the fact that a single employee is upset with the status quo. While discipline and morale in the workplace are related to an agency's efficient performance of its duties, the focus of Myers' questions is not to evaluate the performance of the office but rather to gather ammunition for another round of controversy with her superiors. These questions reflect one employee's dissatisfaction with a transfer and an attempt to turn that displeasure into a cause célèbre.[8]

To presume that all matters which transpire within a government office are of public concern would mean that virtually every remark — and certainly every criticism directed at a public official — would plant the seed of a constitutional case. While as a matter of good judgment, public officials should be receptive to constructive criticism offered by their employees, the First Amendment does not require a public office to be run as a roundtable for employee complaints over internal office affairs.

One question in Myers' questionnaire, however, does touch upon a matter of public concern. Question 11 inquires if assistant district attorneys "ever feel pressured to work in political campaigns on behalf of office supported candidates." We have recently noted that official pressure upon employees to work for political candidates not of the worker's own choice constitutes a coercion of belief in violation of fundamental constitutional rights. *Branti v. Finkel*, [445 U.S. 507, 515-16 (1980); *Elrod v. Burns*, 427 U.S. 347 (1976). . . . [W]e believe it apparent that the issue of

---

7. The inquiry into the protected status of speech is one of law, not fact.

8. This is not a case like *Givhan*, where an employee speaks out as a citizen on a matter of general concern, not tied to a personal employment dispute, but arranges to do so privately. Mrs. Givhan's right to protest racial discrimination — a matter inherently of public concern — is not forfeited by her choice of a private forum. Here, however, a questionnaire not otherwise of public concern does not attain that status because its subject matter could, in different circumstances, have been the topic of a communication to the public that might be of general interest. The dissent's analysis of whether discussions of office morale and discipline could be matters of public concern is beside the point — it does not answer whether *this* questionnaire is such speech.

whether assistant district attorneys are pressured to work in political campaigns is a matter of interest to the community upon which it is essential that public employees be able to speak out freely without fear of retaliatory dismissal.

B

Because one of the questions in Myers' survey touched upon a matter of public concern and contributed to her discharge, we must determine whether Connick was justified in discharging Myers. Here the District Court again erred in imposing an unduly onerous burden on the State to justify Myers' discharge. The District Court viewed the issue of whether Myers' speech was upon a matter of "public concern" as a threshold inquiry, after which it became the government's burden to "clearly demonstrate" that the speech involved "substantially interfered" with official responsibilities. Yet *Pickering* unmistakably states . . . that the State's burden in justifying a particular discharge varies depending upon the nature of the employee's expression. Although such particularized balancing is difficult, the courts must reach the most appropriate possible balance of the competing interests.

C

The *Pickering* balance requires full consideration of the government's interest in the effective and efficient fulfillment of its responsibilities to the public. One hundred years ago, the Court noted the government's legitimate purpose in "[promoting] efficiency and integrity in the discharge of official duties, and [in] [maintaining] proper discipline in the public service." *Ex parte Curtis*, [106 U.S. 371, 373 (1882)]. As Justice Powell explained in his separate opinion in *Arnett v. Kennedy*, 416 U.S. 134, 168 (1974):

> To this end, the Government, as an employer, must have wide discretion and control over the management of its personnel and internal affairs. This includes the prerogative to remove employees whose conduct hinders efficient operation and to do so with dispatch. Prolonged retention of a disruptive or otherwise unsatisfactory employee can adversely affect discipline and morale in the work place, foster disharmony, and ultimately impair the efficiency of an office or agency.

We agree with the District Court that there is no demonstration here that the questionnaire impeded Myers' ability to perform her responsibilities. The District Court was also correct to recognize that "it is important to the efficient and successful operation of the District Attorney's office for Assistants to maintain close working relationships with their superiors." Connick's judgment, and apparently also that of his first assistant Dennis Waldron, who characterized Myers' actions as causing a "mini-insurrection," was that Myers' questionnaire was an act of insubordination which interfered with working relationships. When close working relationships are essential to fulfilling public responsibilities, a wide degree of deference to the employer's judgment is appropriate. Furthermore, we do not see the necessity for an employer to allow events to unfold to the extent that the disruption of the office and the destruction of working relationships is manifest before taking action. We caution that a stronger showing may be necessary if the employee's speech more substantially involved matters of public concern.

. . . Questions, no less than forcefully stated opinions and facts, carry messages and it requires no unusual insight to conclude that the purpose, if not the likely result, of the questionnaire is to seek to precipitate a vote of no confidence in Connick and his supervisors. Thus, Question 10, which asked whether or not the Assistants had confidence in and relied on the word of five named supervisors, is a statement that carries the clear potential for undermining office relations.

Also relevant is the manner, time, and place in which the questionnaire was distributed. . . . Here the questionnaire was prepared and distributed at the office; the manner of distribution required not only Myers to leave her work but others to do the same in order that the questionnaire be completed.[13] Although some latitude in when official work is performed is to be allowed when professional employees are involved, and Myers did not violate announced office policy, the fact that Myers, unlike Pickering, exercised her rights to speech at the office supports Connick's fears that the functioning of his office was endangered.

Finally, the context in which the dispute arose is also significant. This is not a case where an employee, out of purely academic interest, circulated a questionnaire so as to obtain useful research. Myers acknowledges that it is no coincidence that the questionnaire followed upon the heels of the transfer notice. When employee speech concerning office policy arises from an employment dispute concerning the very application of that policy to the speaker, additional weight must be given to the supervisor's view that the employee has threatened the authority of the employer to run the office. . . .

III

Myers' questionnaire touched upon matters of public concern in only a most limited sense; her survey, in our view, is most accurately characterized as an employee grievance concerning internal office policy. The limited First Amendment interest involved here does not require that Connick tolerate action which he reasonably believed would disrupt the office, undermine his authority, and destroy close working relationships. Myers' discharge therefore did not offend the First Amendment. We reiterate, however, the caveat we expressed in *Pickering:* "Because of the enormous variety of fact situations in which critical statements by . . . public employees may be thought by their superiors . . . to furnish grounds for dismissal, we do not deem it either appropriate or feasible to attempt to lay down a general standard against which all such statements may be judged."

Our holding today is grounded in our longstanding recognition that the First Amendment's primary aim is the full protection of speech upon issues of public concern, as well as the practical realities involved in the administration of a government office. Although today the balance is struck for the government, this is no defeat for the First Amendment. For it would indeed be a Pyrrhic victory for the great principles of

13. The record indicates that some, though not all, of the copies of the questionnaire were distributed during lunch. Employee speech which transpires entirely on the employee's own time, and in nonwork areas of the office, bring different factors into the *Pickering* calculus, and might lead to a different conclusion.

free expression if the Amendment's safeguarding of a public employee's right, as a citizen, to participate in discussions concerning public affairs were confused with the attempt to constitutionalize the employee grievance that we see presented here. The judgment of the Court of Appeals is *Reversed.**

NOTES

1. *The* Pickering/Connick *Balancing Test.* In determining whether Myers' termination violated her First and Fourteenth Amendment speech rights, the Court applied an analytical framework that has come to be known as the "*Pickering/Connick* balancing test." For speech in or related to the workplace, the employee must establish that the expression addresses a matter of public concern. As *Connick* demonstrates, aspects of the employee's speech that do not address matters of public concern receive no First Amendment protection. If the speech or portions of it do address matters of public concern, the court then "balances" the employee's interest in speaking on matters of public concern with the employer's interest in promoting workplace efficiency. Finally, even if the employee's interest in free expression prevails in the balance, the employee must also demonstrate causation; that is, the employer disciplined or dismissed the employee because of the employee's speech. This issue was not reached in *Connick*, given the Court's conclusion on the application of the balancing test; had the dissenting opinion been the majority, a remand would likely have been necessary to determine whether the district attorney fired Myers because of her questionnaire or, as the district attorney's office alleged, because of her refusal to accept the transfer.

2. "*A Matter of Public Concern.*" Why does the Court limit employee protection against speech-related adverse employment actions to matters of public concern? Obviously, the distinction is important: Indeed, whether Myers' speech addressed a matter of public concern was dispositive, at least for portions of her questionnaire. Yet what is a matter of public concern? From *Connick*, we have guidance as to what is *not* a matter of public concern: "When employee expression cannot be fairly considered as relating to any matter of political, social, or other concern to the community."

---

* *Editor's Note: Employment Law Trivia.* The defendant in *Connick v. Myers* was Harry Connick, Sr., district attorney for Orleans Parish. You may have heard of his son, musician Harry Connick, Jr. The father became district attorney by beating a famous (or infamous) predecessor in the post, Jim Garrison, who played a role in investigating the Kennedy assassination and, depending on who you believe, either (1) uncovered the true conspiracy only to be foiled by the FBI, (2) bungled a potentially effective investigation, or (3) went on a wild goose chase. Coincidentally, *Garrison v. Louisiana*, cited by the Supreme Court in *Connick* as one of the foundational free speech cases, involved Jim Garrison, who had been found guilty of "criminal defamation" — when he claimed that the large backlog of pending criminal cases was due to the laziness of the judges and that failures of law enforcement were due to their failure to authorize funds for the district attorney. At a press conference, Garrison declared, "The judges have now made it eloquently clear where their sympathies lie in regard to aggressive vice investigations by refusing to authorize use of the DA's funds to pay for the cost of closing down the Canal Street clip joint. . . . This raises interesting questions about the racketeer influences on our eight vacation-minded judges." 379 U.S. at 66. The Supreme Court reversed Garrison's conviction. Undoubtedly, Ms. Myers relied heavily on her boss's predecessor's claims of free-speech rights in pursuing her suit against Connick. In the aftermath, Connick, Sr. continued on as New Orleans District Attorney until 2002, Dennis Waldron became a judge in the Criminal Court, and Sheila Myers is a well-respected criminal defense attorney who litigates frequently against her former employer. Myers' biggest regret, though, is that the decision "is cited as the case against public employees." http://www.freedomforum.org/templates/.

Moreover, the *Connick* majority views speech addressing the internal affairs of the agency and not rising above mere dissatisfaction or displeasure with one's supervisors as not implicating public concern. In other words, mere personal concerns or interests, as opposed to those of the employee as a citizen, are not matters of public concern. *See, e.g., Rodgers v. Banks*, 344 F.3d 587, 599 (6th Cir. 2003) (noting *Connick's* personal interest versus citizen dichotomy).

On the flip side, *Connick* makes clear that employee expression need not be shared with the public to address a matter of public concern. In other words, it may be purely internal, although the fact that it is not shared with the public may affect the analysis of whether it implicates a public concern. *See also Rankin v. McPherson*, 483 U.S. 378 (1987) (finding one worker's statement to a co-worker, after finding out that President Reagan had been shot, that "[i]f they go after him again, I hope they get him" addressed matters of public concern). In terms of content, speech relating to broad public policy issues and improprieties in the agency, as well as public statements questioning the effectiveness of the agency have been recognized as matters of public concern. *See, e.g., Pickering*, 391 U.S. at 571-73; *Rodgers*, 344 F.3d at 600-01 (finding a memo addressing patient care and care deficiencies occurring at a public nursing care facility addressed matters of public concern). In addition, statements about current political events or high-ranking public officials are matters of public concern. *See, e.g., Rankin*, 483 U.S. at 386-87. Moreover, issues or information regarding the functioning, decisions, or initiatives of the department or agency have been found to be matters of public concern where the larger community has shown interest. *See, e.g., Kennedy v. Tangipahoa Parish Library Bd. of Control*, 224 F.3d 359, 373 (5th Cir. 2000) (asserting that "speech made against the backdrop of ongoing commentary and debate in the press involves the public concern"); *Burnham v. Ianni*, 119 F.3d 668 (8th Cir. 1997) (en banc) (holding a display in a public university's history department containing pictures of professors with props associated with their areas of expertise that sparked controversy was a matter of public concern because of the public interest in it). Speech related to the collective bargaining process and other union activities (beyond personal grievances) has been found to be a matter of public concern. *See, e.g., Davignon v. Hodgson*, 524 F.3d 91 (1st Cir. 2008). And, as the majority's citation of *Givhan* indicates, courts have usually found that issues surrounding allegations of discrimination are matters of public concern. *See, e.g., Love-Lane v. Martin*, 355 F.3d 766 (4th Cir. 2004) (finding concerns regarding discriminatory practices in school system to be matter of public concern).

Beyond this, however, there is not much guidance. Indeed, *Connick* emphasized the fact-intensive nature of the inquiry, suggesting that whether the speech addresses a matter of public concern depends on its content, form, and context, along with the time, place, and manner of the speech. What about other matters of public interest not necessarily involving prevailing political issues, government policies, or government officials? For example, although a resulting adverse action against a public employee may seem unlikely in this context, what about obnoxious statements regarding a professional sports event or team? If no, what about a conversation regarding the NFL's "censorship" of the Rolling Stones performance during halftime at the 2006 Super Bowl? What about comments regarding popular but controversial movies — for example, *An Inconvenient Truth, The Passion of the Christ*, or *Brokeback Mountain* —that may anger or offend other employees? Does "public concern" simply mean something that has captured the public's interest or imagination, or is something more required? *See generally* Cynthia L.

Estlund, *Speech on Matters of Public Concern: The Perils of an Emerging First Amendment Category*, 59 GEO. WASH. L. REV. 1 (1990); Randy J. Kozel, *Reconceptualizing Public Employee Speech*, 99 NW. U. L. REV. 1007 (2005); Rodric B. Schoen, Pickering *Plus Thirty Years: Public Employees and Free Speech*, 30 TEX. TECH L. REV. 5 (1999); *see also* George Rutherglen, *Public Employee Speech in Remedial Perspective*, 24 J. L. & POLITICS 129, 130 (2008) (questioning whether the "public concern" test is appropriate in light of its uncertain application).

3. *"Balancing" the Interests.* In balancing the employee's interest against the employer's, the Supreme Court has likewise provided less-than-clear guidance. The Court was unwilling in either *Connick* or *Pickering* to lay down clear parameters for how to engage in the balancing inquiry. *See, e.g., Pickering*, 391 U.S. at 569. Rather than weighing the competing interests, both opinions focused on the employer's interest in efficiency, exploring whether the employee's statements might have actually disrupted the workplace. Indeed, in *Pickering*, the Court's balancing analysis consisted entirely of the following discussion, after which the Court found in favor of the employee:

> The [teacher's] statements are in no way directed towards any person with whom appellant would normally be in contact in the course of his daily work as a teacher. Thus no question of maintaining either discipline by immediate superiors or harmony among coworkers is presented here. Appellant's employment relationships with the Board and, to a somewhat lesser extent, with the superintendent are not the kind of close working relationships for which it can persuasively be claimed that personal loyalty and confidence are necessary to their proper functioning.

Id. at 569-70; *see also Rankin*, 483 U.S. at 388-89 (finding interests of employee outweighed those of employer in the case involving a deputy constable's comments about attempted presidential assassination after rejecting the employer's claims of disruption, public relations problems, and loss in efficiency).

Thus, once the employee has made his or her threshold showing, so-called "balancing" in the speech-in-the-workplace context — as in the privacy-in-the-workplace context — tends instead to be an inquiry into the strength of the employer's proffered justification for taking action against the employee. Occasionally, however, courts have recognized that the importance of the content of the speech increases the burden on the government to show that efficiency concerns ought to prevail. *See, e.g., Love-Lane*, 355 F.3d at 785 (stating that because race discrimination in schools involves a substantial issue of public concern, the government's burden is heightened). Other efficiency interests offered by government employers and recognized by the courts include preserving confidentiality and protecting the public, and, where it is necessary, ensuring loyalty. *See, e.g., Sheppard v. Beerman*, 317 F.3d 351 (2d Cir. 2003) (finding no constitutional violation after the judge terminated a law clerk after outbursts because of the potential disruptiveness of retaining a disloyal and disrespectful clerk in the extremely close and confidential work setting).

The Supreme Court has also indicated that the employer bears the burden of establishing the objective good faith of its proffered efficiency concerns. In other words, it is the employer's obligation to demonstrate that its action was in good faith (not pretextual) and based on a reasonable assessment of the circumstances in terms of whether the speech actually occurred and the extent to which it is likely to lead to disruption or harm efficiency. *See Waters v. Churchill*, 511 U.S. 661, 677-78 (1994).

4. Pickering/Connick *Applied*. Unsurprisingly, this framework has produced mixed results in the lower federal courts, although the defending government institution more often prevails. *Compare Love-Lane*, 355 F.3d at 785 (indicating that "some disharmony" caused by employee's criticisms of allegedly discriminatory practices is not enough to justify adverse employment action), *and Rodgers*, 344 F.3d at 601-02 (rejecting as conclusory the employer's claims that employee complaints about patient care caused disharmony and disruption), *with Vanderpuye v. Cohen*, 94 F. App'x 3 (2d Cir. 2004) (finding that, although city employee's speech regarding conflicts of interest was a matter of public concern, it was outweighed by potential for disruption in functioning of department), *Sheppard*, 317 F.3d at 355 (upholding constitutionality of termination of judicial clerk after outbursts), *and Jeffries v. Harleston*, 52 F.3d 9 (2d Cir. 1995) (holding public university officials did not violate First Amendment rights of professor by reducing his term as department chair because of controversial speech, since they were motivated by reasonable prediction of disruption to university operations).

Public employers tend to prevail in cases in which the speech is offensive, threatening, or harassing to protected groups, including women and minorities, although courts are often unwilling to find that vague or indirect statements, even if hyperbolic, are threatening or harassing. *Compare Pappas v. Giuliani*, 290 F.3d 143 (2d Cir. 2002) (upholding municipality's right to terminate police officer after his anonymous dissemination of racist and anti-Semitic materials), *with Bauer v. Sampson*, 261 F.3d 775 (9th Cir. 2001) (rejecting defendant college's contention that professor's scathing and hyperbolic criticisms of new administrator were threatening or discriminatory and were sufficiently disruptive to warrant discipline). To the extent that the employee's speech might itself violate the law, such as constituting racial or sexual harassment of co-workers, *see* Chapter 9, the employer will obviously have a greater interest in acting. *See, e.g.*, J.M. Balkin, *Free Speech and Hostile Environments*, 99 COLUM. L. REV. 2295 (1999); Cynthia L. Estlund, *Freedom of Expression in the Workplace and the Problem of Discriminatory Harassment*, 75 TEX. L. REV. 687 (1997); Eugene Volokh, *What Speech Does "Hostile Work Environment" Harassment Law Restrict?*, 85 GEO. L. J. 627 (1997).

5. *Speech and Employee Duties*. What if employee speech on a matter of public concern is not only in the workplace, but also in the context of the employee performing his or her particular job duties? The Court took up this issue in the next case.

Garcetti v. Ceballos
547 U.S. 410 (2006)

JUSTICE KENNEDY delivered the opinion of the Court.

It is well settled that "a State cannot condition public employment on a basis that infringes the employee's constitutionally protected interest in freedom of expression." *Connick v. Myers*. The question presented by the instant case is whether the First Amendment protects a government employee from discipline based on speech made pursuant to the employee's official duties.

I

Respondent Richard Ceballos has been employed since 1989 as a deputy district attorney for the Los Angeles County District Attorney's Office. During the period relevant to this case, Ceballos was a calendar deputy in the office's Pomona branch, and in this capacity he exercised certain supervisory responsibilities over other lawyers. In February 2000, a defense attorney contacted Ceballos about a pending criminal case. The defense attorney said there were inaccuracies in an affidavit used to obtain a critical search warrant. The attorney informed Ceballos that he had filed a motion to traverse, or challenge, the warrant, but he also wanted Ceballos to review the case. According to Ceballos, it was not unusual for defense attorneys to ask calendar deputies to investigate aspects of pending cases.

After examining the affidavit and visiting the location it described, Ceballos determined the affidavit contained serious misrepresentations. The affidavit called a long driveway what Ceballos thought should have been referred to as a separate roadway. Ceballos also questioned the affidavit's statement that tire tracks led from a stripped-down truck to the premises covered by the warrant. His doubts arose from his conclusion that the roadway's composition in some places made it difficult or impossible to leave visible tire tracks.

Ceballos spoke on the telephone to the warrant affiant, a deputy sheriff from the Los Angeles County Sheriff's Department, but he did not receive a satisfactory explanation for the perceived inaccuracies. He relayed his findings to his supervisors, petitioners Carol Najera and Frank Sundstedt, and followed up by preparing a disposition memorandum. The memo explained Ceballos' concerns and recommended dismissal of the case. On March 2, 2000, Ceballos submitted the memo to Sundstedt for his review. A few days later, Ceballos presented Sundstedt with another memo, this one describing a second telephone conversation between Ceballos and the warrant affiant.

Based on Ceballos' statements, a meeting was held to discuss the affidavit. Attendees included Ceballos, Sundstedt, and Najera, as well as the warrant affiant and other employees from the sheriff's department. The meeting allegedly became heated, with one lieutenant sharply criticizing Ceballos for his handling of the case.

Despite Ceballos' concerns, Sundstedt decided to proceed with the prosecution, pending disposition of the defense motion to traverse. The trial court held a hearing on the motion. Ceballos was called by the defense and recounted his observations about the affidavit, but the trial court rejected the challenge to the warrant.

[Ceballos sued, claiming that he was subjected to a series of retaliatory employment actions for his March 2 memo. The district court granted defendants summary judgment, but the Ninth Circuit reversed, holding that "Ceballos's allegations of wrongdoing in the memorandum constitute protected speech under the First Amendment."]

II

As the Court's decisions have noted, for many years "the unchallenged dogma was that a public employee had no right to object to conditions placed upon the terms of employment—including those which restricted the exercise of constitutional rights." *Connick.* That dogma has been qualified in important respects. *See id.* The Court has made clear that public employees do not surrender all their First

Amendment rights by reason of their employment. Rather, the First Amendment protects a public employee's right, in certain circumstances, to speak as a citizen addressing matters of public concern. *See, e.g.,* [*Pickering; Connick; Rankin v. McPherson*, 483 U.S. 378, 384 (1987); *United States v. Treasury Employees*, 513 U.S. 454, 466 (1995)]. . . .

[The Court outlined the *Pickering/Connick* balancing test.] A government entity has broader discretion to restrict speech when it acts in its role as employer, but the restrictions it imposes must be directed at speech that has some potential to affect the entity's operations.

To be sure, conducting these inquiries sometimes has proved difficult. . . .

When a citizen enters government service, the citizen by necessity must accept certain limitations on his or her freedom. Government employers, like private employers, need a significant degree of control over their employees' words and actions; without it, there would be little chance for the efficient provision of public services. *Cf. Connick* ("[G]overnment offices could not function if every employment decision became a constitutional matter"). Public employees, moreover, often occupy trusted positions in society. When they speak out, they can express views that contravene governmental policies or impair the proper performance of governmental functions.

At the same time, the Court has recognized that a citizen who works for the government is nonetheless a citizen. The First Amendment limits the ability of a public employer to leverage the employment relationship to restrict, incidentally or intentionally, the liberties employees enjoy in their capacities as private citizens. *See Perry v. Sindermann*, 408 U.S. 593, 597 (1972). So long as employees are speaking as citizens about matters of public concern, they must face only those speech restrictions that are necessary for their employers to operate efficiently and effectively. *See, e.g., Connick*.

The Court's employee-speech jurisprudence protects, of course, the constitutional rights of public employees. Yet the First Amendment interests at stake extend beyond the individual speaker. The Court has acknowledged the importance of promoting the public's interest in receiving the well-informed views of government employees engaging in civic discussion. *Pickering* again provides an instructive example. The Court characterized its holding as rejecting the attempt of school administrators to "limi[t] teachers' opportunities to contribute to public debate." It also noted that teachers are "the members of a community most likely to have informed and definite opinions" about school expenditures. The Court's approach acknowledged the necessity for informed, vibrant dialogue in a democratic society. It suggested, in addition, that widespread costs may arise when dialogue is repressed. The Court's more recent cases have expressed similar concerns. *See, e.g., San Diego v. Roe*, 543 U.S. 77, 82 (2004) *(per curiam)* ("Were [public employees] not able to speak on [the operation of their employers], the community would be deprived of informed opinions on important public issues. The interest at stake is as much the public's interest in receiving informed opinion as it is the employee's own right to disseminate it" (citation omitted)); *cf. Treasury Employees* ("The large-scale disincentive to Government employees' expression also imposes a significant burden on the public's right to read and hear what the employees would otherwise have written and said").

The Court's decisions, then, have sought both to promote the individual and societal interests that are served when employees speak as citizens on matters of public concern and to respect the needs of government employers attempting to perform their important public functions. Underlying our cases has been the premise that while the First Amendment invests public employees with certain rights, it does not empower them to "constitutionalize the employee grievance." *Connick.*

III

With these principles in mind we turn to the instant case. Respondent Ceballos believed the affidavit used to obtain a search warrant contained serious misrepresentations. He conveyed his opinion and recommendation in a memo to his supervisor. That Ceballos expressed his views inside his office, rather than publicly, is not dispositive. Employees in some cases may receive First Amendment protection for expressions made at work. *See, e.g., Givhan v. Western Line Consol. School Dist.*, 439 U.S. 410, 414 (1979). Many citizens do much of their talking inside their respective workplaces, and it would not serve the goal of treating public employees like "any member of the general public," *Pickering*, to hold that all speech within the office is automatically exposed to restriction.

The memo concerned the subject matter of Ceballos' employment, but this, too, is nondispositive. The First Amendment protects some expressions related to the speaker's job. As the Court noted in *Pickering:* "Teachers are, as a class, the members of a community most likely to have informed and definite opinions as to how funds allotted to the operation of the schools should be spent. Accordingly, it is essential that they be able to speak out freely on such questions without fear of retaliatory dismissal." The same is true of many other categories of public employees.

The controlling factor in Ceballos' case is that his expressions were made pursuant to his duties as a calendar deputy. That consideration — the fact that Ceballos spoke as a prosecutor fulfilling a responsibility to advise his supervisor about how best to proceed with a pending case — distinguishes Ceballos' case from those in which the First Amendment provides protection against discipline. We hold that when public employees make statements pursuant to their official duties, the employees are not speaking as citizens for First Amendment purposes, and the Constitution does not insulate their communications from employer discipline.

Ceballos wrote his disposition memo because that is part of what he, as a calendar deputy, was employed to do. It is immaterial whether he experienced some personal gratification from writing the memo; his First Amendment rights do not depend on his job satisfaction. The significant point is that the memo was written pursuant to Ceballos' official duties. Restricting speech that owes its existence to a public employee's professional responsibilities does not infringe any liberties the employee might have enjoyed as a private citizen. It simply reflects the exercise of employer control over what the employer itself has commissioned or created. *Cf. Rosenberger v. Rector and Visitors of Univ. of Va.*, 515 U.S. 819, 833 (1995) ("[W]hen the government appropriates public funds to promote a particular policy of its own it is entitled to say what it wishes"). Contrast, for example, the expressions made by the speaker in *Pickering*, whose letter to the newspaper had no official significance and bore similarities to letters submitted by numerous citizens every day.

Ceballos did not act as a citizen when he went about conducting his daily professional activities, such as supervising attorneys, investigating charges, and preparing filings. In the same way he did not speak as a citizen by writing a memo that addressed the proper disposition of a pending criminal case. When he went to work and performed the tasks he was paid to perform, Ceballos acted as a government employee.

The fact that his duties sometimes required him to speak or write does not mean his supervisors were prohibited from evaluating his performance.

This result is consistent with our precedents' attention to the potential societal value of employee speech. Refusing to recognize First Amendment claims based on government employees' work product does not prevent them from participating in public debate. The employees retain the prospect of constitutional protection for their contributions to the civic discourse. This prospect of protection, however, does not invest them with a right to perform their jobs however they see fit.

Our holding likewise is supported by the emphasis of our precedents on affording government employers sufficient discretion to manage their operations. Employers have heightened interests in controlling speech made by an employee in his or her professional capacity. Official communications have official consequences, creating a need for substantive consistency and clarity. Supervisors must ensure that their employees' official communications are accurate, demonstrate sound judgment, and promote the employer's mission. Ceballos' memo is illustrative. It demanded the attention of his supervisors and led to a heated meeting with employees from the sheriff's department. If Ceballos' superiors thought his memo was inflammatory or misguided, they had the authority to take proper corrective action.

Ceballos' proposed contrary rule, adopted by the Court of Appeals, would commit state and federal courts to a new, permanent, and intrusive role, mandating judicial oversight of communications between and among government employees and their superiors in the course of official business. This displacement of managerial discretion by judicial supervision finds no support in our precedents. When an employee speaks as a citizen addressing a matter of public concern, the First Amendment requires a delicate balancing of the competing interests surrounding the speech and its consequences. When, however, the employee is simply performing his or her job duties, there is no warrant for a similar degree of scrutiny. To hold otherwise would be to demand permanent judicial intervention in the conduct of governmental operations to a degree inconsistent with sound principles of federalism and the separation of powers.

The Court of Appeals based its holding in part on what it perceived as a doctrinal anomaly. The court suggested it would be inconsistent to compel public employers to tolerate certain employee speech made publicly but not speech made pursuant to an employee's assigned duties. This objection misconceives the theoretical underpinnings of our decisions. Employees who make public statements outside the course of performing their official duties retain some possibility of First Amendment protection because that is the kind of activity engaged in by citizens who do not work for the government. The same goes for writing a letter to a local newspaper, see *Pickering*, or discussing politics with a co-worker, see *Rankin*. When a public employee speaks pursuant to employment responsibilities, however, there is no relevant analogue to speech by citizens who are not government employees.

The Court of Appeals' concern also is unfounded as a practical matter. The perceived anomaly, it should be noted, is limited in scope: It relates only to the expressions an employee makes pursuant to his or her official responsibilities, not to statements or complaints (such as those at issue in cases like *Pickering* and *Connick*) that are made outside the duties of employment. If, moreover, a government employer is troubled by the perceived anomaly, it has the means at hand to avoid it. A public employer that wishes to encourage its employees to voice concerns privately retains the option of instituting internal policies and procedures that are receptive to employee criticism.

Giving employees an internal forum for their speech will discourage them from concluding that the safest avenue of expression is to state their views in public.

Proper application of our precedents thus leads to the conclusion that the First Amendment does not prohibit managerial discipline based on an employee's expressions made pursuant to official responsibilities. Because Ceballos' memo falls into this category, his allegation of unconstitutional retaliation must fail.

Two final points warrant mentioning. First, as indicated above, the parties in this case do not dispute that Ceballos wrote his disposition memo pursuant to his employment duties. We thus have no occasion to articulate a comprehensive framework for defining the scope of an employee's duties in cases where there is room for serious debate. We reject, however, the suggestion that employers can restrict employees' rights by creating excessively broad job descriptions. The proper inquiry is a practical one. Formal job descriptions often bear little resemblance to the duties an employee actually is expected to perform, and the listing of a given task in an employee's written job description is neither necessary nor sufficient to demonstrate that conducting the task is within the scope of the employee's professional duties for First Amendment purposes.

Second, Justice Souter suggests today's decision may have important ramifications for academic freedom, at least as a constitutional value. There is some argument that expression related to academic scholarship or classroom instruction implicates additional constitutional interests that are not fully accounted for by this Court's customary employee-speech jurisprudence. We need not, and for that reason do not, decide whether the analysis we conduct today would apply in the same manner to a case involving speech related to scholarship or teaching. . . .

IV

Exposing governmental inefficiency and misconduct is a matter of considerable significance. As the Court noted in *Connick*, public employers should, "as a matter of good judgment," be "receptive to constructive criticism offered by their employees." The dictates of sound judgment are reinforced by the powerful network of legislative enactments — such as whistle-blower protection laws and labor codes — available to those who seek to expose wrongdoing. Cases involving government attorneys implicate additional safeguards in the form of, for example, rules of conduct and constitutional obligations apart from the First Amendment. *See, e.g.*, Cal. Rule Prof. Conduct 5-110 (2005) ("A member in government service shall not institute or cause to be instituted criminal charges when the member knows or should know that the charges are not supported by probable cause"); *Brady v. Maryland*, 373 U.S. 83 (1963). These imperatives, as well as obligations arising from any other applicable constitutional provisions and mandates of the criminal and civil laws, protect employees and provide checks on supervisors who would order unlawful or otherwise inappropriate actions.

We reject, however, the notion that the First Amendment shields from discipline the expressions employees make pursuant to their professional duties. Our precedents do not support the existence of a constitutional cause of action behind every statement a public employee makes in the course of doing his or her job. . . .

Justice Souter, with whom Justice Stevens and Justice Ginsburg join, dissenting.

. . . I agree with the majority that a government employer has substantial interests in effectuating its chosen policy and objectives, and in demanding competence, honesty, and judgment from employees who speak for it in doing their work. But I would hold that private and public interests in addressing official wrongdoing and threats to health and safety can outweigh the government's stake in the efficient implementation of policy, and when they do public employees who speak on these matters in the course of their duties should be eligible to claim First Amendment protection.

I

Open speech by a private citizen on a matter of public importance lies at the heart of expression subject to protection by the First Amendment. At the other extreme, a statement by a government employee complaining about nothing beyond treatment under personnel rules raises no greater claim to constitutional protection against retaliatory response than the remarks of a private employee. *See Connick v. Myers.* In between these points lies a public employee's speech unwelcome to the government but on a significant public issue. Such an employee speaking as a citizen, that is, with a citizen's interest, is protected from reprisal unless the statements are too damaging to the government's capacity to conduct public business to be justified by any individual or public benefit thought to flow from the statements. *Pickering.* Entitlement to protection is thus not absolute.

This significant, albeit qualified, protection of public employees who irritate the government is understood to flow from the First Amendment, in part, because a government paycheck does nothing to eliminate the value to an individual of speaking on public matters, and there is no good reason for categorically discounting a speaker's interest in commenting on a matter of public concern just because the government employs him. Still, the First Amendment safeguard rests on something more, being the value to the public of receiving the opinions and information that a public employee may disclose. "Government employees are often in the best position to know what ails the agencies for which they work." *Waters v. Churchill*, 511 U.S. 661, 674 (1994).

The reason that protection of employee speech is qualified is that it can distract co-workers and supervisors from their tasks at hand and thwart the implementation of legitimate policy, the risks of which grow greater the closer the employee's speech gets to commenting on his own workplace and responsibilities. It is one thing for an office clerk to say there is waste in government and quite another to charge that his own department pays full-time salaries to part-time workers. Even so, we have regarded eligibility for protection by *Pickering* balancing as the proper approach when an employee speaks critically about the administration of his own government employer. In *Givhan v. Western Line Consol. School Dist.* we followed *Pickering* when a teacher was fired for complaining to a superior about the racial composition of the school's administrative, cafeteria, and library staffs, and the same point was clear in *Madison Joint School Dist. No. 8 v. Wisconsin Employment Relations Comm'n*, 429 U.S. 167 (1976) . . . [holding] that a schoolteacher speaking out on behalf of himself and others at a public school board meeting could not be penalized for criticizing pending collective-bargaining negotiations affecting professional employment. . . . In each case, the Court realized that a public employee can wear a citizen's hat when speaking on subjects closely tied to the employee's own job, and *Givhan* stands for the same conclusion even when the speech is not addressed to the public at large.

The difference between a case like *Givhan* and this one is that the subject of Ceballos's speech fell within the scope of his job responsibilities, whereas choosing personnel was not what the teacher was hired to do. The effect of the majority's constitutional line between these two cases, then, is that a *Givhan* schoolteacher is protected when complaining to the principal about hiring policy, but a school personnel officer would not be if he protested that the principal disapproved of hiring minority job applicants. This is an odd place to draw a distinction,[1] and while necessary judicial line-drawing sometimes looks arbitrary, any distinction obliges a court to justify its choice. Here, there is no adequate justification for the majority's line categorically denying *Pickering* protection to any speech uttered "pursuant to . . . official duties."

As all agree, the qualified speech protection embodied in *Pickering* balancing resolves the tension between individual and public interests in the speech, on the one hand, and the government's interest in operating efficiently without distraction or embarrassment by talkative or headline-grabbing employees. The need for a balance hardly disappears when an employee speaks on matters his job requires him to address; rather, it seems obvious that the individual and public value of such speech is no less, and may well be greater, when the employee speaks pursuant to his duties in addressing a subject he knows intimately for the very reason that it falls within his duties.[2]

The majority's response, that the enquiry to determine duties is a "practical one," does not alleviate this concern. It sets out a standard that will not discourage government employers from setting duties expansively, but will engender litigation to decide which stated duties were actual and which were merely formal.

As for the importance of such speech to the individual, it stands to reason that a citizen may well place a very high value on a right to speak on the public issues he decides to make the subject of his work day after day. Would anyone doubt that a school principal evaluating the performance of teachers for promotion or pay adjustment retains a citizen's interest in addressing the quality of teaching in the schools? (Still, the majority indicates he could be fired without First Amendment recourse for fair but unfavorable comment when the teacher under review is the superintendent's daughter.) Would anyone deny that a prosecutor like Richard Ceballos may claim the interest of any citizen in speaking out against a rogue law enforcement officer, simply because his job requires him to express a judgment about the officer's performance? (But the majority says the First Amendment gives Ceballos no protection, even if his judgment in this case was sound and appropriately expressed.) . . .

Indeed, the very idea of categorically separating the citizen's interest from the employee's interest ignores the fact that the ranks of public service include those who

---

1. It seems strange still in light of the majority's concession of some First Amendment protection when a public employee repeats statements made pursuant to his duties but in a separate, public forum or in a letter to a newspaper.

2. I do not say the value of speech "pursuant to . . . duties" will always be greater, because I am pessimistic enough to expect that one response to the Court's holding will be moves by government employers to expand stated job descriptions to include more official duties and so exclude even some currently protectable speech from First Amendment purview. Now that the government can freely penalize the school personnel officer for criticizing the principal because speech on the subject falls within the personnel officer's job responsibilities, the government may well try to limit the English teacher's options by the simple expedient of defining teachers' job responsibilities expansively, investing them with a general obligation to ensure sound administration of the school. Hence today's rule presents the regrettable prospect that protection under *Pickering* may be diminished by expansive statements of employment duties.

share the poet's "object . . . to unite [m]y avocation and my vocation";[3] these citizen servants are the ones whose civic interest rises highest when they speak pursuant to their duties, and these are exactly the ones government employers most want to attract. . . .

Nor is there any reason to raise the counterintuitive question whether the public interest in hearing informed employees evaporates when they speak as required on some subject at the core of their jobs. Two terms ago, we recalled the public value that the *Pickering* Court perceived in the speech of public employees as a class: "Underlying the decision in *Pickering* is the recognition that public employees are often the members of the community who are likely to have informed opinions as to the operations of their public employers, operations which are of substantial concern to the public. Were they not able to speak on these matters, the community would be deprived of informed opinions on important public issues. The interest at stake is as much the public's interest in receiving informed opinion as it is the employee's own right to disseminate it." *San Diego v. Roe* (citation omitted). This is not a whit less true when an employee's job duties require him to speak about such things: when, for example, a public auditor speaks on his discovery of embezzlement of public funds, when a building inspector makes an obligatory report of an attempt to bribe him, or when a law enforcement officer expressly balks at a superior's order to violate constitutional rights he is sworn to protect. (The majority, however, places all these speakers beyond the reach of First Amendment protection against retaliation.)

Nothing, then, accountable on the individual and public side of the *Pickering* balance changes when an employee speaks "pursuant" to public duties. On the side of the government employer, however, something is different, and to this extent, I agree with the majority of the Court. The majority is rightly concerned that the employee who speaks out on matters subject to comment in doing his own work has the greater leverage to create office uproars and fracture the government's authority to set policy to be carried out coherently through the ranks. . . .

But why do the majority's concerns, which we all share, require categorical exclusion of First Amendment protection against any official retaliation for things said on the job? Is it not possible to respect the unchallenged individual and public interests in the speech through a *Pickering* balance without drawing the strange line I mentioned before[?] . . . It is thus no adequate justification for the suppression of potentially valuable information simply to recognize that the government has a huge interest in managing its employees and preventing the occasionally irresponsible one from turning his job into a bully pulpit. Even there, the lesson of *Pickering* (and the object of most constitutional adjudication) is still to the point: when constitutionally significant interests clash, resist the demand for winner-take-all; try to make adjustments that serve all of the values at stake.

Two reasons in particular make me think an adjustment using the basic *Pickering* balancing scheme is perfectly feasible here. First, the extent of the government's legitimate authority over subjects of speech required by a public job can be recognized in advance by setting in effect a minimum heft for comments with any claim to outweigh it. Thus, the risks to the government are great enough for us to hold from the outset that an employee commenting on subjects in the course of duties should not prevail on balance unless he speaks on a matter of unusual importance and satisfies high standards

---

3. R. FROST, TWO TRAMPS IN MUD TIME, COLLECTED POEMS, PROSE, & PLAYS 251, 252 (R. Poirier & M. Richardson eds., 1995).

of responsibility in the way he does it. The examples I have already given indicate the eligible subject matter, and it is fair to say that only comment on official dishonesty, deliberately unconstitutional action, other serious wrongdoing, or threats to health and safety can weigh out in an employee's favor. . . .

My second reason for adapting *Pickering* to the circumstances at hand is the experience in Circuits that have recognized claims like Ceballos's here. First Amendment protection less circumscribed than what I would recognize has been available in the Ninth Circuit for over 17 years, and neither there nor in other Circuits that accept claims like this one has there been a debilitating flood of litigation. . . .

For that matter, the majority's position comes with no guarantee against fact-bound litigation over whether a public employee's statements were made "pursuant to . . . official duties." In fact, the majority invites such litigation by describing the inquiry as a "practical one," apparently based on the totality of employment circumstances. *See* n.2. Are prosecutors' discretionary statements about cases addressed to the press on the courthouse steps made "pursuant to their official duties"? Are government nuclear scientists' complaints to their supervisors about a colleague's improper handling of radioactive materials made "pursuant" to duties?

II

The majority seeks support in two lines of argument extraneous to *Pickering* doctrine. The one turns on a fallacious reading of cases on government speech, the other on a mistaken assessment of protection available under whistle-blower statutes.

A

The majority accepts the fallacy propounded by the county petitioners and the Federal Government as *amicus* that any statement made within the scope of public employment is (or should be treated as) the government's own speech, and should thus be differentiated as a matter of law from the personal statements the First Amendment protects. . . . Some public employees are hired to "promote a particular policy" by broadcasting a particular message set by the government, but not everyone working for the government, after all, is hired to speak from a government manifesto. There is no claim or indication that Ceballos was hired to perform such a speaking assignment. . . .

It is not, of course, that the district attorney lacked interest of a high order in what Ceballos might say. If his speech undercut effective, lawful prosecution, there would have been every reason to rein him in or fire him; a statement that created needless tension among law enforcement agencies would be a fair subject of concern, and the same would be true of inaccurate statements or false ones made in the course of doing his work. But these interests on the government's part are entirely distinct from any claim that Ceballos's speech was government speech with a preset or proscribed content. . . .

This ostensible domain beyond the pale of the First Amendment is spacious enough to include even the teaching of a public university professor, and I have to hope that today's majority does not mean to imperil First Amendment protection of academic freedom in public colleges and universities, whose teachers necessarily speak and write "pursuant to official duties."

B

The majority's second argument for its disputed limitation of *Pickering* doctrine is that the First Amendment has little or no work to do here owing to an assertedly comprehensive complement of state and national statutes protecting government whistle-blowers from vindictive bosses. . . .

To begin with, speech addressing official wrongdoing may well fall outside protected whistle-blowing, defined in the classic sense of exposing an official's fault to a third party or to the public; the teacher in *Givhan*, for example, who raised the issue of unconstitutional hiring bias, would not have qualified as that sort of whistle-blower, for she was fired after a private conversation with the school principal. In any event, the combined variants of statutory whistle-blower definitions and protections add up to a patchwork, not a showing that worries may be remitted to legislatures for relief. Some state statutes protect all government workers, including the employees of municipalities and other subdivisions; others stop at state employees. Some limit protection to employees who tell their bosses before they speak out; others forbid bosses from imposing any requirement to warn. As for the federal Whistleblower Protection Act of 1989, 5 U.S.C. § 1213 *et seq.*, current case law requires an employee complaining of retaliation to show "irrefragable proof" that the person criticized was not acting in good faith and in compliance with the law. And federal employees have been held to have no protection for disclosures made to immediate supervisors, or for statements of facts publicly known already. Most significantly, federal employees have been held to be unprotected for statements made in connection with normal employment duties, *Huffman v. Office of Personnel Management*, 263 F.3d 1341, 1352 (C.A. Fed. 2001), the very speech that the majority says will be covered by "the powerful network of legislative enactments . . . available to those who seek to expose wrongdoing." My point is not to disparage particular statutes or speak here to the merits of interpretations by other federal courts, but merely to show the current understanding of statutory protection: individuals doing the same sorts of governmental jobs and saying the same sorts of things addressed to civic concerns will get different protection depending on the local, state, or federal jurisdictions that happened to employ them.

III

The Court remands because the Court of Appeals considered only the disposition memorandum and because Ceballos charges retaliation for some speech apparently outside the ambit of utterances "pursuant to official duties." When the Court of Appeals takes up this case once again, it should consider some of the following facts that escape emphasis in the majority opinion owing to its focus. [The opinion recounted in some detail the plaintiff's claims of retaliation not only for his written reports but also for his spoken statements to his supervisors, testimony at the hearing in the pending criminal case, and his speech at a meeting of the Mexican-American Bar Association about misconduct of the Sheriff's Department in the criminal case and the failure of the District Attorney's Office to handle allegations of police misconduct.]

Upon remand, it will be open to the Court of Appeals to consider the application of *Pickering* to any retaliation shown for other statements; not all of those statements would have been made pursuant to official duties in any obvious sense, and the claim relating to truthful testimony in court must surely be analyzed independently to protect the integrity of the judicial process.

NOTES

1. *Almost Eroded Away? Connick* was viewed at the time as substantially chipping away at speech protections for employees in the workplace, both because of its more narrow definition of "matters of public concern," and its deferential approach to management's prerogatives in the balancing analysis. Now, in the wake of *Garcetti*, how much genuine protection for public employee speech is left? Not only is there no protection for speech that does not address a matter of public concern, but *all* speech falling within the scope of an employee's official duties is now unprotected. Moreover, where workplace speech does address a matter of public concern and does not fall within the scope of an employee's official duties, it will still be subjected to a balancing of interests and, hence, may be unprotected if it is disruptive or otherwise threatens efficient operation of the agency. Perhaps employees can rest assured that truly non-disruptive speech — that is, speech within the workplace about matters of public concern unrelated to work or the employee's duties — is still safe, but employees engaging in other types of workplace speech or public speech about work must do so at their peril. If this statement is accurate, does the First Amendment afford much protection to government workers? Should it? *Connick* and both *Garcetti* opinions emphasize the important civic interests First Amendment speech protections are supposed to foster. Does the protection actually afforded in the wake of these decisions match this rhetoric?

2. *Deference, Balancing, and Categorical Rules.* As we saw in the privacy context, the focus of the "balancing" inquiry on the employer's interest means that the outcome of a case often hinges on the extent to which the Court is willing to defer to the employer's justification. Indeed, the level of deference was the primary dispute between the majority and the omitted dissent of Justice Brennan in *Connick*. Moreover, the lower federal courts' differing views of how much deference should be accorded to employer claims may explain the uneven application of the *Pickering/Connick* balancing test.

Are the disagreements in *Garcetti* driven by much the same thing? Put another way, although the dispute between the majority and dissent in *Garcetti* involves whether there ought to be a categorical rule governing speech within the scope of an employee's official duties, isn't this disagreement largely about how much deference to the public employer is warranted or needed? Certainly, the majority's language goes further, indicating, for example, that one does not speak as a "citizen" when the speech is pursuant to job duties. But can you identify language in the opinion suggesting that the majority's concern about the practical implications of judicial interference with employer prerogatives makes *no* interference the only option? If so, the bar to judicial review in *Garcetti* may be akin to the various abstention or sovereign immunity doctrines in other areas of the law, which are designed to avoid the downstream disruption and other harmful effects judicial scrutiny may cause. What is the dissent's response to such concerns? Determining which approach is right depends not only on the public import of the employee speech in question, but also the practical consequences — incentives, chilling effects, and so on — of either rule on both employees and employers. Which approach strikes the right balance?

3. *Private Ordering. Connick* and *Garcetti* both state that employees do not waive their constitutional speech and association protections when accepting government work. Although, as discussed in Chapter 6, government employees also cannot be required to jettison prospectively their Fourth Amendment rights, one could contend, at least prior to *Garcetti*, that the Constitution provides more robust protection for speech than for privacy rights. That is because privacy rights may be diminished or eliminated by workplace structures and policies that curtail reasonable expectations of privacy. Speech rights are not "bounded" by any such reasonable expectation requirement.

Post-*Garcetti*, however, acceptance of a particular government position defined by various job duties may impose constraints resulting in the substantial narrowing of one's freedom of expression, at least at work. In fact, the *Garcetti* dissenters express concern that the majority's categorical approach may prompt government employers to manipulate job definitions and duties to capture as much employee speech as possible. *See* Elizabeth M. Ellis, Garcetti v. Ceballos: *Public Employees Left to Decide "Your Conscience or Your Job,"* 41 IND. L. REV. 187 (2008) (arguing that *Garcetti's* threshold "official duties" test should be applied narrowly to prevent employers from broadly defining job descriptions). Is this danger real, or, as the majority suggests, is it overstated?

Suppose a government agency decides to require all employees to "report to their supervisor or other appropriate agency official any acts or omissions by other government employees or officials the employee believes in good faith to be in violation of state or federal law or agency policy or regulations." Failure to do so "may result in suspension, termination, or other disciplinary action." Are all such reports now per se unprotected by the First Amendment? Is the majority's assurance that what matters is not formal policies but actual job practices a sufficient response? If an employee reports misconduct elsewhere — outside the agency or to the public — the First Amendment may be implicated, but then the speech is more likely to be disruptive by straining office morale and working relationships. Also, there may be a need for confidentiality in some contexts, such as when one works with classified or other sensitive information or in an investigatory capacity. Moreover, some government positions may require a public appearance of "neutrality" or the avoidance of conflicts of interest; speech contrary to these demands is unlikely to be protected. Thus, when an employee chooses to "go public," the government's countervailing interest in this area is more likely to trump the worker's interest in expression.

On the "positive" side of private ordering for employees, government employers may agree to carve out areas of expressive freedom for their employees, either through collective bargaining or other express agreements. And, as discussed below, civil service codes may provide protections (i.e., "good behavior" protections) for employee expression within the workplace that fill some of the space left empty by *Garcetti*. Of course, such codes apply to only certain government workers; attorneys such as Ceballos and other professional or discretionary employees typically are not covered. However, an employer's willingness to allow expressive freedom for some employees in some circumstances may give rise to claims of implied-in-fact protections and may cut against its efficiency justifications for limiting otherwise protected speech in similar circumstances.

4. *Whither the Whistleblower?* As the prior note suggests, a paramount concern surrounding *Garcetti* is the plight of government whistleblowers. Indeed, Ceballos was a whistleblower, and his claim is premised on alleged retaliation for both his internal report of illegal activity and for certain external steps he took — that's the point of the dissent's argument as to what should happen on remand. The dissent also argues that *Garcetti* will have a chilling effect on government employees coming forward to report perceived misconduct, while the majority downplays this concern. The dissent and majority further contest whether *Garcetti* will create a perverse incentive for employees to go public with their concerns (report them externally) rather than report them internally up the chain of command within the agency.

Moreover, the dissent suggests that independent whistleblower and antiretaliation protections are inadequate to protect employees attempting to further the public's interest in good government. Recall the discussion in Chapter 4 of whistleblowing and the public policy tort more generally. Isn't the dissent correct that such protections are a patchwork? For a specific example, take a quick look back at *Maimone v. City of Atlantic City*, reproduced at page 216. In that case, the New Jersey Supreme Court upheld a police officer's claim under the state's whistleblower statute, concluding that his (internal) objections to his superiors' decision to terminate enforcement of laws prohibiting prostitution and certain *sexually oriented* businesses was protected conduct under the statute. But as the materials in the notes and elsewhere in the chapter make clear, New Jersey's protections are broader than those in many other jurisdictions. In another state, his claim might have failed for any number of reasons, including that his objection did not involve an actual violation of a statute, that it was internal rather than external, and that he alleged a retaliatory transfer rather than termination or demotion. And some jurisdictions simply have no statutory or common-law public policy protection that would be applicable in these circumstances.

Yet, while this may support the dissent's views of the inadequacy of independent protections, should this concern have affected the outcome in *Garcetti*? Put another way, how is this an argument for enhancing *constitutional* protections for employees?

Also note that many of the same themes that framed the public policy tort discussion in Chapter 4 are present in *Garcetti* — for example, separation of powers, the conflict between social benefits and employer prerogatives, calibrating employer and employee incentives, and floodgates and litigation cost concerns. Similarly, much of the discussion in Chapter 4 involved the balancing of employer, employee, and public interests. Naturally, one aspect of this discussion is how this balance might differ by type of employer — that is, public versus private. Does *Garcetti* shed any light on this? In other words, in the whistleblower context, are there reasons to strike the balance between the interests of employees, employers, and the public differently in the public employer context?

Whatever you think of *Garcetti*, it does not affect statutory or common-law antiretaliation or other public policy protections. Consider Justice Souter's discussion of Ceballos's claims on remand. Recalling the discussion in Chapter 4, might some of the activities Ceballos alleges led to retaliation give rise to state law public policy claims?

5. *The Aftermath.* Public employee free speech claims are now commonly defeated on the basis of *Garcetti* — many of which, like Ceballos's claim, might be characterized as involving whistleblowing. *See, e.g., Weintraub v. Bd. of Educ. of the City of New York*, 593 F.3d 196 (2d Cir. 2010) (holding that a public school teacher's filing of a grievance with the union after the school administrator had refused to discipline a student who had thrown books at him was pursuant to official duties); *Callahan v. Fermon*, 526 F.3d 1040 (7th Cir. 2008) (reversing a pre-*Garcetti* jury verdict in favor of plaintiff after finding, as a matter of law, that all of the speech at issue — including complaints regarding supervisors — was pursuant to plaintiff's official duties as a police officer); *Foraker v. Chaffinch*, 501 F.3d 231 (3d Cir. 2007) (holding as a matter of law that firing range instructors' reports up the chain of command of problems at the range fell within their official duties and therefore are not protected activity under the First Amendment); *Morales v. Jones*, 494 F.3d 590 (7th Cir. 2007) (dismissing a police officer's First Amendment claim after finding that his report to an assistant DA that the police chief was harboring a convicted felon falls within the scope of his official duties). Even when a claim overcomes the barriers *Garcetti* imposes, employee speech claims often fail for other reasons. *See, e.g., Samuelson v. LaPorte Comm. Sch. Corp.*, 526 F.3d 1046 (7th Cir. 2008) (finding, after assuming arguendo, that an employee's speech was not within his official duties, that plaintiff failed to produce sufficient evidence that his nonrenewal as coach was motivated by any of these instances); *Bowers v. Scurry*, No. 07-1382, 2008 WL 1931263 (4th Cir. May 2, 2008) (holding that a state university's interest in providing effective services to the public strongly outweighed a human resources employee's interest in using her university e-mail to disseminate information regarding the potential impact on university employees of pending salary restructuring).

Nevertheless, there are some government employee speech claims that have survived post-*Garcetti*. *See, e.g., Charles v. Grief*, 522 F.3d 508 (5th Cir. 2008) (holding that state lottery commission employee stated viable First Amendment claim because the speech at issue — an e-mail to state legislators complaining about discrimination at the commission — was not directly related to employee's job and addressed a matter of public concern); *Marabel v. Nitchman*, 511 F.3d 924 (9th Cir. 2007) (concluding that plaintiff's complaints about superiors' corrupt overpayments were not related to his official job duties as a ferry engineer and, hence, entitled to First Amendment protection); *Lindsey v. City of Orrick*, 491 F.3d 892 (8th Cir. 2007) (finding that an employee's accusation that the City Council violated Missouri's open meetings law was protected because there was no evidence that raising such matters with the council fell within the employee's official job duties even though he was required to attend council meetings and make reports on other matters).

Scholarly criticisms of the majority opinion in *Garcetti* — as a matter of First Amendment doctrine and in terms of its practical implications for government whistleblowers and others — are legion. *See, e.g.,* Cynthia Estlund, *Free Speech Rights that Work at Work: From the First Amendment to Due Process*, 54 U.C.L.A. L. Rev. 1463 (2007); Orly Lobel, *Citizenship, Organizational Citizenship, and the Laws of Overlapping Obligations*, 97 Cal L. Rev. 433 (2009); Scott A. Moss, *Students and Workers and Prisoners — Oh, My! A Cautionary Note About Excessive Institutional Tailoring of First Amendment Doctrine*, 54 U.C.L.A. L. Rev. 1635 (2007); Sheldon H. Nahmod, *Public Employee Speech, Categorical Balancing, and § 1983: A Critique of* Garcetti v. Ceballos, 42 U. Rich. L. Rev. 561 (2008); Helen Norton, *Constraining Public Employee Speech: Government's Control of Its Workers' Speech to Protect Its Own Expression*, 59 Duke L. J. 1 (2009); Paul M. Secunda, Garcetti *'s Impact on the First Amendment Speech Rights of Federal Employees*, 7 First Amend. L. Rev. 117, 118 (2008); Paul M. Secunda, *The Solomon Amendment, Expressive Associations, and Public Employment*, 54 U.C.L.A. L. Rev. 1767 (2007); Terry Smith, *Speaking Against Norms: Public Discourse and the Economy of Racialization in the Workplace*, 57 Am. U. L. Rev. 523 (2008); Stephen I. Vladeck, *The Espionage Act and National Security Whistleblowing After* Garcetti, 57 Am. U. L. Rev. 1531 (2008). *But see* Lawrence Rosenthal,

The Emerging First Amendment Law of Managerial Prerogative, 77 FORDHAM L. REV. 33 (2008) (defending *Garcetti* as consistent with First Amendment principles).

6. *Freedom of Association.* Beyond the First Amendment's protection for speech is freedom of association. Public sector workers enjoy qualified protections with regard to their political preferences and affiliations, and the Supreme Court has struck down various government requirements that infringe upon such rights. *See, e.g., Rutan v. Republican Party*, 497 U.S. 62 (1990) (holding unconstitutional promotion, transfer, recall, and hiring decisions involving low-level public employees based on political party affiliation and support); *Elrod v. Burns*, 427 U.S. 367 (1976) (holding that a public-sector employee who is not a policy-level decision maker may not be denied employment based on political affiliation); *Cafeteria & Rest. Workers Union v. McElroy*, 367 U.S. 886 (1961) (recognizing that the government could not deny employment because of previous membership in a particular party); *Shelton v. Tucker*, 364 U.S. 479 (1960) (finding unconstitutional an Arkansas requirement that public school teachers file annually an affidavit listing each organization to which they have contributed for five preceding years). Although these employee association cases are 20 or more years old, more recent Supreme Court decisions upholding the right to expressive association suggest they have continued vitality. *See, e.g., Boy Scouts of America v. Dale*, 530 U.S. 640 (2000); *see generally* Paul M. Secunda, *The Solomon Amendment, Expressive Associations, and Public Employment*, 54 U.C.L.A. L. REV. 1767 (2007).

A few courts have also held that employees may not be dismissed because of other personal or familial associations. *See, e.g., Sowards v. Loundon County*, 203 F.3d 426 (6th Cir. 2000) (upholding law enforcement employee's right to political and intimate association in context in which she supported her husband's campaign for sheriff); *see also Roberts v. United States Jaycees*, 468 U.S. 609, 617-18 (1984) (stating that one type of protected freedom of association is the right to maintain certain intimate relationships because of the role such relationships have in safeguarding individual freedom). *But see Shahar v. Bowers*, 114 F.3d 1097 (11th Cir. 1997) (holding that Georgia's Attorney General did not violate attorney's right of association by withdrawing job offer to her based on her lesbian "marriage," even assuming that the attorney had a constitutionally protected right to such a marriage, because the employer's efficiency interests would be jeopardized given the policy-making nature of the position and working relationships within the department).

As in the speech context, employee association rights may be limited when there is a substantial governmental interest for doing so. In *Rutan*, 497 U.S. at 74, the Court struck down an Illinois executive order that established a *de facto* political patronage system ensuring that government agencies would promote and hire only Republican Party members. In so holding, the Court recognized the government's interest in ensuring employee effectiveness and efficiency but found that this interest could be served through the less drastic means of disciplining or discharging staff members whose work is inadequate. *See id.* However, the Court limited strong protection — that is, strict scrutiny — to the treatment of lower-level employees, reaffirming the prerogative of elected officials to fill policy-making positions with like-minded appointees. *See id.; see also Elrod*, 427 U.S. at 366-67.

7. *Worker Rank and Status.* In both the speech and association cases, the worker's rank and status often determine the outcome of the case. Indeed, in both contexts, lower-level employees appear to enjoy greater protection than higher-level workers. At the extreme, the president or a governor or mayor can choose members of his or her

own party for his cabinet, and probably for most "policy making" positions. Beyond this, the greater protection for lower-level employees is a product not of their vulnerabilities, but rather, of the fact that the actions of higher-level employees are more likely to threaten the efficient functioning of the government employer, and thus more likely to justify employer intrusions or prohibitions. Do you think that an assistant district attorney's circulation of a survey on personnel issues (*Connick*) would be more disruptive to the workplace than a deputy's comments to her co-worker expressing a wish that the president had been killed (*Rankin*)? *See also Pickering*, 391 U.S. at 571-72 (noting that because the speaker was a teacher rather than a higher-ranking school district employee, incorrect assertions in his public statements could be easily corrected by the district and any harm done thereby alleviated).

In addition to rank, the nature of the employee's work may affect the analysis. For example, as discussed below, courts seem to accord more deference to employer regulation of employee speech for certain types of workers, including law enforcement officials who interact with the public and teachers. Did Ceballos's position as a prosecuting attorney influence the outcome in the case? What impact did this have on the majority's holding? On the dissent's view? In an omitted separate dissent, Justice Breyer found Ceballos's attorney status to be dispositive in his determination that the speech ought to protected:

> [T]he speech at issue is professional speech — the speech of a lawyer. Such speech is subject to independent regulation by canons of the profession. Those canons provide an obligation to speak in certain instances. And where that is so, the government's own interest in forbidding that speech is diminished. The objective specificity and public availability of the profession's canons also help to diminish the risk that the courts will improperly interfere with the government's necessary authority to manage its work.

Recall the unique treatment of attorneys in the context of the public policy tort in Chapter 4. Are there similar strands of thought running through the *Garcetti* opinions?

8. *Academic Freedom.* One group of workers who may be treated differently with respect to speech rights are academics. Both the majority and dissent acknowledge *Garcetti*'s potential implications for academic freedom, recognizing that speech — expressed through scholarship, commentary, and classroom instruction — is at the center of an academic's work. Previously, the Court had recognized that the preservation of academic freedom is an important First Amendment concern. *See, e.g.,* *Keyishian v. Bd. of Regents*, 385 U.S. 589, 603 (1967) ("The vigilant protection of constitutional freedoms is nowhere more vital than in the community of American schools." (quoting *Shelton v. Tucker*, 364 U.S. 479, 487 (1960)); *see also Rodriguez v. Maricopa County Cmty. Coll. Dist.*, 605 F.3d 703 (9th Cir. 2009) (stating that a college is entitled to substantial deference in choosing not to discipline a professor whose racially charged e-mail offended some employees and expressing doubt that a professor's speech on a matter of public concern directed at the college community could ever form the basis of a hostile work environment claim under Title VII). Given the nature of their work and the social functions educational institutions serve, should academics employed by public colleges or universities receive special constitutional protection? What would be the rationale for such a distinction consistent with the text of the First Amendment? Would you be at all concerned about a constitutional regime that draws such categorical distinctions between types of government workers? If you believe academic speech should not receive such heightened protection, how do you respond to the claim that, without such safeguards, academics will be chilled from engaging in socially useful but controversial or unpopular work, research, or commentary?

Despite the *Garcetti* Court's acknowledgment that academic freedom may raise unique First Amendment issues, some nevertheless are concerned that its analysis may weaken protections for such speech. *See, e.g.*, Sheldon H. Nahmod, *Public Employee Speech, Categorical Balancing and § 1983: A Critique of* Garcetti v. Ceballos, 42 U. Rich. L. Rev. 561 (2008) (asserting that *Garcetti*'s modification of the prior "public concern" test significantly undermines the historical protection afforded to academic freedom). Issues surrounding academic freedom are taken up again in Note 9 at page 422.

Moreover, the availability of a First Amendment claim does not always translate into meaningful protection for professors who make highly unpopular or controversial statements in the course of their work. Consider University of Colorado Professor Ward Churchill, whose controversial essay likening 9/11 victims to Nazis caused an uproar and sparked calls for reevaluating the tenure system. *See* Kyle Henley, *Colorado Case Reopens Debate About Tenure*, Christian Science Monitor, April 11, 2005, *available at* http://www.csmonitor.com/2005/0411/p03s01-ussc.html. The university ultimately terminated Churchill, purportedly for unrelated research misconduct (plagiarism). Churchill then sued, claiming that the university violated his First Amendment rights. The case went to trial, and the jury found in Churchill's favor, concluding that the content of the essay was the university's real reason for terminating him. This victory was a hollow one, however, since the jury awarded only $1.00 in compensatory damages and the judge later determined that Churchill was not entitled to reinstatement. *See, e.g.*, Kirk Johnson & Katherine Seelye, *Jury Says Professor Was Wrongly Fired*, N.Y. Times, Apr. 2, 2009; Tom McGhee, *No Job, No Money for Churchill*, Denver Post, July 7, 2009; *see also* Archive of Postings to The Race to the Bottom Blog, http://www.theracetothebottom.org/ward-churchill/ (containing archive of blog posts on the Churchill trial and its aftermath, and links to court documents and commentary).

* * *

The final broad category of speech claims involves speech or other forms of expression away from work and not primarily about work or directed at work-related issues. The key question in this context is often whether the government employer has a sufficiently substantial interest to justify regulating or prohibiting such off-site speech. In *United States v. National Treasury Employees Union*, 513 U.S. 454 (1995) ("*NTEU*"), the Supreme Court struck down a federal statute banning certain honoraria for expressive activities including published works and presentations by broad classes of federal employees, including activities that bore no direct relation to the nature of the employees' government work. In so doing, the Court found the government's interest in protecting integrity and ethics in government insufficient to support such a broad ban, stating that the "speculative benefits the honoraria ban may provide the Government are not sufficient to justify this crudely crafted burden on respondents' freedom to engage in expressive activities." *See id*. at 477.

The Supreme Court again addressed off-site expressive activity in *City of San Diego v. Roe*, 543 U.S. 77 (2004) (per curiam). In this case, the Court upheld the San Diego Policy Department's termination of one of its officers after discovering that he had sold a video in the adults-only section of eBay of himself stripping off a police uniform and performing a sex act, as well as selling police equipment including official department uniforms. *Id.* at 78. Relying on *NTEU*, the *Roe* Court stated that, first, it must be determined whether there is a relationship between the expression and the workplace, and then, if there is such a relationship, the *Pickering/Connick* analysis applies. Under this approach, the case was easy: Because Roe chose to tie his Internet activities to his status as a police officer and to his department, his expression related to the workplace; the Court thus applied the *Pickering/Connick* analysis, and the City prevailed because Roe's expressive conduct did not address a matter of public concern. *See Roe*, 543 U.S. at 80-82.

In reaching this conclusion, the Court was able to avoid a number of more difficult questions. For example, it did not address whether, in order to receive *any* protection, the off-site expressive conduct must address a matter of public concern. *NTEU* likewise had not addressed this because the Court had found that much of the prohibited expressive activity in that case *did* address matters of public concern. *See* 513 U.S. at 466. Also, the *Roe* Court did not clarify how close the nexus must be between the expressive activity and the person's employment to trigger the *Pickering/Connick* analysis. Moreover, the Court never reached the question of what governmental interest would be sufficient to justify regulation of employees' expressive activities, the content of which is entirely unrelated to the workplace. *NTEU* had held that, where the prohibited expressive activity does not relate directly to the workplace, and involves speech beyond that of highly ranked officials, the government must make some kind of evidentiary showing that the activity actually has a disruptive effect on the workplace. *See* 513 U.S. at 468-74. Again, however, *NTEU* involved a sweeping prohibition on honoraria for entire classes of workers (including workers at lower levels); it had not addressed an adverse employment action with regard to an individual worker. Finally, in reaching its conclusion that the officer's expression in this case does not address a matter of public concern, the *Roe* Court offers another specific example of speech that fails the test while providing little useful guidance for other cases. Each of these issues emerges again in the next case.

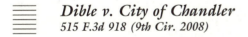

Dible v. City of Chandler
515 F.3d 918 (9th Cir. 2008)

Judge FERNANDEZ delivered the opinion of the Court.

I

Ronald and Megan Dible appeal from the district court's grant of summary judgment against them in their action against the City of Chandler, Arizona, the Chandler Police Department, and the Chandler Police Chief Bobby Joe Harris (collectively "the City"). Principally, the Dibles assert that Ronald Dible was a police officer whose rights under the First Amendment to the United States Constitution were violated when he was terminated for participating in (performing in, recording and purveying) a sexually explicit website with his wife. We affirm.

II

In January of 2002, the Chandler Police Department learned that one of its officers, Ronald Dible, was running a website featuring sexually explicit photographs and videos of his wife. After initially placing Ronald Dible on administrative leave and conducting an internal investigation into his involvement with the website, the City terminated his employment as a police officer.

Ronald Dible and his wife Megan Dible began running the website in September of 2000, after Megan Dible signed a contract with CDM Networks, which operated the website. The Dibles then posted pictures of Megan Dible on the website, under the pseudonym "Katelynn." Those photographs portrayed Megan Dible in various sexual poses and activities with Ronald Dible, another woman, and inanimate objects. The Dibles also posted, among other things, a videotape of Megan Dible masturbating that had been filmed by Ronald Dible. The Dibles did not intend to express any kind of message or engage in social or political commentary through the material they posted on their website. They participated in those activities to make money; it was as simple as that.

. . . Any computer user with internet capability could access the website's home page without charge. The home page featured partially nude pictures of Megan Dible in order to entice customers. If the user wanted to view more pictures of Megan Dible, a fee was required, but before the pictures could be reviewed, the user had to enter into a purported contract with CDM Networks. Once the user accepted the terms of the contract and paid the fee, he was free to view the website's sexually explicit photographs and videos.

The Dibles also offered a CD-ROM for sale on the website. . . . Although the photographs on the website and the CD-ROM generally did not show Ronald Dible's face, one of the photographs did.

The Dibles also promoted their website by attending "barmeets." The purpose of the bar-meets was to have fans of the website meet Megan Dible, although Ronald Dible also attended. The bar-meets, which took place at local bars, were open to the public, and attendees were free to take photographs. They did, and sometimes posted those on their own websites. Although some attendees knew Megan Dible only as Katelynn, others knew her true identity. At those barmeets, both Megan Dible and Ronald Dible posed in sexually suggestive ways with each other and with other people, some of whom were partially nude. The Dibles' photographs from the bar-meets were compiled on a CD-ROM and were then sold through their website.

Ronald Dible believed, indeed most likely knew, that his position in the disreputable sexually explicit website business was not compatible with his position as a police officer and risked violating the City and Police Department rule against engaging "in conduct which might bring discredit to the City service." So he took steps to cover up his participation, and in so doing violated the rule that he could not engage in outside employment unless he first filled out and filed a request to engage in employment outside the department. He did not inform any Department officials about it.[1] He did, however, tell a few people about it, including a fellow police officer, whom he urged to start his own website. The officer eventually did.

---

1. In fact, he lied about his participation when police department people asked.

Sometime in the later part of 2001, rumors about the Dibles' website began circulating among members of the department, and eventually the news of the website filtered up to department officials. Upon learning about it, the police chief on January 25, 2002, ordered Ronald Dible to cease all activity with the website and placed him on administrative leave. The chief then opened an investigation into Ronald Dible's involvement with the website. The investigators questioned Ronald Dible about it, and, in response, he provided several misleading answers. After establishing that he was, in fact, involved in the website, the investigators questioned him about, among other things, whether he and Megan Dible had earned money from the site, and asked to see the contract between Megan Dible and CDM Networks.

By January 25, 2002, the press had also learned about the website and began reporting on it in an unflattering manner. The press reported that the website was run by the Dibles and that he was employed as a city police officer. The record contains no evidence identifying the person who alerted the press to the website's existence or to the Dibles' involvement in it, but, of course, a lot of people already knew. The result of that publicity was disquieting to say the least. A police lieutenant assigned to look into the situation spoke to a large number of officers and others, found that it had severely impacted their working situation, and declared that police officer morale "really hit bottom."

In due course, Ronald Dible's supervisor recommended his dismissal. The supervisor found that Ronald Dible had violated the department's regulation prohibiting its officers from bringing discredit to the city service, and that Ronald Dible had provided false answers to district investigators in the course of their investigation. Chief Harris approved Ronald Dible's dismissal.

Ronald Dible then appealed that decision to the City's Merit Board, which conducted an evidentiary hearing. At the hearing, several officers testified that they had been questioned and ridiculed about the website. A female officer, Amy Hedges, testified that she was called a "porn whore" by an individual she was attempting to arrest. She further testified that she was subjected to derogatory remarks while responding to a bar fight. Specifically, when she arrived at the bar, a patron began gyrating, told her to take off her clothes, and harassed her about the website. Officer Hedges testified that the patron's comments added to the instability of an already fluid field situation and confrontation. Another officer testified to the disrespect that he was shown after the website became publicly known. An investigating officer, who had interviewed many other officers, as well as other people, also testified to the impact of the Dibles' activity on the department. In addition, potential police recruits questioned an officer about the website on each of the five separate recruitment trips that she had conducted after the existence of the site became widely known to members of the public. Assistant Chief Joseph Gaylord testified that he believed the scandal involving Ronald Dible's participation in the sexually explicit website would negatively impact the department's efforts to recruit female officers for years to come. Ultimately, on April 3, 2002, the Merits Board issued a recommendation affirming the decision to discharge Ronald Dible.

IV

The major issue before us [in reviewing the district court's grant of summary judgment] is whether Ronald Dible's First Amendment right to freedom of speech[3] was violated when he was terminated for maintaining and participating in a sexually explicit website with his wife, Megan Dible. In fact, for all practical purposes, the other issues in this case hinge on the decision of that issue. We will, therefore, consider it first and consider the other issues raised by the Dibles thereafter.

Freedom of Speech

. . . The Supreme Court recently took up the issue of employee speech in general and conduct of the sort engaged in by Ronald Dible in particular. *See City of San Diego v. Roe*, 543 U.S. 77 (2004) (per curiam). In that case, a police officer with the City of San Diego, California, made a video of "himself stripping off a police uniform and masturbating." He sold copies on eBay, under a user name of Codestud3@aol.com. While it appears that the uniform was not the specific uniform worn by San Diego police officers, it was "clearly identifiable as a police uniform," and Roe also sold custom videos and official "uniforms of the San Diego Police Department," along with other items of police equipment. "Roe's eBay user profile identified him as employed in the field of law enforcement." When the police department found out, it investigated and ultimately terminated him. He then brought an action in which he claimed that his First Amendment right to freedom of speech had been violated.

The Supreme Court surveyed First Amendment law as it related to government employees, and set forth an analytical framework for consideration of the issue. The Court first recognized that "[a] government employee does not relinquish all First Amendment rights otherwise enjoyed by citizens just by reason of his or her employment." That said, when a government employee's speech is under consideration, there are two paths of analysis, depending on whether the speech is related or unrelated to the person's employment. As the Court put it:

> [A] governmental employer may impose certain restraints on the speech of its employees, restraints that would be unconstitutional if applied to the general public. The Court has recognized the right of employees to speak on matters of public concern, typically matters concerning government policies that are of interest to the public at large, a subject on which public employees are uniquely qualified to comment. See [*Connick v. Myers; Pickering v. Bd. of Ed.*]. Outside of this category, the Court has held that when government employees speak or write on their own time on topics unrelated to their employment, the speech can have First Amendment protection, absent some governmental justification "far stronger than mere speculation" in regulating it. *United States v. Treasury Employees* (*NTEU*). We have little difficulty in concluding that the City was not barred from terminating Roe under either line of cases.

The Court then went on to consider whether Roe's speech activities were related or unrelated to his position as a police officer with the city. It determined that Roe's indecent activity, indeed, related to his employment. In so doing, the Court observed that in *NTEU* the speech in question was not only unrelated but also "had no effect on the mission and purpose of the employer." The Court also emphasized that in *NTEU* "none of the speech at issue 'even arguably [had] any adverse impact' on the employer." It finally pointed out that the City of San Diego had conceded that

---

3. We recognize that the Dibles' conduct was more expression (nudity and sexual activity) than speech as such. That does not change the analysis.

Roe's activities were unrelated in the sense that they were not concerned with the "workings or functioning" of the police department, but, it concluded:

> It is quite a different question whether the speech was detrimental to the SDPD. On that score the City's consistent position has been that the speech is contrary to its regulations and harmful to the proper functioning of the police force. The present case falls outside the protection afforded in *NTEU*. The authorities that instead control, and which are considered below, are this Court's decisions in *Pickering*, *Connick*, and the decisions which follow them.

Of course, as the Court noted, Roe had gone out of his way to identify himself with police work. Perhaps that alone would have sufficed to make his activity related to his employment. If that were the case, it must be said that Ronald Dible did not do what Roe did. Ronald Dible took some pains to keep the police out of the pictures, but because of other clues and information, it became publicly known that he was involved and that he was a police officer. In any event, Ronald Dible's attempts to conceal his activity came to nought and do not distinguish the underlying situation in *Roe*. Many a rule breaker does so clandestinely in the hope that his violations will not come to light and have untoward consequences. When that hope is dashed, the results and consequences for him are the same as they would have been if he had broken the rules overtly. Roe overtly broke his employer's rules (outside employment and immoral conduct) and he properly suffered the consequences by losing his job. Ronald Dible's discovered clandestine activity also broke his employer's rules (outside employment and conduct that brought disrepute) and he properly suffered the consequences by losing his job. In addition, it can be seriously asked whether a police officer can ever disassociate himself from his powerful public position sufficiently to make his speech (and other activities) entirely unrelated to that position in the eyes of the public and his superiors. Whether overt or temporarily hidden, Ronald Dible's activity had the same practical effect — it "brought the mission of the employer and the professionalism of its officers into serious disrepute."

That said, the Court has never explicitly defined what is or is not related, and we need not do so here. As in *Roe*, the result would be the same "under either line of cases." The Dibles cannot prevail. We will explain.

(1) *Related Speech.* If we determined that Ronald Dible's activities were related to his public employment, we would necessarily approach his First Amendment claim as did the Supreme Court in *Roe*. It said:

> To reconcile the employee's right to engage in speech and the government employer's right to protect its own legitimate interests in performing its mission, the *Pickering* Court adopted a balancing test. It requires a court evaluating restraints on a public employee's speech to balance "the interests of the [employee], as a citizen, in commenting upon matters of public concern and the interest of the State, as an employer, in promoting the efficiency of the public services it performs through its employees."

As the Court explained, before an employee is even entitled to have the balancing test applied, the "speech must touch on a matter of 'public concern.'" The Court further pointed out: "*Connick* held that a public employee's speech is entitled to *Pickering* balancing only when the employee speaks 'as a citizen upon matters of public concern' rather than 'as an employee upon matters only of personal interest.'" And, while the borders of the territory of public concern are not entirely defined, they do encompass matters that are "of legitimate news interest; that is, a subject of general interest and of value and concern to the public at the time of publication," and even some private comments in the proper circumstances. So, for example, the Court has said that an employee's quiet statement to a fellow employee at a county constable's office, that she hoped that a future attempt at assassination of the President would succeed, touched on a matter of public concern. *See Rankin v. McPherson.*

No matter. Whatever a periplus of the outer limits of public concern might show, it was pellucid that Roe's vulgar behavior would be discovered to be outside of those borders. As the Court said, "there is no difficulty in concluding that Roe's expression does not qualify as a matter of public concern under any view of the public concern test. He fails the threshold test and *Pickering* balancing does not come into play." *Roe.*

The same is true of Ronald Dible's activities in this case. They did not give the public any information about the operations, mission or function of the police department, and were not even close to the kind of private remarks that the Court has countenanced. His activities were simply vulgar and indecent. They did not contribute speech on a matter of public concern. The Dibles could not prevail if Ronald Dible's speech is deemed to have been related to his employment.

(2) *Unrelated Speech.* If we determined that Ronald Dible's activities were unrelated to his public employment, we would also have to apply a balancing test. Interestingly enough, it is not entirely clear whether the public concern concept would be a necessary threshold to that balancing. In *Roe* the Supreme Court did not exactly say that the public concern concept must be considered, but it also did not expressly hold that the Court of Appeals' determination that public concern was part of the test was incorrect. And in *NTEU*, the Court pointed out that:

> Respondents' expressive activities in this case fall within the protected category of citizen comment on matters of public concern rather than employee comment on matters related to personal status in the workplace. The speeches and articles for which they received compensation in the past were addressed to a public audience, were made outside the workplace, and involved content largely unrelated to their government employment.

Moreover, in *Rankin*, the Court did indicate that a comment about the President was a matter of public concern, but *Rankin* dealt with an unrelated comment made at the workplace itself. We, however, need not resolve whether the public concern test must be satisfied in this instance. *See Locurto v. Giuliani*, 447 F.3d 159, 175 (2d Cir. 2006).

If a statement must be one of public concern when it consists of unrelated activity away from the workplace, Ronald Dible's conduct was no more protected than it would be if the activity were related, and the Dibles' claim would fail on that account. But, suppose passing the public concern test is not required when unrelated expressive activity takes place away from the work setting. What then? Again, we must balance the asserted First Amendment right against the government's justification. *See Roe.* The Dibles' First Amendment claim cannot survive that balance either.

We first note that a number of Supreme Court justices have expressed some dubiety about the strength of the protection offered to activities that can be said to be of the same ilk as those we deal with here, or, perhaps, of an even less indecent ilk. *See City of Erie v. Pap's A.M.*, 529 U.S. 277, 289, (2000) (plurality opinion) (stating that public nude dancing is "only within the outer ambit of the First Amendment protection"). . . . However, this court has said that plurality decisions of the Supreme

Court do not make law and that "the degree of protection the first amendment affords speech does not vary with the social value ascribed to that speech by the courts." *Kev, Inc. v. Kitsap County*, 793 F.2d 1053, 1058 (9th Cir.1986). None of those cases is exactly like the one at hand. We are not dealing with the rights of an ordinary citizen vis-à-vis the government; we are dealing with the rights of a governmental employee (a police officer at that) vis-à-vis his employer. In this context, the reflections of the Justices about the weight of the right to engage in public indecent activity commend themselves to our consideration. As *Roe* suggests, it is a bit difficult to give that activity the same weight as the right to engage in political debate [as in *City of Erie*] or to lecture on religion and black history or to write articles about the environment [as in *NTEU*]. Especially is that true where, as here, the employee admits that he was not interested in conveying any message whatsoever and was engaged in the indecent public activity solely for profit.

In any event, the interest of the City in maintaining the effective and efficient operation of the police department is particularly strong. It would not seem to require an astute moral philosopher or a brilliant social scientist to discern the fact that Ronald Dible's activities, when known to the public, would be "detrimental to the mission and functions of the employer." *Roe*. And although the government's justification cannot be mere speculation, it is entitled to rely on "reasonable predictions of disruption." *Waters v. Churchill*, 511 U.S. 661 (1994) (plurality opinion).

Police departments, and those who work for them, are engaged in a dangerous calling and have significant powers. The public expects officers to behave with a high level of propriety, and, unsurprisingly, is outraged when they do not do so. The law and their own safety demands that they be given a degree of respect, and the sleazy activities of Ronald and Megan Dible could not help but undermine that respect. Nor is this mere speculation.

Almost as soon as Ronald Dible's indecent public activities became widely known, officers in the department began suffering denigration from members of the public, and potential recruits questioned officers about the Dibles' website. Moreover, the department feared that the recruiting of female officers would be affected because of what it seemed to say about the climate at the department. That is not rank speculation. In a similar case involving police officers' public sexual activities, the Eleventh Circuit Court of Appeals noted that this kind of activity by officers, once known, could not help but interfere with the functions and mission of the police department because "it reflected on [deputies'] fitness as deputies and undermined public confidence" in the department. *Thaeter v. Palm Beach County Sheriff's Office*, 449 F.3d 1342, 1356 (11th Cir. 2006). Just so.

We are not gallied by the Dibles' claim that Ronald Dible is being subjected to some kind of heckler's veto. Worries about a heckler's veto have generally dealt with the restriction of a citizen's speech based upon the anticipated disorderly reaction by members of an audience. *See Rosenbaum v. City and County of San Francisco*, 484 F.3d 1142, 1158-59 (9th Cir. 2007). Those worries do not directly relate to the wholly separate area of employee activities that affect the public's view of a governmental agency in a negative fashion, and, thereby, affect the agency's mission. The Dibles' argument ignores the fact that the public can form a negative view of a person due to his particular mode of expression—there is nothing unconstitutional about that. It also ignores the unique and sensitive position of a police department and its necessary and constant interactions with the public.

As the Second Circuit Court of Appeals has pointed out, even where the unrelated expression is a matter of public concern — there a comment on race relations — police officers "are quintessentially public servants" and "part of their job is to safeguard the public's opinion of them." *Locurto.* Thus, said the court, the actions of the police department were not due to a heckler's veto, but rather an example of the government's accounting for the public's perception of the officers' actions when it considered the potential for disruption of the department's functions. *See also Rankin* (taking particular note of the fact that a clerical employee's comments were not made public and, therefore, did not discredit the constable's office).[7]

In fine, whether Ronald Dible's activities were related to his employment or not, the City could discipline him for those activities without violating his First Amendment rights. Thus, the Dibles' claim to the contrary must be rejected.

[The court rejected the Dibles' claim that their First Amendment rights to privacy and freedom of association were violated by the City. It recognized that the First Amendment implicates a right of privacy, which includes a right to make personal decisions and a right to keep personal matters private, and contains a right to the freedom of intimate expression and to associate with others in activities otherwise protected by the First Amendment. Nevertheless, the court found that because the City had not released any information that connected the Dibles to the website, it could not have violated their right to privacy and intimate association by giving them unwanted publicity. The court went on to reject the association claim for the same reasons that it had rejected the speech claim, stating that "a governmental employee cannot avoid the strictures of the balancing tests that we have heretofore described by attempting to resurrect fallen speech claims as privacy and associational claims." It also affirmed the district court's grant of summary judgment on the Dibles' state law right to privacy, intentional infliction of emotional distress, and wrongful termination claims.]

CANBY, Circuit Judge, concurring in the judgment:

I

With all due respect, I am unable to join the majority opinion because I disagree with its resolution of Dible's First Amendment speech claim. Under the facts of this case and the existing precedent, the police department could not discharge Dible for his website expression without violating the First Amendment.

I have no quarrel with some of the majority's analysis. I agree that, if Dible's expressive website activity were properly characterized as employment-related, then his First Amendment claim would fail because his expression, while protected, was not of public concern. The majority opinion correctly reasons that this point is established by [*City of San Diego v. Roe*].

---

7. We have not overlooked *Flanagan v. Munger,* 890 F.2d 1557, 1566-67 (10th Cir. 1989) and *Berger v. Battaglia,* 779 F.2d 992, 1000-01 (4th Cir. 1985). However, to the extent that they minimize the potential for an actual effect on the efficiency and efficacy of police department functions arising from public perceptions of the inappropriate activities of police officers, they are severely undermined by *Roe,* and we decline to follow them.

Dible's website activity was not employment-related, however. As the majority opinion points out, Dible was careful not to identify himself or his website with the police department or with police status at all. That fact differentiates his case from *Roe*. Certainly nothing in the activity Dible portrayed suggested a connection with the police. I am unwilling to conclude, for reasons I will set forth below, that such unrelated expression becomes related to Dible's employment simply because people who disapprove of his expression find out that he is a policeman and make their disapproval or disdain known to the police department in ways that could affect its work.

As the majority opinion points out, the Supreme Court has not, in *Roe* or its antecedents, made perfectly clear whether a governmental employee's expression unrelated to the employment must be of public concern to be protected. In my view it makes little sense to impose the public concern requirement for the protection of unrelated speech. The requirement of public concern comes from *Pickering*. Its usefulness is in making an exception to the right of a public employer to control the expression of employees in matters relating to their employment. One way of limiting the rule to its context, which I would follow, is to hold that there is no requirement that an employee's speech that is unrelated to his employment be of public concern in order to merit First Amendment protection. The Tenth Circuit adopted that rule in *Flanagan v. Munger*, 890 F.2d 1557, 1562-64 (1989). Another way of reaching the same result is to hold, as we did in *Roe v. City of San Diego*, 356 F.3d 1108, 1119 (9th Cir.), *rev'd*, 543 U.S. 77 (2004), that *any* speech by a government employee that is not about his employer, that occurs outside the workplace, and is directed to a segment of the general public, qualifies *ipso facto* as a matter of public concern. As the majority opinion here recognizes, the Supreme Court did not say this approach was incorrect when it reversed *Roe*. Similarly, in *Berger v. Battaglia*, 779 F.2d 992, 998 (4th Cir. 1985), the Fourth Circuit held, in a case of unrelated expression, that *all* such expression was of public concern unless it constituted a private personnel grievance. Either way — whether the public concern requirement is simply dispensed with for expression unrelated to employment, as I prefer, or whether the public concern requirement for unrelated speech is broadened to include virtually the universe of unrelated speech — the outcome is the same. Public concern should not be a hurdle depriving employee speech of First Amendment protection when that speech is unrelated to the employment.

Now, I recognize that pornography, although apparently popular, is not a very respected subject of First Amendment protection in many quarters. The majority opinion here reflects that distaste, variously characterizing Dible's expressive activities as "vulgar," "indecent," "sleazy," and "disreputable." But vigorous enforcement of the free speech guarantee of the First Amendment often requires that we protect speech that many, even a majority, find offensive. Pornography, and sexual expression in general, is protected by the First Amendment when it does not constitute obscenity (and there is no showing that Dible's expression meets that extreme standard). We should accept that fact and accord Dible's expression the constitutional protection to which it is entitled. The majority opinion here falls short of the First Amendment standard in two major respects.

Because Dible's expressive activity was not employment-related, the police department must demonstrate that the alleged harm caused by his expression was "'real, not merely conjectural.'" *NTEU*. The evidence of harm in this case is so insubstantial that it can be characterized as "conjectural." An officer testified that he feared the effect on recruitment of female officers, but no such effect was demonstrated. At least three officers testified that they had been verbally harassed in a manner attributable to the website, but there was no testimony that this seriously interfered with the performance of their duties. In sum, the findings of interference with the mission of the police department are based on the conjecture that Dible's expressive activities might cause some persons to think less well of the police department and that this disfavor might in some ways lead to disruption of police activities. The evidence simply does not meet the *Treasury Employees* standard. It does not outweigh Dible's interest in expression, which is his "interest in engaging in free speech, not the value of the speech itself." *Flanagan.*[1]

A second flaw in the majority's analysis is that it enshrines the "heckler's veto" with respect to *all* conduct of a public employee, or at least of a police department employee. Nothing that Dible did or said in relation to his website activities in itself caused any disruption to police department functions. The alleged (and minimal) disruption was caused by other persons' disapproval of Dible's activities once it became known that he was an officer of the police department. The rule to be drawn from the majority's analysis, apparently, is that police officers may be fired for engaging in expressive activities, unrelated to their employment, when numbers of the public disapprove of the expression vigorously and possibly disruptively. That rule empowers the heckler to veto the speech, and is inconsistent with the First Amendment. *See Terminiello v. Chicago,* 337 U.S. 1, 4-5 (1949). In such a situation, it is the duty of the police department to prevent the disruption by those opposed to the speech, not to suppress or punish the speech. [*See Cohen v. California,* 403 U.S. 15, 23 (1971).]

The heckler's veto applied to sexually expressive activities has disturbing potential for expansive application. A measurable segment of the population, for example, is vigorously antagonistic to homosexual activity and expression; it could easily be encouraged to mobilize were a police officer discovered to have engaged, off duty and unidentified by his activity, in a Gay Pride parade, or expressive cross-dressing, or any number of other expressive activities that might fan the embers of antagonism smoldering in a part of the population. For this reason, it is far better to adopt a rule that protects off-duty speech unrelated to employment when the speech itself causes no *internal* problems, and the only disruption is in the external relations between the police department and the public unhappy with the police officer's expression. The Tenth Circuit adopted just such a rule. *See Flanagan.* The Fourth Circuit avoided adopting an inflexible rule, but held that a police department could not prohibit off-duty, unrelated speech by an officer under circumstances parallel to those in Dible's case: "[N]ot only was the perceived threat of disruption only to external operations and relationships, it was caused not by the speech itself but by threatened reaction to it by offended segments of the public." *Berger.* This public reaction in *Berger* was not inconsequential; it threatened to disrupt the tenuous relationship between the police department and the black community. Even so, "this sort of threatened disruption by others reacting to public employee speech simply may not be allowed to serve as justification for public employer disciplinary action directed at that speech."

---

1. I place no significance at all on Dible's statement that he did not intend to convey any message in his expressive activity. His website constituted expression, and he has raised a First Amendment defense to his termination because of his website activity. It is equally irrelevant to his First Amendment protection that he sought to make money from his expression, as many speakers or writers do. *See, e.g., Smith v. California,* 361 U.S. 147, 150 (1959).

The majority opinion states that to the extent that *Flanagan* and *Berger* "minimize the potential for an actual effect on the efficiency and efficacy of police department functions arising from public perceptions of the inappropriate activities of police officers, they are severely undermined by *Roe*." The rationale of *Flanagan* and *Berger*, however, was not that disruption was minimal, but that as part of the heckler's veto it could not support discipline of the employee. It is true that *Roe* permitted discipline of an officer because of public reaction to his expressive conduct, but that expressive conduct was purposely employment-related. The head of a governmental agency is entitled to control the speech of members of the agency with regard to agency-related matters, unless that speech is a matter of public concern. *Pickering*. But that rule is an exception to the general First Amendment protection of speech. *See NTEU.* To apply the same restriction to off-duty expression by a public employee, unrelated to his employment, is to reject the established principle that public employees may not be required to surrender their constitutional right of free speech as a condition of their employment. *Roe* did not extend to off-duty conduct unrelated to employment, and accordingly it did not undermine *Flanagan* and *Berger*.

In my view, the rationale of *Flanagan* and *Berger* is not only sound, but constitutionally required. We should apply those principles and hold that Dible's expressive website conduct was an unconstitutional ground for his discharge.

II

I concur in the judgment, however, because the record demonstrates that any rational trier of fact would find that Dible would have been discharged for making false statements to police department investigators, had he not been discharged for his website activity. *See Mt. Healthy City Sch. Dist. Bd. of Educ. v. Doyle*, 429 U.S. 274, 287 (1977). There was ample and uncontradicted evidence that, early in the investigation, Dible denied any connection with the website, and later denied that he appeared in any of the videos. He also denied telling anyone to lie about his involvement in the website, when he had told a co-worker to lie. Although some of these statements were later "corrected" or modified, the original deception was clearly established.

Dible contends, however, that his false statements cannot be a ground for discharge because the entire investigation was instituted because of his First Amendment protected activity. [However, the] investigation by the police department in the present case was not illegitimate in its inception. The department was entitled to inquire into Dible's off-duty activity to see whether it was employment-related, which would bring it within the unprotected scope of *Roe*. In addition, the department had a policy requiring police officers to obtain prior approval before engaging in any outside employment, because certain jobs were deemed compromising. The department was entitled to inquire whether this policy had been violated. Nothing in the nature of the investigation entitled Dible to lie. . . .

NOTES

1. *Unresolved Issues Surrounding Off-site Expression*. Recall the issues left unresolved in *NTEU* and *Roe*: (1) Must off-site expression be a matter of public concern to receive *any* protection? (2) How close must the nexus be between the expressive activity and the person's employment to trigger *Pickering/Connick* balancing? (3) What government interests are sufficient to justify regulation of employee expressive activity that is entirely unrelated to work? The *Dible* majority works hard to avoid answering the first two questions, but, in so doing, must answer the third — at least as necessary to support its alternative holding, which assumed the speech was unrelated to work. Look closely at how the majority reaches the conclusion that, regardless of whether Ronald Dible's activities were related to his employment, the City could discipline him for those activities. Under this kind of analysis, the first two unresolved questions often will not matter. Put another way, how likely is it that *any* expressive conduct by a police officer will be protected if it is an embarrassment to, or fosters criticism of, the department?

Now compare this to how the concurring judge would resolve these three matters and how each resolution would affect the analysis of whether the speech is protected. Given how Judge Canby addresses these issues, the relatedness inquiry becomes paramount. Under this alternative framework, how likely is it that off-site expression related to work will be protected? But how about unrelated expression, whether involving a "matter of public concern" or not? What must the department show in order to regulate such unrelated expression? In making the determination that the speech in this case, unlike that in *Roe*, was unrelated to work, Judge Canby does not provide much analysis, but his focus appears to be on the extent to which the police officer made some reference to police work, the department, or his status as an officer. Other matters, including the content of the speech (i.e., how repugnant or embarrassing it might be) and how disruptive it is, are left to the second part of the inquiry, namely whether the department can demonstrate that the speech caused "real" harm. This approach offers a nice, clean analytical framework, but does it serve to protect any speech if one accepts the view that, given the nature of their work, police officers are representatives of the department and city 24/7?

The vast differences between the approaches to analyzing off-site expression claims reflected in the majority and concurring opinions are not merely a matter of academic interest. As their competing citations to other circuits make clear, federal courts are split on these matters. For a host of reasons, defendant police departments and individual supervisors prevail more often than not in these cases, but the *Flanagan* and *Berger* decisions are important counterexamples.

2. *Even More Difficult Facts? Dible* was a more difficult case than *Roe* because Dible had made no reference to his position as a police officer or his police department on his Web site. Nevertheless, the majority did not find this difference to be dispositive. It emphasized that neither Ronald nor Megan Dible made much of an effort to disguise their identity on the Web site or keep these activities secret, and the connection between Ronald's Internet activities and his status as a police officer quickly emerged. He then compounded his problems by not telling the truth about his activities to department officials. Suppose he had taken more pains to hide his identity from the beginning (to avoid the public's drawing the connection with his police work) or to limit access to the site to a more selective group, but the public and his department ultimately found out anyway. Would the outcome on the First Amendment question have been different? Should it have been? If no, does that mean that a police department may prohibit *all otherwise legal*, sexually explicit expressive activity by its police officers? If yes, should a police officer's First Amendment right to expression depend on his or her ability or efforts to remain anonymous or unknown?

3. *Type of Speech.* In *Roe*, the Supreme Court had held that the sexually explicit video at issue in that case did not address a matter of public concern. The Court defined such a matter as "something that is a subject of legitimate news interest; that is, a subject of general interest and of value and concern to the public at the time of publication." 543 U.S. at 83-84. This standard may not provide much guidance for courts assessing very different kinds of speech (see the examples in Note 2 on page 374), thus requiring the periplus around its boundaries so feared by the *Dible* majority. But the speech at issue in *Roe* is similar enough to the expressive activity in *Dible* that the majority had no problem finding that Dible's Web site did not address a matter of public concern. Whether this conclusion is correct or not, are you gallied by the irony — that is, the sexually explicit expression at issue is deemed not a matter of public concern even though the principal reason the government employer wishes to regulate it is because it is a matter of significant concern to the public?

The *Dible* majority emphasized that certain forms of sexually explicit expression enjoy minimal First Amendment protection, Indeed, the majority went out of its way to make clear not only its distaste for such expression, but also the limited social value of sexually explicit materials distributed for profit. But, as the concurrence notes, much expression that may be deemed sexual in nature is still protected by the First Amendment. Can a police department's prohibition on "conduct which might bring discredit to the City service," "conduct unbecoming of an officer," and "immoral conduct" bar all such expression, consistent with the Constitution? How about the (legal) publication of semi-nude photos on an officer's Facebook page, for example, or sexual jokes or banter in off-site conversations, at a comedy club, or in an Internet chat room? *Cf.* Jonathan Casiano, *Stand-Up Gig Could Cost West Orange Cop His Job: 'Club Soda Kenny' Routine Gets Sergeant Suspended Without Pay*, NEWARK STAR-LEDGER, Feb. 9, 2006 (reporting police department action against an officer for his crass and profanity-filled comedy act, even though he did not wear his uniform or identify himself as a police officer in the act). Courts tend to side with police departments in off-site speech and association cases. *See, e.g., Piscottano v. Murphy*, 511 F.3d 247 (2d Cir. 2007) (holding that the Department of Corrections established that the conduct of several officers, expressing their approval of the nature and character of the Outlaws Motorcycle Club, had the potential to disrupt and reflect negatively on its operations, and that its interest in "maintaining the efficiency, security, and integrity of its operations outweighed the associational interests" of the officers). But should they?

4. *Beyond Law Enforcement Officers.* Whatever you might think of the deference courts tend to accord to law enforcement agencies, how free should other types of government employers be in determining what off-site conduct is unbecoming or immoral, or, for that matter, sufficiently embarrassing or scandalous to justify regulation? Certainly, attempts by a government agency to regulate off-site expressive conduct or associations that implicate fundamental rights — religious freedom, intimate relationships, etc. — will be subject to some scrutiny. *See, e.g., Cameron v. Grainger County*, 274 F. App'x. 437 (6th Cir. 2008) (denying summary judgment because a reasonable jury could find that former deputy county clerk's decision to marry into a family that was politically opposed to reelection of her employer was a motivating factor in the employer's decision to fire her); *cf. Flaskamp v. Dearborn Pub. Schs.*, 385 F.3d 935 (6th Cir. 2004) (upholding a school board's decision to disallow tenure to a teacher who had an intimate relationship with a former student). But what about other expressive conduct? Would your answer depend on the type of public employee who engages in the conduct of, for example, teachers, attorneys, public health workers, regulatory inspectors, clerical staff, or janitors? Does the mission of the agency matter, or whether the particular employee is supposed to be a "role model"? Also, would your answer depend as well on the viewpoint or opinions expressed? *See, e.g., Wales v. Bd. of Educ.*, 120 F.3d 82, 85 (7th Cir. 1997) (asserting that "[a] school district is entitled to put in its classrooms teachers who share its educational philosophy"). Should the fact that the speech or association is highly offensive to the community the agency serves be enough to justify the employer's adverse employment action? *See Melzer v. Bd. of Educ.*, 336 F.3d 185 (2d Cir. 2003) (upholding the termination of a teacher after it became known that he was a member of the North American Man/Boy Love Association in part because teachers must respect the views of parents in the community).

5. *Hate Speech.* Should a government agency have greater discretion to regulate off-site, legal expression that might be characterized as "hate speech"—for example, the publication of racist or sexist statements or jokes, anti-Semitic caricatures, or cartoon depictions deeply offensive to Muslims—than expressive conduct that is "merely" irreverent or offensive to some but not within the foregoing categories? *See, e.g., Pappas v. Giuliani*, 290 F.3d 143, 147 (2d Cir. 2002) (noting the importance of maintaining legitimacy in the community in upholding the termination of a police officer who disseminated racist and anti-Semitic writings). If yes, why? Note that much of this expression is more likely than that in *Roe* and *Dible* to address matters of public concern, *see* Note 2, page 374—although again, the extent to which this matters for off-site conduct unrelated to work is unresolved. Recall that the fact that the particular expression would be unacceptable or offensive to most people does not preclude constitutional protection, even if the expression is at work. *See Rankin*, 483 U.S. at 390. So why is "hate speech" and certain other forms of "highly offensive" speech distinguishable? Is greater deference to the employer justified because, at least in some contexts (e.g., employment discrimination) the speech itself might be illegal? If employers did not have broad discretion to regulate such speech might there be troublesome downstream consequences for them, at least in some contexts?

6. *Private Ordering and Deference.* As in Chapter 6, the overarching themes of private ordering and the appropriate level of deference to employer prerogatives are also central to the off-site conduct inquiry. While public employees cannot be required to "waive" prospectively their First Amendment rights, *Roe* and *Dible* demonstrate how a public employer's framing of job responsibilities and conditions, and, accordingly, a worker's decision to accept the position so defined, may limit the freedom the employee has in off-site expression and conduct. Indeed, law enforcement departments and agencies may apply the motto that "you are a police officer twenty-four hours a day, seven days a week" more or less aggressively, and this may ultimately determine the scope of the employee's speech rights. Moreover, as a practical matter, an employee begins litigation in a far weaker position if he or she must concede knowledge of an agreement to department guidelines and practices with regard to off-site and after-hours conduct, whether classified as "unbecoming," "immoral," offensive, or otherwise.

Deference also plays a role if, ultimately, the court seeks to balance the employee's interest in off-site expression against the employer's interest in avoiding harm to its mission or disruption of its operations. Note how the majority and concurring opinions in *Dible* differ on this question. How searching is the majority's review of the reasons given by the department for terminating *Dible*? How is level of scrutiny applied by Judge Canby different? What are the costs and benefits of each approach?

7. *Blogging and Other Web-based Activities.* This discussion brings us back to the high-profile issue of employee blogging and other Web-based activities, discussed more fully at pages 352-55 in Chapter 6. Under the framework in *NTEU* and *Roe*, public employee Internet activity that has a nexus with the workplace — either occurs at work or has work-related content — may have First Amendment protection but will be subject to the *Pickering/Connick* analysis. Internet activity that bears no relationship to work may be more likely to receive protection, although much remains unclear and seemingly depends on the nature of the expression, the worker's position, the role or mission of the agency, and, again, the level of deference courts may be willing to accord the government's justification for its actions. *See generally* Paul M. Secunda, *Blogging While (Publicly) Employed: Some First Amendment Implications*, 47 U. LOUISVILLE L. REV. 679 (2009).

8. *Other Protections for Public Employees.* Public employees may also enjoy certain additional protections for their speech or associational activities. Government restrictions on employee speech and expressive activity may run afoul of the Free Exercise, Equal Protection, and Due Process clauses of the Constitution. Thus, as discussed in Chapter 6, a government employer could not discipline or discharge an employee because of the employee's bona fide religious associations, *see Shrum v. City of Coweta*, 449 F.3d 1132 (10th Cir. 2006), or off-site associations that implicate fundamental rights, including intimate associations, unless the action is the result of a generally applicable policy that is justified by some governmental interest. See Chapter 6, at page 306. Similarly, statutory prohibitions on discrimination will limit a government agency's ability to regulate or prohibit both workplace and off-site conduct. *See id.*

Also, civil service codes and other statutes governing the public workplace often contain prohibitions against termination absent just cause, "good behavior," and other terms that restrict public employers' discretion in — and limit the reasons for — disciplining or terminating their employees. For example, federal law limits employee dismissals for misconduct to situations in which the agency can demonstrate that the misconduct impairs the efficiency of the service it provides and, hence, that a dismissal would promote efficiency. *See* 5 U.S.C. §§ 1101-5 (2006); 5 U.S.C. § 7513(a) (2006). However, this greater substantive protection also has a procedural price: The Supreme Court has held that employees covered by the federal government's comprehensive civil service regime may seek remedies — even for constitutional violations — only within that scheme. *See Bush v. Lucas*, 462 U.S. 367 (1983). State civil service codes do not preclude federal constitutional claims brought under 42 U.S.C. § 1983, but employee remedies for constitutional violations may nevertheless be limited by qualified immunity and other employer defenses. *See generally* Paul M. Secunda, *Whither the Pickering Rights of Federal Employees?* 79 U. COLO. L. REV. 1101 (2007).

In addition, collective bargaining agreements governing some government workers may carve out additional areas of protection and offer additional procedural constraints on agency discretion. Moreover, government agencies certainly may otherwise grant to their employees — unilaterally or by agreement — more protection than the First Amendment affords. *See, e.g., Waters v. Churchill*, 511 U.S. 661, 674 (1994) ("[T]he government may certainly choose to give additional protections to its employees beyond what is mandated by the First Amendment. . . .").

9. *Statutory Restrictions on Political Activity.* The Hatch Act, 5 U.S.C. §§ 7321-7326 (2006), and parallel state statutes, place restrictions on political activities by covered government employees, but also preserve certain freedoms. The Act and comparable state regimes were passed to prevent corruption and undue influence and, hence, impose significant restrictions on the partisan political activities of government workers. Many of these restrictions have been upheld in the face of First Amendment challenges. *See, e.g., United States Civil Serv. Comm'n v. Ass'n of Letter Carriers*, 413 U.S. 548 (1973); *Broadrick v. Oklahoma*, 413 U.S. 601 (1973) (upholding Oklahoma's version of the statute). However, amendments to the Hatch Act in 1993, *see* Pub. L. No. 103-94, 107 Stat. 1001 (1993), and exceptions in state statutes now provide limited rights for employees to take part in campaigns and other political activities while off-duty. Other activities are still banned, including the use of one's position for political influence, soliciting contributions from parties with business before the employee's agency, or engaging in political activities while on duty.

PROBLEMS

7-1. Michael Rasmusson is employed by the City Department of Health Services ("DHS") as a chemist's aide. In late May, DHS's Director of Workplace Diversity ("the Director") alerted all of its employees that June would be designated "Gay, Lesbian, Bisexual, and Transgender ("GLBT") Pride Month."

On June 2, another employee sent an e-mail to all co-workers, including Rasmusson, outlining the history of the gay and lesbian movement in the United States. Rasmusson e-mailed a reply to all recipients, which stated in part:

> I will not participate in gay celebrations because the Bible teaches that homosexuality is a horrible sin and those who practice it will not inherit the Kingdom of God. It is just as wrong for homosexuals to cause civil disorder today as it was in 1969 [the year the movement was founded], and they shouldn't have any more rights today than they did then.

The other employee then complained to the Director, as did other employees. The Director and a human resources officer then informed Rasmusson that sexual orientation is a protected status under state law and that it is unlawful to discriminate against individuals based on this status. He was further informed at the meeting that the DHS considered his e-mail messages to be in violation of this law.

On June 10, Rasmusson sent an e-mail message to one of DHS's high ranking officials, in which he objected to the display of homosexual literature in the lobby of DHS's building and stated that homosexuality is an unhealthy lifestyle that should not be promoted.

On June 17, Rasmusson received an e-mail from another employee inviting members of the department to a voluntary Ellen DeGeneres "coming out" party (at which they would watch together the famous 1997 television episode of *Ellen*, now on DVD). Rasmusson sent the following e-mail in response to this message:

> How could a program such as this where Ellen "comes out" and tells everyone she is a lesbian be humorous? This is nothing for her to be proud of and we should not encourage her in this. Should we also have a party when a man "comes out" and tells everyone he is a child molester?

DHS contends that the employee who sent the invitation, and hence, the recipient of Rasmusson's responsive e-mail, is a lesbian.

Shortly thereafter, Rasmusson was advised by his supervisor that he should not send out any further messages expressing his views on homosexuality. The supervisor further told Rasmusson that, although he is entitled to his personal views, his actions could constitute harassment as defined by DHS's harassment policy. In response, Rasmusson told the supervisor that he should be able to express his opinion on these matters like any other employee and that he intends to do so in response to any further DHS e-mails or activities endorsing homosexuality. At that point, the supervisor terminated Rasmusson.

Assume for purposes of this problem that the relevant state law prohibits employment discrimination based on sexual orientation. Also, assume that Rasmusson has no claim under the Free Exercise Clause or for religious discrimination.

Does Rasmusson have a First Amendment claim? What are Rasmusson's best arguments? How about DHS's? How likely is Rasmusson to prevail? What additional information, if any, would help you assess the likelihood of success? *See Brown v. Minnesota Dep't of Health*, Civ. No. 98-63 (JRT/RLE) (D. Minn. 1998).

If DHS asks for your advice on how it should structure or restructure GLBT Pride Month to reduce the risk of liability (to Rasmusson or others) in the future, what advice would you give? Does this kind of initiative create inherent liability risks, or can it be organized in a way that no speech-related liability is possible?

7-2. Assume the same facts as in 7-1 except, instead of sending the messages described above, Rasmusson was terminated or disciplined by DHS after he responded to GLBT Pride Month in one of the following three ways:

a. Posting information about and criticisms of the event on a socially conservative blog.
b. Criticizing what he called the "perverse gay and lesbian lifestyle" on the blog, but never referring to his employer or the Pride Month event in his postings.
c. Publicly supporting a local campaign pursuing a ballot initiative to repeal the state statute prohibiting discrimination based on sexual orientation and posting campaign flyers in his work cubicle.

Would the change in the facts in each of these three scenarios affect your analysis? If so, how?

B. THE PRIVATE WORKPLACE

In the private workplace, where neither civil service codes nor constitutional protections for expressive activity protect workers from employer actions, the sources of protection for employee speech and associational preferences are very limited. *See* David C. Yamada, *Voices from the Cubicle: Protecting and Encouraging Private Employee Speech in the Post-Industrial Workplace*, 19 BERKELEY J. EMP. & LAB. L. 1 (1998). Indeed, unlike privacy, there are *no* traditional common-law torts that protect employee speech directly. The more recently developed public policy tort may provide some protection, but only in very narrow situations such as speech protected as whistleblowing. Thus, as a general matter, employees in the private sector are left with a limited number of statutory protections for speech. These protections tend to apply only to certain types or categories of speech or association.

First, various statutory protections discussed elsewhere in this text may protect employee speech and expression directly or indirectly. For example, as discussed in Chapter 4, employee statements may be protected due to their content under federal and state statutes that prohibit employer retaliation against whistleblowers and those who testify in judicial or administrative proceedings. Also, as discussed in Chapter 6, federal and state antidiscrimination laws may protect employees from adverse treatment for certain associations, including religious affiliations and interracial intimate relationships, and occasional expressive conduct associated with other protected classifications. See Chapter 6 at page 352. Moreover, some of the privacy protections discussed in that chapter, including the federal wiretapping statute, protect employees from highly intrusive or secret monitoring of their communications, which has the effect of protecting the content of these communications.

In addition, as also discussed in Chapter 6, a number of states have enacted statutes that protect both public- and private-sector employees from adverse employment actions resulting from legal, off-site conduct and personal and political associations. *See, e.g.*, CAL. LAB. CODE §§ 96(k), 98.6 (2009); COL. REV. STAT. § 24-34-402.5 (2009) (prohibiting employers from terminating employees for lawful off-site activities absent job relatedness); MINN. STAT. § 181.938 (2009) (same); N.Y. LAB. LAW § 201-d (2010); S.C. CODE ANN. § 16-175-60 (2009) (providing for a claim of wrongful discharge where an employee is terminated because of his or her exercise of political rights under federal law or state law or because of an individual's political opinions); WASH. REV. CODE § 42.17.680(2) (2010) ("No employer or labor organization may discriminate against an officer or employee in the terms or conditions of employment for (a) the failure to contribute to, (b) the failure in any way to support or oppose, or (c) in any way supporting or opposing a candidate, ballot proposition, political party, or political committee."). Of course, none of these statutes provides absolute protections: Each allows, explicitly or implicitly, employers to defend their actions by showing that they are necessary to serve a legitimate business purpose.

On its face, the most sweeping state protection at present is a Connecticut statute that makes an employer liable for discharging or disciplining an employee on account of the employee's exercise of rights guaranteed in the First Amendment or parallel portions of the state constitution, provided that such exercise does not "materially interfere with the employee's bona fide job performance or the working relationship between the employee and employer." CONN. GEN. STAT. § 31-51q (2010). The Connecticut Supreme Court confirmed that the statute was intended to apply the free speech guarantees of the federal and state constitutions directly to private employers. *See Cotto v. United Technologies Corp.*, 738 A.2d 623 (Conn. 1999). The statute therefore provides potentially significant protection for public and private employee speech and association. *See, e.g., Trusz v. UBS Realty Investors*, 2010 WL 1287148 (D. Conn. March 30, 2010) (upholding portion of discharged employee's § 31-51q speech claim based on allegations that he was terminated for complaining about his employer's "pressuring employees to value properties higher or lower than their actual worth and knowingly misrepresenting such values to investors" because such complaints would be protected in the public employment arena as speech concerning the public). However, given the qualifying language in the statute and, as you have now seen, the qualified nature of employee speech rights under the Constitution, it is not yet clear how meaningful this protection will be. Indeed, in *Cotto* itself, the court found that an employee allegedly terminated for refusing to display at his workstation an American flag distributed by his employer did not state a claim under the statute. The court reasoned that no First Amendment–type interest was implicated because the employer's flag display directive did not require the employee to do or say anything related to his own political beliefs, did not compel him to "assume the risk that others might attribute to him any political beliefs about the flag that he did not share," and, hence, did not constitute coercion of expression or belief. *Id.* at 633-34.

Federal labor law provides another potentially important, albeit limited protection for employee expressive activities regarding workplace terms and conditions, even in the nonunionized context. Section 8(a)(1) of the National Labor Relations Act ("NLRA"), 29 U.S.C. § 158(a)(1) (2006), protects an employee's expressive conduct in two important respects. First, it prohibits discharging an employee for organizing workers. Beyond this, however, it protects all workers in their right under §7 of the NLRA to "concerted activities for the purpose of . . . mutual aid or protection," even apart from the formation of a union. *See* 29 U.S.C. § 157 (2006) ("Employees shall have the right to . . . engage in other concerted activities for the purpose of collective bargaining or other mutual aid or protection, and shall also have the right to refrain from any or all such activities. . . ."). In order to qualify for this protection, the employee activity must be "concerted" — that is, it must involve or be in preparation for group activity and involve a matter of potential common concern among employees, rather than merely activity by the worker solely on his or her own behalf. It must also involve "mutual aid and protection," which requires that it be reasonably work-related, addressing the conditions or terms of employment. Note that while other sources of speech and association rights tend to accord the greatest protection to off-site expressive activities unrelated to work, the "mutual aid and protection" requirement means that the protection under the NLRA applies *only* to work-related expression. Finally, even if the conduct is concerted and has a work-related object, it is protected only if it constitutes "protected activity," a term of art in labor law. Activity is unprotected if it is unlawful, violent, or unduly disruptive to the workplace, but even peaceful but "disloyal" conduct can be unprotected. *See, e.g., NLRB v. Fansteel Metallurgical Corp.*, 306 U.S. 240 (1939) (finding prolonged sit-down strike resulting in seizure of employer's plant and destruction of some of its property to be concerted but unprotected activity).

Consider how this protection for concerted activity might protect employee speech in already familiar fact patterns. First, as discussed in Chapter 6 at page 354, the National Labor Relations Board ("NLRB") has now alleged, in a potentially groundbreaking case, that an employer violated this mandate by terminating an employee after she criticized her supervisor on her Facebook page. In addition, recall *Connick*. Although Myers would have had no concerted activity claim under the NLRA because the act does not apply to public employers; a number of state labor statutes — which may apply to some classes of state and municipal employees — provide parallel protections for such activities. *See, e.g.*, Note, *Free Speech, The Private Employee, and State Constitutions,* 91 YALE L. J. 522, 523-24 & n.12 (1982) (discussing state statutes). Suppose Myers had been working as a prosecutor in one of these states and was covered under the state's statute. If she had circulated a similar questionnaire in her office, might her speech have been entitled to protection? Or was it not "concerted"?

Beyond these provisions, the two other potential, albeit rarely available sources of protection for employees in the private sector are the public policy tort and contract.

Edmondson v. Shearer Lumber Products
75 P.3d 733 (Idaho 2003)

WALTERS, Justice.

This is a wrongful termination of employment case. The employee appeals from the district court's dismissal of the action upon the employer's motion for summary judgment [and later motion to amend his complaint]. We affirm.

Facts

Michael Edmondson was employed by Shearer Lumber Products for twenty-two years at the company's Elk City mill. In 1999, he became a salaried employee and on his most recent performance review, he received a rating of "very good." However, on February 15, 2000, the plant manager, David Paisley, following directions from his superiors fired Edmondson, by reading a statement that informed Edmondson: "Because of your continued involvement in activities that are harmful to the long term interests of Shearer Lumber Products, we are terminating your employment immediately."

It was well known at Shearer Lumber that Edmondson was extensively involved in the community and regularly attended public meetings concerning matters of public interest and concern, such that he was recognized with the Idaho GEM Citizen Award by then Governor Batt. In January of 2000, Edmondson attended a public meeting of a group known as Save Elk City. One of the leaders of the group was the resource manager at Shearer Lumber, Dick Wilhite, who at the group meetings encouraged public support for the proposal that Save Elk City had submitted to the Federal Lands Task Force Working Group for consideration as to how best to manage the Nez Perce National Forest. Edmondson attended the group meetings, but he made no comments on the group's proposal. Nor did he discuss his opinions regarding the Save Elk City proposal at work with other employees.

Shearer Lumber did not openly campaign for the Save Elk City proposal, but Edmondson later learned from Wilhite that the proposal submitted in the name of Save Elk City was the project of Shearer Lumber's owner, Dick Bennett. At that time, Wilhite and Edmondson discussed the various outstanding proposals that might be competing for the Task Force's recommendation to the State Land Board, but Edmondson did not declare a preference for any of the proposals.

Shearer Lumber obtained information that Edmondson had attended meetings of the Task Force, had contacted someone in the administration of the Task Force, and was opposed to the collaborative project that Shearer had sponsored and submitted on behalf of the Save Elk City group. Edmondson was twice called into meetings at

Shearer Lumber, where he claimed he was subjected to intimidation and pressure from Wilhite, Paisley, and John Bennett, Shearer's general manager. It was made clear that Edmondson was *not* to form any opinions on or make any statements to the Federal Lands Task Force. In effect, Edmondson was warned that any opposition to the collaborative project that was contrary to Shearer's interest would lead to serious consequences. Edmondson was informed at the February 2, 2000, meeting that Shearer Lumber wanted all of its employees to support the projects the mill was involved in, if they wanted to avoid serious consequences that would result if the project was derailed or negatively impacted.

John Bennett testified in his deposition that the reason Edmondson was terminated was that Edmondson was opposing the project that Shearer Lumber Products supported, in direct conflict with the company's goals that could ultimately jeopardize a Task Force decision favorable to Shearer's interests. Bennett also attributed to Edmondson contact with the Task Force administration, although it was Edmondson's wife, Jamie, who had made inquiries to the Task Force. Edmondson speculated further as to the reason for his termination, which occurred the day after federal agents impounded some logs stored on the Shearer Mill site, as part of a U.S. Forest Service investigation in which Jamie Edmondson had also played a role. However, John Bennett testified that the logs belonged to a third party, and Shearer had no interest in how the logs were handled.

* * *

[Edmondson sued Shearer Lumber for wrongful termination of employment, but the lower court awarded summary judgment to Shearer because Edmondson's allegations did not fall within Idaho's limited public policy exception.]

Discussion

I . . .

A. The district court did not err in granting summary judgment on the claim of breach of public policy exception to the at-will doctrine.

In Idaho, the only general exception to the employment at-will doctrine is that an employer may be liable for wrongful discharge when the motivation for discharge contravenes public policy. *MacNeil v. Minidoka Memorial Hosp.*, [701 P.2d 208 (Idaho 1985)]; *Jackson v. Minidoka Irrigation Dist.*, 98 Idaho 330, 563 P.2d 54 (1977); *Anderson v. Farm Bureau Mut. Ins. Co. of Idaho*, 732 P.2d 699, 707 (Idaho Ct. App. 1987). The purpose of the exception is to balance the competing interests of society, the employer, and the employee in light of modern business experience. *Crea v. FMC Corp.*, 16 P.3d 272. 275 (Idaho 2000). The public policy exception has been held to protect employees who refuse to commit unlawful acts, who perform important public obligations, or who exercise certain legal rights or privileges. *Sorensen v. Comm Tek, Inc.*, 799 P.2d 70, 74 (Idaho 1990). Public policy of the state is found in the constitution and statutes. *Boise-Payette Lumber Co. v. Challis Indep. Sch. Dist. No. 1*, 268 P. 26 (Idaho 1928). "In the absence of case law or statutory language . . . , the Court finds no basis for expanding the Idaho law that defines the public policy exception to the at-will doctrine." *Lord v. Swire Pacific Holdings, Inc.*, 203 F.Supp. 2d 1175, 1180 (D. Idaho 2002).

Courts have recognized that public policy expressed in the constitution and the statutes of the state may serve as a basis for finding an exception to the employment at-will doctrine. *See generally* 82 AM. JUR. 2d *Wrongful Discharge* § 19, at 692 (1992). The First Amendment prohibits the government from restraining or abridging freedom of speech and assembly. Article I, § 9 of the Idaho Constitution also guarantees the right of free speech: "Every person may freely speak, write and publish on all subjects, being responsible for the abuse of that liberty." Article I, § 10 of the Idaho Constitution guarantees the right of freedom of association: "The people shall have the right to assemble in a peaceful manner, to consult for their common good; to instruct their representatives, and to petition the legislature for the redress of grievances." The First Amendment and Article I, §§ 9 and 10 of the Idaho Constitution do not apply to alleged restrictions imposed by private parties, however. . . .

Edmondson maintains that he was wrongfully terminated because he exercised his constitutionally protected rights of free speech and association. He argues that the public policy at issue prohibits restrictions on free speech and association. He relies on *Gardner v. Evans*, 719 P.2d 1185 (Idaho 1986) and *Lubcke v. Boise City/Ada County Housing Authority*, 860 P.2d 653 (Idaho 1993), which followed the two-step analysis of [*Connick*], in determining initially whether the speech involves a matter of public concern and, if so, applying a balancing test. These cases, however, all deal with governmental restrictions on free speech and associative rights of employees of public agencies, which are inapplicable in the private employment context in which Edmondson worked. The prevailing view among those courts addressing the issue in the private sector is that state or federal constitutional free speech cannot, in the absence of state action, be the basis of a public policy exception in wrongful discharge claims. *See Tiernan v. Charleston Area Med. Ctr., Inc.*, 506 S.E. 578, 589-90 (W. Va. 1998), and cases cited therein.

Edmondson argues that I.C. § 18-7901[1] expresses a public policy extending constitutional free speech protection to relationships between private employers and its employees. The district court did not make a finding specifically addressing I.C. § 18-7901, but even if it had, the facts alleged by Edmondson regarding his termination fall far short of describing conduct that was harassing, intimidating or threatening and based upon the descriptive list set forth in the statute.[2]

Finally, Edmondson urges that public policy is implicated wherever the power to hire and fire is utilized to dictate the terms of an employee's political activities and associations, relying on *Novosel v. Nationwide Ins. Co.*, 721 F.2d 894, 900 (3d Cir. 1983). There the court held that an important public policy was at stake and that Novosel's allegations that the employer coerced political activity stated a wrongful discharge claim. *Id.* However, the public policy adopted in *Novosel* has not been endorsed by any other court, not even the Pennsylvania state courts within the federal district of the Circuit that issued *Novosel*. We likewise decline to extend Idaho's public policy exception through the adoption of *Novosel*.

Accordingly, we hold that an employee does not have a cause of action against a private sector employer who terminates the employee because of the exercise of the

---

1. I.C. § 18-7901 provides as follows: The legislature finds and declares that it is the right of every person regardless of race, color, ancestry, religion or national origin, to be secure and protected from fear, intimidation, harassment, and physical harm caused by the activities of groups and individuals.

2. We do not suggest that the legislature's descriptive list should be deemed to exclude other well-recognized protected classes such as age, gender, or persons with mental or physical disabilities.

employee's constitutional right of free speech. The district court's dismissal of the claim of breach of public policy exception to the at-will doctrine is affirmed. . . .

III.

The district court did not err in denying Edmondson's motion to amend.

Following the decision of the district court on summary judgment, Edmondson filed a motion to amend his complaint to assert a breach of contract claim and a breach of the covenant of good faith and fair dealing. The district court denied the motion after a hearing, holding that the record did not support a claim for breach of an implied-in-fact contract. The district court also held that the record failed to show that the at-will relationship was somehow modified or did not apply to Edmondson.

. . . A limitation of an at-will employment will be implied when, from all the circumstances surrounding the relationship, a reasonable person could conclude that both parties intended that either's party's right to terminate the relationship was limited by the implied-in-fact agreement. *Mitchell v. Zilog, Inc.*, 874 P.2d 520, 523 (Idaho 1994). A plaintiff's subjective understanding is insufficient to establish an express or implied agreement limiting at-will employment. *Arnold v. Diet Center, Inc.*, 746 P.2d 1040 (Idaho Ct. App. 1987). Edmondson's personal belief that the company would not terminate him for attending public meetings, which the company allowed him to attend, or, would not terminate him without good cause, does not create limitations on Shearer's right to terminate him at will.

Unless an employee is hired pursuant to a contract which specifies the duration of the employment or limits the reasons why an employee may be discharged, the employee is at-will and can be terminated for any reason or no reason at all. *Thomas v. Med. Ctr. Physicians, P.A.*, 61 P.3d 557 (Idaho 2002); *Jackson* [*supra*]. Furthermore, as the district court ruled, the employee handbook expressly defined the relationship as at-will and negates Edmondson's claim of intent to restrict the grounds for discharge. *See Moser v. Coca-Cola Nw. Bottling Co.*, 931 P.2d 1227 (Idaho Ct. App. 1997). As a matter of law, therefore, the plaintiff failed to show that an implied contract changed the employee's at-will status. *Raedlein v. Boise Cascade Corp.*, 931 P.2d 621, 624 (Idaho 1996). The district court also held that the covenant of good faith and fair dealing does not prohibit an employer from terminating an employee at-will. We agree. *See Farnworth v. Femling*, 869 P.2d 1378, 1384 (Idaho 1994). We find no error in the district court's decision denying the Edmondson's motion to amend. . . .

* * *

Justice KIDWELL, dissenting.

I wholeheartedly support the presumption that employment in Idaho is "at-will" unless otherwise provided. Unlike the majority, however, I would hold that there is a narrow, but important, public policy exception to the at-will presumption for certain exercises of one's first amendment rights. Therefore, I respectfully dissent. . . .

As the majority has stated, public policy may be imbedded in statutes. *See, e.g., Watson v. Idaho Falls Consol. Hosps., Inc.*, 720 P.2d 632 (Idaho 1986). I believe that statutes are not the only place in which one may find public policy. Indeed, one may find the most significant public policies in this state and our nation in the Idaho Constitution and the Constitution of the United States. Thus, I would hold that certain constitutional public policies deserve protection and vindication through the public policy exception to at-will employment even in the absence of a statutory enactment.

One such policy that deserves protection in the at-will employment context is the policy of encouraging participation and debate regarding issues of public concern. The Idaho Constitution makes clear that "[a]ll political power is inherent in the people. Government is instituted for their benefit, and they have the right to alter, reform, or abolish the same whenever they may deem it necessary. . . ." ID. CONST. Art. 1, §2. In order to exercise the political power inherent in the people, the Idaho and United States constitutions endow individuals with the liberty to speak freely and participate in vigorous public debate. U.S. CONST. Amend. 1; ID. CONST. Art. 1, §9. Allowing employers to terminate employment based on an individual's association and speech regarding public issues that may have little or nothing in connection with the employer's business, invites employers to squelch the association, speech, and debate so necessary to our system of government. This is particularly true in the context of the myriad of small Idaho communities with only one or two prominent employers. Thus, I would hold it against public policy to discharge an employee for constitutionally-protected political speech or activities regarding a matter of public concern, provided that such speech or activity does not interfere with the employee's job performance or the business of the employer.

The majority cites to *Tiernan v. Charleston Area Med. Ctr.*, for the proposition that absent a state action, the constitutional exercise of free speech is not a public policy exception to at will employment. It is my opinion that even absent a state action, a very narrowly drawn public policy exception to the employment at-will doctrine should apply. That narrowly drawn exception would require a two-step analysis. First, did the at-will employee's speech impact the employer's business in *any* manner? If so, was the employee terminated because of his or her speech? The free speech public policy exception would apply to at-will employment in the case where the employee's speech does not impact the employer's business and the employee was terminated for the speech. In *Tiernan* the plaintiff was fired because she wrote a letter to the editor criticizing her employer. Under this proposed public policy exception, the plaintiff's speech clearly impacted her employer and her termination was lawful.

In this case, the evidence in the record clearly creates genuine issues of material fact regarding whether Edmondson was terminated for political speech or activities regarding a matter of public concern. Further, the record shows genuine issues regarding whether Edmondson's speech and activities interfered with his job performance or the business of his employer. On these grounds, I would vacate summary judgment and remand this matter for further proceedings.

NOTES

1. *Freedom of Expression and the Public Policy Tort.* Work your way through Edmondson's public policy claim. Why does the majority reject this theory? Now consider Justice Kidwell's dissent. With which aspects of the majority's reasoning does he take issue, and what dangers does he identify that fail to sway his colleagues?

Both opinions cite *Novosel v. Nationwide Insurance Co.*, 721 F.2d 894 (3d Cir. 1983), undoubtedly the leading case in which a court has found that state and federal constitutional protections for political expression and association are important public policies that can form the basis of an employee's wrongful discharge claim. In that case, a federal circuit panel sitting in diversity held that Novosel stated a claim under Pennsylvania law where he alleged that he was discharged for refusing to participate in his employer's lobbying effort and privately expressing opposition to the company's political stand:

> Although Novosel is not a government employee, the public employee cases do not confine themselves to the narrow question of state action. Rather, these cases suggest that an important public policy is in fact implicated wherever the power to hire and fire is utilized to dictate the terms of employee political activities. In dealing with public employees, the cause of action arises directly from the Constitution rather than from common law developments. The protection of important political freedoms, however, goes well beyond the question whether the threat comes from state or private bodies. The inquiry before us is whether the concern for the rights of political expression and association which animated the public employee cases is sufficient to state a public policy under Pennsylvania law. While there are no Pennsylvania cases squarely on this point, we believe that the clear direction of the opinions promulgated by the state's courts suggests that this question be answered in the affirmative.
>
> Having concluded thereby that an important public policy is at stake, we now hold that Novosel's allegations state a claim [under Pennsylvania law] in that Novosel's complaint discloses no plausible and legitimate reason for terminating his employment, and his discharge violates a clear mandate of public policy.

Id. at 900. Compare this reasoning with that of the majority and dissent in *Edmondson*. Thinking back to the discussion of the public policy tort in Chapter 4, which approach is more consistent with the contours of the theory outlined in that chapter? Which approach is more convincing?

2. *State of the Law on Public Policy Speech Claims.* The *Novosel* decision has generated an enormous amount of attention, often negative. Indeed, Judge Becker of the Third Circuit dissented from the full Third Circuit's denial of an *en banc* rehearing of this decision because, in his view, the panel greatly overreached:

> First, the opinion ignores the state action requirement of first amendment jurisprudence, particularly by its repeated, and, in my view, inappropriate citation of public employee cases, and by its implicit assumption that a public policy against government interference with free speech may be readily extended to private actors in voluntary association with another. Second, the opinion could be read to suggest that an explicit contractual provision authorizing an employer to dismiss a lobbyist for failure to undertake lobbying might be unenforceable or subject to a balancing test. Third, the opinion fails to consider other public policy interests, such as the economic interests of the public in efficient corporate performance, the first amendment interests of corporations, and the legitimate interests of a corporation in commanding the loyalty of its employees to pursue its economic well being.

721 F.2d at 903. There are a few other published cases in which courts have recognized speech or association-based claims under the public policy doctrine. *See, e.g., Chavez v. Manville Prods. Corp.*, 777 P.2d 371 (N.M. 1989). Yet, as *Edmondson* suggests, the courts that have rejected *Novosel*'s reasoning are legion, and, absent a statute, the vast

majority of courts have refused to recognize a public policy claim for employee political, social, or associational choices in private workplaces. *See, e.g., Dixon v. Coburg Dairy, Inc.*, 330 F.3d 250 (4th Cir. 2003) (refusing to extend South Carolina's public policy doctrine to cover termination for the placement of Confederate flag stickers on a tool box); *Grinzi v. San Diego Hospice Corp.*, 14 Cal. Rptr. 3d 893 (Cal. App. 2004) (rejecting *Novosel*'s reasoning and citing to numerous decisions where other courts have done the same); *Tiernan v. Charleston Area Med. Ctr., Inc.*, 506 S.E.2d 578 (W. Va. 1998) (same); *Brunner v. Al Attar*, 786 S.W.2d 784 (Tex. App. 1990) (holding that the termination of an employee because she worked as a volunteer at the AIDS Foundation does not violate public policy).

3. *Comparison to* Borse. Interestingly, the Third Circuit decided both *Borse*, the public policy case involving drug testing set forth in Chapter 6 at page 309, and *Novosel*. And, in both cases, the court, sitting in diversity jurisdiction, attempted to anticipate and apply Pennsylvania law on the public policy doctrine. Broadly speaking, which decision is more consistent with the public policy doctrine cases set forth in Chapter 4? In answering this question, consider what or who the public policy tort is designed to protect. If your answer is that *Novosel* is more in line with the other public policy cases, note the irony, since a number of other courts have adopted the reasoning in *Borse*, while *Novosel* remains an outlier.

4. *Should There Be Stronger Protection for Private-Sector Employees?* Despite the criticism and widespread rejection of *Novosel*'s extension of the public policy doctrine, the power of the court's critique of the employer's conduct ensures its continuing relevance in the debate. Are the *Novosel* court and the dissent in *Edmondson* on to something when they suggest that private employer — coerced political activity is potentially problematic? *See* Lisa B. Bingham, *Employee Free Speech in the Workplace: Using the First Amendment as Public Policy for Wrongful Discharge Actions*, 55 Ohio St. L. J. 341 (1994) (arguing in favor of a *Novosel*-like public policy claim).

Consider that *Novosel* was handed down more than 20 years ago. Are private enterprises today more or less powerful economically and politically? How about employees, individually or collectively? Given that most employees work in the private sector, are the dangers associated with employer conduct like that in *Novosel* and *Edmondson* significant? Indeed, the conduct in *Novosel* and *Edmondson* might be particularly troublesome since the employer in each of these cases sought not only to prohibit employee activities but also to coerce employees into affirmatively participating in political activity on its behalf. If employer-coerced political activity is widespread, did *Novosel* correctly identify a danger to the functioning and legitimacy of our political system? Even if such coercion does not become standard practice, doesn't the prospect of it as well as the chill of employer prohibitions sufficiently threaten aspects of autonomy we view as so fundamental in democratic society that we ought to recognize that such behavior violates public policy?

Justice Kidwell seems deeply troubled by this, noting that the lack of protection for employees "invites employers to squelch the association, speech, and debate so necessary to our system of government[,]" and expressing particular concern "in the context of the myriad of small Idaho communities with only one or two prominent employers." Might this be even more true now in the wake of *Citizens United v. Federal Election Commission*, 130 S.Ct. 876 (2010), in which the Supreme Court held that independent political expenditures by for-profit corporations are protected by the First Amendment and therefore cannot be prohibited? Put another way, now that firms — that is, private employers — have robust protections accompanying their significant resources to influence the political process, shouldn't we be even more concerned about their coercing their employees to support or at least not oppose their policy preferences?

If so, what is the response to Judge Becker's claim that the *Novosel* panel's approach might threaten an employer's ability to terminate a lobbyist? Would there be a workable way to limit such protection such that it would not inhibit, for example, a public relations firm's ability to terminate an employee who refused to speak out against state legislation harmful to the tobacco industry even though he was hired to improve the image and advocate on behalf of clients engaged in cigarette manufacturing?

5. *A Defense of or Threat to the Legislative Process?* As discussed in Chapter 4, a core objection to an expansive common-law public policy tort is that it violates separation of powers principles — that is, the legislature and not the courts ought to decide state public policy and, as importantly, which breaches of such policies should give rise to a private right of action. Even if one generally accepts this proposition, is the argument in favor of the legislative prerogative less strong here, where the concern is the distortion of the political process itself? In other words, should the protection at issue in *Novosel* and *Edmondson* be left to the political process when the public policy supporting the protection is to ensure the legitimacy of that process?

Nevertheless, if, as the *Edmondson* majority and most other courts have concluded, *Novosel* nevertheless went too far, perhaps the employer activity the opinion addresses and the dangers it identifies should be, at minimum, a call for legislative reform to protect both workers and the integrity of the political process. If you agree with this proposition, consider what kind of legislated protections would be appropriate and meaningful. As discussed above, a few states have enacted statutes that may protect employee political activities and associations, although, interestingly, under some of the statutory regimes, off-site political conduct would receive protection while compelled political participation at work, of the type at issue in *Novosel*, would not. Again, the Connecticut statute, as interpreted by the Connecticut Supreme Court in *Cotto*, see page 412, probably would protect employees from such employer demands because it applies constitutional associational protections against private employers, and thereby likely prohibits affirmative coercive measures such as compelled political patronage. Is the Connecticut approach the correct one, or does it also go too far?

6. *Nonpolitical Speech in and Outside the Workplace.* Both *Novosel* and *Edmondson* involve political speech and association. If you believe such activity ought to receive some protection in the private workplace, would you extend the protection to nonpolitical speech addressing a matter of public interest — for example, recent world events, community activities, or entertainment and sports news? Similarly, would you extend associational protections to nonpolitical activities, such as participation in social clubs, corporate boards, nondenominational charities, volunteer organizations, and self-help groups? If so, why? What public policies are served by protecting nonpolitical speech? Is the free exchange of ideas, or at least the exchange of ideas on matters of public concern or importance, a strong enough reason to support such far-reaching protection in the private workplace? Are there other ends to be served by protecting expressive interests in the private workplace? Finally, which of these ends, if any, are worth the costs — for example, litigation costs, counseling and administrative costs, hesitation to fire underperforming workers, the costs of uncertainty — additional restrictions invariably impose on employers?

7. *The Restatement Approach.* Chapter 4 of the draft Restatement (Third) of Employment Law addresses the tort of wrongful discharge in violation of public policy. *See* RESTATEMENT (THIRD) OF EMPLOYMENT LAW (Tentative Draft No. 2, April 3, 2009) §4.02. Advocates of employee speech rights will be disappointed to learn that this draft contains no *Novosel*-like protection for employee speech or association. The draft does contain a "catch-all" provision, *see* §4.02(f) (protecting an employee who "engages in other activity directly furthering a substantial public policy"), but there is no suggestion that this would support a *Novosel*-like claim. Indeed, the Reporters Notes following this section recognize that courts generally have disfavored such claims. *See* §4.02 Reporters Notes cmt. d. Should the ALI attempt to provide more guidance on the difficult issue of determining whether a sufficient public policy basis exists to support a wrongful discharge claim in particular circumstances, including the speech and association context? Or is it too much to expect of a "Restatement" to do anything that flies in the face of so wide a consensus among the courts?

8. *Private Ordering and Employee Expression.* In addition to rejecting Edmondson's public policy claim, the court also rejected his contract theories, finding no express or implicit promise on the part of Shearer that Edmondson's employment was anything but at will. However, other courts have found that contract-based theories are available to employees terminated for speech and associational activities.

For instance, in *Rulon-Miller*, reproduced at page 323, the court upheld an implied-in-fact contract claim arising out of an employee's associational preferences — in that case, involving an employee's intimate association. *See also Novosel*, 721 F.2d *at* 902-03 (concluding that the allegation "that Nationwide's custom, practice or policy created either a contractual just cause requirement or contractual procedures by which defendant failed to abide is a factual matter that should survive a motion to dismiss"). Given the fairly wide acceptance of the theory of implied-in-fact contractual modifications to the at-will relationship, this is a potentially viable theory for employees claiming some right to expression.

Nevertheless, implied just-cause/good-cause terms (such as those alleged in *Edmondson* and *Novosel*) differ from the terms in *Rulon-Miller* in important respects. Recall that the terms enforced against the employer in *Rulon-Miller* addressed the employee's autonomy interests directly; that is, IBM had instituted a general policy of not interfering with its employees' off-site associations and activities. Implied just-cause/good-cause terms do not purport to protect associational rights in particular. In many speech and association cases, such a term may be of limited assistance to employees because it would be fairly easy for employers to articulate a legitimate business reason for terminating employees for their expression or associations. For example, assuming that the employer demands in *Novosel* and *Edmondson* violated no state law, didn't the employers in those cases have just cause/good cause to terminate the employees? Suppose, for instance, that the employer was lobbying for a government contract, which the employee opposed as not in the public interest. Wouldn't the employer be able to terminate the employee without breaching the contract? Recall that *Rulon-Miller* cautioned, "We have concern with an employee's off-the-job behavior only when it reduces his ability to perform regular job assignments, interferes with the job performance of other employees, or if his outside behavior affects the reputation of the company in a major way."

9. *Express Contractual Speech and Association Rights.* In addition to the implied-in-fact contract theory, a few common forms of express contractual provisions protect individual employee expression. Collective bargaining agreements, for example, may include not only just cause provisions, but also specific protections for employee unionizing activity, political activity, and other forms of expression. In addition, high-level workers or those who are in high-demand, including entertainers, sports figures, and executives, may negotiate for terms that give them significant expressive freedom. Such negotiated terms may include the ability to moonlight, the right to engage in philanthropic activities and social causes of one's choosing, and "for cause only" termination, defined so as to shield a great deal of expressive conduct from employer retaliation.

Consider those workers who are hired to express their opinions — for example, editorial writers, political commentators, cartoonists, certain performing artists, and, more and more frequently, bloggers. Obviously, these workers have incentives to negotiate for protections that provide them with sufficient "space" to express their opinions without fear of retribution. But given the many business and legal risks that might arise from such expression, what limitations are their employers likely to demand? These issues have garnered significant, recent attention in the wake of National Public Radio's termination of news analyst Juan Williams (for his remarks regarding Muslims made on Fox News) and MSNBC's short suspension of host Keith Olbermann (for his failure to disclose political contributions pursuant to network policy). However, neither incident resulted in a legal dispute.

The group of employees enjoying perhaps the most robust speech protections is tenured faculty members in academic institutions. The primary policy supporting tenure is academic freedom, although it is intended to serve other values as well, including economic security. *See, e.g.*, American Association of University Professors, *1940 Statement of Principles on Academic Freedom and Tenure*, in AAUP Policy Documents and Reports (1995), *available at* http://www.aaup.org/statements/Redbook/1940stat.pdf. Academic tenure provides protected faculty with guaranteed employment subject to termination only for cause, and, because the aim is to preserve academic freedom, cause generally does not include the views expressed by the faculty member. As discussed above, in the public education context, academic freedom has been recognized as a potentially important First Amendment concern. Academic tenure has generally held strong in both the public and private context. There are, however, economic and political pressures to the contrary, as well as the occasional "spike" in anti-tenure sentiment, *see supra* Note 8, page 393 (discussing the uproar that followed Ward Churchill's statements about 9/11 victims); *see also* James J. Fishman, *Tenure: Endangered or Evolutionary Species*, 38 AKRON L. REV. 771 (2005) (addressing some of the current challenges to tenure).

There are relatively few litigated cases regarding "de-tenuring" or the discharge of tenured employees. Indeed, dismissal of tenured university faculty is relatively rare. *See, e.g.*, James J. Fishman, *Tenure and Its Discontents: The Worst Form of Employment Relationship Save All of the Others*, 21 PACE L. REV. 159, 172-73 (2000).

The most likely expression-related cause for dismissal of a tenured faculty member is sexual or other forms of harassment. *See id.* at 200-01 (stating that the other most frequent causes are other illegal activities, incompetence, and the institution's financial exigency). Another is plagiarism and related forms of research misconduct. Tenure, however, does not typically protect faculty members with regard to administrative positions they also hold, such as deanships and department chairs. *See, e.g., Jeffries v. Harleston*, 52 F.3d 9 (2d Cir. 1995) (holding right to academic freedom does not prevent removal of professor as chair of department). For further discussion of academic tenure, *see generally* Matthew W. Finkin, *"A Higher Order of Liberty in the Workplace": Academic Freedom and Tenure in the Vortex of Employment Practices and Law*, 53 Law & Contemp. Probs. 357 (1990).

Most other workers (i.e., nonunionized, non–high-level, non–civil service, and nontenured) have neither the bargaining power nor inclination at the outset of their employment to negotiate for terms that protect their speech and association prerogatives, and raising such issues at the formation stage may raise unwanted red flags. Such provisions, therefore, are rare and, as a result, the typical nonunionized worker enjoys no express contractual protection for expressive activities. This, combined with the limited availability of other common-law or statutory protections, means that most expressive and associational activity by private-sector employees has no legal protection.

10. *Contractual "Suppression" of Employee Speech.* For most employees, the far more likely kinds of contractual provisions are those designed to suppress or restrict employee speech. A typical example is an employee agreeing as a condition of employment, promotion, or severance not to disclose broad categories of confidential and other work- or employer-related information to third parties during and after his or her term of employment. The enforceability of such provisions — or at least those that purport to limit expression beyond trade secrets, privileged communications, and other traditionally recognized forms of proprietary information — is controversial. One high-profile example is the confidentiality agreement between Jeffrey Wigand and his former employer, Brown & Williamson Tobacco Company ("B & W"), which purported to prohibit Wigand from discussing anything about B & W's business, products, or practices that were not generally known during and after termination of his employment relationship. *See, e.g.*, Terry Morehead Dworkin & Elletta Sangrey Callahan, *Buying Silence*, 36 Am. Bus. L. J. 151, 191 (1998); Bryan Styker Weinstein, *In Defense of Jeffrey Wigand: A First Amendment Challenge to the Enforcement of Employee Confidentiality Agreements Against Whistleblowers*, 49 S.C. L. Rev. 129 (1997). B & W's attempts to enforce this agreement against Wigand and to prevent the CBS show *60 Minutes* from airing interviews with him received significant public attention and were ultimately the subject of the movie *The Insider*. For further discussion of such agreements and their social implications, *see generally* Alan E. Garfield, *Promises of Silence: Contract Law and Freedom of Speech*, 83 Cornell L. Rev. 261 (1998); *see also* Daniel J. Solove & Neil M. Richards, *Rethinking Free Speech and Civil Liability*, 109 Colum. L. Rev. 1650 (2009) (offering a detailed account and critique of how courts confront the clash between free speech and private ordering in the confidentiality agreement context and elsewhere).

11. *Should There Be a Qualified Right to Free Expression in the Private Workplace?* A number of commentators have argued that there ought to be protection for various kinds of employee expression and association in the private workplace. *See, e.g.*, Bruce Barry, Speechless: The Erosion of Free Expression in the American Workplace (2007); Cynthia L. Estlund, *Free Speech and Due Process in the Workplace*, 71 Ind. L.J. 101 (1995); Joseph R. Grodin, *Constitutional Values in the Private Sector Workplace*, 13 Indus. Rel. L.J. 1 (1991); Stephen D. Sugarman, *"Lifestyle" Discrimination in Employment*, 24 Berkeley J. Emp. & Lab. L. 377 (2003); David C. Yamada, *Voices* *from the Cubicle: Protecting and Encouraging Private Employee Speech in the Post-Industrial Workplace*, 19 Berkeley J. Emp. & Lab. L. 1 (1998). Now that you are familiar with the entire legal landscape (statutory, tort, and private ordering) and the practical realities for most workers, does the law treat employee expression appropriately? What reforms, if any, would you advocate?

PROBLEMS

7-3.   Look back at Problems 7-1 and 7-2. This time, however, assume that the employer is not a city agency, but rather the health services department of a private, nonsectarian university, and that Rasmusson is a nontenured employee of the university. Assume all other facts and circumstances remain the same. What are the possible legal theories on which Rasmusson may pursue a claim against his employer for his termination under any of the scenarios described? How probable is it that he will prevail? If there is a risk of liability, how could the university reduce such risk in the future?

7-4.   Patricia Patterson was employed by DollarSave Stores, Inc. ("DSI"), where she had been an accountant working at a large distribution facility for a dozen years. DSI is a large food wholesaler and retailer. Patterson had no written employment contract, although her superiors had always given her very positive work reviews and indicated to her that she had a bright future with DSI. Her job duties required no contact with the public.

After she experienced serious health problems several years ago, Patterson was diagnosed as highly allergic to certain synthetic hormones. These hormones are common in domestic nonorganic beef, poultry, and pork. They also are present in meat byproducts, including stocks, bullions, and lard. To avoid recurring health problems, Patterson's physicians imposed a no–nonorganic meat/meat byproduct dietary restriction on her. As a result, Patterson became a semi-observant vegetarian, read food labels carefully, and purchased organic foods whenever possible. She also became an avid reader of health and organic food journals and a frequent participant in various online discussion groups supporting vegetarianism and organic lifestyles.

Recently, a food-labeling bill began to work its way through the state legislature. This bill would mandate detailed disclosures of both the origins of meat products and byproducts and the hormones and antibiotics used in their production. DSI sells a substantial amount of domestic meat products and other foods containing meat-based ingredients and byproducts, none of which is organic. It therefore opposed further food labeling. DSI informed its workers about its lobbying efforts in a monthly newsletter for employees, but it never asked its own employees to take any action.

On the eve of a legislative hearing on the bill, Patterson was contacted by one of her friends and asked if she could give a statement supporting food labeling. She agreed. At the hearing, she described her health problems, the difficulty she had in determining which foods contained meat byproducts containing hormones, and the corresponding need for better labeling. She never mentioned in her statement that she was employed by DSI. To her surprise, when she arrived at work the next morning, her supervisor terminated her.

First, consider whether Patterson has a cause of action against DSI sounding in tort or contract. What theories may be available to her, and how likely would she be to succeed on such claims? Next, consider whether she would have a viable claim under state statutes like those described at page 412. What barriers to establishing liability might she face? Finally, in your view, should Patterson enjoy any legal protection in this context? Why or why not?

Part Five

WORKPLACE PROPERTY RIGHTS AND RELATED INTERESTS

8

Competition, Employee Loyalty, and the Allocation of Workplace Property Interests

By now you should have a good sense of the rights of employees upon termination. Most employment relationships are at will, and the burden is on the plaintiff-employee to establish additional contractual protection or an available tort or statutory remedy. The cases you read, while proposing different theories of liability, all involved an employee who was involuntarily terminated and sought to prove that the employer had breached a binding promise of job security or violated tort or statutory law. This chapter is different. It looks not at the rights of employees who have been fired, but rather the rights of employers to prevent harm to their business interests by current and former employees. Thus, in the cases that follow, it is typically the employer who is the plaintiff and the employee who is the defendant.

Usually an employer sues a former employee because it believes the employee threatens its business position through competitive behavior. The employee may have left to work for a rival company and may have enticed other employees to join the competitor. The employee's new position might make use of his past work experience in ways that create a competitive advantage for the rival. The employee may rely on knowledge of the former employer's product or business model, or she may solicit customers or clients previously serviced by the employer. In addition, employers may seek to protect their interests or pursue litigation against an employee for strategic reasons. The threat of a lawsuit may deter employees from leaving, and it may induce poorly funded rivals to avoid competition.

Whether the former employee's conduct is illegal is often a complicated question. One of the rationales for the at-will regime in the United States is that in theory it gives employees the freedom to move between jobs. That ability would be compromised if the employee could not meaningfully use her knowledge and skills, including industry-specific ones, upon departure. Moreover, society as a whole benefits from healthy competition between multiple providers of goods and services. On the other hand, many employers spend significant time and money developing their customer base, intellectual property, and other business assets. They may also invest in training their employees. In his seminal article on noncompete agreements, Professor Harlan Blake explained the competing policy considerations:

> From the point of view of the employer, postemployment restraints are regarded as perhaps the only effective method of preventing unscrupulous competitors or employees

from appropriating valuable trade information and customer relationships for their own benefit. Without the protection afforded by such covenants, it is argued, business[es] could not afford to stimulate research and improvement of business methods to a desirably high level, nor could they achieve the degree of freedom of communication within a company that is necessary for efficient operation.

The opposite view is that postemployment restraints reduce both the economic mobility of employees and their personal freedom to follow their own interests. These restraints also diminish competition by intimidating potential competitors and by slowing down the dissemination of ideas, processes, and methods. They unfairly weaken the individual employee's bargaining position vis-à-vis his employer and, from the social point of view, clog the market's channeling of [labor] to employments in which its productivity is greatest.

Harlan M. Blake, *Employee Agreements Not to Compete*, 73 Harv. L. Rev. 625, 627 (1960).

Recognizing these conflicting impulses, the law accords the employer protection against worker competition during the course of the parties' relationship but only limited protection against competition upon termination. This chapter examines those limited rights and the legal tools available to an employer seeking to safeguard what it considers to be its business interests prior to and upon an employee's departure. It looks specifically at three areas: worker recruitment and training; trade secrets and confidential information; and access to customers, clients, and co-workers. As you read, be conscious of how both public law and private ordering play a role in allocating rights in each of these contexts. The rights and obligations of workers who wish to compete are governed by the tort duty of loyalty and statutory protection against the misappropriation of trade secrets, but employers often seek to expand these protections through contract. How do courts treat these different sources of legal protection? Should the source of legal protection make a difference in the outcome in a particular dispute? Does employers' use of written instruments, such as noncompete agreements, point out genuine deficiencies in public protection for employer property rights? Or is this an illustration of the employer unfairly reaching beyond what the law permits to the detriment of its employees?

Throughout the chapter, also keep in mind the inherent conflict between freedom of competition for the employee and protection of employer property interests and investments. How do these competing concerns influence court decisions? Do courts strike a fair balance between employer and employee rights? If not, how can the situation be improved? Do we need clearer rules? More private ordering? A legislative solution?

A. FIDUCIARY DUTIES OF CURRENT EMPLOYEES

Scanwell Freight Express STL, Inc. v. Chan
162 S.W.3d 477 (Mo. 2005)

Limbaugh, Jr., J.

Scanwell Freight Express STL, Inc., sued Stevie Chan for breach of fiduciary duty and Dimerco Express (U.S.A.) Corp. for conspiracy to breach fiduciary duty. Following a jury trial, Scanwell was awarded $54,000 in damages from Chan and $254,000 from Dimerco. . . . The judgment is reversed, and the case is remanded.

I

In brief, and in the light most favorable to the verdict . . . the facts are as follows:

Scanwell, a freight forwarding business, hired Chan in April 1996 to be the general manager of its St. Louis Office. Chan was an at-will employee, and she was not required to sign a noncompete agreement. While serving as Scanwell's general manager, Chan made arrangements with Dimerco, Scanwell's direct competitor, to open a Dimerco office in St. Louis. At Dimerco's request, Chan created a "business proposal" for this purpose. She also arranged for Dimerco to take over the lease of Scanwell's St. Louis office upon its expiration. Chan resigned from Scanwell effective March 1, 2001, and approximately one month later, Dimerco opened its St. Louis office with Chan as its general manager. Dimerco operated in the same premises that Scanwell previously occupied, employed most of the same employees as Scanwell, and for a while even used the same telephone number. Dimerco also acquired a number of Scanwell's customers.

Thereafter, Scanwell filed the suit against Chan and Dimerco that is the subject of this appeal.

II . . .

In the employer-employee relationship, this Court, drawing on the Restatement (2d) of Agency, has implicitly recognized a separate cause of action for breach of the duty of loyalty, *Nat'l Rejectors, Inc. v. Trieman*, 409 S.W.2d 1, 41 (Mo. 1966). . . .

Under *Trieman*, the seminal case on which both sides rely, . . . certain at-will employees were accused of misappropriating trade secrets from their employer in a scheme to compete with the employer. The factual context of the case is especially important because it involves the most common manifestation of the duty of loyalty, and the essence of Scanwell's claim here, which is that an employee has a duty not to compete with his or her employer concerning the subject matter of the employment. This Court described the duty of loyalty in the broad and general terms of section 387 of the Restatement (2d) of Agency, stating, "[an employee] must not, while employed, act contrary to the employer's interests." However, in addressing the corresponding duty not to compete, the Court held, nonetheless, that employees are allowed to "agree among themselves to compete with their then employer upon termination of their employment," and "[t]hey may plan and prepare for their competing enterprises while still employed." Admittedly, the mere decision to enter into competition is "contrary to the employer's interests," but the Court saw the need to balance the duty not to compete with the interest of promoting free competition. As some courts have put it, the law allows employees the privilege to plan and prepare for competition in recognition of the "competing interests of allowing an employee some latitude in switching jobs and at the same time preserving some degree of loyalty owed to the employer." *Cudahy Co. v. Am. Lab., Inc.*, 313 F. Supp. 1339, 1346 (D. Neb. 1970).

Although the *Trieman* Court did not elaborate on the conduct that would constitute a breach of the duty, it necessarily follows that a breach arises when the employee goes beyond the mere planning and preparation and actually engages in direct competition, which, by definition, is to gain advantage over a competitor. The Restatement (2d) of Agency, sec. 393, cmt. e, which this Court cited with favor in *Trieman*, plays on the same idea, further describing the kinds of activities that can constitute a breach of the duty of loyalty. That comment, in pertinent part, states:

> After termination of his agency, in the absence of a restrictive agreement, the agent can properly compete with his principal as to matters for which he has been employed. Even before the termination of the agency, he is entitled to make arrangements to compete, except that he cannot properly use confidential information peculiar to his employer's business and acquired therein. Thus, before the end of his employment, he can properly purchase a rival business and upon termination of employment immediately compete. He is not, however, entitled to solicit customers for such rival business before the end of his employment nor can he properly do other similar acts in direct competition with the employer's business.

III

Applying these standards, this Court concludes that Scanwell presented a submissible case that Chan breached her duty of loyalty. Chan's actions were clearly contrary to Scanwell's interests, and . . . went beyond mere planning and preparation to compete. . . .

First, Chan gave Dimerco confidential information about Scanwell's operations and customers. This included general information on Scanwell's customer base and detailed information on a few of Scanwell's customers. Most of the evidence centered on the fact that Chan gave Dimerco a customer profile of one of Scanwell's largest customers, which included contact information, special handling requirements, rate structure, billing instructions, and other information. At trial, Chan admitted that the customer profile was confidential "[to] some degree" and that it would be helpful to a competitor in soliciting the business of the customer. Dennis Choy, Scanwell's president, also testified that this information was confidential and that, in fact, customer profiles were "the most vital pieces of information for any company to keep within [itself]." Although Chan and Dimerco argue that some of the information in the profile was not confidential because it could be obtained from other sources such as the customers themselves, at least some of the information in the profile, such as Scanwell's air freight rates, was entirely unavailable. Regardless of the extent of the disclosure of confidential information, as other courts have aptly noted, even "slight assistance to a direct competitor can constitute a breach of the employee's duty of loyalty." *Cameco, Inc. v. Gedicke*, 724 A.2d 783, 521-22 (N.J.1999).

A second and more egregious activity was that Chan, while still employed by Scanwell, secured Scanwell's leased premises — Scanwell's business office — for Dimerco. The key testimony on the matter was uncontroverted. [Chan, as office manager, had signed the original and an amended, renewable lease for Scanwell. She forwarded these documents to headquarters, but as the December 1, 2000 renewal deadline approached,] Chan, who was by then preparing to leave Scanwell and open the Dimerco office, took no action to renew the lease for Scanwell and did not notify Scanwell's home office that the renewal deadline was approaching.

Then in early February 2001, while still employed by Scanwell and at a time the Scanwell's premises still could have been relet to Scanwell, Chan, with Dimerco's approval, negotiated and signed a lease of the same premises for Dimerco. Although Chan signed the lease on February 15, 2001, it was on February 20, 2001, that Chan first informed Scanwell that she planned to resign. That same day, she sent a letter to her supervisor at Scanwell, M.B. Hassan, stating, "[t]he new rental lease has been turned back to the landlor[d] and will not be renewed. You can contact [the landlord's agent] if you have [a] different arrangement. Otherwise the lease will end[] [in] March."

While Chan and Dimerco claim that there are no cases holding that an employee owes a "duty to remind" his employer of its legal rights and obligations, they miss the larger issue. Chan did not merely fail to remind Scanwell of the renewal deadline, she arranged for Scanwell's direct competitor to take over the premises, and, in doing so, prevented Scanwell from being able to re-lease the premises after the renewal deadline had passed. As a result of her actions, Scanwell lost its business office, and Scanwell customers who thereafter called or visited the office talked with Dimerco representatives.

IV

Despite this Court's conclusion, [an instructional error requires reversal].

The definitional instruction given in this case stated that "A fiduciary relationship is established when one reposes trust and confidence in another in the handling of certain business affairs." . . . [T]he instruction set out nothing more than the relationship that gives rise to a duty, but without identifying the duty. . . .

Where, as here, an allegation of breach of the duty of loyalty is presented in the context of an employee acting in competition with his or her employer, a proper definitional instruction of the duty of loyalty, consistent with the foregoing analysis, must set out the following elements: 1) In general, an employee must not, while employed, act contrary to the employer's interest; 2) however, an employee may agree with others to compete upon termination of the employment and may plan and prepare for their competing enterprise while still employed; and 3) but an employee may not, while still employed, go beyond mere planning and preparation and act in direct competition with the employer. *See Trieman*; Rest. (2d) Agency, sec. 393, cmt. e. In the absence of such a definitional instruction, the jury was unaware of the conduct that the law prohibits, and prejudice resulted because the jury was allowed to conclude that even mere planning and preparation for competition breached the duty.

This Court also concludes that [the following instruction requires reversal]:

> Your verdict must be for Plaintiff on its claim against Defendant Stevie Chan for breach of fiduciary duties if you believe:
>
> First, Defendant Stevie Chan, the General Manager of Plaintiff, owed a duty of loyalty to Plaintiff, and
>
> Second, during her employment with Plaintiff, Defendant Stevie Chan made arrangements to have defendant Dimerco take over Plaintiff's business operation including securing Plaintiff's business lease for Defendant Dimerco, disclosing confidential information of Plaintiff to Dimerco, and
>
> Third, in so acting, Defendant Stevie Chan breached a duty of loyalty owed to Plaintiff, and
>
> Fourth, as a direct result of Defendant Stevie Chan's conduct Plaintiff was harmed.

. . . Paragraph "Second" is fatally defective. By couching paragraph Second so that the ultimate allegation was that "Chan made arrangements for Dimerco to take over Scanwell's business operation," the verdict director made actionable the aggregate of all of Chan's conduct in making those arrangements, even those arrangements that involved mere "planning and preparation." The jury was not limited to the allegations relating to the lease and the dissemination of confidential information. . . .

NOTES

1. *The Scope of the Duty of Loyalty.* Cases in which employers pursue breach of loyalty claims against employees for pre-departure activities typically involve one of several recurring fact patterns: The employee solicits customers and/or co-workers and opens a competitive business; the employee aids a competitor or discloses information to a competitor; or the employee usurps a corporate opportunity. The privilege to make preparations for departure, described by the court in *Scanwell*, will sometimes insulate the employee from liability for this type of conduct. What particular facts make Chan's behavior egregious enough to submit to a jury? Can you find the lines that she crossed? How would you have advised her had she consulted you about how to transition to Dimerco without running afoul of the law?

2. *Fiduciary Duties of High-Level Employees.* All employees, as agents, owe a duty of loyalty to their employers, as principals, that endures until the termination of the employment relationship. As you probably learned in your Business Associations course, certain employees owe "fiduciary duties" to their employer. It is unclear whether and to what extent fiduciary duties and the employee duty of loyalty differ. Some courts take the view that a fiduciary relationship "establishes a distinct and separate obligation than the duty of loyalty" owing to "the 'peculiar' trust between the employee-agent and his employer-principal." *Rash v. J.Y. Intermediate, Ltd.*, 498 F.3d 1201, 1211 (10th Cir. 2007). From this perspective, fiduciaries are held to a higher standard than ordinary employees and could in theory be found in breach for conduct that would be permissible if perpetrated by a nonfiduciary employee. *See, e.g., id.* (noting that under Texas law a fiduciary must show that she acted with the utmost good faith and most scrupulous honesty toward the principal, including placing the principal's interests before her own). The proposed Restatement of Employment Law appears to take the contrary view. *See* RESTATEMENT OF EMPLOYMENT LAW § 8.01, cmt. a (Council Draft No. 5, Oct. 1, 2010) ("All employees are subject to a duty of loyalty, the obligations of which vary according to . . . the nature of the employee's position. . . . Some courts refer to a 'fiduciary' duty of loyalty when dealing with managerial employees, including corporate officers and other in positions of trust and confidence, but not when dealing with nonmanagerial employees."). Since this language suggests that the contours of the duty of loyalty will vary based on the employee's position, the relative status of the employee or vulnerability of the employer is likely to affect the outcome in particular cases irrespective of whether fiduciary duties are somehow distinct from the general duty of loyalty. At the very least, one would expect courts to look harder at alleged breaches by high-level employees, including corporate executives, employees with long-term or exclusive relationships with customers, employees possessing highly specialized or unique skills or knowledge, and employees who have been entrusted with confidential information upon which their employer's business depends.

3. *Fiduciary Duties and Private Ordering.* The types of employees and executives who are most likely to be held liable as fiduciaries are also those who are likely to be able to bargain for concessions from their companies, including the right to moonlight and provisions in separation agreements authorizing the taking of certain accounts, customers, and opportunities. In addition, when an employee wishes to pursue a business opportunity otherwise "owned" by his or her employer, the employee can do so consistent with her fiduciary obligations by fully disclosing the extent and nature of the opportunity and receiving advance permission to pursue it from the employer. As one court explained:

> [V]arious considerations affect determination of the breach of an employee's duty of loyalty and the appropriate remedy for a breach. . . . One consideration is the possible existence of contractual provisions. A provision might permit an employee to seek a second source of income, whether through a second job or an independent business. Conversely, a non-competition covenant might limit an employee's economic activities both during and after employment. A second consideration is whether the employer knew of or agreed to its employee's secondary profit-seeking activities. An employee's disclosure of an intention to pursue a second source of income alerts the employer to potential problems and protects the employee from a charge of disloyalty. The third consideration concerns the status of the employee and his or her relationship to the employer. An officer, director, or key executive, for example, has a higher duty than an employee working on a production line. Fourth, the nature of the employee's second source of income and its effect on the employer are relevant. . . . Employees should not engage in conduct that causes their employers to lose customers, sales, or potential sales. Nor should they take advantage of their employers by engaging in secret self-serving activities, such as accepting kickbacks from suppliers or usurping their employer's corporate opportunities.

Cameco v. Gedicke, 724 A.2d 783, 521-22 (N.J. 1999); *see also* ALI PRINCIPLES OF CORPORATE GOVERNANCE §5.05 (1994) (addressing the appropriation of corporate opportunities by directors and senior executives).

4. *Solicitation.* A recurring issue in duty of loyalty cases is whether the departing employee solicited co-workers or clients before departure. In *Scanwell*, the competitor company hired most of Scanwell's employees and acquired many of its customers upon taking over its lease. Under the privilege to make preparations articulated in the case, what is an employee permitted to say to potential customers and employees prior to an anticipated departure?

The Colorado Supreme Court wrestled with this issue in *Jet Courier v. Mulei*, 771 P.2d 486 (Colo. 1989). Mulei was the head of the Denver office of an Ohio-based courier service when he decided to establish a competitive business. While still employed by Jet, Mulei met with several of Jet's Denver customers, told them he would be leaving, that he could "give them the same service," and that he "would be in a position, sometime later, to reduce cost." He also met with several of Jet's Denver employees and offered the Denver office staff better working conditions, insurance, and part ownership of his new endeavor if they joined him. In reversing a decision in favor of Mulei, the court held that "an employee may advise current customers of his employer that he will be leaving. However any pretermination solicitation of those customers for a new competing business violates an employee's duty of loyalty." With respect to co-worker solicitation, the court established a multifactored test for determining whether the employee breached the duty of loyalty:

> A court should consider the nature of the employment relationship, the impact or potential impact of the employee's actions on the employer's operations, and the extent

of any benefits promised or inducements made to co-workers to obtain their services for the new competing enterprise. No single factor is dispositive[.]

Id. at 497. How easy is it to draw a line between "advising" and "soliciting"? What if the departing employee asks co-workers about their job satisfaction and desire to stay with their current employer but doesn't actually ask them to defect? *See Kopka, Landau & Pinkus v. Hansen,* 874 N.E.2d 1065 (Ind. Ct. App. 2007) (no breach of duty of loyalty where law firm associate talked to other associates about their salary requirements and willingness to quit but made no offers of employment). What if the departing employee limits her comments to announcing her own departure, but her co-workers express a desire to leave with her? How would you advise such an employee to respond to the co-workers' expressions of interest? If prior to her departure, the employee passes the co-workers' resumes to the new employer at their request, has she breached the duty of loyalty? What if the co-workers are the departing employee's subordinates and the employee actually negotiates with the new employer for them to come with her?

5. *Tortious Interference with Contract.* In addition to breach of the duty of loyalty, solicitation cases sometimes give rise to intentional interference with contract claims against the departing employee. See Chapter 5. However, a former employer may establish interference only in situations where the solicited individual was under an existing or, in some cases, imminent contract of which the departing employee was aware. *See Volt Services v. Adecco Employment Services,* 35 P.3d 329, 333 (Or. App. 2001) ("The elements of . . . intentional interference with economic relations[] are: (1) intentional interference with a proposed or existing economic relationship; (2) with an improper motive or by use of improper means; and (3) damage beyond the fact of interference itself."). Thus, a competitor or departing employee's solicitation of a co-worker employed at will generally does not give rise to an interference claim. In such situations, the employer usually must rely on the broader duty of loyalty claim. *See Jet Courier,* 771 P.2d at 495. On the other hand, a tortious interference claim can arise if the departing employee or the competitor solicits a worker employed under a contract containing restrictive covenants or a fixed term of employment, or a customer who has an existing or prospective service or supply contract. *See, e.g., Volt,* 35 P.3d at 337.

6. *Employer Remedies for the Conduct of "Faithless Servants."* What is the appropriate remedy in a case involving breach of loyalty? It is too late to enjoin the employee's competitive conduct, though it can be enjoined for the future. In cases where an employee usurps clients or a corporate opportunity, the employee may be required to pay for the losses sustained by the employer or to turn over profits gleaned from the competitive behavior. However, the losses or profits sought must be attributable to the disloyal behavior. *See Cameco v. Gedicke,* 724 A.2d 783, 521-22 (N.J. 1999). Another possible remedy, less commonly applied, is forfeiture (sometimes called disgorgement) of benefits obtained during the period of breach: In addition to losses and profits attributable to the breach, the employee is obligated to return any salary or other compensation he received from the employer during his period of disloyalty. *See, e.g., Design Strategies, Inc. v. Davis,* 469 F.3d 284 (2nd Cir. 2006) (requiring former sales manager to pay damages equivalent to salary for two pay periods corresponding to time period in which he promoted competitor company to client interested in obtaining staffing contract). This approach has sometimes been used in situations where the breach of loyalty stems not from competitive behavior but from serious misconduct of the employee. *Astra USA, Inc. v. Bildman,* 914 N.E.2d 36 (Mass. 2009), for instance, involved a CEO who engaged in a pattern of sexual harassment, retaliation, and cover-up, as well as a variety of financial misdeeds over a period of years. Applying New York's "faithless servant" doctrine, the court held that the employee must "forfeit all of his salary and bonuses from Astra for the period of disloyalty" even if the faithless servant "otherwise performed valuable services for his principal." Perhaps most surprisingly, and unlike other situations where a party materially breaches a contract, the wrongdoer was not permitted to recover in restitution for the reasonable value of the other services he rendered during the period of his faithlessness. Does this strike you as an unusually harsh remedy? Although the defendant in *Astra* was a former CEO, the court suggested in dicta that the disgorgement remedy could apply to lower-level employees as well. *Id.* at 49. *But see Rash v. J.Y. Intermediate, Ltd.*, 498 F.3d 1201 (10th Cir. 2007) (forfeiture applicable only to " 'clear and serious' violations of fiduciary duty" considering such factors as the gravity, timing and willfulness of the breach, the harm caused by the breach, and the adequacy of other remedies).

7. *Liability of the New Employer.* As a practical matter, even if a court awards damages to the aggrieved employer, the company may face hurdles trying to recover the judgment. For this reason, employers commonly sue not only the breaching employee but also the company on whose behalf the employee acted. If the defecting employee agreed to a fixed term of employment with her former employer or signed a noncompete agreement, the new employer's actions could constitute tortious interference with contract. But that is not always the case. Chan was not under contract with Scanwell, and the claims against her were based entirely on tort law. In such instances, plaintiff-employers may proceed on the theory that the new employer "aided and abetted" or "conspired with" the employee to breach the duty of loyalty. In *Scanwell*, the lower court held Dimerco liable along with Chan under this theory. While it seems clear that Dimerco and Chan were working together to spin off Scanwell's business, in other cases the competitor's role is less obvious, creating questions as to whether the new employer had the requisite knowledge or intent to justify liability. *Compare Design Strategies*, 469 F.3d at 303-4 (defendant IT Web not liable to former employer despite knowing that co-defendant Davis had been employed by former employer during time that he promoted IT Web's business to Microsoft where Davis had told IT Web that plaintiff was not interested in expanding into web solutions and IT Web had no reason to know Davis had not told his former employer about the Microsoft opportunity) *with Security Title Agency, Inc. v. Pope*, 200 P.3d 977 (Ariz. App. 2008) (defendant title insurance company liable for aiding and abetting defecting branch manager who brought 66 employees to new employer where new employer participated in recruiting sessions with employee, prepared written comparison of two companies' job benefits for distribution, agreed to title and compensation terms to offer solicited workers, and agreed to indemnify defendant employee against former employer). Aiding and abetting liability generally requires that the new employer provide assistance and encouragement with knowledge that the conduct encouraged will constitute a breach of loyalty. *See Security Title* 200 P.3d at 987. Thus, the tort includes a scienter requirement. If you represent a company recruiting an employee from a competitor or undertaking a business venture with an individual employed elsewhere, would you recommend that the client ask about the employee's duties to their current employer? What are the pros and cons of remaining ignorant? What are the ethical implications of this course of action?

8. *Post-employment Contractual Restraints.* The most significant limitation on the duty of loyalty is that it applies only while the employment relationship exists. To extend protection beyond termination, the employer may obtain a contractual

commitment from the employee. Perhaps the most common such agreement, and certainly the broadest, is a covenant not to compete, under which an employee promises not to engage in competition with the employer for a period of time following employment. Employers might also seek, either alone or in conjunction with a noncompete, a commitment not to solicit the employer's clients or other employees (a nonsolicitation agreement) and a commitment not to disclose any confidential information learned during employment (a nondisclosure agreement). The enforceability of restrictive covenants generally and noncompetes in particular is the subject of the next section.

PROBLEM

8-1. Sam Miller was Vice President of H&R Metals, a company that processed scrap metal. He was employed at will with no written contract. On behalf of H&R, Miller investigated the purchase of a high-tech "shredder" from Newell Manufacturing that would increase H&R's operations. Miller negotiated preliminary terms for the purchase; however, H&R's board of directors subsequently voted not to go through with the deal, considering the investment in new technology premature. Dissatisfied with the direction of the business, Miller met with the President of H&R and told him he was planning to leave the company unless H&R made him an equity partner in the business. The President refused. Subsequently, and while still employed by H&R, Miller secured a small business loan from a local bank and contracted with Newell to purchase the shredder himself. He also filed the necessary paperwork to incorporate "Miller's Metals," obtained the state and local permits needed to run a shredding operation, and engaged an advertising company to prepare brochures and other informational materials that he planned to distribute once his business became operational.

One week before tendering his resignation, Miller had lunch with H&R Metals' Operations Manager Georgia Sidway. Miller told Sidway about his disagreement with the President and his plans to open a competitive venture. Sidway asked Miller if he was offering her a job. Miller responded, "Well, at the moment I'm still on company time. But there are options out there. Why don't we have lunch again next week." The following week, Miller quit H&R and Miller's Metals became operational. Due to his extensive advance planning, the business was able to secure its first contract and begin processing metal within a week. Miller met again with Georgia Sidway and offered her a job at a salary that he knew was far above what she had been paid at H&R. Together, Miller and Sidway met with several scrap metal suppliers who had previously provided metal to H&R. One of these suppliers, Packwell Parts, held a one-year contract to supply its scrap output to H&R on a monthly basis. As a result of the meetings, Packwell and three other suppliers decided to shift their business to Miller's Metals.

Suppose H&R learns of Miller's activities and files suit. What causes of action would you expect the former employer to pursue? What defenses would you raise if you were defending Miller? Who is likely to succeed? Regardless of your answer, is there anything you would have told Miller to do differently to avoid this lawsuit? *See generally Metzner v. Maryland Metals*, 382 A.2d 564 (Md. App. 1978).

B. POST-EMPLOYMENT RESTRAINTS ON COMPETITION

By far the most common means by which employers constrain post-employment competition is through contractual agreement. To some extent, trade secret law offers employers a means of restricting the competitive behavior of departing employees absent private agreement. However, except in limited situations described in this section, trade secret law proscribes the use and disclosure of protected information, not competition per se. The creation of contractual covenants — covenants not to compete, nonsolicitation clauses, and nondisclosure clauses — provides employers a more reliable route to protecting their property interests following an employee defection, although, as we will see, the enforceability of such covenants in individual cases is far from certain. The most controversial of these clauses is the noncompetition agreement, under which an employee agrees not to work in a competitive endeavor for a designated period of time, often (though not always) within a designated geographical area. Depending on how broadly they are drafted, these agreements can have the effect of keeping an individual out of the work force (or tied to his or her current employer); they have therefore been subject to significant judicial scrutiny and scholarly debate. As we will see, there is some common ground among many jurisdictions on how to approach noncompete enforcement. However, there is a significant degree of variation in results owing to the fact-specific nature of most courts' approach. There are also outlier jurisdictions such as California, which prohibits enforcement of employee noncompete agreements in that economically important state. The first portion of this section provides an overview of the competing doctrinal approaches and policy issues at stake in enforcing contractual restraints on competition. The next sections explore how those jurisdictions that enforce noncompetes negotiate these tensions in commonly occurring factual scenarios: disputes over skills and training, disputes over trade secrets and information, and disputes over customers and clients.

1. Approaches to Noncompete Enforcement

Cal. Bus. & Prof. Code §§ 16600 et seq.

§ 16600. Void Contracts

[E]very contract by which anyone is restrained from engaging in a lawful profession, trade, or business of any kind is to that extent void.

Restatement (Second) of Contracts

§ 188 Ancillary Restraints on Competition

(1) A promise to refrain from competition . . . is unreasonably in restraint of trade if

(a) the restraint is greater than is needed to protect the promisee's legitimate interest, or

(b) the promisee's need is outweighed by the hardship to the promisor and the likely injury to the public.

Outsource International, Inc. v. Barton
192 F.3d 662 (7th Cir. 1999)

[Defendant Barton was a staffing consultant for Plaintiff Outsource's predecessor company. He signed a noncompete, nonsolicitation and confidentiality agreement upon hire. Six years later, Outsource acquired Barton's employer and Barton resigned. He subsequently opened his own temporary staffing company within the geographic area proscribed by his employment agreement. The Seventh Circuit affirmed the district court's finding that Outsource had presented a prima facie case for a preliminary injunction against Barton under Illinois law.]

POSNER, Chief Judge, dissenting.

I regret my inability to agree with the court's disposition of the case, because it is the right disposition from the standpoint of substantive justice. Mr. Barton is an adult of sound mind who made an unequivocal promise, for which he was doubtless adequately compensated, not to compete with his employer within 25 miles for a year after he ceased being employed. He quit of his own volition — quit in fact to set up in competition with his employer. And all the customers whom he obtained for his new company, before the preliminary injunction which the court affirms today put him temporarily out of business, were customers of his former employer. So he broke his contract. But Illinois law, to which we must of course bow in this diversity suit, is hostile to covenants not to compete found in employment contracts. An Illinois court would not enforce this covenant.

There is no longer any good reason for such hostility, though it is nothing either new or limited to Illinois. The English common law called such covenants "restraints of trade" and refused to enforce them unless they were adjudged "reasonable" in time and geographical scope. *Mitchel v. Reynolds*, 24 Eng. Rep. 347 (K.B. 1711). The original rationale had nothing to do with restraint of trade in its modern, antitrust sense. It was paternalism in a culture of poverty, restricted employment, and an exiguous social safety net. The fear behind it was that workers would be tricked into agreeing to covenants that would, if enforced, propel them into destitution. This fear, though it continues to be cited, has no basis in current American conditions.

Later, however, the focus of concern shifted to whether a covenant not to compete might have anticompetitive consequences, since the covenant would eliminate the covenantor as a potential competitor of the covenantee within the area covered by, and during the term of, the covenant. This concern never had much basis, especially when the covenant was found in an employment contract. It would be unlikely for the vitality of competition to depend on the ability of a former employee to compete with his former employer. So unlikely that it would make little sense to place a cloud of suspicion over such covenants, rather than considering competitive effects on a case by case basis.

At the same time that the concerns behind judicial hostility to covenants not to compete have waned, recognition of their social value has grown. The clearest case for such a covenant is where the employee's work gives him access to the employer's trade secrets. The employer could include in the employment contract a clause forbidding the employee to take any of the employer's trade secrets with him when he left the employment, as in fact the employer did in this case. Such clauses are difficult to enforce, however, as it is often difficult to determine whether the former employee is using his former employer's trade secrets or using either ideas of his own invention or ideas that are in the public domain. A covenant not to compete is much easier to enforce, and to the extent enforced prevents the employee, during the time and within the geographical scope of the covenant, from using his former employer's trade secrets.

A related function of such a covenant is to protect the employer's investment in the employee's "human capital," or earning capacity. The employer may give the employee training that the employee could use to compete against the employer. If covenants not to compete are forbidden, the employer will pay a lower wage, in effect charging the employee for the training. There is no reason why the law should prefer this method of protecting the employer's investment to a covenant not to compete.

I can see no reason in today's America for judicial hostility to covenants not to compete. It is possible to imagine situations in which the device might be abused, but the doctrines of fraud, duress, and unconscionability are available to deal with such situations. A covenant's reasonableness in terms of duration and geographical scope is merely a consideration bearing on such defenses. . . . Had Barton signed a covenant in which he agreed that if he ever left the employ of Outsource he would never again work in the business of providing temporary industrial labor anywhere in the world, there would be at least a suspicion that he had been forced or tricked into signing the covenant and therefore that it should not be enforced. There is no suggestion of that here, and so if I were writing on a clean slate I would agree wholeheartedly with the district court's granting a preliminary injunction against Barton's violating the covenant.

But the Illinois courts approach covenants not to compete in a different way, not radically different perhaps but different enough to require a reversal in this case. Their view is that a covenant not to compete that is contained in an employment contract is enforceable in only two circumstances — either where the covenant protects a "near permanent" relationship between the former employer and his customers, or where it protects "confidential information" (that is, trade secrets) of the former employer. . . .

The Illinois courts appear to place the burden of proving that the covenant meets one of the two criteria of validity on the employer. In effect Illinois requires the employer to prove that the covenant not to compete serves a social purpose. Such a requirement is inconsistent with the idea of freedom of contract, which animates contract law and a corollary of which is that courts do not limit the enforcement of contracts to those the social point of which the court can see. They enforce a contract unless there is some reason to think it imposes heavy costs on third parties, offends the moral code, fails to comply with formal requirements (such as those imposed on some contracts by the statute of frauds), or doesn't embody an actual deal between competent consenting adults.

Still, we must take the Illinois law as we find it, and apply it as best we can to the facts of the case. Barton was employed by Outsource as a salesman, soliciting orders for temporary industrial workers that Outsource would supply. . . . Deciding to go out on his own, he quit Outsource and quickly obtained business from a dozen customers of Outsource with whom he had dealt. There is no question that he violated the covenant not to compete in his employment contract, which barred him for one year after his employment ended from competing with Outsource in the Chicago area. But there is no evidence that he stole any of Outsource's trade secrets. Outsource's customer list [was not secret.] The wages that Outsource pays its workers are not secret either. Barton did not take the list of workers on Outsource's roster, but obtained workers for his customers in the same way that Outsource does, by radio and newspaper advertisements. . . .

[With respect to customers, the] only users of temp labor who testified at the preliminary injunction hearing agreed that such users have no sense of loyalty to particular suppliers. Both witnesses used multiple agencies. It was feasible for Barton to use standard selling techniques, rather than any techniques that he had learned from Outsource or information that he took with him when he left Outsource, to get customers for his new business. . . .

[A]s far as this record shows, all he used in signing up customers for his new venture were the standard sales techniques used in this business.

Since the irreparable harm to Barton from the grant of a preliminary injunction to Outsource exceeds the irreparable harm that Outsource would experience from the denial of the injunction (as a start-up, Barton would find it difficult to prove damages from being frozen out of business for a year as a result of the enforcement of the covenant), Outsource must prove not just that it has a better case than Barton but that it has a much better case. It has a worse case. . . .

NOTES

1. *A Spectrum of Approaches.* The three excerpts—from the California state code, the Restatement (Second) of Contracts, and Judge Posner's dissenting decision in *Outsource v. Barton*—above offer a range of approaches to enforcing noncompetes signed by employees. Judge Posner's opinion offers a pure freedom of contract perspective: Noncompetes are contracts and should be enforced like any other legal agreement. However, Judge Posner acknowledges that this is not the law in Illinois, the state whose law he is charged with applying in the case before him. In fact, it is not the law in any jurisdiction, owing in part to the countervailing policy concerns Posner raises and dismisses.

At the opposite extreme is California, which categorically prohibits noncompete agreements between employers and employees. California has repeatedly defended this position in various cases involving employer attempts to circumvent the rule. *See, e.g., Edwards v. Arthur Andersen*, 189 P.3d 285 (Cal. 2008) (defendant-employer's refusal to release former employee from noncompete agreement except on employee's waiver of claims against the company, resulting in employee not being hired by prospective employer, constituted an "independently wrongful act" that could support employee's claim against former employer for tortious interference with prospective economic advantage); *Silguero v. Cretguard, Inc.* 113 Cal. Rptr. 3d 653 (Cal. App. 2010) (finding employee stated claim for wrongful termination in violation of public policy where new employer fired her upon learning of her noncompete with former employer because of an "understanding" between the two despite acknowledging the agreement was unenforceable under California law); *VL Syst., Inc. v. Unisen, Inc.*, 61 Cal. Rptr. 3d 818, 824 (Cal. App. 2007) (refusing to enforce "no hire" agreement between two firms because "enforcement of th[e] clause would present many of the same problems as covenants not to compete and unfairly limit the mobility of an employee"). One other state, North Dakota, has a similarly restrictive statute. N.D. CENT. CODE § 9-08-06 (2005).

Most jurisdictions (like Illinois) follow some version of the Restatement approach, which enforces "reasonable" noncompetes necessary to protect employers' "legitimate interests." Georgia recently amended its constitution to authorize legislation upholding "reasonable competition agreements," which seems designed to expand the scope of noncompetes in that state. ATLANTA JOURNAL-CONSTITUTION, Nov. 5, 2010, at A17. As we will see, what makes an interest legitimate and agreement reasonable are fodder for much litigation.

2. *Of Paternalism and Employee Bargaining Power.* Posner describes judicial disfavor of noncompetes as rooted in a fear of employee abuse that "has no basis in current American conditions." Do you agree? Certainly employees today are more mobile and have more flexibility than in the eighteenth century when noncompete law developed. Does that mean they are more autonomous? More able to refuse a non-compete agreement? *See* Rachel Arnow-Richman, *Cubewrap Contracts and Worker Mobility: The Dilution of Employee Bargaining Power via Standard Form Noncompetes*, 2006 MICH. ST. L. REV. 963 (asserting that employers frequently present noncompetes to workers in the form of standardized agreements to be signed as routine paperwork after hire when their ability to refuse employment on such terms is highly constrained); Katherine V.W. Stone, *The New Psychological Contract*, 48 UCLA L. REV. 519 (2001) (providing case law examples of employers' use of noncompete agreements with lower-level employees, including manicurists and deliverymen). In assessing the enforceability of noncompetes, courts often seem more willing to find in favor of an employer if the departing employee participated in drafting the agreement or demonstrated bargaining ability in some other capacity. *See, e.g., Campbell Soup Co. v. Desatnik*, 58 F. Supp. 2d 477, 479-81 (D.N.J. 1999) (finding for employer where former senior executive negotiated terms of a prior contract of employment and successfully refused noncompete, but subsequently signed renewal agreement with noncompete without making significant effort to renegotiate); *Delli-Gatti v. Mansfield*, 477 S.E.2d 134 (Ga. Ct. App. 1996) (holding noncompete enforceable against physician who negotiated favorable changes in vacation time and partnership opportunities under employment contract she accepted). Should the current rules of reasonableness be replaced by a heightened examination of employee volition? Some commentators have suggested that such an approach could be useful. *See, e.g.*, Rachel Arnow-Richman, *Bargaining for Loyalty in the Information Age*, 80 OR. L. REV. 1163, 1235-36 (2001); Eileen Silverstein, *Bringing Forth a New World from the Ashes of the Old*, 34 CONN. L. REV. 803, 817-18 (2002).

3. *What Can You Get for Giving Up Your Right to Compete?* In contrast to this view, some scholars believe that judicial refusal to enforce noncompetes deprives employees of the opportunity to freely negotiate the sale of their skills and human capital. *See* Stewart E. Sterk, *Restraints on the Alienation of Human Capital*, 79 VA. L. REV. 383 (1993). From this perspective, employees who sign noncompetes should realize some additional benefits — higher wages, better employment conditions, or enhanced opportunities for training and promotion — in compensation for their concession. However, empirical data suggest otherwise. Studies show that employees who sign noncompetes have lower executive compensation, are less likely to invest in human capital, and are more likely to take "occupational detours" that amount to a step back in their careers. *See* On Amir & Orly Lobel, *Innovation Motivation: Behavioral Effects of Post-Employment Restrictions* (July 13, 2010). San Diego Legal Studies Paper No. 10-32, *available at* http://ssrn.com/abstract=1639367; Mark J. Garmaise, *Ties That Truly Bind: Non-competition Agreements, Executive Compensation and Firm Investment*, working paper, *available at* http://personal.anderson.ucla.edu/mark.garmaise/noncomp7.pdf; Matt Marx, *Good Work if You Can Get It . . . Again: Non-Compete Agreements, "Occupational Detours," and Attainment*, 3 (Mass. Inst. of Tech. Working Paper Series, August 17, 2009), *available at* http://ssrn.com/abstract=1456748; *see generally* Viva R. Moffat, *The Wrong Tool for the Job: The IP Problem with Non-Competition Agreements*, 52 WILL. & MARY L. REV. (forthcoming 2010) (summarizing data).

4. *The Complex Economics of Noncompete Agreements.* Whether individual workers are better or worse off is a different question from whether society as a whole benefits or suffers from noncompete enforcement. On this score, are you surprised to discover that Judge Posner, a pillar of the law and economics school, would advocate for the enforcement of agreements that interfere with interfirm competition?

Noncompete agreements pit two core law and economics principles against one another: freedom of contract for the individual parties to the agreement and freedom of competition generally. Judge Posner expresses what has been the dominant economic view of these agreements — that their anticompetitive effects are minimal and they should be enforced like other contracts. *See* MICHAEL J. TREBILCOCK, THE COMMON LAW OF RESTRAINTS OF TRADE (1986); Maureen Callahan, *Post-Employment Restraint Agreements: A Reassessment*, 52 U. CHI. L. REV. 703, 714-15 (1985); Stewart E. Sterk, *Restraints on the Alienation of Human Capital*, 79 VA. L. REV. 383, 406-7 (1993).

Not everyone agrees. Professor Ronald Gilson has argued that California statutory law prohibiting noncompetes in employment contributed to the vast development of the high-tech industry in Silicon Valley during the late twentieth century by enabling healthy information "spillovers" between firms. He explains:

> From the outset, Silicon Valley developed a business structure that reflected nonlinear career patterns and a special status for entrepreneurs. [Engineers and managers] moved between companies, founded start-ups, supplied former employers, purchased from former employees, and in the course of their careers developed personal and professional relationships that cut across companies and competition. [The result] is a pattern of industrial organization in which firms are remarkably porous to outside influence. . . .
>
> Thus, Silicon Valley's form of industrial organization institutionalized [knowledge spillovers.]
>
> A postemployment covenant not to compete prevents knowledge spillover of an employer's proprietary knowledge . . . by blocking the mechanism by which the spillover occurs: employees leaving to take up employment with a competitor or to form a competing start-up. . . . Given the speed of innovation and the corresponding telescoping of product life cycles, knowledge more than a year or two old likely no longer has significant competitive value. The hiatus imposed by a covenant not to compete thus assures that . . . [t]he value of proprietary tacit knowledge embedded in the employee's human capital . . . will have dissipated over the covenant's term. Nothing of value is left to spill over to a new employer or start-up venture. . . .

Ronald J. Gilson, *The Legal Infrastructure of High Technology Industrial Districts: Silicon Valley, Route 128, and Covenants Not to Compete*, 74 N.Y.U. L. REV. 575, 589-603 (1999); *see also* Charles A. Sullivan, *Revisiting the "Neglected Stepchild": Antitrust Treatment of Postemployment Restraints of Trade*, 1977 U. ILL. L. F. 621, 647-50 (suggesting need for more searching inquiry of anticompetitive effects of noncompetes that considers, among other things, the totality of restraints imposed by an employer or used within an industry). As you read the next set of materials, keep in mind these different views of the costs and benefits of noncompetes, both to individuals and to society.

2. Disputes over Skills and Training

Rem Metals Corporation v. Logan
565 P. 2d 1080 (Or. 1977)

TONGUE, Justice.

This is a suit in equity to enforce "noncompetition" provisions of two employment agreements between plaintiff and defendant, who had been employed by plaintiff as a welder of precision titanium castings. Defendant appeals from a decree enjoining him from engaging in such work for a period of six months in Oregon for Precision Castparts Corporation, a competitor of plaintiff. We reverse.

The primary question presented for decision in this case, according to plaintiff Rem, is whether, as an employer, it had a sufficient "protectable interest" in the skills and knowledge of defendant as a skilled craftsman engaged as a repair welder of precision titanium castings, so as to justify enforcement of such a "noncompetition" agreement as a "reasonable restraint" upon defendant.

The titanium castings on which defendant Logan worked as a repair welder were produced by his employer, the plaintiff, under contract with Pratt & Whitney Aircraft Division for use as bearing housings for jet aircraft engines under exceedingly strict specifications. Only three companies are engaged in the production of such castings for Pratt & Whitney. These include plaintiff, Precision Castparts (its principal competitor) and Misco of Michigan (a smaller company).

In the process of the production of such castings any defects are repaired by welding performed by skilled welders who are "certified" by Pratt & Whitney inspectors as being sufficiently skilled to be entrusted with this important work. There was also some evidence that titanium is a "rare" or "reactive" metal and is difficult to weld.

Defendant was one of two or three "certified" welders employed by plaintiff and was plaintiff's best welder, with a proficiency rating of 98.3 per cent. Other welders rated below 95 per cent. There was testimony, however, that three other welders had been able to become sufficiently qualified so as to be "certified" for Pratt & Whitney work after 20 hours of training and that during 1966 seven of plaintiff's welders (including defendant) were so "certified."

Defendant Logan had been previously employed by Wah Chang Corporation, where he learned to weld electrodes of titanium. He was employed by plaintiff in 1969 and subsequently signed two employment contracts, as did nearly all Rem employees, including provisions to the effect that for a period of one year after termination he would not engage in any business in competition with Rem within the United States, "whether as principal, agent, employer, consultant or otherwise."

In 1972 defendant was transferred to the welding department. He testified that he became "certified" in "less than two weeks," and that no one gave him "any instruction before he took the certification test" for the welding of titanium.

Plaintiff offered testimony describing its training program for welders. When asked whether Rem had any "trade secrets in the welding department that are not generally known in the industry," that witness answered that "Rem was able to do a better job," to ship ahead of its schedules, and with fewer "rejects" from Pratt & Whitney than its competitors, so that "there is something we must be doing that our competitors are not doing." Rem's president testified that defendant received job training at Rem and "extensive written procedures prepared by Rem" which enabled him to weld titanium castings. He also testified, however, that it was nevertheless not surprising that defendant Logan was able to become "certified" within "a matter of a few days," as testified by Logan. Rem's supervisor of welding testified that:

> I don't think it's a matter of disclosing inasmuch as it is its instructional nature. If a welder's in the tank doing the work, we're qualifying it and giving what instructions we are capable of.

There was also testimony by another former Rem titanium welder, since employed by Precision Castparts, that he observed no differences in the welding procedures and techniques at Rem and at PCP except that Rem uses a "vacuum tank," while PCP uses a "plastic bubble," both of which are standard techniques.

On September 18, 1976, defendant Logan, after being refused a wage increase of 50 cents per hour by Rem, went to work at that increased rate for Precision Castparts. Plaintiff offered evidence that, as a result, it was unable for a period of two weeks to ship castings worth approximately $25,000 to Pratt & Whitney and that it then had difficulty in maintaining its shipping schedules of such titanium castings because it did not have welders who were "able to complete the weld repair cycle in a satisfactory manner." It appears, however, that Rem was then able to train two welders who "shortly thereafter were able to pass the qualification test of Pratt & Whitney." Plaintiff's witnesses also testified to their concern over Rem's continued ability to compete with Precision Castparts, its principal competitor, which by then had 14 or 15 titanium welders, including defendant Logan.[2]

[On the subject of the enforcement of noncompetition provisions in employment contracts, the general rule is as follows:]

> Three things are essential to the validity of a contract in restraint of trade: (1) it must be partial or restricted in its operation in respect either to time or place; (2) it must be on some good consideration; and (3) it must be reasonable, that is, it should afford only a fair protection to the interests of the party in whose favor it is made, and must not be so large in its operation as to interfere with the interests of the public.

Eldridge v. Johnson, 245 P.2d 239, 250 (Or. 1952). As also stated in *North Pacific Lbr. v. Moore*, 551 P.2d 431, 434 (1976):

> To be entitled to the protection which a noncompetition covenant purports to provide, the employer must show that he has a legitimate interest entitled to protection.

At the outset, it is important to bear in mind that this is not a case involving an employee whose regular duties involved frequent dealings with customers of his employer and who had access to "customer lists" or other similar confidential information relating to customers. . . .

In our judgment, this case falls within the rule as stated in Blake, *Employee Agreements Not to Compete*, 73 Harv. L. Rev. 625, 652 (1960), as follows:

> . . . It has been uniformly held that general knowledge, skill, or facility acquired through training or experience while working for an employer appertain exclusively to the employee. The fact that they were acquired or developed during the employment does not, by itself, give the employee a sufficient interest to support a restraining covenant, even though the on-the-job training has been extensive and costly. In the absence, of special circumstances the risk of future competition form the employee falls upon the employer and cannot be shifted, even though the possible damages is greatly increased by experience gained in the course of the employment.

To the same effect, although under different facts, it was held in *McCombs v. McClelland*, 354 P.2d 311, 316 (1960) that:

> . . . The fact that defendant may have gained considerable experience while in plaintiff's employ is not grounds for injunctive relief. An employer cannot by contract prevent his

---

2. It also appears that Precision Castparts is "underwriting" the cost of Mr. Logan's defense.

employee upon termination of the employment from using skill and intelligence acquired or increased and improved through experience or through instruction received in the course of employment. . . .

We recognize, however, as does Blake, that on any given set of facts it may be difficult to "draw a line" between "training in the general skills and knowledge of the trade, and training which imparts information pertaining especially to the employer's business" and that this is the "central problem" in such cases. In other words, as stated by Blake:

> Its objective is not to prevent the competitive use of the unique personal qualities of the employee — either during or after the employment but to prevent competitive use, for a time, of information or relationships which pertain peculiarly to the employer and which the employee acquired in the course of the employment. . . . [6]

In such a case, however, the burden of proof is upon the employer to establish the existence of "trade secrets," "information or relationships which pertain peculiarly to the employer," or other "special circumstances" sufficient to justify the enforcement of such a restrictive covenant.

Based upon our examination of this record, which we review de novo, and under the facts and circumstances of this case, we hold that this employer failed to sustain that burden of proof. Although defendant received training and experience while employed by plaintiff which developed his skill as a repair welder of titanium castings, plaintiff did not, in our judgment, establish by sufficient and credible evidence "special circumstances" of such a nature as to entitle Rem to demand the enforcement upon this defendant by injunction of this "noncompetition" clause as a "reasonable restraint."

NOTES

1. *The Threshold Issue.* Rem Metals introduces a critical threshold question in assessing the enforceability of noncompete agreements — does the employer have an underlying interest justifying protection? This inquiry is unique to the law of restrictive covenants in employment. In theory, it protects workers by limiting the situations in which they can be contractually constrained. Is Logan a worker in need of judicial protection? Who is the more vulnerable party in *Rem Metals*, the employer or employee?

In answering that question consider the following: First, it appears uncontradicted that Rem Metals lost $25,000 in the two weeks following Logan's departure before it was able to train replacements. But that damage flowed from Logan's departure, not from his competition. The employer would have suffered the same loss had Logan retired suddenly. Second, Logan is obviously an exceptionally good worker with a skill that is in demand. This may mean he is in a better position than some employees to protect himself in negotiating the terms of his employment, although his inability to secure a raise suggests otherwise. Finally, what would have happened had the employer prevailed? Would you expect Logan to be able to find equally lucrative

---

6. As stated in *Sarkes Tarzin, Inc. v. Audio Devices, Inc., et al.,* 166 F. Supp. 250, 265 (S.D. Cal. 1958): ". . . Trade secrets must be 'the particular secrets of the employer as distinguished from the general secrets of the trade in which he is engaged.' . . ."

employment opportunities if he were precluded from competing with Rem Metals for one year? Do your answers explain the court's application of the "protectable interest" requirement?

2. *Protecting General Training: A Law and Economics View. Rem Metals* articulates the majority rule that an employer may not enforce a noncompete to protect employer investments in general knowledge and training. What is "general training"? After all, the task that Logan performed was highly specialized.

Professor Gary Becker's well-known human capital theory distinguishes between specific training that is useful only to one employer and general training that is useful to many. Professor Becker contends that employers have an incentive to invest in specific training of employees because it benefits their business and cannot be usurped by competitors. On the other hand, employers are unlikely to invest in general training, leaving it to the worker to finance this training herself, either by paying for outside schooling or, in the case of on-the-job training, accepting lower wages during the training period. This theory supports the general rule in *Rem Metals.* Since the employee pays for the training herself, the employer should not be permitted to use a noncompete to prevent use of that general training on behalf of a competitor. *See* GARY S. BECKER, HUMAN CAPITAL: A THEORETICAL AND EMPIRICAL ANALYSIS 19-37 (2d ed. 1975); Edmund W. Kitch, *The Law and Economics of Rights in Valuable Information*, 9 J. LEGAL STUD. 683, 684 (1980) (summarizing Becker's theories).

Several commentators disagree that employees pay for their own general training. Professors Rubin and Shedd note that some forms of general training are too costly for an employee to finance out of her wages, as where an employer imparts to an employee an industry trade secret worth millions of dollars to competitors. In that situation, the employer would require a noncompete agreement to prevent the employee from defecting to another firm willing to pay her a premium in light of her valuable knowledge. Were such noncompetes unenforceable, firms would have limited incentive to invest in acquiring this type of highly valuable information or sharing it with its workforce. *See* Paul H. Rubin & Peter Shedd, *Human Capital and Covenants Not to Compete*, 10 J. LEGAL STUD. 93, 96-7 (1981).

Still, Professors Rubin and Shedd acknowledge that employers may overenforce noncompete agreements. A firm might pay a worker less than the value of her marginal product taking into account its investments, or a firm might seek to enforce the noncompete to preclude the employee's use of all training, including general training paid for in the form of reduced wages. For these reasons, Rubin and Shedd ultimately conclude that noncompetes should not be enforceable to protect general training unless the training includes trade secrets or confidential information. *Id.* at 109-10; *see also* Phillip J. Closius & Henry M. Schaffer, *Involuntary Nonservitude: The Current Judicial Enforcement of Employee Covenants Not to Compete—A Proposal for Reform*, 57 S. CAL. L. REV. 531, 541 (1984). This is the approach that most courts take. *See, e.g., Kelsey-Hayes Co. v. Maleki*, 765 F. Supp. 402, 407-8 (E.D. Mich. 1991) (noncompete not justified where employee was trained in nonproprietary computer language but gained no knowledge of significance of scientific algorithms he translated into program language); *Girtman & Assoc. v. St. Amour*, 26 IER Cases 187 (Tenn. Ct. App. 2007) (enforcement of noncompete against former door and hardware salesman not justified despite fact that employee had no prior experience and company paid for him to attend multiple training sessions leading to industry certification where training provided was not specific to employer and programs were open to anyone in industry); *Tom James Co. v. Mendrop*, 819 S.W.2d 251, 253 (Tex. App. 1991) (measuring methods and tools used in custom tailored men's clothing business were not specific enough to justify protection). *But see* FLA. STAT. ANN. §542.335(1)(b)(5) (recognizing "extraordinary or specialized training" as a legitimate business interest justifying a noncompete). As we will see, employers sometimes try to circumvent this by requiring employees to sign training repayment agreements, an approach that has been sanctioned by at least some jurisdictions. *See, e.g.,* COLO. REV. STAT. 8-2-113(2) (recognizing exception to prohibition on noncompetes to allow enforcement of an agreement "providing for recovery of the expense of educating and training" against an employee who has worked less than two years).

Do these theories about employer and employee investments help explain the result in *Rem Metals*? Who "paid" for Logan's training? Is that a question that can be answered from the facts of the case?

3. *Training and Customer Goodwill.* In holding against the employer, *Rem Metals* distinguishes situations in which the employee has frequent dealings with customers. In some situations employers' asserted interests in training elide with a more particularized interest in preserving client contacts or customer goodwill. This might occur, for instance, where the employee is a salesperson who had no prior experience in the employer's industry and the on-the-job experience and "training" she receives allows her to develop relationships with customers that she may use to her competitive advantage upon departure. *See Roberson v. C.P. Allen Construction Co.,* 30 IER Cases 1242, 1245 (Ala. App. 2010) (enforcing concrete-cutting company's noncompete against salesman who prior to employment "knew nothing about that business" and through his employment "learned the trade" and was provided with "the means to entertain client contacts and to develop relationships with [the employer's] customers"). We will talk about the viability of noncompetes designed to protect this distinct interest beginning at page 474. For now, it is important to be aware that, even if the type of training provided to an employee does not support a noncompete, there may be other justifications for enforcement.

4. *Noncompetes as Alternatives to Fixed-Term Contracts.* If an employer's principal concern is worker retention — and in the case of an interest in employee skills and training, it often is — why use a noncompete? Why doesn't the employer simply obtain a fixed-term employment contract from the desirable employee? Indeed, if the employer fails to secure such a contract, or perhaps chooses to forgo one because it does not want to make an equivalent commitment to retaining the employee for a fixed term, why should it be permitted to use a noncompete to achieve the same result? One possible answer is that because fixed-term contracts cannot be specifically enforced against employees, they do not adequately address employers' concerns about retention. It is also possible that employers are unable to predict in advance the precise length of employment needed to protect their interests, and noncompetes provide greater flexibility. On the other hand, does it trouble you that noncompetes give employers the discretion to seek enforcement based on their unilateral assessment of the circumstance at the time of departure? In part because of such concerns, some commentators have suggested that certain noncompetes should be enforced only if the employer promised the employee some degree of job security in exchange for the covenant. *See* Rachel Arnow-Richman, *Noncompetes, Human Capital, and Contract Formation: What Employment Law Can Learn from Family Law,* 10 TEX. WESLEYAN L. REV. 155 (2003); Tracy L. Staidl, *Enforceability of Noncompetition Agreements When Employment Is At-Will: Reformulating the Analysis,* 2 EMPLOYEE RTS. & EMP. POL'Y J. 95 (1998); *cf.* Kate O'Neill, *Should I Stay or Should I Go? — Covenants*

Not to Compete in a Down Economy: A Proposal for Better Advocacy and Better Judicial Opinions, 6 HASTINGS BUS. L. J. 83 (2010) (suggesting that a "diminution in the quality of employment," as where the former employer's business is deteriorating, should weigh against the failing firm in any subsequent efforts to enforce a noncompete against a worker who left for these reasons).

5. *The Departure Dispute as Morality Play.* Another way of understanding the result in *Rem Metals* is to consider general concepts of fairness. It is hard to feel sorry for an employer who refuses his star welder a $0.50 pay increase. Similarly, it is not surprising to see courts enforcing noncompetes against employees who affirmatively take or destroy documents or otherwise attempt to sabotage the employer's business upon departure. *See, e.g., Pearson v. Visual Innovations Co.*, No. 03-04000563-CV, 2006 WL 903736 (Tex. App. April 6, 2006) (enforcing $250,000 damage award to employer based on breach of noncompete where employee downloaded and deleted employer files, negotiated deals with employer clients while still employed, took employer equipment, and destroyed copies of his and co-workers' noncompete agreements upon departure). In this way, disputes about competition often turn on assessments of fairness and loyalty. *See* ALAN HYDE, WORKING IN SILICON VALLEY: ECONOMIC AND LEGAL ANALYSIS OF A HIGH-VELOCITY LABOR MARKET 37 (2003) (describing the "moralistic" quality of trade secret litigation). Professor Catherine Fisk attributes courts' attention to such matters to the evolution of the law of employment competition in the " 'moral economy' of the early nineteenth century, in which notions of honor, trust, and the moral value of work ('industry') loomed [large]." *See* Catherine Fisk, *Working Knowledge: Trade Secrets, Restrictive Covenants in Employment, and the Rise of Corporate Intellectual Property*, 1800-1920, 52 HASTINGS L. J. 441 (2001). As you read the cases in this chapter, pay attention to how courts' assessment of fault and loyalty correlate with its decisions in favor of or against enforcement of restraints against competition.

6. *The Costs of Litigation.* No matter who is right, disputes over competition can be costly, and that burden weighs more heavily on employees, who are usually less able to bear the expense of defending themselves against a company. Notice how Logan is financing this litigation. At least in reported cases, the new employer is often a co-defendant in litigation over employee competition and/or bearing the cost of defending the defecting employee. Indeed, in the case of a coveted employee, the new employer may well contemplate and plan for the possibility of future litigation in its recruiting and hiring process. *See, e.g., Saks Fifth Ave. v. James, Ltd.*, 630 S.E.2d 304, 307 (Va. 2006) (new employer obtained employees' noncompetes during interview process, referred them to its attorneys, and agreed in writing to defend employees in the event of legal challenge by former employer).

A high-profile example of the new employer's role in noncompetition litigation is the widely publicized 2005 dispute between Google and Microsoft over Google's hiring of former Microsoft Vice President, Kai-fu Lee. Google vigorously defended Mr. Lee against Microsoft's efforts to use its noncompete agreement to prevent him from starting work at Google. The litigation resulted in a ruling permitting Mr. Lee to join Google and begin recruiting for its China office but restricting him from working in the competitive area of search technology or from participating in budgetary or research and development decision making. *See* Kevin J. Delaney & Robert A. Guth, *Ruling Lets Lee Go to Work at Google*, WALL ST. J., Sept. 14, 2005, B2.

Of course, few employees are likely to be in such demand. How might the prospect of litigation influence an ordinary employee's decision whether to leave for a competitor?

7. *Legitimate Interests.* If general training is not a basis for enforcing a noncompete, what is? Can you discern from the court's treatment of Logan's agreement a possible set of facts under which Rem Metals would have had a protectable interest justifying an injunction? Would it have made a difference, for instance, if the certification Rem Metals provided took three months and cost $3,000 to administer? What if Rem Metals had trained Logan on equipment that he had not used in his previous employer? What if Logan had told Rem Metals' contractors that he was leaving Rem Metals and the contractors decided to bring their future business to Logan's new employer? We will explore the two most commonly recognized "legitimate interests" of employers in the next sections.

3. Disputes over Information

≡ **CTI, Inc. v. Software Artisans, Inc.**
≡ *3 F.3d 730 (4th Cir. 1993)*

WILLIAMS, Circuit Judge:

[Comprehensive Technologies International, Inc., "CTI," brought this action against several former employees and Software Artisans, Inc., "SA," asserting trade secret misappropriation and breach of contract in connection with the defendants' development of a computer program called "Transend." The district court entered judgment for the defendants. In 1988, the founder and CEO of CTI, Celestino Beltran, established a Software Product Group, headed by defendant Dean Hawkes, to expand the company in the area of electronic data interchange ("EDI"). EDI is the computer-to-computer transmission of business transactions in proprietary or standard formats. Hawkes was given responsibility for developing software that would enable clients to process and transmit data through EDI technology. Defendant Filippides was hired to market the software, and the other defendant employees wrote the code.]

Each of the Defendant employees except Hawkes signed CTI's standard Confidentiality and Proprietary Information Agreement. Under the Agreement, each employee agreed not to disclose or use, directly or indirectly, during his employment and for three years thereafter any confidential, proprietary, or software-related information belonging to CTI. The Agreement specifically identified the Claims Express and EDI Link projects as confidential. [Hawkes signed] an Employment Agreement that contained similar but more restrictive provisions. In addition to promising confidentiality, Hawkes agreed that during the term of his employment he would not compete with CTI, solicit CTI's customers, or employ CTI's current or former employees.

The Software Products Group undertook to develop two software packages for personal computers. The first, Claims Express, is an electronic medical billing system. Claims Express transmits information that conforms to two specific insurance claims forms [and] has been successfully marketed. CTI's second software package, EDI Link, is not specific to the health care industry. It is designed to permit users to create generic forms, enter data on the forms electronically, test that data for errors, and store both the forms and the data on a computer. Although CTI expended substantial effort on EDI Link, at the time of trial the program had not been completed and had never been sold or marketed. Trial testimony indicated that between 35 and 85 percent of the program had been completed.

In February 1991, all of the Defendant employees left CTI. . . .

In April 1991, the Defendants incorporated Software Artisans, Inc., located in Fairfax, Virginia. By July 1991, SA had developed and begun to market its own program called Transend. According to its User's Manual, Transend creates a "paperless office environment" by enabling its users to process business forms on a computer. Transend is similar to Claims Express and EDI Link in that it is designed to prepare forms for transmission by EDI. Transend permits the user to input data, check the data for errors, and prepare the data for transmission by EDI.

. . . III

Trade Secrets

The district court . . . found that CTI did not prove that the Defendants misappropriated a trade secret. Under Virginia law a "trade secret" is information, including but not limited to, a formula, pattern, compilation, program, device, method, technique, or process, that:

1. Derives independent economic value, actual or potential, from not being generally known to, and not being readily ascertainable by proper means by, other persons who can obtain economic value from its disclosure or use, and
2. Is the subject of efforts that are reasonable under the circumstances to maintain its secrecy.

VA. CODE ANN. § 59.1-336. For purposes relevant to this case, "misappropriation" means the "use of a trade secret of another without express or implied consent by a person who . . . [a]t the time of . . . use, knew or had reason to know that his knowledge of the trade secret was . . . [a]cquired under circumstances giving rise to a duty to maintain its secrecy or limit its use." *Id.*

In denying CTI's claim for trade secret misappropriation, the district court found that CTI did not possess any trade secrets and that, even if CTI did possess trade secrets, the Defendants had not misappropriated them. The court found no evidence that CTI's purported trade secrets—the organization of Claims Express and EDI Link, the database access techniques of the two programs, and the unique identifiers of the two programs—derived independent economic value from not being generally known or were not readily ascertainable by proper means. Consequently, the court concluded that CTI's purported trade secrets failed to satisfy all of the elements necessary to prove a trade secret. The district court also concluded that the Defendants did not "copy" any trade secrets, implying that Defendants did not "use" or otherwise misappropriate them.

CTI argues that in granting judgment for Defendants on its trade secrets claim, the district court misapplied the law. . . .

CTI reads the district court's opinion as ruling as a matter of law that the organization of its database, its database access techniques, and its unique identifiers could not constitute trade secrets because each of their composite elements was in the public domain. CTI argues vociferously (and correctly) that although a trade secret cannot subsist in information in the public domain, it can subsist in a combination of such information, as long as the combination is itself secret. *See Integrated Cash Management v. Digital Transactions*, 920 F.2d 174 (2d Cir. 1990). According to CTI, each of its alleged trade secrets is just such a combination of publicly available information.

In making this argument, CTI misreads the district court's opinion. The district court did not rule that unique combinations or arrangements of publicly available information cannot receive protection as trade secrets. Rather, the district court held that CTI failed to present any evidence that its database organization, its access techniques, and its identifiers were not themselves publicly available. The court specifically found that the arrangement and interaction of the functions of Claims Express and EDI Link were "common to all computer programs of this type." Information that is generally known cannot qualify as a trade secret. Consequently, the district court did not misapply the law; it simply found insufficient evidence to support CTI's claim. The district court correctly concluded that CTI failed to prove that the organization, database access techniques, and identifiers of CTI's software constituted trade secrets.

Even if CTI had demonstrated that these items constituted trade secrets, CTI has not convinced us that the district court clearly erred in finding that the Defendants did not misappropriate any of CTI's alleged trade secrets. CTI points to the short development time and the complete lack of design documentation for Transend as strong circumstantial evidence of misappropriation. Although this evidence does raise some suspicions, Defendants provided a colorable explanation for the absence of design documentation. First, Defendant's expert . . . testified that it was not atypical for small software companies to neglect to prepare extensive design documentation. Second, [Defendant] Sterba testified that he and the others disliked the amount of paperwork involved in documenting their designs, that they preferred to use a "whiteboard" for their design work, and that they placed much of the information that would ordinarily appear in design documentation in the code itself. In light of this testimony, CTI's circumstantial evidence is not enough to convince us that the district court clearly erred in finding that the Defendants did not copy (or "use") any of CTI's alleged trade secret information. . . .

IV

Covenant Not to Compete

CTI next argues that the district court should have enforced Dean Hawkes's covenant not to compete. In his Termination Agreement, Hawkes agreed that, for a period of twelve months following his departure from CTI, he would not engage directly or indirectly in any business within the United States (financially as an investor or lender or as an employee, director, officer, partner, independent contractor, consultant or owner or in any other capacity calling for the rendition of personal services or acts of management, operation or control) which is in competition with the business of CTI. For purposes of this Agreement, the "business of CTI" shall be defined as the design, development, marketing, and sales of CLAIMS EXPRESS and EDI LINK type PC-based software with the same functionality and methodology. . . .

Virginia has established a three-part test for assessing the reasonableness of restrictive employment covenants. Under the test, the court must ask the following questions:

1. Is the restraint, from the standpoint of the employer, reasonable in the sense that it is no greater than is necessary to protect the employer in some legitimate business interest?
2. From the standpoint of the employee, is the restraint reasonable in the sense that it is not unduly harsh and oppressive in curtailing his legitimate efforts to earn a livelihood?
3. Is the restraint reasonable from the standpoint of a sound public policy?

If a covenant not to compete meets each of these standards of reasonableness, it must be enforced. As a general rule, however, the Virginia courts do not look favorably upon covenants not to compete, and will strictly construe them against the employer. The employer bears the burden of demonstrating that the restraint is reasonable.

The district court refused to enforce the covenant not to compete because it concluded that the covenant was broader than necessary to protect CTI's legitimate business interests. First, the court held that the scope of the employment restrictions was too broad because the restrictions precluded Hawkes from working for a competitor in any capacity, even as a janitor. The court implied that CTI did not have a legitimate interest in preventing Hawkes from working for a competitor in a menial capacity. Second, the district court concluded that the geographic scope of the agreement was broader than necessary to protect CTI's interests. The court found that CTI had marketed Claims Express only in Virginia, Nebraska, and perhaps one other state, and therefore CTI did not have a legitimate interest in restricting Hawkes's employment throughout the United States.

Although the district court believed that the covenant was categorically overbroad because it precluded Hawkes from working for a competitor of CTI in any capacity, the Virginia Supreme Court has enforced similarly broad restrictions. . . .

Moreover, as Vice President of CTI's Software Products Group, Hawkes necessarily came in contact with confidential information concerning both CTI's products and its customers. Hawkes's access to such confidential information makes the covenant not to compete more reasonable. As the Virginia Supreme Court has noted,

> [t]he fact that the employment is of such a character as to inform the employee of business methods and trade secrets which, if brought to the knowledge of a competitor, would prejudice the interests of the employer, tends to give an element of reasonableness to a contract that the employee will not engage in a similar business for a limited time after the termination of his employment, and is always regarded as a strong reason for upholding the contract.

Stoneman [*v. Wilson*], 192 S.E. [816, 819 (Va. 1938)]. Similarly, in *Roanoke Engineering* [*v. Rosenbaum*, 290 S.E. 2d 882, 885 (Va. 1982)], an employee had access to confidential financial records, lists of customers and suppliers, and detailed knowledge of overhead factors, pricing policies, and bidding techniques. The Virginia Supreme Court held that this information enabled the employee to become a "formidable competitor" of his former employer, and concluded that a restriction barring the employee from working for competitors in any capacity was no greater than necessary to protect the employer's legitimate business interests.

Hawkes poses a similar danger to CTI's business. As the individual primarily responsible for the design, development, marketing and sale of CTI's software, Hawkes became intimately familiar with every aspect of CTI's operation, and necessarily acquired information that he could use to compete with CTI in the marketplace. When an employee has access to confidential and trade secret information crucial to the success of the employer's business, the employer has a strong interest in enforcing a covenant not to compete because other legal remedies often prove inadequate. It will often be difficult, if not impossible, to prove that a competing employee has misappropriated trade secret information belonging to his former employer. On the facts of this case, we conclude that the scope of the employment restrictions is no broader than necessary to protect CTI's legitimate business interests.

As a second ground for invalidating the covenant not to compete, the district court concluded that the geographic scope of the employment restrictions — "within the United States" — was greater than necessary to protect CTI's business. The district court merely noted that CTI had marketed Claims Express in only three states and therefore did not have a national market for its product.

The district court clearly erred in concluding that CTI did not have a national market for Claims Express. CTI licensed Claims Express in at least ten states. . . . CTI also identified for the district court specific customer prospects in [nineteen states] and the District of Columbia. CTI presented Claims Express and EDI Link (albeit in preliminary form) at national EDIA trade shows in both 1989 and 1990. Finally, CTI presented evidence that it faced direct [and potential] competition from companies located [throughout the country]. Given the breadth of the market for Claims Express, we cannot see how anything less than a nationwide prohibition could conceivably protect CTI's business interests. . . .

Having determined that the covenant not to compete is reasonable from CTI's point of view, we must next determine whether the covenant is reasonable from Hawkes's point of view, i.e., whether the curtailment on Hawkes's ability to earn a living is unduly harsh or oppressive. Although the agreement applies throughout the United States, it restricts Hawkes from engaging in only an extremely narrow category of business. Hawkes may not render personal services to, or perform acts of management, operation, or control for, any business in competition with "the business of CTI," which the agreement defines as "the design, development, marketing and sales of CLAIMS EXPRESS™ and EDI LINK™ type PC-based software with the same functionality and methodology." The agreement therefore permits Hawkes to design, develop, market and sell any software of a type different from Claims Express or EDI Link, any software of the same type having a different functionality or methodology, or any software of the same type having the same functionality and methodology that is not designed to run on personal computers. Hawkes is also free to compete with any other branch of CTI's business. Because Hawkes retains broad employability under the agreement, the agreement is not unduly harsh or oppressive.

In light of the foregoing, we conclude that the covenant not to compete is no greater than necessary to protect CTI's business and is not unduly harsh or oppressive. . . .

NOTES

1. *Trade Secret Defined.* CTI's primary cause of action against its former employees was misappropriation of a trade secret. Virginia, like a majority of states, has adopted the Uniform Trade Secrets Act ("UTSA"), which attempts to standardize the common-law definition of the term. It lists two requirements for a trade secret: The item in question must derive independent economic value from not being generally known and be subject to employer efforts to maintain its secrecy. *See* UTSA, 14 U.L.A. 437 (1990). Older trade secret cases often involved disputes over particular manufacturing processes or the secret ingredients for a particular product. The recipe for Coca-Cola is often cited as the paradigmatic trade secret. Today, however, many employers seek trade secret protection for more general information, either technical information (as is the case in *CTI*) or confidential business information (financial documentation, marketing strategies, etc.). This poses new challenges in identifying what constitutes a trade secret. Although CTI may have made efforts to keep its project under wraps, according to the court the actual components of CTI's programs and their structure followed techniques and configurations that were in common use.

2. *Independently Valuable Information.* Another question that arises in analyzing trade secrets in information is whether that information — even if not generally known — has independent economic value. While few cases discuss this requirement, Professor Arnow-Richman interprets it to mean that information sought to be protected must be useable to competitors outside of the employer's project or business environment. This often is not the case with secret information that is highly technical and company-specific. She explains:

> [I]ndependent value would in most cases be present where the dispute involved a traditional trade secret, like a secret formula or process, that could be used competitively by any other business that happened to obtain it. Moving up the ladder of abstraction, however, value increasingly derives not from information as raw data but from its application in particular contexts. A company's ability to effectively utilize confidential business or customer-related information rests largely on the competency and skills of its employees, who in turn often obtain their expertise from the experience and training provided to them on the job. In such cases it is human capital, or knowledge imbedded in people, that comprises the employer's interest rather than data or information in the traditional sense.

Rachel Arnow-Richman, *Bargaining for Loyalty in the Information Age: A Reconsideration of the Role of Substantive Fairness in Enforcing Employee Noncompetes*, 80 OR. L. REV. 1163, 1190 (2001); *see also* Catherine Fisk, *Working Knowledge: Trade Secrets, Restrictive Covenants in Employment, and the Rise of Corporate Intellectual Property, 1800-1920*, 52 HASTINGS L. J. 441, 503-4 (2001) (from 1890-1930, the "[f]ocus shifted from the drawings of a machine to the design innovations contained in them; from the list of the customers to the knowledge of their identities, locations, needs and their goodwill; and from the precise written formula for a substance to the general knowledge of the process and techniques for making it").

Was this part of the problem in *CTI*? In other words, was the employer trying to protect the work its employees were doing rather than a particular programming technique? If so, is that a good reason for denying CTI trade secret protection, or should the definition of a trade secret be understood to include such interests? How would a broader understanding of trade secret protection affect societal interests, such as the promotion of innovation, competition, and social welfare?

3. *Evidence of Misappropriation.* To succeed on its trade secret claim, CTI had to show not only that its software products were trade secrets, but also that those secrets had been misappropriated. The UTSA offers an expansive definition of misappropriation. The portion most relevant in the competitive employment context defines the concept as

> disclosure or use of a trade secret of another without express or implied consent by a person who . . . at the time of disclosure or use knew or had reason to know that his knowledge of the trade secret was . . . acquired under circumstances giving rise to a duty to maintain its secrecy or limit its use.

14 U.L.A. 437. As *CTI* illustrates, it can be difficult to prove misappropriation of trade secrets. However, the increasing sophistication of computer forensics has made it easier to track the downloading, copying, and e-mailing of files, allowing companies to demonstrate that particular documents were taken by departing employees. *See, e.g, Bimbo Bakeries USA Inc. v. Botticella*, 613 F.3d 102 (3d Cir. 2010) (employer's computer expert identified pattern of accessing multiple documents consistent with copying in the week leading up to former employee's departure and established that portable hard drives had been attached to the computer); *Rapid Temps, Inc. v. Lamon*, 192 P.2d 799 (N.M. App. 2008) (relying on evidence of files found on employee's computer and portable hard drive). But where alleged secrets are intangible and do not exist in written form, or where the employee resorts to less technical means of "copying," the employer must rely on circumstantial evidence of misappropriation. *See, e.g., San Jose Construction, Inc v. S.B.C.C., Inc.*, 67 Cal. Rptr. 3d 54 (Cal. App. 2007) (similarities between project proposals submitted by plaintiff's former construction manager and those he submitted for same projects while in plaintiff's employ and speed with which they were produced created issue of fact on misappropriation of trade secret claim notwithstanding fact that former manager had returned all project files); *Sunbelt Rentals, Inc. v. Head & Engquist Equip.*, 620 S.E.2d 222, 229 (N.C. Ct. App. 2005) (treating as evidence of misappropriation fact that defendant's new company evolved from having no customers to converting several of plaintiff's customers and making extraordinarily high profit in first year of operation following mass defection of plaintiff's employees). If you were representing the employer, what other evidence of misappropriation would you look for and how would you go about obtaining it? If you were counseling an employee about to engage in competition with a former employer, what precautions would you recommend taking to help avoid or potentially defend against a misappropriation claim?

4. *The Role of Contract in Protecting Information.* The preceding notes, as well as the outcome in *CTI*, demonstrate the challenges facing employers in pursuing trade secret misappropriation claims. To avoid these problems, employers often seek contractual protection for information through a nondisclosure or noncompete clause. *See* Ronald J. Gilson, *The Legal Infrastructure of High Technology Industrial Districts: Silicon Valley, Route 128, and Covenants Not to Compete*, 74 N.Y.U. L. Rev. 575 (1999); Gillian Lester, *Restrictive Covenants, Employee Training, and the Limits of Transaction-Cost Analysis*, 76 Indiana L. J. 49, 53 (2001). Do you see the advantages of noncompete agreements reflected in *CTI*, in which the company pursued separate tort and contract theories against Hawkes? If contractual agreements are helpful to employers, why didn't CTI obtain broader restrictive covenants from the other employee-defendants?

A possible criticism of employers' use of noncompetes is that it circumvents the threshold requirements of trade secret law. Recall from *Rem Metals* that employers must make a threshold showing of a legitimate interest in order to enforce a noncompete. What is CTI's "legitimate" interest in enforcing a noncompete against Hawkes if there are no trade secrets to protect? Consider Professor Katherine Stone's perspective:

> The long-standing view has been that to be enforceable, a covenant not to compete must protect an employer's legitimate interest in a trade secret or confidential information. This view creates a paradox, however, because if a court requires a trade secret or confidential information in order to enforce a covenant, the existence of the covenant becomes, at least theoretically, irrelevant. Disclosure of trade secrets and confidential information can be restrained in the absence of such a covenant.
>
> If the law of noncompete covenants merely restates or incorporates the law of trade secrets and confidential relationships, then there is little independent role for the covenant.

Katherine V.W. Stone, *The New Psychological Contract*, 48 UCLA L. Rev. 519, 583-84 (2001). Professor Stone attempts to explain this paradox, noting the possibility that a covenant makes it easier for an employer to obtain injunctive relief before the secret is disclosed.

In contrast to trade secret law, misappropriation is not a prerequisite to noncompete enforcement in most jurisdictions. *See Certainteed Corp. v. Willaims*, 481 F.3d 528 (7th Cir. 2007) (noting in enforcing noncompete that "keeping a business executive with a wealth of information from taking an equivalent position with a rival is [a legitimate interest] when the executive's use of trade secrets would be hard to detect"). But noncompete law does require a threshold showing of the employer's interest in the information to be protected. As Stone puts it: "In theory, the standard of proof for finding a trade secret in the two cases should be no different, unless the court is sub rosa imposing a different test for finding a trade secret where there is a contractual obligation." She goes on:

> . . . A case in point is [*CTI*]. While the court did not find that the knowledge the employee possessed was a trade secret, it justified its decision on the ground that the employee had access to confidential information concerning both the products and customers of the former employer, so that "it will often be difficult . . . to prove that a competing employee has misappropriated trade secret information belonging to his former employer." This rationale suggests that the court acted to protect the trade secret, not to enforce the parties' agreement, but the existence of the covenant enabled it to sidestep the difficult trade secret issue.
>
> When a court requires that there be a trade secret or confidential information in order to enforce a noncompete covenant, employee consent plays only a minor role in the case. [T]he covenant permits the court to enlarge remedies for trade secret misappropriation; in the view of some courts, the covenant permits it to cut corners in its analysis of what constitutes a trade secret.

Id. at 585. The proposed Restatement of Employment Law appears to share Stone's view that the standard for trade secret and noncompete claims should be the same. *See* Restatement of Employment § 8.02, cmt. a (Council Draft No. 5, Oct. 1, 2010) ("The definition of 'confidential information' in this Section is coextensive with the definitions of trade secrets or other protected information used in the Uniform Trade Secrets Act. . . ."), but the case law is far from clear on this point. Do you see why a court might be more inclined to find for an employer on the basis of a noncompete than on a trade secret claim? Do you understand Professor Stone's concern about this practice? What does she mean by "consent plays a minor role" in such decisions?

Consider that a contractual expansion of employer rights beyond that conferred by trade secret law has implications not only for the worker but for society. One criticism of the use of noncompetes in this manner is that it upsets the balance struck by the background intellectual property regime, which is intentionally limited so as to preserve public access to information while still incentivizing creation. *See* Viva R. Moffat, *The Wrong Tool for the Job: The IP Problem with Non-Competition Agreements*, 52 WILL. & MARY L. REV. (forthcoming 2010).

5. *Narrower Restraints as Alternatives.* Do contractual *nondisclosure* agreements pose similar problems to noncompetes? Or does the narrower scope of the prohibition reduce the concern? If the latter, what is the point of having a nondisclosure agreement? Where an employer succeeds in enforcing the broadest restraint in its employment agreement, in Hawkes's case the noncompete provision, such additional language is often irrelevant — an employee who is precluded from competing with his former employer is most likely precluded from disclosing information that will help the competitor compete. However, from a planning perspective, it may be important for the employer to include narrower restrictive covenants in an employment agreement. If the court ultimately refuses to enforce the noncompete agreement, it might still provide a degree of protection to the employer by ordering compliance with the other clauses or even providing damages to the employer based on breach of other clauses. Some courts apply the same rule of reasonableness to lesser restraints like nondisclosure and nonsolicitation clauses. *See, e.g., Ashland Mgmt Incorp. v. Altair Investments*, 869 N.Y.S.2d 465 (1st Dept. 2008). However, because the effects of enforcement of such clauses on the employee tend to be less onerous — for instance, preventing an employee from using certain knowledge or servicing a segment of the market's clientele — application of the same rule may lead to a different assessment of the balance of hardships. In addition, nondisclosure agreements frequently serve an important evidentiary role in trade secret litigation. Revisit the UTSA definition of a trade secret, quoted in *CTI*, and see if you can guess why.

6. *Reasonableness.* Even if an employer is using a noncompete agreement to protect a legitimate interest, the agreement is not enforceable unless it is "reasonable." *CTI* discusses two factors that courts consider in assessing whether a noncompete is reasonable — its geographic reach and the scope of competition prohibited. (A third factor, duration of the restraint, is taken up in the next case.) Note the relationship between the two factors the court considers. The court permits a very broad geographic reach (the whole country) in part because the definition of competition is extremely narrow (only companies developing PC software with the same functionality and methodology). In past decades, courts frequently struck down noncompetes precluding competition throughout the country as categorically overbroad, reflecting the view (and probably the reality in that era) that few businesses could be meaningfully competitive beyond the borders of their state or geographic region. In today's world, however, such geographic provisions are both more common and more commonly enforced, particularly if the scope of prohibited competition is narrowly drawn. *See, e.g., Kramer v. Robec, Inc.*, 824 F. Supp. 508, 512 (E.D. Pa. 1992) (nationwide ban on competition reasonable because computer market is worldwide and Robec distributes throughout the nation and overseas). Indeed, courts have occasionally enforced worldwide restrictions on narrow forms of competitive behavior on behalf of companies operating in an international market. *See, e.g., Superior Consulting Co. v. Walling*,

851 F. Supp. 839, 847 (E.D. Mich. 1994) (finding absence of any geographic term acceptable where former employer did business in 43 states and with foreign nations and scope of competitive behavior could be reduced); *Farr Assocs., Inc. v. Baksin*, 530 S.E.2d 878, 882 (N.C. Ct. App. 2000) (rejecting argument that covenant was overly broad due to absence of defined territorial limit where covenant was limited to not servicing clients of former employer).

Note on Injunctive Relief and the Mechanics of Enforcement

When an important employee departs, employers are most interested in the remedies a court will order if the employee violates the law. If negotiations fail and the employer decides to sue the employee, it will typically seek preliminary injunctive relief from the court. That is, the employer will obtain an immediate, abbreviated hearing at which it will argue that the court should enjoin the employee from disclosing a trade secret and/or breaching his or her noncompete agreement, pending a full trial.

Although the tests vary somewhat among circuits, to obtain a preliminary injunction, an employer must show that there is a danger of irreparable harm, that it is likely to succeed on the merits at trial, that a balance of the equities favors issuing the injunction, and that an injunction will not violate the public interest. *See, e.g., SI Handling Systems, Inc. v. Heisley* 753 F.2d 1244, 1254 (3d Cir. 1985); *see generally* Elizabeth A. Rowe, *When Trade Secrets Become Shackles: Fairness and the Inevitable Disclosure Doctrine*, 7 Tul. J. Tech. & Intell. Prop. 167, 202-7 (2005) (describing preliminary injunction standard and how it affects results in noncompetition cases). During the preliminary injunction stage, the parties can take advantage of a compressed discovery schedule and will often mount a full-blown minitrial at the hearing. The reason for putting so much effort into obtaining or defeating a temporary order is that the preliminary injunction proceeding is often the only step that matters in unlawful competition litigation. By the time the case goes to trial on the merits, months may have passed. From the employer's perspective, any damage to its interests will have already been done. Although an employer who succeeds at trial after losing at the preliminary injunction stage may obtain damages, monetary injury in such cases is often hard to prove and quantify, and damage awards can be difficult to collect from an individual employee.

For the employee, the issuance of a preliminary injunction means that he may be unemployed or underemployed, at least for the period until trial. Even if he ultimately succeeds on the merits, he may not be able to recoup wages lost during the preliminary injunction period, and often the competitive employment opportunity that he sought to pursue will have passed. *See, e.g., FLIR Syst. v. Parrish*, 95 Cal. Rptr. 3d 307 (Cal. App. 2009) (prospective business partner in former employees' new venture broke off discussions and rejected deal upon former employer's initiation of lawsuit). For some high-level employees, a competitor may be willing to wait for the employee to "sit out" the period of his noncompetition agreement. But for many ordinary employees, a preliminary injunction means lost career time, lost income, and lots of legal bills.

If an employer is successful in obtaining injunctive relief, what will the court order say? Where the employer successfully alleges breach of a noncompete, the court will enjoin the employee from competing. The scope of the injunction will reflect the terms of the contract, subject to any modifications the court may fashion to ensure that its effects are not unduly burdensome to the employee. In the case of a trade secret claim, the scope of the injunction is less clear. Trade secret law does not prohibit competition per se; rather, it prohibits misuse of certain information. Therefore, a preliminary injunction in a trade secret case might simply enjoin the employee from using or disclosing that information.

What if the former employer alleges the employee's new job is so closely related to his or her former position that the employee will inevitably use the employer's trade secrets? In *PepsiCo v. Redmond*, 54 F.3d 1262 (7th Cir. 1995), Pepsi sought to enjoin the former General Manager of its California Business Unit from taking a comparable position with rival drink manufacturer Quaker. It argued that Redmond had extensive knowledge of the company's annual operating plan, its pricing architecture, and its marketing and distribution strategies for the upcoming year. Redmond had signed a confidentiality agreement with Pepsi, but not a noncompete. Pepsi nonetheless sought an injunction against competition. The court granted it, finding that "unless Redmond possessed an uncanny ability to compartmentalize information, he would necessarily be making decisions about [Quaker's] Gatorade and Snapple by relying on his knowledge of [Pepsi's] trade secrets." *Id.* at 1269. The court explained:

> Admittedly, PepsiCo has not brought a traditional trade secret case, in which a former employee has knowledge of a special manufacturing process or customer list and can give a competitor an unfair advantage by transferring the technology or customers to that competitor. PepsiCo has not contended that Quaker has stolen the [Pepsi] All Sport formula or its list of distributors. Rather PepsiCo has asserted that Redmond cannot help but rely on PCNA trade secrets as he helps plot Gatorade and Snapple's new course, and that these secrets will enable Quaker to achieve a substantial advantage by knowing exactly how PCNA will price, distribute, and market its sports drinks and new age drinks and being able to respond strategically. . . .
>
> Quaker and Redmond assert that they have not and do not intend to use whatever confidential information Redmond has by virtue of his former employment. . . . They also note with regard to distribution systems that even if Quaker wanted to steal information about PCNA's distribution plans, they would be completely useless in attempting to integrate the Gatorade and Snapple beverage lines.
>
> The defendants' arguments fall somewhat short of the mark. Again, the danger of misappropriation in the present case is not that Quaker threatens to use PCNA's secrets to create distribution systems or co-opt PCNA's advertising and marketing ideas. Rather, PepsiCo believes that Quaker, unfairly armed with knowledge of PCNA's plans, will be able to anticipate its distribution, packaging, pricing, and marketing moves. . . . In other words, PepsiCo finds itself in the position of a coach, one of whose players has left, playbook in hand, to join the opposing team before the big game. Quaker and Redmond's protestations that their distribution systems and plans are entirely different from PCNA's are thus not really responsive.

Id. at 1269-70. Is *PepsiCo* consistent with what *CTI* teaches about the elements of a trade secret claim? Is it consistent with the distinction *Rem Metals* draws between protectable information and an employee's skills and experience? Note that both parties in *PepsiCo* agreed that Redmond had not taken any documents upon departure, nor was he likely to use directly any of the information he remembered at Quaker. Does the risk to Pepsi that Redmond's decisions at Quaker would be informed by his awareness of Pepsi's strategies justify enjoining Redmond from starting his job? Consider Professor Alan Hyde's opinion of the case:

> PepsiCo never identified any specific piece of information that Redmond had and Quaker wanted. PepsiCo did not show that Redmond knew the recipe for All Sport, or

new flavors being worked on secretly, or which athletes had been approached for endorsements, or anything of that sort.

What *did* Redmond know? He was far from the key figure in All Sport. He was one of many regional general managers. He had access, said PepsiCo, to its "Strategic Plan" and "Annual Operating Plan" covering "financial goals, marketing plans, promotional event calendars, growth expectations, and operational changes." He knew which markets Pepsi would focus on, and some aspects of a new delivery system. In other words, he knew what any manager knows.

The *PepsiCo* decision is unusually proplaintiff, [and therefore] not typical. It inhabits a world in which all managers on distribution lists for "strategic plans" and "annual operating plans" serve for life, and may have their departures to work in the area they know enjoined at the option of their employer. It seems not to relate at all to today's world of corporate downsizing and managerial layoffs. It does not rest on any economic analysis of the efficiency advantages of letting Redmond go as against letting PepsiCo enjoin him, even though the Court of Appeals for the Seventh Circuit is famous for its law and economic approach. Nor does it reinforce employment-at-will, to which, in other cases, that court has paid homage. Employees with other options, such as competent managers, may choose not to accept employment at will if, following involuntary termination, they will be unable to work in their area of expertise.

ALAN HYDE, WORKING IN SILICON VALLEY: ECONOMIC AND LEGAL ANALYSIS OF A HIGH-VELOCITY LABOR MARKET 34-35 (2003). Is Professor Hyde suggesting that the PepsiCo decision is out of date? What characteristics of the modern labor market does he identify in his critique? How are they relevant to the policies underlying legal protection of information and other employer interests? Does the law need to better account for employee mobility in what Professor Hyde calls a "high-velocity labor market"? Professor Hyde's views substantially influenced the proposed Restatement of Employment Law. After considerable debate, the current version rejects the inevitable disclosure doctrine, alleging it reaffirms that costs can enjoin employees who expressly or implicitly threaten to describe confidential information. § 8.02, cmt. b (Council Draft No. 5, Oct. 1, 2010).

≡ *EarthWeb, Inc. v. Schlack*
≡ *71 F. Supp. 2d 299 (S.D.N.Y. 1999)*

PAULEY, District Judge.

This diversity action involves claims of breach of contract and misappropriation of trade secrets in the fluid and ever-expanding world of the Internet. Plaintiff EarthWeb, Inc. moves for preliminary injunctive relief enjoining defendant Mark Schiack . . . from: (1) commencing employment with [ITworld.com] and (2) disclosing or revealing EarthWeb's trade secrets to [ITworld.com] or any third parties. For the reasons discussed below, the motion is denied. . . .

Findings of Fact and Conclusions of Law

A. Background

[EarthWeb, which was founded in 1994, provides online products and services to business professionals in the information technology ("IT") industry. Its websites offering IT professionals information, products, and services, EarthWeb obtains its content primarily through licensing agreements with third parties. Advertising is its primary source of revenue, totaling $3.3 million in 1998. Schlack worked in the publishing industry for the past 16 years, including as senior editor and/or editor-in-chief of magazines such as *BYTE* and *Web Builder*. He began at EarthWeb in October 1998 and resigned the following September. His title was Vice President, Worldwide Content.]

Strategic Content Planning

EarthWeb claims that Schlack's primary job responsibilities involved making all significant strategic decisions relating to content. The company also asserts that Schlack either authored or supervised the creation of the content plans for a number of EarthWeb websites launched within the last year. As a result, Schlack knows the specific target audience for each website, how EarthWeb aggregated content on those websites to reach the targeted audience, and how EarthWeb may intend to improve the content and delivery of particular websites.

Schlack does not dispute the extent of his editorial involvement with EarthWeb's websites. Instead, he claims that he had virtually no interaction with senior management and therefore knows little about EarthWeb's overall business goals. He also contends that whatever he knows about EarthWeb's strategic planning is likely to become obsolete rather quickly because the company's websites are constantly changing.

Licensing Agreements and Acquisitions

[Schlack was involved in negotiating at least two licensing agreements with third parties and generally knew the terms and conditions of other agreements. He also knows companies whose content EarthWeb is interested in licensing. But EarthWeb's licensing agreements are frequently revealed by licensors as they search for better deals. EarthWeb does not allege that Schlack retained copies of licensing agreements or other sensitive documents.]

Technical Knowledge

Schlack's job responsibilities required him to be familiar with the software and hardware infrastructure that supports EarthWeb's websites. Thus, Schlack has general knowledge of how EarthWeb customized and deployed the products of outside vendors and consultants in order to fit EarthWeb's programming needs. . . .

However, Schlack had no access to EarthWeb's source codes or configuration files, so his knowledge of EarthWeb's proprietary software and infrastructure is necessarily limited. . . .

EarthWeb's main concern is Schlack's awareness of the trial and error process that EarthWeb undertook in implementing the products and services of outside consultants. Armed with this knowledge, EarthWeb contends that Schlack would be able to solve similar technical problems if they arose at ITworld.com and thereby avoid the mistakes that EarthWeb made in the past. . . .

C. *Schlack's Prospective Position with ITworld.com*

At the moment, ITworld.com does not exist; the website is scheduled to be launched in January 2000. . . . When operational, ITworld.com will be a single website for IT professionals that contains news, product information and editorial opinions written primarily by an internal staff of more than 275 journalists.

Thus, in contrast to EarthWeb's emphasis on obtaining the products and services of third parties through acquisitions and licensing agreements and then making those materials readily accessible on its websites, ITworld.com will rely on original content for over 70% of its website's material. Content such as product reviews and technical research will be created in-house by ITworld.com's staff.

Schlack contends that ITworld.com will also be distinguishable from EarthWeb in the type of audience it targets. While both EarthWeb and ITworld.com are intended to appeal to IT professionals, Schlack argues that the products and services offered by EarthWeb are aimed at programmers and technicians, while ITworld.com will focus on upper level executives, such as technology managers and chief information officers.

Given the dynamics of the Internet, such comparisons may be ephemeral. This underscores the difficulty in assessing the characteristics of ITworld.com, an embryonic business entity that will compete in a nascent industry which is evolving and re-inventing itself with breathtaking speed. . . .

D. *The Employment Agreement*

On October 13, 1998, EarthWeb and Schlack executed an "Employment Agreement" memorializing certain terms and conditions of Schlack's employment. . . .

Specifically, section four of the agreement, titled "Proprietary Information," provides in relevant part:

> (a) [Schlack] will not disclose or use, at any time either during or after the term of employment, except at the request of EarthWeb or an affiliate of EarthWeb, any Confidential Information (as herein defined). "Confidential Information shall mean all proprietary information, technical data, trade secrets, and know-how, including, without limitation, research, product plans, customer lists, markets, software, developments, inventions, discoveries, processes, formulas, algorithms, technology, designs, drawings, marketing and other plans, business strategies and financial data and information, including but not limited to Inventions, whether or not marked as "Confidential." "Confidential Information" shall also mean information received by EarthWeb from customers of EarthWeb or other third parties subject to a duty to keep confidential.

Section five of the employment agreement is titled "Limited Agreement Not to Compete." That section provides in relevant part:

> (c) For a period of twelve (12) months after the termination of Schlack's employment with EarthWeb, Schlack shall not, directly or indirectly:
> (1) work as an employee, employer, consultant, agent, principal, partner, manager, officer, director, or in any other individual or representative capacity for any person or entity that directly competes with EarthWeb. For the purpose

of this section, the term "directly competing" is defined as a person or entity or division on [sic] an entity that is

(i) an on-line service for Information Professionals whose primary business is to provide Information Technology Professionals with a directory of third party technology, software, and/or developer resources; and/or an online reference library, and/or

(ii) an on-line store, the primary purpose of which is to sell or distribute third party software or products used for Internet site or software development[.]

Discussion . . .

B. *Inevitable Disclosure of Trade Secrets, As Irreparable Harm*

In this circuit, irreparable harm may be presumed if a trade secret has been misappropriated. A trade secret, once lost, is lost forever; its loss cannot be measured in money damages.

It is also possible to establish irreparable harm based on the inevitable disclosure of trade secrets, particularly where the movant competes directly with the prospective employer and the transient employee possesses highly confidential or technical knowledge concerning manufacturing processes, marketing strategies, or the like. Such a risk was present in *PepsiCo, Inc. v. Redmond*, 54 F.3d 1262 (7th Cir. 1995). [There] the court effectively converted Redmond's confidentiality agreement into a non-compete agreement by enjoining him from working for a direct competitor of PepsiCo for a sixth month period.

Doubleclick [*v. Henderson*, 1997 WL 731413, at *5-6,] is also instructive. The defendants in *Doubleclick* were two senior executives for an Internet advertising company who were caught misappropriating trade secrets as they surreptitiously plotted to form their own company to compete directly with their former employer. . . . Based on the evidence of actual misappropriation, which was "bolstered by . . . a high probability of 'inevitable disclosure' of trade secrets", the court enjoined the defendants from launching their company, or accepting employment with any competing company, for a period of six months.

While *Doubleclick* appears to represent a high water mark for the inevitable disclosure doctrine in New York, its holding rests heavily on evidence of the defendants' overt theft of trade secrets and breaches of fiduciary duty. Such misconduct has long been recognized as an appropriate ground for enjoining the disclosure of trade secrets, irrespective of any contract between the parties. However, in cases that do not involve the actual theft of trade secrets, the court is essentially asked to bind the employee to an implied-in-fact restrictive covenant based on a finding of inevitable disclosure. This runs counter to New York's strong public policy against such agreements and circumvents the strict judicial scrutiny they have traditionally required. . . .

Thus, in its purest form, the inevitable disclosure doctrine treads an exceedingly narrow path through judicially disfavored territory. Absent evidence of actual misappropriation by an employee, the doctrine should be applied in only the rarest of cases. Factors to consider in weighing the appropriateness of granting injunctive relief are whether: (1) the employers in question are direct competitors providing the same or very similar products or services; (2) the employee's new position is nearly identical to his old one, such that he could not reasonably be expected to fulfill his new job responsibilities without utilizing the trade secrets of his former employer; and (3) the trade secrets at issue are highly valuable to both employers. Other case-specific factors such as the nature of the industry and trade secrets should be considered as well.

While the inevitable disclosure doctrine may serve the salutary purpose of protecting a company's investment in its trade secrets, its application is fraught with hazards. Among these risks is the imperceptible shift in bargaining power that necessarily occurs upon the commencement of an employment relationship marked by the execution of a confidentiality agreement. When that relationship eventually ends, the parties' confidentiality agreement may be wielded as a restrictive covenant, depending on how the employer views the new job its former employee has accepted. This can be a powerful weapon in the hands of an employer; the risk of litigation alone may have a chilling effect on the employee. Such constraints should be the product of open negotiation.

. . . Clearly, a written agreement that contains a non-compete clause is the best way of promoting predictability during the employment relationship and afterwards.

Of course, that is precisely what Schlack got with EarthWeb. Section five of the parties' employment agreement is a "limited" restrictive covenant in which Schlack agrees not to compete with EarthWeb in three narrow categories of employment: companies whose "primary business" is providing IT professionals with (1) "directory" of third party technology, (2) an "online reference library", or (3) an "online store." On the other hand, section four of the employment agreement contains extremely broad language concerning non-disclosure of "proprietary information." Schlack viewed this distinction as critical and says he would not have knowingly agreed to a post-employment restraint on his ability to work in the field of IT journalism on the Internet. EarthWeb, however, appears to gloss over the distinctness of these provisions which it drafted. Under the banner of inevitable disclosure doctrine, EarthWeb contends that Schlack should be enjoined from working for any Internet company that targets IT professionals. . . .

This Court declines to re-write the parties' employment agreement under the rubric of inevitable disclosure and thereby permit EarthWeb to broaden the sweep of its restrictive covenant. . . .

Accordingly, EarthWeb's entitlement to a preliminary injunction enjoining Schlack's future employment must be found to rest, if at all, on the restrictive covenant it drafted, and not on a confidentiality provision conflated with the theory of inevitable disclosure. With this framework in mind, the Court turns to the specific terms of the employment agreement at issue here.

C. *The Non-Compete Provision*

[The court first concluded that ITworld.com was not a directly competitive business, as defined by Schlack's employment agreement because its "primary focus will be to publish news, analysis and product information that is generated daily by its own editorial staff."]

Even if the terms of EarthWeb's restrictive covenant reached Schlack's prospective employment at ITworld.com, EarthWeb would still have to establish that the restraint is reasonable and necessary to protect its legitimate interests. In New York, non-compete covenants will be enforced only if reasonably limited in scope and duration, and only "to the extent necessary (1) to prevent an employee's solicitation or disclosure of trade secrets, (2) to prevent an employee's release of confidential information regarding the employer's customers, or (3) in those cases where the employee's services to the employer are deemed special or unique."

The policy underlying this strict approach rests on notions of employee mobility and free enterprise. "[O]nce the term of an employment agreement has expired, the general public policy favoring robust and uninhibited competition should not give way merely because a particular employer wishes to insulate himself from competition." . . . On the other hand, "the employer is entitled to protection from unfair or illegal conduct that causes economic injury."

Applying these principles here, EarthWeb's restrictive covenant would fail to pass muster even if Schlack's position at ITworld.com fell within the provision's relatively narrow parameters.

1. Duration

As a threshold matter, this Court finds that the one-year duration of EarthWeb's restrictive covenant is too long given the dynamic nature of this industry, its lack of geographical borders, and Schlack's former cutting-edge position with EarthWeb where his success depended on keeping abreast of daily changes in content on the Internet. By comparison, the court in Doubleclick enjoined the defendants for only a six-month period. The Doubleclick court observed that "[g]iven the speed with which the Internet advertising industry apparently changes, defendants' knowledge of DoubleClick's operation will likely lose value to such a degree that the purpose of a preliminary injunction will have evaporated before the year is up." Similar considerations predominate here. . . .

2. Unique and Extraordinary Services

Contrary to EarthWeb's contention, Schlack's services are not "unique and extraordinary." Such characteristics have traditionally been associated with "various categories of employment where the services are dependent on an employee's special talents; such categories include musicians, professional athletes, actors and the like."

However, in order to justify a [sic] enforcement of a restrictive covenant, [m]ore must . . . be shown to establish such a quality than that the employee excels at his work or that his performance is of high value to his employer. It must also appear that his services are of such character as to make his replacement impossible or that the loss of such services would cause the employer irreparable injury.

EarthWeb has not shown that the nature of Schlack's services are unique or that he cultivated the type of special client relationships that the Second Circuit [has] found worthy of protection. . . .

3. Trade Secrets . . .

New York courts consider the following factors in determining whether information constitutes a trade secret: "(1) the extent to which the information is known outside of the business; (2) the extent to which it is known by employees and others involved in the business; (3) the extent of measures taken by the business to guard the secrecy of the information; (4) the value of the information to the business and its competitors; (5) the amount of effort or money expended by the business in developing the information; [and] (6) the ease or difficulty with which the information could be properly acquired or duplicated by others." The most important consideration is whether the information was kept secret. This requires that the owner of a trade secret take reasonable measures to protect its secrecy.

. . . EarthWeb contends that Schlack is intimately familiar with the "strategic thinking" behind the company's websites and its overall business plan. . . .

In some contexts, courts have found that particularized marketing plans, costing and price information may constitute trade secrets. EarthWeb has established, at least at this stage in the proceedings, that Schlack had access to such information. In some respects, however, EarthWeb's proof on this issue is weak. For example, unlike the executive[in PepsiCo], Schlack did not routinely communicate with EarthWeb's upper management.

In addition, a serious question remains as to whether the "strategic thinking" behind EarthWeb's websites is necessarily revealed when those websites are launched on the Internet, and therefore not entitled to trade secret protection. Finally, even if Schlack knows where the "gaps or holes" remain in particular websites EarthWeb has not cited any case law for the proposition that a product's perceived deficiencies are trade secrets.

Based on these facts, the Court finds no imminent risk that Schlack will disclose or use EarthWeb's trade secrets in connection with his employment at ITworld.com. Consequently, EarthWeb has failed to demonstrate a likelihood of irreparable injury entitling it to judicial enforcement of the restrictive covenant, even if that covenant were applicable by its terms and otherwise reasonable in duration. The Court further finds that enforcement of this provision would work a significant hardship on Schlack. When measured against the IT industry in the Internet environment, a one-year hiatus from the workforce is several generations, if not an eternity. . . .

NOTES

1. *Tort versus Contract.* Like CTI, EarthWeb pursued both tort and contract claims against Schlack—inevitable disclosure of trade secrets and breach of noncompete—in attempting to enjoin his employment with ITworld.com. Either of these claims, if successful, could have achieved the result Earthweb sought, yet their elements are slightly different. In addition, there appear to be differences in the court's receptiveness to enjoining future conduct under trade secret law versus a noncompete. Why? Consider the relationship between the scope of the noncompete and Earthweb's trade secret claim. What does the court mean when it says it "declines to re-write the parties' employment agreement under the rubric of inevitable disclosure"? Is the court expressing a preference for noncompetes? If so, why?

2. *Negotiated Term of Employment?* In criticizing the inevitable disclosure doctrine, the court suggests that constraints on competition "should be the product of open negotiation." Do employees generally have the opportunity to negotiate over terms of employment like restrictions on post-employment competition? Did Schlack? How important is the answer to that question in the resolution of this case?

3. *The Demise of Inevitable Disclosure?* EarthWeb expresses hostility toward the doctrine of inevitable disclosure, but it does not reject the theory entirely. A recent

Third Circuit decision, *Bimbo v. Botticella*, 613 F.3d 102 (3d Cir. 2010), suggests that the claim remains viable in at least a subset of cases involving compelling facts. Defendant Botticella was a former senior executive for a large baking conglomerate. He signed a confidentiality agreement upon hire, but not a noncompete. Through his employment with Bimbo, Botticella had access to a wide range of confidential documents containing information on such matters as product lines, cost positions, and promotional strategies. He was also one of a select group of individuals with access to the company's "code books," containing the formulae and process parameters for all of the plaintiff's products, and one of only seven people nationwide to possess all the knowledge necessary to produce the "nooks and crannies" texture of the plaintiff's popular Thomas' English Muffin product. After eight years of employment he accepted a position as a Vice President of Baking Operations for competitor Hostess Brands. Rather than resigning, Botticella continued to work for Bimbo and retain access to its confidential information for several months, during which time he continued to attend strategy meetings about Bimbo's products. He also copied numerous computer files during the weeks leading up to his departure. The court affirmed the issuance of a preliminary injunction against competition, holding that Bimbo was likely to succeed in demonstrating a "substantial threat" of trade secret disclosure. Although it recognized the possibility that a narrow restraint against disclosure might suffice to protect Bimbo's interest, it concluded that Botticellas's "suspicious conduct during his final weeks of employment" justified the district court's decision to provide a "stronger remedy." *Id.* at 118. Does *Bimbo* help you understand the type of unique situations where an inevitable disclosure claim is likely to have teeth?

The proposed Restatement of Employment largely rejects the inevitable disclosure theory. § 8.05, cmt. b (Council Draft No. 5, Oct. 1, 2010) ("'inevitable disclosure' [has proven unworkable in practice, leading to much confusion and uncertainty when high-level employees switch employers. . . . In the absence of an enforceable no-compete covenant, courts should not broadly enjoin all competition by a former employee unless there has been actual use or disclosure of a trade secret or a clear threat [of] use or disclosure [and a more limited injunction] is inadequate."). For more about the controversial nature of the inevitable disclosure doctrine, *See* Elizabeth A. Rowe, *When Trade Secrets Become Shackles: Fairness and the Inevitable Disclosure*, 7 Tul. J. Tech. & Intell. Prop. 167 (2005).

4. *Judicial Scrutiny of Employer Interests.* In comparison to *CTI*, *EarthWeb* offers a more detailed analysis of the information at stake and whether it entitles the employer to protection against competition. There are significant variations both between and within jurisdictions in how much scrutiny courts give to the underlying interests of the employer, both in trade secret and noncompete cases. Is this because the legal definition of what is protectable information is unclear? Or is there inherent uncertainty in assessing what is protectable when the information is technical or complex? *See* Catherine Fisk, *Working Knowledge: Trade Secrets, Restrictive Covenants in Employment, and the Rise of Corporate Intellectual Property*, 1800-1920, 52 Hastings L.J. 441, 535 (2001); Ronald J. Gilson, *The Legal Infrastructure of High Technology Industrial Districts: Silicon Valley, Route 128, and Covenants Not to Compete*, 74 N.Y.U. L. Rev. 575, 599 (1999); Alan Hyde, *Employment Law After the Death of Employment*, 1 U. Pa. J. Lab. & Emp. L. 99, 114-15 (1998). Do you think courts are competent to distinguish between protectable and nonprotectable information? Or does the technical nature of modern trade secret disputes require special expertise? One appellate court decision has rejected entirely the notion of a protectable interest prerequisite to noncompete enforcement in favor of a test based solely on reasonableness. *See Sunbelt Rentals, Inc. v. Ehlers*, 915 N.E.2d 862, 869 (Ill. App. 2009) ("[Courts] should evaluate only the time-and-territory restrictions. [If] they are not unreasonable, then the restrictive covenant should be enforced."). Is this a sensible response to the difficulty of administering the protectable interest rule? Or might such an approach pose other challenges? Is it even possible to assess reasonableness absent some attention to the purpose of the restraint? What determines reasonableness in such cases?

5. *The Value of "Negative Knowledge."* Part of what Earthweb was trying to protect was Schlack's knowledge of the trial and error process Earthweb had undertaken in implementing its products. This is often referred to as "negative knowledge." Why does the court discount this information? Is it not valuable? Or is there simply no way to protect it in a way that does not unfairly disadvantage the employee? Courts take different approaches to this issue, with some reaching results contrary to *EarthWeb*. *See, e.g., Metallurgical Indus. Inc. v. Fourtek, Inc.*, 790 F.2d 1195, 1203 (5th Cir. 1986) (finding no distinction between "positive" and "negative" knowledge because "knowing what not to do often leads to knowing what to do"); *On-line Technologies, Inc. v. Perkin-Elmer Corp.*, 253 F. Supp. 2d 313, 323 (D. Conn. 2003) (finding "negative knowledge" to be a recognized form of "using" a trade secret proscribed under state law).

6. *Reasonable Duration in an Information Economy.* The court states that the one-year duration in Schlack's contract is unreasonably long. The same duration received implicit approval in *CTI*. Why? Is the difference due to the nature of the information being protected? The nature of the subsequent employment? The industry in question? Or is it just a difference in perspective between two courts deciding cases six years apart? In the last decade, courts have generally been stricter in deciding what constitutes a reasonable duration, recognizing that in many dynamic industries, knowledge does not remain secret or valuable for very long. *See, e.g., Estee Lauder Cos., Inc. v. Batra*, 430 F. Supp. 2d. 158 (S.D.N.Y. 2006) (reducing 12-month restraint with international scope to 5 months in recognition of limited long-term utility of marketing information). On the other hand, some courts are willing to enforce noncompetes of as much as three years or more, particularly where the industry in question is more stable or different interests, such as long-term client relationships, are at stake.

7. *Competition Defined.* The court's discussion of the scope of Schlack's noncompete is essentially dicta since the court found that the agreement, by its terms, did not embrace his work at ITworld.com. Using a more general definition of competition can sometimes help employers avoid such a result, but this also creates the risk of uncertainty or overbreadth. If an agreement does not set out a clear definition of competition, the court must reach its own conclusion based on the facts submitted about the nature of the two businesses. *See, e.g., Victoria's Secret Stores, Inc. v. May Dept. Stores Co.*, 157 S.W.3d 256, 261 (Mo. App. 2004) (finding that specialty lingerie store and department store that carried lingerie were not in "material competition" under terms of noncompete). How might Earthweb have redrafted its contract given the result in this case?

PROBLEM

8-2. Julie Hanaco was a biomedical engineer. While in graduate school, she worked for a university-sponsored hospital outreach program as a technical liaison for wheelchair-bound patients. Her job consisted of assessing and translating the medical needs of patients into technical requirements for the production of customized wheelchairs. After graduating, she was hired by Invocare Corp. as a product manager in its sales and marketing department with responsibility for research and development of motorized wheelchairs. Upon hire, she signed a contract prohibiting her "for a period of three years from termination of employment with Invocare, from rendering services as an officer, director, partner or employee, or otherwise providing assistance to, any competitor in the production of custom wheelchairs or other custom medical equipment."

Hanaco worked for Invocare for three years, during which time she was a key employee in the research, testing, and production of Invocare's "Mark V" motorized wheelchair. Although she was not primarily responsible for marketing, she was copied on documents containing the marketing strategy for the Mark V and related financial documentation. One month prior to the public debut of the Mark V, Hanaco left Invocare and opened her own biomedical engineering consulting company. She was immediately approached by Suncare, an Invocare competitor in the end stages of a two-year development process for a new prototype chair. Suncare wants to hire Hanaco as a technical liaison to conduct field trials with potential users of its new chair.

How would you advise Hanaco? Can she take the job with Suncare? If she declines, is she still at risk of liability by running her consulting company? Would it make a difference to know that the typical lead time for developing and producing a new prototype wheelchair is two years? Or that once a new chair debuts, it is common in the industry for competitors to "reverse engineer" the product to discern its technical components?

Note on Employee Creative Works and Inventions

The preceding cases dealt with disputes over information—the employers alleged that the workers had a competitive advantage as a result of the knowledge they obtained or the confidences they received during the course of their employment. In neither case did the employer allege that the defecting employee took his work product with him. In some instances, however, particularly in creative or technically innovative fields, parties will dispute ownership of a particular project or invention that the employee wishes to use subsequent to employment, either herself or on behalf of a competitor. Questions of ownership in such situations can be avoided through private ordering—worker and firm agree in advance how to allocate such rights. When such agreement does not exist, however, intellectual property law, including copyright and patent protection, must dictate the result. We have seen one example of a dispute between workers and firms over ownership and future use of such work product and related works in *Natkin v. Winfrey* in Chapter 1, reproduced at page 17. In that case the plaintiffs were photographers, hired to shoot photos at the *Oprah Winfrey Show*, who claimed the show had violated their copyright rights by using their photos in publicity material. This note provides a brief overview of the legal framework governing claims to such property interests.

A. Employee-Authored Creative Works

The Copyright Act of 1976 provides that copyright protection subsists "in original works of authorship fixed in any tangible medium of expression, now known or later developed, from which they can be perceived, reproduced, or otherwise communicated." 17 U.S.C. § 102. Works of authorship include literary works, artistic works, motion pictures, sound recordings, and other works including some forms of software code. The statute gives copyright owners the exclusive right to reproduce the copyrighted work; to prepare derivative works; to distribute, license, and sell the work; and, in certain circumstances, to display and perform the work. *See Id.* Subject to various qualifications, a copyright owner has the sole prerogative to exercise these rights and to exclude others from doing so during the term of the copyright, which is the life of the author plus 70 years. *See* 17 U.S.C. § 302.

Copyright ownership "vests initially in the author or authors of the work." 17 U.S.C. § 201(a). Generally, the author is the party who actually creates the copyrightable work. The statute provides an important exception, however, for "works made for hire." *See id.* at § 201(b). If the work is for hire, "the employer or other person for whom the work was prepared is considered the author" and owns the copyright, unless there is a written agreement to the contrary. *Id.* A work is for hire if it was "prepared by an employee within the scope of his or her employment" or, in some circumstances, specially ordered or commissioned by written agreement. *See* 17 U.S.C. § 101.

Thus, the operative inquiry in most copyright disputes between firm and worker is whether the worker created the work as an employee acting within the scope of employment, rather than as an independent contractor. As *Natkin* indicated, the Supreme Court set forth a nonexhaustive, 13-factor test for determining employment status for such purposes in *Community for Creative Non-Violence v. Reid*, 490 U.S. 730 (1989). The *Reid* inquiry has resulted in significant litigation, and the contours of the employment relationship therefore may be important in the many areas of the economy in which creative activity is important to business operations, including the creative arts, publishing, advertising, music, media, technology, and communications sectors.

Of course, as the statutory scheme clearly contemplates, the difficulties in distinguishing employees from independent contractors usually may be avoided by contract. The "work for hire" rule is merely the default. The status of the underlying relationship does not matter if the parties have agreed in writing to share one or more rights to the work or allocate all rights to one party. This works both ways: An "employee" can contract to retain her copyright, or an independent contractor can contract to assign it. Again, *Natkin* provides a good example: The entire dispute between the photographers and the production company over employment status could have been avoided if the parties had negotiated and signed a commission or licensing agreement clearly allocating rights regarding the photographs.

The book you are reading was written by law professors as part of their scholarly duties, and with the support of their law schools. Neither of the law schools involved has a specific policy dealing with copyrights. Do Professors Glynn, Arnow-Richman, and Sullivan own the copyright, or do Seton Hall and Denver have a claim? Who else might have an ownership interest? Look at the copyright page to determine one party's (admittedly not disinterested) views on the matter. How do you think this entity (who is neither the employee nor the employer) obtained copyright ownership?

B. Employee Inventions

Under the existing patent regime, *see* 35 U.S.C. § 101 *et seq.*, whoever invents or discovers any new, useful, and nonobvious "process, machine, manufacture, or composition of matter, or any new and useful improvement thereof" may obtain a patent for such invention or discovery, subject to various conditions. The patent holder has the right to exclude others from making, using, or selling the patented invention or discovery during the term of the patent. *See* 35 U.S.C. § 271. Federal law provides that patent rights may be assigned only if the assignment is in writing, *see* 35 U.S.C. § 261, but the enforceability of assignments in the employment context is usually governed by state law. *See, e.g., University Patents, Inc. v. Kligman,* 762 F. Supp. 1212, 1219 (E.D. Pa. 1991); *see also United States v. Dubilier Condenser Corp.,* 289 U.S. 178, 187 (1933) ("The respective rights and obligations of employer and employee, touching an invention conceived by the latter, spring from the contract of employment.").

If a person invents or discovers something patentable during employment, he or she is the presumptive owner of the invention and of the resulting patent. The operative default rule in the patent context is therefore opposite that in copyright, where, again, the employer presumptively owns employee-authored works. As with the copyright regime, however, patent law recognizes the primacy of private ordering through agreements allocating rights between worker and firm. *See Dubilier Condenser Corp.,* 289 U.S. at 187-88. Further, it shifts the default principle in one important way: Even absent an employee's outright assignment of the patent after it is obtained, the employer will own the patent if it hired the employee to invent or discover its subject. *See id.* at 187 ("One employed to make an invention, who succeeds, during his term of service, in accomplishing that task, is bound to assign to his employer any patent obtained."). When the employment contract expressly so provides, the right of assignment and the default rule coincide. *See id.* In the absence of an express agreement, however, the employer may demonstrate from the circumstances of employment an implied agreement by the employee to invent on behalf of the employer. *See id.* at 187-88. Such an agreement may be inferred from employer instructions and employee duties, among other things, although courts sometimes express reluctance to recognize such implied terms. *See, e.g., id.* at 188; *Standard Parts Co. v. Peck,* 264 U.S. 52, 58-59 (1923); *see also Scott Sys., Inc. v. Scott,* 996 P.2d 775, 778 (Colo. Ct. App. 2000) ("If an employee's job duties include the responsibility for inventing or for solving a particular problem that requires invention, any invention created by that employee during the performance of those responsibilities belongs to the employer . . . and the courts will find an implied contract obligation to assign any rights to the employer.").

Obviously then, firms that foresee substantial, innovative activity have a strong incentive to include job descriptions and assignment clauses in employment agreements that clarify ownership rights and the employee's inventive duties. Workers seeking to retain the fruits of their activity have a countervailing incentive to bargain for ownership or co-ownership rights for their inventions or to include language that limits the scope of their duties to the employer. State law often places some restrictions on employee assignments of rights to inventions; for example, some state statutes preclude assignments of inventions unrelated to the employer's business, developed entirely on the employees' own time, or for which no employer equipment or resources were used. *See, e.g.,* CAL. LAB. CODE § 2870; MINN. STAT. ANN. § 181.78; N.C. GEN. STAT. § 66-57.1 (1981); WASH. REV. CODE ANN. § 49.44.140. Nevertheless, employee assignment clauses are standard among firms engaged in research and development, and such assignments are typically enforced if reasonably tied to the nature of the employee's position.

Some employers seek further protection by including so-called "holdover" or "trailer" clauses in their employment agreements. These clauses commonly require an employee to assign to the employer patent rights for inventions created within a defined period after termination of the employment relationship if the invention is related to or conceived as a result of the employee's work for the employer. In determining whether such clauses are enforceable, courts may engage in a "reasonableness" or "balancing" inquiry akin to those applied to restrictive covenants; that is, they assess the extent to which holdover provisions may protect legitimate employer interests, prevent a former employee from seeking other employment, and adversely affect the public interest. *See, e.g., Ingersoll-Rand Co. v. Ciavatta*, 542 A.2d 879, 888 (N.J. 1988).

Even if an employee retains ownership of a patent created during the course of employment, the employer may be entitled to a limited equitable use known as a "shop right." A shop right grants — or compels the employee to grant — the employer a nonexclusive right to practice or use the employee-owned invention when the employee conceived of and perfected the invention during the hours of employment, working with the employer's materials, tools, and other resources. *See Dubilier Condenser Corp.*, 289 U.S. at 187-88; *Francklyn v. Guilford Packing Co.*, 695 F.2d 1158, 1161 (9th Cir. 1983). Some courts have taken a broader view, suggesting that a shop right will exist when, after viewing the circumstances surrounding the development of the patented invention and the inventor's activities, "the facts of a particular case demand, under principles of equity and fairness, a finding that a 'shop right' exists." *McElmurry v. Arkansas Power and Light Co.*, 995 F.2d 1576, 1582-83 (Fed. Cir. 1993). The shop right extends throughout the term of the patent, but, generally, the shop right may not be assigned to third parties. *See, e.g., Wommack v. Durham*, 715 F.2d 962, 965 (5th Cir. 1983).

For further discussion of employee creative works and inventions, and the application of copyright and patent law within the workplace, *see* Dan L. Burk, *Intellectual Property and the Firm*, 71 U. Chi. L. Rev. 3 (2004); Catherine L. Fisk, *Authors at Work: The Origins of the Work-for-Hire Doctrine*, 15 Yale J. L. & Human. 1 (2003); Robert P. Merges, *The Law and Economics of Employee Inventions*, 13 Harv. J. L. & Tech. 1 (1999).

4. Disputes over Customers and Co-workers

Hopper v. All Pet Animal Clinic, Inc.
861 P.2d 531 (Wyo. 1993)

Taylor, Justice.

[This appeal tests the enforceability of a covenant not to compete in an employment contract. The district court found that the covenant was reasonable and enjoined a veterinarian from practicing small animal medicine for three years within a five-mile radius. The veterinarian appealed.]

We hold that the covenant's three year duration imposed an unreasonable restraint of trade permitting only partial enforcement of a portion of that term of the covenant. . . .

II. Facts

Following her graduation from Colorado State University, Dr. Glenna Hopper (Dr. Hopper) began working part-time as a veterinarian at the All Pet Animal Clinic, Inc. (All Pet) in July of 1988. All Pet specialized in the care of small animals; mostly domesticated dogs and cats, and those exotic animals maintained as household pets. Dr. Hopper practiced under the guidance and direction of the President of All Pet, Dr. Robert Bruce Johnson (Dr. Johnson).

Dr. Johnson, on behalf of All Pet, offered Dr. Hopper full-time employment in February of 1989. The oral offer included a specified salary and potential for bonus earnings as well as other terms of employment. According to Dr. Johnson, he conditioned the offer on Dr. Hopper's acceptance of a covenant not to compete, the specific details of which were not discussed at the time. Dr. Hopper commenced full-time employment with All Pet under the oral agreement in March of 1989 and relocated to Laramie, discontinuing her commute from her former residence in Colorado.

A written Employment Agreement incorporating the terms of the oral agreement was finally executed by the parties on December 11, 1989. Ancillary to the provisions for employment, the agreement detailed the terms of a covenant not to compete:

> 12. This agreement may be terminated by either party upon 30 days' notice to the other party. Upon termination, Dr. Hopper agrees that she will not practice small animal medicine for a period of three years from the date of termination within 5 miles of the corporate limits of the City of Laramie, Wyoming. Dr. Hopper agrees that the duration and geographic scope of that limitation is reasonable.

The agreement was antedated to be effective to March 3, 1989.

[The parties subsequently agreed to an Addendum in 1990 which raised Hopper's salary, eliminated the bonus, and added a newly acquired corporate entity, Alpine Animal Hospital, Inc. (Alpine), Laramie, to share Hopper's services. The modified agreement reaffirmed the covenant not to compete.]

One year later, reacting to a rumor that Dr. Hopper was investigating the purchase of a veterinary practice in Laramie, Dr. Johnson asked his attorney to prepare a letter which was presented to Dr. Hopper. The letter, dated June 17, 1991, stated:

> I have learned that you are considering leaving us to take over the small animal part of Dr. Meeboer's practice in Laramie.
> When we negotiated the terms of your employment, we agreed that you could leave upon 30 days' notice, but that you would not practice small animal medicine within five miles of Laramie for a three-year period. We do not have any non-competition agreement for large-animal medicine, which therefore does not enter into the picture.
> I am willing to release you from the non-competition agreement in return for a cash buy-out. I have worked back from the proportion of the income of All-Pet and Alpine which you contribute and have decided that a reasonable figure would be $40,000.00, to

compensate the practice for the loss of business which will happen if you practice small-animal medicine elsewhere in Laramie.

If you are willing to approach the problem in the way I suggest, please let me know and I will have the appropriate paperwork taken care of.

Sincerely,
[Signed]
R. Bruce Johnson,
D.V.M.

Dr. Hopper responded to the letter by denying that she was going to purchase Dr. Meeboer's practice. Dr. Hopper told Dr. Johnson that the Employment Agreement was not worth the paper it was written on and that she could do anything she wanted to do. Dr. Johnson terminated Dr. Hopper's employment and informed her to consider the 30-day notice as having been given. . . .

[Dr. Hopper subsequently purchased a small and large animal practice within the city of Laramie. The practice grew from 368 clients at the time of purchase to approximately 950 at the time of trial, including 187 clients who were also clients of All Pet or Alpine. Small animal work contributed from 51 to 52 percent of Dr. Hopper's gross income in the practice.]

IV. Discussion. . . .

Two principles, the freedom to contract and the freedom to work, conflict when courts test the enforceability of covenants not to compete. There is general recognition that while an employer may seek protection from improper and unfair competition of a former employee, the employer is not entitled to protection against ordinary competition. . . .

A valid and enforceable covenant not to compete requires a showing that the covenant is: (1) in writing; (2) part of a contract of employment; (3) based on reasonable consideration; (4) reasonable in durational and geographical limitations; and (5) not against public policy. *A.E.P. Industries, Inc. v. McClure*, 302 S.E.2d 754, 760 (1983). Wyo. Stat. § 1-23-105 (1988). The reasonableness of a covenant not to compete is assessed based upon the facts of the particular case and a review of all of the circumstances. . . .

Wyoming has previously recognized that the legitimate interests of the employer, covenantee, which may be protected from competition include: (a) the employer's trade secrets which have been communicated to the employee during the course of employment; (b) confidential information communicated by the employer to the employee, but not involving trade secrets, such as information on a unique business method; and (c) special influence by the employee obtained during the course of employment over the employer's customers.

The enforceability of a covenant not to compete using the rule of reason analysis depends upon a determination, as a matter of law, that the promise not to compete is ancillary to the existence of an otherwise valid transaction or relationship. . . .

When Dr. Johnson made the oral promise of employment to Dr. Hopper, the specific terms of the covenant were not discussed. Dr. Johnson testified that no terms for a geographic radius or time restriction on competition were stated during formation of the oral contract of employment. Without terms and without a writing, a promise not to compete at this time failed as ancillary to the creation of the relationship.

The written Employment Agreement Dr. Hopper signed does contain a covenant not to compete which is ancillary to the previously agreed provisions for employment memorialized from the oral contract. RESTATEMENT (SECOND) OF CONTRACTS, *supra*, § 187 cmt. b recognizes that in an ongoing transaction or relationship, a promise not to compete may be made before the termination of the relationship and still be ancillary *as long as it is supported by consideration* and meets other requirements for enforceability. . . .

Wyoming has never determined whether a promise not to compete made during the employment relationship is supported merely by the consideration of continued employment or must be supported by separate contemporaneous consideration. This court's decision in *Ridley* [*v. Krout*, 180 P.2d 124 (Wyo. 1947)] offers useful insight. An employment relationship with a mechanic was formed prior to the execution of the written contract containing the employee's ancillary promise not to compete. *Ridley*. While we did not specifically address the sufficiency of the consideration, the written contract with the mechanic contained separate consideration. In addition to the promise to continue employment for a term of ten years, the employer agreed, as consideration for the promise not to compete, to teach the mechanic new skills as a locksmith and in business operation.

Authorities from other jurisdictions are not in agreement on whether continued employment provides sufficient consideration or whether separate consideration is required to create an ancillary covenant not to compete made during the existence of the relationship. *See* HOWARD A. SPECTER & MATTHEW W. FINKIN, INDIVIDUAL EMPLOYMENT LAW AND LITIGATION § 8.02 (1989) (collecting cases). We believe strong public policy favors separate consideration.

> The better view, even in the at-will relationship, is to require additional consideration to support a restrictive covenant entered into during the term of the employment. This view recognizes the increasing criticism of the at-will relationship, the usually unequal bargaining power of the parties, and the reality that the employee rarely "bargains for" continued employment in exchange for a potentially onerous restraint on the ability to earn a living.

Id., § 8.02 at 450. The separate consideration necessary to support an ancillary promise not to compete made after creation of the employment relationship would include promotion, pay raise, special training, employment benefits or other advantages for the employee.

The written Employment Agreement Dr. Hopper signed contains no evidence of separate consideration, such as a pay raise or other benefit, in exchange for the covenant not to compete. Standing alone, the covenant not to compete contained in the Employment Agreement failed due to lack of separate consideration. However, on June 1, 1990, the parties executed the Addendum to Agreement. In that agreement, Dr. Hopper accepted a pay raise of $550.00 per month. This agreement restates, by incorporation, the terms of the covenant not to compete. We hold that the Addendum to Agreement, with its pay raise, represented sufficient separate consideration supporting the reaffirmation of the covenant not to compete. Therefore, the district court's findings that the covenant was ancillary to an employment contract and that consideration was received in exchange for the covenant are not clearly erroneous. . . .

Employers are entitled to protect their business from the detrimental impact of competition by employees who, but for their employment, would not have had the ability to gain a special influence over clients or customers. . . .

The special interests of All Pet and Alpine identified by the district court as findings of fact are not clearly erroneous. Dr. Hopper moved to Laramie upon completion of her degree prior to any significant professional contact with the community. Her introduction to All Pet's and Alpine's clients, client files, pricing policies, and practice development techniques provided information which exceeded the skills she brought to her employment. While she was a licensed and trained veterinarian when she accepted employment, the additional exposure to clients and knowledge of clinic operations her employers shared with her had a monetary value for which the employers are entitled to reasonable protection. . . .

Enforcement of the practice restrictions Dr. Hopper accepted as part of her covenant not to compete does not create an unreasonable restraint of trade. While the specific terms of the covenant failed to define the practice of small animal medicine, the parties' trade usage provided a conforming standard of domesticated dogs and cats along with exotic animals maintained as household pets. As a veterinarian licensed to practice in Wyoming, Dr. Hopper was therefore permitted to earn a living in her chosen profession without relocating by practicing large animal medicine, a significant area of practice in this state. The restriction on the type of activity contained in the covenant was sufficiently limited to avoid undue hardship to Dr. Hopper while protecting the special interests of All Pet and Alpine.

In addition, as a professional, Dr. Hopper certainly realized the implications of agreeing to the terms of the covenant. While she may have doubted either her employers' desires to enforce the terms or the legality of the covenant, her actions in establishing a small animal practice violated the promise she made. In equity, she comes before the court with unclean hands. If Dr. Hopper sought to challenge the enforceability of the covenant, her proper remedy was to seek a declaratory judgment.

The public will not suffer injury from enforcement of the covenant. . . . While Dr. Hopper provided competent care to All Pet's and Alpine's clients, her services there were neither unique nor uncommon. Furthermore, the services which Dr. Hopper provided in her new practice to small animal clients were available at several other veterinary clinics within Laramie. Evidence did not challenge the public's ability to receive complete and satisfactory service from these other sources. Dr. Hopper's short term unavailability resulting from enforcement of a reasonable restraint against unfair competition is unlikely, as a matter of law, to produce injury to the public. . . .

The geographical limit contained in the covenant not to compete restricts Dr. Hopper from practicing within a five mile radius of the corporate limits of Laramie. As a matter of law, this limit is reasonable in this circumstance. The evidence presented at trial indicated that the clients of All Pet and Alpine were located throughout the county. Despite Wyoming's rural character, the five mile restriction effectively limited unfair competition without presenting an undue hardship. Dr. Hopper could, for example, have opened a practice at other locations within the county.

A durational limitation should be reasonably related to the legitimate interest which the employer is seeking to protect.

In determining whether a restraint extends for a longer period of time than necessary to protect the employer, the court must determine how much time is needed for the risk of injury to be reasonably moderated. When the restraint is for the purpose of protecting customer relationships, its duration is reasonable only if it is no longer than necessary for the employer to put a new [individual] on the job and for the new employee to have a reasonable opportunity to demonstrate his [or her] effectiveness to the customers. If a restraint on this ground is justifiable at all, it seems that a period of several months would usually be reasonable. If the selling or servicing relationship is relatively complex, a longer period may be called for. Courts seldom criticize restraints of six months or a year on the grounds of duration as such, and even longer restraints are often enforced.

[Expert testimony at trial indicated that 70 percent of veterinary clients visit a clinic more than once per year. The remaining 30 percent of the clients use the clinic at least one time per year. In addition,] Dr. Johnson estimated that at All Pet and Alpine, the average client seeks veterinarian services one and one-half times a year. . . . Dr. Johnson admitted that influence over a client disappears in an unspecified "short period of time," but expressed a view that three years was "safe." He also agreed that the number of clients possibly transferring from All Pet or Alpine to Dr. Hopper would be greatest in the first year and diminish in the second year.

We are unable to find a reasonable relationship between the three year durational requirement and the protection of All Pet's and Alpine's special interests. . . . Based on figures of client visits, a replacement veterinarian at All Pet and Alpine would be able to effectively demonstrate his or her own professionalism to virtually all of the clinics' clients within a one year durational limit. . . .

Under the formulation of the rule of reason inquiry, [in] the first Restatement of Contracts, the unreasonableness of any non-divisible term of a covenant not to compete made the entire covenant unenforceable. . . .

The conceptual difficulty of the position taken in the former Restatement of Contracts, *supra*, §518 leads to strong criticism by noted authors and the rejection of this so-called "blue pencil rule" by many courts. In very many cases the courts have held the whole contract to be illegal and void where the restraint imposed was in excess of what was reasonable and the terms to the agreement indicated no line of division that could be marked with a "blue pencil." In the best considered modern cases, however, the court has decreed enforcement as against the defendant whose breach has occurred within an area in which restriction would clearly be reasonable, even though the terms of the agreement imposed a larger and unreasonable restraint. Thus, the seller of a purely local business who promised not to open a competing store anywhere in America has been prevented by an injunction from running such a store with the same block as the one that he sold.

We believe the ability to narrow the term of a covenant not to compete and enforce a reasonable restraint permits public policy to be served in the most effective manner. Businesses function through the efforts of dedicated employees who provide the services and build the products desired by customers. Both the employer and the employee invest in success by expressing a commitment to one another in the form of a reasonable covenant not to compete. For the employer, this commitment may mean providing the employee with access to trade secrets, customer contacts or special training. These assets of the business are entitled to protection. For the employee, who covenants as part of a bargained for exchange, the covenant provides notice of the limits both parties have accepted in their relationship. The employee benefits during his tenure with the employer by his or her greater importance to the organization as a result of the exposure to the trade secrets, customer contacts or special training. When the employer-employee relationship terminates, a reasonable covenant not to compete then avoids unfair competition by the employee against the former employer and the specter, which no court would enforce, of specific performance of the employment agreement. When the parties agree to terms of a covenant, one of which is too broad, the court is permitted to enforce a narrower term which effectuates these public policy goals without arbitrarily invalidating the entire agreement between the parties and creating an uncertain business environment. In those instances where a truly unreasonable covenant operates as a restraint of trade, it will not be enforced.

. . . We, therefore, affirm the district court's conclusions of law that the type of activity and geographic limitations contained in the covenant not to compete were reasonable and enforceable as a matter of law. Because we hold that the covenant's three year durational term imposed a partially unreasonable restraint of trade, we remand for a modification of the judgment to enjoin Dr. Hopper from unfair competition for a duration of one year from the date of termination.

NOTES

1. *Consideration. All Pet* begins with a treatment of contract formalities. Generally, an offer of employment is treated as the requisite consideration for the employee's covenant not to compete. However, where the employee signs an agreement after employment commences, courts take different approaches. Some hold that continued employment is sufficient consideration for the noncompete agreement where the worker is employed at will and could otherwise be terminated. *See, e.g., Lake Land Emp. Group of Akron, LLC v. Columber*, 804 N.E.2d 27, 31-32 (Ohio 2004); *Summits 7, Inc. v. Kelly*, 886 A.2d 365, 372-73 (Vt. 2005). Others, like *All Pet*, require further consideration to support the post-hire agreement. *See, e.g., Lucht's Concrete Pumping, Inc. v. Horner*, 224 P.3d 355, 359 (Colo. App. 2009); *Poole v. Incentives Unlimited, Inc.*, 548 S.E.2d 207, 209 (S.C. 2001); *Labriola v. Pollard Group, Inc.*, 100 P.3d 791 796 (Wash. 2004). *See generally* Tracy L. Staidl, *Enforceability of Noncompetition Agreements When Employment Is At-Will: Reformulating the Analysis*, 2 EMPLOYEE RTS. & EMP. POL'Y J. 95 (1998) (summarizing approaches). Do you recognize this concept of "separate" consideration from courts' treatment of employer modifications of contractually binding handbooks? See Chapter 3.

In this case, Dr. Hopper received a pay raise upon re-executing her employment contract, which included the noncompete. How meaningful is that raise if her employment is at will and she can be fired at any time? What other types of consideration might support a post-hire noncompete? What if Dr. Johnson offered Hopper an All Pet Animal Clinic T-shirt and a free pass to a local movie theater in exchange for her signature? Would the noncompete be enforceable?

2. *Involuntarily Terminated Employees.* A related question is whether noncompetes are enforceable if the at-will employee is terminated involuntarily. Although Dr. Hopper may have been planning to leave, she was fired by Dr. Johnson. Some courts have concluded that an employer who terminates its employee forfeits the right to enforce that employee's noncompete agreement. *See, e.g., Insulation Corp. of Am. v. Brobston*, 667 A.2d 729, 735 (Pa. Super. Ct. 1995) ("The employer who fires an employee for failing to perform in a manner that promotes the employer's business interests deems the employee worthless. . . . [I]t is unreasonable as a matter of law to permit the employer to retain unfettered control over that which it has effectively discarded."). Other courts seem to disregard the manner of termination, focusing solely on the reasonableness of the restraint. *See, e.g., Roberson v. C.P. Allen Const. Co., Inc.*, 30 IER Cases 1242 (Ala. App. 2010); *Twenty Four Collection v. Keller*, 389 So. 2d 1062 (Fla. Dist. Ct. App. 1980). Yet a third approach relies on principles of good faith and fair dealing. In an omitted part of the decision, *All Pet* considered the good faith of Dr. Johnson's actions. Noting that the agreement permitted termination at will, subject to a notice requirement, the court stated:

> Without more, the terms present the potential for an unreasonable restraint of trade. For example, if an employer hired an employee at will, obtained a covenant not to compete, and then terminated the employee, without cause, to arbitrarily restrict competition, we believe such conduct would constitute bad faith. Simple justice requires that a termination by the employer of an at will employee be in good faith if a covenant not to compete is to be enforced.
>
> Under the present facts, we cannot say that the termination of Dr. Hopper occurred in bad faith. Trial testimony presented evidence of increasing tension prior to termination in the professional relationship between Dr. Johnson and Dr. Hopper. This tension, however, did not appear to result in the termination. The notice of termination was given after Dr. Hopper was confronted about her negotiations to purchase a competitive practice and after Dr. Hopper had termed the employment contract worthless. We cannot find in these facts a bad faith termination which would provide a reason to depart from the district court's finding that the contract of employment was valid.

Hopper, 861 P.2d. at 541-42; *see also Rao v. Rao*, 718 F.2d 219, 223 (7th Cir. 1983) (concluding that implied contractual covenant of good faith and fair dealing precludes employer enforcement of noncompete following unjustified termination of employee); RESTATEMENT OF EMPLOYMENT § 8.06(a) (Council Draft No. 5, Oct. 1, 2010) (adopting approach that disallows enforcement where employer "discharges the employee on a "basis that makes enforcement of the covenant inequitable"). In some situations, particularly with executive contracts, the agreement itself will specify what types of termination will give rise to the restraint, in which case the issue of enforceability turns on contract interpretation. *See, e.g., Leach v. Ford Motor Co.*, 299 F. Supp. 2d 763, 773-74 (E.D. Mich. 2004) (termination of executive's employment in context of deteriorating relationship with company did not constitute voluntary termination triggering noncompete where executive indicated unwillingness to resign absent assurance that noncompete would be waived).

3. *Negotiating a Buy-out.* Prior to termination, the employer in *All Pet* offered to release Hopper from the noncompete agreement for $40,000. Private resolution of noncompete disputes, like other legal disputes, is common, and agreeing to a "buy out" is one way to settle. Would accepting this offer have been a better choice for Dr. Hopper? Her decision to reject her employer's offer was apparently based, at least in part, on her belief that the agreement was "not worth the paper it was written on." If that was her belief, and not just a bargaining ploy, what does this tell us about the limits of private ordering? On the one hand, private resolution of noncompete disputes might achieve efficient results, as the parties themselves may be in the best position to identify an amount that compensates the employer for the value of the restraint. On the other hand, it is unlikely that results will be efficient if employees are unaware of their background rights or their employer's. Hopper was a fairly sophisticated employee—a veterinarian and a business owner with several employment options. If she did not appreciate the legal significance of her noncompete agreement, what does this mean for less educated employees?

4. *The Public Interest. All Pet* explicitly takes account of the effects of the employer's restraint on the public. As traditionally articulated, the common-law rule of reason requires the court to weigh the interest of the employer against "hardship to the promisor and the likely injury to the public." RESTATEMENT (SECOND) OF CONTRACTS § 188. However, in most cases, courts do not treat societal interest as a separate factor to be considered in the analysis; rather, the assumption is that a covenant that is reasonable in relation to a protectable interest is unlikely to be harmful to the public. Those instances where courts give societal interest distinct attention tend to involve highly specialized employees engaged in essential services. *See, e.g., Columbus Med. Serv. LLC v. Thomas*, 308 S.W.3d 368 (Tenn. Ct. App. 2009) (noncompete agreement between physical therapists and staffing company that placed therapists in residential facility for disabled was not enforceable despite employer's legitimate interests in training and goodwill where enforcement would interrupt continuity of care for vulnerable patient population); *cf. Merrill Lynch v. de Linier*, 572 F. Supp. 246, 249 (D. Ga. 1983) (noting in denying injunction to enforce noncompete that "[a] stock broker stands in a different relationship to his customers from that of other kinds of salesman [because] of the important role of the broker in protecting the financial welfare of his clients"). Other jurisdictions address public concerns by statutorily prohibiting noncompetes in certain fields, most notably medicine. *See, e.g.,* MASS. GEN. LAW ANN. 112 § 12X (declaring void any restriction on a physician's right to practice in an employment or professional agreement); 6 DEL. C. § 2707 (same). The Model Rules of Professional Conduct similarly prohibit noncompetes between lawyers. *See* MRPC 5.6. Is the protection of public choice as important of a concern with respect to lawyers as it is with respect to doctors? Or is the Model Rule simply an example of lawyers protecting themselves?

5. *Reasonableness Assessments from a Contracts Perspective.* Although judicial assessment of reasonableness is unique to noncompete law, it finds a parallel in the contract defense of unconscionability. You may recall from first-year contracts that an agreement is generally considered unconscionable when it consists of terms unreasonably favorable to one side agreed to under circumstances betraying a lack of meaningful choice on the part of the party seeking to void the agreement. *See, e.g., Williams v. Walker-Thomas*, 350 F.2d 445 (D.C. Cir. 1965); *Ingle v. Circuit City*, 328 F.3d 1165, 1170 (9th Cir. 2003). The focus of the reasonableness inquiry, however, differs from the unconscionability analysis with respect to when terms are evaluated. Most courts look at the reasonableness of the noncompete agreement as of the time of enforcement under the assumption that this approach better protects the employee. In contrast, under basic contract law issues of procedural unconscionability (the circumstances surrounding contract formation) are by definition determined as of time of agreement and an analysis of the substantive fairness of the terms is generally viewed from that vantage point as well. *See Williams*, 350 F.2d at 450; *cf.* U.C.C. § 2-302 (the basic test [of unconscionability] is whether . . . the clauses involved are so one-sided as to be unconscionable under the circumstances existing at the time of the making of the contract).

Another difference is who bears the burden of proof in establishing the fairness of the restraint. Most courts require the employer to demonstrate the reasonableness of its noncompete. *See, e.g., Omniplex World Services Corp. v. U.S. Investigations Services, Inc., et al.*, 618 S.E. 2d 340, 342 (Va. 2005). This is unusual since defendants typically bear the burden of proving any defense to contract, such as unconscionability, once the plaintiff establishes a validly formed contract. Consider the evidence presented as to the reasonableness of the *All Pet* restraint. Do you think allocation of burden of proof was significant in determining the result? Might it be significant to judicial determinations of reasonableness in other cases involving less sophisticated employees with fewer resources?

6. *Reasonable in Relation to What?* Notice that whether a restraint is reasonable with respect to each of the relevant considerations — duration, geography, and definition of competition — depends on an assessment of the value and scope of the particular interest the employer seeks to protect, in this case All Pet's customer base. It is for this reason that the *All Pet* parties sought expert testimony about patient relationships in the veterinary industry. Another common consideration in assessing reasonableness is the nature and extent of the work the former employee performed. This is relevant for purposes of ensuring that the noncompete does not restrain the employee other than in relying on information or contacts he gained on the job. Thus, in the case of an employer's legitimate interest in customers, a restraint that prohibits the employee from competing only in the region where he had customer contact or represented the employer is more likely to be found reasonable than one based broadly, albeit accurately, on the geographic scope of the employer's business. *See, e.g., King v. Head Start Family Hair Salons*, 886 So. 2d 769 (Ala. 2004) (finding noncompete prohibiting hairdresser from working within two miles of any of employer's salons overbroad and modifying geographic scope to a two-mile radius surrounding the location where employee worked); *Robert S. Weiss & Assoc., Inc. v. Wiederlight*, 546 A.2d 216, 220 (Conn. 1988) (provision in noncompete prohibiting commercial insurance salesman from competing within 10 miles of the city where he was employed, but excluding nearby metropolitan area where employer did business, "demonstrated the plaintiff's caution in avoiding an overly broad geographic restriction" and was enforceable as written).

7. *Industry Standards of Reasonableness.* Might industry practices surrounding the use of noncompetes be relevant to the reasonableness inquiry? In *UZ Engineered Products v. Midwest Motor Supply*, 770 N.E.2d 1068 (Ohio. Ct. App. 2001), a salesperson for a metal parts manufacturer accepted employment at a competitor in violation of his two-year noncompetition and nondisclosure agreement. In support of its argument that the agreement was reasonable in duration, the former employer introduced a copy of the noncompete agreement used by the competitor with its own employees, which also contained a two-year restriction. *Id.* at 392-93. In the commercial context, courts routinely look at trade usages and other industry practices in interpreting contracts. *See* U.C.C. § 2-202 (2001) (providing that a final written agreement may be supplemented by usages of trade). Are there reasons to give similar consideration to noncompete practices common to a particular industry? Or could it cut the other way? That is, could the industry's pervasive use of noncompetes be a factor against enforcement because of the generalized effect on competition?

8. *Judicial Responses to Overbroad Agreements.* As *All Pet* illustrates, jurisdictions vary in their response to noncompetes that satisfy the protectable interest requirement but are overbroad in scope. As the First Circuit explains:

> Courts presented with restrictive covenants containing unenforceable provisions have taken three approaches: (1) the "all or nothing" approach, which would void the restrictive covenant entirely if any part is unenforceable, (2) the "blue pencil" approach, which enables the court to enforce the reasonable terms provided the covenant remains grammatically coherent once its unreasonable provisions are excised, and (3) the "partial enforcement" approach, which reforms and enforces the restrictive covenant to the extent it is reasonable, unless the "circumstances indicate bad faith or deliberate overreaching" on the part of the employer.

Ferrofluidics Corp. v. Advanced Vacuum Components, 968 F.2d 1463 (1st Cir. 1992). Which approach does *All Pet* adopt? What are the relative advantages and disadvantages of each? Consider *Team Environmental Services v. Addison*, 2 F.3d 124, 127 (5th Cir. 1993), in which the court expressed concern over the *in terrorem* effects of overbroad agreements:

> An employee barred from plying his trade within 200 miles of his home would be far more hesitant to leave his job than if the proscription affected a substantially smaller area. This increased hesitancy obviously impacts the bargaining relationship with the current employer. Were courts to reform and enforce agreements like those at bar, employers would be free routinely to present employees with grossly overbroad covenants not to compete. While the employer presumptively would know that the agreement would be enforced only to the limit of the law, the employee likely would not.

Id. at 127. Scholars have raised similar concerns. *See, e.g.*, Rachel Arnow-Richman, *Cubewrap Contracts and Worker Mobility: The Dilution of Employee Bargaining Power Via Standard Form Noncompetes*, 2006 MICH. ST. L. REV. 963; Charles A. Sullivan, *The Puzzling Persistence of Unenforceable Contract Terms*, 70 OHIO ST. L. J. 1127 (2009). On the other hand, refusal to enforce any form of restraint in the face of an overbroad agreement penalizes those employers who draft their agreements in good faith, denying even their legitimate rights. As one court put it, "The man who wildly claims that he owns all the cherry trees in the country cannot be denied protection of the orchard in his backyard." *Sidco Paper Co. v. Aaron*, 351 A.2d 250 (Pa. 1976). The proposed Restatement of Employment Law would allow deletion or modification of overbroad covenants if "the employer lacked a reasonable good faith basis for believing the covenant was enforceable," and overbroad alone, "if sufficiently egregious" permits such finding. § 8.08 (Council Draft No. 5, Oct. 1, 2010).

PROBLEMS

8-3. Reexamine the noncompete agreement in Problem 8-2 in light of *All Pet*'s treatment of reasonableness. Assuming Julie Hanaco's former employer has a legitimate interest in protecting the technical and marketing information related to its new wheelchair, is its restraint reasonable in scope? In what respects — duration, geographic scope, and definition of competition — might Hanaco argue it is overbroad? If she were to prevail on such an argument, how would a court respond under each of the three approaches to overbroad agreements discussed above? How would you recommend the employer redraft its agreement to ensure that it is enforceable as written in the maximum number of jurisdictions?

8-4. KFN is a national executive search firm that helps Fortune 500 companies recruit and hire key employees. KFN employs a large number of recruiters whose job it is to pair "prospects" and "talent," that is, to identify job opportunities at top companies and find suitably experienced job seekers to fill them.

Recruiters spend significant time cultivating relationships with top personnel at the "prospect" companies, learning about the operations of the company and getting to know its work culture and hiring patterns in order to maintain that company's consistent business. Recruiters also spend time researching "talent," which includes getting to know candidates who have registered with KFN as well as cold-calling employed executives to see if they might be interested in a job change. Frequently, recruiters develop an area of specialty, such as placing executives with expertise in technology, or servicing companies seeking talent with experience in emerging markets. All of the information that KFN gleans about both its prospects and talent is kept in an extensive database that includes general information about the company or individual, a history of the services KFN has provided to the company or individual, and the recruiters' ideas and impressions about how to best market the individual or assist the company.

Up until now, KFN has never required its recruiters to sign any written agreement upon hire, largely because it feared such an agreement would impede its ability to hire experienced recruiters who bring prior contacts with them to the firm. However, it is revisiting the issue due to recent publicity about large-scale employee defections and data stealing in the job placement industry. Suppose KFN hires you. Would you advise the firm to use a contract containing restrictive covenants? What other practices and precautions would you recommend? If KFN asks you to draft a form contract for use with new recruiters, what would it look like?

C. NEW FRONTIERS IN NONCOMPETITION LITIGATION AND PRIVATE ORDERING

As the previous materials suggest, the laws surrounding competitive behavior of employees offers little certainty, even where the parties have planned for possible post-employment competition through contract. However conscientiously an employer may have drafted a noncompete agreement, it is often unclear whether a court will deem its underlying interests protectable and the terms of the restraint reasonable at the time enforcement is sought. How do parties (and lawyers) manage this type of uncertainty? For employers, one approach is to devise new drafting techniques, or even forge new types of contractual instruments, in an effort to address (or circumvent) judicial hostility to standard noncompetition covenants. Employees, on the other hand, may have limited ability to influence this process. Unless they are exceptionally skilled or highly sought after, employees will often have to accept the terms provided by employers. However, employees may be able to get a leg up in avoiding enforcement of such agreements by seeking to channel disputes into employee-friendly fora, resulting in some cases in a "race to the courthouse." This in turn has led employers to adopt second-order risk management techniques, such as the inclusion of choice-of-law and choice-of-forum clauses in their agreements. The variety of emerging strategies, in both the litigation and drafting contexts, are discussed in this section.

1. The Race to the Courthouse

Advanced Bionics Corp. v. Medtronic, Inc.
59 P. 3d 231 (Cal. 2002)

CHIN, J. . . .

Medtronic, Inc. (Medtronic), a Minnesota corporation with headquarters in Fridley, Minnesota, manufactures implantable neurostimulation devices used to treat chronic pain. In 1995, Medtronic hired plaintiff Mark Stultz in Minnesota as a senior product specialist responsible for spinal cord stimulator lead wires. He was soon promoted to senior product manager in the "Neurostimulation-Pain Division," where he was responsible for managing Medtronic's neurostimulation products.

[Stultz signed the "Medtronic Employee Agreement," which contained a two-year covenant not to compete after employment termination. The Agreement also] included a choice-of-law provision: "The validity, enforceability, construction and interpretation of this Agreement shall be governed by the laws of the state in which the Employee was last employed by Medtronic." For the duration of his employment, Stultz worked for Medtronic's Minnesota office.

On June 7, 2000, Stultz resigned from Medtronic and went to California to work for Advanced Bionics Corporation (Advanced Bionics), a Delaware corporation with headquarters in Sylmar, California. The company, a competitor of Medtronic's, develops and manufactures implantable medical devices used to restore hearing to the profoundly deaf. It hired Stultz as a director of business development to market its own spinal cord stimulation device. On the same day, in Los Angeles County Superior Court, Stultz and Advanced Bionics sued Medtronic for declaratory relief, alleging that Medtronic's covenant not to compete and choice-of-law provisions violate California's law and public policy and are void under Business and Professions Code section 16600. Section 16600 provides in pertinent part that "every contract by which anyone is restrained from engaging in a lawful profession, trade, or business of any kind is to that extent void."

[On June 8, 2000, Stultz and Advanced Bionics notified Medtronic that they were applying for a temporary restraining order to enjoin Medtronic from "taking any action, other than in this court, to enforce its non-competition agreement." Medtronic immediately removed the action to federal court, thus avoiding the scheduled hearing on the TRO. The next day, June 9, it filed an action in Minnesota state court alleging claims for breach of contract against Stultz and tortious interference with contract against Advanced Bionics. Medtronic then obtained a TRO from the Minnesota court enjoining Advanced Bionics from hiring Stultz in any competitive role and barring them "[f]rom making any motion or taking any action or obtaining any order or direction from any court that [would] prevent or interfere in any way with [the Minnesota court's] determining whether it should determine all or any part of the claims alleged in [the Minnesota] lawsuit"

Within a week, the federal court remanded the California action to state court, finding that removal was improper because Medtronic, a Minnesota company, purported to rely on diversity jurisdiction, even though it knew Stultz was still a Minnesota resident. Once back in state court in California, Medtronic moved to dismiss or stay the California action because of the pending Minnesota case. The trial court denied the motion, thus leaving competing actions in both California and Minnesota.]

On August 3, 2000, the Minnesota court issued a preliminary injunction that was similar to its TRO, except it did not include the provision restraining Stultz and Advanced Bionics from pursuing other litigation; it simply restricted Stultz's activities as an Advanced Bionics employee. [Stultz and Advanced Bionics appealed in Minnesota.]

On August 8, 2000, Stultz and Advanced Bionics applied ex parte to the California court for a TRO and order to show cause re preliminary injunction to prohibit Medtronic from taking any further steps in the Minnesota action. The court granted the application, finding there was a "substantial chance" that Medtronic would "go to the Minnesota court [and] attempt to undercut the California court's jurisdiction." Medtronic was "restrained and enjoined from taking any action whatsoever, other than in this Court, to enforce [its covenant not to compete] against . . . Stultz or to otherwise restrain . . . Stultz from working for Advanced Bionics in California, including but not limited to making any appearance, filing any paper, participating in any proceeding, posting any bond, or taking any other action in the second-filed [Minnesota] lawsuit. . . ."

On August 16, 2000, the Minnesota court amended its August 3 preliminary injunction (purportedly nunc pro tunc), stating it had "failed to incorporate language enjoining [Stultz and Advanced Bionics] from obtaining relief in another court that would effectively stay or limit [the Minnesota] action." The court added a provision enjoining Stultz and Advanced Bionics "from seeking any interim or temporary relief from any other court that would effectively stay, limit or restrain [the Minnesota] action," and ordered them to "move to vacate and rescind the August 8, 2000 [TRO] obtained in the California action and refrain from seeking any relief in that action that stays or restrains [the Minnesota] action in any way."[4]

Stultz and Advanced Bionics informed the Los Angeles County Superior Court that the Minnesota court had directed them to seek vacation of the TRO. The superior court refused to vacate its order. . . .

[On appeal, the Second District Court of Appeal held that] (1) the trial court's TRO was necessary and proper to protect plaintiffs' interests pending final disposition of the action . . . (2) notwithstanding the choice-of-law provision in the Agreement, the case would be decided under California law; and (3) because California law would apply and the California action was filed first, California courts should decide the dispute. . . . This appeal followed.

. . . Antisuit TRO's Must Be Granted with Restraint

Although Medtronic acknowledges that, under certain circumstances, a California court has the power to issue a TRO prohibiting a party from taking action in a case pending in another jurisdiction that would interfere with the California court's proceedings, it asserts that the Court of Appeal here erred in concluding

---

4. [T]he Minnesota Court of Appeal affirmed the preliminary TRO, rejecting Stultz and Advanced Bionics contention that the trial court erred by failing to defer to the "first-filed" California action and observing that the "first-filed rule" is not intended to be applied in a rigid or inflexible manner. The court concluded that "Minnesota . . . has a strong interest in having contracts executed in this state enforced in accordance with the parties' expectations."

that the TRO entered in this action was proper. Medtronic claims that the Court of Appeal did not place sufficient emphasis on principles of judicial restraint and comity that strongly inform against issuance of the TRO in this case.

We recognize this is a case of first impression, but note that nearly 100 years ago, this court observed that "[t]he courts of this state have the same power to restrain persons within the state from prosecuting actions in either domestic or foreign jurisdictions which courts of equity have elsewhere." (*Spreckels v. Hawaiian Com. etc. Co.* (1897) [49 P. 35].)

. . . Although *Spreckels* recognized that a California court might have power to issue a TRO to prevent multiple proceedings, and implicitly recognized a forum court's power to restrain proceedings, the court never suggested, implicitly or otherwise, that a court may ignore additional proceedings that arise after the initial action commences. The significant principles of judicial restraint and comity inform that we should use that power sparingly.

Several sister state decisions guide our reasoning. These decisions hold that even if a sister state applies different substantive law than the forum state, that fact alone does not justify the issuance of a TRO enjoining proceedings in the sister state. . . .

. . . The possibility that one action may lead to a judgment first and then be applied as res judicata in another action "is a natural consequence of parallel proceedings in courts with concurrent jurisdiction, and not reason for an injunction." (*Auerbach v. Frank* (D.C. 1996) 685 A.2d 404, 407.) "[T]he possibility of an 'embarrassing race to judgment' or potentially inconsistent adjudications does not outweigh the respect and deference owed to independent foreign proceedings." (*Ibid.*)

Stultz and Advanced Bionics . . . contend that although we should pay deference to foreign state proceedings, California's strong public policy against noncompetition agreements under section 16600 weighs against allowing the action to proceed in Minnesota and provides the exceptional circumstance that warrants our upholding the California court's TRO. As they observe, the law protects Californians, and ensures "that every citizen shall retain the right to pursue any lawful employment and enterprise of their choice." (*Metro Traffic Control, Inc. v. Shadow Traffic Network* (1994) 27 Cal. Rptr. 2d 573.) It protects "the important legal right of persons to engage in businesses and occupations of their choosing." (*Morlife, Inc. v. Perry* (1997) 66 Cal. Rptr. 2d 731.) We have even called noncompetition agreements illegal. (*See, e.g., Armendariz v. Foundation Health Psychcare Services, Inc.* (2000) [6 P.3d 669].) Therefore, according to Stultz and Advanced Bionics, because the noncompetition provision in the Agreement is broad in application and forbids Stultz from working for any competitor on a competitive product for two years after employment termination, it is likely that a California court would conclude the provision is void under section 16600.

We agree that California has a strong interest in protecting its employees from noncompetition agreements under section 16600. But even assuming a California court might reasonably conclude that the contractual provision at issue here is void in this state, this policy interest does not, under these facts, justify issuance of a TRO against the parties in the Minnesota court proceedings. A parallel action in a different state presents sovereignty concerns that compel California courts to use judicial restraint when determining whether they may properly issue a TRO against parties pursuing an action in a foreign jurisdiction.

The comity principle also supports our conclusion. Comity is based on the belief " 'that the laws of a state have no force, *proprio vigore*, beyond its territorial limits, but the laws of one state are frequently permitted by the courtesy of another to operate in the latter for the promotion of justice, where neither that state nor its citizens will suffer any inconvenience from the application of the foreign law. This courtesy, or comity, is established, not only from motives of respect for the laws and institutions of the foreign countries, but from considerations of mutual utility and advantage.' . . . 'The mere fact that state action may have repercussions beyond state lines is of no judicial significance so long as the action is not within that domain which the Constitution forbids.' " (*Estate of Lund* (1945) 159 P.2d 643). The comity principle requires that we exercise our power to enjoin parties in a foreign court sparingly, in line with the policy of judicial restraint discussed above.

Notwithstanding comity principles, Advanced Bionics contends that the first-filed rule provides alternative support for the Court of Appeal's decision to uphold the TRO and to enjoin the litigants from proceeding in Minnesota. We disagree. [The first-filed rule in California applies only to two California courts; it] "was never meant to apply where the two courts involved are not courts of the same sovereignty. Restraining a party from pursuing an action in a court of foreign jurisdiction involves delicate questions of comity and therefore 'requires that such action be taken only with care and great restraint.' " (*Compagnie des Bauxites de Guinea v. Ins. Co. of N. Am.* (3d Cir. 1981) 651 F.2d 877, 887, fn. 10.)

We conclude, therefore, that the Court of Appeal erred in upholding the TRO issued against the parties in the Minnesota proceedings. California courts have the same power as other courts to issue orders that assist in protecting their jurisdiction. However, enjoining proceedings in another state requires an exceptional circumstance that outweighs the threat to judicial restraint and comity principles. As explained, the circumstances of this case do not provide sufficient justification to warrant our court's issuing injunctive orders against parties pursuing the Minnesota litigation. . . .

We hold that the trial court improperly issued the TRO enjoining Medtronic from proceeding in the Minnesota action. We also conclude, however, that the Minnesota action does not divest California of jurisdiction, and Advanced Bionics remains free to litigate the California action unless and until Medtronic demonstrates to the Los Angeles County Superior Court that any Minnesota judgment is binding on the parties. . . .

BROWN, J., concurring.

I agree with most of Justice Moreno's concurrence. . . . I do not, however, agree with the implication in Justice Moreno's opinion that a choice-of-law analysis is irrelevant to determining whether to enjoin parties from litigating a dispute in a foreign jurisdiction. If a careful choice-of-law analysis indicates that the foreign jurisdiction's law applies to the parties' dispute, I think that fact weighs heavily in favor of permitting the foreign proceeding to go forward unimpeded. . . .

This case involves a contract dispute between Medtronic, Inc. (Medtronic), a Minnesota corporation, and Mark Stultz, a former Medtronic employee who worked for Medtronic in Minnesota and, at that time, resided in Minnesota. The parties executed the employment contract in Minnesota, and the choice-of-law provision in the contract designates Minnesota law. Under the terms of the contract, Stultz agreed not to work for a competitor of Medtronic for two years after termination of his employment with Medtronic, and that provision is enforceable under Minnesota law, though not under California law. California had absolutely no interest in this matter until Stultz relocated to California, terminated his employment with Medtronic, and began employment with Advanced Bionics Corporation, a Delaware corporation with headquarters in California. Under these circumstances, where almost all the geographic points of contact in the dispute lie in Minnesota, California's concededly strong interest in promoting competition by encouraging the free movement of personnel laterally across an industry is not " 'materially greater' " than Minnesota's countervailing interest in enforcing bargained-for restrictions on that free movement. (*Nedlloyd Lines B.V. v. Superior Court* (1992) 834 P.2d 1148.) Therefore, the contract's choice-of-law provision, designating Minnesota law, controls. Stultz, having enjoyed the benefits of his contract with Medtronic, should not be free to avoid his side of the agreement and thereby cancel some of the value for which Medtronic legitimately bargained. . . .

Relocating to California may be, for some people, a chance for a fresh start in life, but it is not a chance to walk away from valid contractual obligations, claiming California policy as a protective shield. We are not a political safe zone vis-à-vis our sister states, such that the mere act of setting foot on California soil somehow releases a person from the legal duties our sister states recognize. Rather, we give full faith and credit to the laws of our sister states, and in a case such as this one, I think doing so requires California courts to apply Minnesota law. Moreover, that conclusion is highly relevant to determining whether the trial court's antisuit injunction in this case was appropriate. I see no reason for a trial court to enjoin parties from litigating in a foreign jurisdiction when the foreign jurisdiction's law applies to the dispute and therefore the task of the California courts will ultimately be to discern how the enjoined proceeding would have come out.

MORENO, J., concurring. . . .

In determining which criteria courts of this state should apply when deciding whether to issue an antisuit injunction, I agree with the majority that considerations of comity and judicial restraint should be paramount. . . . I would therefore adopt the restrictive approach [, favored by some federal courts, under which] courts should only issue antisuit injunctions in two situations: if "necessary to protect the jurisdiction of the enjoining court, or to prevent the litigant's evasion of the important public policies of the forum." [N]either exception applies in this case.

[T]he parallel proceeding initiated by Medtronic in Minnesota does not threaten the jurisdiction of the California courts. At the time when the California court issued the TRO at issue here, enjoining Medtronic "from taking any action whatsoever, other than in this Court," the Minnesota court had issued a preliminary injunction restricting Stultz's activities as an Advanced Bionics Corporation employee but not restraining the parties from pursuing other litigation. After the California court issued the antisuit TRO, the Minnesota court revised its preliminary injunction. Notably, however, the Minnesota court did not enjoin the action from proceeding in a California court; instead, the Minnesota injunction was *defensive*; it enjoined the parties "from obtaining relief in another court that would effectively stay or limit [the Minnesota] action." [Unlike situations where the foreign proceedings are designed to rob the alternative court of its jurisdiction by carving out exclusive jurisdiction for the foreign court], the Minnesota injunction did not seek to terminate the litigation in California, but was instituted merely to protect the jurisdiction of the Minnesota court. Further, as courts applying the restrictive approach have held, the possibility that Medtronic may receive a more favorable ruling in a Minnesota court does not threaten the jurisdiction of a California court. . . .

[As for use of an antisuit injunction to protect an important public policy of the forum state, this] exception does not allow for an injunction merely because two states may apply different substantive laws. . . .

The crucial determination is whether the suit was filed in another state for the purpose of *evading* the important policies of the forum state. Such a purpose may be inferred, for example, if neither party has ties to the sister state in which a parallel suit has been initiated. Courts have found that a party's connection to the foreign jurisdiction minimizes the possibility that such a suit was filed for purposes of evading the forum state's law. . . .

In the present case, the issue is not simply whether California has a strong public policy against noncompetition agreements. Instead, the question is whether Medtronic initiated its action in Minnesota for the purpose of *evading* California's public policy. Based on the facts of this case, I conclude that Medtronic did not institute its suit in Minnesota to evade California law. Medtronic is a Minnesota corporation. Medtronic entered into an employment contract with Stultz, a Minnesota resident, in Minnesota. The contract contained a choice-of-law provision that stated: "The validity, enforceability, construction and interpretation of this Agreement shall be governed by the laws of the state in which the Employee was last employed by Medtronic." Stultz worked for Medtronic's Minnesota office for the duration of his employment. Based on these significant ties to a Minnesota forum, as well as the choice-of-law clause designating Minnesota as the chosen forum, I cannot conclude that Medtronic filed suit in Minnesota for the purpose of evading California public policy. . . .

NOTES

1. *Civil Procedure Dream or Nightmare?* Depending on your view of Civil Procedure, *Advanced Bionics* is either an enormous amount of fun or incredibly confusing. It has everything: parallel actions in two states, TROs, removal, interlocutory appeals, comity, choice of law, and so on. But driving all of this seems to be a simple concern of both parties — having the case decided on home turf. Why is it so important to Stuntz and Advanced Bionics that California decide the case? Why is Medtronic so determined to have a Minnesota court hear it?

2. *Choice-of-Forum Clauses.* If Medtronic cared so much about litigating its rights in Minnesota, why didn't it include in its contract a choice-of-forum clause specifying that claims could be pursued only in Minnesota, rather than merely a choice-of-law clause? You might have run into choice-of-forum clauses in Civil Procedure in *Carnival Cruise Lines v. Shute*, 499 U.S. 585 (1991), which upheld a Florida forum clause for a cruise line despite the difficulties litigating in that forum caused the plaintiffs, who were citizens of Washington. The Court found the clause valid under federal law even though plaintiffs had boarded the ship in California, the injury occurred in the waters off Mexico, and the clause was clearly adhesive (it was printed on the back of the cruise ticket).

Litigants' strategies with respect to both choice of law and choice of forum are inextricably intertwined. The Stultz/Advanced Bionics argument against enforcing the Minnesota choice-of-law clause was apparently that, if California public policy prohibited restraints of trade, employers should not be able to end run that prohibition by specifying that some other body of law governed. Obviously, however, a California court is more likely to be persuaded by that argument than is a court in another jurisdiction. This explains the race to the courthouse — while choice of law was what mattered, the validity of the choice-of-law clause likely depended on which forum heard the case.

Suppose the contract *had* contained a choice-of-forum clause limiting actions to Minnesota courts. Would this have solved Medtronic's problems? The enforceability of such clauses, like choice-of-law clauses, is a matter of state contract law. Couldn't Stultz and Advanced Bionics still have sued in California arguing that, under the circumstances, this clause also was invalid because, like the choice-of-law clause, it represented an attempt to frustrate California public policy? For more on the stakes and implications of such interjurisdictional disputes, *see* Timothy P. Glynn, *Interjurisdictional Competition in Enforcing Noncompetition Agreements: Regulatory Risk Management and the Race to the Bottom*, 65 WASH. & LEE L. REV. 1381 (2008).

3. *Odd Planning.* The Medtronic choice-of-law clause provided that the contract "shall be governed by the laws of the state in which the Employee was last employed by Medtronic," which in this case was Minnesota. Is this a good way to draft a clause? It certainly does not guarantee any particular jurisdiction's law will apply. Even if, at the time of drafting, Medtronic had operations only in Minnesota, doesn't this clause create potential problems down the road should it expand to other states? Why do you think it chose this language?

4. *No Holds Barred in the Race to the Courthouse?* After the California case had been "unremoved" from federal court and was back in California state court, Medtronic moved to have it dismissed or stayed because of the pending Minnesota suit. But, of course, the California suit had been filed *before* the Minnesota suit, and any delay in California was due to Medtronic's failed attempt at removal to federal court for the "improper purpose" of avoiding a ruling on the pending TRO. As the lawyer for Medtronic, would you have had the audacity to make a motion to dismiss on these grounds after the case returned to state court?

5. *What's Really Going On?* How important is the fact that Stultz/Advanced Bionics got to the courthouse first? That move may have given them certain procedural advantages in the injunction game, but isn't the real question which of the two jurisdictions has the stronger interest in the case? From Medtronic's perspective, the more "natural" jurisdiction is Minnesota, where the contracting parties were located at all relevant times — both at the time of contract formation and during the course of the employment relationship. Only by bringing a declaratory judgment action did Stultz/Advanced Bionics bring California into the picture. On the other hand, California is the jurisdiction where the alleged breach has occurred, and ultimately the effects of any judgment will be felt there. Maybe there is no "natural" forum.

Interjurisdictional tangles like this are especially likely where one state departs radically from the law operative in other states, as is the case with California's restrictive approach to noncompetition clauses. *Advanced Bionics* simply reflects the collision between the public policy of most states (here, Minnesota), which permit such clauses, and California, which does not. While one could argue that Minnesota has more of an interest in the underlying contract than California, giving effect to Minnesota's public policy means cutting off a California business — Advanced Bionics — from highly valued workers, and thus disadvantaging it in the interstate marketplace in which it seeks to compete.

6. *The Rose Bowl: California v. Minnesota.* The Minnesota court preliminarily enjoined Stultz from competing but did not, initially at least, enjoin Stultz and Advanced Bionics from pursuing their California action. Had this situation continued, the race would have become not a race to the courthouse but rather a race to judgment. That is, Stultz could not engage in competitive employment with Advanced Bionics pending a final judgment (on penalty of contempt), and the first judgment entered would, as a matter of full faith and credit, bind the second court. Thus, Minnesota is leading at this point in the game by virtue of issuing the preliminary injunction in favor of Medtronic; but California could still prevail by deciding the case first. For example, if the California court entered summary judgment for Stultz and Advanced Bionics (disposing of all issues), that judgment would be binding on Minnesota, which would in theory have to dissolve the injunction.

But no one seems content with this scenario. As the second half opens, Stultz and Advanced Bionics (1) appeal the preliminary injunction issued by the Minnesota court, and (2) obtain an order from the California court precluding Medtronic from proceeding in Minnesota, an order that is broad enough to preclude Medtronic from opposing the Minnesota appeal! At this point, California seems to be winning, but Minnesota responds with a razzle-dazzle play—amending its order *nunc pro tunc* to preclude Stultz and Advanced Bionics from getting the order that they had already gotten. At this point, not only are the two states tied, but all parties seem to be in contempt of some court. Not surprisingly, when informed of the Minnesota court order, the California court refused to budge.

One doesn't have to be a sophisticated lawyer to find this situation more than a little absurd. In fact, maybe only sophisticated attorneys wouldn't find this absurd. But, other than the requirement that states give full faith and credit to final judgments of other states, nothing in our federal system prevents situations like this from arising. In theory, antisuit injunctions, like the one issued by the California trial court, offer one "solution" to this problem, but the California Supreme Court is clearly unhappy with this approach. While it affirms the power of its courts to issue such injunctions, it finds that principles of comity sharply limit its ability to exercise that power. Even the risk of frustrating a strong California public policy—prohibiting restraints on employee competition—is not enough, and certainly the mere fact that a party filed first in California does not suffice. Do you agree? Do you think Minnesota would also agree as to its own power to issue antisuit injunction?

7. *Who Wins in Overtime?* Notice that the court's decision does not really resolve the underlying issues. Following *Advanced Bionics*, Medtronic's pursuit of its case in Minnesota is permissible, but the California court on remand might find the noncompetition clause to be invalid as against California public policy. So we seem to be back to the race to judgment situation—whoever gets a final judgment first wins.

Or maybe not. While the full faith and credit clause requires a court to respect a *judgment* entered by a sister state, state courts are rarely required to enforce *injunctions* entered by sister states. *See Baker by Thomas v. GMC*, 522 U.S. 222 (1998). *See generally* Polly J. Price, *Full Faith and Credit and the Equity Conflict*, 84 VA. L. REV. 747 (1998). This might mean that a Minnesota injunction against Stultz and Advanced Bionics will not be enforced in California, suggesting that, as long as Stultz doesn't visit Minnesota again, the Minnesota judgment will be a nullity. Note that the Minnesota court could issue a money judgment that California would be compelled to enforce, but proving damages in cases such as this, not to mention getting them from an employee, is notoriously difficult. And the Minnesota judgment would be preclusive in California, so Stultz and Advanced Bionics could not recover against Medtronic.

If there is no way for Medtronic to win the war, even if it prevails in some important battles, perhaps it should rethink the way it manages the risk of employee competition by a geographically mobile worker. It might, for example, consider utilizing other risk management techniques such as including arbitration clauses in its employment contracts. Such clauses will be addressed in detail in Chapter 13. Nevertheless, it is worth noting that the utility of an arbitration provision might be limited in important respects. An arbitrator may not have the ability to craft the type of relief Medtronic is seeking, and, even if it could, Medtronic might face obstacles in attempting to enforce the arbitral ruling. Maybe it would make more sense to adopt a different type of contract all together. For instance, some employers use compensation — through stock options, deferred compensation, or pay-back agreements — to create incentives for employees to remain with the company rather than going to a competitor. Some examples of these approaches follow.

2. Innovations in Contract Drafting

Heder v. City of Two Rivers
295 F.3d 777 (7th Cir. 2002)

EASTERBROOK, Cir. J.

After the City of Two Rivers decided that all of its firefighters must be certified as paramedics, the City and the firefighters' union agreed [to compensate the firefighters at half of their regular hourly rate for time spent in paramedic training]. The deal between the City and the union included a 3% increase in the wages of firefighters who held certifications, plus an undertaking that any firefighter leaving the City's employ within the next three years would reimburse the City for the cost of the training, which would give each firefighter a portable credential. Two and a half years after beginning his training, Heder quit. Two Rivers withheld all of Heder's pay from his last two pay periods. Heder filed suit under the [Fair Labor Standards Act ("FLSA")], and the City counterclaimed for the remainder of the money that it believes Heder owes under its memorandum of agreement with the union.

[The court first addressed Heder's FLSA claim. The City] concedes that Heder was entitled to compensation that the FLSA specifies as a statutory floor below which no contract may go. That means, in particular, that Heder was entitled to at least the statutory minimum wage for his final two pay periods (leaving the City to collect any residue as an ordinary creditor) and that Heder is entitled to time and a half for any overtime hours for which the FLSA requires that premium. But the parties do not agree on what this means in practice, because the firefighters do not work an ordinary 40-hour week. [Based on the way the City calculated work time, the City was required to pay time and a half for all hours over 204 per 27-day period, even if some of those hours were devoted to training.]

Next we must decide whether the City has a good claim for reimbursement of at least some outlays.

Heder depicts a repayment obligation as a covenant not to compete that is invalid under WIS. STAT. § 103.465. The district judge adopted this characterization; we do not, because in Wisconsin (as in other states) a covenant not to compete must be linked to competition. An agreement to repay Two Rivers if a firefighter goes to work for a rival fire department would be treated as a covenant not to compete. But the agreement between Two Rivers and the firefighters' union does not restrict Heder's ability to compete against the City after leaving its employ. The obligation is unconditional: a firefighter departing before three years have expired must repay training costs even if he goes back to school, changes occupation, or retires. Competition has nothing to do with the matter.

According to Heder, Wisconsin would act as if this were a covenant not to compete, on the ground that repayment induces "involuntary servitude" that is more onerous than the agreements explicitly regulated under § 103.465. Yet this is not what the Supreme Court of Wisconsin said in [*Union Central Life Insurance Co. v. Balistrieri*, 120 N.W.2d 126 (1963)]): there it limited application of § 103.465 to agreements that condition repayment on going to work for the ex-employer's rival. True enough, as the district judge emphasized, Two Rivers' repayment obligation shares with genuine restrictive covenants the feature that it makes changing jobs costly. But that is not enough to throw a contract out the window. Employers offer their workers many incentives to stay, so that they can reap the benefit of training and other productivity enhancers that depend on employees' tenure with the firm. Pay that increases with longevity is one common device; an employee who leaves must start elsewhere at the bottom rung. Firm-specific training (the value of which is lost if the employee changes jobs) likewise penalizes departures. . . . Seniority systems that link duration of service to better assignments, protection against layoffs, and so on, have a similar effect; to quit is to give up accumulated seniority. Private employers give employees profit-sharing plans and stock options that vest later (if the person remains employed) and bonuses that accrue after extra years have been served. Defined-benefit pension systems usually are back-loaded, so that the last years of work before retirement add more to the monthly pension benefit than do earlier years. . . . The common formula that starts with multiplying the final salary by the number of years served produces this effect automatically because salaries tend to rise with inflation and years of service. Yet no one believes that this powerful financial incentive to stick with one's employer until retirement is unlawful, even though it is much larger than the amount Heder must repay Two Rivers for paramedic training. The parties do not cite, and we could not find, any Wisconsin decision that characterizes the kind of incentives mentioned above as restrictive covenants regulated by Wis. Stat. § 103.465. Instead, Wisconsin applies WIS. STAT. § 103.465 only to the extent that a consequence is linked on working for a competitor. . . .

Nor can we see any reason why Wisconsin would want to extend its precedents to block reimbursement agreements such as the one Two Rivers made with its union. Employees received considerable benefits as a result: paramedic training that will be useful for years to come, a 3% increase in compensation starting in 1998 (rising to 3.5% in 1999) for those who are certified paramedics, and extra compensation (at overtime rates) for the training time. Residents of Two Rivers received the benefit of a fire department more likely to save lives. Cities fearing that employees would take their new skills elsewhere would be less likely to provide these benefits. Or they might use other ways to acquire a workforce with better skills. They could, for example, require the employees to undergo and underwrite their own training, with none of the time compensated. This is what law firms do when they limit hiring to persons who already have law degrees, what school systems do when hiring only teachers who hold state certificates. The employer must pay indirectly, through a higher salary, but no court would dream of calling this system (under which employees finance their own training) "involuntary servitude." If an employer may require employees to pay up front, why can't the employer bear the expense but require reimbursement if an early departure deprives the employer of the benefit of its bargain? A middle ground also would be feasible (and lawful): The employer could require the worker to pay for his own training but lend the worker the money and forgive repayment if he sticks around. . . . A worker who left before the loan had been forgiven would have to come up with the funds from his own sources, just as Heder must do. If that system is lawful, as it is, then the economically equivalent system that Two Rivers adopted must be lawful. The cost of training equates to the loan, repayment of which is forgiven after three years.

The district judge objected to the cliff in the repayment system: instead of a slow reduction (equivalent to amortization of a loan), the collective bargaining agreement calls for full repayment before three years and none after. The judge inferred from this that the useful life of paramedic training is three years; as Heder quit with only 1/6 of this time remaining his union could not legally bind him to repay more than 1/6 of these expenses. The inference is unsound: One could as easily infer from the fact that the 3% wage boost is perpetual that paramedic training lasts indefinitely. We know from the record that Heder spent 582 hours undergoing the initial round of training and eight hours to re-certify two years later. This implies that paramedic skills have a useful life that can be extended indefinitely with small recurring investment — and it also implies that the three-year period is generous to workers. Two Rivers could have made the period much longer (say, 10 years). Then even if the debt had been amortized, as the district judge preferred, many workers (all who stayed longer than 3 years but quit or retired before 10) would have been worse off. The actual structure cannot be set aside as onerous — even if Wisconsin had a rule, which it does not, that no onerous term in a collective bargaining agreement is enforceable. The day Heder quit, his paramedic skills were effectively as valuable as the day he received his certification. We do not think that the Supreme Court of Wisconsin is apt to require employers and employees to amortize training costs with precision, to factor in the time value of money (the agreement does not require Heder to pay interest, though it might have done so), or to craft an individual schedule based on the number of years each employee is expected to remain able to work. The collective bargaining agreement is valid under state law, so Heder must repay the full cost of his books and tuition, which came to about $1,400.

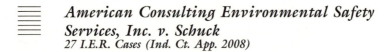

American Consulting Environmental Safety Services, Inc. v. Schuck
27 I.E.R. Cases (Ind. Ct. App. 2008)

FRIEDLANDER, J.

American Consulting Environmental Safety Services, Inc. (American Consulting) appeals from the trial court's judgment in favor of Lynette Schuck and against American Consulting on American Consulting's claim for damages. On appeal, American Consulting presents one issue: Did the trial court err in concluding that Section 12 of an employment contract between American Consulting and Schuck constituted an unenforceable penalty rather than a valid provision for liquidated damages?

We affirm.

American Consulting is an Indiana corporation that provides safety compliance services and materials to customers located within a 200-mile radius of South Bend,

Indiana. To carry out its purpose, American Consulting evaluates the safety and accident prevention policies of businesses and offers programs and courses to bring them into compliance with regulatory agencies' requirements. On January 14, 2005, Schuck was hired by American Consulting as a safety instructor. Schuck signed an employment agreement setting forth the terms and conditions of her employment. Although Schuck had received training in occupational safety and health prior to coming to work for American Consulting, American Consulting required that Schuck undergo additional training. Specifically, Section 12 of the employment agreement provided:

> The Company requires its Employees to be properly trained in safety compliance and state and federal OSHA and EPA standards and the sales, marketing, and other functions of its business. Accordingly, the Company requires each Employee to undergo this training during the initial 180 day probationary period of employment for set [sic] Employee. This training shall cost the Employee the sum of $3,000.00. Set [sic] sum shall be initially due at the first session of training, or when training materials are provided to the Employee, whichever comes first.
>
> However, the Company agrees to pay the cost of this training on the Employees [sic] behalf, but subject to reimbursement by the Employee within the first 12 calendar months of employment. If the Employee remains employed by the Company for 12 continuous calendar months from the first date of hire, the Employee shall not be obligated to reimburse the Company for the cost of training. If, however, the Employee shall voluntarily terminate the employment or if the Employee is terminated by the Employer for good cause, the Employee shall reimburse the Company for the cost of training in accordance with the following schedule:
>
> If Employee terminates employment during the first 0 to 3 months after date of hire, the Employee shall owe the Company $3,000.00.
>
> If the Employee terminates employment during the 4 to 6 months after date of hire, the Employee shall owe the Company $2,160.00.
>
> If the Employee terminates the employment during the 7 to 9 months after date of hire, the Employee shall owe the Company $1,500.00.
>
> If the Employee terminates employment during the 9 to 12 months after the date of hire, the Employee shall owe the Company $750.00.
>
> Any amounts owed by the Employee under this provision shall be deemed a debt to the Company and this contract shall serve as a promissory note. Said amounts owed under this Contract shall become due and payable on the Employees [sic] last day of work. All amounts unpaid from the last day of work on shall accrue interest at the rate of 12 percent per annum.

Schuck's training by American Consulting consisted of spending one day watching videos and taking several short quizzes. The videos were part of a video library American Consulting had accumulated over the course of several years. Additional training included Schuck shadowing another American Consulting employee during visits to existing customers. In total, Schuck completed twelve and one-half days of "shadow training". During the training period, Schuck was paid $9.00 per hour and was not paid overtime.

In June 2005, Schuck informed American Consulting that she had been experiencing medical problems and had found out that she was pregnant. After five months of productive employment, Schuck felt it necessary, due to her pregnancy, to resign from her position. . . .

[American Consulting sued Schuck seeking repayment of $1,500.00 under Section 12 of her employment contract. T]he trial court made the following findings pertinent to our review:

> 13. In considering the facts of this case, the only credible evidence submitted as to the actual loss of the plaintiff is the wages paid to defendant during her training. Defendant testified that her hourly wage was $9.00 per hour and that she had one day of training by watching video tapes [and 12 days of shadow training by following an experienced employee] while that employee was actually earning money for the plaintiff while training employees of customer corporations. Assuming 13 days at 8 hours per day at $9.00 per hour equals $72.00 per day times 13 days equals $936.00. However, the plaintiff's schedule as found in Paragraph 12, provided that because the defendant had already worked six [sic] months at the time of her pregnancy-related request to leave employment, only one-half of that sum would be due, under the intent of the parties. The maximum damages that plaintiff could recover under the actual evidence would be $468.00, assuming that this provision is enforceable. Four Hundred Sixty-Eight Dollars ($468.00) is approximately thirty-one (31%) percent of the amount claimed by the plaintiff.
>
> 15. The lack of reasonableness of the stipulation for repayment of training costs under the circumstances of this case weighs in favor of finding that this is a penalty clause and is unenforceable.

. . . The term "liquidated damages" applies to a specific sum of money that has been expressly stipulated by the parties to a contract as to the amount of damages to be recovered by either party in the event of a breach of the contract by the other. Liquidated damages provisions are useful and generally enforceable in situations where actual damages would be uncertain or difficult to ascertain. To be enforceable, the sum stipulated as liquidated damages must "fairly be allowed as compensation for the breach." Where the stipulated sum is grossly disproportionate to the loss that may result from a breach of contract, we should treat the sum as a penalty rather than as liquidated damages.

As our Supreme Court has noted with regard to the history of litigation of liquidated damage clauses, in cases where actual damages could be readily ascertained and the amount stipulated exceeded the actual damages, then the contract provision has been treated as a "penalty" and only actual damages awarded. "The distinction between a penalty provision and a liquidated damages provision is that a penalty is imposed to secure performance of the contract, and liquidated damages are to be paid in lieu of performance."

In determining whether a stipulated sum payable on a breach of contract constitutes liquidated damages or a penalty, we will consider the facts, the intention of the parties, and the reasonableness of the stipulation under the circumstances of the case. Where there is uncertainty as to the meaning of a liquidated damages provision, classification as a penalty is favored. . . .

Here, Schuck's training consisted of watching videos accumulated over the years by American Consulting. These videos were also used to train other employees. Schuck also shadowed an American Consulting employee for twelve days. American Consulting did not send Schuck for specialized off-site training, seminars, or the like, or bring in specialists to provide on-site training. American Consulting failed to explain how the training it did provide amounted to its stated cost of $3,000.00. American Consulting also failed to demonstrate a reasonable relationship between the reimbursement amounts listed in the Section 12 schedule and the amount of actual damages incurred by the termination of employment.

To be sure, the primary damages American Consulting suffered (if indeed any damages at all) would have been the wage paid to Schuck during her training. This is precisely what the trial court used to compute American Consulting's damages. The trial court calculated Schuck's wage for thirteen days of training at a rate of $9.00 per hour for an eight-hour day and concluded that, at most, American Consulting's loss was $468.00, or thirty-one percent of American Consulting's claimed amount. American Consulting's claimed damages of $1,500.00 is not commensurate with or reasonably related to its actual damages. Furthermore, upon reading the contract, the purpose of Section 12 appears to be to secure performance of the contract for at least a twelve-month period, an earmark of a penalty provision. Based on the foregoing, we can only conclude that Section 12 amounts to an unenforceable penalty.

NOTES

1. *Training Repayment Agreements as an Alternative to Noncompetes.* In what ways might training repayment agreements better serve employers' interests than non-competes? In theory, such agreements circumvent the problem of courts' general disfavor of noncompetes and the particular reluctance to recognize training as a protectable interest. As *Heder* illustrates, at least some courts have taken that view, *see also Pembroke v. Hagin*, 391 S.E.2d 465 (Ga. Ct. App. 1990) (enforcing contract under which peace officer promised to repay city employer for basic training course should he voluntarily terminate employment within 12 months of graduating), as have some state legislatures. *See* COLO. REV. STAT. 8-2-113(2) (permitting enforcement of repayment agreements against employees who serve less than two years). There is also some reason to think that repayment agreements may be more efficient and less likely to overreach than noncompete agreements given that such agreements are tailored to a particular interest and usually apply only if the employee departs within a designated time period. *See* Gillian Lester, *Restrictive Covenants, Employee Training, and the Limits of Transaction-Cost Analysis*, 76 IND. L. J. 49, 75-76 (2001); Brandon S. Long, *Protecting Employer Investment in Training: Noncompetes vs. Repayment Agreements*, 54 DUKE L. J. 1295, 1318-19 (2005).

However, training repayment agreements are hardly a panacea for employers or employees. Where the repayment obligation is tied to post-employment competition, courts are likely to view the agreement as a noncompete and evaluate its reasonableness under comparable standards. *See, e.g., Brunner v. Hand Indus.*, 603 N.E.2d 157 (Ind. Ct. App. 1992) (holding unenforceable agreement obligating former employee to repay costs of training if he joined competitor because employer had no protectable interest in general training and payments were unreasonable). In addition, as *Heder* and *American Consulting* indicate, repayment agreements that do not hinge on non-competition can still run afoul of other laws and doctrines such as restrictions on liquidated damage clauses and state and federal wage payment laws. *See also Sands Appliance Serv. v. Wilson*, 615 N.W.2d 241 (Mich. 2000) (finding training repayment arrangement violated state anti-kickback law prohibiting employer from requiring any form of compensation in exchange for job). From the employee's perspective training repayment agreements might in some instances prove more onerous than noncompetes. Whereas an employee can comply with a noncompete by refraining from competition, a training repayment agreement requires that she have the funds to pay back the company. If the amount is high, it is easy to see how such an agreement can result in a total, if temporary, restraint on mobility.

2. *Liquidated Damages Analysis.* The two cases you read take very different analytical approaches to repayment agreements. *American Consulting* finds the repayment agreement to be an unenforeceable penalty without regard to the law of restrictive covenants. *Heder*, on the other hand, concerns itself with whether the agreement is a noncompete, and upon concluding that it is not, enforces the repayment provision without regard to liquidated damages issues. Although both liquidated damages provisions and restrictive covenants are matters of contract, the law treats the two types of clauses very differently. A liquidated damages provision that is part of a valid contract is presumptively enforceable. The party seeking to avoid payment (the employee in repayment cases) bears the burden of overcoming that presumption by showing that the liquidated amount is disproportionate to probable or actual loss. In contrast, we have seen that in most states, noncompetes are presumed void unless reasonable in relation to the employer's legitimate interests; it is the party seeking enforcement (the employer) who bears the burden of proof.

Why do the employees in *Heder* and *American Consulting* pursue such different legal theories? Is there any reason why the firefighters in *Heder* could not have availed themselves of the penalty argument that persuaded the court in *American Consulting*? Would a liquidated damages analysis lead to a different outcome in *Heder*? Or are competing results in the cases better explained by factual differences? If so, which facts?

Another question is whether a liquidated damages analysis is apt in either case. A typical liquidated damages provision is one that provides for a certain remedy in the event of a party's breach. For instance, an employer might include a repayment clause in a fixed-term contract under which an employee was bound to remain with the company for a set period, a technique you encountered in studying written contracts of high-level employees in Chapter 3. However, neither Heder nor Schuck had any contractual obligation to remain with their employers. Another situation in which employers might seek liquidated damages provisions is in settling claims. You will see an example of this in Chapter 13.

3. *"Garden Leave" Clauses.* Another way in which employers try to circumvent judicial disfavor of noncompetes is by adding clauses to their agreements promising to continue an employee's salary for the duration of the restraint. *See, e.g., Jacono v. Invacare*, No. 86605, 2006 WL 832451 (Ohio. Ct. App. March 30, 2006). Offering pay — sometime referred to as "garden leave" — is a standard feature of noncompete contracts in the United Kingdom. *See generally* Greg T. Lembrich, Note, *Garden Leave: A Possible Solution to the Uncertain Enforceability of Restrictive Employment Covenants*, 102 COLUM. L. REV. 2291, 2292 (2002). A variation on this idea is to give the employee a choice between not competing and receiving some form of compensation or competing and sacrificing that benefit. *See, e.g., Lucente v. IBM*, 310 F.3d 243, 248 (2d Cir. 2002). Under such agreements, the employer essentially pays the worker to temporarily "sit out." Such clauses do not necessarily eliminate all of the harsh effects of noncompetes on employees — in fast-paced industries, skills can atrophy quickly and an employee kept from the field may lose touch with cutting-edge developments. Employers interested in hiring the defecting employee may not be willing to wait out the period of restraint, and the employee might miss out on key opportunities. However, compensating the employee makes the restraint significantly less onerous, which could make some courts more willing to enforce the agreement.

See, e.g., Nike v. McCarthy, 379 F.3d 576, 587 (9th Cir. 2004) (finding fact that agreement obligated Nike to pay employee full salary during period of restriction a factor mitigating potential harm to the employee and supporting issuance of preliminary injunction). *But see Jacono*, 2006 WL 832451, at *7 (finding that clause entitling employee to her base salary if unable to find work due to noncompete "while generous, . . . in and of itself does not make the agreement enforceable").

"Pay to sit out" clauses might increase the employer's chances of prevailing in other ways as well. Such clauses could support the employer's contention that it has a significant legitimate interest underlying the restraint. After all, it is unlikely that an employer would be willing to pay an employee *not* to work absent a significant economic reason to do so. *See* Cynthia L. Estlund, *Between Rights and Contract: Arbitration Agreements and Non-Compete Covenants as a Hybrid Form of Employment Law*, 155 U. Pa. L. Rev. 379, 425 (2006) (suggesting that mandatory garden leave could encourage employer self-policing in determining whether to seek non-compete enforcement). Alternatively, where the agreement is structured to allow the employee to compete or be paid, a court might be convinced that the special rules of noncompete enforcement do not apply. *See, e.g., Fraser v. Nationwide Mut. Ins. Co.*, 334 F. Supp. 2d 755, 760-61 (E.D. Pa. 2004) (describing clause under which insurance agent gave up deferred compensation if he chose to compete post-employment as more akin to incentive program than noncompete in finding contract enforceable without need for balancing of parties' interests). *But see Spiegel v. Thomas, Mann & Smith*, 811 S.W.2d 528, 530 (Tenn. 1991) (clause in law firm's stockholder's agreement under which lawyer who resigned but continued practice of law would forfeit deferred compensation was against public policy and unenforceable under state disciplinary rules prohibiting restriction of practice agreements between lawyers).

4. *No-Hire Agreements.* Still another option for employers is to bypass the employee altogether in favor of contracting directly with customers or competitors. Consulting and placement companies have long required clients to sign "no hire" agreements under which the client agrees that for a period of time it will not hire any employee leased to it by the consulting or placement company. *See, e.g., Blase Indus. v. Anorad Corp.*, 442 F.3d 235 (5th Cir. 2006). In some industries, competitors are adopting a similar technique, entering into mutual "no switching" agreements under which they agree not to "poach" one another's employees. In one sense, these contracts may be less problematic than noncompetes insofar as they are formed between companies possessing roughly equal bargaining power and eliminate only one possible employer for the individual worker. But in another sense, they are more troubling, since there are serious antitrust concerns with such agreements, which could easily be viewed as per se illegal market division (the market being the market for services). *See Palmer v. BRG of Georgia, Inc.*, 498 U.S. 46, 50 (1990) (horizontal market division per se illegal). Further, where such agreements are widely used, or affect an industry that is dominated by a few large entities, no-switching agreements may have even harsher effects on employees than some noncompetes. *See, e.g., Heyde Companies, Inc. v. Dove Healthcare*, 654 N.W.2d 830, 833-34 (Wis. 2002) (finding no-hire agreement used by physical therapist supplier with multiple nursing homes it serviced to be an indirect noncompete that failed statutory reasonableness test). Indeed, such agreements are arguably more objectionable than ordinary noncompetes because the affected workers do not assent to or necessarily even know about them. *Id.* at 836. In addition, the anticompetitive effects of such agreements on society at large may be significant, particularly when made by large rival companies. *See generally*

David Haase, *Agreements Between Employers Not to Hire Each Other's Employees: When Are They Enforceable?*, 21 LABOR LAWYER 277 (2006) (exploring enforceability issues under antitrust and state law).

5. *The Future of Private Ordering.* The legal significance of emerging contractual forms, like those described above, is as yet unknown. Both employers and companies must wait to see how courts and legislatures respond once such agreements start facing more consistent legal challenges. What is certain is that whatever way the law evolves in the area of employee competition, firms are likely to seek out newer and more creative ways of using private ordering to structure their relationships to maximum advantage.

PROBLEM

8-5. Revisit the cases in this chapter in light of the developments in company contracting practices described above. Are there any cases in which it might have been prudent for the employer to use a "pay to sit out" clause, a training repayment agreement, or a "no-switching" contract? Are there other contract forms or clauses that you can think of that might have been appropriate? Choose one case and try your hand at drafting the alternative agreement.

Part Six

STATUTORY PROTECTIONS FOR EMPLOYEES

9

Antidiscrimination

A. THE POLICY BASES FOR ANTIDISCRIMINATION LAW

Federal laws bar discrimination by employers on a number of grounds: race, sex, religion, national origin, age, and disability. In addition, many state laws extend the list of prohibited grounds to marital status, political affiliation, and, increasingly, sexual orientation. What is so bad about discrimination? Employers "discriminate" all the time in the sense that they differentiate between employees for all sorts of reasons. But some bases of differentiation — race, sex, religion, national origin, age, disability — are impermissible, while other bases are perfectly legal. Still other bases, such as sexual orientation, are illegal in only a small, but growing, minority of states. Antidiscrimination laws generally prohibit employers from basing their employment decisions on protected group membership, rather than on an employee's qualifications or some other neutral factor. But reliance on neutral factors that disadvantage protected groups is also sometimes prohibited as discrimination unless the neutral factor is job-related.

The choice to prohibit discrimination emerges from two considerations. Most obviously, discrimination on the basis of certain characteristics, especially race and sex, is viewed as unfair since such characteristics are immutable and, therefore, beyond an individual's control. Because discrimination harms the victim for reasons he or she cannot control, it is also often viewed as immoral. This rationale, however, does not explain the prohibition against discrimination on the basis of religion or other characteristics over which the individual exercises some degree of choice. But discrimination based on religion or other mutable characteristics, such as political affiliation and marital status, is often viewed as wrongful because of deep-rooted concerns about human autonomy and the inalienability of fundamental rights. From this perspective, then, discrimination is wrongful because it damages the dignity of its victims.

Second, there is a socioeconomic agenda to antidiscrimination laws. This emerges most explicitly with respect to the Age Discrimination in Employment Act ("ADEA"), 29 U.S.C. §§ 621 et seq. (2006), and the Americans with Disabilities Act ("ADA"), 42 U.S.C.A. §§ 12101 et seq. (2010), where Congress stressed the waste of human resources caused by discrimination against older workers and workers with disabilities: Such action results not only in individual harm but also in the loss to society of the contributions of those whose abilities are not fully utilized. Although subordinate to dignity values, a concern for the potentially devastating economic consequences of discrimination was also prominent in the enactment of Title VII.

From this perspective, antidiscrimination statutes are united by two simple premises: First, the groups to be protected by the statute are disadvantaged economically; second, the discriminatory conduct of employers causes, or at least contributes to, that disadvantage. Approached this way, the statutes seek to end discrimination in order to improve the economic condition of members of protected groups by allowing them to compete freely for jobs on the basis of their qualifications. Improving the economic condition of such groups can also redound to the benefit of society more generally.

Although equal employment opportunity has received almost unanimous support among all racial groups as an abstract principle, the antidiscrimination laws have often proved controversial in their application. The basic prohibition against express intentional racial discrimination is generally accepted, but a number of specific issues, including affirmative action, pregnancy discrimination, sexual harassment, disparate impact, and discrimination on the basis of sexual orientation, have generated intense national debate. Questions have also been raised about the effectiveness of antidiscrimination laws in raising the standard of living of protected groups.

To begin, not everyone, however, agrees that discrimination should be legally prohibited. Some even question the basic prohibition against express intentional discrimination on account of race. From the beginning, some defended both the wisdom and morality of discrimination or at least questioned the morality of legislating nondiscrimination. While few still subscribe to such views, it has been argued more recently that discrimination may be rational and efficient. Still another view is that, even if discrimination is wrongful, antidiscrimination laws are unnecessary either because market forces will eliminate discrimination without government interference or because discrimination is no longer a significant social problem. An employer that discriminates, after all, must pay a price: Artificially contracting the supply of available labor tends to raise the price of the labor purchased. If many employers discriminate, the price (wages) of their workforce will climb. Competitors will be free to exploit the pool of excluded black (or female) workers at lower wages, thus gaining a competitive advantage. As more employers seek lower-cost black workers, their value will rise. Thus, the market will correct discrimination, without the need for legal intervention. *See* John J. Donohue III, *Advocacy Versus Analysis in Assessing Employment Discrimination Law*, 44 Stan. L. Rev. 1583, 1591 (1992) (recounting such opposition to Title VII's enactment). RICHARD A. EPSTEIN, FORBIDDEN GROUNDS: THE CASE AGAINST EMPLOYMENT DISCRIMINATION LAWS (1992) (adding to the economic argument a strong libertarian critique of government intervention to eliminate discrimination).

Despite these theoretic objections, a variety of statistical studies suggest the continued existence of discrimination in a number of settings, ranging from sports to bankruptcy. In sports, for example, studies of basketball fouls seem to document race bias by referees. *See* Joseph Price & Justin Wolfers, *Racial Discrimination Among NBA Referees* (Nat'l Bureau of Econ. Research Working Paper June 2007), *available*

at http://papers.ssrn.com/sol3/papers.cfm?abstract_id=1136694 ("We find—
even conditioning on player and referee fixed effects [and specific game fixed
effects]—that more personal fouls are called against players when they are officiated
by an opposite-race refereeing crew than when officiated by an own-race crew. These
biases are sufficiently large that we find appreciable differences in whether predominantly black teams are more likely to win or lose, based on the racial composition of the
refereeing crew."). There is also statistical evidence that discrimination exists in
professional baseball coaching, with minorities less likely to be given the more difficult
assignments with more potential for advancement. Michael S. Schmidt & Andrew
Keh, *Baseball's Praised Diversity Is Stranded at First Base*, N.Y. Times, Aug. 11,
2010. ("Among baseball's 30 teams, only 23 percent of the third-base coaches are
members of minorities, compared with 67 percent of its first-base coaches. The disparity has existed for decades but it is now about twice as large as it was in 1990").
In the bankruptcy arena, a recent study suggests that federal judges are more likely to
allow white debtors to reorganize than black debtors, even after holding constant
all relevant factors. Sumit Agarwal et al., *Dismissal with Prejudice? Race and Politics
in Personal Bankruptcy* (Vanderbilt L. & Econs. Research Paper Aug. 25, 2010), *available at* http://papers.ssrn.com/sol3/papers.cfm?abstract_id=1633083 ("[W]hite judges
are 21% more likely to dismiss the chapter 13 petition of an African American debtor
relative to a white debtor."). Perhaps most dramatically, Laura Giuliana, David I.
Levine, & Jonathon Leonard, *Manager Race and the Race of New Hires*, 27 J. Lab.
Econ. 589 (Oct. 2009), use data from a large retailer with frequent employee turnover
to conclude that nonblack managers hire more whites and fewer blacks than do African
American managers; in areas with large Hispanic populations, Hispanic managers hire
more Hispanics and fewer whites than white managers.

This kind of statistical analysis of the persistence of discrimination in the workplace
is confirmed by a number of field experiments. For example, Marianne Bertrand & Sendhil
Mullainathan, *Are Emily and Greg More Employable than Lakisha and Jamal? A Field
Experiment on Labor Market Discrimination*, 94 Am. Econ. Rev. 991 (2004), report
that, when identical fictitious resumes were sent to employers in Boston and Chicago,
those receiving more favorable treatment were those containing non–African American
sounding names. And Claudia Goldin & Cecilia Rouse, *Orchestrating Impartiality: The
Impact of "Blind" Auditions on Female Musicians*, 90 Am. Econ. Rev. 715 (2000), report
that auditions held with the performer behind a screen substantially increased the
likelihood that a female candidate would advance out of the preliminary round in an
orchestra's selection process. *See also* Nilanjana Dasgupta, *Implicit Ingroup Favoritism,
Outgroup Favoritism, and Their Behavioral Manifestations*, 17 Soc. Just. Res. 143
(2004) (collecting research showing biased behavior in employment situations).

Such findings are consistent with older studies showing that, when pairs of black
and white "auditors" applied for jobs, the white applicant was able to advance farther
through the hiring process than an equally qualified black counterpart, in one of five
audits. "In other words, the white was able to either submit an application, receive a
formal interview, or the white was offered a job when the black was not. Overall, in one
out of eight or 15 percent of the audits, the white was offered a job although his equally
qualified black partner was not." Margery Austin Turner, Michael Fix, & Raymond
J. Struyk, Opportunities Denied, Opportunities Diminished: Discrimination in
Hiring 31-32 (1991).

In an attempt to explain the discrepancy between economic theory and the reality
on the ground, Gary Becker in The Economics of Discrimination (2d ed. 1971),

posited that employers have a "taste for discrimination," for which they are willing to pay. Professor David A. Strauss, in *The Law and Economics of Racial Discrimination in Employment: The Case for Numerical Standards*, 79 GEO. L. J. 1619 (1991), notes that the "taste" may be that of the employer itself or of someone whose preferences the employer has to consider — other employees or customers. A version of this argument appeared in Professor Epstein's book FORBIDDEN GROUNDS, in which he argued that homogeneity in a workplace could be conducive to productivity.

> [In employment situations, the increase] in the harmony of tastes and preferences thus works in the long-run interest of all members. To the extent, therefore, that individual tastes are grouped by race, by sex, by age, by national origin — and to some extent they are — then there is a necessary conflict between the commands of any antidiscrimination law and the smooth operation of the firm. Firms whose members have diverse and clashing views may well find it more difficult to make collective decisions than firms with a closer agreement over tastes. . . .

Id. at 66-67. *See also* Devon Carbado & Mitu Galati, *The Law and Economics of Critical Race Theory: Crossroads, Directions, and a New Critical Race Theory*, 112 YALE L. J. 1757, 1762 (2003) (while disagreeing with Professor Epstein's normative view, agreeing that "employers have incentives to screen prospective employees for homogeneity, and, in order to counter racial stereotypes, employees have incentives to demonstrate a willingness and capacity to assimilate."); Scott A. Moss, *Women Choosing Diverse Workplaces: A Rational Preference with Disturbing Implications for Both Occupational Segregation and Economic Analysis of Law*, 27 HARV. WOMEN'S L. J. 1 (2004) (women rationally use the level of diversity as a proxy for discrimination and therefore tend to prefer workplaces with more women).

A related argument that seeks to explain (but not justify) the persistence of discrimination is that some protected characteristics are correlated with ability or other desirable characteristics. For instance, men are statistically more likely than women to have longer job tenure and not terminate or cut back employment after becoming a parent. This theory is sometimes called "statistical discrimination." Strauss, *supra*, at 1622. The logic of statistical discrimination does not require that racial or gender differences be inherent — the correlation between race or gender and productivity could be the result of factors such as past societal discrimination. Further, "statistical discrimination" does not necessarily mean that the employer acts only on the basis of scientifically ascertained differences. Indeed, such discrimination will be more or less "rational" depending on the relationship between the stereotype used and statistical reality.

Is statistical discrimination objectionable even if it is accurate in group terms? Rational or not, relying on generalizations (perhaps better called stereotypes) excludes entire groups without any assessment of individual abilities. This is particularly problematic if the generalization is itself rooted in prior discrimination. *See* Mary Becker, *The Law and Economics of Racial Discrimination in Employment: Needed in the Nineties: Improved Individual and Structural Remedies for Racial and Sexual Disadvantages in Employment*, 79 GEO. L. J. 1659, 1664 (1991); Cass R. Sunstein, *Legal Interference with Private Preferences*, 53 U. CHI. L. REV. 1129 (1986).

Even if perceived productivity differences are real across groups, should employers be free to rely on them? Professor Samuel Issacharoff, in *Contractual Liberties in Discriminatory Markets*, 70 TEX. L. REV. 1219, 1222 (1992), criticizes Epstein's "fundamental assumption that each individual is delivered to the labor market as a more or less intact bundle of skills and abilities." This is "a shockingly static view" of what is, in fact, a dynamic process. Indeed, Issacharoff argues, it is the very "disincentives for optimal acquisition of human capital" brought about by discrimination that justify intervention in the market. Professor Nancy E. Dowd, in *Liberty vs. Equality: In Defense of Privileged White Males*, 34 WM. & MARY L. REV. 429, 442 (1993), views Epstein as a relatively frank apologist for racism and sexism. Quoting Epstein that individual tastes are grouped to some extent by race and sex and that these tastes necessarily conflict with the smooth operation of at least some firms, she states, "These are outrageous statements, filled with stereotypes and race and gender essentialism reduced to implicit biological 'natural' preference, amounting to an outright justification for skin and gender privilege." *See also* Andrew Koppelman, *Feminism & Libertarianism: A Response to Richard Epstein*, 1999 U. CHI. LEGAL F. 115 (1999).

B. INDIVIDUAL DISPARATE TREATMENT DISCRIMINATION

1. Introduction

In order to address the pervasive problem of employment discrimination, Congress enacted a series of statutes dealing with various aspects of the phenomenon. These laws include Title VII of the Civil Rights Act of 1964; the Civil War Reconstruction statutes, especially 42 U.S.C. § 1981; the Age Discrimination in Employment Act of 1967 ("ADEA"); the Rehabilitation Act of 1973; and the Americans with Disabilities Act of 1990 ("ADA"). The avenues of relief under the statutes differ from each other in important ways, but all are concerned with discrimination in employment. The concept of "discrimination," however, has been developed in ways that are not always intuitively obvious. Indeed, "discrimination" is a term of art that embraces several different definitions, each with its own distinctive theory and methods of proof.

Three of the statutes adopt a unitary definition of "disparate treatment" discrimination. The term originated in cases decided under Title VII and has been applied essentially unchanged in both ADEA cases and suits brought under § 1981. Disparate treatment, however, has developed in two distinct ways. Individual disparate treatment is the focus of this section, while systemic disparate treatment is taken up in section C. Individual disparate treatment dominates the cases, at least measured by number filed, in the federal courts.

Title VII, 42 U.S.C. §§ 2000e to 2000e-17 (2006), which embraces almost all employers of 15 or more employees, proscribes discrimination in employment on the basis of race, color, religion, sex, or national origin. Section 703(a), 42 U.S.C.S. § 2000e-2(a)(1), states the basic substantive standard: It is an "unlawful employment practice" for an employer "to fail or refuse to hire or to discharge any individual, or otherwise to discriminate against any individual with respect to his compensation, terms, conditions, or privileges of employment, because of such individual's race, color, religion, sex, or national origin. . . ." The ADEA, 29 U.S.C. §§ 631-34 (2006), applies to employers with 20 or more workers. It tracks Title VII's language but ends each clause with "because of such individual's age." § 623(a).

The ADEA, however, defines "age" to include only those at least 40 years of age. §631(a).

Finally, in its present form, 42 U.S.C. §1981 (2006), guarantees "all persons within the jurisdiction of the United States . . . the same right in every State and Territory to make and enforce contracts . . . as is enjoyed by white citizens. . . ." Section 1981 originated in the Civil War Reconstruction era as one of several statutes intended to protect former slaves. While its success in promoting racial equality was limited for a century, doubts about whether it barred private discrimination ended in 1975 with *Johnson v. Railway Express Agency, Inc.*, 421 U.S. 454, 459-60 (1975), in which the Supreme Court wrote: "§1981 affords a federal remedy against discrimination in private employment on the basis of race."

≡ **Slack v. Havens**
≡ *7 FEP 885 (S.D. Cal. 1973), aff'd as modified, 522 F.2d 1091*
≡ *(9th Cir. 1975)*

THOMPSON, J.

This action is brought by the plaintiffs, four black women, who allege they were discriminatorily discharged, due to their race, in violation of the Civil Rights Act of 1964, specifically 42 U.S.C. §2000e-2(a)(1). . . .

4. On January 31, 1968, plaintiffs Berrel Matthews, Emily Hampton and Isabell Slack were working in the bonding and coating department of defendant Industries' plant, engaged in preparing and assembling certain tubing components for defendant's product. A white co-worker, Sharon Murphy, was also assigned to the bonding and coating department on that day and was performing the same general work as the three plaintiffs mentioned above. The fourth plaintiff, Kathleen Hale, was working in another department on January 31st.

Near the end of the working day, plaintiffs Matthews, Hampton and Slack were called together by their immediate supervisor, Ray Pohasky, and informed that the following morning, upon reporting to work, they would suspend regular production and engage in a general cleanup of the bonding and coating department. The cleanup was to consist of washing walls and windows whose sills were approximately 12 to 15 feet above the floor, cleaning light fixtures, and scraping the floor which was caked with deposits of hardened resin. Plaintiffs Matthews, Hampton and Slack protested the assigned work, arguing that it was not within their job description, which included only light cleanup in their immediate work areas, and that it was too hard and dangerous. Mr. Pohasky agreed that it was hard work and said that he would check to see if they had to do it.

5. On the following work day, February 1, 1968, plaintiffs Matthews, Hampton, and Slack reported to the bonding and coating department along with Sharon Murphy, their white co-worker. However, Mr. Pohasky excused Sharon Murphy to another department for the day, calling in plaintiff Kathleen Hale from the winding department where she had been on loan from the bonding and coating department for about a week. Mr. Pohasky then repeated his announcement that the heavy cleaning would have to be done. The four plaintiffs joined in protest against the heavy cleanup work. They pointed out that they had not been hired to do janitorial type work, and one of the plaintiffs inquired as to why Sharon Murphy had been excused from the cleanup detail even though she had very little seniority among the ladies in the bonding

and coating department. In reply, they were told by Mr. Pohasky that they would do the work, "or else." There was uncontradicted testimony that at sometime during their conversation Pohasky injected the statement that "Colored people should stay in their places," or words to that effect. Some further discussion took place between plaintiffs and Pohasky and then with Gary Helming, plaintiffs' general supervisor, but eventually each of the plaintiffs was taken to the office of Mr. Helming where she was given her final paycheck and fired. Plaintiff Matthews testified without contradiction that on the way to Mr. Helming's office Mr. Pohasky made the comment that "Colored folks are hired to clean because they clean better."

6. The general cleanup work was later performed by newly-hired male employees. Sharon Murphy was never asked to participate in this cleanup before or after the plaintiffs' termination.

7. The day following the plaintiffs' firing a conference was held between plaintiffs and defendant Glenn G. Havens, together with Mr. Helming, Mr. Pohasky and other company officials, but the dispute was not resolved as to the work plaintiffs were expected to do. Apparently, the plaintiffs were offered reinstatement if they would now agree to do the same cleanup work. They refused. . . .

8. Having concluded that defendant Industries is an "employer" under Title VII of the Civil Rights Act for the purposes of this action, we must next consider whether plaintiffs' termination amounted to unlawful discrimination against them because of their race. Defendants deny that the facts support such a conclusion, contending that plaintiffs' case amounts to nothing more than a dispute as to their job classification.

Admittedly, the majority of the discussion between plaintiffs and Industries' management on January 31 and February 1, 1968 centered around the nature of the duties which plaintiffs were ordered to perform. Plaintiffs pointed out that they had not been hired with the understanding that they would be expected to perform more than light cleanup work immediately adjacent to their work stations. They were met with an ultimatum that they do the work — or else. Additionally, no explanation was offered as to why Sharon Murphy, a white co-worker, had been transferred out of the bonding and coating department the morning that the heavy cleaning was to begin there, while plaintiff Hale was called back from the winding department, where she had been working, to the bonding and coating area, specifically for participation in the general cleanup. It is not disputed that Sharon Murphy had less seniority than all of the plaintiffs except plaintiff Hale (having been hired 8 days prior to plaintiff Hale) and no evidence of a bona fide business reason was ever educed by defendants as to why Sharon Murphy was excused from assisting the plaintiffs in the proposed cleaning project.

The only evidence that did surface at the trial regarding the motives for the decisions of the management of defendant Industries consisted of certain statements by supervisor Pohasky, who commented to plaintiff Matthews that "colored folks were hired to clean because they clean better," and "colored folks should stay in their place," or words to that effect. Defendants attempt to disown these statements with the argument that Pohasky's state of mind and arguably discriminatory conduct was immaterial and not causative of the plaintiffs' discharge.

But defendants cannot be allowed to divorce Mr. Pohasky's conduct from that of Industries so easily. First of all, 42 U.S.C. § 2000e(b) expressly includes "any agent" of an employer within the definition of "employer." Secondly, there was a definite causal relation between Pohasky's apparently discriminatory conduct and the firings.

Had Pohasky not discriminated against the plaintiffs by demanding they perform work he would not require of a white female employee, they would not have been faced with the unreasonable choice of having to choose between obeying his discriminatory work order and the loss of their employment. Finally, by backing up Pohasky's ultimatum the top level management of Industries ratified his discriminatory conduct and must be held liable for the consequences thereof. . . .

From all the evidence before it, this Court is compelled to find that defendant Industries, through its managers and supervisor, Mr. Pohasky, meant to require the plaintiffs to perform the admittedly heavy and possibly dangerous work of cleaning the bonding and coating department, when they would not require the same work from plaintiffs' white fellow employee. Furthermore, it meant to enforce that decision by firing the plaintiffs when they refused to perform that work. The consequence of the above was racial discrimination whatever the motivation of the management of defendant Industries may have been. Therefore, the totality of Industries' conduct amounted, in the Court's opinion, to an unlawful employment practice prohibited by the Civil Rights Act, specifically, 42 U.S.C. § 2000e-2(a)(1).

NOTES

1. *Inroad into At Will.* As we have seen, the traditional common-law rule of employment contracts is that any contract not for a definite time is terminable at will by either party — for any reason or for no reason, for good reason or for bad reason. *Slack v. Havens* clearly changes this. How would you state the rule in cases to which Title VII and other antidiscrimination statutes apply?

2. *Proving Discrimination.* Would there be sufficient evidence of discrimination in the case without the statements of Pohasky — that "colored folks are hired to clean because they clean better" — to support a finding that the cleaning assignment was made to plaintiffs because they were African Americans? What other evidence supports the conclusion of race discrimination? Is there any evidence that the assignment was *not* made because of plaintiffs' race? Suppose you represented the defendant in *Slack.* What defenses might you consider when faced with this fact situation? What information would you look for with respect to Sharon Murphy?

3. *The Meaning of "Race."* While "race" seems an intuitive concept (and probably did to Pohasky), "race" as a legal concept is more complicated. In *Saint Francis College v. Al-Khazraji*, 481 U.S. 604 (1987), the Court considered a suit by a U.S. citizen who had been born in Iraq and claimed that he was denied tenure at the college based on his Arab ancestry. The district court rejected his § 1981 claim because Arabs are generally considered Caucasians. The Supreme Court disagreed. While today we tend to think in terms of broader racial groups, many biologists and anthropologists criticize racial classifications as arbitrary and of little use in understanding the variability of human beings. *See, e.g.,* Erik Lillquist & Charles A. Sullivan, *The Law and Genetics of Racial Profiling in Medicine*, 39 Harv. C.R.-C.L. L. Rev. 391 (2004). Current scientific thinking on race, however, was ultimately irrelevant to the *Al-Khazraji* Court. Even if Arabs are now considered Caucasians, that was not the understanding in the nineteenth century when § 1981 was enacted. At that time, "race" was used to include distinct tribes and ethnic groups: "The 1863 version of the New American Cyclopaedia divided the Arabs into a number of subsidiary races; represented the Hebrews as of the Semitic race, and identified numerous other groups as constituting races, including

Swedes, Norwegians, Germans, Greeks, Finns, Italians (referring to mixture of different races), Spanish, Mongolians, Russians, and the like." *See also Shaare Tefila Congregation v. Cobb*, 481 U.S. 615, 617 (1987) (holding that § 1982 suit by a synagogue for defacement of its walls with anti-Semitic slogans is permissible because, when § 1982 was adopted, "Jews and Arabs were among the people then considered to be distinct races and hence within the protection of the statute"). As a result, some "race" discrimination suits under § 1981 are probably better characterized as "national origin" suits under Title VII.

4. *Admissions of Discriminatory Intent.* Pohasky's statements suffice to show his intent to discriminate because they constitute admissions of the state of mind that motivated him to assign the plaintiffs to this job. Where such statements can be proven, they are very powerful indications of discriminatory intent on various grounds:

a. In a race discrimination case, a police officer testified that the chief of police "loudly stated in my presence that he would not allow 'Spics and Niggers' to run his department within very close earshot of me. I know that [he] directed that comment at me and knew I was in the next room." *Perez v. N.J. Transit Corp.*, 341 F. App'x. 757, 761 (3d Cir. 2009).

b. In a sex discrimination case, plaintiff's supervisor "referred to women buyers as 'PMS,' 'menstrual,' and 'dragon lady.' He also stated that most women probably just wanted to stay home." *Passantino v. Johnson & Johnson Consumer Prods.*, 212 F.3d 493 (9th Cir. 2000).

c. In a religious discrimination case, a letter demoting plaintiff because he was a member of a church whose creed was white supremacy (and therefore the employees he supervised would not have confidence in his objectivity) constituted direct evidence of discriminatory intent on the basis of religion. *Peterson v. Wilmur Communications, Inc.*, 205 F. Supp. 2d 1014 (E.D. Wis. 2002).

d. In ADEA age discrimination cases, referring to an older worker as "'an F'n dinosaur.'" *Loveless v. John's Ford, Inc.*, 232 F. App'x 229, 232 n.3 (4th Cir. 2007).

e. In a national origin hostile work environment case, referring to a Mexican-American employee as "'Wetback,' 'Spic,' and 'Mexican Mother F——.'" *Miller v. Kenworth of Dothan Inc.*, 277 F.3d 1269, 1273-74 (11th Cir. 2002).

5. *Animus or Intent?* In these examples, the statement indicates the employer's animus or hostility to the group in question. But Pohasky apparently assigned plaintiffs to the cleaning work in question because he believed them to be better cleaners. Is this pejorative? If so, is it pejorative because it suggests that blacks can do only menial jobs like cleaning? Perhaps it does not matter. While discrimination may be motivated by hate, fear, or revulsion, the statutes do not require such negative impulses. If Pohasky chose the plaintiffs because he thought they were better workers than whites, at cleaning as well as everything else, he would still have been discriminating within the meaning of the statute. He would be intending to assign jobs by race.

6. *Conscious and Unconscious Stereotyping.* Mr. Pohasky was, presumably, aware of the beliefs he had about African Americans. If they were "stereotypes," he thought of them as true generalizations. Many stereotypes are like this — we employ them deliberately because they conform to our view of reality (whether or not that view is correct). But, as we have suggested earlier, there is a different view of how stereotypes operate in today's society. Professor Linda Hamilton Krieger, in *The Content of Our Categories: A Cognitive Bias Approach to Discrimination and Equal Employment Opportunity*, 47 Stan. L. Rev. 1161 (1995), broke ground for a different view of intent to discriminate, one that has come to dominate the academic literature under rubrics such as "cognitive bias," "unreflective discrimination," "subtle bias," and "unconscious" (or "subconscious") "discrimination." *See generally* Marc R. Poirier, *Using Stereotyping and Cognitive Bias Evidence to Prove Gender Discrimination: Is Cognitive Bias at Work a Dangerous Condition on Land?*, 7 Employee Rts. & Emp. Pol'y J. 459 (2003) (offering a taxonomy of these terms). As the diversity of labels indicates, the precise phenomena at issue are often contested, but Professor Krieger offers an excellent place to start. Using the insights provided by cognitive psychology, she concludes that stereotyping by race and gender is far more insidious than is often recognized because it is often an "unintended consequence" of the necessity for humans to categorize their sensory perceptions in order to make any sense of the world:

> [The] central premise of social cognition theory [is] that cognitive structures and processes involved in categorization and information processing can in and of themselves result in stereotyping and other forms of biased intergroup judgment previously attributed to motivational processes. The social cognition approach to discrimination comprises three claims relevant to our present inquiry. The first is that stereotyping . . . is nothing special. It is simply a form of categorization [of our sensory perceptions], similar in structure and function to the categorization of natural objects. According to this view, stereotypes, like other categorical structures, are cognitive mechanisms that all people, not just "prejudiced" ones, use to simplify the task of perceiving, processing, and retaining information about people in memory. They are central, and indeed essential to normal cognitive functioning.
>
> The second claim posited in social cognition theory is that, once in place, stereotypes bias intergroup judgment and decisionmaking. . . . [T]hey function as implicit theories, biasing in predictable ways the perception, interpretation, encoding, retention, and recall of information about other people. These biases are cognitive rather than motivational. They operate absent intent to favor or disfavor members of a particular social group. And, perhaps most significant for present purposes, they bias a decisionmaker's judgment long before the "moment of decision" [when the employment decision in question is made], as a decisionmaker attends to relevant data and interprets, encodes, stores, and retrieves it from memory. These biases "sneak up on" the decisionmaker, distorting bit by bit the data upon which his decision is eventually based.
>
> The third claim follows from the second. Stereotypes, when they function as implicit prototypes or schemas [by which we evaluate each other], operate beyond the reach of decisionmaker self-awareness. Empirical evidence indicates that people's access to their own cognitive processes is in fact poor. Accordingly, cognitive bias may well be both unintentional and unconscious.

Id. at 1187-88. *See also* Tristin K. Green, in *Discrimination in Workplace Dynamics: Toward a Structural Account of Disparate Treatment Theory*, 38 Harv. C.R.-C.L. L. Rev. 91, 128 (2003); Tristin K. Green, *Targeting Workplace Context: Title VII as a Tool for Institutional Reform*, 72 Fordham L. Rev. 659 (2003).

When stereotyping is unintentional and unconscious, should acting based on stereotypes constitute individual disparate treatment discrimination? It is treating people differently based on their race or gender, but is that what antidiscrimination law proscribes? Or does intentional discrimination require a conscious intent to discriminate? For example, Professor Amy Wax argues in *Discrimination as Accident*, 74 IND. L.J. 1129 (1999), that, when discrimination is not conscious, employer efforts to reduce it will likely be unavailing. She therefore opposes liability for this variety of discrimination. *See also* Patrick Shin, *Liability for Unconscious Discrimination? A Thought Experiment in the Theory of Employment Discrimination Law*, 62 HASTINGS L. J, 67 (2010). But even Professor Wax agrees that, from a pure causation perspective, Title VII could be read to bar unconscious discrimination if it could be established as resulting in an adverse employment action. Amy L. Wax, *The Discriminating Mind: Define It, Prove It*, 40 CONN. L. REV. 979, 894 (2008). And others argue against limiting the antidiscrimination statutes to conscious actions. *See* Michael Selmi, *Discrimination as Accident: Old Whine, New Bottle*, 74 IND. L. J. 1234 (1999); Melissa Hart, *Subjective Decisionmaking and Unconscious Discrimination*, 56 ALA. L. REV. 741, 790-91 (2005) (the "judicially imposed requirement of employer dishonesty — with its attendant focus on the consciously intentional nature of prohibited discrimination — was never an element of Title VII, and it should be abandoned."). *See also* Tristin K. Green & Alexandra Kalev, *Discrimination-Reducing Measures at the Relational Level*, 59 HASTINGS L. J. 1435, 1435 (2008) (discrimination-reducing measures should be broadened to address the relational sources of discrimination — social interactions and relations at work that operate to reinforce stereotypes and bias). What do you think? Should disparate treatment discrimination require a conscious intent to discriminate, or is it enough to find that the plaintiff's protected class status caused the decision to occur? If a supervisor honestly believed he was acting for a nondiscriminatory reason, even if his unconscious biases in fact influenced his decision, should liability be imposed? If so, how would a plaintiff prove that, despite the supervisor's "honest belief," racial bias caused the decision?

7. *Are the Bad Old Days Still Around?* While most employment discrimination scholars agree that some variation of the cognitive bias theory explains an increasing percentage of cases in which women and minorities are disadvantaged relative to white males, others have warned against too quickly concluding that "old fashioned" discrimination is not a continuing and serious problem. *See* Michael L. Selmi, *Sex Discrimination in the Nineties, Seventies Style: Case Studies in the Preservation of Male Norms*, 9 EMPLOYEE RTS. & EMP. POL'Y J. 1 (2005) ("[T]here remains a significant amount of discrimination in the workplace that is not properly labeled as subtle but which involves the active and conscious exclusion of women from the workplace."). *See also* Ralph Richard Banks & Richard Thompson Ford, *(How) Does Unconscious Bias Matter?: Law, Politics, and Racial Inequality*, 58 EMORY L. J. 1053, 1059 (2009) ("The unconscious bias approach not only discounts the persistence of knowing discrimination, it elides the substantive inequalities that fuel conscious and unconscious bias alike. While we do not doubt the existence of unconscious bias, we do doubt that contemporary racial bias accounts for all, or even most, of the racial injustice that bedevils our society."). As Selmi documents, discrimination cases are frequently emotionally charged because members of traditionally excluded groups are often resented when they arrive in the workplace or seek to rise above their traditional roles. Discrimination may also be motivated by a desire to subordinate. Mary Becker, *The Law and Economics of Racial Discrimination in Employment: Needed in the Nineties: Improved Individual and Structural Remedies for Racial and Sexual Disadvantages in Employment*, 79 GEO. L. J. 1659, 1667 (1991). Certainly, the continued harassment litigation, challenging explicit sexual and racial harassment, suggests that not all discriminatory biases operate below the level of consciousness.

8. *Intent and the Prohibited Trait.* In *Hazen Paper Co. v. Biggins*, 507 U.S. 604 (1993), a jury found violations under both the ADEA and ERISA when the 62-year-old plaintiff was fired as he approached a critical vesting date for his pension, but the Supreme Court overturned the verdict. *Biggins* introduces us to two important concepts. The first is what has come to be known as the "mixed motives" question, what the law should do when the employer acts because of two separate motives. *Biggins* answered the question by holding that "a disparate treatment claim cannot succeed unless the employee's protected trait actually played a role in that process and had a determinative influence on the outcome." 507 U.S. at 610. This principle continues to operate under the Age Discrimination Act, *see Gross v. FBL Fin. Servs.*, 129 S. Ct. 2343 (2009) (holding that mixed-motive theory is not available under the ADEA and that age must be the "but for" cause of adverse employment action), but we will see that it has been altered under Title VII.

The second important concept in *Biggins* is more central: the meaning of intent to discriminate. The Court held that firing someone to avoid his pension vesting, while a violation of ERISA, was not per se age discrimination.

> It is the very essence of age discrimination for an older employee to be fired because the employer believes that productivity and competence decline with old age. As we explained in *EEOC v. Wyoming*, 460 U.S. 226 (1983), Congress' promulgation of the ADEA was prompted by its concern that older workers were being deprived of employment on the basis of inaccurate and stigmatizing stereotypes.
>
> Although age discrimination rarely was based on the sort of animus motivating some other forms of discrimination, it was based in large part on stereotypes unsupported by objective fact. . . . Moreover, the available empirical evidence demonstrated that arbitrary age lines were in fact generally unfounded and that, as an overall matter, the performance of older workers was at least as good as that of younger workers. . . .
>
> When the employer's decision is wholly motivated by factors other than age, the problem of inaccurate and stigmatizing stereotypes disappears. This is true even if the motivating factor is correlated with age, as pension status typically is. Pension plans typically provide that an employee's accrued benefits will become nonforfeitable, or "vested," once the employee completes a certain number of years of service with the employer. On average, an older employee has had more years in the work force than a younger employee, and thus may well have accumulated more years of service with a particular employer. Yet an employee's age is analytically distinct from his years of service. An employee who is younger than 40, and therefore outside the class of older workers as defined by the ADEA, may have worked for a particular employer his entire career, while an older worker may have been newly hired. Because age and years of service are analytically distinct, an employer can take account of one while ignoring the other, and thus it is incorrect to say that a decision based on years of service is necessarily "age-based."

Id. at 610-11 (citation omitted). The Court did recognize that it would violate the ADEA were the employer to use "[p]ension status [as] a proxy for age, not in the sense that the ADEA makes the two factors equivalent, but in the sense that the employer may suppose a correlation between the two factors and act accordingly." *Id.* at 613 (citation omitted).

But does this approach make sense? Suppose an employer discriminated against workers because they had gray hair. That's pretty highly—but not perfectly—correlated with age. How about wrinkles, which are even more highly (but still not perfectly) correlated with age? And there are many traits that are correlated with, but scarcely essential to, sex and race. We will see that the disparate impact theory to a considerable extent protects against an employer's use of irrational but highly corre-lated factors, but isn't there something odd about saying that discrimination against gray-haired, wrinkled people isn't age discrimination?

9. *Employer Reaction to the Protected Trait. Biggins* focuses our attention on the employer's subjective reaction to the "protected class." In the case itself, of course, that class was older workers. While the Court viewed an employer's belief that "pro-ductivity and competence decline with old age" to be "the very essence of age dis-crimination," surely that cannot be the only impermissible kind of discriminatory intent within the statute: What if the jury found that Biggins was fired because the Hazens thought customers would not like working with older people? Older people are also often seen as "stuck in their ways," resistant to new ideas. If Hazen Paper viewed Biggins as not being sufficiently innovative, might that also indicate age stereotyping?

But *Biggins* can be generalized to other protected classes, most notably race, sex, national origin, or religion under Title VII. For liability to attach, the employer must have some aversion to the class in question. In *Slack*, that aversion was proven in part by Pohasky's remarks. While *Biggins* was remanded for further proceedings, this kind of "direct" evidence was lacking. Without such evidence, could Biggins prevail? How likely is it that the Hazens incorrectly believed Biggins' competence declined? Aren't employers more likely to act on "inaccurate and stigmatizing stereotypes" regarding competence in refusing to hire older workers than in firing them? The Hazens had the opportunity to watch plaintiff perform over almost a decade. If they fired him because they believed his competence was diminishing, how could that be the result of a stereotype? Or does Professor Krieger's article help explain this? To prevail, would Biggins have had to show (a) that they incorrectly evaluated his competence and (b) that they attributed his perceived loss of competence to his age? What if they correctly believed Biggins' performance was declining but also attributed it to his age?

10. *Looking Forward.* Neither *Slack* nor *Biggins* focuses on burdens of proof, but it has become clear that, under the disparate treatment theory, the plaintiff has the burden of establishing discriminatory intent. This raises two distinct problems. *Slack* primarily involved "direct" evidence of intent: Pohasky's statements indicating why he acted as he did. In contrast, *Biggins* primarily involved "circumstantial," or inferential, methods of proof. The next section considers the structure of an inferential case of individual disparate treatment.

2. Proving Discrimination: The Traditional Framework

a. The Plaintiff's Prima Facie Case

McDonnell Douglas Corp. v. Green
411 U.S. 792 (1973)

Justice POWELL delivered the opinion of the Court.

. . . Petitioner, McDonnell Douglas Corp., is an aerospace and aircraft manufac-turer headquartered in St. Louis, Missouri, where it employs over 30,000 people. Respondent, a black citizen of St. Louis, worked for petitioner as a mechanic and laboratory technician from 1956 until August 28, 1964 when he was laid off in the course of a general reduction in petitioner's work force.

Respondent, a long-time activist in the civil rights movement, protested vigorously that his discharge and the general hiring practices of petitioner were racially motivated. As part of this protest, respondent and other members of the Congress on Racial Equality illegally stalled their cars on the main roads leading to petitioner's plant for the purpose of blocking access to it at the time of the morning shift change. The District Judge described the plan for, and respondent's participation in, the "stall-in" as follows:

[F]ive teams, each consisting of four cars would "tie up" five main access roads into McDonnell at the time of the morning rush hour. The drivers of the cars were instructed to line up next to each other completely blocking the intersections or roads. The drivers were also instructed to stop their cars, turn off the engines, pull the emergency brake, raise all windows, lock the doors, and remain in their cars until the police arrived. The plan was to have the cars remain in position for one hour.

Acting under the "stall in" plan, plaintiff [respondent in the present action] drove his car onto Brown Road, a McDonnell access road, at approximately 7:00 a.m., at the start of the morning rush hour. Plaintiff was aware of the traffic problem that would result. He stopped his car with the intent to block traffic. The police arrived shortly and requested plaintiff to move his car. He refused to move his car voluntarily. Plaintiff's car was towed away by the police, and he was arrested for obstructing traffic. Plaintiff pleaded guilty to the charge of obstructing traffic and was fined.

[O]n July 25, 1965, petitioner publicly advertised for qualified mechanics, respondent's trade, and respondent promptly applied for re-employment. Petitioner turned down respondent, basing its rejection on respondent's participation in the "stall-in." . . .

II

The critical issue before us concerns the order and allocation of proof in a private, non-class action challenging employment discrimination. The language of Title VII makes plain the purpose of Congress to assure equality of employment opportunities and to eliminate those discriminatory practices and devices which have fostered racially stratified job environments to the disadvantage of minority citizens. *Griggs v. Duke Power Co.*, 401 U.S. 424, 429 (1971) [reproduced at page 592]. As noted in *Griggs*, "Congress did not intend by Title VII, however, to guarantee a job to every person regardless of qualifications. In short, the Act does not command that any person be hired simply because he was formerly the subject of discrimination, or because he is a member of a minority group. Discriminatory preference for any group, minority or majority, is precisely and only what Congress has proscribed. What is required by Congress is the removal of artificial, arbitrary, and unnecessary barriers to employment when the barriers operate invidiously to discriminate on the basis of racial or other impermissible classification."

There are societal as well as personal interests on both sides of this equation. The broad, overriding interest, shared by employer, employee, and consumer, is efficient and trustworthy workmanship assured through fair and racially neutral employment and personnel decisions. In the implementation of such decisions, it is abundantly clear that Title VII tolerates no racial discrimination, subtle or otherwise. In this case, respondent, the complainant below, charges that he was denied employment "because of his involvement in civil rights activities" and "because of his race and color." Petitioner denied discrimination of any kind, asserting that its failure to re-employ respondent was based upon and justified by his participation in the unlawful conduct against it. Thus, the issue at the trial on remand is framed by those opposing factual contentions. . . .

The complainant in a Title VII trial must carry the initial burden under the statute of establishing a prima facie case of racial discrimination. This may be done by showing (i) that he belongs to a racial minority; (ii) that he applied and was qualified for a job for which the employer was seeking applicants; (iii) that, despite his qualifications, he was rejected; and (iv) that, after his rejection, the position remained open and the employer continued to seek applicants from persons of complainant's qualifications.[13] In the instant case, we agree with the Court of Appeals that respondent proved a prima facie case. Petitioner sought mechanics, respondent's trade, and continued to do so after respondent's rejection. Petitioner, moreover, does not dispute respondent's qualifications[14] and acknowledges that his past work performance in petitioner's employ was "satisfactory."

The burden then must shift to the employer to articulate some legitimate, non-discriminatory reason for the employee's rejection. We need not attempt in the instant case to detail every matter which fairly could be recognized as a reasonable basis for a refusal to hire. Here petitioner has assigned respondent's participation in unlawful conduct against it as the cause for his rejection. We think that this suffices to discharge petitioner's burden of proof at this stage and to meet respondent's prima facie case of discrimination.

. . . Respondent admittedly had taken part in a carefully planned "stall-in," designed to tie up access to and egress from petitioner's plant at a peak traffic hour.[16] Nothing in Title VII compels an employer to absolve and rehire one who has engaged in such deliberate, unlawful activity against it.[17] . . .

Petitioner's reason for rejection thus suffices to meet the prima facie case, but the inquiry must not end here. While Title VII does not, without more, compel rehiring of respondent, neither does it permit petitioner to use respondent's conduct as a pretext for the sort of discrimination prohibited by § 703(a)(1). On remand, respondent must, as the Court of Appeals recognized, be afforded a fair opportunity to show that petitioner's stated reason for respondent's rejection was in fact pretext. Especially relevant to such a showing would be evidence that white employees involved in acts against petitioner of comparable seriousness to the "stall-in" were nevertheless retained or rehired. Petitioner may justifiably refuse to rehire one who was engaged in unlawful,

---

13. The facts necessarily will vary in Title VII cases, and the specification above of the prima facie proof required from respondent is not necessarily applicable in every respect to differing factual situations.

14. We note that the issue of what may properly be used to test qualifications for employment is not present in this case. Where employees have instituted employment tests and qualifications with an exclusionary effect on minority applicants, such requirements must be "shown to bear a demonstrable relationship to successful performance of the jobs" for which they were used, *Griggs v. Duke Power Co.*

16. The trial judge noted that no personal injury or property damage resulted from the "stall-in" due "solely to the fact that law enforcement officials had obtained notice in advance of plaintiff's . . . demonstration and were at the scene to remove plaintiff's car from the highway."

17. The unlawful activity in this case was directed specifically against petitioner. We need not consider or decide here whether, or under what circumstances, unlawful activity not directed against the particular employer may be a legitimate justification for refusing to hire.

disruptive acts against it, but only if this criterion is applied alike to members of all races.

Other evidence that may be relevant to any showing of pretext includes facts as to the petitioner's treatment of respondent during his prior term of employment; petitioner's reaction, if any, to respondent's legitimate civil rights activities; and petitioner's general policy and practice with respect to minority employment. On the latter point, statistics as to petitioner's employment policy and practice may be helpful to a determination of whether petitioner's refusal to rehire respondent in this case conformed to a general pattern of discrimination against blacks. *Jones v. Lee Way Motor Freight, Inc.*, 431 F.2d 245 (C.A. 10 1970); Blumrosen, *Strangers in Paradise:* Griggs v. Duke Power Co., *and the Concept of Employment Discrimination*, 71 MICH. L. REV. 59, 91-94 (1972).[19] In short, on the retrial respondent must be given a full and fair opportunity to demonstrate by competent evidence that the presumptively valid reasons for his rejection were in fact a coverup for a racially discriminatory decision.

NOTES

1. *Rationale for the Proof Structure. McDonnell Douglas* established the structure for litigating cases of individual disparate treatment based on what has been considered "circumstantial evidence" of discrimination, so much so that the case name has become a kind of mantra for analyzing the vast majority of Title VII cases. The first step, the prima facie case, was framed in terms of the four elements. It is obvious, however, that these elements do not fit every fact situation. Indeed, if you think about it, you will see that they describe very few cases: Most employment settings are competitive, which means that an employer hires B instead of A rather than leaving the job vacant. The employer's failure to rehire Green while still seeking other applicants was truly remarkable. How could such an anomalous fact situation become the gold standard in Title VII litigation? In *Teamsters v. United States*, 431 U.S. 324, 358 n.44 (1977), the Court described the rationale for the prima facie case:

> The *McDonnell Douglas* case involved an individual complainant seeking to prove one instance of unlawful discrimination. An employer's isolated decision to reject an applicant who belongs to a racial minority does not show that the rejection was racially based. Although the *McDonnell Douglas* formula does not require direct proof of discrimination, it does demand that the alleged discriminate demonstrate at least that his rejection did not result from the two most common legitimate reasons on which an employer might rely to reject a job applicant: an absolute or relative lack of qualifications or the absence of a vacancy in the job sought. Elimination of these reasons for the refusal to hire is sufficient, absent other explanation, to create an inference that the decision was a discriminatory one.

2. *Generalizing* McDonnell Douglas *to Different Contexts. McDonnell Douglas* is focused on the failure-to-rehire context. Suppose, however, that Green had never

---

19. The District Court may, for example, determine after reasonable discovery that "the [racial] composition of defendant's labor force is itself reflective of restrictive or exclusionary practices." See Blumrosen, *supra*, at 92. We caution that such general determinations, while helpful, may not be in and of themselves controlling as to an individualized hiring decision, particularly in the presence of an otherwise justifiable reason for refusing to rehire. *See generally* Blumrosen, *supra*, n.19, at 93.

worked for the defendant. If you represented him, how would you prove the "qualification" aspect of element (ii)? What if Green had no prior experience in the industry and the employer required experience? Would Green not have a prima facie case? Similarly, what if the job Green sought had not remained open because the employer hired a white worker over Green? This would bar application of the fourth prong as *McDonnell Douglas* formulated it. How could Green then make out a prima facie case? By proving that the white was *less* qualified?

a. In the far more common situation where a plaintiff loses out to a competitor, the Supreme Court has not required plaintiff to prove that she was as well qualified as that competitor in order to make out a prima facie case. In *Patterson v. McLean Credit Union*, 491 U.S. 164, 186-87 (1989), a § 1981 suit in which a black bank employee had been repeatedly passed over for promotions that were given to whites, the Court applied the *McDonnell Douglas* proof structure: "The burden [of establishing a prima facie case] is not onerous. Here, petitioner need only prove by a preponderance of the evidence that she applied for and was qualified for an available position, that she was rejected, and that after she was rejected respondent either continued to seek applicants for the position, or, as is alleged here, filled the position with a white employee." (citations omitted). Thus, to carry her initial burden, plaintiff need only show that she met the minimum qualifications for the job. Of course, if the defendant asserts the successful competitor's superior qualifications as its nondiscriminatory reason, plaintiff will have to challenge that claim at the pretext stage in order to prevail.

b. What are the elements of a prima facie case in a *discharge* case? Most discrimination cases involve discharges, and the lower courts have had to formulate the elements for this context. Indeed, two alternative formulations of *McDonnell Douglas* have emerged — one for individual discharges and the other for discharges in the course of reductions in force. In individual discharge cases, those involving a single employee, courts have tended to require him to show that he was doing "apparently satisfactory" work in order to carry his prima facie case burden. *E.g.*, *Diaz v. Eagle Produce, Ltd.*, 521 F.3d 1201, 1207-8 (9th Cir. 2008); *Rivera v. City & County of Denver*, 365 F.3d 912, 920 (10th Cir. 2004). An alternative approach would allow the plaintiff to show that he was replaced by a person outside the protected class — say, a younger person in the ADEA context. *Wooler v. Citizens Bank*, 274 F. App'x 177, 179-80 (3d Cir. 2008).

c. In contrast, in reductions in force, that is, situations where a number of employees are terminated simultaneously, the "legitimate, nondiscriminatory reason" — the need to reduce expenses — is apparent on its face. Because *positions* are being eliminated, the power of proof that the plaintiff is doing an apparently satisfactory job diminishes. *See Schoonmaker v. Spartan Graphics Leasing, LLC*, 595 F.3d 261 (6th Cir. 2010). Courts have, therefore, tended to require a plaintiff to produce other evidence, such as identifying younger workers who were retained when she was discharged. *Geiger v. Tower Auto.*, 579 F.3d 614 (6th Cir. 2009); *Martino v. MCI Communs. Servs.*, 574 F.3d 447, 454 (7th Cir. 2009). *See generally* Parisis G. Filippatos & Sean Farhang, *The Rights of Employees Subjected to Reductions in Force: A Critical Evaluation*, 6 EMPLOYEE RTS. & EMP. POL'Y J. 263, 326-27 (2002).

d. Suppose a plaintiff is fired but replaced by a member of the same protected class? In *Kendrick v. Penske Transportation Services*, 220 F.3d 1220, 1226

(10th Cir. 2000), the court held that a discharged employee did not have to show that he was replaced by an employee outside of the protected group in order to establish a prima facie case of race discrimination. Indeed, most federal courts of appeals have held that, in a termination case, the plaintiff need not prove as part of the prima facie case that she was replaced by someone outside the relevant class. *E.g., Stella v. Mineta*, 284 F.3d 135, 146 (D.C. Cir. 2002) (holding that plaintiff in a discrimination case need not demonstrate that she was replaced by a person outside her protected class in order to carry her burden of establishing a prima facie case under *McDonnell Douglas*). Why? Even if this is correct for the prima facie case, the same-class replacement may make it extraordinarily difficult to prove pretext when defendant asserts a nondiscriminatory reason for its action. *See generally* Michael J. Zimmer, *A Chain of Inferences Proving Discrimination*, 79 U. COLO. L. REV. 1243, 1279-80 (2008).

3. *Consequences of the Prima Facie Case.* In *Texas Department of Community Affairs v. Burdine*, 450 U.S. 248 (1981), the Court described the consequences of proving a prima facie case:

> Establishment of the prima facie case in effect creates a presumption that the employer unlawfully discriminated against the employee. If the trier of fact believes the plaintiff's evidence, and if the employer is silent in the face of the presumption, the court must enter judgment for the plaintiff because no issue of fact remains in the case.

In accompanying footnote 7, *Burdine* said the use of the term "prima facie case" in *McDonnell Douglas* denoted "the establishment of a legally mandatory, rebuttable presumption"; it did *not* describe "the plaintiff's burden of producing enough evidence to permit the trier of fact to infer the fact at issue." The point of the distinction is that a plaintiff's proof of a prima facie case is not necessarily sufficient to create a jury question, but that plaintiff will nevertheless win if defendant fails to carry its burden of production. *Burdine* made clear, however, that when defendant did introduce into evidence a nondiscriminatory reason, plaintiff had the burden of persuasion as to pretext:

> The burden that shifts to the defendant, therefore, is to rebut the presumption of discrimination by producing evidence that the plaintiff was rejected, or someone else was preferred, for a legitimate, nondiscriminatory reason. The defendant need not persuade the court that it was actually motivated by the proffered reasons. It is sufficient if the defendant's evidence raises a genuine issue of fact as to whether it discriminated against the plaintiff. To accomplish this, the defendant must clearly set forth, through the introduction of admissible evidence, the reasons for the plaintiff's rejection. The explanation provided must be legally sufficient to justify a judgment for the defendant. If the defendant carries this burden of production, the presumption raised by the prima facie case is rebutted, and the factual inquiry proceeds to a new level of specificity. . . .
>
> The plaintiff retains the burden of persuasion. She now must have the opportunity to demonstrate that the proffered reason was not the true reason for the employment decision. This burden now merges with the ultimate burden of persuading the court that she has been the victim of intentional discrimination. She may succeed in this either directly by persuading the court that a discriminatory reason more likely motivated the employer or indirectly by showing that the employer's proffered explanation is unworthy of credence.

450 U.S. at 256. We will see that later cases went further to impose another requirement on the plaintiff: She must prove that the supposed legitimate nondiscriminatory
reason was not only a pretext in the sense that it was untrue but that it was *a pretext for
discrimination*, that is, that it hid a true discriminatory motive.

4. *The Role of Comparators.* "Disparate" treatment, as the phrase suggests,
requires ultimately proving that the plaintiff was treated differently than a person of
a different race or sex was (or would have been) treated. Thus, many disparate treatment cases turn on whether the plaintiff can identify "comparators" who are similarly
situated to her except for her race, sex, and so forth, but were treated differently. The
comparator may enter the analysis at the prima facie case stage or, more commonly, to
show pretext by establishing that the defendant did not apply its supposed nondiscriminatory reason in, for example, a color- or sex-blind manner. *See generally* Charles
A. Sullivan, *The Phoenix from the Ash: Proving Discrimination by Comparators*, 59 ALA.
L. REV. 191 (2009); Ernest F. Lidge III, *The Courts' Misuse of the Similarly Situated
Concept in Employment Discrimination Law*, 67 MO. L. REV. 831 (2002).

The significance of comparators turns on how much similarity courts will require
before dissimilar treatment will give rise to an inference of discrimination. The Supreme
Court's decision in *Ash v. Tyson Foods, Inc.*, 546 U.S. 454 (2006), rejected the most
extreme circuit court approach in the context of comparative qualifications. The Eleventh Circuit overturned a jury verdict for plaintiff and, in the course of its opinion had,
apparently in all seriousness, stated that a plaintiff can use her asserted superior qualifications relative to a comparator to prove discrimination only when "the disparity in qualifications is so apparent as virtually to jump off the page and slap you in the face." *Id.* at
456-57. In reversing, the Supreme Court stressed that its prior decisions established that
"qualifications evidence may suffice, at least in some circumstances, to show pretext," *id.*
at 457 (quoting *Patterson v. McLean Credit Union*, 491 U.S. 164, 187-88 (1989)), and
that plaintiff's proof that the employer "misjudged the qualifications" of the applicants
"may be probative of whether the employer's reasons are pretexts for discrimination."
Id. (quoting *Texas Dep't of Community Affairs v. Burdine*, 450 U.S. 248, 259 (1981)).

Perhaps not surprisingly, the Court then wrote that "[t]he visual image of words
jumping off the page to slap you (presumably a court) in the face is unhelpful and
imprecise as an elaboration of the standard for inferring pretext from superior qualifications." 456 U.S. at 457. While "slap in the face" was too restrictive, the Court felt
this was "not the occasion to define more precisely what standard should govern
pretext claims based on superior qualifications. . . . It suffices to say here that some
formulation other than the test the Court of Appeals articulated in this case would
better ensure that trial courts reach consistent results." *Id.* at 458. The Court did note
other tests, and subsequent lower courts have tended to require plaintiff to show "that
the disparities between the successful applicant's and her own qualifications were 'of
such weight and significance that no reasonable person, in the exercise of impartial
judgment, could have chosen the candidate selected over the plaintiff.'" *Brooks v.
County Comm'n*, 446 F.3d 1160, 1163 (11th Cir. 2006) (citation omitted).

Ash dealt only with comparative *qualifications*, but comparisons can be drawn in
other contexts. Thus, *Fields v. Shelter Mut. Ins. Co.*, 520 F.3d 859 (8th Cir. 2008)
rejected a claim of pay discrimination where putative comparators did not suffice: Two
were hired directly into a claims supervisor position, unlike the employee who was
promoted; two others had worked for the employer for a longer period than had the
plaintiff employee, and one worked in a different office and reported to a different
decision maker. Another example is disparate discipline cases — that is, those in which

plaintiff claims that, although he may have been guilty of misconduct, members of a different race or sex committed similar infractions with lesser or no discipline. In many circuits, the courts require a very close correspondence between the plaintiff and her putative comparator(s) before such proof is given much weight. *Gates v. Caterpillar, Inc.*, 513 F.3d 680 (7th Cir. 2008) (plaintiff, who was discharged for improper telephone and Internet use, was not similarly situated to three male employees who also misused employer's electronic equipment where they had a different supervisor, their conduct was limited to misuse of computers and did not involve telephone use, and they did not continue to engage in misconduct after being initially disciplined). *But see Jackson v. Fedex Corporate Servs.*, 518 F.3d 388, 397 (6th Cir. 2008) ("The district court's narrow definition of similarly situated effectively removed Jackson from the protective reach of the anti-discrimination laws. [Its] finding that Jackson had no comparables from the six other employees in the PowerPad project deprived Jackson of any remedy to which he may be entitled under the law.").

5. *Legitimate Nondiscriminatory Reason.* Defendant may rebut a prima facie case by "articulat[ing] some legitimate, nondiscriminatory reason" for its action. *McDonnell Douglas* established that disloyalty is such a reason. Suppose the court finds as a fact that Green was not rehired because he was a vegetarian. Is this a "legitimate, nondiscriminatory reason"? If so, what does "legitimate" mean? *Biggins* held that a firing to avoid a pension vesting, which would have been an ERISA violation, did not violate the ADEA; it was, therefore, "legitimate" under the latter statute. While the courts continue to speak of the employer's burden of producing a "legitimate nondiscriminatory reason," it seems clear that any reason is "legitimate" if it is "nondiscriminatory." This should not be so surprising in an at-will world.

6. *Retaliation. McDonnell Douglas* was framed as a discrimination case, that is, whether plaintiff was denied reemployment because of his race. You probably noticed that it might have been framed as what we would today call a public policy case — he was not reemployed because of his civil rights activities. The law we studied in Chapter 4 on the public policy tort was largely nonexistent when *McDonnell Douglas* was handed down, but Title VII has its own ban on retaliation. Percy Green raised this issue below, but the Supreme Court did not address it. Retaliation is considered beginning at page 648.

Note on "Adverse Employment Actions"

Refusals to hire (as in *McDonnell Douglas*) and discharges (as in *Slack* and *Biggins*) are obviously sufficient to justify relief if wrongfully motivated. But not all differences in treatment because of race, sex, religion, or age have been viewed as actionable. Some courts, often relying on the notion that the antidiscrimination statutes reach only "terms and conditions" of employment, hold that minor effects do not give rise to a claim. They require "material adverse effects" for a suit to go forward, but often differ on what is material. *Compare Beyer v. County of Nassau*, 524 F.3d 160, 164 (2d Cir. 2008) (a reasonable jury could find that denial of a transfer from a unit that, by objective indications, "had become a disadvantageous place in which to work" to a unit that, "for an officer pursuing a career in police forensics . . . was both highly desirable and objectively preferable" was sufficiently adverse to be actionable), *with Mitchell v. Vanderbilt Univ.*, 389 F.3d 177, 182 (6th Cir. 2004) (deprivation of a summer graduate research assistant, revocation of mentor status in MD/PhD graduate program, removal from position of Medical Director, reduction in lab space, and requirement that research be submitted for internal review were not adverse employment actions when there was no concomitant diminution in material responsibilities or reduction in pay). *See also Nichols v. S. Ill. University-Edwardsville,* 510 F.3d 772, 781 (7th Cir. 2007) (where assignment to a different campus had no effect on plaintiff's "salary, perks, or opportunities for future advancement," it was a lateral transfer and not actionable); *Primes v. Reno,* 190 F.3d 765 (6th Cir. 1999) ("mid-range performance evaluation of 'fully successful'" not actionable); *Williams v. Bristol-Myers Squibb Co.,* 85 F.3d 270 (7th Cir. 1996) (lateral transfer not actionable when any diminution in pay was "indirect and minor").

Some courts seem far more receptive to holding actions with no direct economic consequences to be actionable. *E.g., Crawford v. Carroll,* 529 F.3d 961 (11th Cir. 2008) (denial of merit raise actionable if discriminatory, even if the denial was later reversed by the employer); *Wedow v. City of Kan. City,* 442 F.3d 1027 (8th Cir. 2006) (holding that jury could find an adverse employment action in the lack of adequate protective clothing and private, sanitary shower and restroom facilities for a female firefighter because the conditions jeopardized plaintiff's ability to perform the core functions of her job safely and efficiently); *Holcomb v. Powell,* 433 F.3d 889, 903 (D.C. Cir. 2006) (finding that being put in "professional purgatory" by being assigned duties that were not only far below her grade level but below the level at which plaintiff had entered federal employment ten years earlier was an adverse employment action).

Professor Rebecca Hanner White, in *De Minimis Discrimination,* 47 EMORY L. J. 1121, 1148, 1151 (1998), criticized these kinds of restrictions, arguing that the term "adverse employment action" is not found in the statutory language. The statute's bar on discrimination in connection with hiring, firing, or the "compensation, terms, conditions, or privileges" of employment "is better read as making clear that an employer who discriminates against an employee in a non-job-related context would not run afoul of Title VII, rather than as sheltering employment discrimination that does not significantly disadvantage an employee." *Id. See also* Rosalie Berger Levinson, *Parsing the Meaning of "Adverse Employment Action" in Title VII Disparate Treatment, Sexual Harassment, and Retaliation Claims: What Should Be Actionable Wrongdoing?,* 56 OKLA. L. REV. 623, 674-75 (2003); Tristin K. Green, *Discrimination in Workplace Dynamics: Toward a Structural Account of Disparate Treatment Theory,* 38 HARV. C.R.-C.L. L. REV. 93, 102 (2003); Ernest F. Lidge III, *The Meaning of Discrimination: Why Courts Have Erred in Requiring Employment Discrimination Plaintiffs to Prove That the Employer's Action Was Materially Adverse or Ultimate,* 47 U. KAN. L. REV. 333 (1999); Theresa M. Beiner, *Do Reindeer Games Count as Terms, Conditions or Privileges of Employment Under Title VII?,* 37 B.C. L. REV. 643 (1996).

Note on "Reverse" Discrimination

In *McDonald v. Santa Fe Trail Transportation Co.,* 427 U.S. 273 (1976), the Court held that both Title VII and § 1981 barred discrimination against whites. The plaintiffs, both white, were discharged for their involvement in misappropriating company property while an African American involved in the same incident was retained. The district court ruled that Title VII and § 1981 did not protect white plaintiffs from racial discrimination. The Supreme Court disagreed. The Court focused on the legislative history and the language of Title VII, which prohibits the discharge of "any individual" because of "such individual's race." Turning to the interpretation of § 1981, the Court rejected the employer's assertion that the operation of the phrase "as is enjoyed by white citizens" in the statute precluded its use by whites. To the contrary, the statute explicitly applies to "all persons," including whites. Additionally, the Court acknowledged that the original purpose in enacting § 1981 was to provide protection for African Americans, but it was "routinely viewed, by its opponents and supporters alike, as applying to the civil rights of whites as well as nonwhites." Accordingly, the Court held Title VII and § 1981 protections are available to plaintiffs of all races.

Since *Santa Fe*, whites have been protected against race discrimination under both Title VII and § 1981. It is equally clear that men are protected against sex discrimination in employment under Title VII. Thus, all employees are protected, but they are protected only from discrimination on the prohibited ground. That is, the employer need not have a good reason to discharge as long as its reason is not a prohibited one (e.g., race, sex, or age). While this is the law, employers are well advised to have defensible reasons for firing their workers. In that sense, the enactment of antidiscrimination statutes tends toward a just-cause rule since all workers — African Americans, Caucasians, women, men, older workers, individuals with disabilities, etc. — are free to challenge adverse decisions as discriminatory. While most such challenges will fail, *see* Ann C. McGinley, *The Emerging Cronyism Defense and Affirmative Action: A Critical Perspective on the Distinction Between Color-Blind and Race-Conscious Decision Making Under Title VII*, 39 ARIZ. L. REV. 1003 (1997); Chad Derum & Karen Engle, *The Rise of the Personal Animosity Presumption in Title VII and the Return to "No Cause" Employment*, 81 TEX. L. REV. 1177, 1182 (2003), the costs of litigation can themselves be considerable, and defensible employment decisions conduce to good employee morale. *See* Ann C. McGinley, *Rethinking Civil Rights and Employment at Will*, 57 OHIO ST. L.J. 1443 (1996).

Although *Santa Fe* makes clear that "reverse" discrimination is cognizable under both Title VII and § 1981, the question of the validity of an affirmative action plan, reserved in footnote 8 in *Santa Fe*, was later resolved in favor of the voluntary use of racial and gender preferences. *Johnson v. Transportation Agency of Santa Clara County*, 480 U.S. 616 (1987) (approving affirmative action plan benefiting women); *United Steelworkers v. Weber*, 440 U.S. 969 (1979) (approving affirmative action plan benefiting African Americans). We will discuss these cases at page 585. And, while not explicitly an "affirmative action" case, *Ricci v. DeStefano*, 129 S. Ct. 2658 (2009), reproduced at page 604, may suggest a new approach to the question. After you have read that decision, you will be finally in a position to assess the current status of affirmative action under Title VII.

Putting the affirmative action question aside, how does, say, a white plaintiff prove racial discrimination? *Santa Fe* did not explain how a white or male plaintiff makes out a prima facie case, and the lower courts seem unclear. Suppose that the employer is Harlem Enterprises, Inc., a black-owned and -operated business. *See Lincoln v. Board of Regents*, 697 F.2d 928 (11th Cir. 1983) (affirming judgment against a predominantly black university in an action brought by a white faculty member). Might one also expect that employers will discriminate against males when they attempt to perform traditionally female jobs? In such cases, plaintiffs are "minorities" in the institution or occupation where they sought work. *McDonnell Douglas* applies with little adjustment. But when a predominantly white institution discharges a white worker, how will he establish a prima facie case? In *Santa Fe*, did the plaintiffs make out a prima facie case by showing that they were whites who were fired, while a black was not, although he engaged in the same conduct? Clearly, an African American plaintiff would make out a prima facie case by proving that similarly situated white workers were favored. Does that mean that whites can also?

A number of circuits have adopted some version of a "background circumstances" test — that is, to establish a prima facie case, a "reverse" discrimination, plaintiff must establish "background circumstances" that support an inference that the defendant employer is "that unusual employer who discriminates against the majority." *Parker v. Baltimore & Ohio R.R. Co.*, 652 F.2d 1012, 1017 (D.C. Cir. 1981). In *Iadimarco v. Runyon*, 190 F.3d 151, 161 (3d Cir. 1999), the Third Circuit found the "concept of 'background circumstances' is irremediably vague and ill-defined." It held that a prima facie case in the context of "reverse" discrimination requires merely that the plaintiff present sufficient evidence to allow a factfinder to conclude that the employer is treating some people less favorably than others based upon a trait that is protected under Title VII. But the court then held that this test was not satisfied by showing that the managers who made the challenged decision were African American. *See also Coulton v. Univ. of Pa.*, 237 F. App'x 741 (3d Cir. 2007) (African American decision makers and a manager's predictions by a manager that a white would have problems working in a department with an overwhelming majority of African American did not suffice to prove discrimination where white plaintiff could not show that similarly situated African American employees were treated more favorably). Even in the Third Circuit, is it still harder for a white plaintiff than for an African American to make out a prima facie case? Other circuits continue to use the background circumstances tests. *E.g., Stockwell v. City of Harvey*, 597 F.3d 895, 901 (7th Cir. 2010) (applying "background circumstances" test in reverse discrimination case). *See generally* Charles A. Sullivan, *Circling Back to the Obvious: The Convergence of Traditional and Reverse Discrimination in Title VII Proof*, 46 WM. & MARY L. REV. 1031 (2004).

b. Defendant's Rebuttal and Plaintiff's Proof of Pretext

Assuming that the plaintiff establishes her prima facie case, the next step is for the defendant to put into evidence its nondiscriminatory reason. Given that this is merely a burden of production, employers almost always satisfy it. The *McDonnell Douglas* analysis then proceeds to the third and final step, in which the plaintiff attempts to prove that that reason is a pretext for discrimination. The courts have been rigorous in resisting efforts to collapse the employer's rebuttal case with the plaintiff's prima facie case. For example, *Ruiz v. County of Rockland*, 609 F.3d 486, 493 (2d Cir. 2010), held that defendant's claim of serious misconduct by plaintiff does not bar plaintiff from making out a prima facie case when his performance evaluations showed satisfactory work: "[T]he step at which the court considers such evidence is important" because "no amount of evidence permits a plaintiff to overcome a failure to make out a prima facie case." *See also Lake v. Yellow Transp., Inc.*, 596 F.3d 871, 874 (8th Cir. 2010) (a plaintiff is not required to disprove the asserted reason for firing him at the prima facie stage of the analysis since to do so would collapse the defendant's burden of production into the prima facie case; thus, plaintiff carried its burden by showing that he met the employer's expectations "other than the tardiness and unavailability Yellow offers as its reasons for firing him.").

As a practical matter, the vast majority of individual disparate treatment cases are resolved at the pretext stage, typically on a motion for summary judgment when the court finds that the plaintiff has not adduced sufficient evidence for a jury to determine the defendant's nondiscriminatory reason is pretextual. This is true despite the Supreme Court's permissive approach to proving pretext. In *Patterson v. McLean Credit Union*, 491 U.S. 164 (1989), plaintiff brought a § 1981 suit challenging the defendant's repeated failures to promote her. On appeal, she questioned the district court's instructions to the jury that, in order to prevail, she had to show that she was better qualified than her successful white competitor. The Supreme Court found this to be error. Applying the *McDonnell Douglas/Burdine* proof structure to claims of racial discrimination under § 1981, the Court agreed that plaintiff "retains the final burden of persuading the jury of intentional discrimination" by proving that a defendant's legitimate nondiscriminatory reason was a pretext:

> Although petitioner retains the ultimate burden of persuasion, our cases make clear that she must also have the opportunity to demonstrate that respondent's proffered reasons for its decision were not its true reasons. In doing so, petitioner is not limited to presenting evidence of a certain type. . . . The evidence which petitioner can present in an attempt to establish that respondent's stated reasons are pretextual may take a variety of forms. *McDonnell Douglas.* Indeed, she might seek to demonstrate that respondent's claim to have promoted a better qualified applicant was pretextual by showing that she was in fact better qualified than the person chosen for the position. The District Court erred, however, in instructing the jury that in order to succeed petitioner was required to make such a showing. There are certainly other ways in which petitioner could seek to prove that respondent's reasons were pretextual. Thus, for example, petitioner could seek to persuade the jury that respondent had not offered the true reason for its promotion decision by presenting evidence of respondent's past treatment of petitioner, including the instances of the racial harassment which she alleges and respondent's failure to train her for an accounting position. While we do not intend to say this evidence necessarily would be sufficient to carry the day, it cannot be denied that it is one of the various ways in which petitioner might seek to prove intentional discrimination on the part of respondent. She may not be forced to pursue any particular means of demonstrating that respondent's stated reasons are pretextual.

Earlier in this chapter, we saw that when plaintiff is passed over in favor of another, she need not prove her qualifications were equal or superior to those of the successful competitor to make out a prima facie case; it is enough to show that she has the minimum qualifications for the position. This is clearly the logic of *Patterson:* Plaintiff may establish her prima facie case without showing she is equal or superior to the whites promoted. However, the defendant will typically claim that it promoted the better-qualified persons, who happened to be white. Simply putting into evidence its view that the successful applicant was superior to plaintiff in some respects will suffice to carry the defendant's burden of production. Plaintiff must then prove pretext and, while *Patterson* holds that she may do this in a variety of different ways, the most obvious path is for plaintiff to show that her qualifications were equal or superior to those of the successful competitor. *See generally* Anne Lawton, *The Meritocracy Myth and the Illusion of Equal Employment Opportunity*, 85 MINN. L. REV. 587, 645 (2000). That, of course, brings us back to the whole question of comparators. See Note 4, page 523.

But even this inquiry reveals the complexity of the concept of "pretext." Suppose the plaintiff shows that the defendant's reason is objectively false — for example, the plaintiff proves she has a college degree, while the defendant claims it did not promote her because she did not have a degree. *See Golumb v. Prudential Ins. Co. of Am.*, 688 F.2d 547 (7th Cir. 1982). This would seem to prove pretext, but maybe not: Although the reason is not objectively true, the employer may have believed it to be true and acted on it, rather than on the basis of the employee's protected class. This "honest belief" rule has doomed many claims. *See, e.g., Johnson v. AT&T Corp.*, 422 F.3d 756, 762 (8th Cir. 2005) ("[T]he proper inquiry is not whether AT&T was factually correct in determining that Johnson had made the bomb threats. Rather, the proper inquiry is whether AT&T honestly believed that Johnson had made the bomb threats."); *Ramirez Rodriguez v. Boehringer Ingelheim Pharms., Inc.*, 425 F.3d 67, 77 (1st Cir. 2005) (finding no hearsay problem with statements of physicians criticizing a discharged pharmaceutical representative because the evidence was not offered to prove the truth of the matter asserted "but rather to demonstrate that his superiors had reason, based on a thorough investigation, to believe that he had"). In such cases, the employer's asserted reason is not a "pretext" although it is factually incorrect. Of course, perhaps proof that the employer was objectively wrong is a reason for thinking that something more objectionable than an honest mistake explains the decision.

Alternatively, the defendant's reason might be true but fail to explain the decision. For example, if the employer claims the employee was discharged for tardiness, the female plaintiff might admit that she was frequently late, but claim that men who were also late were not fired. Again, we're discussing comparators: By proving that males were treated more favorably in regard to the asserted reason, the plaintiff undercuts the defendant's explanation. *Anderson v. Savage Lab., Inc.*, 675 F.2d 1221 (11th Cir. 1982). In this case, the reason is true (in the sense that the act or omission it relies on in fact occurred) but nevertheless a pretext (because that was not the real reason for the decision). To add a final layer of complication, a showing that others were guilty of the same act or omission as plaintiff does not necessarily prove that the adverse action taken against plaintiff was a pretext. Most obviously, the employer might have been unaware of the violations by others. *Mechnig v. Sears, Roebuck & Co.*, 864 F.2d 1359 (7th Cir. 1988).

Patterson allows plaintiff to challenge defendant's claimed reason indirectly, "by presenting evidence of respondent's past treatment of petitioner, including the instances of the racial harassment which she alleges and respondent's failure to train her for an accounting position." The partial dissent of Justices Brennan and Stevens argued that the jury instruction below was

> much too restrictive, cutting off other methods of proving pretext plainly recognized in our cases. We suggested in *McDonnell Douglas*, for example, that a black plaintiff might be able to prove pretext by showing that the employer has promoted white employees who lack the qualifications the employer relies upon, or by proving the employer's "general policy and practice with respect to minority employment." And, of particular relevance given petitioner's evidence of racial harassment and her allegation that respondent failed to train her for an accounting position because of her race, we suggested that evidence of the employer's past treatment of the plaintiff would be relevant to a showing that the employer's proffered legitimate reason was not its true reason.

Id. at 217. How is this proof relevant to the ultimate issue of whether the plaintiff was discriminated against?

1. Proving that the employer promoted whites without the asserted qualifications tends to show that the qualifications are unnecessary, even in the employer's own view.

2. Showing the employer's "general policy and practice with respect to minority employment" suggests that, if the employer generally discriminates, it is more likely it discriminated as to the particular plaintiff.
3. While harassment itself, if sufficiently severe, violates Title VII, *see* Section D, perhaps a company that condones racial harassment is more likely to be discriminatory in promotions.
4. Defendant's failure to train plaintiff, and its general past treatment of her may be probative of discrimination — unless the reason for adverse treatment was peculiar to plaintiff and unrelated to her race.

Will plaintiff at least get to the jury if she adduces evidence sufficient to raise a material issue of fact on one of these claims?

Patterson held it error to limit the jury's consideration of pretext. Does the jury need to be instructed about the effect to be given a finding that the employer's reason is pretextual? If so, what should that instruction be? A simple "false in one, false in all," or something more tailored to the case being considered? The courts of appeal have split on this. *Compare Townsend v. Lumbermens Mut. Cas. Co.*, 294 F.3d 1232, 1238 (10th Cir. 2002) ("[D]istrict courts must instruct juries that they can infer discriminatory intent from disbelief of defendants' explanations."), *with Gehring v. Case Corp.*, 43 F.3d 340, 343 (7th Cir. 1994) (while the jury could infer age discrimination from its disbelief of defendant's reason, such an instruction was not required since "a judge need not deliver instructions describing all valid legal principles."). Conversely, is it error not to instruct the jury that the employer has the right to make business judgments that are free of discrimination? *Walker v. AT&T Technologies*, 995 F.2d 846 (8th Cir. 1993) (yes). *But see Kelley v. Airborne Freight Corp.*, 140 F.3d 335 (1st Cir. 1998).

Suppose defendant puts into evidence more than one nondiscriminatory reason. Some lower courts have required the plaintiff to adduce proof of the pretextual nature of *all* the reasons, *e.g., Kautz v. Met-Pro Corp.*, 412 F.3d 463 (3d Cir. 2005) (granting summary judgment against employee who could not show that all of employer's nondiscriminatory reasons were pretextual). Other courts believe that proof that any reason is pretextual will usually permit the jury to infer that the pretext conceals a discriminatory motive. *See generally* Lawrence D. Rosenthal, *Motions for Summary Judgment When Employers Offer Multiple Justifications for Adverse Employment Actions: Why the Exceptions Should Swallow the Rule*, 2002 UTAH L. REV. 335, 335-36 (2002). Of course, sometimes an employer's multiple reasons will conflict, or change over time, thus providing another basis to infer pretext. *E.g., Jones v. Nat'l Am. Univ.*, 608 F.3d 1039 (8th Cir. 2010) (a change in the employer's reasons for its action between those offered the Equal Employment Opportunity Commission ("EEOC") and those adduced at trial can be evidence of pretext sufficient to uphold a jury verdict, at least in the context of other evidence of age bias); *Juarez v. AGS Gov't Solution Group*, 314 F.3d 1243 (10th Cir. 2003) (proof that manager's evaluation contained fraudulent data and the employer offered conflicting reasons for discharge is sufficient to establish pretext in a race discrimination case).

Employers have also attempted to buttress their nondiscriminatory reason with what is sometimes called the "same actor defense." Courts have often declined to infer a discriminatory intent when the person who hired an older worker also discharged him within a relatively short period of time. The rationale is that, had the employer held stereotypical views, he would not have hired the plaintiff in the first place.

Brown v. CSC Logic, Inc. 82 F.3d 651 (5th Cir. 1996); *Proud v. Stone*, 945 F.2d 796 (4th Cir. 1991) Several circuits have applied this inference to discrimination cases outside the ADEA. *See, e.g., Jaques v. Clean-Up Group, Inc.*, 96 F.3d 506 (1st Cir. 1996) (disability discrimination); *Jiminez v. Mary Washington College*, 57 F.3d 369 (4th Cir. 1995) (race and national origin discrimination). The conditions for the "same actor" defense are restrictive: Obviously, the same supervisor must make both decisions, and the decisions must be in tension with one another. For example, a person who hires an older worker or a woman for one position might be expected not to discriminate in discharging that person, but could easily hold stereotypic views about the limitations of such persons with respect to higher-level jobs. The strength of the inference will also vary depending on the circumstances. *EEOC v. Boeing Co.*, 577 F.3d 1044, 1052 (9th Cir. 2009) ("Although a termination is rarely motivated by bias when it is initiated by the same actors who recently selected the same employee for the job or promotion in the first place, the logic differs when applied to less overtly 'positive' employment decisions, such as refraining from firing an employee at the earliest opportunity or giving an employee a lukewarm evaluation, rather than a poor one."). *See generally* Natasha T. Martin, *Immunity for Hire: How the Same-Actor Doctrine Sustains Discrimination in the Contemporary Workplace*, 40 CONN. L. REV. 1117 (2008); Ross B. Goldman, Note, *Putting Pretext in Context: Employment Discrimination, the Same-Actor Inference, and the Proper Roles of Judges and Juries*, 93 VA. L. REV. 1533 (2007).

Patterson was not the Supreme Court's last encounter with the question of pretext. *St. Mary's Honor Center v. Hicks*, 509 U.S. 502 (1993), involved a race discrimination claim. At the bench trial, the plaintiff established a prima facie case under *Burdine*, thus triggering the *McDonnell Douglas* presumption. Defendant, in turn, produced two alternative explanations to rebut the presumption, but both were rejected by the judge. Since he credited neither explanation, one might have thought that the judge would have necessarily found them to be "pretexts" for discrimination. However, that was not his conclusion. Rather, the trial judge believed that the action was taken on the basis of personal animosity by the supervisor toward the plaintiff, something the supervisor had denied on the stand. The court therefore determined that the plaintiff had not met his burden of persuasion that the adverse actions were based on race. The Court of Appeals reversed, reasoning that, since the judge disbelieved the proffered explanations, the defendants were in "no better position than if they had remained silent."

The Supreme Court disagreed. The *McDonnell Douglas* presumption shift did not shift the plaintiff's ultimate burden of persuasion. To this point, the opinion was consistent with *Burdine*. But the majority went further. Looking to statements in prior opinions that the plaintiff always carries the burden of persuading the trier of fact that the defendant intentionally discriminated against him because of his race, the majority held that mere disbelief of the defendant's asserted nondiscriminatory reason was not enough to find for plaintiff. Rather, the trier of fact had to find that the rejected reasons were not just a pretext for some hidden motivation but were a pretext for discrimination. *See also DeFreitas v. Horizon Inv. Mgmt. Corp.*, 577 F.3d 1151 (10th Cir. 2009) (although plaintiff presented evidence that the employer's supposed reasons for firing her were pretextual, she did not present evidence that would allow the inference that her predominantly Mormon employer fired her because she was a Catholic when her religion was known through her tenure and she was given promotions and raises).

The dissent argued that the Court's decision would encourage employers to perjure themselves to defeat the *McDonnell Douglas* presumption. The Court responded by pointing out other procedural devices that gave the defendant an "advantage" even if ultimately proved to be false.

After *Hicks*, a prima facie case creates a mandatory presumption in favor of the plaintiff, but one that disappears as soon as the defendant carries its burden of production. But what is the effect of the proof that established the prima face case? In the wake of *Hicks*, there was considerable uncertainty as to whether plaintiff had to produce *additional* evidence of discrimination, that is, evidence beyond the prima facie case and any proof of pretext. This was called the "pretext plus" reading of *Hicks*. The alternative reading, the "pretext only" view, was that the trier of fact's disbelief of the purported nondiscriminatory reason permitted, although it did not require, a finding of discrimination. The Court resolved this dispute in the next case.

Reeves v. Sanderson Plumbing Products, Inc.
530 U.S. 133 (2000)

Justice O'CONNOR delivered the opinion of the Court.

This case concerns the kind and amount of evidence necessary to sustain a jury's verdict that an employer unlawfully discriminated on the basis of age. Specifically, we must resolve whether a defendant is entitled to judgment as a matter of law when the plaintiff's case consists exclusively of a prima facie case of discrimination and sufficient evidence for the trier of fact to disbelieve the defendant's legitimate, nondiscriminatory explanation for its action. We must also decide whether the employer was entitled to judgment as a matter of law under the particular circumstances presented here.

I

In October 1995, petitioner Roger Reeves was 57 years old and had spent 40 years in the employ of respondent, Sanderson Plumbing Products, Inc., a manufacturer of toilet seats and covers. Petitioner worked in a department known as the "Hinge Room," where he supervised the "regular line." Joe Oswalt, in his mid-thirties, supervised the Hinge Room's "special line," and Russell Caldwell, the manager of the Hinge Room and age 45, supervised both petitioner and Oswalt. Petitioner's responsibilities included recording the attendance and hours of those under his supervision, and reviewing a weekly report that listed the hours worked by each employee.

In the summer of 1995, Caldwell informed Powe Chesnut, the director of manufacturing and the husband of company president Sandra Sanderson, that "production was down" in the Hinge Room because employees were often absent and were "coming in late and leaving early." Because the monthly attendance reports did not indicate a problem, Chesnut ordered an audit of the Hinge Room's timesheets for July, August, and September of that year. According to Chesnut's testimony, that investigation revealed "numerous timekeeping errors and misrepresentations on the part of Caldwell, Reeves, and Oswalt." Following the audit, Chesnut, along with Dana Jester, vice president of human resources, and Tom Whitaker, vice president of operations, recommended to company president Sanderson that petitioner and

Caldwell be fired. In October 1995, Sanderson followed the recommendation and discharged both petitioner and Caldwell.

At trial, respondent contended that it had fired petitioner due to his failure to maintain accurate attendance records, while petitioner attempted to demonstrate that respondent's explanation was pretext for age discrimination. Petitioner introduced evidence that he had accurately recorded the attendance and hours of the employees under his supervision, and that Chesnut, whom Oswalt described as wielding "absolute power" within the company had demonstrated age-based animus in his dealings with petitioner.

[The jury returned a verdict in favor of petitioner of $35,000 in compensatory damages, which the judge doubled as liquidated damages pursuant to the jury's finding that the employer's age discrimination was "willful." The judge also awarded plaintiff $28,490.80 in front pay for two years' lost income. The Fifth Circuit reversed], holding that petitioner had not introduced sufficient evidence to sustain the jury's finding of unlawful discrimination. After noting respondent's proffered justification for petitioner's discharge, the court acknowledged that petitioner "very well may" have offered sufficient evidence for "a reasonable jury [to] have found that [respondent's] explanation for its employment decision was pretextual." The court explained, however, that this was "not dispositive" of the ultimate issue — namely, "whether Reeves presented sufficient evidence that his age motivated [respondent's] employment decision." Addressing this question, the court weighed petitioner's additional evidence of discrimination against other circumstances surrounding his discharge. Specifically, the court noted that Chesnut's age-based comments "were not made in the direct context of Reeves's termination"; there was no allegation that the two other individuals who had recommended that petitioner be fired (Jester and Whitaker) were motivated by age; two of the decision makers involved in petitioner's discharge (Jester and Sanderson) were over the age of 50; all three of the Hinge Room supervisors were accused of inaccurate record keeping; and several of respondent's management positions were filled by persons over age 50 when petitioner was fired. On this basis, the court concluded that petitioner had not introduced sufficient evidence for a rational jury to conclude that he had been discharged because of his age. . . .

II

Under the ADEA, it is "unlawful for an employer . . . to fail or refuse to hire or to discharge any individual or otherwise discriminate against any individual with respect to his compensation, terms, conditions, or privileges of employment, because of such individual's age." When a plaintiff alleges disparate treatment, "liability depends on whether the protected trait (under the ADEA, age) actually motivated the employer's decision." *Hazen Paper Co. v. Biggins.* That is, the plaintiff's age must have "actually played a role in [the employer's decision making] process and had a determinative influence on the outcome." Recognizing that "the question facing triers of fact in discrimination cases is both sensitive and difficult," and that "there will seldom be 'eyewitness' testimony as to the employer's mental processes," *Postal Service Bd. of Governors v. Aikens,* the Courts of Appeals, including the Fifth Circuit in this case, have employed some variant of the framework articulated in *McDonnell Douglas* to analyze ADEA claims that are based principally on circumstantial evidence. . . . This Court has not squarely addressed whether the *McDonnell Douglas* framework, developed to assess claims brought under §703(a)(1) of Title VII of the Civil Rights Act of 1964, also applies to ADEA actions. Because the parties do not dispute the issue, we shall assume, arguendo, that the *McDonnell Douglas* framework is fully applicable here.

[Under this framework, petitioner established a prima facie case and respondent rebutted it.] Although intermediate evidentiary burdens shift back and forth under this framework, "the ultimate burden of persuading the trier of fact that the defendant intentionally discriminated against the plaintiff remains at all times with the plaintiff." And in attempting to satisfy this burden, the plaintiff—once the employer produces sufficient evidence to support a nondiscriminatory explanation for its decision—must be afforded the "opportunity to prove by a preponderance of the evidence that the legitimate reasons offered by the defendant were not its true reasons, but were a pretext for discrimination." That is, the plaintiff may attempt to establish that he was the victim of intentional discrimination "by showing that the employer's proffered explanation is unworthy of credence." Moreover, although the presumption of discrimination "drops out of the picture" once the defendant meets its burden of production, the trier of fact may still consider the evidence establishing the plaintiff's prima facie case "and inferences properly drawn therefrom . . . on the issue of whether the defendant's explanation is pretextual."

In this case, the evidence supporting respondent's explanation for petitioner's discharge consisted primarily of testimony by Chesnut and Sanderson and documentation of petitioner's alleged "shoddy record keeping." Chesnut testified that a 1993 audit of Hinge Room operations revealed "a very lax assembly line" where employees were not adhering to general work rules. As a result of that audit, petitioner was placed on 90 days' probation for unsatisfactory performance. In 1995, Chesnut ordered another investigation of the Hinge Room, which, according to his testimony, revealed that petitioner was not correctly recording the absences and hours of employees. Respondent introduced summaries of that investigation documenting several attendance violations by 12 employees under petitioner's supervision, and noting that each should have been disciplined in some manner. Chesnut testified that this failure to discipline absent and late employees is "extremely important when you are dealing with a union" because uneven enforcement across departments would keep the company "in grievance and arbitration cases, which are costly, all the time." He and Sanderson also stated that petitioner's errors, by failing to adjust for hours not worked, cost the company overpaid wages. Sanderson testified that she accepted the recommendation to discharge petitioner because he had "intentionally falsified company pay records."

Petitioner, however, made a substantial showing that respondent's explanation was false. First, petitioner offered evidence that he had properly maintained the attendance records. Most of the timekeeping errors cited by respondent involved employees who were not marked late but who were recorded as having arrived at the plant at 7 A.M. for the 7 A.M. shift. Respondent contended that employees arriving at 7 A.M. could not have been at their workstations by 7 A.M., and therefore must have been late. But both petitioner and Oswalt testified that the company's automated timeclock often failed to scan employees' timecards, so that the timesheets would not record any time of arrival. On these occasions, petitioner and Oswalt would visually check the workstations and record whether the employees were present at the start of the shift. They stated that if an employee arrived promptly but the timesheet contained no time of arrival, they would reconcile the two by marking "7 A.M." as the employee's arrival time, even if the employee actually arrived at the plant earlier. On cross-examination, Chesnut acknowledged that the timeclock sometimes malfunctioned, and that if "people were there at their work stations" at the start of the shift, the supervisor "would write in seven o'clock." Petitioner also testified that when employees arrived before or stayed after their shifts, he would assign them additional work so they would not be overpaid.

Petitioner similarly cast doubt on whether he was responsible for any failure to discipline late and absent employees. Petitioner testified that his job only included reviewing the daily and weekly attendance reports, and that disciplinary write-ups were based on the monthly reports, which were reviewed by Caldwell. Sanderson admitted that Caldwell, and not petitioner, was responsible for citing employees for violations of the company's attendance policy. Further, Chesnut conceded that there had never been a union grievance or employee complaint arising from petitioner's record keeping, and that the company had never calculated the amount of overpayments allegedly attributable to petitioner's errors. Petitioner also testified that, on the day he was fired, Chesnut said that his discharge was due to his failure to report as absent one employee, Gina Mae Coley, on two days in September 1995. But petitioner explained that he had spent those days in the hospital, and that Caldwell was therefore responsible for any overpayment of Coley. Finally, petitioner stated that on previous occasions that employees were paid for hours they had not worked, the company had simply adjusted those employees' next paychecks to correct the errors.

Based on this evidence, the Court of Appeals concluded that petitioner "very well may be correct" that "a reasonable jury could have found that [respondent's] explanation for its employment decision was pretextual." Nonetheless, the court held that this showing, standing alone, was insufficient to sustain the jury's finding of liability: "We must, as an essential final step, determine whether Reeves presented sufficient evidence that his age motivated [respondent's] employment decision." And in making this determination, the Court of Appeals ignored the evidence supporting petitioner's prima facie case and challenging respondent's explanation for its decision. The court confined its review of evidence favoring petitioner to that evidence showing that Chesnut had directed derogatory, age-based comments at petitioner, and that Chesnut had singled out petitioner for harsher treatment than younger employees. It is therefore apparent that the court believed that only this additional evidence of discrimination was relevant to whether the jury's verdict should stand. That is, the Court of Appeals proceeded from the assumption that a prima facie case of discrimination, combined with sufficient evidence for the trier of fact to disbelieve the defendant's legitimate, nondiscriminatory reason for its decision, is insufficient as a matter of law to sustain a jury's finding of intentional discrimination.

In so reasoning, the Court of Appeals misconceived the evidentiary burden borne by plaintiffs who attempt to prove intentional discrimination through indirect evidence. This much is evident from our decision in *St. Mary's Honor Center.* There we held that the factfinder's rejection of the employer's legitimate, nondiscriminatory reason for its action does not compel judgment for the plaintiff. The ultimate question is whether the employer intentionally discriminated, and proof that "the employer's proffered reason is unpersuasive, or even obviously contrived, does not necessarily establish that the plaintiff's proffered reason . . . is correct." In other words, "it is not enough . . . to disbelieve the employer; the factfinder must believe the plaintiff's explanation of intentional discrimination."

In reaching this conclusion, however, we reasoned that it is permissible for the trier of fact to infer the ultimate fact of discrimination from the falsity of the employer's explanation. Specifically, we stated:

> The factfinder's disbelief of the reasons put forward by the defendant (particularly if disbelief is accompanied by a suspicion of mendacity) may, together with the elements of the prima facie case, suffice to show intentional discrimination. Thus, rejection of the defendant's proffered reasons will permit the trier of fact to infer the ultimate fact of intentional discrimination.

Proof that the defendant's explanation is unworthy of credence is simply one form of circumstantial evidence that is probative of intentional discrimination, and it may be quite persuasive. [*St. Mary's Honor Center.*] ("Proving the employer's reason false becomes part of (and often considerably assists) the greater enterprise of proving that the real reason was intentional discrimination"). In appropriate circumstances, the trier of fact can reasonably infer from the falsity of the explanation that the employer is dissembling to cover up a discriminatory purpose. Such an inference is consistent with the general principle of evidence law that the factfinder is entitled to consider a party's dishonesty about a material fact as "affirmative evidence of guilt." *Wright v. West*, 505 U.S. 277 (1992); 2 J. Wigmore, EVIDENCE § 278(2), p. 133 (J. Chadbourn rev. ed. 1979). Moreover, once the employer's justification has been eliminated, discrimination may well be the most likely alternative explanation, especially since the employer is in the best position to put forth the actual reason for its decision. *Cf. Furnco Constr. Corp. v. Waters*, 438 U.S. 567, 577 (1978) ("When all legitimate reasons for rejecting an applicant have been eliminated as possible reasons for the employer's actions, it is more likely than not the employer, who we generally assume acts with some reason, based his decision on an impermissible consideration"). Thus, a plaintiff's prima facie case, combined with sufficient evidence to find that the employer's asserted justification is false, may permit the trier of fact to conclude that the employer unlawfully discriminated.

This is not to say that such a showing by the plaintiff will always be adequate to sustain a jury's finding of liability. Certainly there will be instances where, although the plaintiff has established a prima facie case and set forth sufficient evidence to reject the defendant's explanation, no rational factfinder could conclude that the action was discriminatory. For instance, an employer would be entitled to judgment as a matter of law if the record conclusively revealed some other, nondiscriminatory reason for the employer's decision, or if the plaintiff created only a weak issue of fact as to whether the employer's reason was untrue and there was abundant and uncontroverted independent evidence that no discrimination had occurred. *See Fisher v. Vassar College*, 114 F.3d 1332, 1338 (2d Cir. 1997) ("If the circumstances show that the defendant gave the false explanation to conceal something other than discrimination, the inference of discrimination will be weak or nonexistent"). To hold otherwise would be effectively to insulate an entire category of employment discrimination cases from review under Rule 50, and we have reiterated that trial courts should not "treat discrimination differently from other ultimate questions of fact." *St. Mary's Honor Center*.

Whether judgment as a matter of law is appropriate in any particular case will depend on a number of factors. Those include the strength of the plaintiff's prima facie case, the probative value of the proof that the employer's explanation is false, and any other evidence that supports the employer's case and that properly may be considered on a motion for judgment as a matter of law. For purposes of this case, we need not — and could not — resolve all of the circumstances in which such factors would entitle an employer to judgment as a matter of law. It suffices to say that, because a prima facie case and sufficient evidence to reject the employer's explanation may permit a finding of liability, the Court of Appeals erred in proceeding from the premise that a plaintiff must always introduce additional, independent evidence of discrimination.

III . . .

A

The remaining question is whether, despite the Court of Appeals' misconception of petitioner's evidentiary burden, respondent was nonetheless entitled to judgment as a matter of law. Under Rule 50, a court should render judgment as a matter of law when "a party has been fully heard on an issue and there is no legally sufficient evidentiary basis for a reasonable jury to find for that party on that issue." . . .

[In entertaining a motion for judgment as a matter of law, the court should review all of the evidence in the record.] In doing so, however, the court must draw all reasonable inferences in favor of the nonmoving party, and it may not make credibility determinations or weigh the evidence. *Lytle v. Household Mfg., Inc.*, 494 U.S. 545, 554-55 (1990). "Credibility determinations, the weighing of the evidence, and the drawing of legitimate inferences from the facts are jury functions, not those of a judge." *Anderson v. Liberty Lobby*, 477 U.S. 242 (1986). Thus, although the court should review the record as a whole, it must disregard all evidence favorable to the moving party that the jury is not required to believe. See Wright & Miller 299. That is, the court should give credence to the evidence favoring the nonmovant as well as that "evidence supporting the moving party that is uncontradicted and unimpeached, at least to the extent that that evidence comes from disinterested witnesses."

B

Applying this standard here, it is apparent that respondent was not entitled to judgment as a matter of law. In this case, in addition to establishing a prima facie case of discrimination and creating a jury issue as to the falsity of the employer's explanation, petitioner introduced additional evidence that Chesnut was motivated by age-based animus and was principally responsible for petitioner's firing. Petitioner testified that Chesnut had told him that he "was so old [he] must have come over on the Mayflower" and, on one occasion when petitioner was having difficulty starting a machine, that he "was too damn old to do [his] job." According to petitioner, Chesnut would regularly "cuss at me and shake his finger in my face." Oswalt, roughly 24 years younger than petitioner, corroborated that there was an "obvious difference" in how Chesnut treated them. He stated that, although he and Chesnut "had [their] differences," "it was nothing compared to the way [Chesnut] treated Roger." Oswalt explained that Chesnut "tolerated quite a bit" from him even though he "defied" Chesnut "quite often," but that Chesnut treated petitioner "in a manner, as you would . . . treat . . . a child when . . . you're angry with [him]." Petitioner also demonstrated that, according to company records, he and Oswalt had nearly identical rates of productivity in 1993. Yet respondent conducted an efficiency study of only the regular line, supervised by petitioner, and placed only petitioner on probation. Chesnut conducted that efficiency study and, after having testified to the contrary on direct examination, acknowledged on cross-examination that he had recommended that petitioner be placed on probation following the study.

Further, petitioner introduced evidence that Chesnut was the actual decision-maker behind his firing. Chesnut was married to Sanderson, who made the formal decision to discharge petitioner. Although Sanderson testified that she fired petitioner because he had "intentionally falsified company pay records," respondent only introduced evidence concerning the inaccuracy of the records, not their falsification. A 1994 letter authored by Chesnut indicated that he berated other company directors, who were supposedly his co-equals, about how to do their jobs. Moreover, Oswalt testified that all of respondent's employees feared Chesnut, and that Chesnut had exercised "absolute power" within the company for "as long as [he] can remember."

In holding that the record contained insufficient evidence to sustain the jury's verdict, the Court of Appeals misapplied the standard of review dictated by Rule 50. Again, the court disregarded critical evidence favorable to petitioner — namely, the evidence supporting petitioner's prima facie case and undermining respondent's non-discriminatory explanation. The court also failed to draw all reasonable inferences in favor of petitioner. For instance, while acknowledging "the potentially damning nature" of Chesnut's age-related comments, the court discounted them on the ground that they "were not made in the direct context of Reeves's termination." And the court discredited petitioner's evidence that Chesnut was the actual decision maker by giving weight to the fact that there was "no evidence to suggest that any of the other decision makers were motivated by age." Moreover, the other evidence on which the court relied — that Caldwell and Oswalt were also cited for poor record keeping, and that respondent employed many managers over age 50 — although relevant, is certainly not dispositive. In concluding that these circumstances so overwhelmed the evidence favoring petitioner that no rational trier of fact could have found that petitioner was fired because of his age, the Court of Appeals impermissibly substituted its judgment concerning the weight of the evidence for the jury's.

The ultimate question in every employment discrimination case involving a claim of disparate treatment is whether the plaintiff was the victim of intentional discrimination. Given the evidence in the record supporting petitioner, we see no reason to subject the parties to an additional round of litigation before the Court of Appeals rather than to resolve the matter here. The District Court plainly informed the jury that petitioner was required to show "by a preponderance of the evidence that his age was a determining and motivating factor in the decision of [respondent] to terminate him." The court instructed the jury that, to show that respondent's explanation was a pretext for discrimination, petitioner had to demonstrate "1, that the stated reasons were not the real reasons for [petitioner's] discharge; and 2, that age discrimination was the real reason for [petitioner's] discharge." Given that petitioner established a prima facie case of discrimination, introduced enough evidence for the jury to reject respondent's explanation, and produced additional evidence of age-based animus, there was sufficient evidence for the jury to find that respondent had intentionally discriminated. The District Court was therefore correct to submit the case to the jury, and the Court of Appeals erred in overturning its verdict.

Justice GINSBURG, concurring.

The Court today holds that an employment discrimination plaintiff may survive judgment as a matter of law by submitting two categories of evidence: first, evidence establishing a "prima facie case," as that term is used in *McDonnell Douglas Corp. v. Green*, and second, evidence from which a rational factfinder could conclude that the employer's proffered explanation for its actions was false. Because the Court of Appeals in this case plainly, and erroneously, required the plaintiff to offer some evidence beyond those two categories, no broader holding is necessary to support reversal.

I write separately to note that it may be incumbent on the Court, in an appropriate case, to define more precisely the circumstances in which plaintiffs will be required to submit evidence beyond these two categories in order to survive a motion for judgment as a matter of law. I anticipate that such circumstances will be uncommon. As the Court notes, it is a principle of evidence law that the jury is entitled to treat a party's dishonesty about a material fact as evidence of culpability. Under this commonsense principle, evidence suggesting that a defendant accused of illegal discrimination has chosen to give a false explanation for its actions gives rise to a rational inference that the defendant could be masking its actual, illegal motivation. Whether the defendant was in fact motivated by discrimination is of course for the finder of fact to decide; that is the lesson of *St. Mary's Honor Center v. Hicks.* But the inference remains — unless it is conclusively demonstrated, by evidence the district court is required to credit on a motion for judgment as a matter of law, that discrimination could not have been the defendant's true motivation. If such conclusive demonstrations are (as I suspect) atypical, it follows that the ultimate question of liability ordinarily should not be taken from the jury once the plaintiff has introduced the two categories of evidence described above. Because the Court's opinion leaves room for such further elaboration in an appropriate case, I join it in full.

NOTES

1. *Beyond Pretext Plus.* Professor Michael Zimmer, *Slicing & Dicing of Individual Disparate Treatment Law*, 61 LA. L. REV. 577 (2001), views *Reeves* as broader than merely rejecting the lower court's "pretext-plus" rule. He argues that the Court rejected the underpinning for that rule, which was that the probative value of the evidence supporting plaintiff's prima facie case "drops out of the picture" once defendant introduces evidence of its nondiscriminatory reason for its action. *Id.* at 587-88. *Reeves* also made clear that all the evidence in the record needs to be reviewed in deciding motions for summary judgment or judgment as a matter of law: "That evidence includes evidence supporting the prima facie case, evidence tending to prove the defendant's proffered reason to be false, and all other circumstantial evidence such as age-related comments of decision makers that supports plaintiff's case. Slicing and dicing away plaintiff's evidence to leave only evidence supporting defendant's case is inconsistent with the true nature of the *McDonnell Douglas* method of analyzing individual disparate treatment cases." *Id.* at 591-92.

2. *In the Wake of* Reeves. While most circuits appear to be following *Reeves* by focusing on the evidence in the record and the inferences that can be drawn from that evidence in deciding motions for summary judgment and judgment as a matter of law, several circuits appear to be going their own way. At one extreme, the Seventh Circuit has arguably reincarnated the pretext-plus rule by framing the question as whether the defendant is lying. *Faas v. Sears, Roebuck & Co.*, 532 F.3d 633, 642 (7th Cir. 2008) ("Pretext means a dishonest explanation, a lie rather than an oddity or an error. . . . Pretext is more than a mistake on the part of the employer; it is a phony excuse.") (citations and internal quotations omitted). However, consistent with *Reeves*, other circuits appear to be finding that "stray comment" evidence is sometimes sufficient evidence that the factfinder may consider in deciding whether the employer acted with an intent to discriminate. *E.g., Santiago-Ramos v. Centennial P.R. Wireless Corp.*, 217 F.3d 46, 55 (1st Cir. 2000); Laina Rose Reinsmith, Note, *Proving an Employer's Intent: Disparate Treatment Discrimination and the Stray Remarks Doctrine After* Reeves v. Sanderson Plumbing Products, 55 VAND. L. REV. 219, 255 (2002) (arguing that stray remarks evidence should be treated the same as other circumstantial evidence).

3. *"Unreasonable" Decision versus Business Judgment.* Courts have often recognized that the more unusual and idiosyncratic a decision is — in terms of the way business is normally conducted — the more appropriate it is to infer discrimination. This principle is in obvious tension with what has sometimes been called the "business judgment" rule, which is that courts should not second-guess business decisions. One illustration of the conflict is *White v. Baxter Healthcare Corp.*, 533 F.3d 381, 393 (6th Cir. 2008), in which the majority reaffirmed that "the plaintiff may also demonstrate pretext by offering evidence which challenges the reasonableness of the employer's decision 'to the extent that such an inquiry sheds light on whether the employer's proffered reason for the employment action was its actual motivation'" (citation omitted). It went on:

> [O]ur Circuit has never adopted a "business-judgment rule" which requires us to defer to the employer's "reasonable business judgment" in Title VII cases. Indeed, in most Title VII cases the very issue in dispute is whether the employer's adverse employment decision resulted from an objectively unreasonable business judgment, i.e., a judgment that was based upon an impermissible consideration such as the adversely-affected employee's race, gender, religion, or national origin. In determining whether the plaintiff has produced enough evidence to cast doubt upon the employer's explanation for its decision, we cannot . . . unquestionably accept the employer's own self-serving claim that the decision resulted from an exercise of "reasonable business judgment." Nor can we decide "as a matter of law" that "an employer's proffered justification is reasonable." The question of whether the employer's judgment was reasonable or was instead motivated by improper considerations is for the jury to consider. . . .

Id. at 394 n.6.

4. *"Me, Too" Proof of Pretext.* In *Sprint/United Management Co. v. Mendelsohn*, 552 U.S. 379 (2007), a reduction-in-force case, plaintiff wanted to call as witnesses five other older workers who claimed that they, too, were discriminated against because of their age in the downsizing. Defendant objected because none of these potential witnesses worked under the same supervisor as the plaintiff. The trial court excluded the testimony, and the jury found for the defendant. The court of appeals reversed because, as it saw it, the district court had relied on a per se rule of exclusion of all such so-called "me too" evidence.

The Supreme Court, in a unanimous opinion by Justice Thomas, vacated the circuit court's judgment finding the evidence admissible and remanded the case to the district court to determine admissibility on a case-by-case basis since "such evidence is neither *per se* admissible nor *per se* inadmissible." *Id.* at 381. Emphasizing the broad discretion accorded trail courts' evidentiary rulings — reviewable under a deferential abuse of discretion standard — the trial court should make the admissibility determination: "With respect to evidentiary questions in general [including "relevance" under federal Rule of Evidence 401] and Rule 403 [as to "prejudice"] in particular, a district court virtually always is in the better position to assess the admissibility of the evidence in the context of the case before it." *Id.* at 387. Discrimination cases are well suited to this generally applicable approach since:

> [t]he question whether evidence of discrimination by other supervisors is relevant in an individual ADEA case is fact based and depends on many factors, including how closely related the evidence is to the plaintiff's circumstances and theory of the case. Applying Rule 403 to determine if evidence is prejudicial also requires a fact-intensive, context-specific inquiry.

Id. at 388. Indeed, discrimination cases may be especially fact sensitive. One scholar has argued that the focus on "insular individualism" of supervisors and managers is inconsistent with how workplaces operate in practice, with any particular decision being influenced by a web of other decisions and practices, sometimes influencing individual actors in ways they do not themselves understand. Tristin Green, *Insular Individualism: Employment Discrimination Law After* Ledbetter v. Goodyear, 43 Harv. C.R-C.L. L. Rev. 353 (2008).

After *Mendelsohn* the determination in every case will be contextual, taking into account the requirements of Fed. R. Evid. 401 and 403. As to Rule 401, Sprint claimed that any discrimination by other supervisors was simply irrelevant to the question at issue: Did plaintiff's supervisor pick her for discharge because of her age? If the intent of a single individual is the touchstone, isn't that right? Is that still true even if there is some umbrella policy that allowed each supervisor freedom to make such decisions? And what about the possibility that a supervisor would feel freer to discriminate if others were so acting, and then the actions of others would be admissible (at least if they happened before the challenged action and the supervisor knew about them).

As for prejudice under Rule 403, "[a]lthough relevant, evidence may be excluded if its probative value is substantially outweighed by the danger of unfair prejudice, confusion of the issues, or misleading the jury, or by considerations of undue delay, waste of time, or needless presentation of cumulative evidence." Thus, a low level of relevance may not be sufficient to justify admission of evidence if it is likely to prejudice the jury. *See Mattenson v. Baxter Healthcare Corp.*, 438 F.3d 763, 770-71 (7th Cir. 2006) (in a division of 7,000 employees with hundreds of executives, the fact that some may dislike old workers and even fire old workers because of their age is weak evidence that a particular older employee was fired because of his age; absent proof of a pervasive culture of prejudice, such evidence may be excluded under Rule 403, although it not reversible error to admit it). Isn't there a real danger that a jury would punish Sprint for being a "bad employer" if all this evidence were admitted, even if the decision as to Mendelsohn herself was not discriminatory?

The significance of *Mendelsohn* will, of course, ultimately depend on how the district courts apply their discretion. As a practical matter, this means that "me too" evidence will largely disappear from the radar screen, becoming less a question of "law" than a question of how a particular district court views the evidence in the context of the case before it. Whatever the results in the district courts, the determinations will be reviewed only under the highly deferential abuse of discretion standard, which means that few questions of admissibility will be overturned. Commentary on *Mendelsohn* can be found by Professors Mitchell Rubenstein, Paul Secunda, and David Gregory, Sprint/United Management Co. v. Mendelsohn: *The Supreme Court Appears to Have Punted on the Admissibility of "Me Too" Evidence of Discrimination. But Did It?*, 102 Nw. U. L. Rev. Colloquy 264, 374, 382, 387 (2008).

3. Proving Discrimination: Mixed Motive Analysis

Price Waterhouse v. Hopkins
490 U.S. 228 (1989)

Justice Brennan announced the judgment of the Court and delivered an opinion, in which Justice Marshall, Justice Blackmun, and Justice Stevens join. . . .

. . . At Price Waterhouse, a nationwide professional accounting partnership, a senior manager becomes a candidate for partnership when the partners in her local office submit her name as a candidate. All of the other partners in the firm are then invited to submit written comments on each candidate — either on a "long" or a "short" form, depending on the partner's degree of exposure to the candidate. Not every partner in the firm submits comments on every candidate. After reviewing the comments and interviewing the partners who submitted them, the firm's Admissions Committee makes a recommendation to the Policy Board. This recommendation will be either that the firm accept the candidate for partnership, put her application on "hold," or deny her the promotion outright. The Policy Board then decides whether to submit the candidate's name to the entire partnership for a vote, to "hold" her candidacy, or to reject her. The recommendation of the Admissions Committee, and the decision of the Policy Board, are not controlled by fixed guidelines: a certain number of positive comments from partners will not guarantee a candidate's admission to the partnership, nor will a specific quantity of negative comments necessarily defeat her application. Price Waterhouse places no limit on the number of persons whom it will admit to the partnership in any given year.

Ann Hopkins had worked at Price Waterhouse's Office of Government Services in Washington, D.C., for five years when the partners in that office proposed her as a candidate for partnership. Of the 662 partners at the firm at that time, 7 were women. Of the 88 persons proposed for partnership that year, only 1 — Hopkins — was a woman. Forty-seven of these candidates were admitted to the partnership, 21 were rejected, and 20 — including Hopkins — were "held" for reconsideration the following year. Thirteen of the 32 partners who had submitted comments on Hopkins supported her bid for partnership. Three partners recommended that her candidacy be placed on hold, eight stated that they did not have an informed opinion about her, and eight recommended that she be denied partnership.

In a jointly prepared statement supporting her candidacy, the partners in Hopkins' office showcased her successful 2-year effort to secure a $25 million contract with the Department of State, labeling it "an outstanding performance" and one that

Hopkins carried out "virtually at the partner level." Despite Price Waterhouse's attempt at trial to minimize her contribution to this project, Judge Gesell specifically found that Hopkins had "played a key role in Price Waterhouse's successful effort to win a multimillion dollar contract with the Department of State." Indeed, he went on, "[n]one of the other partnership candidates at Price Waterhouse that year had a comparable record in terms of successfully securing major contracts for the partnership."

The partners in Hopkins' office praised her character as well as her accomplishments, describing her in their joint statement as "an outstanding professional" who had a "deft touch," a "strong character, independence and integrity." Clients appear to have agreed with these assessments. At trial, one official from the State Department described her as "extremely competent, intelligent," "strong and forthright, very productive, energetic and creative." Another high-ranking official praised Hopkins' decisiveness, broadmindedness, and "intellectual clarity"; she was, in his words, "a stimulating conversationalist." Evaluations such as these led Judge Gesell to conclude that Hopkins "had no difficulty dealing with clients and her clients appear to have been very pleased with her work" and that she "was generally viewed as a highly competent project leader who worked long hours, pushed vigorously to meet deadlines and demanded much from the multidisciplinary staffs with which she worked."

On too many occasions, however, Hopkins' aggressiveness apparently spilled over into abrasiveness. Staff members seem to have borne the brunt of Hopkins' brusqueness. Long before her bid for partnership, partners evaluating her work had counseled her to improve her relations with staff members. Although later evaluations indicate an improvement, Hopkins' perceived shortcomings in this important area eventually doomed her bid for partnership. Virtually all of the partners' negative remarks about Hopkins — even those of partners supporting her — had to do with her "interpersonal skills." Both "[s]upporters and opponents of her candidacy," stressed Judge Gesell, "indicated that she was sometimes overly aggressive, unduly harsh, difficult to work with and impatient with staff."

There were clear signs, though, that some of the partners reacted negatively to Hopkins' personality because she was a woman. One partner described her as "macho"; another suggested that she "overcompensated for being a woman"; a third advised her to take "a course at charm school." Several partners criticized her use of profanity; in response, one partner suggested that those partners objected to her swearing only "because it[']s a lady using foul language." Another supporter explained that Hopkins "ha[d] matured from a tough-talking somewhat masculine hard-nosed mgr to an authoritative, formidable, but much more appealing lady ptr candidate." But it was the man who, as Judge Gesell found, bore responsibility for explaining to Hopkins the reasons for the Policy Board's decision to place her candidacy on hold who delivered the coup de grace: in order to improve her chances for partnership, Thomas Beyer advised, Hopkins should "walk more femininely, talk more femininely, dress more femininely, wear make-up, have her hair styled, and wear jewelry."

Dr. Susan Fiske, a social psychologist and Associate Professor of Psychology at Carnegie-Mellon University, testified at trial that the partnership selection process at Price Waterhouse was likely influenced by sex stereotyping. Her testimony focused not only on the overtly sex-based comments of partners but also on gender-neutral remarks, made by partners who knew Hopkins only slightly, that were intensely critical of her. One partner, for example, baldly stated that Hopkins was "universally disliked" by staff, and another described her as "consistently annoying and irritating"; yet these were people who had had very little contact with Hopkins. According to Fiske,

Hopkins' uniqueness (as the only woman in the pool of candidates) and the subjectivity of the evaluations made it likely that sharply critical remarks such as these were the product of sex stereotyping—although Fiske admitted that she could not say with certainty whether any particular comment was the result of stereotyping. Fiske based her opinion on a review of the submitted comments, explaining that it was commonly accepted practice for social psychologists to reach this kind of conclusion without having met any of the people involved in the decisionmaking process.

In previous years, other female candidates for partnership also had been evaluated in sex-based terms. As a general matter, Judge Gesell concluded, "[c]andidates were viewed favorably if partners believed they maintained their femin[in]ity while becoming effective professional managers"; in this environment, "[t]o be identified as a 'women's lib[b]er' was regarded as [a] negative comment." In fact, the judge found that in previous years "[o]ne partner repeatedly commented that he could not consider any woman seriously as a partnership candidate and believed that women were not even capable of functioning as senior managers—yet the firm took no action to discourage his comments and recorded his vote in the overall summary of the evaluations."

Judge Gesell found that Price Waterhouse legitimately emphasized interpersonal skills in its partnership decisions, and also found that the firm had not fabricated its complaints about Hopkins' interpersonal skills as a pretext for discrimination. Moreover, he concluded, the firm did not give decisive emphasis to such traits only because Hopkins was a woman; although there were male candidates who lacked these skills but who were admitted to partnership, the judge found that these candidates possessed other, positive traits that Hopkins lacked.

The judge went on to decide, however, that some of the partners' remarks about Hopkins stemmed from an impermissibly cabined view of the proper behavior of women, and that Price Waterhouse had done nothing to disavow reliance on such comments. He held that Price Waterhouse had unlawfully discriminated against Hopkins on the basis of sex by consciously giving credence and effect to partners' comments that resulted from sex stereotyping. Noting that Price Waterhouse could avoid equitable relief by proving by clear and convincing evidence that it would have placed Hopkins' candidacy on hold even absent this discrimination, the judge decided that the firm had not carried this heavy burden. . . .

II . . .

In passing Title VII, Congress made the simple but momentous announcement that sex, race, religion, and national origin are not relevant to the selection, evaluation, or compensation of employees. Yet, the statute does not purport to limit the other qualities and characteristics that employers may take into account in making employment decisions. The converse, therefore, of "for cause" legislation, Title VII eliminates certain bases for distinguishing among employees while otherwise preserving employers' freedom of choice. This balance between employee rights and employer prerogatives turns out to be decisive in the case before us.

Congress' intent to forbid employers to take gender into account in making employment decisions appears on the face of the statute. In now-familiar language, the statute forbids an employer to "[discriminate] *because of* such individual's . . . sex." (emphasis added). We take these words to mean that gender must be irrelevant to employment decisions. To construe the words "because of" as colloquial shorthand for "but-for causation," as does Price Waterhouse, is to misunderstand them.

But-for causation is a hypothetical construct. In determining whether a particular factor was a but-for cause of a given event, we begin by assuming that that factor was present at the time of the event, and then ask whether, even if that factor had been absent, the event nevertheless would have transpired in the same way. The present, active tense of the operative verbs of § 703(a)(1) ("to fail or refuse"), in contrast, turns our attention to the actual moment of the event in question, the adverse employment decision. The critical inquiry, the one commanded by the words of § 703(a)(1), is whether gender was a factor in the employment decision *at the moment it was made.* Moreover, since we know that the words "because of" do not mean "solely because of,"[8] we also know that Title VII meant to condemn even those decisions based on a mixture of legitimate and illegitimate considerations. When, therefore, an employer considers both gender and legitimate factors at the time of making a decision, that decision was "because of" sex and the other, legitimate considerations — even if we may say later, in the context of litigation, that the decision would have been the same if gender had not been taken into account.

To attribute this meaning to the words "because of" does not, as the dissent asserts, divest them of causal significance. A simple example illustrates the point. Suppose two physical forces act upon and move an object, and suppose that either force acting alone would have moved the object. As the dissent would have it, neither physical force was a "cause" of the motion unless we can show that but-for one or both of them, the object would not have moved; to use the dissent's terminology, both forces were simply "in the air" unless we can identify at least one of them as a but-for cause of the object's movement. Events that are causally overdetermined, in other words, may not have any "cause" at all. This cannot be so.

[Congress did not intend to require a plaintiff "to identify the precise causal role played by legitimate and illegitimate motivations"; it meant only to require her "to prove that the employer relied upon sex-based considerations" in its decision.]

To say that an employer may not take gender into account is not, however, the end of the matter, for that describes only one aspect of Title VII. The other important aspect of the statute is its preservation of an employer's remaining freedom of choice. We conclude that the preservation of this freedom means that an employer shall not be liable if it can prove that, even if it had not taken gender into account, it would have come to the same decision regarding a particular person. The statute's maintenance of employer prerogatives is evident from the statute itself and from its history, both in Congress and in this Court. . . .

The central point is this: while an employer may not take gender into account in making an employment decision . . . , it is free to decide against a woman for other reasons. We think these principles require that, once a plaintiff in a Title VII case shows that gender played a motivating part in an employment decision, the defendant may avoid a finding of liability only by proving that it would have made the same decision even if it had not allowed gender to play such a role. This balance of burdens is the direct result of Title VII's balance of rights.

Our holding casts no shadow on *Burdine*, in which we decided that, even after a plaintiff has made out a prima facie case of discrimination under Title VII, the burden

---

8. Congress specifically rejected an amendment that would have placed the word "solely" in front of the words "because of." 110 Cong. Rec. 2728, 13837 (1964).

of persuasion does not shift to the employer to show that its stated legitimate reason for the employment decision was the true reason. We stress, first, that neither court below shifted the burden of persuasion to Price Waterhouse on this question, and in fact, the District Court found that Hopkins had not shown that the firm's stated reason for its decision was pretextual. Moreover, since we hold that the plaintiff retains the burden of persuasion on the issue whether gender played a part in the employment decision, the situation before us is not the one of "shifting burdens" that we addressed in *Burdine*. Instead, the employer's burden is most appropriately deemed an affirmative defense: the plaintiff must persuade the factfinder on one point, and then the employer, if it wishes to prevail, must persuade it on another. *See NLRB v. Transportation Management Corp.*, 462 U.S. 393 (1983).[12]

Price Waterhouse's claim that the employer does not bear any burden of proof (if it bears one at all) until the plaintiff has shown "substantial evidence that Price Water-house's explanation for failing to promote Hopkins was not the 'true reason' for its action" merely restates its argument that the plaintiff in a mixed-motives case must squeeze her proof into *Burdine*'s framework. Where a decision was the product of a mixture of legitimate and illegitimate motives, however, it simply makes no sense to ask whether the legitimate reason was "the 'true reason'" for the decision — which is the question asked by *Burdine*.[13] . . .

In saying that gender played a motivating part in an employment decision, we mean that, if we asked the employer at the moment of the decision what its reasons were and if we received a truthful response, one of those reasons would be that the applicant or employee was a woman. In the specific context of sex stereotyping, an employer who acts on the basis of a belief that a woman cannot be aggressive, or that she must not be, has acted on the basis of gender.

. . . As to the existence of sex stereotyping in this case, we are not inclined to quarrel with the District Court's conclusion that a number of the partners' comments showed sex stereotyping at work. As for the legal relevance of sex stereotyping, we are beyond the day when an employer could evaluate employees by assuming or insisting that they matched the stereotype associated with their group. . . . An employer who objects to aggressiveness in women but whose positions require this trait places women in an intolerable and impermissible Catch-22: out of a job if they behave aggressively and out of a job if they don't. Title VII lifts women out of this bind.

Remarks at work that are based on sex stereotypes do not inevitably prove that gender played a part in a particular employment decision. The plaintiff must show that

---

12. [Contrary to the dissent, it is] perfectly consistent to say both that gender was a factor in a particular decision when it was made and that, when the situation is viewed hypothetically and after the fact, the same decision would have been made even in the absence of discrimination. . . . [W]here liability is imposed because an employer is unable to prove that it would have made the same decision even if it had not discriminated, this is not an imposition of liability "where sex made no difference to the outcome." In our adversary system, where a party has the burden of proving a particular assertion and where that party is unable to meet its burden, we assume that that assertion is inaccurate. Thus, where an employer is unable to prove its claim that it would have made the same decision in the absence of discrimination, we are entitled to conclude that gender did make a difference to the outcome.

13. [A case need not be labeled either a "pretext" case or a "mixed motives" case from the beginning; plaintiffs often will allege both. At some point, however, the district court must decide whether mixed motives are involved.] If the plaintiff fails to satisfy the factfinder that it is more likely than not that a forbidden characteristic played a part in the employment decision, then she may prevail only if she proves, following *Burdine*, that the employer's stated reason for its decision is pretextual. The dissent need not worry that this evidentiary scheme, if used during a jury trial, will be so impossibly confused and complex as it imagines. Juries long have decided cases in which defendants raise affirmative defenses. . . .

the employer actually relied on her gender in making its decision. In making this showing, stereotyped remarks can certainly be evidence that gender played a part. In any event, the stereotyping in this case did not simply consist of stray remarks. On the contrary, Hopkins proved that Price Waterhouse invited partners to submit comments; that some of the comments stemmed from sex stereotypes; that an important part of the Policy Board's decision on Hopkins was an assessment of the submitted comments; and that Price Waterhouse in no way disclaimed reliance on the sex-linked evaluations. This is not, as Price Waterhouse suggests, "discrimination in the air"; rather, it is, as Hopkins puts it, "discrimination brought to ground and visited upon" an employee. By focusing on Hopkins' specific proof, however, we do not suggest a limitation on the possible ways of proving that stereotyping played a motivating role in an employment decision, and we refrain from deciding here which specific facts, "standing alone," would or would not establish a plaintiff's case, since such a decision is unnecessary in this case. But see [O'Connor, J., at page 549, concurring in the judgment].

As to the employer's proof, in most cases, the employer should be able to present some objective evidence as to its probable decision in the absence of an impermissible motive.[15] Moreover, proving "that the same decision would have been justified . . . is not the same as proving that the same decision would have been made." An employer may not, in other words, prevail in a mixed-motives case by offering a legitimate and sufficient reason for its decision if that reason did not motivate it at the time of the decision. Finally, an employer may not meet its burden in such a case by merely showing that at the time of the decision it was motivated only in part by a legitimate reason. The very premise of a mixed-motives case is that a legitimate reason was present, and indeed, in this case, Price Waterhouse already has made this showing by convincing Judge Gesell that Hopkins' interpersonal problems were a legitimate concern. The employer instead must show that its legitimate reason, standing alone, would have induced it to make the same decision.

III

The courts below held that an employer who has allowed a discriminatory impulse to play a motivating part in an employment decision must prove by clear and convincing evidence that it would have made the same decision in the absence of discrimination. We are persuaded that the better rule is that the employer must make this showing by a preponderance of the evidence. . . .

IV

[Price Waterhouse challenged as clearly erroneous the district court's findings both that stereotyping occurred and that it played any part in the decision to place Hopkins' candidacy on hold. The plurality disagreed.]

---

15. Justice White's suggestion that the employer's own testimony as to the probable decision in the absence of discrimination is due special credence where the court has, contrary to the employer's testimony, found that an illegitimate factor played a part in the decision, is baffling.

In finding that some of the partners' comments reflected sex stereotyping, the District Court relied in part on Dr. Fiske's expert testimony. Without directly impugning Dr. Fiske's credentials or qualifications, Price Waterhouse insinuates that a social psychologist is unable to identify sex stereotyping in evaluations without investigating whether those evaluations have a basis in reality. This argument comes too late. At trial, counsel for Price Waterhouse twice assured the court that he did not question Dr. Fiske's expertise and failed to challenge the legitimacy of her discipline. Without contradiction from Price Waterhouse, Fiske testified that she discerned sex stereotyping in the partners' evaluations of Hopkins and she further explained that it was part of her business to identify stereotyping in written documents. We are not inclined to accept petitioner's belated and unsubstantiated characterization of Dr. Fiske's testimony as "gossamer evidence" based only on "intuitive hunches" and of her detection of sex stereotyping as "intuitively divined." Nor are we disposed to adopt the dissent's dismissive attitude toward Dr. Fiske's field of study and toward her own professional integrity.

Indeed, we are tempted to say that Dr. Fiske's expert testimony was merely icing on Hopkins' cake. It takes no special training to discern sex stereotyping in a description of an aggressive female employee as requiring "a course at charm school." Nor, turning to Thomas Beyer's memorable advice to Hopkins, does it require expertise in psychology to know that, if an employee's flawed "interpersonal skills" can be corrected by a soft-hued suit or a new shade of lipstick, perhaps it is the employee's sex and not her interpersonal skills that has drawn the criticism.

Price Waterhouse also charges that Hopkins produced no evidence that sex stereotyping played a role in the decision to place her candidacy on hold. As we have stressed, however, Hopkins showed that the partnership solicited evaluations from all of the firm's partners; that it generally relied very heavily on such evaluations in making its decision; that some of the partners' comments were the product of stereotyping; and that the firm in no way disclaimed reliance on those particular comments, either in Hopkins' case or in the past. Certainly a plausible — and, one might say, inevitable — conclusion to draw from this set of circumstances is that the Policy Board in making its decision did in fact take into account all of the partners' comments, including the comments that were motivated by stereotypical notions about women's proper deportment. . . .

Nor is the finding that sex stereotyping played a part in the Policy Board's decision undermined by the fact that many of the suspect comments were made by supporters rather than detractors of Hopkins. A negative comment, even when made in the context of a generally favorable review, nevertheless may influence the decisionmaker to think less highly of the candidate. . . . The additional suggestion that the comments were made by "persons outside the decisionmaking chain" — and therefore could not have harmed Hopkins — simply ignores the critical role that partners' comments played in the Policy Board's partnership decisions.

Price Waterhouse appears to think that we cannot affirm the factual findings of the trial court without deciding that, instead of being overbearing and aggressive and curt, Hopkins is in fact kind and considerate and patient. If this is indeed its impression, petitioner misunderstands the theory on which Hopkins prevailed. The District Judge acknowledged that Hopkins' conduct justified complaints about her behavior as a senior manager. But he also concluded that the reactions of at least some of the partners were reactions to her as a woman manager. Where an evaluation is based on a subjective assessment of a person's strengths and weaknesses, it is simply not true that each evaluator will focus on, or even mention, the same weaknesses. Thus, even if we knew that Hopkins had "personality problems," this would not tell us that the partners who cast their evaluations of Hopkins in sex-based terms would have criticized her as sharply (or criticized her at all) if she had been a man. It is not our job to review the evidence and decide that the negative reactions to Hopkins were based on reality; our perception of Hopkins' character is irrelevant. We sit not to determine whether Ms. Hopkins is nice, but to decide whether the partners reacted negatively to her personality because she is a woman.

V

We hold that when a plaintiff in a Title VII case proves that her gender played a motivating part in an employment decision, the defendant may avoid a finding of liability only by proving by a preponderance of the evidence that it would have made the same decision even if it had not taken the plaintiff's gender into account. . . .

Justice O'CONNOR, concurring in the judgment.

I agree with the plurality that on the facts presented in this case, the burden of persuasion should shift to the employer to demonstrate by a preponderance of the evidence that it would have reached the same decision concerning Ann Hopkins' candidacy absent consideration of her gender. I further agree that this burden shift is properly part of the liability phase of the litigation. I thus concur in the judgment of the Court. My disagreement stems from the plurality's conclusions concerning the substantive requirement of causation under the statute and its broad statements regarding the applicability of the allocation of the burden of proof applied in this case. . . .

I

. . . The legislative history of Title VII bears out what its plain language suggests: a substantive violation of the statute only occurs when consideration of an illegitimate criterion is the "but-for" cause of an adverse employment action. The legislative history makes it clear that Congress was attempting to eradicate discriminatory actions in the employment setting, not mere discriminatory thoughts. Critics of the bill that became Title VII labeled it a "thought control bill," and argued that it created a "punishable crime that does not require an illegal external act as a basis for judgment." Senator Case . . . responded:

> The man must do or fail to do something in regard to employment. There must be some specific external act, more than a mental act. Only if he does the act because of the grounds stated in the bill would there be any legal consequences.

Thus, I disagree with the plurality's dictum that the words "because of" do not mean "but-for" causation; manifestly they do. We should not, and need not, deviate from that policy today. . . .

The evidence of congressional intent as to which party should bear the burden of proof on the issue of causation is considerably less clear. . . . [In the area of tort liability,] the law has long recognized that in certain "civil cases" leaving the burden of persuasion on the plaintiff to prove "but-for" causation would be both unfair and destructive of the deterrent purposes embodied in the concept of duty of care. Thus, in multiple causation cases, where a breach of duty has been established, the common law of torts has long shifted the burden of proof to multiple defendants to prove that their negligent actions were not the "but-for" cause of the plaintiff's injury. *See, e.g., Summers v. Tice*, 199 P.2d 1 (Cal. 1948). The same rule has been applied where the effect of a defendant's tortious conduct combines with a force of unknown or innocent origin to produce the harm to the plaintiff. *See Kingston v. Chicago & N.W.R. Co.*, 211 N.W. 913, 915 (Wis. 1927). . . . *See also* 2 J. Wigmore, SELECT CASES ON THE LAW OF TORTS, § 153, p. 865 (1912). . . .

[At times, however, the but-for] "test demands the impossible. It challenges the imagination of the trier to probe into a purely fanciful and unknowable state of affairs. He is invited to make an estimate concerning facts that concededly never existed. The very uncertainty as to what might have happened opens the door wide for conjecture. But when conjecture is demanded it can be given a direction that is consistent with the policy considerations that underlie the controversy."

. . . There is no doubt that Congress considered reliance on gender or race in making employment decisions an evil in itself. . . . Reliance on such factors is exactly what the threat of Title VII liability was meant to deter. While the main concern of the statute was with employment opportunity, Congress was certainly not blind to the stigmatic harm which comes from being evaluated by a process which treats one as an inferior by reason of one's race or sex. . . . At the same time, Congress clearly conditioned legal liability on a determination that the consideration of an illegitimate factor caused a tangible employment injury of some kind.

Where an individual disparate treatment plaintiff has shown by a preponderance of the evidence that an illegitimate criterion was a substantial factor in an adverse employment decision, the deterrent purpose of the statute has clearly been triggered. More importantly, as an evidentiary matter, a reasonable factfinder could conclude that absent further explanation, the employer's discriminatory motivation "caused" the employment decision. The employer has not yet been shown to be a violator, but neither is it entitled to the same presumption of good faith concerning its employment decisions which is accorded employers facing only circumstantial evidence of discrimination. Both the policies behind the statute, and the evidentiary principles developed in the analogous area of causation in the law of torts, suggest that at this point the employer may be required to convince the factfinder that, despite the smoke, there is no fire. . . .

[The plurality, however, goes too far by holding that the burden shifts when "a decisional process is 'tainted' by awareness of sex or race in any way."] In my view, in order to justify shifting the burden on the issue of causation to the defendant, a disparate treatment plaintiff must show by direct evidence that an illegitimate criterion was a substantial factor in the decision. . . .

NOTES

1. *The Holding of* Price Waterhouse. Understanding the significance of *Price Waterhouse* is complicated by the lack of a majority opinion for the Court. There was a four-judge plurality opinion written by Justice Brennan with separate concurrences by Justices O'Connor and White. In such circumstances, the holding of the Court is said to be the narrowest point on which five justices concurring in the judgment agree. *See Marks v. United States*, 430 U.S. 188 (1977). Although Justice White had also concurred, the narrowest holding was generally accepted by the lower courts to be found in the opinion of Justice O'Connor. In contrast, Justice Stevens's dissent in *Gross v. FBL Fin. Servs.*, 129 S. Ct. 2343 (2009), argues that Justice White's opinion generated the controlling rule.

To put it simply, the trial judge had found that Price Waterhouse had relied on Hopkins' gender in putting her application for partnership on "hold," but it also found that legitimate objections to plaintiff's interpersonal skills were a factor in the decision. The plurality held that in a situation where a defendant's motives were mixed — that is, where legitimate and illegitimate considerations were both present — a plaintiff need only prove by a preponderance of the evidence that her race, gender, or other protected characteristic was "a motivating factor" for the challenged decision. Upon that showing, the burden of persuasion shifted to the defendant to avoid liability by proving as an affirmative defense that it would have made the same decision absent the discrimination.

If Justice O'Connor's concurrence controlled, it narrowed the plurality's rule in two ways: First, she raised the bar by requiring the plaintiff to show that the impermissible factor, such as plaintiff's sex, was a "substantial," not just a "motivating," factor. And, second, to trigger the *Price Waterhouse* shift in the burdens, she required plaintiff to introduce "direct" evidence of discrimination. Finding this concurrence to be the narrowest holding, the lower courts generally read *Price Waterhouse* to apply when the plaintiff had sufficient direct evidence to determine that discrimination was a "substantial" factor. If the trier of fact so found, plaintiff would prevail unless defendant carried the burden of persuasion that it would have made the same decision even if the prohibited trait was not a substantial factor.

2. *Direct Evidence.* What is "direct" evidence anyway? If the term means anything, it refers to evidence that, if believed, would establish a fact at issue without the need to draw any inferences. In disparate treatment cases, the fact at issue is whether the employer relied on a prohibited characteristic in making its decision. An evidence purist would say that there can be no direct evidence of the state of mind of a person because intent is internal and cannot be directly observed. *See generally* Charles A. Sullivan, *Accounting for* Price Waterhouse: *Proving Disparate Treatment Under Title VII*, 56 Brook. L. Rev. 1107 (1991). As used by Justice O'Connor, "direct evidence" would seem to require a statement by the decision maker that showed he was motivated by illegitimate considerations with respect to the at-issue decision.

Analytically, this raises at least two questions. First, what did the decision maker actually say? The decision maker may, of course, testify as to his reasons. But testimony of out-of-court statements will be allowed even if the party allegedly making the statement now denies that he did so. *EEOC v. Warfield-Rohr Casket Co.*, 364 F.3d 160, 163-64 (4th Cir. 2004) ("[T]here is no requirement that an employee's testimony be corroborated in order to apply the mixed-motive framework."). Second, does the comment reflect illegitimate considerations? Obviously some comments are explicitly racist or sexist, but less explicitly racist comments have also been held to be capable of being found to be racist. *Ash v. Tyson Foods, Inc.*, 546 U.S. 454 (2006), held that a manager's use of "boy" to refer to an African American man could reveal discriminatory intent: "The speaker's meaning may depend on various factors including context, inflection, tone of voice, local custom, and historical usage. Insofar as the Court of Appeals held that modifiers or qualifications are necessary in all instances to render the disputed term probative of bias, the court's decision is erroneous." *Tyson,* 546 U.S. at 456. *See also McGinest v. GTE Serv. Corp.,* 360 F.3d 1103, 1116-17 (9th Cir. 2004) (the use of "code words" for race, like "drug dealer," can indicate discrimination). *But see Putman v. Unity Health Sys.,* 348 F.3d 732 (8th Cir. 2003) (comments about plaintiff not being "humble enough" and being "too prideful" not clearly linked to race).

3. *Lower Court Confusion About "Direct" Evidence.* Some lower-court cases applied the direct evidence requirement for the *Price Waterhouse* case with little difficulty. *See Fuhr v. Sch. Dist. of Hazel Park,* 364 F.3d 753, 759 (6th Cir. 2004). But the circuits evolved a range of definitions of "direct evidence." Some courts read *Price Waterhouse* as applying only in cases involving "direct evidence," in the classic evidentiary sense of the term, that is, that the evidence proves the fact at issue without need to draw any inferences. *See, e.g., Fuller v. Phipps,* 67 F.3d 1137 (4th Cir. 1995). These cases demanded a very close connection between the evidence and the alleged discriminatory decision. A startling example is *Shorter v. ICG Holdings, Inc.,* 188 F.3d 1204 (10th Cir. 1999), which held that defendant's manager referring to plaintiff as an "incompetent nigger" within a day or two of having fired her was not direct evidence of discriminatory intent. The statement was merely a matter of personal opinion.

As we will see in the next principal case, "direct" evidence is no longer a meaningful category under Title VII, since the Supreme Court has held that the Civil Rights Act of 1991 overturned any requirement of direct evidence for what we have termed mixed-motive cases. And the Court's decision in *Gross v. FBL Fin. Servs.,* 129 S. Ct. 2343 (2009), rejecting any "mixed-motive" burden-shifting under the ADEA altogether, rendered the concept of "direct" evidence inapplicable under that statute. However, the "directness" of the evidence at issue, that is, how closely it was linked to the decision in question and how probative it is of discriminatory motivation, can be expected to continue to influence courts in deciding more "gestalt" questions — such as whether a reasonable jury could find discrimination on the available evidence.

4. *Causation.* Perhaps the most significant aspect of *Price Waterhouse* was the Court's conclusion that an employer could be liable even if the discriminatory intent *did not actually cause* an employment action. All that was necessary is that such intent be a motivating factor. Even Justice O'Connor would impose liability without proof of causation where discriminatory intent was a "substantial factor." But this description of causation may be somewhat deceptive — if the employer established it would have made the same decision in any event, the employer is not liable. Thus, the plaintiff need not show but-for causation to win a judgment, but plaintiff will lose if the defendant shows no such causation. In that sense, *Price Waterhouse* can still be said to be consistent with *Biggins'* requirement that discrimination be a "determinative influence." After *Price Waterhouse,* the question was not so much causation as who proves causation.

5. *No Harm, No Foul?* This requirement of causation, however, did not last long. Ironically, the one point on which all nine justices agreed in *Price Waterhouse* — that the discriminatory intent had to cause harm before Title VII liability attached — was legislatively rejected by the Civil Rights Act of 1991, which added a new §703(m), 42 U.S.C. §2000e-2(m) (2006). That section provides that "an unlawful employment practice is established when the complaining party demonstrates that race, color, religion, sex, or national origin was a motivating factor for any employment practice, even though other factors also motivated the practice." Thus, the "motivating factor" test of the *Price Waterhouse* plurality is accepted, as is the corollary of "mixed-motive" violations. Perhaps even more significant, the amendment also modifies *Price Waterhouse* by establishing that the plaintiff's proof of an illegitimate "motivating factor" does not merely shift the burden of proving no causation to the defendant, but actually establishes a violation, without regard to what the defendant can prove on rebuttal. "But-for" or "determinative factor" causation has been replaced by "motivating factor" causation.

The new statute, however, offers an opportunity for defendants to limit plaintiff's remedies even if a violation has been established. A new paragraph was added to §706(g), 42 U.S.C. §2000e-5(g), which provides that, in §703(m) cases, if a respondent can "demonstrate" that it "would have taken the same action in the absence of the impermissible motivating factor," plaintiff's remedies are limited. Thus, a court

> (i) may grant declaratory relief, injunctive relief (except as provided in clause (ii)), and attorney's fees and costs demonstrated to be directly attributable only to the pursuit of a claim under section 703(m); and (ii) shall not award damages or issue an order requiring any admission, reinstatement, hiring, promotion, or payment. . . .

In such a situation, then, the plaintiff is essentially limited to a declaration of defendant's liability plus attorney's fees. She is not entitled to any monetary damages.

While this scheme continues to govern discrimination cases under Title VII, the Supreme Court rejected such analysis for the ADEA in *Gross v. FBL Fin. Servs.*, 129 S. Ct. 2343 (2009), where plaintiff's burden is to prove that age was a determinative factor in all cases. It is not clear whether the *Gross* approach will control retaliation cases under Title VII. *See Smith v. Xerox Corp.*, 602 F.3d 320, 327-32 (5th Cir. 2010) (2-1) (despite *Gross*, retaliation cases under Title VII are subject to Title VII's motivating factor analysis for burden-shifting, and direct evidence of discrimination is not necessary). As for the ADA, *Serwatka v. Rockwell Automation, Inc.*, 591 F.3d 957 (7th Cir. 2010), held that *Gross* requires applying determinative factor causation to the ADA, although some have argued that the ADA's incorporation by reference of VII procedures and remedies requires a different result under that statute. *See* Catherine T. Struve, *Shifting Burdens: Discrimination Law Through the Lens of Jury Instruction*, 51 B.C. L. Rev. 279 (2010); Melissa Hart, *Procedural Extremism: The Supreme Court's 2008-2009 Employment and Labor Cases*, 13 Emp. Rts. & Emp. Pol'y J. 253 (2010).

6. *No Blacks Need Apply.* Suppose an employer places a sign outside its personnel office, saying, "No blacks need apply." Is that a violation of §703? Surprisingly, the plurality opinion in *Price Waterhouse* suggests that the answer is "not necessarily" because the sign might not be a causative factor in any particular decision. What is the law now that §703(m) and (g) have been added? Wouldn't plaintiff still need to prove that race was a motivating factor in denying her a job in order to establish a violation?

7. *Expert Testimony on Stereotyping and Cognitive Bias.* Can expert testimony be used to prove that ambiguous comments reflect bias? What were the various views in

Price Waterhouse about Dr. Susan Fiske? In his dissent, Justice Kennedy wrote that "Fiske purported to discern stereotyping in comments that were gender neutral — e.g., 'overbearing and abrasive' — without any knowledge of the comments' basis in reality and without having met the speaker or subject." Is this criticism valid? May not certain statements be susceptible of varying meanings, with expert testimony helping the factfinder in deciding whether the statements are likely to reflect stereotyping? *See generally* Melissa Hart & Paul M. Secunda, *A Matter of Context: Social Framework Evidence in Employment Discrimination Class Actions*, 78 FORDHAM L. REV. 37 (2009); David L. Faigman, Nilanjana Dasgupta, & Cecilia L. Ridgeway, *A Matter of Fit: The Law of Discrimination and the Science of Implicit Bias*, 59 HASTINGS L. J. 1389, 1426-27 (2008).

8. *Carrying the Employer's Burden of Proof.* How can an employer shoulder its burden to prove "same decision" under amended § 706(g)? The employer could try to extract from the pattern of its other decisions a kind of template of requirements for advancement. The employer might introduce expert testimony of the factors that operated in its decision making and how they would have netted out in the plaintiff's case. Another method would be a "customs of the trade" approach, again employing expert testimony, but this time to establish how a "reasonable" employer would have evaluated the candidate. In the abstract, this evidence is less probative than proof of how the employer treated favored workers because the issue is what the defendant, not a hypothetical employer, would have done absent bias. After all, the defendant might be stricter or more liberal than others in the industry and is entitled to be so. But trade practice is nevertheless relevant because it seems appropriate to assume that a particular employer conforms to industry standards or general practice until it is shown otherwise.

9. *Multiple Decision Makers.* While disparate treatment is often discussed in terms of the intent of the "employer," employers typically are corporations or other business organization. Where entities are concerned, the intent that matters is presumably that of the actual decision maker. But many decisions involve not a single decision maker, but multiple deciders, in a collegial or hierarchical structure, or some combination of the two. Multiple decision makers will be found where the decision is made collegially (as by a board or a committee) and where it is made by a hierarchical process (A recommends to B, who recommends to C, who "decides").

If the factfinder decides that one person in the process acted with intent to discriminate, does that establish that discrimination was a "motivating factor" under § 703(m), or must more be shown to establish liability? *See Barbano v. Madison County*, 922 F.2d 139 (2d Cir. 1990). And what if the actual decision maker is unwittingly influenced by a prejudiced person with no formal part in the process? *Staub v. Proctor Hosp.*, 560 F.3d 647 (7th Cir. 2009), *cert. granted*, 130 S. Ct. 2089 (2010) (rejecting liability in a case involving uniformed service personnel's employment rights when a reasonable jury could not have found that the decision maker was influenced by others' biases since she conducted an independent investigation). *See generally* Stephen Befort & Alison Olig, *Within the Grasp of the Cat's Paw: Delineating the Scope of Subordinate Bias Liability Under Federal Antidiscrimination Statutes*, 60 S.C. L. REV. 383 (2008); Rebecca Hanner White & Linda Hamilton Krieger, *Whose Motive Matters? Discrimination in Multi-Actor Employment Decision Making*, 61 LA. L. REV. 495, 534 (2001).

10. *The Jury.* The plurality in *Price Waterhouse* notes that at "some point in the proceedings . . . the District Court must decide whether a particular case involves mixed motives." At what point in the trial does this decision take place? How would you prepare jury instructions on *McDonnell Douglas/Burdine* and *Price Waterhouse?* If the instructions accurately stated the law, would jurors be likely to understand them? The next case might help.

Desert Palace, Inc. v. Costa
539 U.S. 90 (2003)

Justice THOMAS delivered the opinion of the Court.

The question before us in this case is whether a plaintiff must present direct evidence of discrimination in order to obtain a mixed-motive instruction under Title VII of the Civil Rights Act of 1964, as amended by the Civil Rights Act of 1991. We hold that direct evidence is not required.

I

A

Since 1964, Title VII has made it an "unlawful employment practice for an employer . . . to discriminate against any individual . . . , *because of* such individual's race, color, religion, sex, or national origin." (emphasis added). In *Price Waterhouse v. Hopkins*, the Court considered whether an employment decision is made "because of" sex in a "mixed-motive" case, *i.e.*, where both legitimate and illegitimate reasons motivated the decision. The Court concluded that, under §2000e-2(a)(1), an employer could "avoid a finding of liability . . . by proving that it would have made the same decision even if it had not allowed gender to play such a role." The Court was divided, however, over the predicate question of when the burden of proof may be shifted to an employer to prove the affirmative defense.

Justice Brennan, writing for a plurality of four Justices, would have held that "when a plaintiff . . . proves that her gender played a *motivating* part in an employment decision, the defendant may avoid a finding of liability only by proving by a preponderance of the evidence that it would have made the same decision even if it had not taken the plaintiff's gender into account." The plurality did not, however, "suggest a limitation on the possible ways of proving that [gender] stereotyping played a motivating role in an employment decision."

Justice White and Justice O'Connor both concurred in the judgment. Justice White would have held that the case was governed by *Mt. Healthy City Bd. of Ed. v. Doyle*, 429 U.S. 274 (1977), and would have shifted the burden to the employer only when a plaintiff "showed that the unlawful motive was a *substantial* factor in the adverse employment action." Justice O'Connor, like Justice White, would have required the plaintiff to show that an illegitimate consideration was a "substantial factor" in the employment decision. But, under Justice O'Connor's view, "the burden on the issue of causation" would shift to the employer only where "a disparate treatment plaintiff [could] show by *direct evidence* that an illegitimate criterion was a substantial factor in the decision."

Two years after *Price Waterhouse*, Congress passed the 1991 Act "in large part [as] a response to a series of decisions of this Court interpreting the Civil Rights Acts of 1866 and 1964." *Landgraf v. USI Film Products*, 511 U.S. 244 (1994). In particular, § 107 of the 1991 Act, which is at issue in this case, "responded" to *Price Waterhouse* by "setting forth standards applicable in 'mixed motive' cases" in two new statutory provisions.[1] The first establishes an alternative for proving that an "unlawful employment practice" has occurred:

> Except as otherwise provided in this subchapter, an unlawful employment practice is established when the complaining party demonstrates that race, color, religion, sex, or national origin was a motivating factor for any employment practice, even though other factors also motivated the practice.

42 U.S.C. § 2000e-2(m)

The second provides that, with respect to " 'a claim in which an individual proves a violation under section 2000e-2(m),' " the employer has a limited affirmative defense that does not absolve it of liability, but restricts the remedies available to a plaintiff. The available remedies include only declaratory relief, certain types of injunctive relief, and attorney's fees and costs. In order to avail itself of the affirmative defense, the employer must "demonstrate that [it] would have taken the same action in the absence of the impermissible motivating factor."

Since the passage of the 1991 Act, the Courts of Appeals have divided over whether plaintiff must prove by direct evidence that an impermissible consideration was a "motivating factor" in an adverse employment action. Relying primarily on Justice O'Connor's concurrence in Price Waterhouse, a number of courts have held that direct evidence is required to establish liability under § 2000e-2(m). In the decision below, however, the Ninth Circuit concluded otherwise.

B

Petitioner Desert Palace, Inc., dba Caesar's Palace Hotel & Casino of Las Vegas, Nevada, employed respondent Catharina Costa as a warehouse worker and heavy equipment operator. Respondent was the only woman in this job and in her local Teamsters bargaining unit.

Respondent experienced a number of problems with management and her co-workers that led to an escalating series of disciplinary sanctions, including informal rebukes, a denial of privileges, and suspension. Petitioner finally terminated respondent after she was involved in a physical altercation in a warehouse elevator with fellow Teamsters member Herbert Gerber. Petitioner disciplined both employees because the facts surrounding the incident were in dispute, but Gerber, who had a clean disciplinary record, received only a 5-day suspension.

. . . At trial, respondent presented evidence that (1) she was singled out for "intense 'stalking'" by one of her supervisors, (2) she received harsher discipline than men for the same conduct, (3) she was treated less favorably than men in the

---

1. This case does not require us to decide when, if ever, § 107 applies outside of the mixed-motive context.

assignment of overtime, and (4) supervisors repeatedly "stacked" her disciplinary record and "frequently used or tolerated" sex-based slurs against her.

Based on this evidence, the District Court denied petitioner's motion for judgment as a matter of law, and submitted the case to the jury with instructions, two of which are relevant here. First, without objection from petitioner, the District Court instructed the jury that "the plaintiff has the burden of proving . . . by a preponderance of the evidence" that she "suffered adverse work conditions" and that her sex "was a motivating factor in any such work conditions imposed upon her."

Second, the District Court gave the jury the following mixed-motive instruction:

> You have heard evidence that the defendant's treatment of the plaintiff was motivated by the plaintiff's sex and also by other lawful reasons. If you find that the plaintiff's sex was a motivating factor in the defendant's treatment of the plaintiff, the plaintiff is entitled to your verdict, even if you find that the defendant's conduct was also motivated by a lawful reason.
>
> However, if you find that the defendant's treatment of the plaintiff was motivated by both gender and lawful reasons, you must decide whether the plaintiff is entitled to damages. The plaintiff is entitled to damages unless the defendant proves by a preponderance of the evidence that the defendant would have treated plaintiff similarly even if the plaintiff's gender had played no role in the employment decision.

Petitioner unsuccessfully objected to this instruction, claiming that respondent had failed to adduce "direct evidence" that sex was a motivating factor in her dismissal or in any of the other adverse employment actions taken against her. The jury rendered a verdict for respondent, awarding backpay, compensatory damages, and punitive damages. The District Court denied petitioner's renewed motion for judgment as a matter of law.

The Court of Appeals upheld the District Court's judgment after rehearing the case en banc. The en banc court saw no need to decide whether Justice O'Connor's concurrence in *Price Waterhouse* controlled because it concluded that Justice O'Connor's references to "direct evidence" had been "wholly abrogated" by the 1991 Act. And, turning "to the language" of § 2000e-2(m), the court observed that the statute "imposes no special [evidentiary] requirement and does not reference 'direct evidence.'" Accordingly, the court concluded that a "plaintiff . . . may establish a violation through a preponderance of evidence (whether direct or circumstantial) that a protected characteristic played 'a motivating factor.'" Based on that standard, the Court of Appeals held that respondent's evidence was sufficient to warrant a mixed-motive instruction and that a reasonable jury could have found that respondent's sex was a "motivating factor in her treatment."

II

This case provides us with the first opportunity to consider the effects of the 1991 Act on jury instructions in mixed-motive cases. Specifically, we must decide whether a plaintiff must present direct evidence of discrimination in order to obtain a mixed-motive instruction under 42 U.S.C. § 2000e-2(m). Petitioner's argument on this point proceeds in three steps: (1) Justice O'Connor's opinion is the holding of *Price Waterhouse*; (2) Justice O'Connor's *Price Waterhouse* opinion requires direct evidence of discrimination before a mixed-motive instruction can be given; and

(3) the 1991 Act does nothing to abrogate that holding. Like the Court of Appeals, we see no need to address which of the opinions in *Price Waterhouse* is controlling: the third step of petitioner's argument is flawed, primarily because it is inconsistent with the text of § 2000e-2(m).

Our precedents make clear that the starting point for our analysis is the statutory text. And where, as here, the words of the statute are unambiguous, the "judicial inquiry is complete." Section 2000e-2(m) unambiguously states that a plaintiff need only "demonstrate" that an employer used a forbidden consideration with respect to "any employment practice." On its face, the statute does not mention, much less require, that a plaintiff make a heightened showing through direct evidence. Indeed, petitioner concedes as much.

Moreover, Congress explicitly defined the term "demonstrates" in the 1991 Act, leaving little doubt that no special evidentiary showing is required. Title VII defines the term " 'demonstrates' " as to "meet the burdens of production and persuasion." § 2000e(m). If Congress intended the term " 'demonstrates' " to require that the "burdens of production and persuasion" be met by direct evidence or some other heightened showing, it could have made that intent clear by including language to that effect in § 2000e(m). Its failure to do so is significant, for Congress has been unequivocal when imposing heightened proof requirements in other circumstances, including in other provisions of Title 42. . . . 42 U.S.C. § 5851(b)(3)(D) (providing that "relief may not be ordered" against an employer in retaliation cases involving whistleblowers under the Atomic Energy Act where the employer is able to "*demonstrate by clear and convincing evidence* that it would have taken the same unfavorable personnel action in the absence of such behavior") (emphasis added); *cf. Price Waterhouse* ("Only rarely have we required clear and convincing proof where the action defended against seeks only conventional relief.").

In addition, Title VII's silence with respect to the type of evidence required in mixed-motive cases also suggests that we should not depart from the "conventional rule of civil litigation [that] generally applies in Title VII cases." That rule requires a plaintiff to prove his case "by a preponderance of the evidence," using "direct or circumstantial evidence," *Postal Service Bd. of Governors v. Aikens*, 460 U.S. 711, 714, n.3 (1983). We have often acknowledged the utility of circumstantial evidence in discrimination cases. For instance, in *Reeves v. Sanderson Plumbing Products, Inc.* we recognized that evidence that a defendant's explanation for an employment practice is "unworthy of credence" is "one form of *circumstantial evidence* that is probative of intentional discrimination." (emphasis added). The reason for treating circumstantial and direct evidence alike is both clear and deep-rooted: "Circumstantial evidence is not only sufficient, but may also be more certain, satisfying and persuasive than direct evidence." *Rogers v. Missouri Pacific R. Co.*, 352 U.S. 500, 508, n.17 (1957).

The adequacy of circumstantial evidence also extends beyond civil cases; we have never questioned the sufficiency of circumstantial evidence in support of a criminal conviction, even though proof beyond a reasonable doubt is required. And juries are routinely instructed that "the law makes no distinction between the weight or value to be given to either direct or circumstantial evidence." 1A K. O'MALLEY, J. GRENIG, & W. LEE, FEDERAL JURY PRACTICE AND INSTRUCTIONS, CRIMINAL § 12.04 (5th ed. 2000); *see also* 4 L. SAND, J. SIFFERT, W. LOUGHLIN, S. REISS, & N. BATTERMAN, MODERN FEDERAL JURY INSTRUCTIONS P74.01 (2002) (model instruction 74-2). It is not surprising, therefore, that neither petitioner nor its *amici curiae* can point to any other circumstance in which we have restricted a litigant to the presentation of direct evidence absent some affirmative directive in a statute.

Finally, the use of the term "demonstrates" in other provisions of Title VII tends to show further that § 2000e-2(m) does not incorporate a direct evidence requirement. *See, e.g.*, 42 U.S.C. §§ 2000e-2(k)(1)(A)(i), 2000e-5(g)(2)(B). For instance, § 2000e-5(g)(2)(B) requires an employer to "demonstrate that [it] would have taken the same action in the absence of the impermissible motivating factor" in order to take advantage of the partial affirmative defense. Due to the similarity in structure between that provision and § 2000e-2(m), it would be logical to assume that the term "demonstrates" would carry the same meaning with respect to both provisions. But when pressed at oral argument about whether direct evidence is required before the partial affirmative defense can be invoked, petitioner did not "agree that . . . the defendant or the employer has any heightened standard" to satisfy.

Absent some congressional indication to the contrary, we decline to give the same term in the same Act a different meaning depending on whether the rights of the plaintiff or the defendant are at issue.

For the reasons stated above, we agree with the Court of Appeals that no heightened showing is required under § 2000e-2(m).

In order to obtain an instruction under § 2000e-2(m), a plaintiff need only present sufficient evidence for a reasonable jury to conclude, by a preponderance of the evidence, that "race, color, religion, sex, or national origin was a motivating factor for any employment practice." Because direct evidence of discrimination is not required in mixed-motive cases, the Court of Appeals correctly concluded that the District Court did not abuse its discretion in giving a mixed-motive instruction to the jury. Accordingly, the judgment of the Court of Appeals is affirmed. . . .

Justice O'CONNOR, concurring.

I join the Court's opinion. In my view, prior to the Civil Rights Act of 1991, the evidentiary rule we developed to shift the burden of persuasion in mixed-motive cases was appropriately applied only where a disparate treatment plaintiff "demonstrated by direct evidence that an illegitimate factor played a substantial role" in an adverse employment decision. *Price Waterhouse v. Hopkins* (O'Connor, J., concurring in judgment). This showing triggered "the deterrent purpose of the statute" and permitted a reasonable factfinder to conclude that "absent further explanation, the employer's discriminatory motivation 'caused' the employment decision." (O'Connor, J., concurring in judgment).

As the Court's opinion explains, in the Civil Rights Act of 1991, Congress codified a new evidentiary rule for mixed-motive cases arising under Title VII. I therefore agree with the Court that the District Court did not abuse its discretion in giving a mixed-motive instruction to the jury.

NOTES

1. *What Was the Fuss About?* If you were a newcomer to discrimination law and had not been steeped in the intricacies of *McDonnell Douglas* and *Price Waterhouse* proof structures, you might wonder what all the fuss was about in *Desert Palace* and why the Court was so focused on questions of proof more than 40 years after Title VII was enacted. After all, what is so remarkable about a case holding that "[i]n order

to obtain an instruction under § 2000e-2(m), a plaintiff need only present sufficient evidence for a reasonable jury to conclude, by a preponderance of the evidence, that 'race, color, religion, sex, or national origin was a motivating factor for any employment practice.' "? This seems simple to the point of banality.

However, having struggled with the prior cases, you should understand that *Desert Palace* made a profound difference in at least one branch of the prior law. Congress had modified *Price Waterhouse* in the Civil Rights Act of 1991 by adopting Justice Brennan's "motivating factor" articulation of plaintiff's burden and, indeed, expanded on the plurality's holding by providing that plaintiff's proof of a motivating factor was sufficient for liability. While, as under *Price Waterhouse*, defendant could still carry its burden of persuasion that it would have made the same decision even absent the illegitimate consideration, that proof no longer negates liability; the 1991 amendments narrow the "same decision" defense to reducing plaintiff's remedies.

Congress, however, did not explicitly address Justice O'Connor's "direct" evidence threshold for applying this method of analysis, and we have seen that the lower courts generally continued to require some version of "direct evidence" in order to trigger *Price Waterhouse* burden-shifting. In this light, the significance of *Desert Palace* is to eliminate the direct evidence barrier to burden-shifting and avoid the complicated inquiry into whether evidence is sufficiently "direct." If a plaintiff can prove, by any kind of evidence, that a particular factor motivated the at-issue decision, the plaintiff prevails — although the defendant may limit the plaintiff's remedies if it establishes it would have made the same decision anyway.

2. *Have O'Connor's Worst Fears Been Realized?* In *Price Waterhouse*, Justice O'Connor expressed concern about not imposing liability on the employer, or even shifting a burden of persuasion, because of inconclusive indications of discrimination:

> Thus, stray remarks in the workplace . . . cannot justify requiring the employer to prove that its hiring or promotion decisions were based on legitimate criteria. Nor can statements by nondecisionmakers, or statements by decisionmakers unrelated to the decisional process itself suffice to satisfy the plaintiff's burden in this regard. In addition, in my view testimony such as Dr. Fiske's in this case, standing alone, would not justify shifting the burden of persuasion to the employer. Race and gender always "play a role" in an employment decision in the benign sense that these are human characteristics of which decisionmakers are aware and may comment on in a perfectly neutral and nondiscriminatory fashion. For example, in the context of this case, a mere reference to "a lady candidate" might show that gender "played a role" in the decision, but by no means could support a rational factfinder's inference that the decision was made "because of" sex. What is required is what Ann Hopkins showed here: direct evidence that decisionmakers placed substantial negative reliance on an illegitimate criterion in reaching their decision.

In the wake of *Desert Palace*, can "stray remarks" be sufficient to get to the jury on a claim that sex or race was a motivating factor? *See generally* Michael J. Zimmer, *A Chain of Inferences Proving Discrimination*, 79 U. COLO. L. REV. 4 (2008) ("Direct, direct-lite, or circumstantial evidence" (or any combination) can be used to prove individual disparate treatment discrimination; discriminatory motivation can be shown by unequal treatment, defendant's admissions that it discriminated, actions based on stereotypes, and the *McDonnell Douglas* approach).

3. *Does* Desert Palace *Destroy* McDonnell Douglas? While there is no dispute that *Desert Palace* eliminates direct evidence as a precondition to what used to be called a *Price Waterhouse* case, is it even more radical in that it eliminates the whole *McDonnell*

Douglas proof structure? *Desert Palace* can be read narrowly. For example, footnote 1 indicates that the Court was not deciding the impact of this decision "outside of the mixed-motive context." But prior to *Desert Palace*, one boundary between *Price Waterhouse* and *McDonnell Douglas* was "direct" evidence. With direct evidence gone, is there still a boundary between these two methods of proof or have the two been collapsed into one? Put another way, even though *Desert Palace* does not explicitly purport to do so, has it destroyed the *McDonnell Douglas* approach?

After *Price Waterhouse*, the distinction between the *Price Waterhouse* and *McDonnell Douglas* cases had been framed in two ways. First, *Price Waterhouse* governed "direct evidence" cases, while *McDonnell Douglas* applied to "circumstantial evidence" proof. Second, *Price Waterhouse* was viewed as involving "mixed motives," while *McDonnell Douglas* was viewed as involving a single motive. If circumstantial evidence can be used to prove liability using §703(m)'s "motivating factor" standard of liability, *Price Waterhouse*—or, more accurately, §703(m) cases—cannot be viewed as a "direct" evidence proof structure in contrast to *McDonnell Douglas's* "circumstantial" or "indirect" evidence structure.

The second way the two methods of proof have been distinguished is by viewing *McDonnell Douglas* as involving proof of a "single motive," while *Price Waterhouse* involves "mixed motives." Finding a "single motive" based on the process of elimination is the core of *McDonnell Douglas*—plaintiff proves that the normal nondiscriminatory reasons do not apply to her case, thereby establishing a prima facie case; defendant introduces evidence of a nondiscriminatory reason in rebuttal; plaintiff then introduces evidence that defendant's reason is not the true reason in order to establish that such a reason is a pretext for discrimination. This process leads to the factfinder thinking about the case as an either/or proposition: either the defendant's reason explains the decision or the plaintiff's claim of discrimination explains it. That makes the method seem to be about "single motives." However, *Price Waterhouse* also held that Congress did not establish a sole cause standard under Title VII. Rather, a but-for or determinative factor standard would permit plaintiff to prevail with a showing that is less than sole cause, that is, less than that discrimination was the "single motive." She wins even if the factfinder finds that another reason is involved, as long as discrimination is the but-for reason or the determinative influence. Is that possible in a traditional *McDonnell Douglas* case? Has the description of *McDonnell Douglas* as involving a "single motive" always been metaphorical?

St. Mary's Honor Center v. Hicks may shed some light here. As you will recall, in *Hicks*, the trial had determined that personal animosity, not discrimination, explained the adverse decision, even though the individual defendant denied such animosity. Thus, the court found a fact claimed by neither party. The narrow holding of *Hicks* is that disbelief of the supposed nondiscriminatory reason was not necessarily sufficient: The trier had to find not merely that the defendant's reason was pretextual but that it was a pretext for discrimination. But the broader holding of the case is that the trier of fact can make any determination justified by the record before it. This would seems to point toward letting the jury reach the motivating factor question even in a pure *McDonnell Douglas* setting if the factfinder so determined from the record. A jury could find that both impermissible and permissible reasons motivated a decision, even though the parties each claim only one motivation—plaintiff's claim of discrimination and defendant's claim of a nondiscriminatory reason. Thus, after *Desert Palace*, a jury could disbelieve both plaintiff's claim that discrimination entirely explained the challenged decision and defendant's claim that nondiscrimination entirely explained it.

Or does *McDonnell Douglas* survive *Desert Palace*? When faced with a motion for summary judgment, will plaintiffs still be able to rely on the process of elimination of nondiscriminatory reasons that then support the drawing of an inference that the reason for defendant's action was discrimination? If so, *McDonnell Douglas* appears to live, at least at that procedural level. Can plaintiff use this process of elimination argument before the jury?

4. *Splitting the Baby.* Is there a downside for plaintiffs if *Desert Palace* becomes the uniform method of analyzing individual disparate treatment cases? While § 703(m) provides the "motivating factor" standard for liability, it is subject to § 706(g)(2)(B)'s same decision defense. On the one hand, a jury finding that defendant discriminated may be unlikely to believe defendant's proof that it would have made the same decision even if it had not discriminated; on the other, a jury may be tempted to "split the baby," that is, accept both the plaintiff's proof that discrimination was a motivating factor *and* the defendant's proof that it would have made the same decision regardless. That would substantially limit the remedies plaintiff would get. Might *McDonnell Douglas* survive at least in cases where a risk-preferring plaintiff and a risk-preferring defendant both choose not to invoke *Desert Palace* by asking for the instruction approved in that case but rather place all their eggs in the *McDonnell Douglas* either/or basket? Should courts defer to parties' request of jury instructions based on *McDonnell Douglas* if they believe they mischaracterize the facts?

5. *Lower Courts and Commentators.* Will the lower courts continue to maintain the single-versus-mixed-motive distinction after *Desert Palace*? So far, they have been reluctant to inter so long standing and powerful a doctrine as the *McDonnell Douglas* framework, although they have not persuasively justified its survival. One decision summarized the confusion:

> Since *Desert Palace*, the federal courts of appeals have, without much, if any, consideration of the issue, developed widely differing approaches to the question of how to analyze summary judgment challenges in Title VII mixed-motive cases. The Eighth Circuit has explicitly held that the *McDonnell Douglas/Burdine* burden-shifting framework applies to the summary judgment analysis of mixed-motive claims after *Desert Palace*. See *Griffith v. City of Des Moines*, 387 F.3d 733, 736 (8th Cir. 2004). The Eleventh Circuit seems to have joined the Eighth Circuit in this regard. *See Burstein v. Emtel, Inc.*, 137 Fed. Appx. 205, 209 n.8 (11th Cir. 2005) (unpublished).
>
> The Fifth Circuit, in contrast, has adopted a "modified *McDonnell Douglas*" approach, under which a plaintiff in a mixed-motive case can rebut the defendant's legitimate non-discriminatory reason not only through evidence of pretext (the traditional *McDonnell Douglas/Burdine* burden), but also with evidence that the defendant's proffered reason is only one of the reasons for its conduct (the mixed-motive alternative). *See Machinchick v. PB Power, Inc.*, 398 F.3d 345, 352 (5th Cir. 2005).
>
> Adopting a sort of middle ground between these two positions are the Fourth and Ninth Circuits which permit a mixed-motive plaintiff to avoid a defendant's motion for summary judgment by proceeding either under the "pretext framework" of the traditional *McDonnell Douglas/Burdine* analysis or by "presenting direct or circumstantial evidence that raises a genuine issue of material fact as to whether an impermissible factor such as race motivated [, at least in part,] the adverse employment decision." *Diamond v. Colonial Life & Accident Ins. Co.*, 416 F.3d 310, 318 (4th Cir. 2005); *McGinest v. GTE Serv. Corp.*, 360 F.3d 1103, 1122 (9th Cir. 2004) The D.C. Circuit appears to have recently joined this middle ground approach. *See Fogg v. Gonzales*, 3 492 F.3d 447, 451 & n* (D.C. Cir. 2007).

White v. Baxter Healthcare Corp., 533 F.3d 381, 399-400 (6th Cir. 2008) (some citations and all parentheticals omitted). According to *Baxter*, the other circuits have either refused to decide the issue or it has not arisen. Turning to the appropriate rule, the Sixth Circuit wrote:

> [T]he *McDonnell Douglas/Burdine* burden-shifting framework does not apply to the summary judgment analysis of Title VII mixed-motive claims. We likewise hold that to survive a defendant's motion for summary judgment, a Title VII plaintiff asserting a mixed-motive claim need only produce evidence sufficient to convince a jury that: (1) the defendant took an adverse employment action against the plaintiff; and (2) "race, color, religion, sex, or national origin was a *motivating factor*" for the defendant's adverse employment action. 42 U.S.C. §2000e-2(m) (emphasis added). This burden of producing some evidence in support of a mixed-motive claim is not onerous and should preclude sending the case to the jury only where the record is devoid of evidence that could reasonably be construed to support the plaintiff's claim. Moreover, as it is irrelevant, for purposes of a summary judgment determination, whether the plaintiff has presented direct or circumstantial evidence in support of the mixed-motive claim, see *Desert Palace*, we direct that this summary judgment analysis just described, rather than the *McDonnell Douglas/Burdine* burden-shifting framework, be applied in all Title VII mixed-motive cases regardless of the type of proof presented by the plaintiff.

Id. at 400 (citations omitted). But this apparent clarity was offset by a footnote:

> However, . . . the *McDonnell Douglas/Burdine* framework continues to guide our summary judgment analysis of single-motive discrimination claims brought pursuant only to Title VII's general anti-discrimination provision, 42 U.S.C. §2000e-2(a)(1), and not pursuant to 42 U.S.C. §2000e-2(m). We decline to adopt the view, proposed by some courts and commentators, that the *McDonnell Douglas/Burdine* framework has ceased to exist entirely following *Desert Palace*. Indeed, post-*Desert Palace*, the Supreme Court has continued to apply the *McDonnell Douglas/Burdine* analysis to summary judgment challenges in single-motive Title VII cases. *See Raytheon Co. v. Hernandez*, 540 U.S. 44, 53-54, (2003).

Id. The court, however, did not notice that *Raytheon* was brought under the ADA, which does not have, explicitly at least, a parallel to 703(m). As suggested by the footnote, the commentators have generally read *Desert Palace* as destroying *McDonnell Douglas*, in effect if not in theory. *E.g.*, Michael J. Zimmer, *The New Discrimination Law:* Price Waterhouse *is Dead, Whither* McDonnell Douglas?, 53 Emory L. J. 1887 (2004); Kenneth R. Davis, Price-*Fixing: Refining the* Price Waterhouse *Standard and Individual Disparate Treatment Law*, 31 Fla. St. U. L. Rev. 859, 861 (2004); William R. Corbett, McDonnell Douglas, *1973-2003: May You Rest in Peace?*, 6 U. Pa. J. Lab. & Emp. L. 199, 212-13 (2003); Henry L. Chambers, Jr., *The Effect of Eliminating Distinctions Among Title VII Disparate Treatment Cases*, 57 SMU L. Rev. 83, 102-3 (2004); Jeffrey A. Van Detta, *"Le Roi Est Mort; Vive Le Roi!": An Essay on the Quiet Demise of* McDonnell Douglas *and the Transformation of Every Title VII Case After* Desert Palace, Inc. v. Costa *into a "Mixed-Motives" Case*, 52 Drake L. Rev. 71, 79 (2003).

Even if the commentators are correct and *McDonnell Douglas* is doctrinally no longer required, the case law applying it will continue to have utility. Even if a court *need* no longer pursue the three-step ritual of that line of cases, it will still have to decide whether evidence of a motivating discriminatory reason is sufficient for a jury to find for plaintiff. This includes assessing whatever evidence the plaintiff adduces to exclude the nondiscriminatory reasons — whether those would have been the "most common" legitimate reasons that in the past were negated as part of plaintiff's prima facie case or the more specific reason articulated in defendant's case. While plaintiff will not need to exclude all potential nondiscriminatory reasons, she may have to cast sufficient doubt on innocent reasons to allow the jury to find in her favor by a preponderance of the evidence that an impermissible reason was a motivating factor. Some would say that this is *McDonnell Douglas* in substance if not form.

In practice, then, we might expect to see courts continue to use the *McDonnell Douglas/Reeves* structure as a way of implementing the more gestalt "sufficient evidence" approach of *Desert Palace.* But a court that wished to save itself time in granting summary judgment to defendant might summarize the evidence and conclude that it was not sufficient for a reasonable jury to find intent to discriminate motivating the challenged decision. Nevertheless, such a court would be well advised to find "sufficient evidence" in a case such as *Reeves,* where the Supreme Court has held that proof of a prima facie case plus proof of pretext will generally be sufficient at least to allow the trier of fact to decide that discrimination occurred.

6. *Back to "Intent" and "Motivating Factor."* Aside from its effect on proof structures, *Desert Palace* may lead to a refocus on the meaning of intent. Although the initial reaction to the case was to look to the adjectives — single vs. mixed — the decision may put the noun "motive" back on center stage. If courts define motive to embrace less conscious or even unconscious impulses and attitudes, the case may offer new opportunities for plaintiff's to prove discrimination through cognitive bias theory. On the other hand, conservative courts may seize this opportunity to define motive itself in terms of conscious decision making.

Further, the linchpin of *Desert Palace* is an undefined and perhaps incoherent concept: discriminatory intent as a "motivating factor" even when it does not necessarily change any decision. The lower courts have shown agility in avoiding the import of much clearer terms, and it may be that *Desert Palace* will founder on renewed attention to what it means to be a motivating factor. As we have seen, the term originated in the plurality opinion in *Price Waterhouse,* where something might be a "factor" in a decision even though it made no difference to the result. Maybe like plus or minus "0" in a mathematical formula. Of course, the plurality used the concept essentially for burden shifting, seeming to mean merely that a factor was motivating when it appeared likely to make a difference in a particular decision, leaving the defendant the ability to avoid liability by proving that it did not do so because the same decision would have been made had the factor not been present. But § 703(m) makes a motivating factor a basis for liability, not merely burden shifting. While a motivating factor can be less than a but-for cause, it is not clear how much less it can be and still count.

Note on Age Discrimination Variations on the Individual Disparate Treatment Theme

To some extent, the law developed under Title VII, § 1981, and the ADEA is similar. For example, in describing the core violation, *Hazen Paper Co v. Biggins,* 507 U.S. 604 (1993), drew heavily on Title VII precedents establishing the disparate treatment theory. After quoting from the *Teamsters v. United States*, 431 U.S. 324, 335 n.15 (1977), description of disparate treatment, the Court went on to state that "[t]he disparate treatment theory is of course available under the ADEA, as the language of that statute makes clear." *Id.* at 609. Implementing this perception, the Supreme Court has assumed the *McDonnell Douglas* framework applies to age discrimination claims, although it has inexplicably refused to so hold. *Reeves v. Sanderson Plumbing Prods., Inc.*, 530 U.S. 133, 142 (2000) ("This Court has not squarely addressed whether the *McDonnell Douglas* framework . . . also applies to ADEA actions. Because the parties do not dispute the issue, we shall assume, arguendo, that the *McDonnell Douglas* framework is fully applicable here.").

Although the Court has not explicitly revisited the *McDonnell Douglas* framework's applicability to cases under the ADEA, it recently drove a wedge between the analysis of Title VII claims and ADEA claims. In *Gross v. FBL Fin. Serv.*, 129 S. Ct. 2343 (2009), the Supreme Court not only rejected the application of Title VII's motivating factor analysis under § 703(m) to cases under the ADEA, but also refused to apply *Price Waterhouse* analysis to ADEA cases, reaffirming that a plaintiff claiming age discrimination must prove that discrimination was a determinative factor in a challenged decision.

The majority adopted a three-step rationale. First, it held that the amendment of Title VII in the 1991 to add the "motivating factor" standard of liability in § 703(m) did not apply to the ADEA. Thus, *Desert Palace* is limited to Title VII cases. Given the decision in *Smith v. City of Jackson*, 544 U.S. 228 (2005), which focused on differences between the ADEA's language and Title VII's as a result of the 1991 amendment to Title VII, this step was not surprising. The second step, however, was startling, which was to also hold that the burden-shifting approach established by the Court for Title VII in *Price Waterhouse* did not apply. Given the Court's stress on statutory language in *City of Jackson*, and the fact that *Price Waterhouse* interpreted identical language in the pre-1991 version of Title VII and the ADEA, the Court's analysis is inexplicable. The third step in rejecting applying *Price Waterhouse* to the ADEA was even more bizarre: *Gross* appeared to overrule *Price Waterhouse* even though it had just found it inapplicable to the ADEA, and, as to Title VII, it had already been superseded by the 1991 amendments to Title VII. If there is a point to this, it might be to foreclose the application of *Price Waterhouse* to § 1981 and, perhaps, to retaliation cases under Title VII that are not explicitly subject to § 703(m), *See generally* Martin J. Katz, Gross *Disunity*, 114 Penn St. L. Rev. 857 (2010); Michael C. Harper, *The Causation Standard in Federal Employment Law: Gross v. FBL Financial Services, Inc., and the Unfulfilled Promise of the Civil Rights Act of 1991*, 58 Buffalo L. Rev. 69 (2010).

From a practical standpoint, following *Gross*, plaintiffs claiming both age and, say, sex discrimination will now have two very different sets of instructions to the jury (or standards of liability for the trial judge). While direct and/or circumstantial evidence apparently can be used to support both claims, plaintiff must prove her age claim with evidence strong enough to support drawing the inference that age was the but-for cause of the action. Failing to establish that means there is no liability under the ADEA. But, even if the factfinder finds but-for linkage as to age, she might still also prevail if the factfinder is convinced that sex was also "a motivating factor." It is logically possible to find that sex was implicated even though age was the but-for reason, since a but-for finding allows other reasons to be implicated. The plaintiff, however, might claim that sex was the but-for reason. If the factfinder would find that, then it would be logically impossible to find liability under the ADEA since there can be only one but-for reason for some action. *See* Catherine T. Struve, *Shifting Burdens: Discrimination Law Through the Lens of Jury Instructions*, 51 B.C. L. Rev. 279 (2010).

The circuit courts have so far read *Gross* not to affect the application of *McDonnell Douglas* analysis in ADEA cases. *E.g.*, *Smith v. City of Allentown*, 589 F.3d 684, 691 (3d Cir. 2009) ("*Gross* stands for the proposition that it is improper to shift the burden of persuasion to the defendant in an age discrimination case. *McDonnell Douglas*, however, imposes no shift in that particular burden" since it shifts only a burden of production); *Leibowitz v. Cornell Univ.*, 584 F.3d 487, 498 n.2 (2d Cir. 2009) (applying *McDonnell Douglas* after *Gross* requires the plaintiff to prove that age was the but-for cause of the defendant's adverse employment action). They have also continued to look to something like "direct evidence" — not as a burden-shifting device but rather as a reason to find that age was a determinative factor. *Mora v. Jackson Mem'l Found., Inc.*, 597 F.3d 1201 (11th Cir. 2010); *Baker v. Silver Oak Senior Living Mgmt. Co.*, 581 F.3d 684 (8th Cir. 2009).

While *Gross* creates a formal split between the analysis of cases under both statutes, the ADEA also differs in other respects from Title VII. For example, *Biggins* itself noted that "age discrimination rarely was based on the sort of animus motivating some other forms of discrimination," although the Court recognized that "it was based in large part on stereotypes unsupported by objective fact." *Id.* at 610-11 (quoting *EEOC v. Wyoming*, 460 U.S. 226, 231 (1983)). Some commentators have agreed that age discrimination is different but warn that it may actually be worse because of "opportunistic" conduct by employers. In Governing the Workplace: The Future of Labor and Employment Law 64-65 (1988), Professor Paul Weiler argued that workers tend to be paid less than they are worth when first hired and more than they are worth in the later stages of their careers. Compensation tends to be linked to seniority in the firm, and workers with greater seniority receive more than their increased productivity would justify. This structure tends to keep employees loyal to the firm throughout their working lives but also creates a potential for "opportunistic" employer behavior, that is, taking advantage of the situation by replacing senior employees with younger, lower-paid workers. Older discharged workers rarely will be able to command the same compensation from another employer because their skills tend to be firm-specific. By narrowly defining what it means to discriminate on account of age, *Biggins* freed employers to make productivity-based judgments and perhaps resurrected the problem of opportunistic behavior. When you study disparate impact discrimination, see page 591, consider whether that theory offers a better way to challenge this phenomenon than disparate treatment.

Another dramatic difference between Title VII and the ADEA flows from the fact that, given the limitation of the ADEA to those 40 and older, age discrimination against individuals below the cutoff is legal. *Cf. Bergen Commer. Bank v. Sisler*, 723 A.2d 944 (N.J. 1999) (state antidiscrimination law protects young workers from discrimination on account of their youth). Further, the Supreme Court has held that, even within the protected class of those over 40, it is permissible to discriminate against younger workers in favor of older workers (although not vice versa). *General Dynamics Land Systems, Inc. v. Cline*, 540 U.S. 581, 586 (2004) (while the ADEA's language could be read as flatly barring all "age" discrimination, "Congress's interpretive clues speak almost unanimously to an understanding of discrimination as directed against workers who are older than the ones getting treated better.").

Still another difference between the ADEA and Title VII arises because, unlike race and sex, which tend to be viewed as discrete points, age is a continuum. Inferring age discrimination from differences in treatment, therefore, is more or less plausible depending on the size of the age disparity at issue. In *O'Connor v. Consolidated Coin Caterers Corp.*, 517 U.S. 308, 311-12 (1996), the lower court had found that a 56-year-old plaintiff had not made out a prima facie case of age discrimination under *McDonnell Douglas/Burdine* because he was replaced by a worker over age 40 and thus in the same protected group as plaintiff. The Supreme Court rejected this approach:

> As the very name "prima facie case" suggests, there must be at least a logical connection between each element of the prima facie case and the illegal discrimination for which it establishes a "legally mandatory, rebuttable presumption." The element of replacement by someone under 40 fails this requirement. The discrimination prohibited by the ADEA is discrimination "because of [an] individual's age," though the prohibition is "limited to individuals who are at least 40 years of age." This language does not ban discrimination because they are aged 40 or over; it bans discrimination against employees because of their age, but limits the protected class to those who are 40 or older. The fact that one person in the protected class has lost out to another person in the protected class is thus irrelevant, so long as he has lost out because of his age. Or to put the point more concretely, there can be no greater inference of age discrimination (as opposed to "40 or over" discrimination) when a 40 year-old is replaced by a 39 year-old than when a 56 year-old is replaced by a 40 year-old.

Id. O'Connor held that an inference of age discrimination "cannot be drawn from the replacement of one worker with another worker insignificantly younger. Because the ADEA prohibits discrimination on the basis of age and not class membership, the fact that a replacement is substantially younger than the plaintiff is a far more reliable indicator of age discrimination than is the fact that the plaintiff was replaced by someone outside the protected class." 517 U.S. at 313. How large an age discrepancy is necessary to infer age discrimination from a comparison? *See Ramlet v. E.F. Johnson Co.*, 507 F.3d 1149 (8th Cir. 2007) (one year's and five years' age difference between plaintiff and comparators insufficient to establish a prima facie case); *Barber v. CSX Distribution Servs.*, 68 F.3d 694, 699 (3d Cir. 1995) (eight years sufficient); *Grosjean v. First Energy Corp.*, 349 F.3d 332 (6th Cir. 2003) (six years not sufficient). Obviously, this is highly contextual, depending on what other evidence is available.

Note on Pleading

In 2002, the Supreme Court reversed a Second Circuit decision that had required plaintiff to plead at least a *McDonnell Douglas* claim in order to survive a Rule 12(b)(6) motion to dismiss for failure to state a claim. *Swierkiewicz v. Sorema, N.A.*, 534 U.S. 506 (2002). The plaintiff had alleged that he had been first demoted and ultimately fired by his employer because of his national origin and age in violation of Title VII of the Civil Rights Act of 1964 and the ADEA. He did plead his age (49) and national origin (Hungarian) and the younger age (32) and different national origin (French) of the favored co-worker. He also alleged that he had 25 years' more experience than the co-worker. For the Second Circuit that was not enough — he had to at least plead a prima facie case under the *McDonnell Douglas* proof structure.

In a unanimous opinion written by Justice Thomas, the Supreme Court reversed, reaffirming the traditional view of notice pleading under the Federal Rules of Civil

Procedure. Put simply, the plaintiff's complaint gave the defendant employer adequate notice of both the act being challenged — plaintiff's discharge — and of the legal bases upon which he was suing — national origin discrimination in violation of Title VII and age discrimination in violation of the ADEA. Since the employer knew what adverse actions were being charged, who the supposed favored employee was, and what statutory requirements were allegedly violated, it had all the information that notice pleading requires. As for the failure to plead a prima facie case under *McDonnell Douglas*, the Court noted that *McDonnell Douglas* provides "an evidentiary standard, not a pleading requirement"; therefore, "under a notice pleading system, it is not appropriate to require a plaintiff to plead facts establishing a prima facie case." 534 U.S. at 511. Whatever hurdles employment discrimination plaintiffs had to face in their quest for vindication, pleading problems appeared to be a thing of the past. For example, in *Bennett v. Schmidt*, 153 F.3d 516, 518 (7th Cir. 1998), the Seventh Circuit wrote "[b]ecause racial discrimination in employment is 'a claim upon which relief can be granted,' this complaint could not be dismissed under Rule 12(b)(6). 'I was turned down for a job because of my race' is all a complaint has to say."

In the past few years, however, this certainty has been severely shaken. In two remarkable cases, *Bell Atlantic Corp. v. Twombly*, 550 U.S. 544 (2007), and *Ashcroft v. Iqbal*, 129 S. Ct. 1937 (2009), the Court adopted a "plausible pleading" standard for Rule 12(b)(6) motions, a standard whose operational meaning remains unclear but that many believe has radically changed pleading requirements under the Federal Rules.

The *Iqbal* opinion essentially sets out an analytic structure that suggest that a court analyze a complaint under "[t]wo working principles." 129 S. Ct. at 1949. Drawing on *Twombly*, *Iqbal* requires a court deciding a Rule 12(b)(6) motion to identify the "factual" allegations as distinct from legal conclusions in a complaint. "Facts" plead must be taken as true, but allegations that do not state "facts" need not be credited: "[T]he tenet that a court must accept as true all of the allegations contained in a complaint is inapplicable to legal conclusions. Threadbare recitals of the elements of a cause of action, supported by mere conclusory statements, do not suffice." *Id.* Obviously, what counts as a "fact" as opposed to a legal conclusion is key to understanding this first prong of *Iqbal*. For purposes of this course, one critical question is whether a complaint alleging "discrimination" pleads a fact or a conclusion.

Once the facts alleged are identified, the second *Iqbal* step is to determine whether, accepting such allegations as true, the "complaint that states a plausible claim for relief." Quoting heavily from *Twombly*, the Court explained:

> To survive a motion to dismiss, a complaint must contain sufficient factual matter, accepted as true, to "state a claim to relief that is plausible on its face." A claim has facial plausibility when the plaintiff pleads factual content that allows the court to draw the reasonable inference that the defendant is liable for the misconduct alleged. The plausibility standard is not akin to a "probability requirement," but it asks for more than a sheer possibility that a defendant has acted unlawfully. Where a complaint pleads facts that are "merely consistent with" a defendant's liability, it "stops short of the line between possibility and plausibility of 'entitlement to relief.'"

Id. This is "a context-specific task that requires the reviewing court to draw on its judicial experience and common sense." *Id.* If a plaintiff's allegations of "discrimination" are only conclusions, the court must look to the rest of the complaint for "facts" that show that the claim of discrimination is plausible." *Iqbal* itself was a discrimination claim, albeit one arising under the Constitution, not Title VII, and the Court found implausible the plaintiff's claim that he was subjected to especially harsh conditions of incarceration because of his nationality and religion. While it might have been plausible that lower-level officials acted from such motives, it was not plausible that Attorney General Ashcroft and Federal Bureau of Investigation Director Mueller did so when other motives — such as a desire to protect national security by keeping "suspected terrorists in the most secure conditions available until the suspects could be cleared of terrorist activity" — were more apparent. *Id.* at 1952.

The $64 question is whether *Swierkiewicz* survives the new regime. *Twombly* cited it with apparent approval, but *Iqbal* did not cite it at all. Some commentators argue that *Swierkiewicz* remains good law, and therefore that plausible pleading, properly understood, will have relatively little effect on employment discrimination claims. *E.g.*, Joseph A. Seiner, *After* Iqbal, 45 WAKE FOREST L. REV. 179, 194 (2010); Joseph A. Seiner, *Pleading Disability*, 51 B.C. L. REV. 95 (2010); Joseph A. Seiner, *The Trouble with* Twombly: *A Proposed Pleading Standard for Employment Discrimination Cases*, 2009 U. ILL. L. REV. 1011. Others are more skeptical. *E.g.*, Suzette M. Malveaux, *Front Loading and Heavy Lifting: How Pre-Dismissal Discovery Can Address the Detrimental Effect of* Iqbal *on Civil Rights Cases*, 14 LEWIS & CLARK L. REV. 65, 82 (2010); Suja A. Thomas, *The New Summary Judgment Motion: The Motion to Dismiss Under* Iqbal *and* Twombly, 14 LEWIS & CLARK L. REV. 15 (2010). And one commentator, looking at the worst-case scenario, offers suggestions for effectively pleading claims under the new pleading standard. Charles A. Sullivan, *Plausibly Pleading Employment Discrimination*, WILL. & MARY L. REV. (forthcoming), *abstract available at* http:// ssrn.com/abstract=1657872.

PROBLEM

9-1. In response to a help-wanted ad, Jane Armstrong, a 38-year-old woman, applies for a job as a cab driver at the Hacker Cab Company. She has a valid driver's license and has driven extensively, but not for pay, for 20 years. She is a vegetarian and a Capricorn. After a brief interview, at which all these facts emerge, she is rejected by "Tip" O'Neill, Hacker's president. Armstrong comes to you for legal counsel. You do some investigation. The first call you make is to O'Neill, who admits that the job is still open, but explains that he rejected Armstrong because "Capricorns make lousy drivers; besides she's too old to adjust to the rigors of cab driving, especially since she doesn't eat meat." When asked whether Armstrong's gender played a part in the decision, O'Neill replied, "Hell no. Some of my best friends are women. I don't care if my brother marries one. Har, har." A "windshield survey" of the Hacker Cab Company at shift-changing times reveals an almost total absence of women drivers. It is common knowledge that there is a heavy turnover in the cab-driving business.

How would you analyze this case based on *Price Waterhouse*, *McDonnell Douglas*, and *Desert Palace*?

C. SYSTEMIC DISCRIMINATION

We have seen that individual challenges to adverse employment decisions require the courts to focus on how a particular plaintiff has been treated by a defendant. But employment policies that sweep more broadly can also be challenged — for example, an employer's policy to hire only men, to fire older workers, or to separate employees by race, gender, or age. Challenges might also be mounted against employer practices that are not consciously designed to exclude, but that have the effect of disproportionately disadvantaging employees with protected characteristics. Such policies and practices raise systemic issues that may be addressed through one of the two concepts of systemic discrimination presently governing Title VII actions: systemic disparate treatment and disparate impact.

1. Systemic Disparate Treatment

Systemic disparate treatment can be proven in two ways. First, the plaintiff may simply demonstrate that the employer has an announced, formal policy of discrimination. Second, the plaintiff who fails to prove a formal policy may nevertheless establish that the employer's pattern of employment decisions reveals that a policy of disparate treatment operates. In both cases, intent is critical, but it is obvious from the facial discrimination in a formal policy and inferable from the impact of the practices.

a. *Formal Policies of Discrimination*

Historically, formal systems excluding women and minority group members or segregating them into inferior jobs were common. While there were rarely "white only" signs outside workplaces in the same way such signs were posted near public restrooms and drinking fountains in the South, many employers, particularly in the South, formally segregated jobs by race, with blacks typically consigned to lower-paying, less-attractive jobs. For example, Duke Power in North Carolina limited African Americans to the "Labor Department," the lowest-level jobs in the company. *See Griggs v. Duke Power Co.*, 401 U.S. 424 (1971). Most employers also segregated many jobs by gender, again with lower-level jobs assigned to female workers. It was common for newspaper classified employment advertisements to be separately listed under "help wanted male" and "help wanted female."

With the passage of Title VII in 1964, most formal discriminatory policies of race or sex discrimination ended. Similarly, prior to the passage of the ADEA, employers typically imposed mandatory retirement at age 65. Since the ADEA now generally bars age discrimination for those over 40, most such formal discriminatory policies have disappeared.

Nevertheless, not all formal policies were rescinded without court intervention. An example is *Trans World Airlines, Inc. v. Thurston*, 469 U.S. 111 (1985), in which the defendant airline permitted pilots disqualified from serving in that capacity for reasons other than age to transfer automatically to the position of flight engineer but barred those who were required by a federal regulation to stop flying as pilots at age 60 from doing so. The Court had no trouble finding the policy facially discriminatory. "Since [the policy] allows captains who become disqualified for any reason other than age to 'bump' less senior flight engineers, Trans World Airline's ("TWA") transfer policy is discriminatory on its face." *Id.* at 121. Because the policy drew an age line, it necessarily reflected an intent to discriminate on that basis. *But see Ky. Ret. Sys. v. EEOC*, 128 S.Ct. 2361 (2008) (permitting a retirement plain to explicitly take age into account when there was no reason to believe it systematically disadvantaged older workers).

Today, most employers understand the requirements of the antidiscrimination laws and would not normally adopt a facially discriminatory plan unless the employer believed that the plan did not violate the statute, either because it was not technically discrimination or because it believed the policy to be permissible under a statutory exception. The first possibility is not as far-fetched as one might think. Sex distinctions in employer dress and grooming codes generally have been held not to constitute illegal sex discrimination under Title VII when they treat male and female employees separately but equally. See page 643. We will also encounter racial and gender preferences that are sometimes permissible under Title VII as part of valid affirmative action plans. See page 585. As for exceptions to the statute, several are possible. Police and fire departments continue to have age restrictions because of an exception written into the ADEA. And with respect to gender, age, and national origin, the bona fide occupational qualification ("BFOQ") defense permits classification on these bases in limited circumstances where the protected characteristic is strongly enough related to success on the job. In *Thurston*, the court rejected the airline's attempt to use this defense because many pilots over age 60 continued to work as flight engineers for TWA, thus undercutting the claim that being younger than 60 was a BFOQ. As we will see, the BFOQ defense generally requires that all members of one sex or all persons over a certain age be unable to perform the position in question.

b. Systemic Practices

Trans World Airlines v. Thurston involved a formal policy that facially treated older workers differently. There was no need, therefore, to search further for intent to discriminate. But the systemic disparate treatment theory goes beyond formal policies to reach pervasive practices rooted in intentional discrimination. Thus, the second type of systemic disparate treatment arises where no formal, announced policy of using race or gender can be established, but the plaintiff nevertheless shows a pattern of decisions explainable only if such a policy exists covertly.

In short, the plaintiff can establish a prima facie case of such treatment by showing that the employer's personnel practices reveal a de facto policy of discrimination. This showing is usually by statistical evidence of a gross and long-lasting disparity between, say, the racial or gender composition of the employer's workforce and the composition that would be expected, given the labor market from which the defendant picks its workers. The statistical evidence can be buttressed by anecdotal evidence supporting the inference that the employer had a policy of discriminating. For example, in *Teamsters v. United States*, 431 U.S. 324 (1977), the plaintiff showed that almost no black or Hispanic workers had been assigned to the "line driver" job despite their availability in the lower-status "city driver" jobs and in the general population from which the employer selected its employees. Buttressing this "inexorable zero" in minority representation in the line driver jobs was testimony by workers that supervisors had told them that the company was not ready for black and Hispanic line drivers. The Court undertook a similar analysis in *Hazelwood School District v. United States*, 433 U.S. 299 (1977), although there the question was whether a school district could be shown to have discriminated in hiring when the representation of minority teachers was compared to the racial composition of the relevant labor market for teachers.

Where plaintiff's case is based primarily on statistical evidence, as in *Teamsters*, determining whether there is disparate treatment often leads to a battle between the parties' statistical experts. The defendant may challenge the plaintiff's prima facie case by introducing evidence showing that plaintiff's statistical data or techniques are flawed. For instance, a common tactic is to challenge the labor pool on which the expectancy for female or minority work force representation was based. Alternatively, the employer may admit the disparity but offer an alternative explanation for the statistics that negate its intent to discriminate. Perhaps the most famous example of this defense is *EEOC v. Sears, Roebuck & Co.*, 839 F.2d 302 (7th Cir. 1988). Women constituted some 60 percent of the applicants for full-time sales jobs at Sears (both commissioned and noncommissioned) but only 27 percent of the newly hired commissioned salespeople. Median hourly wages were about twice as high for commissioned as for noncommissioned salespeople. The EEOC argued that, given the desirability of the commissioned jobs, this disparity could be explained only by an inference of intentional discrimination by Sears and that, even though the Commission had the burden of proving such intent, the statistics were a sufficient basis to carry that burden.

The employer, however, successfully blunted the EEOC's statistical showing by convincing the trial court that the large disparity between men and women in commission sales jobs was explained by women generally lacking interest in those jobs, in part because of the competitive nature of the work. To be more precise, the district court found that the EEOC had not sustained its burden because, in light of the lack of interest argument, it had not established that the disparity resulted from Sears' discrimination. Ironically, Sears based its defense on a school of feminist thinking that stresses the differences between men and women, reasoning that the divergent life experiences of men and women lead them to develop different perspectives and attitudes. Thus, Sears argued it was the women's lack of interest in commission sales jobs, not the employer's discrimination, that resulted in underrepresentation of women in those jobs. While *Sears* illustrates the upsides and downsides of even apparently strong statistical showings, it may be equally indicative of a major failure of trial strategy by the EEOC, which produced not a single female employee or applicant to testify as to having been denied a commissioned position. *See also EEOC v. Consolidated Service Systems*, 989 F.2d 233 (7th Cir. 1993) (while finding a statistically significant overrepresentation of Koreans at the employer, the court found that this resulted from the employer's reliance on word-of-mouth recruiting, not intent to prefer Koreans).

Sears was a major setback for the systemic disparate treatment, but the theory is currently being deployed against an even larger retailer. In *Dukes v. Wal-Mart Stores, Inc.*, 603 F.3d 571 (9th Cir. 2010), the en banc Ninth Circuit certified a class action on behalf of half a million female workers against Wal-Mart, claiming pay and promotion discrimination. Although that opinion focused largely on whether the requirements for a class action were met (an inquiry that is not necessary when the EEOC sues, as in *Sears*), the court did recognize the substantial overlap between the merits question (Did Wal-Mart engage in systemic disparate treatment?) and the procedural questions as to whether a class could be certified. In the process, it reviewed voluminous evidence including statistical evidence of the relative success of male and female workers within Wal-Mart (as in *Sears*) and statistical evidence of female success at Wal-Mart compared to how women fared at other large retailers. Perhaps most interesting was the "social framework" expert testimony that sought to link the statistics to company policies, which was critical for certifying a nationwide class action.

The systemic theory is usually asserted either in a government enforcement action (as in *Teamsters* or *Hazelwood*) or in a private class action. In these settings, the establishment of a prima facie of systemic disparate treatment has been held to result in a *Price Waterhouse*—like shifting of the burden of persuasion. That is, when systemic disparate treatment toward the class is proven, and an individual plaintiff is shown to be a member of that class, discrimination as to the individual is established — subject to the defendant carrying a burden of proof that the individual was not harmed by the pattern of discrimination. *See Teamsters*; *Franks v. Bowman Transp. Co.*, 424 U.S. 747, 772 (U.S. 1976) ("petitioners here have carried their burden of demonstrating the existence of a discriminatory hiring pattern and practice by the respondents and, therefore, the burden will be upon respondents to prove that individuals who reapply were not in fact victims of previous hiring discrimination."). May an individual plaintiff, not in the class action context, employ the theory to obtain the advantage of the shift in burdens? Some courts have been reluctant to permit plaintiffs in individual actions to assert the systemic theories, particularly systemic disparate treatment. *E.g.*, *Williams v. Giant Food, Inc.*, 370 F.3d 423 (4th Cir. 2004) (individual plaintiff cannot pursue Title VII or §1981 suit based solely on pattern-or-practice discrimination; such allegations do not change nature of alleged failures to promote, which remain discrete discriminatory acts). *Accord Davis v. Coca-Cola Bottling Co. Consol.*, 516 F.3d 955, 967 (11th Cir. 2008).

c. *Bona Fide Occupational Qualifications*

Section 703(e) of Title VII provides:

> Notwithstanding any other provision of this title . . . it shall not be an unlawful employment practice for an employer to hire and employ employees . . . on the basis of religion, sex, or national origin in those certain instances where religion, sex, or national origin is a bona fide occupational qualification reasonably necessary to the normal operation of that particular business or enterprise.

The ADEA also provides a BFOQ defense that uses language identical to Title VII. This defense, while a potentially large loophole in the antidiscrimination statutes' prohibitions, has been read very narrowly as to sex, age, and national origin. The Title VII provision does not by its terms allow race discrimination to be a BFOQ. *See Chaney v. Plainfield Healthcare Ctr.*, 612 F.3d 908 (7th Cir. 2010) (holding that honoring a patient's request for white caregivers was not a justification for discrimination in job assignments, even if the employer had a good faith belief that it was required by state law to honor such requests). *See also Ferrill v. The Parker Group, Inc.*, 168 F.3d 468 (11th Cir. 1999) (rejecting, in a §1981 case, a BFOQ for racially segregating telemarketers aimed at getting out the vote for an election, with blacks calling blacks and whites calling whites).

The Supreme Court's first meaningful treatment of the BFOQ defense was in *Dothard v. Rawlinson*, 433 U.S. 321 (1977), in which the Court upheld a rule requiring prison guards in "contact" positions to be the same gender as the inmates they guarded. The majority stressed that Alabama's penitentiaries had been held unconstitutional because of their dangerous and inhumane conditions. Since inmates were not segregated according to dangerousness, the 20 percent of male prisoners who were sex offenders were scattered throughout the dormitories. While characterizing the BFOQ defense as "an extremely narrow exception to the general prohibition of discrimination on the basis of sex," the Court recognized that in an "environment of violence and disorganization, it would be an over-simplification to characterize [the rule against women] as an exercise in 'romantic paternalism.' " *Id.* at 334-35. Title VII normally allows individual women to decide whether jobs are too dangerous for them, but the Alabama prisons conditions made it likely that women could not perform the essence of the correctional counselor's job — to maintain security:

> A woman's relative ability to maintain order in a male, maximum-security, unclassified penitentiary of the type Alabama now runs could be directly reduced by her womanhood. There is a basis in fact for expecting that sex offenders who have criminally assaulted women in the past would be moved to do so again if access to women were established within the prison. There would also be a real risk that other inmates, deprived of a normal heterosexual environment, would assault women guards because they were women.

Id. at 336. Thus, an employee's "very womanhood" could undermine her ability to do the job. The dissent by Justice Marshall protested this analysis as justifying discrimination by the barbaric state of the prisons. Those conditions violate the Constitution and, therefore, cannot constitute "the normal operation of that particular business or enterprise" required by the BFOQ defense. Further, the notion that the employee's "very womanhood" makes assaults more likely

> regrettably perpetuates one of the most insidious of the old myths about women — that women, wittingly or not, are seductive sexual objects. The effect of the decision, made I am sure with the best of intentions, is to punish women because their very presence might provoke sexual assaults. It is women who are made to pay the price in lost job opportunities for the threat of depraved conduct by prison inmates. Once again, "[t]he pedestal upon which women have been placed has . . . , upon closer inspection, been revealed as a cage." It is particularly ironic that the cage is erected here in response to feared misbehavior by imprisoned criminals.

Id. at 345 (Marshall, J., dissenting).

The Supreme Court's next encounter with the BFOQ defense was in a suit under the ADEA. *Western Air Lines v. Criswell*, 472 U.S. 400 (1985), involved whether an airline could limit flight engineer positions to pilots no older than 60 under the BFOQ exception to the ADEA. Flight engineers monitored side-facing instrument panels in commercial aircraft of that era such as the Boeing 727. A Federal Aviation Administration ("FAA") regulation banned those over age 60 from the other two pilot jobs — captain and first officer — but did not set any standard for flight engineers.

Defendant's evidence focused on the possibility that flight engineers would suffer a heart attack, the risks of which generally increase with age. Plaintiff's evidence established that physiological deterioration was individualized and could be ascertained through physical examinations that the FAA required for all flight engineers. Further, other airlines allowed flight engineers over age 60 to continue to fly without any apparent safety problems.

The Court upheld a jury instruction that included a "two-part inquiry [, which] properly identifies the relevant considerations for resolving a BFOQ defense to an age-based qualification purportedly justified by considerations of safety." *Id.* at 416. That test was whether it was (1) highly impractical to make individualized determinations as to ability to perform the job safely; and (2) some persons over the defined age possess "traits of a physiological, psychological or other nature which preclude safe and efficient job performance that cannot be ascertained by means other than knowing their age." *Id.*

The Court later elaborated on this test and applied it in the sex discrimination context in *International Union, UAW v. Johnson Controls, Inc.*, 499 U.S. 187 (1991), which involved a "fetal protection policy" that broadly excluded women from jobs that exposed them to lead. Lower courts had reached conflicting results in deciding whether such policies even distinguished workers on the basis of sex, as opposed to a neutral characteristic, such as fetal safety. However, the Supreme Court had no difficulty with that question: "The bias in Johnson Controls' policy is obvious. Fertile men, but not fertile women, are given a choice as to whether they wish to risk their reproductive health for a particular job." *Id.* at 197. Further, "the absence of a malevolent motive does not convert a facially discriminatory policy into a neutral policy with a discriminatory effect." *Id.* at 199. While a discriminatory policy can nevertheless be justified as a bona fide occupational qualification, Johnson Controls' policy did not meet the strict requirements of this exception:

> The wording of the BFOQ defense contains several terms of restriction that indicate that the exception reaches only special situations. The statute thus limits the situations in which discrimination is permissible to "certain instances" where sex discrimination is "reasonably necessary" to the "normal operation" of the "particular" business. Each one of these terms — certain, normal, particular — prevents the use of general subjective standards and favors an objective, verifiable requirement. But the most telling term is "occupational"; this indicates that these objective, verifiable requirements must concern job-related skills and aptitudes.

Id. at 201. The majority rejected the argument that "occupational" merely meant "related to a job," holding, rather, that the term related to "qualifications that affect an employee's ability to do the job." *Id.* Since susceptibility of a fetus to lead poisoning was entirely unconnected to whether its mother could make batteries, this approach effectively foreclosed the BFOQ defense.

The Court recognized that the safety of third parties had been important in cases such as *Criswell* but drew a distinction, observing that in those cases

> safety concerns were not independent of the individual's ability to perform the assigned tasks, but rather involved the possibility that, because of age-connected debility, a flight engineer might not properly assist the pilot, and might thereby cause a safety emergency. Furthermore, although we considered the safety of third parties in *Dothard* and *Criswell*, those third parties were indispensable to the particular business at issue. In *Dothard*, the third parties were the inmates; in *Criswell*, the third parties were the passengers on the plane. We stressed that in order to qualify as a BFOQ, a job qualification must relate to the "essence," or to the "central mission of the employer's business."

Id. at 202-3. While the health of future children was a deep social concern, the BFOQ did not render it essential to battery making.

The *Johnson Controls* reasoning was reinforced by the Pregnancy Discrimination Act, which had amended Title VII in 1978 to declare that pregnancy discrimination was sex discrimination. The Court described the PDA as "contain[ing] a BFOQ standard of its own: Unless pregnant employees differ from others 'in their ability or inability to work,' they must be 'treated the same' as other employees 'for all employment-related purposes.'" *Id.* at 204. This meant that "women as capable of doing their jobs as their male counterparts may not be forced to choose between having a child and having a job." *Id.*

While the Court was not persuaded that tort liability to fetuses was a real danger, it did note that "[w]e, of course, are not presented with, nor do we decide, a case in which costs would be so prohibitive as to threaten the survival of the employer's business. We merely reiterate our prior holdings that the incremental cost of hiring women cannot justify discriminating against them." Finally, the majority specifically noted that its decision did not suggest that sex could not constitute a BFOQ when privacy interests are implicated.

In the wake of *Johnson Controls,* most BFOQ claims have arisen in the institutional context, most often prisons, as in the next principal case, but also in hospitals, *Slivka v. Camden-Clark Mem'l Hosp.*, 594 S.E.2d 616 (W. Va. 2004), and psychiatric facilities, *Healey v. Southwood Psychiatric Hospital*, 78 F.3d 128 (3d Cir. 1996). Can you guess why?

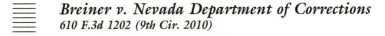 ### Breiner v. Nevada Department of Corrections
610 F.3d 1202 (9th Cir. 2010)

BERZON, Circuit Judge:

The Nevada Department of Corrections (NDOC) hires only female correctional lieutenants at a women's prison. The district court granted summary judgment upholding NDOC's discriminatory employment policy, concluding that the policy imposed only a "de minimis" restriction on male prison employees' promotional opportunities and, alternatively, that the policy falls within Title VII's exception permitting sex discrimination in jobs for which sex is a bona fide occupational qualification, 42 U.S.C. § 2000e-2(e)(1). We reverse as to both holdings.

Factual & Procedural Background

In September 2003, NDOC's Inspector General learned that a female inmate at the Southern Nevada Women's Correctional Facility (SNWCF) had been impregnated by a male guard. At the time, SNWCF was operated by a private company, Corrections Corporation of America (CCA). The pregnant inmate alleged that her relationship with the guard stemmed from CCA's refusal to provide the psychotropic medications she had long been prescribed to treat her schizophrenia. NDOC Director Jackie Crawford acknowledged that her office had received a number of complaints concerning medical issues at SNWCF. At Crawford's direction, the Inspector General interviewed approximately 200 inmates about "their personal experiences with the medical function at [SNWCF]." Nearly all the inmates reported receiving substandard medical treatment.

In the course of the investigation, the Inspector General also discovered that SNWCF had become "an uninhibited sexual environment." He noted "frequent instances of inappropriate staff/inmate interaction," "flirtatious activities between staff and inmates," and "widespread knowledge" of "long-term inmate/inmate sexual relationships." In exchange for sex, prison staff "routinely introduce[d] . . . contraband into the institution, including alcohol, narcotics, cosmetics, [and] jewelry." The inmates' sexual behavior — which they freely admitted was designed to "compromise staff and enhance inmate privileges" — was, in the Inspector General's view, "predictable." The Inspector General attributed the guards' misconduct to "a lack of effective supervisory management oversight and control. . . . There is no evidence that supervisors or managers recognize this risky behavior or do anything to stop it." To address this "leadership void," the Inspector General recommended that "line supervisors undergo leadership training" and that "subordinate staff undergo re-training with emphasis on inmate con games and ethical behavior."

In the wake of the Inspector General's report, which ignited "very high profile" media coverage, CCA announced that it was terminating its contract to operate SNWCF. NDOC resumed control of the facility and, according to Crawford, faced intense political pressure to "mitigate the number of newspaper articles" and to "assure the State of Nevada that we would not be embarrassed like this again." To achieve this goal, Crawford decided to restaff the facility so that seventy percent of the front line staff at SNWCF would be women.

Crawford also decided to hire only women in SNWCF's three correctional Lieutenant positions. The correctional lieutenants are shift supervisors and are the senior employees on duty seventy-five percent of the time. Correctional lieutenants report to wardens or deputy wardens and are responsible for supervising the prison's day-to-day operations, including directing the work of subordinate staff, inspecting the facility and reporting infractions, and monitoring inmates' activities and movement through the facility. There is one correctional lieutenant assigned to SWNCF per shift. Although the correctional lieutenant posting specified that "only female applicants will be accepted for these positions," several males applied for the positions, which were eventually filled by three women.

[Three male Nevada correctional officers brought suit although they had not applied for the lieutenant positions. They challenged only the gender limitation with respect to that position; the "seventy-percent-female restriction on front line guards" was, therefore, not at issue in this litigation. The district court granted NDOC's motion for summary judgment, holding, first, that the gender restriction "had a 'de minimis' impact on the plaintiffs' overall promotional opportunities," and, second, it in any event fell within Title VII's BFOQ exception. The Ninth Circuit first found that, despite not having applied for the positions at issue, at least one plaintiff had standing to bring suit because he was discouraged from applying by the employer's conduct and was otherwise qualified. It then reversed the district court on both grounds.]

A. The "De Minimis" Theory

NDOC asserts that the three SNWCF positions were the only correctional lieutenant promotions in the NDOC system as a whole restricted to women applicants and that twenty-nine out of thirty-seven correctional lieutenant positions filled over a four year period went to men. Relying on these statistics, NDOC maintains that the concededly discriminatory policy of excluding men from the SNWCF correctional lieutenant positions had only a "de minimis" impact on the plaintiffs and so did not violate Title VII with regard to them. This conclusion reflects a fundamental misunderstanding of the basic precepts of Title VII and is not supported by our case law.

[The court stressed the desirability of the positions at issue, and noted "[t]hat another opportunity may later arise for which the applicant is eligible does not negate the injury of being denied an earlier position on the basis of one's sex, with the resulting loss of pay for a period and delayed eligibility for another promotion." Further, positions are not fungible, and some may be more desirable for individuals than others, for example, because of location. Cases like *Robino v. Iranon*, 145 F.3d 1109 (9th Cir. 1998), were inapposite. That decision approved assigning only female guards to certain posts to protect female inmate privacy, but involved only assignments within the prison, not positions.] *Robino*'s premise, then, was necessarily that a minor impact on job assignments was too minimal to be actionable. This very limited concept has no application to NDOC's policy. An employer's "fail[ure] or refus[al] to hire" on the basis of sex is, without limitation, actionable under Title VII. 42 U.S.C. § 2000e-2(a)(1). NDOC's refusal to hire men in the correctional lieutenant positions therefore violates Title VII unless NDOC can demonstrate that gender is a BFOQ for the positions. NDOC cannot meet that burden, as we now explain.

B. Gender as a Bona Fide Occupational Qualification . . .

NDOC has not explicitly articulated the "job qualification" for correctional lieutenants for which it claims sex is a legitimate proxy. We are left to try to adduce what that "qualification" might be from the declarations by NDOC officials on which the defendants rely in their briefs as justification for the facially discriminatory policy. . . .

From this panoply of explanations, it appears that NDOC administrators sought to "reduce the number of male correctional employees being compromised by female inmates," and that they believed the gender restriction on shift supervisors would accomplish this because (1) male correctional lieutenants are likely to condone sexual abuse by their male subordinates; (2) male correctional lieutenants are themselves likely to sexually abuse female inmates; and (3) female correctional lieutenants possess an "instinct" that renders them less susceptible to manipulation by inmates and therefore better equipped to fill the correctional lieutenant role.[5]

The first theory fails because NDOC has not shown that "all or nearly all" men would tolerate sexual abuse by male guards, or that it is "impossible or highly impractical" to assess applicants individually for this qualification. As to the second theory,

---

5. NDOC also suggests that privacy and rehabilitation were among the "factors . . . considered important" in implementing the gender restriction. Neither in its briefs nor at oral argument, however, was NDOC able to direct the court to any evidence that Crawford or other administrators actually considered privacy or rehabilitation in developing the policy. This void is not surprising, as it is the guards who have direct daily contact with the inmates, not the correctional lieutenants. As noted, NDOC, in a separate policy not here challenged, restricts the number of front line guards in female prisons. As there is no evidence in this record to indicate that concern about privacy or rehabilitation was a basis for the decision to preclude men from serving in the supervisory positions, we do not consider those rationales in our BFOQ analysis.

there is no "basis in fact," *Dothard*, for believing that individuals in the correctional lieutenant role are particularly likely to sexually abuse inmates. The third theory — and, to a significant degree, the first two — relies on the kind of unproven and invidious stereotype that Congress sought to eliminate from employment decisions when it enacted Title VII.

[The court reviewed *Dothard*, concluding that its finding of a BFOQ] was premised on a level of violence among inmates atypical even among maximum security facilities. *See Gunther v. Iowa State Men's Reformatory*, 612 F.2d 1079, 1085 (8th Cir. 1980).

Appellate courts, including this court, have followed *Dothard* in requiring prison administrators to identify a concrete, logical basis for concluding that gender restrictions are "reasonably necessary."[6] In *Everson v. Michigan Department of Corrections*, 391 F.3d 737 (6th Cir. 2004), the Sixth Circuit upheld a gender restriction imposed by the Michigan Department of Corrections (MDOC) to eradicate "rampant sexual abuse of female prisoners." MDOC had "pledged . . . to minimize access to secluded areas and one-on-one contact between male staff and female inmates" pursuant to settlement of two lawsuits, one brought by the United States Department of Justice, alleging that the failure to protect female inmates from ongoing sexual abuse violated their constitutional rights. To effectuate the settlement agreements, MDOC employed only female guards in the housing units of women's prisons. MDOC data showed that most allegations of sexual abuse, and all of the sustained allegations, involved male employees, and that sexual abuse occurred most frequently in the housing units. This data, the court held, "established that the exclusion of male [guards] will decrease the likelihood of sexual abuse."

In *Henry v. Milwaukee County*, 539 F.3d 573 (7th Cir. 2008), a juvenile detention center decided to staff each housing "pod" with at least one guard of the same sex as the juveniles housed on that pod, to achieve a "direct role model/mentoring form of supervision." During the day, one of the two guards on each male "pod" could be female, but the sole night shift slot on each pod had to be staffed by a man. The Seventh Circuit accepted the administrator's "professional judgment" that same-gender mentoring was "necessary to achieve the [facility's] mission of rehabilitation." Yet, the court found no factual support for the administrator's conclusion that the program's effectiveness required same-sex staff at all times, including on the night shift, when the juvenile inmates were sleeping.

In *Robino*, we held that even had the gender-based restriction on assignments been actionable under Title VII, it fell within the BFOQ exception. The prison, based on "a study conducted by a specially appointed task force in compliance with an EEOC settlement agreement," designated as female only those posts that "require[d] the [guard] on duty to observe the inmates in the showers and toilet areas . . . or provide[d] unsupervised access to the inmates." Because "a person's interest in not being viewed unclothed by members of the opposite sex survives incarceration," we held that protecting inmate privacy and preventing sexual misconduct warranted the restriction.

These cases illustrate that, even in the unique context of prison employment, administrators seeking to justify a BFOQ must show "a high correlation between sex and ability to perform job functions." *Johnson Controls*. Moreover, the particular staffing restriction at issue must match those "job functions" with a high degree of

---

6. Judgments by prison administrators that "are the product of a reasoned decision-making process, based on available information and experience," are entitled to some deference. *Robino*.

specificity to be found reasonably necessary. *See id.*; *Robino*. In *Henry*, for example, the application of the gender restriction on the night shift would not address privacy concerns, as "the vast majority of the time that the juveniles were unclothed occurred during [ ] daytime shifts" when women were permitted to staff the pods, and was not justified by the mentoring objective because "the opportunity . . . to interact with the juveniles on the [night] shift [wa]s very minimal."

Applying this "high correlation" requirement, NDOC's first rationale for restricting the supervisory correctional lieutenant positions to women cannot suffice. Crawford's testimony suggests that because the supervisors employed by CCA were male and had failed to prevent sexual abuse, NDOC was entitled to conclude that men as a class were incapable of adequately supervising front line staff in female prisons. While we must defer to the reasoned judgment of prison administrators, *see Robino*, CCA's acknowledged leadership failure falls far short of providing "a factual basis for believing that all or substantially all [men] would be unable to safely and effectively perform the duties of the job," or that it would be "impossible or highly impracticable to determine job fitness" — here, the ability to enforce workplace rules prohibiting sexual misconduct — "on an individualized basis." *Williams v. Hughes Helicopters, Inc.*, 806 F.2d 1387, 1391 (9th Cir. 1986) [ADEA]. The fundamental switch in operational responsibility to NDOC, moreover, made any inference from the experience under CCA's extremely poor management all the weaker.

NDOC's second rationale fares no better. There is no evidence indicating that any correctional lieutenant at SNWCF had sexual relationships with an inmate. In contrast, in *Everson*, copious data about the actual incidence of sexual abuse in Michigan's women's prisons supported the conclusion that the gender restriction on guards in the housing units would be effective. In *Robino*, prison administrators used "a study by a specially appointed task force" and "an extensive inventory of post duties" to limit the gender restriction to those posts that "provide[d] unsupervised access to the inmates." NDOC, however, offers neither data nor logical inferences about the opportunities for abuse inherent in the correctional lieutenant position to support the restriction.

In fact, the one substantiated case of sexual abuse Crawford mentioned was the front line guard who impregnated an inmate, yet NDOC continues to employ men in thirty percent of these positions. *See Everson*. When asked why the complete prohibition on the hiring of men was limited to correctional lieutenants, Crawford stated, "We did not want to go globally on this. We wanted to be specifically, what can we do to bring this thing under control . . . ? And it was the recommendation that we just look at . . . not the line level, but the supervisor level." This explanation falls short of the "reasoned decision-making process, based on available information and experience," *Robino*, that can support a BFOQ.

Even if there were a factual basis to believe that any correctional lieutenant sexually abused any inmate, there is no basis to presume that sexual abuse, by correctional lieutenants or by guards with their supervisors' tacit permission, would continue after the state resumed control over the prison. CCA's lax oversight provided male correctional lieutenants "the opportunity not to take action against male correctional subordinates that sexually abused female inmates." That opportunity cannot be presumed to exist after the wholesale change of SNWCF's leadership, designed precisely to cure wholesale management defects going well beyond the sexual abuse issue.

To hold otherwise would be to absolve NDOC from their fundamental responsibility to supervise their staff, from wardens to front-line guards. In *Dothard*, the inmates' violent behavior, which prison administrators could not directly control, rendered the gender restriction reasonably necessary. Neither *Dothard* nor any of the cases on which NDOC relies support finding a BFOQ based on the bald assertion that it would be "impossible . . . to ensure that any given male correctional lieutenant will take action to prevent and stop sexual misconduct." Where, as here, the problem is *employee* behavior, prison administrators have multiple resources, including background checks, prompt investigation of suspected misconduct, and severe discipline for infractions, to ensure compliance with institutional rules.

NDOC has not demonstrated that these alternative approaches — including the Inspector General's suggestion of enhanced training for both supervisors and front-line guards — are not viable. *See Henry; Forts v. Ward*, 621 F.2d 1210, 1216 (2d Cir. 1980) (upholding a district court order "prohibit[ing] the stationing of male guards at locations where inmates could be viewed . . . unclothed" but reversing a ban on male guards during the night shift because inmate privacy could be protected by means that did not infringe on employment rights); *Gunther* (holding that gender was not a BFOQ where administrative changes in job functions and procedures would adequately protect inmate privacy). [One witness's] conclusory assertion that "more training is not a cure for this serious issue" is, without more, wholly inadequate. Even the NIC report, on which NDOC purportedly relied, recommends "improving training programs to heighten staff awareness of [sexual abuse] and its consequences."

Disturbingly, in suggesting that all men are inherently apt to sexually abuse, or condone sexual abuse of, female inmates, NDOC relies on entirely specious gender stereotypes that have no place in a workplace governed by Title VII. NDOC's third theory, that women are "maternal," "patient," and understand other women, fails for the same reason. To credit NDOC's unsupported generalization that women "have an instinct and an innate ability to discern . . . what's real and what isn't" and so are immune to manipulation by female inmates would violate "the Congressional purpose to eliminate subjective assumptions and traditional stereotyped conceptions regarding the . . . ability of women to do particular work." *Rosenfeld v. S. Pac. Co.*, 444 F.2d 1219, 1225 (9th Cir. 1971). "The harmful effects of occupational cliches," *Gerdom v. Continental Airlines*, 692 F.2d 602, 607 (9th Cir. 1982), are felt no less strongly when invoked as a basis for one gender's unique suitability for a particular job than when relied on to exclude members of that sex from employment. Simply put, "we are beyond the day when an employer could . . . insist[ ] that [employees] matched the stereotype associated with their group." *Price Waterhouse v. Hopkins.*

A BFOQ can be established only by "objective, verifiable requirements [that] concern job-related skills and aptitudes." *Johnson Controls.* Though the professional judgment of prison administrators is entitled to deference, *see Robino*, "[t]he refusal to hire a [man] because of [his] sex based on assumptions of the comparative employment characteristics of [men] in general" will not support a BFOQ. 29 C.F.R. § 1604.2(a)(1).

In sum, NDOC has not met its burden of showing "a basis in fact," *Dothard*, for concluding that all male correctional lieutenants would tolerate sexual abuse by their subordinates; that all men in the correctional lieutenant role would themselves sexually abuse inmates; or that women, by virtue of their gender, can better understand the behavior of female inmates. Nor has it refuted the viability of alternatives that would achieve that goal without impeding male employees' promotional opportunities. . . .

NOTES

1. *Adverse Employment Action?* The court's rejection of the de minimis argument might suggest that any sex discrimination is impermissible unless justified by a BFOQ. But a closer reading suggests that this is not true. As we saw on page 524, a "de minimis" exception seems alive and well under Title VII, although it is framed in terms of whether the at-issue decision constitutes an "adverse employment action." For many courts, a "lateral transfer," that is, one that does not result in loss of pay or a demotion, is not actionable. In jurisdictions with stringent definitions of adverse employment action, an employer may be able to assign individuals by sex, age, or even race without having to establish a BFOQ. *See Tipler v. Douglas County*, 482 F.3d 1023, 1025 (8th Cir. 2007 ("a bona fide occupational qualification analysis is unnecessary if (1) the policy requiring female-only supervision of female inmates is reasonable, and (2) such a policy imposes only a 'minimal restriction' on the employee"). *But see Piercy v. Maketa*, 480 F.3d 1192 (10th Cir. 2007) (facial discrimination might be actionable when it was not clear that assignments were purely lateral). *See generally* Rebecca Hanner White, *De Minimis Discrimination*, 47 EMORY L. J. 1121, 1148, 1172-73 (1998) ("When there is direct evidence of a discriminatory act, or when a fact finder has concluded the discrimination was motivated by the protected characteristic, the 'de minimis' nature of the discrimination should not serve as a basis for dismissing the claim. That the discrimination may be viewed as 'trivial' or 'de minimis' goes merely to remedies and not to liability.").

2. *Avoiding Sexual Harassment and Exploitation.* Although it could be described in "privacy" terms, *Breiner* is about more than privacy in the sense of an interest in not being seen unclothed by members of the opposite sex. The scandal that gave rise to the policy at issue indicates the serious problems that can arise in custodial settings, which may explain why employers in such settings often resort to such policies. And, while the court struck down the sex-limitation for lieutenants, it made clear that the policy as to the sex of the front-line guards themselves was not at issue. In purely numerical terms, the number of positions reserved for female guards undoubtedly dwarfed the three supervisory slots at issue in the case. If a male guard sued the prison, would he win? It's safe to assume that avoiding harassment and exploitation of female inmates is an appropriate goal, but is a gender line reasonably necessary to achieve it? *See generally* Kim Shayo Buchanan, *Beyond Modesty: Privacy in Prison and the Risk of Sexual Abuse*, 88 MARQ. L. REV. 751 (2005) ("the modesty critics' concern about stereotyping is misguided. [W]hen women prisoners are sexually exploited by guards, they are victims of sexual aggression; feminists do them no favor by pretending that they are not.").

3. *Rehabilitation.* The court finds that neither rehabilitation nor privacy concerns were proffered as justifications for the sex limitation. In some cases, however, courts have found rehabilitation to be a legitimate basis for a BFOQ. In *Healey v. Southwood Psychiatric Hospital*, 78 F.3d 128, 132-33 (3d Cir. 1996), plaintiff challenged a gender-specific rule for assigning childcare specialists at a hospital for emotionally disturbed children and adolescents, some of whom had been sexually abused. The court upheld summary judgment for the employer based on the BFOQ defense:

> The "essence" of Southwood's business is to treat emotionally disturbed and sexually abused adolescents and children. Southwood has presented expert testimony that staffing both males and females on all shifts is necessary to provide therapeutic care. "Role modeling," including parental role modeling, is an important element of the staff's job, and a

male is better able to serve as a male role model than a female and vice versa. A balanced staff is also necessary because children who have been sexually abused will disclose their problems more easily to a member of a certain sex, depending on their sex and the sex of the abuser. If members of both sexes are not on a shift, Southwood's inability to provide basic therapeutic care would hinder the "normal operation" of its "particular business." Therefore, it is reasonably necessary to the normal operation of Southwood to have at least one member of each sex available to the patients at all times.

See also *Torres v. Wisconsin Dep't of Health & Social Services*, 859 F.2d 1523 (7th Cir. 1988) (rehabilitation in a prison context).

4. *Privacy.* While *Breiner* is about much more than "privacy" as it usually conceived, the court cites *Rubino* for the proposition that an individual's interest in not being seen unclothed by a member of the opposite sex survives incarceration. A number of cases have concurred, but they have often stressed, as in *Robino* itself, that measures short of denying individuals jobs because of their sex can suffice. *E.g., Henry v. Milwaukee County*, 539 F.3d 573 (7th Cir. 2008)? What about the privacy of patients and clients? *See Olsen v. Marriott Int'l, Inc.*, 75 F. Supp. 2d 1052, 1068 (D. Ariz. 1999) (rejecting sex as BFOQ for massage therapists since customers' requests for females "is based neither on inability of men to fulfill core job functions nor on the notion that core job functions intrude upon privacy interests and require assignment of clients to massage therapists of the same sex). The *Johnson Controls* majority denied that its opinion would do away with privacy protections. But how would a privacy-based policy be defended? *See generally* Amy Kapczynski, Note, *Same-Sex Privacy and the Limits of Antidiscrimination Law*, 112 YALE L.J. 1257 (2003); Deborah A. Calloway, *Equal Employment and Third Party Privacy Interests: An Analytical Framework for Reconciling Competing Rights*, 54 FORDHAM L. REV. 327 (1985).

5. *Deference.* Many BFOQ cases turn on the level of deference courts accord the professional judgment of employers. Particularly in the prison context, the cases tend to at least claim to be deferring to some extent. In *Breiner* itself, the prison officials' cavalier rationale for their own rule probably was largely responsible for the opinion's evident disdain. But the Ninth Circuit at least claimed that some deference was due. How much? *See also Henry*, 539 F.3d 580-81 ("We agree that the administrators of juvenile detention facilities, like the administrators of female correctional facilities, are entitled to substantial deference when fashioning policies to further the goals of the facility. We do not agree, however, that the discretion accorded to these individuals in either context is effectively unlimited.").

6. *Essence of the Business.* Although not at issue in *Breiner* some BFOQ cases have turned not on whether one gender was better than another in some respect but rather whether such superiority went to the " 'essence' of the business." This test originated in *Diaz v. Pan American Airways, Inc.*, 442 F.2d 385 (5th Cir. 1971), holding that sex was not a BFOQ for the job of flight attendant — despite the asserted superiority of women in being sexually attractive to male passengers and comforting to female passengers — because those characteristics are peripheral to the airline's essential concern with safe transportation. *Johnson Controls* confirms the importance of "essence" analysis in applying the BFOQ. However, the fact that a policy relates to an essential function, and even promotes it, is not sufficient to establish a BFOQ: "Title VII's standard is not satisfied simply because a policy promotes an essential function of an institution. Although sex-based assignments might be helpful in pursuing [the goals of rehabilitation, security, and privacy], in order to satisfy the

anti-discrimination strictures of Title VII, [the employer] must show that the contested sex classifications are " 'reasonably necessary.' " *Henry*, 539 F.3d 581. In *Henry*, the court held that "Although reducing the number of opposite-sex staff on the pods may *help* to promote security, efficient risk management and privacy, Milwaukee County has failed to establish that its policy was *reasonably necessary* for these goals." *Id.* at 581.

7. *Customer Preference*. Whatever the correct view of privacy, it would support relatively narrow inroads into Title VII's proscriptions. It does, however, tend to merge into a larger question: When, if ever, is "customer preference" a basis for a BFOQ? So framed, the courts have not been sympathetic. For example, the Ninth Circuit rejected a BFOQ claim in *Fernandez v. Wynn Oil Co.*, 653 F.2d 1273 (9th Cir. 1981), where the defendant argued that the plaintiff could not be made vice president of international operations because Latin American clients would react negatively to a woman in such a position. Although finding the defense not factually supported, the Ninth Circuit also held the defense inadequate as a matter of law because customer preference cannot justify gender discrimination. *Id. See also EEOC v. HI 40 Corp.*, 953 F. Supp. 301 (W.D. Mo. 1996) (being female was not a BFOQ for counselors at weight-loss centers, despite the centers' mostly female customers' preference for female counselors). *But see EEOC v. University of Texas Health Science Ctr.*, 710 F.2d 1091, 1095 (5th Cir. 1983) (upholding as a BFOQ an age-45 limitation on initial hiring of campus police in part because of testimony that "younger officers are better able to handle frequent confrontational episodes on campus because of their ability to relate to youthful offenders."). What does *Johnson Controls* suggest about this question? *See* Ernest F. Lidge III, *Law Firm Employment Discrimination in Case Assignments at the Client's Insistence: A Bona Fide Occupational Qualification?*, 38 CONN. L. REV. 159 (2005).

8. *Sex Appeal as a BFOQ*. Is selling sex appeal a BFOQ? In *Frank v. United Airlines*, 216 F.3d 845 (9th Cir. 2000), female flight attendants challenged the airlines' maximum weight requirements requiring women to meet a standard for medium body frames while the standard for men corresponded to standards for large body frames. Women were required to weigh 14 to 25 pounds less than male colleagues of the same height and age. The court found this to be a formal policy of sex discrimination and struck it down because the airline failed to justify it as a BFOQ:

> United made no showing that having disproportionately thinner female than male flight attendants bears a relation to flight attendants' ability to greet passengers, push carts, move luggage, and, perhaps most importantly, provide physical assistance in emergencies. . . . Far from being "reasonably necessary" to the "normal operation" of United's business, the evidence suggests that, if anything, United's discriminatory weight requirements may have inhibited the job performance of female flight attendants.

Id. at 855. Why would United adopt such a policy? Is it to satisfy customer preference for conventional views of attractiveness? *See also Wilson v. Southwest Airlines Co.*, 517 F. Supp. 292 (N.D. Tex. 1981) (being female was not a BFOQ for defendant who marketed itself as "love airline," using the female allure and sex appeal of its employees).

A current example is Hooters, a chain of restaurants that hires only women, who are clad in provocative outfits, to serve food to customers. In an investigation by the EEOC in the mid-1990s, the company defended its practice by arguing that "[a] lot of places serve good burgers. The Hooters' Girls, with their charm and All-American sex appeal, are what our customers come for." *Restaurant Chain to Resist Hiring Men,*

N.Y. TIMES, Nov. 16, 1995, at A20, col. 5. The EEOC dropped its investigation against Hooters after the company's massive public relations campaign. A private action was then settled, under terms that allowed Hooters to continue to hire only women as waitpersons. The men who were discriminated against by this company policy did, however, receive monetary compensation. *Hooters to Pay $3.75 Million in Sex Suit*, USA TODAY, Oct. 1, 1997, at 1A. *See generally* Kimberly A. Yuracko, *Private Nurses and Playboy Bunnies: Explaining Permissible Sex Discrimination*, 92 CAL. L. REV. 147, 191 (2004) (differentiating approaches taken by courts to cases raising issues of patient privacy versus sexual titillation). *See also* Russell Robinson, *Casting and Caste-ing: Reconciling Artistic Freedom and Antidiscrimination Norms*, 95 CAL. L. REV. 1, 5 (2007) ("when it comes to casting, an entire industry effectively disregards Title VII. . . . [C]asting discrimination therefore provides a reminder that society's tastes for certain race and gender-based conventions, such as the expectation that women — but not men — appear frontally nude in film, temper Title VII's capacious language and confine its impact.").

d. Voluntary Affirmative Action

As we have seen, Title VII and § 1981 bar race discrimination, not merely discrimination against African Americans and other racial minorities. Title VII also bars sex discrimination, not merely discrimination against women. Accordingly, discrimination against whites and males is as impermissible as discrimination against minorities and women, although we have also seen that "reverse" discrimination may be harder to prove. One kind of reverse discrimination that is subject to somewhat different rules are racial and gender preferences pursuant to a valid affirmative action plan.

The Supreme Court first encountered this problem in *United Steelworkers of America v. Weber*, 443 U.S. 193 (1979), where a five-to-two majority upheld an employer's use of a voluntary affirmative action plan benefiting unskilled black workers. Kaiser Aluminum had negotiated with the union representing its workers to create a training program for incumbent, unskilled workers to fill skilled job categories. Until this plan was adopted, craft positions were filled by people with craft experience, typically learned in craft unions that had historically excluded blacks from membership. In order to address the resultant lack of trained minorities, the plan reserved for black employees 50 percent of the openings in these newly created in-plant training programs until the percentage of skilled black craft workers approximated the percentage of blacks in the local labor force. While the plan provided as many training openings for whites as for blacks, African Americans with less seniority than whites were admitted to it because there were far fewer of them available.

After holding that Title VII's prohibition against racial discrimination does not condemn all private, voluntary, race-conscious affirmative action plans, the Court upheld the particular plan in the instant case and rejected the plaintiffs' discrimination claim.

> We need not today define in detail the line of demarcation between permissible and impermissible affirmative action plans. It suffices to hold that the challenged Kaiser-USWA affirmative action plan falls on the permissible side of the line. The purposes of the plan mirror those of the statute. Both were designed to break down old patterns of

racial segregation and hierarchy. Both were structured to "open unemployment opportunities for Negroes in occupations which have been traditionally closed to them."

At the same time, the plan does not unnecessarily trammel the interests of the white employees. The plan does not require the discharge of white workers and their replacement with new black hires. . . . Nor does the plan create an absolute bar to the advancement of white employees; half of those trained in the program will be white. Moreover, the plan is a temporary measure; it is not intended to maintain racial balance, but simply to eliminate a manifest racial imbalance.

Id. at 208.

The Court reaffirmed *Weber* in *Johnson v. Transportation Agency, Santa Clara County, California,* 480 U.S. 616 (1987), and extended its application to affirmative action on behalf of women. The employer had promoted Diane Joyce to the position of road dispatcher, making her the first woman included among the 238 skilled craft worker jobs. A male, who had scored two points higher on an interview, sued, claiming reverse discrimination. Although Diane Joyce was qualified for the job, the district court found that the woman's sex was the determining factor in her selection.

When the case reached the Supreme Court, it used the opportunity to broadly approve affirmative action plans. As to the litigation structure of such cases, the Court held that, when a defendant claims it has acted in accordance with an affirmative action plan, the plaintiff has the burden of persuasion in establishing the invalidity of that affirmative action plan. Interestingly, the Court used the inferential method of proof established in *McDonnell Douglas Corp. v. Green,* even though the decision maker admitted that sex was a factor in the selection decision. But the employer's explanation that it had relied upon its affirmative action plan was viewed by the Court as a "legitimate, nondiscriminatory reason," leaving it up to the male plaintiff to prove the plan invalid. Thus, in a reverse discrimination case, the plaintiff bears the burden of persuasion to prove discrimination, either because the challenged action was not taken pursuant to an affirmative action plan, see page 525, or because it was taken pursuant to an invalid plan. As to the substantive standard, *Weber* and *Johnson* specify two requirements: the "manifest imbalance" requirement and the "not unduly trammel" requirement.

Manifest Imbalance. The plan's use of race or sex must be aimed at remedying a "manifest imbalance in a traditionally segregated job category." Such an imbalance brings the affirmative action plan into alignment with the purposes of Title VII, which include breaking down historic patterns of discrimination. Justice Blackmun's concurrence in *Weber* demonstrated how broad this first factor is: "[T]he Court considers a job category to be 'traditionally segregated' when there has been a societal history of purposeful exclusion of blacks from the job category, resulting in a persistent disparity between the proportion of blacks in the labor force and the proportion of blacks among those who hold jobs within the category." *Weber,* 443 U.S. at 212.

This approach is cast in terms of statistical disparity alone, without regard to the underlying cause of the disparity. *Weber* made clear that an employer may adopt an affirmative action plan in the absence of any prior discrimination on its own part; remedying the effects of societal discrimination will suffice. *See id.* at 214. As for determining whether a manifest imbalance in a traditionally segregated job category exists, the *Johnson* Court observed that the proper comparison is between the percentage of minorities or women in the job category in the employer's work force and the percentage of those workers in the *relevant labor pool. Johnson,* 480 U.S. at 632.

A comparison with general population figures is appropriate only when the job involves no skills or skills easily acquired by the general population, as in *Weber*. *Id*. For skilled jobs, the appropriate comparison is to the skilled labor pool. *See Hazelwood Sch. Dist. v. United States*, 433 U.S. 299 (1977). Because *Johnson* involved skilled trade positions, the Court viewed the appropriate comparison to be that between the percentage of skilled craft workers in the employer's work force (zero) and the percentage of women in the relevant labor market having the requisite skills. *Johnson*, 480 U.S. at 632. Once the proper comparison is established, it is still necessary to determine whether the imbalance is great enough to justify the affirmative action remedy.

An important, and as yet unresolved, issue is whether a voluntary affirmative action plan must be "remedial" to be lawful under Title VII. The affirmative action plans in both *Weber* and *Johnson* were aimed at remedying a manifest imbalance in a traditionally segregated job category, and the Court's decisions in those cases addressed when such a remedial interest would support an affirmative action plan. But when no such manifest imbalance exists, may a voluntary affirmative action plan yet be permissible? *Taxman v. Board of Education of Township of Piscataway*, 91 F.3d 1547 (3d Cir. 1996) (en banc) involved a claim by a white school teacher who had been laid off while an equally qualified black teacher was retained. The Third Circuit rejected the school district's use of race under its affirmative action plan to choose between two equally qualified teachers when one needed to be laid off. Since there was no underrepresentation of blacks in the Piscataway school system, the board did not assert a remedial purpose for the plan but instead relied upon a diversity rationale, reasoning that students would benefit from a racially diverse teaching staff. The Third Circuit, however, held that a nonremedial interest would not support an affirmative action plan under Title VII. The Supreme Court granted certiorari, and many expected a decision affirming *Taxman* and thus narrowing the affirmative action exception under Title VII. In a very unusual move, recounted in Michael J. Zimmer, Taxman: *Affirmative Action Dodges Five Bullets*, 1 U. PA. J. LAB. & EMP. L. 229 (1998), civil rights groups underwrote a settlement that resulted in dismissal of the writ as moot. In the wake of the Supreme Court's decision approving nonremedial affirmative action under the Equal Protection Clause in the context of higher education in *Grutter v. Bollinger*, 539 U.S. 306 (2003), the lower courts might be more open to such justifications in the context of Title VII, but the Court's decision in *Parents Involved in Community Schools v. Seattle School Dist. No. 1*, 551 U.S. 701 (2007), cuts the other way. See page 590.

Not Unduly Trammel. The second prong for determining the legitimacy of an affirmative action plan under *Weber* and *Johnson* is that the plan must not "unduly trammel" the interests of majority group members. A common criticism of affirmative action by its opponents is that such programs disadvantage majority workers. In *Weber*, the Court described three possible concerns of white workers, but it thought none of these were at stake in the *Weber* plan:

> The plan does not require the discharge of white workers and their replacement with new black hires. . . . Nor does the plan create an absolute bar to the advancement of white employees; half of those trained in the program will be white. Moreover, the plan is a temporary measure; it is not intended to maintain racial balance, but simply to eliminate a manifest racial imbalance.

Weber, 443 U.S. at 209. Consequently, when a plan does not deprive an employee of a vested right, when it is not an absolute bar to majority workers' advancement, and when it is aimed at attaining, not maintaining, racial balance, it will satisfy this second prong.

Most affirmative action plans focus on hiring and promotion, making them more easily defensible under the second prong of the *Weber/Johnson* standard. *Weber* itself involved a training program to which no one had automatic entitlement. Similarly, in *Johnson*, the male plaintiff had no entitlement to the position but was one of several qualified applicants for the job. Moreover, the plan did not block plaintiff from being promoted in the future, and he in fact received a promotion when another opening arose. *Johnson*, 480 U.S. at 639, n.15. The Court emphasized that no rigid quotas had been set; instead, sex was only one factor out of several considered by the employer in deciding whom to promote. An affirmative action plan used to determine layoffs, as opposed to hiring or promotion, would likely find more difficulty satisfying this prong.

Again, the *Taxman* case provides a useful comparison. Using race as a tiebreaker to decide which teacher to lay off when seniority and qualifications were equal was viewed by the Third Circuit as unduly trammeling the interests of Taxman, who lost her job and was unemployed for some time. In *Weber* and *Johnson*, no one lost a job or any position to which they were otherwise entitled. Upholding a layoff for affirmative action purposes is particularly unlikely when the interest asserted for the plan is not a remedial one. Even if the Court were to approve adoption of voluntary affirmative action plans for nonremedial purposes, upholding the application of such plans in a layoff context seems unlikely.

Although the Supreme Court has not decided a Title VII affirmative action case since *Johnson*, *Ricci v. DeStefano*, 29 S. Ct. 2658 (2009), reproduced at page 604, may have cast doubt on *Weber* and *Johnson*. *Ricci* arose from a promotion test administered by the fire department in New Haven, Connecticut, which yielded racially skewed results. The rate of white candidates who passed the test was significantly higher than the rate of minority candidates. When the city decided not to certify the test results because of potential disparate impact liability, white firefighters sued the city, alleging that the refusal to certify constituted disparate treatment based on race under Title VII. In a sharply divided opinion, the Supreme Court determined that the city's actions amounted to intentional disparate treatment discrimination against white firefighters and granted them summary judgment. The fact that the racial disparity in the test results created a prima facie case for disparate impact was not a defense to the disparate treatment claim unless the employer had a "strong basis in evidence" to believe that it would be liable for disparate impact discrimination. *Id.* at 2664. In order to meet this requirement, an employer had to demonstrate a strong basis to believe that the test was not a business necessity or job-related or that no practices with less discriminatory impact on minorities were available. *Id.* at 2678.

The meaning of *Ricci* for affirmative action is unclear. On the one hand, the majority never cited either *Johnson* or *Weber*, perhaps suggesting that there are simply two lines of authority governing two different situations. This is bulwarked by the fact that the city did not articulate the usual justifications for affirmative action but rather simply argued that its refusal to certify results was justified by its fear of disparate impact liability. On the other hand, *Ricci* takes a more stringent approach to practices designed to help minorities, and many suspect that the majority that decided *Ricci* would take a much more stringent approach to the issue of affirmative action under Title VII than prior cases. When you have read *Ricci*, ask whether its approach to disparate treatment discrimination is consistent with the prior cases.

Note on Voluntary Affirmative Action Plans of Public Employers

A public employer's affirmative action plan may be lawful under Title VII but still fall afoul of the Equal Protection Clause when a constitutional claim is brought. As you learned in Constitutional Law, all racial classifications by the state, local, or federal government are to be measured by strict scrutiny. Under this test, "such classifications are constitutional only if they are narrowly tailored measures that further compelling governmental interests." *Adarand Constr. v. Pena*, 515 U.S. 200 (1995); *Richmond v. J.A. Croson*, 488 U.S. 469 (1989). According to the Supreme Court, providing a remedy for the victims of proven discrimination is a sufficiently important governmental interest to withstand constitutional attack, but remedying the effects of societal discrimination is not. *Wygant v. Jackson Bd. of Educ.*, 476 U.S. 262 (1986). Thus, to withstand a reverse equal protection claim, an employer must have convincing evidence of prior discrimination before embarking on an affirmative action program.

The Court's most definitive word on race-conscious decision making emerged in five-to-four decisions in two nonemployment cases, *Grutter v. Bollinger*, 539 U.S. 306 (2003), and *Gratz v. Bollinger*, 539 U.S. 244 (2003). In considering challenges by white students denied admission to the University of Michigan, the Supreme Court upheld diversity, at least for an educational institution, as a compelling governmental interest. Justice O'Connor, speaking for the Court in *Grutter*, implied that diversity may be a compelling governmental interest in areas beyond higher education by citing favorably the amici briefs of large corporations and the brief of military leaders arguing in favor of racially diverse workforces.

The Court disagreed, however, about whether the programs at issue were narrowly tailored to achieving that diversity interest. In *Grutter*, the Court upheld the law school admissions program as narrowly tailored to the diversity objective; however, in *Gratz*, dealing with undergraduate admissions, the Court struck down that program as being not tailored enough. The essential difference between the two programs was that the law school assessed the complete admissions file of each individual applicant, including membership in underrepresented minority groups, while the undergraduate program mechanically gave applicants who were members of underrepresented minority groups certain points.

In the wake of the Michigan cases, the Seventh Circuit revisited the "diversity" question in a challenge to the Chicago police department's practice of "standardizing" test scores racially to increase the number of African Americans and Hispanics promoted within the force. In rejecting a challenge by white officers, the court held that "there is an even more compelling need for diversity in a large metropolitan police force charged with protecting a racially and ethnically divided major American city like Chicago. Under the *Grutter* standards, we hold, the City of Chicago has set out a compelling operational need for a diverse police department." *Petit v. Chicago*, 352 F.3d 1111, 1117-18 (7th Cir. 2003).

Despite *Petit*, the impact of *Grutter* and *Gratz* on affirmative action in the employment context is uncertain. A number of circuits "sustained Title VII challenges to race-conscious diversity programs used by the cities of Milwaukee, Newark, Shreveport, Chicago, and Omaha, as well as at least one major private employer, Xerox Corporation. And, perhaps surprisingly, the courts cited *Grutter* as compelling the conclusion that the challenged diversity programs violated Title VII." These include *Alexander v. City of Milwaukee*, 474 F.3d 437 (7th Cir. 2007); *Lomack v. City of Newark*, 463 F.3d 303 (3d Cir. 2006); *Frank v. Xerox Corp.*, 347 F.3d 130, 133, 137 (5th Cir. 2003). And the tendency was only confirmed by the Supreme Court's latest word on the subject in *Parents Involved in Community Schools v. Seattle School Dist. No. 1*, 551 U.S. 701 (2007), Although not an employment case, *Parents Involved* struck down the use of race to achieve greater diversity in elementary and secondary schools in Seattle and Louisville school districts. Most assignments honored student choice, but, for example, "tie-breakers" were used for the more popular schools, one of which was the race of the student in an attempt to maintain a white/nonwhite racial balance.

Chief Justice Roberts wrote an opinion for a plurality: "The way to stop discrimination on the basis of race is to stop discriminating on the basis of race." *Id.* at 748. Applying traditional analysis, the plurality noted that only two interests had been recognized as compelling in the school context, remedying past intentional discrimination (but not de facto segregation) and "diversity in higher education." *Id.* at 720. Neither applied to either of the cases before the Court — there was discrimination to remedy and, as for diversity, race was "not considered as part of a broader effort to achieve 'exposure to widely diverse people, cultures, ideas, and viewpoints.' . . . [Race] is not simply one factor weighed with others in reaching a decision, as in *Grutter*; it is *the* factor." *Id.* at 723.

Because Roberts spoke for only four justices, Justice Kennedy's concurring opinion provides the governing rule. Kennedy voted to invalidate the race-based assignment but in a less sweeping fashion than the majority, leaving room for taking race into account in decision making by differentiating hope from reality: "The enduring hope is that race should not matter; the reality is that too often it does." *Id.* at 787. For him, what the school districts did wrong was to assign "to each student a personal designation according to a crude system of individual racial classifications." *Id.* at 789. That did not mean that a school district cannot take race into account as one component in its decision-making process, because "avoiding racial isolation" is a compelling governmental interest. *Id.* He wrote:

> Race may be one component of that diversity, but other demographic factors, plus special talents and needs, should also be considered. What the government is not permitted to do, absent a showing of necessity not made here, is to classify every student on the basis of race and to assign each of them to schools based on that classification. Crude measures of this sort threaten to reduce children to racial chits valued and traded according to one school's supply and another's demand.

Id. at 798.

What does *Parents Involved* say about affirmative action plans enacted by public employers? It would seem that the tiebreaker approach of the Piscataway School District, in *Taxman* referred to above, would not be permissible. But, would a public employer in making an employment decision be acting constitutionally if it considered race as long as it made the decision in the context of looking at additional factors that might be relevant to the job?

Adarand, Grutter/Gratz, and *Parents Involved* are all constitutional, not statutory decisions, but public employers' affirmative action plans must fall within both constitutional and statutory limits. That the Court found diversity to be a compelling state interest in the context of university admissions in *Grutter* does not necessarily mean it will be viewed as a compelling state interest in the employment setting, were a constitutional challenge brought. It seems likely, however, that in at least some employment contexts, public employers will be able to contend successfully that a compelling state interest in diversity exists. A public elementary or high school, for example, may have a compelling state interest in employing a racially diverse faculty much as the University of Michigan had a compelling interest in a diverse student body. Thus it is possible that cases like *Taxman* might come out differently in the future.

Of course, in cases involving race-based decision making by governmental actors, courts apply the highest level of constitutional scrutiny, or strict scrutiny. Traditionally, sex-based classifications have been judged by a less demanding level of scrutiny under the Fourteenth Amendment, sometimes called "intermediate scrutiny." *United States v. Virginia,* 518 U.S. 515 (1996). It would thus seem that affirmative action in favor of women would be easier to constitutionally justify than affirmative action based on race.

2. Systemic Disparate Impact Discrimination

While disparate treatment discrimination is the purposeful exclusion of minorities or women from jobs, disparate impact discrimination exists when employment policies, regardless of intent, adversely affect one group more than another and cannot be justified. This section briefly outlines the structure of disparate impact analysis, the policies subject to disparate impact analysis, and defenses to a disparate impact case.

As we will see, the disparate impact theory clearly applies under Title VII of the Civil Rights Act of 1964 and under the ADA. It also operates under the ADEA, although in a very diluted form. *See Meacham v. Knolls Atomic Power Lab.,* 554 U.S. 84 (2008); *Smith v. City of Jackson,* 544 U.S. 228 (2005). See page 620. The Supreme Court has held that disparate impact is *not* available under 42 U.S.C. § 1981 (2006). *See Gen. Bldg. Contractors Ass'n v. Pennsylvania,* 458 U.S. 5 (2002), or under 42 U.S.C. § 1983 (2006) in suits enforcing the equal protection clause of the United States Constitution. *See, e.g., Personnel Admin. of Mass. v. Feeney,* 442 U.S. 256, 272 (1979).

Even under Title VII, where disparate impact originated as a theory of liability, recent developments have altered the landscape. The theory originated in 1971 in *Griggs v. Duke Power Co.,* 401 U.S. 424 (1971), and was elaborated on in a number of Supreme Court decisions until 1989. In that year, *Wards Cove Packing Co. v. Atonio,* 490 U.S. 642 (1989), radically reconceptualized the law. Congress, in turn, revived disparate impact analysis as the centerpiece (and most controversial part) of the Civil Rights Act of 1991. Most recently, the Supreme Court decided *Ricci v. DeStefano,* 29 S. Ct. 2658 (2009), which at least limited the disparate impact theory and which some believe signals its end.

Griggs v. Duke Power Co.
401 U.S. 424 (1971)

Chief Justice BURGER delivered the opinion of the Court.

[Prior to the effective date of Title VII, Duke Power explicitly discriminated on the basis of race. "Negroes were employed only in the Labor Department where the highest paying jobs paid less than the lowest paying jobs in the other four 'operating' departments in which only whites were employed." With the enactment of Title VII, the Company abandoned its prior policy and allowed blacks to be hired into, or transfer to, any other department. However, Duke Power applied to these workers a high school diploma requirement that had applied for a decade to white workers seeking operating jobs. Further, on the effective date of Title VII, Duke Power for the first time required satisfactory scores on two professionally prepared aptitude tests for initial employment (although for current employees only the high school diploma was required for transfer). Shortly thereafter, Duke Power permitted incumbent employees who lacked a high school education to transfer by passing the two tests, the Wonderlic Personnel Test, which purports to measure general intelligence, and the Bennett Mechanical Comprehension Test. The district court found neither test directed or intended to measure the ability to learn to perform a particular job or category of jobs. The requisite scores used for both initial hiring and transfer approximated the national median for high school graduates.][3]

[Both the district court and the Fourth Circuit found that, despite the prior policy of overt racial discrimination, there was no showing of a racial purpose or invidious intent in the adoption of the high school diploma requirement or general intelligence test and that these standards had been applied fairly to whites and Negroes alike.]

The objective of Congress in the enactment of Title VII is plain from the language of the statute. It was to achieve equality of employment opportunities and remove barriers that have operated in the past to favor an identifiable group of white employees over other employees. Under the Act, practices, procedures, or tests neutral on their face, and even neutral in terms of intent, cannot be maintained if they operate to "freeze" the status quo of prior discriminatory employment practices.

The Court of Appeals' [judges] agreed that, on the record in the present case, "whites register far better on the Company's alternative requirements" than Negroes.[6] This consequence would appear to be directly traceable to race. Basic intelligence must have the means of articulation to manifest itself fairly in a testing process. Because they are Negroes, petitioners have long received inferior education in segregated schools and this Court expressly recognized these differences in Gaston County v. United States, 395 U.S. 285 (1969). There, because of the inferior education received by Negroes in North Carolina, this Court barred the institution of a literacy test for voter registration on the ground that the test would abridge the right to vote indirectly on

---

3. The test standards are thus more stringent than the high school requirement, since they would screen out approximately half of all high school graduates.

6. In North Carolina, 1960 census statistics show that, while 34% of white males had completed high school, only 12% of Negro males had done so. U.S. Bureau of the Census, U.S. Census of Population: 1960, Vol. 1, Characteristics of the Population, pt. 35, Table 47.

Similarly, with respect to standardized tests, the EEOC in one case found that use of a battery of tests, including the Wonderlic and Bennett tests used by the Company in the instant case, resulted in 58% of whites passing the tests as compared with only 6% of the blacks. Decision of EEOC, CCH Empl. Prac. Guide, ¶ 17,304.53 (Dec. 2, 1966). See also Decision of EEOC 70-552, CCH Empl. Prac. Guide, ¶ 6139 (Feb. 19, 1970).

account of race. Congress did not intend by Title VII, however, to guarantee a job to every person regardless of qualifications. In short, the Act does not command that any person be hired simply because he was formerly the subject of discrimination, or because he is a member of a minority group. Discriminatory preference for any group, minority or majority, is precisely and only what Congress has proscribed. What is required by Congress is the removal of artificial, arbitrary, and unnecessary barriers to employment when the barriers operate invidiously to discriminate on the basis of a racial or other impermissible classification.

Congress has now provided that tests or criteria for employment or promotion may not provide equality of opportunity merely in the sense of the fabled offer of milk to the stork and the fox. On the contrary, Congress has now required that the posture and condition of the job-seeker be taken into account. It has—to resort again to the fable—provided that the vessel in which the milk is proffered be one all seekers can use. The Act proscribes not only overt discrimination but also practices that are fair in form, but discriminatory in operation. The touchstone is business necessity. If an employment practice which operates to exclude Negroes cannot be shown to be related to job performance, the practice is prohibited.

On the record before us, neither the high school completion requirement nor the general intelligence test is shown to bear a demonstrable relationship to successful performance of the jobs for which it was used. Both were adopted, as the Court of Appeals noted, without meaningful study of their relationship to job-performance ability. Rather, a vice president of the Company testified, the requirements were instituted on the Company's judgment that they generally would improve the overall quality of the work force.

The evidence, however, shows that employees who have not completed high school or taken the tests have continued to perform satisfactorily and make progress in departments for which the high school and test criteria are now used. The promotion record of present employees who would not be able to meet the new criteria thus suggests the possibility that the requirements may not be needed even for the limited purpose of preserving the avowed policy of advancement within the Company. In the context of this case, it is unnecessary to reach the question whether testing requirements that take into account capability for the next succeeding position or related future promotion might be utilized upon a showing that such long-range requirements fulfill a genuine business need. In the present case the Company has made no such showing.

The Court of Appeals held that the Company had adopted the diploma and test requirements without any "intention to discriminate against Negro employees." We do not suggest that either the District Court or the Court of Appeals erred in examining the employer's intent; but good intent or absence of discriminatory intent does not redeem employment procedures or testing mechanisms that operate as "built-in headwinds" for minority groups and are unrelated to measuring job capability.

The Company's lack of discriminatory intent is suggested by special efforts to help the undereducated employees through Company financing of two-thirds the cost of tuition for high school training. But Congress directed the thrust of the Act to the *consequences* of employment practices, not simply the motivation. More than that, Congress has placed on the employer the burden of showing that any given requirement must have a manifest relationship to the employment in question.

The facts of this case demonstrate the inadequacy of broad and general testing devices as well as the infirmity of using diplomas or degrees as fixed measures of capability. History is filled with examples of men and women who rendered highly effective performance without the conventional badges of accomplishment in terms of certificates, diplomas, or degrees. Diplomas and tests are useful servants, but Congress has mandated the common sense proposition that they are not to become masters of reality.

[The Court also rejected the defendant's argument that § 703(h), which authorizes the use of "any professionally developed ability test" that is not "designed, intended or used to discriminate because of race," justified the test requirements. Looking to EEOC guidelines and the legislative history of the statute, "the conclusion is inescapable that the EEOC's construction of § 703(h) to require that employment tests be job related comports with congressional intent."]

Nothing in the Act precludes the use of testing or measuring procedures; obviously they are useful. What Congress has forbidden is giving these devices and mechanisms controlling force unless they are demonstrably a reasonable measure of job performance. Congress has not commanded that the less qualified be preferred over the better qualified simply because of minority origins. Far from disparaging job qualifications as such, Congress has made such qualifications the controlling factor, so that race, religion, nationality, and sex become irrelevant. What Congress has commanded is that any tests used must measure the person for the job and not the person in the abstract. . . .

NOTES

1. *Disparate Impact History in a Nutshell.* The disparate impact theory was refined by the Court in a number of decisions from 1971 until 1989, at which point the Supreme Court decided *Wards Cove Packing Co. v. Atonio*, 490 U.S. 642 (1989), which most observers viewed as essentially gutting the theory. *Wards Cove* generated a national controversy about the disparate impact theory that was ultimately resolved by the enactment of the Civil Rights Act of 1991, whose centerpiece was a debate over "quotas," *Wards Cove*, and the appropriate structure of the disparate impact theory. During the debates, proponents argued that a strong impact theory was needed to open up job opportunities to minorities and women. Opponents vociferously claimed that disparate impact would result in quotas by encouraging employers to hire minorities and women, without regard to qualifications, merely to avoid potential liability. What do you think of the argument? Did *Griggs* encourage quota hiring?

In any event, since 1991 disparate impact has largely been framed in terms of the meaning of the amendments made by the Civil Rights Act. As we will see, however, those amendments refer back to prior law, so that some of the history of disparate impact must be revisited to determine what the present statute prohibits and permits. And the Supreme Court's 2009 decision in *Ricci v. DeStefano* once again cast doubt on the viability of the theory.

2. *Rationales for Disparate Impact.* Why should a showing of adverse impact alone, without intent to discriminate, be sufficient to establish illegal discrimination? Is it because defendants may be acting with intent to discriminate, but proof of such intent is not available to plaintiff? Duke Power imposed the challenged rules just as Title VII became effective. Was the Supreme Court merely trying to get around the lower court's finding of no intent to discriminate?

Or perhaps the North Carolina school system was responsible. *Griggs* dealt with an educational prerequisite as well as test results, which probably correlate highly with increased level and quality of education. These requirements were imposed in a state that segregated African Americans in underfunded and inferior school systems. Is it this de jure discrimination in education that caused blacks in North Carolina to be disproportionately affected by Duke Power's rule? If so, why should the employer be responsible? Ramona L. Paetzold & Steven L. Willborn, in *Deconstructing Disparate Impact: A View of the Model Through New Lenses*, 74 N.C. L. REV. 325, 353-54 (1995), argue that the cause of impact is irrelevant to the disparate impact theory since "[t]he law treats the employer's criterion as the cause of a disparity, even though it may be only one of a wide array of factors necessary to produce the disparity." *See also* Kathryn Abrams, *Title VII and the Complex Female Subject*, 92 MICH. L. REV. 2479, 2524 (1994).

Another rationale for employer liability in such cases is grounded in efficiency. Professor Paulette Caldwell believes that Title VII was designed to increase productive efficiency by allowing individuals to achieve their full economic potential. *See* Paulette Caldwell, *Reaffirming the Disproportionate Effects Standard of Liability in Title VII Litigation*, 46 U. PITT. L. REV. 555 (1985). Caldwell's point is that, in the long run, efficiency will be improved if the pool of potential workers is widened by adding persons whose full potential would never be developed if denied entry-level positions. Is this what Chief Justice Burger meant when he wrote in *Griggs* that "[h]istory is filled with examples of men and women who rendered highly effective performance without the conventional badges of accomplishment in terms of certificates, diplomas, and degrees?" If so, does it have anything to do with intent to discriminate?

At first blush, whatever the underlying justifications, disparate impact seems in tension with the basic premise of antidiscrimination legislation: because members of protected groups are indistinguishable from similarly situated members of the majority, they ought not be treated differently in the workplace. While group differences may exist, disparate treatment ignores those differences and focuses instead on members of the protected group who are similarly situated to nonprotected individuals. In contrast, impact analysis not only acknowledges, but also focuses on, differences between groups. Individuals will be entitled to a remedy precisely because they are members of a group that is different.

The impact approach, however, does not abandon the equality principle. The business necessity defense permits the employer to rely on differences between employees when those differences are relevant to the job. Employers are prohibited from considering only differences that are not related to job performance. Thus, for purposes of qualifying for work, the underlying premise remains true: Protected group members should be treated equally when their work qualifications are the same.

Disparate impact liability effectively creates a duty for employers to identify and eliminate employment practices that unnecessarily operate as "built-in headwinds" for protected groups that have not yet achieved economic parity with white males. Viewed in this light, disparate impact can be considered a form of liability for negligence — an employer who does not intend to discriminate may nonetheless be liable for failing to exercise its duty of care toward protected group members. *See* David Benjamin Oppenheimer, *Negligent Discrimination*, 141 U. PA. L. REV. 899 (1993).

3. *Proving Impact.* The Court's use of statistics in *Griggs* is unsophisticated — even naive — compared with later refinements. The impact statistics on high school diplomas and tests were not linked in any direct way to the defendant's practices. Nevertheless, *Griggs* is a landmark case because it validates a statistical approach to discrimination litigation. Further, the decision establishes another critical point: When data that relates directly to the practices of the defendant itself is not available, a plaintiff may make out a prima facie case with more general statistics, leaving the defendant to show the inapplicability of those statistics to its practices.

In contrast, in *Wards Cove Packing Co. v. Atonio*, 490 U.S. 642 (1989), the Supreme Court undertook a much more sophisticated view of statistical proof. At issue in that case was a remote, seasonal salmon-canning facility with two main classes of workers — cannery jobs (almost all Native Alaskan and Filipino) and noncannery jobs (almost all white). The comparison between the racial breakdown of those working in cannery jobs and those in noncannery jobs was more dramatic than the comparative pass rates in *Griggs*, and the plaintiffs in *Wards Cove* sought to prove the discriminatory impact of a number of neutral hiring practices, including "nepotism, a rehire preference, a lack of objective hiring criteria, separate hiring channels, [and] a practice of not promoting from within." *Id*. at 647. Consider how the plaintiffs could establish disparate impact based on the employer's use of the practices in hiring. If the unskilled noncannery workforce is predominantly white, nepotism and rehire preferences are likely to yield predominantly white hiring. But to what group should the workforce numbers be compared to determine whether the results are disparate?

Wards Cove held that the "proper comparison [is] between the racial composition of [the at-issue jobs] and the racial composition of the qualified . . . population in the relevant labor market." The concept of the relevant labor market is borrowed from systemic disparate treatment law. Is the relevant labor market concept as used in disparate treatment cases appropriate for disparate impact analysis? Consider two systemic disparate treatment cases discussed in the previous section. In *Teamsters v. United States* (see page 571), the relevant labor market was the general population, while in *Hazelwood*, it was persons certified to teach in the relevant geographic area. In *Teamsters*, there was no reason to believe that the subset of those interested in and otherwise qualified for truck-driving jobs varied much from the general population. That was obviously not true in *Hazelwood*, which involved school teachers. In both cases, however, the issue was whether the statistics supported an inference of discriminatory intent. The Court was seeking to identify the pool from which the employer drew its employees so it could compare that group with the group selected in order to determine whether the difference between the two was significant enough to suggest intentional discrimination.

The question in a disparate impact case is not whether the statistics provide an inference of discriminatory intent but whether the employer's neutral employment practice has a disparate impact on a statutorily protected group. For purposes of this inquiry, what is the "relevant labor market"? Is it the applicant pool, the labor pool from which the employer recruited, the labor pool in the geographic area surrounding the workplace, or the general population — and, if the last, the general population where? Each of these options creates potential problems. The applicant pool is perhaps the most relevant comparison group because it is directly affected by the employer's practices. The applicant pool, however, might be distorted by the employer's choice of recruitment sources, or posted qualifications, or reputation for discrimination. Similarly, the employer's choice of labor pool may not be appropriate because that pool may be distorted by the employer's practices. The geographic area "around" the workplace may not be appropriate because the job in question may require a broader search. Is the best choice the labor pool from which a reasonable nondiscriminatory employer would draw its employees? But a reasonable employer who had no intention to discriminate might select a labor pool that is very homogenous just because it is convenient. Should that pool be compared with the most diverse pool of qualified applicants available in order to determine whether there is a disparate impact? Does impact analysis impose on employers a duty to seek out the most diverse labor pool?

4. *Who Can Use the Disparate Impact Theory?* The cases invoking disparate impact have almost all involved minorities or women. Can whites or males invoke the theory? *See* Charles A. Sullivan, *The World Turned Upside Down?: Disparate Impact Claims by White Males*, 98 Nw. U. L. Rev. 1505 (2004) (exploring possible uses of disparate impact by these groups and concluding that while as a matter of pure statutory interpretation, Title VII is better read not to permit such suits, it should be construed to permit them because of equal protection concerns).

As we have seen, disparate impact has gone through a kind of legal roller coaster, reaching a highpoint in *Griggs*, a nadir in *Wards Cove*, and some kind of intermediate position in the Civil Rights Act of 1991. And we'll soon see another plunge in *Ricci v. DeStefano*, reproduced at page 604. Students and practicing attorneys are understandably less interested in this history than in what the statute presently requires, but the 1991 Civil Rights Act itself incorporates by reference some pieces of that history. As a result, while the following discussion focuses on the statute as it now exists, *Wards Cove* and Supreme Court decisions between *Griggs* and *Wards Cove* are cited where relevant. At the end of this discussion, we'll examine *Ricci's* impact on disparate impact.

a. Plaintiff's Proof of a Prima Facie Case

Section 703(k)(1)(A)(i) states the general rule for a disparate impact case: Plaintiff carries the burden of persuasion that the employer "uses a particular employment practice that causes disparate impact on the basis of race, color, religion, sex, or national origin." This embraces two questions that arose before the 1991 Amendments: (1) Is every employment-related action of an employer a qualifying "employment practice"? (2) How does a plaintiff establish that a disparate impact resulted from a "particular" practice as opposed to a congeries of causes?

The point can be illustrated by *Connecticut v. Teal*, 457 U.S. 440 (1982), which involved a two-part selection process: a written test and a more subjective assessment of the candidates who passed the written test. The employer attempted to avoid disparate impact analysis of its written test on the ground that the "bottom line"—the end product of the employer's total selection procedure—did not have a disparate racial impact, even though the test considered by itself had such an impact. The Supreme Court rejected that approach, focusing on the right of individual black applicants to be free from barriers in the employment process that impact blacks as a group. While blacks were not disproportionately screened out of jobs in *Teal*, they were disproportionately screened out of the opportunity to compete for those jobs by the test. The 1991 Civil Rights Act, by requiring the plaintiff to prove "a particular employment practice that causes disparate impact," essentially codifies *Teal*.

Teal, however (like *Griggs*), involved a challenge to an objective, pass/fail requirement. The plaintiffs in *Griggs* challenged the employer's requirements for a high school diploma and a passing score on two standardized tests. The *Teal* plaintiffs also challenged a test. Thus, the practices being challenged in both cases, and in other Supreme Court disparate impact decisions, were objective requirements, and the impact of each could be readily measured. What would have happened if the test in *Teal* did not have a disparate impact but plaintiffs had been able to show that the subjective portion of the selection process resulted in the disproportionate exclusion of African Americans? Can subjective components comprise "a particular employment practice" under the amended statute? The answer seems clearly yes. In *Watson v. Fort Worth Bank & Trust*, 487 U.S. 977 (1988), the Court unanimously held that subjective employment practices could also be attacked under the disparate impact theory. *Id.* at 989. Watson's employer relied upon supervisors' subjective assessments of employees in deciding who would receive promotions, a subjective evaluation process that allegedly had resulted in a disparate impact on black employees. Rejecting the employer's argument that subjective practices did not lend themselves to disparate impact analysis, the Court determined that its "decisions in *Griggs* and succeeding cases could largely be nullified if disparate impact analysis were applied only to standardized selection practices." *Id.* at 990. The Court was persuaded that "disparate impact analysis is in principle no less applicable to subjective employment criteria than to objective or standardized tests. In either case, a facially neutral practice, adopted without discriminatory intent, may have effects that are indistinguishable from intentionally discriminatory practices." *Id.* Accordingly, the Court held that disparate impact claims may be brought to attack either objective or subjective practices. In light of *Watson*, §703(k) will undoubtedly be read to include subjective practices that have an impact.

This suggests that the disparate impact theory will sweep very broadly, but there are some statutory and judicially crafted exceptions. Thus, §703(k)(3) exempts employer rules prohibiting the employment of an individual who currently, knowingly, and illegally uses or possesses a controlled substance. Additional limitations may be created by the courts. An example of a "volitional exception" is *Garcia v. Spun Steak Co.*, 998 F.2d 1480 (9th Cir. 1993), where the employer required its bilingual employees to speak only English while on the job. Although the impact of the rule would fall more harshly on employees of Hispanic origin, the Ninth Circuit found the rule immune from impact attack: Bilingual employees could comply with the rule and thus could avoid discipline through choosing to follow the rule. The court, moreover, found that employees have no affirmative right to speak their language of choice or otherwise to express their cultural heritage at work. *See also Lanning v. SEPTA*, 308 F.3d 286, 293 (3d Cir. 2002) (suggesting that the ability of women to improve their performance on a physical fitness test by training for it was relevant to assessing the test's validity). *But see Maldonado v. Altus*, 433 F.3d 1294, 1304-5 (10th Cir. 2006) (holding that English-only rules can create or contribute to a hostile work environment under disparate treatment and disparate impact theories).

Another judge-made exception may be employer passivity: At least one circuit has held that, for a disparate impact claim, the practice being challenged must be affirmatively adopted by the employer. In *EEOC v. Chicago Miniature Lamp Works*, 947 F.2d 292 (7th Cir. 1991), the employer relied upon a word-of-mouth recruiting method for hiring new employees. Although the EEOC contended this resulted in a disparate impact on blacks, the court refused to permit an impact claim to proceed, reasoning it was the employees' actions of referring their friends and relatives, not any employer policy, that had caused the impact. "Passive reliance" on employee action is not an employer policy for purposes of disparate impact analysis, said the court.

While these kinds of limitations on disparate impact may be significant, the most difficult problem for plaintiffs is likely to be identifying the "particular" employment practice that causes an impact. We have seen that in *Connecticut v. Teal*, the Supreme Court rejected the "bottom line" defense to disparate impact claims, reasoning that if a particular component of a selection process had a disparate impact, that component could be challenged even if the overall result of the selection process produced no impact. *Teal*, 457 U.S. 440. In *Wards Cove v. Atonio*, the Court confronted the flip side of *Teal*, and held that plaintiffs could *not* mount a disparate impact challenge to the bottom line results of the employer's hiring practices: "[A] Title VII plaintiff does not make out a case of disparate impact simply by showing that, 'at the bottom line' there is racial *imbalance* in the work force. As a general matter, a plaintiff must demonstrate that it is the application of a specific or particular employment practice that has created the disparate impact under attack." *Wards Cove*, 490 U.S. at 657. *See generally* Charles A. Sullivan, *Disparate Impact: Looking Past the* Desert Palace *Mirage*, 47 Wm. & Mary L. Rev. 911 (2005).

In the 1991 Civil Rights Act, Congress essentially codified this aspect of *Wards Cove*. Section 703(k)(1)(A) provides that an unlawful employment practice based on disparate impact is established under this title only if "(i) a complaining party demonstrates that a respondent uses a particular employment practice that causes a disparate impact. . . ." Importantly, however, the statute provides an exception: Plaintiffs may attack the bottom line if they can show that the individual components of the whole process are not capable of separation. § 703(k)(1)(B)(i).

Thus, if more than one employment practice is involved in a selection process (as in *Teal*), plaintiff must identify the component or components that are causing the disparate impact and must prove the impact of each. This is not a dramatic change in the law. *Griggs*, after all, involved a challenge to both standardized testing and to the high school diploma requirement. Evidence of the impact of each was presented to and relied upon by the Court. Discovery of employer records and testimony may produce evidence to support a showing of impact. If the plaintiff cannot prove the impact of each separate practice of the overall selection process, how can a plaintiff prove that the multiple components are not capable of separation for analysis? The answer should be a pragmatic one: Has the plaintiff taken all reasonable steps to establish the impact of the separate practices? If plaintiff shows she did her best and still could not separate out the impact of each practice, then the case should be analyzed by looking at the bottom line outcome of the total of the employer's selection procedures. *See Allen v. Highlands Hosp. Corp.*, 545 F.3d 387, 404 (6th Cir. 2008) ("[T]he plaintiffs have at best alleged that HHC desired to reduce costs associated with its highly paid workforce, including those costs associated with employees with greater seniority. But the plaintiffs have not established that this corporate desire evolved into an identifiable practice that disproportionately harms workers who are at least 40 years old").

Yet another question is how much disparity must the plaintiff show to establish disparate impact? In *Griggs*, for example, the disparate pass rates on the tests of whites and blacks were substantial. Even with respect to high school diplomas, the white graduation rate was three times that of the blacks. Might some practices have a real impact, but one that is not large enough to satisfy the statute? The answer is unclear. The EEOC uses a "four-fifths rule" as evidence of impact — that is, it regards "a selection rate for any race, sex, or ethnic group which is less than four-fifths (4/5) (or eighty percent) of the rate for the group with the highest rate" as sufficient and "a greater than four-fifths rate" as generally insufficient. The Supreme Court has neither adopted nor rejected the four-fifths rule, see *Connecticut v. Teal*, 457 U.S. 440, 453 n.12 (1982) (stressing that the rule was designed to allocate government enforcement resources, not to define liability). It has been cited by a number of courts, even when recognized only as a rule of thumb. *See EEOC v. Joint Apprenticeship Committee*, 186 F.3d 110 (2d Cir. 1998); *Bullington v. United Air Lines, Inc.*, 86 F.3d 1301 (10th Cir. 1999). *But see Bew v. City of Chicago*, 252 F.3d 891 (7th Cir. 2001) (upholding a finding of a prima facie case of disparate impact even though 98.24 percent of blacks and 99.96 percent of whites had passed a test because there was a statistical correlation between race and test failure).

Once the plaintiff has made such a showing, the statute further provides that:

> If the respondent demonstrates that a specific employment practice does not cause the disparate impact, the respondent shall not be required to demonstrate that such practice is required by business necessity.

Section 703(k)(B)(ii); 42 U.S.C. § 2000e-2(k)(B)(ii). The new Act does not further define this "no cause" defense.

PROBLEM

9-2.   The Naperville police department chief wants to replace the traditional police revolver used as standard equipment with the much more powerful Smith & Wesson Model 59 service revolver. The Model 59 is very powerful and is quite large, with a wide hand grip. National data show that over 50 percent of all women and about 10 percent of all men would be unable to handle the gun because of the size of the hand grip. Assume the police chief asks you if there would be any legal problem with the department adopting the Model 59. What additional facts would you like to know before you render an opinion? Could you recommend that the department take any steps before requiring that the Model 59 be used by all department officers that might help insulate the department from disparate impact liability?

---

b. Defendant's Rebuttal

There are several rebuttal possibilities available to the employer to respond to a prima facie case of disparate impact discrimination. The most obvious is simply for employers to try to undermine the plaintiff's showing of a prima facie case by introducing evidence that the data on which plaintiff relied were flawed. The second is for the employer to attempt to carry the burden of persuasion that the practice at issue is within the statutory business necessity/job-related defense. *Griggs* provides one example of a failed effort: The fact that the employer had legitimate, and even plausible, justifications for its policies was not sufficient absent some kind of empirical demonstration that its policies conduced to greater productivity. Other Supreme Court cases have taken a hard line toward what suffices where testing is concerned. *See Albemarle Paper Co. v. Moody*, 422 U.S. 405 (1975); *but see Washington v. Davis*,

426 U.S. 229 (1976). We will encounter a taste of the complications of testing validation and, indeed, of business necessity in *Ricci*, but a brief recounting of one recent case suggests some of the complications.

Lanning v. Southeastern Pennsylvania Transportation Authority, 181 F.3d 478 (3d Cir. 1999) (*Lanning I*), involved a physical fitness test instituted by SEPTA, to upgrade the quality of its transit police force. Designed by an expert exercise physiologist with extensive experience in designing physical fitness tests for various law enforcement agencies, the test required applicants to complete a 1.5 mile run within 12 minutes. This would require an aerobic capacity of 42.5 mL/kg/min, the aerobic capacity the expert determined would be necessary to perform the job of SEPTA transit officer. Implementation of the test had a strongly disparate impact on women: Between 6 and 12 percent of women applicants passed it as compared to 55 to 60 percent of male applicants. While SEPTA rigorously applied the test to new applicants, it did not impose similar requirements on incumbents, merely offering incentives for current officers to meet such aerobic levels. Most did, but many did not, and SEPTA never attempted to measure the performance of those who failed to keep fit. Indeed, some "unfit" incumbent officers were promoted and also given special recognition, commendations, and satisfactory performance evaluations.

Turning to the meaning of business necessity, *Lanning I* pursued a complex analysis that began by recognizing that the 1991 Act instructed the courts that in interpreting that language, "[n]o statements other than the interpretive memorandum . . . shall be considered legislative history of, or relied upon in any way as legislative history. . . ." Pub. L. 102-66, Sec. 105 (1991), 105 Stat. 1071, 1074. The interpretive memorandum, in turn, stated: "The terms 'business necessity' and 'job related' are intended to reflect the concepts enunciated by the Supreme Court in *Griggs*, and in the other Supreme Court decisions prior to *Wards Cove*. 137 Cong. Rec. 28, 680 (1991)." This meant, according to *Lanning I*, that Congress endorsed the business necessity standard enunciated in *Griggs* (and not *Wards Cove*'s watering down of that standard). It concluded:

> Taken together, *Griggs, Albemarle* and *Dothard* teach that in order to show the business necessity of a discriminatory cutoff score an employer must demonstrate that its cutoff measures the minimum qualifications necessary for successful performance of the job in question. Furthermore, because the Act instructs us to interpret its business necessity language in conformance with *Griggs* and its pre-*Wards Cove* progeny, we must conclude that the Act's business necessity language incorporates this standard.

Lanning I, 181 F.3d at 489. Thus, what you learned about business necessity from reading *Griggs* seems largely applicable.

But if the *Lanning I* approach to the proper standard is simply a return to *Griggs*, the application of that standard generated greater difficulties. The aerobic test at issue was "job related" in the sense that everyone who passed it will be fit, at least aerobically, for the job. It might not be "job related" if that term means that those who fail the test are not fit to be police officers. The majority in *Lanning I* believed that the aerobic test must measure only the *minimum* qualifications necessary for the job. What is wrong with the "more is better" approach? Is it that more may be *better* for business but not *necessary*? Since SEPTA did not require aerobic fitness of current employees, although it did encourage such fitness, how could the specified aerobic level be "necessary"?

Lanning I, thus, took a very stringent approach to business necessity and seemed to presage a victory for plaintiffs. However, the court remanded, and on remand the district court found that the test satisfied the Third Circuit's requirements. In *Lanning II*, 308 F.3d 286 (3d Cir. 2002), the court of appeals affirmed:

> SEPTA argued that the run test measures the "minimum qualifications necessary" because the relevant studies indicate that individuals who fail the test will be much less likely to successfully execute critical policing tasks. For example, the District Court credited a study that evaluated the correlation between a successful run time and performance on 12 job standards. The study found that individuals who passed the run test had a success rate on the job standards ranging from 70% to 90%. The success rate of the individuals who failed the run test ranged from 5% to 20%. The District Court found that such a low rate of success was unacceptable for employees who are regularly called upon to protect the public. In so doing, the District Court implicitly defined "minimum qualifications necessary" as meaning "likely to be able to do the job."
>
> Plaintiffs argued, however, that within the group that failed the run test, significant numbers of individuals would still be able to perform at least certain critical job tasks. They argued that as long as some of those failing the run test can do the job, the standard cannot be classified as a "minimum." In essence, plaintiffs proposed that the phrase "minimum qualifications necessary" means "some chance of being able to do the job." Under this logic, even if those failing the test had a 1% chance of successfully completing critical job tasks, the test would be too stringent.
>
> We are not saying, as our distinguished brother in dissent suggests we are saying, that "more is better." While, of course, a higher aerobic capacity will translate into better field performance — at least as to many job tasks which entail physical capability — to set an unnecessarily high cutoff score would contravene *Griggs*. It would clearly be unreasonable to require SEPTA applicants to score so highly on the run test that their predicted rate of success be 100%. It is perfectly reasonable, however, to demand a chance of success that is better than 5% to 20%. . . .
>
> [W]e reject without more the argument that applicants — male and female — should not be tested until they have graduated from the police academy, perhaps two and one-half years after they first applied to SEPTA; indeed, the dissent recognizes but relegates to a footnote the increase in SEPTA's costs and the uncertainty in planning and recruitment this would occasion. [And] all incumbents — male and female — are now required to take a physical fitness test every six months, another step toward improving the workforce. In this connection, it bears mention that SEPTA is unable to discipline incumbents who do not pass the test only because of the patrol officers' union's challenge, sustained by an arbitrator. With the union's blessing, however, SEPTA offers financial incentives to those officers who do pass.
>
> One final note. While it is undisputed that SEPTA's 1.5 mile run test has a disparate impact on women, it is also undisputed that, in addition to those women who could pass the test without training, nearly all the women who trained were able to pass after only a moderate amount of training. It is not, we think, unreasonable to expect that women — and men — who wish to become SEPTA transit officers, and are committed to dealing with issues of public safety on a day-to-day basis, would take this necessary step.

Lanning II, 308 F.3d at 291-93. Are you convinced that it is a "business necessity" to require only recruits to be fit? Is the last paragraph the real basis for the result, that the impact could easily have been avoided by the female candidates? If so, how does that fit into the statutory analysis?

A number of commentators have addressed the meaning of business necessity and job relation after the 1991 Act. Susan S. Grover, *The Business Necessity Defense in*

Disparate Impact Discrimination Cases, 30 GA. L. REV. 387 (1996) (arguing for a uniform, high standard); Michael Garvin, *Disparate Impact Claims Under the New Title VII*, 68 NOTRE DAME L. REV. 1153 (1993) (claiming that § 703(k) did not really change *Wards Cove*); Andrew C. Spiropoulos, *Defining the Business Necessity Defense to the Disparate Impact Cause of Action: Finding the Golden Mean*, 74 N.C. L. REV. 1479, 1485 (1996) (arguing that the Supreme Court has articulated strict and lenient different versions of the business necessity defense and that the 1991 Amendments should be read to allow more flexibility for positions that, because of their difficulty, great responsibility, or special risks to the public, require skills or intangible qualities that cannot be measured empirically).

PROBLEM

9-3. Rath Packing had a rule prohibiting the employment of spouses of current employees. The plaintiff has succeeded in establishing that the no-spouse rule has a disparate impact on the employment of women. Rath asserts that the rule is necessary to promote optimum production and employee performance because spousal relationships in the workplace create problems of efficiency, productivity, and ease of management. It says that its no-spouse rule resulted from past problems that occurred when married couples worked at Rath. These included dual absenteeism, vacation scheduling, supervision, and pressure to hire spouses. However, during a three-year period for which information on absenteeism is available, employees with spouses working at Rath exhibited a lower absentee rate than did those without spouses working there. Rath was able to point to one incident of habitual dual absenteeism, which was perceived by Rath management as having a significant disruptive effect on plant operations. *See EEOC v. Rath Packing Co.*, 787 F.2d 318 (8th Cir. 1986).

Is Rath's policy legal?

---

c. *Alternative Employment Practices*

The Civil Rights Act of 1991 permits a plaintiff to prevail by showing a particular employment practice with a disparate impact if the employer fails to establish job relation and business necessity. But a disparate impact violation also exists when, despite the employer's successful proof of job relation and business necessity, the plaintiff shows that there exists an alternative employment practice "and the [employer] refuses to adopt such alternative employment practice." § 703(k)(1)(A).

However, proving an "alternative employment practice" may not be easy and there is no case law holding an employer liable under this alternative path and little explaining it in any detail. *See IBEW v. Miss. Power & Light Co*, 442 F.3d 313 (5th Cir. 2006) (noting plaintiffs did not offer meaningful alternative); *Allen v. City of Chicago*, 351 F.3d 306 (7th Cir. 2003) (plaintiffs did not prove that merit promotions alone were an effective alternative).

Among unanswered questions is whether the alternative practice need be non-discriminatory or merely less discriminatory in effect. A second question is whether this path to liability exists when the alternative devices are effective, but not *equally* effective, or more costly. Under the statute, a successful alternative selection practice claim also requires that the employer "refuse" to adopt the alternative practice. Does the plaintiff have the burden of proving that the employer refused? "Refuse" seems to mean more than mere failure to use the alternative practice. Would proof that the employer knew of the existence of the practice and failed to adopt it suffice? What if an employee proposed an alternative practice by placing it in the employer's suggestion box? What if the alternative practice is offered during discovery or at trial and the employer fails or "refuses" to adopt it?

d. Another Defense

Ricci v. DeStefano
129 S. Ct. 2658 (2009)

Justice KENNEDY delivered the opinion of the Court.

. . . In 2003, 118 New Haven firefighters took examinations to qualify for promotion to the rank of lieutenant or captain. Promotion examinations in New Haven (or City) were infrequent, so the stakes were high. The results would determine which firefighters would be considered for promotions during the next two years, and the order in which they would be considered. Many firefighters studied for months, at considerable personal and financial cost.

When the examination results showed that white candidates had outperformed minority candidates, the mayor and other local politicians opened a public debate that turned rancorous. Some firefighters argued the tests should be discarded because the results showed the tests to be discriminatory. They threatened a discrimination lawsuit if the City made promotions based on the tests. Other firefighters said the exams were neutral and fair. And they, in turn, threatened a discrimination lawsuit if the City, relying on the statistical racial disparity, ignored the test results and denied promotions to the candidates who had performed well. In the end the City took the side of those who protested the test results. It threw out the examinations.

Certain white and Hispanic firefighters who likely would have been promoted based on their good test performance sued the City and some of its officials. Theirs is the suit now before us. The suit alleges that, by discarding the test results, the City and the named officials discriminated against the plaintiffs based on their race, in violation of both Title VII and the Equal Protection Clause of the Fourteenth Amendment. The City and the officials defended their actions, arguing that if they had certified the results, they could have faced liability under Title VII for adopting a practice that had a disparate impact on the minority firefighters. The District Court granted summary judgment for the defendants, and the Court of Appeals affirmed.

We conclude that race-based action like the City's in this case is impermissible under Title VII unless the employer can demonstrate a strong basis in evidence that, had it not taken the action, it would have been liable under the disparate-impact statute. The respondents, we further determine, cannot meet that threshold standard. As a result, the City's action in discarding the tests was a violation of Title VII. In light of our ruling under the statutes, we need not reach the question whether respondents' actions may have violated the Equal Protection Clause.

I . . .

A . . .

[The City's promotion process was governed by its charter, which included a civil service merit system as determined by job-related tests, as well as by a collective bargaining agreement with the firefighters' union and state and federal law. The charter imposed a "rule of three"—whoever was promoted had to be among the top three scorers. The CBA with the union required that, for promotion eligibility, a written examination would account for 60% and an oral examination 40% of each applicant's total score.]

After reviewing bids from various consultants, the City hired Industrial/Organizational Solutions, Inc. (IOS) to develop and administer the examinations, at a cost to the City of $100,000. IOS is an Illinois company that specializes in designing entry-level and promotional examinations for fire and police departments. In order to fit the examinations to the New Haven Department, IOS began the test-design process by performing job analyses to identify the tasks, knowledge, skills, and abilities that are essential for the lieutenant and captain positions. IOS representatives interviewed incumbent captains and lieutenants and their supervisors. They rode with and observed other on-duty officers. Using information from those interviews and ride-alongs, IOS wrote job-analysis questionnaires and administered them to most of the incumbent battalion chiefs, captains, and lieutenants in the Department. At every stage of the job analyses, IOS, by deliberate choice, oversampled minority firefighters to ensure that the results—which IOS would use to develop the examinations—would not unintentionally favor white candidates.

With the job-analysis information in hand, IOS developed the written examinations to measure the candidates' job-related knowledge. For each test, IOS compiled a list of training manuals, Department procedures, and other materials to use as sources for the test questions. IOS presented the proposed sources to the New Haven fire chief and assistant fire chief for their approval. Then, using the approved sources, IOS drafted a multiple-choice test for each position. Each test had 100 questions, as required by CSB rules, and was written below a 10th-grade reading level. After IOS prepared the tests, the City opened a 3-month study period. It gave candidates a list that identified the source material for the questions, including the specific chapters from which the questions were taken.

IOS developed the oral examinations as well. These concentrated on job skills and abilities. Using the job-analysis information, IOS wrote hypothetical situations to test incident-command skills, firefighting tactics, interpersonal skills, leadership, and management ability, among other things. Candidates would be presented with these hypotheticals and asked to respond before a panel of three assessors.

IOS assembled a pool of 30 assessors who were superior in rank to the positions being tested. At the City's insistence (because of controversy surrounding previous examinations), all the assessors came from outside Connecticut. IOS submitted the assessors' resumes to City officials for approval. They were battalion chiefs, assistant chiefs, and chiefs from departments of similar sizes to New Haven's throughout the country. Sixty-six percent of the panelists were minorities, and each of the nine three-member assessment panels contained two minority members. IOS trained the panelists for several hours on the day before it administered the examinations, teaching them how to score the candidates' responses consistently using checklists of desired criteria.

Candidates took the examinations in November and December 2003. Seventy-seven candidates completed the lieutenant examination — 43 whites, 19 blacks, and 15 Hispanics. Of those, 34 candidates passed — 25 whites, 6 blacks, and 3 Hispanics. Eight lieutenant positions were vacant at the time of the examination. As the rule of three operated, this meant that the top 10 candidates were eligible for an immediate promotion to lieutenant. All 10 were white. Subsequent vacancies would have allowed at least 3 black candidates to be considered for promotion to lieutenant.

Forty-one candidates completed the captain examination — 25 whites, 8 blacks, and 8 Hispanics. Of those, 22 candidates passed — 16 whites, 3 blacks, and 3 Hispanics. Seven captain positions were vacant at the time of the examination. Under the rule of three, 9 candidates were eligible for an immediate promotion to captain — 7 whites and 2 Hispanics.

B

[Although the City's contract with IOS contemplated "a technical report" by IOS after the examinations, City officials, including its counsel, Thomas Ude, met in early 2004 with IOS Vice President Chad Legel, who had led the IOS team that developed and administered the tests. They] expressed concern that the tests had discriminated against minority candidates. Legel defended the examinations' validity, stating that any numerical disparity between white and minority candidates was likely due to various external factors and was in line with results of the Department's previous promotional examinations.

Several days after the meeting, Ude sent a letter to the CSB [New Haven Civil Service Board] purporting to outline its duties with respect to the examination results. Ude stated that under federal law, "a statistical demonstration of disparate impact," standing alone, "constitutes a sufficiently serious claim of racial discrimination to serve as a predicate for employer-initiated, voluntar[y] remedies-even . . . race-conscious remedies."

1

The CSB first met to consider certifying the results on January 22, 2004. Tina Burgett, director of the City's Department of Human Resources, opened the meeting by telling the CSB that "there is a significant disparate impact on these two exams." She distributed lists showing the candidates' races and scores (written, oral, and composite) but not their names. Ude also described the test results as reflecting "a very significant disparate impact," and he outlined possible grounds for the CSB's refusing to certify the results.

Although they did not know whether they had passed or failed, some firefighter-candidates spoke at the first CSB meeting in favor of certifying the test results. Michael Blatchley stated that "[e]very one" of the questions on the written examination "came from the [study] material. . . . [I]f you read the materials and you studied the material, you would have done well on the test." Frank Ricci stated that the test questions were based on the Department's own rules and procedures and on "nationally recognized" materials that represented the "accepted standard[s]" for firefighting. Ricci stated that he had "several learning disabilities," including dyslexia; that he had spent more than

$1,000 to purchase the materials and pay his neighbor to read them on tape so he could "give it [his] best shot"; and that he had studied "8 to 13 hours a day to prepare" for the test. "I don't even know if I made it," Ricci told the CSB, "[b]ut the people who passed should be promoted. When your life's on the line, second best may not be good enough."

Other firefighters spoke against certifying the test results. They described the test questions as outdated or not relevant to firefighting practices in New Haven. Gary Tinney stated that source materials "came out of New York. . . . Their makeup of their city and everything is totally different than ours." And they criticized the test materials, a full set of which cost about $500, for being too expensive and too long.

[There was a second CSB meeting on February 5, at which both proponents and opponents of the test appeared. Some asked for a validation study to determine whether the tests were job-related, while others suggested that "the City could 'adjust' the test results to 'meet the criteria of having a certain amount of minorities get elevated to the rank of Lieutenant and Captain.' "]

3

At a third meeting, on February 11, Legel addressed the CSB on behalf of IOS. Legel stated that IOS had previously prepared entry-level firefighter examinations for the City but not a promotional examination. He explained that IOS had developed examinations for departments in communities with demographics similar to New Haven's, including Orange County, Florida; Lansing, Michigan; and San Jose, California.

Legel explained the exam-development process to the CSB. . . . Near the end of his remarks, Legel "implor[ed] anyone that had . . . concerns to review the content of the exam. In my professional opinion, it's facially neutral. There's nothing in those examinations . . . that should cause somebody to think that one group would perform differently than another group."

4

At the next meeting, on March 11, the CSB heard from three witnesses it had selected to "tell us a little bit about their views of the testing, the process, [and] the methodology." The first, Christopher Hornick, spoke to the CSB by telephone. Hornick is an industrial/organizational psychologist from Texas who operates a consulting business that "direct[ly]" competes with IOS. Hornick, who had not "stud[ied] the test at length or in detail" and had not "seen the job analysis data," told the CSB that the scores indicated a "relatively high adverse impact." He stated that "[n]ormally, whites outperform ethnic minorities on the majority of standardized testing procedures," but that he was "a little surprised" by the disparity in the candidates' scores — although "[s]ome of it is fairly typical of what we've seen in other areas of the countr[y] and other tests." Hornick stated that the "adverse impact on the written exam was somewhat higher but generally in the range that we've seen professionally."

When asked to explain the New Haven test results, Hornick opined in the telephone conversation that the collective-bargaining agreement's requirement of using written and oral examinations with a 60/40 composite score might account for the statistical disparity. He also stated that "[b]y not having anyone from within the [D]epartment review" the tests before they were administered — a limitation the City had imposed to protect the security of the exam questions — "you inevitably get things in there" that are based on the source materials but are not relevant to New Haven. Hornick suggested that testing candidates at an "assessment center" rather than using written and oral examinations "might serve [the City's] needs better." Hornick stated that assessment centers, where candidates face real-world situations and respond just as they would in the field, allow candidates "to demonstrate how they would address a particular problem as opposed to just verbally saying it or identifying the correct option on a written test."

Hornick made clear that he was "not suggesting that [IOS] somehow created a test that had adverse impacts that it should not have had." He described the IOS examinations as "reasonably good test[s]." He stated that the CSB's best option might be to "certify the list as it exists" and work to change the process for future tests, including by "[r]ewriting the Civil Service Rules." Hornick concluded his telephonic remarks by telling the CSB that "for the future," his company "certainly would like to help you if we can."

[The Court then described at length further proceedings, including (1) statements by a Homeland Security fire program specialist who viewed the questions as job-relevant, and (2) statements by a Boston College professor specializing in "race and culture as they influence performance on tests," who had not reviewed the tests themselves but viewed the racial impact as consistent with results across the country. The City's counsel argued against the tests, claiming that they "had one of the most severe adverse impacts that he had seen" and that "there are much better alternatives to identifying [firefighting] skills." He offered his "opinion that promotions . . . as a result of these tests would not be consistent with federal law." The mayor's representative took a similar tack. Ultimately, the CSB voted 2 to 2 on the use of the test results, which meant that the results would not be certified.]

II . . .

A . . .

As enacted in 1964, Title VII's principal nondiscrimination provision held employers liable only for disparate treatment. That section retains its original wording today. It makes it unlawful for an employer "to fail or refuse to hire or to discharge any individual, or otherwise to discriminate against any individual with respect to his compensation, terms, conditions, or privileges of employment, because of such individual's race, color, religion, sex, or national origin." §2000e-2(a)(1). Disparate-treatment cases present "the most easily understood type of discrimination," *Teamsters* v. *United States*, and occur where an employer has "treated [a] particular person less favorably than others because of" a protected trait. *Watson* v. *Fort Worth Bank & Trust*. A disparate-treatment plaintiff must establish "that the defendant had a discriminatory intent or motive" for taking a job-related action.

The Civil Rights Act of 1964 did not include an express prohibition on policies or practices that produce a disparate impact. But in *Griggs v. Duke Power Co.*, the Court interpreted the Act to prohibit, in some cases, employers' facially neutral practices that, in fact, are "discriminatory in operation." The *Griggs* Court stated that the "touchstone" for disparate-impact liability is the lack of "business necessity": "If an employment practice which operates to exclude [minorities] cannot be shown to be related to job performance, the practice is prohibited." Under [*Griggs* and its progeny], if an employer met its burden by showing that its practice was job-related, the plaintiff was required to show a legitimate alternative that would have resulted in less discrimination.

Twenty years after *Griggs*, the Civil Rights Act of 1991 was enacted. The Act included a provision codifying the prohibition on disparate-impact discrimination. That provision is now in force along with the disparate-treatment section already noted. Under the disparate-impact statute, a plaintiff establishes a prima facie violation by showing that an employer uses "a particular employment practice that causes a disparate impact on the basis of race, color, religion, sex, or national origin." An employer may defend against liability by demonstrating that the practice is "job related for the position in question and consistent with business necessity." Even if the employer meets that burden, however, a plaintiff may still succeed by showing that the employer refuses to adopt an available alternative employment practice that has less disparate impact and serves the employer's legitimate needs.

B

Petitioners allege that when the CSB refused to certify the captain and lieutenant exam results based on the race of the successful candidates, it discriminated against them in violation of Title VII's disparate-treatment provision. The City counters that its decision was permissible because the tests "appear[ed] to violate Title VII's disparate-impact provisions."

Our analysis begins with this premise: The City's actions would violate the disparate-treatment prohibition of Title VII absent some valid defense. All the evidence demonstrates that the City chose not to certify the examination results because of the statistical disparity based on race — *i.e.*, how minority candidates had performed when compared to white candidates. As the District Court put it, the City rejected the test results because "too many whites and not enough minorities would be promoted were the lists to be certified." Without some other justification, this express, race-based decisionmaking violates Title VII's command that employers cannot take adverse employment actions because of an individual's race.

The District Court did not adhere to this principle, however. It held that respondents' "motivation to avoid making promotions based on a test with a racially disparate impact . . . does not, as a matter of law, constitute discriminatory intent." And the Government makes a similar argument in this Court. It contends that the "structure of Title VII belies any claim that an employer's intent to comply with Title VII's disparate-impact provisions constitutes prohibited discrimination on the basis of race." But both of those statements turn upon the City's objective — avoiding disparate-impact liability — while ignoring the City's conduct in the name of reaching that objective. Whatever the City's ultimate aim — however well intentioned or benevolent it might have seemed — the City made its employment decision because of race. The City rejected the test results solely because the higher scoring candidates were white. The question is not whether that conduct was discriminatory but whether the City had a lawful justification for its race-based action.

We consider, therefore, whether the purpose to avoid disparate-impact liability excuses what otherwise would be prohibited disparate-treatment discrimination.

Courts often confront cases in which statutes and principles point in different directions. Our task is to provide guidance to employers and courts for situations when these two prohibitions could be in conflict absent a rule to reconcile them. In providing this guidance our decision must be consistent with the important purpose of Title VII — that the workplace be an environment free of discrimination, where race is not a barrier to opportunity.

With these principles in mind, we turn to the parties' proposed means of reconciling the statutory provisions. . . . Petitioners would have us hold that, under Title VII, avoiding unintentional discrimination cannot justify intentional discrimination. That assertion, however, ignores the fact that, by codifying the disparate-impact provision in 1991, Congress has expressly prohibited both types of discrimination. We must interpret the statute to give effect to both provisions where possible. We cannot accept petitioners' broad and inflexible formulation.

Petitioners next suggest that an employer in fact must be in violation of the disparate-impact provision before it can use compliance as a defense in a disparate-treatment suit. Again, this is overly simplistic and too restrictive of Title VII's purpose. The rule petitioners offer would run counter to what we have recognized as Congress's intent that "voluntary compliance" be "the preferred means of achieving the objectives of Title VII." *Firefighters v. Cleveland*, 478 U.S. 501, 515 (1986); see also *Wygant v. Jackson Bd. of Ed.*, 476 U.S. 267, 290 (1986) (O'Connor, J., concurring in part and concurring in judgment). Forbidding employers to act unless they know, with certainty, that a practice violates the disparate-impact provision would bring compliance efforts to a near standstill. Even in the limited situations when this restricted standard could be met, employers likely would hesitate before taking voluntary action for fear of later being proven wrong in the course of litigation and then held to account for disparate treatment.

At the opposite end of the spectrum, respondents and the Government assert that an employer's good-faith belief that its actions are necessary to comply with Title VII's disparate-impact provision should be enough to justify race-conscious conduct. But the original, foundational prohibition of Title VII bars employers from taking adverse action "because of . . . race." § 2000e-2(a)(1). And when Congress codified the disparate-impact provision in 1991, it made no exception to disparate-treatment liability for actions taken in a good-faith effort to comply with the new, disparate-impact provision in subsection (k). Allowing employers to violate the disparate-treatment prohibition based on a mere good-faith fear of disparate-impact liability would encourage race-based action at the slightest hint of disparate impact. A minimal standard could cause employers to discard the results of lawful and beneficial promotional examinations even where there is little if any evidence of disparate-impact discrimination. That would amount to a *de facto* quota system, in which a "focus on statistics . . . could put undue pressure on employers to adopt inappropriate prophylactic measures." *Watson*. Even worse, an employer could discard test results (or other employment practices) with the intent of obtaining the employer's preferred racial balance. That operational principle could not be justified, for Title VII is express in disclaiming any interpretation of its requirements as calling for outright racial balancing. § 2000e-2(j). The purpose of Title VII "is to promote hiring on the basis of job qualifications, rather than on the basis of race or color." *Griggs*.

In searching for a standard that strikes a more appropriate balance, we note that this Court has considered cases similar to this one, albeit in the context of the Equal Protection Clause of the Fourteenth Amendment. The Court has held that certain government actions to remedy past racial discrimination — actions that are themselves based on race — are constitutional only where there is a " 'strong basis in evidence' " that the remedial actions were necessary. *Richmond v. J. A. Croson Co.*, 488 U.S. 469, 500 (1989). This suit does not call on us to consider whether the statutory constraints under Title VII must be parallel in all respects to those under the Constitution. That does not mean the constitutional authorities are irrelevant, however. Our cases discussing constitutional principles can provide helpful guidance in this statutory context. . . .

The same interests [as operated in *Wygant* and *Croson*] are at work in the interplay between the disparate-treatment and disparate-impact provisions of Title VII. Congress has imposed liability on employers for unintentional discrimination in order to rid the workplace of "practices that are fair in form, but discriminatory in operation." *Griggs*. But it has also prohibited employers from taking adverse employment actions "because of" race. Applying the strong-basis-in-evidence standard to Title VII gives effect to both the disparate-treatment and disparate-impact provisions, allowing violations of one in the name of compliance with the other only in certain, narrow circumstances. The standard leaves ample room for employers' voluntary compliance efforts, which are essential to the statutory scheme and to Congress's efforts to eradicate workplace discrimination. And the standard appropriately constrains employers' discretion in making race-based decisions: It limits that discretion to cases in which there is a strong basis in evidence of disparate-impact liability, but it is not so restrictive that it allows employers to act only when there is a provable, actual violation.

Resolving the statutory conflict in this way allows the disparate-impact prohibition to work in a manner that is consistent with other provisions of Title VII, including the prohibition on adjusting employment-related test scores on the basis of race. *See* § 2000e-2(*l*). Examinations like those administered by the City create legitimate expectations on the part of those who took the tests. As is the case with any promotion exam, some of the firefighters here invested substantial time, money, and personal commitment in preparing for the tests. Employment tests can be an important part of a neutral selection system that safeguards against the very racial animosities Title VII was intended to prevent. Here, however, the firefighters saw their efforts invalidated by the City in sole reliance upon race-based statistics.

If an employer cannot rescore a test based on the candidates' race, § 2000e-2(*l*), then it follows *a fortiori* that it may not take the greater step of discarding the test altogether to achieve a more desirable racial distribution of promotion-eligible candidates — absent a strong basis in evidence that the test was deficient and that discarding the results is necessary to avoid violating the disparate-impact provision. Restricting an employer's ability to discard test results (and thereby discriminate against qualified candidates on the basis of their race) also is in keeping with Title VII's express protection of bona fide promotional examinations. *See* § 2000e-2(h) ("[N]or shall it be an unlawful employment practice for an employer to give and to act upon the results of any professionally developed ability test provided that such test, its administration or action upon the results is not designed, intended or used to discriminate because of race"); *cf. AT&T Corp. v. Hulteen*, 129 S. Ct. 1962 (2009).

For the foregoing reasons, we adopt the strong-basis-in-evidence standard as a matter of statutory construction to resolve any conflict between the disparate-treatment and disparate-impact provisions of Title VII.

Our statutory holding does not address the constitutionality of the measures taken here in purported compliance with Title VII. We also do not hold that meeting the strong-basis-in-evidence standard would satisfy the Equal Protection Clause in a future case. As we explain below, because respondents have not met their burden under Title VII, we need not decide whether a legitimate fear of disparate impact is ever sufficient to justify discriminatory treatment under the Constitution.

Nor do we question an employer's affirmative efforts to ensure that all groups have a fair opportunity to apply for promotions and to participate in the process by which promotions will be made. But once that process has been established and employers have made clear their selection criteria, they may not then invalidate the test results, thus upsetting an employee's legitimate expectation not to be judged on the basis of race. Doing so, absent a strong basis in evidence of an impermissible disparate impact, amounts to the sort of racial preference that Congress has disclaimed, § 2000e-2(j), and is antithetical to the notion of a workplace where individuals are guaranteed equal opportunity regardless of race.

Title VII does not prohibit an employer from considering, before administering a test or practice, how to design that test or practice in order to provide a fair opportunity for all individuals, regardless of their race. And when, during the test-design stage, an employer invites comments to ensure the test is fair, that process can provide a common ground for open discussions toward that end. We hold only that, under Title VII, before an employer can engage in intentional discrimination for the asserted purpose of avoiding or remedying an unintentional disparate impact, the employer must have a strong basis in evidence to believe it will be subject to disparate-impact liability if it fails to take the race-conscious, discriminatory action.

C

The City argues that, even under the strong-basis-in-evidence standard, its decision to discard the examination results was permissible under Title VII. That is incorrect. Even if respondents were motivated as a subjective matter by a desire to avoid committing disparate-impact discrimination, the record makes clear there is no support for the conclusion that respondents had an objective, strong basis in evidence to find the tests inadequate, with some consequent disparate-impact liability in violation of Title VII.

On this basis, we conclude that petitioners have met their obligation to demonstrate that there is "no genuine issue as to any material fact" and that they are "entitled to judgment as a matter of law." Fed. Rule Civ. Proc. 56(c). . . .

[The majority agreed with the City that the adverse racial impact here was significant, which required it "to take a hard look at the examinations to determine whether certifying the results would have had an impermissible disparate impact." But] a prima facie case of disparate-impact liability — essentially, a threshold showing of a significant statistical disparity, *Connecticut v. Teal,* and nothing more — is far from a strong basis in evidence that the City would have been liable under Title VII had it certified the results. That is because the City could be liable for disparate-impact discrimination only if the examinations were not job related and consistent with business necessity, or if there existed an equally valid, less-discriminatory alternative that served the City's needs but that the City refused to adopt. We conclude there is no strong basis in evidence to establish that the test was deficient in either of these respects. . . .

1

There is no genuine dispute that the examinations were job-related and consistent with business necessity. The City's assertions to the contrary are "blatantly contradicted by the record" [including the statements of Chad Legel and city officials outlining the detailed steps taken to develop and administer the examinations. The only outside witness who reviewed the examinations in any detail was the only one with any firefighting experience, and he stated that the "questions were relevant for both exams."].

2

Respondents also lacked a strong basis in evidence of an equally valid, less-discriminatory testing alternative that the City, by certifying the examination results, would necessarily have refused to adopt. Respondents raise three arguments to the contrary, but each argument fails. First, respondents refer to testimony before the CSB that a different composite-score calculation — weighting the written and oral examination scores 30/70 — would have allowed the City to consider two black candidates for then-open lieutenant positions and one black candidate for then-open captain positions. (The City used a 60/40 weighting as required by its contract with the New Haven firefighters' union.) But respondents have produced no evidence to show that the 60/40 weighting was indeed arbitrary. In fact, because that formula was the result of a union-negotiated collective-bargaining agreement, we presume the parties negotiated that weighting for a rational reason. Nor does the record contain any evidence that the 30/70 weighting would be an equally valid way to determine whether candidates possess the proper mix of job knowledge and situational skills to earn promotions. Changing the weighting formula, moreover, could well have violated Title VII's prohibition of altering test scores on the basis of race. *See* § 2000e-2(*l*). On this record, there is no basis to conclude that a 30/70 weighting was an equally valid alternative the City could have adopted.

Second, respondents argue that the City could have adopted a different interpretation of the "rule of three" [such as "banding, which is "rounding scores to the nearest whole number and considering all candidates with the same whole-number score as being of one rank." However, had] the City reviewed the exam results and then adopted banding to make the minority test scores appear higher, it would have violated Title VII's prohibition of adjusting test results on the basis of race. § 2000e-2(*l*); *see also Chicago Firefighters Local 2 v. Chicago*, 249 F. 3d 649, 656 (CA7 2001) (Posner, J.) ("We have no doubt that if banding were adopted in order to make lower black scores seem higher, it would indeed be . . . forbidden"). As a matter of law, banding was not an alternative available to the City when it was considering whether to certify the examination results.

Third, and finally, respondents refer to statements by Hornick in his telephone interview with the CSB regarding alternatives to the written examinations. Hornick stated his "belie[f]" that an "assessment center process," which would have evaluated candidates' behavior in typical job tasks, "would have demonstrated less adverse impact." But Hornick's brief mention of alternative testing methods, standing alone, does not raise a genuine issue of material fact that assessment centers were available to the City at the time of the examinations and that they would have produced less adverse impact. . . .

3

On the record before us, there is no genuine dispute that the City lacked a strong basis in evidence to believe it would face disparate-impact liability if it certified the examination results. In other words, there is no evidence — let alone the required strong basis in evidence — that the tests were flawed because they were not job-related or because other, equally valid and less discriminatory tests were available to the City. Fear of litigation alone cannot justify an employer's reliance on race to the detriment of individuals who passed the examinations and qualified for promotions. The City's discarding the test results was impermissible under Title VII, and summary judgment is appropriate for petitioners on their disparate-treatment claim.

* * *

The record in this litigation documents a process that, at the outset, had the potential to produce a testing procedure that was true to the promise of Title VII: No individual should face workplace discrimination based on race. Respondents thought about promotion qualifications and relevant experience in neutral ways. They were careful to ensure broad racial participation in the design of the test itself and its administration. As we have discussed at length, the process was open and fair.

The problem, of course, is that after the tests were completed, the raw racial results became the predominant rationale for the City's refusal to certify the results. The injury arises in part from the high, and justified, expectations of the candidates who had participated in the testing process on the terms the City had established for the promotional process. Many of the candidates had studied for months, at considerable personal and financial expense, and thus the injury caused by the City's reliance on raw racial statistics at the end of the process was all the more severe. Confronted with arguments both for and against certifying the test results — and threats of a lawsuit either way — the City was required to make a difficult inquiry. But its hearings produced no strong evidence of a disparate-impact violation, and the City was not entitled to disregard the tests based solely on the racial disparity in the results.

Our holding today clarifies how Title VII applies to resolve competing expectations under the disparate-treatment and disparate-impact provisions. If, after it certifies the test results, the City faces a disparate-impact suit, then in light of our holding today it should be clear that the City would avoid disparate-impact liability based on the strong basis in evidence that, had it not certified the results, it would have been subject to disparate-treatment liability. . . .

Justice SCALIA, concurring.

I join the Court's opinion in full, but write separately to observe that its resolution of this dispute merely postpones the evil day on which the Court will have to confront the question: Whether, or to what extent, are the disparate-impact provisions of Title VII of the Civil Rights Act of 1964 consistent with the Constitution's guarantee of equal protection? The question is not an easy one. *See generally* Primus, *Equal Protection and Disparate Impact: Round Three*, 117 HARV. L. REV. 493 (2003).

The difficulty is this: Whether or not Title VII's disparate-treatment provisions forbid "remedial" race-based actions when a disparate-impact violation would *not* otherwise result — the question resolved by the Court today — it is clear that Title VII not only permits but affirmatively *requires* such actions when a disparate-impact violation *would* otherwise result. But if the Federal Government is prohibited from discriminating on the basis of race, *Bolling v. Sharpe*, 347 U. S. 497, 500 (1954), then surely it is also prohibited from enacting laws mandating that third parties — *e.g.*, employers, whether private, State, or municipal — discriminate on the basis of race. As the facts of these cases illustrate, Title VII's disparate-impact provisions place a racial thumb on the scales, often requiring employers to evaluate the racial outcomes of their policies, and to make decisions based on (because of) those racial outcomes. That type of racial decisionmaking is, as the Court explains, discriminatory. . . .

The Court's resolution of these cases makes it unnecessary to resolve these matters today. But the war between disparate impact and equal protection will be waged sooner or later, and it behooves us to begin thinking about how — and on what terms — to make peace between them.

Justice ALITO, with whom Justice SCALIA and Justice THOMAS join, concurring.

[The concurrence "join[ed] the Court's opinion in full" but wrote separately to correct important omissions in Justice GINSBURG's dissent. The major thrust of this concurrence was that, even were the Court to accept the dissent's "good cause" standard, the facts of the case required a trial as to whether the avoidance of disparate impact liability was a pretext because there was a fact question, even under that lower standard, as to whether "the City's real reason was illegitimate, namely, the desire to placate a politically important racial constituency."]

Justice GINSBURG, with whom Justice STEVENS, Justice SOUTER, and Justice BREYER join, dissenting.

[The dissent started with the observation that, when Title VII was applied to public employment in 1972 "municipal fire departments across the country, including New Haven's, pervasively discriminated against minorities." She noted that in the early 1970's, "African-Americans and Hispanics composed 30 percent of New Haven's population, but only 3.6 percent of the City's 502 firefighters. The racial disparity in the officer ranks was even more pronounced: '[O]f the 107 officers in the Department only one was black, and he held the lowest rank above private.'" While some progress had been made, "[b]y order of this Court, New Haven, a city in which African-Americans and Hispanics account for nearly 60 percent of the population, must today be served — as it was in the days of undisguised discrimination — by a fire department in which members of racial and ethnic minorities are rarely seen in command positions." . . .]

Neither Congress' enactments nor this Court's Title VII precedents (including the now-discredited decision in *Wards Cove*) offer even a hint of "conflict" between an employer's obligations under the statute's disparate-treatment and disparate-impact provisions. Standing on an equal footing, these twin pillars of Title VII advance the same objectives: ending workplace discrimination and promoting genuinely equal opportunity. *See McDonnell Douglas Corp. v. Green.*

Yet the Court today sets at odds the statute's core directives. When an employer changes an employment practice in an effort to comply with Title VII's disparate-impact provision, the Court reasons, it acts "because of race" — something Title VII's disparate-treatment provision generally forbids. This characterization of an employer's compliance-directed action shows little attention to Congress' design or to the *Griggs* line of cases Congress recognized as pathmarking. . . . [Because a court is bound to read the provisions of any statute as harmonious] Title VII's disparate-treatment and disparate-impact proscriptions must be read as complementary.

In codifying the *Griggs* and *Albemarle* instructions, Congress declared unambiguously that selection criteria operating to the disadvantage of minority group members can be retained only if justified by business necessity. In keeping with Congress' design, employers who reject such criteria due to reasonable doubts about their reliability can hardly be held to have engaged in discrimination "because of" race. A reasonable endeavor to comply with the law and to ensure that qualified candidates of all races have a fair opportunity to compete is simply not what Congress meant to interdict. I would therefore hold that an employer who jettisons a selection device when its disproportionate racial impact becomes apparent does not violate Title VII's disparate-treatment bar automatically or at all, subject to this key condition: The employer must have good cause to believe the device would not withstand examination for business necessity. *Cf. Faragher v. Boca Raton*, 524 U. S. 775, 806 (1998) (observing that it accords with "clear statutory policy" for employers "to prevent violations" and "make reasonable efforts to discharge their duty" under Title VII). . . .

This litigation does not involve affirmative action. But if the voluntary affirmative action at issue in *Johnson* [*v. Transportation Agency, Santa Clara Cty.*] does not discriminate within the meaning of Title VII, neither does an employer's reasonable effort to comply with Title VII's disparate-impact provision by refraining from action of doubtful consistency with business necessity. . . .

NOTES

1. *Putting It All Together or Tearing It All Apart?* If you want an opportunity to think about big concepts spread across this entire chapter, *Ricci* has it all: systemic disparate treatment, disparate impact, testing, and affirmative action from a statutory or constitutional perspective. What more could a professor (or student) ask for? The other perspective on *Ricci*, however, is that it tears apart quite a lot of what you've learned to this point. Indeed, there are those who think that it is the end of disparate impact liability. That may be an overstatement, but *Ricci* is at least a sea change that will reverberate in a variety of ways.

2. *The Holding.* The majority was clear: Defendants' decision to not use test results because their use would have meant no promotions for African Americans and only two for Hispanics, who together made up over half of the test takers, was intentional disparate treatment discrimination against the white test takers who would have been promoted had the test been certified. That the test results amounted to a prima facie case of disparate impact discrimination was not a defense to a disparate treatment case unless the employer also had a strong basis in evidence to believe that it would be liable for disparate impact discrimination, which means that it would have no business necessity/job relation defense and that there is no viable alternative employment practice.

3. *Relation to Affirmative Action.* Only Justice Ginsburg in dissent puts *Ricci* in context with the Court's Title VII affirmative action decisions. Recall that under *Weber/Johnson*, see page 505, a prima facie case of disparate treatment is not required in order to justify an affirmative action plan; all that is necessary is a manifest imbalance in a traditionally segregated job category and no unnecessary trammeling of majority rights. In *Ricci*, however, even an uncontested prima facie case of disparate impact (a clear manifest imbalance in terms of the test itself) is not enough to permit the employer to take steps to reduce or eliminate the impact.

The parallels between affirmative action analysis under Title VII and *Ricci's* approach to the intersection of disparate treatment and disparate impact are obvious. In both, race may influence an employer's decision, but only under certain circumstances. For a valid affirmative action plan, there must be a manifest imbalance, and majority interests must not be unduly trammeled. In the case of tests with a disparate impact, the test may be thrown out precisely because of that impact, but only under a strong basis in evidence test. So both doctrines allow disparate treatment under more-or-less tight constraints.

Prior to *Ricci*, some wondered if the Roberts Court would overrule *Weber/Johnson's* approval of voluntary affirmative action. Does *Ricci* suggest that the answer is no because it allows some systemic disparate treatment? On the other hand, *Ricci* was not an affirmative action case, at least as that term is normally used. No one was preferred over anyone else, although white firefighters lost promotions they would otherwise have gotten. Since the majority condemned actions taken for racial reasons absent a strong basis in evidence for disparate impact liability, *Ricci* can be viewed as harsher than the affirmative action cases. And the "strong basis in evidence test" seems to require more in the way of proof than "manifest imbalance" does in the affirmative action context.

4. *Does Knowledge Equal Intentional Discrimination?* The majority finds intent to discriminate against whites because the City acted to avoid disparate impact liability to blacks (absent the "strong evidence" defense). But does the fact that the City acted because it knew of a "statistical disparity based on race" necessarily lead to the conclusion that it rejected the test "solely because the higher scoring candidates were white"? Is there a difference between intending not to disadvantage African American and Hispanic candidates and intending to discriminate against the white candidates? Did New Haven invalidate the test in order to deprive whites of promotions? Or was that merely a foreseeable consequence? Or does it matter? *See generally* Michael J. Zimmer, *Ricci's Color-Blind Standard in a Race Conscious Society: A Case of Unintended Consequences? available at* http://papers.ssrn.com/sol3/papers.cfm?abstract_id=1529438 ("In short, the Court appears to have established essentially a 'color-blind' standard of disparate treatment liability for Title VII. This new standard allows a civil rights plaintiff to prove her disparate treatment case by proof that (1) the defendant knew the racial or gender consequences of its decision and (2) it then made that decision in light of that knowledge, which made the decision 'because of race,' and (3) the plaintiff suffered an adverse employment action as a result."); Helen Norton, *The Supreme Court's Post-Racial Turn Towards a Zero-Sum Understanding of Equality*, 52 WM. & MARY L. REV. 197 (2010) ("*Ricci's* redefinition of culpable mental state for antidiscrimination purposes thus destabilizes the longstanding premise that the Court does not view decisionmakers' attention to race to address patterns of racial hierarchy as itself suspicious.").

5. *A Hierarchy of Theories?* The majority thinks that disparate treatment is the main evil that Congress proscribed; disparate impact is a late addition to the statute and must be tailored to minimize any conflict with the disparate treatment bar. Justice Ginsburg takes an opposite view — *Griggs* made clear that disparate impact was implicit in Title VII from the beginning. This difference influences the approach of each side: Disparate treatment can be sacrificed to disparate impact, for the majority, only if the "strong basis in evidence" test is met, thus ensuring that disparate treatment is generally avoided. (You might also wonder, from a legislative intent perspective, why it matters to the majority that disparate impact was added only in the 1991 Civil Rights Act. Doesn't the application of the theory, no matter when, require trying to reconcile both in a nongrudging manner?).

But let's probe Justice Ginsburg's view a bit more. She sees no conflict between disparate treatment and disparate impact claims. Disparate treatment prohibits intentional discrimination but, even if the employer's practices were not intentionally discriminatory, there is a duty to not use practices with a disparate impact unless the practices were justified as job-related and consistent with business necessity. By enacting both theories, Congress thus intended to allow race consciousness to avoid an unjustified racial impact. To put it another way, such race consciousness could not be the kind of disparate treatment Title VII meant to proscribe. For the dissent, the *Ricci* Court's invalid equation of consciousness of race with intent to discriminate creates the tension that it then resolves with its new hierarchy of theories.

6. *What's the Disagreement on the Standard?* The various opinions disagree about a lot, especially the application of the appropriate standard to the facts of the case. But Supreme Court decisions are usually more about law than facts, and, on the law, is there much difference between the majority and the Ginsburg dissent? The majority articulates the "strong basis in evidence" standard. Justice Ginsburg found no violation if the employer has "good cause to believe the device would not withstand examination for business necessity." So the difference is "strong basis" versus "good cause." A tempest in a teapot?

At one point, Justice Ginsburg argues against the majority's standard because "[i]t is hard to see how these requirements differ from demanding that an employer establish 'a provable, actual violation' *against itself*." (emphasis in original). In the affirmative action cases, some justices sought to avoid requiring an employer, in defending an affirmative action plan favoring minorities, having to adduce proof that would make it liable to minorities. This would, obviously, discourage the adoption of such plans. But how does this argument apply here? By definition, if there is such a "strong basis," the employer can scrub the test. There will then be no disparate impact liability because the test is never used, and there will be no disparate treatment liability because of the strong basis for disparate impact liability.

7. *Isn't There Strong Basis for Disparate Impact Liability?* The Court wrote "a prima facie case of disparate-impact liability — essentially a threshold showing of a significant statistical disparity and nothing more — is far from a strong basis in evidence that the City would have been liable under Title VII had it certified the results." Can that be true in light of § 703(k), which shifts the burden of persuasion to the defendant upon the showing of disparate impact? In other words, if black firefighters were to mount a disparate impact attack, they would win upon showing the fact of impact — unless the employer carried its burden of showing business necessity/job relation defense. *Ricci*, however, requires the employer seeking to avoid disparate impact liability in the first place to show that it has no business necessity, or at least show that it has a strong basis in evidence that it has no business necessity. *Wards Cove* shifted the burden of proving no business necessity to black plaintiffs. Is *Ricci* a very convoluted

way of doing the same thing, with the employer acting as a kind of proxy for potential black plaintiffs?

8. *Was the Test Job-Related/Business Necessity as a Matter of Law?* Given (a) the majority's strong basis in evidence test, (b) its acknowledgment of the existence of a prima facie case, and (b) its grant of summary judgment to the white firefighters, it must follow that the test was valid as a matter of law. While we haven't explored test validation in detail, is it so clear that the test was valid? The mere fact that effort is put into test design isn't necessarily enough to validate it under governing principles. Indeed, the *Ricci* majority does not address the jurisprudence associated with the test exception in original §703(h). Why?

9. *Alternative Employment Practices.* The Court agrees that even a valid test can't be used if there's an alternative employment practice that achieves the same purposes with lesser racial impact. The record before the CSB showed alternatives that were less discriminatory — simply altering the ratio of written to oral scores (as did Bridgeport, a city just down the interstate from New Haven), using "assessment centers," or altering the "rule of three" to a banding approach — all were alternatives that may have had less impact and that may have equally served the employer's needs. So why not remand on this question?

10. *Suppose Minority Test Takers Claim Disparate Impact?* Pursuant to *Ricci* decision, the City certified the test results, and a black plaintiff brought suit challenging the promotions in the *Ricci* case. He wasn't a party to the *Ricci* litigation, which means that under normal principles of res judicata, he wasn't technically bound by the result, *Martin v. Wilks*, 490 U.S. 755 (1989), although admittedly a provision added to Title VII by the 1991 CRA, 42 U.S.C. §2000e-2(n) (2006) might foreclose his suit. Charles A. Sullivan, Ricci v. DeStefano: *End of the Line or Just Another Turn on the Disparate Impact Road?*, 104 Nw. U. L. Rev. 411, 424-25 (2010). But, civil procedure principles aside, Justice Kennedy concluded the opinion for the Court with a rather enigmatic statement about a subsequent disparate impact suit:

> If, after it certifies the test results, the City faces a disparate-impact suit, then in light of our holding today it should be clear that the City would avoid disparate-impact liability based on the strong basis in evidence that, had it not certified the results, it would have been subject to disparate-treatment liability.

Relying heavily on this sentence, the district court dismissed the suit. *Briscoe v. City of New Haven*, 2010 U.S. Dist. LEXIS 69018, *22 (D. Conn. July 12, 2010) ("If, as he contends, Briscoe is denied his day in court or is bound by a decision in a case to which he was not a party, it is because the Supreme Court decided as much, and this court is bound by the decisions of the high court.").

11. *The End of Disparate Impact?* Is the disparate impact theory of liability gone? In other words, while the *Ricci* majority *allows* an employer to take race into account when it has the requisite strong basis in fact, does this sentence suggest that the employer can *choose* never to apply disparate impact because doing so will always be disparate treatment? Under this view, avoidance of disparate treatment is always a complete defense to disparate impact. Or does the sentence make sense only when the employer does not (as New Haven didn't) have a strong basis to believe that it was subject to disparate impact liability? Under this view, an employer *must* avoid a practice with a disparate impact, even if it results in disparate treatment, so long as it has the requisite strong basis in evidence. But hold it — that can't be right. Before *Ricci*, an employer could prevail in a suit by black firefighters only by proving that it had a business necessity for its practice, not by showing that it had a strong basis in evidence that it had a business necessity. *See generally* Joseph Seiner & Benjamin Gutman, *Does* Ricci *Herald a New Disparate Impact?* 90 B.U. L. Rev. 2181 (2010) (arguing that the sentence suggests the creation of yet another affirmative defense to disparate impact discrimination).

12. *Or Maybe It Matters When?* *Ricci* focuses on New Haven's decision whether to certify the test. At that point, the CSB had to favor either those who were successful or those who were not, with obvious racial consequences. As Kennedy wrote, "[t]he problem, of course, is that *after the tests were completed*, the raw racial results became the predominant rationale for the City's refusal to certify the results." (emphasis added). He went on to stress that "[t]he injury arises in part from the high, and justified, expectations of the candidates who had participated in the testing process on the terms the City had established for the promotional process." Elsewhere, he spoke of "competing expectations."

But the majority seems to recognize that, in deciding whether or what to test, and before the competing expectations crystallized, potential racial effects can be taken into account:

> Title VII does not prohibit an employer from considering, before administering a test or practice, how to design that test or practice in order to provide a fair opportunity for all individuals, regardless of their race. And when, during the test-design stage, an employer invites comments to ensure the test is fair, that process can provide a common ground for open discussions toward that end.

This strongly suggests, consistent with Justice Kennedy's stance in *Parents Involved in Community Schools v. Seattle School District No. 1*, 551 U.S. 701 (2007), see page 587, that an employer need not be color-blind in its approach to test design.

13. *1989 Redux?* It has been 20 years, but has a new conservative majority in the Roberts Court been able to undermine Title VII just as the Rehnquist Court majority did in 1989? Is the fear that employers would have an incentive to use racial quotas what drives the *Ricci* decision, just as it drove the decision in *Wards Cove*? If Congress were to act to create a statutory defense less stringent than strong basis in evidence, would this new majority take the step suggested by Justice Scalia to embed *Ricci* in the Constitution by striking down disparate impact analysis as unconstitutional?

14. *The Scholarship.* Perhaps needless to say, many scholars have tried to understand the implication of *Ricci*. In addition to the articles already cited, *see* Charles A. Sullivan, Ricci v. DeStefano: *End of the Line or Just Another Turn on the Disparate Impact Road?*, 104 Nw. U. L. Rev. 411 (2010); Cheryl I. Harris & Kimberly West-Faulcon, *Reading* Ricci: *Whitening Discrimination, Racing Test Fairness*, 58 U.C.L.A. L. Rev. 73 (2010); Kerri Stone, *The Unexpected Appearance of Transferred Intent in Title VII*, 55 Loyola L. Rev. 752 (2010).

Note on Impact Analysis Under the ADEA

In *Smith v. City of Jackson*, 544 U.S. 228 (2005), the Supreme Court held that disparate impact is available under ADEA but in a considerably diluted form. *City of Jackson* involved a challenge by older police officers to raises that disparately favored younger workers. The Court reasoned that the ADEA should be interpreted identically to Title VII to the extent that both statutes were identical. However, two textual differences between the ADEA and Title VII combined to lead the Court to conclude that the scope of the disparate-impact theory is narrower under the ADEA. The first textual difference is ADEA §4(f)(1), 29 U.S.C. §623(f)(1), which lacks any Title VII analog. That section expressly permits differentiations "based on reasonable factors other than age." This indicated to the Court that Congress viewed age, unlike race or other classifications protected by Title VII, as sometimes a relevant factor in employment. *See* Judith J. Johnson, *Rehabilitate the Age Discrimination in Employment Act: Resuscitate the "Reasonable Factors Other Than Age" Defense and the Disparate Impact Theory*, 55 HASTINGS L. J. 1399 (2004).

Further developing the significance of the reasonable factor other than age ("RFOA") language, *Meacham v. Knolls Atomic Power Lab.*, 554 U.S. 84 (2008), held that the RFOA was an affirmative defense as to which the defendant bore the burden of persuasion. Further, *Meacham* ruled that the RFOA defense superseded the normal business necessity/job relation defense for disparate impact claims under Title VII: "[W] are now satisfied that the business necessity test should have no place in ADEA disparate-impact cases." *Id.* at 97. Rather, the only question is whether a non-age factor that produces an age impact is "reasonable," although what that means and how it might differ from normal business necessity/job relation analysis is not clear.

The second difference is the Civil Rights Act of 1991, which amended Title VII but not the ADEA with respect to refining disparate impact. In short, the 1991 CRA was widely seen as restoring disparate impact law to its state under *Griggs v. Duke Packing*, following the Court's more limiting decision in *Wards Cove Packing Co. v. Atonio*. Since that amendment did not apply to the ADEA, the Court concluded that the *Wards Cove* version of disparate impact applies in age discrimination cases.

Applying this standard to the case, the *City of Jackson* majority found that the plaintiffs had not sufficiently identified the challenged practice to satisfy *Wards Cove*. *See also Allen v. Highlands Hosp. Corp.*, 545 F.3d 387, 404 (6th Cir. 2008) ("the plaintiffs have at best alleged that HHC desired to reduce costs associated with its highly paid workforce, including those costs associated with employees with greater seniority. But the plaintiffs have not established that this corporate desire evolved into an identifiable practice that disproportionately harms workers who are at least 40 years old"). *City of Jackson* also stated that, in any event, the City's decision to grant raises based on seniority and positions was reasonable given the City's goal of raising employees' salaries to match those in surrounding communities.

D. SEXUAL AND OTHER DISCRIMINATORY HARASSMENT

In this section, we consider employees' rights to a workplace in which they are free from sexual and other discriminatory harassment. Under Title VII, the ADEA, and the ADA, employees have a cause of action for harassment when the harassment is on the basis of membership in a protected group. Harassment poses different challenges than the theories of discrimination discussed previously in this chapter. For example, much conduct underlying sexual harassment, unlike other discriminatory behavior, is unobjectionable, even desired, in contexts outside the workplace. Further, sexual harassment, like other kinds of discriminatory harassment, typically does not result in any adverse economic impact on the victim, even if the emotional distress is severe. The decision to find a violation of the discrimination laws under such circumstances is in sharp contrast to efforts by courts in other antidiscrimination contexts to limit suits to cases where there is an "adverse employment action." In addition, discriminatory harassment frequently occurs in violation of, rather than in compliance with, company policy, and harassers often are satisfying their own personal interests, rather than seeking to further their employer's interests. This attribute of discriminatory harassment raises a new issue: What is the employer's liability for harassment by supervisors and co-workers in violation of company policy? Finally, because controlling discriminatory harassment in the workplace by disciplining harassing employees may relieve an employer of liability, discriminatory harassment raises questions about the rights of employees who perpetrate this form of discrimination.

Although the lower federal courts were originally dismissive of sexual harassment as a theory of liability under Title VII, the Supreme Court decision in *Meritor Savings Bank v. Vinson*, 477 U.S. 57 (1986), signaled a sea change in the acceptance of this theory. The facts in *Meritor* were extreme. Sidney Taylor, a vice president of Meritor and manager of one of its branch offices, hired Michelle Vinson and became her supervisor. Vinson started as a trainee but ultimately was promoted to assistant branch manager, working at the same branch until her discharge in 1978. While her advancement at the bank was based on merit, she alleged that she had been constantly harassed by Taylor during her four years of employment. According to Vinson's testimony, Taylor "invited her out to dinner and, during the course of the meal, suggested that they go to a motel to have sexual relations. At first she refused, but out of what she described as fear of losing her job she eventually agreed. . . . Taylor thereafter made repeated demands upon her for sexual favors, usually at the branch, both during and after business hours; she estimated that over the next several years she had intercourse with him some 40 or 50 times. In addition, Taylor fondled her in front of other employees, followed her into the women's restroom when she went there alone, exposed himself to her, and even forcibly raped her on several occasions." *Meritor*, 477 U.S. at 60.

The Supreme Court declared that: "Without question, when a supervisor sexually harasses a subordinate because of the subordinate's sex, that supervisor 'discriminate[s]' on the basis of sex." *Id.* at 64. As importantly, the Court rejected the argument that harassment was limited to economic losses. Looking in large part to EEOC Guidelines on Sexual Harassment, 29 C.F.R. § 1604.11, the Court held that "a plaintiff may establish a violation of Title VII by proving that discrimination based on sex has created a hostile or abusive work environment." *Meritor*, 477 U.S. at 66. It did caution, however, that "not all workplace conduct that may be described as 'harassment' affects a 'term, condition, or privilege' of employment within the meaning of Title VII. For sexual harassment to be actionable, it must be sufficiently severe or pervasive 'to alter the conditions of [the victim's] employment and create an abusive working environment.'" *Id.* at 67. The Court also made clear that "the fact that sex-related conduct was 'voluntary,' in the sense that the complainant was not forced to participate against her will, is not a defense to a sexual harassment suit brought under Title VII. The gravamen of any sexual harassment claim is that the alleged sexual advances were 'unwelcome.' 29 C.F.R. § 1604.11(a) (1985)." *Id.* at 68.

Meritor established what was essentially a new cause of action under Title VII, one that is in many ways very different than the kind of discrimination we have studied to this point. However, it left a myriad of questions to be answered. Two of the most important were when the offensive conduct was "because of sex" and what conduct is sufficiently "severe or pervasive" to be actionable.

Oncale v. Sundowner Offshore Services, Inc.
523 U.S. 75 (1998)

Justice SCALIA delivered the opinion of the Court.

This case presents the question whether workplace harassment can violate Title VII's prohibition against "discrimination . . . because of . . . sex," when the harasser and the harassed employee are of the same sex.

I

The District Court having granted summary judgment for respondent, we must assume the facts to be as alleged by petitioner Joseph Oncale. The precise details are irrelevant to the legal point we must decide, and in the interest of both brevity and dignity we shall describe them only generally. In late October 1991, Oncale was working for respondent Sundowner Offshore Services on a Chevron U.S.A., Inc. oil platform in the Gulf of Mexico. He was employed as a roustabout on an eight-man crew which included respondents John Lyons, Danny Pippen, and Brandon Johnson. Lyons, the crane operator, and Pippen, the driller, had supervisory authority. On several occasions, Oncale was forcibly subjected to sex-related, humiliating actions against him by Lyons, Pippen and Johnson in the presence of the rest of the crew. Pippen and Lyons also physically assaulted Oncale in a sexual manner, and Lyons threatened him with rape.

Oncale's complaints to supervisory personnel produced no remedial action; in fact, the company's Safety Compliance Clerk, Valent Hohen, told Oncale that Lyons and Pippen "picked [on] him all the time too," and called him a name suggesting homosexuality. Oncale eventually quit — asking that his pink slip reflect that he "voluntarily left due to sexual harassment and verbal abuse." When asked at his deposition why he left Sundowner, Oncale stated "I felt that if I didn't leave my job, that I would be raped or forced to have sex."

[The district court held that "Mr. Oncale, a male, has no cause of action under Title VII for harassment by male co-workers." The Fifth Circuit affirmed.]

II

Title VII's prohibition of discrimination "because of . . . sex" protects men as well as women, *Newport News* [*Shipbuilding & Dry Dock Co. v. EEOC*, 462 U.S. 669, 678 (1983)], and in the related context of racial discrimination in the workplace we have rejected any conclusive presumption that an employer will not discriminate against members of his own race. "Because of the many facets of human motivation, it would be unwise to presume as a matter of law that human beings of one definable group will not discriminate against other members of that group." *Castaneda v. Partida*, 430 U.S. 482 (1977). In *Johnson v. Transportation Agency*, Santa Clara County, 480 U.S. 616 (1987), a male employee claimed that his employer discriminated against him because of his sex when it preferred a female employee for promotion. Although we ultimately rejected the claim on other grounds, we did not consider it significant that the supervisor who made that decision was also a man. If our precedents leave any doubt on the question, we hold today that nothing in Title VII necessarily bars a claim of discrimination "because of . . . sex" merely because the plaintiff and the defendant (or the person charged with acting on behalf of the defendant) are of the same sex.

Courts have had little trouble with that principle in cases like *Johnson*, where an employee claims to have been passed over for a job or promotion. But when the issue arises in the context of a "hostile environment" sexual harassment claim, the state and federal courts have taken a bewildering variety of stances. Some, like the Fifth Circuit in this case, have held that same-sex sexual harassment claims are never cognizable under Title VII. Other decisions say that such claims are actionable only if the plaintiff can prove that the harasser is homosexual (and thus presumably motivated by sexual desire). Still others suggest that workplace harassment that is sexual in content is always actionable, regardless of the harasser's sex, sexual orientation, or motivations.

We see no justification in the statutory language or our precedents for a categorical rule excluding same-sex harassment claims from the coverage of Title VII. As some courts have observed, male-on-male sexual harassment in the workplace was assuredly not the principal evil Congress was concerned with when it enacted Title VII. But statutory prohibitions often go beyond the principal evil to cover reasonably comparable evils, and it is ultimately the provisions of our laws rather than the principal concerns of our legislators by which we are governed. Title VII prohibits "discrimination . . . because of . . . sex" in the "terms" or "conditions" of employment. Our holding that this includes sexual harassment must extend to sexual harassment of any kind that meets the statutory requirements.

Respondents and their amici contend that recognizing liability for same-sex harassment will transform Title VII into a general civility code for the American workplace. But that risk is no greater for same-sex than for opposite-sex harassment, and is adequately met by careful attention to the requirements of the statute. Title VII does not prohibit all verbal or physical harassment in the workplace; it is directed only at "discrimination . . . because of . . . sex." We have never held that workplace harassment, even harassment between men and women, is automatically discrimination because of sex merely because the words used have sexual content or connotations. "The critical issue, Title VII's text indicates, is whether members of one sex are exposed to disadvantageous terms or conditions of employment to which members of the other sex are not exposed." *Harris* [*v. Forklift Systems, Inc.*, 510 U.S. 17 (1993)].

Courts and juries have found the inference of discrimination easy to draw in most male-female sexual harassment situations, because the challenged conduct typically involves explicit or implicit proposals of sexual activity; it is reasonable to assume those proposals would not have been made to someone of the same sex. The same chain of inference would be available to a plaintiff alleging same-sex harassment, if there were credible evidence that the harasser was homosexual. But harassing conduct need not be motivated by sexual desire to support an inference of discrimination on the basis of sex. A trier of fact might reasonably find such discrimination, for example, if a female victim is harassed in such sex-specific and derogatory terms by another woman as to make it clear that the harasser is motivated by general hostility to the presence of women in the workplace. A same-sex harassment plaintiff may also, of course, offer direct comparative evidence about how the alleged harasser treated members of both sexes in a mixed-sex workplace. Whatever evidentiary route the plaintiff chooses to follow, he or she must always prove that the conduct at issue was not merely tinged with offensive sexual connotations, but actually constituted "discrimination . . . because of . . . sex."

And there is another requirement that prevents Title VII from expanding into a general civility code: As we emphasized in *Meritor* and *Harris*, the statute does not reach genuine but innocuous differences in the ways men and women routinely interact with members of the same sex and of the opposite sex. The prohibition of harassment on the basis of sex requires neither asexuality nor androgyny in the workplace; it forbids only behavior so objectively offensive as to alter the "conditions" of the victim's employment. "Conduct that is not severe or pervasive enough to create an objectively hostile or abusive work environment—an environment that a reasonable person would find hostile or abusive—is beyond Title VII's purview." *Harris*. We have always regarded that requirement as crucial, and as sufficient to ensure that courts and juries do not mistake ordinary socializing in the workplace—such as male-on-male horseplay or intersexual flirtation—for discriminatory "conditions of employment."

We have emphasized, moreover, that the objective severity of harassment should be judged from the perspective of a reasonable person in the plaintiff's position, considering "all the circumstances." *Harris*. In same-sex (as in all) harassment cases, that inquiry requires careful consideration of the social context in which particular behavior occurs and is experienced by its target. A professional football player's working environment is not severely or pervasively abusive, for example, if the coach smacks him on the buttocks as he heads onto the field—even if the same behavior would reasonably be experienced as abusive by the coach's secretary (male or female) back at the office. The real social impact of workplace behavior often depends on a constellation of surrounding circumstances, expectations, and relationships which are not fully captured by a simple recitation of the words used or the physical acts performed. Common sense, and an appropriate sensitivity to social context, will enable courts and juries to distinguish between simple teasing or roughhousing among members of the same sex, and conduct which a reasonable person in the plaintiff's position would find severely hostile or abusive. . . .

NOTES

1. *Sex-as-Conduct versus Gender. Oncale* makes clear that, regardless of the gender of the harasser and victim, the central issue for purposes of establishing liability under Title VII is whether the terms and conditions of the victim's employment were altered because of "sex." This term has generated some confusion because "sex" is sometimes used to refer to sexual conduct and sometimes to refer to biological sex. Although *Oncale* establishes that same-sex harassment is actionable under Title VII, the question remains: When is harassment because of or on the basis of sex? The Court confirms prior opinions that the gender of the target must cause the harassment. Thus, an inference of sex-based discrimination was often drawn by the lower courts based on sexual advances made by a heterosexual toward a victim of the opposite sex. Consistent with this logic, the Court indicates that sexual advances by a homosexual toward an individual of the same sex also may give rise to the inference that such action is "because of sex." *See* Rebecca Hanner White, *There's Nothing Special About Sex: The Supreme Court Mainstreams Sexual Harassment*, 7 Wm. & Mary Bill Rts. J. 725, 734 (1999) ("The fact that harassment is sexual in nature may (and often will) be powerful evidence that the victim is suffering harassment because of her sex. The defendant may, however, avoid liability if the fact finder is convinced that the victim was not a target of harassment because of her sex, whether or not the harassment was sexual in nature."); Steven Willborn, *Taking Discrimination Seriously:* Oncale *and the Fate of Exceptionalism in Sexual Harassment Law*, 7 Wm. & Mary Bill Rts. J. 677 (1999). In contrast, David S. Schwartz, *When is Sex Because of Sex? The Causation Problem in Sexual Harrassment Law*, 150 U. Pa. L. Rev. 1697 (2002), argues for a "sex per se" rule that would go beyond a presumption and find sexual conduct sufficient to satisfy the "because of sex" requirement.

Another approach is to find harassment to be sexual when it is predicated on a plaintiff's failure to conform to gender norms. The paradigm example is an "effeminate" male or a "butch" woman. A handful of cases have recognized this theory of harassment. *See, e.g., Nichols v. Azteca Rest. Enters., Inc.*, 256 F.3d 864 (9th Cir. 2001) (discrimination against male for acting too feminine is actionable under Title VII); *Smith v. Salem*, 378 F.3d 566, 572 (6th Cir. 2004) (transsexual stated a Title VII claim by alleging that he was a victim of discrimination because his conduct and mannerisms "did not conform with his employers' and co-workers' sex stereotypes of how a man should look and behave"). In this regard, consider the relevance of the Court's recognition in *Price Waterhouse* (reproduced at page 542) that gender stereotyping is direct evidence of sex discrimination under Title VII.

This theory comes very close to finding discrimination on the basis of sexual orientation to be actionable. Although courts often go to great lengths to distinguish between sex discrimination and sexual orientation discrimination, *e.g., Dawson v. Bumble & Bumble*, 398 F.3d 211 (2d Cir. 2005), a number of commentators argue that such discrimination is properly viewed as sex discrimination within the meaning of Title VII. *See* Katherine M. Franke, *What's Wrong with Sexual Harassment?*, 49 Stan. L. Rev. 691, 732 (1997); Zachary A. Kramer, *The Ultimate Gender Stereotype: Equalizing Gender-Conforming and Gender-Nonconforming Homosexuals Under Title VII*, 2004 U. Ill. L. Rev. 465, 465 (2004); Camille Hébert, *Sexual Harassment as Discrimination "Because of . . . Sex": Have We Come Full Circle?* 27 Ohio N.U. L. Rev. 439 (2001) (plaintiff harassed for failure to conform to gender stereotypes would meet the "because of . . . sex" requirement).

2. *Gender Harassment. Oncale*'s notion that sexual harassment is only a subset of sex discrimination is underscored by cases in which women complain not of unwelcome sexual advances but of environments that are hostile to women in other ways. For example, recall *Desert Palace*, reproduced at page 555. This was a discriminatory discharge case, not a contaminated work environment case, and thus, the Supreme Court apparently did not find it necessary to include some of the comments directed at and about plaintiff. But consider the facts as recounted in the Ninth Circuit's opinion from the hostile environment perspective:

> Costa also presented evidence that she was penalized for her failure to conform to sexual stereotypes. Although her fellow Teamsters frequently lost their tempers, swore at fellow employees, and sometimes had physical altercations, it was Costa, identified in one report

as "the lady Teamster," who was called a "bitch," and told "you got more balls than the guys." Even at trial, and despite testimony that she "got along with most people" and had "few arguments," Caesars' managers continued to characterize her as "strong willed," "opinionated," and "confrontational," leading counsel to call her "bossy" in closing argument. Supervisor Karen Hallett, who later signed Costa's termination order, expressly declared her intent to "get rid of that bitch," referring to Costa.

Supervisors frequently used or tolerated verbal slurs that were sex-based or tinged with sexual overtones. Most memorably, one co-worker called her a "fucking cunt." When she wrote a letter to management expressing her concern with this epithet, which stood out from the ordinary rough-and-tumble banter, she received a three-day suspension in response. Although the other employee admitted using the epithet, Costa was faulted for "engaging in verbal confrontation with co-worker in the warehouse resulting in use of profane and vulgar language by other employee."

Costa v. Desert Palace, 299 F.3d 838, 845-46 (9th Cir. 2002) (en banc). These epithets were not hurled at plaintiff because her co-workers desired to have sex with Costa — they wanted to drive her out of the workplace. One inference is that they did so because she was a woman — the only woman in that position. The courts have found that harassing conduct of a nonsexual nature can constitute sexual harassment, sometimes called gender harassment. *See, e.g., EEOC v. Nat'l Educ. Ass'n, Alaska*, 422 F.3d 840, 842 (9th Cir. 2005) ("[O]ffensive conduct that is not facially sex-specific nonetheless may violate Title VII if there is sufficient circumstantial evidence of qualitative and quantitative differences in the harassment suffered by female and male employees."); *Haugerud v. Amery Sch. Dist.*, 259 F.3d 678 (7th Cir. 2001) (conduct was not sexual, but sole female custodian presented sufficient evidence that it was directed toward her because of her sex); *Smith v. Sheahan*, 189 F.3d 529 (7th Cir. 1999) (physical assault created hostile work environment for female jail guard).

Vicki Schultz, in *Reconceptualizing Sexual Harassment*, 107 YALE L. J. 1683, 1686-87, 1689 (1998), argues against the "sexual desire-dominance paradigm" for sexual harassment because that paradigm "has served to exclude from legal understanding many of the most common and debilitating forms of harassment faced by women (and many men) at work each day." One of Schultz's solutions is for courts to employ a rebuttable presumption of illegal harassment when the harassment is directed at women who work in traditionally segregated job categories. *See also* Rebecca Hanner White, *There's Nothing Special About Sex: The Supreme Court Main-streams Sexual Harassment*, 7 WM. & MARY BILL RTS. J. 725, 735-6 (1999) ("[Schultz's] approach makes sense intuitively, and is consistent with *Oncale*, provided that courts keep in mind that only an inference of sex-discrimination is created, not a conclusive method of proof. After all, a woman in a male-dominated workplace may be harassed because she is a woman, or she may be harassed because she is a jerk."). Given that Costa was the only woman in her workplace, how would the trier of fact decide the abuse aimed at her was because she was a woman doing "men's work" or because she was "a jerk"?

3. *Sex, Not Sexual Orientation.* If Oncale's employer can establish that his co-workers harassed him because he is a homosexual, can he nonetheless establish an actionable claim under Title VII? We will see that discrimination on the basis of sexual orientation is not generally actionable under Title VII. See page 646. The law thus requires courts to distinguish between harassment on the basis of sexual orientation (legal) and harassment on the basis of sex (illegal), and rejects the argument that harassment on the basis of sexual orientation is necessarily on the basis of sex.

Shepherd v. Slater Steel Corp., 168 F.3d 998 (7th Cir. 1999), read *Oncale* to establish two prongs by which same-sex harassment may be gender discrimination:

> (1) credible evidence that the harasser is gay or lesbian — in which case it is reasonable to assume that the harasser would not harass members of the other sex (or at least not with "explicit or implicit proposals of sexual activity"); and (2) proof that the plaintiff was harassed in "such sex-specific and derogatory terms" as to reveal an antipathy to persons of plaintiff's gender.

168 F.3d at 1009. The first prong obviously tracks heterosexual harassment where the harasser is interested in engaging in sexual conduct with the victim. The second prong suggests hostility to a gender, not to sexual orientation. But does it make sense to you? Since same-sex harassment is involved, the second prong posits that the harasser has "antipathy" to the gender he (or she) shares with the victim. When will this occur? When the antipathy is to the individual's orientation? *See generally* L. Camille Hébert, *Transforming Transsexual and Transgender Rights*, 15 WM. & MARY J. WOMEN & L. 535 (2009) (the term "sex" should be defined more broadly than courts have seen fit to do with respect to sexual minorities, to extend protection not only on biological status but gender-linked traits, including gender identity). *See also* Zachary A. Kramer, *Heterosexuality and Title VII*, 103 NW. U. L. REV. 205, 208-9 (2009) ("there is a double standard at work in employment discrimination cases. For lesbian and gay employees, sexual orientation is a burden because courts are primed to reject otherwise actionable discrimination claims on the theory that such claims are an attempt to bootstrap protection for sexual orientation into Title VII. However, rather than being burdened by their sexual orientation in employment discrimination cases, heterosexual employees are not affected by theirs.").

4. *The Equal-Opportunity Harasser.* To understand how the law can distinguish between sexual harassment and sexual orientation harassment, suppose a harasser targets both gays and lesbians, that is, he harasses anyone that he considers to be "deviant." Obviously, there is no sex discrimination here — he's an equal opportunity harasser. While the harassment is on the basis of orientation, that is not actionable under Title VII.

The equal opportunity harasser appears often in the literature and sometimes in the cases. In the heterosexual context, female plaintiffs have encountered the sometimes successful defense that the harasser directs his offensive conduct and remarks against both men and women and therefore does not violate Title VII. *See Reine v. Honeywell Int'l Inc.*, 362 F. App'x 395 (5th Cir. 2010) (recognizing equal opportunity harasser defense when both men and women were treated badly and only a few of the harassing comments related to sex). *But see Beckford v. Dep't of Corr.*, 605 F.3d 951, 960 (11th Cir. 2010) ("That the close management inmates are typically crude and even obscene does not mean that their harassment was indiscriminate. The employees presented evidence that the inmates called them cunts, whores, bitches, and sluts, and we have ruled that these gender-specific and highly offensive epithets evidence sex-based harassment under Title VII"); *Venezia v. Gottlieb Mem'l Hosp., Inc.*, 421 F.3d 468, 473 (7th Cir. 2005) (harassment of both husband and wife by different individuals did not necessarily mean that there was no sex discrimination). *See generally* Martin J. Katz, *Reconsidering Attraction in Sexual Harassment*, 79 IND. L.J. 101, 125-39 (2004); Ronald Turner, *Title VII and the Inequality-Enhancing Effects of the Bisexual and Equal Opportunity Harasser Defenses*, 7 U. PA. J.

Lab. & Emp. L. 341, 342, 345 (2005); Charles R. Calleros, *The Meaning of "Sex":* *Homosexual and Bisexual Harassment Under Title VII*, 20 Vt. L. Rev. 55, 70-78 (1995).

5. *Disparate Impact Theory.* If a court concludes that harassment was not because of sex in the intent sense but nevertheless had a greater effect on women than on men, perhaps because it occurred in a sex-segregated workplace, the disparate impact theory suggests a possible way to attack the mistreatment. *See* Camille Hébert, *The Disparate* *Impact of Sexual Harassment: Does Motive Matter?*, 53 Kan. L. Rev. 341 (2004) (arguing that disparate impact should be applicable to sexual harassment cases because women as a group are disproportionately disadvantaged by sexually harassing conduct in the workplace); Kelly Cahill Timmons, *Sexual Harassment and Disparate Impact:* *Should Non-Targeted Workplace Sexual Conduct be Actionable Under Title VII?*, 81 Neb. L. Rev. 1152, 1155 (2003) (concluding "that non-targeted sexual conduct in the workplace should be actionable only if the conduct's disproportionate impact on women is great").

EEOC v. Sunbelt Rentals, Inc.
521 F.3d 306 (4th Cir. 2008)

Wilkinson, Circuit Judge:

This case arises from a Title VII action brought by the United States Equal Employment Opportunity Commission on behalf of Clinton Ingram, a Muslim American, against Sunbelt Rentals, Inc. The EEOC alleges that Ingram, while working at Sunbelt, was subjected to a religiously hostile work environment in violation of Title VII. The district court granted summary judgment for Sunbelt and dismissed the claim.

Title VII extends the promise that no one should be subject to a discriminatorily hostile work environment. In the wake of September 11th, some Muslim Americans, completely innocent of any wrongdoing, became targets of gross misapprehensions and overbroad assumptions about their religious beliefs. But the event that shook the foundations of our buildings did not shake the premise of our founding — that here, in America, there is no heretical faith. Because the evidence, if proven, indicates that Ingram suffered severe and pervasive religious harassment in violation of Title VII, we reverse the district court's grant of summary judgment and remand with directions that this case proceed to trial.

I.

A.

Sunbelt is a company that rents and sells construction equipment. In October 2001, a month after the September 11th attacks, it hired Ingram to work at its Gaithersburg, Maryland store. After initially working as a truck driver, Ingram was later promoted to the position of rental manager, a position he held until his termination in February 2003. As a rental manager, Ingram primarily worked at a rental counter located inside the store's showroom and was responsible for assisting customers with equipment rentals.

Ingram worked in close quarters with several other Sunbelt employees. In addition to Ingram, there were three other rental managers at the Gaithersburg location: David Gray, John "Hank" Parater, and Barry Fortna. Gray and Parater had work stations on either side of Ingram at the office's rental counter, and Fortna, the "lead rental manager," worked at a desk behind the counter.

In addition to his fellow rental managers, Ingram frequently interacted with Mike Warner, the store's shop foreman, and Steve Riddlemoser, the overall manager of the Gaithersburg office. When Riddlemoser was not in the office, Warner served as the "acting manager." If both Riddlemoser and Warner were absent, then Fortna was left in charge. The regional manager for the Gaithersburg location was Eddie Dempster.

Prior to joining Sunbelt, Ingram, who is an African American, converted to Islam while serving in the United States Army. It is undisputed that Sunbelt, as well as Ingram's coworkers, knew Ingram was a Muslim. In fact, Sunbelt permitted Ingram to use a private, upstairs room for short prayer sessions that were required by Ingram's faith. In addition, Sunbelt allowed Ingram to attend a weekly congregational prayer session that took place from 1:00-1:45 p.m. on Friday afternoons. Ingram also observed tenets of his faith at the workplace by keeping a beard and wearing a kufi, a traditional headgear worn by Muslim men. Notably, Ingram was the only Muslim employee at the Gaithersburg office.

During his time at Sunbelt, Ingram claims he was subjected to a hostile work environment on the basis of his religion. According to Ingram, the abusive environment was marked by a steady stream of demeaning comments and degrading actions directed against him by his coworkers — conduct that went unaddressed and unpunished by Sunbelt supervisors.

For instance, coworkers used religiously-charged epithets and often called Ingram names such as "Taliban" and "towel head." In addition, fellow employees frequently made fun of Ingram's appearance, challenged his allegiance to the United States, suggested he was a terrorist, and made comments associating all Muslims with senseless violence. Sometimes Ingram's supervisors personally participated in the harassment. Sunbelt responds, in turn, that Ingram also used profane and derogatory language in the workplace.

Additionally, Ingram was the victim of several religiously charged incidents. For instance, on one occasion, Gray held a metal detector to Ingram's head and, after the detector did not go off, called Ingram a "fake ass Muslim want-to-be turbine wearing ass." In a separate incident, Gray showed Ingram a stapler and said that "if anyone upsets you pretend this stapler is a model airplane [and] just toss it in the air, just repeatedly catch it, [and] don't say anything." Ingram understood this to be a reference to the September 11 attacks and another attempt by Gray to equate Ingram with terrorists. Finally, a cartoon was posted in the store's dispatch area depicting persons "dressed in Islamic or Muslim attire" as suicide bombers. [In the cartoon, an instructor with a bomb strapped to his body tells the others: "okay, pay attention" because "I'm only showing you . . . how this works once."] Taking offense, Ingram complained about the cartoon to the dispatcher and eventually tore it down.

In addition to these explicitly religious incidents, Ingram suffered from other forms of harassment. For example, his timecard, which was used to punch time in and out, was frequently hidden, especially on Fridays when he went to congregational prayer. Likewise, coworkers constantly unplugged his computer equipment and, on one occasion, defaced his business card by writing "dumb ass" over his name.

After nearly every incident of harassment, Ingram verbally complained to Rid-dlemoser, and sometimes Dempster and Warner. [These complaints did not resolve the matter and ultimately Ingram complained to Sunbelt's Human Resources Department. This, too, failed to stop the harassment. Although there was] a short period of relative improvement, the religious harassment and pranks "just basically started up again." For instance, Gray continued to harass Ingram about his appearance and his faith. After Ingram informed Dempster that the harassment was "starting to happen again," Dempster accused Ingram of "being paranoid," "seeing things," and "trying to build a case against" Sunbelt. The harassment allegedly continued until Ingram's termination in February 2003.

B.

[The district court granted summary judgment to Sunbelt, finding the harassment not sufficiently severe or pervasive to establish a prima facie case of a hostile work environment. The district court stated] "[t]here's a lot of coarse behavior that goes on in the workplace," and Sunbelt was "a little more rough and ready than, let us say, the Century Club of New York of which fine ladies are members." Second, the court stated that several of the incidents that Ingram complained about, such as the hiding of his timecard, lacked a direct "nexus with religion." Third, the court explained that if the explicitly religious incidents involving his coworkers were sufficiently severe or pervasive, Ingram would have included them in his written complaint to Human Resources. Because he did not, the district court presumed they must not have been sufficiently severe or pervasive. . . .

II . . .

In order to prove that Ingram suffered from a "discriminatorily hostile or abusive work environment," *Harris v. Forklift Systems, Inc.*, 510 U.S. 17 (1993), the EEOC must demonstrate that the harassment was (1) unwelcome, (2) because of religion, (3) sufficiently severe or pervasive to alter the conditions of employment and create an abusive atmosphere, and (4) imputable to the employer, *see Gilliam v. South Carolina Dep't of Juvenile Justice*, 474 F.3d 134, 142 (4th Cir. 2007).

[The court had no difficulty finding the conduct "unwelcome," given Ingram's response to his co-workers and his complaints to management. Nor did it have any difficulty with the religious nature of the comments, given that, for example, "Taliban" or "towel head" would not have been applied to a non-Muslim employee, and the co-workers "teased [him] about his appearance, particularly his kufi and beard."]

C.

The main area of contention here is whether the harassment alleged by Ingram was "sufficiently severe or pervasive to alter the conditions of [his] employment and create an abusive working environment." *Harris* (quoting *Meritor*). Viewed on summary judgment, the evidence establishes that Ingram persistently suffered from religious harassment of the most demeaning, degrading, and damaging sort. The district court erred when it held the EEOC had failed to satisfy this requirement.

1.

The "severe or pervasive" element of a hostile work environment claim "has both subjective and objective components." *Ocheltree v. Scollon Prods., Inc.*, 335 F.3d 325, 333 (4th Cir. 2003) (en banc) (citing *Harris*). First, the plaintiff must show that he "subjectively perceive[d] the environment to be abusive." *Harris*. Next, the plaintiff must demonstrate that the conduct was such that "a reasonable person in the plaintiff's position" would have found the environment objectively hostile or abusive. *Oncale v. Sundowner Offshore Servs., Inc.*. Because Sunbelt does not, and could not, challenge the EEOC's contention that the harassment seemed severe and pervasive to Ingram personally, we focus our attention on the element's objective component.

This objective inquiry "is not, and by its nature cannot be, a mathematically precise test." *Harris*. Rather, when determining whether the harassing conduct was objectively "severe or pervasive," we must look "at all the circumstances," including "the frequency of the discriminatory conduct; its severity; whether it is physically threatening or humiliating, or a mere offensive utterance; and whether it unreasonably interferes with an employee's work performance." *Id.*; *Ocheltree*. "[N]o single factor is" dispositive, *Harris*, as "[t]he real social impact of workplace behavior often depends on a constellation of surrounding circumstances, expectations, and relationships which are not fully captured by a simple recitation of the words used or the physical acts performed," *Oncale*.

While this standard surely prohibits an employment atmosphere that is "permeated with discriminatory intimidation, ridicule, and insult," *Harris*, it is equally clear that Title VII does not establish a "general civility code for the American workplace," *Oncale*. This is because, in order to be actionable, the harassing "conduct must be [so] extreme [as] to amount to a change in the terms and conditions of employment." *Faragher v. City of Boca Raton*, 524 U.S. 775, 788 (1998). Indeed, as the Court observed, "simple teasing, offhand comments, and isolated incidents (unless extremely serious) will not amount to discriminatory changes in the terms and conditions of employment." *Id.; see also Clark County Sch. Dist. v. Breeden*, 532 U.S. 268, 270-71 (2001).

Our circuit has likewise recognized that plaintiffs must clear a high bar in order to satisfy the severe or pervasive test. Workplaces are not always harmonious locales, and even incidents that would objectively give rise to bruised or wounded feelings will not on that account satisfy the severe or pervasive standard. Some rolling with the punches is a fact of workplace life. Thus, complaints premised on nothing more than "rude treatment by [coworkers]," *Baqir v. Principi*, 434 F.3d 733, 747 (4th Cir. 2006), "callous behavior by [one's] superiors," *Bass v. E.I. DuPont de Nemours & Co.*, 324 F.3d 761, 765 (4th Cir. 2003), or "a routine difference of opinion and personality conflict with [one's] supervisor," *Hawkins v. PepsiCo, Inc.*, 203 F.3d 274, 276 (4th Cir. 2000), are not actionable under Title VII.

The task then on summary judgment is to identify situations that a reasonable jury might find to be so out of the ordinary as to meet the severe or pervasive criterion. That is, instances where the environment was pervaded with discriminatory conduct "aimed to humiliate, ridicule, or intimidate," thereby creating an abusive atmosphere. *Jennings v. Univ. of North Carolina*, 482 F.3d 686, 695 (4th Cir. 2007) (en banc) (citing *Meritor*). With these principles in mind, we examine whether a reasonable person in Ingram's position would have found the environment to be sufficiently severe or hostile.

2.

The evidence indicates that Ingram suffered religious harassment that was "persistent, demeaning, unrelenting, and widespread." *Harris v. L & L Wings, Inc.*, 132 F.3d 978, 984 (4th Cir. 1997). It is impossible as an initial matter to ignore the context in which the harassment took place. In the time immediately following September 11th, religious tensions ran higher in much of the country, and Muslims were sometimes viewed through the prism of 9/11, rather than as the individuals they were. Sunbelt's Gaithersburg office was no exception. After the terrorist attacks took place, there was lots of talk amongst Sunbelt employees, especially by Gray, about how the "Muslim religion is bad." Likewise, after it was publicized that the D.C. snipers were Muslim, anti-Islam sentiment rose in the Sunbelt workplace. Ingram, the lone Muslim employee, was left to bear the verbal brunt of anti-Islamic sentiment.

Specifically, Ingram was subject to repeated comments that disparaged both him and his faith. Several coworkers, including one with supervisory authority, referred to Ingram in harshly derogatory terms. Mike Warner, the store's shop foreman, called Ingram "Taliban" "over and over again," as well as "towel head." Likewise, Sal Rindone, a Sunbelt mechanic, told Ingram that he thought Ingram was a member of the Taliban. This same coworker also challenged Ingram's allegiance to the United States, asking Ingram "are you on our side or are you on the Taliban's side," and telling him that if "you don't like America or where we stand, you can just leave." Ingram, a veteran of the United States Army, responded that he was not a member of the Taliban but rather "an American and a Muslim."

In addition, Ingram was persistently harassed about his appearance, particularly his kufi and beard. For example, Warner, when making fun of Ingram's appearance, "would make it known that" he thought Ingram actually "look[ed] like a Taliban." On at least one occasion, Gray called Ingram a "fake Muslim" because of his beard. As Gray later admitted, such "comments were made often." According to Ingram, the harassment by Gray was "an ongoing thing, daily."

Ingram was also harassed about his short, Sunbelt-sanctioned prayer sessions. Gray told Ingram "several times" that he had a "problem" with Ingram leaving his desk to pray. In addition, Ingram's timecard was often hidden on Fridays, the day he went to congregational prayer. Even more severe was a comment made by Warner to another coworker, which was later related to Ingram. Warner said that if he ever caught Ingram praying upstairs, that would be "the end of him."

In addition to the abusive comments made to and about Ingram personally, several coworkers made hostile remarks about Islam generally. For instance, rental manager Hank Parater told Ingram that the United States should go to Saudi Arabia and "kill them all," referring to Muslims in the Arab world. Parater also said that he wanted to be a Muslim so he could have eight wives. After it was announced on a television in the store's showroom that the D.C. snipers had been apprehended, another coworker stared at Ingram and shouted, "I should have known they were Muslims." Gray admitted that the treatment of Ingram likely stemmed from "the events of September 11th and the sniper attacks in our area."

Ingram was also the object of anti-Muslim crudities that associated Ingram, and the Muslim faith, with violence and terrorism. [The court repeated the metal detector, staple, and cartoon incidents. While focusing primarily on Ingram's "personal experience," the court also noted the affidavits of two Sunbelt customers who were Muslims, one of whom attested that Sunbelt employees called him a litany of derogatory names, including "Bin Laden," "Hezbullah," "Ayatollah," "Kadaffi," "Saddam Hussein," "terrorist," and "sun nigger."]

Ingram also was forced to endure harassment lacking a direct religious nexus. Coworkers frequently hid Ingram's timecard, unplugged his computer equipment, and defaced his business card with terms such as "dumb ass." Although similar pranks were played on other Sunbelt employees, there is evidence suggesting that Ingram suffered such harassment more often than others and more likely because of his religion. For instance, Ingram's timecard was hidden most frequently on Fridays, the day he went to congregational prayer. On the Friday before Ingram filed the written complaint, his timecard was hidden on at least five separate occasions. In light of the extensive, explicitly religious harassment by the same coworkers, a reasonable jury could infer that other harassing incidents were also motivated by a disdain for Ingram's faith.

Sunbelt makes much of the fact that those who participated in the harassment were merely Ingram's coworkers, and not anyone with supervisory authority over him. However, the evidence presented creates at least a triable issue in that regard. Warner, the store's shop foreman and a primary harasser of Ingram's, served as the acting manager whenever Riddlemoser was absent. At the very least, he was viewed as a "higher up" within the office. Similarly, Fortna, the lead rental manager, supervised Ingram's work and even signed the "supervisor" line on Ingram's disciplinary forms. As a result, a jury could infer that the harassment by Warner and Fortna had a greater impact given their supervisory status. *See Faragher.*

Likewise, Sunbelt insists the harassment could not have been sufficiently severe because, *inter alia*, it was never "physically threatening." While the presence of "physical threats undeniably strengthens a hostile work environment claim," we have not held that such evidence is required. *White v. BFI Waste Servs.*, 375 F.3d 288, 298 n.6 (4th Cir. 2004). Names can hurt as much as sticks and stones, and the Supreme Court has never indicated that the humiliation so frequently attached to hostile environments need be accompanied by physical threat or force.

While the district court suggested that the harassment might be discounted because the environment was inherently coarse, Title VII contains no such "crude environment" exception, and to read one into it might vitiate statutory safeguards for those who need them most. Of course, if Sunbelt's environment was somehow so universally crude that the treatment of Ingram was nothing out of the ordinary, the jury would be entitled to take that into account. However, the evidence here suggests that the jury could also take the opposite view — that the harassment of Ingram was unique.

Any of the above incidents, viewed in isolation, would not have been enough to have transformed the workplace into a hostile or abusive one. No employer can lightly be held liable for single or scattered incidents. We cannot ignore, however, the habitual use of epithets here or view the conduct without an eye for its cumulative effect. Our precedent has made this point repeatedly. *See Amirmokri v. Baltimore Gas & Elec. Co.,* 60 F.3d 1126, 1131 (4th Cir. 1995) (finding the alleged harassment was sufficiently severe or pervasive because an Iranian plaintiff was called "names like 'the local terrorist,' a 'camel jockey' and 'the Emir of Waldorf'" on an almost daily basis).

Companies cannot, of course, be charged with cleansing their workplace of all offensive remarks. Such a task would be well-nigh impossible, and would encourage companies to adopt authoritarian traits. But we cannot regard as "merely offensive," and thus "beyond Title VII's purview," *Harris*, constant and repetitive abuse founded upon misperceptions that all Muslims possess hostile designs against the United States, that all Muslims support jihad, that all Muslims were sympathetic to the 9/11 attack, and that all Muslims are proponents of radical Islam.

If Americans were forced to practice their faith under the conditions to which Ingram was subject, the Free Exercise Clause and the embodiment of its values in the Title VII protections against workplace religious prejudice would ring quite hollow. Title VII makes plain that religious freedom in America entails more than the right to attend one's own synagogue, mosque, or church. Free religious exercise would mean little if restricted to places of worship or days of observance, only to disappear the next morning at work. In this regard, Title VII helps ensure the special nature of American unity, one not premised on homogeneity but upon the common allegiance to and customary practice of our constitutional ideals of mutual respect.

D.

[The court finally turned to the basis of the employer's liability for the actions of its workers and managers, finding that the standards for such liability were met.]

NOTES

1. *Other Bases of Discriminatory Harassment.* As *Sunbelt* illustrates, harassment claims under the antidiscrimination statutes have not been limited to sexual harassment. While sexual harassment predominates among the hostile environment cases under Title VII, the first case to recognize hostile environment as a basis for liability under Title VII, *Rogers v. EEOC*, 454 F.2d 234 (5th Cir. 1971), concerned an employer who "created an offensive work environment for employees by giving discriminatory service to its Hispanic clientele." Sexual harassment cases such as *Meritor* revived litigation over work environments contaminated by racial, national origin, or age discrimination. *See Tademy v. Union Pac. Corp.*, 520 F.3d 1149 (10th Cir. 2008) (a life-size noose hung prominently in an outside area of the workplace when coupled with racist graffiti on plaintiff's locker and on restroom walls and racist cartoons posted on company billboards as well as racist reference may be sufficiently pervasive to violate Title VII); *Jackson v. Flint Ink N. Am. Corp.*, 382 F.3d 869 (8th Cir. 2004) (trial warranted when, in addition to a number of other incidents, plaintiff's "name was written in a shower at his workplace and . . . there was an arrow connecting his name with a burning cross and a KKK sign [since] an objective observer would regard this combination of figures as a threat of serious bodily harm if not death to Mr. Jackson"). The Seventh Circuit has also ruled that a white district sales manager's use of the word "nigger" on just two occasions constituted racial harassment even though black employees in the same workplace sometimes used the word. *Rodgers v. Western-Southern Life Ins. Co.*, 12 F.3d 668 (7th Cir. 1993). *Sunbelt* was itself a religious harassment case under Title VII, but there have also been successful claims under the ADA, *Arrieta-Colon v. Wal-Mart P.R., Inc.*, 434 F.3d 75 (1st Cir. 2006) (upholding jury verdict of disability discrimination for plaintiff who was harassed because his penile implants left him in a constant state of semi-erection), and presumably age-based harassment would also be actionable.

2. *Harris.* The *Sunbelt* court repeatedly refers to *Harris v. Forklift Systems, Inc.,* 510 U.S. 17 (1993), where a unanimous Court, building on *Meritor*, established the standards for "severe or pervasive." Although the district court had recognized the severity of the harassment, it had dismissed because the comments were not "so severe as to be expected to seriously affect [Harris'] psychological well-being." Quoting *Meritor*, the Court wrote:

> When the workplace is permeated with "discriminatory intimidation, ridicule, and insult," that is "sufficiently severe or pervasive to alter the conditions of the victim's employment and create an abusive working environment," Title VII is violated.
>
> This standard, which we reaffirm today, takes a middle path between making actionable any conduct that is merely offensive and requiring the conduct to cause a tangible psychological injury. As we pointed out in *Meritor*, "mere utterance of an . . . epithet which engenders offensive feelings in an employee," does not sufficiently affect the conditions of employment to implicate Title VII. Conduct that is not severe or pervasive enough to create an objectively hostile or abusive work environment — an environment that a reasonable person would find hostile or abusive — is beyond Title VII's purview. Likewise, if the victim does not subjectively perceive the environment to be abusive, the conduct has not actually altered the conditions of the victim's employment, and there is no Title VII violation.
>
> But Title VII comes into play before the harassing conduct leads to a nervous breakdown. A discriminatorily abusive work environment, even one that does not seriously affect employees' psychological well-being, can and often will detract from employees' job performance, discourage employees from remaining on the job, or keep them from advancing in their careers. Moreover, even without regard to these tangible effects, the very fact that the discriminatory conduct was so severe or pervasive that it created a work environment abusive to employees because of their race, gender, religion, or national origin offends Title VII's broad rule of workplace equality. The appalling conduct alleged in *Meritor*, and the reference in that case to environments " 'so heavily polluted with discrimination as to destroy completely the emotional and psychological stability of minority group workers,' " quoting *Rogers v. EEOC*, merely present some especially egregious examples of harassment. They do not mark the boundary of what is actionable.

530 U.S. at 21-22. Thus, while Title VII certainly "bars conduct that would seriously affect a reasonable person's psychological well-being, . . . the statute is not limited to such conduct. So long as the environment would reasonably be perceived, and is perceived, as hostile or abusive, there is no need for it also to be psychologically injurious." *Id.* at 22.

The *Harris* Court stressed that "[t]his is not, and by its nature cannot be, a mathematically precise test," *id*. Rather, it requires "looking at all the circumstances. These may include the frequency of the discriminatory conduct; its severity; whether it is physically threatening or humiliating, or a mere offensive utterance; and whether it unreasonably interferes with an employee's work performance." *Id.* The employee's "psychological well-being" is relevant, but by no means the only factor.

3. *Applying* Harris. As *Sunbelt* well illustrates, *Harris* provides little in the way of answers even if it sets the governing analytic structure. The divergent views of the same conduct by the district court and the Fourth Circuit illustrate how indeterminate the "severe or pervasive" concepts are even after *Harris*. You might find a parallel in the tort of intentional infliction of emotional distress in Chapter 5, but courts in discriminatory harassment cases have tended to find claims stated far more often than under the common law. Is that because it's somehow more harmful to make an employee's life miserable for reasons related to her protected status than for other reasons?

In any event, many courts have applied the *Harris* standard, and the results are anything but consistent. *Compare EEOC v. Prospect Airport Servs.*, 2010 U.S. App. LEXIS 18447 (9th Cir. Sept. 3, 2010) (while the first two advances by a female co-worker to a male did not amount to an abusive environment, her continued advances in the face of plaintiff's making clear his lack of interest could be found by a jury to create an environment that the plaintiff reasonably perceived as hostile and abusive), *with Paul v. Northrop Grumman Ship Systems*, 309 F. App'x 825 (5th Cir. 2009) (single incident of "chesting up" to plaintiff and rubbing pelvic region across her hips and buttocks in confrontation lasting approximately 90 seconds is not sufficiently severe or pervasive to constitute actionable Title VII claim); *Hensman v. City of Riverview*, 316 F. App'x 412 (6th Cir. 2009) (calling plaintiff "voluptuous" twice, hugging her three times, and grabbing her arm once over the course of six weeks, though inappropriate, is not severe or pervasive enough to create a hostile working environment). *See generally* Ann Juliano & Stewart Schwab, *The Sweep of Sexual Harassment Cases*, 86 CORNELL L. REV. 548 (2001).

4. *A Few Comments Not Enough?* Courts have sometimes resisted finding actionable harassment based only on offensive comments. In *Clark County School District v. Breeden*, reproduced at page 648, the Supreme Court held that no reasonable person could believe that telling a single joke with a sexual innuendo constituted actionable harassment. *See also Ladd v. Grand Trunk Western R.R.*, 552 F.3d 495, 501 (6th Cir. 2009) (where no actual touching took place and plaintiff testified to only one specific incident of a sex- or race-based epithet directed at her, a "total lack of specificity" as to other verbal abuse directed at her justified summary judgment for the employer despite evidence of other epithets — "lesbian," "dyke," and "gay" — that were not directed at her); *Skouby v. Prudential Ins. Co.*, 130 F.3d 794 (7th Cir. 1997) (male employees' banter about attending striptease club and presentation to plaintiff of eight to ten drawings with sexual themes not severe or pervasive); *Sprague v. Thorn Americas, Inc.*, 129 F.3d 1355 (10th Cir. 1997) (sporadic comments over 16-month period, including joking request that plaintiff undo her top button, staring down her dress and joking about it, and referring to a jewelry item as "kinky," did not create a hostile environment). As in *Sunbelt*, courts have been more open to finding a hostile environment based on verbal harassment when the comments are alleged to be "commonplace," "ongoing," and "continuing" over a long period of time. *E.g., Pucino v. Verizon Communs., Inc.*, 2010 U.S. App. LEXIS 16749 (2d Cir. Aug. 13, 2010) (constant use of "bitch" over several years). However, in *McCowan v. All Star Maintenance*, 273 F.3d 917 (10th Cir. 2001), the court found a jury question in a racially hostile work environment claim, even though the plaintiffs worked for only three weeks. Throughout their employment, they were subjected to vulgar and offensive speech, including such terms as "burrito-eating motherfuckers" and "stupid fucking Mexicans." The court overturned the lower court's grant of summary judgment, leaving it to the jury to determine whether the conduct was sufficiently severe or pervasive. And sometimes a claim can be stated with neither touching nor comments. *See Billings v. Town of Grafton*, 515 F.3d 39 (1st Cir. 2008) (even absent touching, sexual advances, or overtly sexual comments, a manager's repeatedly staring at his subordinate's breasts could constitute actionable harassment).

5. *Blue Collar versus White Collar.* In discussing the requirement that conduct be severe or pervasive to be actionable, the *Oncale* court states, "in same-sex (as in all) harassment cases, that inquiry requires careful consideration of the social context in which particular behavior occurs and is experienced by its target." One possible meaning of this is that actions that may be severe in one context are mild in another. We saw a variation on this in *Sunbelt* where the employer argued that the religion-based comments were somehow less objectionable because of the general atmosphere of workers riding each other. In *Williams v. General Motors*, 187 F.3d 553 (6th Cir. 1999), the court held that the standard for establishing sexual harassment does not vary with the work environment. The same standard applies, therefore, whether the complaint is asserted in a coarse blue-collar environment or in a more refined professional environment. Is this holding consistent with *Oncale?* Consider the following:

> It is true that the severity of alleged harassment must be assessed in light of the social mores of American workers and workplace culture, see *Oncale*, but nothing in *Oncale* even hints at the idea that prevailing culture can excuse discriminatory actions. Employers who tolerate workplaces marred by exclusionary practices and bigoted attitudes cannot use their discriminatory pasts to shield them from the present-day mandate of Title VII.

See generally Michael J. Frank, *The Social Context Variable in Hostile Environment Litigation*, 77 NOTRE DAME L. REV. 437 (2002).

6. *Is "Unwelcome" Still a Requirement?* *Harris* framed the core question for harassment cases as whether "the environment would reasonably be perceived, and is perceived, as hostile or abusive." This formulation conspicuously omitted any reference to whether particular conduct had to be "unwelcome" in order to be actionable, a requirement that *Meritor* had explicitly imposed. And many believe that *Harris* modified *sub silentio* that part of *Meritor*. If conduct is subjectively experienced by the subject as hostile or abusive, it can scarcely be "welcomed" by the subject. *See, e.g., Carr v. Allison Gas Turbine Div., Gen. Motors Corp.*, 32 F.3d 1007, 1008 (7th Cir. 1994) ("'Welcome sexual harassment' is an oxymoron"). Such a view of *Harris* also avoided one of the few aspects of *Meritor* that feminists found objectionable: the Court's statement that evidence of "a complainant's sexually provocative speech or dress" is "obviously relevant" to deciding "whether he or she found particular sexual advances unwelcome." The Court did recognize the possibility that such evidence would be unduly prejudicial as compared to its probative value but stressed that "there is no per se rule against its admissibility." *Meritor*, 477 U.S. at 69. The concept of assessing a plaintiff's sexual history or her personal style in order to resolve a case, whether it be a criminal prosecution for rape or a civil suit for sexual harassment, is profoundly disturbing and has resulted in amendments to the Rules of Evidence to restrict such inquiries. *See* Jane H. Aiken, *Protecting Plaintiffs' Sexual Pasts: Coping with Preconceptions Through Discretion*, 51 EMORY L. J. 559 (2002) (exploring the civil application of Rule 412).

But is unwelcomeness truly gone? Not according to the *Sunbelt* court, although it had no trouble in finding the religious comments to be unwelcome to Ingram. Some argue that this aspect of *Meritor* is alive and well, together with *Meritor*'s authorization of an inquiry into plaintiff's "dress and personal fantasies." Under this view, welcomeness is not a question of the victim's subjective reaction but, rather, what a reasonable person in the shoes of the alleged harasser would believe she wanted, welcomed, or would otherwise find unobjectionable. Even under such a view, some courts have been resolute in sharply restricting inquiries into the plaintiff's life. An extreme example is *Burns v. McGregor Electronic Industries*, 989 F.2d 959 (8th Cir. 1993), where the Eighth Circuit twice had to reverse the district court, which clearly disapproved of plaintiff's lifestyle. The Eighth Circuit held that a woman's *off-work* dress and activities were irrelevant to whether she welcomed advances at work. Similarly, the fact that she might welcome advances from some individuals does not mean that any man was free to make them:

> The plaintiff's choice to pose for a nude magazine outside work hours is not material to the issue of whether plaintiff found her employer's work-related conduct offensive. This is not a case where Burns posed in provocative and suggestive ways at work. Her private life, regardless how reprehensible the trier of fact might find it to be, did not provide lawful acquiescence to unwanted sexual advances at her work place by her employer. To hold otherwise would be contrary to Title VII's goal of ridding the work place of any kind of unwelcome sexual harassment. . . .

Burns, 989 F.2d at 963. The trial court made explicit findings that the conduct was not invited or solicited despite her posing naked for a nationally distributed magazine The court believed, however, that because of her outside conduct, including her "interest in having her nude pictures appear in a magazine containing much lewd and crude sexually explicit material," the uninvited sexual advances of her employer were not "in and of [themselves] offensive to her." *Id.* The trial court also explained that Burns "would not have been offended if someone she was attracted to did or said the same thing," but the appeals court rejected this approach: "This rationale would allow a complete stranger to pursue sexual behavior at work that a female worker would accept from her husband or boyfriend. This standard would allow a male employee to kiss or fondle a female worker at the workplace." *Id.* at 963.

But notice that even *Burns*, which essentially excludes off-work conduct, did not reject the welcomeness inquiry explicitly. Had plaintiff "posed in provocative and suggestive ways at work," it presumably would have admitted that evidence, although it may run afoul of Rule 412. *See Jaros v. LodgeNet Entm't Corp.*, 171 F. Supp. 2d 992 (D.S.D. 2001), *aff'd*, 294 F.3d 960 (8th Cir. 2002). While *Burns* was decided before *Harris*, post-*Harris* cases, like *Sunbelt*, continue to ask whether conduct was invited or welcomed. *E.g., Hocevar v. Purdue Frederick Co.*, 223 F.3d 721, 728-29 (8th Cir. 2000) ("In determining whether conduct is 'unwelcome,' we should consider whether the plaintiff indicated, by her conduct, that the alleged harassment was unwelcome."). Such cases seem to put a burden on plaintiff to rebuff sexual advances or otherwise object to sexualized conduct before the harasser can be held responsible and therefore seem to provide harassers a free bite at the apple. *See generally* Susan Estrich, *Sex at Work*, 43 STAN. L. REV. 813 (1991) (arguing for the elimination of the welcomeness inquiry); Mary F. Radford, *By Invitation Only: The Proof of Welcomeness in Sexual Harassment Cases*, 72 N.C. L. REV. 499 (1994) (arguing that defendants should bear the burden of proving welcomeness).

7. *When Is Severe or Pervasive Harassment OK?* Can harassment ever be justified? Establishments such as Hooters restaurants hire females as waitresses, dress them in outfits designed to be provocative, and advertise not just the food, but also the sexually attractive personnel. If a Hooters waitress complains of sexual harassment by customers, can the employer justify it, perhaps as a BFOQ? The only decided case to raise this issue starkly is *Lyle v. Warner Brothers Television Productions*, 132 P.3d 211,

225-26 (Cal. 2006), where a writer for the "Friends" sitcom failed to recover under the state's fair employment law for the sexually oriented atmosphere in the studio:

> There is no dispute Friends was a situation comedy that featured young sexually active adults and sexual humor geared primarily toward adults. Aired episodes of the show often used sexual and anatomical language, innuendo, wordplay, and physical gestures to create humor concerning sex, including oral sex, anal sex, heterosexual sex, gay sex, "talking dirty" during sex, premature ejaculation, pornography, pedophiles, and "threesomes." The circumstance that this was a creative workplace focused on generating scripts for an adult-oriented comedy show featuring sexual themes is significant in assessing the existence of triable issues of facts regarding whether the writers' sexual antics and coarse sexual talk were aimed at plaintiff or at women in general, whether plaintiff and other women were singled out to see and hear what happened, and whether the conduct was otherwise motivated by plaintiff's gender.
>
> Here, the record shows that the instances of sexual antics and sexual discussions identified ante did not involve and were not aimed at plaintiff or any other female employee. It further confirms that such "nondirected" conduct was undertaken in group sessions with both male and female participants present, and that women writers on the Friends production also discussed their own sexual experiences to generate material for the show. That the writers commonly engaged in discussions of personal sexual experiences and preferences and used physical gesturing while brainstorming and generating script ideas for this particular show was neither surprising nor unreasonable from a creative standpoint. Indeed, plaintiff testified that, when told during her interview for the Friends position that "the humor could get a little lowbrow in the writers' room," she responded she would have no problem because previously she had worked around writers and knew what to expect. Although plaintiff contends the writers "sorely understated the actual climate" of the writers' room in her interview, these types of sexual discussions and jokes (especially those relating to the writers' personal experiences) did in fact provide material for actual scripts. The fact that certain discussions did not lead to specific jokes or dialogue airing on the show merely reflected the creative process at work and did not serve to convert such nondirected conduct into harassment because of sex.

8. *Nontargeted Harassment.* There has been some question as to whether harassment must be targeted at women in order to be actionable. *See Ocheltree v. Scollon Prods.*, 335 F.3d 325, 327 (4th Cir. 2003) (en banc). But the cases have generally not found the absence of targeting to be fatal to a claim. *See Patane v. Clark*, 508 F.3d 106 (2d Cir. 2007) (sexual harassment claim stated as to professor's watching of pornographic videotapes even though plaintiff, his secretary, did not see them when her complaint alleged she regularly observed the professor viewing pornographic videos and she had to handle such videos while opening and delivering his mail; the mere presence of pornography in the workplace can alter the status of women); *Reeves v. C.H. Robinson Worldwide, Inc.*, 525 F.3d 1139 (11th Cir. 2008) (even if not directed at a female employee, daily fare of a sex-themed radio show could satisfy the "based on" element in a sexual harassment hostile work environment case when it resulted in continuous conversation and jokes relating to sexual anatomy, masturbation, and female pornography and discussed in a manner more degrading to women than men); *Gallagher v. C.H. Robinson Worldwide, Inc.*, 567 F.3d 263, 274 (6th Cir. 2009) ("Whether the offensive conduct was intentionally directed specifically at Gallagher or not, the fact remains that she had no means of escaping her co-workers' loud insulting language and degrading conversations; she was unavoidably exposed to it.").

Further, when harassment is targeted at the plaintiff, harassment of other women may be relevant to establishing that the conduct is actionable. After recognizing that its precedents permitted the factfinder to "consider similar acts of harassment of which a plaintiff becomes aware during the course of his or her employment, even if the harassing acts were directed at others or occurred outside of the plaintiff's presence," *Hawkins v. Anheuser-Busch, Inc.*, 517 F.3d 321, 336 (6th Cir. 2008), went on:

> The degree to which a past act of harassment is relevant to the determination of whether a plaintiff's work environment is hostile is a fact-specific inquiry that requires courts to determine the relevancy of past acts on a case-by-case basis. In general, however, the appropriate weight to be given a prior act will be directly proportional to the act's proximity in time to the harassment at issue in the plaintiff's case. The further back in time the prior act occurred, in other words, the weaker the inference that the act bears a relationship to the current working environment. On the other hand, more weight should be given to acts committed by a serial harasser if the plaintiff knows that the same individual committed offending acts in the past. This is because a serial harasser left free to harass again leaves the impression that acts of harassment are tolerated at the workplace and supports a plaintiff's claim that the workplace is both objectively and subjectively hostile.

Id. at 336-37. *See also Ziskie v. Mineta*, 547 F.3d 220 (4th Cir. 2008) (district court erred in refusing to consider affidavits of plaintiff's female co-workers regarding harassment merely because it was not experienced firsthand by plaintiff; evidence that her co-workers experienced treatment similar to that claimed by the plaintiff could lend credence to her mistreatment claims, show the harassment was pervasive, or support a finding that she was treated poorly by co-workers because of her sex, and not some other reason).

9. *Harassment in Splitsville.* The recurring problem of consensual relationships gone bad has troubled harassment law. Even if welcomeness is, generally speaking, not a viable defense separate and apart from the *Harris* requirements, there is one situation where it might arise — where a consensual relationship goes bad. Although firing one's former lover seems analytically indistinguishable from discharging a person who will not have sex with the harasser in the first place, some courts have been more ambivalent about this scenario. *Compare Pipkins v. Temple Terrace*, 267 F.3d 1197, 1201 (11th Cir. 2001) (stating that, construing plaintiff's allegations in the light most favorable to her, "she merely portrays any action by Klein to have been taken because of his disappointment in their failed relationship. Again, such a motivation is not 'because of . . . sex.'") *with Green v. Adm'rs of the Tulane Educ. Fund*, 284 F.3d 642, 657 (5th Cir. 2002) ("[I]t was only after the relationship ended that Richardson began to harass her. This fact alone supports a jury's inference that he harassed her because she refused to continue to have a casual sexual relationship with him. As such, we conclude that there was sufficient evidence to support the jury's finding of sexual harassment."). *See also Forrest v. Brinker Int'l Payroll Co., LP*, 511 F.3d 225, 229 (1st Cir. 2007) ("In cases involving a prior failed relationship between an accused harasser and alleged victim, reasoning that the harassment could not have been motivated by the victim's sex because it was instead motivated by a romantic relationship gone sour establishes a false dichotomy. Presumably the prior relationship would never have occurred if the victim were not a member of the sex preferred by the harasser, and thus the victim's sex is inextricably linked to the harasser's decision to harass.").

Believe it or not, some management attorneys recommend a "love contract" for couples entering consensual relationships. Sharon Rabin-Margalioth, *Love at Work*,

13 Duke J. Gender L. & Pol'y 237, 253 n.98 (2006), writes that a typical love contract will be written something like this:

> We hereby notify the Company that we wish to enter into a voluntary and mutual consensual social relationship. In entering into this relationship, we both understand and agree that we are both free to end the social relationship at any time. Should the social relationship end, we both agree that we shall not allow the breakup to negatively impact the performance of our duties. Prior to signing this Consensual Relationship Contract, we received and reviewed the Company Sexual Harassment Policy, a copy of which is attached hereto. By signing below, we acknowledge that the social relationship between us does not violate the Company's Sexual Harassment Policy, and that entering into the social relationship has not been made a condition or term of employment.

See also Vicki Schultz, *The Sanitized Workplace*, 112 Yale L.J. 2061, 2126-28 (2003). Do you think this would exonerate an employer of liability? Might it create other problems even if it did?

10. *Harassment Meets the First Amendment.* Hostile environment sexual harassment liability frequently is based on sexually offensive, obscene, or denigrating speech. Some harassment cases, however, have involved speech that is not sexually explicit and more clearly political in nature. An individual is free to get on a soap box and argue that women belong in the kitchen, not the workplace. Can that same individual bring his soapbox into the workplace and argue the same thing there? *See Lipsett v. University of Puerto Rico*, 864 F.2d 881, 903-4 (1st Cir. 1988) (female resident stated a Title VII claim by alleging that she was subjected to comments that women should not be surgeons). Is harassment law limited by the First Amendment? *See* David Bernstein, You Can't Say That!: The Growing Threat to Civil Liberties from Antidiscrimination Laws (2003); Miranda Oshige McGowan, *Certain Illusions About Speech: Why the Free-Speech Critique of Hostile Work Environment Harassment Is Wrong*, 19 Const. Comment. 391 (2002); Helen L. Norton, *You Can't Ask (or Say) That: The First Amendment Implications of Civil Rights Restrictions on Decisionmaker Speech*, 11 Wm. & Mary Bill Rts. J. 727, 729, 777 (2003); Eugene Volokh, *What Speech Does "Hostile Work Environment" Harassment Law Restrict?*, 85 Geo. L.J. 627 (1997); Kingsley R. Browne, *Zero Tolerance for the First Amendment: Title VII's Regulation of Employee Speech*, 27 Ohio N.U. L. Rev. 563 (2001); Charles R. Calleros, *Title VII and the First Amendment: Content-Neutral Regulation, Disparate Impact, and the "Reasonable Person,"* 58 Ohio St. L.J. 1217 (1997); Cynthia L. Estlund, *Freedom of Expression in the Workplace and the Problem of Discriminatory Harassment*, 75 Tex. L. Rev. 687 (1997).

Despite the outpouring of scholarship on the subject, few cases have raised First Amendment problems with such suits, and the Supreme Court has, in dicta in *R.A.V. v. City of St. Paul, Minnesota*, 505 U.S. 377 (1992), suggested that there is no free speech concern:

> [S]ince words can in some circumstances violate laws directed not against speech but against conduct (a law against treason, for example, is violated by telling the enemy the nation's defense secrets), a particular content-based subcategory of a proscribable class of speech can be swept up incidentally within the reach of a statute directed at conduct rather than speech. Thus, for example, sexually derogatory "fighting words," among other words, may produce a violation of Title VII's general prohibition against sexual discrimination in employment practices, 42 U.S.C. §2000e-2;

29 C.F.R. § 1604.11 (1991). *See also* 18 U.S.C. § 242; 42 U.S.C. §§ 1981, 1982. Where the government does not target conduct on the basis of its expressive content, acts are not shielded from regulation merely because they express a discriminatory idea or philosophy.

R.A.V., 505 U.S. at 389. Since *R.A.V.*, the Court decided *Harris* in which the sexually harassing behavior was primarily evidenced by offensive remarks. Although the constitutionality of imposing liability on the employer for those remarks was raised in briefs submitted in that case, the Court did not address the issue in its opinion. Does the dictum in *R.A.V.* explain why Hardy's statements in *Harris* are not protected?

11. *Constructive Discharge.* In many harassment cases, the plaintiff, unable to resolve the matter internally, quits. That was true, for example, in *Harris*. Assuming the sexual harassment was actionable, and the employer liable, can such a plaintiff recover for lost future earnings, or is she limited to the emotional distress caused by the harassment during the time she was employed? The question is one of "constructive discharge," that is, situations in which an employee's formal quitting is viewed as equivalent to being fired. The Supreme Court has held that the fact that harassment is sufficiently severe or pervasive to contaminate the work environment and thus be actionable is not necessarily sufficient to establish a constructive discharge. *Pennsylvania State Police v. Suders*, 542 U.S. 129 (2004), held that "A hostile-environment constructive discharge claim entails something more: A plaintiff who advances such a compound claim must show working conditions so intolerable that a reasonable person would have felt compelled to resign." Had Ingram quit, would he have been constructively discharged?

12. *Employer Liability.* Conduct by a supervisor, co-worker, or even customer may be harassment without making the employer liable for such conduct. In *Sunbelt* itself, the court, having found a triable claim of harassment, still had to go on to decide whether the employer was liable for such conduct. Because they are part and parcel of more general employer efforts to comply with the law and reduce legal exposure, issues of employer liability are treated in Chapter 13 on risk management.

Note on Grooming and Dress Codes

Perhaps the most blatant remaining form of gender discrimination in employment is employer dress and grooming codes, which frequently have disparate standards for males and females. How can such standards survive Title VII's prohibition of gender discrimination? In *Willingham v. Macon Telegraph Publ'g Co.*, 507 F.2d 1084, 1091-92 (5th Cir. 1975) (en banc), the Fifth Circuit denied a man's challenge to an employer's rule prohibiting male (but not female) employees from having hair longer than shoulder length:

Equal employment *opportunity* may be secured only when employers are barred from discriminating against employees on the basis of immutable characteristics, such as race and national origin. Similarly, an employer cannot have one hiring policy for men and another for women *if* the distinction is based on some fundamental right. But a hiring policy that distinguishes on some other ground, such as grooming codes or length of hair, is related more closely to the employer's choice of how to run his business than to equality of employment opportunity. . . . [A] line must be drawn between distinctions grounded on such fundamental rights as the right to have children or to marry and those interfering with the manner in which an employer exercises his judgment as to the way to operate a business. Hair length is not immutable and in the situation of employer vis à vis employee enjoys no constitutional protection. If the employee objects to the grooming code he has the right to reject it by looking elsewhere for employment, or alternatively he may choose to subordinate his preference by accepting the code along with the job. . . .

We adopt the view, therefore, that distinctions in employment practices between men and women on the basis of something other than immutable or protected characteristics do not inhibit employment *opportunity* in violation of Sec. 703(a). Congress sought only to give all persons equal access to the job market, not to limit an employer's right to exercise his informed judgment as to how best to run his shop.

We are in accord also with the alternative ground. . . . "From all that appears, equal job opportunities are available to both sexes. It does not appear that defendant fails to impose grooming standards for female employees; thus in this respect each sex is treated equally."

Willingham has received general acceptance: gender-specific differences in dress and grooming codes do not per se violate Title VII. *See, e.g., Harper v. Blockbuster Entm't Corp.*, 139 F.3d 1385 (11th Cir. 1998) (different hair length standards for men and women do not violate Title VII); *Tavora v. New York Mercantile Exch.*, 101 F.3d 907 (2d Cir. 1997) (same).

No one seems to doubt that permitting female, but not male, employees to have shoulder-length hair is sex discrimination in an analytic sense. What, then, is the justification for permitting it? Does *Willingham* establish a de minimis test under which trivial sex distinctions do not warrant federal court intervention? That would explain the court's distinction between cases involving hair length and cases involving "fundamental rights," a concept that seems to have been borrowed from equal protection doctrine. Remember, also, that some courts have required different treatment to have material adverse effects in order to constitute discrimination. Maybe hair length requirements are not material. Or is *Willingham* an example of a "volition" exception to Title VII: Employer requirements that can easily be met by an employee are not within the statutory proscription?

Declining protection because the different treatment is trivial is consistent with the courts' treatment of sexual harassment that is not sufficiently serious or pervasive to create a hostile environment. But even a minor incident of sexual harassment becomes actionable as a quid pro quo case when job benefits are contingent on acceptance of the discriminatory remarks or conduct. What if an employee is threatened with the loss of his job on the ground that his hair is too long? How can this be viewed as trivial? Recently, a dress question made the headlines when a former Citigroup business banking officer sued the company because she claims she was fired her for being "too hot." Her supervisors told her she must refrain from wearing turtleneck tops, pencil skirts, high-heeled shoes, and fitted business suits. Although other females were permitted to wear such items, this attire on her allegedly made her "too distracting" to her supervisors. Dareh Gregorian, *Woman Says She Was Fired from Citibank for Being Too Hot*, N.Y. POST, June 3, 2010, *available at* http://www.nypost.com/p/news/local/manhattan/too_S00LEBs0JUIl9OhB6xTBVI. If her allegations are true, does she have a claim? Could the employer's actions also be defended as reasonable steps to prevent harassment?

Many commentators look on grooming cases as sui generis, that is, that they shouldn't be read to have much meaning beyond the context in which they arise, perhaps because the issues they address are perceived by many to be insignificant.

But don't these cases reflect stereotypes so ingrained that they are not even recognized as such? *See* Karl E. Klare, *Power/Dressing: Regulation of Employee Appearance*, 26 New Eng. L. Rev. 1395 (1992). Why is it that an employer can legally prohibit males from wearing dresses or eye shadow? Is it because there is something wrong with males assuming "female" roles? Is a man wrong to assume such roles in turn because females are inferior and a man demeans himself by aping them? Is it merely coincidence that society looks more favorably on women who appropriate "male" attire (e.g., the pants suit) than the other way around? Or perhaps the courts are simply applying what they perceive as legislative intent: Whatever Congress *said*, it did not *mean* to bar this kind of employer rule. Isn't it clear that the 1964 Congress did not intend Title VII to require a unisex dress code?

Several decisions have found Title VII violated when the employer's dress code did not treat women equally. In *Carroll v. Talman Federal Savings & Loan Ass'n*, 604 F.2d 1028 (7th Cir. 1979), the court considered a dress code allowing males to wear "customary business attire" but requiring women to wear uniforms. Although disclaiming any intent to pass on the reasonableness of general employer dress regulations, the court distinguished the case before it where the disparate treatment was demeaning to women: "While there is nothing offensive about uniforms per se, when some employees are uniformed and others not there is a natural tendency to assume that the uniformed women have a lesser professional status than their male colleagues attired in normal business clothes." *Id*. at 1033. *See also Frank v. United Air Lines*, 216 F.3d 845 (9th Cir. 2000) (an airline's differential weight standards for flight attendants were facially discriminatory because they imposed unequal burdens on men and women in how they were calculated). Expectations that there would be a sea change in this area were, however, dashed by *Jespersen v. Harrah's Operating Co.*, 444 F.3d 1104 (9th Cir. 2006) (7-4), which rejected a claim that sex-differentiated grooming policies were illegal because they placed an unequal burden on women.

The issue of appearance restrictions, whether framed as a discrimination issue or as a matter of personal autonomy has generated considerable attention in the law reviews. The *Duke Journal of Gender & Law* devoted an entire symposium issue to it in 2007. *See also* Angela Onwuachi-Willig, *Another Hair Piece: Exploring New Strands of Analysis Under Title VII*, 98 Geo. L. J. 1079 (2010); Devon Carbado, Mitu Gulati & Gowri Ramachandran, The Story of Jespersen v. Harrah's: Makeup and Women at Work in Employment Discrimination Stories (Joel Wm. Friedman ed., 2006); Gowri Ramachandran, *Intersectionality as "Catch 22": Why Identity Performance Demands Are Neither Harmless Nor Reasonable*, 69 Alb. L. Rev. 299, 303 (2005); Catherine L. Fisk, *Privacy, Power, and Humiliation at Work: Re-Examining Appearance Regulation as an Invasion of Privacy*, 66 La. L. Rev. 1111 (2006).

PROBLEM

9-4. You work as an employment lawyer. A young woman has come to see you seeking advice. She tells you that she works at a nearby mid-sized law firm. She is a relatively young associate, and this is her first job after her clerkship. She tells you she made a "big mistake" by getting "involved" with a partner at the firm. While she does not work in his practice group, she is sometimes assigned out to work with that group, which is how she got to know him. From her point of view, the relationship "didn't work out" and "wasn't that big a deal." However, she is beginning to be concerned that it's a much bigger deal for him.

She broke up with him two weeks ago, sending him an e-mail from her G-mail account, telling him the usual stuff. He responded with a series of three e-mails ranging from confused to hurt to angry. His last e-mail stated, "You'll be sorry about this. We had a very good thing going." (If you want to see all the e-mails, log on to the casebook website and follow the instructions.) He has not since communicated with her directly, but he snubs her when they meet in the halls, and she has heard from a senior associate that "Joe's badmouthing you with the partners big-time."

Your client will not be considered for partner for several years, but her annual review was last week, and she received a 7 (out of a scale of 10). In last year's annual review, she was rated an 8.5. The reviewing partner, who is in charge of her group, told her, "Don't worry about it, I'm sure you'll bounce back and there's no impact on salary or bonus." But she did not find her explanations for the slippage very satisfactory.

How would you advise her?

Note on Sexual Orientation Discrimination

Sexual orientation is not listed as a protected characteristic under Title VII, and discrimination on the basis of sexual orientation per se is not actionable under federal law. Although it is easy to frame sexual orientation discrimination as simple disparate treatment (a male, say, is discriminated against for engaging in conduct — sexual relations with males — that would not be a problem were he female), courts have not been willing to read Title VII to reach this result. *See, e.g., DeSantis v. Pac. Telephone & Telegraph Co.* 608 F.2d 327 (9th Cir. 1979); *see generally* Mary Anne C. Case, *Disaggregating Gender from Sex and Sexual Orientation: The Effeminate Man in the Law and Feminist Jurisprudence*, 105 YALE L. J. 1, 2-3 (1995).

It is possible, however, to frame discrimination on the basis of sexual orientation as a problem of gender stereotyping. Similar arguments can be made with respect to transgender or transsexual individuals. Early cases, however, rejected such a theory. *See, e.g., Smith v. Liberty Mutual Ins. Co.*, 569 F.2d 325 (5th Cir. 1978) (finding discrimination against a male on the basis of his perceived "effeminacy" not within the statute); *DeSantis* (finding that male could be legally fired for being effeminate, even if he was not gay). However, the authority of such cases was radically undercut by *Price Waterhouse v. Hopkins* (reproduced at page 542), which held it impermissible to discriminate against a woman because she is too masculine. It would seem that discrimination against a male for "effeminancy" or other failures to conform to male stereotypes would also be impermissible, and some courts have so held. In *Nichols v. Azteca Restaurant Enterprises, Inc.*, 256 F.3d 864 (9th Cir. 2001), the court found plaintiff had stated a claim under Title VII when he alleged he was discriminated against for acting "too feminine." It said *Price Waterhouse* prohibits discrimination based on sex stereotyping and thus to the extent *DeSantis* conflicts with *Price Waterhouse*, it is no longer good law. *See also Prowel v. Wise Bus. Forms, Inc.*, 579 F.3d 285 (3d Cir. 2009) (although the plaintiff might have been subjected to harassment because of his sexual orientation per se, there was enough basis to suspect that the harassment was because of his failure to conform to gender stereotypes to warrant a trial). *But see Hamm v. Weyauwega Milk Prods.*, 332 F.3d 1058, 1068 (7th Cir. 2003) (Posner, J., concurring) (" 'Sex stereotyping' should not be regarded as a form of sex discrimination, though it will sometimes, as in the *Hopkins* case, be evidence of sex discrimination."). Is it a very long step to prohibit discrimination on the basis of sexual orientation—the most extreme way in which members of one sex demonstrate a characteristic usually associated with the other sex? *See generally* Zachary A. Kramer, *Heterosexuality and Title VII*, 103 Nw. U. L. Rev. 205, 227-30 (2009); L. Camille Hébert, *Transforming Transsexual and Transgender Rights*, 15 Wm. & Mary J. Women & L. 535 (2009).

The absence of a federal statute prohibiting discrimination on the basis of sexual orientation has led to a number of other legal theories attacking such conduct. In public employment, sexual orientation discrimination has been challenged on the basis of the right of privacy, due process, free speech, and equal protection. Until recently, these constitutional attacks had very limited success, but developments such as *Lawrence v. Texas*, 539 U.S. 558 (2003) (striking down Texas same-sex sodomy law) and *Romer v. Evans*, 517 U.S. 620 (1996) (striking down Colorado law as discriminating against gays) augur more success for such claims.

One significant setback for what Justice Scalia describes pejoratively as the "homosexual agenda," was *Boy Scouts of America v. Dale*, 530 U.S. 640 (2000), where the Court overturned a state court decision requiring the Boy Scouts to admit a gay scoutmaster under the state's law barring discrimination in public accommodations on the basis of sexual orientation. The Court held that so applying New Jersey's public accommodations law violated the Boy Scouts' "First Amendment right of expressive association." *Id.* at 644. Although *Dale* involved a state law relating to sexual orientation discrimination in public accommodations, some have warned that it might undercut antidiscrimination statutes like Title VII. *But see Rumsfeld v. Forum for Academic & Institutional Rights, Inc.*, 547 U.S. 47 (2006) (limiting the right of expressive association to situations where compliance with the at-issue law would indicate to the world that the association was endorsing a position).

Further, challenges based on state constitutions have also been successful. On the same day and in the same city where *DeSantis* was handed down, the Supreme Court of California decided *Gay Law Students Ass'n v. Pacific Telephone & Telegraph Co.*, 595 P.2d 592 (Cal. 1979), holding that homosexuals could sue a public utility for employment discrimination under the equal protection clause of the California Constitution. *See also Goodridge v. Dep't of Pub. Health*, 798 N.E.2d 941 (Mass. 2003) (holding the state could not "deny the protections, benefits, and obligations conferred by civil marriage to two individuals of the same sex who wish to marry"); *Witt v. Dep't of the Air Force*, 527 F.3d 806, 819 (9th Cir. 2008) (2-1) (in assessing a challenge to the military's Don't Ask, Don't Tell policy "when the government attempts to intrude upon the personal and private lives of homosexuals, in a manner that implicates the rights identified in *Lawrence*, the government must advance an important governmental interest, the intrusion must significantly further that interest, and the intrusion must be necessary to further that interest. In other words, for the third factor, a less intrusive means must be unlikely to achieve substantially the government's interest.").

More broadly, a number of states have enacted their own civil rights legislation expressly covering sexual orientation. Such statutes typically protect against discrimination on the basis of sexual orientation, normally defined as including heterosexuality, bisexuality, and homosexuality. For a comprehensive listing, see http://www.lambdalegal.org. *See generally* Roberta Achtenberg & Karen Moulding, Sexual

Orientation and the Law §§ 5.01-.07 (2008); Peter M. Cicchino, Bruce R. Deming & Katherine M. Nicholson, Note, *Sex, Lies and Civil Rights: A Critical History of the Massachusetts Gay Civil Rights Bill*, 26 HARV. C.R.-C.L. L. REV. 549, 556-57 (1991). While versions of an Employment Nondiscrimination Act ("ENDA") have been perennially introduced in Congress, it has yet to pass.

E. RETALIATION

In addition to prohibiting discrimination on the grounds of race, sex, religion, national origin, and age, Title VII, § 1981, and the ADEA create a remedy for certain retaliatory conduct. Retaliation is also prohibited by the ADA in somewhat different terms.

Section 704(a) of Title VII, 42 U.S.C. § 2000e-3(a), provides:

> It shall be an unlawful employment practice for an employer to discriminate against any of his employees or applicants for employment . . . because he has opposed any practice made an unlawful employment practice by this title, or because he has made a charge, testified, assisted, or participated in any manner in an investigation, proceeding, or hearing under this title.

The ADEA prohibits retaliation in substantially identical language. 29 U.S.C. § 623(d). Even though § 1981 does not expressly prohibit retaliation, it has been held to do so through its prohibition of discrimination on account of race. *CBOCS West, Inc. v. Humphries*, 553 U.S. 442 (2008); *see also Jackson v. Birmingham Bd. of Educ.*, 544 U.S. 167 (2005) (retaliation for opposing sex discrimination was sex discrimination within the meaning of Title IX).

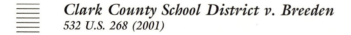

Clark County School District v. Breeden
532 U.S. 268 (2001)

PER CURIAM.

[Plaintiff sued her employer, the Clark County School District, alleging that the District had taken two separate adverse employment actions against her in response to two different protected activities in which she had engaged.]

On October 21, 1994, [Ms. Breeden's] male supervisor met with [her] and another male employee to review the psychological evaluation reports of four job applicants. The report for one of the applicants disclosed that the applicant had once commented to a co-worker, "I hear making love to you is like making love to the Grand Canyon." At the meeting [Ms. Breeden's] supervisor read the comment aloud, looked at [her] and stated, "I don't know what that means." The other employee then said, "Well, I'll tell you later," and both men chuckled. [Ms. Breeden] later complained about the comment to the offending employee, to Assistant Superintendent George Ann Rice, the employee's supervisor, and to another assistant superintendent of petitioner. Her first claim of retaliation asserts that she was punished for these complaints.

The Court of Appeals for the Ninth Circuit has applied § 2000e-3(a) to protect employee "opposition" not just to practices that are actually "made . . . unlawful" by Title VII, but also to practices that the employee could reasonably believe were unlawful. We have no occasion to rule on the propriety of this interpretation, because even assuming it is correct, no one could reasonably believe that the incident recounted above violated Title VII.

Title VII forbids actions taken on the basis of sex that "discriminate against any individual with respect to his compensation, terms, conditions, or privileges of employment." 42 U.S.C. § 2000e-2(a)(1). Just three Terms ago, we reiterated, what was plain from our previous decisions, that sexual harassment is actionable under Title VII only if it is "so 'severe or pervasive' as to 'alter the conditions of [the victim's] employment and create an abusive working environment.'" (Only harassing conduct that is "severe or pervasive" can produce a "constructive alteration in the terms or conditions of employment"); *Faragher v. Boca Raton*, 524 U.S. 775 (1998), quoting *Meritor*; *Oncale v. Sundowner Offshore Services, Inc.*, [reproduced at page 623] (Title VII "forbids only behavior so objectively offensive as to alter the 'conditions' of the victim's employment"). Workplace conduct is not measured in isolation; instead, "whether an environment is sufficiently hostile or abusive" must be judged "by 'looking at all the circumstances,' including the 'frequency of the discriminatory conduct; its severity; whether it is physically threatening or humiliating, or a mere offensive utterance; and whether it unreasonably interferes with an employee's work performance.'" *Faragher v. Boca Raton* (quoting *Harris*). Hence, "[a] recurring point in [our] opinions is that simple teasing, offhand comments, and isolated incidents (unless extremely serious) will not amount to discriminatory changes in the 'terms and conditions of employment.'" *Faragher v. Boca Raton*.

No reasonable person could have believed that the single incident recounted above violated Title VII's standard. The ordinary terms and conditions of [Ms. Breeden's] job required her to review the sexually explicit statement in the course of screening job applicants. Her co-workers who participated in the hiring process were subject to the same requirement, and indeed, in the District Court [she] "conceded that it did not bother or upset her" to read the statement in the file. Her supervisor's comment, made at a meeting to review the application, that he did not know what the statement meant; her co-worker's responding comment; and the chuckling of both are at worst an "isolated incident" that cannot remotely be considered "extremely serious," as our cases require, *Faragher v. Boca Raton*. The holding of the Court of Appeals to the contrary must be reversed.

Besides claiming that she was punished for complaining to [the School District's] personnel about the alleged sexual harassment, [Ms. Breeden] also claimed that she was punished for filing charges against petitioner with the Nevada Equal Rights Commission and the Equal Employment Opportunity Commission (EEOC) and for filing the present suit. [She] filed her lawsuit on April 1, 1997; on April 10, 1997, [her] supervisor, Assistant Superintendent Rice, "mentioned to Allin Chandler, Executive Director of plaintiff's union, that she was contemplating transferring plaintiff to the position of Director of Professional Development Education"; and this transfer was "carried through" in May. In order to show, as her defense against summary judgment required, the existence of a causal connection between her protected activities and the transfer, [Ms. Breeden] "relied wholly on the temporal proximity of the filing of her complaint on April 1, 1997 and Rice's statement to plaintiff's union representative on April 10, 1997 that she was considering transferring plaintiff to the

[new] position." The District Court, however, found that [Ms. Breeden] did not serve [the School District] with the summons and complaint until April 11, 1997, one day after Rice had made the statement, and Rice filed an affidavit stating that she did not become aware of the lawsuit until after April 11, a claim that [Ms. Breeden] did not challenge. Hence, the court concluded, [she] "had not shown that any causal connection exists between her protected activities and the adverse employment decision."

The Court of Appeals reversed, relying on two facts: The EEOC had issued a right-to-sue letter to [Ms. Breeden] three months before Rice announced she was contemplating the transfer, and the actual transfer occurred one month after Rice learned of [her] suit. The latter fact is immaterial in light of the fact that [the School District] concededly was contemplating the transfer before it learned of the suit. Employers need not suspend previously planned transfers upon discovering that a Title VII suit has been filed, and their proceeding along lines previously contemplated, though not yet definitively determined, is no evidence whatever of causality.

As for the right-to-sue letter: [Ms. Breeden] did not rely on that letter in the District Court and did not mention it in her opening brief on appeal. Her demonstration of causality all along had rested upon the connection between the transfer and the filing of her lawsuit — to which connection the letter was irrelevant. When, however, [the School District] answering brief in the Court of Appeals demonstrated conclusively the lack of causation between the filing of [Ms. Breeden's] lawsuit and Rice's decision, [she] mentioned the letter for the first time in her reply brief. The Ninth Circuit's opinion . . . suggests that the letter provided [the School District] with its first notice of [her] charge before the EEOC, and hence allowed the inference that the transfer proposal made three months later was [its] reaction to the charge. This will not do.

First, there is no indication that Rice even knew about the right-to-sue letter when she proposed transferring respondent. And second, if one presumes she knew about it, one must also presume that she (or her predecessor) knew *almost two years earlier* about the protected action (filing of the EEOC complaint) that the letter supposedly disclosed. . . . The cases that accept mere temporal proximity between an employer's knowledge of protected activity and an adverse employment action as sufficient evidence of causality to establish a prima facie case uniformly hold that the temporal proximity must be "very close," *Neal v. Ferguson Constr. Co.*, 237 F.3d 1248, 1253 (CA10 2001). *See, e.g., Richmond v. Oneok, Inc.*, 120 F.3d 205, 209 (CA10 1997) (3-month period insufficient); *Hughes v. Derwinski*, 967 F.2d 1168, 1174-1175 (CA7 1992) (4-month period insufficient). Action taken (as here) 20 months later suggests, by itself, no causality at all. . . .

NOTES

1. *Public Policy Tort.* Recall the public policy discussion in Chapter 4. Retaliation under the antidiscrimination statutes is simply a version of the rule that an employee cannot be discharged in violation of public policy. However, as will be explained in these Notes, the doctrine has developed under the antidiscrimination laws in sometimes more elaborate but not always intuitive ways.

2. *Prima Facie Case of Retaliation.* A standard formulation of the prima facie case for retaliation is found in *Shelton v. Trs. of Columbia University*, 369 F. App'x 200, 201 (2d Cir. 2010): the plaintiff must show that "(1) he was engaged in a protected activity, (2) the institution was aware of that activity, (3) he suffered an adverse action, and (4) there was a causal connection between the protected activity and the adverse action." If plaintiff is able to establish such a case, the burden of production shifts to the employer to put into evidence a nonretaliatory reason for its action. At that point, the plaintiff may still prevail by proving that reason is a pretext for retaliation. *Jute v. Hamilton Sundstrand Corp.*, 420 F.3d 166, 179 (2d Cir. 2005). At issue in *Breeden* were the first and third prongs.

3. *Opposition and Participation.* Shirley Breeden presented two distinct claims of protected conduct. One was for opposition conduct (her internal complaints), while the other was for participation conduct (her filing of charges to the state agency and the EEOC). Many courts and commentators perceive a sharp distinction between the protections of the "opposition" clause and the "participation" clause. While a plaintiff invoking the opposition clause must demonstrate a reasonable, good faith belief that the conduct complained of is unlawful, the participation clause may protect conduct without regard to its basis. One of the first "participation" cases, *Pettway v. American Cast Iron Pipe Co.*, 411 F.2d 998 (5th Cir. 1969), set the tone for these decisions by finding actionable retaliation when a worker was fired for filing an allegedly false and malicious charge with the EEOC — namely, that the employer had bought off an EEOC investigator. The court wrote: The purpose of §704(a) "is to protect the employee who utilizes the tools provided by Congress to protect his rights. The Act will be frustrated if the employer may unilaterally determine the truth or falsity of charges and take independent action." *Id.* at 1004-5; *see also Glover v. S. Carolina Law Enf.*, 170 F.3d 411 (4th Cir. 1999) (unreasonable deposition testimony protected by participation clause). *But see Fine v. Ryan Int'l* 305 F.3d 746 (7th Cir. 2002) (improper to retaliate against employee for filing lawsuit that was based on reasonable, good faith belief; improper to retaliate unless claim is "completely groundless").

After the *Breeden* Court disposed of the plaintiff's "opposition clause" claim by deciding that no reasonable person could believe that she had been sexually harassed, it went on to consider the causation issue on her "participation" clause claim. It would have had no need to do so if filing of an "unreasonable" charge was unprotected. Does *Breeden* thus confirm the lower courts that have held that the participation clause prohibits retaliation even where the underlying discrimination claim lacks a reasonable basis? Would even a charge filed in bad faith be protected? *See* Lawrence D. Rosenthal, *Reading Too Much into What the Court Doesn't Write: How Some Federal Courts Have Limited Title VII's Participation Clause's Protections After* Clark County School District v. Breeden, 83 WASH. L. REV. 345 (2008) (arguing that some courts are incorrectly applying the reasonable belief standard to participating clause claims).

4. *Reasonable Belief.* While the reasonableness of a plaintiff's belief in the illegality of the challenged conduct may be irrelevant for participation, that does not seem to be true where opposition is at stake. *Breeden* assumed, but did not decide, that the opposition clause's protections attach if the challenged practice is not in fact unlawful. In other words, a reasonable, good faith belief that the employer has acted unlawfully may or may not suffice under the opposition clause. While the statutory language supports limiting the statute's protections only to opposition to conduct that is in fact unlawful, would such an interpretation be consistent with the policy objectives of §704? *See Robinson v. Shell Oil*, 519 U.S. 337 (1997) (the policy of §704 furthered by including former employees within the protections of the statute). Assuming a reasonable, good faith belief is necessary, there are certain to be problems as to when an employee's perceptions are reasonable. *See* Terry Smith, *Everyday Indignities: Race,*

Retaliation, and the Promise of Title VII, 34 COLUM. HUM. RTS. L. REV. 529 (2003) (criticizing judicial reactions to opposition to "subtle discrimination"). *See also* B. Glenn George, *Revenge*, 83 TUL. L. REV. 439 (2008); Deborah L. Brake & Joanna L. Grossman, *The Failure of Title VII as a Rights Claiming System*, 86 N.C. L. REV. 859 (2008); Lawrence D. Rosenthal, *To Report or Not to Report: The Case for Elim-inating the Objectively Reasonable Requirement for Opposition Activities Under Title VII's Anti-Retaliation Provision*, 39 ARIZ. ST. L.J. 1127 (2007).

5. *Temporal Proximity.* Assuming protected conduct, the plaintiff must still show an adverse action and a causal link between the protected conduct and the adverse action. Does *Breeden* mean that the plaintiff always loses on summary judgment where the employer has denied retaliation and the only evidence of causation is that the adverse employment action occurred three months or more after the decision maker learned of the protected activity? What if the decision maker began contem-plating such action within three months of learning of the protected activity? *See Franzoni v. Hartmarx Corp.*, 300 F.3d 767 (7th Cir. 2002) (six-month time lapse between charge of discrimination and termination, standing alone, insufficient proof of causation). *But see Pinkerton v. Colorado Dept. of Transp.*, 563 F.3d 1052 (10th Cir. 2009) (termination within a few days of verification of the complaint plain-tiff filed with employer, together with evidence that employer's reasons for firing plaintiff may not have been credible, held sufficient); *Mickey v. Zeidler Tool & Die Co.*, 516 F.3d 516 (6th Cir. 2008) (termination the day employer received notice of EEOC charge sufficed).

6. *Balancing Opposition and Employer Interests.* Opposition conduct may be less protected than participation conduct in another way. Where participation is concerned, the courts have not been sympathetic to countervailing employer interests. For example, courts have found employers guilty of unlawful retaliation when they treat differently an employee who files a discrimination charge, even if the employer's action seems justified from a business perspective. *See, e.g., EEOC v. Bd. of Governors of State Colls. and Univs.*, 957 F.2d 424 (7th Cir. 1992) (invalidating a collective bar-gaining agreement provision terminating grievance proceedings when a lawsuit is filed). *But see Richardson v. Comm'n on Human Rights & Opportunities*, 532 F.3d 114 (2d Cir. 2008) (election-of-remedies provision in a collective bargaining agree-ment, which provided that employee alleging discrimination may not arbitrate a dis-pute as a grievance if she filed a charge did not violate Title VII when the employee remained free to file a charge with the EEOC and pursue an action in federal court). That the employer is invoking a neutral rule that would have been applied to employ-ees engaging in other forms of litigation does not mean those rules may be applied to persons who have engaged in participation activities under employment discrimination statutes. In a sense, §704's participation clause entitles plaintiffs to special treatment.

But what about the opposition clause? Can the form the employee's opposition takes remove her from the protections of the Act? As should be obvious from *McDonnell Douglas Corp. v. Green*, reproduced at page 517, the answer is yes. Recall that Green had engaged in a "stall in" to protest alleged discrimination by the company, and the company had asserted his participation in those activities as the explanation for why Green was not rehired. Although *McDonnell Douglas* did not directly rule on §704(a), as that claim was not before the Court, it wrote, in language broad enough to embrace §704(a): "Nothing in Title VII compels an employer to absolve and rehire one who has engaged in such deliberate, unlawful activity against it." *McDonnell Douglas*, 411 U.S. at 803. How far does *McDonnell Douglas* go in allowing an employer to discriminate because of the nature or form of an employee's "opposition"? Is it merely a "law and order" decision in that it permits retaliation where the opposition violates criminal statutes, or can it be read more broadly?

Rather than establishing a "disloyalty" bright line, the lower courts may be employing a balancing test in this area. *See, e.g, Niswander v. Cincinnati Ins. Co.*, 529 F.3d 714, 722 (6th Cir. 2008) (plaintiff's turning over confidential employment documents to her attorney was not protected under the participation clause when the documents were irrelevant to her claim); *Vaughn v. Epworth Villa*, 537 F.3d 1147 (10th Cir. 2008) (plaintiff engaged in protected conduct when she submitted unredacted medical records to the EEOC to support her charge, but employer could terminate her for this conduct when other employees engaging in similar conduct unrelated to a charge of discrimination would also have been terminated); *Argyropoulos v. City of Alton*, 539 F.3d 724 (7th Cir. 2008) (employee who secretly recorded meeting with supervisors not protected). If so, what goes on the scales? *See Cruz v. Coach Stores, Inc.*, 202 F.3d 560 (2d Cir. 2000) (slapping co-worker in response to sexual harassment not a protected activity, certainly when other options were available to plaintiff); *Douglas v. DynMcDermott Petro. Oper. Co.*, 144 F.3d 364 (5th Cir. 1998) (unethical disclosure by attorney justified discharge even if that conduct was in opposition to discrimination). What if the employee is a high-level affirmative action official? *Johnson v. Univ. of Cincinnati*, 215 F.3d 561 (6th Cir. 2000) (Title VII protects VP for Human Resources advocating on behalf of women and minorities). Is the validity of the allegation or the employer's reaction a factor? What about the extent of any resulting disruption? *See Robbins v. Jefferson Cty. Sch. Dist.*, 186 F.3d 1253 (10th Cir. 1999). Could even substantial disruption be outweighed by employer provocation? Should the court consider whether the plaintiff was more disruptive than necessary or whether the plaintiff had ulterior motivations?

7. *Distinguishing Opposition from Participation.* Because the opposition and participation clauses offer different degrees of protection, it is important to distinguish between the two. In *Crawford v. Metro Gov't of Nashville & Davidson Counties*, 129 S. Ct. 846 (2008), the Supreme Court held that an employee's involvement in an employer's internal investigation into possible harassment was protected under the opposition clause:

> "Oppose" goes beyond "active, consistent" behavior in ordinary discourse, where we would naturally use the word to speak of someone who has taken no action at all to advance a position beyond disclosing it. Countless people were known to "oppose" slavery before Emancipation, or are said to "oppose" capital punishment today, without writing public letters, taking to the streets, or resisting the government. And we would call it "opposition" if an employee took a stand against an employer's discriminatory practices not by "instigating" action, but by standing pat, say, by refusing to follow a supervisor's order to fire a junior worker for discriminatory reasons. There is, then, no reason to doubt that a person can "oppose" by responding to someone else's question just as surely as by provoking the discussion, and nothing in the statute requires a freakish rule protecting an employee who reports discrimination on her own initiative but not one who reports the same discrimination in the same words when her boss asks a question.

129 S. Ct. at 852 (citation omitted). The *Crawford* Court did not reach the question of whether it was also protected under the participation clause. The result was to assure a minimum level of protection but leave open whether the employee reasonably believed that the conduct she reported was harassment. Suppose she didn't.

For example, suppose she just answered her employer's question without even thinking about whether the conduct was illegal. If that's not opposition, might it still be "participation," or does the statute require at least a formal charge or suit by somebody?

8. *Expanding Protection Against Retaliation. Crawford* expanded protection against retaliation. But it is not the only case that has done so. In two other recent decisions, the Court has held that the antidiscrimination provisions of 42 U.S.C. § 1981, *CBOS West, Inc. v Humphries*, 553 U.S. 442 (2008), and the federal employee sections of Title VII, *Gomez-Perez v. Potter*, 553 U.S. 474 (2008), implicitly bar retaliation. *See generally* Michael J. Zimmer, *A Pro-Employee Supreme Court?: The Retaliation Decisions*, 60 S.C. L. Rev. 917 (2009). Other commentators have argued for greater reliance on state antiretaliation provisions to correct holes in federal protection. Alex B. Long, *Viva State Employment Law! State Law Retaliation Claims in a Post-Crawford/Burlington* Northern *World*, 77 Tenn. L. Rev. 253, 257 (2010).

9. *Third-party Retaliation*: The Sixth Circuit recently held that Title VII does not bar third-party retaliation, that is, situations where the individual alleging retaliation did not personally engage in any protected activity. In *Thompson v. North Am. Stainless, LP*, 567 F.3d 804 (6th Cir. 2009), *cert. granted*, 130 S. Ct. 3542 (2010), the plaintiff was terminated after his fiancé, a co-worker, filed a sex discrimination claim with the EEOC. *See generally* Alex B. Long, *The Troublemaker's Friend: Retaliation Against Third Parties and the Right of Association in the Workplace*, 59 Fla. L. Rev. 931 (2007) (asserting that employees often suffer for associating with "troublemaking" employees; one goal of the antiretaliation statutes should be to encourage employees to continue to associate with each other).

≡
≡ *Burlington Northern & Santa Fe Ry. Co. v. White*
≡ *548 U.S. 53 (2006)*

Breyer, J.

Title VII of the Civil Rights Act of 1964 forbids employment discrimination against "any individual" based on that individual's "race, color, religion, sex, or national origin." A separate section of the Act — its anti-retaliation provision — forbids an employer from "discriminating against" an employee or job applicant because that individual "opposed any practice" made unlawful by Title VII or "made a charge, testified, assisted, or participated in" a Title VII proceeding or investigation. . . .

We conclude that the anti-retaliation provision does not confine the actions and harms it forbids to those that are related to employment or occur at the workplace. We also conclude that the provision covers those (and only those) employer actions that would have been materially adverse to a reasonable employee or job applicant. In the present context that means that the employer's actions must be harmful to the point that they could well dissuade a reasonable worker from making or supporting a charge of discrimination.

[Shortly after Sheila White, the only woman working in her department at the Railroad's Tennessee yard, complained of harassment by her supervisor, she was reassigned from her position operating a forklift to a track laborer job, a more physically demanding and dirtier job. The pay and benefits, however, were the same. After White filed a charge of discrimination with the EEOC, she was suspended without pay for 37 days, a suspension that would have become a termination had she not filed a grievance. The company contended White had been suspended because she was insubordinate.

White did grieve her suspension, and the hearing officer found she had not been insubordinate and ordered her reinstated with backpay. White filed suit, alleging that the change in her job responsibilities and her suspension constituted actionable retaliation under Title VII. A jury agreed with White. The Sixth Circuit, en banc, affirmed the judgment in White's favor.]

II

Title VII's anti-retaliation provision forbids employer actions that "discriminate against" an employee (or job applicant) because he has "opposed" a practice that Title VII forbids or has "made a charge, testified, assisted, or participated in" a Title VII "investigation, proceeding, or hearing." No one doubts that the term "discriminate against" refers to distinctions or differences in treatment that injure protected individuals. *See Jackson v. Birmingham Bd. of Ed.*, 544 U.S. 167, 174 (2005); *Price Waterhouse v. Hopkins*, (plurality opinion); *see also* 4 OXFORD ENGLISH DICTIONARY 758 (2d ed. 1989) (def. 3b). But different Circuits have come to different conclusions about whether the challenged action has to be employment or workplace related and about how harmful that action must be to constitute retaliation. . . .

A

Petitioner and the Solicitor General both argue that the Sixth Circuit is correct to require a link between the challenged retaliatory action and the terms, conditions, or status of employment. They note that Title VII's substantive anti-discrimination provision protects an individual only from employment-related discrimination. They add that the anti-retaliation provision should be read *in pari materia* with the anti-discrimination provision. And they conclude that the employer actions prohibited by the anti-retaliation provision should similarly be limited to conduct that "affects the employee's 'compensation, terms, conditions, or privileges of employment.'"

We cannot agree. The language of the substantive provision differs from that of the anti-retaliation provision in important ways. Section 703(a) sets forth Title VII's core anti-discrimination provision in the following terms:

> It shall be an unlawful employment practice for an employer—
>
> (1) *to fail or refuse to hire or to discharge* any individual, or otherwise to discriminate against any individual *with respect to his compensation, terms, conditions, or privileges of employment*, because of such individual's race, color, religion, sex, or national origin; or
> (2) to limit, segregate, or classify his employees or applicants for employment in any way *which would deprive or tend to deprive any individual of employment opportunities or otherwise adversely affect his status as an employee*, because of such individual's race, color, religion, sex, or national origin. (emphasis added).

Section 704(a) sets forth Title VII's anti-retaliation provision in the following terms:

> It shall be an unlawful employment practice for an employer *to discriminate against* any of his employees or applicants for employment . . . because he has opposed any practice

made an unlawful employment practice by this subchapter, or because he has made a charge, testified, assisted, or participated in any manner in an investigation, proceeding, or hearing under this subchapter. (emphasis added).

The underscored words in the substantive provision — "hire," "discharge," "compensation, terms, conditions, or privileges of employment," "employment opportunities," and "status as an employee" — explicitly limit the scope of that provision to actions that affect employment or alter the conditions of the workplace. No such limiting words appear in the anti-retaliation provision. Given these linguistic differences, the question here is not whether identical or similar words should be read *in pari materia* to mean the same thing. Rather, the question is whether Congress intended its different words to make a legal difference. We normally presume that, where words differ as they differ here, " 'Congress acts intentionally and purposely in the disparate inclusion or exclusion.' " *Russello v. United States*, 464 U.S. 16, 23 (1983).

There is strong reason to believe that Congress intended the differences that its language suggests, for the two provisions differ not only in language but in purpose as well. The anti-discrimination provision seeks a workplace where individuals are not discriminated against because of their racial, ethnic, religious, or gender-based status. *See McDonnell Douglas Corp. v. Green*, [reproduced at page 517]. The anti-retaliation provision seeks to secure that primary objective by preventing an employer from interfering (through retaliation) with an employee's efforts to secure or advance enforcement of the Act's basic guarantees. The substantive provision seeks to prevent injury to individuals based on who they are, *i.e.*, their status. The anti-retaliation provision seeks to prevent harm to individuals based on what they do, *i.e.*, their conduct.

To secure the first objective, Congress did not need to prohibit anything other than employment-related discrimination. The substantive provision's basic objective of "equality of employment opportunities" and the elimination of practices that tend to bring about "stratified job environments," would be achieved were all employment-related discrimination miraculously eliminated.

But one cannot secure the second objective by focusing only upon employer actions and harm that concern employment and the workplace. Were all such actions and harms eliminated, the anti-retaliation provision's objective would *not* be achieved. An employer can effectively retaliate against an employee by taking actions not directly related to his employment or by causing him harm *outside* the workplace. *See, e.g., Rochon v. Gonzales*, 438 F.3d [1211, 1213 (CADC 2006)] (FBI retaliation against employee "took the form of the FBI's refusal, contrary to policy, to investigate death threats a federal prisoner made against [the agent] and his wife"); *Berry v. Stevinson Chevrolet*, 74 F.3d 980, 984, 986 (CA10 1996) (finding actionable retaliation where employer filed false criminal charges against former employee who complained about discrimination). A provision limited to employment-related actions would not deter the many forms that effective retaliation can take. Hence, such a limited construction would fail to fully achieve the anti-retaliation provision's "primary purpose," namely, "maintaining unfettered access to statutory remedial mechanisms." *Robinson v. Shell Oil Co.*, 519 U.S. 337 (1997).

Thus, purpose reinforces what language already indicates, namely, that the anti-retaliation provision, unlike the substantive provision, is not limited to discriminatory actions that affect the terms and conditions of employment. . . .

Finally, we do not accept the petitioner's and Solicitor General's view that it is "anomalous" to read the statute to provide broader protection for victims of retaliation than for those whom Title VII primarily seeks to protect, namely, victims of race-based, ethnic-based, religion-based, or gender-based discrimination. Congress has provided similar kinds of protection from retaliation in comparable statutes without any judicial suggestion that those provisions are limited to the conduct prohibited by the primary substantive provisions. [The Court cited several decisions under the National Labor Relations Act.]

In any event, as we have explained, differences in the purpose of the two provisions remove any perceived "anomaly," for they justify this difference of interpretation. Title VII depends for its enforcement upon the cooperation of employees who are willing to file complaints and act as witnesses. "Plainly, effective enforcement could thus only be expected if employees felt free to approach officials with their grievances." *Mitchell v. Robert DeMario Jewelry, Inc.*, 361 U.S. 288 (1960). Interpreting the anti-retaliation provision to provide broad protection from retaliation helps assure the cooperation upon which accomplishment of the Act's primary objective depends.

For these reasons, we conclude that Title VII's substantive provision and its anti-retaliation provision are not coterminous. The scope of the anti-retaliation provision extends beyond workplace-related or employment-related retaliatory acts and harm. We therefore reject the standards applied in the Courts of Appeals that have treated the anti-retaliation provision as forbidding the same conduct prohibited by the anti-discrimination provision and that have limited actionable retaliation to so-called "ultimate employment decisions."

B

The anti-retaliation provision protects an individual not from all retaliation, but from retaliation that produces an injury or harm. As we have explained, the Courts of Appeals have used differing language to describe the level of seriousness to which this harm must rise before it becomes actionable retaliation. We agree with the formulation set forth by the Seventh and the District of Columbia Circuits. In our view, a plaintiff must show that a reasonable employee would have found the challenged action materially adverse, "which in this context means it well might have 'dissuaded a reasonable worker from making or supporting a charge of discrimination.' " *Rochon.* We speak of *material* adversity because we believe it is important to separate significant from trivial harms. Title VII, we have said, does not set forth "a general civility code for the American workplace." *Oncale v. Sundowner Offshore Services, Inc.*, [reproduced at page 623]; see *Faragher* (judicial standards for sexual harassment must "filter out complaints attacking 'the ordinary tribulations of the workplace, such as the sporadic use of abusive language, gender-related jokes, and occasional teasing' "). An employee's decision to report discriminatory behavior cannot immunize that employee from those petty slights or minor annoyances that often take place at work and that all employees experience. *See* 1 B. LINDEMANN & P. GROSSMAN, EMPLOYMENT DISCRIMINATION LAW 669 (3d ed. 1996) (noting that "courts have held that personality conflicts at work that generate antipathy" and " 'snubbing' by supervisors and co-workers" are not actionable under §704(a)). The anti-retaliation provision seeks to prevent employer interference with "unfettered access" to Title VII's remedial mechanisms. *Robinson.* It does so by prohibiting employer actions that are likely "to deter victims of discrimination from complaining to the EEOC," the courts, and their employers. *Ibid.*

And normally petty slights, minor annoyances, and simple lack of good manners will not create such deterrence. *See* 2 EEOC 1998 MANUAL §8, p. 8-13.

We refer to reactions of a *reasonable* employee because we believe that the provision's standard for judging harm must be objective. An objective standard is judicially administrable. It avoids the uncertainties and unfair discrepancies that can plague a judicial effort to determine a plaintiff's unusual subjective feelings. We have emphasized the need for objective standards in other Title VII contexts, and those same concerns animate our decision here. *See, e.g., Pennsylvania State Police v. Suders,* 542 U.S. 129 (2004) (constructive discharge doctrine); *Harris v. Forklift Systems, Inc.* (hostile work environment doctrine).

We phrase the standard in general terms because the significance of any given act of retaliation will often depend upon the particular circumstances. Context matters. "The real social impact of workplace behavior often depends on a constellation of surrounding circumstances, expectations, and relationships which are not fully captured by a simple recitation of the words used or the physical acts performed." A schedule change in an employee's work schedule may make little difference to many workers, but may matter enormously to a young mother with school age children. *Cf., e.g., Washington* [*v. Ill. Dep't of Revenue,* 420 F.3d 658 (CA7 2005)] (finding flex-time schedule critical to employee with disabled child). A supervisor's refusal to invite an employee to lunch is normally trivial, a nonactionable petty slight. But to retaliate by excluding an employee from a weekly training lunch that contributes significantly to the employee's professional advancement might well deter a reasonable employee from complaining about discrimination. *See* 2 EEOC 1998 MANUAL §8, p. 8-14. Hence, a legal standard that speaks in general terms rather than specific prohibited acts is preferable, for an "act that would be immaterial in some situations is material in others." *Washington.*

Finally, we note that contrary to the claim of the concurrence, this standard does *not* require a reviewing court or jury to consider "the nature of the discrimination that led to the filing of the charge." Rather, the standard is tied to the challenged retaliatory act, not the underlying conduct that forms the basis of the Title VII complaint. By focusing on the materiality of the challenged action and the perspective of a reasonable person in the plaintiff's position, we believe this standard will screen out trivial conduct while effectively capturing those acts that are likely to dissuade employees from complaining or assisting in complaints about discrimination.

III

Applying this standard to the facts of this case, we believe that there was a sufficient evidentiary basis to support the jury's verdict on White's retaliation claim. . . . Burlington does not question the jury's determination that the motivation for these acts was retaliatory. But it does question the statutory significance of the harm these acts caused. The District Court instructed the jury to determine whether respondent "suffered a materially adverse change in the terms or conditions of her employment," and the Sixth Circuit upheld the jury's finding based on that same stringent interpretation of the anti-retaliation provision (the interpretation that limits §704 to the same employment-related conduct forbidden by §703). Our holding today makes clear that the jury was not required to find that the challenged actions were related to the terms or conditions of employment. And insofar as the jury also found that the actions were "materially adverse," its findings are adequately supported.

First, Burlington argues that a reassignment of duties cannot constitute retaliatory discrimination where, as here, both the former and present duties fall within the same job description. We do not see why that is so. Almost every job category involves some responsibilities and duties that are less desirable than others. Common sense suggests that one good way to discourage an employee such as White from bringing discrimination charges would be to insist that she spend more time performing the more arduous duties and less time performing those that are easier or more agreeable. That is presumably why the EEOC has consistently found "retaliatory work assignments" to be a classic and "widely recognized" example of "forbidden retaliation." 2 EEOC 1991 MANUAL §614.7, pp. 614-31 to 614-32. . . .

To be sure, reassignment of job duties is not automatically actionable. Whether a particular reassignment is materially adverse depends upon the circumstances of the particular case, and "should be judged from the perspective of a reasonable person in the plaintiff's position, considering 'all the circumstances.'" *Oncale.* But here, the jury had before it considerable evidence that the track labor duties were "by all accounts more arduous and dirtier"; that the "forklift operator position required more qualifications, which is an indication of prestige"; and that "the forklift operator position was objectively considered a better job and the male employees resented White for occupying it." Based on this record, a jury could reasonably conclude that the reassignment of responsibilities would have been materially adverse to a reasonable employee.

Second, Burlington argues that the 37-day suspension without pay lacked statutory significance because Burlington ultimately reinstated White with backpay. Burlington says that "it defies reason to believe that Congress would have considered a rescinded investigatory suspension with full back pay" to be unlawful, particularly because Title VII, throughout much of its history, provided no relief in an equitable action for victims in White's position.

We do not find Burlington's last mentioned reference to the nature of Title VII's remedies convincing. After all, throughout its history, Title VII has provided for injunctions to "bar like discrimination in the future," *Albemarle Paper Co. v. Moody*, 422 U.S. 405 (1975) (internal quotation marks omitted), an important form of relief. And we have no reason to believe that a court could not have issued an injunction where an employer suspended an employee for retaliatory purposes, even if that employer later provided backpay. In any event, Congress amended Title VII in 1991 to permit victims of intentional discrimination to recover compensatory (as White received here) and punitive damages, concluding that the additional remedies were necessary to "'help make victims whole.'" *West v. Gibson*, 527 U.S. 212 (1999). We would undermine the significance of that congressional judgment were we to conclude that employers could avoid liability in these circumstances.

Neither do we find convincing any claim of insufficient evidence. White did receive backpay. But White and her family had to live for 37 days without income. They did not know during that time whether or when White could return to work. Many reasonable employees would find a month without a paycheck to be a serious hardship. And White described to the jury the physical and emotional hardship that 37 days of having "no income, no money" in fact caused. ("That was the worst Christmas I had out of my life. No income, no money, and that made all of us feel bad. . . . I got very depressed"). Indeed, she obtained medical treatment for her emotional distress. A reasonable employee facing the choice between retaining her job (and paycheck) and filing a discrimination complaint might well choose the former. That is to say, an indefinite suspension without pay could well act as a deterrent, even if the suspended employee eventually received backpay. . . . Thus, the jury's conclusion that the 37-day suspension without pay was materially adverse was a reasonable one. . . .

[Justice Alito's concurring opinion omitted.]

NOTES

1. *Retaliation Outside the Workplace.* Prior to *Burlington*, the Court had held that former employees were protected from retaliation in terms of unfavorable references. *Robinson v. Shell Oil Co.*, 519 U.S. 337 (1997) (former employee given inaccurate references). In some sense, of course, that case involved retaliation outside the workplace. *Burlington* confirms that, holding that, while § 703 reaches only actions that affect employment or that alter the conditions of the workplace, § 704 is *not* limited to discriminatory acts that affect the terms and conditions of employment.

Occasionally a question has arisen as to whether an employer violates the retaliation provisions of the antidiscrimination statutes by bringing suit against the employee in retaliation for protected conduct. For example, would it be permissible for an employer to bring defamation charges against an employee who has alleged discrimination? The Supreme Court addressed a similar issue under the National Labor Relations Act. *BE&K Construction Co. v. NLRB*, 536 U.S. 516 (2002), held, in light of First Amendment concerns, that the NLRA did not prohibit reasonably based but unsuccessful lawsuits filed with a retaliatory purpose. A baseless suit would lack this justification and, after *Burlington*, would seem actionable.

2. *Adverse Employment Actions Under § 703?* Given that the actions White complained of clearly affected her employment, why do you think the Court felt it necessary to decide whether § 704 applied to actions that did not affect the terms and conditions of employment? Perhaps the Court reached out to resolve this question because it did not believe the actions, even though arising from the workplace, would have stated a claim under § 703? Obviously, this would have important implications for the concept of "adverse employment action" we discussed at page 524. In his concurring opinion in *Burlington*, Justice Alito disagreed with the majority's analysis, believing that the scope of §§ 703 and 704 are the same and both reach only materially adverse employment actions. But he found the actions White challenged to be materially adverse within the meaning of either section. As applied to § 703, this would be a more pro-plaintiff position in discrimination cases than many predicted of Justice Alito. *See generally* Lisa Durham Taylor, *Parsing Supreme Court Dicta and the Example of Non-Workplace Harms*, 57 DRAKE L. REV. 75 (2008); Lisa Durham Taylor, *Adding Subjective Fuel to the Vague-Standard Fire: A Proposal for Congressional Intervention After* Burlington Northern & Santa Fe Railway Co. v. White, 9 U. PA. J. LAB. & EMP. L. 533 (2007); Ernest F. Lidge III, *What Types of Employer Actions Are Cognizable Under Title VII?: The Ramifications of* Burlington Northern & Santa Fe Railroad Co. v. White, 59 RUTGERS L. REV. 497, 535 (2007).

3. *Catch-22?* Some courts seem to believe that the employee's persistence in opposition conduct is at least a factor, and perhaps a weighty one, in determining that the claimed action was not likely to deter a reasonable employee from engaging in protected conduct. *Somoza v. Univ. of Denver*, 513 F.3d 1206, 1214 (10th Cir. 2008) ("[T]he fact that an employee continues to be undeterred in his or her pursuit of a remedy, as here was the case, may shed light as to whether the actions are sufficiently material and adverse to be actionable."). Does this impermissibly shift the focus from the reasonable employee to the actual employee? *Wells v. Gates*, 336 F. App'x 378, 384 (4th Cir. 2009) ("Although 'the fact that an employee continues to be undeterred in his or her pursuit of a remedy . . . may shed light as to whether the actions are sufficiently material and adverse to be actionable,' [citing Somoza] the court ultimately must apply an objective standard").

F. DISABILITY DISCRIMINATION

Protecting individuals with disabilities from discrimination in employment poses difficult problems. Legally, disability discrimination poses the threshold question of who is protected, that is, who is a "disabled" individual. Further, disabilities are sometimes relevant to an individual's ability to work. While many disabilities would not affect the performance of particular jobs at all, some disabilities deprive people of the physical and/or mental prerequisites to perform essential job functions. Prohibiting "discrimination" against such individuals would unduly interfere with employers' ability to select a qualified workforce. Other disabled individuals may be qualified to work but only if the employer accommodates their disability in some way. Such individuals, unlike most other statutorily protected groups, require some form of different treatment in order to enjoy equal access to employment opportunities and benefits. Merely guaranteeing equal treatment for similarly situated individuals in those situations does not adequately respond to the problem of promoting employment of the disabled.

The ADA seeks to deal with these problems in two separate ways. First, while generally barring disability discrimination, the statute broadens the defenses available to employers as compared with other antidiscrimination statutes. Employers are permitted to engage in disparate treatment on the basis of disability if the disabled employee is unable to perform the essential functions of the job. In addition, employers are free to use qualification standards that screen out disabled individuals if those qualifications are job-related and consistent with business necessity.

Counterbalancing this, disabled individuals have rights beyond those guaranteed to other groups protected by antidiscrimination legislation. The centerpiece of disability discrimination law is the employer's affirmative duty to provide reasonable accommodation to ensure that individuals with disabilities secure equal employment opportunities and benefits. The focus of the duty to accommodate is on equal employment opportunity, not merely equal treatment.

As a result, employers are legally obligated to treat covered employees equally or differently depending on the circumstances — employers must treat individuals with disabilities equally to nondisabled persons if they are qualified and their disabilities do not require accommodation; employers are permitted to treat such individuals differently, that is, to discriminate against them, if their disabilities cannot be accommodated; and employers are required to treat such individuals differently, and better than other workers, if reasonable accommodations are necessary to ensure equal employment opportunity and benefits.

Further, accommodation providing equal opportunity for individuals with disabilities can be costly for employers. The ADA, therefore, includes an "undue hardship" defense, which makes cost, usually irrelevant under the disparate treatment provisions of other antidiscrimination statutes, an expressly enumerated statutory defense to discrimination based on the duty to accommodate.

The focus of this section will be Title I of the ADA, which deals with employment, although other parts of the statute deal with important issues beyond employment. The ADA and associated regulations borrows extensively from the Rehabilitation Act of 1973, 29 U.S.C. §§ 701-95 (2006), which was a narrower federal statute covering only federal contractors and federal executive agencies. The Rehabilitation Act continues to operate in its original sphere, and its precedents influence ADA decisions, and the ADA regulations and Interpretive Guidance of the (EEOC) borrow from regulations under the earlier act.

The ADA was passed in 1990, but the first decade and a half of its life proved profoundly disappointing to disability advocates. The amorphous definition of disability permitted the courts to narrowly circumscribe the statute's reach. While we will examine the details of this development, the net result was that most cases under Title I of the ADA were dismissed because the plaintiffs were either not disabled within the meaning of the statute (as construed by the courts) or too disabled to perform the essential functions of the jobs they sought. The result of increasing dissatisfaction with a number of Supreme Court decisions was the Americans with Disabilities Act Amendment Act of 2008, Pub. L. 110-325, signed into law in on September 2008 and effective January 1, 2009. *See generally* Alex B. Long, *Introducing the New and Improved Americans with Disabilities Act: Assessing the ADA Amendments Act of 2008*, 103 Nw. U. L. Rev. Colloquy 217 (2008). This section focuses on the amended statute, although an understanding of the original ADA is critical to appreciating the potential of the current law.

1. The Meaning of "Disability"

In contrast to other statutes prohibiting discrimination in employment, establishing membership in the ADA's protected classification often requires extensive legal and factual analysis. Generally speaking, to claim protection under the ADA, a plaintiff must be "a qualified individual with a disability"; that is, the plaintiff must be an individual with a disability who can perform essential job functions with or without reasonable accommodation. Section 3(1) provides three definitions of "disability":

    A. a physical or mental impairment that substantially limits one or more of the major life activities of . . . [an] individual;
    B. a record of such an impairment; or
    C. being regarded as having such an impairment.

This definition requires three inquiries. First, whether the individual has an impairment. The first part of the definition, § 3(2)(A), deals with an individual who has an actual impairment. It contains three elements, each of which is further defined in the EEOC's ADA regulations. Section 1630.2(h) of the regulations defines physical or mental *impairment* as:

    1. Any physiological disorder or condition, cosmetic disfigurement, or anatomical loss affecting one or more of the following body systems: neurological, musculoskeletal, special sense organs, respiratory (including speech organs), cardiovascular, reproductive, digestive, genitor-urinary, hemic and lymphatic, skin, and endocrine; or

2. Any mental or psychological disorder, such as mental retardation, organic brain syndrome, emotional or mental illness, and specific learning disabilities.

The second inquiry is whether a "major life activity" is limited by the impairment. Originally, the definition of such activities was left to the EEOC's regulations, but the ADAAA added a statutory definition that both incorporated the EEOC's approach and broadened it. For purposes of determining whether an individual has an actual disability,

(A), major life activities include, but are not limited to, caring for oneself, performing manual tasks, seeing, hearing, eating, sleeping, walking, standing, lifting, bending, speaking, breathing, learning, reading, concentrating, thinking, communicating, and working.

(B) . . . a major life activity also includes the operation of a major bodily function, including but not limited to, functions of the immune system, normal cell growth, digestive, bowel, bladder, neurological, brain, respiratory, circulatory, endocrine, and reproductive functions.

42 U.S.C. § 12102 (2).

The third inquiry is whether the limitation is "substantial." As you might guess, this was a major point of debate both under the original ADA and in framing the Americans with Disabilities Act Amendments Act ("ADAAA"), and Congress's solution was less than elegant.

ADA coverage, however, does not depend on establishing an actual, present disability. As noted, § 3(2)(B) also reaches individuals with a "record" of an impairment, and § 3(2)(C) protects those that the employer "regards" as having an impairment. Once you have a better sense of what constitutes an actual disability, we will explore the "record" and "regarded as" prongs of the statutory prohibition.

a. Actual Impairment

The Supreme Court first considered the meaning of disability in *School Board of Nassau County v. Arline*, 480 U.S. 273 (1987). *Arline* was a Rehabilitation Act case construing the definition of "handicapped individual," which is identical to the ADA's definition of individual with a disability. The school board fired Arline, an elementary school teacher, because it believed her active tuberculosis posed a threat to the health of others. When she sued, the board contended that a person with a contagious disease was not protected by the Rehabilitation Act if the adverse employment action was based on the employee's contagiousness and not on the condition itself. The Supreme Court disagreed. In finding Arline to be a handicapped individual, the Court refused to allow the school to disassociate the contagious effects of the teacher's impairment from the impairment itself. As the Court stated, "Arline's contagiousness and her physical impairment each resulted from the same underlying condition, tuberculosis. It would be unfair to allow an employer to seize upon the distinction between the effects of a disease on others and the effects of a disease on a patient and use that distinction to justify discriminatory intent."

In light of *Arline*'s holding, is a person who tests positively for HIV, the virus that causes AIDS, an "individual with a disability"? Given that a contagious disease can be a "disability," a person who has developed AIDS is undoubtedly an "individual with a disability" under both the Rehabilitation Act and the ADA. That is, active AIDS clearly qualifies as a physical impairment and also substantially limits major life activities. But *Arline* left open the question whether an asymptomatic person can be considered "handicapped" solely on the basis of contagiousness.

In *Bragdon v. Abbott*, 524 U.S. 624 (1998), the plaintiff, infected with HIV, sued her dentist for disability discrimination when he required her cavity to be filled in a hospital instead of in his office as usual. She sued under Title II of the statute, which prohibits discrimination in public accommodations; however, the definition of discrimination under the Title II is the same as that under Title I, thus rendering *Bragdon* relevant to employment. Applying the three-step analysis we have sketched, the Court first asked whether the condition at issue was a "physical impairment." *Id.* at 632. The Court decided that HIV is a "physical impairment" from the moment of infection, regardless of the presence of symptoms. *Id.* Second, the Court asked whether the impairment affected a major life activity. *Id.* at 637. The plaintiff in this case relied successfully on the major life activities of reproduction and child bearing, but the Court noted that HIV affects many other major life activities. *Id.* at 638-39. Third, the Court examined whether the impairment's effect on reproduction was "substantial," *id.* at 639, concluding that HIV substantially limits the plaintiff's ability to bear children because of the risk of transmitting the disease. *Id.* The Court elaborated that, "the Act addresses substantial limitations on major life activities, not utter inabilities." *Id.* at 641. Accordingly, *Bragdon* upheld the plaintiff's claim under the ADA since HIV infection is a physical impairment that substantially limits the major life activity of reproduction. *Id.*

In a passage that has influenced numerous later cases, the Court stressed that "whether respondent has a disability covered by the ADA is an individualized inquiry." *Id.* at 657. Thus, what is a disability for one person may not be disabling for another. Thus, the Court did not rule on whether HIV infection is a per se disability under the ADA, irrespective of its limiting effects on the activities of the particular plaintiff. *Id.* at 642.

Bragdon was not only the first case decided by the Court but it was also the high point of jurisprudence under the original ADA in terms of broadly reading the statute's coverage. Every other Court decision under Title I restricted the reach of the statute. One of the most significant retrenchments was in *Toyota Motor Mfg., Kentucky, Inc. v. Williams*, 534 U.S. 184 (2002). At issue there was a plaintiff employed on a Toyota assembly line, where she worked with pneumatic tools. Ms. Williams developed carpal tunnel syndrome and related impairments that restricted her ability to perform manual tasks at her job. Toyota initially modified her job duties to accommodate her condition but ultimately refused to provide her the accommodation she sought; it then discharged her after her condition had worsened to the extent that she could not work at all. Williams sued under the ADA, claiming Toyota failed to reasonably accommodate her disability and terminated her employment.

The central issue before the Court was what major life activities counted. Williams claimed that the activity at stake was performing manual tasks, and the Court held that "to be substantially limited in performing manual tasks, an individual must have an impairment that prevents or severely restricts the individual from doing activities that are of central importance to most people's daily lives." 534 U.S. at 187. Thus, the opinion simultaneously broadened what counted as a major life activity and broadened what was necessary to be substantially limited. Do you see how that double play would dramatically narrow the ADA's reach? The narrower an activity may be defined and still count as major, the more likely it is that a plaintiff can prove she is substantially limited. Conversely, the broader the activity is defined, the less likely the plaintiff is substantially limited in performing it. For example, suppose a person is unable to walk long distances. If "walking" is a major life activity, the individual would be limited but perhaps not substantially limited; on the other hand, walking long distances is less likely to be viewed as a major life activity, but the person is more likely to be considered substantially limited.

In justifying its decision, the Court wrote that "substantially limited and major life activities" both "need to be interpreted strictly to create a demanding standard for qualifying as disabled" to implement Congress's goals in passing the ADA. 534 U.S. at 197. Congress didn't agree, and expressed that disagreement in a variety of ways in the ADAAA. Thus, it commanded that '[t]he definition of disability in this Act shall be construed in favor of broad coverage of individuals under this Act, to the maximum extent permitted by the terms of this Act," 42 U.S.C.A. § 12102(4)(A), in the process explicitly rejecting the *Williams* strict interpretation language. More specifically, as we have seen, the new statute defined major life activities very broadly.

As for "substantially limited," the ADAAA was more circuitous although very clear in its thrust. Thus, the amendments do not directly define the term. However, the ADAAA states that *Toyota* "has created an inappropriately high level of limitation necessary to necessary to obtain coverage under the ADA." Congress then went on to disapprove the then-effective EEOC regulations by expressing its "expectation" that the EEOC "will revise that portion of its current regulations that define the term 'substantially limits' as "significantly restricted' to be consistent with this Act" and its amendments. The ADAAA simultaneously answered a question the Supreme Court had raised by explicitly providing authority to the EEOC to issue regulations defining disability, and the agency has in fact issued proposed regulations, http://edocket .access.gpo.gov/2009/E9-22840.htm.* Finally, Congress commanded that "[t]he term "substantially limits" shall be interpreted consistently with the findings and purposes" of the ADAAA. § 12102(4)(B).

Note on Impairments

The threshold requirement for a disability is an impairment, and with the ADAAA's broadening of "major life activities" and its watering down of "substantially

---

*The extent to which courts should defer to EEOC regulations was more than a little confused before the ADAAA, and some uncertainty remains. Title I of the originally ADA conferred substantive rule-making authority on the EEOC, 42 U.S.C.A. § 12116, which would seem to require the courts to accord substantial deference under *Chevron U.S.A., Inc. v. Nat. Resources Defense Council, Inc.*, 467 U.S. 837 (1984), and its progeny. However, two problems arose. First, the EEOC carried out that mandate by issuing both regulations and an "Interpretive Guidance," and there has been question as to whether the Guidance is due the same deference as the regulations. Rebecca Hanner White, *Deference and Disability Discrimination*, 9 MICH. L. REV. 532 (2000)

Secondly, *Sutton v. United Air Lines, Inc.*, refused to defer to the EEOC because the agency at that time had authority only to interpret Title I, and the interpretation at issue involved the prefatory umbrella provisions of the statute. This question seems to have been resolved by the ADAAA, which expressly gives the EEOC (and other agencies charged with administering other Titles of the ADA) the authority to issue regulations relating to the definition of disability. 42 U.S.C.A. § 12205a. And deference to EEOC regulations now seems mandated by *Chevron U.S.A., Inc. v. Echazabal*, 536 U.S. 73 (2002) (deferring to EEOC interpretation of the "direct threat" defense even though it was broader than the statutory language).

limited," that threshold question is increasingly central to the determination of whether there is an actual disability. *Bragdon* found HIV to be an impairment from the moment of infection, and *Toyota* assumed that plaintiff's carpal tunnel condition constituted an impairment; rather the question was whether that impairment substantially limited a major life activity. But whether a condition is an impairment is not always easy. Foreseeing some problems, the ADAAA explicitly provided that "[a]n impairment that is episodic or in remission is a disability if it would substantially limit a major life activity when active." § 12102(4)(D). Does that mean, for instance, that multiple sclerosis is an impairment, even though, in its early stages, it can be relatively asymptomatic? The EEOC's proposed regulations list multiple sclerosis as an example of "Impairments that Will Consistently Meet the Definition of Disability." § 1630.2(j).

Despite this broad approach, the Act and its regulations specifically exclude certain conditions from the definition of impairment. ADA Sections 508 and 511 expressly exclude certain sex-related practices or conditions, such as homosexuality, bisexuality, transvestism, pedophilia, transexualism, and exhibitionism. Also excluded are compulsive gambling, kleptomania, pyromania, and disorders resulting from the current illegal use of psychoactive drugs. Further, the EEOC's Interpretive Guidance, 29 C.F.R. Part 1630 Appendix, provides that the term "physical or mental impairment" does not include physical characteristics, such as weight, height, and eye color, that are in the "normal range" and are not the result of a physiological disorder. § 1630.2(h). The Interpretive Guidance also excludes common personality traits, illiteracy, economic disadvantages, and advanced age, although physical and mental impairments associated with aging may be covered. *See* 29 C.F.R. pt. 1630, app. § 1630.2(h), (j).

Although pregnancy shares many of the characteristics of a disability as defined by the ADA, the EEOC Interpretive Guidance states that pregnancy per se is not a disability covered by the statute because pregnancy is not an impairment. *See* 29 C.F.R. pt. 1630, app. § 1630.2(h); *see generally* Melissa Cole, *Beyond Sex Discrimination: Why Employers Discriminate Against Women with Disabilities When Their Employee Health Plans Exclude Contraceptives from Prescription Coverage*, 43 ARIZ. L. REV. 501, 521 (2001) ("For most women, pregnancy does not involve the sorts of substantial limitations that rise to the level of a disability. For those women who face grave health risks in pregnancy, however, the very potential of pregnancy constitutes a disability, a substantial limitation on the major life activity of reproduction.").

Interestingly, the proposed regulations are similar to the earlier regulations in suggesting that temporary conditions can be impairments, although it views them as unlikely to be disabilities: "Temporary, non-chronic impairments of short duration with little or no residual effects (such as the common cold, seasonal or common influenza, a sprained joint, minor and non-chronic gastrointestinal disorders, or a broken bone that is expected to heal completely) usually will not substantially limit a major life activity." § 1630.2(j). *See also Pollard v. High's of Baltimore, Inc.*, 281 F.3d 462 (4th Cir. 2002) (nine-month absence from work for back surgery not a disability because only temporary).

Is any physical characteristic outside what is considered the normal range an "impairment"? Consider unusual strength or high intelligence. Are these impairments (because they are out of the normal range), but not disabilities (because they do not substantially impair life activities)? Or are they not impairments at all because they are out of the normal range on the "positive," rather than the "negative," side? Is being left-handed an impairment?

What about individuals with genetic propensities but no actual disease at the moment? It seems unlikely that such individual are currently actually disabled within the meaning of the ADA. This is in part because such an individual will not ordinarily be substantially limited in a major life activity—although like *Bragdon*, some such conditions may limit reproduction for fear of passing on the condition to offspring. But genetic propensities will likely not be viewed as impairments because they are not certain to eventuate. A few diseases, like Huntington's, are inevitable for those with the allele, although they may not manifest the symptoms until late in life. Most "genetic diseases," however, simply make individuals more susceptible to the condition (although sometimes increasing the risk factor enormously). Is someone with the Huntington's allele but no symptoms impaired? If so, does this impairment substantially limit any major life activity? Even if the answer is yes, what about those genetic diseases whose appearance is not inevitable? *See generally* John V. Jacobi, *Genetic Discrimination in a Time of False Hopes*, 30 FLA. ST. U.L. REV. 363 (2003).

The Genetic Information Non-Discrimination Act ("GINA"), 22 Stat. 881, codified at 42 U.S.C.A. § 2000ff, was enacted in May 2008, and its employment provisions took effect on November 21, 2009. It does not amend the ADA but does provide a separate source of protection against certain kinds of genetic discrimination. GINA prohibits discrimination by employers and health insurers based on genetic information. The EEOC is charged with enforcement of the employment provisions of the act and has promulgated proposed regulations to carry out Title II, the employment chapter. 74 FED. REG. 9056 (Mar. 2, 2009). In a nutshell, Title II of GINA prohibits the use of genetic information in employment, prohibits the intentional acquisition of genetic information about applicants and employees, and imposes strict confidentiality requirements. It applies to employers, public and private, with 15 or more employees. The EEOC's proposed regulations regard the protections of GINA as absolute when it comes to an employer's *use* of genetic information; any use is strictly prohibited. Moreover, acquisition of genetic information by employers is restricted. *See generally* Jessica Roberts, *Preempting Discrimination: Lessons from the Genetic Information Nondiscrimination Act*, 63 VAND. L. REV. 439 (2010), (examining the justifications for passing preemptive genetic information discrimination legislation and concluding that Congress had twin objectives: a research justification and an antidiscrimination justification).

A final question about impairments relates to physical conditions caused at least in part by voluntary conduct. The First Circuit considered whether such conditions constitute impairments in *Cook v. Rhode Island Dept. of Mental Health*, 10 F.3d 17 (1st Cir. 1993). Bonnie Cook was morbidly obese, meaning that she weighed either more than twice her optimal weight or more than 100 pounds over her optimal weight. In response to her claim of discrimination under the Rehabilitation Act, the defendant argued that " 'mutable' conditions are not the sort of impairments" covered by the Act because Cook could "simply lose weight and rid herself of any concomitant disability." *Id.* at 23. Although the court questioned whether "immutability is a prerequisite to the existence" of an "impairment," it found evidence in the record to support a finding that the dysfunctional metabolism underlying morbid obesity is permanent. The defendant also argued that morbid obesity cannot be an impairment because it is "caused, or at least exacerbated, by voluntary conduct." The court responded:

> The Rehabilitation Act contains no language suggesting that its protection is linked to how an individual became impaired, or whether an individual contributed to his or her

impairment. On the contrary, the Act indisputably applies to numerous conditions that may be caused or exacerbated by voluntary conduct, such as alcoholism, AIDS, diabetes, cancer resulting from cigarette smoking, heart disease resulting from excesses of various types, and the like. Consequently, voluntariness, like mutability, is relevant only in determining whether a condition has a substantially limiting effect.

Id. at 24. *See generally* Jane Byeff Korn, *Fat*, 77 B.U. L. Rev. 25 (1997). Does the ADAAA's command to broadly construe the definition of disability resolve this? *See* Jane Byeff Korn, *Too Fat*, 17 Va. J. Soc. Pol'y & L. 209, 211 (2010) ("While the ADAAA appears to provide more protection for most people with disabilities, this amendment will probably not protect people who are obese absent a significant change in our thinking about obesity.").

≣ ## Horgan v. Simmons
≣ *704 F. Supp. 2d 814 (N.D. Ill. 2010)*

Ruben Castillo, J.

[Plaintiff sued his supervisor, Timothy Simmons, and his employer, Morgan Services, Inc. for invasion of privacy and disability discrimination. The defendants moved to dismiss under Rule 12(b)(6), but the court denied the motion as to both ADA claims.]

Plaintiff has been diagnosed as HIV positive for the past ten years, but kept his status confidential, disclosing his medical condition only to his close friends. In February 2001, he began working for Morgan, a linen and uniform rental services company, as a sales manager in Los Angeles. In January 2008, Defendants promoted him to General Manager of the Chicago facility. Plaintiff claims that his HIV positive status never interfered with his ability to perform the essential functions of his job and that he "has always met or exceeded Morgan's legitimate expectations." Specifically, in 2009, Plaintiff claims he brought in a lucrative account with the company's "biggest customer in the country."

Simmons is Morgan's president and was Plaintiff's supervisor in Chicago. On July 15, 2009, Plaintiff alleges that Simmons asked to meet with him for what Simmons termed a "social visit." During their visit, Plaintiff alleges that Simmons "told plaintiff that he was really worried about him." When Plaintiff responded by discussing his work performance, Plaintiff claims that Simmons cut him off saying "this is not about results." Plaintiff alleges that Simmons then "demanded" to know what was going on with him, telling Plaintiff that "if there was something medical going on, [he] needed to know." Plaintiff insisted that there was nothing that affected his ability to work. However, Plaintiff claims that Simmons "continued to insist there was something physical or mental that was affecting [Plaintiff]." Plaintiff claims he was "compelled to tell Simmons that he was HIV positive," but he assured Simmons that his status did not affect his ability to do his job.

Plaintiff alleges that Simmons then asked him about his prognosis. Plaintiff responded that "he had been HIV positive for a long time and that the condition was under control and that his T-cell count was over 300." Next, Plaintiff alleges that Simmons asked "what would happen if his T-cell count went below 200," and Plaintiff replied that he would then have AIDS. After urging Plaintiff to inform his family about his condition, Plaintiff alleges that Simmons asked him "how he could ever perform his job with his HIV positive condition and how he could continue to work with a terminal illness." Additionally, [Plaintiff claims that Simmons told him "that a General Manager needs to be respected by the employees and have the ability to lead," and indicated that he "did not know how [Plaintiff] could lead if the employees knew about his condition."

Simmons allegedly ended the meeting by telling Plaintiff that he needed "to recover" and that he should "go on vacation" and "leave the plant immediately." Simmons then told Plaintiff that he would discuss the situation with Morgan's owner. The next day, Plaintiff alleges that he received a copy of an email sent to all general managers and corporate staff indicating that "effective immediately" Plaintiff was "no longer a member of Morgan [ ]." . . .

The ADA makes it unlawful for an employer to "discriminate against a qualified individual on the basis of disability in regard to . . . terms, conditions, and privileges of employment." 42 U.S.C. § 12112(a). "To prevail on an ADA claim, the plaintiff must show (1) he is disabled; (2) he is qualified to perform the essential function of the job with or without accommodation; and (3) he suffered an adverse employment action because of his disability." *EEOC v. Lee's Log Cabin*, 546 F.3d 438, 442 (7th Cir. 2008), *amended by, reh'g en banc denied by*, 554 F.3d 1102 (7th Cir. 2009) (internal citation omitted). The ADA defines "disability," with respect to an individual, as: (1) "a physical or mental impairment that substantially limits one or more major life activities of such individual"; (2) "a record of such an impairment"; or (3) "being regarded as having such an impairment." 42 U.S.C. § 12102(1). Plaintiff alleges that he was terminated on the basis of his disability: being HIV positive. Although Defendants acknowledge that being HIV positive is a physical impairment, they argue that Plaintiff has not pled "a limitation of a major life activity," and thus fails to state a claim of disability under the ADA.

Effective January 1, 2009, Congress amended the ADA to "[reinstate] a broad scope of protection." Specifically, Congress found that the Supreme Court had "narrowed" the protection intended to be afforded by the ADA, and through the ADAAA rejected the holdings of *Sutton v. United Air Lines, Inc.* and *Toyota Motor Manufacturing, Kentucky, Inc., v. Williams*. Although the ADAAA left the ADA's three-category definition of "disability" intact, significant changes were made to how these categories were interpreted.

As relevant to this case, the ADAAA clarified that the operation of "major bodily functions," including "functions of the immune system," constitute major life activities under the ADA's first definition of disability. In addition, "an impairment that is episodic or in remission is a disability if it would substantially limit a major life activity when active." Congress also instructed that "[t]he term 'substantially limits' shall be interpreted consistently with the findings and purposes of the [ADAAA]." *Id.* Noting that courts had "created an inappropriately high level of limitation," the ADAAA states that "it is the intent of Congress that the primary object of attention in cases brought under the ADA should be whether entities covered under the ADA have complied with their obligations. . . ." Therefore, the "question of whether an individual's impairment is a disability under the ADA should not demand extensive analysis." *Id.*

Defendants claim that even with the additional language of the ADAAA, Plaintiff fails to plead a disability sufficient to state an actionable ADA claim. This Court disagrees. Drawing all inferences in Plaintiffs favor, it is certainly plausible — particularly, under the amended ADA — that Plaintiff's HIV positive status substantially limits a major life activity: the function of his immune system. Such a conclusion is consistent with the EEOC's proposed regulations to implement the ADAAA which lists HIV as an impairment that will consistently meet the definition of disability. *See* Proposed Rules, Regulations To Implement the Equal Employment Provisions of the Americans with Disabilities Act, As Amended, 74 FR 48431, at *48441 (Sept. 23, 2009) ("Interpreting the definition of disability broadly and without extensive analysis as required under the [ADAAA], some types of impairments will consistently meet the definition of disability. Because of certain characteristics associated with these impairments, the individualized assessment of the limitations on a person can be conducted quickly and easily, and will consistently result in a determination that the person is substantially limited in a major life activity.").

Relying primarily on the decision in *Lee's Log Cabin*, Defendants argue that a substantial limitation of an identifiable major life activity is "an essential basis" to establish a claim for relief under the ADA. In that case, the Seventh Circuit "decline[d] to adopt" a rule that HIV is a *per se* disability under the ADA.[1] *Lee's Log Cabin*. However, the court explicitly stated that its decision, which was decided at the summary judgment stage, should not "be read to suggest that the EEOC's complaint failed to state a claim." *Lee's Log Cabin*. The Court finds that the level of pleading which Defendants argue is not required at this stage. *See* Fed. R. Civ. P. 8(a)(2); *Bell Atlantic Corp. v. Twombly*, 550 U.S. 544, 570 ("we do not require heightened fact pleading of specifics, but only enough facts to state a claim to relief that is *plausible* on its face") (emphasis added).[2]

Accordingly, this Court finds that Plaintiff has overcome the "two easy-to-clear hurdles" necessary to survive a motion to dismiss: (1) Defendants have notice of the claims and the grounds on which they rest; and (2) the allegations suggest that Plaintiff has a right to relief. Defendants' motion to dismiss Plaintiff's first claim is therefore denied.

B. Count II — Impermissible Medical Inquiry

. . . The ADA prohibits "inquiries of an employee as to whether [an] employee is an individual with a disability or as to the nature or severity of the disability, unless such examination or inquiry is shown to be job-related and consistent with business necessity." 42 U.S.C. §12112(d)(4). Here, Plaintiff alleges that Simmons demanded to know whether "something medical [was] going on" and "continued to insist there was something physical or mental that was affecting [Plaintiff]." Plaintiff claims that based

---

1. Other courts, however, have found that as a matter of law, being HIV positive is a *per se* disability under the ADA. *See e.g. Rivera v. Heyman*, 157 F.3d 101, 103 (2d Cir. 1998) ("HIV infection is a disability under the [ADA]").

2. Further, although Plaintiff does not argue it in his brief, the complaint also establishes a disability under the third definition set forth by the ADA because he was regarded as having an impairment. "An individual meets the requirement of 'being regarded as having such an impairment' if the individual establishes that he or she has been subjected to an action prohibited under [the ADA] because of an actual or perceived physical or mental impairment whether or not the impairment limits or is perceived to limit a major life activity." 42 U.S.C. §12102(3)(A). Here, Plaintiff alleges that when he told Simmons that he was HIV positive, Simmons asked "how [Plaintiff] could ever perform his job with his HIV positive condition and how he could continue to work with a terminal illness." In addition, Simmons allegedly told Plaintiff that "a General Manger needs to be respected by the employees and have the ability to lead" and that Simmons "did not know how [Plaintiff] could lead if the employees knew about his condition." The next day, Plaintiff alleges that he was terminated. This Court finds that such allegations are sufficient to plausibly suggest that Plaintiff was terminated because Defendants regarded his HIV positive status as an impairment.

on this questioning, he was "compelled to tell Simmons that he was HIV positive." Further, Simmons allegedly asked Plaintiff about his prognosis and what would happen if his T-cell count fell below 200. Such questioning constitutes an inquiry as to whether Plaintiff had a disability and the nature and severity of the disability, and is thus prohibited by the ADA.[3] *See* 42 U.S.C. § 12112(d)(4); *Coffman v. Indianapolis Fire Dep't*, 578 F.3d 559, 565 (7th Cir. 2009).

Nevertheless, Defendants argue that after Plaintiff disclosed his HIV positive status, they were "entitled to ask questions about the stage to which the virus had progressed because it related to [Plaintiff's] possible fitness to work both presently and in the future," and that such questioning was "job-related and consistent with business necessity." Again, Plaintiff alleges that he was "compelled to tell Simmons that he was HIV positive," and disclosed this information only after an impermissible inquiry under the ADA. Further, Plaintiff's allegation that he repeatedly insisted that nothing (including his HIV status) affected his ability to perform his duties directly rebuts Defendants' assertion that the questioning was necessary to discern whether Plaintiff could "cope with the demands and responsibilities of his job."

Thus, Plaintiff has sufficiently pled a claim for an impermissible inquiry under the ADA and Defendants' motion to dismiss on this basis is denied.

[The court dismissed plaintiff's state law tort claim of intrusion on seclusion, finding "even if the disclosure of Plaintiff's HIV status was not voluntary, Defendants' questioning does not give rise to the level of intrusion actionable under the tort."]

NOTES

1. *First-Generation ADAAA Case.* Since the ADAAA did not become effective until January 1, 2009, and it is clear that it is not retroactive, *see, e.g., Lytes v. DC Water & Sewer Auth.*, 572 F.3d 936 (D.C. Cir. 2009); *Milholland v. Sumner County Bd. of Educ.*, 569 F.3d 562 (6th Cir. 2009), it is not surprising that there are very few cases interpreting it, or that the cases thus far are, like *Horgan*, decided on motions to dismiss. It is, of course, perilous to draw conclusions from so few data points, but *Horgan* suggests the radical impact that the ADAAA might have.

2. *Major Life Activity.* First consider the amendments' effect on major life activities. You might wonder why, long after *Bragdon*, there was still a question as to whether HIV affected a major life activity. But recall that, in *Bragdon*, the activity was reproduction, and the plaintiff was a female who claimed to be substantially limited in her ability to bear a child because of the risk of passing on the disease to it. In *Horgan*, however, the plaintiff was male, which meant that he was in no danger in fathering a child with HIV. Under the original ADA, plaintiff could have claimed that his condition substantially limited him in having sex because of the aversion of potential sexual partners. But notice how the ADAAA short circuits the whole

---

3. Defendants argue that Simmons' alleged use of the conditional "if" when initiating his questions signals that Plaintiff's medical problems were not the exclusive subject matter of the questioning. The EEOC guidelines, however, indicate that questions that are *likely* to elicit information regarding a disability are prohibited under the ADA. "Enforcement Guidance: Disability-Related Inquiries and Medical Examinations of Employees Under the ADA" at 3 (emphasis added). Accordingly, it is of no concern that such questioning could also elicit information regarding non-disability related issues.

question — major life activities now "include the operation of a major bodily function," and specifically lists the immune system.

3. *Substantially Limits.* The fact that the immune system is compromised by HIV does not, of course, necessarily mean that there is a substantial limitation. HIV can now be well controlled by a drug regimen. But here, again, the ADAAA changes the analysis. First, the language requiring an impairment that is "episodic or in remission" be treated as though it were active might well answer the question. Second, the ADAAA requires a condition to be assessed in its unmitigated state. Isn't it pretty clear that HIV would develop into AIDS without appropriate treatment? Does that mean that plaintiff should be treated as if he had full-blown AIDS, certainly a substantial limitation on many life activities? Even those possibilities aside, the court stresses that Congress disapproved of *Toyota's* "inappropriately high level of limitation." In ordinary life, wouldn't someone with HIV be considered substantially limited?

4. *Regarded as Disabled.* Even if these arguments don't resolve the question, didn't Simmons "regard" Horgan as disabled under the new statute? See footnote 2. After all, the "regarded as" definition requires only that the employer discriminate against an employee on the basis of an impairment, and *Bragdon* held that HIV was an impairment. If plaintiff proves what he alleges, is there any doubt as to defendant's liability? By the way, the plaintiff's failure to argue what the court describes as an obvious basis for a claim under the ADAAA suggests just how much views will have to be reoriented to take the amendments into account.

5. *Privacy.* The principal case offers both a refresher of the limits of the common law of privacy, see Chapter 6, and an indication of how the ADA may protect privacy interests, even if that is not its main thrust. While the state claim failed, apparently because aggressive questioning is not actionable, the ADA claim on inquiry into disability prevailed.

Note on Major Life Activities

As *Horgan* suggests, the ADAAA's amendment of the statute to include a definition of major life activities should significantly reduce the need to interpret that term. But it might be useful to survey some of the pre-ADAAA decisions to appreciate the confusion. Some of these decisions remain good law; many do not. For example, *Pack v. Kmart Corp.*, 166 F.3d 1300 (10th Cir. 1999), held that sleep is a major life activity, but concentration is not. The ADAAA lists both. *Head v. Glacier Northwest, Inc.*, 413 F.3d 1053, 1058 (9th Cir. 2005), viewed thinking, reading, interacting with others, and sleeping as major life activities. The ADAAA embraces all of these except "interacting with others," and it does include "communicating," which might or might not be the same thing. *Reeves v. Johnson Controls World Servs., Inc.*, 140 F.3d 144 (2d Cir. 1998), wrote that "everyday mobility" is not a major life activity where agoraphobia restricted plaintiff's ability to cross bridges and overpasses, enter tunnels, and board trains. The ADAAA doesn't list "everyday mobility" as a major life activity, but its list is not exhaustive. For discussions of pre-ADAAA cases, *see* Curtis D. Edmonds, *Snakes and Ladders: Expanding the Definition of "Major Life Activity" in the Americans with Disabilities Act*, 33 TEX. TECH. L. REV. 321 (2002). Wendy F. Hensel, *Interacting with Others: A Major Life Activity Under the Americans with Disabilities Act?*, 2002 WIS. L. REV. 1139.

Arline, Bragdon, and Williams all had physical disabilities, but as some of the cases we've just surveyed indicate, the ADA encompasses mental and emotional disabilities as well as physical ones. According to Ann Hubbard:

> There can be no doubt that Congress intended major life activities to reach beyond what makes life merely possible to what makes it enjoyable and meaningful. An activity's importance must be assessed in light of the full array of aspirations and opportunities our modern society offers. These include the everyday activities that allow an individual to participate in every aspect of our modern society: civic, social, educational, economic, vocational, professional, political, commercial, recreational and cultural. Activities in all of these public spheres, as well as in personal and family life, must therefore be included in the category of "major."

The Major Life Activity of Belonging, 39 Wake Forest L. Rev. 217, 224-25 (2004); *see also* Ann Hubbard, *Meaningful Lives and Major Life Activities*, 55 Ala. L. Rev. 997 (2004); Ann Hubbard, *The Major Life Activity of Caring*, 8 Iowa J. Gender, Race & Just. 327 (2004); Ann Hubbard, *The Myth of Independence and the Major Life Activity of Caring*, 8 J. Gender Race & Just. 327 (2004).

Prior to the ADAAA, there was also considerable confusion about whether working could be considered a major life activity. Both *Sutton* and *Toyota* explicitly reserved this question. The ADAAA resolves one bone of contention by explicitly including "working" in its list of major life activities. Nevertheless, *Sutton* looked to the EEOC regulations providing that, where the major life activity of working is alleged, plaintiffs are substantially limited only if they establish that they are excluded from "either a class of jobs or a broad range of jobs" as compared to persons with "comparable training, skills and abilities." 527 U.S. at 491, quoting § 1630.2(j)(3)(i). "The inability to perform a single, particular job does not constitute a substantial limitation in the major life activity of working." *Id.*

The EEOC's proposed regulations would radically change this approach:

> An impairment substantially limits the major life activity of working if it substantially limits an individual's ability to perform, or to meet the qualifications for, the type of work at issue. Whether an impairment substantially limits the major life activity of working must be construed broadly to the maximum extent permitted under the ADA and should not demand extensive analysis

20 C.F.R. § 1630.2(j)((7)(ii)). This means that the prior case law is suspect. In *Sutton* itself, the plaintiffs were found not substantially limited with respect to working because other airline positions were open to them. But isn't "global airline pilot" a "type" of work? Similarly, firefighting was held not to be a class of jobs, *Bridges v. City of Bossier*, 92 F.3d 329 (5th Cir. 1996), but seems clearly a type of work. And prior authority that looked to the plaintiff's location in deciding substantial limitations on working, for example, *Fjellestad v. Pizza Hut*, 188 F.3d 944 (8th Cir. 1999), will need to be reconsidered if the proposed regulations are promulgated.

Note on Substantially Limited

Once a major life activity is defined, the remaining question is whether the impairment substantially limits plaintiff's participation in it. The primary question before the

Toyota court was whether Williams' impairment substantially limited her major life activity of performing manual tasks. The Court answered that question by stating that only if the impairment "prevents or severely restricts the individual from doing activities that are of central importance to most people's daily lives" will it be considered substantially limiting. Moreover, the Court required that the impairment's impact must also be permanent or long term. 534 U.S. at 198.

The ADAAA explicitly disapproved of *Toyota's* approach as setting "an inappropriately high level of limitation," and for good measure it also disapproved of the extant EEOC regulations: "Congress finds that the current Equal Employment Opportunity Commission ADA regulations defining the term 'substantially limits' as 'significantly restricted' are inconsistent with congressional intent, by expressing too high a standard." 42 U.S.C.A. § 12101.

Responding to this concern, § 1630.2(j)(1) of the EEOC's proposed regulations would provide:

> In general. An impairment is a disability within the meaning of this section if it "substantially limits'" the ability of an individual to perform a major life activity as compared to most people in the general population. An impairment need not prevent, or significantly or severely restrict, the individual from performing a major life activity in order to be considered a disability.

The proposal would also include other "rules of construction" intended to avoid a narrow interpretation of "substantially limited":

> (v) . . . An impairment may substantially limit a major life activity even if it lasts, or is expected to last, for fewer than six months.
>
> (vi) In determining whether an individual has a disability, the focus is on how a major life activity is substantially limited, not on what an individual can do in spite of an impairment.

The proposed regulations go on to add that "[t]he comparison of an individual's limitation to the ability of most people in the general population often may be made using a common-sense standard, without resorting to scientific or medical evidence." This seems to bulwark some court cases to that effect, *e.g.*, *Gribben v. UPS*, 528 F.3d 1166 (9th Cir. 2008) (no comparator evidence on an "average person in the general population" required; plaintiff's testimony of his limitations sufficient for jury to determine whether he was disabled), and disapprove of more restrictive decisions. *See generally* Cheryl L. Anderson, *Comparative Evidence or Common Experience: When Does "Substantial Limitation" Require Substantial Proof Under the Americans with Disabilities Act?*, 57 AM. U. L. REV. 409 (2007).

If the proposed regulations are promulgated, much of the prior case law will be abrogated, and limitations will have to be much less "substantial" than before to meet the ADA's threshold.

Note on Mitigating Measures

One of the targets of the ADAAA was *Sutton v. United Airlines, Inc.* 527 U.S. 471 (1999), a case that held that individuals who used mitigating or ameliorative measures to deal with their impairment should be assessed in their mitigated state. While *Sutton* itself involved pilots rejected by an airline because they needed glasses for 20/20 vision, the opinion and two companion cases—*Murphy v. UPS*, 527 U.S. 516 (1999) (plaintiff's high blood pressure should be considered in his medicated state to assess substantial limitation), and *Albertson's, Inc. v. Kirkingburg*, 527 U.S. 555 (1999) (plaintiff's subconscious adjustments to his monocular vision should be considered in assessing substantial limitation)—threatened to radically cut back on the protected class. Indeed, Justice Stevens's dissent in *Sutton* argued that the majority's approach would permit an employer to discriminate against a veteran who lost a leg if his prosthesis was effective. 527 U.S. 497-98.

The ADAAA explicitly disapproved of *Sutton* and provides that "the determination of whether an impairment substantially limits a major life activity shall be made *without regard* to the ameliorative effects of mitigating measures," listing a number of mitigating measures such as medication, prosthetics, hearing aids, etc. However, the amended statute goes on to provide that "the ameliorative effects of the mitigating measures of ordinary eyeglasses or contact lenses shall be considered in determining whether an impairment substantially limits a major life activity." Accordingly, while Congress amended the statute in direct response to the result in *Sutton*, it essentially agreed that the *Sutton* plaintiffs were not to be considered persons with *actual* disabilities within the meaning of the ADA.

In the wake of the ADAAA, there remains a problem regarding those who do not use measures when they are available. Such individuals will be disabled (a matter that divided the courts prior to the ADAAA), but the failure to mitigate may sometimes make them unqualified. As we will see, a disabled person is otherwise qualified if she can perform the essential functions of the position with or without reasonable accommodation. The obvious question that will arise is the extent to which an employer must accommodate an individual who does not use mitigating measures to enable her to do the job at issue. *See generally* Jeannette Cox, *"Corrective" Surgery and the Americans with Disabilities Act*, 46 SAN DIEGO L. REV. 113 (2009); Reagan S. Bissonnette, Note, *Reasonably Accommodating Nonmitigating Plaintiffs After the ADA Amendments Act of 2008*, 50 B.C. L. REV. 859, 859 (2009).

Finally, there is the question of whether the use of a mitigating measure might itself create a disability where none previously existed. *Sulima v. Tobyhanna Army Depot*, 602 F.3d 177, 187 (3d Cir. 2010), held that the side effects from medical treatment may themselves constitute an impairment under the ADA even if the condition treated is not itself disabling; however, since " 'disability' connotes an involuntary condition," a plaintiff seeking protection on this theory must show both that the treatment was required in the "prudent judgment" of the medical profession and that there is not an equally efficacious available alternative that lacks similarly disabling side effects.

PROBLEMS

9-5.   Sarah Smith is an assembly-line worker who is diabetic and dependent on insulin injections to maintain her glucose level. She must inject up to four times a day to maintain ideal glucose levels. If her glucose level drops too low, she will become hypoglycemic and go into a coma. If her glucose level is too high, it will cause long-term physical deterioration of numerous body systems. Since eating increases glucose levels, Sarah needs to inject one half hour before eating larger meals. Her doctor has recommended that she eat smaller and more frequent meals to help modulate variations in her glucose levels. Outside of work, Sarah leads an active life and exercises regularly. She must be careful to time her injections depending on her exercise and eating patterns. Exercise reduces glucose levels on a short-term basis and can upset the balance of insulin and glucose in the body, possibly resulting in a hypoglycemic reaction. Because Sarah is careful about her eating, exercise, and treatment regimen, her diabetes is reasonably well controlled. She does not yet exhibit any physical damage related to excess glucose levels. She carries small amounts of sugar with her to minimize the incidence of hypoglycemic reactions. Assembly-line workers operate on a very rigid schedule. Sarah wants to seek accommodations from her employer to make it easier for her to maintain her glucose levels while at work. Was Sarah an individual with a disability under the original ADA? What about under the ADA as amended?

9-6. Alpha-1 antitrypsin ("AAT") is a serum protein that protects the lungs from proteolytic enzymes. Approximately 80 percent of individuals who inherit an AAT deficiency from both parents develop chronic obstructive pulmonary disease ("COPD"). Individuals who inherit the deficiency from only one parent have an increased risk of developing COPD (one in ten), especially if they smoke or work in dusty environments. Tuan Lee, who inherited AAT deficiency from both of his parents, does not yet suffer from any symptoms of COPD. Is Tuan impaired? If so, is he substantially limited with respect to a major life activity and, therefore, protected under the ADA as amended?

---

b. Record of Such an Impairment

Section 3(2) of the ADA defines disability to include having a record of an impairment that substantially limits a major life activity. A variety of "records" contain such information, including employment records, medical records, and education records. However, "[t]he impairment indicated in the record must be an impairment that would substantially limit one or more of the individual's major life activities." 29 C.F.R. pt. 1630, app. § 1630.2(k). *See Colwell v. Suffolk County Police Dept.*, 158 F.3d 635, 645 (2d Cir. 1998) (hospitalization for cerebral hemorrhage was too vague and too short to be record of impairment); *Sherrod v. American Airlines, Inc.*, 132 F.3d 1112, 1120-21 (5th Cir. 1998) (hospitalization for back surgery was not a record of an impairment that would substantially limit a major life activity). *See generally* Alex B. Long, *(Whatever Happened to) The ADA's "Record of" Prong(?)*, 81 WASH. L. REV. 669 (2006).

Both the original and proposed regulations view the ADA as protecting cancer survivors from discrimination on the basis of their medical history. See proposed § 1630.2(k), Example 1. *See generally* Jane Byeff Korn, *Cancer and the ADA: Rethinking Disability*, 74 S. CAL. L. REV. 399 (2001) (focusing on breast cancer survivors).

PROBLEM

9-7. Reconsider Problems 9-5 and 9-6. Could you make a "record of impairment" argument on behalf of Sarah or Tuan?

c. *Regarded as Having Such an Impairment*

We saw earlier that individuals are protected by the ADA even if they are not actually impaired or if they are "regarded" by their employers as being impaired. *Sutton* read this provision of the statute as addressing two situations: "(1) a covered entity mistakenly believes that a person has a physical impairment that substantially limits one or more major life activities, or (2) a covered entity mistakenly believes that an actual, nonlimiting impairment substantially limits one or more major life activities." 527 U.S. at 489. The Court quoted EEOC regulations as indicating that such misperceptions often 'result from stereotypic assumptions not truly indicative of . . . individual ability.' " For example, *Brown v. Lester E. Cox Medical Center*, 286 F.3d 1040 (8th Cir. 2002), upheld a jury verdict for plaintiff on her "regarded as" claim when evidence showed that the employer regarded plaintiff's multiple sclerosis as substantially limiting her ability to think. The court rejected the employer's argument that it regarded plaintiff as only below average for a surgical nurse since the employer apparently believed plaintiff's multiple sclerosis made her unfit for further employment in any capacity at the medical center. But stereotyping is not necessary for a "regarded as" claim. A good-faith or "innocent misperception" can still result in liability under the "regarded as" prong. *See School Bd. of Nassau County v. Arline*, 480 U.S. 273 (1987) (threat posed by teacher with tuberculosis must be assessed in terms of medical evidence).

Although not directly addressed in *Sutton*, the original ADA regulations defining "regarded as impaired" allow a plaintiff with a physical or mental impairment to argue that the impairment is substantially limiting "as a result of the attitudes of others toward such impairment." The Interpretive Guidance further explains this provision:

> For example, an individual may have a prominent facial scar or disfigurement, or may have a condition that periodically causes an involuntary jerk of the head but does not limit the individual's major life activities. If an employer discriminates against such an individual because of the negative reactions of customers, the employer would be regarding the individual as disabled and acting on the basis of that perceived disability.

29 C.F.R. pt. 1630, app. § 1630.2(l). Reconsider discrimination based on obesity. Might an obese person have a claim if he is denied employment because of the feared negative reactions of customers?

"Regarded as" discrimination may be more common than might first appear. Professor Michelle Travis, in *Perceived Disabilities, Social Cognition, and "Innocent Mistakes,"* 55 VAND. L. REV. 481 (2002), contends that "at least some perceived disabilities are likely to result not from consciously held, group-based prejudices or generalizations, but from nonmotivational cognitive processing errors," *id.* at 491, that is, errors that do not derive from conscious prejudices or even conscious group-based decision making. She asserts that social cognition research can help to determine when such mistakes have occurred. She concludes that "courts should apply the ADA's perceived disability prong to claims involving nonmotivational mistakes, but she argues that such mistakes should not trigger the same extent of liability as mistakes that are invidiously motivated or otherwise the product of conscious, group-based decisionmaking." *Id.* She advocates a "middle ground" approach to liability that would fashion the remedies awarded to the employer's conduct.

While *Sutton* set the structure for analyzing regarded as claims, it also cut back on the potential sweep of the "regarded as" prong by reading it literally: A person was regarded as having a disability only if she was regarded as having an impairment that substantially limited a major life activity. In other words, plaintiff must be regarded as having an actual disability. An example is *Tockes v. Air-Land Transp. Serv. Inc.*, 343 F.3d 895 (7th Cir. 2003), holding that plaintiff failed to establish that his employer regarded him as disabled, even though he was told by his manager, when he was fired, that it had been a "mistake" to hire someone who was "handicapped" and that manager called him crippled and disabled. While plaintiff established that his employer regarded him as disabled, he did not establish that the employer regarded him as disabled within the meaning of the ADA. This can't be right, can it?

The ADAAA legislatively overruled *Sutton* in this respect, but did so by creating a two-tiered structure for disability claims. For actual (and presumably "record of") disabilities, the statute continue to both forbid discrimination and mandate accommodation. But for "regarded as" claims, the ADAAA bars discrimination only; it does not mandate accommodation.

Thus, the ADAAA provides:

> (A) An individual meets the requirement of 'being regarded as having such an impairment' if the individual establishes that he or she has been subjected to an action prohibited under this Act because of an actual or perceived physical or mental impairment whether or not the impairment limits or is perceived to limit a major life activity.
>
> (B) Paragraph 1(C) [the "regarded as" prong] shall not apply to impairments that are transitory and minor. A transitory impairment is an impairment with an actual or expected duration of 6 months or less.

As we saw in *Horgan*, the "regarded as" prong now provides the broadest protection—whether or not the plaintiff was disabled by his HIV, the mere fact that the employer acted on the basis of it violated the statute since HIV has been held to be an impairment. Thus, for this claim, there need be no finding that the impairment, real or perceived, was regarded as substantially limiting a major life activity. Rather, plaintiff need show merely that the employer took a prohibited action because of the impairment, real or perceived, and that the impairment was not "transitory and minor." Not a heavy lift for Mr. Horgan.

How would this apply to the *Sutton* plaintiffs? They presumably have no actual disability under the ADA, originally or as amended, since their corrective lenses may be taken into account in determining whether their visual impairments substantially limit one or more major life activities. But, corrected or not, they do have myopia, an impairment. And their prospective employer denied them employment because of their myopia. They thus would be considered individuals with a disability under the "regarded as" prong under the amended statute, although the "qualification standard" defense might avoid liability for United.

While extending the statute's "regarded as" prong to protect against discrimination on the basis of an impairment, the ADAAA partially counterbalanced this expansion by providing that "regarded as" plaintiffs are not entitled to reasonable accommodation: an employer "need not provide a reasonable accommodation . . . to an individual who meets the definition of disability solely under" the regarded as prong. Thus, if an individual is merely regarded as disabled, and not also actually disabled, she is protected from discrimination but not entitled to any accommodation. *See generally* Stephen F. Befort, *Let's Try This Again: The ADA Amendments Act of 2008 Attempts to Reinvigorate the "Regarded As" Prong of the Statutory Definition of Disability,* *** UTAH L. REV. ***, *** (forthcoming). Mr. Horgan cannot be discriminated against because of his HIV but no accommodation need be made, say for treatment purposes.

2. The Meaning of "Qualified Individual with a Disability"

Establishing the existence of a disability is necessary but not sufficient to bring an individual within Title I's protections since that statute prohibits discrimination only against "a *qualified* individual with a disability because of the disability of such individual." 42 U.S.C. § 12112(a) (2006) (emphasis added). In turn, Title I in § 12111(8) defines a "qualified individual with a disability" as:

> an individual with a disability who, with or without reasonable accommodation, can perform the essential functions of the employment position that such individual holds or desires. For the purposes of this title, consideration shall be given to the employer's judgment as to what functions of a job are essential, and if an employer has prepared a written description before advertising or interviewing applicants for the job, this description shall be considered evidence of the essential functions of the job.

This definition protects disabled individuals who can perform the essential tasks of their jobs and thus prevents employers from denying employment because a disability precludes the performance of nonessential or relatively unimportant aspects of the job. On the other hand, denying employment to someone who cannot perform the essential functions of the job with or without reasonable accommodation is perfectly legal. *See Kinneary v. City of New York*, 601 F.3d 151 (2d Cir. 2010) (when an individual who was denied his captain's license because shy bladder syndrome prevented him from urinating for random drug tests, he was not otherwise qualified to perform the essential functions of his job). Accordingly, to determine whether an individual is qualified, it is necessary to distinguish the essential functions of the job from those that are not.

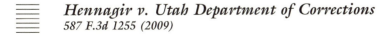

Hennagir v. Utah Department of Corrections
587 F.3d 1255 (2009)

LUCERO, Circuit Judge.

This case requires us to determine whether a job function that is rarely required in the normal course of an employee's duties may nonetheless be an essential job function under the Americans with Disabilities Act. We conclude that when the potential consequences of employing an individual who is unable to perform the function are sufficiently severe, such a function may be deemed essential. We further conclude that it is unreasonable for an employee to demand identical job duties less the disputed essential job requirement, regardless of the label given to the proposed accommodation.

Plaintiff Barbara Hennagir was employed as a physician's assistant ("PA") by the Utah Department of Corrections ("DOC"). Following several years of successful work by Hennagir, DOC added a physical safety training requirement to medical and clinical positions that required inmate contact, including Hennagir's position. Unable to complete the training because of a number of physical impairments, Hennagir complained of disability discrimination and requested that she be able to continue in her position without fulfilling the new requirement. DOC refused, leading to this lawsuit. . . .

I

From April 1997 until August 2005, Hennagir was employed as a PA at DOC's Central Utah Correctional Facility in Gunnison, Utah ("Gunnison"). When she was hired, DOC did not require Peace Officer Standards and Training ("POST") certification for medical and clinical staff at Gunnison. In 2001, however, DOC sought to enter such staff into Utah's Public Safety Retirement system ("PSR"). To enroll in PSR, all covered positions in the agency must be POST certified. POST certification includes an assessment of physical strength, flexibility, and endurance.

DOC considered the POST certification requirement for medical staff for several years. As early as September 1998, a DOC division director recommended POST certification to the executive director. In 1999, a medical technician was attacked by a Gunnison inmate, and the victim sued DOC and a number of its employees, leading the State Risk Management Division to echo the POST certification recommendation. The following year, DOC clinical services administrators met to discuss POST certification. At that meeting, questions were raised as to whether incumbent employees could be "grandfathered" in — that is, exempted from the POST requirement based on their status as current employees.

In 2001, DOC contacted Utah Retirement Systems ("URS") regarding its plan to enroll medical and clinical personnel in PSR. URS advised that workers could be eligible for PSR only if every employee in a given position was POST certified. In 2002, DOC applied for PSR for all its clinical personnel whose job duties required contact with inmates. Because Hennagir's PA position at Gunnison included inmate contact, it was approved for PSR, and thus POST certification was mandated.

Gunnison medical staff began attending a POST "academy" in October of 2002. Hennagir attended, but was given permission not to participate in the physical activities because of her medical conditions. Hennagir complains of a number of impairments, including lupus, osteoarthritis, rheumatism, avascular necrosis, Sjogren's syndrome, and fibromyalgia. She has had both hips replaced and undergone surgery on her left shoulder. As a result of these maladies, Hennagir is limited in activities such as sitting, bathing, sleeping, lifting, bending and flexing, climbing stairs, running, and biking.

DOC eventually opted to require POST certification for incumbent employees. In October 2003, Hennagir was notified that she would be unable to continue working as a PA at Gunnison because she was unable to meet the POST certification requirement.

[As a result of her internal grievance, DOC's Director of the Division of Institutional Operations, told plaintiff that he did not have the power to exempt her from POST certification, but he offered her a PA position at another facility that did not require such certification. The other facility was, however, over 100 miles from plaintiff's home. Ultimately, Hennagir was told to choose between the transfer or termination. Rather, she took medical leave under the Family and Medical Leave Act. When this leave was exhausted, she went on long-term disability leave, which lasted nearly a year, during which DOC retained her position at Gunnison. During these events, Hennagir had filed charges of discrimination and retaliation with the EEOC. The agency found reasonable cause to believe that she had been the victim of disability discrimination and that DOC's offer to transfer her was not a reasonable accommodation. The agency initiated conciliation efforts, and DOC made a final offer to Hennagir of a medical position at Gunnison auditing, reviewing, coordinating, and monitoring the contract care of inmates at the same salary. Hennagir declined, and DOC terminated her employment.]

II ...

A ...

Hennagir bears the burden of showing that she is able to perform the essential functions of her job, with or without reasonable accommodation. *Mason* [*v. Avaya Commc'ns, Inc.*, 357 F.3d 1114, 1116 (10th Cir. 2004) (citing *US Airways, Inc. v. Barnett*, 535 U.S. 391, 400 (2002))]. To determine whether POST certification is an essential job function, we begin by deciding "whether [DOC] actually requires all employees in the particular position to satisfy the alleged job-related requirement." *Davidson v. Am. Online, Inc.*, 337 F.3d 1179, 1191 (10th Cir. 2003). If it does, we look to whether POST certification is fundamental to the Gunnison PA position. *Id.; see also* 29 C.F.R. § 1630.2(n)(1). Among the factors we consider in this inquiry are:

(i) The employer's judgment as to which functions are essential;
(ii) Written job descriptions prepared before advertising or interviewing applicants for the job;
(iii) The amount of time spent on the job performing the function;
(iv) The consequences of not requiring the incumbent to perform the function;
(v) The terms of a collective bargaining agreement;
(vi) The work experience of past incumbents in the job; and/or
(vii) The current work experience of incumbents in similar jobs.

29 C.F.R. § 1630.2(n)(3); *see also Mason*. However, this analysis "is not intended to second guess the employer or to require him to lower company standards. . . . Provided that any necessary job specification is job-related, uniformly enforced, and consistent with business necessity, the employer has a right to establish what a job is and what is required to perform it." *Davidson*.

The undisputed evidence shows that all PAs at Gunnison must become POST certified. Under URS rules, all employees in a position must achieve POST certification once that position is approved for PSR enrollment. Further, Medical Director Garden testified that every medical doctor, registered nurse, and PA at Gunnison had become POST certified. Hennagir does not attempt to controvert this evidence. Instead, she argues that POST certification was not required when she was hired, that she successfully performed her job duties for years without being POST certified, and that the POST certification requirement was added to the PA position in order to qualify for PSR, not because it is essential.

We begin by noting that the essential function inquiry is not conducted as of an individual's hire date. "The ADA does not limit an employer's ability to establish or change the content, nature, or functions of a job." *See Milton v. Scrivner, Inc.*, 53 F.3d 1118, 1124 (10th Cir. 1995). We must look instead to whether a job function was essential at the time it was imposed on Hennagir. *See id.* We conclude it was.

We weigh heavily the employer's judgment regarding whether a job function is essential. *See Mason*; 29 C.F.R. § 1630.2(n)(3)(i) (listing "[t]he employer's judgment as to which functions are essential" as a factor to be considered). DOC decision-makers are unanimous regarding the importance of POST certification. As early as 1998, a DOC division director sought to implement POST certification for medical staff because "[t]he institutional setting requires, first and foremost, that all employees have a security mission," and the lack of certification "tends to create a conflict amongst our staff as to who's [sic] responsibility it is to ensure safety and control." Michael Chabries, DOC's Executive Director when the POST certification requirement was implemented, explained that, "like certified corrections officers, the medical staff often had daily, direct inmate contact and thus daily exposure to the myriad risks of working with an inmate population." By enrolling these employees in PSR, Chabries stated, "the Department could require these employees to become fully trained and certified as peace officers and thus better able to handle, directly, the risks and dangers found at the prison's facilities." Garden opined that "POST certification is important in terms of training, insuring that the staff are not injured, [and] that the staff understand the danger of working in that environment."

Further, the risks involved in direct inmate contact strike at the heart of another factor used to determine whether a job function is essential: the consequences of not requiring an employee to perform the function. *See* 29 C.F.R. § 1630.2(n)(3)(iv). Sadly, DOC's fears regarding the physical safety of its medical and clinical staff were realized in 1999, when a medical technician was attacked by an inmate during the course of her duties. That incident led the State Risk Management Division to recommend a POST certification requirement. The common sense nature of this recommendation is patent: Because the potential consequences of an inmate attack are severe, it is reasonable to require employees who have direct contact with inmates to undergo training on responding to these dangerous scenarios.

Hennagir acknowledges that she spent much of her time meeting with prison inmates, taking their medical histories, and physically examining them. She contends, however, that she never had to employ emergency training during her eight years at Gunnison, and that other employees have had similar experiences. This argument goes to a number of properly weighed factors: the amount of time spent on the job performing the function, the work experience of past incumbents, and the current work experience of incumbents in similar jobs. *See* 29 C.F.R. § 1630.2(n)(3)(iii), (vi), (vii). In light of the undisputed evidence described in the preceding paragraphs, however, we find this argument insufficient to create a material issue of fact.

The Sixth Circuit faced a similar set of circumstances when it addressed whether the ability to restrain an inmate was an essential job function of a sheriff's deputy. *Hoskins v. Oakland County Sheriff's Dep't*, 227 F.3d 719, 727 (6th Cir. 2000). As our sibling circuit explained, "Although a deputy [sheriff] may be required physically to restrain inmates only infrequently, the potential for physical confrontation with inmates exists on a daily basis, and the consequence of failing to require a deputy to perform this function when the occasion arises could be a serious threat to security." *Id.* (citation omitted); *see also Frazier v. Simmons*, 254 F.3d 1247, 1260 (10th Cir. 2001) ("Even viewing the evidence in the light most favorable to [plaintiff] and assuming that an investigator may be required to perform these physical activities infrequently, the potential for physical confrontation with a suspect exists any time [plaintiff] conducts a crime scene investigation."); 29 C.F.R. pt. 1630, app. ("[A]lthough a firefighter may not regularly have to carry an unconscious adult out of a burning building, the consequence of failing to require the firefighter to be able to perform this function would be serious."). Like the sheriff's deputy in *Hoskins*, Hennagir came face to face with inmates on a daily basis. We agree with the Sixth Circuit that, in such circumstances, completion of emergency response training is an essential job function.

B

[The fact that plaintiff could not perform an essential job function without accommodation did not end the inquiry since it was still possible that she could perform that function with a reasonable accommodation. However, the burden of proposing such an accommodation is on plaintiff, *Mason*, and each accommodation she proposed, "although labeled differently, demands an identical modification: waiver of the POST certification requirement. According to Hennagir, she should be permitted to retain the same job duties (perhaps with a different title) without completing POST certification." This was unreasonable since it amounted to requesting that DOC eliminate an essential job function. Further, plaintiff's claim that DOC refused to engage in an interactive process to explorer a reasonable accommodation failed since such a claim is dependent on plaintiff showing that a reasonable accommodation was possible.]

NOTES

1. *Essential Functions.* What makes a job function "essential"? The EEOC's regulations define the term to mean the "fundamental job duties," as opposed to the "marginal functions" of the job. Factors to consider in making that distinction are whether the position exists to perform the function, the number of employees available to perform the function, and/or whether the function is highly specialized, thus requiring special expertise. In addition to the employer's job description, other evidence to consider includes, although it is not limited to, the employer's judgment, the amount of time spent performing the function, the work experience of people previously or currently in the job or similar jobs, and the terms of any collective bargaining agreement. *See* 29 C.F.R. § 1630.2(n). *See Shannon v. New York City Transit Auth.*, 332 F.3d 95 (2d Cir. 2003) (color-blind bus driver unable to perform essential functions of the job, which included recognizing traffic signals).

2. *Who Proves What?* A plaintiff is not protected by the ADA unless she can perform the essential functions of the job. That would suggest that she has to establish what the essential functions are and her ability to perform them. On the other hand, a plaintiff has an incentive to minimize the essential functions, which suggests that, as a practical matter, the defendant will be urging such proof — and, of course, it's likely to be in the best position to establish the point. *See Bates v. UPS*, 511 F.3d 974 (9th Cir. 2007) (en banc) (although the plaintiff has the ultimate burden of persuading the factfinder that he can perform the job's essential functions, an employer who disputes the plaintiff's claim that he can perform those functions must put forth evidence of what the essential functions are).

3. *Changing Essential Functions.* The *Hennagir* court concludes that the fact that a particular function is rarely performed does not prevent it from being essential. *See also Richardson v. Friendly Ice Cream Corp.*, 594 F.3d 69, 78 (1st Cir. 2010) (stating that the essential functions of a position "are not limited to the 'primary' function of the position). Further, the court relies heavily on the employer's view of what's now essential, even though the function at issue had not been deemed essential by that employer for years. Is such deference appropriate or does it create the possibility of an end run around the reasonable accommodation duty? *See also Gratzl v. Office of the Chief Judges*, 601 F.3d 674 (7th Cir. 2010) (job reclassification rendered plaintiff unable to perform the essential functions of the new position).

4. *Job Descriptions.* Does the ADA itself suggest such deference? Recall that §12111(8) states that "consideration shall be given to the employer's judgment as to what functions of a job are essential" and that written job descriptions prepared prior to advertising or interviewing applicants "shall be considered evidence of the essential functions of the job." But such documentation is only "evidence" — doesn't that term suggest that the court can look behind what the employer says is essential?

To some extent this is certainly true. What is important is not necessarily what the employer claims to be an essential function but rather whether the employer treats a function as essential. *See Carmona v. Sw. Airlines Co.*, 604 F.3d 848 (5th Cir. 2010) (although plaintiff, who had psoriatic arthritis, was not able to work regularly, he was able to perform the essential functions of his job as a flight attendant when he did work, and the employer's lenient policy regarding attendance allowed the jury to find that that was sufficient).

5. *Showing Up.* Woody Allen famously said, "Eighty percent of success is showing up." That seems to be true in ADA cases, since numerous courts have held that regular and timely attendance at work is an essential job function, and, therefore, a disabled individual who cannot meet that requirement is not "qualified." *See, e.g., Vandenbroek v. PSEG Power Conn. LLC*, 356 F. App'x 457, 460 (2d Cir. 2009) (an alcoholic whose resultant absenteeism caused his discharge was not within the statute's protection, even if the discharge could have been viewed as caused by his disability, since he was not otherwise qualified, given that attendance at scheduled shifts was an essential function of a boiler utility operator at the power plant); *Brenneman v. Medcentral Health Sys.*, 366 F.3d 412 (6th Cir. 2004) (regular attendance was an essential function of pharmacy technician position); *Spangler v. Federal Home Loan Bank*, 278 F.3d 847 (8th Cir. 2002) (same for bank employee). Other circuits, however, have recognized that particular jobs may not require uninterrupted attendance at the workplace. *See Carmona v. Sw. Airlines Co.*, 604 F.3d 848 (5th Cir. 2010) (flight attendant); *Cehrs v. Northeast Ohio Alzheimer's Research Ctr.*, 155 F.3d

775 (6th Cir. 1998) (nurse). *See generally* Michelle A. Travis, *Recapturing the Transformative Potential of Employment Discrimination Law*, 62 WASH. & LEE L. REV. 3 (2005). Is there a difference between an employee whose disability results in sporadic absences and one whose disability requires a medical leave? Attendance and leave as a reasonable accommodation is discussed further in Chapter 10.

    6. *Essential Only for Some?* What are the essential functions of a job when not all incumbents in the job perform the same work? In *Stone v. City of Mount Vernon*, 118 F.3d 92 (2d Cir. 1997), the city argued that it could not hire a paraplegic in the fire department's fire alarm bureau because he could not engage in firefighting or fire-suppression activities. The court indicated that, even if it would be an undue hardship to hire five or ten disabled individuals in the bureau, it might not be an undue hardship to hire one. *Id.* at 101. *But see Dargis v. Sheahan*, 526 F.3d 981 (7th Cir. 2008) (corrections officer was not qualified because of his inability to rotate through positions requiring inmate contact, despite claim that some co-workers were assigned to no-contact positions).

    7. *Quality and Quantity of Work as Essential.* Suppose an individual can perform all the essential job tasks, but cannot meet the speed or quality standards set by the employer. The Interpretive Guidance provides:

> [T]he inquiry into essential functions is not intended to second guess an employer's business judgment with regard to production standards, whether qualitative or quantitative, nor to require employers to lower such standards. . . . If an employer requires its typists to be able to accurately type 75 words per minute, it will not be called upon to explain why an inaccurate work product, or a typing speed of 65 words per minute, would not be adequate. . . . However, if an employer does require accurate 75 word per minute typing . . , it will have to show that it actually imposes such requirements on its employees in fact, and not simply on paper.

29 C.F.R. pt. 1630, app. §1630.2(n); *see Milton v. Scrivner, Inc.*, 53 F.3d 1118 (10th Cir. 1995) (pace set by employer's new production standard constituted an essential function of grocery selector job). What arguments would you make on essential functions on behalf of a dyslexic lawyer who produces a good work product but is denied partnership on the basis of (relatively) low productivity? Is she a qualified individual with a disability? Note that the statute prohibits discriminatory qualification standards unless job-related for the position in question and consistent with business necessity and the duty of reasonable accommodation. *See* 42 U.S.C. §12112(b)(6) (2006). Is the Interpretive Guidance consistent with this statutory provision?

    Put another way, is it appropriate to judge disabled workers by the standards of the status quo, standards that were developed for an "abled" world? According to the "social model" of disability, on which the ADA was largely erected, "inequalities foisted upon the disabled because of their exclusion from social interaction (including work) have been the result of socially constructed practices rather than the outgrowth of natural phenomena." Michael Ashley Stein, *Labor Markets, Rationality, and Workers with Disabilities*, 21 BERKELEY J. EMP. & LAB. L. 314, 330-31 (2000). The paradigmatic example is architecture "not accessible to wheelchair users, [that] may be viewed as a 'natural' condition by the majority non-disabled class. Yet, because there is no absolute reason why a 'universal design' which can give access to a restroom for all users should not equally be the norm, the social model perceives the distinction as artificial and the result of an unjust social arrangement." *Id*. While the social construction of restrooms may be readily apparent, the social construction of workplace practices may seem both natural and necessary to efficiency. Does the ADA require a reconsideration of such practices when they impede the opportunities of the disabled, or does the ADA's transformative potential stop because these are "essential functions"?

8. *Associational Discrimination*. Even if an employee is not herself disabled under any of the three prongs, she may still not be discriminated against because of her relationship with a person who is disabled. 42 U.S.C. § 12112(b)(4) bars discrimination against "a qualified individual because of the known disability of an individual with whom the qualified individual is known to have a relationship or association." In this scenario, the protected person must be qualified, but the disabled person need not be.

For example, in *Dewitt v. Proctor Hosp.*, 517 F.3d 944 (7th Cir. 2008), a claim of discrimination on account of the plaintiff's association with her disabled husband was allowed to proceed where there was evidence that her discharge was an effort to avoid the high costs of her husband's cancer treatment; her supervisor's comments about "creative" cost-cutting and her suggestion that less expensive hospice care be considered, coupled with plaintiff's discharge shortly after review of medical claims, allowed inference that employer was concerned that husband might require treatment indefinitely. *See also Trujillo v. PacifiCorp*, 524 F.3d 1149 (10th Cir. 2008) (married employees raised factual issue as to whether the alleged reason for their discharges was a pretext for avoiding the high costs of their son's medical expenses). In *Dewitt*, Judge Posner concurred, suggesting, however, that, if the employer would have discriminated against anyone who ran up such high medical bills, there would have been no discrimination on the basis of disability. What do you think of that argument?

3. The Duty of Reasonable Accommodation

A qualified individual with a disability is one who can perform the essential functions of the job she holds or desires—with or without reasonable accommodation. The concept of reasonable accommodation distinguishes the ADA from other antidiscrimination statutes. Under the ADA, it is not enough for an employer to treat its disabled employees the same—no better and no worse—than it treats its nondisabled employees. In appropriate circumstances, the employer must take affirmative steps that will allow disabled employees to perform their jobs—it must provide a "reasonable accommodation" where that will not result in "undue hardship." Failing to provide reasonable accommodations constitutes one form of discrimination under the statute.

In *Hennagir*, the plaintiff lost her claim because she could not identify a reasonable accommodation that would not modify an essential function. But she was disabled, so, had she been qualified, she would have been entitled to reasonable accommodations for her disabilities. The question of what precisely is a "reasonable accommodation" under the ADA is deferred to Chapter 10, which discusses that question together with the Family and Medical Leave Act, the other major statute requiring employers to accommodate certain personal needs of their employees.

4. Discriminatory Qualification Standards

The ADA prohibits the use of discriminatory standards or selection criteria in hiring and classifying employees. Section 102(b) provides that "discriminate" includes

3. utilizing standards, criteria, or methods of administration . . . that have the effect of discrimination on the basis of disability, . . .

6. using qualification standards, employment tests, or other selection criteria that screen out or tend to screen out an individual with a disability or a class of individuals with disabilities unless the standard, test or other selection criteria, as used by the covered entity, is shown to be job-related for the position in question and is consistent with business necessity. . . .

Employers have at least three possible defenses to an allegation of discrimination under this definition. First, the language of the prohibition on discriminatory standards and selection criteria is reminiscent of disparate impact under Title VII; not surprisingly, ADA regulations indicate that both paragraphs are subject to a job-relatedness and business necessity defense similar to that permitted in disparate impact cases. *See* 29 C.F.R. §§ 1630.7, 1630.10. However, § 103(a), which sets forth defenses, provides that the use of criteria with a disparate impact on the basis of disability must also be consistent with the employer's duty to provide reasonable accommodation. *See* 29 C.F.R. § 1630.15(b)(1), (c). Second, standards or selection criterion may also be defended on the basis that they are permitted or required by another federal statute or regulation. *See* 29 C.F.R. § 1630.15(e). Third, ADA § 103(b) provides that "[t]he term 'qualification standards' may include a requirement that an individual shall not pose a direct threat to the health or safety of other individuals in the workplace."

In short, qualification standards that are either facially discriminatory or that have a disparate impact on disabled individuals can violate the ADA, but all discriminatory qualification standards may be defended as job-related and consistent with business necessity, permitted or required by another federal statute or regulation, or necessary to prevent a direct threat to health and safety.

Most challenges to qualification standards do not raise significant factual issues about whether the challenged standard or criteria actually screens out disabled individuals. Challenged standards frequently are facially discriminatory, such as vision requirements for drivers. Even standards or criteria that do not expressly implicate a disabling impairment are generally challenged on the ground that a disabled individual cannot meet the standard because of his or her disability. Thus, the fact that the standard or criteria screens out an individual with a disability is obvious. The primary issue in these cases, therefore, is whether the discriminatory standard or criteria can be defended.

This section first examines the direct threat defense. Second, it considers the job-relatedness and business necessity defense as applied to qualification standards that screen out disabled individuals, including those promulgated by the federal government. Finally, it addresses the disparate impact theory in disability discrimination cases.

a. Direct Threat

ADA § 103(b) provides that "[t]he term 'qualification standards' may include a requirement that an individual shall not pose a direct threat to the health or safety of other individuals in the workplace." Direct threat is defined by § 101(3) as a "significant risk to the health or safety of others" that cannot be eliminated by a reasonable accommodation. The EEOC requires the "direct threat" determination to be based on a reasonable medical judgment that considers such factors as the duration of the risk, the nature and severity of the potential harm, the likelihood of the potential harm, and the imminence of the potential harm. *See* 29 C.F.R. § 1630.2(r). Direct threat is simultaneously relevant to whether the individual with a disability is "qualified" to perform essential functions, whether the employer is justified in basing an employment decision on the individual's disability, and whether the employer has a duty to accommodate the individual's disability. It is unclear whether the plaintiff or defendant has the burden of proof as to whether an employee posed a direct threat. *EEOC v. Wal-Mart Stores, Inc.*, 477 F.3d 561 (8th Cir. 2007) (employer bears the burden of persuasion). *See generally* Rene L. Duncan, Note, *The "Direct Threat" Defense Under the ADA: Posing a Threat to the Protection of Disabled Employees*, 73 Mo. L. Rev. 1303 (2008) (arguing that the legislative history of the ADA indicates that the employer has the burden of proof on this defense).

The ADA's "direct threat" provision is derived from the Supreme Court's decision in *School Board of Nassau County v. Arline*, 480 U.S. 273 (1987), which was decided under § 504 of the Rehabilitation Act. The Court held that an individual with tuberculosis was not otherwise qualified to be an elementary school teacher if she posed a significant risk of transmitting the disease to others and if that risk could not be eliminated through reasonable accommodation. In *Bragdon v. Abbott*, 524 U.S. 624 (1998), the defendant, a dentist, asserted that whether a risk is significant is to be assessed from the point of view of the person denying the service. The Court, however, stated that such assessments are to be made on the basis of medical or other objective evidence available at the time that the allegedly discriminatory action occurred. A good-faith belief that a significant risk exists is not enough, nor would any special deference be afforded a defendant who is himself a medical professional.

The EEOC's regulation interpreting "direct threat" defines the term to include "a significant risk of substantial harm to the health or safety *of the individual or others* that cannot be eliminated or reduced by reasonable accommodation." 29 C.F.R. § 1630.2(r) (emphasis added). The validity of that regulation was at issue in *Chevron U.S.A. Inc. v. Echazabal*, 536 U.S. 73 (2002). Echazabal suffered from Hepatitis C, which caused severe liver damage. Chevron had refused to hire him because the position in question involved exposure to toxins in Chevron's refinery that posed elevated risk of harm to his damaged liver. The trial court granted summary judgment for Chevron based on the EEOC's regulation, but the Ninth Circuit invalidated that regulation. Since the ADA specifically provided for a "threat to others" defense, but was silent on the issue of "threat to self," the Ninth Circuit reasoned that Congress intended to exclude "threat to self."

The Supreme Court disagreed, since the text of the statute suggests that an employer's qualification standards "may include," but not be limited to, harm to others. Second, the Court held that there is no evidence that Congress made a deliberate choice to omit "threat to self" from the affirmative defense's scope. Third, the Court noted the slippery slope of limiting the direct-threat defense to situations that would harm others in the workplace. Referring to the risk of injury to others *outside* the workplace, the Court posited, "If Typhoid Mary had come under the ADA, would a meat packer have been defenseless if Mary had sued after being turned away?" *See generally* Samuel R. Bagenstos, *The Supreme Court, The Americans with Disabilities*

Act, and Rational Discrimination, 55 ALA. L. REV. 923 (2004); D. Aaron Lacy, *Am I My Brother's Keeper: Disabilities, Paternalism, and Threats to Self*, 44 SANTA CLARA L. REV. 55 (2003).

While *Echazabal* involved one direct-threat issue, others often arise in the workplace. Thus, courts assessing the risk of hiring HIV-infected individuals have reached different results depending on the nature of the work involved. *Compare Chalk v. United States Dist. Court*, 840 F.2d 701 (9th Cir. 1988) (teacher with AIDS did not pose a "significant risk" in the workplace and his condition could be monitored to ensure that any secondary infections he contracted also would not pose a significant risk), *with Waddell v. Valley Forge Dental Assocs.*, 276 F.3d 1275 (11th Cir. 2001) (HIV-positive dental hygienist posed a direct threat to the health and safety of others); *see generally* Katrina Atkins & Richard Bales, *HIV and the Direct Threat Defense*, 91 KY. L. J. 859 (2002-3).

The direct-threat defense is often raised in the context of employees with mental disabilities. In *The ADA, The Workplace, and the Myth of the "Dangerous Mentally Ill,"* 34 U.C. DAVIS L. REV. 849, 850-51 (2001), Professor Ann Hubbard notes that public fears concerning persons with mental disabilities are strikingly disproportionate to the risk of violence actually posed and cautioned that a direct-threat defense may not be based on erroneous risk assessments. *See also* Ann Hubbard, *Understanding and Implementing the ADA's Direct Threat Defense*, 95 Nw. U. L. REV. 1279 (2001); Jane Byeff Korn, *Crazy (Mental Illness Under the ADA)*, 36 U. MICH. J.L. REFORM 585 (2003).

Another issue that arises in connection with a direct-threat situation is whether the risk can be reasonably accommodated. For instance, can an accommodation that would reduce health or safety risks be unreasonable because of the burden it would place on co-workers? For example, what if co-workers can protect themselves against an individual's contagious disease by being vaccinated, wearing face masks and plastic gloves, or avoiding close contact with the person with a disability? *See Treadwell v. Alexander*, 707 F.2d 473 (11th Cir. 1983) (a proposed accommodation that would result in substantially increased workloads for co-workers was unreasonable); *cf.* 29 C.F.R. pt. 1630, app. § 1630.15(d) (describing accommodations that are an undue hardship).

b. *Job-related and Consistent with Business Necessity*

If a qualification standard excludes disabled individuals, it may still be permissible when it is "job-related and consistent with business necessity." In *Albertsons, Inc. v. Kirkingburg*, 527 U.S. 555 (1999), Albertsons fired Kirkingburg from his job as a commercial truck driver because he failed to meet federal vision standards. Kirkingburg sued his employer under the ADA when it failed to rehire him after he attained a waiver from the Department of Transportation ("DOT") that would have licensed him despite his condition. Kirkingburg contended that the ADA forbids an employer from requiring as a job qualification that an employee meet a federal standard when that employee obtained a waiver of the applicable standard. The Supreme Court held that "it was error to read the regulations establishing the waiver program as modifying the content of the basic visual acuity standard in a way that disentitled an employer like Albertsons to insist on it." The Court added that the waiver program was an "experiment" without "empirical evidence," and it would not require an employer to participate. Justice Thomas concurred in the judgment on the grounds that Kirkingburg was not a "qualified individual with a disability" since he did not meet the minimum visual acuity level required by the government.

Kirkingburg thus holds that employers hiring drivers covered by DOT's regulations may adopt blanket rules excluding drivers who do not meet DOT's physical requirements. In other words, individualized assessments are not required in this context, and the employer need not present evidence of the job-relatedness or business necessity of the qualification. *Cf.* 29 C.F.R. § 1630.15(e) (1998) (providing that compliance with another federal law or regulation is a defense to liability under the ADA).

Bates v. UPS, 511 F.3d 974 (9th Cir. 2007) (en banc), approached the questions of justification more generally. It first rejected a BFOQ analysis (which the court had previously adopted). Instead:

> To show "job-relatedness," an employer must demonstrate that the qualification standard fairly and accurately measures the individual's actual ability to perform the essential functions of the job. When every person excluded by the qualification standard is a member of a protected class — that is, disabled persons — an employer must demonstrate a predictive or significant correlation between the qualification and performance of the job's essential functions.
>
> To show that the disputed qualification standard is "consistent with business necessity," the employer must show that it "substantially promote[s]" the business's needs. "The 'business necessity' standard is quite high, and is not to be confused with mere expediency." For a safety-based qualification standard, "[i]n evaluating whether the risks addressed by . . . [the] qualification standard constitute a business necessity, the court should take into account the magnitude of possible harm as well as the probability of occurrence."
>
> Finally, to show that "performance cannot be accomplished by reasonable accommodation," the employer must demonstrate either that no reasonable accommodation currently available would cure the performance deficiency or that such reasonable accommodation poses an "undue hardship" on the employer.

Id. at 996 (citations and footnotes omitted). The court then turned to the qualification standard allocation of burdens of proof, which it viewed as parallel to those for the direct-threat defense. It explained:

> Because UPS has linked hearing with safe driving, UPS bears the burden to prove that nexus as part of its defense to use of the hearing qualification standard. The employees, however, bear the ultimate burden to show that they are qualified to perform the essential function of safely driving a package car. . . .
>
> By requiring UPS to justify the hearing test under the business necessity defense, but also requiring plaintiffs to show that they can perform the essential functions of the job, we are not saying, nor does the ADA require, that employers must hire employees who cannot safely perform the job, particularly where safety itself is an essential function. Nor are we saying that an employer can never impose a safety standard that exceeds minimum requirements imposed by law. However, when an employer asserts a blanket safety-based qualification standard — beyond the essential job function — that is not mandated by law and that qualification standard screens out or tends to screen out an individual with a disability, the employer — not the employee — bears the burden of showing that the higher qualification standard is job-related and consistent with business necessity, and that performance cannot be achieved through reasonable accommodation.

Id. at 992.

c. Disparate Impact

Disparate impact discrimination is applicable under the ADA. For example, in *Raytheon Company v. Hernandez*, 540 U.S. 44 (2003), plaintiff was forced to resign from defendant's employ after testing positive for cocaine. Two years later, he reapplied for employment, but his application was denied. The company contended it had a policy of refusing to rehire anyone who had been terminated for violation of workplace conduct rules. The Supreme Court ruled the Ninth Circuit had mistakenly treated this as a disparate treatment claim when it was at most a disparate impact analysis. To the extent that a neutral policy (no rehiring of discharge workers) resulted in not rehiring addicts, it was not because of intentional discrimination against the disabled but because a neutral rule disproportionately affected them. While the Court recognized that disparate impact is viable under the ADA, its opinion left unexamined whether the defendant's "no rehire" policy would run afoul of the statute under disparate impact analysis because the plaintiff had not properly plead the disparate impact claim. *See* Elizabeth Roseman, Comment, *A Phoenix from the Ashes? Heightened Pleading Requirements in Disparate Impact Cases*, 36 SETON HALL L. REV. 1043 (2006). It also did not reach the question of whether the ADA requires an employer to bend neutral rehiring policies as a form of reasonable accommodation of a disabled worker. *See generally* Christine Neylon O'Brien, *Facially Neutral No-Rehire Rules and the Americans with Disabilities Act*, 22 HOFSTRA LAB. & EMP. L.J. 114 (2004).

Framing reasonable accommodation claims as disparate impact claims can in some cases raise difficult policy issues. Consider, for example, the request of a covered individual for extra sick leave to deal with medical problems. Restricting sick leave would not directly exclude the person from work, but it might make it more difficult for her to schedule doctor's appointments, or more expensive because she must take unpaid personal days to see the doctor. As a consequence this type of policy could result in fewer disabled persons being employed. This policy would "impact" individuals with disabilities because their needs differ from those of other individuals. Should disparate impact liability apply to claims like this?

The closest the Court has come to answering this is *Alexander v. Choate*, 469 U.S. 287 (1985), decided under the Rehabilitation Act. There, the Court rejected the claim that the Tennessee Medicaid Program's 14-day limitation on inpatient coverage would have an unlawful disparate impact on the disabled. How might *Choate* affect a claim by an individual with a disability for more sick leave than other individuals receive? Under the ADA, can such an employee attack a sick leave policy that restricts paid leave to 14 days on the ground that the policy has a disparate impact on employees with disabilities? The EEOC suggests that such a claim is not viable, but that an employee affected by such a policy may be entitled to leave as a reasonable accommodation:

> It should be noted, however, that some uniformly applied employment policies or practices, such as leave policies, are not subject to challenge under the adverse impact theory. "No-leave" policies (e.g., no leave during the first six months of employment) are likewise not subject to challenge under the adverse impact theory. However, an employer, in spite of its "no-leave" policy, may, in appropriate circumstances, have to consider the provision of leave to an employee with a disability as a reasonable accommodation, unless the provision of leave would impose an undue hardship.

29 C.F.R. pt. 1630, app. § 1630.15(c). Does this mean that the policy is legal but that accommodation is always required unless it is an undue hardship? Is there much difference between that view and declaring the policy illegal vis-à-vis the disabled except where undue hardship exists, which would then make the policy a business necessity?

Note on a Rock and a Hard Place

When a disabled worker is discharged, she often needs to seek disability benefits, typically Social Security disability. Eligibility for such benefits is generally contingent on inability to work. This creates a tension between the disabled worker's claim that she is sufficiently disabled to be eligible for those benefits and her possible ADA challenge to the discharge, which requires that she be a "qualified individual." In *Cleveland v. Policy Management Systems Corporation*, 526 U.S. 795 (1999), the plaintiff lost her job after suffering a stroke. She then filed a Social Security Disability Insurance ("SSDI") claim since she was "unable to work" because of her "condition." *Id.* at 798. After receiving those benefits, the plaintiff filed an ADA claim against her employer for failing to provide her with "reasonable accommodations" so that she could have continued to perform her essential job functions. *Id.* Although the lower courts had held that a plaintiff cannot maintain two inconsistent positions for the purposes of SSDI and the ADA, the Supreme Court determined that a plaintiff's claim of total disability under the SSDI does not necessarily bar the plaintiff from filing an ADA claim for failure to make reasonable accommodations. *Id.* at 803. The Court stated that a plaintiff can be "unable to work" for purposes of the SSDI, and still may have been able to work if the employer had made "reasonable accommodations." *Id.* The Court noted that factual or legal inconsistencies must be explained by the plaintiff for the claim to survive summary judgment. *Id.* at 806.

After *Cleveland*, courts no longer presume that a claim for disability benefits is necessarily inconsistent with an ADA claim but instead closely examine the factual statements made in the benefits proceedings. *See, e.g., DeRosa v. Nat'l Envelope Corp.*, 595 F.3d 99, 104 (2d Cir. 2010) ("Fairly construed, [plaintiff's] statements related to his social interactions, not his capability to perform the essential functions of his job if permitted to work from home. With the context of the statements thus understood, the apparent contradiction between DeRosa's statements that he is limited in social circumstances, but still able to perform the conditions of his employment with a no-longer-available accommodation, is reconcilable."); *Kiely v. Heartland Rehabilitation Services Inc.*, 359 F.3d 386 (6th Cir. 2004) (legally blind former employee's application for Social Security disability benefits did not estop him from establishing claim under state disability law where he alleged that he applied for benefits on basis of his legal blindness, not inability to work). Suppose an employer requires employees who seek employer-provided disability benefits to sign a statement asserting, "I cannot perform the essential functions of any job with or without reasonable accommodation." Will signing such a statement bar a subsequent ADA claim?

If you were advising a discharged employee who you believe has a viable claim for disability discrimination, would you advise him to seek disability benefits? What factors would go into your advice?

G. PROCEDURES AND REMEDIES

Title VII creates an amalgam of methods — administrative and judicial — for enforcement of its substantive proscriptions, which both the ADA and ADEA follow with a few variations. The basic Title VII procedures for enforcement of the substantive rights it creates are found in 42 U.S.C. § 2000e-5 (2006) and are very complicated, especially for unrepresented individuals. Many of the complications arise from two distinct periods of limitation, which together mean that it is relatively easy for a plaintiff to finally get to court out of time. *See generally* CHARLES A. SULLIVAN & LAUREN WALTER, EMPLOYMENT DISCRIMINATION LAW & PRACTICE (2008), ch. 12.

Title VII time limitations were forced onto the national stage by *Ledbetter v. Goodyear Tire & Rubber Co.*, 550 U.S. 618 (2007), which held that Title VII's charge filing period begins to run when the employee is notified of an adverse employment decision. In the case itself, the plaintiff, who had won a jury verdict, had learned about her raise (but not the raises of her male co-workers) years before she filed her charge. *Ledbetter's* rejection of her claim struck a nerve both on the Court and in Congress. Justice Ginsburg read a strong dissent from the bench in which she called on Congress to override the majority, and Congress responded with the Lilly Ledbetter Fair Pay Act of 2009 ("FPA"), Pub. L. No. 111-2, § 3, 123 Stat. 5, 5-6 (2009) (to be codified at 42 U.S.C. § 2000e-5(e)(3)(A)). However, the FPA, while both retroactive and applicable to other antidiscrimination laws, is limited to expanding the governing limitations period only for "a discriminatory compensation decision or other practice," thus leaving other acts of discrimination still subject to very complex and very rigorous limitations periods. *See generally* Charles A. Sullivan *Raising the Dead?: The Lilly Ledbetter Fair Pay Act*, 84 TUL. L. REV. 499 (2010) (examining the statutory scheme and arguing for a "causation-only" interpretation of the FPA).

Most suits under the antidiscrimination laws are individual disparate treatment claims brought by private persons. But the EEOC may also sue, and, as we saw in connection with the two systemic theories, class actions are often invoked to prosecute systemic claims. In such settings, the complications of discrimination law are magnified by the complications of class action law. All of this may come to a head before the Supreme Court in the near future as a result of *Dukes v. Wal-Mart Stores, Inc.*, 603 F.3d 571 (9th Cir. 2010) (en banc), in which a sharply divided court upheld the certification of a class of some half-million women employed by Wal-Mart. Needless to say, certiorari has been sought. *See generally* Tristin Green, *Targeting Workplace Context: Title VII as a Tool for Institutional Reform*, 72 FORDHAM L. REV. 659 (2003); Melissa Hart, *Will Employment Discrimination Class Actions Survive?*, 37 AKRON L. REV. 813, 814-15 (2004); Michael Selmi, *The Price of Discrimination: The Nature of Class Action Employment Discrimination Litigation and Its Effects*, 81 TEX L. REV. 1249 (2003); Nantiya Ruan, *Bringing Sense to Incentives: An Examination of Incentive Payments to Named Plaintiffs in Employment Discrimination Class Actions*, 10 EMP. RTS. & EMP. POL'Y J. 395, 426 (2006).

Title VII, § 1981, the ADEA, and Title I of the ADA have similar, but distinct, remedial schemes. *See generally* Sullivan & Walter, ch. 13. As a result, the availability of, and limitations on, different forms of relief varies from statute to statute. Generally speaking, however, the statutes offer a successful plaintiff the possibility of instatement or reinstatement (with appropriate seniority) as well as back pay and attorneys' fees.

In appropriate cases, front pay (the same as back pay but measured from the time of judgment to the time the plaintiff resumes her rightful position) is also available. *See Pollard v. E. I. du Pont de Nemours & Co.*, 532 U.S. 843 (2001). However, back pay awards under all the statutes are to be reduced by amounts that were earned and could have been earned with reasonable diligence through alternative employment.

Title VII, the ADA, and § 1981 also offer compensatory and punitive damages, although both are capped under Title VII and the ADA. *See Pollard v. E. I. du Pont de Nemours & Co.*, 532 U.S. 843 (2001); Rebecca Hollander-Blumoff & Matthew T. Bodie, *The Effects of Jury Ignorance About Damage Caps: The Case of the 1991 Civil Rights Act*, 90 IOWA L. REV. 1365 (2005), but neither is available under the ADEA, which instead offers something called "liquidated damages." Where available, compensatory damages include emotional injury.

Punitive damages may be awarded only upon a showing of "malice" or "reckless indifference" by an employer. *Kolstad v. American Dental Ass'n*, 527 U.S. 526 (1999). *See generally* Stacy A. Hickox, *In Reduction of Punitive Damages for Employment Discrimination: Are Courts Ignoring Our Juries?*, 54 MERCER L. REV. 1081, 1121 (2003); Catherine M. Sharkey, *Punitive Damages as Societal Compensatory Damages*, 113 YALE L.J. 347, 352 (2003); Joseph Seiner, *The Failure of Punitive Damages in Employment Discrimination Cases: A Call for Change*, 50 WM. & MARY L. REV. 735 (2008).

A final remedial issue is whether the person who committed the discriminatory act has personal liability or whether liability is limited to the employer. *Miller v. Maxwell's Int'l, Inc.*, 991 F.2d 583 (9th Cir. 1993), held that neither Title VII nor the ADEA imposes personal liability. The court reasoned that these statutes are addressed to "employers," and even though this term is defined to include "agents" of the employer, this inclusion was intended to incorporate the doctrine of respondeat superior. Moreover, because both statutes exempt small employers from coverage, the court thought it "inconceivable" that Congress would have intended to impose liability on individual employees. Other appellate decisions have agreed that supervisory employees do not have personal liability to the discriminatee under Title VII and ADA Title I and the ADEA. But employees do have personal liability to the discriminatee under § 1981 and may be reachable under state law analogs to the federal discrimination laws. *See generally* Rebecca Hanner White, *Vicarious and Personal Liability for Employment Discrimination*, 30 GA. L. REV. 509 (1996).

10

Accommodating Workers' Lives

This chapter addresses the obligations that arise when employees require some accommodation in order to meet the demands of the employer's workplace. Of course, many familiar employment practices can be viewed as accommodating the needs of some classes of workers while also meeting the needs of employers. For example, part-time work may allow some workers — for instance, parents of young children, and mothers in particular — more flexibility while enabling employers to tailor labor costs more closely to demand. "Seasonal" work also allows matching the needs of employees who cannot work all year (e.g., students or those employed in other seasonal jobs) to fill employer needs at times of peak demand. "Temporary" work (a word that reflects actual expectations rather than legal status given the ubiquity of the at-will rule) also allows a better matching of employer needs and employee availability than the more traditional full-time, full-year job. Finally, working from home, which has grown substantially with the advent of technology enabling telecommuting, reduces employer overhead and may maximize worker convenience especially for workers who are unable to commute to the traditional workplace due to physical problems or family commitments. Literally millions of individuals work in each of these statuses. *See generally* Katherine V.W. Stone, *Legal Protections for Atypical Employees: Employment Law for Workers Without Workplaces and Employees Without Employers*, 27 Berkeley J. Emp. & Lab. L. 251, 255-56 (2006) (reporting estimates of the millions of employees in the United States engaged in these kinds of work in recent years).

However, such employment structures are not without their problems. In Chapter 1, for example, we saw that "temp" help has morphed in some areas from its traditional form — rather than an agency providing truly short-term workers, the agency provides "leased" workers on a long-term basis. In such structures neither the employee nor the workplace at which she labors views the arrangement as temporary. Rather, the relationship is recast to shift costs and risks from the firm at which the contingent workers labor to the "employer" who leases them to that firm. And part-time employment has been criticized as frequently a device used to reduce labor costs not only by paying workers (usually female) lower rates than full-time workers but also by denying them fringe benefits such as health insurance. Similarly, seasonal work, while a useful mechanism for matching the needs of employers and employees in many sectors of the economy, also generates huge social problems as "migrant workers" crisscross the country as employment opportunities open and close. Finally, working from home has strong positives and strong negatives; we will see that telecommuting has tended to employ both very high-value employees and very low-value workers, such as telemarketers.

Beyond such structures, and the focus of this chapter, is the question of the extent to which the law does, or should, require employers to "accommodate" the differing needs of individuals who aspire to be as "normal" or "regular" as their circumstances permit. The two primary examples are workers with family caretaking responsibilities, in particular pregnant women and mothers, and disabled individuals, who may be able to perform effectively if the employer accommodates their disabilities. While a pregnant worker will usually be physically incapacitated for a relatively short time, the intermittent disruption caused by several pregnancies and the continuing demands of childcare create difficulties for many women far beyond any period of physical incapacity. Some of these difficulties may be traced to employer perceptions about the "commitment" of mothers or the "distractions" children place on mothers, but many women face significant challenges in managing their professional and personal lives beyond those addressed by the antidiscrimination mandates. Put simply, treating mothers equally with fathers will often not result in equality of outcomes.

As for the disabled, until its amendment in 2008, the courts narrowly construed the definition of "disability" under the Americans with Disabilities Act ("ADA"), meaning that the duty of accommodation imposed by that Act reached relatively few individuals. With the passage of the ADAAA — the Americans with Disabilities Amendments Act — the protected class in terms of those with actual disabilities was greatly expanded, even though the new statute also made clear that there was no need to accommodate those who were merely "regarded as" disabled rather than actually disabled. See Chapter 9. The result is that there is certain to be renewed focus on accommodating individuals who have difficulty meeting the normal demands of a workplace but who could provide effective work if they were accommodated.

Similarly, feminists argue that Title VII's prohibition of pregnancy discrimination has had limited success because it is less the demands of pregnancy and the first few months of infant care that pose problems for the success of women than the continuing demands on women's time and attention from raising a family and, increasingly, taking care of elderly parents. *See also* Peggie R. Smith, *Elder Care, Gender, and Work: The Work-Family Issue of the 21st Century*, 25 BERKELEY J. EMP. & LAB. L. 351 (2004). While some men face similar challenges in reconciling the demands of home and the workplace, such responsibilities still fall disproportionately on women.

The law's response to this problem has been very limited but nevertheless highly controversial. The Family and Medical Leave Act ("FMLA") ensures 12 weeks of *unpaid* leave a year for a variety of purposes related to child-rearing and care for ill family members. The FMLA, however, covers larger employers only, applies to only relatively unusual life events (i.e., it does not permit leave for many garden-variety demands on worker time), and, in the end, provides only for unpaid leave, thus exacting a high price from the workers it protects.

Underlying this entire problem is the question of whether the traditional structure of most workplaces, which relies on permanent workers employed in a "full-time face-time" fashion, is necessary to productivity. *See* Michelle Travis, *Recapturing the Transformative Potential of Employment Discrimination Law*, 62 WASH. &

LEE L. REV. 3, 6 (2005). The business world's resistance to the FMLA, and the courts' narrow construction of both Title VII's prohibition of pregnancy discrimination and the ADA's definition of disability are predicated to a large extent on the perception that the traditional model of employment is not only natural but also necessary for American businesses to continue to be competitive in a global economy.

This chapter attempts to grapple with the questions of accommodating various needs relating to workers' lives. While the focus will be on current legal regimes, the student should keep in mind two points. First, for their own business reasons firms may well take a more accommodationist stance than the law requires. To the extent that demands for good workers can be met by a more flexible approach to firm policies, such as the slow but steady growth of "flextime," the law may prove ultimately to be far less important than economics. *See* GREGORY FETTERMAN ET AL., THE LEGAL FRAMEWORK FOR STATES AS EMPLOYERS-OF-CHOICE IN WORKPLACE FLEXIBILITY: A CASE STUDY OF ARIZONA AND MICHIGAN (2009), http://www.twigafoundation.org/documents%5CTwiga WhitePaper.AZ.MI.Final.pdf (flextime programs largely help businesses' bottom lines); WorldatWork, *Attraction and Retention: The Impact and Prevalence of Work-Life and Benefit Programs* (2007), http://www.worldatwork.org/waw/adimLink ?id=21945 (flextime programs positively influence attraction and retention of talented employees). Second, whatever the current state of the law, there is an increasing concern that it is not proactive enough in dealing with the legitimate life-cycle needs of the current workforce. Legal change may well be in the offing.

Section A deals with how the antidiscrimination laws bear on workers needing certain types of accommodations, briefly discussing the Title VII duty of reasonable accommodation of religion and then focusing on the more robust ADA duty of reasonable accommodation of disability. This sets the stage for section B, which considers the extent to which the general prohibition of sex discrimination under Title VII and the Pregnancy Discrimination Act may assist mothers in the workplace. It then turns to the FMLA, which protects both men and women whose health problems or family issues collide with the demands of the workplace.

A. ACCOMMODATION UNDER THE AMERICANS WITH DISABILITIES ACT

Title VII imposes very limited obligations on employers to address the needs of employees seeking accommodations. As we will see, the statute bars discrimination on the basis of pregnancy, but it merely requires equal treatment of pregnant workers — there is no requirement that pregnancy or childbirth, much less child-rearing, be accommodated.

One provision of Title VII does mandate that employers "reasonably accommodate" the religious practices and beliefs of their employees, but this command has been read so narrowly as to pose few demands on employers. Section 701(j) provides:

> The term "religion" includes all aspects of religious observance and practice, as well as belief, unless an employer demonstrates that he is unable to reasonably accommodate to an employee's or prospective employee's religious observance or practice without undue hardship on the conduct of the employer's business.

Despite the apparent sweep of this provision, the Supreme Court has interpreted this language to minimize its effect. Thus, *Trans World Airlines, Inc. v. Hardison*, 432 U.S. 63 (1977), upheld the discharge of an employee whose religion forbade him to work on his Sabbath. It rejected a variety of possible accommodations, including alterations in the seniority system established by a collective agreement. As for accommodations that would have left the seniority system intact, they, too, were not required since each involved some cost to the employer, and "[t]o require TWA to bear more than a de minimis cost in order to give Hardison Saturdays off is an undue hardship." *Id.* at 84. While the employee was free to seek shift-swaps from co-workers, honoring such swaps may satisfy the employer's duty. *See also Ansonia Bd. of Educ. v. Philbrook*, 479 U.S. 60, 68 (1986) ("[W]here the employer has already reasonably accommodated the employee's religious needs, the statutory inquiry is at an end. The employer need not further show that each of the employee's alternative accommodations would result in undue hardship.").

The ADA, although using basically the same language as Title VII's religion clause, nevertheless imposes a more robust duty of accommodation. Thus, it declares as discriminatory

> not making reasonable accommodations to the known physical or mental limitations of an otherwise qualified individual with a disability who is an applicant or employee, unless such covered entity can demonstrate that the accommodation would impose an undue hardship on the operation of the business of such covered entity. . . .

§ 12112(b)(5)(A). While the ADA is treated in more detail in Chapter 9, our present concern is not with the protected class (qualified individuals with disabilities) but with the employer's duty of accommodation. Under the current statute, qualified persons with actual disabilities must be accommodated; those who are only "regarded as" disabled may not be discriminated against on the basis of their impairment but need not be accommodated

It is important to note, however, that the ADA's complicated structure makes reasonable accommodation relevant both to establishing and to defending against a discrimination claim based on the failure to accommodate. As we saw in Chapter 9, a person with a statutory "disability" is protected only if he or she is a "qualified individual," which is in turn defined as "an individual with a disability who, with or without reasonable accommodation, can perform the essential functions of the employment position that such individual holds or desires." § 12111(8). If a disabled individual can perform essential functions only with reasonable accommodation, the employer has a duty to provide those accommodations. *Cf. Hoffman v. Caterpillar, Inc.*, 256 F.3d 568 (7th Cir. 2001) (employer has no duty to accommodate employees with respect to nonessential functions). But if the disabled individual cannot perform the job without accommodations that are not reasonable or that impose an undue hardship, she or he is not a "qualified individual," and therefore disparate treatment on the basis of disability is permitted and accommodating the disability is not required.

What, then, is a "reasonable accommodation"? The statute provides that such accommodations include the following:

> (A) making existing facilities used by employees readily accessible to and usable by individuals with disabilities; and

(B) job restructuring, part-time or modified work schedules, reassignment to a vacant position, acquisition or modification of equipment or devices, appropriate adjustment or modifications of examinations, training materials or policies, the provision of qualified readers or interpreters, and other similar accommodations for individuals with disabilities.

How far does "job restructuring" or "reassignment to a vacant position" go?

U.S. Airways, Inc. v. Barnett
535 U.S. 391 (2002)

Justice BREYER delivered the opinion of the Court.

The Americans with Disabilities Act of 1990 prohibits an employer from discriminating against an "individual with a disability" who, with "reasonable accommodation," can perform the essential functions of the job. This case, arising in the context of summary judgment, asks us how the Act resolves a potential conflict between: (1) the interests of a disabled worker who seeks assignment to a particular position as a "reasonable accommodation," and (2) the interests of other workers with superior rights to bid for the job under an employer's seniority system. In such a case, does the accommodation demand trump the seniority system?

In our view, the seniority system will prevail in the run of cases. As we interpret the statute, to show that a requested accommodation conflicts with the rules of a seniority system is ordinarily to show that the accommodation is not "reasonable." Hence such a showing will entitle an employer/defendant to summary judgment on the question — unless there is more. The plaintiff remains free to present evidence of special circumstances that make "reasonable" a seniority rule exception in the particular case. And such a showing will defeat the employer's demand for summary judgment.

I

In 1990, Robert Barnett, the plaintiff and respondent here, injured his back while working in a cargo-handling position at petitioner U.S. Airways, Inc. He invoked seniority rights and transferred to a less physically demanding mailroom position. Under U.S. Airways' seniority system, that position, like others, periodically became open to seniority-based employee bidding. In 1992, Barnett learned that at least two employees senior to him intended to bid for the mailroom job. He asked U.S. Airways to accommodate his disability-imposed limitations by making an exception that would allow him to remain in the mailroom. After permitting Barnett to continue his mailroom work for five months while it considered the matter, U.S. Airways eventually decided not to make an exception. And Barnett lost his job.

Barnett then brought this ADA suit claiming, among other things, that he was an "individual with a disability" capable of performing the essential functions of the mailroom job, that the mailroom job amounted to a "reasonable accommodation" of his disability, and that U.S. Airways, in refusing to assign him the job, unlawfully discriminated against him.

[The District Court granted summary judgment to U.S. Airways, stressing the decades-old use of a seniority system by USAir and that such seniority policies were common in the airline industry. In this context, "USAir employees were justified in relying upon the policy. As such, any significant alteration of that policy would result in undue hardship to both the company and its nondisabled employees." The Ninth Circuit reversed en banc, finding that a seniority system was merely a factor in a fact-intensive undue hardship analysis. On U.S. Airways's petition, the Supreme Court granted certiorari on the question whether "the [ADA] requires an employer to reassign a disabled employee to a position as a 'reasonable accommodation' even though another employee is entitled to hold the position under the employer's bona fide and established seniority system."]

II

In answering the question presented, we must consider the following statutory provisions. First, the ADA says that an employer may not "discriminate against a qualified individual with a disability." 42 U.S.C. § 12112(a). Second, the ADA says that a "qualified" individual includes "an individual with a disability who, *with* or without *reasonable accommodation*, can perform the essential functions of" the relevant "employment position." § 12111(8) (emphasis added). Third, the ADA says that "discrimination" includes an employer's "*not making reasonable accommodations* to the known physical or mental limitations of an otherwise qualified . . . employee, *unless* [the employer] can demonstrate that the accommodation would impose an *undue hardship* on the operation of [its] business." § 12112(b)(5)(A) (emphasis added). Fourth, the ADA says that the term "'reasonable accommodation' may include . . . reassignment to a vacant position." § 12111(9)(B).

The parties interpret this statutory language as applied to seniority systems in radically different ways. In US Airways' view, the fact that an accommodation would violate the rules of a seniority system always shows that the accommodation is not a "reasonable" one. In Barnett's polar opposite view, a seniority system violation never shows that an accommodation sought is not a "reasonable" one. Barnett concedes that a violation of seniority rules might help to show that the accommodation will work "undue" employer "hardship," but that is a matter for an employer to demonstrate case by case. . . .

A

U.S. Airways' claim that a seniority system virtually always trumps a conflicting accommodation demand rests primarily upon its view of how the Act treats workplace "preferences." Insofar as a requested accommodation violates a disability-neutral workplace rule, such as a seniority rule, it grants the employee with a disability treatment that other workers could not receive. Yet the Act, U.S. Airways says, seeks only "equal" treatment for those with disabilities. *See, e.g.*, 42 U.S.C. § 12101(a)(9). It does not, it contends, require an employer to grant preferential treatment. *Cf.* H. R. Rep. No. 101-485, pt. 2, p. 66 (1990); S. Rep. No. 101-116, pp. 26-27 (1989) (employer has no "obligation to prefer *applicants* with disabilities over other *applicants*" (emphasis added)). Hence it does not require the employer to grant a request that, in violating a disability-neutral rule, would provide a preference. . . .

While linguistically logical, this argument fails to recognize what the Act specifies, namely, that preferences will sometimes prove necessary to achieve the Act's basic equal opportunity goal. The Act requires preferences in the form of "reasonable accommodations" that are needed for those with disabilities to obtain the same work-place opportunities than those without disabilities automatically enjoy. By definition any special "accommodation" requires the employer to treat an employee with a disability differently, i.e., preferentially. And the fact that the difference in treatment violates an employer's disability-neutral rule cannot by itself place the accommodation beyond the Act's potential reach.

Were that not so, the "reasonable accommodation" provision could not accomplish its intended objective. Neutral office assignment rules would automatically prevent the accommodation of an employee whose disability-imposed limitations require him to work on the ground floor. Neutral "break-from-work" rules would automatically prevent the accommodation of an individual who needs additional breaks from work, perhaps to permit medical visits. Neutral furniture budget rules would automatically prevent the accommodation of an individual who needs a different kind of chair or desk. Many employers will have neutral rules governing the kinds of actions most needed to reasonably accommodate a worker with a disability. *See* 42 U.S.C. § 12111(9)(b) (setting forth examples such as "job restructuring," "part-time or modified work schedules," "acquisition or modification of equipment or devices," "and other similar accommodations"). Yet Congress, while providing such examples, said nothing suggesting that the presence of such neutral rules would create an automatic exemption. Nor have the lower courts made any such suggestion. *Cf. Garcia-Ayala v. Lederle Parenterals, Inc.*, 212 F.3d 638, 648 (CA1 2000) (requiring leave beyond that allowed under the company's own leave policy); *Hendricks-Robinson v. Excel Corp.*, 154 F.3d 685, 699 (CA7 1998) (requiring exception to employer's neutral "physical fitness" job requirement).

In sum, the nature of the "reasonable accommodation" requirement, the statutory examples, and the Act's silence about the exempting effect of neutral rules together convince us that the Act does not create any such automatic exemption. The simple fact that an accommodation would provide a "preference"—in the sense that it would permit the worker with a disability to violate a rule that others must obey—cannot, in and of itself, automatically show that the accommodation is not "reasonable." As a result, we reject the position taken by U.S. Airways and Justice Scalia to the contrary. . . .

B

Barnett argues that the statutory words "reasonable accommodation" mean only "effective accommodation," authorizing a court to consider the requested accommodation's ability to meet an individual's disability-related needs, and nothing more. On this view, a seniority rule violation, having nothing to do with the accommodation's effectiveness, has nothing to do with its "reasonableness." It might, at most, help to prove an "undue hardship on the operation of the business." . . . Barnett adds that any other view would make the words "reasonable accommodation" and "undue hardship" virtual mirror images — creating redundancy in the statute. And he says that any such other view would create a practical burden of proof dilemma.

The practical burden of proof dilemma arises, Barnett argues, because the statute imposes the burden of demonstrating an "undue hardship" upon the employer, while the burden of proving "reasonable accommodation" remains with the plaintiff, here the employee. This allocation seems sensible in that an employer can more frequently and easily prove the presence of business hardship than an employee can prove its absence. But suppose that an employee must counter a claim of "seniority rule violation" in order to prove that an "accommodation" request is "reasonable." Would that not force the employee to prove what is in effect an absence, i.e., an absence of hardship, despite the statute's insistence that the employer "demonstrate" hardship's presence?

These arguments do not persuade us that Barnett's legal interpretation of "reasonable" is correct. For one thing, in ordinary English the word "reasonable" does not mean "effective." It is the word "accommodation," not the word "reasonable," that conveys the need for effectiveness. An ineffective "modification" or "adjustment" will not accommodate a disabled individual's limitations. Nor does an ordinary English meaning of the term "reasonable accommodation" make of it a simple, redundant mirror image of the term "undue hardship." The statute refers to an "undue hardship on the operation of the business." 42 U.S.C. § 12112(b)(5)(A). Yet a demand for an effective accommodation could prove unreasonable because of its impact, not on business operations, but on fellow employees — say because it will lead to dismissals, relocations, or modification of employee benefits to which an employer, looking at the matter from the perspective of the business itself, may be relatively indifferent.

Neither does the statute's primary purpose require Barnett's special reading. The statute seeks to diminish or to eliminate the stereotypical thought processes, the thoughtless actions, and the hostile reactions that far too often bar those with disabilities from participating fully in the Nation's life, including the workplace. See generally §§ 12101(a) and (b). These objectives demand unprejudiced thought and reasonable responsive reaction on the part of employers and fellow workers alike. They will sometimes require affirmative conduct to promote entry of disabled people into the workforce. They do not, however, demand action beyond the realm of the reasonable. . . .

Finally, an ordinary language interpretation of the word "reasonable" does not create the "burden of proof" dilemma to which Barnett points. Many of the lower courts, while rejecting both U.S. Airways' and Barnett's more absolute views, have reconciled the phrases "reasonable accommodation" and "undue hardship" in a practical way.

They have held that a plaintiff/employee (to defeat a defendant/employer's motion for summary judgment) need only show that an "accommodation" seems reasonable on its face, i.e., ordinarily or in the run of cases. *See, e.g., Reed v. Lepage Bakeries, Inc.*, 244 F.3d 254, 259 (CA1 2001) (plaintiff meets burden on reasonableness by showing that, "at least on the face of things," the accommodation will be feasible for the employer).

Once the plaintiff has made this showing, the defendant/employer then must show special (typically case-specific) circumstances that demonstrate undue hardship in the particular circumstances. *See Reed* (" 'undue hardship inquiry focuses on the hardships imposed . . . in the context of the particular [employer's] operations' ").

Not every court has used the same language, but their results are functionally similar. In our opinion, that practical view of the statute, applied consistently with ordinary summary judgment principles, *see* Fed. Rule Civ. Proc. 56, avoids Barnett's burden of proof dilemma, while reconciling the two statutory phrases ("reasonable accommodation" and "undue hardship").

III

The question in the present case focuses on the relationship between seniority systems and the plaintiff's need to show that an "accommodation" seems reasonable on its face, i.e., ordinarily or in the run of cases. We must assume that the plaintiff, an employee, is an "individual with a disability." He has requested assignment to a mail-room position as a "reasonable accommodation." We also assume that normally such a request would be reasonable within the meaning of the statute, were it not for one circumstance, namely, that the assignment would violate the rules of a seniority system. *See* § 12111(9) ("reasonable accommodation" may include "reassignment to a vacant position"). Does that circumstance mean that the proposed accommodation is not a "reasonable" one?

In our view, the answer to this question ordinarily is "yes." The statute does not require proof on a case-by-case basis that a seniority system should prevail. That is because it would not be reasonable in the run of cases that the assignment in question trump the rules of a seniority system. To the contrary, it will ordinarily be unreasonable for the assignment to prevail.

A

Several factors support our conclusion that a proposed accommodation will not be reasonable in the run of cases. Analogous case law supports this conclusion, for it has recognized the importance of seniority to employee-management relations. [The Court cited its Title VII *Hardison* opinion and numerous lower court decisions under the Rehabilitation Act, and the ADA, holding that seniority systems found in collective bargaining agreements trump requested accommodations. The Court then noted that the advantages and disadvantages posed by violating seniority systems did not belong to collectively bargained systems alone.]

For one thing, the typical seniority system provides important employee benefits by creating, and fulfilling, employee expectations of fair, uniform treatment. These benefits include "job security and an opportunity for steady and predictable advancement based on objective standards." They include "an element of due process," limiting "unfairness in personnel decisions." And they consequently encourage employees to invest in the employing company, accepting "less than their value to the firm early in their careers" in return for greater benefits in later years.

Most important for present purposes, to require the typical employer to show more than the existence of a seniority system might well undermine the employees' expectations of consistent, uniform treatment — expectations upon which the seniority system's benefits depend. That is because such a rule would substitute a complex case-specific "accommodation" decision made by management for the more uniform, impersonal operation of seniority rules. Such management decision making, with its inevitable discretionary elements, would involve a matter of the greatest importance to employees, namely, layoffs; it would take place outside, as well as inside, the confines of a court case; and it might well take place fairly often. *Cf.* ADA, 42 U.S.C. § 12101(a)(1) (estimating that some 43 million Americans suffer from physical or mental disabilities). We can find nothing in the statute that suggests Congress intended to undermine seniority systems in this way. And we consequently conclude that the employer's showing of violation of the rules of a seniority system is by itself ordinarily sufficient.

B

The plaintiff (here the employee) nonetheless remains free to show that special circumstances warrant a finding that, despite the presence of a seniority system (which the ADA may not trump in the run of cases), the requested "accommodation" is "reasonable" on the particular facts. That is because special circumstances might alter the important expectations described above. The plaintiff might show, for example, that the employer, having retained the right to change the seniority system unilaterally, exercises that right fairly frequently, reducing employee expectations that the system will be followed—to the point where one more departure, needed to accommodate an individual with a disability, will not likely make a difference. The plaintiff might show that the system already contains exceptions such that, in the circumstances, one further exception is unlikely to matter. We do not mean these examples to exhaust the kinds of showings that a plaintiff might make. But we do mean to say that the plaintiff must bear the burden of showing special circumstances that make an exception from the seniority system reasonable in the particular case. And to do so, the plaintiff must explain why, in the particular case, an exception to the employer's seniority policy can constitute a "reasonable accommodation" even though in the ordinary case it cannot.

IV

[We conclude that "ordinarily" the ADA does not require] an employer to assign a disabled employee to a particular position even though another employee is entitled to that position under the employer's "established seniority system." ... Hence, a showing that the assignment would violate the rules of a seniority system warrants summary judgment for the employer—unless there is more. The plaintiff must present evidence of that "more," namely, special circumstances surrounding the particular case that demonstrate the assignment is nonetheless reasonable. ...

Justice O'CONNOR, concurring.

... Although a seniority system plays an important role in the workplace, ... I would prefer to say that the effect of a seniority system on the reasonableness of a reassignment as an accommodation for purposes of the ADA depends on whether the seniority system is legally enforceable. ...

Justice SCALIA, with whom Justice THOMAS joins, dissenting. ...

I

The Court begins its analysis by describing the ADA as declaring that an employer may not "discriminate against a qualified individual with a disability." In fact the Act says more: an employer may not "discriminate against a qualified individual with a disability *because of the disability* of such individual." 42 U.S.C. § 12112(a) (emphasis added). It further provides that discrimination includes "not making reasonable accommodations *to the known physical or mental limitations* of an otherwise qualified individual with a disability." § 12112(b)(5)(A) (emphasis added).

Read together, these provisions order employers to modify or remove (within reason) policies and practices that burden a disabled person "because of [his] disability." In other words, the ADA eliminates workplace barriers only if a disability prevents an employee from overcoming them — those barriers that would not be barriers but for the employee's disability. These include, for example, work stations that cannot accept the employee's wheelchair, or an assembly-line practice that requires long periods of standing. But they do not include rules and practices that bear no more heavily upon the disabled employee than upon others — even though an exemption from such a rule or practice might in a sense "make up for" the employee's disability. It is not a required accommodation, for example, to pay a disabled employee more than others at his grade level — even if that increment is earmarked for massage or physical therapy that would enable the employee to work with as little physical discomfort as his co-workers. That would be "accommodating" the disabled employee, but it would not be "making . . . accommodation to the known physical or mental limitations" of the employee, § 12112(b)(5)(A), because it would not eliminate any workplace practice that constitutes an obstacle because of his disability.

So also with exemption from a seniority system, which burdens the disabled and nondisabled alike. In particular cases, seniority rules may have a harsher effect upon the disabled employee than upon his co-workers. If the disabled employee is physically capable of performing only one task in the workplace, seniority rules may be, for him, the difference between employment and unemployment. But that does not make the seniority system a disability-related obstacle, any more than harsher impact upon the more needy disabled employee renders the salary system a disability-related obstacle. When one departs from this understanding, the ADA's accommodation provision becomes a standardless grab bag — leaving it to the courts to decide which workplace preferences (higher salary, longer vacations, reassignment to positions to which others are entitled) can be deemed "reasonable" to "make up for" the particular employee's disability. . . .

[These dissenters would have affirmed summary judgment for the defendant without providing the plaintiffs an opportunity to show that creating an exception to the seniority system was reasonable in the circumstances.]

[Justice SOUTER, with whom Justice GINSBURG joined, dissented.]

NOTES

1. *Collectively Bargained versus Unilaterally Created Seniority Systems.* The *Barnett* decision is reminiscent of the Supreme Court's refusal in *Hardison* to read Title VII's duty of religious accommodation to require modifications in the employer's seniority system. However, in at least two ways, *Barnett* is more dramatic. First, the ADA lacks Title VII's language privileging seniority systems. *See* 42 U.S.C. § 2000e-2(h) ("[I]t shall not be an unlawful employment practice for an employer to apply . . . different terms, conditions, or privileges of employment pursuant to a bona fide seniority . . . system"). Second, unlike TWA, the employer in *Barnett* was not caught between a

rock and a hard place by virtue of a contractually enforceable collective bargaining agreement. Was the Supreme Court correct in its assumption that such a system generally confers the same advantages on workers as do those that result from collective bargaining? Justice O'Connor believed that a system could grant such advantages if it were legally enforceable; thus, she would have preferred to limit the presumption in favor of seniority systems to those the employer was contractually obligated to follow. She joined the Court's opinion, however, observing that the majority's rule and her preferred one will generally reach the same result. *See generally* Seth D. Harris, *Rethinking the Economics of Discrimination:* U.S. Airways v. Barnett, *the ADA, and the Application of Internal Labor Market Theory,* 89 Iowa L. Rev. 123, 126 (2003) ("Justice Breyer's *Barnett* opinion can be best explained with reference to the view that an employer's seniority system can play an important role in shaping and protecting the employer's sunk investments/delayed dividends contract with its employees").

2. *Accommodation as Preference.* The *Barnett* Court expressly acknowledged that the ADA will sometimes require that the disabled worker receive a preference. "By definition any special 'accommodation' requires the employer to treat an employee with a disability differently, i.e., preferentially. And the fact that the difference in treatment violates an employer's disability-neutral rule cannot by itself place the accommodation beyond the Act's potential reach." The notion that the ADA requires employers to favor disabled individuals in at least some circumstances, and therefore to incur greater costs for such persons than for their nondisabled co-workers, has generated considerable debate about the normative and economic justifications for this mandate. In short, why has Congress defined unlawful "discrimination" to include failing to accommodate?

The Equal Employment Opportunity Commission's ("EEOC") Interpretive Guidance describes reasonable accommodation in terms of according individuals with a disability "equal employment opportunity," which means "an opportunity to attain the same level of performance, or to enjoy the same level of benefits and privileges of employment as are available to the average similarly situated employee without a disability." 29 C.F.R. pt. 1630, app. § 1630.9. As you will see, this is the same argument made for pregnant women: Formal equality, in the sense of treating such individuals the same as other workers, will not allow them to participate equally in the workplace given the special demands placed on them by their family responsibilities. Is the argument stronger for the disabled? Why?

Failure to accommodate is discrimination by definition under the ADA, but there is an obvious difference between discrimination per se and a failure to accommodate. This has led to a lively literature on whether the duty to accommodate is consistent with the antidiscrimination commands of other statutes we have studied. Some of this literature views the disparate impact theory under Title VII as providing a rough analog to the ADA's duty to accommodate and therefore finds little difference between accommodation and antidiscrimination. *See, e.g.,* Samuel R. Bagenstos, *"Rational Discrimination," Accommodation, and the Politics of (Disability) Civil Rights,* 89 Va. L. Rev. 825 (2003); Samuel R. Bagenstos, *Subordination, Stigma, and "Disability,"* 86 Va. L. Rev. 397 (2000); Mary Crossley, *Reasonable Accommodation as Part and Parcel of the Antidiscrimination Project,* 35 Rutgers L. J. 861 (2004); Christine Jolls, *Antidiscrimination and Accommodation,* 115 Harv. L. Rev. 642 (2001); Mark Kelman, *Market Discrimination and Groups,* 53 Stan. L. Rev. 833 (2001); Stewart J. Schwab & Steven L. Willborn, *Reasonable Accommodation of Workplace Disabilities,* 44 Wm. & Mary L. Rev. 1197 (2003); Michael Ashley Stein, *Same*

Struggle, Different Difference: ADA Accommodations as Antidiscrimination, 153 U. PA. L. REV. 579 (2004); J.H. Verkerke, *Disaggregating Antidiscrimination and Accommodation*, 44 WM. & MARY L. REV. 1385 (2003).

3. *Accommodation Beyond Seniority Systems.* Although *Barnett* was decided in the context of a seniority system dispute, the issue raised by the case is much broader. Roughly speaking, accommodations can impose costs on the employer, fellow workers, both, or neither. *Barnett* seemed to be only about imposing costs on co-workers — although the employer could perhaps face productivity problems if employee morale suffered. The Court held that, where a seniority system exists, such costs need not be imposed. But suppose there's no seniority system?

When, if ever, will a disabled employee's request for reassignment to a vacant position entitle him to the job over other qualified (or better qualified) applicants? Recall that the Court "assumed" that plaintiff's request for reassignment to a vacant position would "normally . . . be reasonable within the meaning of the statute" but for the seniority system, which specified that seniority-based bidding would fill such vacancies. The lower courts had sharply disagreed on their answer to this question. *Compare Huber v. Wal-Mart Stores, Inc.*, 486 F.3d 480, 483 (8th Cir. 2007), *cert. dismissed*, 552 U.S. 1136 (2008) ("[T]he ADA is not an affirmative action statute and does not require an employer to reassign a qualified disabled employee to a vacant position when such a reassignment would violate a legitimate nondiscriminatory policy of the employer to hire the most qualified candidate."), *with Smith v. Midland Brake, Inc.*, 180 F.3d 1154, 1164-65 (10th Cir. 1999) (en banc) ("[I]f the reassignment language merely requires employers to consider on an equal basis with all other applicants an otherwise qualified existing employee with a disability for reassignment to a vacant position, that language would add nothing to the obligation not to discriminate, and would thereby be redundant."). The core of that disagreement is reflected in *Barnett's* majority and dissenting opinions. What is the rule advocated by the majority? The dissent?

In the case where the disabled worker is qualified but less qualified than a nondisabled worker, requiring reassignment to a vacant position will presumably impose costs on both co-workers and the employer. *See generally* Stacy M. Hickox, *Transfer as an Accommodation: Standards from Discrimination Cases and Theory*, 62 ARK. L. REV. 195 (2009); Nicole B. Porter, *Reasonable Burdens: Resolving the Conflict Between Disabled Employees and Their Coworkers*, 34 FLA. ST. U. L. REV. 313 (2007); Cheryl L. Anderson, *"Neutral" Employer Policies and the ADA: The Implications of* U.S. Airways Inc. v. Barnett *Beyond Seniority Systems*, 51 DRAKE L. REV. 1 (2002); Alex B. Long, *The ADA's Reasonable Accommodation Requirement and "Innocent Third Parties,"* 68 MO. L. REV. 863, 905 (2003). But surely the question of whether an accommodation is reasonable (or an undue hardship) can't turn solely on whether it involves costs. Or can it? We'll explore the cost question below. Reconsider this question after you read the next case.

4. *Knowing About the Need for Accommodation.* The employer's duty of accommodation is normally triggered by an employee's request. "In general . . . it is the responsibility of the individual with a disability to inform the employer that an accommodation is needed." 29 C.F.R. pt. 1630, app. § 1630.9. As we will see, the regulations envision an "interactive process" in which possible accommodations are considered. But the accommodation duty is in tension with the notion that an employer normally should not inquire into the existence of a disability. Obviously, when the employee raises her disability in a request for accommodation, the employer can ask for further information as part of the interactive process. But is it ever appropriate for the employer to raise the accommodation question on its own initiative? The regulations provide that "[i]f an employee with a known disability is having difficulty performing his or her job, an employer may inquire whether the employee is in need of a reasonable accommodation." 29 C.F.R. pt. 1630, app. §1630.9. *Compare Bultemeyer v. Fort Wayne Cmty. Schs.*, 100 F.3d 1281 (7th Cir. 1996) (even though employee did not personally ask for an accommodation, the employer was sufficiently aware of his disability that it was required to engage in an interactive process about reasonable accommodations), *with Gaston v. Bellingrath Gardens & Home, Inc.*, 167 F.3d 1361 (11th Cir. 1999) (when employee informed employer of her disability and of her inability to perform new job functions but never requested accommodation, employer had no obligation to accommodate). Suppose you represent an employer who suspects, but does not know, that an employee's deteriorating job performance is related to a disability. Do you advise your client to inquire about it? Wouldn't that elevate the risk of a disability discrimination claim if an adverse employment action was later taken against the individual?

* * *

Although the ADA is now two decades old, there have been relatively few cases developing the duty of reasonable accommodation. That is largely because, as explored in Chapter 9, most of the action in the courts was devoted to the threshold question of whether the plaintiff was protected by the statute in the first place, with the courts taking such a strict view of disability that plaintiffs were usually found either not to be disabled or to be so disabled as to be unqualified to do the essential functions of the job. The 2008 passage of the ADAAA promises to change that and bring reasonable accommodation back to center stage.

In that endeavor, two aspects of the ADA duty intersect. One is procedural, the "interactive process" that the governing regulations require when an accommodation is requested. The second is substantive: What makes an accommodation "reasonable"? When is hardship on the employer "undue"? This question is complicated by the fact that, although one could view hardship as merely one factor in the question of whether an accommodation was reasonable, *Barnett* divides them into two separate inquiries, with the burden of persuasion varying depending on what inquiry is the focus of concern. Thus, the *Barnett* Court endorsed the lower courts that "have held that a plaintiff/employee (to defeat a defendant/employer's motion for summary judgment) need only show that an 'accommodation' seems reasonable on its face, i.e., ordinarily or in the run of cases. . . . Once the plaintiff has made this showing, the defendant/employer then must show special (typically case-specific) circumstances that demonstrate undue hardship in the particular circumstances."

Let's see how these questions play out in a garden-variety accommodation case.

Lowe v. Independent School District No. 1 of Logan County, Oklahoma
363 F. App'x 548 (10th Cir. 2010)

[Plaintiff Terianne Lowe filed suit against her former employer, Independent School District No. 1 of Logan County, Oklahoma, for failure to reasonably accommodate her post-polio condition in violation of the ADA. The district court granted summary judgment in favor of the District, but the Tenth Circuit reversed.]

Ms. Lowe had polio as a child and, as a result, has worn leg braces for most of her life and has had several knee replacements. She has been advised by her physician that she will have to be in a wheelchair at some point and that walking and standing for long periods will accelerate the deterioration of her leg muscles.

Ms. Lowe was certified to teach a variety of science courses for grades seven through twelve and had experience as a classroom teacher. Since the 1988-89 school year, Ms. Lowe had been employed by the District as a high school counselor. Because a counselor is a "teacher" under state law, Ms. Lowe was employed under a standard teacher's contract with counseling duties added pursuant to a separate "extra duty" contract. Ms. Lowe's counselor position was sedentary and required no accommodation for her disability.

In the fall of 2005, as a result of complaints from parents and staff about Ms. Lowe's performance as a counselor at Guthrie High School, Terry Simpson, the District Superintendent, determined that Ms. Lowe's extra-duty contract as a counselor would not be renewed for the 2006-07 school year and that Ms. Lowe would, instead, be reassigned as a classroom teacher. Ms. Lowe was informed of this decision in March 2006 by Jan Chadwick, the principal of Guthrie High School. Ms. Lowe understood that her base salary as a teacher would not be affected by the reassignment but that she would lose the approximately $5700.00 in additional income she earned under the extra-duty contract as a counselor.

In May 2006, the temporary teaching contract of Mary Rhinehart expired and was not renewed by the District. Ms. Rhinehart had taught physical science at the high school in one of the smallest and most crowded classrooms that, as then configured, would not accommodate a walker or a wheelchair in the aisles between the lab tables. The physical science class, and all other science classes at the high school, were laboratory classes. The physical science class was the only opening for a science teacher at the high school for the 2006-07 school year.

Ms. Lowe, for reasons explained below, eventually came to understand that she would be reassigned to teach physical science in Ms. Rhinehart's small, crowded classroom. In order to plan for that contingency, Ms. Lowe met with Lori Allen, head of the Guthrie High School science department, to share with Ms. Allen her concerns about the reassignment in light of her disability. Ms. Allen did not question the need for such a meeting because she had learned from a school board member that Ms. Rhinehart was not retained in order to open up a teaching slot for Ms. Lowe in Ms. Rhinehart's former classroom. Together, Ms. Lowe and Ms. Allen compiled a list of accommodations they believed necessary in order for Ms. Lowe to teach physical science in the laboratory science classroom formerly used by Ms. Rhinehart. Before the end of the 2005-06 school year, Ms. Lowe presented the list of accommodations and a letter from her physician to principal Chadwick, her immediate supervisor, to Don Bowman, the District's human resources director, and to Superintendent Simpson. Shortly thereafter, Ms. Chadwick was told by Don Bowman that no accommodation would be made and that Ms. Lowe should be assigned to a non-laboratory science class.[2] Ms. Chadwick passed this information along to Ms. Lowe.

By August 2006, Ms. Lowe had heard nothing from the District regarding her request for accommodation, other than the message from Mr. Bowman, relayed by Ms. Chadwick, that no accommodation would be made. Two weeks before school was

---

2. Apparently at this point, Mr. Bowman, like Superintendent Simpson, did not know that all high-school science classes were laboratory classes.

to begin, Mary Pratz, an advocacy specialist and representative with the Oklahoma Education Association, set up a meeting attended by Superintendent Simpson, Ms. Lowe, Michelle Redus, president of the Guthrie Association of Classroom Teachers, and herself. The purpose of the meeting was to discuss the accommodations Ms. Lowe believed she would need in order to teach physical science in Ms. Rhinehart's former classroom. It is clear that, at the time of the August meeting, Ms. Lowe believed that such would be her assignment come the start of the new school year.

As we will discuss below, there is significant disagreement among those present at the August meeting as to what actually was said. One thing is clear: Ms. Lowe was dissatisfied with the result of the meeting and submitted her resignation two days later. . . .

III. DISCUSSION . . .

In order "[t]o establish her claim under the ADA, [Ms. Lowe] must show: (1) she is a disabled person within the meaning of the ADA; (2) she is able to perform the essential job functions with or without reasonable accommodation; and (3) [defendant] discriminated against her because of her disability." *Albert v. Smith's Food & Drug Ctrs., Inc.*, 356 F.3d 1242, 1249 (10th Cir. 2004).

There is no dispute as to the first two requirements. The issue is whether the District discriminated against Ms. Lowe because of her disability. "The ADA defines the term 'discriminate' to include 'not making *reasonable accommodations* to the known physical or mental limitations of an otherwise qualified individual with a disability who is an applicant or employee, unless such covered entity can demonstrate that the accommodation would impose an undue hardship on the operation of the business of such covered entity. . . .'"

[In *Smith v. Midland Brake, Inc.*, 180 F.3d 1154 (10th Cir. 1999) (en banc)] "[w]e noted that the employer and employee must engage in an interactive process to determine what [accommodation] would be appropriate." "The obligation to engage in an interactive process is inherent in the statutory obligation to offer a reasonable accommodation to an otherwise qualified disabled employee."

Once the District was in receipt of Ms. Lowe's list of possible accommodations and the letter from her doctor regarding the reassignment, it was required to proceed "in a reasonably interactive manner" with Ms. Lowe to determine what reasonable accommodation might be made to the physical-science-teaching job in order for her to perform it successfully. *Id.* "The interactive process is typically an essential component of the process by which a reasonable accommodation can be determined," and "includes good-faith communications between the employer and employee." *Id.* "Neither party may create or destroy liability by causing a breakdown of the interactive process." *Albert.* A question of fact as to whether an employer has failed to interact in good faith and thus failed to reasonably accommodate will preclude summary judgment for the employer.

Defendant argues that "the interactive process is merely a means to achieve a reasonable accommodation rather than an independent substantive requirement." While that is true, *see Rehling v. City of Chicago*, 207 F.3d 1009, 1015-16 (7th Cir. 2000) (recognizing that the interactive process the ADA contemplates is not an end in itself), a plaintiff can prevail if she can "show that the result of the inadequate interactive process was the failure of the [employer] to fulfill its role in determining what specific actions must be taken . . . in order to provide the qualified individual a reasonable accommodation." In other words, a plaintiff must show "that the employer's failure to engage in an interactive process resulted in a failure to identify an appropriate accommodation for the qualified individual."

The first step in analyzing Ms. Lowe's failure-to-accommodate claim is to determine whether her ultimate resignation was, as the district court concluded, based merely on her speculation as to where she would be reassigned. Contrary to the district court, we think that, given the information available to Ms. Lowe, she could have reasonably concluded that she would be assigned to teach a physical science class in a small and crowded classroom.

Given all the evidence available to Ms. Lowe, much of it coming from defendant's agents, we think the district court erred in concluding that Ms. Lowe's view of the situation was based merely on her personal speculation. The fact that, even after the August meeting, Superintendent Simpson never informed Ms. Lowe that she would not have to teach in Ms. Rhinehart's classroom justified Ms. Lowe in her belief that she would not be able to resume duties as a classroom science teacher at Guthrie High School. Further, the District's late-advanced theory that it could have placed Ms. Lowe in a junior high science class was never conveyed to her.

We turn now to the facts relative to the interactive process. Early on, as mentioned above, Ms. Lowe learned from Principal Chadwick that no accommodation would be made. Ms. Chadwick had been told this by the District's human resources director, Don Bowman, shortly after the District received the letter from Ms. Lowe's doctor outlining necessary accommodations. After this indirect contact by Mr. Bowman, the District failed for at least four months to respond directly to Ms. Lowe's suggestions for accommodation and only did so when prodded to act by Mary Pratz, an official from the Oklahoma Education Association.

When a meeting was finally convened at Ms. Pratz's behest, even Superintendent Simpson admitted that he did not prepare for it, had not reviewed Ms. Lowe's list of suggested accommodations, and did not know coming into the meeting that all science classes at the high school were lab classes. There is no dispute that Ms. Redus stated that the master schedule for the upcoming year at the high school indicated that Ms. Lowe would be teaching physical science, although there is also evidence that master schedules are sometimes changed at the last minute.

The pivotal issue is whether Ms. Lowe was told, at any time, that she would either be accommodated to teach the physical science class or that she would not have to teach a lab science class at all. The evidence on this point is contradictory [and thus raises a genuine issue of material fact. Most of those present thought that Lowe was told no accommodation would be made although Superintendent Simpson testified, "I believe I indicated that there was a possibility she would not be in a lab science."]

In addition to concluding that Ms. Lowe's failure-to-accommodate claim was too speculative, the district court held that "[b]ecause plaintiff resigned before classes started, she cannot show that the defendant failed to accommodate her disability." We think this is wrong for two reasons.

First, Ms. Lowe's resignation did not preclude her failure-to-accommodate claim. In *Albert v. Smith's Food & Drug Ctrs., Inc.*, the plaintiff's severe asthma prevented her from continuing her job as a cashier. She applied unsuccessfully for other jobs with the defendant and worked for three weeks in customer service. The defendant then told her there were no more hours for her in customer service, but she could have her old cashier job back if her physician would approve. When he would not, the plaintiff stopped working and filed for unemployment. The fact that plaintiff had stopped working for the defendant did not preclude her from pursuing her failure-to-accommodate claim. Indeed, this court held that because the material facts about the interactive process were in dispute, it was error to grant summary judgment to the defendant.

To the extent the District implies that, had Ms. Lowe not resigned, it would have continued to work with her toward a reasonable accommodation, we note that the existence of a dispute concerning the status of the interactive process raises a genuine issue of material fact as to whether the District failed in its duty to reasonably accommodate Ms. Lowe.

Second, Ms. Lowe has raised a genuine issue of material fact on her constructive discharge claim. "Constructive discharge occurs when an employer unlawfully creates working conditions so intolerable that a reasonable person in the employee's position would feel forced to resign." *Strickland v. United Parcel Serv., Inc.*, 555 F.3d 1224, 1228 (10th Cir. 2009) (quotation omitted). "The standard is objective: the employer's subjective intent and the employee's subjective views on the situation are irrelevant. Whether a constructive discharge occurred is a question of fact." We conclude that a genuine issue of material fact exists as to whether a reasonable person, faced with a teaching assignment that will require much standing and moving about, and knowing that such activity will hasten her muscular degeneration and the need for a wheelchair, would have no other choice but to resign. *See Sanchez v. Denver Pub. Schs.*, 164 F.3d 527, 534 (10th Cir. 1998) (holding that the conditions of the job must be objectively intolerable and that the plaintiff must show that she had no other choice but to quit). . . .

IV. CONCLUSION

The evidence produced by Ms. Lowe raises a genuine issue of material fact as to whether, by failing to engage in the interactive process in good faith, the District failed to identify an appropriate accommodation and thus violated the ADA. It also raises a genuine issue of material fact as to whether a reasonable person, under the circumstances, would have felt compelled to resign. . . .

O'Brien, J., concurring.

[Although joining in the Order and Judgment, the concurrence stressed that Lowe was not happy to hear that she would be reassigned from her counselor position to that of a classroom teacher because she preferred being a counselor and did not want to return to the classroom. In April she applied for a position with Guthrie Job Corps, citing the reason for wanting to leave her position with the school district as "retirement." She was offered full-time employment by the Job Corps, which she accepted on June 12, 2006. While Lowe's assumptions about where and what she would teach may have been reasonable, she also knew that teachers were often reassigned at the last minute before school started. Further, Simpson may have simply wanted to keep his options open.]

On August 4, two days after the meeting and without requesting a definitive answer from Simpson as to what he would do in response to her concerns, Lowe sent her resignation letter, saying only, "Consider this my resignation. I am retiring." The letter gave no notice she was resigning due to the School District's failure to make reasonable accommodations, nor did she condition her resignation on such a failure. An employer is not liable for failing to assure an employee reasonable accommodations will be made. The statute imposes liability for "*not making* reasonable accommodations to the known physical or mental limitations of an otherwise qualified individual with a disability who is an applicant or employee. . . ." 42 U.S.C. § 12112(b)(5)(A) (emphasis added). Lowe's resignation may have short-circuited the process by not giving the School District an adequate time to respond. We cannot know whether a reasonable accommodation would or would not have been forthcoming. . . .

The School District argues, correctly, I think, that the interactive process is merely a method of facilitating statutory goals. It is a recommendation, not a statutory requirement. *White v. York Int'l Corp.*, 45 F.3d 357, 363 (10th Cir. 1995). "The federal regulations implementing the ADA 'envision an interactive process that requires *participation by both parties.*'" *Templeton v. Neodata Servs., Inc.*, 162 F.3d 617, 619 (10th Cir. 1998) (quoting *Beck v. Univ. of Wis. Bd. of Regents*, 75 F.3d 1130, 1135 (7th Cir. 1996)) (emphasis added). While it may be an essential component to understand the employee's needs, "a plaintiff cannot base a reasonable accommodation claim solely on the allegation that the employer failed to engage in an interactive process." *Rehling v. City of Chicago*, 207 F.3d 1009, 1016 (7th Cir. 2000) ("[T]he interactive process is a means and not an end in itself."). Clearly an employer could, with impunity, ignore the interactive process so long as it reasonably accommodated employee needs.

This case comes down to whether the School District would have accommodated Lowe's needs by reassignment to a non-laboratory classroom (as it could have done) had she not resigned in a huff.[7] Since the record does not supply an answer to that question with reasonable certainty this case must be tried.

NOTES

1. *Not Getting to the Merits.* Are you surprised that the court never determined whether the proposed accommodations were reasonable/not an undue hardship? Or did it? *Lowe* does say that the mere failure to pursue the interactive process is not a violation of the ADA. In this regard, the Tenth Circuit agrees with most other circuits that have been unwilling to impose liability on an employer solely for failure to engage in the interactive process. There must also be a showing that a reasonable accommodation could have been found had the process been pursued. *See Lucas v. W. W. Grainger, Inc.*, 257 F.3d 1249, 1256 n.2 (11th Cir. 2001); *Kvorjak v. Maine*, 259 F.3d 48 (1st Cir. 2001). But does that mean that the *Lowe* court necessarily found at least a genuine issue of material fact that plaintiff could have been reasonably

---

7. The School District's behavior is not a model for interactive engagement. However, the interactive process creates a duty on both parties to act in good faith. *Smith v. Midland Brake, Inc.* Lowe's good faith in the process is equally as questionable as the School District's. It was no secret Lowe resented her removal from the counseling position and did not want to return to the classroom. Lowe testified "[t]here were some places that they could have put me and that were discussed with Mary Pratz and with Lori Allen [head of high school science department] and with Michelle Redus. There were places that they could have put me." But Lowe never presented these alternatives to Simpson. Lowe also testified there were some science classrooms at the high school where she could teach which would only require the lowering of the blackboard. The record does not indicate Lowe suggested she be assigned to these classrooms. Under these circumstances, it seems rather arbitrary to mention only the School District's shortcomings in the process.

accommodated without undue hardship? How could that be when it never discussed either the accommodations or the hardship?

2. *A Two-Way Street?* By definition, an "interactive process" involves both sides working together toward an accommodation. The *Lowe* concurrence suggests that plaintiff might have failed to do her part, which implies a downside to the interactive process requirement for employees: An employee who fails to participate in discussions about accommodation may forfeit protection against failure-to-accommodate discrimination. *E.g., Beck v. Univ. of Wis. Bd. of Regents*, 75 F.3d 1130 (7th Cir. 1996). In *Reed v. LePage Bakeries, Inc.*, 244 F.3d 254 (1st Cir. 2001), the court ruled that LePage had no obligation to accommodate Reed's disability because Reed had failed to provide LePage with the information necessary to create a suitable means to accommodate her bipolar disorder. *See also Templeton v. Neodata Servs., Inc.*, 162 F.3d 617 (10th Cir. 1998) (terminating employee for refusing to provide reasonably requested medical information does not violate the ADA). Is that the point of the concurrence — especially footnote 7 — that at trial, plaintiff may have somehow waived her rights by not participating in the process? But the majority says, "[n]either party may create or destroy liability by causing a breakdown of the interactive process." In any event, if the employer's failure to interact is not a violation of the ADA unless there was a reasonable accommodation possible, perhaps the employee's failure is not a bar to suit if such participation would have been futile.

3. *The Effect of Plaintiff's Resignation.* The *Lowe* court had to dispose of three threshold issues to get to the merits. The first was whether plaintiff's resignation was based on mere speculation or rather her reasonable belief that she would not be accommodated. The second was whether, even if her belief were reasonable, her resignation somehow mooted her failure to accommodate claim. And the third issue was whether the failure to accommodate resulted in a constructive discharge. Plaintiff survived all three challenges, but suppose Ms. Lowe had consulted you after the August meeting. Given the duty to cooperate in the interactive process and the risks posed by resignation, would you have counseled her that she could resign and still sue? Wouldn't it be better advice to her to continue working, at least until the school year started? The denial of an accommodation will frequently make it difficult, but not impossible, for a disabled employee to continue to work, which means that some hard choices may have to be made. Given the demanding standard for constructive discharge, it is certainly possible that an employee who quits when she is not accommodated will have forfeited any ADA claim.

4. *What Accommodations?* In ADA accommodation cases, the devil is often in the details. Ms. Lowe's treating doctor wrote that his patient "has a functional limitation which requires sedentary work only. She is unable to repetitively climb stairs; is unable to kneel, squat, or crawl." Appendix. Given those limitations, these were Ms. Lowe's proposed "Laboratory Safety Modifications for Physical Disabilities":

> Classroom will need to be modified so teacher can be accessible to each table. (Wider aisles to allow wheel chair/walker access)
> - Lab stations will need to be lowered.
> - Chalkboards/whiteboards will need to be lowered so are accessible from a sitting position.
> - Overhead cart and screen will need to be modified to accommodate a sitting position.

- Eyewash station will need to be added that is accessible.
- Fume hood will need to be added that is accessible.
- Safety Shower will need to be added that is accessible.
- Fire extinguisher and fire blanket need to be lowered.
- Chemical and flammable storage will need to be modified so it is accessible.
- General lab equipment storage will need to be modified so it is accessible.
- Teacher aide will be needed to gather lab equipment, transport chemicals, and monitor safety issues during labs.

5. *Costs of Accommodation.* It's pretty clear that making all of these changes to the classroom would have entailed some direct costs, and there is also the possibility of indirect costs — such as potential lost student space. Of course, maybe some of them could have been eliminated had there been an interactive process. But suppose Bowman and Sampson called you for advice before the meeting, and suppose that they told you that their physical plant staff had estimated the costs of the accommodation at $10,000. Is this reasonable? An undue hardship? The language of the statute suggests that real costs may have to be incurred in order to accommodate. Thus, §101(9) provides that qualified readers or interpreters may be a reasonable accommodation. Further, the Interpretive Guidance suggests that reasonable accommodations include providing personal assistants such as a page turner for an employee with no hands or a travel attendant for an employee who is blind. 29 C.F.R. pt. 1630, app. §1630.2(o). *See generally* Mark C. Weber, *Unreasonable Accommodation and Due Hardship*, 62 FLA. L. REV. 1119 (2010) ("The duty to accommodate is a substantial obligation, one that may be expensive to satisfy, and one that is not subject to a cost-benefits balance, but rather a cost-resources balance; it is also subject to increase over time.").

The cases have not yet gone so far. *Vande Zande v. Wis. Dep't of Admin.*, 44 F.3d 538 (7th Cir. 1995), is the seminal reasonable accommodation case, and it involves a paraplegic plaintiff, who was employed by the state for three years. In order to enable her to perform her job duties, the State Department "made numerous accommodations" but refused her request for an at-home computer when pressure ulcers forced her to stay home. Despite this refusal, the plaintiff was able to complete all but 16.5 hours of work during her eight-week home confinement. The remaining time was covered by her paid sick leave reserves. She filed suit under the ADA alleging that her employer failed to reasonably accommodate her disability.

The Seventh Circuit, in an opinion written by Judge Posner, held that "[t]he employee must show that the accommodation is reasonable in the sense both of efficacious and proportionate to costs," 44 F.3d at 543, the approach later approved by *Barnett.* The court elaborated that an employer is not required to accommodate a disability by allowing the disabled worker to work, unsupervised, from home, since productivity would inevitably be reduced. *Id.* at 544-45. Accordingly, the employer's action was deemed reasonable as a matter of law. *Id.* at 545. The court also rejected the plaintiff's claim that the State Department was required to lower the communal kitchen sink by two inches so that she could use it instead of the bathroom sink. *Id.* at 546. "The duty of reasonable accommodation is satisfied when the employer does what is necessary to enable the disabled worker to work in *reasonable comfort*." *Id.* (emphasis added).

If we assume that Lowe could show that her proposals were "efficacious," can she also show that the hypothetical $10,000 is proportionate? Professor Sunstein critiques Posner's opinion for not providing any real content to the concept of "proportionate."

Cass R. Sunstein, *Cost-Benefit Analysis Without Analyzing Costs or Benefits: Reasonable Accommodation, Balancing, and Stigmatic Harms,* 74 U. Chi. L. Rev. 1895, 1904-05 (2007). With respect to Posner's statement that employees can't be accommodated by working from home because of concerns about supervision, he writes:

> Talk about casual empiricism! If the question is whether the costs of the accommodation are disproportionate to the benefits, we might want to make some kind of serious inquiry into both costs and benefits. What is the evidence that if workers telecommute, "their productivity will inevitably be greatly reduced"? In assessing benefits, do we ask how much disabled people are willing to pay to telecommute? Or do we ask how much they would have to be paid to be denied the right to telecommute? More particularly, what is the evidence that Vande Zande's own productivity was reduced? Did her productivity fall during the eight-week period in which she worked at home? What, in fact, is the nature of her job, such that "team work under supervisors" is required? It would seem important to ask and answer that question to assess her request to telecommute. But Judge Posner does not inquire.

Indeed, Sunstein suggests that *Vande Zande's* analysis boils down to nothing more than a judge's intuitions. Given the risk of a judge's reaction being negative, would you err on the side of granting the accommodation if you were advising the school district in *Lowe*?

Finally, to the extent that costs have to be "proportionate" to benefits, some scholars have argued that benefits for nondisabled workers ought to be factored in. *See* Michelle A. Travis, *Lashing Back at the ADA Backlash: How the Americans with Disabilities Act Benefits Americans Without Disabilities,* 76 Tenn. L. Rev. 311 (2009); Elizabeth F. Emens, *Integrating Accommodation,* 156 U. Pa. L. Rev. 839 (2008). That doesn't seem applicable in *Lowe*, but suppose installation of a ramp or elevator benefits not only the disabled worker but also other workers and improves their productivity?

6. *Looking at Undue Hardship.* Suppose that, as the district's counsel, you conclude that the accommodation Lowe seeks may well be reasonable. *Barnett* nevertheless allows an employer to prevail if such an accommodation would be an undue hardship, a question that is analyzed separately. Section 101(10) of the ADA provides that "undue hardship" means "an action requiring significant difficulty or expense, when considered in light of" the following factors:

(i) the nature and cost of the accommodation needed under this Act;

(ii) the overall financial resources of the facility or facilities involved in the provision of the reasonable accommodation; the number of persons employed at such facility; the effect on expenses and resources, or the impact otherwise of such accommodation upon the operation of the facility;

(iii) the overall financial resources of the covered entity; the overall size of the business of a covered entity with respect to the number of its employees; the number, type, and location of its facilities; and

(iv) the type of operation or operations of the covered entity, including the composition, structure, and functions of the workforce of such entity; the geographic separateness, administrative, or fiscal relationship of the facility or facilities in question to the covered entity.

42 U.S.C. § 12111(10) (2006).

In *Borkowski v. Valley Cent. Sch. Dist.*, 63 F.3d 131 (2d Cir. 1995), the court discussed these criteria, concluding that the issue of "undue hardship" is one of degree: "[E]ven this list of factors says little about how great a hardship an employer must bear before the hardship becomes undue." The court held that employers are not required to show that they would be driven to the brink of insolvency. It relied on ADA legislative history rejecting a provision that would have defined an undue hardship as one that threatened the continued existence of the employer. *Id.* at 139. "Where the employer is a government entity, Congress could not have intended the only limit on the employer's duty to make reasonable accommodation to be the full extent of the tax base on which the government entity could draw." *Id.; see generally* Steven B. Epstein, *In Search of a Bright Line: Determining When an Employer's Financial Hardship Becomes "Undue" Under the Americans with Disabilities Act*, 48 VAND. L. REV. 391 (1995) (proposing a mathematical model for determining undue hardship). *See also Vande Zande*, 44 F.3d at 543 (an accommodation is an undue hardship when it is unduly costly "in relation to the benefits of the accommodation to the disabled worker as well as to the employer's resources."). Do you understand how undue hardship might help the district in *Lowe*?

7. *Putting the Two Terms Together.* As a practical matter, one would expect that a plaintiff would typically be able to prove that a proposed accommodation was efficacious. The more serious question is likely to be whether its costs are proportionate to its benefits (although you should note that employees have incentives to propose less costly accommodations whose costs are, therefore, more likely to be proportionate). Costs, then, will tend to be the determinative factor as to the reasonableness of an accommodation. And they will, at least in extreme cases, be relevant to the undue hardship question. Despite the different burdens, aren't these the same question? Judge Posner's grand synthesis in *Vande Zande* was as follows:

> [C]osts enter at two points in the analysis of claims to an accommodation to a disability. The employee must show that the accommodation is reasonable in the sense both of efficacious and of proportional to costs. Even if this prima facie showing is made, the employer has an opportunity to prove that upon more careful consideration the costs are excessive in relation either to the benefits of the accommodation or to the employer's financial survival or health. . . . One interpretation of "undue hardship" is that it permits an employer to escape liability if he can carry the burden of proving that a disability accommodation reasonable for a normal employer would break him.

And *Barnett* seems to endorse this approach of looking to costs twice.

8. *Back to* Lowe. Now that you know what reasonable accommodation and undue hardship mean as a matter of law, was there a reasonable accommodation available in *Lowe*? It might have been costly to modify the classroom in question, especially if the result was space for fewer students. But why could the school not just assign Lowe to another, less cramped classroom? It might require bumping another teacher into Ms. Rheinhart's cramped space, but is that a problem? Does your answer depend on whether there's a seniority system in place regarding classrooms? And what about assigning her to junior high classes?

9. *Full-time Face-time.* As *Vande Zande* suggests, a frequent question is whether an employer need accommodate by allowing an employee to work at home. Most circuits, in agreement with Posner, have found regularly and timely

attendance at work to be an essential job function for most positions, thus foreclosing any need to accommodate individuals whose disabilities prevent them from working more or less normal schedules. If such individuals are unable to come to work regularly, they are not "otherwise qualified." If they are able to come to work but request an accommodation, that accommodation will not be reasonable to the extent that it deviates substantially from regular and timely attendance. *See, e.g., Mason v. Avaya Commc'ns, Inc.,* 357 F.3d 1114 (10th Cir. 2004). Employers, therefore, generally are not required to accommodate disabled individuals by allowing numerous absences or by granting leaves of absence of indefinite duration. *See, e.g., Krensavage v. Bayer Corp.,* 314 F. App'x 421, 426 n.1 (3d Cir. 2008) (indefinite leave is not reasonable accommodation since employee's need to be absent for so long meant he was no longer qualified for the job); *Wood v. Green,* 323 F.3d 1309 (11th Cir. 2003) (indefinite leave of absence is not a reasonable accommodation). Despite the "full-time face-time" norm, a short-term leave of absence often will be viewed as a reasonable accommodation, particularly when the employer's own policies provide for paid or unpaid leave as great as that requested by the disabled employee. *See, e.g., Nunes v. Wal-Mart Stores, Inc.,* 164 F.3d 1243 (9th Cir. 1999) (jury question on reasonableness when plaintiff was terminated before leave period under employer's policy expired); *Rascon v. U.S. W. Commc'ns, Inc.,* 143 F.3d 1324 (10th Cir. 1998) (request for 4- to 5-month leave not unreasonable when employer's policy provided for leaves ranging from 6 to 12 months); *see generally* Stephen F. Befort, *The Most Difficult Reasonable Accommodation Issues: Reassignment and Leave of Absence,* 37 Wake Forest L. Rev. 439 (2002). Do you think that the continued judicial skepticism about the reasonableness of working from home is justified in light of changes in American work patterns and the increased availability of technology enabling individuals to work remotely?

10. *"Voluntary" Accommodations.* Wisconsin provided Vande Zande with a number of accommodations. For example, it had bathrooms modified, had a step ramped, and bought adjustable furniture for plaintiff. *Vande Zande,* 44 F.3d at 544. These may or may not have been required in light of the court's opinion. The ADA Interpretive Guidance indicates that an employer is permitted to provide accommodations beyond those required. *See* 29 C.F.R. pt. 1630, app. § 1630.9 ("nothing in this part [relating to reasonable accommodation] prohibits employers or other covered entities from providing accommodations beyond those required by this part"). If an employer provides a noncompulsory accommodation, can the employer withdraw the accommodation or refuse to extend it to other similarly situated disabled individuals? This might seem like a rhetorical question since providing the accommodation would seem to establish both that it is reasonable and not an undue hardship. But some courts suggest the answer may be yes! *See Phelps v. Optima Health, Inc.,* 251 F.3d 21, 26 (1st Cir. 2001) (employers providing employees an accommodation does not obligate them to continue providing it); *Holbrook v. City of Alpharetta, Ga.,* 112 F.3d 1522, 1528 (11th Cir. 1997) (police department did not violate ADA when it ceased to make noncompulsory accommodations for employee); *Myers v. Hose,* 50 F.3d 278, 284 (4th Cir. 1995) ("the fact that certain accommodations may have been offered . . . to some employees as a matter of good faith does not mean that they must be extended to Myers as a matter of law"). However, the fact that an employer provides nonmandated accommodations to a disabled male employee may have implications for its duty to provide accommodations to pregnant women under the nondiscrimination commands of Title VII.

11. *Norms Trumping Law.* Many employers, often counseled by attorneys, have taken the initiative in developing protocols for engaging proactively with disabled employees about their need for accommodation. Such internal procedures often apply whenever an individual suffers a physical or mental limitation, whether or not that condition constitutes a recognized disability. This means that other workers may reap a benefit from the reasonable-accommodation requirement and that, in at least some instances, voluntary accommodations are achieved without the need for a protracted legal dispute. According to Professor Stephen Befort:

> The ADA's interactive process [for accommodating claimed disabilities] has launched a quiet revolution that gets little coverage in the case reporter system. All over the United States, disabled employees and human resources managers are joining together to invent mutually acceptable workplace solutions in the form of reasonable accommodations. The alternative dispute resolution format of the interactive process facilitates a creative and cooperative search for win-win outcomes. The prospect of litigation in the absence of a voluntary resolution provides a powerful incentive for both parties to conduct this search in good faith. The interactive process, in short, has significantly transformed procedural structures and norms impacting the disabled.

Accommodation at Work: Lessons from the Americans with Disabilities Act and Possibilities for Alleviating the American Worker Time Crunch, 13 CORNELL J. L. & PUB. POL'Y 615, 628 (2004); *see also* Rachel Arnow-Richman, *Public Law and Private Process: Toward an Incentivized Organizational Justice Model of Equal Employment Quality for Caregivers*, 2007 UTAH L. REV. 25 (2007). With the ADAAA's expansion of the actual "disability" category, employers are likely to have a renewed concern for accommodation.

PROBLEMS

10-1. Sam is hearing impaired. He has applied and has been turned down for a secretarial job that included answering phones. He comes to you for advice, informing you that he told the interviewer that he could perform all aspects of the job, except for answering the phone, without any accommodation. With respect to answering the phone, he proposed two alternatives at the interview: (1) eliminating the phone responsibilities or (2) providing a telecommunications device (TDD) that would allow him to answer the phone. The interviewer rejected Sam because neither alternative was "feasible."

In advising Sam, first focus on whether he is qualified for this job. What arguments can he make? What arguments can the employer make? If you conclude that Sam is qualified, which, if either, of the two alternatives is reasonable and not an undue hardship? What further information would you need to answer this question?

10-2. About five years ago, Jan developed a violent, and potentially fatal, food allergy to paprika. She is so sensitive that aromas from co-workers' food can trigger an attack, and an attack can, unless treated immediately, kill her. To avoid exposure, Jan uses a service dog named Penny, who has been trained at a cost of $10,000 to Jan to sniff paprika and warn Jan of its presence. Jan takes Penny everywhere, including to work. There was never a problem until recently, when a co-worker claimed that he was allergic to Penny and asked that she be removed from the workplace. You are advising the employer. What advice do you give? *See* Steven Greenhouse, *When Treating One Worker's Allergy Sets Off Another's*, N.Y. TIMES, May 11, 2010, Section A-10. *See generally* Kelly Cahill Timmons, *Accommodating Misconduct Under the American with Disabilities Act*, 57 FLA. L. REV. 187 (2005).

B. ANTIDISCRIMINATION, ACCOMMODATION, AND THE PROBLEM OF WORK-FAMILY BALANCE

In addition to needs that arise as a result of disability, many employees have family responsibilities that impact their ability to work. Perhaps the most common problem is the conflict faced by many workers, particularly women, in attempting to balance the demands of work and the responsibilities of caring for young children. But workers face a variety of life demands that can have such effects, ranging from obligations to aging parents, to family emergencies and sudden illnesses, to personal needs relating to their own health and well-being.

The legal obligations of employers in responding to such life needs are modest. Unlike disability, there is no general duty to accommodate workers' family and personal responsibilities. However, because most workers can expect to face such demands at some point in their lives, the limited rights that they have in such situations are profoundly important. For the same reason, employers can expect to face difficult questions about whether and when to accommodate the life needs of its workforce, both as a legal compliance problem and as a strategic business matter. This section considers two laws that apply to workers facing a subset of life events that can affect work: Title VII, as amended by the Pregnancy Discrimination Act, which prohibits discrimination on the basis of pregnancy; and the FMLA, which provides up to 12 weeks of unpaid leave to workers who need such leave for the birth or care of a new child or for their own illness or that of a family member. It goes on to consider perspectives on whether the law can and should be expanded in this area to require greater accommodation of workers' lives in light of the diversified needs of the modern workforce.

1. Pregnancy Under Title VII: The Limits of Formal Equality

In one of its first decisions under Title VII, the Supreme Court determined that discrimination against women on account of parentage, a quality they share with males, was illegal. In *Phillips v. Martin Marietta Corp.*, 400 U.S. 542 (1971), the employer barred the employment of women who were parents of preschool age children while similarly situated men were hired. The Supreme Court held such conduct illegal. While *Phillips* did recognize that such discrimination might be permissible if the employer could prove that not having preschool children was within the narrow "bona fide occupational qualification" ("BFOQ") exception for sex discrimination, see Chapter 9, the case has come to stand for the bedrock employment discrimination proposition that individuals must be treated as such and cannot be stereotyped as members of the sex or race to which they belong. Even if it were true, as Martin Marietta claimed, that, as a group, mothers of small children had worse attendance records than fathers, Title VII would render it illegal to treat individual mothers adversely on the basis of their gender.

Phillips was an easy case — it prohibited discrimination on account of a woman's status as a parent, a condition mothers shared with fathers. But the question of whether employers could treat women differently on account of pregnancy — a female physical condition that has no analog for males — proved more difficult for the Court. The Supreme Court's initial encounter with this problem was in *General Electric Co. v. Gilbert*, 429 U.S. 125 (1976), which held that discrimination on account of pregnancy was not per se sex discrimination within the meaning of Title VII. The case involved a fringe benefit plan for employees who could not work as a result of disabilities, but it excluded pregnancy-related disabilities. The Court rejected the plaintiff's claims, relying on its prior decision in *Geduldig v. Aiello*, 417 U.S. 484 (1974), which had upheld a similar state disability insurance plan against an equal protection challenge. In deciding *Gilbert*, the Court held that a pregnancy classification is not per se disparate treatment because of sex:

> The lack of identity between the excluded disability and gender as such under this insurance program becomes clear upon the most cursory analysis. The program divides potential recipients into two groups — pregnant women and nonpregnant persons. While the first group is exclusively female, the second includes members of both sexes.

429 U.S. at 135 (quoting *Geduldig*, 417 U.S. at 496-97 n.20). Thus, under *Gilbert* employers not only had no duty to accommodate pregnancy or motherhood but could also freely discriminate against "pregnant people."

In 1978, Congress responded by enacting the Pregnancy Discrimination Act ("PDA"), which added §701(k) to Title VII. That section begins: "The terms 'because of sex' or 'on the basis of sex' include, but are not limited to, because of or on the basis of pregnancy, childbirth or related medical conditions. . . ." This sentence overruled *Gilbert* and promised more restrictions on how employers could treat women, at least during their pregnancies. It appears to proscribe all explicit pregnancy classifications that cannot be justified under the BFOQ defense, see Chapter 9, which allows sex discrimination in highly exceptional circumstances. *See Harris v. Pan Am. World Airways*, 649 F.2d 670 (9th Cir. 1980) (at a certain point in pregnancy, an employer's policy restricting employment of flight attendants may be justified by BFOQ concerns for passenger safety).

While some hoped that that the PDA would not only proscribe discrimination but also trigger a broader duty to accommodate pregnancy, those hopes were frustrated. After defining "sex" to include pregnancy and related conditions, the PDA goes on to impose the following standard for the treatment of pregnant women by employers: "Women affected by pregnancy, childbirth, or related medical conditions shall be treated the same for all employment-related purposes, including receipt of benefits under fringe benefit programs, as other persons not so affected but similar in their ability or inability to work." The circuit courts have cut back on the breadth of the proscription of pregnancy discrimination in the first clause of § 701(k) by viewing this second clause as limiting the first. Under this reading, the key is whether a woman "affected by pregnancy" is "treated the same" as a similarly situated man would be, that is, a man facing similar physical restrictions and limitations due to a different medical condition. If so, there is no violation of the statute even if pregnancy actually disadvantages a woman. *See generally* Joanna L. Grossman, *Pregnancy, Work, and the Promise of Equal Citizenship*, 98 GEO. L.J. 567, 570 (2010) ("The PDA . . . is modeled on a basic formal equality framework, which provides no absolute right to accommodation necessitated by pregnancy"); Kimberly A. Yuracko, *Trait Discrimination as Sex Discrimination: An Argument Against Neutrality*, 83 TEX. L. REV. 167 (2004) (in the PDA, "Congress renamed the trait at issue from pregnancy per se to the more generalized trait of physical disability and then reframed the cross-sex comparison in terms of this non-sex-specific trait.").

An early case so holding was *Marafino v. St. Louis County Circuit Court*, 707 F.2d 1005 (8th Cir. 1983), which found that the failure to hire the plaintiff as a law clerk for a state judge because she was pregnant did not violate § 701(k). The court reasoned that the employer would not have hired anyone requiring a leave of absence shortly after beginning a short-term position. Thus, the employer did not discriminate against pregnant women but rather against persons (including but not limited to pregnant women) who would have to take a leave in the foreseeable future. *Marafino* has come to be the law.

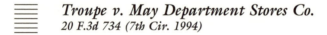

Troupe v. May Department Stores Co.
20 F.3d 734 (7th Cir. 1994)

POSNER, Chief Judge.

The plaintiff, Kimberly Hern Troupe, was employed by the Lord & Taylor department store in Chicago as a saleswoman in the women's accessories department. She had begun working there in 1987, initially working part time but from July 1990 full time. Until the end of 1990 her work was entirely satisfactory. In December of that year, in the first trimester of a pregnancy, she began experiencing morning sickness of unusual severity. The following month she requested and was granted a return to part-time status, working from noon to 5:00 p.m. Partly it seems because she slept later under the new schedule, so that noon was "morning" for her, she continued to experience severe morning sickness at work, causing what her lawyer describes with understatement as "slight" or "occasional" tardiness. In the month that ended with a warning from her immediate supervisor, Jennifer Rauch, on February 18, she reported late to work, or left early, on nine out of the 21 working days. The day after the warning she was late again and this time received a written warning. After she was tardy three days in a row late in March, the company on March 29 placed her on probation for 60 days. During the probationary period Troupe was late eleven more days; and she was fired on June 7, shortly after the end of the probationary period. She testified at her deposition that on the way to the meeting with the defendant's human resources manager at which she was fired, Rauch told her that "I [Troupe] was going to be terminated because she [Rauch] didn't think I was coming back to work after I had my baby." Troupe was due to begin her maternity leave the next day. We do not know whether it was to be a paid maternity leave but at argument Lord & Taylor's counsel said that employees of Lord & Taylor are entitled to maternity leave with half pay. We must assume that after Troupe was fired she received no medical benefits from Lord & Taylor in connection with her pregnancy and the birth of her child; for she testified without contradiction that she received no monetary benefits of any kind, other than unemployment benefits, after June 7, 1991. We do not know whether Lord & Taylor was less tolerant of Troupe's tardiness than it would have been had the cause not been a medical condition related to pregnancy. There is no evidence on this question, vital as it is.

. . . The great, the undeniable fact is the plaintiff's tardiness. Her lawyer argues with great vigor that she should not be blamed — that she was genuinely ill, had a doctor's excuse, etc. That would be pertinent if Troupe were arguing that the Pregnancy Discrimination Act requires an employer to treat an employee afflicted by morning sickness better than the employer would treat an employee who was equally tardy for some other health reason. This is rightly not argued. If an employee who (like Troupe) does not have an employment contract cannot work because of illness, nothing in Title VII requires the employer to keep the employee on the payroll.

Against the inference that Troupe was fired because she was chronically late to arrive at work and chronically early to leave, she has only two facts to offer. The first is the timing of her discharge: she was fired the day before her maternity leave was to begin. Her morning sickness could not interfere with her work when she was not working because she was on maternity leave, and it could not interfere with her work when she returned to work after her maternity leave because her morning sickness would end at the latest with the birth of her child. Thus her employer fired her one day before the problem that the employer says caused her to be fired was certain to end. If the discharge of an unsatisfactory worker were a purely remedial measure rather than also, or instead, a deterrent one, the inference that Troupe wasn't really fired because of her tardiness would therefore be a powerful one. But that is a big "if." We must remember that after two warnings Troupe had been placed on probation for sixty days and that she had violated the implicit terms of probation by being as tardy during the probationary period as she had been before. If the company did not fire her, its warnings and threats would seem empty. Employees would be encouraged to flout work rules knowing that the only sanction would be a toothless warning or a meaningless period of probation.

Yet this is only an interpretation; and it might appear to be an issue for trial whether it is superior to Troupe's interpretation. But what is Troupe's interpretation? Not (as we understand it) that Lord & Taylor wanted to get back at her for becoming pregnant or having morning sickness. The only significance she asks us to attach to the timing of her discharge is as reinforcement for the inference that she asks us to draw from Rauch's statement about the reason for her termination: that she was terminated because her employer did not expect her to return to work after her maternity leave was up. We must decide whether a termination so motivated is discrimination within the meaning of the pregnancy amendment to Title VII.

Standing alone, it is not. (It could be a breach of contract, but that is not alleged.) Suppose that Lord & Taylor had an employee named Jones, a black employee scheduled to take a three-month paid sick leave for a kidney transplant; and whether thinking that he would not return to work when his leave was up or not wanting to incur the expense of paying him while he was on sick leave, the company fired him. In doing so it might be breaking its employment contract with Jones, if it had one, or violating a state statute requiring the payment of earned wages. But the company could not be found guilty of racial discrimination unless (in the absence of any of the other types of evidence of discrimination that we have discussed) there was evidence that it failed to exhibit comparable rapacity toward similarly situated employees of the white race. We must imagine a hypothetical Mr. Troupe, who is as tardy as Ms. Troupe was, also because of health problems, and who is about to take a protracted sick leave growing out of those problems at an expense to Lord & Taylor equal to that of Ms. Troupe's maternity leave. If Lord & Taylor would have fired our hypothetical Mr. Troupe, this implies that it fired Ms. Troupe not because she was pregnant but because she cost the company more than she was worth to it.

The Pregnancy Discrimination Act does not, despite the urgings of feminist scholars, *e.g.*, Herma Hill Kay, *Equality and Difference: The Case of Pregnancy*, 1 Berkeley Women's L. J. 1, 30-31 (1985), require employers to offer maternity leave or take other steps to make it easier for pregnant women to work, *cf. Cal. Fed. Savs. & Loan Ass'n v. Guerra*, 479 U.S. 272, 286-87 (1987); 29 C.F.R. § 1604.10(b) and App. to Pt. 604 (EEOC Guidelines on Discrimination Because of Sex: Questions and Answers on the Pregnancy Discrimination Act)—to make it as easy, say, as it is for their spouses to continue working during pregnancy. Employers can treat pregnant women as badly as they treat similarly affected but nonpregnant employees, even to the point of "conditioning the availability of an employment benefit on an employee's decision to return to work after the end of the medical disability that pregnancy causes." *Maganuco v. Leyden Cmty. High Sch. Dist. 212*, 939 F.2d 440, 445 (7th Cir. 1991). *Maganuco* and other cases hold that disparate impact is a permissible theory of liability under the Pregnancy Discrimination Act, as it is under other provisions of Title VII. But, properly understood, disparate impact as a theory of liability is a means of dealing with the residues of past discrimination, rather than a warrant for favoritism. *Finnegan v. Trans World Airlines, Inc.*, 967 F.2d 1161, 1164 (7th Cir. 1992).

The plaintiff has made no effort to show that if all the pertinent facts were as they are except for the fact of her pregnancy, she would not have been fired. So in the end she has no evidence from which a rational trier of fact could infer that she was a victim of pregnancy discrimination. . . . The Pregnancy Discrimination Act requires the employer to ignore an employee's pregnancy, but . . . not her absence from work, unless the employer overlooks the comparable absences of nonpregnant employees—in which event it would not be ignoring pregnancy after all. Of course there may be no comparable absences, but we do not understand Troupe to be arguing that the reason she did not present evidence that nonpregnant employees were treated more favorably than she is that . . . there is no comparison group of Lord & Taylor employees. What to do in such a case is an issue for a case in which the issue is raised. (We do not even know how long Troupe's maternity leave was supposed to be.) We doubt that finding a comparison group would be that difficult. Troupe would be halfway home if she could find one nonpregnant employee of Lord & Taylor who had not been fired when about to begin a leave similar in length to hers. She either did not look, or did not find. Given the absence of other evidence, her failure to present any comparison evidence doomed her case.

NOTES

1. *Firing a Woman for Being Pregnant Is Sometimes OK.* Like *Marafino*, *Troupe* interprets the PDA to prohibit only conduct that treats pregnant women differently than "similarly situated" nonpregnant people. That means that it is OK to fire a woman because she is pregnant—as long as a similarly situated male (or nonpregnant woman) would be fired. *See also Spees v. James Marine, Inc.*, 617 F.3d 380 (6th Cir. 2010) (plaintiff survived summary judgment as to employer's transferring her to a less desirable position when it learned of her pregnancy; but she lost her claim of discrimination related to her subsequent discharge since the employer terminated her after receipt of her doctor's note saying she should be given light duty confined to bed, which mean she was fired for inability to work, not pregnancy). Does this make sense? In *Newport News Shipbuilding & Dry Dock Co. v. E.E.O.C.*, 462 U.S. 669 (1983), the Supreme Court held illegal an employer's policy restricting medical insurance for pregnancy to female employees, and therefore excluding the wives of male employees. The Court wrote that the PDA establishes the following:

> [F]or all Title VII purposes, discrimination based on a woman's pregnancy is, on its face, discrimination because of her sex. . . . By making clear that an employer could not discriminate on the basis of an employee's pregnancy, Congress did not erase the original prohibition against discrimination on the basis of an employee's sex.

Id. at 684-85. Is *Troupe* consistent with this view?

Troupe further narrows the statute's protection by adopting restrictive rules about proving different treatment based on pregnancy. How exactly is a pregnant employee to prove what her employer would do for a hypothetical similarly situated male employee? In finding Troupe's evidence insufficient, does Posner overlook the significance of the employer's disability and maternity leave policy? By adopting a leave policy, hasn't the employer acknowledged that disabled employees will receive leave if they meet the stated requirements? If so, is depriving Troupe of her leave inconsistent with the written policy, leaving no explanation for her termination other than her pregnancy?

2. *A Throwback? Troupe* seems to accept as nondiscriminatory the employer's concern that Troupe might not come back after her leave. Scholars have argued that "Kimberly Troupe appears to have fallen victim to sex stereotyping" because Lord & Taylor would probably not have concluded that a similarly situated employee, about to take disability leave, would fail to return to work after the leave. *See* Ann C. McGinley & Jeffrey W. Stempel, *Condescending Contradictions: Richard Posner's Pragmatism and Pregnancy Discrimination*, 46 FLA. L. REV. 193, 221 (1994). Permitting the defendant to act on the assumption that Troupe would not return to work after her baby was born validates exactly the type of stereotype about women, especially pregnant women, that the PDA was intended to overcome. *Id.*

In *Maldonado v. U.S. Bank*, 186 F.3d 759 (7th Cir. 1999), a bank fired an employee upon learning she was pregnant, reasoning that her due date would render her unable to work during the summer, a particularly busy time of the year. The Seventh Circuit reversed summary judgment in the bank's favor, holding that an "employer cannot take anticipatory action unless it has a good faith basis, supported by sufficiently strong evidence, that the normal inconveniences of an employee's pregnancy will require special treatment." *Id.* at 767. Does this decision at least cut back on the more troubling aspects of the Seventh Circuit's decision in *Troupe*? One commentator describes the case as standing only for "the right of pregnant workers not to be *presumed* incapable." Joanna L. Grossman, *Pregnancy, Work, and the Promise of Equal Citizenship*, 98 GEO. L. J. 567, 607 (2010) (emphasis in original).

3. *No Accommodation Required.* Posner reads the statute as adopting a strict equal treatment rule and consequently imposing no duty to accommodate pregnant employees in any respect. The employer can discriminate against pregnancy to the extent that pregnancy has characteristics shared by other conditions (such as a temporary disability). That Ms. Troupe's morning sickness caused her absences is simply irrelevant if the employer would have discharged someone who was late for other reasons. As Posner explains, "The Pregnancy Discrimination Act does not, despite the urgings of feminist scholars, require employers to offer maternity leave or take other steps to make it easier for pregnant women to work." Of course, from the critics' perspective, that is precisely the problem with the statute. Because of pregnancy, and motherhood more generally, many women find it harder than men, including fathers, to maintain consistent work performance and workforce attachment. This is due at least in part to the way American society is presently constructed, with women still assuming the bulk of child-rearing responsibilities. The Family and Medical Leave Act, which we will explore shortly, attempts to address some of these issues with varying degrees of success.

4. *Equal Treatment in Benefits.* While *Marafino* and *Troupe* use the second clause of the PDA to narrow the rights that might be granted by the first clause, the second clause of § 701(k) also plays an important role in ensuring that pregnant women are treated fairly by employers. If the statute consisted of the first clause only, employers would be required, at most, not to discriminate against women because of their pregnancies, leaving unresolved whether insurance coverage and leaves of absence could exclude pregnancy from coverage. Congress was unwilling to require employers to provide such benefits to pregnant women but did mandate, through the second clause, that employers who do provide such benefits to nonpregnant workers must extend them to women similarly situated "in their ability or inability to work."

Questions sometimes arise, however, about the extent to which employers can exclude fertility treatments and birth control from coverage, which could be viewed as pertaining to pregnancy-related conditions. *See Saks v. Franklin Covey Co.*, 316 F.3d 337 (2d Cir. 2003) (rejecting a claim that denial of fertility treatments violated Title VII). *But see Hall v. Nalco Co.*, 534 F.3d 644 (7th Cir. 2008) (finding denial of in vitro fertilization to be sex discrimination against women). *See generally* Stephen F. Befort & Elizabeth C. Borer, *Equitable Prescription Drug Coverage: Preventing Sex Discrimination in Employer-Provided Health Plans*, 70 LA. L. REV. 205 (2009); Ernest F. Lidge III, *An Employer's Exclusion of Coverage for Contraceptive Drugs Is Not per se Sex Discrimination*, 76 TEMPLE L. REV. 533 (2003).

5. *Disparate Impact.* Judge Posner in *Troupe* states that disparate impact is a viable theory under the PDA although "properly understood, disparate impact as a theory of liability is a means of dealing with the residues of past discrimination, rather than a warrant for favoritism." What does he mean by this? In Chapter 9 we learned that some employment practices can be challenged not because they are intentionally discriminatory but because they have disproportionate adverse effects on protected groups and are not justified as a business necessity. What if an employer provides no leave to its employees and the impact of this "no leave" policy falls more harshly on women because of their need for pregnancy-related leaves? Would an impact claim be viable? Some think that the command of the PDA that pregnant workers be treated the same as similarly situated, nonpregnant workers limits the PDA to only disparate treatment. If so, does the codification of the disparate impact theory in the Civil Rights Act of 1991 alter that conclusion? Certainly it would seem that if a practice disproportionately impacted *women*, even if it were because of pregnancy, disparate impact theory would be available. But would a disparate impact claim be stated if the practice disproportionately impacted *pregnant women*, as opposed to *women* as a group? *Compare Garcia v. Woman's Hosp. of Tex.*, 97 F.3d 810, 813 (5th Cir. 1996) (disparate impact claim available if plaintiff can show that employer's lifting requirement affects substantially all pregnant women and is not a bona fide job duty) *with Stout v. Baxter Healthcare Corp.*, 282 F.3d 856, 861 (5th Cir. 2002) (no disparate impact claim available where "plaintiff's only challenge is that the amount of sick leave granted to employees is insufficient to accommodate the time off required in a typical pregnancy"). *See generally* Joanna L. Grossman, *Pregnancy, Work, and the Promise of Equal Citizenship*, 98 GEO. L. J. 567, 616 (2010) ([the disparate impact theory] "has proved decidedly ineffectual thus far. The reality is that plaintiffs almost never prevail on such claims in the pregnancy context.").

6. *The Bottom Line.* Suppose an employer has no leave policy for anyone. Does Title VII require that employer to provide leave to pregnant women? *Troupe* would say no from a disparate treatment perspective — since there are no nonpregnant people being given leave, there can be no sex discrimination. The case would also seem to bar disparate impact for such a policy. *See Stout v. Baxter Healthcare Corp.*, 282 F.3d 856, 861 (5th Cir. 2002) ("To hold otherwise would be to transform the PDA into a guarantee of medical leave for pregnant employees, something we have specifically held that the PDA does not do"). The bottom line, then, is that Title VII imposes no duty to accommodate pregnancy. Accordingly, most scholars believe that Title VII's protections do not address the fundamental problem posed by women's family caretaking responsibilities. *See generally* Kathryn Abrams, *Cross-Dressing in the Master's Clothes*, 109 YALE L. J. 745 (2000); Laura T. Kessler, *The Attachment Gap: Employment Discrimination Law, Women's Cultural Caregiving, and the Limits of Economic and Liberal Legal Theory*, 34 U. MICH. J. L. REFORM 371, 457 (2001); Martha Chamallas, *Mothers and Disparate Treatment: The Ghost of* Martin Marietta, 44 VILL. L. REV. 337 (1999).

However, others have argued that Title VII can often be deployed to address some of these problems.

≡ *Walsh v. National Computer Systems*
≡ *332 F.3d 1150 (8th Cir. 2003)*

National Computer Systems, Inc. (NCS) appeals from a judgment of the district court awarding Shireen A. Walsh compensatory damages, punitive damages, prejudgment interest, attorneys' fees, and costs totaling $625,526. . . .

We review the facts in the light most favorable to the jury's verdict. Walsh worked as an account representative in the customer service division of NCS from May 1993 through October 30, 1998. She was a salaried ("exempt") employee whose duties included selling and renewing service contracts on scanners sold to NCS customers. She was considered a "top performer." Walsh received multiple promotions, regular raises, and consistently favorable performance evaluations throughout her employment at NCS.

In March 1997, Barbara Mickelson became Walsh's supervisor. Walsh was pregnant at the time and experienced medical complications related to her pregnancy, requiring frequent medical attention. NCS maintained a policy that entitled exempt employees to take unlimited sick leave for doctor appointments for themselves or their children, but Mickelson repeatedly asked Walsh for advance notification and documentation of Walsh's doctor appointments. Other account representatives were not required to provide the same information about their appointments.

Walsh took full-time medical leave from April 7, 1997 until the birth of her son on May 9, 1997. She returned to work on August 4, 1997 after her maternity leave, and immediately experienced hostility from Mickelson. When Walsh was showing co-workers pictures of her son on her first day back to work, Mickelson told her to stop disrupting the office and to get back to work. Mickelson gave Walsh's coworkers the afternoon off to go to a craft fair as a reward for having covered Walsh's workload while she was on leave, but Walsh was told to stay in the office and watch the phones. One morning when Walsh arrived at 7:37 a.m. instead of 7:30 because she was delayed by her son's illness, she found an email sent from Mickelson at 7:33 that suggested that Mickelson was scrutinizing Walsh's hours. When Walsh asked if she could change her schedule to leave work at 4:30 p.m. instead of 5:00 because her son's daycare closed at 5:00, Mickelson told Walsh that her territory needed coverage until 5:00 and that "maybe she should look for another job." Other account representatives left work at 3:45 on a regular basis, and Mickelson testified at trial that Walsh's territory did not need to be covered through 5:00. Walsh was required to submit a vacation form when other workers were not. Mickelson attached signs ("Out — Sick Child") to Walsh's cubicle when Walsh had to care for her son, yet notes typically were not placed on other absent employees' cubicles. Mickelson reprimanded Walsh for "chit-chatting" in the cubicle section, when she was actually discussing work with a co-worker. Mickelson referred to Walsh's son as "the sickling." Mickelson placed a note in Walsh's personnel file regarding a minor incident involving Walsh's retrieval of a personal fax intended for a co-worker, as requested by the co-worker. Mickelson informed Walsh that she must make up "every minute" that she spent away from the office for doctors [sic] appointments for herself or her son and time spent caring for her son. No other employee was required to make up work for time missed due to appointments and other personal matters. At one point, Mickelson threw a phone book on Walsh's desk and told her to find a pediatrician who was open after hours. When Walsh told Mickelson she needed to pick her son up from daycare because he was ill, Mickelson replied, "Is this an April Fool's joke? If so, it's not at all funny." Walsh fainted at work as a result of stress and was brought to the hospital. The next day, Mickelson stopped at Walsh's cubicle and told her, "you better not be pregnant again."

In October 1997, Walsh reported to NCS's human resources representative, Mike McRath, that she was being treated differently than other account representatives and was required to make up time spent taking her son to the doctor. In the same month, Walsh's workload was increased without an increase in salary. McRath told her that if she was "accusing management of doing something unethical, she better have proof." In June 1998, when Walsh confronted Mickelson about the way she treated account representatives at a meeting, Mickelson swore at Walsh and pounded on the table. The next day Walsh told Mickelson that she wanted to be treated fairly, and Mickelson responded that it was an issue of manager's discretion. When Walsh reported Mickelson's behavior to Bruce Haseley, human resources manager, he appeared disinterested and told Walsh he could not take sides in the matter. Soon, department changes increased Walsh's responsibilities, which required her to work overtime. Walsh protested and Mickelson yelled at her. They went to Haseley's office for mediation, and Haseley offered no assistance. No investigation occurred either before or after Walsh's departure.

[Walsh ultimately began looking for another job and accepted employment with West Group. She submitted a letter of resignation to NCS but then reconsidered. She called Haseley to see if the situation with Mickelson could be worked out, but Haseley said he did not think that was possible. He did say he would speak with Mickelson, but later called Walsh back to tell her that Mickelson wished to continue with her termination.

At trial, the jury found that Walsh had been subjected to a hostile work environment and had been constructively discharged on the basis of pregnancy or gender discrimination. It awarded Walsh $11,000 for wage and benefit loss, $45,000 for other damages, and $382,145 in punitive damages. A judgment for Walsh of $438,145.40 was reduced by the district court as a result of Title VII's cap on compensatory and punitive damages and the court also reduced the punitive award to $300,000. However, it added attorneys' fees, and the final judgment of $625,525.90 was entered for Walsh.]

2. The Merits of the Case: Gender Discrimination on the Basis of Pregnancy

Even if NCS had preserved its right to appeal the jury's verdict on the hostile work environment claim, the facts of the case support Walsh's claim that she was a member of a protected class and was discriminated against on the basis of her pregnancy. . . . NCS argues that Walsh is alleging parent or caretaker discrimination, which is not proscribed by Title VII. *See Piantanida v. Wyman Ctr., Inc.*, 116 F.3d 340, 342 (8th Cir. 1997) (holding that childcare is not gender specific in the way that pregnancy and childbearing are, and that any discrimination experienced on the basis of a parent's decision to care for a child is not actionable because parenthood is not a protected class). Walsh asserts that she was discriminated against not because she was a new parent, but because she is a woman who had been pregnant, had taken a maternity leave, and might become pregnant again. "Potential pregnancy . . . is a medical condition that is sex-related because only women can become pregnant." *Krauel v. Iowa Methodist Med. Ctr.*, 95 F.3d 674, 680 (8th Cir. 1996). Because Walsh presented evidence that it was her potential to become pregnant in the future that served as a catalyst for Mickelson's discriminatory behavior, we will not disturb the jury verdict.

Once Walsh returned to work from her maternity leave, Mickelson made several discriminatory remarks to her. During a discussion about Walsh's coworker's pregnancy, Mickelson sarcastically commented to Walsh, "I suppose you'll be next." On another day, Walsh took a half-day vacation to go on a boat trip with her husband. After she returned, Mickelson stated, "Well, I suppose now we'll have another little Garrett [the name of Walsh's son] running around." On April 23, 1998, Walsh fainted at work and had to go to the hospital. The following day Mickelson stopped by Walsh's cubicle and said, "You better not be pregnant again!" Furthermore, when Walsh was pregnant, Mickelson asked Walsh for advanced [sic] notification and documentation of her doctor appointments, while other account representatives were not required to provide the same information concerning their appointments. Mickelson's comments, combined with the conduct detailed above . . . , provide ample support for the jury's finding that Walsh was discriminated against on the basis of her pregnancy.

C. Punitive Damages

Title VII allows for an award of punitive damages if the defendant committed illegal discrimination "with malice or with reckless indifference to the federally protected rights of an aggrieved individual." 42 U.S.C. § 1981a(b)(1). "Reckless indifference" means that the defendant had "knowledge that it may be acting in violation of federal law." *Kolstad v. Am. Dental Ass'n*, 527 U.S. 526, 535 (1999). Reckless indifference may be imputed to the employer if an employee commits a discriminatory act while serving in a managerial capacity and acts within the scope of employment. We have upheld punitive damages awards in cases where the employer has deliberately turned a deaf ear to discriminatory conduct. *Beard v. Flying J, Inc.*, 266 F.3d 792, 804 (8th Cir. 2001) (punitive damages appropriate where specific complaints about sexual assault were made and the company failed to take action).

The record shows that NCS had knowledge that it may have been acting in violation of federal law by not investigating Walsh's complaints that she was being treated unfairly. [Although a variety of managers admitted to knowing about NCS's nondiscrimination and antiharassment corporate policies, and there were at least ten separate reports to human resources that Walsh was being treated unfairly, NCS did not investigate the reported complaints.] Walsh told Haseley she would consider staying with NCS if he could assure her that her working conditions under Mickelson would improve. Haseley refused. Although Walsh may not have specifically stated to management that Mickelson's conduct rose to the level of a federal violation, she need not have made such a specific complaint. Mickelson, Haseley, Sherck and McRath were aware that NCS's nondiscrimination policy, consistent with federal law, prohibited comments and conduct that disparaged pregnancy and potential pregnancy. In light of these facts, we hold there is sufficient evidence that NCS demonstrated reckless indifference to the numerous allegations of pregnancy discrimination reported by several women, including Walsh.

[The court affirmed the verdict that NCS acted with the requisite reckless indifference to justify punitive damages and rejected the defendant's contention that the amount awarded was excessive and unconstitutional.]

NOTES

1. *Accommodation as an Equal Treatment Issue.* The *Walsh* case suggests a fine line that both employers and employees must walk. An employee can be fired for allowing childcare responsibilities to intrude too much into work time, but the employer must treat mothers and fathers the same in this regard. Thus, the absence of a duty to accommodate may, to some extent, be counterbalanced by a heightened concern for treating pregnant workers (and perhaps those with caregiving responsibilities) differently than other workers. Thus, a plaintiff may be successful in proving disparate treatment if she is able to show that, while an employer's failure to accommodate is not itself illegal, the particular failure to accommodate her was discriminatory. Some litigants have been successful with such claims, particularly in the context of accommodations needed for the physical demands of pregnancy. *See, e.g., Orr v. City of Albuquerque*, 531 F.3d 1210 (10th Cir. 2008) (upholding jury verdict for plaintiffs in light of evidence that they were required to use sick leave for their maternity leave when the employer's regulations permitted the use of vacation time and other employees

were routinely allowed to use vacation or compensatory time for leave for purposes unrelated to a pregnancy); *see also Back v. Hastings on Hudson Union Free Sch. Dist.*, 365 F.3d 107 (2d Cir. 2004) (denying an employer summary judgment based on evidence that the employer stereotyped the "qualities of mothers" when it presumed the young mother would not be devoted to her job and when it implied that she could not be a good mother if she continued to work).

Nevertheless, there is a significant difference in theory between a duty to accommodate pregnancy and childbirth and the lesser duty of nondiscrimination. An employer can avoid liability for failing to accommodate pregnant women and mothers with childcare responsibilities by having inflexible work rules and not accommodating anyone. For example, an employer that had no "light work" policy for nonpregnant workers would have no duty to provide any light work to a pregnant employee. *See Reeves v. Swift Transp. Co., Inc.*, 446 F.3d 637 (6th Cir. 2006) (employer's policy of granting light-duty assignments only to workers with work-related injuries and not to pregnant employees did not violate the PDA). And, needless to say, if an employer does not have to accommodate the pregnancy of its female workers, it certainly does not have to accommodate childcare responsibilities.

In addition, the success of claims of discriminatory failure to accommodate may depend on evidence of preferential treatment of workers with personal needs unrelated to caregiving or pregnancy. Such comparators may not exist in a particular workplace, and, even if they do, the employer can always defend by demonstrating the absence of pretext, in other words, that there is a nondiscriminatory business reason for treating the comparators differently. *See, e.g., Tysinger v. Police Dep't of City of Zanesville*, 463 F.3d 569, 574 (6th Cir. 2006) (while two male officers suffered temporary incapacity like plaintiff, neither sought an accommodation of any kind and continued working in their usual assigned capacities; thus, they were not similarly situated to plaintiff).

2. *Accommodation from a Planning Perspective.* The risk of liability tied to the differential treatment of workers needing accommodations requires that employers be conscientious in deciding how to respond to workers' requests for deviations from regular work practices. If you were an employer, what type of policy would you institute? Would you (1) accommodate everyone; (2) accommodate no one; (3) trust your supervisors to make "appropriate" accommodation decisions? With respect to the last option, what kind of considerations should influence whether a particular accommodation was appropriate? If you were the supervisor, wouldn't your decision depend on the kind of work involved? The cost of the requested accommodations? The value of the particular employee to your team or the business as a whole? The anticipated duration of the accommodation? The need for managerial consistency? Do these questions point up some of the difficulties an employer might have in devising a policy or set of protocols for dealing with workers' individual needs and requests?

3. *Proof of Bias.* Walsh's case was obviously far stronger than many because of the statements of her supervisor. She was able to present not only evidence of more favorably treated workers, but also evidence reflecting hostility toward her pregnancy and potential to become pregnant. Absent those statements by the supervisor, would the disparate application of work policies to Walsh as a mother have given rise to liability? Are you surprised that the person who seemed most hostile to Walsh was herself a woman? Can you explain it?

4. *Meet FReD.* Professor Joan Williams has used the terms "Family Responsibilities Employment Discrimination (FReD)," Joan C. Williams & Stephanie Bornstein *The Evolution of "FReD": Family Responsibilities Discrimination and Developments in* *the Law of Stereotyping and Implicit Bias*, 59 HASTINGS L. J. 1311 (2008), and the "maternal wall," Joan C. Williams & Nancy Segal, *Beyond the Maternal Wall: Relief for Family Caregivers Who Are Discriminated Against on the Job*, 26 HARV. WOMEN'S L. J. 77 (2003), to describe situations like that in *Walsh* and, more generally, to refer to barriers that impede the workplace advancement of women with childcare responsibilities, including differential accommodation, hostility, and stereotyping. While Walsh's success is by no means typical of cases where mothers have claimed sex discrimination, Professor Williams argues that Title VII has been more effective in dealing with these kinds of cases than is often realized, and she details a number of other legal theories under existing law that may be brought to bear in workplaces that do not accommodate mothers. *Id.* at 124, 151-60; *see also* Joan C. Williams, *The Social Psychology of Stereotyping: Using Social Science to Litigate Gender Discrimination Cases and Defang the "Cluelessness" Defense*, 7 EMP. RTS. & EMP. POL'Y J. 401 (2003). *But see* Julie C. Suk, *Are Gender Stereotypes Bad for Women? Rethinking Antidiscrimination Law and Work-Family Conflict*, 110 COLUM. L. REV. 1, 57 (2010) (while the law protects women against stereotyped responses, "when employers make the same demands on women and men, without regard for their caregiving responsibilities, people who are primary caregivers (usually women) will find it more difficult to meet the employer's expectations than people who are not primary caregivers (usually men).").

5. *A Disparate Impact Transformation?* Some scholars have attempted to read Title VII to be even more responsive to the problems of working mothers. One of the most dramatic efforts would require restructuring of the workplace under Title VII's disparate impact theory. Professor Michelle Travis deploys this theory to challenge what she calls the "full-time face-time" norm for most American workplaces, that is, "traditional methods of organizing the when, where, and how of work performance, including the default preferences for full-time positions, unlimited hours, rigid work schedules, an uninterrupted worklife, and performance of work at a central location." Michelle A. Travis, *Recapturing the Transformative Potential of Employment Discrimination Law*, 62 WASH. & LEE L. REV. 3, 6 (2005). She argues:

> Under the transformative approach, judges would distinguish a job's actual required tasks from the malleable organizational norms governing the when, where, and how of task performance, and they would treat the latter as particular practices regarding the former. When women challenge an exclusionary default structure, such as the full-time face-time norm, this approach would characterize the default workplace structure as a proper subject for disparate impact review. The employer would be required to eliminate the organizational structure and replace it with a less discriminatory alternative workplace design unless the employer could defend the conventional design as "job related" and "consistent with business necessity" (which often will not be possible). This approach would force employers to demonstrate a business justification in order to resist workplace restructuring and retain an exclusionary workplace norm.

Id. at 38-39. Professor Travis believes that such an approach is well-based legally, but she concedes that most courts have not pursued it, largely because of what she calls "workplace essentialism," the notion that full-time face-time is not merely descriptive of present reality but "both normative and definitional. In other words, full-time face-time has become not just the way that successful companies currently are designed, but also the way that they *should* and *must* be designed." *Id.* at 10.

In short, if Professor Travis's views were to find their way into the case law, at least some workplaces would become more flexible and attuned to the needs of women, not only pregnant women but women with childcare responsibilities that limit their ability to participate in workplaces as they are presently structured. Accommodation would be achieved under the banner of disparate impact. As we have seen, there are doctrinal problems with this theory, including the argument that the specific command in the second clause of §701(k) that pregnant workers be treated the same as nonpregnant workers in their ability to work excludes by negative inference the disparate impact theory in pregnancy discrimination cases by adopting a pure equal treatment model for pregnant and nonpregnant persons. But, doctrine aside, do you think courts should adopt Professor Travis' theory? Do you think judges are prepared to read Title VII as broadly as she urges? When you consider the FMLA in the next section, ask yourself if the shortcomings of that statute reflect limited political will to intrude very far on traditional employer prerogatives.

6. *Title VII No Obstacle to Some Accommodation.* While employers are not required to accommodate pregnant workers, they are permitted to do so, at least to some extent. *California Federal Savings & Loan Ass'n v. Guerra*, 479 U.S. 272 (1987), held that employers could provide some preferential treatment to pregnant workers without violating Title VII's prohibition of sex discrimination. In that case, the Court found no conflict between Title VII's prohibition of sex discrimination and a California statute which, in effect, created a right to unpaid maternity leave by granting women a right to return to comparable employment after delivery. The PDA was "a floor beneath which pregnancy disability benefits may not drop — not a ceiling above which they may not rise." *Id.* at 280. But the limits to such preferences are not clear. *Schafer v. Bd. of Pub. Educ. of the Sch. Dist. of Pittsburgh, Pa.*, 903 F.2d 243 (3d Cir. 1990), struck down a policy giving women one year's maternity leave while denying comparable paternity leave for men. Since the leave far exceeded the normal period of disability related to child-*bearing*, it was really child-*rearing* leave. According to the court, *Guerra* did not justify preferring mothers over fathers for this purpose since either parent could care for the child. *Id. But see Johnson v. Univ. of Iowa*, 431 F.3d 325 (8th Cir. 2005) (allowing biological mothers, but not fathers, to use accrued paid sick leave for absences after birth of a child is not gender discrimination because additional paid leave is provided to women for pregnancy-related disability, not child-rearing purposes). Issues of "preferential" treatment of mothers sometimes arise in cases brought by fathers with caregiving responsibilities who are denied accommodations or face hostility at work owing to stereotypes about caregiving as "women's work." *See generally* Martin H. Malin, *Fathers and Parental Leave*, 72 Tex. L. Rev. 1047 (1994). But there is reason to believe that differential treatment of mothers and fathers in terms of paid leave is quite common. *See* Christen Linke Young, *Childbearing, Childrearing, and Title VII: Parental Leave Policies at Large American Law Firms*, 118 Yale L.J. 1182, 1185 (2009) (finding that "some firms provide mothers with extremely extended maternity leave — well in excess of their pregnancy-related disability — while offering fathers little or no paid time off when their children are born.").

7. *Employer Initiatives to Accommodate Family Caretaking.* While courts have been slow to require employers to significantly restructure work under the mantle of Title VII, some employers have been proactive. For example, Professor Susan Sturm reports on several large organizations that have viewed it as good business to make the workplace more hospitable to women:

> Deloitte & Touche, America's third largest accounting, tax, and management consulting firm, implemented a major Women's Initiative that dramatically increased women's advancement in the company and reduced the turnover rate of women in

particular and employees in general. The firm accomplished this by forming ongoing, participatory task forces with responsibility for determining the nature and cause of a gender gap in promotion and turnover, making recommendations to change the conditions underlying these patterns, developing systems to address those problems and to make future patterns transparent, and monitoring the results. . . .

The Women's Initiative resulted not from the threat of litigation, but rather from the CEO's perception that a gender gap in the promotion and turnover rate signaled a problem with the firm's capacity to compete effectively for talent. In 1991, Mike Cook, Chairman and CEO of Deloitte & Touche, discovered that, although Deloitte had been hiring women at an aggressive rate — 50% or more — for more than ten years, the rate of promotion for women hovered at around 10%. The data also revealed "a significant and growing gap in turnover" between the percentage of women and men. This gender gap coincided with a series of changes that "made hiring and training professionals a strategic imperative."

Susan Sturm, *Second Generation Employment Discrimination: A Structural Approach*, 101 COLUM. L. REV. 458, 492-93 (2001). The author also cites Home Depot and Intel Corporation as examples of companies that have made great strides in accommodating working mothers.

8. *The ADA and the PDA.* As we saw in the previous section, the ADA requires employers to accommodate the disabilities of their workers. While §701(k) does not impose an obligation to give special treatment or otherwise accommodate pregnant workers, leave policies have proliferated under the impetus of the ADA, which means there is an increased number of employees granted leave for reasons other than pregnancy that may serve as comparators for a potential disparate treatment claim. Might an employee like Walsh claim a right to equal treatment with a disabled worker? Or does the fact that the employer grants leave to the disabled worker in order to comply with the ADA provide a nondiscriminatory justification for treating that worker more favorably?

9. *Beyond Antidiscrimination.* Because the protection provided by Title VII is limited, commentators have suggested a variety of responses beyond proposals like those of Professors Travis and Williams for reinterpreting existing statutes. The closest the nation has come to developing new law requiring work-family accommodations is the FMLA, which is treated next.

2. The Family and Medical Leave Act

Partly in response to some of the limits of discrimination law discussed in the previous section, Congress enacted the Family and Medical Leave Act ("FMLA") in 1993. The statute is administered by the Department of Labor, which issued final regulations in 1995 and then amended those regulations effective January 1, 2009. 29 C.F.R. §825 (2010). *See generally* Ashley Hawley, Comment, *Taking a Step Forward or Backward?: The 2009 Revisions to the FMLA Regulations*, 25 WIS. J. L. GENDER & SOC'Y 137 (2010). The FMLA differs from the PDA, Congress's previous effort to address work-family conflict, in several ways. The statute goes beyond issues of gender discrimination and the challenges posed by pregnancy in an attempt to target the problem of work-family balance more broadly. It seeks to do this by extending rights to workers both for family care and for self-care. Thus, leave is required not only in connection with the birth of a child and to deal with serious family illnesses (family care) but also to deal with the worker's own serious illness (self-care). It protects workers in gender-neutral terms, providing the same rights to men and women workers with family responsibilities.

At the same time, the FMLA raises many of the same issues associated with existing discrimination law, including concerns about the limits of equality and the problem of preferential treatment. In addition, it has been subject to significant criticism, both by employers, who believe it improperly intrudes on managerial prerogative, and by advocates and feminists, who find it insufficient in addressing workers' needs, particularly those of mothers.

29 U.S.C. § 2612. Leave Requirement

(a) In general.

(1) *Entitlement to leave.* Subject to section 103, an eligible employee shall be entitled to a total of 12 workweeks of leave during any 12-month period for one or more of the following:

(A) Because of the birth of a son or daughter of the employee and in order to care for such son or daughter.

(B) Because of the placement of a son or daughter with the employee for adoption or foster care.

(C) In order to care for the spouse, or a son, daughter, or parent, of the employee, if such spouse, son, daughter, or parent has a serious health condition.

(D) Because of a serious health condition that makes the employee unable to perform the functions of the position of such employee. . . .

(c) *Unpaid leave permitted.* Except as provided in subsection (d) [pertaining to the ability of the employer require or employee to elect to substitute existing paid leave for FMLA leave], leave granted under subsection (a) may consist of unpaid leave. . . .

29 U.S.C. § 2614. Employment and Benefits Protection

(a) Restoration to position

(1) In general

[A]ny eligible employee who takes leave under section 2612 of this title for the intended purpose of the leave shall be entitled, on return from such leave —

(A) to be restored by the employer to the position of employment held by the employee when the leave commenced; or

(B) to be restored to an equivalent position with equivalent employment benefits, pay, and other terms and conditions of employment.

(2) Loss of benefits

The taking of leave under section 2612 of this title shall not result in the loss of any employment benefit accrued prior to the date on which the leave commenced.

(3) Limitations

Nothing in this section shall be construed to entitle any restored employee to . . .

(B) any right, benefit, or position of employment other than any right, benefit, or position to which the employee would have been entitled had the employee not taken the leave. . . .

NOTES

1. *FMLA Coverage.* The FMLA has far more limited coverage than most of the other statutory schemes we treat in this book. For example, Title VII and the ADA reach all employers with 15 or more employees. By contrast, the FMLA applies only to employers with 50 or more employees. Further, unlike the antidiscrimination statutes, not all employees of covered employers are protected. Part-time employees, first-year employees, and even employees who work for small offices of larger employers are not entitled to leave under the FMLA. This is because the statute requires "eligible" employees to have worked for the employer for at least 12 months, § 2611(2)(A)(1), and for at least 1,250 hours during the year preceding the start of the leave, § 2611(2)(A)(ii), and to be employed at a worksite where the employer employs at least 50 employees within a 75-mile radius. § 2611(2)(B)(ii). *See Babcock v. BellSouth Adver. & Publ'g Corp.*, 348 F.3d 73 (4th Cir. 2003) (employee was entitled to extension of leave after being employed for one year, even though the employer would not have violated the statute had it denied leave when she first applied before her first anniversary); *Staunch v. Cont'l Airlines, Inc.*, 511 F.3d 625 (6th Cir. 2008) (flight attendant not entitled to FMLA leave when she had worked fewer than 1,250 hours).

2. *FMLA Benefits.* The statute's basic command is *unpaid* leave, which is defined as reinstating the employee to the same or an equivalent job when the leave ends. Elsewhere, the statute permits the employee to elect, or the employer to require, the use of any paid leave the employee may have accrued under the employer's other policies (vacation, paid sick time, etc.) during FMLA leave. *See* 29 U.S.C. § 2612(d)(2). As a practical matter, most employers insist on this, in part for administrative convenience and in part to ensure that employees do not take 12 weeks of FMLA leave and existing paid leave consecutively, resulting in a longer absence from work. The other principal advantage conferred by the FMLA is the requirement that employers maintain pre-existing benefits, including health insurance, while the employee is on FMLA leave. However, the employee is obligated to continue paying his or her portion of the premiums, which can be onerous during a time in which the employee is not receiving a salary.

The fact that FMLA leave is unpaid is the key limitation and source of criticism of the statute. Only a relatively privileged class of workers is likely to be able to take full advantage of its benefits. A number of commentators have called for the provision of paid family/medical leave, funded by either the employer or government sources. *See, e.g.*, Samuel Issacharoff & Elyse Rosenblum, *Women and the Workplace: Accommodating the Demands of Pregnancy*, 94 COLUM. L. REV. 2154 (1994); Gillian Lester, *A Defense of Paid Family Leave*, 28 HARV. J. L. & GENDER 1 (2005); Michael Selmi, *Family Leave and the Gender Wage Gap*, 78 N.C. L. REV. 707, 770-73 (2000). There have also been initiatives to require paid leave at the state level. Currently California and New Jersey are the only states in which such a program has been implemented; in both cases, leave is funded through the state's temporary disability insurance program. *See* California Family Temporary Disability Insurance Program, CAL. UNEMP. INS. CODE § 3301 (2004); N.J. STAT. ANN. §§ 43:21-25-31 (West 2010). Washington is scheduled to provide paid leave in 2012. WASH. REV. CODE ANN. § 49.86.030 (West 2010).

3. *Limitations on FMLA Rights.* Despite the FMLA's general authorization of leave, the statute does have some limitations. For example, the statute expressly provides that seniority need not accrue during any statutory-mandated leave. §2614(a)(3). Further, §2614(b) creates an exception to the reinstatement right for "highly compensated employees" (the top ten percent of all employees in a designated geographic area), but only if reinstatement would cause "substantial and grievous economic injury." 29 C.F.R. §825.218; *see Kephart v. Cherokee County, N.C.*, 229 F.3d 1142 (4th Cir. 2002). Finally, an employee who takes leave for her own health condition may be asked to provide a doctor's certification of her ability to resume work. §2614(a)(4); *Hatchett v. Philander Smith Coll.*, 251 F.3d 670, 677 (8th Cir. 2001) ("[A]n employee is not entitled to restoration if, at the end of the FMLA leave period, the employee is still unable to perform an essential function of the job.").

4. *Resistance and Reaction to Enactment of the FMLA.* The relatively narrow coverage of the FMLA and its limited unpaid benefit reflect a strong resistance to the statute on the part of corporate America. *See* Cristina Duarte, *The Family and Medical Leave Act of 1993: Paying the Price for an Imperfect Solution*, 32 U. LOUISVILLE J. FAM. L. 833, 853-62 (1994). The first President Bush vetoed two earlier versions of the statute, but the bill gained momentum when it was framed as addressing a "family" issue rather than a feminist one. Opponents of the FMLA argued that it started down the slippery slope of government-mandated policies, reducing corporate control over employee benefit programs. *See generally* Joseph Willis, *The Family and Medical Leave Act of 1993: A Progress Report*, 36 J. FAM. L. 95 (1997/1998). Employers worried about the effectiveness of temporary replacements and/or morale problems resulting from redistribution of work to cover FMLA leaves. Small business owners, in particular, complained of administrative costs, especially the statute's record-keeping and notice provisions. *See generally* G. John Tysse & Kimberly L. Japinga, *The Federal Family and Medical Leave Act: Easily Conceived, Difficult Birth, Enigmatic Child*, 27 CREIGHTON L. REV. 361, 375-77 (1994).

5. *Impact of the FMLA.* In the almost two decades since the FMLA has been in effect, many employees have taken advantage of the rights it provides. A 2008 Department of Labor report noted an employer survey that indicated that 6.1 million persons, or eight percent of employees, utilized FMLA leave in 2005. http://www.dol.gov/whd/FMLA2007Report/Chapter11.pdf. Of these, 1.5 million used intermittent leave. The Employment Policy Foundation estimated the direct costs of such leave to employers to be $21 billion in terms of lost productivity, health benefits, and net labor replacement costs. But a 2007 survey by Human Resource Management found that 71 percent of respondents reported no noticeable productivity harm. It is true that co-workers of the statute's beneficiaries have noted concomitant increased coverage responsibilities: Two-thirds of employers reassign the absent worker's tasks to a co-worker, and assigning work to co-workers occurred more frequently from 2000-2003. http://www.policyarchive.org/handle/10207/bitstreams/12252.pdf; http://www.protectfamilyleave.org/research/2003_SHRM_FMLA_Survey.pdf. Thus, the high costs that corporations believed would come from compliance with the FMLA have apparently not materialized. Is that because other workers have largely been required to pick up the slack? Indeed, there is reason to think that the statute has resulted in some benefits to employers in improved staff retention, morale, and productivity. *See* Jane Waldfogel, *Family-Friendly Policies for Families with Young Children*, 5 EMP. RTS. & EMP. POL'Y J. 273, 290-91 (2001). Of course, this success is perhaps attributable to the very limited protections afforded by the FMLA. A more aggressive statute, such as one requiring paid leave, might generate a very different response.

6. *FMLA Irony.* There has been no constitutional challenge to the statute as far as it reaches private employment, but the Supreme Court has considered a claim that the FMLA could not constitutionally apply to the states because of the Eleventh Amendment. In *Nevada Department of Human Resources v. Hibbs*, 538 U.S. 721 (2003), the Court rejected that argument in an opinion replete with irony. The plaintiff in that case, William Hibbs, worked for the Department's Welfare Division. He sought, and was granted, leave under the FMLA to care for his ailing wife, who was recovering from a car accident, but he and the Department disagreed about the amount of leave. He was terminated when he failed to report to work when the Department required him to do so. He sued, and the Department interposed a claim of Eleventh Amendment immunity.

While the Eleventh Amendment generally bars private suits against the state without their consent, *Board of Trustees of Univ. of Ala. v. Garrett*, 531 U.S. 356 (2001) (barring ADA suits); *Kimel v. Fla. Bd. of Regents*, 528 U.S. 62 (2000) (barring ADEA suits), Congress may "abrogate such immunity in federal court if it makes its intention to abrogate unmistakably clear in the language of the statute and acts pursuant to a valid exercise of its power under §5 of the Fourteenth Amendment." 538 U.S. at 726. Since there was no doubt that Congress had intended to abrogate states' immunity, *Hibbs* turned on whether Congress acted within its §5 power in either attacking equal protection violations or enacting "prophylactic legislation that proscribes facially constitutional conduct, in order to prevent and deter unconstitutional conduct." *Id.* at 721-22. The Court held yes.

In enacting the FMLA, Congress looked to evidence that states continued to rely on invalid gender stereotypes in the employment context, specifically in the administration of leave benefits. That evidence, however, was not of continued discrimination against women but rather of discrimination against male workers. For example, one survey stated that 37 percent of surveyed private-sector employees were covered by maternity leave policies, while only 18 percent were covered by paternity leave policies. *Id.* at 730. Further, there was also evidence of "differential leave policies [for men and women that] were not attributable to any differential physical needs of men and women, but rather to the pervasive sex-role stereotype that caring for family members is women's work." *Id.* at 731. Finally, "even where state laws and policies were not facially discriminatory, they were applied in discriminatory ways." *Id.* at 732. The Court concluded that "the States' record of unconstitutional participation in, and fostering of, gender-based discrimination in the administration of leave benefits is weighty enough to justify the enactment of prophylactic §5 legislation." *Id.* at 735. *But see, e.g., McKlintic v. 36th Judicial Circuit Court*, 508 F.3d 875 (8th Cir. 2007) (rejecting a private FMLA suit against a state court under the self-care provisions of the statute: Although Congress had adduced sufficient evidence of gender-based discrimination in leave benefits under the family-care provision of the statute, there was no such evidence with respect to self-care leave).

The irony of *Hibbs*, then, is that although the gender-neutral statute was largely designed to address the work-life concerns of women, it was upheld because of evidence of Congress's concern about discrimination against men. The next excerpt also suggests that not only are employers' attitudes toward men as caregivers part of the problem, but male attitudes themselves also must change if women are to play a more central role in the workplace.

Michael Selmi, *Family Leave and the Gender Wage Gap*
78 N.C. L. Rev. 707, 708-12 (2000)

In large measure, [gender inequality] persists because men have not yet changed their employment-related behavior, and employers exact penalties on women not only because of their actual behavior, which differs from men's, but also because of the presumption that women will leave the workforce when they have children. Thus, increasing workplace equality will require persuading men to behave more like women, rather than trying to induce women to behave more like men. Achieving this objective would create a new workplace norm where all employees would be expected to have and spend time with their children, and employers would adapt to that reality.

[American society remains] conflicted about the role that women should play both in the workplace and the home. Although the United States has one of the highest female labor force participation rates among industrialized countries, it also has done the least to assist those women with the demands of work and family. The United States was one of the last of the industrialized countries to adopt a family leave law and even today offers the least generous family leave benefits of any such country. . . .

Increasing our societal commitment to family leave issues is critically important for at least two closely related reasons. First, if we are to make greater progress on gender equality in the workplace . . . , we must challenge the existing stereotypes surrounding family leave, which invariably impact women negatively. [E]mployers generally assume that women's work in the home will adversely affect their performance in the workplace and make employment decisions accordingly. To close the gender gap further, we need to take steps to disrupt both the reality and the expectations of how women's relation to their children affects their labor market behavior. Second, creating a workplace where it is expected that workers will have, and take care of, children is essential to furthering our societal interest in the family. . . .

[The gender wage gap contributes to and perhaps explains the bulk of workplace disparities based on gender and is rooted in] a fact that stubbornly resists change: women overwhelmingly continue to be primarily responsible for child care and child rearing. . . . As a result, things have continued for the most part as they were: women have less of an attachment to the labor force than men (though the differences are narrowing), miss more work than men, take more time off when they have children, and generally work fewer hours. All of these factors contribute to a cumulative workplace disadvantage that exacts a heavy price in terms of salary, promotions, and responsibility. Economist Claudia Goldin recently estimated that only about 13% of college educated women successfully attained both family and career by midlife.

Even those women who do not have children, or who exit the labor market only for a very brief period when they do have children, are affected adversely by what often is labeled statistical discrimination—the use of group statistics as a proxy for information, in this instance the likelihood that more women than men will leave the workforce to have children with the further assumption that the accompanying labor force disruption will negatively impact productivity.

If we are to progress further toward workplace equality, it will be necessary for men to change their behavior in the labor market by, at a minimum, taking more leave around the birth or adoption of their children. . . .

NOTES

1. *Explaining* Hibbs? Does Professor Selmi's account help explain the Court's rationale in *Hibbs*? Does it offer a practical strategy for addressing the disadvantages faced by women? Or do you find it somewhat troubling that the premise for the validity of the FMLA, at least in the sovereign immunity context, is discrimination against men?

2. *Has It Worked?* Hibbs provides a powerful account of the history of stereotypes and discrimination surrounding work/family issues. While passage of the FMLA is often viewed as a major, if very limited, advance in requiring employers to become more "family friendly" in gender-neutral terms, not all commentators are so sure. Professor Selmi concludes as follows:

> [The Act] failed to ease the burden on women, and indeed the Act's effects likely have been more negative than positive. For example, the passage of the FMLA in 1993 appears to have curtailed a trend at the state level toward implementing family leave policies that were often more generous than the FMLA. In addition, recent data indicate that very few workers utilize the federal legislation, and women are considerably more likely than men to take advantage of the law. Accordingly, at least in the eyes of employers, family leave remains a woman's issue, one for which all women are being penalized in the marketplace.

Selmi, *supra*, at 711.

Professor Selmi's solution is to create greater incentives for men to take leave for the birth or adoption of a child. He proposes amendments to the FMLA varying "from forcing men to take six weeks of paid leave to creating a governmental contract set-aside program aimed at rewarding employers who succeed in encouraging their employees to take family leave. [C]reating ways for men to become more involved in child rearing could help transform the workplace so that the female model of the worker, rather than the male model, becomes the norm. If men begin to act more like women in terms of their responsibilities toward their children, employers may come to expect that all of their employees will take part in child rearing and may become more willing to accommodate that responsibility." *Id*. at 712-13. Does Selmi go too far in urging that men be pressured or incentivized into taking leave? Is he too optimistic about the ability of the law to assist societal change? For more on the social and institutional constraints that affect male caregivers, see generally Martin H. Malin, *Fathers and Parental Leave*, 72 Tex. L. Rev. 1047, 1049-50 (1994); Martin H. Malin, *Fathers and Parental Leave Revisited*, 19 N. Ill. U. L. Rev. 25 (1998).

3. *Pregnancy and Motherhood Under the FMLA.* Turning to the obstacles faced by pregnant women and working mothers, the FMLA's principal contribution is that it supplements Title VII's prohibition of pregnancy discrimination by requiring accommodation of at least some of the more exigent demands of pregnancy and motherhood. Today, Ms. Troupe could take FMLA leave rather than lose her job. The statute guarantees employees who could otherwise be legally discharged under Title VII the right to return to their jobs after taking time off to give birth or care for their children. But even viewed together, the FMLA and Title VII provide a relatively limited accommodation regime for mothers. Normal childcare responsibilities are not addressed by the FMLA, and even caring for an ill child is not protected if a "serious health condition" is not in play. What constitutes a "serious health condition" is sometimes complicated, but most routine aliments that keep children home from school, such as colds and earaches, are not FMLA leave–eligible.

As a result, there have been calls for expanded accommodation of caregiving, including proposals for FMLA leave for more quotidian childrearing, mandated accommodation in the form of required workplace flexibility, and accommodation tailored to individual caregiving needs similar to that granted religion and disability under other laws. *See, e.g.*, Laura T. Kessler, *The Attachment Gap: Employment Discrimination Law, Women's Cultural Caregiving, and the Limits of Economic and Liberal Legal Theory*, 34 U. Mich. J. L. Reform 371, 386-87 (2001); Debbie N. Kaminer, *The Work-Family Conflict: Developing a Model of Parental Accommodation in the Workplace*, 54 Am. U. L. Rev. 305 (2004); Peggie R. Smith, *Accommodating Routine Parental Obligations in an Era of Work-Family Conflict: Lessons from Religious Accommodations*, 2001 Wis. L. Rev. 1443 (2001). *Cf.* Rachel Arnow-Richman, *Incenting Flexibility: The Relationship Between Public Law and Voluntary Action in Enhancing Work-Life Balance*, 42 Conn. L. Rev. 1081, 1099 (2010) (arguing that reasons such as "lack of information, cognitive biases, transaction costs, and other impediments" lead to suboptimal decisions with respect to leave: "In the context of workplace accommodations, this may mean that employers are under-serving caregivers (and in some instances themselves) by failing to make cost-neutral and even mutually advantageous accommodations."). A few states have responded by going further than the federal law in mandating unpaid leave. For example, Massachusetts prohibits small employers from terminating female employees for taking maternity leave for not more than eight weeks. Mass. Gen. Laws Ann., Ch. 149, § 105D (West 2010). That state also mandates 24 hours of school-related leave per year for parents to do such things as attend parent-teacher conferences. Ch. 149, § 52D(a)-(b)(1); *see generally* Kirsten K. Davis, *Extending the Vision: An Empowerment Identity Approach to Work-Family Regulation as Applied to School Involvement Leave Statutes*, 16 Wm. & Mary J. of Women & L. 613 (2010). Given the history of the passage of the FMLA, such measures would likely face serious political obstacles in most states.

Might further measures also, at some point, create problems of theoretic consistency? Does privileging pregnancy, childbirth, and the early months of childrearing reinforce the notion that women's primary role is childrearing? Would extending such rights in a gender-neutral fashion solve that problem if, as Professor Selmi argues, women will be the primary ones to invoke such benefits? And, to the extent that benefits are used exclusively or primarily by women and are costly for employers, would imposing such requirements lead employers to avoid hiring women in the first place? While such conduct would violate Title VII, it might frequently be impossible to detect.

In part as a result of such concerns, some commentators have urged moving the focus away from enabling caregiving to making work more accessible to people of all backgrounds and family situations, for instance by reducing the work week and eliminating mandatory overtime. *See, e.g.*, Marion Crain, *"Where Have All the Cowboys Gone?": Marriage and Breadwinning in Postindustrial Society*, 60 Ohio St. L. J. 1877 (1999); Vicki Schultz, *Life's Work*, 100 Colum. L. Rev. 1881 (2000). Might such proposals be more likely to garner public and political support? Are they likely to be as helpful to women with caregiving responsibilities? The Great Recession has led some employers, largely in terms of saving money, to institute different work arrangements, most notably, the 4/40 workweek (four days of ten hours each). But there is reason to doubt that such changes will contribute substantially to better work-family balance, especially for women. Michelle A. Travis, *What a Difference a Day Makes, or Does It? Work/Family Balance and the Four-Day Work Week*, 42 CONN. L. REV. 1223 (2010); Rachel Arnow-Richman, *Incenting Flexibility: The Relationship Between Public Law and Voluntary Action in Enhancing Work-Life Balance*, 42 CONN. L. REV. 1081, 1099 (2010).

4. *Substantive Benefits and Redistributive Concerns.* The FMLA contains an affirmative directive — eligible employees must receive a specific substantive benefit — making it more of an accommodation statute like the ADA than a nondiscrimination statute like Title VII. Any kind of accommodation requirement raises redistribution concerns, particularly where the laws in question impose the costs of redistribution not on society generally but on the employers who are required to accommodate the workers in question. *See* Samuel R. Bagenstos, *The Future of Disability Law*, 114 YALE L. J. 1 (2004) (arguing that, because the ADA may serve as an open-ended tool of redistribution to people with disabilities, courts have attempted to constrain the mandate through antidiscrimination principles, such as employer fault, resulting in the law's failure to undo deep-rooted structural barriers to employment for people with disabilities).

Professor Arnow-Richman argues that the history of the ADA, and in particular courts' narrow interpretation of its accommodation mandate, bode poorly for the future of work-family accommodation. This is particularly true, she suggests, in what she describes as the contemporary "Me, Inc." economy:

> The desirability of employer-supported accommodation rests on two assumptions: (i) basic features of the contemporary workplace represent choices about work structure that can and should be changed; and (ii) it is reasonable to expect employers to absorb the costs associated with making those changes or with providing necessary benefits to employee caregivers.
>
> These assumptions are . . . especially problematic when examined against the history of government intervention in the workplace and the nature of modern employment relationships. [V]oluntarily-provided employer benefits . . . have been the dominant mode of addressing employee lifecycle needs for the majority of the twentieth century. Such an allocation of rights and responsibilities at work was enabled by a particular "social contract" of employment, one in which employers and employees anticipated a long-term symbiotic relationship often governed by a collective bargaining agreement. In contrast, today's work relationships are defined by a "Me, Inc." work culture — an employment environment in which workers are increasingly independent, short-term employment relationships predominate, collective action is all but absent, and employer reliance on contingent labor has dramatically expanded. In an economy where employees' futures depend not on their current employer but on the value of their human capital within the external labor market, the incentives for voluntary accommodation of employees' lifecycle needs are generally absent.
>
> These changes at work complicate the call for employer accommodation of caregiving. To the extent that private mechanisms have failed to adequately respond to workers' needs, it is tempting to fill the gap with government mandates. But that top-down approach shows insufficient consideration for contemporary expectations about the way people work.
>
> [C]orresponding developments in work culture . . . foster a sentiment of individualism among workers and raise the bar on performance standards in ways that are likely to undermine accommodation efforts. In the new economy, employers have a significant interest in obtaining the maximum contribution and commitment from their employees for the length of their tenure. . . . Companies expect their employees to self-educate,

initiate new ideas, and assist their employers in achieving better products, services, and methods of production. . . .

This means that while employment relationships are becoming shorter in duration, they are simultaneously becoming more demanding. In such an environment, principles of equality and merit-based treatment are likely to intensify to the detriment of employees balancing caregiving responsibilities. . . .

See Rachel Arnow-Richman, *Accommodation Subverted: The Future of Work/Family Initiatives in a "Me, Inc." World*, 12 TEX. J. WOMEN & L. 345, 373-88 (2003). She concludes that responding to the problem of insufficient accommodation of caregiving through government mandates

> shows insufficient consideration for contemporary expectations about the way people work. The emerging "Me, Inc." workplace makes it harder, not easier, for employers (and employees) to relinquish the particular structures that are most detrimental to care-givers, and it creates an environment where tensions between "ideal workers" and those with caregiving needs are likely to be exacerbated. The imposition of extensive employer-funded accommodation in this context may overreach and spawn backlash.

Id. at 374. Are you convinced by these concerns, or is Arnow-Richman's account overly pessimistic? Rather than caving to the "Me, Inc." work culture, should the law make wider efforts to dismantle what might appear to some observers as a race to the bottom?

5. *Hurting the People We Are Trying to Help?* Separate from concerns about fairness for employers are concerns about the impact of accommodation mandates on the group intended to benefit from them. Some authorities have raised questions about the consequences of statutes such as the FMLA and ADA. Christine Jolls, *Accommodation Mandates*, 53 STAN. L. REV. 223, 225, 291 (2000), writes:

> Legal requirements that employers provide specified benefits to their workers, such as . . . family leave, are virtually omnipresent in modern employment law. Some mandates are directed to workers as a whole, and many of these date back to the early part of the twentieth century (workers' compensation, for instance). But other, newer mandates are directed to discrete, identifiable groups of workers, such as the disabled. These mandates are intended to accommodate the unique needs of those workers.
>
> [For the FMLA], with significant occupational segregation the effect of an accom-modation mandate will be to lower the relative wages of disadvantaged workers and to increase or decrease their relative employment levels depending on whether the value of the mandated accommodation exceeds or falls short of its cost.
>
> A caveat to this conclusion, however, relates to the cognitive psychology argument [which] suggests that employment adjustments may be more likely, and wage adjustments less likely, if the costs of a mandated accommodation are difficult to monetize. [Since the cost of unpaid leave is likely to be ambiguous, an employer is not confronted with a specific increase in cost.] Rather it faces the hard-to-monetize disruption of losing an employee temporarily and having either to replace the employee or to reassign the individual's tasks to others. For reasons of cognitive psychology, accommodation mandates that impose such hard-to-monetize costs may be more likely to be reflected in reductions in the relative employment levels of disadvantaged workers and less likely to be reflected in reductions in their relative wages.

See also John J. Donohue III, *Understanding the Reasons for and Impact of Legislatively Mandated Benefits for Selected Workers*, 53 STAN. L. REV. 897 (2001); *cf.* Cass R.

Sunstein, *Human Behavior and the Law of Work*, 87 Va. L. Rev. 205, 206-8 (2001) (supporting mandates as a default rule but allowing them to be waived). If Professor Jolls is correct, more accommodation would mean less employment for women (mothers) but more accommodating employment for those who obtain jobs. Is that a worthwhile trade-off? Who should decide?

6. *A Procedural Approach?* Is there a middle road that can expand caregiver rights while avoiding the pitfalls of accommodation mandates? Professor Arnow-Richman offers a proposal that would require new legislation but not create a new substantive right. She argues that voluntary accommodation of caregiving would be more prevalent if employers acted not on the basis of stereotype but with greater awareness and understanding of employees' accommodation needs, which often have limited impact on the workplace. She then proposes that employers should have a duty to discuss caregiving accommodations with their employees, somewhat along the lines of the ADA's interactive process. Unlike the ADA, however, there would be no substantive duty to accommodate. She explains:

> A simple and potentially fruitful change to the statutory [canon] can be achieved by amending the FMLA to include an interactive process requirement similar to that which exists under the ADA. In addition to providing twelve weeks of unpaid leave, the Act could require employers to engage in a good-faith, interactive process with qualifying employees to consider ways of altering their work schedules (or work requirements) to effect a needed accommodation. At a minimum this procedural obligation would be triggered in two circumstances: when an employee experiences a qualifying caregiving-related event or when an employee returns from FMLA leave taken for such purposes.
>
> Such an approach represents an initial step toward addressing what is perhaps the strongest criticism of the FMLA: that the Act is event-centered, treating birth, adoption and family illness as discrete moments rather than life-long experiences. A procedural requirement imposed on the employer upon the conclusion of FMLA leave recognizes, for instance, that an employee who gives birth or adopts a new child cannot be expected to seamlessly return to full-time work upon the conclusion of the child's third month. Rather, such a law supposes that any time a qualifying event occurs, additional accommodations beyond leave may well be necessary and can potentially be achieved through mutual agreement where parties meet in a meaningful attempt to assess the employee's situation and any limitations that he or she might face upon returning to work.
>
> Similarly, an interactive process can refine, in some situations, the blunt effect of a one-size-fits-all mandated benefit. By engaging in a good-faith process at the onset of a qualifying event, parties may be able to identify alternative accommodations that are more closely tailored to the employee's situation and just as viable for the employer. For instance, there may be situations in which a relatively simple job modification will enable a pregnant employee to continue working and allow the employer to avoid the disruption of a temporary replacement. It may also be possible to work out a flexible schedule that enables an employee caring for a seriously ill family member to maintain close to full-time employment and avoid the administrative difficulties associated with the use of intermittent leave.
>
> Of course, the right described here would be limited to the right to request and discuss; it would not compel the employer to accommodate the worker, but merely facilitate voluntary solutions. This is critical to the political viability of the proposal both in terms of congressional adoption and the reliability of judicial enforcement. By the same token, the absence of an underlying substantive right to accommodation means that care must be taken to ensure employer accountability under the amendment. The worker's procedural rights must be enforced by a monetary penalty sufficient to deter noncompliance.

A violation of the procedural obligation could also result in a presumption of employer liability on a substantive claim under the FMLA or the PDA. [Where employers] fail to engage in an interactive process under the FMLA . . . the court should assume that the employer unlawfully took account of the employee's pregnancy, use of leave, or invocation of rights in rendering the adverse employment decision. In addition, the law could go further by affirmatively shifting the burden of proof to the defendant in such cases, requiring the employer to prove that the employer's asserted non-discriminatory rationale was in fact the reason (or a sufficient reason) for its decision.

Rachel Arnow-Richman, *Public Law and Private Process: Toward an Incentivized Organizational Justice Model of Equal Employment Quality for Caregivers*, 2007 UTAH L. REV. 25, 56-58 (2007). She adds, "[a]s a further incentive, an employer's procedural failures could result in a presumption of employer liability on certain substantive claims under the FMLA and Title VII." *Id.* at 58. *See also* Rachel Arnow-Richman, *Incenting Flexibility: The Relationship Between Public Law and Voluntary Action in Enhancing Work-Life Balance*, 42 CONN. L. REV. 1081 (2010) (arguing that mandated "interactive process" regarding accommodation is more likely to yield better results than such general policies as the 4/40 workweek, adopted by some employers). To what extent do procedural protections assist employees in the absence of mandates? In other words, does an employer have any incentive to accommodate an employee if the law does not so require? If not, do the litigation incentives proposed by Professor Arnow-Richman help? Might they impose additional risks?

≡ *Goelzer v. Sheboygan County, Wisconsin*
≡ *604 F.3d 987 (7th Cir. 2010)*

WILLIAMS, Circuit Judge.

After two decades of employment with her county government, Dorothy Goelzer was fired from her job. Her supervisor informed her of the termination decision two weeks before she was scheduled to begin two months of leave under the Family and Medical Leave Act (FMLA). This leave did not mark the first time Goelzer was away from work on FMLA leave, as Goelzer had taken a significant amount of authorized FMLA leave during the four preceding years to deal with her own health issues and those of her mother and husband. After she lost her job, Goelzer brought this suit and alleged that her employer had interfered with her right to reinstatement under the FMLA and had retaliated against her for taking FMLA leave. The defendants contend that her supervisor simply decided to hire another person with a larger skill set. [The district court granted summary judgment against plaintiff, but the Seventh Circuit reversed.]

I. BACKGROUND

[Sheboygan County hired Dorothy Goelzer in 1986 as Clerk Typist in its office of the Register of Deeds. By 1999, she was the administrative assistant to Adam Payne, the Board's Administrative Coordinator. Payne consistently gave Goelzer good performance reviews and merit increases. In some of his evaluations, he praised her for rarely being absent.]

Goelzer began to have significant health issues in 2002. She had eye surgery in July and took approximately a month of FMLA leave during her surgery and recovery. She also had multiple doctors' appointments in the months before and after her surgery. All in all, she used 312.50 hours of sick leave in 2002, the equivalent of nearly eight forty-hour weeks. Payne wrote in Goelzer's 2002 performance evaluation that, "[t]hough Dorothy has had an excellent record in the past, (36 hours of sick leave in 2001), she utilized 312 hours or 39 days of sick leave in 2002."

Goelzer continued to have health problems in 2003. She . . . took time off on thirty-two different days during 2003 for her health issues and used a total of 176.50 hours of leave. Payne commented on Goelzer's use of sick leave again in that year's performance evaluation, stating: "Dorothy utilized 176.50 hours or 22 days of sick leave in 2003." He gave her an overall rating of 3.36, with a 3.5 in the attendance category. He did not award her a merit pay increase. [When Goelzer disagreed with Payne about no merit increase, Payne responded with a February 5, 2004 memorandum that again referred to her leave: "In fact, the past two years, use of sick leave and vacation combined, you were out of the office 113 days. As the only support person in the office, this has presented challenges in the functionality and duties associated with the office."]

Goelzer used 94 hours of sick leave in 2004. She received a merit increase of 1.5% after her 2004 evaluation. The next year, Goelzer's health was stable, but her mother's health was not. Goelzer took FMLA leave on nine days in 2004 for appointments related to her mother or husband, and her 2005 FMLA applications included requests for intermittent leave to care for her mother. Goelzer received a 1.25% merit increase after 2005. Goelzer stated in an affidavit that when she asked why she did not receive a higher merit pay increase, Payne responded that she had missed a lot of time at work due to appointments with her mother.

Goelzer learned in 2006 that she would need foot surgery that year. On May 10, 2006, Goelzer submitted an FMLA leave request for time away from work from September 22, 2006 to November 20, 2006 for her foot surgery and recovery. At Payne's request, Goelzer provided a medical certification for the foot surgery to Human Resources Director Michael Collard on June 1, 2006. Collard wrote directly to Goelzer's doctor five days later and asked whether Goelzer could return to light duty office work before November 19, 2006, and if so, when. Goelzer's doctor responded that she would be totally disabled and unable to work during that time period. The County eventually approved Goelzer's FMLA leave request on August 8.

On August 15, 2006, the Sheboygan County Board passed an ordinance that converted the position of County Administrative Coordinator to that of County Administrator. The Board also appointed Payne to serve as County Administrator. With this change, Payne now had the power under Wisconsin Statute § 59.18(3) to discharge Goelzer on his own, a power he did not previously have. Within the next ten days, Payne told Collard that he wanted to meet to discuss options for terminating Goelzer's employment. In preparation for the August 25, 2006 meeting, Collard prepared notes related to options, with a list that included "term outright, just need to change," "eliminate position," "Change T/O — reshuffle — create new position not qualified for," "Raise expectations & evaluate," and "Retaliation for FMLA?".

On September 8, 2006, two weeks before Goelzer was to commence FMLA leave for her foot surgery, Payne discharged Goelzer with an effective date of November 30, 2006. (Payne placed Goelzer on paid leave until November 30, 2006 so that she would receive the FMLA leave that had been previously approved.) At the time, Goelzer had used 67 hours of leave in 2006 and was scheduled to take an additional 328 hours related to her foot surgery. . . .

Payne did not immediately replace Goelzer. Instead, he first utilized an unpaid college intern. On January 16, 2007, the County Board enacted an ordinance that eliminated Goelzer's former position and replaced it with the position of "Assistant to the Administrator." It also increased the pay grade for the role from Grade 6 to Grade 8. Payne hired Kay Lorenz as the Assistant to the Administrator on March 19, 2007. . . .

II. ANALYSIS . . .

The FMLA allows an eligible employee with a serious health condition that renders the employee unable to perform her position to take twelve workweeks of leave during each twelve-month period. 29 U.S.C. § 2612(a)(1)(D). An employee may also utilize this leave to care for certain immediate relatives, including a parent or spouse, with a serious health condition. *Id.* § 2612(a)(1)(C). Under the FMLA, an employee on leave is entitled to the right to be restored to the same or an equivalent position that she had before she took qualifying leave. *Id.* § 2614(a)(1)-(2). An employer may not "interfere with, restrain, or deny the exercise of or the attempt to exercise" any FMLA rights. *Id.* § 2615(a)(1).

In addition, the FMLA affords protection to employees who are retaliated against because they exercise rights protected by the Act. *Lewis v. Sch. Dist. #70*, 523 F.3d 730, 741 (7th Cir. 2008). Pursuant to 29 U.S.C. § 2615(a)(2), it is "unlawful for any employer to discharge or in any other manner discriminate against any individual for opposing any practice made unlawful by this subchapter." The Act also makes it unlawful to "discharge" or "discriminate" against a person for taking part in proceedings or inquiries under the FMLA. 29 U.S.C. § 2615(b). We have construed these provisions as stating a cause of action for retaliation.

[The court looked to Goelzer's complaint to see if it alleged both interference and retaliation, concluding that it did. One paragraph cited 29 U.S.C. § 2614(a)(1), the FMLA provision barring interference, while a different used the language of § 2615(a)(2), prohibiting retaliation.]

A. FMLA Interference

We first address Goelzer's interference argument. The plaintiff carries the burden of proving an FMLA interference claim. *Darst v. Interstate Brands Corp.*, 512 F.3d 903, 908 (7th Cir. 2008). To establish such a claim, an employee must show that: (1) she was eligible for the FMLA's protections; (2) her employer was covered by the FMLA; (3) she was entitled to take leave under the FMLA; (4) she provided sufficient notice of her intent to take leave; and (5) her employer denied her FMLA benefits to which she was entitled. *Burnett Burnett v. LFW, Inc.*, 472 F.3d 471, 477 (7th Cir. 2006). There is no dispute regarding the first four requirements; it is clear that the FMLA allowed Goelzer to take the leave that she did. The only issue is whether the defendants fired her to prevent her from exercising her right to reinstatement to her position. *See Simpson v. Office of the Chief Judge of the Circuit Court of Will County,*

559 F.3d 706, 712 (7th Cir. 2009) ("Firing an employee to prevent her from exercising her right to return to her prior position can certainly interfere with that employee's FMLA rights.").

An employee's right to reinstatement is not absolute. The FMLA allows an employer to refuse to restore an employee to the "former position when restoration would confer a 'right, benefit, or position of employment' that the employee would not have been entitled to if the employee had never left the workplace." *Kohls v. Beverly Enters. Wis., Inc.*, 259 F.3d 799, 805 (7th Cir. 2001) (citing 29 U.S.C. § 2614(a)(3)(B)); *see also* 29 C.F.R. § 825.216(a) ("An employee has no greater right to reinstatement or to other benefits and conditions of employment than if the employee has been continuously employed during the FMLA leave period."). In other words, an employee is not entitled to return to her former position if she would have been fired regardless of whether she took the leave.

The question at this stage of the proceedings, then, is whether a jury could find that the defendants did not reinstate Goelzer because she exercised her right to take FMLA leave. Payne and the County maintain that the answer is "no," as their position is that Goelzer's employment would have been terminated regardless of whether she took FMLA leave. They maintain that after Payne received a promotion to County Administrator, he simply exercised his new authority to replace Goelzer on his own with a person of his choosing. They stress that before his promotion, Payne would have needed the approval of the County through its Executive Committee before he could terminate Goelzer's employment. With the promotion to County Administrator, however, Payne could now make the termination decision on his own. And three weeks after he assumed his new role, Payne notified Goelzer she was losing her job, a decision he says had nothing to do with Goelzer's use of FMLA leave.

Michael Collard, the County's Human Resources Director, supports Payne's account. Collard asserts that Payne had expressed frustration for some time that Goelzer was not performing the tasks Payne had envisioned for her, and Collard also says that Payne had expressed a desire for an assistant with a greater skill set. In addition, although Payne did not immediately replace Goelzer and instead first utilized a college intern, Payne maintains that in the longer term he wanted the position to be enhanced to allow him to assign more sophisticated tasks beyond those that he says Goelzer could handle.

The defendants' account provides one possible explanation for the termination decision, and a jury might well choose to believe it. But there is another possibility as well. Goelzer contends that she lost her job because Payne and the County were not happy that she had exercised her right to take FMLA leave. . . . Even though the leave was authorized, we conclude that the evidence Goelzer introduced in response to the defendants' motion for summary judgment could lead a jury to find that she was denied reinstatement not because Payne simply wanted a different assistant, but because she had exercised her right to take leave under the FMLA.

A jury might be swayed by comments Payne made that could suggest frustration with Goelzer's use of FMLA leave. In her 2002 performance evaluation, for instance, Payne explicitly contrasted Goelzer's use of FMLA leave with her past "excellent" attendance, saying, "[t]hough Dorothy has had an excellent attendance record in the past, (36 hours of sick leave in 2001), she utilized 312 hours or 39 days of sick leave in 2002." Payne gave her a 3.5 rating in the "attendance" category in 2002. He noted her use of sick leave in the following year's performance evaluation as well, stating "Dorothy utilized 176 hours of 22 days of sick leave in 2003," and he gave her an overall rating of 3.36 that year but did not award a merit increase. Notably too, when Goelzer asked Payne in 2006 why she did not receive a higher merit increase based on her 2005 performance, she says that Payne responded that she had missed too much time from work to attend to appointments with her mother.

A jury might also look to the memorandum Payne wrote in 2004 in response to Goelzer's view that she should have received a merit increase, where he said in part: "you were out of the office having eye surgery in 2002 and 2003. In fact, the past two years, use of sick leave and vacation combined, you were out of the office 113 days. As the only support person in the office, this has presented challenges in the functionality and duties associated with the office." A jury might view this memorandum as evidence that Goelzer lost her job because she exercised her right to take FMLA leave, as it might Payne's comments in an evaluation he wrote in January 2006: "On occasion, I have been concerned with office and phone coverage. Dorothy had numerous appointments the past year and needs to be more cognitive of the time she is away from her desk or corresponding with others on non-related work activities." The defendants do not dispute that the FMLA protected Goelzer's attendance at these appointments, and a jury could look to those comments as indication that Payne was not pleased Goelzer had been absent for many FMLA-covered appointments, even though she was permitted to take them by the Act and an employer is not to interfere with that right.

Moreover, although Payne now maintains he had concerns about Goelzer's skill set and performance, he consistently gave her favorable performance reviews. He says now that her satisfactory performance ratings reflect his "lowered expectations" of her abilities, but the performance ratings themselves do not speak of lowered expectations, and a jury would not be compelled to credit this explanation. In fact, just over seven months before Payne told Goelzer she was being terminated, he had conducted Goelzer's annual performance review and concluded that her performance met or exceeded expectations in all areas.

A factfinder might also consider that, if Payne had serious problems with Goelzer's performance, he could have asked the County Board to terminate Goelzer's employment before he received the promotion, yet he did not do so. In addition, although Payne asserts that he wanted an assistant with a larger skill set, there are no documents evidencing a plan to restructure the assistant position before Goelzer's termination. And, of course, Payne told Goelzer that she was losing her job two weeks before she was scheduled to take two months of FMLA leave. In short, we are left with two competing accounts, either of which a jury could believe. So summary judgment is not appropriate, and we reverse its grant.

B. FMLA Retaliation

Goelzer also contends her FMLA retaliation theory should proceed to trial. The FMLA provides that it is unlawful for an employer "to discharge or in any manner discriminate against" any employee for opposing any practice the FMLA makes unlawful. 29 U.S.C. § 2615(a)(2). The difference between a retaliation and interference theory is that the first "requires proof of discriminatory or retaliatory intent while [an interference theory] requires only proof that the employer denied the employee his or her entitlements under the Act." *Kauffman* [*v. Fed. Express Corp.*, 426 F.3d 880, 884 (7th Cir. 2005)]. To succeed on a retaliation claim, the plaintiff does not need to prove that "retaliation was the *only* reason for her termination; she may establish an FMLA retaliation claim by 'showing that the protected conduct was a substantial or motivating factor in the employer's decision'" *Lewis.*

A plaintiff may proceed under the direct or indirect methods of proof when attempting to establish an FMLA retaliation claim. *Burnett.* Under the direct method, the only method Goelzer employs, a plaintiff must present evidence that her employer took a materially adverse action against her because of her protected activity. If the plaintiff's evidence is contradicted, the case must proceed to trial unless the employer presents unrebutted evidence that it would have taken the adverse action against the plaintiff even if it did not have a retaliatory motive. That is, the plaintiff survives summary judgment by " 'creating a triable issue of whether the adverse employment action of which she complains had a discriminatory motivation.' " *Lewis.*

Payne and the County maintain that a jury could not conclude that they intentionally discriminated against Goelzer for using FMLA leave. In addition to the evidence to which she pointed in support of her interference claim, Goelzer also directs our attention to Human Resources Director Collard's inquiry to Goelzer's physician that asked "[w]hether Ms. Goelzer would be physically able to work light duty in an office environment prior to November 19, 2006, and if so, when would be an appropriate time that we would expect her to return." [This inquiry likely violated the regulations which, at the time, prohibited an employer contacting an employee's physician without his permission. 29 C.F.R. § 825.307. As since amended, the regulation allows an employer to "contact the health care provider for purposes of clarification and authentication of the medical certification . . . after the employer has given the employee an opportunity to cure any deficiencies. . . ." While the FMLA does not appear to provide a right to relief unless a violation of this regulation results in interference with the employee's rights under the statute, plaintiff] asserts that Collard's inquiry to her doctor supports her claim that the defendants had retaliated against her for using her FMLA leave.

Even if Collard's inquiry is put to the side, there is enough evidence in the record for a jury to find that the defendants fired Goelzer because she had utilized FMLA leave and not because Payne wanted to hire a new person with more skills. For example, Goelzer had received positive performance reviews, and none suggest on their face that they were the result of any "lowered expectations" from Payne. Payne denies that he made any oral derogatory comments regarding Goelzer's FMLA use, but that is for the jury to decide, and in any event the jury might view his written comments on Goelzer's performance evaluations regarding her use of FMLA leave as evidence that her use of FMLA leave motivated the termination decision. Payne also communicated the termination decision after he knew Goelzer planned to be out for two months on FMLA leave, and she had utilized a significant amount of FMLA leave in the years preceding the decision. Although the defendants disclaim any causal connection between Goelzer's requests for and use of FMLA leave and her firing, we conclude that a jury could find otherwise. As is the case with her interference theory, then, summary judgment is not appropriate on her retaliation action, and we reverse its grant in the defendants' favor. . . .

NOTES

1. *Qualifying Conditions.* There was no dispute in *Goelzer* that plaintiff's various leaves were both authentic and qualifying. That is, the defendant did not challenge either the genuineness of plaintiff's reasons for seeking leave or that these reasons satisfied the FMLA's requirements. The genuineness of employee claims is obviously often a difficult question for human resource departments, and the problem is made more difficult by the FMLA's limitations on contacting the plaintiff's doctor. Do you see why an employer might be satisfied with a doctor's note, and not wish to inquire further?

As for whether a particular set of circumstances qualifies for FMLA leave, that is often a complicated question. Perhaps the most difficult arises with respect to whether the plaintiff (or a family member) has a "serious health condition."

2. *Serious Health Conditions.* As you might expect, "serious health condition" is a term of art under the statute, and one that is extensively addressed by Department of Labor regulations. To appreciate some of the complexities, consider *Russell v. N. Broward Hosp.*, 346 F.3d 1335 (11th Cir. 2003). There, the defendant did not deny that Russell was out for medical reasons, but it argued that her absences nonetheless were not protected leave under the FMLA. Although Russell was badly injured (she fell at work, and was diagnosed with a fractured right elbow and a sprained ankle and related problems), the court found that her injury did not constitute a "serious health condition" under the FMLA. That was because the statute defines a "serious health condition" as "an illness, injury, impairment, or physical or mental condition that involves—(A) inpatient care in a hospital, hospice, or residential medical care facility; or (B) continuing treatment by a health care provider." *Id.* § 2611(11). Russell was not admitted to a hospital, so eligibility turned on whether she had undergone continuing treatment. While the statute itself does not define that term, the Department of Labor provided a detailed definition:

> (2) *Continuing Treatment* by a health care provider. A serious health condition involving continuing treatment by a health care provider includes any one or more of the following:
>
> (i) A period of incapacity (i.e., inability to work, attend school or perform other regular daily activities due to the serious health condition, treatment therefor, or recovery therefrom) of more than three consecutive calendar days, and any subsequent treatment or period of incapacity relating to the same condition, that also involves:
>
> (A) Treatment two or more times by a health care provider, by a nurse or physician's assistant under direct supervision of a health care provider, or by a provider of health care services (e.g., physical therapist) under orders of, or on referral by, a health care provider; or
>
> (B) Treatment by a health care provider on at least one occasion which results in a regimen of continuing treatment under the supervision of the health care provider. . . .

29 C.F.R. § 825.113(a)(2)(i). Because Ms. Russell was not incapacitated for "more than three consecutive days," she was not entitled to FMLA leave. Although she was partially incapacitated for a number of days over a ten-day period, she was not fully incapacitated for the requisite time. While the regulations also provide for other varieties of "continuing treatment," such as incapacity due to pregnancy or prenatal care or due to a chronic serious health condition such as asthma, diabetes, or epilepsy, § 825.113, none of these alternatives was applicable to plaintiff's situation.

3. *Denial of Merit Raises.* Plaintiff in the principal case seemed to challenge only her dismissal. What if she had challenged the denial of a merit raise? Payne's own statements would seem to establish that her leave was a factor in denying a raise. That would mean that she should win on such a claim, regardless of the reason for her ultimate termination. Or is there something odd about having to factor in as much as 12 weeks of absenteeism in making merit determinations?

4. *Interference.* Do you understand the difference between the "interference" and "retaliation" claims at issue in *Goelzer*? Section 2615(a)(1) of the Act sets out the interference claim, providing:

> Exercise of rights. It shall be unlawful for any employer to interfere with, restrain, or deny the exercise of or the attempt to exercise, any right provided under this subchapter.

The paradigm cases under this provision are an employer's denial of a leave in the first place or its refusal to reinstate the employee to a comparable position when the leave is over. These disputes, then, typically boil down to whether the employee is leave-eligible. Thus, while the plaintiff has the burden of persuasion, carrying it does not require any proof of employer intent. As *Goelzer* frames it, "an employee must show that: (1) she was eligible for the FMLA's protections; (2) her employer was covered by the FMLA; (3) she was entitled to take leave under the FMLA; (4) she provided sufficient notice of her intent to take leave; and (5) her employer denied her FMLA benefits to which she was entitled."

However, the statute expressly provides that a restored employee is not entitled to "any right, benefit, or position of employment other than any right, benefit, or position to which the employee would have been entitled had the employee not taken the leave." 29 U.S.C. 2614(a)(3)(B). Thus, as recognized in the regulations, an employer may deny reinstatement to an employee on FMLA leave if that employee would have been terminated or her job eliminated had she continued working. *See* 29 C.F.R. 825.216; *Batacan v. Reliant Pharms., Inc.*, 228 F. App'x 702, 704 (9th Cir. 2007) (since an employee on leave has no greater right to reinstatement than if she had been continuously employed, "an employee taking FMLA leave may be terminated pursuant to a legitimate reduction in force.").

As applied to Ms. Goelzer, the only question was whether she would have been discharged in any event, and the Seventh Circuit has placed the burden of persuasion under the interference clause on the employee. *Rice v. Sunrise Express, Inc.*, 209 F.3d 1008, 1018 (7th Cir. 2000) ("the employee always bears the ultimate burden of establishing the right to the benefit" under the interference clause).

It is true that *Goelzer* quotes the Department of Labor regulations that appear to place a burden on the employer when it claims that the employee would have been terminated in any event: "An employer must be able to show that an employee would not otherwise have been employed at the time reinstatement is requested in order to deny restoration to employment." 29 C.F.R. § 825.216(a)(1). But the Seventh Circuit does not view this as justifying burden shifting; rather, it reads it as simply stating the substantive law. The other circuits to have squarely addressed the question have concluded the contrary. *Phillips v. Matthews*, 547 F.3d 905, 911 (8th Cir. 2008) ("The burden is on the employer to prove the reason for termination was unrelated to FMLA."); *Smith v. Diffee Ford-Lincoln-Mercury, Inc.*, 298 F.3d 955, 963 (10th Cir. 2002) ("[T]he regulation validly shifts to the employer the burden of proving that an employee, laid off during FMLA leave, would have been dismissed regardless of the employee's request for, or taking of, FMLA leave."); *see also O'Connor v. PCA Family Health Plan, Inc.*, 200 F.3d 1349, 1354 (11th Cir. 2000) ("[T]he employer has an opportunity to demonstrate it would have discharged the employee even had she not been on FMLA leave"). At any rate, the court finds a jury trial on the issue — although Payne had "skill set" reasons for replacing Goelzer, there was genuine issue of material fact as to whether her past use of leave and her currently being "on track to use nearly 400 hours" influenced his decision. *See generally* Rachel Arnow-Richman, *Accommodation Subverted: The Future of Work/Family Initiatives in a "Me, Inc." World*, 12 Tex. J. Women & L. 345, 371 (2003) (criticizing *Rice* as contradicting the FMLA's accommodation-oriented approach to caregiving). *See also* Martin H. Malin, *Interference with the Right to Leave Under the Family and Medical Leave Act*, 7 Emp. Rts. & Emp. Pol'y J. 329 (2003).

5. *Retaliation.* Section 2615(a)(2) provides that it is unlawful for an employer "to discharge or in any other manner discriminate against any individual for opposing any practice made unlawful by this subchapter." The paradigm case for this is the employer who grants leave and reinstates the employee but then later discharges her for taking such leave. The critical issue is whether a plaintiff making a retaliation claim must demonstrate not only a right to leave but also that the employer had a discriminatory reason for denying reinstatement. The courts generally apply Title VII proof structures to determine whether the requisite intent exists. *See, e.g., Brungart v. BellSouth Telecomms., Inc.* 231 F.3d 791, 798 (11th Cir. 2000).

6. *Role of the Regulations.* Given the vagueness of the statute and the (comparative) specificity of the regulations, a frequent question under the FMLA will be the meaning and validity of the Department of Labor's regulations. *See Russell v. N. Broward Hosp.*, 346 F.3d 1335 (11th Cir. 2003) (finding that the regulations required three consecutive full days of incapacity for a serious health condition and upholding them as valid against plaintiff's attack that they were an unreasonable interpretation of the statute). The FMLA delegated to the Secretary of Labor the authority to "prescribe such regulations as are necessary to carry out" the FMLA's general requirements for leave. 29 U.S.C. § 2654. Under familiar principles of administrative law, that means substantial deference to the agency's interpretation of the statute. The *Russell* court found no reason to question the Department of Labor's view, even though the result was that someone who had what would intuitively be viewed as a serious health condition was left unprotected by the statute.

We have encountered the "*Chevron* question" of the validity of administrative agency regulations in the context of the ADA in Chapter 9 where we saw that the pattern of deference was pretty checkered; indeed, the ADAAA was passed in part to reinforce EEOC authority. See page 665. Neither has the Department of Labor gotten a free pass from the Court. *Ragsdale v. Wolverine World Wide, Inc.*, 535 U.S. 81 (2002), rejected a Department of Labor regulation providing that leave may not count against an employee's FMLA entitlement unless the employer promptly notified the employee that the leave has been designated as FMLA leave. The Court viewed the regulation as inconsistent with the statutory requirement of only 12 weeks of leave a year. Importantly, Ragsdale could not show that she had been prejudiced or harmed by the employer's failure to give notice. The Court did not decide what would happen in a case when an employee could show harm flowing from the employer's failure to provide notice.

7. *Intermittent Leave.* Notice that in *Goelzer*, the plaintiff often took "intermittent leave," typically for doctors' appointments. While leave is frequently thought of in extended terms, FMLA leave may be taken intermittently in blocks as small as an hour at a time (and, as discussed in the next note, without prior notice if the need for leave is unforeseeable). Obviously, some triggers for FMLA leave do not raise the question of intermittent leave (for example, illness for three days), while others invariably will (continuing treatment by a health care provider). Intermittent leave is required only when it is medically necessary, *Haggard v. Levi Strauss & Co.*, 8 F. App'x 599 (8th Cir. 2001) (physician's note for employee working half-days did not trigger right to intermittent leave because it did not state the medical necessity for the leave), which distinguishes it from other kinds of leave under the statute.

Because of the scheduling difficulties and potential disruption of such leave (and, perhaps because there is less of a pay "hit" for employees availing themselves of intermittent leave), some employers assert that this one is of the most onerous requirements of the FMLA. *See* Eric Paltell, *Intermittent Leave Under the Family and Medical Leave Act of 1993: Job Security for the Chronically Absent Employee?*, 10 LAB. LAW. 1 (1994). Do you think such concerns are legitimate or are they likely overstated? Do the facts in *Goelzer* influence your opinion?

Responding to these kinds of concerns, the statute and its regulations allow an employer to transfer an employee who seeks intermittent leave from a job where attendance is vital to an equivalent position where the employee's periodic absences will be less burdensome. 29 U.S.C. § 2612(b)(2); 29 C.F.R. § 825.204; *see Spangler v. Fed. Home Loan Bank of Des Moines*, 278 F.3d 847, 853 (8th Cir. 2002); *see also Carmona v. Sw. Airlines Co.*, 604 F.3d 848, 860 n.3 (5th Cir. 2010) ("[W]hile the FMLA can excuse an employee from his employer's ordinary attendance requirements, it does not do so where the employee requests the right to take intermittent leave without notice indefinitely. The FMLA also does not prevent the employee from being transferred to a different job with equivalent pay and benefits where his periodic absences will do less damage to the business."). *See generally* S. Elizabeth Wilborn Malloy, *The Interaction of the ADA, the FMLA, and Workers' Compensation: Why Can't We Be Friends?*, 41 BRANDEIS L.J. 821, 837 (2003).

8. *Employee Notice Requirements.* Another compliance issue that frequently arises in FMLA litigation concerns the law's notice requirements. The statute provides that, when the need for leave is foreseeable, an employee must generally give her employer no less than 30 days' advance notice, although there is some flexibility built into the regulations when it is not possible to do so. *See* 29 U.S.C. § 2612(e)(1) & (2)(B); 29 C.F.R. § 825.302. Goelzer apparently met these requirements, but not all employees are so careful. *See Cruz v. Publix Super Mkts., Inc.*, 428 F.3d 1379 (11th Cir. 2005) (employee did not provide employer with sufficient notice of the reasons why she would need to assist her pregnant daughter).

While the statute does not address notice requirements when leave is unforeseeable, the regulations provide that notice be given to the employer "as soon as practicable," and that should generally be "within the time prescribed by the employer's usual and customary notice requirements applicable to such leave." 29 C.F.R. § 825.303(a). The regulations go on to detail to whom notice may be given, by whom notice may be given, and how it may be provided. 29 C.F.R. § 825.303(b). "The employee need not expressly assert rights under the FMLA or even mention the FMLA, but need state only that leave is needed. The employer will be expected to obtain any additional required information through informal means." *Id.*

This can create some compliance challenges for the employer who must determine when it is appropriate to seek such additional information. While the employer will want to know if the leave is FMLA-eligible, most routine illnesses and common injuries do not trigger statutory protection. The employer may wish to balance its desire for certainty against administrative convenience issues as well as the potential awkwardness (and other liability risks) that may result from probing into an employee's personal situation. Recall from *Goelzer* that the regulations do not give the employer a blank check in following up with a health care provider.

The notice provisions can also create pitfalls for employees. Although the regulations are very generous to employees, particularly with respect to unforeseen needs, employees will not be entitled to FMLA leave unless they provide their employer information "sufficient to reasonably apprise it of the employee's request to take time off for a serious health condition." The point is that, even if the employee has what constitutes a qualifying condition, there is a further obligation to adequately inform the employer. *Compare Collins v. NTN-Bower Corp.*, 272 F.3d 1006 (7th Cir. 2001) (telling employer that employee was "sick" not sufficient); *Carter v. Ford Motor Co.*, 121 F.3d 1146 (8th Cir. 1997) (notice insufficient when Carter informed Ford that he was sick and did not know when he could return to work but did not offer further information regarding his condition), *with Spangler v. Fed. Home Loan Bank*, 278 F.3d 847 (8th Cir. 2002) (requesting time off for "depression again" is possibly a valid request when employer knew employee suffered from depression); *Price v. City of Fort Wayne*, 117 F.3d 1022 (7th Cir. 1997) (notice sufficient when employee filled out employer-provided leave request form, indicated that cause was medical need, and attached doctor's note requiring her to take the time off).

9. *Perfect Attendance Programs.* The effect of the FMLA on incentive programs to reward attendance generated considerable controversy. A plain language reading of the statute would seem to make individuals on FMLA leave eligible, but such incentive programs arguably substantially improve productivity. The amended regulations make clear that such programs are permissible, even when they exclude participation by those taking FMLA leave. 29 C.F.R. §215(c)(2).

10. *The FMLA and the ADA.* The ADA and the FMLA overlap to some extent. Individuals who are covered by both statutes have more than one option for dealing with an impairment that necessitates frequent absences. Even if leave would not be a reasonable accommodation given their employer's needs, leave without pay under the FMLA is a statutory right as long as the employer is provided with adequate notice. In addition, employees with attendance problems that are health related, but who are not disabled within the meaning of the ADA, will still be entitled to leave without pay if their health problem is a "serious health condition" under the FMLA. The overlap between the ADA and FMLA can create tricky compliance issues for the employer, as well. For example, while an employee with a serious health condition will max out her FMLA entitlement after 45 weeks, if the employee's condition qualifies disability and she requests additional leave, the employer must consider whether granting it would be a reasonable accommodation.

11. *Individual Liability.* Unlike the antidiscrimination statutes but similar to the Fair Labor Standards Act (FLSA), the FMLA has been held to provide for individual liability for individuals acting for the employer. *But see Modica v. Taylor*, 465 F.3d 174 (5th Cir. 2006) (suggesting that, unlike in the private sector, public employees may be entitled to qualified immunity). For example, Goelzer sued Adam Payne personally. *See generally* Sandra F. Sperino, *Under Construction: Questioning Whether Statutory Construction Principles Justify Individual Liability Under the Family and Medical Leave Act*, 71 Mo. L. Rev. 71 (2006); Sandra F. Sperino, *Chaos Theory: The Unintended Consequences of Expanding Individual Liability Under the Family and Medical Leave Act*, 9 Emp. Rts. & Emp. Pol'y J. 175 (2005). Given what you know about the two statutes, does it make sense to hold individuals liable for FMLA and minimum wage violations and leave violations but not gender discrimination?

12. *Counseling the Employer.* Prior to her health problems, Goelzer was frequently praised by Payne for her good attendance. In hindsight, was that a mistake? It certainly helped plaintiff establish that her later attendance problems were likely to be viewed as very problematic by him. Or was the problem not the earlier praise but Payne's repeated references to her absences after she began using her leave? And what about "the problem employee," the one who frequently misses work for questionable reasons? In *Russell*, the plaintiff had had attendance problems well before the accident that led to her discharge. It's possible, even probable, that the hospital believed she was malingering, or at least making a mountain out of a molehill. Of course, the hospital might be right or wrong in this belief, but, in an at-will world, it would be free to discharge such workers without fear of liability. Does the FMLA unduly restrict employers' ability to deal with such problems? *See* Sara Schlaefer Muoz, *A Good Idea, But . . . : Some Businesses Complain That the Family and Medical Leave Act Should Be More Aptly Named the Slackers Protection Act*, WALL ST. J., Jan. 24, 2005. To what extent do problems like this suggest attorney involvement in what seem like normal human resources processes?

* * *

While a casebook tends to focus on cases, employers tend to view statutes like the FMLA as requiring systemic changes in employment policies. Thus, almost all covered employers have overhauled their leave policies in response to the passage of the statute. Attorneys representing employers will, therefore, frequently be involved in the task of drafting such policies and occasionally in the task of interpreting them when particularly problematic situations arise. One skill of the employer's lawyer, when wearing her drafting hat, is to create policies that are both legal and administrable by the Human Resources Department. The next problem asks you to do just that.

PROBLEMS

10-3. You are U.S. counsel for Ocyllis, Inc., a Canadian firm that has just acquired an American corporation. The Canadian general counsel, your boss, has asked you to review the possible application of several of Ocyllis's personnel policies for possible application and/or modification in the United States. The first such policy is reproduced below:

1. *Intent.* This policy is designed to facilitate reasonably flexible arrangements at the time of birth or adoption of children. The policy will enable both parents to combine a productive career with family responsibilities with minimal impact on the corporation.
2. *Eligibility.* Full-time and part-time employees, who have at least 13 weeks' continuous employment at the Corporation prior to the birth or adoption of a child are eligible for pregnancy, paternity, and/or parental leave. To be eligible for financial benefits from the Corporation, employees must have 26 weeks of continuous service prior to birth or adoption.

3. *Pregnancy Leave.* Pregnancy leave is available only to natural mothers. An eligible employee is entitled to paid pregnancy leave for up to 19 weeks at 85 percent of full pay. In exceptional circumstances, a pregnancy leave may be extended beyond the 19-week period, at the discretion of the Ocyllis Board of Directors. An employee is normally expected to give four weeks' notice of the date of return to work, should this be different from the previously agreed date.

4. *Paternity Leave.* Paternity leave is available only to natural fathers. An eligible employee is entitled to two weeks' leave with full salary, pay and benefits. Leave must be taken within the first 26 weeks after the birth of the child.

5. *Parental Leave.* Parental leave is available to all parents, natural and adoptive. An eligible employee is entitled to unpaid leave for up to 35 weeks. For natural mothers and fathers, parental leave is in addition to pregnancy or paternity leave. For natural mothers, parental leave commences when pregnancy leave ends. For natural fathers and adoptive parents, parental leave must begin no later than 52 weeks after the birth of the child or the date the adopted child first comes into the custody, care, and control of the employee.

6. *Benefits During Leave.* Employees who take advantage of these provisions will incur no loss in salary level and will be entitled to pension, health disability, and other benefits provided the employee contributes the necessary amount of the cost of benefits. Vacation and sick leave shall continue to accrue during leave.

Advise Ocyllis to what extent United States law requires changes in this policy. Note also where the policy may be more generous than U.S. law requires and advise Ocyllis on whether extending those provisions to its American operations is desirable.

10-4. You have now learned some of the basic nuts and bolts of FMLA coverage and enforcement and have had the opportunity to try your hand at implementing the law through a workplace policy. In light of this knowledge, imagine that you are a legislative aide to a U.S. Senator who has a strong interest in work/family issues and has publicly committed to introducing legislation to redress some of the perceived shortcomings of current law. She has asked you to do preliminary research and advise her about possible approaches. What would you recommend? Would you amend existing legislation like the FMLA or the PDA? Or might you propose new legislation? Who would your proposal protect and what would it require? Would it apply to all businesses and all workers, and, if not, how would you limit it? To the extent your proposal would generate costs, how should they be allocated among employers, workers, and/or taxpayers? Are there ways of framing your proposal that might be responsive to potential political and social resistance?

11

Wages and Benefits

This chapter provides an introduction to direct regulation of employee compensation, which includes wages, in-kind wage substitutes, and "fringe benefits," most notably health coverage, retirement benefits, and profit-sharing plans. This contrasts with some of the mandates discussed in the previous chapters that can protect compensation, but less directly. For example, because worker pay and benefits are "terms and conditions of employment," the discriminatory behavior we studied in Chapter 9 that adversely affects these conditions is prohibited. In addition, in Chapter 10 we learned that the Family and Medical Leave Act mandates that employers maintain health benefits for employees during periods of leave covered by the statute, and the Pregnancy Discrimination Act requires employers to treat pregnancy-related leave the same as other types of short-term disability-based leave. Moreover, there are other employer-funded benefits or protections, such as mandated workers' compensation for work-related injuries and unemployment insurance.

Despite these limitations and the laws treated below, most compensation received by most workers is the result of private ordering. The vast majority of workers in the United States earn in excess of the wages mandated by the Fair Labor Standards Act ("FLSA"), 29 U.S.C.A. § 201-19 (2010), and state labor laws. These wages, therefore, are a result of individual employee-employer negotiation, collective bargaining, or, more generally, labor market forces, rather than regulation. In addition, as discussed in Chapter 1, to the extent that workers and firms may structure their relationships to avoid "employment" (usually through firm-independent contractor relationships), most of the protections discussed in this chapter do not apply at all. And, as we will address below, many employees are exempt from the FLSA's wage requirements.

Similarly, with very few exceptions, employers historically have not been obligated to provide their workers with health or retirement benefits. It is only their decision to do so that triggers the mandates of the Employee Retirement Income Security Act ("ERISA"), 29 U.S.C. § 1001-1461 (2006). However, as part of the health care reform package Congress passed in 2010, large employers will be subject to tax penalties beginning in 2014 if they fail to provide health insurance coverage or provide coverage that is unaffordable, and their full-time employees qualify for subsidized coverage elsewhere. *See* 26 U.S.C. § 4980H (2006).

This chapter focuses primarily on wage and hour protections and, in particular, the scope and limitations of the FLSA. Along the way, it will also touch on state wage and hour mandates. The chapter will conclude with a brief introduction to benefits regulation, outlining the broad contours of ERISA and the employer provisions of the new health care reform package.

A. WAGE PROTECTIONS

Wage protections for workers have a mixed history in the United States. Long before federal labor statutes favoring collective bargaining, *see* National Labor Relations Act, codified as amended at 29 U.S.C. § 151-69 (2006), there were attempts to regulate directly abuses by employers. Some of the earliest efforts were state laws restricting child labor. Although a number of jurisdictions also passed statutes controlling the hours of employment of adults, the most far-reaching were frequently struck down by the Supreme Court in the substantive due process period when the Supreme Court interpreted the Fourteenth Amendment to prohibit states from "interfering" with employment contracts. *See e.g., Lochner v. New York*, 198 U.S. 45 (1905). One major exception to Supreme Court hostility to such regulation was with respect to women. The famous Brandeis Brief provided the Supreme Court in *Muller v. Oregon*, 208 U.S. 412 (1908), with a basis for upholding legislation "protecting" women by limiting their hours of employment, while similar statutes applied to men were being struck down.

With the demise of substantive due process, *see, e.g., Opp Cotton Mills Inc. v. Adm'r of Wage & Hour Div.*, 312 U.S. 126 (1941); *W. Coast Hotel Co. v. Parrish*, 300 U.S. 379 (1937), statutes directly regulating hours worked and wages paid became the norm in the United States. At the federal level, the FLSA is the primary mechanism for dealing with perceived employer abuses. However, a number of other federal, state, and local laws also directly regulate worker pay.

Of course, government control of wage levels has always had its critics. Some claim that establishing a minimum wage above market rates harms social welfare and has adverse effects on the working poor, including artificially reducing the demand for labor. David Neumark & William Wascher, *Minimum Wages and Low-Wage Workers: How Well Does Reality Match the Rhetoric?* 92 MINN. L. REV. 1296 (2008); Daniel Shaviro, *The Minimum Wage, the Earned Income Credit and Optimal Subsidy Policy*, 64 U. CHI. L. REV. 405 (1997); *see also* John Foley, *Questioning the Merits of Federal Minimum Wage Legislation*, 5 GEO. J. L. & PUB. POL'Y 679 (2007) (arguing that the minimum wage increases unemployment, leads to higher inflation, and produces other detrimental effects on the poor). Others support the minimum wage on traditional and not-so-traditional grounds. *See, e.g.,* DAVID CARD & ALAN B. KRUEGER, MYTH AND MEASUREMENT: THE NEW ECONOMICS OF THE MINIMUM WAGE (Princeton Univ. Press 1995) (presenting evidence that the minimum wage has minimal or no negative effect on employment); Richard A. Ippolito, *The Impact of the Minimum Wage If Workers Can Adjust Effort*, 46 J. LAW & ECON. 207 (2003) (contending that the minimum wage has little effect on employment, output, and profits); Bruce E. Kaufman, *Institutional Economics and the Minimum Wage: Broadening the Theoretical and Policy*

Debate, 63 Ind. & Lab. Rel. Rev. 427 (2010) (offering a number of justifications for the minimum wage, including addressing unequal bargaining power, promoting economic stability and long-term economic efficiency, and reducing labor market externalities); Noah D. Zatz, *The Minimum Wage as a Civil Rights Protection: An Alternative to the Antipoverty Arguments?*, 1 U. Chi. Legal F. 1 (2009) (arguing that the minimum wage is justified not only as a poverty reduction tool, but also as a civil rights protection); Fiscal Policy Institute, States with Minimum Wages Above the Federal Level Have Had Faster Small Business and Retail Job Growth (March 30, 2006), *available at* http://www.fiscalpolicy.org/FPISmallBusinessMinWage.pdf (finding employment in the retail sector showed greater improvement in areas of the country with higher state and local minimum wage requirements, possibly due to the greater spending power of low-wage workers). Globalization, which has made it easier for many firms to export production to parts of the world where labor costs are substantially cheaper, has added fuel to both sides of the debate.

The issue of the government's role in regulating wages is debated cyclically in Congress when efforts are made to increase the FLSA minimum wage. *See* William P. Quigley, *Full-Time Workers Should Not Be Poor: The Living Wage Movement*, 70 Miss. L. J. 889, 909-19 (2001). And, as explored in Chapter 1, discussions of wage regulation and wages generally are tied to other hot-button issues, including immigration "reform." Perhaps unsurprisingly, although the basic protections afforded by the FLSA have persisted, the opponents of government regulation of wages have gained the upper hand at times, at least at the national level. For example, after an increase in 1997, the minimum wage remained at $5.15 an hour for a decade — reflecting a sharp decline in real wages. Moreover, as discussed below, some believe that the practical effect of new Department of Labor ("DOL") regulations promulgated in 2004 is to exempt more workers from the FLSA's overtime protections.

However, in May 2007, Congress enacted legislation increasing the minimum wage in three steps, culminating in 2009 at $7.25 an hour. *See* 29 U.S.C.A. § 206(a)(1)(C) (2010). This increase also has had an impact on state law, which may provide protection for classes of workers excluded from coverage under the FLSA. For example, the federal increase boosted minimum wage levels in those jurisdictions that tie their wage requirements to federal law. The federal mandate now exceeds the minimum wage in some states, although other states have enacted a wage floor above the federal level. *See* U.S. Department of Labor Employment Standards Administration Wage and Hour Division, Minimum Wage Laws in the States, January 1, 2010, *available at* http://www.dol.gov/esa/minwage/america.htm (listing state minimum wage requirements).

1. The FLSA

The original purposes of the FLSA were to prevent certain historic employer abuses of labor — including child labor — and to ensure that every covered employee received at least a basic minimum wage and a premium for work exceeding the standard number of hours per week. The statute was also designed — through its overtime pay provisions — to create incentives to spread employment over a greater number of workers. Thus, the FLSA requires covered employers to pay covered employees a minimum wage (again, currently $7.25 for most covered workers); it also requires employers to pay workers an overtime premium at one half their "regular rate of pay" for hours worked in excess of 40 hours per week. *See* 29 U.S.C.A. §206(a)-(b), 207(a)(1) (2010). It is worth noting, however, that the FLSA's overtime provisions do not limit the number of hours an employee may be required to work and thus the statute does not protect from discharge workers who refuse to work overtime.

The FLSA also contains the Equal Pay Act, a very limited ban on sex discrimination in pay, *see id.* at §206(d), and provisions designed to curtail oppressive child labor and protect children's safety and educational opportunities, particularly for children under 16 years of age, *see id.* at §212(c). Finally, it establishes certain wage-related record-keeping requirements for employers. *See id.* at §211. Most of the planning, litigation, and public policy issues relate to the minimum wage and overtime requirements.

With some exceptions, the substantive requirements of the FLSA are straightforward; in other words, when they are applicable, the FLSA's wage and hour requirements are fairly simple to apply. They are also mandatory and, hence, for the most part, cannot be waived via contract. Thus, private ordering plays a relatively small role where the FLSA operates. Of course, this raises an interesting, overarching policy question: Should the requirements of the FLSA be mandatory, or should employees and employers be allowed to waive these requirements, at least in some circumstances?

Nevertheless, given the current statutory and regulatory framework, FLSA litigation usually focuses on the statute's coverage — that is, issues surrounding who constitutes an "employee," who constitutes a covered employer, and who is otherwise exempt from the FLSA's protections or mandates. A few application issues have led to significant litigation, including determining what constitutes hours "worked" and calculating "rate of pay" for purposes of overtime.

a. Scope of Coverage

i. Employee and Employer

Because the FLSA broadly governs "employees" engaged in interstate commerce, the first step in determining whether the act applies at all is to determine whether a worker is an "employee" rather than another kind of worker — in most circumstances, an independent contractor. This definition of "employee" was addressed at length in Chapter 1, and its application in the FLSA context in particular was addressed in *Ansoumana v. Gristede's Operating Corp.*, reproduced at page 30.

Ansoumana also discussed aspects of who qualifies as an "employer" for FLSA purposes. Recall that there may be more than one "employer": a separate entity may be liable under the FLSA as a "joint employer." Moreover, supervisory personnel with direct control over employees may qualify as "employers" and, hence, may be individually liable for violations along with the firm or entity they control. Such personal liability for statutory violations is not unique but is quite rare. As *Ansoumana* indicated, extending liability to individual officers or controlling persons ensures that responsible parties have strong incentives to comply with the statute's mandates.

The *Ansoumana* decision, however, did not address the FLSA's "commerce" and "enterprise" coverage provisions. Any *employee* "engaged in commerce or in the production of goods for commerce" is covered by the Act, whether or not the employer is an enterprise engaged in commerce as statutorily defined. 29 U.S.C. §206(a), 207(a)(1) (2006); *see Brennan v. Arnheim & Neely, Inc.*, 410 U.S. 512, 516-17 (1973). To be engaged in commerce, individual employees must be "performing work involving or related to the movement of persons or things (whether tangibles or intangibles, and including information and intelligence)" between states. 29 C.F.R. §779.103. In addition, an employee is engaged in commerce when regularly engaging in interstate communication (such a using the mails or telephone) or when regularly traveling across state lines while working. Substantial, rather than sporadic or de minimis, interstate activities are required. Whether an employee's interstate activities are sufficiently substantial is a fact-intensive inquiry. *See, e.g., Locke v. St. Augustine's Episcopal Church*, 690 F. Supp. 2d 77 (E.D.N.Y. 2010) (holding after a detailed factual analysis that a church janitor was not an employee engaged in commerce under the FLSA, nor was his employer an enterprise engaged in commerce); *Bowrin v. Catholic Guardian Society*, 417 F. Supp. 2d 449 (S.D.N.Y. 2006) (finding that employees of a charitable organization were not engaged in commerce in most tasks they performed, but some tasks involving interstate travel were covered activities).

On the other hand, even an employee who is not individually engaged in such commerce will be covered if he or she is "employed in an enterprise engaged in commerce or in the production of goods for commerce." 29 U.S.C. §206(a), 207(a)(1). The most difficult and litigated aspect of this requirement is what constitutes an "enterprise." Indeed, the scope of the employing enterprise is important for several other reasons. First, the FLSA has a minimum dollar volume limitation; it currently does not apply to employing enterprises whose annual gross volume of sales is less than $500,000. 29 U.S.C. §203(s)(1)(A)(ii). In addition, whether several operations or entities constitute a single enterprise may be dispositive of whether the statute's overtime mandates have been satisfied; for example, if an employee works for two separate entities that constitute a single enterprise, the sum of the hours the employee works for both entities during a week will determine whether the employee is entitled to an overtime premium. Finally, if liability under the FLSA is established, recovery may depend on the scope of the enterprise when one part of or entity within it is insolvent.

The FLSA defines "enterprise" as follows:

> "Enterprise" means the related activities performed (either through unified operation or common control) by any person or persons for a common business purpose, and includes all such activities whether performed in one or more establishments or by one or more corporate or other organizational units including departments of an establishment operated through leasing arrangements, but shall not include the related activities performed for such enterprise by an independent contractor.

29 U.S.C. §203(r). Certain relationships or arrangements are exempted from enterprise treatment, including exclusive-dealership arrangements and franchises. *See id.* In *Brennan v. Arnheim & Neely, Inc.*, 410 U.S. 512, 518 (1973), the Supreme Court stated that the three main elements of this statutory definition are "related activities, unified operation or common control, and common business purpose."

See also 29 C.F.R. §779.202 ("[T]he enterprise includes all such related activities which are performed through 'unified operation' or 'common control' . . . even if they are performed by more than one person, or in more than one establishment, or by more than one corporate or other organizational unit."). Obviously, these elements overlap, and various pieces of evidence may be relevant to more than one. "Activities are 'related' when they are the same or similar." *Arnheim & Neely, Inc.*, 410 U.S. at 518; *see also Chao v. A-One Med. Servs., Inc.*, 346 F.3d 908 (9th Cir. 2003) (holding two companies to be one enterprise because both provided home health care services even though they serviced different types of patients under different levels of care with differing eligibility requirements); *Pierce v. Coleman Trucking, Inc.*, 2005 WL 2338822 (N.D. Ohio Sept. 23, 2005) (finding related activities when two companies engaged in identical asbestos removal activities and differed only in their union relationships).

According to DOL regulations, "common control"

> includes the power to direct, restrict, regulate, govern, or administer the performance of the activities. "Common" control includes the sharing of control and it is not limited to sole control or complete control by one person or corporation. "Common" control therefore exists where the performance of the described activities are [sic] controlled by one person or by a number of persons, corporations, or other organizational units acting together.

29 C.F.R. §779.221; *see also Arnheim & Neely, Inc.*, 410 U.S. at 518 (finding that operations controlled through a fully integrated central office constituted a unified operation subject to common control). Common ownership is one factor in determining common control, but it is not dispositive. *See, e.g., Dole v. Odd Fellows Home Endowment Bd.*, 912 F.2d 689 (4th Cir. 1990).

Another regulation broadly defines common business purpose:

> Generally, the term "common business purpose" will encompass activities whether performed by one person or by more than one person, or corporation, or other business organization, which are directed to the same business objective or to similar objectives in which the group has an interest. The scope of the term "enterprise" encompasses a single business entity as well as a unified business system which performs related activities for a common business purpose.

29 C.F.R. §779.213. This definition is consistent with the Supreme Court's treatment in *Arnheim & Neely, Inc.*, 410 U.S. at 518, finding a real estate management company's operations at a number of different, separately owned buildings had a common business purpose because the "activities at the several locations are tied together by the common business purpose of managing commercial properties for profit."

Finally, in 1974, Congress extended the definition of "employer" under the FLSA to include virtually all public employers. *See* Pub. L. 93-259, §6, 88 Stat. 58-62 (1974); 29 U.S.C. §203(d) (2006). The Supreme Court ultimately found this extension to be a proper exercise of Congress's Commerce Clause power and not inconsistent with the strictures of the Tenth Amendment. *See Garcia v. San Antonio Metro. Transit Auth.*, 469 U.S. 528 (1985). However, the combined effect of two subsequent Supreme Court decisions, *Seminole Tribe v. Florida*, 517 U.S. 44 (1996), and *Alden v. Maine*, 527 U.S. 706 (1999), renders states immune from *private* suits for damages under the FLSA. The Department of Labor may still enforce the

FLSA against the states, and municipalities and other political subdivisions do not enjoy such sovereign immunity, and are, thus, frequently the target of private FLSA suits, *see, e.g., Acton v. City of Columbia*, 436 F.3d 969 (8th Cir. 2006).

ii. Exemptions

Even if a worker is a covered employee employed by one or more covered employers, the employee may nevertheless be exempt from the FLSA's protections. The FLSA and implementing DOL regulations contain a significant number of exemptions excluding certain categories of employees from the minimum wage requirements, the overtime provisions, or both. Many of the exemptions apply to employees in specific industries or subsectors of specific industries, or those holding jobs in certain, defined job categories. For example, some workers under 20 years of age may receive wages as low as $4.25 for the first 90 days of employment. In addition, various categories of transportation, domestic, and agricultural workers are exempt from the FLSA's overtime requirements, and the statute contains separate overtime requirements for firefighters and law enforcement officials. Also, some seasonal employees and agricultural workers are exempt from both the minimum wage and overtime requirements. Moreover, public employees are subject to a number of unique provisions. Most notably, section 7(o) of the statute, 29 U.S.C. § 207(o), allows public employers to compensate employees who work overtime with compensatory time — that is, one and one half hours off for every hour worked in excess of 40 hours per week — instead of overtime pay. A frequently debated policy question is whether that same option should be available to private sector employees. Currently, the provision of "comp time" in lieu of overtime is not permitted even if both parties would prefer it.

When you encounter FLSA in practice, the first place to begin is to ascertain whether the situation you are confronting falls within one of the many exceptions to the general coverage provisions we have sketched. This chapter does not attempt to cover all of the various exemptions in the statute, *see, e.g.*, 29 U.S.C. § 213, but it does convey the flavor of the analysis while treating some of the more important exemptions in terms of numbers of workers excluded from the FLSA's protections.

The "White Collar" Exemptions

The best-known exemptions tend to be labeled generically as the "white collar" exemptions. Section 13(a)(1) of the FLSA completely exempts "any employee employed in a bona fide executive, administrative, or professional capacity." *See* 29 U.S.C. § 213(a)(1). In subsequent amendments to the FLSA, Congress also added a special exemption for certain "computer employees" and "highly compensated" employees. *See* 29 U.S.C. § 213(a)(17).

The goal underlying the white-collar exemptions, at least historically, was to exclude from coverage those workers not engaged directly in production but rather involved in management, administration, and the learned or creative professions. The § 13(a)(1) exemptions were "premised on the belief that the workers exempted typically earned salaries well above the minimum wage, and they were presumed to enjoy other compensatory privileges such as above average fringe benefits and better opportunities for advancement, setting them apart from the nonexempt workers entitled to overtime pay." *See* 69 Fed. Reg. 22,122, 22,123-24 (April 23, 2004). In addition, Congress believed that the work such employees performed was "difficult to standard-ize to any time frame and could not be easily spread to other workers after 40 hours in a week, making compliance with the overtime provisions difficult and generally preclud-ing the potential job expansion intended by the FLSA's time-and-a-half overtime premium." *Id.* at 22,123. Such distinctions may be less meaningful today, as the American economy shifts from manufacturing to the provision of services, technology and communications, and creative professions. Views differ on whether this is a reason to expand or contract the exemptions.

DOL regulations govern the exemptions. *See* 20 C.F.R. § 541. These regulations — which were first promulgated in the 1940s and remained largely unchanged until 2004 — contained requirements that had to be satisfied in order for an employee to be treated as exempt. To qualify, an employee's compensation had to exceed a defined salary floor ($155 per week, or $8,060 annually) and had to be in the form of a set "salary," rather than an hourly wage subject to reductions based on the quality or quan-tity of work performed. In addition, an employee qualified for such exempt status only if his or her "primary duties" were "administrative," "professional," or "executive" in nature. Each of these duty classifications, in addition to the term "primary duty" was defined, although inexactly and, hence, was subject to widespread litigation.

In 2004, the DOL altered portions of the white-collar exemption regime. *See* Defining and Delimiting the Exemptions for Executive, Administrative, Professional, Outside Sales and Computer Employees, 29 C.F.R. § 541 (2010). These changes generated great controversy in the mainstream media and in political circles because of their anticipated net effect; according to many commentators, they would signif-icantly increase the number of workers exempt from the FLSA's protections wage and overtime protections.

The ultimate effect of the revised regulations is complex. In one way, the new rules benefit employees: They raise the qualifying salary level for these exemptions to $455 a week or $23,660 per year, meaning more workers are now nonexempt based on their wages alone, irrespective of their responsibilities. On the other hand, other provisions clearly exempt more employees. For example, the new rules exempt from coverage an employee "who leads a team of other employees assigned to complete major projects for the employer," without regard to whether the employee has direct supervisory authority over other team members. *See* 29 C.F.R. § 541.203(c). In addition, more workers with only *some* executive duties are now exempt because the new "primary duty" test does not limit the amount of nonexempt work an employee can perform and still be considered an "executive." *See id.* Finally, the new regulations contain an additional exemption for employees earning more than $100,000 a year ("highly compensated employees"), without regard to primary duties; such an employee must perform only a single exempt task "customarily and regularly" in order to be exempt. *See* 29 C.F.R. § 541.601. Since the $100,000 trigger is not inflation-indexed, more and more employees will reach this status over time.

A primary purpose of these rules was to reduce the uncertainty the prior regulations produced and the litigation that resulted. *See* 69 Fed. Reg. 22,122 (Apr. 23, 2004). Various aspects of the exemptions do provide greater clarity. For instance, "salary" and the effect of reductions in pay for various purposes are now defined more clearly. *See* 29 C.F.R. § 541.602. Similarly, some exemptions are now better defined, including the computer employee, outside salesperson, and education exemptions. And new provi-sions set out categorical exclusions from the exemptions, including those for emergency response personnel, "blue collar" and other workers engaged only in manual or repetitive labor, *see* 29 C.F.R. § 541.3(a), (b), and nurse practitioners, *see* 29 C.F.R. 541.301(e)(2). Moreover, the new regulations provide a single primary duty test, abandoning the prior approach, which contained two different tests — the "long" and "short" tests — based on salary level. *See id.* at § 541.700.

Nevertheless, much in the new regulations parrots or parallels the prior regulations. For example, the purposes of the exemptions remain the same, and the basic distinction between production and administrative work continues to be paramount. Moreover, the definitions and terms that govern applicability of the exceptions are generally quite similar to those under the prior regime.

Also, determining whether an employee is exempt as an executive, administrator, or professional remains a highly fact-sensitive inquiry. And how the general rules governing these exemptions and the somewhat altered "primary duty test" may apply in particular situations continues to pose planning difficulties. Indeed, whether an employee who was nonexempt before is now exempt as an executive, administrator, or professional may not be clear. Few courts have applied the new regulations, and developing a guiding body of case law will take years. Employers and employees, therefore, will need to rely not only on the new regulations and the examples they provide in assessing exempt/nonexempt status but also on older case law, at least where the operative standards have not changed significantly.

The best way to appreciate the challenges facing employers, employees, and courts is to see how the white-collar exemptions are applied in relatively close cases. Thus, as a starting point, read the following case involving employees classified as "assistant managers" by their employers.

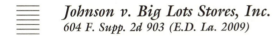

Johnson v. Big Lots Stores, Inc.
604 F. Supp. 2d 903 (E.D. La. 2009)

SARAH S. VANCE, District Judge.

From January 26-27, 2009, the Court conducted a bench trial in this overtime pay and misclassification collective action brought under the Fair Labor Standards Act (FLSA), 29 U.S.C. § 201, et seq. After considering all the evidence presented at trial and deposition testimony that the Court reviewed after the live trial concluded, the Court rules as follows. . . .

I. Findings of Fact and Conclusions of Law

A. *Procedural and Factual Background*

Defendant Big Lots Stores, Inc. is a nationwide retailer of "closeout" and "overstock" merchandise. It operates approximately 1,400 stores in 46 states across the country. Big Lots sells consumer goods ranging from futons to food and utilizes second- and third-generation retail space.

At each store, Big Lots typically employs a salaried store manager, at least one salaried assistant store manager (ASM), an hourly associate store manager, a customer service specialist (CSS), associate hourly employees such as cashiers and stockers, and an office manager or bookkeeper. Depending on a store location's size, sales volume, number of employees, and performance history, two ASMs and only one associate manager may be employed, or the store will employ only one ASM and two associate managers. Some stores also include furniture departments and employ a furniture sales manager. Big Lots classifies both store managers and ASMs as exempt executive employees for purposes of the overtime pay provisions of the FLSA. Thus ASMs do not receive overtime pay when they work more than 40 hours in a week. ASMs are eligible for quarterly and annual bonuses based on store sales, the average amount of a purchase within their store, and controllable profit. With the exception of the furniture sales manager, none of Big Lots' nonexempt associates is eligible for bonuses.

Big Lots' formal description of the ASM job position states that ASMs are responsible for interviewing and hiring hourly associate employees, supervising the work of hourly associates, and providing for the safety of persons in the store and security of Big Lots' property. Depending on whether someone is an ASM for Merchandising or Operations, that individual's job description also includes either overseeing freight delivery and the unloading and stocking of merchandise known as the "Dock-to-Stock" (DTS) process, or supervising the work of hourly associates in the store and the cashiering operation, respectively. Big Lots stores are supposed to operate on a management model in which there is always a member of management in the store, known as the manager on duty, and in which the managers work in overlapping shifts. Big Lots' model management schedule provides that ASMs are to work a minimum of five, nine-hour shifts per week, opening and closing the store depending on the hours of their shifts.

On November 23, 2004, a group of plaintiffs sued Big Lots, asserting that it misclassified ASMs as executive employees and thereby unlawfully denied them overtime pay in violation of § 207(a)(1) of the FLSA. Plaintiffs styled their complaint as a collective action under § 216(b) of the FLSA and brought their overtime pay and misclassification claims on behalf of themselves and all other similarly situated individuals. Plaintiffs specifically contended that although their formal job descriptions included managerial responsibilities, their actual managerial duties were de minimis and did not meet the criteria for exempt executive employees. Plaintiffs asserted that in reality they consistently worked more than 40 hours per week and that they spent the vast majority of their time performing, under strict corporate guidelines, nonexempt tasks that had little to do with managing the store, such as unloading merchandise from delivery trucks, organizing storerooms, stocking merchandise on shelves, operating cash registers, and cleaning their stores.

[The court conditionally certified the matter as collective action, and the parties sent notices to ASM employees of Big Lots, which ultimately resulted in an opt-in nationwide class of 936 current and former ASMs. At an initial bench trial, the court found that Big Lots "did not maintain a nationwide de facto policy of misclassifying ASMs and that an ASM's duties often varied from store to store." That meant that the matter was not fit for adjudication as a nationwide collective action. Accordingly, it was decertified, and the court decided the claims of two named plaintiffs at a second bench trial.]

B. The Executive Exemption

The FLSA requires that employers pay their employees at a rate of at least one and one-half times their regular rate for the hours an employee works in excess of a 40-hour workweek. 29 U.S.C. § 207(a)(1). But employers do not have to pay time-and-a-half to individuals "employed in a bona fide executive, administrative, or professional capacity." *Id.* § 213(a)(1). The FLSA itself does not further define these "white-collar" exemptions. Instead it delegates authority to the Secretary of Labor to promulgate rules that define these exemptions. *Id.* The white-collar exemptions are affirmative defenses to overtime pay claims. The employer bears the burden of proving that a plaintiff is properly classified as an exempt employee. *See Corning Glass Works v. Brennan*, 417 U.S. 188 196-97 (1974).

Two sets of regulations are pertinent to this case: those in effect before August 23, 2004 (the "pre-2004 regulations" or "old regulations"), and those that went into effect on August 23, 2004 (the "post-2004 regulations" or "current regulations"). Under the so-called "short test" of the old regulations, an employee who was paid a salary of at least $250 per week (which was true of both remaining plaintiffs) qualified as an executive if his primary job duties (1) consisted of the management of the enterprise and (2) included the customary and regular direction of the work of two or more other employees. 29 C.F.R. 541.1(f) (pre-2004). In 2004, the Secretary of Labor revised the criteria for the executive exemption. Now, to qualify as an executive, an employee must (1) be paid on a salaried basis at least $455 per week (which was true of both remaining plaintiffs); (2) have management of the enterprise as his or her primary duty; (3) "customarily and regularly" direct the work of two or more other employees; and (4) have the authority to hire or fire other employees or make recommendations about the hiring, firing, advancement, promotion or any other change of status of other employees that are given "particular weight." 29 C.F.R. § 541.100(a).

The Secretary of Labor has also promulgated regulations that define the terms used in the executive criteria. The definitions identify numerous, non-exclusive factors that courts should consider in analyzing whether an employee qualifies as an exempt executive. Several courts have observed that any determination about whether an employee's job duties satisfy the regulatory criteria is a highly fact-intensive inquiry that must be made on a case-by-case basis in light of the totality of the circumstances. As the ultimate issue here is whether plaintiffs are misclassified, a fact-intensive inquiry into their respective employment experiences is required.

1. Management as Primary Duty

The current regulations include the following illustrative list of management activities:

> interviewing, selecting, and training of employees; setting and adjusting their rates of pay and hours of work; directing the work of employees; maintaining production or sales records for use in supervision or control; appraising employees' productivity and efficiency for the purposes of recommending promotions or other changes in status; handling employee complaints and grievances; disciplining employees; planning the work; determining the techniques to be used; apportioning the work among the employees; determining the type of materials, supplies, machinery, equipment or tools to be used or merchandise to be bought, stocked and sold; controlling the flow and distribution of materials or merchandise and supplies; providing for the safety and security of the employees or the property; planning and controlling the budget; and monitoring or implementing legal compliance measures.

29 C.F.R. § 541.102 (post-2004). The old regulations contained a similar list. *See* 29 C.F.R. § 541.102(b) (pre-2004). Under the regulations, management entails performing tasks included in the other executive exemption criteria, i.e., directing the work of other employees and having the authority to hire or fire and make influential recommendations that affect others' employment status.

An employee's "primary duty" is management if it is the "principal, main, major or most important duty that the employee performs." 29 C.F.R. § 541.700(a) (post-2004). Both the old and the current regulations make clear that the determination of an employee's primary duty must be based on the totality of the circumstances. As the current regulations put it, the determination of an employee's primary duty "must be based on all the facts in a particular case, with the major emphasis on the character of the employee's job as a whole." *Id.; see also* 29 C.F.R. § 541.103 (pre-2004). The old regulations set forth five non-exclusive factors to consider: (1) the amount of time spent in the performance of managerial duties; (2) the relative importance of the managerial duties as compared with other types of duties; (3) the frequency with which the employee exercises discretionary powers; (4) the employee's relative freedom from supervision; and (5) the relationship between the employee's salary and the wages paid other employees for nonexempt work performed. 29 C.F.R. § 541.103 (2003). The current regulations set forth only four factors: (1) the relative importance of the exempt duties as compared with other types of duties; (2) the amount of time spent performing exempt work; (3) the employee's relative freedom from direct supervision; and (4) the relationship between the employee's salary and the wages paid to other employees for the kind of nonexempt work performed by the employee. 29 C.F.R. § 541.700(a) (post-2004). Both the old and current versions recognize that "the amount of time spent performing exempt work can be a useful guide in determining whether exempt work" is an employee's primary duty, and that, as a general rule, if an employee spends a majority of her time on management activities, then management is her primary duty. 29 C.F.R. § 541.700(b) (post-2004); 29 C.F.R. § 541.103 (pre-2004). But they also stress that "nothing . . . requires that exempt employees spend more than 50 percent of their time performing exempt work," 29 C.F.R. § 541.700(b) (post-2004). Rather, "[t]ime alone . . . is not the sole test, and in situations where the employee does not spend over 50 percent of his time in managerial duties, he might nevertheless have management as his primary duty if the other pertinent factors support such a conclusion." 29 C.F.R. § 541.103 (pre-2004).

The current regulations also explicitly recognize that an employee may perform exempt and nonexempt duties concurrently. Although the old regulations did not address the concept of concurrent duties specifically, courts that interpreted the earlier version acknowledged that an employee could have management as his primary duty even if he concurrently performed nonexempt duties. *See, e.g., Thomas v. Speedway SuperAmerica, LLC,* 506 F.3d 496, 504-05 (6th Cir. 2007). . . . Indeed, in the preamble to the 2004 version, the Secretary commented that the new regulations "are consistent with current case law which makes clear that the performance of both exempt and nonexempt duties concurrently or simultaneously does not preclude an employee from qualifying for the executive exemption." 69 Fed. Reg. 22136 (Apr. 23, 2004). That view is now codified in the regulations: "Concurrent performance of exempt and nonexempt work does not disqualify an employee from the executive exemption if the [other regulatory criteria] are otherwise met." 29 C.F.R. § 541.106(a).

"Whether an employee meets the [executive exemption criteria] when the employee performs concurrent duties is determined on a case-by-case basis." *Id.* The regulations distinguish between exempt and nonexempt employees who both perform nonexempt work based on whether the exempt employee retains supervisory and managerial responsibility even while performing nonexempt work: "Generally, exempt executives . . . [decide] when to perform nonexempt duties and remain responsible for the success or failure of business operations under their management while performing the nonexempt work. In contrast, the nonexempt employee generally is directed by a supervisor to perform the exempt work or performs the exempt work for defined periods." *Id.* To illustrate how an employee may retain her exempt status while concurrently performing exempt and nonexempt duties, the regulations specifically point to the multitasking of an assistant manager in a retail establishment. Such an employee may perform work such as serving customers, cooking food, stocking shelves and cleaning the establishment, but performance of such nonexempt work does not preclude the exemption if the assistant manager's primary duty is management. An assistant manager can supervise employees and serve customers at the same time without losing the exemption. An exempt employee can also simultaneously direct the work of other employees and stock shelves. 29 C.F.R. §541.106(b) (post-2004). Thus, even though an assistant retail manager might "not spend more than 50 percent of [her] time performing exempt duties [she] may nonetheless meet the primary duty requirement if the other factors support such a conclusion." 29 C.F.R. §541.700(b) (post-2004). *See also* 29 C.F.R. §541.700(c) (post-2004) (An assistant retail manager who "perform[s] exempt executive work such as supervising and directing the work of other employees, ordering merchandise, managing the budget and authorizing payment of bills may have management as [her] primary duty," even if a majority of her time is spent on nonexempt work). Factors to consider in determining whether management is still an employee's primary duty when that individual is, say, stocking shelves alongside the employees whom she simultaneously supervises include to what extent the assistant manager herself is closely supervised and what the pay difference is between the assistant manager and the nonexempt hourly employees. 29 C.F.R. §541.700(c).

2. Directing the Work of at Least Two Other Employees

Under both the old, short test and the current test, an employee must "customarily and regularly direct[ ] the work of two or more other employees" in order to qualify as an exempt executive. 29 C.F.R. 541.100(a)(3) (post-2004); 29 C.F.R. §541.1(b) (pre-2004). The old regulations did not define "customarily and regularly." The current regulations explain that the phrase means "a frequency that must be greater than occasional but which, of course, may be less than constant. Tasks or work performed 'customarily and regularly' include work normally and recurrently performed every workweek; it does not include isolated or one-time tasks." 29 C.F.R. §541.701 (post-2004).

Determining whether someone directs the work of at least two employees is more complicated than just counting heads. An individual qualifies as an executive only if she customarily and regularly supervises the work of two or more "full-time employees or their equivalent." 29 C.F.R. §541.104(a) (post-2004); 29 C.F.R. §541.105(a) (pre-2004). Of particular importance here are the terms "full-time" and "equivalent." The regulations do not expressly define what "full-time" means. But with certain exceptions that apply to the financial and banking industries where so-called "banker's hours" sometimes apply, full-time generally means 40 hours per week. The regulations also account for the supervision of full-time and part-time employees, clarifying that "[o]ne full-time and two half-time employees, for example are equivalent to two full-time employees" and that "[f]our half-time employees are also equivalent" to two full-time employees. 29 C.F.R. §541.104(a) (post-2004). *See also* 29 C.F.R. §541.105(a) (pre-2004). The regulations do not require that an employee supervise the work of the same employees day in and day out to qualify as exempt, and they contemplate situations in which supervisors might share or split the supervision of subordinate employees. *See* 29 C.F.R. §541.104(b) (post-2004). But the rules prohibit double-counting of employee-hours for supervision purposes. *See* 29 C.F.R. §541.104(d). Perhaps the clearest way to make sense of these rules is the Department of Labor's "80- hour" rule, which generally requires an exempt supervisor to "direct a total of 80 employee-hours of work each week." 69 Fed. Reg. 22135.

3. The Authority to Hire or Fire or Make Recommendations That Are Given Particular Weight

Whether an employer gives "particular weight" to an employee's recommendations as to the hiring, firing, advancement, promotion or any other change of status of other employees depends on "whether it is part of the employee's job duties to make such suggestions and recommendations; the frequency with which such suggestions and recommendations are made or requested; and the frequency with which the employee's suggestions and recommendations are relied upon." 29 C.F.R. §541.105 (post-2004). The Department of Labor further recognizes that a court's determination as to whether a particular employee's recommendations are given particular weight may rest on evidence that is extrinsic to the employee's testimony. In the Preamble to the regulations enacted in 2004, the Secretary explained that evidence of "particular weight" could include "witness testimony that recommendations were made and considered; the exempt employee's job description listing responsibilities in this area; the exempt employee's performance reviews documenting the employee's activities in this area; and other documents regarding promotions, demotions or other change of status that reveal the employee's role in this area." 69 Fed. Reg. 22135.

In general, "an executive's suggestions and recommendations must pertain to employees whom the executive customarily and regularly directs." 29 C.F.R. §541.105 (post-2004). An "occasional suggestion" does not qualify. *Id.* But an employee's recommendations "may still be deemed to have 'particular weight' even if a higher level manager's recommendation has more importance and even if the employee does not have authority to make the ultimate decisions as to the employee's change in status." *Id.*

Neither the pre- nor post-2004 regulations define "change of status." But the Secretary of Labor explains in the Preamble that this phrase should "be given the same meaning as that given by the Supreme Court in defining the term 'tangible employment action' for purposes of Title VII liability." 69 Fed. Reg. 22131. The Supreme Court has explained that a tangible employment action "constitutes a significant change in employment status, such as hiring, firing, failing to promote, reassignment with significantly different responsibilities, or a decision causing a significant change in benefits." *Burlington Industries, Inc. v. Ellerth*, 524 U.S. 742, 761 (1998). And generally speaking, "only a supervisor, or other person acting with the authority of the company" can effect a tangible employment action. It is also recognized that an individual may still effect a tangible employment action even if the decision or recommendation is "subject to review by higher level supervisors." With these regulatory criteria and illustrative, multi-factor definitions in mind, the Court now turns to analyzing whether Big Lots properly classified the plaintiffs as exempt.

C. *John Johnson*

Johnson began working at Big Lots on July 28, 2002 and worked for the company for about two years. For the first 11 months of his employment, Johnson worked for Big Lots' Store 529 in Venice, Florida, which employed between16 to 24 workers during the non-holiday season. During Johnson's tenure as an ASM at Store 529, the store employed Ken Williams as the Store Manager and Patti Hecker as a second ASM. In June 2003, Williams left and a new store manager was brought in to Store 529. Johnson then transferred to Store 561 in Port Charlotte, Florida, which employed about 14 to 25 workers during the non-holiday season. There, Johnson worked with Store Manager Cliff Baer and ASM Robert Burden, his co-plaintiff. Blanca Lopez, who testified for Big Lots in this case, was the District Manager for both stores. Johnson worked at Store 561 until he suffered a heart attack on July 21, 2004. After returning from medical leave in November 2004, Johnson worked for about two weeks at Store 1545 in Fort Myers, Florida. Big Lots formally terminated Johnson's employment on February 12, 2005 after he exhausted the amount of time Big Lots allows for a leave of absence. While employed with Big Lots, Johnson's annual salary ranged from $29,000 to $30,866 a year. Johnson also received 10 bonuses during his tenure of employment, ranging from $125 to $500 each. Johnson was never paid any overtime.

Johnson testified that he usually worked Monday through Saturday, between 10 to 12 hours a day, which would result in a 60-72 hour workweek. Johnson's schedule varied, but he typically closed the store four days a week and opened the store two days a week. Johnson testified that when he opened or closed, other managers, like the furniture manager, associate manager or another ASM, might be present. At times the Store Manager worked from open to close. When Johnson was the only salaried manager in the store, between six to eight hourly employees, including hourly managers such as customer service specialists (CSS's), associate managers, and bookkeepers, would also be working.

D. *Primary Duty*

As discussed, supra, the former and current regulations, both of which apply here, set forth several factors to consider in deciding whether management is an employee's primary duty. Under both sets of regulations, the Court considers: the relative importance of the exempt duties as compared with other types of duties; the amount of time the employee spends performing exempt work; the employee's relative freedom from direct supervision; and the relationship between the employee's salary and the wages paid to other employees for the kind of nonexempt work performed by the employee. *See* 29 C.F.R. § 541.103 (2003); 29 C.F.R. § 541.700(a). Under the old regulations, courts also look to the frequency with which the employee exercises discretionary powers.

Because the executive exemption is an affirmative defense to an overtime action, Big Lots has the burden of proving that the exemption applies. *See Morgan v. Family Dollar Stores, Inc.*, 551 F.3d 1233, 1269 (11th Cir. 2008). The Court has considered all of the factors, and for the following reasons finds that Big Lots has not shown that management was Johnson's primary duty.

1. The Amount of Time Spent Performing Exempt Work

In most cases, an employee has management as his primary duty if he spends over 50% of his time performing exempt work. *Murray v. Stuckey's, Inc.*, 939 F.2d 614, 618 (8th Cir.1991). No circuit courts have found management was a primary duty when the employee spent 80 to 90% of his time performing nonexempt tasks. *See Morgan v. Family Dollar Stores, Inc.*, 551 F.3d 1233, 1272 (11th Cir.2008). But "time alone . . . is not the sole test, and in situations where the employee does not spend over 50 percent of his time in managerial duties, he might nevertheless have management as his primary duty if the other pertinent factors support such a conclusion." *Murray*.

Johnson performed few management activities most days. On a typical day, although he might briefly perform some managerial duties in opening the store, Johnson spent the majority of his shift stocking shelves with merchandise, and he saw this task as his most important duty. Johnson also performed janitorial duties daily. He swept. He mopped. He cleaned the bathrooms. Customer service tasks, such as helping customers, retrieving shopping carts from the parking lot, and carrying purchases to customers' cars, were a part of Johnson's daily duties. On most days, Johnson performed recovery, which is essentially a task where the worker finds out-of-place merchandise and returns it to its proper location. In addition, he ran the cash register, sometimes for up to three hours a day.

On "truck day," the day the company truck delivered merchandise to the store, Johnson's work was similarly non-managerial. The stores had one truck day per week, and on that day, a team of employees unloaded and stocked merchandise under a highly routinized procedure called "Dock-to-Stock" (DTS). The DTS process was under the overall direction of the Store Manager, but Johnson was designated "DTS Lead." Although, on paper, Johnson's duties as DTS Lead included training associates on the DTS process and ensuring that performance standards were met, in reality, Johnson largely did the same work as the stockers. He unloaded freight from the truck, working side by side with the stockers. He moved the freight from the truck to pallets. He moved the pallets from the stockroom to the floor with a pallet jack. He moved the merchandise from the pallets to the shelves. He ticketed merchandise in accordance with Big Lots' detailed corporate procedures (i.e., he put the tickets on the top right corner of the merchandise).

Johnson occasionally told the stockers to "pick up the pace," move a pallet, or build an endcap. But as Big Lots' witness Gary Vellenkamp testified, these instructions were "rarely" given because the stockers generally knew how to do their jobs. This is corroborated by the fact that each step in the DTS process was described in the minutest detail in Big Lots' DTS manual and DTS checklist. Ultimately, Johnson was the "Lead" in name only. The highly routinized DTS process needed little management, and thus Johnson spent the vast majority of his truck days performing the same manual labor as the rest of the DTS crew.

Johnson never performed many common managerial duties. Johnson testified that he never set hours or created schedules for other employees. He did not regularly direct the work of other employees. He did not conduct huddle meetings with employees. He did not regularly hire, fire, or promote employees. He did not approve vacations or sick leave. He did not interview potential employees or evaluate employment applications. He did not order merchandise. He did not have any discretionary authority over prices, advertising, or where merchandise was placed in the store. He did not plan or control the store's budget or administer payroll. He was not consulted about the store's operations.

Johnson did open and close the store regularly, using the procedures outlined in Big Lots' detailed opening and closing checklists. The other managerial duties Johnson performed were done rarely or often amounted to little more than filling out forms at the direction of a supervisor. Big Lots produced three employee appraisals signed by Johnson. Johnson filled out the forms, in which the managers rated four different aspects of employee performance on a scale of 0-3, with the help of Williams or Lopez. These three forms were the only ones he completed during his two years at Big Lots. The ratings on the performance appraisals determined whether an employee was entitled to a raise, and if the employee was to receive the raise, a member of management had to fill out an Action Request Form. Big Lots produced eight Action Request Forms signed by Johnson. Lopez testified that these forms took no more than a minute to fill out. Johnson also was involved in disciplining employees through Big Lots' Progressive Counseling program. Big Lots produced ten Progressive Counseling forms signed by Johnson, and the forms showed that Johnson disciplined employees for various reasons, such as being short on their tills, failing to show up, or insubordination. Johnson explained that, for most of the counseling, Williams directed him to fill out the forms and told him what to write. Johnson did not do any Progressive Counseling at Store 561.

Big Lots concedes that Johnson spent the majority of his time performing nonexempt work, but contends that management was still his primary duty since he performed his nonexempt duties concurrently with his exempt ones. The Court rejects this argument for a number of reasons. For one, the evidence that Johnson directed and supervised the work of other employees is scant. Big Lots' witness Vellenkamp described the frequency with which Johnson gave him instructions as "rarely" and "seldomly." He admitted that he and Johnson generally performed the same tasks most days. Further, Johnson's ability to supervise was limited by his non-managerial work, which mostly consisted of manual labor. Johnson could not easily stock shelves and simultaneously supervise employees in all parts of the 30,000 square-foot store. See *Morgan*. Cleaning the bathrooms would similarly impede Johnson from supervising the work of others. The mere title of "assistant manager" coupled with manual labor does not show that Johnson was concurrently supervising other employees. Because there is only the thinnest of evidence that Johnson actually supervised other employees, the Court finds that he was not performing exempt duties concurrently with his nonexempt tasks.

Even if the Court found that Johnson concurrently performed managerial and non-managerial duties, the analysis would not end. The regulations provide that, "[w]hen an employee performs exempt and nonexempt work concurrently, whether the exemption is met is determined on a case-by-case basis." 29 C.F.R. § 541.106(a). Exempt executives typically decide when to perform nonexempt duties, while nonexempt employees are directed by a supervisor to perform exempt work. *Id*. If an assistant manager in a retail establishment is closely supervised and earns little more than nonexempt employees, the assistant manager generally does not satisfy the primary duty requirement. 29 C.F.R. §541.700(c).[2] The Court will consider these factors, infra, under the freedom from supervision prong of the regulations.

Further, that Johnson was the "manager on duty" a portion of his time does not affect this factor. First, the courts are split as to whether a manager on duty of the store necessarily has management as her primary duty. The First Circuit has held that "the person 'in charge' of a store has management as his primary duty, even though he spends the majority of his time on non-exempt work and makes few significant decisions." *Donovan v. Burger King Corp. (I)*, 672 F.2d 221, 227 (1st Cir. 1982); *see also Donovan v. Burger King Corp. (II)*, 675 F.2d 516, 522 (2d Cir. 1982) (assistant managers that are "solely in charge" of their restaurants for the great bulk of their working time are relatively free from supervision). But other courts have held that the title "manager on duty" is not a talisman for finding management a primary duty. *See Ale v. Tennessee Valley Auth.*, 269 F.3d 680, 691 (6th Cir. 2001) ("The words 'in charge' are not a magical incantation that render an employee a bona fide executive regardless of his actual duties."). As explained by the Eleventh Circuit, "[C]ourts cannot rely solely on whether an employee was 'in charge' of the store. Rather, they must evaluate the employee's actual job duties." *Morgan*, 551 F.3d at 1272 n. 60; *see also Thomas* (the court cannot rely solely upon plaintiff's statements that she was "the person ultimately in charge of [her] store," and must instead look to her actual job duties). This Court agrees with the Sixth and Eleventh Circuits that an inquiry into what the "manager in charge" actually did during his shift is required. Here, Johnson was not free to decide when to perform nonexempt work because the amount of nonexempt work required of him took up the vast majority of his time, and the nominal amount of exempt work he performed was tightly controlled from above.

But even if management was Johnson's primary duty when he was "in charge" of the store, he was not manager on duty for the majority of his workweek. Johnson testified that he was "manager in charge" for only 10-12 hours of his 70-hour workweek, thus roughly 15 to 18 percent of the week. Even using Big Lots' witness Patti Hecker's estimate that Johnson was manager on duty 40% of the week, Johnson was still below a 50% threshold.

In the other cases where the courts found that the "manager in charge" had management as his primary duty, the plaintiffs were "managers in charge" for all or the great majority of their workweek. *See Burger King I*, 672 F.2d at 227; *Burger King II*, 675 F.2d at 522; *Murray v. Stuckey's, Inc.*, 939 F.2d 614, 618 (8th Cir.1991). That is not the case here. Even if the Court presumes Johnson was performing managerial duties when he was manager on duty, he was not manager on duty for most of his workweek.

In sum, the evidence shows that Johnson spent the great majority of his time performing non-managerial duties. That Johnson performed managerial duties less than 50% of his workweek is not dispositive, see *Burger King I*, but this factor suggests his primary duty was not management.

---

2. While this subsection of the regulation became effective in 2004 and is thus applicable only to a brief period of the plaintiffs' employment, the Court nevertheless finds it instructive as to whether management was their primary duty.

2. Relative Importance of the Exempt Duties as Compared to the Nonexempt Duties

Under this factor, the Court weighs the importance of plaintiff's managerial duties with the importance of his non-managerial duties, keeping in mind the overall goal of running a successful company.

Here, Johnson's non-managerial duties included unloading freight, stocking shelves, running the cash register, performing recovery, cleaning up, and assisting customers, while his managerial duties included opening and closing the store and a limited amount of evaluating employee performance and disciplining employees. The evidence does not show that Johnson's managerial duties were more important than his non-managerial duties. *See* 29 C.F.R. § 541.700(a). Johnson's primary value to Big Lots was his job of moving freight from the backroom to the sales floor. District Manager Lopez explained the importance of this task to Johnson in his job interview, when she took him to the back room of a Big Lots Store, showed him the freight, and asked him "if [he] felt that [he] could unload the backroom." Johnson felt that his most important duty was stocking shelves and making sure all of the freight was placed on sale. Johnson's disdainful statements in his 2004 performance appraisal further attest that putting out freight was his primary function: "I wished I had known that all I was going to be used for was just 'stocking' only. If that were the case things could have been much easier. Now that I know where I stand my position is easier, just keep putting out freight."

Part of the reason Johnson spent so much time stocking and performing other non-managerial tasks was because of Big Lots' policy of avoiding overtime payments to its hourly workers. Big Lots' corporate offices set the number of payroll hours available to the stores, and the stores were not allowed to exceed the budgeted hours. If the hourly workers could not perform the tasks within the budgeted hours, the tasks fell to salaried workers like Johnson. Big Lots' policy made it difficult to delegate tasks to associates. Because of this policy, Johnson routinely worked 60-plus hours a week to accomplish non-managerial tasks that could have been assigned to hourly workers if Big Lots was willing to pay overtime. Johnson's completion of these tasks was essential to the functioning of the store. *See Morgan* (finding that store managers [sic] non-exempt duties were more important than their exempt ones when "[a] large amount of manual labor by store managers was a key to Family Dollar's business model given each store's limited payroll budget").

Further, many of Johnson's "managerial tasks" were also performed by non-salaried employees, such as furniture managers, CSS's, office coordinators, and associate managers, who were also considered part of the management team. For instance, associate managers could open and close the store when a salaried manager was on vacation. Office coordinators would often open the safe, count the cash inside, prepare the deposit, and take it to the bank. CSS's and associate managers performed balance checks on cash registers. Huddle meetings could be performed by anyone. And all employees trained other employees in their respective positions (i.e., stockers trained stockers; cashiers trained cashiers).

In sum, the evidence shows that Johnson's primary value to Big Lots was for his performance of non-managerial tasks such as moving and stocking freight. Most of the managerial duties at Johnson's stores were performed by the Store Manager. The few "managerial" duties Johnson performed involved being told exactly what to do by the

Store Manager or by Big Lots' corporate policies and checklists. If Johnson failed to perform his managerial duties, Big Lots would still function in much the same manner because the Store Manager, and even non-salaried managers such as the associate manager or the CSS, could and did perform many of these tasks. *Cf. Thomas* (finding that a Speedway store manager was critical to the gas station's success because if the manager failed to perform her duties of hiring, training, and assigning work schedules, no one else would perform these tasks). If Johnson did not perform his non-managerial tasks, however, operations at the store could suffer because there were not enough payroll hours for hourly associates to accomplish these tasks. Because Johnson's non-managerial duties were relatively more important than his managerial duties, this factor favors a finding that Johnson's primary duty was not management.

3. Freedom from Direct Supervision and Exercise of Discretionary Authority

Both the new and old regulations list "freedom from direct supervision" as a factor to consider in deciding whether management is an employee's primary duty. The old regulations also list "the frequency with which the employee exercises discretionary powers," but the new regulations omit this factor. Because the frequency with which an employee exercises discretionary power is part and parcel of freedom from supervision, the Court will consider these factors jointly. *See Morgan.*

Johnson rarely exercised discretionary authority. Johnson's actions were strictly controlled by corporate directives, emails from the District Manager, and orders from the Store Manager. The Big Lots stores received Weekly Action Plans, Plan-O-Grams, and Plan-O-Guides that dictated which items were to go on sale and where the merchandise was to be placed in the store. As Hecker explained, "[Big Lots] tell[s] us what they want, where they want it and how they want it." A Big Lots checklist governed the procedures in opening and closing the store. Further, Big Lots' store operating procedures controlled virtually all aspects of the store operations, from the proper way to stock merchandise ("use both hands") to the stretches stockers should perform to warm up, to the specific bills and change to put in the money drawer of the cash register, to the places to put tags on merchandise.

Johnson's discretion was further cabined by the District Manager and Store Manager. Johnson received instructions on where to place merchandise from the Store Manager, and only the Store Manager would deviate from the Weekly Action Plans. The instructions Johnson gave to Big Lots' associates were pursuant to the direction of the Store Manager. Johnson would also receive emails, sometimes daily, from the District Manager that would assign specific tasks to the ASMs. As Hecker explained, "[Johnson's] management functions were very limited . . . all assistant managers had to ask or be told what to do and when to do it."

As an ASM, Johnson was also closely supervised. The Big Lots Store Managers worked nearly every day, at times from open to close, and micromanaged the ASMs when they were both in the store. Although Johnson was the only salaried manager in the store for some portion of the week, he still had to comply with the written instructions of the Store Managers or emails from the District Manager. Even when Johnson was the "manager on duty," he had no meaningful supervisory role. He told associates "good job" or to "hurry up," generally disciplined employees at the behest of others, and had no role in hiring decisions.

As such, Big Lots has not shown that this factor weighs in favor of a finding that management was Johnson's primary duty.

4. Relationship Between the Employee's Salary and the Wages Paid to Nonexempt Employees Performing Similar Work

Finally, the Court will look to the relationship between Johnson's salary and the wages paid other employees for nonexempt work. The parties dispute whether the Court should compare Johnson's weekly salary to that of his subordinates or Johnson's effective hourly rate to the hourly rate of his subordinates. The Sixth Circuit has utilized the comparison of hourly rates urged by plaintiffs. *See Thomas.* There, the Court reduced the store manager's weekly salary to an hourly rate of pay by dividing the salary by the number of actual hours worked. The Court then compared that rate to the hourly rate of subordinate employees. The Eleventh Circuit also used this method in *Morgan.*

The Court holds that the relevant comparison is the effective hourly wage of Johnson with the hourly wage of his subordinates. Plaintiffs have provided evidence that Big Lots ASMs regularly worked over forty-hour weeks performing the tasks of hourly workers so that Big Lots could avoid paying hourly workers overtime compensation. To compare the wages an hourly worker earned in a 40- hour workweek with the salary an ASM earned in a 60- to 70-hour workweek would ignore the huge discrepancy in work time caused by Big Lots' policy. The fair comparison is the effective hourly wage of an ASM with the hourly wage of someone doing the non-exempt work he regularly performed. If Johnson worked 60 hours a week for 50 weeks a year, his initial salary of $29,000 per year, plus an average quarterly bonus of $250, would give him an effective hourly wage of $10 per hour. His later salary of $30,866, plus an average quarterly bonus of $250, would give him an effective hourly wage of $10.62 per hour. Johnson's hourly wage is therefore only about $1 higher than the hourly wages of the associate managers ($8.97-$9.67 per hour) and the highest paid CSS's ($8.70-$9.82 per hour) at Store 529 and Store 561. Johnson's wage is less than that of the furniture department manager ($10.74-$12.62), an hourly employee, at both stores. Given the relatively small difference between these hourly rates, this factor is neutral as to whether Johnson's primary duty was management. *See Morgan* (noting that because the store managers' rate was only $2-$3 higher than that of the assistant managers, this factor was neutral as to whether management was the store managers' primary duty).

5. Witness Credibility

The Court finds that overall, Johnson was a credible witness. . . . The Court therefore finds that the substance of Johnson's testimony, i.e., that he spent the great majority of his time on nonexempt tasks and a comparatively inconsequential amount of time performing management duties, is more probably true than not true.

The Court did not find the testimony of Lopez, Big Lots' most favorable witness, to be particularly relevant to Johnson's daily duties. As District Manager, Lopez oversaw 15 stores, which would mean 15 Store Managers, 30 ASMs, and about 300-500 total employees depending on the time of year. Lopez did not work with Johnson on a daily basis. Her testimony was largely based on the general duties of Big Lots ASMs. . . . Because Lopez's testimony largely was not based on her direct experience with Johnson, the Court finds Lopez's testimony only minimally relevant to whether Johnson's primary duty was management.

6. Summary

Taken together, the factors suggest that management was not Johnson's primary duty. Since Big Lots must establish each element, Big Lots has failed to meet its burden of proving that Johnson meets the executive exemption. Because the Court finds that management was not Johnson's primary duty, the Court will not consider the other requirements of the executive exemption.

[After performing a similar analysis and reaching similar conclusions as to the other plaintiff, Robert Burden, the court turned to remedies. It found that Big Lots had not acted "willfully" in misclassifying the plaintiffs as exempt executives, and therefore did not extend recovery back beyond the FLSA's standard two-year statute of limitations. However, the court nevertheless found that Big Lots had not shown that it had acted in good faith and on reasonable grounds in classifying the plaintiffs as exempt. It noted that after the California lawsuit was filed, Big Lots was on notice that its ASM position might be improperly classified. Its failure to conduct studies or surveys to ascertain whether all of its ASMs were actually performing managerial duties left open the distinct possibility that ASMs were misclassified on an individual basis. "Furthermore, Big Lots' no overtime policy had a natural tendency to cause District and Store Managers to demand the last bit of extra manual labor from the ASMs, leaving them little time or opportunity to delegate or supervise. As such, Big Lots should have been more proactive in finding out what was actually going on on the ground." Thus, Big Lots failed to show that it should be exempted from the liquidated damage award.

The court then calculated damages for unpaid overtime and doubled the amount to reflect liquidated damages. It awarded $63,587.60 in damages to Johnson and $63,847.40 to Burden, and ordered the parties to submit an accounting of attorney's fees and costs.]

NOTES

1. *Initial Impressions.* The employees at issue in *Johnson* had the title of manager, had at least some supervisory duties, and had the authority to exercise judgment in their work. Stepping back from legal doctrine, wouldn't you consider these employees to be white collar? Indeed, one of the lingering problems with these exemptions is that both employees and employers have often failed to understand their scope. For example, many employees who view themselves as "white collar" — perhaps in part because they receive a "salary" rather than "hourly wages" — may simply assume that they are exempt and thus not demand overtime pay. Such employees may instinctively prefer the exempt designation insofar as they associate that categorization with

professional status, and may well view it as a proxy for the importance of their jobs and their value to the company. Employers, too, may be mistaken about the law or share similar perceptions about the relationship between exempt status and employee value. Consider as well that the FLSA places significant record-keeping responsibilities on employers with respect to the hours and compensation levels of nonexempt workers. This can create administrative burdens for the employer and negatively affect morale among employees who must keep track of and regularly report all of their work time.

2. *Certainty and the "Old" and "New" Regulations.* As discussed above, a major criticism of the "old" regulations governing the exemptions for executive, administrative, and professional employees was how little guidance they provided. In *Johnson*, the court considers the executive exemption under both the pre- and post-2004 rules. Do you see much distinction between them in terms of certainty of outcomes or ease of application? Also, the two circuit opinions on which *Johnson* relies heavily, *Morgan v. Family Dollar Stores*, Inc., 551 F.3d 1233 (11th Cir. 2008), and *Thomas v. Speedway SuperAmerica, LLC*, 506 F.3d 496 (6th Cir. 2007), applied the pre-2004 rules in whole or in part, further suggesting that the 2004 changes may not have altered the analysis significantly. Considering the purpose of the executive exemption inquiry — determining whether the workers at issue really do exercise significant authority — could it be any less fact-intensive? Greater certainty would be an upside, but what might be the downside of bright-line rules that seek to categorize workers *ex ante*?

3. *Right Result?* Do you think the *Johnson* court reached the right result? Are the distinctions the court draws between Johnson and those that are exempt under the executive exemption meaningful? Are you satisfied with the tests the court articulated for making these determinations? Although the opinion is replete with detail, are there factors that should have been considered that were not?

4. *"Managers." Johnson* is far from the only case in which employees identified as "managers" by their employers have successfully claimed that they are nonexempt. While *Johnson* addressed assistant store managers, some of these cases have involved the highest-ranking employees at their respective facilities. For example, in *McKinney v. United Stor-All Centers LLC*, 656 F. Supp. 2d 114 (D.D.C. 2009), the court denied the employer's motion for summary judgment on the issue of whether employees hired as "primary managers" of its self-storage facilities — which leased storage units and rental trucks to customers — were exempt from the FLSA's overtime mandates under the administrative and executive employee exemptions. After engaging in a detailed analysis akin to that in *Johnson*, the court concluded that, despite their rank at the firm's local facilities, there were genuine issues of material fact as to whether these employees' primary duties were executive (exercising significant authority) or administrative (exercising significant discretion) in nature. In recent years, misclassification of store managers has been a particularly fertile area for litigation and large settlements. *See, e.g.*, http://www.lawyersandsettlements.com/settlements/employment-settlements/ (discussing a preliminary $42 million settlement between Staples, Inc., and a class of assistant store managers, and a $9 million settlement between BJ's Wholesale Club and certain mid-level managers); Michael R. Triplett, *Jury Awards $19.1 Million to Family Dollar Managers in Nationwide Collective Action*, DAILY LABOR REPORT BANNER, No. 4, p. A-8, March 7, 2006.

5. *Administrative Employees.* As *McKinney* suggests, determining whether a worker is covered by the exemption for administrative employees, like the executive employee exemption, is often a highly fact-intensive inquiry. The DOL regulations provide that an "employee employed in a bona fide administrative capacity" means any employee:

> (1) Compensated on a salary or fee basis at a rate of not less than $455 per week . . . exclusive of board, lodging or other facilities;
> (2) Whose primary duty is the performance of office or non-manual work directly related to the management or general business operations of the employer or the employer's customers; and
> (3) Whose primary duty includes the exercise of discretion and independent judgment with respect to matters of significance.

29 C.F.R. § 541.200. As the regulations recognize, this exemption overlaps with the one for executive employees. *See* 29 C.F.R. § 541.201. The key distinction is that administrative employees need not manage or supervise others — they must simply exercise discretion and independent judgment on important business matters. The exercise of discretion and independent judgment encompasses "the comparison and the evaluation of possible courses of conduct, and acting or making a decision after the various possibilities have been considered." 29 C.F.R. § 541.202. The employee must have the "authority to make an independent choice, free from immediate direction or supervision," although one can exercise discretion and independent judgment even if his or her decisions or recommendations are reviewed at a higher level. The regulations list a number of factors to consider in determining whether an employee exercises discretion and independent judgment. *See id.*

"Matters of significance" refers to the level of importance or consequence of the work performed. Areas in which work might qualify for the exemption include "tax; finance; accounting; budgeting; auditing; insurance; quality control; purchasing; procurement; advertising; marketing; research; safety and health; personnel management; human resources; employee benefits; labor relations; public relations, government relations; computer network, internet and database administration; legal and regulatory compliance; and similar activities." *See* 29 C.F.R. § 541.201. A number of specific examples of qualifying work are set forth in Note 7 below.

6. *Professional Employees.* Another exemption is for "professional employees," but the framework for determining which employees are exempt as "professionals" parallels, in many cases, the tests for determining executive or administrative employee status. The regulations provide that an "employee employed in a bona fide professional capacity" under the FLSA means an employee:

> (1) Compensated on a salary or fee basis at a rate of not less than $455 per week . . . exclusive of board, lodging, or other facilities; and
> (2) Whose primary duty is the performance of work:
> (i) Requiring knowledge of an advanced type in a field of science or learning customarily acquired by a prolonged course of specialized intellectual instruction; or
> (ii) Requiring invention, imagination, originality or talent in a recognized field of artistic or creative endeavor.

29 C.F.R. § 541.300. Note, however, that certain categories of licensed professionals are exempt regardless of their salary. *See, e.g.,* 29 C.F.R. § 541.304 (exempting

employees who have "a valid license or certificate permitting the practice of law or medicine or any of their branches and is actually engaged in the practice thereof" as well as residents and interns pursuing such a profession). Yet courts tend to construe these categories narrowly. *See, e.g., Belt v. Emcee, Inc.* 444 F.3d 403 (5th Cir. 2006) (holding that nurse practitioners and physician assistants fell outside of the "practice of medicine" exception to the salary-basis test for determining professional exemption from overtime-pay requirements).

7. *Guidance and Planning Implications.* Employment counsel are frequently called upon to make *ex ante* assessments of whether employees are exempt. Now that you are familiar with the tests for determining whether an employee is exempt under the executive and administrative exemptions, how comfortable would you be in making such assessments? Do the standards articulated facilitate category-wide treatment, or, as an attorney, would you feel it necessary to evaluate each person in each job? Further, to the extent that jobs often vary in reality from the corresponding job description, might you find it useful to visit each location to discuss the work with supervisors or even employees? Can you anticipate some problems in doing that?

There are some additional sources of guidance available beyond judicial decisions applying the regulations. Individual employers can seek feedback from the DOL on the exempt status of their employees. Upon such request, the DOL will issue a nonbinding opinion letter regarding the employees' status based on the facts the employer provided. In addition, the regulations themselves provide some particularized examples of workers who are or are not exempt. Consider, for instance, some of the examples provided in the regulations on the administrative exemption:

> (a) Insurance claims adjusters generally meet the duties requirements for the administrative exemption, whether they work for an insurance company or other type of company, if their duties include activities such as interviewing insured's, witnesses and physicians; inspecting property damage; reviewing factual information to prepare damage estimates; evaluating and making recommendations regarding coverage of claims; determining liability and total value of a claim; negotiating settlements; and making recommendations regarding litigation. . . .
>
> (c) An employee who leads a team of other employees assigned to complete major projects for the employer (such as purchasing, selling or closing all or part of the business, negotiating a real estate transaction or a collective bargaining agreement, or designing and implementing productivity improvements) generally meets the duties requirements for the administrative exemption, even if the employee does not have direct supervisory responsibility over the other employees on the team.
>
> (d) An executive assistant or administrative assistant to a business owner or senior executive of a large business generally meets the duties requirements for the administrative exemption if such employee, without specific instructions or prescribed procedures, has been delegated authority regarding matters of significance.
>
> (e) Human resources managers who formulate, interpret or implement employment policies and management consultants who study the operations of a business and propose changes in organization generally meet the duties requirements for the administrative exemption. However, personnel clerks who "screen" applicants to obtain data regarding their minimum qualifications and fitness for employment generally do not meet the duties requirements for the administrative exemption. . . .
>
> (g) Ordinary inspection work generally does not meet the duties requirements for the administrative exemption. Inspectors normally perform specialized work along

standardized lines involving well-established techniques and procedures which may have been catalogued and described in manuals or other sources. Such inspectors rely on techniques and skills acquired by special training or experience. They have some leeway in the performance of their work but only within closely prescribed limits.

29. C.F.R. § 541.203

Although employers' counsel ought to scrutinize carefully such examples, the guidance they provide may still be of limited assistance since they focus on relatively few of the thousands of positions in the American workplace. Moreover, as *Johnson* and the qualifying language in each of the foregoing examples suggest, individual variations in the nature and scope of employees' duties can be dispositive even within an individual job category established by an employer. Seemingly "easy" determinations may not be so easy in light of such variations, and employers and their attorneys therefore must be careful not to rely too much on either category-based examples or earlier judicial decisions and opinion letters.

8. *Overtime Pay.* Given the higher social standing of white-collar workers, why would the plaintiffs want to *not* be exempt? While it may be too obvious to stress, they were not concerned with whether they were paid $7.25 an hour — undoubtedly, they received more than that. These are not "minimum wage" cases at all, but illustrate that the FLSA can play an important role for higher-status employees who are asked to work overtime. Big Lots violated the law, but the court held it did not do so "willfully." Can you understand how easy it might be for an employer dealing with "white collar" or even "professional" workers not to focus on problems such as those raised in these cases? And what about the policy questions — assuming that the plaintiffs are being paid well above the $7.25 minimum wage after all their hours are counted, is it appropriate to require premium pay for "overtime"?

9. *Harms and Remedies.* Uncertainty is not the only reason that white-collar exemptions are frequently litigated: The amount of money potentially at stake provides an obvious incentive for these claims. This is particularly true for those cases brought as "collective" actions, a form of representative action (similar to a class action) expressly provided for in the FLSA, *see* 29 U.S.C. § 216(b), in which large numbers of employees may join together to seek relief. *Johnson* is fairly typical — the litigation was pursued at least initially as a collective action involving many employees who were not paid overtime over long periods of time. In these kinds of cases, if the employer turns out to be wrong, liability for unpaid overtime compensation alone may climb into the millions of dollars. Indeed, the damages in *Johnson* — almost $130,000 for only two employees — gives you a sense of these stakes. The case also illustrates that employers may be subject to "liquidated damages" — an additional amount equal to the amount of unpaid wages — for violations of the FLSA's overtime and minimum wage mandates. *See* 29 U.S.C. § 216(b). The court may, however, in its discretion award lesser or no liquidated damages if it finds that the employer's actions giving rise to FLSA liability were in good faith and that the employer had reasonable grounds for believing that his act or omission was not a violation. *See* 29 U.S.C. § 260; 29 C.F.R. § 790.22. Moreover, prevailing FLSA plaintiffs are also awarded their reasonable attorneys' fees. *See* 29 U.S.C. § 216(b). Finally, any person who willfully violates the provisions of the FLSA may be subject to criminal fines and imprisonment. *See* 29 U.S.C. § 216(a).

This potential liability accounts for the many high-profile cases, verdicts, and settlements in these cases in recent years. For example, like the "manager" cases discussed above, there has been a recent wave of overtime suits by employees in the financial industry. *See, e.g.*, Posting of Paul M. Second to WorkplaceProfBlog, http://lawprofessors.typepad.com/laborprof_blog/2006/05/smith_barney_ov.html (May 31, 2006) (discussing Citigroup's settlement with employees for $98 million). And there have been many suits brought by other kinds of workers resulting in large payouts. *See, e.g.*, http://www.lawyersandsettlements.com/settlements/employment-settlements/ (discussing a $22.5 million settlement between Cintas — a uniform provider — and delivery drivers it misclassified as exempt, and a $4 million settlement between Polo Ralph Lauren and commissioned sales employees).

As discussed in the notes following the *Ansoumana* case in Chapter 1, page 30, there have also been a number of successful and high-profile minimum-wage suits. However, as also mentioned, enforcement of wage and hour laws at the low end of the labor market is difficult and rare. *See id.* For this reason, wage and hour violations — sometimes referred to as "wage theft" — are widespread. *See, e.g.*, Brishen Rogers, *Toward Third-Party Liability for Wage Theft*, 11 Berkeley J. Empl. & Lab. L. 1, 10 n.33 (citing numerous recent studies showing that violations are common); *see also* Annette Bernhardt et al., The Gloves-Off Economy: Workplace Standards at the Bottom of the Labor Market 7-8 (2008) (same). Chapter 1 discusses a number of phenomena that contribute to this underenforcement problem, including "employer" coverage questions, insolvency of fly-by-night labor contractors, and the socioeconomic vulnerability and immigrant status of workers. Insufficient remedies to incentivize private attorneys to bring these claims is another reason, since, in contrast to claims for overtime by higher-wage workers, the potential damages for lost wage claims for low-wage workers often do not add up to much. Still another factor is the array of procedural hurdles workers must overcome to obtain relief under the FLSA, including the statute's collective action mechanism for consolidating claims, 29 U.S.C. § 216(b), which, unlike ordinary class actions, require workers to opt into the suit. *See* Craig Becker and Paul Strauss, *Representing Low-Wage Workers in the Absence of a Class: The Peculiar Case of Section 16 of the Fair Labor Standards Act and the Underenforcement of Minimum Labor Standards*, 92 Minn. L. Rev. 1317 (2006); Nantiya Ruan, *Facilitating Wage Theft: How Courts Use Procedural Rules to Undermine Substantive Rights of Low-Wage Workers*, 63 Vand. L. Rev. 727 (2010). Due to a chronic lack of resources, the DOL and state agencies traditionally have been unable to fill the enforcement gap. *See* Gloves Off, *supra*, at 13.

10. *Erring on the Side of Safety?* Unlike mistakenly classifying an employee as exempt, mistakenly classifying an employee as nonexempt is unlikely to harm the employee. Since erroneously treating the employee as exempt poses great risks to the employer in terms of unpaid overtime plus interest, liquidated damages, and paying its own attorneys' fees and litigation costs and those of the plaintiff, it would seem that employers might choose to err on the side of classifying workers as nonexempt. But employers might discount the risks of liability by the (un)likelihood that the employee or the DOL will actually bring suit and prevail. Depending on the employer's view of the risks, the employer may be willing to accept the possibility of downstream liability to avoid paying overtime in the near term. And erring on the side of nonexempt status has its own obvious problem: the risk of substantial overtime payments. However, an employer who chooses this path could also limit such costs by avoiding overtime and hiring additional workers. Can you appreciate how complex a legal and business decision it is to decide whether positions are exempt or not? Realize too that over the course of time, even correct decisions may have to be reconsidered in light of changing workplace practices.

11. *Private Ordering Again.* We started our discussion of the FLSA by saying that there is relatively little role for private ordering. That's certainly true with respect to the substantive provisions — the workers could not prospectively waive their rights to overtime compensation in order to, say, get more overtime hours. But the exemptions analyzed in these cases can be viewed as opening a door to private ordering. An employer's structuring a job in certain ways will bring the employee within or without the exemption. Of course, there are real, if not legal, constraints on this type of planning. Hiring subordinates might result in exemption for the supervisor, but it also results in two more workers protected by the FLSA.

PROBLEM

11-1. Suppose you are an attorney at a large law firm. You have been asked by the firm's managing partner to give her advice on whether various "paralegals" are exempt employees. You are confident that the vast majority of paralegals are not exempt as "learned professionals," given that the new regulations explicitly provide that only paralegals possessing specialized degrees in other professional fields and applying that knowledge are exempt as such professionals. *See* 29 C.F.R. §541.301(e)(7). But might some paralegals be administrative employees?

You know that most paralegals in your firm — like the bulk of paralegals elsewhere — simply assist attorneys in completing various tasks, including drafting and filing legal documents and forms, preparing for trial, reviewing documents, communicating with clients, organizing documents and materials, performing basic compilations, and engaging in basic legal research. As to whether paralegals whose primary duties fit this description are exempt under the administrative exemption, your research reveals a recent Department of Labor Opinion Letter — providing a nonbinding legal opinion based on the facts provided by the employer — that offers a fairly definitive "no," indicating that such employees do not exercise the level of judgment and discretion necessary to satisfy the exemption's requirements:

> It continues to be our opinion that the duties of paralegal employees do not involve the exercise of discretion and independent judgment of the type required by section 541.200(a)(3) of the final regulations, thus an analysis of whether their work is related to management or general business operations is not necessary. The outline of the duties of the paralegal employees you provide describes the use of skills rather than discretion and independent judgment. The paralegals typically are drafting particular documents to assist attorneys on a particular case or matter. The paralegals are not themselves formulating or implementing management policies, utilizing authority to waive or deviate from established policies, providing expert advice, or planning business objectives in accordance with the dictates of 29 C.F.R. §541.202(b). Thus, . . . the paralegal employees appear to fit more appropriately into that category of employees who apply particular skills and knowledge in preparing assignments. Employees who apply such skills and knowledge generally are not exercising independent judgment, even if they have some leeway in reaching a conclusion. In addition, most jurisdictions have strict prohibitions against the unauthorized practice of law by laypersons. Under the American Bar

Association's Code of Professional Responsibility, a delegation of legal tasks to a lay person is proper only if the lawyer maintains a direct relationship with the client, supervises the delegated work, and has complete professional responsibility for the work produced. The implication of such strictures is that the paralegal employees you describe would not have the amount of authority to exercise independent judgments with regard to legal matters necessary to bring them within the administrative exemption.

Wage and Hour Division, U.S. Department of Labor, Opinion Letter FLSA2005-54, 2005 WL 3638473 (December 16, 2005).

Despite the Opinion Letter, you know that paralegal duties vary enormously in your firm, and there is no formal job description for any of them. Indeed, some of the more experienced and successful paralegals in your firm have responsibilities requiring a significant amount of judgment. Accordingly, you inquire further and learn some pertinent information with regard to four such paralegals. In addition to performing the basic duties described above:

> Adrianne works in the Family Law group and is largely responsible for initial client screening and intake decisions;
>
> Boris, who has worked in the firm's Corporate Group for 15 years, has authority to update and edit the department's library of standard forms;
>
> Carlos is the person primarily responsible for pretrial document management in several multimillion-dollar cases for the Commercial Litigation group; and
>
> Devon, who works in your firm's human resources department, exercises fairly broad de facto authority to make various types of regulatory compliance decisions.

Under any of these circumstances, would the paralegal be exempt as an administrative employee? Do the examples from the regulations discussed in Note 7 above help? Does the Department's Opinion letter determine the outcome for any of them, or does its discussion of the discretion and independent judgment factor suggest rather that the outcome is far from clear? What other information, if any, might be helpful in making your assessment?

---

b. FLSA Application Problems

When an employee is entitled to the FLSA's minimum wage protections, overtime protections, or both, application of the requirements is often straightforward. Nevertheless, a few application issues have produced litigation. One set of these issues involves the calculation of hours or compensable time, and another involves rate-of-pay determinations.

i. Compensable Time

In applying the FLSA's minimum wage and overtime mandates, one must determine the number of hours an employee has worked. The original statute contained no definition of "work," "compensable time," or any other term addressing what counts as work or working hours. In a series of early cases, the Supreme Court held that the statute's definition of "employ" — "to suffer or permit to work" — means that employers must pay employees for productive activities they control or require and are for the employer's primary benefit. *See Tennessee Coal, Iron, & R.R. Co. v. Muscoda Local No. 123*, 321 U.S. 590 (1944); *Armour & Co. v. Wantock*, 323 U.S. 126 (1944); *Skidmore v. Swift & Co.*, 323 U.S. 134 (1944). The Court also held, however, that time spent in "incidental" activities is also compensable. *See Skidmore, supra.* This lack of clarity led Congress to pass the Portal-to-Portal Act of 1947, *see* 29 U.S.C. § 254 (2006), which explicitly *excludes* from compensable time (1) travel to and from work and the work site prior to or after the workday or principal work activities and (2) activities that are "preliminary to or postliminary to said principal activity or activities," unless such travel or activities are included as compensable time pursuant to custom or contract.

What constitutes "preliminary or postliminary" activities, however, has been the subject of a fair amount of litigation. In general, an employee's activities preparing for work or after ending work, such as putting on or taking off work clothes, are noncompensable. However, where such activities are "an integral and indispensable part of the principal activities," they remain compensable. *Mitchell v. King Packing Co.*, 350 U.S. 260, 262-63 (1956). Thus, while donning work clothes is normally noncompensable, putting on and taking off uniforms at work pursuant to employer requirements or industry custom, or for safety reasons, is compensable. *See, e.g., IBP, Inc. v. Alvarez*, 546 U.S. 21 (2005) (finding that where putting on and taking off required work gear and uniforms are integral and indispensable activities, time spent moving to and from changing areas to work areas constitutes compensable time as does time waiting to doff gear). Also compensable is preparing necessary tools or equipment. *Mitchell*, 350 U.S. at 262-63 (finding knife-sharpening in a meat-packing plant is integral and indispensable to employee's principal activity of butchering); *see also* 29 C.F.R. § 790.8(c) (protective clothing for workers in a chemical plant).

Various other questions with regard to compensable time are addressed by detailed Department of Labor regulations. These include rules that distinguish compensable break times, sleep time, lunch and other meal times, and other "down" times from nonproductive portions of the day that are not compensable. In recent years, lawsuits over uncompensated break, meal, and other time have received significant attention. Perhaps most noteworthy is the recent wave of FLSA and state wage-and-hour lawsuits against Wal-Mart Stores, Inc., alleging various compensable time-related violations. Wal-Mart's total exposure in judgments and settlements was in the hundreds of millions of dollars. *See, e.g.,* Wage and Hour Lawsuits against Wal-Mart Settled for over $350 Million, December 30, 2008, *available at* http://www.aboutlawsuits.com/wage-and-hour-lawsuits-against-wal-mart-settled-2211/ (discussing Wal-Mart's agreement to pay between $352 million and $640 million to settle 63 wage and hour lawsuits filed in 42 states). *See generally* Michael Orey, *Wage Wars*, Businessweek, October 1, 2007, *available at* http://www.businessweek.com/magazine/content/07_40/b4052001.htm.

The status of "on-call" time is another area in which there is much controversy and litigation. This issue has produced many disputes in certain job categories — for example, emergency response personnel, automated equipment and information systems maintenance personnel, and nonexempt medical workers. This is unsurprising considering the number of hours at issue and, hence, the enormous economic stakes for both employees and employers.

≡ Pabst v. Oklahoma Gas & Electric Co.
228 F.3d 1128 (10th Cir. 2000)

LUCERO, Circuit Judge.

[W]e conclude that plaintiffs' on-call duties requiring them to continually monitor automated alarms by pager and computer were compensable under the FLSA. In so holding, we reject the argument that on-call monitoring time is not compensable unless contemporaneously reported to the employer as overtime. Further, we uphold the district court's determination that the employer's FLSA violation was not willful, and affirm both the award of prejudgment interest and the denial of liquidated damages. . . .

I

Plaintiffs are Electronic Technicians in Oklahoma Gas & Electric's ("OG&E") Facility Operations Department. Plaintiffs Pabst and Gilley were Electronic Technician I's ("Tech 1s") and plaintiff Barton was an Electronic Technician II ("Tech 2"). The three plaintiffs, along with two other employees, monitored automated heat, fire, and security systems in several OG&E buildings. Prior to an August 1994 reduction in force, these duties required twelve on-site employees working three eight-hour shifts.

Plaintiffs were on call to monitor OG&E building alarms weekdays from 4:30 p.m. to 7:30 a.m. and twenty-four hours a day on weekends. During these hours, alarms went to computers at Pabst's and Gilley's homes, as well as to pagers for all plaintiffs. After October 1994, Barton began to receive alarms at home via lap-top computer. Plaintiffs were required to respond to the alarms initially within ten minutes, then, after October 1996, within fifteen minutes. Failure to respond within the time limit was grounds for discipline. Each plaintiff was assigned, and required always to carry, an alpha-numeric pager. These pagers were only 70% reliable. The short response time, coupled with unreliable pagers, forced plaintiffs to remain at or near their homes while on call.

The district court found that plaintiffs received an average of three to five alarms per night, not including pages for security issues. Although not all alarms required plaintiffs to report to the office — it appears many could be fixed by remote computer — the district court found it took an average of forty-five minutes to respond to each alarm. Neither party disputes those findings on appeal.

[The district court also found that the employer did not utilize a rotational on-call schedule. A rotation "would not have been feasible because of the frequency of alarms and plaintiffs' differing areas of expertise."]

According to plaintiffs, their supervisor instructed them to report only on-call time spent responding to an alarm. OG&E paid plaintiffs for at least one hour for each alarm to which they responded, and two hours if they had to return to OG&E facilities. Plaintiffs apparently reported some, but not all, of the alarms they answered, but did not claim as overtime the remainder of their time spent on call.

Considerable testimony was presented regarding the extent to which monitoring interfered with plaintiffs' personal activities. Most significantly, an average of three to five alarms per night, each requiring on average forty-five minutes of work, severely disrupted plaintiffs' sleep habits; indeed, they testified to rarely experiencing more than five hours of uninterrupted sleep per night. In addition, even during waking hours, plaintiffs were unable to pursue many personal activities while on call because of the need to come into their homes to check their computers every fifteen minutes.

The district court found plaintiffs' on-call time compensable under the FLSA and awarded them compensation for fifteen hours per weekday and twenty-four hours per Saturday and Sunday, less any hours already paid for responding to alarms. . . .

II . . .

"Employ" is defined as including "to suffer or permit to work." § 203(g). The pertinent question, and one with which courts have struggled, is whether on-call time is "work" for purposes of the statute. The FLSA does not explicitly address the issue of on-call time.[1] Courts, however, have developed a jurisprudence of on-call time, based on the Supreme Court cases of *Armour & Co. v. Wantock*, 323 U.S. 126 (1944), and *Skidmore v. Swift & Co.*, 323 U.S. 134 (1944). Those cases determine the relevant inquiry to be whether an employee is "engaged to wait" or "waiting to be engaged," *Skidmore*, or, alternatively, whether on-call time is spent predominantly for the benefit of the employer or the employee, *see Armour*. Necessarily, the inquiry is highly individualized and fact-based, and "requires consideration of the agreement between the parties, the nature and extent of the restrictions, the relationship between the services rendered and the on-call time, and all surrounding circumstances," *Boehm v. Kansas City Power & Light Co.*, 868 F.2d 1182, 1185 (10th Cir. 1989) (citing *Skidmore*). We also focus on the degree to which the burden on the employee interferes with his or her personal pursuits. *See Armitage v. City of Emporia*, 982 F.2d 430, 432 (10th Cir. 1992). Several facts are relevant in assessing that burden: number of calls, required response time, and ability to engage in personal pursuits while on call. *See id.; Renfro v. City of Emporia*, 948 F.2d 1529, 1537-38 (10th Cir. 1991).

A

OG&E argues that it did not know plaintiffs were working the entire time they were on call and thus did not "suffer or permit" them to work. 29 U.S.C. § 203(g). Its theory goes as follows: Plaintiffs were responsible for reporting their own overtime;[2] because they reported only time spent responding to calls (and apparently not even all of that), rather than *all* of their on-call time, OG&E lacked knowledge that they were

---

1. Although regulations promulgated by the Department of Labor address that issue, they are unhelpful to our analysis because they fail to anticipate a scenario, like that in the present case, in which an on-call employee is able to perform his or her duties from a location away from the employer's premises. *See* 29 C.F.R. § 785.17 (stating that an "on call" employee is working if "required to remain on call on the employer's premises or so close thereto that he cannot use the time effectively for his own purposes"). More helpful are those regulations applicable to fire protection and law enforcement employees. *See* 29 C.F.R. § 553.221(d) (stating that time spent on call is compensable if "the conditions placed on the employee's activities are so restrictive that the employee cannot use the time effectively for personal pursuits").

2. Plaintiffs worked a forty-hour week in addition to their time on call. Thus, to the extent on-call time was working time, it was compensable at the overtime rate. *See* 29 U.S.C. § 207.

working and therefore did not suffer or permit them to work. This argument misinterprets the nature of the on-call time inquiry and borders on the disingenuous.

As a factual matter, OG&E's purported lack of actual knowledge is dubious. Plaintiffs cite record testimony detailing a reprimand Pabst received for attempting to report the entire time spent monitoring systems as overtime. . . . More significantly, OG&E's policy informed plaintiffs they would be compensated only for on-call time spent responding to an alarm. The only logical inference was that they would not be compensated for time spent monitoring their computers and pagers, unless they took some specific action responding to an alarm. To claim, then, that OG&E did not know plaintiffs were working because they did not report every hour of their evenings and weekends as overtime is misleading. While OG&E arguably may have lacked knowledge of the legal proposition that the FLSA required compensating plaintiffs for their on-call time under the system at issue, OG&E certainly knew that plaintiffs were performing the duties they had been assigned.

OG&E relies heavily on *Davis v. Food Lion*, 792 F.2d 1274, 1276 (4th Cir. 1986) for its knowledge theory. In *Davis*, the court found that "Food Lion has an established policy which prohibits employees from working unrecorded, so-called 'off-the-clock', hours." Davis argued that Food Lion's "Effective Scheduling" system required him to work such off-the-clock hours in order to perform his required duties and avoid reprimand. The Fourth Circuit held the FLSA "required Davis to prove Food Lion's actual or constructive knowledge of his overtime work," and found no clear error in the district court's "factual finding that Food Lion has no actual or constructive knowledge of Davis's off-the-clock work."

Davis is not applicable to the case before us. First, there is no evidence of anything like an explicit prohibition on plaintiffs' performing after-hours monitoring duties; on the contrary, such was the very essence of their responsibilities. Moreover, *Davis* was not, as plaintiffs correctly note, an on-call time case. In the on-call context, an employer who creates an on-call system obviously has constructive, if not actual, knowledge of employees' on-call duties. An employer must evaluate whether those duties are compensable under the FLSA, and if the employer concludes they are not, the employees do not bear the burden of submitting overtime requests for hours that fall outside the definition of what the employer classifies as compensable. Plaintiffs reported (apparently with some omissions) the hours to which they were entitled under OG&E's policy. That they did not report the entirety of their remaining on-call hours does not preclude the obvious conclusion that OG&E had knowledge of their on-call status.

[OG&E argued that its rotating on-call schedule meant that it had neither actual nor constructive knowledge of the full extent of plaintiffs' on-call hours. The argument was that OG&E believed only one plaintiff to be on call during a given week, and thus it did not know of the other two. But the district court noted that there was strong evidence against any such rotational schedule and that even OG&E conceded that there were weeks when two employees recorded time despite the supposed rotation. There was no clear error in the district court's findings.]

B

Whether a particular set of facts constitutes compensable "work" under the FLSA is a legal question we review de novo. *See Berry v. County of Sonoma*, 30 F.3d

1174, 1180 (9th Cir. 1994). In *Renfro*, we granted FLSA compensation to firefighters for their on-call time. *Renfro*'s facts include the following:

> the firefighter must be able to report to the stationhouse within twenty minutes of being paged or be subject to discipline; that the on-call periods are 24-hours in length; and primarily that the calls are frequent-a firefighter may receive as many as 13 calls during an on-call period, with a stated average frequency of 3-5 calls per on-call period.

OG&E emphasizes that all but one published Tenth Circuit case addressing on-call time have found it non-compensable. Counting published cases, however, is meaningless in resolving a fact-intensive question such as the compensability of on-call time. Rather, the proper question is which case is most analogous. . . . In sum, this case is far more analogous to *Renfro* than to the more numerous precedents cited by OG&E.

Although OG&E complains bitterly against having to compensate plaintiffs for working twenty-four hours a day, seven days a week, the cost to an employer of an "always on call" arrangement does not mean that such a system is not cognizable under the FLSA, so long as the on-call time qualifies as work under the relevant FLSA precedents. While one circuit has held that always being on call, while extremely burdensome, does not in and of itself make the on-call time compensable for FLSA purposes, *see Bright v. Houston Northwest Med. Ctr. Survivor, Inc.*, 934 F.2d 671, 678-79 (5th Cir. 1991) (en banc), another circuit found that requiring employees to monitor and respond all day, every day is a factor weighing in favor of compensability, *see Cross v. Arkansas Forestry Comm'n*, 938 F.2d 912, 916-17 (8th Cir. 1991) (holding that on-call time is compensable under the FLSA because employees were required to continuously monitor transmissions and respond within thirty minutes, and because they were subject to on-call status twenty-four hours per day for every day of a work period). We agree with both *Bright* and *Cross*: Although always being on call is not dispositive, such an added burden is relevant in assessing the extent to which all-the-time on-call duty deprives employees of the ability to engage in personal activities.

The only significant difference between the burden on the plaintiffs in *Renfro* and the burden on Pabst, Gilley, and Barton is that plaintiffs here often did not have to report to the employer's workplace in order to respond to calls. This lighter burden, however, is offset by the fact that plaintiffs, unlike the firefighters in *Renfro*, were not on call for "six shifts of twenty-four hours each in a 19-day cycle," but rather during *all* of their off-premises time. The frequency of calls here actually is greater than in *Renfro* because plaintiffs' calls during weekdays occurred during a fifteen hour, rather than a twenty-four hour, period. Additionally, in *Renfro*, we found on-call time compensable despite the fact that the firefighters "had participated in sports activities, socialized with friends and relatives, attended business meetings, gone shopping, gone out to eat, babysitted, and performed maintenance or other activities around their home." *Renfro* controls the application of the FLSA to the facts before us, and leads us to hold that the district court was correct in finding plaintiffs' on-call time compensable.

III

We next consider OG&E's claims that the award of overtime compensation should be reduced by subtracting out several time periods.

We reject, as a matter of law, OG&E's argument that time spent in personal pursuits should be subtracted. The relevant inquiry in on-call cases is not whether plaintiffs' duties prevented them from engaging in any and all personal activities during on-call time; rather it is "whether 'the time is spent predominantly for the employer's benefit or the employee's.'" *Boehm* (quoting *Armour*). This is a yes-no inquiry—whose benefit predominated? OG&E cites no authority for the proposition that a court must determine whose benefit predominated during each on-call hour. *Cf. Renfro* (holding firefighters' on-call time compensable even though they engaged in some personal pursuits during that time). OG&E's other arguments for reductions in the damages award, which pertain to individual plaintiffs, are factual issues subject to clear error review.

OG&E argues that Barton should not have been awarded overtime compensation from October 1994 through October 1, 1996 because during that time he was monitoring alarms only by pager and not by computer. OG&E primarily focuses on the comparatively small amount of remote overtime Barton charged during that period, as compared to Gilley and Pabst. However, we are persuaded the district court did not clearly err in determining that Barton, like Gilley and Pabst, received between three and five pages per night during this period, despite the comparatively smaller amount of overtime Barton recorded. . . .

[The court affirmed the district court's denial of liquidated damages, finding that the court did not abuse its discretion in concluding that OG&E's actions were reasonable and in good faith, despite its mistaken belief that the on-call time was noncompensable.]

NOTES

1. *A Costly Mistake.* Although this case was brought by only three employees, and the court ultimately rejected their bid for liquidated damages, OG&E's liability was still significant, given that these employees consistently worked a 24/7 schedule. Had OG&E known that the FLSA required overtime compensation for this time, how might it have structured its on-call regime to limit the amount it would have to pay out to its technicians? Could it have instituted a rotation system? Might it have been cheaper to hire a fourth tech for a night shift than to pay overtime? Might knowledge of potential liability also have influenced how OG&E ran its operations—for example, what equipment it uses, what times of day this equipment should be running, how many resources it puts into daytime maintenance? The possibility of more reliable pagers jumps off the page.

2. *Disparate Outcomes and Planning Implications.* The *Pabst* court recognizes the differing views of the various circuit courts on when on-call time is compensable. Indeed, these differences are even more profound when one digs a little deeper. For example, *Bright v. Houston Northwest Medical Center Survivor, Inc.*, 934 F.2d 671 (5th Cir. 1991) (en banc), did not simply hold, as *Pabst* suggests, that always being on-call "does not in and of itself make the on-call time compensable for FLSA purposes." Rather, the *Bright* court held as a matter of law that a biomedical equipment repair technician on-call around the clock was not entitled to compensation for on-call periods except those in which he actually worked because (1) he was not required to remain at or very near the hospital where he worked, (2) he was free to be at his home or at any place he chose without advising his employer, and (3) he was "subject only to the restrictions that he be reachable by beeper, not be intoxicated, and be able to arrive at the hospital in 'approximately' twenty minutes." *Id.* at 676; *see also Adair v. Charter Cty. of Wayne*, 452 F.3d 482 (6th Cir. 2006) (finding officers employed by county airport were not entitled to overtime pay for off-duty time during which they were required to carry pagers and remain relatively near to work because they could engage in regular activities).

In light of these differing approaches and outcomes, the issue of on-call time provides a nice example of the planning difficulties for employers with operations in more than one part of the country. Should such an employer treat similarly situated employees differently based on local circuit law? Are there other reasons or constraints that might lead an employer not to make such distinctions?

3. *From Pagers to PDAs.* Pabst involved a pager, technology that is so last-millennium. In an era of smart phones, employees are increasingly expected to respond during what are, in theory, nonworking hours. Even when such responses are not expected, employees often do answer e-mails or calls off hours. *See, e.g.,* Cheryl Corley, *Using Your BlackBerry Off-Hours Could Be Overtime*, NPR.org, August 14, 2010, http://www.npr.org/templates/story/story.php?storyId=129184907 (discussing a suit brought by a Chicago police officer for unpaid overtime because he felt obligated to log in to the Blackberry his department provided often after his shift was over). The employer might or might not know of the activity, or, at least, the extent of it. But, as we saw in Chapter 6, employers typically have the legal freedom and technological ability to track employee use of employer equipment 24/7. How should the law deal with this reality? *See generally* Sean L. McLaughlin, Comment, *Controlling Smart-Phone Abuse: The Fair Labor Standards Act's Definition of "Work" in Non-exempt Employee Claims for Overtime*, 58 U. Kan. L. Rev. 737 (2010). If you were an employer's attorney would you consider advising employees not to use company e-mail, phone, or other electronic devices during nonwork hours? That seems extreme, but the risks of liability might be pretty high. The alternative of monitoring such use and reacting on a more individual basis also seems problematic.

4. *Line Drawing.* Compensation for on-call time provides yet another example of the difficultly of drawing lines under the FLSA and the corresponding costs and risks for employers and employees trying to determine *ex ante* what the terms of their relationship will be. Congress may be institutionally incapable of drawing finer distinctions to avoid such problems. But, why can't or why doesn't the DOL attempt to make things clearer? In answering this question, consider the potential costs and risks of clarity. For example, are unforeseen loopholes and other unintended consequences more likely? Also, does greater specificity increase the need for more frequent regulatory amendments?

5. *Computer Personnel.* One obvious growth area in the "on-call" context in recent years involves information technology ("IT") and computer personnel. Given that virtually all public and private employers use such technology, and many, if not most, need their systems to operate 24 hours a day, employees are needed who can respond when there are software, hardware, and other problems. However, these employees pose an additional wrinkle to the "on-call" question. As mentioned above, some computer personnel are exempt under the special exemption for computer employees. *See* 29 U.S.C.A. §213(a)(17). The new governing regulation, which closely tracks the statutory language, provides as follows:

29 C.F.R. §541.400 General Rule for Computer Employees. . . .

(b) The section 13(a)(1) exemption applies to any computer employee compensated on a salary or fee basis at a rate of not less than $455 per week . . . , exclusive of board, lodging or other facilities, and the section 13(a)(17) exemption applies to any computer employee compensated on an hourly basis at a rate not less than $27.63 an hour. In addition, under either section 13(a)(1) or section 13(a)(17) of the Act, the exemptions apply only to computer employees whose primary duty consists of:

(1) The application of systems analysis techniques and procedures, including consulting with users, to determine hardware, software or system functional specifications;

(2) The design, development, documentation, analysis, creation, testing or modification of computer systems or programs, including prototypes, based on and related to user or system design specifications;

(3) The design, documentation, testing, creation or modification of computer programs related to machine operating systems; or

(4) A combination of the aforementioned duties, the performance of which requires the same level of skills.

The exemption does not include employees primarily engaged in the manufacture or repair of computer hardware and related equipment or those who merely use computers in their work. *See* 29 C.F.R. §541.401.

In light of this exemption, think about the various kinds of computer or information employees with whom you have worked at school or while employed. Are any or all of your school's or your employer's IT employees exempt? Recall, of course, that some may already be exempt under the administrative or executive exemptions. Is this easy to determine or would you require more detail regarding duties to make an assessment? *Cf.* Wage and Hour Division, U.S. Department of Labor, Opinion Letter FLSA FLSA2006-42, 2006 WL 3406603 (October 26, 2006) (opining that an IT Support Specialist position in which the employee is primarily responsible for "installing, configuring, testing, and troubleshooting computer applications, networks, and hardware" does not involve the exercise of sufficient discretion to qualify for the administrative exemption and does not involve the "application of systems analysis techniques and procedures, including consulting with users, to determine hardware, software or system functional specifications" necessary to qualify for the computer employee exemption).

Among computer employees, how many are "on-call," at least some of the time? What about the *Pabst* plaintiffs? The employer never argued that these employees were exempt, only that their on-call time was not compensable. Do you see why?

In terms of policy, does it make sense to exempt these computer employees from the FLSA's strictures, including the overtime provisions that might mandate premium compensation for when they are on-call (assuming such time would otherwise satisfy the test articulated in *Pabst*)? In other words, are these computer employees more like learned and creative professionals or more like the technicians in *Pabst*? In answering this question consider not only what such computer employees do, but also their relative ability to protect themselves in the market. Is your answer today different than it might have been in 2000, at the height of the Internet and technology boom?

PROBLEM

11-2.   Oops, I Did It [Violated the FLSA?] Again. . . . This item appeared in Yahoo! News on March 30, 2006:

Former Spears Bodyguards Sue for Overtime

Three men hired to guard pop star Britney Spears have filed a lawsuit claiming they worked long hours and were not paid overtime.

The lawsuit, filed Tuesday in Superior Court, names three companies — Britney Brands Inc., Britney Touring Inc. and Team Tours Inc. — as responsible for not properly compensating former bodyguards Lonnie Jones, Randy Jones and Silas Dukes.

Together, the three men are seeking damages exceeding $25,000 for unpaid wages and benefits, their attorney Daniel Emilio said Wednesday. Messages left at the office of Spears' publicist Leslie Sloane Zelnick were not immediately returned.

Randy Jones and Dukes worked 12- to 16-hour shifts and were required to be on call 24 hours a day during trips with Spears, according to the lawsuit. Lonnie Jones worked 12-hour shifts, the suit said.

The trio claimed they were only paid a "straight salary," missed meals and didn't receive overtime pay.

Hired in 2004, the men claim they were laid off on Nov. 30, 2005 without receiving a final paycheck.

http://news.yahoo.com/s/ap/20060330/ap_on_en_mu/people_spears.

Suppose you were contacted by Ms. Spears' legal team and asked to assist in determining the risk of liability under the FLSA and preparing a possible defense. They send you the complaint, which, under California's liberal pleading regime, provides little detail in addition to what is set forth above. Their two questions for you are (1) whether these bodyguards might be exempt under the white-collar exemptions and (2) if not, whether their "on-call" time might constitute compensable hours. As to the first question, what additional information would you need to make this determination? Given what you know at this point, how likely is it that these bodyguards are exempt? As to the second question, what information would you need to determine whether the on-call time is compensable? Again, given what you know at this point, how likely is it that this time is compensable? Additionally, based on the facts provided so far, is there a possible further line of defense here? Hint: Take a look back at *Ansoumana. But see Schultz v. Capital Intern. Security, Inc.,* 460 F.3d 595 (4th Cir. 2006) (holding workers hired to provide security for Saudi prince were "employees" covered by FLSA because, among other things, prince and security company exercised nearly complete control over their jobs, they were paid a set rate per shift, some worked for the prince for several years, and he preferred workers who would stay over the long term).

Finally, switch gears and consider the plaintiffs' perspective. Although the complaint appears not to have done so at this point, could and should the plaintiffs have named Ms. Spears as a defendant in her personal capacity? After all, she's "not that innocent." Wouldn't that up the settlement value of the case?

---

ii. Calculating "Regular Rate of Pay"

As we have seen, the FLSA's overtime provisions require employers to pay covered workers "time and a half," that is, one and one-half times their "regular rate of pay" for hours in excess of 40 hours in any given week. *See* 29 U.S.C. § 207 (2006). What constitutes an employee's "regular rate of pay" is a fairly easy calculation when an employee receives only hourly wages or receives a salary and has a work week with standard hours. Thus, for example, an employee who receives a weekly salary of $1,000 for 40 hours of work has a regular rate of pay of $25 per hour. If the employee works 50 hours in a given week, the employer will have to pay the employee $1,375 for that week—$1,000 weekly salary for the first 40 hours plus $375 for the additional 10 hours ($25 multiplied by the 10 additional hours multiplied by the one-and-one-half overtime premium rate).

If the employee's salary compensates for fewer than 40 hours a week, then the employee is entitled to his or her regular rate for additional hours up to 40 hours, and the premium rate thereafter. Thus, for example, an employee who receives a weekly salary of $750 for 30 hours of work a week has a regular rate of $25 dollars per hour. If the employee works 50 hours in a given week, the employer will have to pay the employee $1,375 for that week—$750 weekly salary for 30 hours, plus $250 for 10 additional hours ($25 multiplied by 10), plus $375 for the remaining 10 hours ($25 multiplied by the 10 additional hours plus one-half that amount, representing the overtime premium).

The regular rate of pay calculation becomes more difficult, however, when the employee receives a salary for hours that are contemplated to fluctuate week-to-week or receives forms of compensation in addition to his or her hourly wage or salary. If the employee is so employed, a DOL regulation allows the employer to use a fluctuating workweek computation method to determine the regular rate and overtime pay. *See* 29 C.F.R. § 778.114. This method still guarantees an overtime premium for each overtime hour worked, but, by allowing a recomputation of the regular rate each week based on the total hours worked, it in effect allows the employer to pay less of a premium per hour the more hours the employee works in any given week.

However, this calculation method is available only when (1) there is "a clear mutual understanding of the parties" that the salary is compensation for "the hours worked each workweek, whatever their number, rather than for working 40 hours or some other fixed weekly work period"; (2) the salary is sufficient to ensure a rate not less than the applicable minimum wage rate for every hour worked in any week (regardless of the number of hours worked); and (3) the employee actually receives the extra compensation, in addition to the base salary, for all overtime hours worked at a rate not less than one-half the employee's regular rate of pay. Thus, this is one context in which private ordering can alter an employee's rights under the FLSA, although the statute limits the potential impact of such ordering and its requirements provide baseline protections against employer abuse.

In terms of determining the employee's regular rate of pay when the employee receives compensation in addition to a regular wage or salary, the FLSA provides that this rate shall include "all remuneration for employment paid to, or on behalf of, the employee," unless the type of additional compensation falls within one of eight exclusions such as Christmas or birthday gifts, vacation pay, bonuses, and fringe benefits. *See* 29 U.S.C. § 207(e). Determining the meaning of "remuneration for employment" and interpreting and applying the exclusions have proven difficult in some circumstances.

Acton v. City of Columbia
436 F.3d 969 (8th Cir. 2006)

LAY, Circuit Judge.

Chris N. Acton and ninety-nine current and former firefighters (the "firefighters") employed by the City of Columbia, Missouri (the "City") brought suit against the City for failing to include a series of payments in the firefighters' regular rate of pay, in violation of 29 U.S.C. § 207(e) (the Fair Labor Standards Act or "FLSA").

[The district court granted the firefighters' summary judgment] motion in part, ruling that sick leave buy-back monies should be included in the firefighters' regular rate of pay. However, the district court also denied the firefighters' motion in part, ruling that monies received under the City's meal allowance program were excluded from the regular rate. Finally, the district court found no evidence that the City willfully violated the FLSA. . . .

IV.   Sick Leave Buy-Back

Under the City's sick leave buy-back program, firefighters who work twenty-four hour work shifts during the course of one year accumulate ten days of sick leave. Firefighters who fail to use their sick leave are entitled to "sell back" any of the ten unused sick days to the City in exchange for a lump sum payment equal to 75% their regular hourly pay, provided the firefighter has amassed at least six months sick leave. The firefighters contend that all monies received from the sale of sick leave should be included in their regular rate of pay. The regular rate of pay calculation is critical because it provides the base point from which the firefighters' overtime compensation is calculated.

A.   *The Fair Labor Standards Act*

Section 207(e) of the FLSA provides, in relevant part, that "all remuneration for employment paid to, or on behalf of, the employee" must be included in the employee's regular rate of pay, provided such remuneration is not prohibited by one of eight statutory exclusions listed under § 207(e)(1)-(8). 29 U.S.C. § 207(e). There is a statutory presumption "that remuneration in any form is included in the regular rate calculation. The burden is on the employer to establish that the remuneration in question falls under an exception." *Madison v. Res. for Human Dev. Inc.*, 233 F.3d 175, 187 (3d Cir. 2000).

Before beginning our analysis, we must clarify a preliminary matter of statutory construction under the FLSA that has been a point of confusion between the parties. First, the City argues sick leave buy-back monies do not constitute remuneration for employment. Next, the City contends sick leave buy-back monies are also excluded under § 207(e)(2) because they "are not made as compensation for [the employee's] hours of employment." *Id*. However, the language "not made as compensation for [the employee's] hours of employment" posited in § 207(e)(2) is but a mere re-articulation of the "remuneration for employment" requirement set forth in the preambulary language of § 207(e). Section 207(e)(2), properly understood, operates not as a separate basis for exclusion, but instead clarifies the types of payments that do not constitute remuneration for employment for purposes of § 207. Therefore, we treat the City's "remuneration for employment" and § 207(e)(2) arguments under the same mode of analysis. Finally, because both provisions modify one other, we must necessarily consider the express requirements of § 207(e)(2) and the federal regulations interpreting it when determining if sick leave buy-back monies constitute remuneration for employment.

1. Remuneration for Employment

Regulation 29 C.F.R. § 778.223 provides the touchstone for our inquiry because it addresses the scope of § 207(e)(2). Specifically, regulation § 778.223 addresses whether monies paid to employees for remaining on call are excluded from the regular rate under § 207(e)(2). The regulation concludes that monies paid to employees to remain on call, while not related to "any specific hours of work," are nevertheless awarded as "compensation for performing a duty involved in the employee's job" — namely, the employee's willingness and commitment to work unscheduled hours if requested. *See* 29 C.F.R. § 778.223. The plain language of the regulation makes clear that all monies paid as compensation for either a general or specific work-related duty should be included in the regular rate. The critical question before this court is whether sick leave buy-back monies compensate the firefighters for some specific or general duty of employment.

In order to qualify for sick leave buy-back payments, firefighters must come to work regularly for a period of several years in order to amass the requisite six month sick leave reserve. Then, the firefighters must also accrue additional sick leave in the present year in order to be eligible for buy-back. Thus, the primary effect of the buy-back program is to encourage firefighters to come to work regularly over a significant period of their employment tenure. We recognize consistent workplace attendance to be a general duty of employment and, therefore, rule that sick leave buy-back monies constitute remuneration for employment.[10]

The City sets forth three primary arguments to support its conclusion that sick leave buy-back payments are not remuneration for employment. First, the City argues its buy-back program was intended to promote two objectives unrelated to employee compensation. On the one hand, the sick leave buy-back program was intended to

---

10. We also note that sick leave buy-back monies do not resemble any of the payments expressly excluded under § 207(e)(2). *See* 29 C.F.R. § 778.224(a) (noting that payments excluded from the regular rate under § 207(e)(2) must "be 'similar' in character to the payments specifically described" in (e)(2)). Sick leave buy-back monies, in contrast to § 207(e)(2) payments, are awarded to employees for coming to work consistently, not for work that was never performed.

provide firefighters with a form of short-term disability insurance because the City does not have a disability policy covering employee illness or disability lasting six months or less. The sick leave buy-back program, with its six-month accrued sick leave requirement, was devised as a mechanism for employees to self-insure against personal illness or disability. Alternatively, the City argues its sick leave buy-back program discourages employees from treating sick leave as another form of vacation or personal leave because the program creates a money incentive for employees to accrue, but not use, their sick leave.

These arguments are not compelling. Even if the sick leave buy-back program was intended to provide employees with a form of short-term disability insurance and to discourage misuse of sick leave, one plain effect of the program is to reward regular workplace attendance through a non-discretionary, year-end, lump sum payment. The City's proffered justifications do not change the undisputed fact that the firefighters are plainly rewarded for regularly showing up for work over a period of years.

Second, the City also cites 29 C.F.R. § 825.125, a Department of Labor opinion letter, and a decision from a federal district court in the Northern District of Illinois to support its claim that bonuses awarded for perfect attendance do not require performance by the employee, but rather contemplate the absence of occurrences. 29 C.F.R. § 825.215 ("Bonuses for perfect attendance and safety do not require performance by the employee but rather contemplate the absence of occurrences."); Opinion Letter from Maria Echaveste, Administrator, U.S. Department of Labor (Mar. 21, 1994) ("Bonuses premised on 'perfect attendance' or 'perfect safety' are rewards not for work or production, but for compliance with rules."); *Dierlam v. Wesley Jessen Corp.*, 222 F. Supp. 2d 1052, 1057 (N.D. Ill. 2002) (noting that a bonus that does not require its recipient to meet production goals or quality standards "simply contemplates the non-occurrence of an event — [the recipient's] absence from work").

However, none of these three authorities address the applicability of § 207. Instead, each confronts the issue of whether an employee is entitled to a bonus for good attendance upon returning to work under the Family Medical Leave Act. The City's attempt to cite language taken out of context from authorities interpreting another federal statute in no way binds us in this case. To the extent the City uses these authorities to argue that consistent workplace attendance does not "require performance by the employee," we flatly disagree. We believe consistent workplace attendance *does* require performance. In the modern workplace, regular and prompt workplace attendance is a valued commodity, one for which the City appropriately rewards its employees.

Finally, the City cites the Sixth Circuit's decision in *Featsent v. City of Youngstown*, 70 F.3d 900 (6th Cir. 1995), to support its argument that sick leave buy-back monies do not constitute remuneration for employment. In *Featsent*, the Sixth Circuit ruled that monies paid to employees who did not submit medical claims and failed to use accrued sick leave were excluded from the regular rate of pay under § 207(e)(2) because such payments are "unrelated to the [employee's] compensation for services and hours of service."

We decline to follow the Sixth Circuit's decision in *Featsent*. The *Featsent* court failed to articulate any basis for its reasoning. The court did not distinguish regulation § 778.223 in reaching its conclusion, nor did it recognize and explain how payments awarded to an employee for not using accrued sick leave, which necessarily requires employees to work more days than they are required, is not tantamount to payment for services rendered. Because we are unpersuaded by the Sixth Circuit's analysis, we reject its conclusion.

2. Statutory Exceptions. . . .

Section 207(e)(5) provides:

> [E]xtra compensation provided by a premium rate paid for certain hours worked by the employee in any day or workweek because such hours are hours worked in excess of eight in a day or in excess of the maximum workweek applicable to such employee under subsection (a) or in excess of the employee's normal working hours or regular working hours, as the case may be[.]

The dissent argues sick leave monies should be excluded under § 207(e)(5) because they constitute premium payments for specific hours worked. This analysis fails for several reasons. First, sick leave monies are not paid for specific hours worked. Instead, these payments compensate employees for a record of consistent attendance over the course of several years, not simply for working days during a given year they are otherwise entitled to take off.

Second, in order for payments to be excluded under § 207(e)(5), they must be "paid for certain hours worked by the employee in any day or workweek because such hours are hours worked in excess of eight in a day or in excess of the maximum [required in a] workweek." *Id.* Even assuming, as the dissent does, that sick leave buy-back payments are paid in sole recognition for the specific days a firefighter chooses to work instead of calling in sick, there is still no basis to exclude such payments under § 207(e)(5). Section 207(e)(5), by its own terms, limits its applicability to payments made for certain hours worked in excess of the employee's normal daily or weekly schedule. Under the dissent's approach, buy-back payments are, at best, premium payments for working normally scheduled hours.

Finally, § 207(e)(5) plainly excludes only "premium" payments — that is, payments no less than one and one-third the employee's regular rate. *See* 29 C.F.R. § 778.308(b). The dissent creatively "compounds" sick leave buy-back payments, which are awarded at the sub-premium rate of 75% the firefighters' hourly wage, with the firefighters' base hourly wage. This ignores the fact that the premium payments themselves must be at least one and one-third the employee's hourly rate. *See id.* Be this as it may, the dissent's approach, taken to its logical conclusion, yields unsettling results. Under the dissent's theory, all extra monies paid to employees for specific hours worked may be "compounded" with the employee's regular hourly rate and excluded under § 207(e)(5), in contravention of the express requirements of 29 C.F.R. § 778.207(b). *See* 29 C.F.R. § 778.207(b) (stating that non-overtime premiums for specific hours worked, such as nightshift differentials and hazard pay, must be included in the regular rate). Therefore, we rule that § 207(e)(5) does not exclude sick leave buy-back payments from the regular rate of pay. . . .

LOKEN, Chief Judge, dissenting. . . .

Sick leave buy-back payments admittedly do not fit comfortably within the exclusion in 29 U.S.C. § 207(e)(2) for "payments made for occasional periods when no work is performed." But the court is wrong to suggest that such payments "are not related to specific duties or hours worked." In my view, sick leave buy-back payments are functionally equivalent to premium overtime pay that is expressly excluded from an employee's regular rate. Like overtime, and unlike true attendance bonuses, these payments relate to specific hours *worked* — the days that the employee chose to work rather than to use paid sick leave.

As the Supreme Court said in the FLSA's formative years, "[t]o permit overtime premium to enter into the computation of the regular rate would be to allow overtime premium on overtime premium — a pyramiding that Congress could not have intended." *Bay Ridge Operating Co. v. Aaron*, 334 U.S. 446, 464 (1948). This principle was codified in 1949. *See* 29 U.S.C. § 207(e)(5)-(e)(7). If sick leave buy-back payments fit awkwardly under § 207(e)(2) because they relate to hours worked, rather than to hours not worked, these payments are squarely within the purview of the three exclusions found in subsections (e)(5)-(e)(7) that apply to "extra compensation provided by a premium rate paid for certain hours worked."[14]

Section 207(e)(5) excludes "extra compensation provided by a premium rate paid for certain hours worked . . . because such hours are hours worked . . . in excess of the employee's . . . regular working hours." A firefighter who works one or more paid sick leave days has worked in excess of his "regular working hours." If otherwise eligible under the City's program, he may sell unused sick leave to bring his total pay for sick leave hours worked up to 175% of his regular rate. The related exclusion in § 207(e)(6) applies to "extra compensation provided by a premium rate paid for work by the employee on . . . regular days of rest" if the premium rate is not less than one and one-half times the regular rate. These exclusions were intended to prevent the pyramiding of "overtime on overtime." They have been applied to a variety of overtime compensation programs.

In response, the court asserts that sick leave buy-back payments are not compensation at a premium rate. This ignores economic reality. The City agreed to pay the plaintiff firefighters for ten days of sick leave each year. If sick leave is used, the City must pay another employee to do the work, presumably at a rate at least equal to the regular rate of the firefighter on sick leave. If the firefighter instead works, leaving his sick leave unused, the City through the buy-back program pays, on top of the regular rate already paid, a premium equal to 75% of the firefighter's regular rate. Thus, for those days worked, the firefighter is paid 175% of his regular rate. This premium is greater than and functionally no different than the premium the FLSA requires employers to pay for overtime work — not less than one and one-half times (150%) the employee's regular rate. *See* 29 U.S.C. § 207(a). And like overtime, extra compensation paid for unused sick leave is offset by the employer not incurring the expense of hiring additional workers or paying other employees to fill in.

It may make little difference whether the City's sick leave buy-back payments are excluded from a firefighter's regular rate under § 207(e)(2) because they are "similar to payments made when no work is performed due to illness," *Featsent*, or under § 207(e)(5) or (6) as overtime compensation paid at a premium rate. But the contrary decision of the district court and this court to include those payments in the regular rate both distorts FLSA principles and discourages use of a creative overtime payment device that benefits both employers and employees. I respectfully dissent from this decision.

---

14. Unlike the exclusion in § 207(e)(2) for payments for hours not worked, compensation excluded from the employee's regular rate under subsections (e)(5)-(e)(7) "shall be creditable toward overtime compensation payable pursuant to this section." § 207(h). . . .

NOTES

1. *Remuneration and Exclusions.* The majority engaged in a two-step inquiry. First, it had to decide whether the sick leave buy-back payments are "remuneration." That seems pretty clear, doesn't it? Why the fuss? Second, the court had to determine whether the payments, although remuneration, fell within one of the exclusions in the statute. The majority's explanation makes sense, doesn't it? But so does the dissent's! They come at the question using different paradigms. Who has the better approach? Why?

2. *Seeing the Forest.* Although the interpretation of the language of the statute and underlying regulations dominates the discussion, what are the real stakes in this case? In other words, now that the firefighters have prevailed, what effect will it have on their compensation? Who, in the buy-back program circumstance, may be benefiting under the surface? If you were the employer's counsel, would you recommend eliminating this or adjusting the employees' base rate of pay? Think about whether, going forward, this result is likely to be good, bad, or neutral for employees and employers.

3. *Planning Problems Continued.* Far more important than the particulars of the analysis in this case are the broader lessons for employment law counselors and human resources personnel. This case and the others in this chapter suggest that there are a number of traps for the unwary, and that each compensation decision must be analyzed from a number of perspectives to ensure the FLSA is not violated. Given the complexity and how costly mistakes may be, personnel and compensation decisions with potential FLSA implications ought to be undertaken with great care.

2. Other Wage Protections

At the federal level, the FLSA is the primary mechanism for dealing with perceived wage and hour abuses. However, federal law provides a number of other more narrowly drawn protections in certain contexts. For example, prevailing wage laws require various firms contracting with the federal government to compensate their workers at the prevailing minimum wage for like workers in the local labor market. *See, e.g.,* 40 U.S.C. §§ 3141-44, 3146, 3147 (Davis-Bacon Act); 41 U.S.C. §§ 35-43, 43a, 43b, 44, 45 (Walsh-Healey Act). Moreover, as mentioned previously, the Equal Pay Act mandates that male and female employees doing equal work in a workplace receive the same pay, absent some justification unrelated to sex.

But, as *Ansoumana* illustrates, there are also state and local wage and hour protections. This is because, unlike ERISA, discussed below, the FLSA does not preempt the field; that is, its protections are not exclusive. Thus, state and local governments may provide for wage and hour protections that exceed those in the FLSA. For example, many states have enacted their own prevailing wage laws for government contractors. Most states also have wage payment laws (including so-called "theft of service" statutes) that provide for civil and criminal liability for failure to pay promised wages. *See, e.g.,* Rita J. Verga, *An Advocate's Toolkit: Using Criminal "Theft of Service" Laws to Enforce Workers' Right to Be Paid,* 8 N.Y. City L. Rev. 283 (2005). Indeed, to ensure wages are paid, New York and Wisconsin have taken the extraordinary step of imposing pro rata liability on certain shareholders for unpaid wages (if and when the corporation does not meet its wage obligations). *See* N.Y. Bus. Corp. § 630; Wis. Stat. § 180.0622.

States also impose what might be deemed "procedural" wage and hour protections; for instance, a California statute requires that commission agreements with certain sales representatives be in writing, and that the writing contain various information, including how the commission is computed. The statute also requires documentation of how payment is calculated when an employee's commissions are paid. *See* CAL. CIV. CODE §§ 1738.10-.16 (2010); *Baker v. American Horticulture Supply, Inc.* 111 Cal. Rptr.3d 695 (Cal. Ct. App. 2010) (discussing the statute).

In addition, many states have their own minimum wage and overtime protections. These laws vary greatly. *See* U.S. Department of Labor Employment Standards Administration Wage and Hour Division, Minimum Wage Laws in the States — July 1, 2010, *available at* http://www.dol.gov/esa/minwage/america.htm (listing state minimum wage and overtime protections). According to the DOL, as of July 1, 2010, five states have no minimum wage and five states have minimum wage requirements that are lower than the federal minimum. *See id.* Of course, the FLSA minimum wage governs most workers in these jurisdictions, and, thus, lower minimum wage standards will provide the floor only for those not within the FLSA. Approximately half of the states track the federal mandate, although their coverage may be broader. Fourteen states — including several northeastern states and all states touching the Pacific Ocean — and the District of Columbia have passed higher minimum wage requirements. The State of Washington currently has the highest basic minimum wage — $8.55 per hour — although Oregon is a close second at $8.40, followed by Connecticut, the District of Columbia, Illinois, and Nevada at $8.25. *See id.* These significantly higher wage floors and their periodic increases indicate that, although minimum wage increases happen only sporadically at the federal level, proponents continue to enjoy success in particular regions of the country.

Several states also have their own overtime regulations. California, for example, requires that firms pay workers double-time (twice the regular rate) for hours worked in excess of 12 hours per day or 48 hours per week. *See id.* It is worth noting that such a double-overtime regime could have profound effects on litigation awards and, hence, employer incentives and planning. Consider, for example, how the bodyguards' potential recovery in the Spears case — *see* Problem 11-2 — might differ under the California statute.

When possible under state law, municipalities may also regulate wages of employees within their borders. For example, as of January 1, 2010, San Francisco mandates a wage of $9.79. *See* City and County of San Francisco Labor Standards Enforcement, Minimum Wage Ordinance, Jan. 1, 2010, *available at* http://www.sfgsa.org/index .aspx?page=411. Another effort in this direction is the movement to have cities enact "living wage" laws governing municipal contractors. *See generally* Scott L. Cummings & Steven A. Boutcher, *Mobilizing Local Government Law for Low-Wage Workers*, 1 CHI. LEGAL F. 187, 195 (2009) (discussing the broad reach of the Los Angeles Living Wage Ordinance, which imposes wage obligations above the federal and state minimums on employers that receive financial benefits from the municipality); Clayton P. Gillette, *Local Redistribution, Living Wage Ordinances, and Judicial Intervention*, 101 Nw. U. L. REV. 1057 (2007) (discussing the growing number of local living wage ordinances and legal challenges to them); William Quigley, *Full-Time Workers Should Not Be Poor: The Living Wage Movement*, 70 MISS. L. J. 889 (2001); Jon Gertner, *What Is a Living Wage?*, N.Y. TIMES, Jan. 15, 2006, *available at* http://www.nytimes.com/2006/01/ 15/magazine/15wage.html (discussing the history of the living wage moment). For a more critical view of the effects of living wage ordinances, see David Neumark, *Living Wages: Protection for or Protection from Low-Wage Workers?*, 58 Indus. & Lab. Rev. 27 (2004) (suggesting that living wage laws may protect unionized workers from low-wage workers, rather than benefitting low-wage workers generally).

B. FRINGE BENEFIT PROTECTIONS

An increasingly important aspect of employment compensation is fringe benefits, a term that includes everything from pensions and medical insurance to tuition reimbursement programs to free parking spaces. Unlike other industrialized nations, which tend to provide substantial government retirement, health, and insurance benefits through social legislation, the American approach to fringe benefits begins with a legally mandated but limited safety net or base of protection. As discussed in Chapter 12, federal law mandates that the states provide a scheme of workers' compensation for injuries on the job, and it also mandates an unemployment insurance regime. Social security law provides for limited retirement and disability benefits; Medicare finances health insurance for the elderly; and Medicaid provides health coverage for some of those not able to pay. 42 U.S.C. § 1396 *et seq.* (2006) ("Medicaid Act"); 42 U.S.C. § 426 *et seq.* (2006) ("Medicare Act"); 42 U.S.C. § 301 *et seq.* (2006) ("Social Security Act"). Some states supplement that "safety net" with additional programs.

Above this floor, the law leaves the decision to provide fringe benefits to employers' discretion. Employers may do so unilaterally, by individual contract, or as a result of collective negotiations with representatives of the workers. Not only do the federal and state governments provide only minimal retirement, disability, and health benefits, but federal law historically has not mandated that employers provide such benefits, beyond their contributions to unemployment insurance and workers' compensation; with a few exceptions, neither has state law. However, as part of the health care reform package Congress passed in 2010, *see generally* Patient Protection and Affordable Care Act, Pub. L. No. 111-148, 124 Stat. 119 (2010) (as modified by the Health Care and Education Reconciliation Act of 2010 (Pub. L. 111-152, 124 Stat. 1029 (2010)) (hereinafter "PPACA") (codified principally in various sections of 26, 29, and 42 U.S.C.A.), a large employer will face tax penalties beginning in 2014 if it does not offer health care coverage or offers coverage that is not "affordable," *see* 26 U.S.C.A. § 4980H (2010).

Nevertheless, at present, many employers provide no fringe benefits. Minimum-wage employers, for example, rarely provide health insurance benefits. Even "sick days" and vacation days are often unavailable, or are offered to employees only after a long probationary period. Thus, the decision to leave these terms of employment almost entirely to private ordering means that many workers lack basic benefits.

Rather than requiring fringe benefits, the federal government's approach traditionally has been to utilize various tax incentives to encourage employers to provide some fringe benefits. The Internal Revenue Code excludes specified employee benefits from what would otherwise be taxable income to the employee. Employees (and hence their employers) generally prefer such benefits to standard wages because they are not taxable to the employee at all or are at least tax-deferred. For example, a parking space may not be taxable at all; pension benefits will normally be taxable only at retirement.

Of course, the exclusion of certain compensation from employee income by casting it as a fringe benefit makes sense for the employer only if it gets to deduct the cost of the benefit as a business expense, as it could deduct wages. The Tax Code permits employers to do so, but in order to qualify, employers must observe certain principles, including those involving "nondiscrimination," a term of art in benefits law that will be discussed below. With regard to pension plans, the employer may deduct contributions to tax-qualified retirement plans, but the employees need not recognize any income based on that contribution until receipt of the benefit. Further, the investment income from accumulated contributions is tax-free at the time it is earned. As a result, compensation in fringe benefits is more valuable to employees who have a greater than zero effective tax rate than is base rate compensation, which is fully taxable when received.

Once an employer provides certain fringe benefits, federal law regulates their operation through the requirements for exclusion set forth in the Tax Code and, for some schemes, through the Employee Retirement Income Security Act ("ERISA"), 29 U.S.C. §§ 1001-1461 (2006). These laws do not, however, determine the level or kind of benefits; that is left to the employer setting up the benefit plan.

The legal treatment of fringe benefits is so complex that it is a world unto its own. Indeed, "Employee Benefits" is both a specialty area of practice and a specialized law school course. Thus, this chapter will not provide comprehensive coverage of this subject. It will, however, give, a brief overview of ERISA's basic structure, some other benefits regulations, and the employer mandates of the PPACA.

1. ERISA

Prior to the enactment of ERISA in 1974, "regulation" of fringe benefit plans in the United States was almost an accidental by-product of tax treatment and thus was tied to the Tax Code and the regulations and rulings of the Internal Revenue Service. This system was viewed by many as inadequate: "Horror" stories were told of older employees fired shortly before becoming eligible for benefits and of employers unable to pay employees and retirees the benefits promised, and neither the Tax Code nor the common law provided adequate remedies. Thus, ERISA's primary purpose was to protect employees' justified expectations with regard to certain benefits their employers promised them. In enacting ERISA, Congress maintained the parallel provisions of the Internal Revenue Code but created an entirely separate structure to regulate employee benefit plans. Accordingly, as amended, ERISA is codified at 29 U.S.C. §§ 1001-1461 (2006), and in scattered sections of the Internal Revenue Code.

ERISA does not mandate that employers establish employee benefit plans, nor does it dictate what kinds of benefits they may ultimately provide. It regulates such plans and benefits only once the employer has chosen to provide them. However, once the employer "opts in" to ERISA, the statute's mandates may affect the scope and the nature of the benefits offered. Despite the absence of legal compulsion to do so, many employers offer various kinds of benefit plans covered by ERISA. For example, according to the Bureau of Labor Statistics, in March 2010, retirement benefits were available to 74 percent of full-time workers in private industry, while access to medical care and paid sick leave was available to 86 percent and 74 percent of such workers, respectively. *See* Bureau of Labor Statistics, *Economic News Release* (July 27, 2010), *available at* http://www.bls.gov/news.release/ebs2.nr0.htm. However, part-time workers receive far fewer benefits: Only 39 percent of part-time workers had retirement benefits, and medical care and paid sick leave were provided to 24 and 26 percent, respectively. *See id.* Note also that participation numbers have declined from prior years, and the types of medical and retirement benefits employers are now offering may be less favorable to employees than in the past.

ERISA contains a complex statutory regime that is supplemented by agency regulations and a tremendous amount of case law on a number of issues of great import — including the statute's preemptive scope and the scope of judicial review of plan administrators' decisions. Although we must leave the bulk of these matters to an Employee Benefits course, what follows is a cursory glance at ERISA's key features.

a. Coverage

ERISA covers a broad array of employer fringe benefit plans. An "employee benefit plan" is within the statute if the plan is established or maintained by an "employer" or "union," although plans maintained by government employers, churches, and certain private plans are excluded. *See* 29 U.S.C. § 1003(a) and (b)(1)-(5). In addition to the threshold question of which individuals are "employees" (*see Yates v. Hendon*, reproduced at page 51 and *Vizcaino v. Microsoft Corporation*, discussed on page 27), there are issues about what qualifies as a "benefit plan" and who qualifies as a "participant."

Among employee benefit plans, the central distinction in the statute is between employee "welfare" benefit plans and employee "pension" benefit plans. The basic difference is the nature of the benefit: An employee pension benefit plan provides retirement income and an employee welfare benefit plan provides fringe benefits for nonretirement purposes such as medical insurance. To say it another way, a pension plan's benefits are payable only after the termination of covered employment, while a welfare plan is everything that is not a pension plan. This distinction is critically important: Consistent with its original purposes, ERISA mandates far more controls on pension plans than on welfare plans, and, as discussed below, because ERISA broadly preempts state regulation of employee benefit plans, this often results in a regulatory "void" — that is, an absence of legal protections — for welfare benefits.

ERISA contemplates two basic types of employee pension benefit plans: defined benefit and defined contribution plans. A defined benefit plan is what most people think of as a "pension": a promise by the employer to provide employees a guaranteed monthly retirement benefit defined by some formula based on the amount of the employee's compensation and her length of service. The alternative is the increasingly common defined contribution plan, which provides for an individual account for each participant and for benefits based solely upon the amount contributed to the participant's account, and any investment gains or losses in such account. A popular type of defined contribution plan is the "401(k)." The basic difference between the two types of plans is risk: In defined benefit plans, the employer bears the risks of investment since it guarantees a certain level of payment when employees retire; in defined contribution plans, the employee bears these risks since she makes the investment decisions and, upon retirement, gets only what has accumulated. Obviously, employees generally prefer the guaranteed benefit that a defined benefit plan affords, and employee advocates have emphasized their social benefits. But defined contribution plans are the choice of pragmatic employers wanting to avoid the risks of defined benefit plans, and the regulatory constraints ERISA and tax regulations place on such plans. Indeed, for these reasons and others, defined benefit plans are a dying breed: Private employers have rarely chosen to establish defined benefit plans in the last two decades, and many have recently "frozen" their defined benefit plans (i.e., barred new entrants or ceased accruals) or converted them to defined contribution plans.

b. Statutory Structure

The differences between the two types of pension plans providing retirement income, and between pension and welfare plans covering other fringe benefits, have profound effects on employer obligations under ERISA. These obligations can best be understood by describing the statutory structure. ERISA is divided into four subchapters: Title I provides protection for employee benefit rights by imposing reporting and disclosure requirements as well as fiduciary responsibilities on all benefits plans, establishing participation and vesting standards for pension plans, setting forth funding requirements for defined benefit plans, and providing an administrative and enforcement scheme. *See generally* 29 U.S.C. §§ 1002, 1102-06. Title I also contains newer provisions that address welfare benefit plans specifically, including requirements regarding worker loss of health insurance benefits upon termination, insurance portability, long-term care insurance, and health information privacy. Consolidated Omnibus Budget Reconciliation Act of 1985, 29 U.S.C. § 1181 *et seq.* (2006); Health Insurance Portability and Accountability Act of 1996, 29 U.S.C. § 1181-82 (2006); the Newborns' and Mothers' Health Protection Act of 1996, 29 U.S.C. § 1185 (2006); the Mental Health Parity Act of 1996, 29 U.S.C. § 1185a (2006); Women's Health and Cancer Rights Act of 1998, 29 U.S.C. § 185b (2006).

Title II amended the Tax Code to accommodate ERISA. Title III deals primarily with the relationship between ERISA and the Internal Revenue Code and their enforcement agencies, the DOL and the IRS. In order for employers and employees to be entitled to the tax advantages accorded to many fringe benefits under the Tax Code, the tax provisions must be satisfied. The requirements of ERISA must also be satisfied for those employee benefit plans that fall within its coverage. While retirement plans were first regulated through the Tax Code, many of those tax qualification standards were incorporated into ERISA, resulting in mirror-image rules applying under ERISA and the Tax Code.

There are, however, some important provisions dealing with tax-qualified pension plans found only in the Tax Code. The most important are the rules against "discrimination" in favor of highly compensated employees. Many of the Code sections providing tax preferences for different fringe benefits allow some, but not too much, discrimination in favor of the high and mighty. 26 U.S.C. §§ 401 and 414. The goal of the nondiscrimination provisions is to ensure that the tax subsidy does not benefit only or mostly higher-paid employees or business owners. The decision makers of employers want these benefits for themselves, for their families, and for those employees with the ability to demand such benefits from their employers. Pressure to protect the bottom-line profitability, however, gives these decision makers an incentive to withhold such benefits from most employees. Congress tried to encourage extension of benefits but rejected a flat rule prohibiting all discrimination, ostensibly because it would have caused too many employers to not provide certain fringe benefits at all.

Title IV regulates plan termination and establishes an insurance scheme for defined benefit plans, guaranteeing that participants in those plans are provided their benefits should their plan terminate. It creates the Pension Benefit Guaranty Corporation ("PBGC") to administer this insurance program. As suggested above, the fees for the PBGC insurance, the prerequisites to terminate a plan, and the potential residual liability established in Title IV create substantial disincentives to employers to create defined benefit retirement plans. In recent years, the preponderance of underfunded plans and the significant payouts the PBGC has made upon plan defaults have received significant public attention and led to calls for legal reform. The stricter funding requirements included in the Pension Protection Act of 2006, Pub. L. No. 190-280, 120 Stat. 780 (codified in various sections of 26 & 29 U.S.C.) were designed in part to address this concern, although whether these requirements are adequate remains the subject of controversy.

c. Preemption

There are few areas of the law more bedeviled by abstruse legal reasoning, and inconsistent judicial decisions than ERISA preemption. The decisions on the subject — including those issued by the Supreme Court — are legion, as is the legal commentary, and even ERISA experts have difficulty navigating the resulting uncertain and peculiar framework. At the most general level, ERISA preemption involves both "field" and "conflict" preemption under ERISA's regulatory scheme. In terms of the former, ERISA preempts any state law that "relates to" an "employee benefit" plan; thus, ERISA's enforcement regime and substantive obligations are exclusive, even where ERISA does not mandate or otherwise regulate benefits. 29 U.S.C. § 1144; *see, e.g., New York State Conference of Blue Cross & Blue Shield Plans v. Travelers Ins., Inc.*, 514 U.S. 645 (discussing the breadth and history of ERISA preemption although ultimately finding a state law imposing surcharges on commercial insurers not preempted); *Egelhoff v. Egelhoff ex rel. Breiner*, 532 U.S. 141 (2001) (striking down a state statute that revoked automatically upon divorce the designation of a spouse as a beneficiary to the extent the law applied to ERISA benefit plans). The only exceptions are those matters — insurance, banking, or securities — that are expressly saved from ERISA's preemptive scope, unless such regulation is swept back into ERISA's coverage under the statute's "deemer" clause, which essentially preempts those state laws that affect self-funded (noninsured) welfare benefit plans. 29 U.S.C. § 1144 (b)(2); *see, e.g., Metropolitan Life Ins. Co. v. Massachusetts*, 471 U.S. 724 (1985) (upholding a state law mandating mental health care benefits in group health insurance policies under the savings clause and not swept back into ERISA's scope under the deemer clause).

Leaving the considerable details aside, field preemption is of greatest import in the welfare benefit context because, although ERISA's welfare benefit provisions are relatively weak, preemption may preclude employer-related health care and other reforms at the state level. For example, in 2006, a federal court struck down as preempted under ERISA a 2006 Maryland law, popularly known as the "Walmart Bill," requiring that employers with more than 10,000 workers in Maryland pay a penalty to the state's health insurance program if they fail to devote at least 8 percent of their state payroll to health insurance for their employees. *See Retail Indus. Leaders Ass'n v. Fielder*, 435 F. Supp. 2d 481 (D. Md. 2006), *aff'd*, 475 F.3d 180 (4th Cir. 2007); *see generally* Edward A. Zelinsky, *Maryland's Wal-Mart Act: Policy and Preemption*, 28 CARDOZO L. REV. 847 (2007) (agreeing with the preemption decision and finding the statute ill-conceived as a matter of policy).

Conflict preemption centers on the exclusiveness of ERISA's enforcement scheme under 29 U.S.C. § 1132. As the Supreme Court has repeated a number of times, ERISA preempts any state-law cause of action that duplicates, supplements, or supplants the ERISA civil enforcement remedies. *See, e.g., Aetna Health, Inc. v. Davila*, 542 U.S. 200 (2004) (finding preempted plaintiffs' state-law causes of action against their health maintenance organizations for failure to exercise ordinary care in coverage decisions). As discussed below, because the remedies provided by ERISA are limited, this kind of preemption sometimes precludes participants and beneficiaries harmed by plan administrators' or fiduciaries' breaches of duty from obtaining adequate relief. ERISA preemption therefore is highly controversial because it creates a kind of regulatory vacuum: State attempts to provide greater employee benefits protections are often preempted even though ERISA provides no substantive protection at all, and state-law remedies necessary to make harmed parties whole are unavailable because of the exclusivity of ERISA's remedial regime.

d. Enforcement and Remedies

ERISA's primary enforcement provision, 29 U.S.C. § 1132, authorizes civil actions by participants, beneficiaries, fiduciaries, employee benefit plans, and the Secretary of Labor. This section provides for a wide range of claims against plan administrators and other fiduciaries, but the remedies available are limited to the recovery of benefits, certain statutory penalties for nondisclosure, and equitable relief on behalf of the plan. Most types of compensatory damages (emotional distress, mental anguish, and other consequential damages) are unavailable, as are punitive damages. The remedies ERISA affords, therefore, may be inadequate to make the aggrieved party whole. For example, a participant in an employer-sponsored health care plan has no state-law tort claim against the plan or plan administrator for an erroneous coverage decision that results in the failure to treat a medical condition, and equitable relief and the recovery of benefits ERISA affords fall far short of compensating the harm caused. *See, e.g., Corcoran v. United Health Care, Inc.*, 965 F.2d 1321 (5th Cir. 1992) (finding preempted state-law claims against a plan administrator for failure to exercise due care in denying certification of hospitalization to a woman, which resulted in the death of her fetus, in spite of the fact that damages for emotional injuries are not available under ERISA). Thus, although § 1132's coverage is broad, its remedies are narrow, which has led to significant criticism of the regime and calls for reform. On a positive note for plaintiffs, ERISA does provide for recovery of attorneys' fees for prevailing parties, *see* § 1132(e), which are typically not available for state common-law causes of action.

Denial-of-benefits claims are the most common claims against administrators of welfare benefit plans. A key and often-litigated issue in many such cases is the standard of review the court should apply to the administrator's decision to deny benefits. Where the employee benefit plan has granted the administrator discretion to make benefits decisions, courts normally will afford these decisions substantial deference, although an administrator conflict of interest is a factor to consider in determining whether the administrator abused its discretion. *See, e.g. Metropolitan Life Ins. Co. v. Glenn*, 554 U.S. 105 (2008); *see also Conkright v. Frommert*, 130 S. Ct. 1640 (2010) (holding that deference ought to be accorded to an ERISA plan administrator despite the administrator's prior mistake in construing provisions of the plan).

Finally, ERISA contains an antidiscrimination and antiretaliation provision that makes it unlawful for any person to "discharge, fine, suspend, expel, discipline, or discriminate against a participant or beneficiary for exercising any right to which he is entitled under the provisions of an employee benefit plan . . . or for the purpose of interfering with the attainment of any right to which such participant may become entitled under the plan. . . ." 29 U.S.C. § 1140. This protection is integral to ERISA because the statute was in large part a response to employers terminating employees just prior to their becoming vested under retirement plans. Again, although the scope of this section is broad, the remedies are limited to those set forth in § 1132.

2. Employment-Related Benefits Not Governed by ERISA

Some employment-related benefits are not governed by ERISA. As discussed above, benefits that do not require the establishment of a "plan" — an administrative or processing scheme — or are not accumulated over time and payable upon a contingency beyond the employer's control are not governed by ERISA. In addition, some types of benefit plans are expressly excluded from ERISA's reach. One example we have already seen is an Employee Stock Purchase Plan ("ESPP"), one of two benefit plans at issue in *Vizcaino v. Microsoft Corp.*, discussed in Chapter 1, page 27. The ESPP is a supplemental benefit plan that, if qualified, is afforded favorable tax treatment but is excluded from ERISA coverage and therefore governed by state benefits law. *See* 26 U.S.C. § 423.

Moreover, other types of benefits are governed by separate legal regimes. Two examples are workers' compensation and state-sponsored unemployment compensation. The former, which each state has established, is addressed in Chapter 12. Each state has also enacted a scheme of unemployment compensation. These programs originated in the 1930s when, through the Social Security Act, Congress provided incentives for states to adopt compulsory programs. They operate under federal standards, are federally funded, and are financed by a payroll tax on covered employers. As a result, the basic parameters of unemployment compensation regimes are similar in all states, although the details may vary widely.

To be eligible for such compensation, workers typically must have had a prior employment relationship (as opposed to some other type of relationship), must meet minimum earnings or working time standards, and must have been terminated involuntarily without fault. Obviously, whether a termination is involuntary and without fault is sometimes in controversy. An employee who is fired for work-related misconduct is ineligible, as is an employee who voluntarily quits without good cause. The concept is that employees need to be protected by insurance from economic dislocations over which they have no control. The "moral hazard" implicit in unemployment insurance is limited by excluding those employees who are fired for good reason or who quit without justification. Because employer payroll taxes are linked to claims experience, employers frequently contest employee claims of involuntary or no-fault termination. However, and consistent with the moral hazard approach, an employee who quits may still be entitled to coverage if he or she can demonstrate some kind of "good cause" for doing so. *See* Deborah Maranville, *Workplace Mythologies and Unemployment Insurance: Exit, Voice and Exhausting All Reasonable Alternatives to Quitting*, 31 Hofstra L. Rev. 459 (2002). These include medical conditions and physical limitations. The question of whether a particular condition should be treated as the employee's choice or covered by insurance is reflected in the differing state approaches to when and whether pregnancy-related termination of employment should be covered. *See* Martin H. Malin, *Unemployment Compensation in a Time of Increasing Work-Family Conflicts*, 29 U. Mich. J. L. Reform 131, 142 n.48 (1996). Of course, while former employees who are unable to work are ineligible for unemployment insurance, they may be eligible for other types of benefits (e.g., workers' compensation, private disability insurance, or state or federal disability benefits).

Unemployment compensation benefits tend to be based on the recipient's former wages but top out at a predetermined level, which is relatively low. They are also payable for only a fixed period of time (typically no longer than six months), although Congress has extended the period after certain dramatic occurrences, including Hurricane Katrina. *See* U.S. Department of Labor, Hurricane Recovery Assistance, *available at* http://www.dol.gov/opa/hurricane-recovery.htm; Press Release, Office of the House Democratic Leader Nancy Pelosi, Tens of Thousands of Katrina Survivors Are Still Suffering and the Future of Gulf Coast Remains Unclear (Feb. 28, 2006) (discussing a Senate bill extending unemployment benefits for 150,000 survivors of Hurricane Katrina). Congress has also extended benefits during recessions, including several extensions during the Great Recession, although they have proven to be politically controversial. *See, e.g.*, Carl Hulse, *Jobless Benefit Extension Clears Senate Hurdle*, N.Y. Times A16 (July 20, 2010) (discussing the heated debate over the further extension of benefits for those out of work six months or more).

Other limitations are imposed to encourage workers to find new employment, including requirements that recipients look for and accept suitable work. State unemployment compensation schemes are administered by state commissions, although these administrative regimes and their procedures must satisfy certain criteria in order to be entitled to federal reimbursements for their expenses. Some have urged that unemployment compensation schemes be reimagined to serve broader goals than the traditional short-term alleviation of economic dislocation. *See* Gillian Lester, *Unemployment Insurance and Wealth Redistribution*, 49 UCLA L. Rev. 335 (2001).

3. Health Care Reform: Employee Benefits–Related Provisions of the PPACA

Enacted in 2010, the PPACA imposes a complex array of additional mandates and limitations on health insurance plans. These include tighter restrictions on eligibility requirements for health insurance plans; standards regarding administrative costs, pricing, and services offered; additional disclosures in tax returns and to employees; and new provisions regarding employer "cafeteria" plans. The PPACA also imposes a number of new taxes relating to the provision of health insurance and provides for new subsidies and tax credits for employers.

Perhaps the most significant change involving employee benefits are the provisions governing large employers and health care coverage. The PPACA does not mandate that employers offer employees health insurance. However, beginning in 2014, an employer with at least 50 full-time employees (or equivalents) will face tax penalties if one or more of its full-time employees obtains subsidized coverage — that is, a premium credit or cost-sharing reduction for coverage — through a "qualified health insurance plan" (a nonemployer health plan established pursuant to the terms of the PPACA). Put another way, the law's penalty provisions will apply if at least one full-time employee opts into a qualified health insurance plan and receives subsidized coverage because his or her qualifying employer (1) does not provide health insurance coverage or (2) provides coverage that is not affordable. Some of the key provisions regarding large employers and their employees are as follows:

- An "applicable large employer" is defined as having "at least fifty full-time employees during the preceding calendar year." Full-time employees are those working 30 or more hours per week, excluding full-time seasonal employees who work for less than 120 days during the year. The hours worked by part-time employees are included in the calculation for determining whether the employer is covered. *See* 26 U.S.C.A. §4980H.
- Regardless of whether an applicable large employer offers coverage, it will be liable for a tax penalty only if one or more of its full-time employees obtains coverage through a "qualified health insurance plan" (established elsewhere by the PPACA) and the coverage is subsidized through a premium credit or cost-sharing reduction. Part-time workers are not included in penalty calculations, and an employer will not pay a penalty for any part-time employees, even if one or more receives subsidized coverage. *See* 26 U.S.C.A. §4980H.
- As a general matter, an employee who is not offered employer-sponsored minimal essential health care coverage (as defined in 26 U.S.C.A. §5000A) and who is not eligible for Medicaid or other programs may be eligible for premium credits for coverage through a qualified health plan when the employee's family income is between 133 percent and 400 percent of the federal poverty level. Employees who are offered employer-sponsored coverage can obtain such premium credits only if, in addition to the criteria above, they also are not enrolled in their employer's coverage because it is unaffordable — that is, either the employee's required contribution toward the plan premium would exceed 9.5 percent of their household income or the plan pays for less than 60 percent, on average, of covered health care expenses. *See* 26 U.S.C.A. §36B.
- An applicable large employer that does not offer health insurance coverage will be subject to a penalty if one or more of its full-time employees receives subsidized coverage in a qualified health insurance plan. The monthly penalty assessed to employers who do not offer coverage will be equal to the number of full-time employees minus 30 multiplied by one-twelfth of $2,000. *See* 26 U.S.C.A. §4980H.
- Employers that do offer health coverage will not be treated as meeting the employer requirements if at least one full-time employee obtains subsidized coverage in a qualified health insurance plan because, in addition to meeting the other eligibility criteria, the coverage is unaffordable. The monthly penalty assessed to the employer for each full-time employee who receives subsidized

coverage will be one-twelfth of $3,000 for any applicable month. However, the total monthly penalty for an employer will not exceed the total number of the firm's full-time employees minus 30 multiplied by one-twelfth of $2,000. *See* 26 U.S.C.A. § 4980H.

- Employers with more than 200 full-time employees that offer coverage must automatically enroll new full-time employees in a plan (and continue enrollment of current employees). Automatic enrollment programs will be required to include adequate notice and the opportunity for an employee to opt out. *See* 29 U.S.C.A. § 218a.

Because these and many of the other provisions in the PPACA will not become effective for years, and there will likely be an enormous amount of intervening agency rule-making and some litigation regarding its key provisions, its impact on the nature, cost, and availability of employer-provided health coverage will not be known for some time. Moreover, because health care reform remains controversial, Congress may amend the statute before some of the mandates become effective.

12

Worker Safety and Health

From industrial accidents to occupational diseases, safety and health are pervasive problems in the workplace. The causes range from debatable dangers to evident perils, and emanate from physical surroundings, machinery, vehicles, chemicals, and, of course, other humans. Some risks are inherent in certain occupations (at least given present technology), but others can be reduced or even eliminated. For a host of reasons, the American workplace, as a whole, appears to be getting safer. For example, workplace fatalities declined 17 percent in 2009. U.S. DEPARTMENT OF LABOR, BUREAU OF LABOR STATISTICS (hereinafter "DOL, BLS"), 2009 CENSUS OF FATAL OCCUPATIONAL INJURIES (1992-2009), *available at* http://www.bls.gov/iif/oshcfoi1.htm. Similarly, the rate of occupational injury and illness cases in private industry declined from 5.0 per 100 full-time equivalent workers in 2003 to 3.9 in 2008. DOL, BLS, OCCUPATIONAL INJURIES AND ILLNESSES: INDUSTRY DATA, *available at* http://www.bls.gov/iif/oshwc/osh/os/ostb2071.pdf; http://www.bls.gov/iif/oshwc/osh/os/ostb1355.pdf.

Nevertheless, there remain industries and sectors—for example, construction, farming, trucking, mining, and commercial fishing—that are relatively dangerous. And general improvements in safety do not assure that any particular worker or work-place will be injury-free. For example, in 2008, 4.1 million workers suffered some kind of job-related injury, and 2.0 million injuries resulted in days away from work, transfer, or work restrictions. DOL, BLS, INDUSTRY INJURY AND ILLNESS DATA, *available at* http://www.bls.gov/iif/oshwc/osh/os/ostb2071.pdf; *see also* DOL, BLS, LOST-WORKTIME INJURIES AND ILLNESSES: CHARACTERISTICS AND RESULTING TIME AWAY FROM WORK, 2004, *available at* http://www.bls.gov/news.release/archives/osh2_12132005.pdf. Moreover, work-related sickness and illness continue to raise significant public policy concerns: according to the National Institute for Occupational Safety and Health ("NIOSH"), 49,000 annual deaths are attributed to work-related diseases (about 134 per day), NIOSH, *About NIOSH*, *available at* http://www.cdc.gov/niosh/about.html, and there were approximately 249,000 newly reported cases of occupational illnesses reported in 2004, *see* INDUSTRY INJURY AND ILLNESS DATA, *supra*. In addition, occasionally high-profile incidents produce many injuries or deaths. In 2010, for example, the explosion of BP's Deepwater Horizon platform in the Gulf of Mexico killed 11 workers and injured 17, and the disaster at Massey Energy's Upper Big Branch Mine in West Virginia resulted in the death of 29 miners.

The reported numbers also may significantly understate the incidence of workplace injury, disease, and death. *See, e.g.,* Steven Greenhouse, *Work-Related Injuries Underreported,* N.Y. TIMES, November 16, 2009, *available at* http://www.nytimes.com/2009/11/17/us/17osha.html?_r=3&hp; Orly Lobel, *Interlocking Regulatory and Industrial Relations: The Governance of Workplace Safety,* 57 ADMIN. L. REV. 1071, 1079 n.31 (2005). And, despite the declining numbers, the direct costs of disabling workplace injuries are enormous—approximately $52 billion in 2009. Liberty Mutual Research Inst. for Safety, Annual Report (2009), *available at* http://www.libertymutual.com. Indirect costs are much greater.

The problems of worker safety and health can be addressed in various ways. One is through private ordering. Health and safety issues are a frequent subject of collective bargaining agreements, and most such agreements, in addition to providing for health insurance, deal with at least some workplace safety issues, including safety standards and leave policies for injuries and illnesses. But collective bargaining is an imperfect means of improving worker safety and health, not only because such bargaining does not guarantee employer concessions or significant improvements, but also because the vast majority of workers are nonunionized. In theory, employees could bargain for health and safety protections individually, but, with the exception of health and disability insurance, terms addressing these issues directly are rarely part of individual employment agreements even where such agreements exist.

The statutory and other mandates discussed throughout this casebook address aspects of the problem in a variety of ways, albeit neither directly nor comprehensively. For example, as discussed in Chapter 4, whistleblower statutes and the public policy tort protect employees who have reported suspected safety hazards, refused to engage in dangerous activities, or otherwise assisted government officials in addressing safety concerns. We also saw in Chapter 7 that the National Labor Relations Act ensures even nonunionized workers the right to engage in "concerted activity" for a variety of ends, one of which is workplace health and safety. *See NLRB v. Washington Aluminum Co.,* 370 U.S. 9 (1962) (holding that a group of workers leaving their employment because of extreme cold was protected activity). Moreover, as covered in Chapters 9 and 10, fostering workplace safety and health plays an important role under the Americans with Disabilities Act, as either a by-product of the employer's obligation to reasonably accommodate disabled workers or, conversely, as a reason for refusing to provide certain accommodations. Likewise, other antidiscrimination provisions and the Family and Medical Leave Act implicate safety and health in various ways, including health- or injury-related leave policies and real or perceived gender-related health or safety risks, as addressed in a number of bona fide occupational qualification cases. Finally, as considered in Chapter 11, the Fair Labor Standards Act's ("FLSA") child labor provisions are premised on protecting the health and safety of this particularly vulnerable group. In addition, ERISA's regulation of welfare benefit plans was originally designed to protect worker benefits, including health insurance, although that law does not require the provision of such benefits. In fact, its preemption doctrine defeats many state attempts to enhance health-related benefits.

Despite the pervasiveness of concerns over the safety and health of workers, the law has developed only two major regimes that deal directly and primarily with the question. One is state workers' compensation systems; the other is the federal Occupational Safety and Health Act ("OSHA"), 29 U.S.C. §§ 651 *et seq.* (2006). Much like pension law, workers' compensation has become its own discipline: Most law schools offer a separate course on it and many attorneys practice primarily or exclusively in this area. Nevertheless, because it is important that you have at least some acquaintance with workers' compensation and OSHA, both regimes are addressed briefly below.

The two systems have proven to be both important and, unsurprisingly, controversial. As mentioned in Chapter 5, in the early twentieth century, the workers' compensation system replaced the common-law tort of negligence with an administrative regime of strict liability for work-related injuries and diseases. This system provides more certain recovery for employees for physical injuries in accidents arising out of their employment, but subject to a trade-off: Workers' compensation restricts the amount of recovery and preempts others claims through workers' compensation exclusivity. There is some question as to whether the costs of this system create adequate incentives for employers to reduce safety hazards. Limitations on employer liability might reduce incentives to eliminate workplace hazards below the point a tort system would set and perhaps below what is acceptable from a societal perspective. *See generally* Emily A. Spieler, *Perpetuating Risk? Workers' Compensation and the Persistence of Occupational Injuries*, 31 HOUS. L. REV. 119 (1994). On the other hand, despite exclusivity, employers face substantial costs under workers' compensation, either directly as self-insurers or more commonly in terms of their compensation insurance premiums, which will reflect, at least to some extent, a company's claim history. *See* MICHAEL J. MOORE & W. KIP VISCUSI, COMPENSATION MECHANISMS FOR JOB RISKS: WAGES, WORKERS' COMPENSATION, AND PRODUCT LIABILITY 151-78 (1990). The cost of the workers' compensation system has increased to the point where there has been recurrent talk of a compensation crisis. *See generally* Martha T. McCluskey, *Insurer Moral Hazard in the Workers' Compensation Crisis: Reforming Cost Inflation, Not Rate Suppression*, 5 EMP. RTS. & EMPLOY. POL'Y J. 55 (2001); Martha T. McCluskey, *The Illusion of Efficiency in Workers' Compensation "Reform,"* 50 RUTGERS L. REV. 657 (1998).

The other major legal regime addressing workplace safety is OSHA, which was enacted by Congress in 1970 and remains the most direct attack on the problem. Together with state counterparts and a few other federal safety regimes covering specific industries (such as the Mine Safety and Health Administration), OSHA seeks to prevent (instead of merely compensate) workplace injuries. *See generally* MARK ROTHSTEIN, OCCUPATIONAL SAFETY AND HEALTH LAW (2010 ed.). However, while the workplace has grown somewhat safer, it is not clear that OSHA gets much of the credit. Over time, many have questioned whether that regime, which consists largely of a regulatory scheme enforced by periodic agency inspection of worksites, rather than lawsuits brought by affected workers, is an effective means of ensuring safety and compliance. *See generally* THOMAS O. MCGARITY & SIDNEY A. SHAPIRO, WORKERS AT RISK: THE FAILED PROMISE OF THE OCCUPATIONAL SAFETY AND HEALTH ADMINISTRATION (1993); Lobel, *supra*, at 1079-81, 1097-99. And there has been a wave of highly critical assessments of OSHA's performance in the last decade. *See* CTR. FOR PUB. INTEGRITY, BROKEN GOVERNMENT: AN EXAMINATION OF EXECUTIVE BRANCH FAILURES SINCE 2000 10-11 (2008); Susan Bisom-Rapp, *What We Learn in Troubled Times: Deregulation and Safe Work in the New Economy*, 55 WAYNE L. REV. 1097, 1231-39 (2009); Stephen Labaton, *OSHA Leaves Worker Safety Largely in Hands of Industry*, N.Y. TIMES, April 25, 2007; Lynn Rhinehart, *Workers at Risk: The Unfulfilled Promise of the Occupational Safety and Health Act*, 111 W. VA. L. REV. 117, 121-23 (2008); R. Jeffrey Smith, *Under Bush, OSHA Mired in Inaction*, WASH. POST, Dec. 29, 2008 at A1; *see also* David C. Vladeck, *The Failed Promise of Workplace Health*

Regulation, 111 W. Va. L. Rev. 15 (2008) (discussion of recent coal mine disasters and the failure of federal workplace health and safety regimes to protect workers).

A. WORKERS' COMPENSATION

1. The History of Workers' Compensation

In the late nineteenth and early twentieth centuries, workers often could not recover compensation for workplace injuries because of the "unholy trinity" of common-law defenses: the fellow-servant rule (which provided that the employer was not vicariously liable for worker injuries caused by negligent co-workers), assumption of risk, and contributory negligence. As courts gradually began removing these barriers, employers' fears of liability for workplace injuries grew. This, along with a number of other factors, ultimately led to the universal adoption of workers' compensation schemes. In summarizing the origins of workers' compensation, Price Fishback and Shawn Kantor write:

> . . . The first decade of the twentieth century saw dramatic changes in the economic and legal environment surrounding workplace accident compensation, and these changes facilitated the formation of a political coalition in favor of workers' compensation. . . .
>
> The American movement for compensation legislation began in 1898, when the New York Social Reform Club presented the New York legislature with a compensation bill emulating the 1897 British law. The bill was killed in committee and deemed "too radical to pass" by the bill's legislative sponsor. As the economic and political environment changed over the next decade, the legislation obtained increasing support in response to an increase in employment in dangerous industries, an increased public awareness of workplace accident problems, and employers' worries about an increasingly unfavorable liability climate.
>
> Public awareness of workplace accidents during the period increased as shifts in employment across industries led to an increase in the share of workers in more dangerous jobs in manufacturing and mining and as the reporting of accident risk increased sharply. . . . [T]here was increased public awareness of workplace accidents because state labor departments, with their increasing budgets, improved their reporting of workplace injuries; therefore, the reported level of accident risk was rising. Reformers used these statistics to publicize the dangers and consequent financial hardships associated with workplace accidents.
>
> The greater attention paid to accident risk added to the consternation of employers because it occurred within an increasingly unfavorable liability climate. . . . [T]he number of states with employers' liability laws that restricted one or more of the employers' [common law tort] defenses for nonrailroad accidents rose from 7 in 1900 to 25 by 1913. The courts also modified the common-law defenses, which further exacerbated employers' uncertainty about the negligence liability system. Greater uncertainty about the law led employers and injured workers to accept the relatively high costs of litigation and test the bounds of the law more often, which in turn led to an increase in court cases at every level. In fact, the increased uncertainty was associated with a more than threefold rise in the number of state supreme court cases related to nonrailroad workplace accident litigation from 154 in 1900 to 490 in 1911. [Expanded liability combined with legal uncertainty] contributed to an increase in the liability insurance premiums that employers

paid. . . . This was not merely an artifact of an ever-increasing insurance industry because liability insurance out-paced other forms of insurance. . . . While part of the increase in liability insurance premiums may have been caused by increases in coverage, anecdotal evidence from several states suggests that increases in insurance rates also played a significant role.

Employers' worsening accident liability status in the early 1900s encouraged employer-supported lobbying groups to explore the possibility of a switch to a no-fault compensation system. Between 1908 and 1910 the National Civic Federation, which was composed of leaders from major corporations and conservative unions, devoted substantial time in their meetings to developing and promoting a workers' compensation bill. Meanwhile, the National Association of Manufacturers in 1910 called on its members to provide voluntary accident insurance, but then in 1911 the National Association of Manufacturers fully endorsed workers' compensation as a solution to the accident compensation problem. After forming in 1907 the American Association of Labor Legislation became one of the leading advocates for workers' compensation. The federal government, which often preceded most employers in offering relatively generous workplace benefits, established workers' compensation for federal workers in 1908 as a result of Theodore Roosevelt's strong support.

Employers' shift in interest toward workers' compensation coincided with changing sentiments among organized labor, whose ranks expanded from 868,000 in 1900 to 2.14 million in 1910, growing nearly three times faster than the labor force. The attitudes of major labor organizations went through a substantial change as they gained more experience with the results of employers' liability laws. Around the turn of the century, the American Federation of Labor believed that better accident compensation could be achieved by stripping employers of their three [tort] defenses. Organized labor's reluctance to embrace workers' compensation was part of a more general opposition to government regulation of the workplace on the theory that business interests controlled politics, and, thus, better benefits for workers could be achieved only through the voluntary organization of workers. But organized labor harshly criticized the fact that large numbers of injured workers were left uncompensated by the negligence system and that a large percentage of the insurance premiums that employers paid for liability never reached injured workers. In 1909, therefore, the American Federation of Labor switched its position and passed four resolutions supporting workers' compensation legislation, and the organization, at the federal level and through its state affiliates, became a vocal proponent of no-fault accident compensation.

The support from major employers' groups and organized labor led to the widespread adoption of workers' compensation after a couple of experiments in Maryland in 1902 and Montana in 1909 were declared unconstitutional. In the second decade of the century . . . 43 states adopted workers' compensation. By 1930 all the states except Arkansas, Florida, Mississippi, and South Carolina had enacted the legislation. As Harry Weiss noted, "No other kind of labor legislation gained such general acceptance in so brief a period in this country."

The Adoption of Workers' Compensation in the United States, 1900-30, 41 J. L. & ECON. 305, 315-19 (1998); *see also* ARTHUR A. LARSON & LEX K. LARSON, LARSON'S WORKERS' COMPENSATION LAW §§ 2.07-.08 (Matthew Bender and Co., Inc., 2010). Fishback and Kantor go on to explain that the basic trade-offs between employer and employee interests continue to define workers' compensation regimes today:

Instead of being imposed by one interest group at the expense of other groups, workers' compensation was enacted because a broad-based coalition of divergent interests saw gains from reforming the negligence liability system. Employers anticipated a reduction in labor friction, a reduction in the uncertainty of their accident and court costs, and a reduction in the gap between what they paid for insurance and what injured workers received. In addition, they were able to pass at least some of the additional costs of workers' compensation benefits on to their workers in the form of lower real wages. Workers, on average, anticipated higher post-accident benefits from the new legislation. Even if they "bought" the better benefits through lower wages, they anticipated better "insurance" coverage against workplace accident risk. Further, insurers believed that the shift to workers' compensation would reduce problems with adverse selection, and thus they could expand their coverage of workplace accidents.

2. The Basic Structure of Workers' Compensation Statutes

Today, all states have workers' compensation regimes. Since their enactment in the early part of the last century, the basic structure of these statutes has remained the same. Because workers' compensation is a creature of state law, there are important variations; however, these regimes contain the same core components:

1. Insurance. A WC [workers' compensation] statute requires employers to secure and provide insurance for their employees against the losses suffered by reason of workplace injuries. Such insurance must come either from approved carriers or from the employer's own resources for self-insurance, as certified by a state agency.

2. Entitlement. Unlike the tort system, in which recovery against the employer (and its liability insurer) depends upon proof of both the employer's fault (and also the absence of worker fault), the injured employee may draw upon WC insurance if the injury was in any way caused by the job — i.e., if it "arose out of and in the course of employment."

3. Benefits. While a WC regime expands the basis of employer responsibility to encompass all job-related injuries, it reduces correspondingly the extent of the employer's legal responsibility for any particular injury. Rather than award full tort compensation for all economic and noneconomic losses suffered by each victim, the typical WC benefit scheme reimburses the victim [for medical costs and some portion of net wages lost due to temporary and permanent disabilities].

4. Administration. Primary responsibility for administering a WC scheme is conferred upon an administrative tribunal: the expectation is that this process will give workers quicker, easier, and less expensive access to the above benefit structure. Ideally, such ready access is also facilitated by substituting "cause" for "fault" as the precondition for recovery, and by replacing at-large damages tailored to each victim with the schedule formula designed for the average worker.

5. Exclusivity. The tacit assumption of the no-fault model is that victims as a group are better protected, ex ante, by such a guarantee of more limited redress for crucial financial losses from workplace injuries, even granting that in particular cases, viewed ex post, the individual worker who can establish fault would likely be able to collect more substantial tort compensation for all the economic and noneconomic consequences of the injury. Having made such an assumption and required the employer to provide and pay for this preferred WC system, the legislature then grants employers the *quid pro quo* of statutory immunity from any liability for these workplace injuries under the background tort system. . . .

Paul C. Weiler, *Workers' Compensation and Product Liability: The Interaction of a Tort and Non-Tort Regime*, 50 OHIO ST. L.J. 825, 826-30 (1989). While the core elements persist despite local variations, these laws have not been static over time; for example, benefits were liberalized in the 1970s, and, as a result of rising insurance costs many states retrenched in the late 1990s, enacting reforms limiting workers' compensation benefits and recoveries. *See generally* McCluskey, *The Illusion of Efficiency in Workers' Compensation "Reform," supra*, at 683-98.

Assuming a worker's injury is a compensable one to begin with, a topic that is addressed in the next section, workers' compensation laws provide benefits for physical injuries and illnesses — that is, medical benefits and wage-loss benefits for disabling conditions — and limited death benefits. Although medical expenses are normally completely covered, lost wages are subject to a statutory cap. Critically, workers' compensation also excludes pain and suffering damages and some emotional distress damages. Most states finance such benefits by requiring employers to self-insure (and satisfy the state that they are solvent enough to do so), purchase private workers' compensation insurance, or participate in a state-provided insurance plan.

The standard set of benefits generally includes:

- *Medical Expenses.* Workers' compensation regimes usually require complete coverage of all medical expenses reasonably required to cure or relieve the effects of workplace injuries and covered occupational diseases. These ordinarily include not only direct medical services, but also necessary incidental services such as transportation and medical equipment.

- *Temporary Disability Benefits.* All states' regimes provide for temporary disability benefits for a period of recovery after a worker has been injured. These benefits, which cover both total and partial disabilities, normally run from the time of the injury plus a waiting period (three to seven days) until the conclusion of the healing period. The healing period ends when the worker is able to return to work or has reached maximum medical improvement and must seek permanent disability benefits. Temporary benefits tend to be calculated based on a percentage (normally two-thirds, but sometimes only half) of the employee's lost wages, which in turn is based on the worker's average weekly wage for a preceding period — often 3, 6, or 12 months. However, such benefits are capped at a particular level per week, and the cap varies by jurisdiction.

- *Permanent Disability Benefits.* Permanent disabilities normally are broken into two categories: unscheduled and scheduled. *Scheduled disabilities* refers to permanent disabilities listed in a statutorily adopted schedule of possible injuries to designated parts of the body. These are compensated according to predetermined statutory amounts for the loss of particular body parts — that is, the actual loss of the limb or part or, in many cases, the loss of the use of that limb or part. The statute mandates a fixed rate that is paid for a specific number of weeks. These scheduled benefits are supposed to reflect roughly the standard amount of earning capacity lost from the injury. *Unscheduled disabilities* refer to those injuries not listed in the existing schedule. They are compensated based on the loss of earning capacity, normally determined after a fact-finding investigation by a vocational expert and capped at a statutory maximum. The amount awarded may be calculated based on a variety of factors, including prior average earnings, the loss of physical functions to the injured body part, the education and employment history of the worker, and the worker's ability to continue employment. If the worker can return to work, only functional impairment will be taken into account, and there is a cap (varying by state) on the amount that can be received. Although the method differs by state, a standard calculation provides the worker with his/her average salary for the time period he/she was completely incapacitated up to a maximum amount, and, thereafter, a percentage of the maximum amount allowed tied to the percentage of earning capacity lost (i.e., if the worker lost 40 percent of earning capacity, he/she would receive 40 percent of the maximum benefits). Given the calculation method, unscheduled benefits are specific to the worker and the injury suffered. States have allowed separate recovery for scheduled and unscheduled injuries if the employee can demonstrate that the loss of earning capacity is separate for the two injuries.

- *Vocational Rehabilitation Services.* Vocational services are aimed at getting the injured worker back to work in some capacity.
- *Death Benefits.* All states provide death benefits for spouses and dependents of employees who suffer fatal work-related injuries, although the benefits vary widely in both amount and duration. These benefits tend to be based on a percentage of the employee's average weekly wage, tied to the number of dependents, capped at a statutory maximum amount, and limited to a specified statutory period. Many states also provide limited benefits for funeral expenses. Some states have separate statutory provisions that increase the amount of death benefits for the dependents of certain types of workers, including police officers, firefighters, and paramedics.

Obviously, disputes may arise over what medical expenses are necessary and reasonable, whether and to what the extent an employee is disabled, the average weekly wages the employee earned prior to injury or death, who is a "dependent," and a host of other issues. Given their standardized structure, however, the amount of benefits owed in a particular case is far more predictable and certain than tort damages, facilitating efficient resolution of many potential disputes.

3. Coverage and Compensable Injuries

Given the structure of workers' compensation regimes, and in particular the fact that workers' compensation is no-fault and its benefits structure standardized, disputes that do arise as a result of workplace injuries and illnesses typically involve coverage and compensability — that is, whether the worker, employer, and particular injury fall within the scope of the regime. For example, take a moment to look back at *Fitzgerald v. Mobil Oil Corp.* in Chapter 1, page 9. In that case, Fitzgerald was hurt while working, and the disputed issue was whether he was an "employee" of Mobil Oil at the time: If so, his remedies against Mobil were limited to workers' compensation; if not, he could bring claims against Mobil in tort. In light of the benefits described above, why did Mobil Oil argue vigorously for employee status and Fitzgerald argue against it? Recall, however, that whether being an "employee" is in fact beneficial to a worker depends on the circumstances. Employment status (and hence, workers' compensation coverage) is beneficial where the worker might have difficulties recovering against the firm in tort — for instance, difficulty in establishing negligence or causation. What does this tell you about the circumstances surrounding the accident in *Fitzgerald*?

When worker and firm are found to be employee and employer, participation in the state's workers' compensation scheme is mandatory for the employer in all states except Texas, although very small employers are sometimes exempted, and many states exempt or limit coverage for certain agriculture and domestic workers. Nevertheless, the vast majority of employees are covered.

Where these threshold issues of employment and statutory coverage are satisfied, the next issue is whether the injury or illness is compensable. Compensable injuries are accidental injuries that occur in the course of employment and arise out of employment. The concept of "accident," the notion of "course of employment," and the requirement that an injury "arise out" of employment have each raised questions as to the reach of workers' compensation coverage. Further, some workplace illnesses, including occupational diseases, are subject to separate statutory treatment since they may not be accidental in the sense that they were not sudden or unexpected. This section considers each of these concepts.

a. Injuries Sustained "in the Course of" Employment

In most cases, determining whether a worker sustains an injury in the course of employment or outside of employment is easy. However, sometimes this issue is far from clear-cut because the worker's conduct or actions are outside of or inconsistent with the worker's job duties and are not for the benefit of the employer. Most cases falling into this gray area involve situations in which worker injuries occurred while the worker was traveling to or from work, on a "frolic or detour," engaging in "horseplay" or unauthorized conduct at work, participating in extracurricular activities somehow related to work, or acting in pursuit of personal interest. As you read, keep in mind that, while the "in the course of" employment inquiry is similar to the one courts use to determine whether an employer is liable for an employee's tort under the doctrine of respondeat superior (something you may have studied in your torts class and this book touched on in Chapter 1), the law governing this issue in the workers' compensation context is somewhat different, embodying its own set of considerations.

Kindel v. Ferco Rental, Inc.
899 P.2d 1058 (Kan. 1995)

LOCKETT, Judge.

A worker was killed on his return trip home from work. The worker's surviving spouse and minor children claimed death benefits. The Administrative Law Judge (ALJ) denied their claim, finding that the worker had abandoned his employment and therefore the accident did not arise out of and in the course of his employment. On review, the Workers Compensation Board (the Board) reversed the ALJ, finding that the worker's death arose out of and in the course of his employment. The employer appealed . . .

Donald L. Kindel was employed by Ferco Rental, Inc. (Ferco). On October 11, 1991, Kindel was transported in a company pickup truck from his home in Salina,

Kansas, to a construction job site in Sabetha, Kansas. James Graham, Kindel's supervisor, was the driver of the truck. The company truck had been checked out to Graham to transport Kindel and other employees to and from the job site.

On the way to Sabetha, Graham and Kindel passed a former employee of Ferco. Kindel held up a note inviting the former co-worker to join them at the Outer Limits, a "striptease" bar adjacent to Interstate 70 on the west side of Topeka. At approximately 3:30 p.m., after completing the day's work at the job site in Sabetha, Graham and Kindel proceeded back toward Salina. On the way, the two men stopped at the Outer Limits for approximately four hours, where they became inebriated.

Graham suffers from amnesia and cannot recall any of the events occurring after they stopped at the Outer Limits. Graham testified, however, that it was Kindel's idea to stop at the Outer Limits; that Kindel made the arrangements to meet the former co-worker at the Outer Limits after work that day; and that if Kindel would have wanted to proceed straight home, Graham would have done so.

At approximately 8:50 p.m., the Kansas Highway Patrol received a call of a motor vehicle accident on Interstate 70. . . . When Trooper McCool arrived at the accident scene, he observed the Ferco truck overturned and lying in the south ditch of the westbound lane near an entrance to a rest area. Graham, who was driving, and Kindel had been partially ejected out of the truck's windshield. Kindel was deceased. Subsequent tests determined that Graham and Kindel had blood alcohol levels of .225 and .26, respectively.

Prior to the accident, Graham and Kindel were aware that Ferco had a policy that, except to obtain food or fuel, company vehicles were to be used only to go directly from the shop to the job site. Company vehicles were not to be used for personal pleasure or business. Ferco had a comprehensive drug and alcohol policy in place at the time of the accident which, among other things, prohibited workers from using the company equipment while under the influence of alcohol. Employees were not authorized to use a company vehicle to stop at a bar to consume alcohol. Kindel signed off on this policy on December 8, 1990. The employer asserted that when the employees stopped at the bar, authorization to use the company vehicle ceased and any further use of the company vehicle was not part of their employment.

At the time of the accident on October 11, 1991, Graham possessed a valid Kansas driver's license. Ferco was aware of Graham's propensity for drinking and driving. Graham had been charged with DUI some six days prior to this incident and had a previous conviction for which he had had his driver's license suspended. Graham understood that he was prohibited from drinking while using company equipment. Graham testified that the reason for stopping at the Outer Limits was to pursue pleasure and to have a good time. He said it was his understanding that when he pulled up at the Outer Limits, his work was over for the day.

Kindel's surviving spouse and minor children filed a workers compensation claim, seeking death benefits pursuant to K.S.A.1991 Supp. 44-510b. The ALJ found "that the deviation was so substantial and there is not a causal connection between the deviation and the purpose of employment, nor a causal nexus between the resulting accident and death as to say that the claimant had ever returned to the scope of his employment. . . . The subsequent death, therefore, did not arise out of and in the course of his employment."

The ALJ made no findings as to whether Kindel's death resulted substantially from his intoxication. The claimants appealed.

After reviewing the record, the Board reached the opposite conclusion, finding that Kindel's death arose out of and in the course of his employment. The Board acknowledged case law from other jurisdictions supporting the ALJ's decision, but found case law supporting a finding of compensability to be more persuasive. The Board first noted that Kindel's trip to and from Sabetha, absent the detour, would have been considered a part of his employment. The Board stated that even if it assumed that the deviation from employment increased the risk of injury, the injury and resulting death resulted from the combined personal and work-related risks. The Board concluded that, under Kansas law, the increased risk attributable to the deviation did not, by itself, bar recovery. . . .

[The Board went on to conclude that "this case is not materially different from any other where a claimant deviates from his employment but has returned at the time of the accident. The Appeals Board therefore finds that claimant's death arose out of and in the course of his employment."]

The Board reversed the decision of the ALJ and remanded the case for a determination of the appropriate benefits. The employer appealed. . . .

Arising out of and in the Course of Employment

Although K.S.A.1991 Supp. 44-508(f), a codification of the longstanding "going and coming" rule, provides that injuries occurring while traveling to and from employment are generally not compensable, there is an exception which applies when travel upon the public roadways is an integral or necessary part of the employment. *See Blair v. Shaw*, 233 P.2d 731 (Kan. 1951); *Messenger v. Sage Drilling Co.*, 680 P.2d 556 (Kan. App. 1984). Because Kindel and other Ferco employees were expected to live out of town during the work weeks, and transportation to and from the remote site was in a company vehicle driven by a supervisor, this case falls within the exception to the general rule.

In any employment to which workers compensation laws apply, an employer is liable to pay compensation to an employee where the employee incurs personal injury by accident arising out of and in the course of employment. Whether an accident arises out of and in the course of the worker's employment depends upon the facts peculiar to the particular case.

The two phrases arising "out of" and "in the course of" employment, as used in our Workers Compensation Act, K.S.A. 44-501 *et seq.*, have separate and distinct meanings; they are conjunctive, and each condition must exist before compensation is allowable. The phrase "out of" employment points to the cause or origin of the accident and requires some causal connection between the accidental injury and the employment. An injury arises "out of" employment when there is apparent to the rational mind, upon consideration of all the circumstances, a causal connection between the conditions under which the work is required to be performed and the resulting injury. Thus, an injury arises "out of" employment if it arises out of the nature, conditions, obligations, and incidents of the employment. The phrase "in the course of" employment relates to the time, place, and circumstances under which the accident occurred and means the injury happened while the worker was at work in the employer's service.

Both the ALJ and the Board acknowledge the separate considerations inherent in the determination whether the death arose "out of" and "in the course of" employment.

The ALJ concluded that the length of time Kindel spent at the Outer Limits and his substantial consumption of alcohol removed his subsequent activity from arising "in the course of" his employment, notwithstanding the fact he was on his homeward route at the time of the accident. The Board, on the other hand, determined that Kindel's injury and death resulted from combined risks attributable to his personal deviation *and* his employment, and held that the increased risk factor attributable to the deviation should not bar recovery. The point of disagreement between the ALJ and Board is whether the deviation was so substantial as to permanently remove the worker from the course of his employment, even though he later continued his homeward route. The parties cite various cases for support of their respective positions.

Two Kansas cases address a somewhat similar situation and determined whether the worker had abandoned his employer's business. They are *Angleton v. Starkan, Inc.*, 828 P.2d 933 (Kan. 1992), and *Woodring v. United Sash & Door Co.*, 103 P.2d 837 (Kan. 1940). . . . Angleton, who was employed as a truck driver for Starkan, was hauling a load of cattle when a pair of hijackers began following him in another truck. By conversation over the citizens band radio, one of the hijackers persuaded Angleton to pull off the highway to smoke marijuana. Angleton stopped his truck and got into the hijackers' truck. While Angleton was smoking a marijuana cigarette, one of the hijackers shot and killed him. . . .

The *Angleton* court first determined that absent the alleged marijuana episode, the accident occurred in the course of Angleton's employment. The court noted that at the time of his death, Angleton was en route to deliver his load of cattle to a feedlot on the route designated by his employer and that at the time Angleton pulled off the highway, he was driving his load in fulfillment of his employment obligations. The court further observed that Angleton was killed because he was responsible for the Starkan truck and cattle and his employment for Starkan transporting valuable cargo exposed him to an increased risk of injury of being robbed while on the highway.

The *Angleton* court then examined whether the alleged use of marijuana changed the district court's conclusion that the accident resulting in Angleton's death arose out of and in the course of his employment. The district court had noted that the only testimony that Angleton pulled off the highway to smoke marijuana was the testimony by one of the hijackers and found that testimony to be inherently unreliable. . . . The *Angleton* court determined that the record supported the district court's finding that the hijacker's testimony was unreliable and held that the testimony was not sufficient or reliable to support a finding that the worker's conduct constituted a deviation from his employment. The court found that Angleton's death arose in the course of and out of his employment.

In *Woodring* . . . , the claimant was a traveling salesman who lived in Salina. Woodring was sent by his employer to meet a client in Enterprise, Kansas, to further the employer's business. Prior to arriving at Enterprise, the claimant went to Minneapolis, Kansas, and picked up three friends who made the journey to Enterprise with him. When the worker arrived at Enterprise, he discovered the man he was supposed to meet was in Abilene. The claimant made no further attempts to contact the client, and instead proceeded to a local drinking establishment with his friends for "an hour or so" where he imbibed intoxicating liquor. Thereafter, while driving recklessly on his return journey to Salina, claimant was injured when his car overturned. . . .

The *Woodring* court then observed that where a business errand is the purpose of a worker's journey, the social incident of taking a few guests along for the pleasure of their company would not affect the worker's right to compensation for an injury sustained in the performance of that errand. The *Woodring* court noted that an intruding question was whether a worker, engaged in the employer's service, could be permitted to recover compensation for an injury sustained while operating an automobile on the public highway under the influence of intoxicating liquor in violation of a Kansas statute which made such an act a criminal offense punishable by fine or imprisonment or both. It found that because the district court had determined the business errand was finished or abandoned and that the worker had set about the pursuit of his own pleasure or indulgence, there was no theory of law or of justice which would impose on the employer the obligation to pay compensation for any injury sustained by the worker under such circumstances.

The claimants rely heavily on *Angleton* . . . for support of a finding of compensability in this case. The claimants seek to distinguish *Woodring*, noting that Kindel was a passenger being driven home by his supervisor in a company vehicle and that the supervisor was required to return his employer's vehicle. The employer fails to address the *Angleton* precedent, but contends that the rationale of *Woodring* should be applied to this case. It is important to note that in *Angleton* and *Woodring* there were allegations that the worker was violating the law. Here, although Kindel was intoxicated, the fact he drank was not a violation of the law nor was he violating a law, at the time he was killed.

In support of their arguments, both parties cite numerous cases from outside of Kansas. The most favorable case for the employer is *Calloway v. Workmen's Comp.*, 268 S.E.2d 132 (W. Va. 1980). In *Calloway*, the West Virginia Supreme Court found the claimant salesman's activity of drinking and tavern-hopping from midafternoon until 11 p.m. amounted to an abandonment of any business purpose such that the injuries he received in an accident shortly thereafter while being transported home were not compensable. The *Calloway* court acknowledged that workers compensation laws generally recognize that an employee is entitled to compensation for an injury received while travelling on behalf of his employer's business.

The court noted that where an employee deviates from the employer's business, the employee may be denied compensation if the injury occurs during the deviation and that once the employee ceases the deviation and returns to the employer's business, a subsequent injury is ordinarily compensable. The court then observed:

> In the case of a major deviation from the business purpose, most courts will bar compensation recovery on the theory that the deviation is so substantial that the employee must be deemed to have abandoned any business purpose and consequently cannot recover for injuries received, even though he has ceased the deviation and is returning to the business route or purpose. [Citations omitted.]
>
> . . . A deviation generally consists of a personal or nonbusiness-related activity. The longer the deviation exists in time or the greater it varies from the normal business route or in purpose from the normal business objectives, the more likely that it will be characterized as major.

The *Calloway* court then reviewed a number of cases in which various courts have characterized an employee's deviations to be sufficiently major to deny compensation. The *Calloway* court concluded:

> In the present case, there is no dispute that the claimant was initially traveling on behalf of his employer in an attempt to solicit new business in the Logan County area. However, even under the facts liberally construed in his behalf, he had completed any company

business in the midafternoon when he and his fellow employee began to frequent taverns. The continuation of this activity until 11:00 p.m. was a major deviation, not only in time but also in its nature. It can only be viewed as an abandonment of any business purpose.

The most favorable case for the claimants is *Rainear v. C.J. Rainear & Co.*, 307 A.2d 72 (N.J. 1973). In *Rainear*, the New Jersey Supreme Court held that where an automobile accident had occurred while the decedent was on his way home from work along a proper and permissible route, decedent's 10-hour stop at a restaurant and bar to eat and drink did not amount to such a departure from the decedent's reasonable sphere of employment as to bar a compensation award. In that case, the decedent's travel expenses were being paid by his employer. There was nothing in the record to confirm that drinking caused the accident. The *Rainear* court reviewed a number of cases awarding compensation to employees injured following a deviation. The court stated:

> There is nothing in the compensation law which fixes an arbitrary limit to the number of hours of deviation which may be terminated with travel coverage resumed. Thus if the decedent ate dinner at [the restaurant and bar] en route home and stayed there simply watching television for hours before continuing on his intended travel home, there clearly would be no rational basis for failing to apply the broad remedial principles embraced in [other New Jersey workers compensation cases]. While the fact that he also did some drinking there may have influenced the Appellate Division's negative result, the drinking really has no legal bearing here since there was no proof that the accident or death resulted from intoxication.

A deviation from the employer's work generally consists of a personal or nonbusiness-related activity. The longer the deviation exists in time or the greater it varies from the normal business route or in purpose from the normal business objectives, the more likely that the deviation will be characterized as major. In the case of a major deviation from the business purpose, most courts will bar compensation recovery on the theory that the deviation is so substantial that the employee must be deemed to have abandoned any business purpose and consequently cannot recover for injuries received, even though he or she has ceased the deviation and is returning to the business route or purpose.

Is there substantial evidence to support the Board's finding of compensability, *i.e.*, that Kindel's death arose in the course of his employment? The employer provided transportation. Kindel was a passenger and not the driver. He was being transported home after completion of his duties. Despite approximately four hours at the Outer Limits, the distance of the deviation was less than one quarter of a mile. Kindel was killed after resuming the route home. Under the facts, even though the worker was intoxicated, as a passenger in his employer's vehicle, he was not committing a violation of Kansas law. Kindel was killed while engaging in an activity contemplated by his employer while traveling on a public interstate highway. The fact he had been drinking has no legal bearing on the present compensation determination since there was no proof that the accident or Kindel's death resulted from Kindel's intoxication.

The workers compensation statutes are to be liberally construed to effect legislative intent and award compensation where it is reasonably possible to do so. We note that the workers compensation law does not fix an arbitrary limit on the number of hours of deviation, which may be terminated with travel coverage resumed. Whether there was a deviation, and if that deviation had terminated, is a question of fact to be determined by the administrative law judge or the Workers Compensation Board. Under our standard of review, we find that the Board did not act unreasonably, arbitrarily, or capriciously and there is substantial evidence to support the Board's conclusion that the fatal injury occurred in the course of Kindel's employment.

Did Death Result Substantially from Intoxication?

K.S.A. 1991 Supp. 44-501(d) provides:

If it is proved that the injury to the employee results . . . substantially from the employee's intoxication, any compensation in respect to that injury shall be disallowed.

Employer contends that Kindel's intoxication was a substantially causative factor in bringing about his death. . . .

To defeat a workers compensation claim based on the worker's intoxication, an employer must prove not only that the worker was intoxicated, but also that such intoxication was the substantial cause of the injury. The presumption of intoxication provided for under the Kansas criminal statute is inapplicable in workers compensation cases. Evidence of the blood alcohol concentration of a workers compensation claimant is relevant to the issue of the cause of the accident in which the claimant is injured but does not give rise to a presumption of intoxication. . . .

To this court, the employer asserts that Kansas courts have recognized that a passenger owes a duty to exercise that care which a reasonably careful person would use for his or her own protection under the existing circumstances. . . .

Common-law defenses to tort theories of negligence do not apply to workers compensation claims. . . .

Because Kindel was covered by workers compensation, these defenses are not available to the employer; therefore, Kindel had no common-law duty as a passenger.

In addition, the employer failed to prove that Kindel's intoxication was a substantial cause of the injury. The testimony of Trooper McCool was that the alcohol level of the driver was a substantial cause of the accident. Neither the ALJ nor the Board concluded that the accident substantially resulted from Kindel's intoxication. The fact that Kindel was a passenger, and not the driver, defeats the employer's claim. . . .

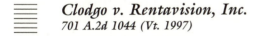

Clodgo v. Rentavision, Inc.
701 A.2d 1044 (Vt. 1997)

GIBSON, Justice.

Defendant Rentavision, Inc. appeals a decision of the Commissioner of the Vermont Department of Labor and Industry awarding workers' compensation benefits to claimant Brian Clodgo. Rentavision argues the Commissioner erred in awarding compensation for an injury sustained while claimant and another employee were engaged in horseplay. We reverse.

On July 22, 1995, claimant was working as manager of Rentavision's store in Brattleboro. During a lull between customers, claimant began firing staples with a staple gun at a co-worker, who was sitting on a couch watching television. The co-worker first protested, but then, after claimant had fired twenty or thirty staples at him, fired three staples back at claimant. As claimant ducked, the third staple hit him in the eye. Claimant eventually reported the injury and filed a claim for workers' compensation benefits. Rentavision contested the award, arguing that claimant was engaged in noncompensable horseplay at the time of the injury. Following a hearing in March 1996, the Commissioner awarded permanent partial disability and vocational rehabilitation benefits, medical expenses, and attorney's fees and costs. This appeal followed. . . .

Compensable injuries under Vermont's Workers' Compensation Act are those received "by accident arising out of and in the course of . . . employment." 21 V.S.A. §618. Although only work-related injuries are compensable, we recognize that "even [employees] of maturer years [will] indulge in a moment's diversion from work to joke with or play a prank upon a fellow [employee]." *Leonbruno v. Champlain Silk Mills*, 128 N.E. 711, 711 (N.Y. 1920). For such a horseplay-related injury to be compensated, however, claimant must show that it both (1) arose out of the employment, and (2) occurred in the course of the employment. A nonparticipant injured by the horseplay of others will nearly always be able to meet this test, *see* 2 A. LARSON & L. LARSON, WORKERS' COMPENSATION LAW §23.61, at 5-199 (1997), while a participant may or may not recover. *See* 2 LARSON & LARSON, *supra*, §23.20, at 5-182 to 5-183.

In setting forth the applicable standard, the Commissioner stated that nothing short of specific intent to injure falls outside the scope of the Act. This overly broad statement was borrowed, however, from a case analyzing the exclusive-remedy aspects of workers' compensation law, made in the context where an employee attempts to prove specific intent by the employer to injure the employee. *See Kittell v. Vermont Weatherboard, Inc.*, 417 A.2d 926, 927 (Vt. 1980). Whether a horseplay participant is entitled to recover usually hinges on whether the injury occurred in the course of employment, which, in turn, depends on the extent of the employee's deviation from work duties. . . .

The question certified for review is whether claimant's horseplay bars him from recovery for the resulting injury under Vermont's Workers' Compensation Act. Rentavision contends the Commissioner misapplied the law in concluding that claimant's horseplay-related injury was compensable. We agree. An injury arises out of employment if it would not have occurred but for the fact that the conditions and obligations of the employment placed claimant in the position where he or she was injured. Thus, claimant must show that "but for" the employment and his position at work, the injury would not have happened.

Although the accident here would not have happened but for claimant's participation in the horseplay and therefore was not exclusively linked to his employment, it also was not a purely personal risk that would have occurred regardless of his location and activity on that day. He was injured during work hours with a staple gun provided for use on the job, and thus the findings support a causal connection between claimant's work conditions and the injury adequate to conclude that the accident arose out of his employment.

Nonetheless, claimant must also show that the injury occurred in the course of the employment. An accident occurs in the course of employment when it was within the period of time the employee was on duty at a place where the employee was reasonably expected to be *while fulfilling the duties of the employment contract*. Thus, while some horseplay among employees during work hours can be expected and is not an automatic bar to compensation, the key inquiry is whether the employee deviated too far from his or her duties.

The Commissioner must therefore consider (1) the extent and seriousness of the deviation; (2) the completeness of the deviation (i.e., whether the activity was commingled with performance of a work duty or was a complete abandonment of duty); (3) the extent to which the activity had become an accepted part of the employment; and (4) the extent to which the nature of the employment may be expected to include some horseplay. The Commissioner found that although shooting staples was common among employees, such activity was not considered acceptable behavior by Rentavision. She made no finding concerning whether Rentavision knew that staple-shooting occurred at work, but did find that claimant made material misrepresentations of fact designed to avoid an inference of horseplay or inappropriate behavior in order that he might obtain workers' compensation benefits. Claimant makes no showing that shooting staples at fellow employees was an accepted part of claimant's employment or furthered Rentavision's interests.

The facts show that the accident was unrelated to any legitimate use of the staplers at the time, indicating there was no commingling of the horseplay with work duties. The Commissioner focused on the slack time inherent in claimant's job, but this factor alone is not dispositive. Although some horseplay was reasonably to be expected during idle periods between customers, the obvious dangerousness of shooting staples at fellow employees and the absence of connection between duties as a salesperson and the horseplay events indicates the accident occurred during a substantial deviation from work duties. Therefore, we reverse the Commissioner's award.

Reversed.

MORSE, Justice, dissenting.

I respectfully dissent. The Court reverses a decision of the Commissioner of the Vermont Department of Labor and Industry awarding workers' compensation benefits for an injury sustained while claimant was engaged in "horseplay" with another employee. The basic criteria of analysis utilized by the Commissioner are not disputed by the Court. Rather, the Court disagrees with the Commissioner's application of the law to the facts, holding that the horseplay constituted a substantial deviation from the course of employment and therefore was not compensable.

Under settled standards of review, the Court has stepped out of its proper role. The Court is not to second-guess the Commissioner's conclusions. . . .

With respect to the extent and seriousness of the deviation, as well as its completeness, the Commissioner found that claimant and his fellow employee had completed virtually all the work that needed to be done in the absence of customers and that business was very slow that day. When the injury occurred, claimant and his fellow employee were in a period of enforced idleness while they waited for customers. They were not actively pursuing any specific tasks and were passing the time as required by their jobs. As Larson points out, when there is a lull in work, there are no duties to abandon. During such periods, the deviation can be more substantial than at other times when an employee may be actively pursuing a task directly related to employment. *Id.* § 23.65, at 5-219, 5-226 to 5-227. The Commissioner could thus reasonably conclude that the horseplay in this case did not constitute an abandonment of duties or even a serious deviation from the demands of work at that time of day.

Regarding the extent to which such horseplay had become an accepted activity, the Commissioner found that it had been a commonplace occurrence at the store.

Although the executive assistant to defendant's president testified that claimant's horseplay was not considered acceptable behavior, he acknowledged that an employee would not be fired for engaging in such activity. The Commissioner thus reasonably concluded that the horseplay as engaged in by claimant, while not condoned by the employer, was a tacit part of employment.

Finally, the Commissioner could reasonably conclude that work in a retail establishment might be expected to include such horseplay. The Commissioner characterized the claimant and his fellow employee as "suffering through a very slow day in a retail establishment," having quoted Larson as noting that "idleness breeds mischief, so that if idleness is a fixture of the employment, its handmaiden mischief is also." (Quoting 2 LARSON & LARSON, *supra*, §23.65, at 5-219.) Retail work necessitates passing time if there are no customers demanding attention. . . . The Commissioner's determination that the nature of the business lent itself to the horseplay in question was fairly and reasonably supported by the facts.

In sum, the Commissioner applied the proper legal standard to the facts, and the evidence fairly and reasonably supports the Commissioner's conclusion, a conclusion that, I might add, is a reasonable one given the policy of the law to help alleviate the consequences of injury in the workplace. . . .

NOTES

1. *A Sufficient Connection with Employment?* Ultimately, the "in the course of" and "arises out of" requirements seek to ensure that the injury was sufficiently connected with work or the workplace to justify shifting the risk of loss to the employer and the workers' compensation system. Based on your reading of *Kindel* and *Clodgo*, what is the legal standard for determining if an injury occurs "in the course of" employment? Why do the courts reach opposite conclusions on whether the injuries in question satisfied this standard? One could strongly argue that the horseplay at issue in *Clodgo* was not as significant a deviation from the workers' duties as conduct at issue in *Kindel*, which involved spending several hours at an off-site location. How can the cases be reconciled, if at all?

As discussed above, there is an ongoing debate about the efficiency and efficacy of workers' compensation — a system that costs billions of dollars a year. If rising costs and cost containment are legitimate concerns, why should the employer be responsible for injuries sustained outside the workplace and outside an employee's specified work duties and tasks? Why might such broad coverage be socially beneficial (i.e., worth the costs)? Even if you conclude that the employer's responsibility ought to extend beyond the scope of workplace duties in some circumstances, can the result in *Kindel* be justified?

2. *The Journey to and from Work.* Under the "going and coming rule," an injury occurring during a worker's journey to and from work — before and after work, or during the lunch break — is not compensable, unless it occurs on the work premises or in the employer's vehicle. *See* LARSON & LARSON, *supra*, at §§13.01, 15.01. However, there are a number of exceptions to this principle. Most importantly, travel to and from work is compensable if the journey itself is a substantial part of the worker's service or if, based on the employer's needs or requests, the journey is made with a special degree of inconvenience or urgency. Thus, for example, where travel to different locations is part of the job, the employee travels on a "special errand" for the employer, or the employee must travel to remote sites, such travel is often considered in the course of employment. *See id.* at §§ 13.01, 14.01-.06. Of increasing importance in the era of telecommuting, travel between home and work may be in the course of employment if home is a regular "second office." Why did the court find that the commute from work at issue in *Kindel* was in the course of employment?

3. *Worker Intoxication and Misconduct.* Injuries resulting from or relating to the use or abuse of alcohol or drugs are common subjects of controversy in the workers' compensation context. As we saw in *Kindel,* many states now limit recovery for injuries sustained as a result of intoxication, although the extent to which alcohol must have "caused" the injuries varies by statute and is a frequently litigated issue. *See, e.g., Cyr v. McDermott's, Inc.* 996 A.2d 709 (Vt. 2010) (reversing and remanding the labor commissioner's denial of workers' compensation benefits after finding that, although the worker was intoxicated when he ingested chemicals from a soda bottle that had been given to him while at work, there remained an issue whether the intoxication caused his resulting injuries). *See generally* LARSON & LARSON, *supra,* at §§ 36.01, 36.03. Why were Kindel's wife and children still able to recover benefits despite the intoxication provision in the Kansas statute? Were Graham's injuries compensable?

Some states also provide a statutory defense for "willful misconduct." Although this kind of defense could be interpreted broadly, courts generally have limited its application to deliberate or intentional violations of regulations designed to prevent serious injury or intentional and knowing violations of statutes designed to prevent the type of injury that occurred. *See* LARSON & LARSON, *supra,* at §§ 34.01-.03, 37.03. Thus, mere horseplay like that at issue in *Clogdo* would not constitute willful misconduct, although, as that case makes clear, such conduct may still fall outside the course of employment. Does the narrow reading of willful misconduct make sense in light of what you know about the purpose of the workers' compensation system and the "trade-offs" that it embodies?

Finally, note that the *Kindel* court rejects the employer's attempt to use common-law tort defenses, including the defense that a passenger is obliged to take reasonable care to ensure his or her own safety under the circumstances. Here again we see the trade-off underlying workers' compensation: Just as injured employees cannot bring common-law tort claims, employers cannot escape workers' compensation liability by presenting common-law defenses.

4. *Work-related Recreational or "Extracurricular" Activities.* A recurrent issue involving the connection between the injury and employment is whether recreational and social activities — for example, sports, exercising, games, social gatherings — are within the course of employment. As a general matter, they are — if they occur on the employers' premises during normal work breaks or otherwise incident to employment. In addition, such activities are within the course of employment when required by the employer or when the employer derives some direct benefit from the activity beyond mere enhancement of employee health or morale. *See generally* LARSON & LARSON, *supra,* at §§ 22.01-.05. The more tenuous the nexus between the activity and the workplace, work terms and hours, and direct employer sponsorship or support, the less likely it is that it will be found to be "in the course of" employment. *Compare Bender v. Dakota Resorts Mgmt., Inc.,* 700 N.W.2d 739 (S.D. 2005) (finding compensable injury sustained by employee of ski resort injured while skiing at the resort during his break, which he and other employees did on a regular basis); *E.C. Styberg Engineering Co., Inc. v. Lab. and Indus. Rev. Comm'n,* 692 N.W.2d 322 (Wis. Ct. App. 2004) (same for softball injury sustained during paid break) *with Montgomery County v. Smith,* 799 A.2d 406 (Md. Ct. App. 2002) (denying workers' compensation benefits to a worker injured while playing basketball after his workday in gym at

detention center where he worked where employer did not require or sponsor activity). Courts remain deeply split over whether injuries occurring during employer-sponsored parties, picnics, and other events are within the course of employment, although distinctions sometimes hinge on the degree of employer pressure to attend or participate. *See*, LARSON & LARSON, *supra*, at § 22.04; *see, e.g.*, *Young v. Taylor-White, LLC*, 181 S.W.3d 324 (Tenn. 2005) (rejecting claim for benefits where injury occurred in a voluntary "three-legged race" at an employer-sponsored picnic); *State v. Dalton*, 878 A.2d 451 (Del. 2005) (awarding benefits where worker was hurt in charity softball game where evidence suggested that participation by police officers like claimant was expected). Some states have statutorily barred workers' compensation benefits for injuries sustained during recreational activities absent employer compulsion to participate. *See* LARSON & LARSON, *supra*, at § 22.02.

5. *"Personal Comfort" Doctrine.* Another issue that arises often in "in the course of" employment cases is the extent to which injuries that occur during employee deviations from work tasks to seek "personal comfort"—for example, eating, using the restroom, washing, resting, getting warm, and so forth—are compensable. The so-called "personal comfort" doctrine provides that such deviations are in the course of employment unless the departure is sufficiently great that it constitutes an intent to abandon the job temporarily or unless the method chosen is unusual or unreasonable, such that it cannot be considered incidental to employment. *See generally* LARSON & LARSON, *supra*, at §§ 21.01-.08. Although the inquiry is fact-specific, injuries are usually compensable in run-of-the-mill cases involving breaks for personal comforts at work during work hours. *See, e.g.*, *Illinois Consol. Tel. Co. v. Indus. Comm'n*, 732 N.E.2d 49 (Ill. Ct. App. 2000) (awarding benefits to worker who was injured in a fall down the stairs while returning to work from the restroom). Greater deviations, however, often are not compensable. *See, e.g.*, *Galaida v. Autozone, Inc.*, 882 So.2d 1111 (Fla. Ct. App. 2004) (finding that, although an authorized cigarette break might qualify under the doctrine, a gunshot wound an employee received during such a break was not compensable because the employee's conduct—dropping a firearm while reaching for a cigarette out of his car—and resulting injury were not a foreseeable consequence of the break); *In re Estate of Fry*, 620 N.W.2d 449 (Wis. Ct. App. 2000) (estate of worker killed in traffic accident while en route to a medical appointment with employer's permission not entitled to recovery under personal comfort doctrine). Indeed, the doctrine applies only to injuries occurring on work premises or other areas where workers are authorized to be during work hours.

b. *"Arises out of" Employment*

Odyssey/Americare of Oklahoma v. Worden
948 P.2d 309 (Ok. 1997)

HODGES, Justice.

Odyssey/Americare of Oklahoma (Employer) and its insurer seek vacation of a Court of Civil Appeals opinion in this matter which sustained an order of the Workers' Compensation Court awarding benefits to Cheryl Worden (Claimant). The trial tribunal found that Claimant's injury arose out of her employment. This Court finds that there was not competent evidence to support that determination.

Claimant was a field nurse for Employer. She lived approximately twenty miles away from Employer's office. She went to Employer's office about once a week. Otherwise, she worked out of her home scheduling appointments with patients and traveling to visit them. At trial, the parties submitted a stipulation that Claimant was Employer's employee covered under the Workers' Compensation Act. Claimant testified that as she was walking to her car to go to a patient appointment, she slipped on wet grass in her yard and fell injuring her foot and ankle. The grass was wet from rain. But for the patient appointment, she would not have left the house.

The trial tribunal originally denied the claim, finding that her injury did not arise out of and in the course of her employment. According to the court, "the claimant's injuries were as a result of a risk which was purely personal to the claimant and not as a result of a hazardous risk associated with the claimant's employment." . . .

Oklahoma law requires that an employer pay compensation only for "accidental personal injury sustained by the employee arising out of and in the course of his employment, without regard to fault. . . ." OKLA. STAT. tit. 85, §11 (1991). The term "in the course of employment" relates to the time, place, or circumstances under which the injury is sustained. The term "arise out of employment" contemplates the causal connection between the injury and the risks incident to employment. The two requirements are distinct and are not synonymous. *Id.* Only the "arise out of" requirement is at issue in this matter. The parties agree that Claimant was in the course of her employment at the time of injury.

There are three categories of injury-causing risk an employee may encounter while in the course of employment: risks solely connected with employment, which are compensable; personal risks, which are not compensable; and neutral risks, such as weather risks, which are neither distinctly connected with employment nor purely personal. *See* 1 LARSON'S WORKERS' COMPENSATION LAW §7.30 (1997). Whether a neutral risk that causes an injury is employment-related or personal is a question of fact to be decided in each case.

Nationwide, there have been five lines of interpretation of the "arising out of" requirement. 1 LARSON *supra* at §6. The "peculiar risk" doctrine required the claimant "to show that the source of the harm was in its nature peculiar to his occupation." *Id.* at §6.20. At one time the peculiar risk doctrine was the dominant test in American Workers' Compensation jurisprudence but it was gradually replaced by the "increased risk" doctrine.

The "increased risk" test "differs from the peculiar-risk test in that the distinctiveness of the employment risk can be contributed by the increased *quantity* of a risk that is *qualitatively* not peculiar to the employment." *Id.* The rule is often stated as a determination of whether the claimant's employment exposed the worker to more risk than that to which the general public was exposed.

An easier test for a claimant to meet is that of "actual risk." "Under this doctrine, a substantial number of courts are saying, in effect, 'We do not care whether the risk was also common to the public, if in fact it was a risk of *this* employment.'" *Id.* at §6.40.

A number of courts now apply the "positional risk" doctrine. It states that "[a]n injury arises out of employment if it would not have occurred *but for* the fact that the conditions on the employment placed claimant in the position where he was injured." *Id.* at §6.50.

A rarely used line of interpretation is that of "proximate cause." This test demands "that the harms be foreseeable as a hazard of this kind of employment, and that the chain of causation be not broken by any independent intervening cause, such as an act of God." *Id.* at § 6.60. This line of authority is "encountered occasionally in opinions and old texts." *Id.*

Prior to the 1986 amendments to Oklahoma's Workers' Compensation Act, Oklahoma cases relied primarily on the increased risk doctrine to determine whether a risk arose out of a worker's employment. However, the peculiar risk and positional risk tests had also been applied. *See, e.g., Halliburton Services v. Alexander*, 547 P.2d 958, 961 (Okla. 1976) ("where accidental injury results from risk factor peculiar to task performed, it arises out of employment. . . ."); *Fox v. Nat'l Carrier*, 709 P.2d 1050, 1053 (Okla. 1985) (but for claimant's employment as truck driver he would not have been exposed to risk of choking on food at restaurant). But in 1986, the Oklahoma Legislature amended section 3(7) of title 85 to require that "only injuries having as their source a risk not purely personal but one that is reasonably connected with the conditions of employment shall be deemed to arise out of employment." The Legislature also repealed the provision which required an employer to produce "substantial evidence" to overcome a presumption that an injury was compensable under the Workers' Compensation Act. *See* OKLA. STAT. tit. 85, § 27 (1981) (repealed). The presumption and its corresponding burdens of production and persuasion were abolished.

These statutory changes to the analysis of the "arise out of" requirement were explained in *Am. Mgmt. Sys., Inc. v. Burns*, 903 P.2d 288 (Okla. 1995). In *Burns*, a worker visiting Oklahoma City on a business trip for his employer was murdered in his hotel room by an unknown assailant with unknown motive. This Court explained that a claimant now has the burden of establishing the causal connection between injury and employment. "To establish injury or death as attributable to an employment-related risk, the operative force of a hazard, other than that which affects the public in general, must be identified." This Court specifically held that the positional risk test is now "unavailable for proving an injury's causal nexus to employment." Burn[s'] widow failed to establish that her husband's death arose out of his employment rather than from the ever-present risk of crime faced by the general public.

Despite the holding in *Burns*, the Court of Civil Appeals in this matter held that "because the risk responsible was clearly presented by the requirements of her employment, it does not matter whether the risk of injury to her was no greater than the risk to the general public." Thus, it applied essentially the positional risk test rejected in the 1986 amendments to the Workers' Compensation Act as explained in *Burns*.

The Court of Civil Appeals read two post-*Burns* cases as controlling this controversy, *Darco Transp. v. Dulen*, 922 P.2d [591 (Okla. 1996)] and *Stroud Mun. Hosp. v. Mooney*, 933 P.2d 872 (Okla. 1996). It noted that in each case compensation was allowed for traffic collision injuries even though the employee was exposed to the same street risk faced by the general motoring public. That is true, but for reasons that are not present in the instant claim.

In *Darco*, a cross-country truck driver was injured when the tractor-trailer rig he was driving was struck by a train at a crossing where the warning equipment had malfunctioned. The test this Court applied was the same increased risk test that had been applied in *Burns*. However, the accident risk the truck driver encountered in *Darco* arose out of his employment "because the perils of this servant's travel for his master [were] co-extensive with the risks of employment." *Darco*. Thus, for that truck driver the risk of traffic accident arose from the very nature of his employment.

The Court of Civil Appeals also read *Stroud Mun. Hosp. v. Mooney*, as modifying the rule in *Burns*. *Mooney* involved an exception to the "general rule that an injury sustained while going to or from an employer's premises is not one arising out of and in the course of employment." There, the special mission exception applied because the employee was instructed to return immediately from his lunch break at home to the emergency room of his employer's hospital in order for him to perform emergency blood work. The employee was injured in an automobile accident while he was attempting to comply with his employer's instruction. . . .

In this matter, there are no facts to indicate that Claimant was on a special mission outside regular working hours for her employer. In fact, the record demonstrated that she was within her regular working hours performing her usual tasks. *Mooney*'s special mission exception was not asserted by Claimant nor does it apply to these facts.

Neither *Darco* nor *Mooney* abrogate or modify the increased risk test required by the Workers' Compensation Act and described in *Burns*. . . .

This case is controlled by the increased risk test for the arising out of element of coverage provided in the Workers' Compensation Act. . . . The question is whether Claimant's employment subjected her to a risk that exceeded the ordinary hazards to which the general public is exposed. It did not.

Claimant encountered the neutral risk of wet and therefore slippery grass due to rain. Her employment exposed her to no more risk of injury from wet grass than that encountered by any member of the general public. No evidence was presented linking the risk to her employment. Although Claimant was undeniably in the course of her employment at the time of her injury, the injury did not arise from her employment. The trial tribunal's initial order denying coverage was correct. The order allowing compensation was error.

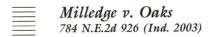

Milledge v. Oaks
784 N.E.2d 926 (Ind. 2003)

RUCKER, Justice.

Case Summary

This case presents the question of when and to what extent an injury resulting from an unexplained accident occurring in the workplace is compensable under Indiana's Worker's Compensation Act. We conclude that an unexplained accident represents a "neutral risk" and that the "positional-risk" doctrine applies. Under which, an injury is compensable if it would not have occurred but for the fact that the condition or obligation of the employment put the employee in the position at the time of injury.

Facts and Procedural History

In 1983 Phyllis Milledge began working as a housekeeper at a nursing home known as "The Oaks, A Living Center." On October 21, 1994, she arrived at work shortly before 7 a.m. to begin her usual shift and parked her car in the nursing home parking lot. After closing the door upon exiting the car Milledge twisted her ankle. She proceeded to her job and completed the majority of her shift but the pain in her ankle prevented Milledge from finishing her duties. Leaving work early, Milledge went to the emergency room of a local hospital where x-rays revealed a sprained ankle. However, her ankle still bothered her a week after the injury. Among other things she suffered swelling in her right leg, and her right foot was severely discolored. In addition, a large blister had developed on her ankle, which her husband lanced on two occasions. Milledge returned to the hospital on November 6, 1994, where she was treated with antibiotics. On November 14, 1994, after surgical procedures failed to control the infection that had developed, Milledge's right leg was amputated below the knee. Subsequently, she was fitted with a prosthesis.

When The Oaks' worker's compensation insurance carrier denied her claim for benefits on March 3, 1995, Milledge filed an Application for Adjustment of Claim before the Worker's Compensation Board. On July 21, 1999, a hearing was conducted before a single-member hearing officer who denied the claim concluding in part:

> The record shows [Milledge's] injury may have occurred in the course of her employment, but fails to show any causal connection between her ankle sprain and her work duties for [The Oaks]. Thus, [Milledge's] injury did not arise out of and in the course of her employment with [The Oaks] for the purposes of the [Indiana Worker's Compensation] Act.

[The full Board adopted the hearing officer's decision, and the Court of Appeals affirmed. The Supreme Court reversed.]

Discussion . . .

There is no question that the injury Milledge sustained in this case occurred in the course of her employment. She sprained her ankle on the parking lot of her employer while arriving for work at her regularly scheduled time. [The governing case was *Outlaw v. Erbrich Prods. Co., Inc.*, 742 N.E.2d 526, 530 (Ind. Ct. App. 2001), holding that "an accident occurs 'in the course of employment' when it takes place within the period of employment, at a place where the employee may reasonably be, and while the employee is fulfilling the duties of employment or while engaged in doing something incidental thereto."] Rather, the question is whether Milledge's injury arose out of her employment. Highlighting the Board's finding that the parking lot was "clean, dry, level and clear of debris" the Court of Appeals concluded the injury Milledge sustained did not arise out of her employment. This was so because the facts of this case lacked the requisite causal connection between the injury and the employment.

Commenting on the causal connection necessary to show that an accidental injury arises out of employment, this Court has said "[the] nexus is established when a reasonably prudent person considers the injury to be born out of a risk incidental to the employment, or when the facts indicate a connection between the injury and the circumstances under which the employment occurs." *Wine-Settergren v. Lamey*, 716 N.E.2d 381, 389 (Ind. 1999).

The "risks incidental to employment" fall into three categories: (1) risks distinctly associated with employment, (2) risks personal to the claimant, and (3) risks of neither distinctly employment nor distinctly personal in character. Risks that fall within categories numbered one and three are generally covered under the Indiana Worker's Compensation Act. However risks personal to the claimant, those "caused by a pre-existing illness or condition unrelated to employment," are not compensable. . . . In this case there was nothing inherent in The Oaks' parking lot that either caused or contributed to Milledge's injury. As such her injury was not born out of a risk categorized as distinctly associated with employment.

As for category number two, the record does not show that Milledge's injury to her ankle was the result of a pre-existing illness or condition. To the contrary, although the Board made no finding on this point, uncontroverted evidence of record reveals that prior to the accident of October 21, 1994, Milledge experienced no problems with her right leg in general or to her ankle in particular. The record also shows, that although Milledge suffered from diabetes for thirty years, at the time of the accident she was taking medication for her diabetes and she reported having no trouble with the illness; additionally, she noted that diabetes had never prevented her from fulfilling her job responsibilities. In this case Milledge simply has no explanation of what caused her to twist her ankle; nor does the record give any indication of causation. The facts here are thus analogous to those cases involving injuries suffered by an employee as the result of an "unexplained" fall. As the Court of Appeals has observed:

> Workplace falls can result from either an employment, personal or neutral risk, or from a combination thereof. Some falls clearly result from risks personal to the employee; that is, they are caused by a pre-existing illness or condition, unrelated to employment. As a general matter, these "idiopathic" falls are not compensable. In contrast, some falls are "unexplained" in that there is no indication of causation. Most jurisdictions compensate such falls, classifying them as neutral risks.

Courts have taken three approaches in addressing the "arising out of" element in unexplained fall cases. One approach requires the worker to rule out idiopathic causes for the fall. If the worker carries that burden, then an inference arises that the fall arose out of employment. Using this approach the Oregon Supreme Court has applied a "work-connection" test to determine whether an injury arises out of and in the course of employment. *Phil A. Livesley Co. v. Russ*, 672 P.2d 337, 339, 340 (Or. 1983). The "work-connection" test focuses on whether the relationship between the injury and the employment is sufficient for the injury to be compensable. If the "in the course of" element is fully met, then it will satisfy the "arising out of" element, provided the employee rules out idiopathic causes. *See also Waller v. Mayfield*, 524 N.E.2d 458, 464-65 (Ohio 1988) ("Where the course of employment test is fully met, where cause-in-fact cannot be directly established, and where the claimant has met his burden of eliminating idiopathic causes, we interpret the Workers' Compensation Act to allow the inference that the unexplained fall arose out of employment."). Although this is an attractive approach, it nonetheless places the employee in the position of attempting to prove a negative. This is not a burden we believe the employee should have to bear. *See, e.g., Town of Montezuma v. Downs*, 685 N.E.2d 108, 116 n.9 (Ind. Ct. App. 1997) ("To require the Downs to affirmatively prove that the pipeline was not inspected would require them to prove a negative, something which we refuse to do."), *trans. denied; Jackson v. Warrum*, 535 N.E.2d 1207, 1218 (Ind. Ct. App. 1989) (describing as "impossible" the "burden of proving a negative fact"). We therefore decline to adopt this view.

A second approach leaves the burden on the employee to show a causal connection between the injury and the employment. This is the most difficult burden to meet when an injury occurs without explanation. And although it is especially well suited for injuries that result from risks distinctly associated with employment, as discussed in more detail below, it is problematic for risks that are neither distinctly employment related nor distinctly personal in character. This is essentially the approach adopted by the Court of Appeals in this case.

A third approach involves applying the "positional risk test" also referred to as the "positional risk doctrine." *See Smith v. Bob Evans Farms, Inc.*, 754 N.E.2d 18, 26 n.1 (Ind. Ct. App. 2001) (observing that under Indiana law "the positional risk doctrine is generally applied to neutral risks"); *accord K-Mart Corp. v. Novak*, 521 N.E.2d 1346, 1348-49 (Ind. Ct. App. 1988). Under this doctrine "an injury arises out of the employment if it would not have occurred *but for* the fact that the conditions and obligations of the employment placed claimant in the position where he was injured." Larson, *supra*, § 3.05, at 3-6. This but for reasoning is the foundation of the positional risk doctrine, under which if the "in the course of" employment element is met, then there is a rebuttable presumption that the injury "arises out of" employment. Although similar to the "work connection" test mentioned above, here the burden is on the employer to demonstrate that the injury was actually the result of a cause personal to the claimant.

The positional risk doctrine is generally applied in those instances where injuries result from risks that are categorized as neutral. . . .

We acknowledge, as has the Court of Appeals, that neutral risks present risk of loss problems. This is so because the risk does not fall clearly upon the employer or the employee. Responding to the question of who should bear this risk, Professor Larson observes:

> The usual answer in the past has been to leave this loss on the employee, on the theory that he or she must meet the burden of proof of establishing affirmatively a clear causal connection between the conditions under which the employee worked and the occurrence of the injury. More recently, some courts have reasoned in the following vein: Either the employer or the employee must bear the loss; to show connection with the employment, there is at least the fact that the injury occurred while the employee was working; to show connection with the employee there is nothing; therefore, although the work connection is slender, it is at least stronger than any connection with the claimant's personal life.

LARSON, *supra*, § 4.03, at 4-3.

We believe the positional risk doctrine is the appropriate analytical tool for resolving questions concerning injuries that result from neutral risks. It has been adopted by a majority of jurisdictions that have spoken on the subject. And it is consistent with the underlying purpose of the Worker's Compensation Act: to provide compensation to workers suffering from work-related injuries without meeting the liability requirements of tort law. Worker's compensation is for the benefit of the employee, and the Act should "be liberally construed . . . so as not to negate the Act's humane purposes." *Frampton v. Cent. Ind. Gas Co.*, 297 N.E.2d 425, 427 (Ind. 1973).

In this case the injury to Milledge's ankle is without explanation. It is thus classified as a neutral risk in that the cause of the injury is neither personal to Milledge nor distinctly associated with her employment. The injury would not have occurred but for the fact that the conditions and obligations of her employment placed Milledge in the parking lot where she was injured. In turn, The Oaks has not carried its burden of demonstrating that this unexplained accident, which precipitated the ankle injury, was the result of idiopathic causes. Milledge is thus entitled to compensation under the Indiana Worker's Compensation Act.

This does not however end our analysis. Milledge sought worker's compensation not for her ankle injury alone, but also, and primarily, for the disability arising from the injury including the surgery that led to the amputation of her leg. Whether Milledge was entitled to such compensation was fiercely contested before the single-member hearing officer. However, determining that Milledge failed to show any causal connection between her ankle injury and her employment, neither the hearing officer nor the full Board ever reached the question of whether Milledge's infection and subsequent amputation were causally connected to her ankle injury. Therefore this cause is remanded to the Board for consideration of this issue. . . .

NOTES

1. *Comparing the Cases and the "Arising Out of" Tests.* The "arising out of" employment test is concerned with the causal connection between employment and the injury. Work your way through the *Worden* and *Milledge* analyses. First, consider how similar the analyses are in terms of the focus of the inquiry and categorization of risks. What types of risks are universally compensable and what types clearly are not? Then turn to the differences in the tests the courts articulate for assessing the causal connection to employment with regard to neutral risks. Did these differences matter in these two cases? In other words, were the outcomes different because of the tests the courts articulated or because of distinguishable facts?

2. *The Five Approaches. Worden* lists the five traditional approaches to assessing a causal connection in cases involving neutral or mixed risks of injury. As the court indicates, the most stringent of the five, the proximate-cause test (requiring foreseeability and no intervening cause), is now largely obsolete. *See* LARSON & LARSON, *supra*, at §§ 3.01, 3.06. The peculiar-risk doctrine, also fairly stringent, has largely been abandoned as well. *See id.* at §§ 3.01-.02. A growing group of jurisdictions have moved to the most permissive of the approaches, the positional-risk test, as adopted by the *Milledge* court. However, despite the fact that *Milledge* is among the well-known positional-risk decisions, its approach is in serious doubt within its own jurisdiction since the Indiana legislature later amended the underlying statute to state that employees retain the burden of persuasion in workers' compensation cases. *See* IND. CODE. 22-3-2-2 (2010) ("The burden of proof is on the employee. The proof by the employee of an element of a claim does not create a presumption in favor of the employee with regard to another element of the claim."); *Pavese v. Cleaning Solutions*, 894 N.E.2d 570 (Ind. Ct. App. 2008) (discussing the statutory change and concluding that it abrogates the burden shift in *Milledge*). While this amendment seemingly rejects *Milledge's* burden-shifting framework, it did not address the court's adoption of a "but for" inquiry, and the Indiana Supreme Court has not considered anew the status of the positional-risk test.

Nevertheless, with the facts of *Worden* and *Milledge* as a backdrop, consider how the three viable approaches — actual risk, increased risk, and positional risk — might affect the outcome in close cases. In light of this, and the purposes of the workers' compensation regime, which of the three is the most appropriate? To test your understanding, what would have happened had Worden slipped on wet grass on arriving at a patient's home rather than on leaving her own home?

Now look back at *Kindel* and *Clodgo*. In both cases, the courts found that the employee's injuries arose out of employment. Why? Would it matter which of the three approaches the court had adopted?

3. *Milledge's Disability.* The *Milledge* court never reached the question of whether Milledge's "downstream" disability due to the amputation was causally connected to her employment and, hence, compensable. Obviously, Milledge will have won the battle but lost the war if she is denied compensation for that disability on remand. Fortunately for Milledge and other injured workers, most of the time when the primary injury has arisen from employment, all the consequences, including worsening injuries, complications, and even aggravation caused by medical malpractice are also compensable, absent an intervening cause attributable to the worker's own conduct. *See* LARSON & LARSON, *supra*, at §§ 10.01-.12. Why do you suppose workers' compensation regimes take this liberal approach? In other words, what is to be gained by making the employer — via greater insurance premiums — bear the risk for all such downstream consequences, including even tortious medical treatment? Do these social benefits justify "charging" the employer for the injurious consequences of others?

4. *Workplace Assaults.* Whether an assault in the course of employment — by a co-worker or other third-party — "arises out of" employment has been the subject of much litigation and legislation. Assaults normally arise out of employment if, at a minimum, the risk of an assault is increased by the nature of the job or the work setting or if it was precipitated by a work-related dispute (e.g., an assault upon a supervisor). This means that, generally, assaults by co-workers or other third parties that are motivated by personal or private reasons do not arise out of employment, unless employment facilitates an assault that would not otherwise be made — for example, where the dangerous nature of the job increases the risk of an assault or, at least sometimes, where work friction and proximity are a contributing factor. *See, e.g., Sanderson Farms, Inc. v. Jackson*, 911 So. 2d 985 (Miss. Ct. App. 2005) (holding that employee's injuries from assault by co-employee following argument over personal loan did not arise out of employment); *see generally* LARSON & LARSON, *supra*, at §§ 8.01-.03. However, some courts have held that an assault in the workplace (or during work hours) by a co-worker or third party is enough to establish that it arose out of employment. *See, e.g., Wal-Mart Stores, Inc. v. Reinholtz*, 955 P.2d 223 (Okla. 1998) (finding compensable injuries an employee sustained by rape by her supervisor because employment itself put claimant at greater risk of injury than the general public); *Redman Indus., Inc. v. Lang*, 943 P.2d 208 (Or. 1997) (same); *K-Mart Corp. v. Herring*, 188 P.3d 140 (Ok. 2008) (affirming the lower court's finding that a worker's injuries arose during the course of employment when, during a continuous seven-hour shift as night watchman with no scheduled breaks, he left the employer's premises to use the bathroom, decided to go to a fast food restaurant, and was shot outside the restaurant). The "assault exception" to workers' compensation coverage is sometimes separately codified rather than simply a variation of the "arising out of" employment analysis. *See, e.g.,* MINN. STAT. § 176.011, subd. 16 ("Personal injury does not include an injury caused by the act of a third person or fellow employee intended to injure the employee because of personal reasons, and not directed against the employee as an employee, or because of the employment.").

5. *In the Course of and Arising out of Employment.* Now that we have seen four cases addressing either the "in the course of" "arising out of" employment requirements, take a moment to consider what each element addresses. What type of connections with employment, specifically, is each requirement designed to test? For instance, why is it that, while the "arising out of" issue was hotly contested in both *Worden* and *Milledge*, the "in the course of" issue was not? Although these tests are distinct, keep in mind that, in many circumstances, the facts and analyses underlying the resolution of each are not so easily separated. For example, consider how a finding that an injury occurred in the course of employment is likely to affect the "arising out of" analysis under the positional risk doctrine. Similarly, in most jurisdictions, the "street-risk doctrine" provides that street- or highway-related injuries for employees — for example, delivery and sales people — whose duties increase their exposure to the hazards of "the street" arise out of employment. *See* LARSON & LARSON, *supra*, at §§ 6.01-.06. Thus, if an employee is consistently on the road in the course of his or her employment, any injuries he or she might sustain during such travels are likely to also "arise out of" employment.

The leading treatise on workers' compensation suggests that there is interplay between the two inquiries: Where there is a weak "in the course of" connection, courts may require a stronger "arising out of" connection to support a finding of compensability, and vice versa. *See* LARSON & LARSON, *supra*, at § 29.01. Might this sliding scale or "balancing out" process account for the varying results in the four cases we have read in this section?

c. "Accidental" or "By Accident"

In addition to the requirements that an injury arise in the course of employment and out of employment to be compensable, most state statutes also require that it normally be "accidental" or "by accident." The touchstone for whether the injury is "accidental" is unexpectedness: "an unlooked for mishap or an untoward event which is not expected or designed." *See* LARSON & LARSON, *supra*, at § 42.02 (quoting the seminal English case of *Fenton v. Thorley & Co.*, [1903] A.C. 443). A further element of "accidental" recognized in many jurisdictions — although a highly criticized one — is that the injury must be traceable to a definite time, place, and occasion or cause, at least within reasonable limits. In other words, courts read "accident" or "by accident" to require that "an accident" be shown to have given rise to the injury. *See id.*

The main fault line running through the cases analyzing this element involves whether the notion of unexpectedness inherent in "accidental" requires an accidental cause or merely an accidental result. *Id.* at §§ 42.02, 43.01. The leading treatise provides the classic example of a situation in which the work-related cause is expected but the result is not: "A worker who, for years, has lifted hundred-pound sacks many times a day suffers a heart attack while lifting one in the usual way, and medical testimony confirms that the heavy lift did in fact cause the attack." *Id.* at § 42.02. Whether unexpected injuries resulting from such "usual" exertion or exposure are compensable varies by jurisdiction and the nature and definiteness of the injury. The vast majority of courts have found that sudden mechanical or structural changes in the body, such as something breaking, rupturing, or herniating, are accidental — even where the exertion causing the change is usual. Similarly, courts almost always find usual exposure causing freezing or sunstroke to be accidental. A less sizable majority find "generalized conditions" — for example, heart attacks, back injuries, muscle strains, and other similar problems — resulting from usual exertion to be accidental. The other jurisdictions require the injured worker to demonstrate that some kind of unusual or abnormal exertion or exposure (including, for example, excessive strain or work, or sudden shocks or falls) caused the injury. *See generally id.* at §§ 43.01-03. Of course, determining what constitutes a sufficiently unusual or abnormal exertion often poses difficult issues.

It is worth noting that workplace assaults may be "accidental." A workplace assault or battery by a co-worker or third-party, although intentional on the part of the perpetrator, may be sudden and unexpected by the employee and unexpected and unintended by the employer. Obviously, if the assault or other injurious action is intended by or attributable to the employer, then the injury is not accidental, and the employee may sue the employer in tort. In addition, even if deemed accidental, a co-worker or third-party assault resulting from a personal or private motive may nevertheless be excluded from workers' compensation coverage because it does not arise out of employment or is otherwise subject to a statutory "assault exception."

Relatedly, as discussed at the end of Chapter 5, a frequent subject of litigation is whether sexual harassment and other forms of discrimination are covered under workers' compensation or excluded as intentional or quasi-intentional conduct. The question typically arises not when the plaintiff files a compensation claim but rather when a harassed worker sues in tort or under a state antidiscrimination statute because the remedies that are available under such regimes — in particular those addressing mental and emotional distress — are unavailable under workers' compensation. Normally, if there is no physical injury associated with such conduct, the victim will not be covered under the workers' compensation regime, and hence there will be no exclusivity. Where, however, the harassing or discriminatory behavior caused some type of physical injury — for example, a sexually motivated assault or battery — the question is much closer, and, as discussed in Chapter 5, courts have not agreed on the answer. Of course, workers' compensation law does not preempt federal discrimination law, and thus, if the conduct rises to the level of actionable discrimination against the employer under Title VII or another federal antidiscrimination statute (see Chapter 9), the employee may bring such claims.

Another particularly troublesome category of "accident" cases involves diseases, including infectious diseases acquired through exposure at work, diseases aggravated by work exertion, diseases brought on or made worse by the work environment or temperature, and "occupational diseases" caused by exposure — sometimes over long periods — to harmful conditions tied to particular types of employment. There are circumstances in which diseases are clearly compensable, such as when the disease follows as a natural consequence of a work-related injury that is accidental or when it is a direct result of a particular workplace mishap, malfunction, or other unusual event. *See* LARSON & LARSON, *supra*, at § 42.03.

In many other contexts, however, the disease inquiry has proven difficult. One problem is the cause-result issue discussed above, and courts have been divided over whether routine exposure to conditions causing or aggravating diseases is compensable. Beyond this, some diseases, including occupational ones, are not unexpected at all — think of, for example, "black lung" disease, a condition not only expected but in fact anticipated when one works for extended periods in coal mines. Another concern involves indefiniteness, given the frequent difficulty of tracing diseases to particular occasions and causes or showing that they developed suddenly and unexpectedly. With diseases that are common in the general population, simply establishing a connection to work can be difficult. The employee may need to show that the disease was caused by work conditions rather than by routine or normal exposure to germs, toxins, or the actions of the worker herself. Consider, for instance, a worker whose job exposes him to toxins associated with lung cancer but who is also a smoker. Finally, the time element — that is, the delay in manifestation of the disease — also raises a host of potential proof and other problems, most notably in the occupational disease context.

All states have addressed aspects of these problems statutorily, and there are some federal regimes addressing particular diseases or industries. All state statutes include specific sections covering occupational diseases, and many are general in scope, covering all employment-related diseases. Others contain lists of covered conditions, but typically these statutes also include catchall provisions that extend to nonspecified diseases. Such statutes do *not* require evidence of unexpected or sudden triggering events. Rather, occupational disease coverage depends on whether there is a sufficiently recognizable link between the disease and the particular type of work at issue — work that at least increases the risk of such disease.

Note on Compensability of "Mental Injuries"

Whether work-related injuries that may be characterized as "mental," "stress-related," or "psychological" in nature are compensable under workers' compensation has produced an enormous amount of litigation and controversy. Early on, only "physical injuries" were contemplated under workers' compensation regimes, and thus, emotional distress and mental injuries were not compensable absent some corresponding physical injury or disorder. Over time, however, greater recognition has developed not only of the seriousness of various "mental injuries" but also of the need to compensate at least some such ailments. In addressing the physical-mental divide, courts and commentators have separated claims into four general categories: (1) physical stimuli causing physical injuries, (2) mental stimuli causing physical injuries (so-called "mental-physical"), (3) physical stimuli causing mental injuries ("physical-mental"), and (4) mental or nervous injuries caused by mental stimulus ("mental-mental"). *See generally* LARSON & LARSON, *supra*, at §§ 56.01-.04.

Provided the injury is sufficiently connected to work and is accidental, category 1 claims have always been compensable. There is now general agreement that claims in categories 2 and 3 (mental-physical and physical-mental) are compensable as well, although states and courts may impose various proof requirements and limit recovery for mental injuries in a number of ways. A common example of a category 2 claim is a stress-induced heart attack; category 3 includes claims for psychological conditions that result from or are exacerbated by a physical injury.

Thus, currently, the controversy focuses largely on the final category — mental-mental claims. This group of workers' compensation claims raises the same types of concerns as emotional distress claims in tort, including floodgates issues, causation and diagnostic problems, and questions of proof. They also raise concerns about the cost of the workers' compensation system. Although most states now provide workers' compensation coverage for mental-mental claims, some do not. *See id.* at § 56.06[3]-[4]. Of the states that accept such claims, some require no greater showing than that required for claims for physical injuries; others require a showing that a sudden stimulus caused the psychological or mental injury; and still others require a showing that the mental stress was unusual in the given context. *See id. at* § 56.06[2]-[7]. Some state legislatures have amended their statutes to limit such claims in various ways, including requiring a heightened level or particular type of stress or mental impairment, increasing the burden of proof, imposing specific diagnostic guidelines, altering causation standards, limiting the amount of benefits, or excluding benefits altogether. *See id.* at § 56.06. Of course, compensability for such claims would benefit many employees, but those who prefer to sue in tort or some other state-law theory would be barred from doing so due to workers' compensation exclusivity.

Note on Exclusivity

Exclusivity is a core component of all workers' compensation regimes, and, as we have seen, the scope of the bar is frequently litigated in contexts in which tort or other remedies would otherwise be available and would be superior for the worker (e.g., offering greater damages for lost wages, damages for emotional and mental stress, and the potential for punitive damages). Whether workers' compensation provides the exclusive remedy normally depends on resolution of the various scope questions addressed above — that is, whether the worker is a covered "employee," whether the injury or illness arose in the course of and out of employment, whether the injury was accidental or the illness was an otherwise covered occupational disease, and whether the type of injury — for example, mental-mental — is compensable. In a few cases, however, courts have found that exclusivity extends beyond the scope of covered injuries, although these holdings are highly controversial. *See, e.g., Bias v. E. Associated Coal Corp.*, 640 S.E.2d 540 (W. Va. 2006) (holding that a common-law negligence claim for stress-related injuries employee sustained at work is preempted by workers' compensation exclusivity even though a statute precluding benefits for mental-mental injuries bars recovery under the state's workers' compensation regime).

Note, however, that even if workers' compensation is the exclusive remedy vis-à-vis the employer or employers, see Chapter 1, the worker may have a viable tort claim against third-parties whose conduct contributed to the injury. Furthermore, in many contexts in which an employee is injured or becomes ill, counsel will pursue additional remedies against third-party tortfeasors with resources, including manufacturers of defective products used by the employee, landowners, and other firms whose actions may affect the safety of the employee or workplace. Co-employees, customers, or other individuals whose negligent or intentional conduct causes the harm also may be liable, but often such tortfeasors lack sufficiently deep pockets to be worth suing. Finally, a few courts have recognized that employers are in some cases effectively "third parties" and subject to tort suit under the "dual capacity" doctrine, which provides that an employee may recover in tort against an employer if the employer caused or aggravated the injury while acting in a non-employer capacity. For example, an employer may be subject to a tort suit for providing negligent medical care for the employee that aggravated the employee's condition or for manufacturing a defective product that harms the employee at work.

B. OSHA

Workers' compensation regimes are supposed to create incentives for employers to improve workplace safety by mandating compensation for occupational injuries and diseases. In contrast, OSHA, the Occupational Safety and Health Act of 1970, 29 U.S.C. §§ 651-78 (2006), is designed to address safety directly by setting and enforcing standards to prevent workplace injuries and diseases. It does so through a top-down regulatory structure rather than through private enforcement or injury claims. OSHA is therefore an entirely different type of legal regime than workers' compensation. As a result, it produces a different kind of litigation — mostly addressing the setting of standards — and its own unique set of problems and controversies.

1. A Glance at OSHA's History and Structure

Prior to adoption of OSHA, state legislation had long regulated some workplace health and safety matters and federal legislation had addressed particular industries with a notorious history of safety problems, such as coal mines. Yet OSHA marked the first comprehensive national effort to deal with workplace safety. It is sweeping in its coverage, excluding only state and local government employers, employers covered by other safety regimes, and workplaces in states with approved safety plans. State occupational safety laws are preempted by OSHA unless the state adopts a plan approved by the Occupational Safety and Health Administration in which case the state plan precludes federal activity. Nevertheless, more general state and local laws, such as those relating to fire safety, continue unaffected by OSHA, and workers' compensation regimes are expressly saved from preemption, despite their obvious relationship to workplace safety.

The statute created an elaborate administrative mechanism for its enforcement. The acronym OSHA is often used both to mean the Act itself and the agency within the Labor Department — the Occupational Safety and Health Administration — charged with implementing the statute. The administrative structure created by the statute is more complicated than those governing many other federal agencies, but the Secretary of Labor, acting through OSHA, is charged with promulgating and enforcing safety standards.

a. Safety Standards

Under §5(a) of the Act, 29 U.S.C. §654, safety standards come in two basic forms: the statute's "general duty clause" and specific standards promulgated by OSHA. The general duty clause is a catchall provision requiring a safe workplace even in the absence of more specific standards. However, it is residual in that it governs a potential workplace hazard only if no specific promulgated standard addresses the hazard.

The general duty provision states that an employer "shall furnish to each of his employees employment and a place of employment which are free from recognized hazards that are causing or are likely to cause death or serious physical harm to his employees." To prove a violation of the clause, the Secretary of Labor must establish that the employer failed to keep the workplace free of a hazard to which employees were exposed, that the hazard was "recognized" based on standard knowledge in the industry, that the hazard was likely to cause death or serious physical harm, and that there are feasible methods or measures for addressing the hazard. An employer, therefore, may violate the clause even though no employee has yet been harmed. The various elements of a violation of this clause have been the subject of occasional controversy, as has its application to particular hazards arguably addressed by specific standards.

Most of the debate, however, has focused on OSHA's promulgation of specific standards. The Act requires that employers "comply with occupational safety and health standards" promulgated by OSHA. There are three kinds of specific standards contemplated under the Act: interim standards, new or permanent standards, and temporary standards. In deriving specific standards, OSHA is assisted by a research agency, the National Institute for Occupational Safety and Health ("NIOSH"), located in the Department of Health and Human Services. NIOSH has no power to adopt standards; it simply advises OSHA.

Temporary standards are, in essence, emergency standards that OSHA may adopt with minimal procedures if it finds that a particular substance or new hazard poses a grave danger to employees and that an emergency measure is necessary to protect employees from such danger. *See* 29 U.S.C. §655(c). Given the high bar, OSHA has rarely adopted such emergency standards.

OSHA was also authorized to adopt so-called interim standards, which were intended to be placeholders for more considered efforts. These provisions were largely based on federal standards existing prior to OSHA or "consensus" (lowest common denominator) standards of various standards-producing institutions. OSHA adopted thousands of such standards shortly after the statute was enacted, creating a storm of controversy, in part because they imposed an immediate and complex array of new safety requirements on many employers. Many of these provisions were later abolished by statute, but, 35 years later, "interim" standards continue to make up the bulk of specific standards under OSHA.

After the initial period in which interim standards were to be adopted, OSHA was authorized to promulgate new or permanent standards (which may be completely new, or modify or revoke interim standards). Enactment of such standards, however, is subject to more rigorous administrative procedures and greater substantive limits than apply to interim standards. The substantive limits in particular have been the subject of legal challenges to proposed standards and the basis for criticism of the OSHA workplace safety regime.

Part of the difficulty stems from the generality of the statutory delegation. For example, §6(b)(5) of the statute states that the Secretary, in dealing with toxic or harmful physical agents, "shall set the standard which most adequately assures, to the extent feasible, on the basis of the best available evidence, that no employee will suffer material impairment of health or functional capacity." It also states that that "other considerations shall be the latest available scientific data in the field, the feasibility of the standards, and the experience gained under this and other health and safety laws." Section 3(8) of the statute defines a health and safety standard as one that is "reasonably necessary and appropriate to safe or healthful employment."

Through judicial refinement, some clearer requirements now have emerged. For example, to promulgate any permanent standard, OSHA must demonstrate that the regulation will reduce or eliminate a "significant risk" to worker health or safety. *Indus. Union Dep't v. Am. Petroleum Inst.*, 448 U.S. 607, 641 (1980). This risk must be sufficiently quantified to enable OSHA to characterize it as significant. *See id.* at 656. In addition, OSHA must demonstrate that the risk to health or safety is "material," *AFL-CIO v. OSHA*, 965 F.2d 962, 973 (11th Cir. 1992), and that the proposed standard is feasible — that is, "capable of being done, executed, or effected" by the regulated industry, both technologically and economically. *Am. Textile Mfrs. Inst. v. Donovan* ("*ATMI*"), 452 U.S. 490, 508-09 (1981). However, OSHA usually need not engage in a cost-benefit analysis — a determination of whether the costs of compliance with the proposed standard are reasonable when compared to its benefits. *See ATMI*, 452 U.S. at 506-22.

The agency's determinations with regard to risk, materiality, and feasibility are conclusive if they are "supported by substantial evidence in the record considered as a whole," 29 U.S.C. § 655(f), a standard that is not as deferential as "arbitrary and capricious" review but still falls far short of requiring scientific certainty or allowing de novo judicial inquiry. Nevertheless, these requirements do mandate that OSHA demonstrate that its standards are premised on available scientific evidence of probable benefits to worker health or safety — a significant hurdle in certain occupational disease and chemical exposure contexts.

Although not insurmountable, this need for substantial scientific support in a world of scientific uncertainty, combined with challenges by industry, other procedural hurdles, and resistance or delays within OSHA itself has resulted in few permanent standards actually being promulgated. *See generally* David Michaels & Celeste Monforton, *Scientific Evidence in the Regulatory System: Manufacturing Uncertainty and the Demise of the Formal Regulatory System*, 13 J. L. & POL'Y 17 (2005). For example, since its inception, OSHA has promulgated comprehensive standards for only about 30 chemical toxins, *see id.* at 28, sometimes only after being compelled to do so following judicial challenges by labor or workplace safety advocates. Consider how all of these factors combined to delay promulgation of standards at issue in the next case, which involves exposure to a particular toxin (hexavalent chromium) that clearly threatens worker health.

Public Citizen Research Health Group v. Chao
314 F.3d 143 (3d Cir. 2002)

BECKER, Chief Judge.

This opinion addresses a Petition by Public Citizen Health Research Group ("Public Citizen") to review the inaction of [OSHA], and to require OSHA to commence a rulemaking that would lower the permissible exposure limit for hexavalent chromium. It is not disputed that hexavalent chromium, which is widely used in various industries and which has been classified as a carcinogen, can have a deleterious effect on worker health. [NIOSH] has for several decades recommended that OSHA adopt a far more stringent permissible exposure limit ("PEL") for hexavalent chromium than the consensus [interim] standard it promulgated in 1971. In response to a 1993 petition for rulemaking, OSHA agreed that there was clear evidence that exposure to hexavalent chromium at the consensus level can result in excess risk of lung cancer and other chromium-related illnesses, and announced that it was initiating a rulemaking that it expected would conclude in 1995. However, nearly a decade after this announcement, nothing has happened, evincing a clear pattern of delay.

This matter was before us once before. . . . In that [1998] case, we declined Public Citizen's request to compel agency action. . . . At that time, OSHA represented that it intended to issue a proposed rule by September 1999, and we found such a deadline permissible in light of alleged competing policy priorities. . . . Yet, at the time of oral argument in this case, which was nine years after OSHA initially announced its intention to begin the rulemaking process, no rulemaking had yet been initiated, and it appeared that none would be in the foreseeable future. Indeed, at oral argument, OSHA's counsel admitted the possibility that OSHA might not promulgate a rule for another ten or twenty years, if at all.

We concluded that the delay had become unreasonable, and that while competing policy priorities might explain slow progress, they could not justify indefinite delay and recalcitrance in the face of an admittedly grave risk to public health. We therefore determined to grant the petition and to direct OSHA to proceed expeditiously with its hexavalent chromium rulemaking process. This opinion was drafted on an expedited basis . . . when we received OSHA's announcement that it had instituted the long-sought rulemaking process, stating that: "The health risks associated with occupational exposure to hexavalent chromium are serious and demand serious attention. . . . We are committed to developing a rule that ensures proper protection to safeguard workers who deal with hexavalent chromium."

This notice appears to have been prompted by the displeasure clearly evidenced by the panel during oral argument, especially the question posed to counsel whether they would be receptive to mediation regarding the timeframe for a judicially-ordered rulemaking. [In any event, the notice does not render the case moot because] the agency's action does not resolve an important facet of the case, namely Public Citizen's request that we order OSHA to issue a proposed rule within 90 days and supervise OSHA's progress.

Accordingly, we will publish the opinion that had been prepared to resolve the remedy issue, and will direct that Public Citizen and OSHA submit to a course of mediation for sixty days before The Honorable Walter K. Stapleton. If the parties cannot agree to a workable timetable during that period, the panel will issue and enforce a schedule of its own device. . . .

I. Facts and Procedural Posture

Hexavalent chromium is a compound found only rarely in nature but used widely in industry — for chrome plating, stainless steel welding, alloy production, and wood preservation. The dangers of exposure to it have long been recognized, and include ulceration of the stomach and skin, necrosis, perforation of the nasal septum, asthma, and dermatitis. More significantly, there is strong evidence that inhaled hexavalent chromium is carcinogenic. Since 1980, the Department of Health and Human Service's National Toxicology Program has designated various hexavalent chromium compounds as human carcinogens. The Environmental Protection Agency has been in accord since 1984. . . . Disturbingly, the primary evidence of hexavalent chromium's carcinogenicity comes not from animal studies, but from epidemiological studies of workers exposed to it; in short, as Public Citizen states, "the principal evidence is actual human body counts."

Soon after [OSHA] took effect in 1970, OSHA established a 100 $\mu g/m^3$ [a weight-to-volume ratio that can be converted to "parts per billion" by multiplying by the chemical weight of the compound] permissible exposure limit ("PEL") for inhalation exposure to hexavalent chromium. That level did not reflect OSHA's independent judgment about the appropriate standard, but rather constituted a "lowest common denominator" consensus standard to provide workers some measure of protection pending OSHA's consideration of the optimal long-term standard. The 1971 standard remains in effect. However, although today's foremost health concern regarding hexavalent chromium is its carcinogenicity, OSHA did not take that into account when promulgating the standard. . . .

Shortly after OSHA promulgated the consensus standard, NIOSH . . . urged OSHA to adopt a PEL of 1.9 $\mu g/m^3$, a level 1/52 of the existing standard. At that time, NIOSH concluded that the evidence of the carcinogenicity of a few specified hexavalent chromium compounds was lacking, but that all other forms were carcinogenic. Subsequently, however, NIOSH concluded that all forms of hexavalent chromium should be considered carcinogenic, and it recommended that the 1.9 $\mu g/m^3$ standard be applied to all such compounds.

In 1993, Public Citizen petitioned OSHA to issue an emergency temporary standard that would set a PEL of 0.5 $\mu g/m^3$ as an 8-hour weighted average. The Occupational Safety and Health Act requires OSHA to issue an emergency temporary standard without the usual notice-and-comment procedures if it finds that such action is needed to protect employees against grave danger. 29 U.S.C. § 655(c). OSHA denied the petition because it contended that "the extremely stringent judicial and statutory criteria for issuing" an emergency standard were not met. It did, however, acknowledge that its existing standard was inadequate. . . . It therefore announced that [it would begin rulemaking on the matter and anticipated notice would be published in March 1995].

This timetable was short-lived. Only a month after its response to Public Citizen's rulemaking petition, OSHA reported that the date for issuance of a proposed standard had slipped from March to May 1995, and by May 1995 the anticipated issuance date had been pushed back again to December 1995. Thus began a pattern of delay. . . .

Amidst this ongoing delay, OSHA commissioned a comprehensive risk assessment of hexavalent chromium. This assessment, which became known as the "Crump Report," concluded that exposure at the current PEL (100 $\mu g/m^3$) over a 45-year working lifetime could be expected to result in between 88 and 342 excess cancer deaths per thousand workers. Moreover, the Crump Report concluded that significant numbers of excess cancer deaths could be expected even at much lower levels of exposure. . . .

OSHA's November 1996 semiannual regulatory agenda endorsed the Crump analysis, and OSHA explicitly acknowledged that "[t]here appears to be no dispute that the current PEL is too high" and "must be greatly reduced." Accordingly, OSHA stated that it was considering a new standard 10 to 100 times lower than the existing one. . . . Even at that level, it noted, there would be significant risk of excess cancer deaths.

Addressing these events in its present brief, OSHA contends that it was then concerned with methodological imperfections in the available data. For example, the Crump Report did not control for the effects of smoking or asbestos, factors obviously related to lung cancer incidence; if the studied populations of chromium-exposed workers smoked more than the general population, smoking could have accounted for some of the excess deaths. Industry groups therefore pressured OSHA to wait for the results of the then-forthcoming Johns Hopkins study, which, in the industry's view, was "expected to be the most accurate and complete database on chromium exposure and mortality available." OSHA also represents that budget cuts, government shutdowns, and new responsibilities under the Small Business Regulatory Enforcement Fairness Act of 1996 limited the resources available for hexavalent chromium rulemaking. In August 1997, OSHA explained to Public Citizen that work on the rule was continuing, but that these considerations had delayed progress and prevented it from expediting the rulemaking.

Public Citizen, discouraged by what it viewed as a pattern of inaction, urged OSHA in March 1997 to commit to a timetable for rulemaking. [OSHA did not so commit and, in 1997, Public Citizen sought review of OSHA's allegedly unreasonable delay before this Court.]

We declined Public Citizen's request to compel agency action, for we concluded that the facts did not yet "demonstrate that inaction is . . . unduly transgressive of the agency's own tentative deadlines." Key to our decision [were] our observation[s] that the Secretary of Labor has "quintessential discretion . . . to allocate OSHA's resources and set its priorities," [that the delays might be reasonable, and that the intervenors raised serious questions about the data underlying Public Citizen's calculations]. Given these scientific questions, OSHA's superior technical expertise, and its professed plan to issue a deadline for proposed rulemaking in September 1999, we concluded that OSHA's delay was not yet unreasonable.

Following our ruling, OSHA adhered to its September 1999 pledge in each of its regulatory agendas published through April 1999. But it in fact issued no proposed rule in September 1999, and in its November 1999 agenda it announced that its new target date was June 2001. . . .

Meanwhile, August 2000 saw the release of the long-awaited Johns Hopkins study on hexavalent chromium.[3] . . . [The Hopkins Study confirmed the elevated lung cancer risk from hexavalent chromium exposure observed in other studies.]

Although the Hopkins Study explicitly sought to address the shortcomings in previous empirical research, namely the lack of controls for smoking, asbestos, and other environmental factors, its release did not spur OSHA into action. The study was released in August 2000, but OSHA's November 2000 agenda pushed the date for a proposed rule back to September 2001. OSHA's second-most-recent agenda, issued December 3, 2001, reflected another, more radical departure from previous plans: for the first time since 1994, the hexavalent chromium rulemaking was denominated a "long-term action," and the timetable for action stated that the date for a proposed rule was "to be determined."

OSHA offers a number of explanations for the delay that has now become indefinite. It notes that "[t]he day the [Bush] Administration took office, it instructed the agencies that any new regulatory actions must be reviewed and approved by a department or agency head appointed after January 20, 2001." As it was not headed by a presidential appointee until August 3, 2001, OSHA contends that it could not begin to set its new regulatory priorities until that time. Even then, it asserts, two extraordinary unforeseen events — the attacks on the World Trade Center and Pentagon and the anthrax mailings — required it immediately to divert significant resources to safety efforts.

Even amidst these distractions, OSHA represents, it has continued to evaluate the need for a new hexavalent chromium rule. . . .

In OSHA's submission, the problem is that it "believes that the information now available is inconclusive on important issues, such as whether the epidemiological studies . . . apply to all Cr VI compounds and the utility of the data to establish a dose-response relationship." Although the Hopkins Study was a step forward, OSHA points out that its authors acknowledged certain limitations, particularly in estimating the cumulative exposure for the different individuals in the cohort. The study also did not resolve the dispute over whether all hexavalent chromium compounds present the same degree of risk. Because OSHA has decided that it would benefit

---

3. Public Citizen alleges that many of the Hopkins study's results, if not its actual data, had been available to OSHA since 1995.

from public input and expert criticism on these issues, it has published a request for information (RFI) in its August 2002 regulatory agenda. After the time for response, OSHA states, it will evaluate all of the information available and decide how to proceed.

Public Citizen brought the present petition for review alleging that "[d]eference to an agency's priorities and timetables only goes so far," and arguing that, "at some point, a court must tell an agency that enough is enough." The Administrative Procedure Act, 5 U.S.C. § 706(1), creates a right of action by an aggrieved party to compel unreasonably delayed agency action. When the action sought is the promulgation of an occupational exposure standard under 29 U.S.C. § 655, the federal courts of appeals have exclusive jurisdiction under 29 U.S.C. § 655(f), which we have interpreted to provide "jurisdiction to conduct judicial review over the health and safety standards issued by the Secretary of Labor, as well as over claims in which the Secretary has not yet acted but where her delay is allegedly unreasonable." [*Oil, Chem. & Atomic Workers Union v. OSHA*, 145 F.3d 120, 122 (3d Cir. 1998).]

II.   Discussion

. . . Our polestar is reasonableness, and while in 1997 we found reasonable OSHA's delay in the face of scientific uncertainty and competing regulatory priorities, we now find ourselves further from a new rule than we were then. We examine each of OSHA's justifications in turn.

A.   Has OSHA's Delay Been Excessive?

In 1993, OSHA acknowledged that the existing hexavalent chromium standard is inadequate and "that there is clear evidence that exposure to Cr VI at the current PEL of 100 μg/m3 can result in an excess risk of lung cancer and other Cr VI-related illnesses." That was fully nine years ago, and its first target date for a proposed rule — March 1995 — is now more than seven years past. OSHA has missed all ten of its self-imposed deadlines, including the September 1999 target it offered to this Court in *Oil Workers*. Far from drawing closer to a rulemaking, all evidence suggests that ground is being lost. OSHA's December 2001 regulatory agenda demoted the rulemaking from a "high priority" to a "long term action" with a timetable "to be determined." In fact, at oral argument, OSHA's counsel admitted the possibility that another ten or even twenty years might pass before it issues a rule, if it ever does.

OSHA responds that Public Citizen's concerns about the missed deadlines and recent reclassification are misconceived. It explains that under the Regulatory Flexibility Act, 5 U.S.C. § 602, agencies must publish regulatory agendas that include all rules the agency intends to propose or promulgate that are "likely to have a significant economic impact on a substantial number of small entities." A rule's inclusion in an agency's agenda does not, however, require the agency to consider or act on that item. *See* 5 U.S.C. § 602(d). . . .

Regarding hexavalent chromium's recent downgrade to a "long-term project," OSHA clarifies that this is a reflection of whether the rulemaking will be completed in a short period of time and represents that the designation carries no implication about a rulemaking's relative importance to other matters OSHA is considering. The items listed as "high priority" in the December 2001 agenda, it says, were simply those on which OSHA intended to take action in fiscal 2002. It therefore contends that the priority downgrade was more a clarification than a change in the agency's priorities.

We find neither of these explanations satisfactory. We agree with OSHA insofar as its failure strictly to follow its published agenda is not actionable, but this defense misses the point: OSHA's persistent failure to meet deadlines is not the disease itself, but rather a symptom of its dilatory approach to the hexavalent chromium rulemaking process. Similarly, even if OSHA's decision to downgrade the project's priority truly represents a clarification rather than a change, it still gives clear evidence that at least another year will pass before OSHA takes even the first formal step toward promulgating a rule. . . .

Section 6(b) of the Occupational Safety and Health Act requires the Secretary of Labor to "set the standard which most adequately assures, to the extent feasible, on the basis of the best available evidence, that no employee will suffer material impairment of health or functional capacity even if such employee has regular exposure to the hazard dealt with by such standard for the period of his working life." 29 U.S.C. §655(b). The Supreme Court has found that this language compels action: "Both the language and structure of the Act, as well as its legislative history, indicate that it was intended to require the elimination, as far as feasible, of significant risks of harm." *Indus. Union Dep't, AFL-CIO v. Am. Petroleum Inst.*, 448 U.S. 607, 641 (1980). As such, the agency's priorities are judicially reviewable, and this Court and others have compelled OSHA to take action to address significant risks. . . .

We find extreme OSHA's nine-year (and counting) delay since announcing its intention to begin the rulemaking process, even relative to delays other courts have condemned in comparable cases. Indeed, in no reported case has a court reviewed a delay this long without compelling action. . . .

OSHA contends that [among the various reported cases, in only one] did a court compel the agency to issue a *proposed* rule; the others dealt with situations where the agency had issued a proposed rule but was allegedly dilatory in issuing a final regulation. It further notes that [that one case was later characterized as exceptional and the project at issue was conceded to be urgent].

While we acknowledge that . . . the other cases are in some ways distinguishable from this one, we nonetheless regard them as valuable precedent. . . . At all events, we think it "exceptionally rare" that an agency would for years classify an action as a "high priority," only to demote it to a "long term project" upon the release of a study that provides more convincing evidence of the danger than had previously existed.

We are satisfied that OSHA's delay in this case is objectively extreme, and we find its regression alarming in the face of its own 1996 statement that "there appears to be no dispute that the current PEL is too high." We therefore conclude that, absent a scientific or policy-based justification for its delay, we must compel it to act.

B. Does Scientific Uncertainty Justify OSHA's Delay?

In . . . the first installment of this case, Public Citizen relied upon the Crump Report's finding that between 88 and 342 out of every 1,000 workers exposed to hexavalent chromium will die from cancer attributable to that exposure. We recognized, however, that there were "serious questions about the validity of the data and assumptions underlying Petitioner's calculations." For example, . . . it was "wrong to assume that all workers in industries dealing with chromium in some way or another are exposed to 100 µg/m³ hexavalent chromium, every working day for 45 years." We likewise observed that some workers breathe through respirators that protect them from exposure to chromium, and that Public Citizen's calculations failed to distinguish between lead chromate and other hexavalent chromium compounds with potentially different carcinogenicities. Finally, and most importantly, we were troubled by the Crump Report's failure to control for smoking and asbestos inhalation, two factors likely related to lung cancer incidence.

Based on this imperfect science and our recognition that "OSHA . . . possesses enormous technical expertise we lack," we concluded that we were "not in a position to tell the Secretary how to do her job." OSHA offers several reasons for us to continue that deferential posture. First, OSHA allegedly "has not yet completed its evaluation of the Hopkins study." It points out that the study's authors acknowledged certain limitations of their data, particularly in estimating the cumulative exposure for different individuals in the cohort, and also that the study did not address the previous dispute over whether all hexavalent chromium compounds present the same degree of risk. OSHA summarizes that, "even assuming the Hopkins study is the most useful single study available, it does not answer all of the technically complex questions about carcinogenicity and other health effects that OSHA would need to resolve in developing a Cr VI rule."

Second, OSHA alleges that "Public Citizen virtually ignores the other critical components of a Cr VI rulemaking." One of OSHA's requirements is that a standard must be technologically feasible, and given that one governing hexavalent chromium would apply to numerous industries, the feasibility analysis is quite complex. While it admits that it has successfully addressed issues of comparable complexity in the past, it notes that "these efforts have not been successful where courts have found insufficient rigor in the agency's analysis of scientific and economic issues." *See, e.g.,* Indus. Union *Dep't; AFL-CIO v. OSHA,* 965 F.2d 962 (11th Cir. 1992). The bottom line, OSHA states, is that "[t]he belief that a chemical may be carcinogenic does not lead easily to the appropriate PEL for that chemical," and forcing it to issue a rule prematurely will likely result in that rule being overturned in court.

We agree with OSHA that the evidence may be imperfect, that the feasibility inquiry is formidable, and that premature rulemaking is undesirable. But given the history chronicled above, we find these concerns insufficient to justify further delay in regulating hexavalent chromium. First, while it is true that the Hopkins study's authors recognized certain limitations of their data, the epidemiological data as of the mid-1990s were sufficient for EPA, ATSDR, NIOSH, the National Toxicology Program, and the International Agency for Research on Cancer to find hexavalent chromium carcinogenic; for OSHA to commence a rulemaking proceeding; and for OSHA's contractor to estimate that exposures at a fraction of the current PEL would result in significant excess cancer deaths.

Moreover, OSHA based its delay on its professed desire to consider that study because of its superior data and ability to control for smoking. It was released in August 2000, more than two years ago, but it has hardly facilitated the rulemaking process.[5] OSHA now offers it as a justification for further inaction, claiming that it has not completed its evaluation of the study's findings and that the study's conclusions "can be much better assessed when experts in the field have had the opportunity to review and criticize it."

---

5. Indeed, the Hopkins study's results were first presented publicly in 1995.

We are unconvinced. Public Citizen points out that, as the study was published in a peer-reviewed journal, experts in the field have already had the opportunity to criticize it. Notably, in the two years since its publication, "no response or letter criticizing it has been published." Especially since many of the study's findings have been available since 1995, the time for examining it has passed; we also note that, if further professional criticism is absolutely necessary, the notice-and-comment process will provide an ample opportunity.

Nor do we find persuasive OSHA's broad assertion that the Hopkins study "does not answer *all* of the technically complex questions . . . that OSHA would need to resolve in developing a Cr VI rule." This is obviously true, but without more it is irrelevant, for the Occupational Safety and Health Act does not *require* scientific certainty in the rulemaking process. Indeed, read fairly, the Act virtually forbids delay in pursuit of certainty—it requires regulation "on the basis of the best *available* evidence," 29 U.S.C. §655(b)(5) (emphasis added), and courts have warned that "OSHA cannot let workers suffer while it awaits the Godot of scientific certainty." *United Steelworkers of Am. v. Marshall*, 647 F.2d 1189, 1266 (D.C. Cir. 1980).

OSHA points to one specific shortcoming of the Hopkins study—that it "did not address the previous dispute over whether all hexavalent chromium compounds present the same degree of risk." That is indeed a question it did not resolve, and this uncertainty is the principal topic of [the brief filed by the intervenor, an industry advocate], which argues that the lead chromate used in pigments is not as carcinogenic as other hexavalent chromium compounds. The Hopkins study casts no light on this issue because its test population did not work in the pigment industry, but even without better data than that which existed in *Oil Workers* in 1997, we find this uncertainty insufficient to delay rulemaking further. Even if the chromate in pigments is not carcinogenic, an argument that, tellingly, OSHA itself does not offer, requiring concrete findings on this distinction would effectively hold hostage the thousands of workers who are exposed to non-pigment hexavalent chromium. We will not sanction that result when [OSHA flagged this issue in the prior litigation four years ago].

Finally, while we are sympathetic to OSHA's claim that a thorough feasibility analysis is both highly important and quite difficult, we cannot allow an imperfect analysis to justify indefinite delay. OSHA first announced a rulemaking nine years ago, and by its own account it has been examining the issue through NIOSH for at least four years. OSHA does not explain why this particular feasibility determination requires an extreme length of time, and it does not offer even a projection of how much time it might ultimately require. In such a situation, our traditional agency deference begins to resemble judicial abdication, and we conclude that scientific uncertainties and technical complexities, while no doubt considerable, can no longer justify delay. Judges on this court are not paid to decide the easy cases, and neither is OSHA. Difficult challenges go with the territory, and courts and agencies regularly surmount them. The notice-and-comment process should itself provide a fertile forum for gathering information on feasibility.

C. Do Competing Priorities Justify OSHA's Delay?

[OSHA argues that it exercised its discretion to concentrate its resources elsewhere. For example, in 1999 and 2000, OSHA "focused most of its rulemaking resources on issuing an ergonomics standard before the end of the former Administration's term."

Because the Clinton Administration placed such great emphasis on quickly finalizing those standards, the process was remarkably compressed; OSHA issued a proposed rule on November 23, 1999, and a final rule less than a year later, on November 14, 2000, "a timetable that required tremendous agency resources."]

OSHA represents that the delays became worse when the Bush administration took office, [given the administration's directive not to approve new standards without approval of the new agency head, the delay in the appointment of an agency head, and the September 11 attacks and anthrax mailings].

We do not lightly discount these admittedly significant competing priorities . . . [but] we reach the ineluctable conclusion that hexavalent chromium has progressively fallen by the wayside. This is unacceptable. . . .

D. What Is the Proper Remedy?

Public Citizen requests that we direct OSHA to issue a proposed rule within 90 days, and to submit a schedule for finalizing the rule within 12 months thereafter. Neither OSHA's brief nor its recent announcement contains a proposed timetable, but it insists that Public Citizen's proposed pace of rulemaking "is unrealistic in light of the procedural, consultative, and analytical duties that constrain OSHA rulemaking and the historical time frames required for OSHA to develop a toxic chemical standard." For example, the Regulatory Flexibility Act, 5 U.S.C. §§ 601-12, requires it to prepare a regulatory flexibility analysis if the rule will have a "significant economic impact upon a substantial number of small entities," a mandate this rulemaking is sure to trigger. Also, the Small Business Regulatory Enforcement Fairness Act, 5 U.S.C. § 609(b), requires it to convene a review panel to address the rule's potential impacts on small entities. Finally, Executive Order 12866 requires that OSHA submit its proposal, including a detailed economic analysis, to the Office of Management and Budget, which is to review it within 90 days.

While we are certain that the time for action has arrived, we are cognizant of our lack of expertise in setting permissible exposure limits, and we recognize the damage that an ill-considered limit might cause. At oral argument, we presented the parties with a somewhat novel possibility: that they would submit to a course of mediation, conducted by a senior judge of this Court, in which they might work together toward a realistic timetable that we would then enforce. Both sides stated their willingness to engage in this process, and we think it the most promising way to develop a reasonable and workable schedule. We are, however, highly aware that this presents yet another opportunity for potentially indefinite bargaining and delay. We will therefore submit the matter to mediation for a period not to exceed sixty days, after which time, if the parties have not reached an accord, the panel will promulgate a schedule it deems appropriate. . . .

NOTES

1. *Even More Delays.* The Third Circuit's decision by no means ended the matter. When the parties could not agree, the Court adopted the mediator's recommendation and directed OSHA to publish a proposed rule no later than October 4, 2004, and to publish a final standard no later than January 18, 2006. The Court subsequently granted OSHA an extension to February 28, 2006. *See* National Metal Finishing Resource Center, *OSHA Hexavalent Chromium PEL Page*, *available at* http://www.nmfrc.org/compliance/pel2.cfm. OSHA published its final rule that day, *see* 71 Fed. Reg. 10099-10385 (Feb. 28, 2006), some 13 years after OSHA agreed that there was evidence that the level of exposure to hexavalent chromium allowed by the 1971 interim standard posed an excessive risk to worker health. The final standard provides for a PEL of 5.0 $\mu g/m^3$, as opposed to the 0.5 $\mu g/m^3$ for which Public Citizen had petitioned. Thereafter, both Public Citizen and industry representatives filed suit challenging the final standard. OSHA issued corrections to the rule on June 23, 2006, and an amendment on October 30, 2006, reflecting a settlement agreement with various parties. *See* 71 Fed. Reg. 36,008 (June 23, 2006); 71 Fed.Reg. 63,238 (Oct. 30, 2006). Nevertheless, litigation continued on both the standard and OSHA's decision to alter certain employee notification requirements. Ultimately, the Third Circuit upheld the promulgated rules, except for the change in the notification requirements, which it remanded back to OSHA for further consideration. *See Public Citizen Health Research Group v. U.S. Dept. of Labor*, 557 F.3d 165 (3d Cir. 2009). There were yet further delays in implementing inspection and compliance programs; for example, the National Emphasis Program targeting hexavalent chromium did not go into effect until February 2010. *See* OSHA, *National Emphasis Program — Hexavalent Chromium*, Directive No. CPL 02-02-076 (Feb. 23, 2010), *available at* http://www.osha.gov/OshDoc/Directive_pdf/CPL_02-02-076.pdf.

2. *A Rare, Hard-Fought Victory.* As the history of this case and the tone of the court's opinion suggests, federal courts are loath to order agencies, including OSHA, to promulgate rules. *See* Sidney A. Shapiro & Richard W. Murphy, *Eight Things Americans Can't Figure Out About Controlling Administrative Power*, 61 ADMIN. L. REV. 5, 27 (2009) ("An agency's assertion that it has not had time to respond becomes less persuasive after a significant amount of time. Nevertheless, the courts normally do not force a response before the expiration of at least several years."); Alan B. Morrison, *Administrative Agencies Are Just Like Legislatures and Courts — Except When They're Not*, 59 ADMIN. L. REV. 79, 96 (2007) (stating that, although courts recognize they have the power to require agencies to reach a final decision on a request for rulemaking, they have been reluctant to do so except in extreme cases). Indeed, courts view themselves as far better equipped to review and reject agency actions, although, even in that context, they must be deferential to the agency's determinations. And inaction by OSHA is common.

So why, ultimately, did the Third Circuit take such an exceptional step in this case and order OSHA to act? Do you think the court overstepped? Certainly, some question whether a court should ever interfere when an agency chooses not to regulate, absent a clear congressional directive to act. What reasons, if any, justify court interference with an agency's discretion to determine whether to engage in the rulemaking process? In thinking about this question, recall the discussion of deference to administrative agencies in Chapter 9, page 665.

3. *The Role of Scientific and Technological Uncertainty.* Assuming OSHA's concerns about scientific and technological uncertainty were not simply a *post hoc* justification for dragging its feet, this case demonstrates how uncertainty arguments from regulated industries have deterred OSHA from acting, particularly with regard to allegedly harmful chemicals and substances. Consider how the substantial evidence requirement, combined with scientific and technological uncertainty regarding health risks and feasibility, may affect OSHA's decision making. First, developing the science to determine risk and feasibility takes time and resources. Given the nature of the inquiry, OSHA itself may have good-faith doubts about the science even after accumulating greater knowledge. For example, it may question the causal connection between exposure and disease, the levels of exposure that pose a danger, whether all forms of the substance pose equal problems, and so forth. Beyond this, OSHA officials know what to expect downstream—if the agency forges ahead with the rule-making process where any doubt exists, industry groups will challenge the scientific and technological bases for the proposed standards during the notice and comment period. *See generally* Michaels & Monforton, *supra*. If these challenges fail, these groups can seek relief from Congress and, if that fails, they may bring suit challenging the final version of the rule.

That said, what is the alternative? Should the requirements for OSHA to promulgate specific standards be more lenient? There are alternative approaches to rule making or judicial review that might strike the balance in favor of greater regulation to the benefit of workers. For example, Congress could amend the statute to provide for more deferential "arbitrary and capricious" review or to streamline procedures by reducing opportunities for public comment and participation. On the other hand, given the substantial costs on regulated employers, might it be good policy to require OSHA both to engage in a full notice and comment process and to make the rigorous showing of significant risk and feasibility that the law currently requires?

4. *Other Factors Contributing to Agency Inaction.* Uncertainty clearly was not the only reason for OSHA's inaction on hexavalent chromium. The various other reasons—limited resources, unforeseen events, other priorities, new procedural hurdles, changing agency leadership, and ideological preferences—played critical roles. Won't at least one of these factors always be present as OSHA attempts to regulate workplace hazards? If so, is this simply a story of a lack of political will or, alternatively, "capture" of the agency or Congress by powerful interest groups? Is it naive to think that OSHA can ever overcome industry attempts to delay or prevent standards promulgation? In other words, perhaps OSHA's approach to promulgating standards cannot be fixed. If it can be, how and by whom?

b. Enforcement

OSHA enforcement historically has been largely of the "command and control" variety. That is, OSHA inspectors issue citations for violations of specific standards or of the general duty clause. These citations, may range from "de minimis" ones with no penalty to "serious," and "willful" violations whose penalties can range up to $70,000. For a failure to abate violations, a $7,000 a day penalty is possible. Citations are not initially enforced in court. Rather, if contested, they are adjudicated administratively by the Occupational Safety and Health Review Commission ("OSHRC"), composed of three commissioners appointed by the president. Only after the OSHRC decision can an employer seek there review in the appropriate court of appeals. Criminal sanctions are also available, but only when an employer makes false statements to an inspector, intentionally interferes with an inspection, or has actual knowledge of a dangerous condition that leads to a fatality.

OSHA engages in regular inspections and will also inspect employers in response to employee complaints. Generally, inspections are conducted without advance notice, but, absent OSHA obtaining a warrant, an employer can refuse to allow access to its establishment. OSHA need not demonstrate probable cause of a criminal violation to obtain an administrative search warrant, but rather must have specific evidence of a violation or show satisfaction of reasonable standards for conducting the particular inspection. *See Marshall v. Barlow's, Inc.*, 436 U.S. 307 (1978). In many instances, however, employers waive the warrant requirement. Why do you think that is? *See generally* Note, *The Permissible Scope of OSHA Complaint Inspections*, 49 U. CHI. L. REV. 203 (1982).

In 2009, OSHA conducted 39,004 inspections and found 87,663 violations of OSHA's standards and regulations. About three quarters were "serious," but only a small percentage were "willful." *See* OSHA, OSHA Enforcement: Ensuring Safe and Healthy Workplaces, *available at* http://www.osha.gov/dep/2009_enforcement _summary.html. Although the number of inspections and cited violations has held fairly constant in recent years, *see id.*, and have increased over historic lows in the mid-1990s, both total inspections and found violations are down dramatically from earlier years. *See* Public Citizen Health Research Group, *Report Detailing Occupational Safety and Health Administration Enforcement Actions from 1972 through 1998* (HRG Publication #1494), *available at* http://www.citizen.org/publications/release.cfm?ID=6693. OSHA also provides some ancillary protections, including anti-retaliation and disclosure provisions.

A very important aspect of OSHA's structure is what it does not permit: Unlike statutes such as Title VII and the FLSA, OSHA does not authorize private enforcement. As *Public Citizen* suggests, private parties may be able in extreme cases to compel OSHA to promulgate standards, but they cannot compel it to enforce those standards against particular violators. Occasionally, OSHA standards have been used to establish a standard of care in suits based on other theories, such as negligence. *See generally* ROTHSTEIN, *supra*, §§ 501, 502, and 513. Nevertheless, given the general absence of private enforcement, the significance of administrative enforcement (or the lack thereof) cannot be overstated.

2. OSHA's Troubled Past and Present, and Its Uncertain Future

The implementation and enforcement of OSHA have been much criticized from all sides. Employers have complained about the burdensomeness of the regulations, the "nitpickiness" of inspectors and excessiveness of citations, and the lack of recognition for good-faith efforts to comply. These types of criticisms and related advocacy efforts have had an impact, including the repeal of some of the interim regulations, the limited promulgation of new and permanent standards, successful challenges to certain OSHA initiatives, and reductions in OSHA's enforcement resources. In addition, as discussed in the *Public Citizen* case above, various changes in the law—including the Regulatory Flexibility Act and the Small Business Regulatory Enforcement Fairness Act—have imposed constraints on OSHA's ability to promulgate and enforce new standards. Moreover, as discussed below, partially in response to industry pressure, OSHA has shifted toward a model of greater self-regulation—that is, allowing employers to avoid an ordinary inspection schedule if they demonstrate their ability to comply with health and safety standards and improve their safety records. Currently all of these programs are voluntary. Industry groups were able to defeat the one compelled self-regulation program—the Cooperative Compliance Program—that they viewed as imposing obligations that were too onerous. Orly Lobel, *Interlocking Regulatory and Industrial Relations: The Governance of Workplace Safety*, 57 ADMIN. L. REV. 1071, 1124-28 (2005).

On the other hand, labor and work safety advocates have bemoaned OSHA's ineffectiveness in purging the workplace of preventable safety hazards. Many have expressed concern about the various substantive and procedural barriers to OSHA's promulgation of new specific regulations. But most critics have focused on enforcement, arguing that OSHA's efforts and the penalties resulting from violations are woefully inadequate. They argue, for example, that there are far too few inspections and resulting sanctions to create sufficient incentives for employers to comply with OSHA's mandates, particularly given the relatively weak penalties for most violations. *See, e.g.*, Cynthia Estlund, *Rebuilding the Law of the Workplace in an Era of Self-Regulation*, 105 COLUM. L. REV. 319, 360 (2005) (discussing OSHA's chronic underfunding and weak penalties); Susan Bisom Rapp, *What We Learn in Troubled Times: Deregulation and Safe Work in the New Economy*, 55 WAYNE L. REV. 1197, 1211, (2009) ("AFL-CIO Associate General Counsel Lynn Rhinehart recently noted that given its current level of resources, OSHA can conduct inspections of 'each workplace under its jurisdiction on average once every 133 years.'"); *see also* Secretary of Labor Hilda L. Solis, *Remarks as Prepared for Delivery OSHA Latino Safety Conference Houston, TX*, April 14, 2010, *available at* http://www.dol.gov/_sec/media/speeches/20100414_OSHALSC.htm ("OSHA only has about 1,000 inspectors. States running their own state plans have about the same number. That means it would take more than 130 years to inspect every single one of the 8 million workplaces in this country just once."). In the eyes of critics, the long-term trend toward reduced enforcement in the OSHA context and deregulation more generally have simply made things worse.

As of its first two years, the Obama Administration had, contrary to this trend, emphasized greater enforcement, including implementing a number of new regulatory initiatives, modestly increasing OSHA's budget, and hiring additional inspectors. *See, e.g.*, Laura Walter, *DOL 2011 Budget Request Includes OSHA Increase, Focus on Enforcement*, EHS Today, Feb. 1, 2010, *available at* http://ehstoday.com/standards/osha/dol-budget-request-osha-increase-focus-enforcement-2414/. However, the overall effect of these changes remains to be seen.

The vexing questions, then, are the extent to which the critiques of OSHA, from either side, are valid, and if so, whether realistic reforms might make the regime more effective. While scholarly commentaries on OSHA's history and problems are legion, the following article offers one particularly instructive summary of the regime's failings.

≡ ### Interlocking Regulatory and Industrial Relations:
≡ ### The Governance of Workplace Safety
Orly Lobel, 57 ADMIN. L. REV. 1071, 1077-97 (2005)

Debates and battles fraught with irony and illusion exist at the center of a field in which death and injury are very real. OSHA is an agency immersed in paradox. Companies criticize OSHA for being outrageously intrusive and unreasonable, while labor criticizes the agency for being exceptionally slow and ineffective. In self-reflective moments, OSHA is deeply critical of its legal mandate and organizational structure. OSHA insiders assert that the agency is dangerously under-staffed, under-funded, under-appreciated, and overly-attacked by all sides.

Congress adopted [OSHA] to "assure so far as possible every working man and woman in the Nation safe and healthful working conditions and to preserve our human resources." The OSH Act passed after considerable struggle in a unique constellation of interests, when a series of fatal occupational construction and mining accidents captured popular attention in the activist climate of the late 1960s. Congress empowered OSHA to prescribe standards to improve safety and health in the workplace. But soon after the enactment of the OSH Act, Congress made multiple attempts to weaken the agency's authority. Since its establishment, the agency and its regulatory practices have been the source of debate, litigation, and conflict. For over three decades, legal scholars have repeatedly invoked OSHA as the paradigmatic case of bureaucratic inefficiency and regulatory failure. The agency's opponents have described its actions to regulate workplace safety as "paternalistic government at its most intrusive," a bureaucracy that cultivates "a culture of regulatory excess that eats away at the vitality of our economy." In an environment of abundant critique of the regulatory state, OSHA has become the prime example of all that is unreasonable and pathological about administrative agencies. It has been described as "an ill-conceived, poorly executed regulatory regime."

A. The Persistence and Costs of Occupational Risks

In the world at large, more people die at work than in wars. In the United States, over a dozen workers are killed daily in on-the-job accidents, and over a hundred more die every day from work-related disease. Many more suffer from occupational injury and disease, which impacts the lives of millions of workers each year. The risk is distributed unequally across sectors and segments of the labor market and the most vulnerable, low-skilled, and disorganized workers bear the risks of the most serious injuries. For example, in recent years, the number of fatal work injuries among foreign-born Hispanic workers has risen steadily.

High injury and illness rates are not only morally wrong but also tremendously expensive. The direct costs for occupational injuries in the United States are estimated at over $40 billion, with indirect costs exceeding $200 billion per year. The further magnitude of occupational disease (on top of injury) is rarely considered. For example, occupational exposures to toxic substances account for approximately one-fifth of all cancer cases, which is more than all other environmental exposures combined.

Occupational disease also kills more people each year than other preventable causes of death, including motor vehicle accidents, diabetes, and homicides. From both macro and micro perspectives, soaring health insurance premiums present further pressures on workplace risk prevention, which negatively impact the ability of employers to hire new workers and pay for health care benefits. This, in turn, increases the level of unemployment and the number of the uninsured people. Yet, government spending on worker safety has never reached the level of other social issues, and OSHA's budget continues to steadily decline.

B. OSHA's Reach: Limited Resources and Inspection Rates

Despite an image of intrusiveness and omnipresence, OSHA is actually a low-budget, understaffed, overextended agency. In today's American labor market, OSHA is responsible for the safety of more than 115 million workers at over eight million worksites. The agency currently has a staff of over 2,000 employees, which is actually fewer workers than the agency had at its inception. . . . In effect, OSHA is able to inspect every workplace that it oversees less than once each century. OSHA manages to investigate only one-quarter of the workplaces with reported fatalities. Even the most at-risk industries, such as construction sites, are inspected, on average, once every ten years.

C. Doing Business While Endangering Lives: The Penalties

The penalty under the OSH Act for willfully endangering workers is a misdemeanor. Simply stated, if an employer intentionally disregards or is plainly indifferent to safety standards and a fatal accident results, the maximum penalty is six months imprisonment. In contrast, the maximum penalty for willfully endangering a protected fish under the Clean Water Act is fifteen years of imprisonment. A serious violation of OSHA—a citation for hazards that pose a substantial probability to cause serious physical harm or death to an employee—carries a maximum penalty of $7,000. By comparison, the unlawful importation of a wild bird entails a penalty of $25,000, while an employment discrimination act can carry a penalty of $50,000. The maximum sentence in the OSH Act, six months imprisonment, is half the penalty for harassing a wild burro on federal lands. A serious occupational safety violation carries less than the fine for shooting a moose out of season.

. . . Worker safety is a readily available example used by behavioral scholars to describe inconsistencies in the pattern of civil penalties across regulatory contexts. For example, Cass Sunstein, Daniel Kahneman, and their co-authors have described the disparity between the penalties of the OSH Act and the Wild Bird Conservation Act as a "serious anomaly." [Cass Sunstein et al., *Predictably Incoherent Judgments*, 54 STAN. L. REV. 1153, 1190-91 (2002).]

D. The Incredible Threat of Prosecution

A 1988 congressional report on worker safety calculated that "a company official who willfully and recklessly violates federal OSHA laws stands a greater chance of winning a state lottery than being criminally charged." According to more recent studies, the comparison with lotteries overstates the odds. In the past two decades, approximately 170,000 workplace fatalities occurred in the United States. OSHA investigated less than one-quarter of these deaths. Of the investigated cases, OSHA found 1,798 cases (2,197 deaths) eligible for prosecution, that is, cases in which workers were killed because of an occupational safety standards violation. Of these cases, OSHA referred less than 200 cases to the Department of Justice for criminal prosecution, despite, or perhaps because of, the fact that the maximum penalty for the most severe cases is a misdemeanor. Federal prosecutors have declined to pursue two-thirds of these cases and only eight of them have resulted in prison sentences for company officials. . . . Even repeat violators have been rarely prosecuted. In effect, since the enactment of the OSH Act over 33 years ago, less than one dozen employers have been imprisoned under federal laws for causing a worker's death.

The monetary fines are equally troubling. In 2003, serious violations of the OSH Act carried an average penalty of less than $900. For the 2,197 worker deaths in the past two decades that OSHA investigated, employers faced a total of $106 million in civil fines, a shockingly meager sum in comparison to finance-related corporate crimes. . . .

II.   The New World of Regulation

OSHA practices and the limits of its reach epitomize the relative power of industry and the weakness of labor. However, they also signify more general failures of the traditional top-down command-and-control model employed by regulatory agencies, as well as the changing circumstances of the new world of work. The thin nature of the administrative process has failed to fulfill the promise of safety to all workers in all industries.

A.   Over-Regulation Causes Under-Regulation

In its early days of existence, OSHA promulgated hundreds of pages of regulation. Rules were often too complex, ambiguous, or simply unsuited to fit the realities of production and work. The sea of regulation had a self-destructive effect. Even proponents of OSHA standard-setting agreed that many of OSHA's regulatory standards were "hopelessly vague [or needlessly detailed and some] . . . were plainly ridiculous." Even the most conscientious employers were unable to comply with the heavily detailed safety code. Businesses felt that the substantive safety rules were overly intrusive, leading OSHA to issue fines for failure to comply with standards that were unreasonable, unnecessarily complicated, or simply trivial. For example, standards about the color of ladders and the height and number of bathroom toilets seemed pointless and were ill-suited for ordering the heterogeneous market. Such standards were particularly burdensome on small workplaces. More disturbingly, the connection between such standards and the real risks workers faced on the job was tenuous. OSHA's substantive standards have been pervasively incapable of fully addressing the realities of safety management. In the past two decades, industrial organization studies have repeatedly indicated that standards frequently diverge from the major sources of fatalities and injuries in the workplace. Even with perfect compliance, studies predict that uniform occupational safety regulation can only prevent less than 25 percent of occupational injury. In effect, at least in certain industries, violations of OSHA standards account for less than 20 percent of fatal accidents. At the same time, most accidents can in fact be prevented by state action.

The most controversial of OSHA's rules have been those that demanded high costs of compliance when estimates about the projected benefits are substantially low. The image of OSHA since its early years quickly became that of a zealous regulator that exaggerates the benefits of its rules and is insensitive about its costs. In the early 1980s, industry litigated against OSHA's universal standards on exposure to toxic substance, resulting in the famous Supreme Court benzene decision [*Indus. Union Dep't v. Am. Petroleum Inst.*, 448 U.S. 607, 641 (1980)] that struck down exposure standards and held that OSHA must first establish the existence of a "significant risk" before it regulates preventative standards. . . .

B. *Over-Enforcement Causes Under-Enforcement*

. . . Since its inception, OSHA's traditional regulatory action consisted of top-down enforcement of substantive rules by quasi-random inspections of various work-sites and prosecution and sanctions upon the finding of a violation. In the regulatory process, the compliance officer arrives unannounced and informs management and workers about their rights and about the proceedings of the inspection. Then, the officer conducts a tour of the worksite, which, depending on the size of the workplace, can take between a day and several weeks, involving one or more inspectors. Traditionally, an inspector is obliged to cite every identified violation. Each violation cited is subject to a fine, but inspectors may negotiate compliance deals to reduce the fines.

The first wave of OSHA's enforcement activities has had positive effects upon the hard conditions of work, primarily in large industrial firms. But a sole focus on adversarial enforcement also produces counterproductive effects. A substantial number of empirical and comparative studies have pointed to the negative effects of regulatory adversarialism. Eugene Bardach and Robert Kagan, in their seminal study on "regulatory unreasonableness," found that the combination of OSHA's dense rules and surprise inspections deters employers from compliance. [citing EUGENE BARDACH & ROBERT A. KAGAN, GOING BY THE BOOK: THE PROBLEM OF REGULATORY UNREASONABLE-NESS 106-16 (1982)] Counterproductive enforcement can be explained by several interrelated reasons. First, punishment in the case of good faith efforts to comply is likely to demoralize and reduce the willingness of firms to consider safety beyond mere compliance. . . . Second, confrontational enforcement diminishes the willingness of firms to cooperate and learn. . . . Finally, an adversarial framework misses the opportunity to leverage long-term incentives of firms to avoid noncompliance, including such factors as increased productivity, reputation, and good working relations. All of these complex incentives vary across industries, in which size, rapidity of change, technology, cycles of organizational life, branding, and the mobility of workers all structure the balance between firms' short and long term goals.

After a social field becomes an established area of regulatory intervention, policy strategies must be diversified in order to best ratchet up private behavior. In evolutionary terms, as OSHA enters its fourth decade, the agency's ability to improve compliance through direct top-down enforcement in some industries is now substantially limited. This is in part a result of earlier accomplishment and in part the result of earlier blind spots. . . .

Perhaps the most important aspect of the problem with over-enforcement, along with the coexistence of under-enforced contexts, is that of resource allocation. Universal one-dimensional interactions between regulators and regulated parties deplete the limited resources of public agencies. Agencies are less likely to engage in sophisticated targeting when the vast sea of regulated entities simply swims before their eyes. The result is a de facto unrealistic threat of inspection for most industries. . . .

III.   The New World of Work . . .

At the same time that the role of the state in regulating the market is evolving, occupational risks are posing new challenges for regulators. The new global economy has dramatically altered the nature of work and employment. In the past several decades, firms have shifted from mass production both to post-industrial manufacturing and to service markets. The typical economic enterprise of the industrial era was a large and long-term firm. Production was relatively stable, menial tasks were narrowly defined, and roles were segmented. By contrast, production today is more heterogeneous, volatile, and includes complex contractual chains. These changes present difficulties for a centralized agency to promulgate and enforce universal top-down rules that will fit all firms.

A. Accelerated Production

In a time of "radicalized modernity" and "just-in-time" production, the law must recognize market demands of rapid change and adaptability. As technological, social, and economic conditions change quickly, production and employment patterns need to adjust rapidly. Firms experience heightened pressures of competition and profitability. Substantive standards quickly become outdated as production conditions constantly change within firms. Accelerated production patterns also entail variability across firms and industries. As a result, the private sector is often better positioned to determine the particular details about tools and techniques required for production. Under such conditions, the goal of public ordering cannot and should not be the displacement of the judgment of the regulated entity. Rather, public policy should aim to direct responsible decisionmaking processes and support the increased market demands for continuous improvement through trial and error problem solving.

B. Firm Size, Longevity, and Capabilities

As described above, large industrial firms are now entering their fourth decade of interaction with OSHA. Many of these firms have established a safety infrastructure and processes to control occupational risks. In order to improve the safety conditions in these firms, OSHA must creatively adopt new approaches that can leverage these efforts and support industry-wide long-term learning. By contrast, the increase in small firms has proven particularly challenging for OSHA, as well as for other regulatory agencies. In the context of occupational safety, fatal and serious accidents are more likely to occur in small and mid-size businesses for three reasons. First, smaller employers typically lack the in-house expertise and resources to improve practices. Small scale production can also reduce incentives to invest in machinery, training, and a safe infrastructure. Second, smaller firms are likely to have shorter life-cycles. Longevity of a firm's existence is a factor in its ability and willingness to learn about safe processes and improve its infrastructure. Finally, smaller and less stable firms are less sensitive to bad publicity and consumer awareness efforts.

C. Safety Chains and Employment Contingencies

Workplaces are increasingly connected by multiple contractual and subsidiary ownership links. Complex chains of authority can create disorganization and uncertainty about responsibilities. In the past decade, OSHA investigations have revealed that a number of serious safety violations, for example in a series of explosions in the petrochemical industry, were the result of outsourcing. Outsourcing is likely to divide responsibilities and create confusion and ambiguity about accountability. It provides firms new opportunities to evade legal responsibility and introduces increased competitive pressures on subcontractors to obtain the contract. Lengthy and complex production chains also allow managers to rationalize and distance themselves psychologically from work-related injuries. . . .

Complex production chains coincide with the increased contingency of employment relations. Businesses seek to employ part-time, temporary, leased, and subcontracted day laborers and seasonal workers. Like in other areas of employment regulation, duties are contested through the ambiguities of employer/employee legal definitions. Under the OSH Act, employers only have a duty toward those they legally "employ." Initially, OSHA attempted to take a broad view of the responsibility of contractors and their subcontractors. However, courts have narrowed OSHA's citations, reasoning that Congress had not intended to impose the burden of controlling risk on firms who did not have appropriate control over workers to abate hazards.

D. *Automation and New Hazards*

The industrial era's physical hazards of operating heavy machinery continue to exist today, but these hazards are supplemented by a range of new occupational risks. New manufacturing patterns and the rise of the service sector have introduced a myriad of new risks. New technologies, including increased automation and computation, account for the rise in musculoskeletal injury. . . . The regulation of ergonomics has been an especially contentious issue in recent years. In today's workplaces, musculoskeletal disorders, repetitive trauma, and stress-related injury are the largest category of occupational risk, accounting for more than one-third of all injuries and illnesses. After years of research and development on ergonomics, when OSHA finally promulgated an ergonomic standard in 2001, Congress rescinded the standard. . . .

NOTES

1. *A Troubled Past and Present.* Although aspects of her account are contestable, Professor Lobel provides a comprehensive portrait of OSHA's problems, the real-life (and death) consequences, scholarly criticisms, and possible root causes. Is there anything in her account that surprises you? Why? With this history of regulatory failure as a backdrop, the question going forward is whether and how to fix the existing workplace safety regime.

2. *A Third Way?* The discussion of how to improve OSHA and, more generally, workplace safety and health, has shifted away from the traditional bilateral debate between more or less regulation. For example, Professor Lobel goes on to discuss recent OSHA reforms that focus on neither top-down enforcement nor further deregulation but rather on promoting safety and health compliance or "self-regulation" efforts within regulated firms. One example of this "third way" is OSHA's Voluntary Protection Program ("VPP"):

> The Voluntary Protection Program . . . exempts employers with exemplary safety records from routine inspections. VPP has three levels of participation status, "Star,"

"Merit," and "Demonstration," certifying the level of safety achievement of participating members. To achieve Star status, signifying the highest level of health and safety, a firm must maintain below industry average injury rates. The central requirements for participation are the adoption of an approved written safety program, an established feedback system to notify management of hazards, and a planned system of responses to those hazards. In order to adopt an internal safety plan, employers must conduct thorough analyses of the safety hazards in their worksites and have clear procedures for prevention and control. Two other requirements are the encouragement of employee involvement in the execution of the program and the provision of adequate training.

. . . As long as this program of audited self-regulation proves to effectively reduce accidents, the agency does not intervene in the processes. The VPP has attracted mainly larger worksites, which is in part a result of the capability of large businesses to design a comprehensive safety and health program.

Id. at 1105-06 (footnotes and citations omitted).

A second approach is the Safety and Health Achievement Recognition Program ("SHARP"), which Professor Lobel describes as equivalent to VPP but "designed for small firms in high hazard industries." Like participation in VPP, SHARP exempts companies from general, scheduled inspections although SHARP participants are still subject to inspections following worker complaints or serious safety and health occurrences. *See id.* at 1106. A third approach is the Strategic Partnership Program ("SPP"), which is designed to encourage employers in hazardous industries to develop measures for eliminating specific risks by helping employers integrate lessons from multiple worksites. Unlike VPP and SHARP, the SPP does not exempt participants from inspections but limits inspections to the most serious hazards. *See id.* at 1106-07.

Early studies — including one conducted by the Government Accounting Office, ("GAO") showed these programs to be successes. *See id.* at 1108 noting that the GAO study "found that participation in the programs has considerably reduced injury and illness rates, improved relationships with OSHA, improved productivity, and decreased worker compensation costs." In her 2005 article, Professor Lobel argued for such compliance-centered regimes, although she cautioned that, to prevent such public/private cooperation from becoming merely deregulation in disguise, steps must be taken to ensure that OSHA will indeed return to direct enforcement where firms fail to comply or improve safety through self-governance and that workers — the stakeholders OSHA is supposed to protect — have a voice in the governance. *See id.* at 1112-15.

Unfortunately, OSHA seems not to have heeded such warnings. A more recent GAO report found that, while VPP programs expanded significantly during the last years of the Bush Administration, OSHA failed to develop adequate internal controls and mechanisms for assessing the programs' performance. The agency therefore was unable to ensure that only qualified worksites were allowed to participate in the program and that participants remained compliant with health and safety standards. The GAO also found significant rates of noncompliance among certain types of participating firms. *See generally* GAO, OSHA's VOLUNTARY PROTECTIONS PROGRAM: IMPROVED OVERSIGHT AND CONTROLS WOULD BETTER ENSURE PROGRAM QUALITY (May 2009), *available at* http://www.gao.gov/new.items/d09395.pdf. In light of these findings and other enforcement priorities, the Obama Administration has sought to shift resources away from voluntary compliance to other OSHA programs. *See* Steve Tuckey, *OSHA's Deeper Bite: The Obama Administration Injects New Power into the Occupational Safety Agency as Employers Find Themselves on the Defensive*, CBS

Money Watch.com, April 1, 2010, *available at* http://findarticles.com/p/articles/mi_m0BJK/is_3_21/ai_n53519363/.

3. *Incentives to Participate.* To the extent voluntary programs are at all effective in promoting workplace safety, what are the incentives for firms to participate? Obviously, enlightened firms might find it in their self-interest in part to avoid the costs of workers' compensation. But if a firm has made a cold-blooded, cost-benefit judgment that injuries are less expensive than safety, will cooperative approaches be attractive? Isn't the biggest incentive to participate reduced inspections? And doesn't Professor Lobel say that inspections are rare and violations not expensive in any event?

Once a firm participates in one of these programs and attains a safety record and status that reduces the chances of inspections and penalties, what incentives are there to remain truly compliant (as opposed to simply appearing compliant on paper) over the long term? The development of a culture of compliance within a firm is undoubtedly a good thing, particularly when, as Professor Lobel advocates, a firm engages workers in the compliance process. OSHA's self-governance programs may promote such development where it would not have otherwise existed, and, perhaps, the resulting benefits — for example, fewer workplace injuries and improved employee morale — will convince firms that prioritizing such compliance is in their long-term interest.

Yet, in times when there are strong incentives to reduce costs, such as during economic downturns or where the firm faces stiff competition, such cultures and programs can erode very quickly, something we have witnessed occasionally in other areas, such as in compliance with corporate and securities mandates. In the current economic environment, one might predict that firms — or at least individual managers or officials under pressure to "make their numbers" — are more likely to avoid or delay safety improvements if inspections and sanctions are unlikely. Doesn't this suggest that OSHA must, even while promoting self-governance, play an ongoing and active oversight role? If so, doesn't this lead right back to the same basic problem, namely, that, to be truly effective, OSHA needs greater resources and the power to impose more biting sanctions?

4. *Perfecting Self-governance.* Professor Cynthia Estlund also critiques the new self-governance approach under OSHA, albeit in the context of exploring the evolution of workplace regulation more generally — from collective bargaining to command and control to self-regulation. *See generally* Cynthia Estlund, *Rebuilding the Law of the Workplace in an Era of Self-Regulation*, 105 Colum. L. Rev. 319 (2005). Like Lobel, she sees both potential promise in self-regulation and the dangers of insufficient corresponding government oversight and the lack of worker involvement. Professor Estlund asserts that, for the governance approach to be effective in achieving statutory goals, it must be "monitored self-regulation":

> The basic template for effective self-regulation would be based on an explicit code of conduct encompassing at least employers' substantive legal obligations and employees' right, free from retaliation, to communicate with each other and with monitors and regulators regarding code compliance; code compliance would be the responsibility of specified managerial officials and would be monitored by independent outside monitors accountable in part to workers. Entry into the system would be encouraged by public and private enforcement mechanisms — targeted public enforcement and the threat of potent sanctions against the worst lawbreakers, and private rights of action on behalf of aggrieved employees, including whistleblowers — the full force of which would be mitigated or held in abeyance for employers engaged in a system of effective self-regulation.

See id. at 379. In other words, Professor Estlund envisions self-regulation under OSHA and elsewhere being truly effective only if it embodies tripartite involvement of workers, employers, and government regulators. In addition, appropriate incentives must be sustained through ongoing monitoring by independent outsiders, the threat of sanctions and civil lawsuits for noncompliance with safety standards, and meaningful anti-retaliation protection for whistleblowers. *See id.*

Whether this kind of approach would prove successful in furthering OSHA's purposes more efficiently and effectively is uncertain, although reforms in the direction Professor Estlund envisions might very well promote far greater buy-in — and, hence, efforts that promote compliance — by both workers and firms. Still, regardless of its merits, are there reasons to doubt whether policy makers would ever be willing and able to craft, fund, and maintain such a regime?

Case Study: The Horrors of McWane

In light of what you have seen in this chapter, consider the plight of the workers at various divisions and subsidiaries of McWane, Inc., the subject of a three-part expose in the *New York Times*. As you read, remember that this is a story not from the early twentieth century, but from the early *twenty-first* century. Thus, all of this occurred nearly a century after the establishment of workers' compensation regimes and decades after OSHA was first enacted. Ask yourself how this happened and what reforms (if any) might have helped prevent all or some of the tragedies described.

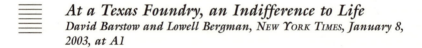

At a Texas Foundry, an Indifference to Life
David Barstow and Lowell Bergman, NEW YORK TIMES, January 8, 2003, at A1

TYLER, TEX. — It is said that only the desperate seek work at Tyler Pipe, a sprawling, rusting pipe foundry out on Route 69, just past the flea market. Behind a high metal fence lies a workplace that is part Dickens and part Darwin, a dim, dirty, hellishly hot place where men are regularly disfigured by amputations and burns, where turnover is so high that convicts are recruited from local prisons, where some workers urinate in their pants because their bosses refuse to let them step away from the manufacturing line for even a few moments.

Rolan Hoskin was from the ranks of the desperate. His life was a tailspin of unemployment, debt and divorce. A master electrician, 48 years old, he had retreated to a low-rent apartment on the outskirts of town and taken an entry-level maintenance job on the graveyard shift at Tyler Pipe.

He would come home covered in fine black soot, utterly drained and dreading the next shift. "I don't know if I'm going to last another week," his twin brother recalls him saying. The job scared him; he didn't know what he was doing. But the pay was decent, almost $10 an hour, and his electricity was close to being cut off. "He was just trying to make it," his daughter said.

On June 29, 2000, in his second month on the job, Mr. Hoskin descended into a deep pit under a huge molding machine and set to work on an aging, balky conveyor belt that carried sand. Federal rules require safety guards on conveyor belts to prevent workers from getting caught and crushed. They also require belts to be shut down when maintenance is done on them.

But this belt was not shut down, federal records show. Nor was it protected by metal safety guards. That very night, Mr. Hoskin had been trained to adjust the belt while it was still running. Less downtime that way, the men said. Now it was about 4 a.m., and Mr. Hoskin was alone in the cramped, dark pit. The din was deafening, the footing treacherous under heavy drifts of black sand.

He was found on his knees. His left arm had been crushed first, the skin torn off. His head had been pulled between belt and rollers. His skull had split. "If he fought that machine I know his last thought was me," said his daughter, April Hoskin-Silva, her dark eyes rimmed with tears.

It was not just a conveyor belt that claimed Mr. Hoskin's life that warm summer night. He also fell victim to a way of doing business that has produced vast profits and, as the plant's owners have admitted in federal court, deliberate indifference to the safety of workers at Tyler Pipe.

Mr. Hoskin worked for McWane Inc., a privately held company based in Birmingham, Ala., that owns Tyler Pipe and is one of the world's largest manufacturers of cast-iron sewer and water pipe. It is also one of the most dangerous employers in America, according to a nine-month examination by The New York Times, the PBS television program "Frontline" and the Canadian Broadcasting Corporation.

Since 1995, at least 4,600 injuries have been recorded in McWane foundries, many hundreds of them serious ones, company documents show. Nine workers, including Mr. Hoskin, have been killed. McWane plants, which employ about 5,000 workers, have been cited for more than 400 federal health and safety violations, far more than their six major competitors combined.

No McWane executive would be interviewed on the record. But in a series of written responses, the company's president, G. Ruffner Page, acknowledged "serious mistakes" and expressed deep regret for Mr. Hoskin's death. "Our intensified focus on safety speaks to lessons learned," he wrote. At the same time, he sought to explain and strongly defend the company's business methods.

"Over the years, McWane has grown by the acquisition of troubled companies that had become uncompetitive," he wrote. "Through substantial investment in new plant and equipment and more disciplined management practices, McWane transformed these underperforming companies into efficient and viable operations." Disciplined management, he said, has allowed McWane to stave off foreign competitors who have no regard for safety.

In the last decade, many American corporations have embraced such a vision of capitalism — cutting costs, laying off workers and pressing those who remain to labor harder, longer and more efficiently. But top federal and state regulators say McWane has taken this idea to the extreme. Describing the company's business, they use the words "lawless" and "rogue."

The company's managers call it "the McWane way."

The story of Tyler Pipe, drawn from company and government documents and interviews with dozens of current and former workers and managers, is a case study in the application of the McWane way. It is the anatomy of a workplace where, federal officials and employees say, nearly everything — safety programs, environmental controls, even the smallest federally mandated precautions that might have kept Rolan Hoskin alive — has been subordinated to production, to the commandment to keep the pipe rolling off the line.

Federal safety inspectors tried to make a difference. They cited and fined and cajoled. But for years, records show, little changed.

"You put people at risk," a former senior plant manager at Tyler Pipe said. "We did every day."

Which is why even now the toughest of Tyler Pipe veterans remember the day McWane came to town as the day they were, as one of them put it, "kicked into hell."

Introducing "the McWane Way" . . .

The pipe foundry occupies several hundred acres northwest of downtown. Its smokestacks rise high above a north and south plant, each with its own cupola, a multistory furnace that melts tons of scrap metal to produce smoky white rivers of molten iron. The molten iron is poured into spinning cylinders to form pipes, into molds of packed black sand to make fittings. The company would not let a reporter tour the plant. But employees describe simply stepping inside as an overwhelming experience. First is the heat, wave upon wave of it, sometimes in excess of 130 degrees. Then there is the noise — of pipe slamming into pipe, of pneumatic tools that grind and cut, of massive machines that shudder and shake, of honking forklifts and roaring exhaust systems. Dust and fumes choke the lungs and coat the lights, leaving the plant floor a spectral labyrinth of glowing pipes and blackened machinery.

[In the early 1990s, Tyler Pipe employed about 2,800 people and did about $200 million in business a year; it was modestly profitable. In 1995, the Tyler Corporation sold the foundry to McWane.] In one stroke, McWane had bought one of its main rivals and acquired its largest plant.

Within weeks, senior executives flew in from Birmingham and set about executing a plan of stunning audacity: Over the next two years, they cut nearly two-thirds of the employees, yet insisted that production continue apace. They eliminated quality control inspectors and safety inspectors, pollution control personnel and relief workers, cleaning crews and maintenance workers. . . .

To keep up production, McWane eliminated one of three shifts; instead of three shifts of eight hours, there were two 12-hour shifts. At the end of a shift, supervisors often marched through yelling, "Four more hours!" So employees worked 16-hour days, sometimes seven days a week.

Men who operated one machine were ordered to operate three. Breaks were allowed only if a relief worker was available, but McWane had reduced the number of relief workers and forbade supervisors to fill in for hourly workers. The policy hit hardest near iron-pouring stations, where workers had to drink plenty of fluids to withstand the heat. The humiliating result, six workers said in separate interviews, was that men were sometimes forced to urinate in their pants or risk heat exhaustion.

Even the most basic amenities did not survive. The barbecues and 401(k) plan were easy enough targets. But items like soap, medicated skin cream and hand towels were eliminated from the stockroom as "luxuries," company records show. If available at all, they had to be specially ordered with approval from top managers. . . .

Restrictions were placed on safety equipment. Protective aprons, safety boots and face shields were no longer stocked and readily available. Heavy, heat-resistant $17 gloves were replaced by $2 cloth ones. As a result, workers wrapped their hands in duct tape to protect from burns.

[The union was helpless to resist.] Morale plummeted, but profits soared. Senior managers say they were told that Tyler Pipe earned more than $50 million in 1996 — double the reported profits for the five-year period before McWane arrived.

Four years after the takeover, inspectors from the federal Occupational Safety and Health Administration spent several days taking the measure of the new regime. They found more than 150 safety hazards. They found poorly maintained equipment. They found a work force that was poorly trained, ill equipped, overworked.

"Throughout the plant, molten metal is seen spilling from the cupolas, bulls and ladles," their report said. "The forklift trucks transport the metal, and the ground behind the trucks often smokes with puddles of molten metal. Workers are covered with black residue from the foundry sand. Many work areas are dark, due to poor lighting and clouds of sand. Despite all the ignition and fuel sources, exit paths are not obvious. Many workers have scars or disfigurations which are noticeable from several feet away. Burns and amputations are frequent."] . . .

Talking Safety, Walking Danger

Any foundry is filled with dangers seen and unseen. For three of the last four years, the cast-iron foundry industry has recorded the nation's highest injury rates. But the inspectors said they were drawn to Tyler Pipe because its rate was so much higher than the industry average, records show. Even with far fewer workers at Tyler in 1996 than in 1995, more workdays were lost because of injuries, records show.

On paper, the company emphasized safety. "You are expected to work efficiently and as quickly as possible without compromising safety rules or safe practices in any way," the employee handbook states.

But inspectors and workers alike called the safety program a charade. "In essence, they are doing it in 'form' but not with substance," the inspectors wrote.

The company prepared extensive written safety rules. But even the most senior supervisors let employees work in clear violation of those rules, the inspectors found. And while the company promised twice-a-week safety inspections, the same hazards showed up week after week.

Ultimately, the inspectors wrote, it came down to incentives: "They have never developed a mechanism to hold supervisors accountable for safety while, on the other hand, they have mastered a system for holding supervisors accountable for production downtime." . . .

Experienced workers left in droves. Many were fired under a new "no fault" attendance policy that assessed points for each sick day and half points for arriving late or leaving early. Ten points resulted in dismissal. Others quit because of sudden demotions and pay cuts. Mr. Fowler, the personnel director, said he quit because he tired of being seen as a "monster."

New employees are called "pumpkin heads" because of the orange hard hats they must wear, and each week waves of pumpkin heads arrived. But it was not until pumpkin heads started showing up with electronic monitoring bracelets that people realized the company was recruiting at Texas prisons. Many of the newly released prisoners did not last. They worked up to 16 hours a day, sometimes for 14 days straight, then were fired or quit before they qualified for benefits or union protection.

According to interviews and company documents, turnover at times approached 100 percent. Many rookie employees got hurt and left. It was a vicious cycle: injuries fueled turnover; turnover fueled injuries.

The plant was filled with workers who barely knew their way around, let alone grasped the dangers they faced. In April 1996, a crew of outside contract workers was sent up onto the roof to clean gutters. One worker, Juan Jimenez, stepped through a skylight and plunged 55 feet to his death. Mr. Page said that Tyler Pipe's safety director had pointed out the skylight to Mr. Jimenez, but OSHA inspectors said the death "could have been avoided" if the skylight had safety rails as required under OSHA rules. . . .

Losing Limbs But Not Pipes

On Jan. 22, 1997, another maintenance worker, Ira Cofer, descended alone into a machine pit. "Downsizing had ended the earlier practice of entering the pits with a buddy," OSHA investigators later wrote. When Mr. Cofer's sleeve snagged in an unguarded conveyor belt, he struggled desperately to free himself. It was nearly three hours before his screams were heard.

"Eyewitnesses said that the friction of the belt had sanded his arm away, so that even his elbow joint was worn smooth and flat," investigators wrote.

Mr. Cofer's arm had to be amputated.

"I was mad for a while, then I was praying," he said of the ordeal. "There was nothing there but the Lord."

In their accident report, plant managers put the blame squarely on Mr. Cofer: "Keep hand away from belt and do not work alone," they wrote.

Within months, four more maintenance workers suffered amputation injuries at Tyler Pipe. In 1999, OSHA cited the plant for 31 instances of inadequate guarding on machines. By 2000, according to OSHA, 60 percent of the north plant's 70 maintenance workers had been hurt.

Senior managers knew all this, OSHA records show. They knew that guards were frequently left off for weeks at a time. They knew that maintenance mechanics were working on running conveyor belts, entering treacherous machine pits alone.

And so in June 2000, Rolan Hoskin, afraid of the job but too desperate for work to quit, took his turn in the pit. . . .

Burn the Tires, Scrub the Toilet

McWane's senior executives, including C. Phillip McWane, the chairman and chief executive, received regular reports from all their plants. The reports measured seemingly everything — injuries, lost work hours, dismissals, operating margins. By 2000, it was clear that Tyler Pipe had become an exceedingly profitable enterprise.

It was also clear that something was very wrong. Red flags were everywhere.

There had been three deaths since the takeover. The injury rate was climbing, the company's own reports showed. "Safety is without a doubt one of our worst areas," Mr. Stoker wrote in a confidential memorandum to top supervisors. "I have failed in this area, but I can promise you that we will not fail to improve in this area come 2001." . . .

Texas workers' compensation laws give McWane broad immunity from negligence lawsuits. But they also required it to pay medical bills and lost wages for injured workers. Company executives complained that they were "hemorrhaging" money on workers' compensation — many millions of dollars a year and rising.

Once again, the company chose a minimalist approach, according to company and OSHA records and former safety and health employees. It devised a system of "workers' compensation cost control techniques" that shifted responsibility for safety problems onto the workers themselves.

It was a system that assumed widespread fraud and often subjected workers reporting injuries to disciplinary action, and sometimes firing, for violating safety rules.

"Whether the employee is 100 percent or 5 percent at fault is irrelevant," wrote Stephen A. Smith, then president of the McWane subsidiary that owns Tyler Pipe.

In 2000 and 2001, company records show, more than 350 workers were subjected to disciplinary actions — known as D.A.'s — after reporting injuries. "All disciplines short of termination is [sic] administered with the intent and purpose to teach," the plant's employee handbook explained.

But OSHA inspectors concluded that the system was used not to teach but to punish. Disciplinary action was meted out if it was the fault of the employee or not, they said.

"The true significance of a D.A. is that they move an employee along a track for termination," the inspectors wrote. Even longtime employees with exemplary work records could be fired for a single D.A. Employees say they learned to keep injuries a secret whenever possible.

In his response, the McWane president, Mr. Page, said no Tyler Pipe worker had been fired in retaliation for reporting an injury. He said managers were encouraged to enforce safety rules "so that there would be no doubt about management's commitment to the safety program." He added, "No judge or jury has ever concluded that Tyler Pipe acted improperly." . . .

"We Do Not Send Flowers"

Michelle Sankowsky, a nurse, was hired in January 2002 as Tyler Pipe's occupational health and compensation manager. It was a new position, overseeing all workers' compensation cases. She met daily with Boyd T. Collier III, the human resources manager, and other senior executives. She quit after four months, she said, because she concluded that the company routinely targeted injured workers for dismissal.

"You've got to understand," she said. "The mentality is that if it weren't for people looking for a free ride, looking for the paid vacations, if it wasn't for the malingerers, if it wasn't for the fakers, if it wasn't for people being careless and reckless, then they wouldn't have the numbers."

Ms. Sankowsky said she suggested a variety of low-cost ideas to reduce rampant ergonomic complaints. She proposed conducting warm-up exercises and wrapping brush handles in foam. "Not cost effective," she says she was told.

In Texas, injured workers have the right to choose their own doctors. At Tyler Pipe, this right came with an important qualification. "We require every employee injured at work to see the company-approved physician if a doctor is necessary," the employee handbook says. "NO EXCEPTIONS!" The labor contract said the same. In a memorandum to all workers, Mr. Collier said he wanted injured workers to see the company doctor first to "ensure the very best care in Smith County for our employees."

Ms. Sankowsky sees it differently. "It all boiled down to that they wanted to be in control," she said. Controlling the care, she said, was viewed as the key to saving money and reducing injury numbers reported to OSHA. And the key to controlling the care, she said, was Occu-Safe, a tiny medical company hired in 1999 to run the plant dispensary and care for injured workers at its downtown clinic.

Occu-Safe was an unlikely choice for the job. Established only months before, it had no track record and few other clients. It was owned by Mike Adams, whose prior business experience, court records show, included a bankrupt air-conditioning venture. In an interview, Mr. Adams said he won the contract by promising deep reductions in workers' compensation claims.

Mr. Adams also shared Tyler Pipe's skepticism about injury claims; he says he believes that up to 50 percent are fraudulent, and that "overutilization" of doctors is a "huge problem." At his clinic, he said, doctors are under strict orders to avoid "hope so, think so, want so medicine."

Tyler Pipe was by far Mr. Adams's largest client, paying him $615,000 in 2001, records show, and Mr. Adams began most days discussing injury cases with Mr. Collier, the human resources manager. Occu-Safe, Ms. Sankowsky said, was simply too small to assert unbiased medical judgment.

"One of the benefits of having Occu-Safe as your medical provider is that people were not taken off work," she said.

Mr. Adams denies that Mr. Collier has tried to influence medical decisions. "The day he does, I'll walk away," he said.

Still, records suggest that Occu-Safe was responsive to Mr. Collier. When a supervisor punctured his arm late one Friday night, emergency room doctors put him on Vicodin, a strong painkiller, and told him to stay off work a week. But according to internal e-mail, Mr. Collier wanted him back right away; Occu-Safe representatives ordered him to switch to a less potent drug and report to work on Tuesday.

Workers who insisted on seeing their own doctors were assumed to be malingerers. It was called "jumping ship," and employees who did it, Ms. Sankowsky said, were targeted for disciplinary action and termination.

Mr. Collier's hostility toward outside doctors was apparent in an e-mail message on Feb. 19, 2002, to Ms. Sankowsky, who had asked about sending flowers to an employee who had had surgery for a workplace injury.

"Michelle: Typically we do not send flowers to hourly ee's," he wrote. "And the only time we send flowers to salaried ee's is death in the immediate family; I'd entertain a proposal to fund flowers for cases like Brian but we need to scope it very narrow so it didn't apply for cases that were referred by CARPENTER and his band of outlaws."

Mr. Collier was referring to Dr. Robert Carpenter, a chiropractor with union ties who has treated approximately 60 injured Tyler Pipe workers over the last two years. About 40 of them have since been fired, said Dr. Carpenter, who has filed a defamation suit against Mr. Collier. He said he no longer gets new patients who work at Tyler Pipe.

"If I was an injured worker, then I would think that perhaps I might get fired if I went to see Dr. Carpenter," he said.

A Broken Back and a Bass Boat

Marcos Lopez crossed the Mexican border and found work at Tyler Pipe at the age of 17. He was used to tough work, and he saw plenty of men get hurt. But nothing on earth, he said, prepared him for McWane.

"You reach this point that you just don't care about you," said Mr. Lopez, who is now 45. "And you set your mind on work. And that's what they want. And that's how people get hurt."

On March 2, 2002, it happened to him. He was working on some machinery, stretching awkwardly in a tight space, when he slipped and fell. His back slammed into metal. He heard a snap, he said, and felt dizzying waves of pain and nausea. In the dispensary, records show, he was pale and weeping and showing signs of shock. He said his pain — a "burning in the bone" — was so intense that it was a challenge just to breathe.

Had he been sent to a hospital, had an X-ray been done, it would have been clear that Mr. Lopez had suffered a terrible injury, a severe compression fracture in his spine.

But he was not sent to a hospital. "They just tell me to sit down and wait for the safety man," he recalled. Ms. Sankowsky, in the dispensary that day, recalls that senior safety managers were deeply suspicious of Mr. Lopez. He had a prior back injury, in 2000. Worse still, he had "jumped ship" and been kept off work for months.

Then, in questioning Mr. Lopez, the managers discovered that he had recently bought a bass boat. They found this highly significant, Ms. Sankowsky recalls. Might he be faking injury to get his boat paid off with disability insurance? When she argued that shock was difficult to fake, Ms. Sankowsky said, the safety manager brushed her aside: "Michelle, don't you think that you could sweat and cry a little bit if you thought you were going to get a free boat and paid vacation?"

Mr. Lopez was sent by van to the Occu-Safe clinic where, after a brief examination, he was given pain medicine and sent home, records show. The clinic doctor diagnosed a back strain and told the plant to expect Mr. Lopez back in three days. In fact, he was getting worse. He felt a creeping numbness in his legs and hands.

At Tyler Pipe, Ms. Sankowsky said, Mr. Collier and the safety managers were "really circling their wagons around Mr. Lopez, that he's a fraud, he's a fake, and, you know, we're going to get him before he gets us." At a meeting on March 13, the managers approved a plan to place Mr. Lopez under surveillance, corporate records show.

The next day, on his third visit to Occu-Safe, Mr. Lopez asked for an X-ray. It showed a "bad compression fracture," medical records state. Still, he was sent home. Nobody informed him of the new findings, he said, and according to Ms. Sankowsky, this was deliberate.

"Why do you not tell this gentleman that he's got a compression fracture of the spine?" she said she asked an Occu-Safe manager. "And he said to me, 'Well, then he'd know how hurt he was.'"

The clinic, she said, quietly began to explore the possibility that Mr. Lopez had cancer that had weakened his spine. Mr. Collier, she said, welcomed the news. "So we can deny the claim because it's cancer?" she recalls him asking. . . .

McWane kept Mr. Lopez under surveillance this year, determined to prove him a malingerer. In his response, Mr. Page said Mr. Lopez had been filmed "lifting heavy loads into his car" — proof, he said, that Mr. Lopez has not suffered any serious disability. A doctor for the Texas Workers Compensation Commission, however, recently determined that despite surgery and months of rehabilitation, Mr. Lopez has a permanent partial disability.

NOTES

1. *A Complete and Systemic Regulatory Failure.* As an epilogue to this story and later reports indicate, McWane and certain company officials ultimately were held accountable civilly and criminally for various safety and environmental violations. *See id.* ("[T]he company pleaded guilty in federal court to deliberately ignoring safety rules that could have saved Mr. Hoskin's life. In the fall [2002], McWane reached a settlement with OSHA, admitting that it had willfully violated safety rules a dozen times.")

But the plight of the workers at Tyler Pipe is but one piece of a larger tragedy. As the later portions of the *New York Times* exposé detail, similar violations, injuries, and deaths occurred at other McWane plants and foundries around the country. The regulatory failures that allowed this to happen occurred at all levels and in various locations. In the last part of the exposé, the authors summarize the systemic lapses in regulatory and legal oversight that allowed McWane officials to avoid safety and health mandates for so long:

> In plant after plant, year after year, McWane workers have been maimed, burned, sickened and killed by the same safety and health failures. Flammable materials are mishandled; respirators are not provided; machines are missing safety guards; employees are not trained. The evidence spills forth from hundreds of regulatory files scattered in government offices around the country — more than 400 safety violations and 450 environmental violations since 1995 alone.
>
> Yet regulators and law enforcement officials have never joined forces to piece this record together, never taken a coordinated approach to end patterns of transgression. Their responses, piecemeal and disjointed, bring into sharp relief weaknesses in government's ability to take on corporations with operations spread far and wide.
>
> "The current law is inadequate to deal with serious violators, repetitive violators, situations where people are put at risk day after day," said Charles N. Jeffress, who headed the Occupational Safety and Health Administration in the late 1990's.
>
> Nine workers have been killed in McWane plants since 1995. OSHA investigators concluded that three of those deaths resulted directly from McWane's deliberate violations of federal safety standards, records show. Safety lapses at least contributed to five other deaths, investigators found.
>
> Yet those deaths rarely received more than cursory attention from state and local law enforcement authorities. The police often did little more than photograph the body and call the coroner. Local district attorneys, if they were informed, generally deferred to OSHA.

David Barstow & Lowell Bergman, *Deaths on the Job, Slaps on the Wrist*, N.Y. TIMES, Jan. 10, 2003, at A1. As the article indicates, one big problem was that there was little coordination between various state and federal regulators and law enforcement officials; in other words, prior to the exposé, McWane's enterprise (and its business practices and culture) as a whole was never subjected to scrutiny or oversight. Yet, beyond this, each legal regime that was supposed to deter such conduct through incentives and sanctions failed to do so.

2. *Criminal Sanctions.* While McWane itself and certain McWane officials were ultimately held accountable criminally, the risk of such sanctions failed to deter the firm for a variety of reasons. First, under OSHA and most other regimes, criminal sanctions are available only for certain deliberate or knowing violations of particular standards. Liability therefore can be difficult to establish, particularly for decision makers high up in the corporate hierarchy, even though they are the ones who set the tone and foster the practices that create the unsafe environment. According to the Times article, McWane officials escaped criminal liability for workers' deaths for this reason. In addition, criminal sanctions imposed on the company as an entity may not deter owners or high-ranking officials not only because the penalties or settlements may be insufficient but because, in the unlikely event that the firm ultimately ceases to exist as a result, these individuals may be able to walk away with their gains. Moreover, under political pressure from the firm and fearful of destroying local jobs, prosecutors may be reluctant to file charges. The *New York Times* piece details how this happened in the McWane context: The firm and its allies pressured local prosecutors and New York's attorney general, convincing them not to act and to resist prosecuting until pressed to do so by federal prosecutors.

3. *OSHA Inspections and Sanctions.* OSHA's regulatory regime also failed to deter McWane. In part this was the result of a cost-benefit analysis by McWane's management, reinforcing the views of those critics who claim OSHA sanctions are far too infrequent and small to deter safety violations:

> McWane, current and former managers said, viewed the burden of regulatory fines as far less onerous than the cost of fully complying with safety and environmental rules. At the time of Mr. Wagner's death, company budget documents show, McWane calculated down to the penny per ton the cost of OSHA and environmental fines, along with raw materials. Since Mr. Wagner's death at the Kennedy Valve plant here, 85 miles southeast of Rochester, the company has paid less than $10 million in fines and penalties for its safety and environmental violations and three criminal convictions — less than 1 percent of its annual revenues.

4. *Slaps on the Wrist.* Indeed, at various points, the *Times* article discusses how serious or ongoing violations, including some that resulted in serious injuries and deaths, resulted in relatively modest sanctions. In addition, McWane often found ways to avoid the scrutiny of OSHA personnel and state investigators, and, ultimately, significant sanctions:

> Resistance starts the moment an inspector shows up at the gate, say managers and workers at McWane plants across the country and in Canada. Several senior managers said their plants followed a set procedure.
>
> Step 1, they said, was to stall the inspectors outside as alarms went out to supervisors to fix or cover up violations. Machines operating without required pollution controls would be shut down. Machines with obvious and irreparable safety defects would be hidden behind stacks of pallets. Chemical spills would be mopped up. Safety guards, often left off for weeks at a time, would be reattached.
>
> Clyde E. Dorn, former safety director at a plant in Anniston, Ala., said he simply lied. Once, he recalled, he withheld test results that showed workers were severely overexposed to silica, which can cause the lung disease silicosis. Robert S. Rester, a former plant manager in Birmingham, said his workers fooled environmental regulators by submitting samples from the city water supply. It was just that simple, he said. . . .
>
> In violation of OSHA rules, McWane managers have also altered workplace death scenes before investigators arrived, police and OSHA records show.
>
> One such case occurred at the Atlantic States foundry in Phillipsburg, N.J. Not only was a possible criminal investigation undermined, but the case also yielded a picture of persistent safety problems disregarded there and at other McWane plants.

At 6 a.m. on March 24, 2000, an Atlantic States worker named Alfred E. Coxe was run over by a forklift. Patrol officers arrived within minutes, and as Mr. Coxe was being airlifted to a hospital, they set about preserving the scene. Using chalk, they marked the position of the forklift and tire marks, their reports show. Meanwhile, detectives from the county prosecutor's office and the Police Department were summoned, along with officials from the medical examiner's office and OSHA. The detectives arrived first, within two hours.

The forklift was gone.

In their reports, the detectives said plant officials were evasive about its whereabouts. What is more, they wrote, plant workers had repeatedly run a street sweeper over the area, wiping away chalk marks and tire marks. Workers told a local newspaper reporter that supervisors had rushed to "clean up" before OSHA arrived. . . .

[Mr. Coxe died of his injuries. The police were told by the driver of the forklift that its brakes had failed when he tried to stop and that supervisors knew of the problem. OSHA inspectors arrived only four and a half hours after Mr. Coxe was struck and tested the forklift. Its brakes appeared fine. In light of this, the county prosecutor, John Laky, did not pursue charges, but he acknowledged that he was not aware of a variety of aspects at the time.]

Contrary to the skid tests witnessed by OSHA, photographs and notes taken by the first officers at the scene neither showed nor described any skid marks from the front tires, the only ones with brakes. According to those records, the only tire marks at all were behind the rear tires, a discrepancy that remains unexplained.

Mr. Laky said he had assumed that the marks were skids caused by applying brakes on the rear tires. He was shocked when told that the forklift's only brakes were on the front.

Mr. Laky was also unaware of persistent forklift problems at Atlantic States, a pattern that OSHA inspectors began to discover in the weeks after Mr. Coxe's death.

The first clue came from another driver assigned to the forklift that struck Mr. Coxe. That driver told OSHA inspectors that it had been having brake problems for more than a month, that he had reported those problems and that nothing had been done.

With a little more digging, OSHA inspectors found that defects reported by drivers were routinely ignored, in part because there was only one mechanic for 14 forklifts in 24-hour use. They also discovered that neither the mechanic nor the drivers were authorized to take forklifts out of service for safety defects. Only senior supervisors could do that, they found.

There were problems with the drivers, too. Mr. De Los Santos was not certified to operate a forklift; the year before, he had struck his supervisor with a forklift, breaking the man's foot. What is more, managers had assigned at least six other uncertified workers to drive forklifts. . . .

Several weeks after Mr. Coxe's death, OSHA officials returned to inspect the foundry's forklifts. They examined forklift inspection sheets filled out each day by the drivers. The sheets indicated safety defects on all 14 machines—including No. 24, the one that had killed Mr. Coxe.

Its brakes were not working properly. . . .

Moreover, although OSHA inspectors concluded that three deaths were the result of deliberate violations of OSHA standards, only one case was referred to the Justice Department, and that case resulted in only a misdemeanor charge against the company.

Finally, it is worth noting that, just prior to publication of the exposé, OSHA informed McWane that it did not qualify as an "OSHA partner" because it had not yet shown sufficient commitment to workplace safety. McWane made overtures regarding its compliance efforts at various times, but, from all outward appearances, it never had any intention of cooperating in good faith with regulatory officials.

5. *Private Ordering.* Certainly no one would expect that the kinds of economically vulnerable workers who were subjected to McWane's workplaces could have bargained individually with the firm for greater protection. But at least some of the workers at Tyler Pipe were unionized at the time McWane took over. The *Times* article does not explore that issue, but why do you suppose collective bargaining likewise failed to protect these workers? In answering this question, recall the nature and flexibility of the labor market Tyler Pipe was willing to draw from and the lack of alternatives for at least some, if not many, of its workers. In what circumstances might worker empowerment through collective bargaining or otherwise be more effective in preventing or reducing workplace hazards?

6. *Workers' Compensation, Intimidation, and Retaliation.* Workers' compensation regimes are supposed to create incentives for employers to improve workplace conditions. Although McWane could not escape the pervasive reach of workers' compensation laws, it nevertheless found ways to reduce its costs under these regimes. Look back at McWane's practices at Tyler Pipe: How did the company keep workers' compensation costs down? Assuming many of its methods violated state health and workers' compensation laws, how was it able to get away with this course of conduct for so long?

Similarly, some of the ways McWane treated its employees might have supported antiretaliation and public policy claims. Again, why was McWane nevertheless willing to engage in this type of conduct? Note that OSHA's antiretaliation regime has been the subject of much criticism, including in a recent GAO report. *See* GAO, WHISTLEBLOWER PROTECTION: SUSTAINED MANAGEMENT ATTENTION NEEDED TO ADDRESS LONG-STANDING PROGRAM WEAKNESSES (August 2010), *available at* http://www.gao.gov/new.items/d10722.pdf; *see also* Jarod S. Gonzalez, *A Pot of Gold at the End of the Rainbow: An Economic Incentives-Based Approach to OSHA Whistleblowing* (Texas Tech. Sch. of Law Legal Studies Research Paper No. 2010-11, May 11, 2010), *available at* http://papers.ssrn.com/sol3/papers.cfm?abstract_id=1538336&download=yes (discussing the weaknesses and limitations of OSHA's existing antiretaliation regime).

One further consideration is whether OSHA and workers' compensation ought to be viewed as interdependent rather than as entirely separate and distinct regimes. For example, might the social utility of the trade-off underlying workers' compensation depend to some extent on the quality of the OSHA regime?

7. *Tort Suits for Injuries Resulting from Unsafe Working Conditions.* Based on what you have learned in this chapter, why, as a general matter, was McWane unconcerned about civil lawsuits arising from workplace injuries and deaths? If injured employees or the families of deceased workers were able to bring such suits, might this have deterred McWane to a greater extent? Can you think of reasons why the tort system (or a tort-like statutory private right of action) might provide a more effective deterrent than criminal sanctions, a command-and-control regulatory regime like OSHA, or workers' compensation? What are the potential social costs of allowing tort suits against employers like McWane premised on unreasonably dangerous working conditions? On balance, would the benefits outweigh these costs?

Keep in mind that the legal availability of private enforcement mechanisms would not ensure that all workers have access to such mechanisms nor that firms would not avoid at least some of the liability risks. Recall, for example, the discussion of private enforcement of the FLSA in Chapter 1, page 38, following the *Ansoumana* case. In light of that discussion, how might an enterprise like McWane attempt to blunt the effectiveness of private suits? What types of liability rules might frustrate such avoidance techniques?

8. *Just a Bad Apple?* At least in terms of the depth of the safety problems and the sheer scale of the tragedy, McWane was among the worst of the worst. But that does not mean the horrors described are unique to McWane plants and foundries, or that the McWane story should be written off as merely a tale of an aberrational "bad apple." Stories of other firms that frequently or habitually fail to comply with workplace safety and health standards occasionally bubble to the surface, sometimes in the wake of tragedy. Massey Energy—the owner of the mine where 29 workers died in 2010—is one example. Howard Berkes and Robert Benincasa, *Other Massey Mines Show a Pattern of Violations*, NPR.com, April 13, 2010, *available at* http://www.npr .org/templates/story/story.php?storyId=125864847; Steven Mufson, *Massey Energy has Litany of Critics, Violations*, WASH. POST, Apr. 6, 2010, *available at* http://www .washingtonpost.com/wp-dyn/content/article/2010/04/06/AR2010040601531 .html.

In what circumstances might other firms possess similar incentives? And how often might company officials, supervisors, workers, regulators, and policy makers face similar choices, pressures, and constraints?

PROBLEM

12-1. Suppose you work for the Workplace Safety and Health Institute, a nonpartisan "think tank" devoted to developing and advocating innovative and efficient ways to improve workplace safety and reduce work-related injuries and diseases. Given what you have seen in this chapter, what kinds of legal reforms might you advocate? In thinking about solutions, consider all possibilities, including, *inter alia*, greater direct regulation and enforcement of the "command and control" variety (more regulations and inspections, and greater sanctions); alternative regulatory arrangements that seek to promote "third way" self-regulation; greater protection against retaliation for whistleblowers or injured workers; reintroduction of tort liability for employer negligence; enhanced civil and criminal liability for responsible supervisors or officers; and employee empowerment, including greater protections for collective bargaining and bargaining units. At a general level, what are the costs and benefits of these various approaches? In light of the nature of the modern workplace, what are the practical impediments to implementation? Which methods might work in combination, and which would not?

Part Seven

RISK
MANAGEMENT

13

Managing the Risks and Costs of Liability in Employment Disputes

To a considerable extent, this entire book has been about "risk management." Private ordering allows parties to structure their relationship as they see fit, creating certain legal obligations and limiting others. Chapters 1 through 3 dealt with the initial choice to create an employment relationship and on what terms. We saw that contracting parties can sometimes avoid "employment" altogether, a strategy often pursued by firms seeking to avoid the legal liabilities associated with that status. Even where an employment relationship exists, the ability to set terms contractually—coupled with the at-will presumption—often permits employers to limit their obligations to employees, for instance, by disclaiming contractual right to job security. Alternatively, in situations where the employer is willing to provide security, it can offset such provisions against other terms of the relationship.

Such risk management is largely in the hands of employers. Many if not most workers face a take-it-or-leave-it choice as to whether a particular job carries employment status and the terms of any relationship that may be offered. Chapter 3 dealt primarily with the rather exceptional, highly valued worker, who may be able to trade salary and other benefits for enhanced job security or other favorable employment terms. More often, however, freedom of contract merely affords workers an ability to take or reject what the employer offers; they must then work with the tools that the public law regime provides to "employees," assuming they can establish that status, to maximize their position.

This does not mean, however, that the employer has free rein in structuring work relationships. Any decision it makes involves trade-offs. We saw in Chapters 1, 5, and 12 that the employer that avoids tort liability to workers by structuring its relationships as "employment" thereby assumes tort liability to third parties for its workers' actions and subjects itself to the workers' compensation regime. It also undertakes a host of other statutory risks and duties to its employees, including the antidiscrimination laws and the Family and Medical Leave Act, treated in Chapters 9 and 10, and the wage and benefits laws discussed in Chapter 11.

Moreover, employers cannot always be confident that their election of a particular status or set of terms will actually determine their legal obligations. We saw in

Chapter 1 that the test for employment status is multi-factored and dependent on circumstances beyond the intent of the parties. Similarly, although employers may designate a particular relationship at will, alterations in at-will status may occur due to the promises and assurances of supervisors, written employment manuals, or implicit company policies and practices. Thus, despite the availability of contract law, and regardless of the ultimate structure chosen, both employers and employees often find their legal relationship ambiguous.

Perhaps most importantly, there are significant limits on the extent to which the law permits private ordering in workplace relationships. For instance, we saw in Chapter 8 that employers can use noncompetition agreements and related contract mechanisms to enhance their property rights and to insulate themselves against the risk of employee defection that arises when employment is at will. However, the enforceability of such agreements is constrained by public policy, and employers are often unable to predict whether such contracts will provide the protection they seek. In addition, employers have very limited ability to structure or restructure terms of employment mandated by statutory law. An employer may not, for instance, limit its liability under state workers' compensation law in exchange for larger payments, nor may it substitute time off for overtime pay under federal wage and hour law, even if both parties would prefer that arrangement. And, of course, employers have no — or very limited — ability to "waive" substantive obligations arising under constitutional, tort, and antidiscrimination laws discussed in Chapters 4, 5, 7, 9, and 10.

In sum, the patchwork of laws governing workplace relationships — a combination of contract law principles operating against a backdrop of tort rules and general and employment-specific statutes and regulations — presents serious challenges to the cost-conscious, compliance-oriented employer. Thus, an important question to think about as you complete your study of employment law is the interaction between firms and workers in what might be described as "second level" efforts at risk management. These techniques are "second" level because they attempt to reduce employers' risks entailed by the initial policy choice as to whether to offer employment at all and in what form. They include efforts to ensure compliance with the law, prevent disputes, and reduce the costs associated with legal disputes when they inevitably arise. Larger employers frequently consult with attorneys and human resource experts before implementing policies or making personnel decisions to try to avoid not only running afoul of the law but also appearing to do so for fear of drawing a costly (even if ultimately unsuccessful) lawsuit. Similarly, where an employee may contest a decision, employers frequently seek cost-effective ways of dealing with the dispute short of litigation, such as private resolution or settlement.

This chapter explores several ways in which employers respond to the risk of litigation and legal liability and employee responses to such efforts. It begins in Section A with employer efforts to prevent and resolve disputes in-house, with particular emphasis on sexual harassment. As a result of two seminal Supreme Court decisions on vicarious liability for hostile work environment claims, employers have strong incentives to take precautions against harassment and respond aggressively if it occurs.

The chapter then turns in Section B to employer termination practices and the use of severance and release agreements to avoid possible litigation. Particularly in large layoff situations, employers typically promise post-termination pay, and perhaps other benefits, in exchange for the employee's promise not to sue the employer.

Section C then considers several mechanisms that employers have used to reduce risks in litigation. The first is the increasingly common practice of requiring employees to sign pre-dispute arbitration agreements. Under such agreements, parties do not waive or settle the merits of claims but rather agree that, should a dispute arise, they will resolve it through a private arbitration process rather than through traditional litigation. The second is the use of stipulated damages clauses to safeguard employer interests by ensuring a monetary remedy is available in the event that an employee breaches its obligations to the employer.

Section D turns to yet another kind of risk management — passing the risk to others. It addresses the use of insurance as a means of managing the costs of liability to employees. Finally, Section E very briefly considers bankruptcy, which might be viewed, at least in some contexts, as the ultimate risk-management technique of employers.

As you read, you will understand that the study of risk management begins with techniques employers implement, but, as in the rest of this book, the focus quickly shifts to the responses of employees and the policy choices implicated in deciding how far the law should permit private ordering in this setting. From the employer's perspective, consider whether these risk management tools are effective in achieving employer goals and, if not, how they might be made more effective. Equally important, consider the effects of such measures on employees' ability to vindicate their rights. How should courts respond to second-level private ordering designed to avoid liability and public disputes? Is there a way to balance the employer's concerns about liability and costs of compliance with the employee's substantive and procedural rights? Are there places where private ordering has gone too far?

A. PREVENTIVE MEASURES AND CORRECTIVE ACTION

1. Anticipating and Responding to Hostile Work Environment Harassment

The best way to avoid litigation expenses is to resolve disputes internally, and employers use a variety of methods to do this. A very common technique is to develop internal procedures through which employees can air or report concerns before they develop into a legal problem. For instance, many companies have written complaint procedures under which employees are directed to report their concerns to particular personnel and follow up with reports to successively higher levels of management if the employee remains dissatisfied. A less formal approach is to establish an "open door" policy which invites employees to speak to any manager, or particular management personnel, on an as-needed basis. Depending on the employer, these approaches may be adopted in tandem and may have a greater or lesser degree of formality and structure.

For example, a Publix Supermarket Policy provides:

> It is just a fact of life that occasionally there will be problems and misunderstandings among people. If something bothers you, or if you need clarification of a Publix policy or procedure, please talk to a manager about it. Always remember, as a Publix associate you

can talk to anyone in management. Experience has shown, however, that many problems can best be worked out by the following steps:

1. Discuss your problem or raise your question directly with your immediate Supervisor/ Manager/Department Head.
2. If the matter is not resolved or you still have a question or concern, go to the next highest level of management (for example, Store Manager, District Manager, Regional Director of Retail Operations, or a Vice-President).
3. Just remember — you can discuss your problem with anyone in management all the way to the top level. Also, your Divisional Human Resources Department is available to assist you with any matter at any time, and you may contact the Employee Assistance Department in Lakeland for confidential counseling.

Madray v. Publix Supermarkets, Inc., 208 F.3d 1290, 1295 (11th Cir. 2000); *see also Parker v. Hahnemann Univ. Hosp.*, 7 Wage & Hour Cas. 2d (BNA) 88 (D.N.J. 2001) (five Open Door Policy steps are: (1) Submit Dispute to Supervisor; (2) Appeal Supervisor's Decision to the Department Head; (3) Appeal Decision of the Department Head to Administration; (4) Appeal Administration's Decision to the FTP Committee; and (5) Final and Binding Arbitration).

Adopting a policy like Publix's is not without some risk to employers. Employees have sometimes attempted to use open door policies as the basis of a contract claim when they are discharged. They might allege, for instance, that the employer failed to follow or participate in all steps of its process or that they were retaliated against for invoking the policy. While the Publix policy does not explicitly promise nonretaliation, it may impliedly do so, and some grievance policies are more explicit in immunizing employees who invoke company procedures. Thus, an occasional court has recognized a cause of action where the employee can show that she was retaliated against for pursuing open door avenues. *See, e.g., Holt v. Home Depot, U.S.A., Inc.*, 2004 U.S. Dist. LEXIS 824, 3-4 (D. Conn. 2004) ("[T]he jury could reasonably find that Home Depot's promise not to retaliate against employees for using the open-door procedure was so clear, emphatic, highly touted, and widely proclaimed that plaintiff could reasonably believe it was inviolable and thus not covered by general disclaimers in the handbook and application."); *Vida v. El Paso Employees' Fed. Credit Union*, 885 S.W.2d 177 (Tex. App. 1994) (cause of action if employer retaliated against plaintiff for use of its grievance procedure when the employee manual explicitly assured that no retaliation would occur). However, most courts have rejected such claims, in some cases because of language disclaiming the binding nature of the policy and in other instances because the policy did not constitute a sufficiently definite promise. *See, e.g., Haynes v. Level 3 Communs., LLC*, 167 F. App'x 712 (10th Cir. 2006) (employer's open-door policy too vague to constitute a contract or support a claim of promissory estoppel); *Stefano v. Micron Tech., Inc.*, 65 F. App'x 139, 142 (9th Cir. 2003) (existence of open-door policy did not bring plaintiff within any exception to at-will employment).

As a result, there is relatively little legal downside in adopting such policies, and they have significant advantages. In addition to limiting costly litigation, they may result in more favorable outcomes for both employees and employers. While litigation often entails a permanent severing of the employment relationship, successful internal resolution can enable the aggrieved employee to continue working. If the attempted resolution is not successful and the dispute winds up in litigation (whether court or arbitration), the employer's internal response can be a critical aid in its defense.

This is most true with respect to employment discrimination. In the Title VII context, the Supreme Court decided two cases in 1998 dealing with a sexual hostile work environment created by a supervisor in which employer efforts to prevent and respond to harassment figured prominently. In *Burlington Industries, Inc. v. Ellerth*, 524 U.S. 742 (1998), the harassment took place while the supervisor and victim were away from the office on a business trip. In the other, *Faragher v. Boca Raton*, 524 U.S. 775 (1998), the victims were lifeguards who were harassed at a beach remote from the city employer. In both cases, the employees failed to complain about the harassment until after leaving their jobs. It was assumed for the purposes of the case that the conduct in question, if attributable to the employers, would have constituted actionable hostile environment harassment under Title VII, an issue you considered in Chapter 9. The employers essentially defended by arguing that they were not liable for the harassing conduct of the supervisors because the harassment did not result in any tangible employment action by the supervisor, such as a termination or demotion, and because the employees had not complained before leaving the company. Thus, the question before the Court was when an employer should be liable for harassing conduct, given its lack of knowledge of the behavior. This question is critical under Title VII since personal liability does not attach to an individual actor under the federal discrimination laws. *See* Rebecca Hanner White, *Vicarious and Personal Liability for Employment Discrimination*, 30 GA. L. REV. 509, 545-61 (1996) (summarizing conflicting authority and concluding that expanding personal liability could undercut positive incentives created by vicarious liability approach). While some state antidiscrimination statutes provide for individual liability, and state courts sometimes find in favor of claims against harassers in their personal capacity, *see, e.g., Elezovic v. Ford Motor Co.*, 697 N.W.2d 851, 861 (Mich. 2005), it can be difficult for plaintiffs to collect on those judgments. As a result, an employee typically has no recovery — despite having proven harassment in the workplace — if the employer is not liable for the actions of the harasser.

Drawing on agency principles, the *Ellerth* and *Faragher* opinions laid out the structure for employer liability for supervisory harassment. First, there is automatic employer liability when a supervisor subjects plaintiff to "a tangible employment action, such as discharge, demotion, or undesirable reassignment." *Faragher* at 808. In such cases, the employer's liability is absolute and not subject to any defense. Second, when a supervisor subjects plaintiff to conduct that is *not* a tangible employment action, such as a contaminated work environment, the employer is liable but subject to an affirmative defense. The Court explained:

> When a supervisor makes a tangible employment decision, there is assurance the injury could not have been inflicted absent the [supervisor's] agency relation [with the employer]. A tangible employment action in most cases inflicts direct economic harm. As a general proposition, only a supervisor, or other person acting with the authority of the company, can cause this sort of injury. A co-worker can break a co-worker's arm as easily as a supervisor, and anyone who has regular contact with an employee can inflict psychological injuries by his or her offensive conduct. But one co-worker (absent some elaborate scheme) cannot dock another's pay, nor can one co-worker demote another. . . .
>
> Tangible employment actions are the means by which the supervisor brings the official power of the enterprise to bear on subordinates. A tangible employment decision requires an official act of the enterprise, a company act. . . . The supervisor often must obtain the imprimatur of the enterprise and use its internal processes.

For these reasons, a tangible employment action taken by the supervisor becomes for Title VII purposes the act of the employer. Whatever the exact contours of the aided in the agency relation standard, its requirements will always be met when a supervisor takes a tangible employment action against a subordinate. . . .

Whether the agency relation aids in commission of supervisor harassment which does not culminate in a tangible employment action is less obvious. . . . On the one hand, a supervisor's power and authority invests his or her harassing conduct with a particular threatening character, and in this sense, a supervisor always is aided by the agency relation. On the other hand, there are acts of harassment a supervisor might commit which might be the same acts a co-employee would commit, and there may be some circumstances where the supervisor's status makes little difference. . . .

In order to accommodate the agency principles of vicarious liability for harm caused by misuse of supervisory authority, as well as Title VII's equally basic policies of encouraging forethought by employers and saving action by objecting employees, we adopt the following holding. . . . An employer is subject to vicarious liability to a victimized employee for an actionable hostile environment created by a supervisor with immediate (or successively higher) authority over the employee. When no tangible employment action is taken, a defending employer may raise an affirmative defense to liability or damages. . . . The defense comprises two necessary elements: (a) that the employer exercised reasonable care to prevent and correct promptly any sexually harassing behavior, and (b) that the plaintiff employee unreasonably failed to take advantage of any preventive or corrective opportunities provided by the employer or to avoid harm otherwise. While proof that an employer had promulgated an antiharassment policy with complaint procedure is not necessary in every instance as a matter of law, the need for a stated policy suitable to the employment circumstances may appropriately be addressed in any case when litigating the first element of the defense. And while proof that an employee failed to fulfill the corresponding obligation of reasonable care to avoid harm is not limited to showing any unreasonable failure to use any complaint procedure provided by the employer, a demonstration of such failure will normally suffice to satisfy the employer's burden under the second element of the defense. No affirmative defense is available, however, when the supervisor's harassment culminates in a tangible employment action, such as discharge, demotion, or undesirable reassignment.

Ellerth, at 761-65.

Notice that the Court also alluded to a third scenario where employer liability for hostile work environment may be implicated — sexual harassment by a nonsupervisor, such as a co-worker (or even a customer). While *Ellerth* and *Faragher* did not address that situation directly, the majority of lower court cases hold that the employer is liable for nonsupervisory harassment only if the employer is negligent. Thus, a hostile environment resulting from the activities of co-workers will not result in any liability unless the employer knew or should have known of the problem and did not reasonably address it. This is viewed as a form of direct liability for the employer's own negligence as opposed to vicarious liability for the conduct of the harasser. However, the employer's policies and practices are still relevant to this assessment, insofar as negligence may occur where the employer fails to have processes in place to discover and reasonably respond to harassing behavior. As a practical matter, then, the employer's mechanisms to prevent and correct harassment apply both in the supervisor harassment and co-worker harassment cases, although the burdens of proof are reversed in the two situations.

Needless to say, this structure offers both benefits and burdens to employers. An employer who reacts reasonably to harassment in situations where there is no supervisor involved will avoid direct liability, no matter how extreme the co-worker or customer harassment. And, absent a tangible employment action, an employer who takes appropriate steps to "prevent and correct" violations by supervisors will have satisfied the first prong of the affirmative defense and be halfway to avoiding vicarious liability. Thus, *Ellerth* and *Faragher* understandably generated a cottage industry among lawyers and employment relation specialists about appropriate prevention and correction strategies. In the cases that follow, consider which employer actions are effective and which are not. Does the result in each case correspond to the effectiveness of the employer's response? In other words, does the existence of the affirmative defense encourage good employer practices, or does it encourage superficial efforts that simply make the employer look good in court, what has been dubbed "paper compliance" with the law? How could the employer have been more successful in avoiding and/or responding in each case?

Watson v. Home Depot USA, Inc.
2003 U.S. Dist. LEXIS 13406 (N.D. Ill. Aug. 1, 2003)

Leinenweber, J.

I. Background . . .

1. *Watson's Employment and Orientation*

In August 1999, Home Depot hired Watson as a sales associate for its North Avenue store in Chicago, Illinois. Shortly after being hired, Watson participated in Home Depot's orientation program, which lasted for about two weeks. Like all Home Depot employees, Watson received Copies of Home Depot's Respect, Harassment/Discrimination, Equal Employment Opportunity, and Open Door Policies as well as training on those polices. The Harassment/Discrimination Policy prohibits harassment or discrimination and states that "anyone who condones or fails to take appropriate action to address a violation of Home Depot's harassment/discrimination policy will be subject to disciplinary action up to and including termination." It further "prohibits retaliation against any associate who comes forward to report harassment and/or discrimination." The policy emphasizes the importance of reporting any harassing or disrespectful behavior and sets forth resources that an employee may use if they feel that the policy has been violated. These resources include contacting a member of management, the Store Manager, District Manager, Human Resource Manager, or Division Vice President of Human Resources, or using the Alert Line, a phone line that enables employees to report harassment anonymously. Watson also participated in a Respect for All People training program, which further addressed workplace harassment and discrimination issues and which again informed employees about procedures available at Home Depot for resolving harassment or discrimination concerns. A few months after hiring Watson, Home Depot transferred her to the Pro Sales Department, where her responsibilities included building relationships with and selling products to industrial, commercial, and other business customers. She appears to have performed her job satisfactorily and received a raise on July 3, 2000.

2. The Performance Notice

In the afternoon of July 13, 2000, however, Watson received an Associate Performance Notice for allegedly violating company policies or procedures. According to the Performance Notice, Watson's supervisors Victor Terrell, who served as Assistant Store Manager, and Ford Neubert, the Department Supervisor, found Watson in a friend's car in the Home Depot parking lot while she was supposed to be at her desk. Terrell and Neubert prepared the Performance Notice, which warned Watson to stay at her desk in the future and Terrell asked Watson to "clock out and go home." The Performance Notice was placed in Watson's file, but Home Depot took no further disciplinary action for this incident. Indeed, despite the fact that Watson had only worked for part of that day, Home Depot paid her for a full shift.

3. Events After July 13, 2000

Watson's relationship with Home Depot changed swiftly in the wake of the parking lot incident. Before leaving the store on July 13, she complained to Co-Store Manager, Al Stermer, about the confrontation and about being sent home for the day. Watson also contacted Home Depot's Midwest Region Human Resources Manager, James Owens ("Owens"), that day to complain that Terrell had belittled her and disciplined her unfairly.

[O]n July 14, Watson learned that her work schedule had been changed. Instead of working Monday to Friday from 8:00 a.m. to 5:00 p.m., she was now expected to work on the weekends with two weekdays off. As a single mother, Watson found this change burdensome and also complained about it to Owens.

On July 20, 2000, Owens called Jay Tippieconnic the Store Manager, to tell him that Watson had complained about a write-up she received. The next day, after a week of confusion about Watson's new schedule, Tippieconnic met with Watson to discuss the entire situation. During their conversation, Watson broke down and explained that the situation went beyond the write-up. She described how on April 6, 2000, Terrell had followed her home during lunch, had asked to come into her apartment, and had then forced her into having sex with him. In Watson's statement, she alleges that she also described Terrell's poor treatment of her, but it is unclear what poor treatment she described. After hearing Watson's story, Tippieconnic sent Watson home, telling her he would pay her for the rest of that day and for the weekend and assuring Watson that he would have Michelle Williams, a Loss Prevention Specialist with whom Watson appeared to be comfortable, contact her over the weekend. Tippieconnic next called Owens and District Manager Ron Johnston to set up a meeting with Watson for the following Monday. Over the weekend, he spoke with Watson twice, reassuring her that Home Depot would not abandon her.

The following Monday, Owens, Williams, and Tippieconnic waited to meet with Watson. Watson arrived several hours late, and handed them the sworn statement in which she detailed her interactions with Terrell prior to, including, and after the alleged April 6 sexual encounter. Watson stated that Terrell had kissed her on January 27, 2000, while they were having lunch together, and that he continued to flirt with her throughout February and March 2000. She also contended that during those months, Terrell failed to support her professionally, yelled at her at work, and was physical with her, at times grabbing her arm to move her from one spot to another. Watson stated that she complained to Terrell about his behavior and that he promised to improve. On April 6, however, Watson alleged that during her lunch hour, Terrell followed her home and, despite being told not to come into her apartment, entered Watson's home and raped her repeatedly. After the alleged rape, Watson stated that Terrell had become increasingly hostile toward her. Watson conceded that she was in a friend's car when Terrell and Neubert issued the Performance Notice. She claimed, however, that the friend was also her customer and had asked Watson to walk with her to explain Home Depot's credit and sales programs. She asserted that Terrell had punished her for the parking lot incident and changed her schedule in retaliation for Watson's refusal to engage in a sexual relationship with him.

After reading Watson's statement, Owens attempted to ask Watson questions about what she had written. Watson refused to provide additional information or to answer his questions and replied that everything she had to say was in the statement itself. Watson did express concern that she would be terminated and that Terrell would harm her, however, Owens assured Watson that Home Depot would immediately begin a complete investigation of her allegations and that she would not lose her job. He also asked Watson to think about whether she wished to continue to work at the North Avenue store, or whether she would prefer to be transferred elsewhere. During the investigation, Home Depot placed Watson on paid administrative leave and suspended Terrell.

4. *The Investigation*

At the end of July, Watson contacted the Chicago Police Department to report the April 6 incident. Meanwhile, as promised, Owens began the investigation of Watson's claim. Together with EEO Specialist Doris Stephenson and Associate Relations Manager Chris Nichols, Owens interviewed twenty-one people, including Terrell, Home Depot managers, supervisors, and employees, and non-Home Depot personnel whom Watson had identified as witnesses. None of the relevant witnesses corroborated Watson's allegations that Terrell had acted inappropriately toward her or had mistreated her. Owens, Stephenson, and Nichols interviewed Terrell twice, once on July 27 and again on August 9. Terrell denied all of Watson's allegations regarding inappropriate behavior. He denied ever having visited Watson's home and contended that he was at his apartment on April 6 at the time of the alleged assault. Although Watson had described Terrell as leaving her apartment at 5:15 p.m. on April 6, Terrell's landlady told Home Depot that she had spoken with Terrell between 4:30 p.m. and 5:00 p.m. that day. Watson's landlord also contested Watson's allegation that he had met Terrell when Terrell was entering Watson's apartment on April 6. The landlord showed Owens, Nichols, and Stephenson a copy of his own calendar that indicated that he was not at Watson's apartment building that afternoon.

With regard to the parking lot incident, the investigation team spoke with Deborah Crawford, who confirmed that she was with Watson in the parking lot on July 13 when Watson was reprimanded. They also spoke with Neubert, who told the investigators that Watson had become angry, yelled and threw the Performance Notice at Terrell when Terrell reprimanded her.

Owens also investigated Watson's allegations that Terrell had changed her schedule to punish her for not engaging in a sexual relationship with him. Ivan

Justiano, an associate in the North Avenue store, told the investigation team that *he* was in charge of writing Watson's schedule and that he had previously scheduled her to work weekends. Owens reviewed all of Watson's time and payroll records and found no support for Watson's claim that she worked a set weekday schedule and never worked weekends.

Finally, Tippieconnic told the investigators that prior to July 21, 2000, Watson had never complained about Terrell and stated that he had been unaware of any of the events described in Watson's statement. Throughout the investigation, Watson repeatedly refused to discuss her statement with Owens or with any other members of the investigation team.

5. *After the Investigation*

On August 18, 2000, Home Depot concluded its investigation and determined that Watson's allegations of sexual harassment could not be substantiated. Despite its findings, Home Depot offered Watson the option of transferring to a different store in the same position and at the same pay. Home Depot also transferred Terrell to another store on July 31, 2000, so that Watson could remain at the North Avenue location if she wished. Instead of returning to Home Depot, however, Watson requested an unpaid medical leave of absence due to depression and temporary psychological distress, which Home Depot granted. Home Depot provided Watson with its medical leave policy, which explained that her employment would be terminated if she did not return to work after a one-year absence. After Watson failed to return to work upon expiration of her medical leave . . . she was terminated from active employment. . . .

II.   Discussion . . .

[In *Burlington Industries, Inc. v. Ellerth* and *Faragher v. City of Boca Raton*,] the Supreme Court created a distinction between "cases in which the supervisor takes a tangible employment action against the subordinate and those in which he does not." *Molnar v. Booth*, 229 F.3d 593, 600 (7th Cir. 2000). The Supreme Court explained that an employer was vicariously liable "to a victimized employee for an actionable hostile environment created by a supervisor with immediate (or successively higher) authority over the employee" where "the supervisor's harassment culminates in a tangible employment action, such as discharge, demotion, or undesirable reassignment." In cases where the supervisor took no tangible employment action, however, the Supreme Court permitted the defending employer to raise an affirmative defense to liability or damages. . . .

[Watson does not contest] that Home Depot terminated Watson for failing to return from medical leave pursuant to company policy and that Terrell had been transferred to another Home Depot at the time Watson was terminated. Watson has failed to [establish] that there is a genuine issue for trial as to whether Terrell took tangible employment action against her [and therefore Home Depot may raise the affirmative defense to liability.] To defend itself successfully, Home Depot must establish: (a) that it exercised reasonable care to prevent and correct promptly any sexually harassing behavior, and (b) that Watson unreasonably failed to take advantage of any preventive or corrective opportunities provided by Home Depot or to avoid harm otherwise.

a. Home Depot's Exercise of Reasonable Care

To avoid liability, Home Depot must first demonstrate that it exercised "reasonable care to prevent and correct promptly any sexually harassing behavior." The existence of "an appropriate anti-harassment policy will often satisfy this first prong, because Title VII is designed to encourage the creation of anti-harassment policies and effective grievance mechanisms." *Shaw v. AutoZone, Inc.*, 180 F.3d 806, 811 (7th Cir. 1999). In this case, it is undisputed that Home Depot had numerous written policies in place throughout Watson's employment prohibiting sexual harassment. These policies included a Harassment/Discrimination Policy, a Respect Policy, and an Equal Employment Opportunity Policy. While the Harassment/Discrimination Policy could have been more tailored to address sexual harassment specifically, it stated clearly that "Home Depot does not tolerate harassment or discrimination" based on sex and directed employees to complain about conduct they found offensive, harassing or disrespectful.

These policies also established multiple procedures for employees to follow in the event that they experienced any harassment, thereby permitting employees to bypass the harassing supervisor in the complaint process. These procedures included contacting various managers, human resources personnel, or using the Alert Line, a phone line that enabled employees to report harassment anonymously. Home Depot also maintained an Open Door Policy, which emphasized that supervisors' doors were "always open" and that if a Department Supervisor or Assistant Manager could not help an employee, the problem "should be taken" up the chain of command. The Open Door Policy also reminded employees that the Human Resource Manager "is always available to help you with concerns and issues." Watson acknowledges that she received copies of these policies and underwent extensive training on the policies and procedures during her orientation.

Home Depot also acted swiftly and decisively to correct the harassment once it learned of Watson's allegations. After his initial meeting with Watson, Tippieconnic, the Store Manager, immediately gave her the weekend off with pay. He also set up a meeting the following Monday to discuss Watson's allegations. At that meeting, Owens assured Watson that Home Depot would investigate her allegations and offered Watson the choice of continuing to work at the North Avenue store, or of being transferred elsewhere with the same pay and position. Home Depot also immediately placed Watson on paid administrative leave and suspended Terrell. It then proceeded to do a thorough and extensive investigation of Watson's claims. Even though the investigation failed to substantiate Watson's allegations of sexual harassment, Home Depot transferred Terrell to another store so that Watson could remain at the North Avenue store if she wished. It also granted Watson's request for a one-year unpaid medical leave of absence.

In spite of these actions, Watson still contends that Home Depot did not take reasonable care to prevent and correct the harassment "until after the fact." The undisputed evidence establishes, however, that Home Depot had promulgated its policies and procedures regarding harassment before Watson began at Home

Depot and before any alleged harassment occurred. Watson also appears to argue that Home Depot failed to correct the harassment by reneging on alleged promises to relocate her to another apartment and to assist her in dealing with the rape. Yet she places this argument in a paragraph dealing with her negligent retention claim, which the Court has dismissed. Moreover, she fails to adduce any evidence to support her contention that Home Depot made these promises. There is certainly nothing in the company policies to suggest that such actions are part of Home Depot standard procedures as Watson appears to suggest.

Regardless, the facts establish that Home Depot took reasonable steps to prevent sexual harassment and that, when faced with allegations of harassment, also took extensive steps to correct the violation. As a matter of law, Home Depot has satisfied the first prong of the *Ellerth/Faragher* affirmative defense.

b. Watson's Unreasonable Failure to Report Harassment

Home Depot must also establish that Watson "unreasonably failed to take advantage of any preventive or corrective opportunities provided by the employer or to avoid harm otherwise." According to Watson, the harassment began when Terrell kissed her on January 27, 2000. It continued through February and March 2000 when Terrell flirted with her, failed to give her professional support, yelled at her, and was physically aggressive with her. On April 6, Terrell allegedly raped her repeatedly. Despite her escalating problems with Terrell, Watson did not complain to anyone until she spoke to Owens on July 21, 2000. Home Depot argues that given Watson's knowledge of the harassment policies and procedures, that her delay in complaining about Terrell's behavior was unreasonable.

In her Response, Watson argues that she failed to complain about the harassment because she feared Terrell. It is, of course, asking a great deal to require a victim of sexual harassment to come forward and reveal what they have endured to their employer. But as the Supreme Court explained, "a victim has a duty to use such means as are reasonable under the circumstances to avoid or minimize[] damages." *Faragher.* This duty exists even if the employee fears confrontation, unpleasantness or retaliation in return for speaking out. In this case, Home Depot had established a variety of reasonable mechanisms for employees to report harassment, including the anonymous tip line and open-door policy that permitted employees to bypass the offending supervisor in reporting the harassment. Moreover, even if the alleged rape made Watson's fears of Terrell reasonable, she endured several months of harassment prior to the rape without alerting Home Depot. During this time, Watson complained directly to Terrell about his behavior and he promised to improve. When those promises proved hollow, Watson still chose not to use Home Depot's mechanisms for reporting the harassment.

"While proof that an employee failed to fulfill the corresponding obligation of reasonable care to avoid harm is not limited to showing an unreasonable failure to use any complaint procedure provided by the employer, a demonstration of such failure will normally suffice to satisfy the employer's burden under the second element of the defense." *Faragher.* Watson's failure to use Home Depot's procedures to report *any* of the harassment she allegedly suffered, despite her knowledge of those procedures, was unreasonable. Home Depot has satisfied the second element of the affirmative defense and, as a result, the Court grants summary judgment. . . .

NOTES

1. *Prong 1: Employer Preventive and Corrective Action.* Pay close attention to the risk management choices Home Depot made both before and after Watson's harassment complaint. According to *Ellerth* and *Faragher*, in order to satisfy the first prong of the affirmative defense the employer must exercise reasonable care both to prevent and to correct harassing behavior. What did Home Depot do to *prevent* harassment? Is the sexual harassment policy the only evidence of its prevention, or did it take other measures as well? What aspects of the policy itself convince the court that it is an effective preventive tool? Can you come up with a checklist of features, based on the court's opinion, that you would advise a future client to include in drafting its own harassment policy?

With respect to *correction*, the reasonableness of the employer's response depends on its ability to end the harassing behavior. Although the employer is not required to ensure that no harassment continues, it must take reasonable steps toward that end. A recurring factual question is whether the employer's response was adequate under the circumstances. Here Home Depot was not able to corroborate that harassment had occurred, which may make its position more difficult. If the employer does nothing in that situation and the harassment reoccurs, it may appear that it did not take the victim's complaint seriously, and it will probably have a hard time establishing the affirmative defense. However, if the employer takes action against the alleged harasser, it risks penalizing an innocent employee, which can itself have legal consequences. How did Home Depot handle this sensitive situation?

2. *Prong 2: The Victim's Unreasonable Failure to Report.* The second prong of the affirmative defense focuses not on the employer's actions but on the victim's. Is this an appropriate consideration? On the one hand, an employer arguably should not be responsible for behavior for which it genuinely could not have known. On the other, victims often — understandably — do not complain at the outset of harassment, hoping they can "handle" it themselves. *See* Linda Hamilton Krieger, *Employer Liability for Sexual Harassment — Normative, Descriptive, and Doctrinal Interactions: A Reply to Professors Beiner and Bisom-Rapp*, 24 U. Ark. Little Rock L. Rev. 169, 180-83 (2001) (demonstrating that women rarely report harassment initially through formal channels and more frequently respond by ignoring the behavior, re-attributing it to benign motives, or attempting to confront or appease the harasser). Indeed, because a hostile-work-environment claim requires severe or pervasive conduct, victims are probably correct in thinking that a few minor incidents do not constitute illegal behavior. *See Clark County Sch. Dist. v. Breeden*, reproduced at page 648. Does the requirement that the victim not unreasonably delay in reporting suffice to handle this problem? How much time is unreasonable? In *Watson*, the victim waited approximately three months after the alleged assault (which was itself two months after the first inappropriate incident) before reporting. Courts have reached widely different results on this question. *Compare Mota v. Univ. of Tex. Houston Health Sci. Ctr.*, 261 F.3d 512 (5th Cir. 2001) (nine-month delay was reasonable) *with Pinkerton v. Colorado DOT*, 563 F.3d 1052 (10th Cir. 2009) (two-month delay was unreasonable);

Conatzer v. Medical Prof. Bldg. Serv., 255 F. Supp. 2d 1259, 1270 (N.D. Okla. 2003) (17-day delay was unreasonable).

3. *Prompt Complaint Followed by Effective Remedial Action.* What would have happened had Watson reported her supervisor immediately and all other facts were identical? Would Home Depot still have prevailed? Because the two prongs of the affirmative defense are conjunctive, an employer should be held vicariously liable in that situation under a literal reading of the Court's language: It can establish the first prong (the employer took reasonable preventive and corrective action), but not the second required element (the victim unreasonably failed to complain). *See, e.g,* *Chapman v. Carmike Cinemas*, 307 F. App'x 164 (10th Cir. 2009) (summary judgment for employer improper where plaintiff immediately reported sexual assault despite the fact that employer terminated perpetrator because employer cannot establish unreasonable failure to report). Yet several courts have resisted that result, finding *Ellerth* and *Faragher*—cases involving inadequate policies and victims who did not report—factually distinguishable from cases involving prompt reporting and responsive action. *See, e.g, McCurdy v. Ark. State Police*, 375 F.3d 762 (8th Cir. 2004). Other courts avoid a direct attack on the conjunctive requirements by going to some lengths to find the victim's reporting to be unreasonably delayed, thus allowing an employer who satisfies prong one to also satisfy prong two. *See Conatzer, supra.*

What *should* the result be? Some commentators argue that, for policy reasons, the affirmative defense should remain available to employers who respond effectively, whether or not the employee unreasonably delays reporting. *See generally* David Sherwyn et al., *Don't Train Your Employees and Cancel Your "1-800" Harassment Hotline: An Empirical Examination and Correction of the Flaws in the Affirmative Defense to Sexual Harassment Charges*, 69 FORDHAM L. REV. 1265, 1280-84 (2000-01) (arguing that affirmative defense requirement that victim unreasonably fail to report creates incentive for employers to discourage reporting and recommending elimination of second prong of defense). On the other hand, is there a competing rationale for finding liability despite the employer's admirable response? *See* Joanna L. Grossman, *The First Bite Is Free: Employer Liability for Sexual Harassment*, 61 U. PITT. L. REV. 671, 711-15 (2000) (arguing that decisions focusing solely on employer corrective action impermissibly substitute a negligence standard for the Supreme Court's vicarious liability rule); John H. Marks, *Smoke, Mirrors, and the Disappearance of "Vicarious" Liability: The Emergence of a Dubious Summary-Judgment Safe Harbor for Employers Whose Supervisory Personnel Commit Hostile Environment Workplace Harassment*, 38 HOUS. L. REV. 1401, 1442 (2002) (arguing that judicial approaches to "rapid-onset harassment" that disregard the second prong of the defense overlook Supreme Court's plain language and defy Title VII's compensatory agenda, which should not reward an innocent employer over an equally innocent victim); Krieger, *supra*, at 169, 196-97 (suggesting that harassment is a reasonably foreseeable harm flowing from the operation of a business whose costs should be internalized).

4. *Victim Requests for Confidentiality.* What if the victim promptly reports but insists that the matter be kept confidential? Several courts have found in favor of employers in those situations, treating the victim's complaint as ineffective. *See, e.g., Hardage v. CBS Broad., Inc.*, 427 F.3d 1177, 1185-88 (9th Cir. 2005) (affirmative defense established where employee made "vague" complaints and insisted on confidentiality, saying he would handle the situation himself); *Olson v. Lowe's Home Ctrs. Inc.*, 130 F. App'x 380, 390 (11th Cir. 2005) (suggesting that, if plaintiff had stated she "did not want [the harasser]'s comments reported or acted upon, then [the employer] would not have been placed on proper notice of harassment). However, there is also contrary authority:

> [A]n employer's investigation of a sexual harassment complaint is not a gratuitous or optional undertaking; under federal law, an employer's failure to investigate may allow a jury to impose liability on the employer. . . . Nor is the company's duty to investigate subordinated to the victim's desire to let the matter drop. Prudent employers will compel harassing employees to cease all such conduct and will not, even at a victim's request, tolerate inappropriate conduct that may, if not halted immediately, create a hostile environment.

Malik v. Carrier Corp., 202 F.3d 97, 105-06 (2d Cir. 2000); *see also* Equal Employment Opportunity Commission ("EEOC") Enforcement Guidance: Vicarious Employer Liability for Unlawful Harassment by Supervisors, §V.C.1.d, No. 915.002 (June 18, 1999) (inaction by supervisor in response to confidential report could result in liability).

Suppose you are an employer who wishes to provide harassment training to its workforce. How should you advise your supervisors to handle a "confidential" complaint of harassment? One of the underlying concerns for employers is that, while the particular employee demanding confidentiality may thereby be precluded from suit, future employees who are harassed will be able to show the employer knew that there was a problem and failed to deal with it; in other words, as to potential victims, the employer will not be able to show reasonable steps to prevent the harassment.

5. *Complaints Outside the Chain of Command.* Another question pertaining to the second prong is whether the employer will be deemed to be on notice of the harassing behavior despite the failure to make a "formal" complaint through an established sexual harassment reporting procedure. "Open door" policies have sometimes backfired on employers in this regard. Several courts have held that an employer's open door policy justified an employee in concluding that she had satisfied her responsibility to complain about harassment by reporting the problem to any person authorized to hear general problems under such a policy. In one case the court rejected the defendant's argument that plaintiff had failed to utilize its complaint process:

> We recognize that Lowe's provided several means to report sexual harassment, such as calling a toll-free number or writing to Lowe's Internal Audit Department. However, these are alternative means by which Olson could have put Lowe's on notice of the harassment. The fact remains that Hall was a manager and Lowe's Open Door Program clearly allows employees to complain to "any member of management." Consequently, the district court erred in concluding that Olson did not complain to an appropriate person under Lowe's policies.

Olson v. Lowe's Home Ctrs. Inc., 130 F. App'x 380, 390 (11th Cir. 2005).

A related issue is whether an employee reasonably reports where she or he complains to the harassing supervisor but does not go up the chain of command. Some courts have held that victims satisfy their reporting obligations in such situations, at least where the offending supervisor is designated as a proper recipient for complaints under the policy. *See, e.g., Gorzynski v. JetBlue Airways Corp.*, 596 F.3d 93 (2d Cir. 2010) ("We do not believe that the Supreme Court . . . intended that victims of sexual harassment . . . must go from manager to manager until they find someone who will address their complaints."). Others hold that employees who do not escalate their complaint up the chain of command or bypass the offending manager by using other channels designated in the employer's harassment policy failed to satisfy their reporting obligations. *See, e.g., Chapman, supra* (employee did not adequately avail herself of employer's remedial measures where she complained about hostile comments only to offending managers and failed to use company hotline or contact off-site managers designated in employer policy); *Madray v. Publix*, 208 F.3d 1290, 1301-02 (11th Cir. 2000) (finding unreasonable failure to report by employee harassed by store manager where policy required employee to report either to store manager, district manager, or division manager, and employee reported only to assistant managers within her store); *Peoples v. Marjack Co.*, 108 Fair Emp Prac. Cas. (BNA) 1331 (D. Md. 2010) (plaintiff failed to take advantage of employer's corrective opportunities where she reported only to her direct supervisor and harassment policy stated that the "executive team" and human resources department were the proper authorities to receive complaints).

6. *Strategic Employer Reporting Restrictions.* Might rulings that find employees to have failed to pursue proper employer reporting policies encourage employers to narrow their reporting procedures to foreclose suits? One possibility is for an employer to designate only one or two individuals to whom complaints can be made. *See* Anne Lawton, *Operating in an Empirical Vacuum: The* Ellerth *and* Faragher *Affirmative Defense*, 13 COLUM. J. GENDER & L. 197 (2005) (critiquing judicial deference to employer's designation of appropriate persons to handle complaints). Another possibility is that employers will discourage complaints or at least place the employee in a bad light by requiring complaints to be made within a very short time of the harassment. *See Rennard v. Woodworker's Supply, Inc.*, 101 F. App'x 296, 300 (10th Cir. 2004) (plaintiff disciplined for failing to report sexual harassment within one week as required by employer policy); Anne Lawton, *The Bad Apple Theory in Sexual Harassment*, 13 GEO. MASON L. REV. 817, 850-55 (2005) (criticizing this practice for creating a private statute of limitations that trumps victims' federal rights). On the other hand, does the first prong of the defense limit the extent to which employers can use such strategies successfully? In other words, can a policy that significantly limits the manner and time frame in which a victim is required to report harassment still satisfy the preventive action component of the defense?

7. *Tangible Employment Actions.* The *Ellerth/Faragher* defense applies only to hostile work environment claims. The Supreme Court made clear in both cases that, where the supervisor engages in a tangible employment action that adversely affects the victim, vicarious liability is automatic. For this reason, plaintiffs will often argue that the harassment they endured culminated in some more tangible adverse action. Could that argument have been made in *Watson*? The implication from Watson's complaint is that both the reprimand she received and the undesirable change in schedule were tied to the harassing behavior. If she could establish that causal connection, would the acts she complained of constitute tangible employment actions sufficient to impose vicarious liability?

Courts disagree as to the definition of tangible employment act. Some hold that a tangible employment act means an "ultimate" employment decision, such as a discharge. *See, e.g., Lutkewitte v. Gonzales*, 436 F.3d 248, 252 (D.C. Cir. 2006) (finding no tangible employment action in supervisor requiring subordinate to attend off-site conference or in victim's general fear that she would lose her job if she did not attend). Others take the view that any act that substantially affects a term or condition of employment suffices. *See, e.g., Green v. Administrators of Tulane Educational Fund*, 284 F.3d 642, 654-55 (5th Cir. 2002) (finding that "demotion, together with the substantial diminishment of her job responsibilities, was sufficient to constitute a tangible employment action" despite absence of any economic loss).

A parallel debate in the retaliation context was resolved by the Supreme Court, which rejected lower court holdings making retaliation actionable only when it resulted in an "ultimate employment action." *See Burlington Northern & Santa Fe Ry. v. White*, 126 S. Ct. 2405 (2006) (the anti-retaliation provision "covers those (and only those) employer actions that would have been materially adverse to a reasonable employee or job applicant."). Does this holding suggest a relaxed standard for tangible employment actions is appropriate in the sexual harassment context, or are these two different doctrines?

What is clear is that the act in question must be an official exercise of managerial judgment. In *Pennsylvania State Police v. Suders*, 542 U.S. 129 (2004), the Supreme Court addressed the question whether the *Ellerth/Faragher* defense was available to employers in situations where harassment culminated in a constructive discharge. The Third Circuit had held a constructive discharge, as the equivalent of a termination, constituted a tangible employment action, rendering the employer strictly liable for the victim's harassment. The Supreme Court reversed, explaining:

> Like the harassment considered in our pathmarking decisions [*Ellerth* and *Faragher*], harassment so intolerable as to cause a resignation may be effected through co-worker conduct, unofficial supervisory conduct, or official company acts. Unlike an actual termination, which is *always* effected through an official act of the company, a constructive discharge need not be. A constructive discharge involves both an employee's decision to leave and precipitating conduct: The former involves no official action; the latter, like a harassment claim without any constructive discharge assertion, may or may not involve official action.
>
> To be sure, a constructive discharge is functionally the same as an actual termination in damages-enhancing respects. . . . But when an official act does not underlie the constructive discharge, the *Ellerth* and *Faragher* analysis, we here hold, calls for extension of the affirmative defense to the employer. As those leading decisions indicate, official directions and declarations are the acts most likely to be brought home to the employer, the measures over which the employer can exercise greatest control. Absent "an official act of the enterprise," as the last straw, the employer ordinarily would have no particular reason to suspect that a resignation is not the typical kind daily occurring in the work force. And as *Ellerth* and *Faragher* further point out, an official act reflected in company records — a demotion or a reduction in compensation, for example — shows "beyond question" that the supervisor has used his managerial or controlling position to the employee's disadvantage. Absent such an official act, the extent to which the supervisor's misconduct has been aided by the agency relation, as we earlier recounted, is less certain. That uncertainty, our precedent establishes, justifies affording the employer the chance to establish, through the *Ellerth/Faragher* affirmative defense, that it should not be held vicariously liable.

Id. at 147-48. Do you agree with the Court's analysis? Does its resolution of the constructive discharge question shed any light on how it might resolve the outstanding question whether a tangible employment action requires an "ultimate" employment decision?

8. *Liability to the Putative Harasser?* The structure of the affirmative defense clearly encourages employers to discipline, even discharge, harassers. In *Watson*, Home Depot suspended Terrell during the investigation and later, despite concluding that Watson's allegations "could not be substantiated," transferred him to another store "so that Watson could remain at the North Avenue location if she wished." Did Home Depot risk liability to Terrell?

Since he was likely an at-will employee, contractual liability seems foreclosed, and the public policy tort is inapposite. In contrast, had there been a governing collective bargaining agreement, there would typically have been constraints on the employer's action, including limitations on the discipline that may be meted out even to a person properly found to have been guilty of harassment was proportionate to the offense. *See Westvaco Corp. v. United Paperworkers Int'l Union*, 171 F.3d 971, 977 (4th Cir. 1999) ("the general public policy against sexual harassment is not sufficient to supplant labor arbitration of employee disciplinary sanctions"). Similarly, civil service laws and academic tenure protections might limit employer responses to harassment and other wrongful conduct by supervisors or co-workers in government and university settings.

What about privacy concerns and defamation? Suppose Terrell were in fact innocent of any wrongful conduct but word of the charges against him went around the workplace? Might the employer be responsible if its conduct caused rumors? Might it be liable for defamation? Would the mere fact of transferring Terrell have carried a defamatory message that he was guilty? Revisit Chapter 5 for these issues. Finally, what about sex discrimination? Might an employer's response to a charge of harassment be viewed as a violation of Title VII? *See Sassaman v. Gamache*, 566 F.3d 307 (2d Cir. 2009) (discharge of male on the basis that men had a propensity to harass, subjecting employer to potential liability by female claiming harassment, was actionable).

Williams v. Spartan Communications
No. 99-1566, 2000 U.S. App. LEXIS 5776 (4th Cir. March 30, 2000)

MOTZ, C.J.

Veneal Williams sold advertising from 1989 to 1995 for Spartan Communications, Incorporated, which runs a television station in Spartanburg, South Carolina. Her immediate supervisor was Local Sales Manager Mitchell Maund, who was promoted to that position in 1992. Williams alleges that between 1992 and 1995 Maund sexually assaulted her three times during business trips that the two took together. The second assault assertedly occurred in Williams' van, while the two were watching an R-rated movie rented on Maund's instructions.

On May 24, 1995, Williams reported Maund's assaults to Spartan General Sales Manager Greg Rose and Spartan Personnel Manager Donna Groothedde. Maund was out of town that day, but Rose, Groothedde and Spartan Vice President and General Manager Jack West met with him the following day, May 25. At that time, Maund admitted to renting and watching the movie in Williams' van. That afternoon, Maund, Rose, Groothedde, and West met again; as a result of Maund's admitted rental of the movie, he resigned. Maund received five months severance pay in return for releasing Spartan from liability for his dismissal. Due to the distress of continued sexual harassment, Williams left her job with Spartan and is now unemployed and in counseling.

[A magistrate judge granted summary judgment to Spartan. On appeal, the issue] is whether Spartan has established, as a matter of law, its entitlement to an affirmative defense to Williams' hostile environment claim. The Supreme Court has explained that "when no tangible employment action is taken, a defending employer may raise an affirmative defense" to a claim of "vicarious liability . . . for an actionable hostile environment created by a supervisor with immediate . . . authority over the employee." *Faragher v. Boca Raton*, 524 U.S. 775, 807 (1998); *Burlington Indus. v. Ellerth*, 524 U.S. 742, 765 (1998). To do so an employer must demonstrate by the "preponderance of the evidence" that (1) it "exercised reasonable care to prevent and correct promptly any sexually harassing behavior" and (2) "the plaintiff employee unreasonably failed to take advantage of any preventative [sic] or corrective opportunities provided by the employer or to avoid harm otherwise." The magistrate judge held that Spartan had satisfied both elements of the affirmative defense as a matter of law and so granted the company summary judgment.

We believe that this ruling was error. We need only discuss the first prong of the defense — whether Spartan has established, as a matter of law, that it "exercised reasonable care to prevent and correct promptly" the sexually harassing behavior.

The magistrate judge found that the following evidence demonstrated that Spartan had indisputably satisfied this prong: (1) Williams admitted that she knew of Spartan's anti-harassment policy, had attended a meeting at which it was discussed, and saw a posted notice of it, which identified persons to whom she could report improper conduct, and (2) Spartan forced Maund to resign as soon as it learned of Williams' allegations.

This rationale fails to recognize that while the existence of an antiharassment policy and prompt corrective action pursuant to it provides important evidence that an employer has acted to meet the first prong of the affirmative defense, such evidence does not compel this conclusion. Rather, any anti-harassment policy offered to satisfy the first prong of the *Faragher-Ellerth* defense must be "both reasonably designed and reasonably effectual." *Brown v. Perry*, 184 F.3d 388, 396 (4th Cir. 1999). Moreover, a prompt response to complaints of harassment made pursuant to a policy banning harassment does not necessarily establish the first prong of the affirmative defense.

The magistrate judge also entirely ignored substantial relevant evidence submitted by Williams that could lead a factfinder to conclude that Spartan's anti-harassment policy was not an effective preventive program. This evidence included: (1) Maund's deposition testimony that he received no training on sexual harassment and did not even recall any specific discussion of the anti-harassment policy; (2) senior Spartan management's toleration of and participation in lewd conversations and publication of sexually explicit jokes and cartoons in the workplace; (3) evidence that an employee's complaint to a Spartan manager about foul language and sexist jokes in the workplace produced no corrective action; (4) General Sales Manager Rose's comment that a secretary had been fired because "she didn't give him a blow job"; (5) Vice President and General Manager West's remark to male managers looking at female participants in a management training function, "Boys, I've stepped over better than that just to jack off"; (6) General Sales Manager West's comment after a sexual harassment training meeting, "does this mean we can't fuck the help any more"; (7) the close relationship between Maund (the alleged harasser) and West, Rose, and other senior managers at Spartan; and (8) the anti-harassment policy's failure, in contravention of EEOC guidelines, to assure those reporting harassment that they would not be subject to retaliation, particularly when the policy provided that "an employee who in bad faith falsely accuses another employee of harassment will be subject to disciplinary action up to and including termination."

In *Faragher*, the Supreme Court found a city was vicariously liable for harassment by lifeguard supervisors, despite the existence of a sexual harassment policy, when the plaintiff beach employees were "completely isolated from the City's higher management" and the city "failed to disseminate its policy against sexual harassment among the beach employees." In *Smith v. First Union National Bank*, 202 F.3d 234, 245 (4th Cir. 2000), we held that even though the employer's anti-harassment policy had been disseminated to employees it did not demonstrate, as a matter of law, that the employer had satisfied the first prong of the *Faragher* defense because the policy referred only to sexual conduct and was read by the plaintiff not to include nonsexual, gender-based harassment. We also emphasized that "employers cannot satisfy the first element of the *Faragher-Ellerth* affirmative defense if its management-level employees are discouraging the use of the complaint process."

Here Spartan disseminated an anti-harassment policy which failed to provide that complainants would be free from retaliation, and yet warned that false reports of harassment would subject a complainant to disciplinary action, "including termination." Although these features do not, in themselves, render the policy ineffective, when considered in conjunction with the conduct of most senior Spartan management, a policy with such features could be found to be ineffective. The outrageous comments by Vice President and General Manager West ("does this mean we cannot fuck the help anymore") and General Sales Manager Rose (a secretary was terminated because "she didn't give him a blow job") suggest not only that a complaint made pursuant to this anti-harassment policy might fall on deaf ears, but also that such a complaint might cause the complainant's termination. Indeed, Williams produced evidence that a Spartan employee decided not to complain of harassment because of fear of being fired. The long and close personal relationships between those managers who made the denigrating comments, West and Rose, and the alleged harasser, Maund, were so well known that several of the witnesses described them as members of the "Augusta Boys Club." Given these relationships, a factfinder could conclude that a complaint about Maund would receive a particularly skeptical response from Spartan management.

We note that Spartan's policy states that "any employee who feels they are being subjected to any form of harassment in violation of this policy should bring their complaint to the attention" of one of four members of management: "[1] the[ ] immediate supervisor, [2] the General Manager, [3] the appointed liaison, or [4] the Manager of Corporate Human Resources." Providing an employee recourse to multiple members of management is commendable. But Williams produced evidence that could lead a factfinder to determine that the extra protection seemingly afforded by this provision was illusory in her case. This is so because one of the four suggested recipients of harassment complaints was the harasser himself, Maund; another was his good friend, Vice President and General Manager West (the source of the "does this mean we can't fuck the help any more" and the "I've stepped over better than that just to jack off" remarks); and the remaining two managers reported to West, the General Manager of the station and Vice President of the entire company. Thus, the conduct of Spartan's senior management could be found to have isolated Williams from effective channels of complaint. A factfinder could conclude that the language in the anti-harassment policy together with the conduct of Spartan's most senior management "discouraged complaining about a supervisor's harassing behavior." *Smith*.

This is not to say that Williams has demonstrated that Spartan cannot establish the first prong of Faragher's affirmative defense. A factfinder may well ultimately conclude that Spartan's anti-harassment policy and prompt corrective action do establish this prong. However, we believe that when Williams' evidence is considered in the light most favorable to her, Spartan has not established the first prong as a matter of law. For these reasons, we reverse the district court's grant of summary judgment to Spartan.

REVERSED.

WILKINSON, C.J., dissenting.

I agree with the district court that Spartan Communications has established both prongs of the affirmative defense under *Faragher* and *Ellerth*. I would therefore uphold the grant of summary judgment. . . .

As to the first prong of the defense, Spartan exercised reasonable care to prevent and correct the sexually harassing behavior that Williams reported. Spartan put in place a strong anti-harassment policy that states the "working environment should be free of intimidation and harassment." The policy defines and prohibits sexual harassment and encourages employees to come forward with complaints. A complaint may be reported to any one of at least four different people, including the department head, general manager, appointed EEO liaison, and the manager of corporate human resources. Williams admits that she was aware of this policy. She attended a meeting at which the policy was discussed by the corporate personnel director and saw a posted notice prohibiting sexual harassment and identifying various persons to whom she could report any improper conduct. Spartan also took swift action to correct the alleged harassment. When Williams finally reported Maund's inappropriate behavior, Spartan immediately conducted an investigation and asked Maund to resign only two days after receiving Williams' complaint.

Though the existence of an anti-harassment policy is not sufficient to satisfy the first part of the affirmative defense, the policy here is "both reasonably designed and reasonably effectual." *Brown v. Perry*, 184 F.3d 388, 396 (4th Cir. 1999). The majority attempts to discredit the effectiveness of the policy by referring to lewd statements by management and to the fact that Spartan's policy did not contain an explicit anti-retaliation provision. Yet the majority does not assert that the policy was ineffective when complaints were reported or that Spartan had retaliated against any employee who made a complaint. There is simply "no evidence that [the] employer adopted or administered an anti-harassment policy in bad faith or that the policy was otherwise defective or dysfunctional." There is only the evidence that Spartan immediately terminated Maund when it learned of his misconduct. Because it had an effective policy, Spartan has satisfied the first part of the affirmative defense.

The majority's litany of crude remarks attributed to management does not under-mine Spartan's affirmative defense. It is a rare case when some remarks could not be dredged up or alleged in order to challenge management's reasonableness. The affirmative defense focuses not on remarks, however, but on the conduct of employers and employees in preventing and addressing sexual harassment complaints. A collec-tion of off-hand remarks unrelated to the harassment simply does not preclude Spartan from establishing the first prong of the affirmative defense on summary judgment. Indeed, the remarks related by the majority were not directed toward Williams. She was not even present when most of them were made. While no one would approve of the comments, Title VII is not intended to allow courts to act as censors of workplace speech or impose a general workplace civility code.

As to the second prong of the defense, Williams failed to take advantage of the opportunities provided by Spartan to avoid the sexual harassment. "[A] demonstration of such failure will normally suffice to satisfy the employer's burden under the second element of the defense." *Faragher.* In *Montero v. Agco Corp.*, the Ninth Circuit held that where the plaintiff knew about the company's policy, knew whom to contact with harassment complaints, and yet waited almost two years to report the harassment, the company "successfully established the second prong of the *Faragher* defense" and was entitled to judgment as a matter of law. 192 F.3d 856, 863 (9th Cir. 1999). Similarly, Williams knew about Spartan's policy, knew whom to contact with grievances, and yet waited three years to report the harassment. During this time, plaintiff was allegedly assaulted twice more, once while watching an R-rated movie in her van with Maund and again while with Maund in her hotel room. *Faragher* and *Ellerth* encourage employees to report such conduct precisely to avoid continued harassment. Spartan has established that Williams unreasonably failed to take advantage of the company's preventive and corrective measures. Williams "should not recover damages that could have been avoided if she had done so." *Faragher.*

By denying summary judgment in a case where the affirmative defense has been clearly established, the majority simply indicates an aversion to the Supreme Court's mandate in *Faragher* and *Ellerth*. In doing so, the majority creates the worst of all possible worlds. Despite the existence of a reasonable and effective complaint procedure, the employee continues to be harassed for nearly three years because no misconduct was reported. The company in turn has no opportunity to rectify unacceptable behavior. Such an outcome is the antithesis of Title VII's primary objective, which is "not to provide redress but to avoid harm." *Faragher.* The Supreme Court has explained that employer liability is limited to encourage the creation of effective anti-harassment policies and also to "encourage employees to report harassing conduct before it becomes severe or pervasive." *Ellerth.* Spartan attempted to prevent and acted to correct sexually harassing behavior. It should not be held liable when an employee fails to use the available channels for reporting harassment. As this court stated in Brown, "The law requires an employer to be reasonable, not clairvoyant or omnipotent."

I would affirm the judgment.

NOTES

1. *"Paper Compliance?" Williams* raises an important question—does a sexual harassment policy actually prevent harassment? More importantly, should the existence of such a policy absolve an employer of liability for harassment that occurs nevertheless? Many commentators have criticized the Supreme Court's decisions in *Ellerth* and *Faragher* for granting too much deference to employer policies and practices. *See, e.g.*, Susan Bisom-Rapp, *An Ounce of Prevention Is a Poor Substitute for a Pound of Cure: Confronting the Developing Jurisprudence of Education and Prevention in Employment Discrimination Law*, 22 BERKELEY J. EMP. & LAB. L. 1 (2001); Susan D. Carle, *Acknowledging Informal Power Dynamics in the Workplace: A Proposal for Further Development of the Vicarious Liability Doctrine in Hostile Environment Sexual Harassment Cases*, 13 DUKE J. GENDER L. & POL'Y 85 (2006); Joanna L. Grossman, *The Culture of Compliance: The Final Triumph of Form Over Substance in Sexual Harassment Law*, 26 HARV. WOMEN'S L.J. 3 (2003); Anne Lawton, *Operating in an Empirical Vacuum: The* Ellerth *and* Faragher *Affirmative Defense*, 13 COLUM. J. GENDER & L. 197 (2005). These commentators argue that the affirmative defense creates incentives for employers to go through the motions of being tough on

harassment, establishing strongly worded policies and implementing training programs, but that such practices do not get at the root cause of harassing behavior. Indeed, some have suggested that those practices come at the expense of more aggressive efforts to equalize the workplace and to respond to acts of discrimination. Consider Professor Lawton's take:

> [T]he courts are asking employers the wrong questions. Why are employers not required to show evidence of their efforts to evaluate and assess the impact of their organization's culture on the incidence of workplace harassment? If role models, such as supervisors, set the tone in the workplace . . . then should the employer not evaluate its supervisors, in part, on their efforts to enforce and comply with the employer's anti-harassment policy?
>
> Why are employers with highly sex-segregated workplaces not required to demonstrate their efforts to decrease sex segregation within jobs? Noting the connection between high levels of harassment and low numbers of women in the workplace, [empirical research suggests] "that strong affirmative action programs and moving (large numbers of) women into jobs traditionally held by men may prove a reasonable organizational strategy for reducing harassment." If harassment is more likely to occur in "male bastions" then should employers in those fields not be held to a higher standard of prevention? . . .
>
> Finally, if employers depend on their anti-harassment policies and procedures to deter workplace harassment, should they not be required to evaluate those policies and procedures? Why do federal courts not require an employer to ask its own employees about their perceptions of the employer's procedure? If employees believe the employer does not punish harassers and penalizes victims who come forward with complaints of sexual harassment, why would an employer be allowed to prevail on the affirmative defense for simply drafting a policy and procedure that workers are reluctant to use?

13 COLUM. J. GENDER & L. at 233-35 (2005). She concludes that courts' equating policies with prevention essentially shifts the burden of proof to the employee on the reasonableness of the employer's prevention efforts. *Id.* at 235; *see also* Vicki Schultz, *The Sanitized Workplace*, 112 YALE L.J. 2061, 2174-77 (2003) (suggesting that liability for hostile work environment sexual harassment should turn on the extent of sex segregation in the particular workplace rather than employer's aggressiveness in policing sexual conduct).

    Williams certainly demonstrates that it is possible for an employer to have a policy on the books and at the same time tolerate a work culture in which objectionable behavior endures. The question is whether courts will hold such employers accountable. *Williams* and other decisions find that an employer must do more than institute a policy or a training program to prevent and correct harassment. *See, e.g., Herndon v. City Manchester*, 284 S.W.3d. 682 (Mo. App. 2009) (concluding under state law version of affirmative defense that police department failed to take preventative measures despite its harassment policy where department failed to adequately examine offending officer's disciplinary record in past position and was aware that officer had previously engaged in harassment of nonemployee); *cf. Hawkins v. Anheuser-Busch, Inc.* 517 F.3d 321 (6th Cir. 2008) (concluding for purposes of co-worker harassment claim that "an employer's responsibility to prevent future harassment is heightened where it is dealing with a known serial harasser and is therefore on clear notice that the same employee has engaged in inappropriate behavior in the past"). However, the *Williams* decision provoked a strong dissent, and other courts have adopted the dissenting judge's more deferential view of employer practices.

See, e.g., Barrett v. Applied Radiant Energy Corp., 240 F.3d 262 (4th Cir. 2001) ("Distribution of an anti-harassment policy provides 'compelling proof' that the company exercised reasonable care in preventing and promptly correcting sexual harassment. The only way to rebut this proof is to show that the 'employer adopted or administered an anti-harassment policy in bad faith or that the policy was otherwise defective or dysfunctional.' "); David Sherwyn et al., *Don't Train Your Employees and Cancel Your "1-800" Harassment Hotline: An Empirical Examination and Correction of the Flaws in the Affirmative Defense to Sexual Harassment Charges*, 69 FORDHAM L. REV. 1265, 1285-86 (2000-01) (finding that among reported sexual harassment decisions between 1998 and 2000, all but one held that the employer satisfied the reasonable care requirement by maintaining a sexual harassment policy that allowed the victim the opportunity to report to someone other than a harassing supervisor).

2. *Conjunctive Elements.* The *Williams* court deals only with the first prong of the defense, and only with its first element—whether the employer engaged in preventive action. Since a reasonable jury could find that the employer failed to reasonably prevent harassment, the other aspects of the defense were irrelevant; if the jury so finds, the employer will be liable. Assume, however, that the court went on to complete the analysis. How would the employer fare? Prompt and effective *corrective* action was taken: immediately after Williams reported Maund's behavior, he resigned. As for the second prong, the harassment perpetrated against Williams continued for three years before she reported, which strongly suggests she was unreasonable in failing to report. Given these facts, the court's willingness to look beyond the employer's policy on harassment in assessing prevention was critical to the plaintiff's success.

3. *Reasonable Failures to Report.* Alternatively, could Williams successfully argue that her significant delay in reporting Maund's harassing behavior (as measured from his first act) was reasonable? Note the employer's sexual harassment policy did not offer assurances of nonretaliation, and as the court makes clear, the past comments of senior managers could give an employee good reason to fear that her complaint of harassment would not be taken seriously. Courts often are reluctant to find a failure to report reasonable where the victim cites only general fear and embarrassment. *See, e.g., Matvia v. Bald Head Isle Mgmt.*, 259 F.3d 261, 270 (4th Cir. 2001) (finding that general fear of negative reactions from co-workers, which ultimately came to fruition, did not justify failure to report; a retaliation claim is the proper avenue for dealing with retaliatory behavior should it occur). Other courts, however, have found that a victim's failure to report promptly could be reasonable in similar circumstances, as where the employer's work culture discouraged reporting or the victim had a specific basis for fearing retaliation. *See, e.g., Reed v. MBNA Mktg. Sys.*, 333 F.3d 27, 36-37 (1st Cir. 2003) (finding 17-year-old victim's failure to report reasonable where harasser told her his family had significant influence in the company and she would be fired for reporting); *Mota v. Univ. of Tex. Houston Health Sci. Ctr.*, 261 F.3d 512 (5th Cir. 2001) (finding untenured professor's delay in reporting harassment by prominent department head reasonable where harasser stated that people working in his department had to "get along" with him and that victim's immigration status could be jeopardized if he no longer worked as university employer).

4. *Supervisor versus Co-worker.* Both *Watson* and *Williams* involve harassment by a supervisor. Whether the harasser has authority over the victim is an important threshold question for purposes of employer liability. If the harasser does not have supervisory authority, the presumption of vicarious liability, and therefore the need for the *Ellerth/Faragher* defense, does not apply, and the victim must affirmatively establish employer negligence. Thus, where harassment is perpetrated by a co-worker or a third party, such as a customer, the employee must show as an element of her prima facie case of hostile work environment that the employer knew or should have known that the harassment was taking place and failed to take remedial action. *See, e.g., Breda v. Wolf Camera & Video*, 222 F.3d 886, 889 (11th Cir. 2000). As this test suggests, courts will look at many of the same factors that are relevant under the affirmative defense in determining negligence. Reports to a supervisor are among the ways an employer might know or be deemed to know about co-worker harassment, and the extent to which the employer exercises reasonable care in response to the co-worker's behavior largely replicates the inquiry under the corrective action prong of *Ellerth/Faragher*. Thus the critical distinction between the two tests is primarily the burden of proof.

Whether a person is a "supervisor" can be difficult to determine, particularly in modern professional workplaces where employees may work with relative independence or in nonhierarchical teams with co-workers. In a variety of employment settings, employees "report" to a higher-ranked employee on their day-to-day work but that person does not have meaningful control over most aspects of the employee's position, like salary or termination. Faced with these realities, courts take different approaches in determining whether a harasser is a supervisor. Some interpret "supervisor" narrowly to mean someone with authority to make ultimate economic decisions with respect to terms and conditions of employment, like hiring and firing decisions. *See, e.g., Parkins v. Civil Constructors of Illinois*, 163 F.3d 1027, 1034 (7th Cir. 1998) ("[T]he essence of supervisory status is the authority to affect the terms and conditions of the victim's employment. This authority primarily consists of the power to hire, fire, demote, promote, transfer, or discipline an employee. Absent entrustment of at least some of this authority, an employee does not qualify as a supervisor for purposes of imputing liability to the employer."). Others take a broader view, focusing on whether the harasser possessed employer-delegated authority that aided him or her in creating the hostile work environment. *See, e.g., Mack v. Otis Elevator Co.*, 326 F.3d 116 (2d Cir. 2003) (factual question existed as to whether "mechanic in charge," who had authority under union contract to schedule work and ensure safety, was victim's supervisor for purposes of affirmative defense). Note that the definition of supervisor is relevant not only in determining the status of the harasser (and consequently whether a negligence or vicarious liability framework applies) but also in determining what the employer knew of the harassment and whether the employee took advantage of the employer's complaint policy. If those employees who observe or hear about the harassment are co-workers without managerial authority, the employer is likely to escape liability under either framework. *See, e.g., Blevins v. Famous Recipe Co. Operations*, 107 Fair Emp. Prac. Cas. (BNA) 1855 (M.D. Tenn. 2009) (factual issue existed as to whether "shift leader" to whom plaintiff reported harassment was a supervisor whose knowledge could be imputed to management). In theory, an employee who is harassed by a supervisor ought to have an easier time obtaining relief than one harassed by a co-worker, since in the former case liability is automatic subject to the employer's defense. Ironically, in jurisdictions that defer significantly to the employer's policies, that is not always the case. Suppose that a visibly upset employee asks her supervisor for a shift change in order to avoid another employee who has "been giving [her] problems." If the employee declines to elaborate, a court that strictly reads the second prong of *Ellerth/Faragher* might conclude that the employee unreasonably failed to report the harasser's behavior. Yet depending on the facts, a jury might reasonably conclude that the supervisor should have known about the harassing behavior, the standard applicable to co-worker claims. *See Duch v. Jakubek*, 588 F.3d 757 (2d Cir. 2009) (jury could conclude that supervisor had constructive knowledge of co-worker harassment where employee requested shift change, employer observed employee "teary and red" when asked about the harasser, and supervisor knew harasser had engaged in past misconduct toward female employees). Does such a result suggest courts should rethink the way they have interpreted the *Ellerth/Faragher* defense?

5. *Beyond Sexual Harassment.* Although the Supreme Court's decisions in *Ellerth* and *Faragher* involved sexual harassment in particular, most courts have assumed that the affirmative defense applies to hostile work environment claims based on other protected characteristics and arising under sources of law other than Title VII's prohibition on sex discrimination. *See, e.g., Oleyar v. County of Durham*, 336 F. Supp. 2d 512 (M.D.N.C. 2004) (hostile work environment under ADEA); *Allen v. McPhee*, 240 S.W.3d 803 (Tenn. 2007) (state law sexual harassment claim). Might the concept of employer prevention and corrective action have bearing on employer liability for other forms of discrimination as well? We saw in Chapter 10 that the ADA is widely understood to impose an obligation on employers to engage in a good faith "interactive process" with disabled workers in need of an accommodation, although it is unclear what the ramifications are for failing to do so. Proactive employer behavior can also limit the employee's damage award upon a successful showing of discrimination. *See Kolstad v. American Dental Ass'n*, 527 U.S. 526, 545 (1999) ("[I]n the punitive damages context, an employer may not be vicariously liable for the discriminatory employment decisions of managerial agents where these decisions are contrary to the employer's 'good-faith efforts to comply with Title VII.'").

Perhaps the ultimate risk management question in this context is whether positive employer behavior will influence courts in their assessment of employer liability for discrimination generally. In *Pruitt v. Metcalf & Eddy*, No. 03 Civ. 4780 (DF), 2006 WL 39621 (S.D.N.Y. Jan. 6, 2006), a file clerk had a dispute with his supervisor about his not assisting in dismantling the office Christmas tree on the basis of his religious beliefs, culminating in an altercation in which the supervisor believed she had been threatened. The employer made several efforts to resolve the situation but ultimately terminated the clerk. In the plaintiff's subsequent suit for failure to accommodate and discriminatory termination on the basis of race and religion, the court awarded summary judgment to the employer. Regarding the accommodation claim, the court stressed that the employer had made efforts to respond to plaintiff's complaints:

> [Plaintiff's] argument that his beliefs were not accommodated because Arvay "made [him] take the Christmas tree down upon threat of . . . disciplinary treatment" is misplaced. It was only after Arvay allegedly forced Plaintiff to take down the tree that, in accordance with Defendants' internal procedure, he complained to Human Resources about any purported religious discrimination, and the evidence shows that Montminy then promptly commenced an investigation. As part of this investigation, Montminy held a meeting within one week of receiving Plaintiff's formal complaint to discuss, *inter alia*, the conflict between Plaintiff's religious beliefs and holiday decorating. The evidence reflects that, at that meeting, Montminy, Arvay and Plaintiff resolved the issue by agreeing that Plaintiff would no longer be involved in holiday decorating. Further, there is no indication that Plaintiff found this particular resolution to be "an unsatisfactory compromise" with respect to his religious beliefs.

Id. at *11. According to the court, plaintiff's claim that the supervisor should have been reprimanded and required to undergo counseling or attend "religious tolerance sessions" missed the point because the only question was whether plaintiff's religion had been reasonably accommodated. Is the court's consideration of the employer's complaint procedure and its corrective efforts appropriate in this context?

6. *Treatment of the Harasser.* The *Williams* court noted that "as a result of Maund's admitted rental of the movie, he resigned. Maund received five months severance pay in return for releasing Spartan from liability for his dismissal." The majority does not further explore this, and the dissent seems to think that the employer did as much as could be expected when it "fired" Maund. Thus, the terms of the alleged harasser's termination apparently do not affect the adequacy of the employer's "correct" response. But why pay an admitted harasser severance? Is it because the admitted conduct was not necessarily harassment? Even so, what claims do you think Maund waived in return for his severance pay? If you were the employer's counsel, would you have recommended paying him five months' salary? Reconsider your answer when you have finished Section B.

PROBLEMS

13-1. Spectrum Stores, a regional convenience store chain, asks you to review its policy on sexual harassment. Spectrum owns approximately 25 stores and 2 warehouses across two states and employs over 300 employees. Approximately 20 of those employees, including its officers and human resources personnel, work in Spectrum's corporate headquarters. Orientation for all store personnel is conducted at the headquarters, and the following policy is distributed to all employees at that time:

> Spectrum Stores does not and will not tolerate harassment of our employees, applicants or customers. The term "harassment" includes but is not limited to: slurs, jokes and other verbal, graphic or physical conduct relating to an individual's race, color, sex, sexual orientation, or religion. "Harassment" also includes sexual advances, requests for sexual favors, unwelcome touching and other verbal, graphic or physical conduct of a sexual nature.
>
> VIOLATION OF THIS POLICY WILL SUBJECT THE EMPLOYEE TO DISCIPLINARY ACTION.
>
> If you feel that you are being harassed in any way you should notify your immediate supervisor. If you believe that a supervisor or a member of management has acted inconsistently with this policy and you are not comfortable bringing a complaint regarding harassment to your immediate supervisor or if you believe that your complaint concerning a co-worker, a customer, or a vendor has not been handled to your satisfaction, please immediately contact either the Vice President of Human Resources or the Executive Vice President.
>
> Please do not assume Spectrum is aware of your problem. Please bring your complaints and concerns to our attention so that we can resolve them.

Is there anything you would recommend adding to or changing in this policy? Are there any other practices or procedures you would recommend that Spectrum adopt? If you need further information to answer, what questions would you ask Spectrum's management before offering advice?

13-2. Terri Munroe was a shipping and receiving clerk in one of Spectrum Stores' warehouses and the only female employee at her worksite. Reed Gilbelt, a co-worker, frequently subjected Terri to sexual comments and lewd behavior. Among other things, he referred to her as "luscious" and "sweet cheeks," and on two occasions he suggested that Terri accompany him to the Red Roof Inn during a break. He frequently sent suggestive e-mails to her.

After enduring this behavior for six months, Terri reported Reed's conduct to her supervisor, Vincent Sing. Vincent laughed when he read the e-mails Terri showed him and told Terri that she should "resolve the problem on her own." Over the next three months, Sing engaged in suggestive behavior as well. He told Terri that he "had a job for her under his desk," remarked that Terri should wear shorter shorts on one occasion when he saw her standing on high equipment, and invited Terri out with him on three occasions. Once when Terri asked to be permitted to clock out early due to illness, Vincent told her she could only leave if she came home with him. When Terri refused, Vincent forced her to work until the end of her regular shift.

Three months after first reporting Reed's behavior to Vincent, Terri reported the behavior of both employees to Diane O'Connor, Spectrum's Human Resources Vice President. O'Connor placed Terri on paid leave and launched an immediate investigation, during which she interviewed over a dozen employees during the course of two weeks. As a result of the investigation, Spectrum terminated Reed, and Vincent resigned. O'Connor informed Terri of this outcome and Terri returned to work. She did not experience any further harassment upon her return; however, she resigned from employment one month later citing her distress at the behavior she had endured prior to the investigation and being "shunned" upon her return to work by some co-workers who were upset about the departures of Reed and Vincent.

Assume that Spectrum maintains the sexual harassment policy laid out in problem 13-1 above and that the company provides sexual harassment training to all its employees. Suppose you represent Terri. Enumerate all of the discrimination claims and theories of liability that you can pursue against Spectrum. If Terri's experience amounts to severe and pervasive hostile behavior based on sex, can she establish that Spectrum should be vicariously liable for Reed's conduct? What about for Vincent's conduct? Think about how you would go about establishing this element of her claim(s), anticipate what arguments Spectrum is likely to make, and explain how you would respond to them.

2. Employer Investigations of Workplace Misconduct

Internal investigations of sexual harassment complaints are now standard practice among sophisticated employers, and they are used not only in dealing with allegations of discrimination, but in ensuring compliance with regulatory and criminal laws and dealing with civil liability on many fronts. Some internal investigations receive a great deal of media attention, such as former Senator George Mitchell's investigation of the steroid question on behalf of Major League Baseball. They may be conducted by line managers, compliance officers, corporate counsel, or, as in Mitchell's case, outside counsel.

A firm might wish to have an attorney, often an outside attorney, conduct its internal investigation for a number of reasons. Foremost is the fact that investigations do not normally trigger privilege protections when conducted by non-lawyers. *See* Theodore R. Lotchin, Note, *No Good Deed Goes Unpunished? Establishing a Self-Evaluative Privilege for Corporate Internal Investigations*, 46 Wm. & Mary L. Rev. 1137 (2004). There is the additional advantage of the perception of impartiality when an investigation is conducted by someone without a direct stake in the outcome. *See* Joanna L. Grossman, *The Culture of Compliance: The Final Triumph of Form over Substance in Sexual Harassment Law*, 26 Harv. Women's L. J. 3, 57-63 (2003) (discussing institutional and other biases in internal investigations). *But see Morin v. Me. Educ. Ass'n*, 993 A.2d 1097 (Me. 2010) (rejecting disqualification of law firm on the basis that one of its attorneys conducted the investigation). For the latter reason, there is also a tendency to have special counsel retained to investigate serious cases, especially when a higher-level official is the subject of a complaint. Using special counsel also avoids disqualification that may result from the same law firm both conducting the investigation and litigating any suit that ensues if the investigating attorney becomes a necessary witness. *See* Jeffrey A. Van Detta, *Lawyers as Investigators: How Ellerth and Faragher Reveal a Crisis of Ethics and Professionalism Through Trial Counsel Disqualification and Waivers of Privilege in Workplace Harassment Cases*, 24 J. Legal Prof. 261 (1999/2000).

At the same time, investigations have generated difficult ethical questions for lawyers, who may be faced with conflicts of interest or even risk criminal liability should their work help hide client wrongdoing or obstruct investigations by outside authorities. *See* Peter J. Henning, *Targeting Legal Advice*, 54 Am. U. L. Rev. 669, 694 (2005) (quoting the SEC's Director of Enforcement, Stephen Cutler, "One area of particular focus for us is the role of lawyers in internal investigations of their clients or companies. We are concerned that, in some instances, lawyers may have conducted investigations in such a manner as to help hide ongoing fraud, or may have taken actions to actively obstruct such investigations.").

a. Representing the Employer in an Investigation

From the employer's perspective, the purpose of an internal investigation is to ascertain the facts in order to determine the optimal course of action — while trying to avoid making matters worse. The resulting choices might include making no changes after finding no wrongdoing, improving procedures to avoid even the perception of future problems despite a finding of no wrongdoing, self-reporting violations to enforcement authorities or regulators, taking steps to remedy the situation by disciplining or discharging those responsible for illegal or unwise conduct, and making settlement offers to aggrieved persons. Of course, the employer's response will usually itself be constrained by various legal doctrines. For example, the antidiscrimination laws prohibit retaliation against those who participate in legal proceedings and even those who oppose discrimination. The Supreme Court recently reaffirmed this in *Crawford v. Metropolitan Gov't of Nashville & Davidson County*, 129 S. Ct. 846 (2009) (holding that an employee's response to questions during a harassment investigation constituted protected "opposition" conduct under Title VII's antiretaliation principle).

Whatever the ultimate action taken, the first step is to ascertain the facts. Practitioners have developed a number of strategies for maximizing the efficacy of fact seeking in these investigations while minimizing the risks the investigations themselves may create. For example, it is both common sense and standard practice to identify and safeguard electronic files and relevant documents since employees may well wish to hide or destroy them to protect themselves and/or the corporation. It is also important to have a set of protocols for conducting witness interviews. One set of commentators recommends two rounds of interviews, the first and more informal is "designed to stake out the field of inquiry," and the second round is more focused:

> The purposes of the preliminary round of interviews is to: (a) introduce the investigating attorney, explain what is happening, and secure the witness's cooperation and understanding of the need for confidentiality; (b) learn the witness's background and connection to the matter under investigation; (c) give each witness an idea of what is going to happen in the investigation; and (d) attempt to identify the universe of witnesses and pertinent documents.
>
> In the initial interview, every effort should be made to put the witness at ease and convey the notion that the investigating attorney views the witness as a collaborator in a joint effort to find out exactly what happened. The initial interview should be a conversation — *not* an examination. The less the investigating attorney professes to know about the client and the client's industry during the initial interview, the better. Ideally, the investigating attorney assumes the role of student and asks the witness to assume the role of teacher. The investigating attorney should ask who *the witness* thinks the investigating attorney should interview and what documents *the witness* thinks the investigating attorney should review in order to find out what happened. The witness will probably end up telling the investigator the witness's version of what happened without much additional prompting. If the witness is not forthcoming, the investigating attorney will have to proceed to a second, more adversarial interview, as described below. The initial interview should end with the investigating attorney explaining that the investigation is ongoing and it is possible that the witness will have to be interviewed again. If the witness asks what is going to happen at the conclusion of the investigation, the only truthful answer is that the investigating attorney is simply gathering the facts, and that until those facts are unearthed, there is no way to predict the results of the investigation. . . .
>
> [I]f there is some material disagreement between witnesses, or between witnesses and available documents, the investigating attorney will need to conduct a second round of interviews with those witnesses whose stories seem to conflict with those of other witnesses or with available documents. In contrast to the preliminary interview, the second interview should be more in the nature of an examination than a conversation. . . .
>
> [T]he investigating attorney may want to employ a professional court reporter for this purpose. A verbatim transcript will remove any doubt as to what the witness actually said during the interview. An employee witness in fear of losing his or her job, or perhaps even of prosecution, may later deny having made crucial disclosures. . . . Another reason a court reporter may be beneficial in taking statements of crucial witnesses is that, in the event the government is notified of the facts discovered in the investigation, it will be in the company's best interest for the government to be satisfied that the company has engaged in a serious and professional effort to discover and document the facts. . . .
>
> However, creating a verbatim transcript of witness interviews is contrary to the conventional wisdom of many practitioners. This conventional wisdom counsels against creating a verbatim transcript to protect against disclosure of such materials in the event a decision is made to voluntarily disclose the results of an internal investigation to the government. Instead, investigating attorneys often prepare post-interview memoranda that include the attorney's mental impressions and opinions so the memoranda will be

protected by the work product doctrine. . . . [P]reserving applicable privileges is vitally important in conducting witness interviews. However, the government is requesting waiver of privileged materials with increasing frequency as a condition for the disclosing entity to receive credit for full cooperation. Therefore, preservation of privileges is ultimately uncertain, and may be less important than ensuring the accuracy of the testimony of critical witnesses. . . .

Ames Davis & Jennifer L. Weaver, *A Litigator's Approach to Interviewing Witnesses in Internal Investigations,* 17 HEALTH LAWYER 8, 9 (2005).

This passage suggests a number of the problems with internal investigations, including the very controversial practice of the Department of Justice and other state and federal regulatory authorities to demand (they might say "request") waivers of attorney-client privilege and work product protection as a condition of settlement discussions. Although the Department of Justice has retreated somewhat from a harsh position articulated in the so-called Thompson Memorandum, the current "McNulty Memorandum," Memorandum from Deputy Att'y Gen. Paul J. McNulty for Heads of Dep't Components and U.S. Attorneys (Dec. 12, 2006), *available at* http://www.usdoj.gov/dag/speeches/2006/mcnulty_memo.pdf, leaves the privilege still very much at risk. *See* American College of Trial Lawyers, *Recommended Practices For Companies and Their Counsel in Conducting Internal Investigations,* 46 AM. CRIM. L. REV. 73 (2009). As Davis and Weaver suggest, the attorney investigator should make every effort to preserve these protections. Other commentators recommend a series of steps to maximize the probability of protecting privileges, including:

- Early lawyer involvement
- Explicit corporate request for legal (as opposed to business) advice
- Documenting the confidentiality of communications
- Restricting the internal flow of information
- Obtaining information from highest possible sources
- Labeling documents judiciously to avoid diluting protection for sensitive material
- Interposing legal conclusions, mental impressions, and strategies in all notes
- Treating former employee contacts as confidential for work product protection
- Deciding whether to release the report to a governmental agency, underwriter's counsel, accountants, or the press in light of the effect on privileges
- Express legal conclusions, opinions, and recommendations in the report to the board of directors

Thomas R. Mulroy & Eric J. Munoz, *The Internal Corporate Investigation,* 1 DEPAUL BUS. & COMM. L. J. 49, 82-84 (2002).

While the careful attorney will do her best to ensure that the privilege applies, she will also be aware that the protections may well be waived should a prosecutor threaten criminal charges or a regulator threaten a civil enforcement action. *See* David M. Zornow & Keith D. Krakaur, *On the Brink of a Brave New World: The Death of Privilege in Corporate Criminal Investigations,* 37 AM. CRIM. L. REV. 147 (2000). Further, the corporation may well choose to waive its privilege even if not pressed by a government agency. For example, while the EEOC does not demand privilege waivers as part of its investigations, an employer seeking to allay Commission doubts about the effectiveness of its sexual harassment or antidiscrimination policies might want to provide such reports.

One of the central problems of the internal investigation is the relationship of the investigator to the employee being questioned. That individual may not understand that the investigator is in no sense that person's attorney — especially if the investigation begins with a version of informal "conversation" described by Davis and Weaver. The potential for misunderstanding of the role of the attorney is especially great if (as is often the case) the attorney investigating the matter on behalf of the employer has previously represented the individual being questioned in matters in which the interests of the employer and employee were aligned.

New Jersey saw this play out recently in a high-profile case, *Speeney v. Rutgers*, 369 F. App'x 357 (3d Cir. 2010), which started with sexual harassment complaints by several students against a Rutgers University professor. Rutgers retained what was then Carpenter, Bennett & Morrissey both to represent it in the university's internal de-tenuring proceeding against the harasser and to defend it against a suit by him. Ultimately, both proceedings were resolved before any conclusion, with the professor leaving Rutgers. The plaintiffs were apparently unhappy with the settlement and/or with any compensation to be paid to them on their own claims.

They were also unhappy with the law firm. In its representation of Rutgers, the firm interviewed the students who later became key witnesses in the internal proceedings and, presumably, would have been key to Rutgers's defense of the professor's suit. When the students brought suit, they not only pursued claims against Rutgers for the harassment, but also sued Carpenter for malpractice, asserting that they were not mere witnesses but rather clients of the firm. And, for good measure, they sought to have the firm disqualified from representing Rutgers in their suit against it.

The Third Circuit's decision was scarcely definitive. Since the plaintiffs ultimately settled their claims against Rutgers, the disqualification motion was moot when the matter reached the Third Circuit. But there was still the plaintiffs' malpractice claim against "their" lawyers, the Carpenter firm. While the district court had found that there was no attorney-client relationship, the Third Circuit remanded for another determination in light of new evidence the plaintiffs claim to have had.

As *Speeney* suggests, the safest course of action is for the investigating attorney to inform the employee explicitly that the investigator is not representing him and get a signed acknowledgment of that notification. Again, this is in some tension with the informal initial approach to investigation some urge. Such an explanation also avoids the risk that the employee will later attempt to claim that the conversation was privileged because the employee reasonably (if wrongly) believed the attorney to be representing him. *See generally* Sarah Helene Duggin, *Internal Corporate Investigations: Legal Ethics, Professionalism and the Employee Interview*, 2003 COLUM. BUS. L. REV. 859. Professor Duggin reproduces Judge Frederick Lacey's suggested warning for use at the outset of all employee interviews conducted as part of internal corporate investigations:

> I am not your lawyer[;] I represent the corporation. It is the corporation's interests I have been retained to serve. You are entitled to have your own lawyer. If you cannot afford a lawyer, the corporation may or may not pay his fee. You may wish to consult with him before you confer with me. Among other things, you may wish to claim the privilege against self-incrimination. You may wish not to talk to me at all.
>
> What you tell me, if it relates to the performance of your duties, and is confidential, will be privileged. The privilege, however, requires explanation. It is not your privilege to claim. It is the corporation's privilege. Thus, not only can I tell, I must tell, others in the

corporation what you have told me, if it is necessary to enable me to provide the legal services to the corporation that has retained it has retained me to provide.

Moreover, the corporation can waive its privilege and thus, the president, or I, or someone else, can disclose to the authorities what you tell me if the corporation decides to waive its privilege.

Also, if I find wrongdoing, I am under certain obligations to report it to the Board of Directors and perhaps the stockholders.

Finally, the fact that our conversation is privileged does not mean that what you did or said is protected from disclosure just because you tell me about it. You may be subpoenaed, for example, and required to tell what you did, or said or observed, even though you told me about it.

Do you understand?

Id. at 945-46. Judge Lacey dubbed this an "Adnarim" warning — "Miranda" spelled backward. While it is not constitutionally required (certainly not outside the public sector), it is ethically required in some circumstances and will usually be good practice. Those who resist any standard warning agree that it dispels any possible confusion about the relationship of the investigator to the witness but stress the risk is that it will discourage frank disclosure by the employee. Do you think that Davis and Weaver would favor providing such a warning? Wouldn't the warning tend to raise witness defenses, especially in the first, putting-the-witness-at-ease stage they recommend? Which approach would you use?

b. The Employee as Witness or Target

In the typical internal investigation, the individuals interviewed will be current employees, although former employees and "outsiders" such as suppliers or independent contractors may sometimes be asked to provide information. With outsiders, the biggest problem for the investigator is obtaining cooperation when she has neither legal process nor a command-and-control relationship. With current employees, the attorney likely has the necessary leverage to obtain cooperation, simply because the employer can require the witness' participation. That leverage, however, creates its own risks, most notably the possibility that the employee participating under compulsion will not be truthful.

Some employees, of course, have incentives to cooperate or, at least, few disincentives. The person alleging sexual harassment, for example, will need to cooperate because of her responsibility to take advantage of her employer's mechanisms for correcting problems. True "innocent bystanders" in the firm may see no reason not to cooperate simply because they have little stake in the dispute and cooperation will clearly be expected as part of the job. But the person accused of wrongdoing or anyone who fears that he or she will be accused or blamed by the target, has more to worry about; and coworkers, subordinates, or supervisors of targets may be concerned about the consequences for them — whichever way the investigation proceeds.

Suppose an employee has been given Judge Lacey's Adnarim warning and has concerns about either being (or becoming) a target or risking the ire of the target or of those close to him. Can the warned worker refuse to cooperate, or at least demand that an attorney be present? In the union setting, federal labor law often accords members the right to have a union representative present. *See* Michael D. Moberly & Andrea G. Lisenbee, *Honing Our* Kraft?: *Reconciling Variations in the Remedial Treatment of*

Weingarten *Violations*, 21 Hofstra Lab. & Emp. L. J. 523 (2004). It is possible some such rights exist outside the union context, but the National Labor Relations Board has vacillated on this issue and currently does not recognize such a right. *See* Ann C. Hodges, *The Limits of Multiple Rights and Remedies: A Call for Revisiting the Law of the Workplace*, 22 Hofstra Lab. & Emp. L. J. 601 (2005); Christine Neylon O'Brien, *The NLRB Waffling on* Weingarten *Rights*, 37 Loy. U. Chi. L. J. 111 (2005). As a result, it is not uncommon for employers to prohibit witnesses from bringing their own representative to an investigation.

There is, of course, no legal compulsion for the employee to answer questions, and the employee could refuse to appear without her attorney. Further, at least in circumstances where criminal liability is possible (rare in sexual harassment investigation, but common in a wide range of other investigations such as investigations into embezzlement), the employee's statements — particularly untruthful or misleading ones — can be used against her in subsequent criminal proceedings. *See, e.g.*, Timothy P. Harkness & Darren LaVerne, *Lying to In-House Counsel May Lead to Prosecution*, Nat'l L. J. (July 27, 2006). Thus, a refusal to cooperate is sometimes the employee's wisest course of conduct. *See Hopp & Flesch, LLC v. Backstreet*, 123 P.3d 1176 (Colo. 2005) (attorney did not commit malpractice by advising employee not to participate in internal investigation because her statements could be used in subsequent criminal proceedings).

On the other hand, employees who do not cooperate risk discipline or termination and likely have little legal recourse against their employer. In the Mitchell investigation of Major League Baseball, for example, there was resistance from ballplayers for fear that information obtained would be subpoenaed by federal prosecutors and then used against the witness. Because of this risk, Senator Mitchell reportedly sought that MLB agree to sanction players who refused cooperation. *See* Chass, *supra*, at D1. Generally speaking, there is no exception to the at-will rule that would prevent an employer from discharging an employee who refuses to cooperate. *Merkel v. Scovill, Inc.*, 787 F.2d 174 (6th Cir. 1986); *Costello v. St. Francis Hosp.*, 258 F. Supp. 2d 144 (E.D.N.Y. 2003). Indeed, it might even be good cause sufficient to justify firing even where an employee has some preexisting right to job security. *Lybarger v. City of Los Angeles*, 206 Cal. Rptr. 727 (Ct. App. 1984).

Privacy claims are also likely unavailing since the employer's need to ascertain whether there was a violation of law or company policy will almost always trump any privacy concerns, provided the inquiry is not overly broad. These issues will be front and center in many sexual harassment investigations. Of course, limitations on how information is gathered during an investigation still apply, such as the general prohibition on polygraph tests and any constraints imposed by tort law. Thus, an employer could be subject to claims of false imprisonment or intentional infliction of emotional distress in the case of egregious employer misconduct. *But see Jones v. Dep't of Pub. Safety & Corr.*, 923 S. 2d 699 (La. Ct. App. 2005) (upholding discharge based in part on refusal of corrections officer to take a polygraph examination as part of a sexual harassment investigation).

The one situation where an employee could have greater legal protection is in a public employment setting. While a demand for cooperation on threat of dismissal seems permissible in the private sector, there is a split in authority as to whether a public entity's threat to discharge an employee who does not cooperate means any resulting statements were inadmissible as coerced self-incrimination. *See People v. Sapp*, 934 P.2d 1367, 1374 (Colo. 1997) (if the state created a belief that employees might be discharged for asserting the privilege against self-incrimination other than by stating that a witness was expected to testify truthfully, the resulting statement cannot be used against him). *But see Debnam v. North Carolina Dep't of Correction*, 432 S.E.2d 324 (N.C. 1993) (employer did not violate employee's right against self-incrimination by terminating him for refusing to answer questions; employer was not required to affirmatively inform employee of the law of use immunity before discharging him for refusing to answer questions that could have incriminated him).

c. Employee Right to Indemnification or a Defense?

Another issue raised by Judge Lacey's suggested warning is who will pay for the attorneys' fees of an employee who does seek the advice of counsel. The Adnarim warning assures the employee of the right to counsel, but goes on, "If you cannot afford a lawyer, the corporation may or may not pay his fee." This vagueness was probably intentional since prosecutors sometimes frown on advances of legal fees and even indemnification of employees, Duggin, *supra*, at 914-15, and internal investigators therefore tend to avoid committing on this issue prior to the conclusion of the investigation. For employees who cannot afford their own counsel, corporate punting on reimbursement may be the equivalent of saying no.

At any rate, problems can arise when the employer considers whether to provide for representation. First, assume the employer decides to do so, whether or not it feels obligated to take that step. Court Rule 1.8(f) controls cases in which an attorney "accept[s] compensation for representing a client from one other than the client,"[1] and, as indicated by the recent New Jersey Supreme Court case *In re State Grand Jury Investigation*, 983 A.2d 1097 (N.J. 2009), arranging for such representation can be problematic. In that case, the state sought to disqualify attorneys representing employees of a target firm because of how the firm had arranged for representation.

After reviewing Rule 1.8(f) and other ethical rules, the court ultimately rejected disqualification on the facts before it. However, it set forth six principles to govern such situations: (1) informed consent of the client, (2) barring the payer from "directing, regulating or interfering with the lawyer's professional judgment in representing his client," (3) no current attorney-client relationship between the lawyer and the payer, (4) prohibiting the lawyer from communicating with the payer "concerning the substance of the representation of his client," (5) processing payment of all attorney invoices as the payer would for its own counsel, and (6) barring the payer from ceasing to pay "without leave of court brought on prior written notice to the lawyer and the client." *Id.* at 495-97.

Although *In re State Grand Jury Investigation* arose in the criminal context, Rule 1.8(f) presumably applies to all situations where an employer pays the litigation expenses of its workers. Thus, attorneys would be well advised to take the Court's six factors into account when entering into any such relationship.

---

1. The rule provides:
　　　(f) A lawyer shall not accept compensation for representing a client from one other than the client unless:
　　　　　(1) the client gives informed consent;
　　　　　(2) there is no interference with the lawyer's independence of professional judgment or with the lawyer-client relationship; and
　　　　　(3) information relating to representation of a client is protected as required by RPC 1.6.

Assuming the employer is not willing to pay for counsel, the question is whether it has an obligation to do so. Whether any employee who does retain counsel, either for the investigation itself or any subsequent proceedings against him, has a right to indemnification is a complicated question, and may depend on whether the employer is in the public or private sector. In the public sector, state statutes often set the ground rules. *See, e.g., Prado v. State*, 186 N.J. 413, 895 A.2d 1154 (2006) (state statute required Attorney General to defend employees unless the Attorney General determined that challenged conduct was "not within the scope of employment," was due to "actual fraud, willful misconduct or actual malice," or would "create a conflict of interest between the State and the employee").

In the private sector, many state corporate statutes require mandatory indemnification, but they are usually limited to corporate "officers." Some statutes, however, are broad enough to reach ordinary employees. For example, an Illinois statute provides:

> To the extent that a present or former director, officer or *employee* of a corporation has been successful, on the merits or otherwise, in the defense of any action, suit or proceeding . . . such person shall be indemnified against expenses (including attorneys' fees) actually and reasonably incurred by such person in connection therewith, if the person acted in good faith and in a manner he or she reasonably believed to be in, or not opposed to, the best interests of the corporation.

805 ILCS 5/8.75(c) (emphasis added). Other states reach similar results under common-law principles. The RESTATEMENT (SECOND) OF AGENCY, for example, would impose on a principal a duty to indemnify the agent if there is an agreement to do so. RESTATEMENT (SECOND) OF AGENCY § 438; *see also Harris v. Howard Univ., Inc.*, 28 F. Supp. 2d 1, 14 (D.D.C. 1998) (finding pursuant to university by-laws that employer was required to indemnify plaintiff vice president for acts committed in good faith but not for those attributable to gross negligence); Kevin Oates, *Professor Defend Thyself: The Failure of Universities to Defend and Indemnify Their Faculty*, 39 WILLAMETTE L. REV. 1063 (2003).

But a formal agreement is not necessary. The Restatement goes on:

> (2) In the absence of terms to the contrary in the agreement of employment, the principal has a duty to indemnify the agent where the agent
>> (a) makes a payment authorized or made necessary in executing the principal's affairs or, unless he is officious, one beneficial to the principal, or
>> (b) suffers a loss which, because of their relation, it is fair that the principal should bear.

Section 439 of the Restatement is even more specific, providing that a

> principal is subject to a duty to exonerate an agent who is not barred by the illegality of his conduct to indemnify him for . . . (c) payments of damages to third persons which he is required to make on account of the authorized performance of an act which constitutes a tort or a breach of contract; (d) expenses of defending actions by third persons brought because of the agent's authorized conduct, such actions being unfounded but not brought in bad faith.

The underlying notion is akin to unjust enrichment. That is, to the extent that an employee is sued for pursuing the interests of his employer, the costs of defense are ones that are expended on behalf of that employer, and the employer has been unjustly enriched to the extent the employee, not the employer, has incurred them.

Notice, however, that the Restatement's requirement to repay the costs of a defense is subject to the limitation that the agent not be "barred by the illegality of his conduct." *Id.*; *see also* § 440 (no duty to indemnify agent for negligent behavior, conduct known by agent to violate law, or losses resulting in no benefit to principal). Other sections of the Illinois statute *permit*, but do not *require* indemnification even if the employer is found to have committed wrong. Thus, under both state statutory and common-law indemnification, it may be critical to indemnification that the employee prevails in defending himself on the underlying claim. *See, e.g., Farmers Ins. Group v. County of Santa Clara*, 906 P.2d 440, 450-51 (Cal. 1995) (indemnification of harasser not required under state statute requiring indemnification by public employers when harassment not within employee's scope of employment and does not serve employer's interests).

A further problem is whether the employer is required to *advance* attorneys' fees, as opposed to repaying such fees when they have been incurred. As a practical matter, an employer refusing to pay fees until the conclusion of the litigation will put enormous pressure on most employees, and, in complex cases, it may well result in the employee being unable to retain an attorney. Thus, where the employer and employee's interests align, it is in the employer's interest to advance fees, as in the New Jersey *Grand Jury* case, although there is little legal compulsion on employers to do so. The exception is where the obligation to indemnify stems from a contractual commitment or a provision of the company's by-laws, as is sometimes the case with officers and high-level employees. *See Homestore, Inc. v. Tafeen*, 888 A.2d 204, 211-14 (Del. 2005) (upholding advancement of litigation expenses to former officer required by corporate by-laws and rejecting argument that company need not advance litigation expenses because employee personally profited by alleged wrongdoing and had taken steps that made it harder for the corporation to collect on his undertaking); *International Airport Ctrs., L.L.C. v. Citrin*, 455 F.3d 749 (7th Cir. 2006) (rejecting an employer's effort to enjoin an employee's action seeking advancement under Delaware law). Since in most cases advancement of fees is voluntary, employers may condition their commitment on an undertaking of the employee to repay the moneys advanced if he is ultimately determined to have committed wrongdoing.

Finally, it is not clear that any of these principles would apply when an employee who seeks recovery of costs of the counsel in the course of an internal investigation. The indemnification issue is cast in terms of shifting the costs from the agent to the principal when a third party sues. While the right might apply even in the absence of formal proceedings, such as a settlement for "nuisance value," the internal investigation pits the employee-witness against the employer, not against any third party. This is particularly true where the investigation is in response to a harassment complaint. In such instances, the employer conducts the investigation with hopes of taking corrective action that will enable it to avoid vicarious liability in a subsequent lawsuit by the complaining party.

Should the internal investigation result in the discharge of the employee, who is then sued by the third party whose complaint may have triggered the investigation, a statutory or common law right of indemnification may well apply but may be dependent upon the employee being exonerated in the course of the proceedings. Further, to the extent the former employer refuses to advance attorneys' fees and costs, the former employee will be in a very difficult situation — regardless of the theoretic right to indemnification.

The bottom line, of course, is that the employee who is interviewed during, or is even the target of, an internal investigation is often faced with a number of unpalatable alternatives. The employee can refuse to cooperate and risk discipline or dismissal; the employee can cooperate and risk discipline, dismissal, and even the use of statements she makes in later criminal proceedings against her. The employee can insist on an attorney to help her decide on her course of action, and will probably (but not certainly) have the request accommodated, but she may well be responsible for the attorneys' fees involved. Should the investigation result in her discharge, she will probably have no right against her former employee, except perhaps a right to indemnification should she prevail in any suit brought against her.

PROBLEMS

13-3. You have been consulted by an individual you know slightly from the local gym. He tells you that he is a midlevel manager at the local branch of Pal-Mart, a chain of superstores. He has had some recent disagreements with a female subordinate. Yesterday, he was told by a Human Resource specialist that he was being suspended temporarily with pay pending Pal-Mart's investigation of a complaint of sexual harassment. He was told to expect a call from an attorney with a large firm in the nearby city, who would be handling the investigation.

He has not been provided any further information, but he is sure that the complaint was made by his subordinate. He wants to know how to proceed. What further questions do you have for him? Log on to the Web site, ask your questions, and advise him in light of the answers you receive.

13-4. You have been retained by Pal-Mart as special counsel to investigate the matter raised in Problem 13-1. You have received a "demand letter." Log on to the Web site to obtain a copy of the complaint. Sketch out your strategy for investigating the matter.

B. CONDUCTING LAYOFFS AND OBTAINING RELEASE AGREEMENTS

One important risk management technique for employers is to obtain contractual releases of liability from terminated employees. It is generally understood that employees cannot prospectively waive substantive claims under any of the federal employment statutes; such legislation would be rendered wholly inoperative if employees could be required to waive or release rights as a condition of employment. *See Alexander v. Gardner-Denver Co.*, 415 U.S. 36, 51 (1974) ("[W]e think it clear that there can be no prospective waiver of an employee's rights under Title VII."). However, once a cause of action arises, the employee may release any claims he or she may have subject to certain conditions. Effective release agreements are typically obtained by providing terminated employees with severance pay contingent upon signing a waiver of rights.

We saw a variation on this in *Watson*, where Home Depot obtained the alleged harasser's "resignation" by providing him five months of severance pay.

Such "buy outs" often occur in cases of individual terminations, and they can be notorious when high-level executives leave major companies with "golden handshakes." *See In re the Walt Disney Co. Deriv. Litig.*, 906 A.2d 27 (Del. 2006) (rejecting breach of duty claims against board of directors for decisions to hire and shortly thereafter, fire the CEO with multimillion-dollar buy-out). However, much more modest packages are particularly common in the context of large-scale reductions in force ("RIFs"). RIFs pose many legal and practical challenges for employers. Companies must ensure they do not select employees for layoff based on an impermissible criterion, such as age. In addition, they must comply with certain statutory requirements, such as providing advance notice of layoffs. For example, the federal Workers Adjustment and Retraining Act, 29 U.S.C. § 2101 et seq. (2006) ("WARN"), requires covered employers engaging in "plant closings" or "mass layoffs" to usually provide 60 days' notice to affected workers. Perhaps most importantly, employers must be cognizant that the financial, social, and emotional effects of layoffs can be devastating to the affected employees and in the case of a closing, may have repercussions throughout the community where the company is located. Even smaller-scale layoffs may negatively affect the morale and productivity of those workers who remain employed. For all of these reasons, careful advance planning can be critical in maintaining a successful working environment post-layoff as well as avoiding liability to those who are "let go."

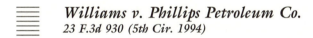

Williams v. Phillips Petroleum Co.
23 F.3d 930 (5th Cir. 1994)

WILLIAMS, J.

[In 1992, Phillips Petroleum Company, Phillips Gas Holding Company, Inc. ("PGHC"), and Phillips 66 Company, a division of Phillips Petroleum Company, reduced their work forces at their Houston Chemical Complex ("HCC") and laid off over 500 employees at their Bartlesville, Oklahoma, location. PGHC provided the Bartlesville workers 60 days' notice prior to the reduction in force. The defendants also laid off 27 workers at several locations in Houston to whom they did not provide notice. Six of the laid off Houston workers (the "original plaintiffs") brought suit alleging that defendants had violated WARN by failing to provide 60 days' notice. Subsequently, four of the workers laid off from the Bartlesville location (the "Bartlesville plaintiffs") sought to join the suit. All of the original and Bartlesville plaintiffs signed releases in connection with their terminations in exchange for what the employer described as enhanced layoff benefits. The district court refused to permit joinder of the Bartlesville plaintiffs and awarded summary judgment to the employer on the original plaintiffs' claims.]

III

A

The district court rendered summary judgment because no mass layoff occurred at the single sites of employment where the original plaintiffs worked. . . .

WARN requires covered employers to provide "affected employees" notice of a mass layoff. "Affected employees" include "employees who may reasonably be expected to experience an employment loss as a consequence of a proposed plant closing or mass layoff by their employer." 29 U.S.C. § 2101(a)(5). A "mass layoff" is defined as any employment loss at a single site of employment that involves one-third of the employees at that site and at least fifty employees, or at least 500 employees. 29 U.S.C. § 2101(a)(3); 20 C.F.R. § 639.3(c). If a "mass layoff" occurs, the employer must provide written notice to each affected employee at least sixty days prior to the layoff and inform various state and local officials of the mass layoff. 29 U.S.C. § 2102. An employer who violates WARN is liable for back pay, lost benefits, civil penalties, and attorneys' fees. 29 U.S.C. § 2104.

The statute does not define a "single site of employment." The rules promulgated by the Secretary of Labor provide that "[n]on-contiguous sites in the same geographic area which do not share the same staff or operational purpose should not be considered a single site." 20 C.F.R. § 639.3(i)(4). . . .

The Houston and Bartlesville layoffs cannot be aggregated to bootstrap the Houston plaintiffs over the WARN minimum required for a mass layoff. . . . It is not plausible, under any reasonable or good-faith reading of the regulations, that the Houston and Bartlesville plants — located in different states and hundreds of miles apart — could be considered a "single site" for purposes of WARN.

Employees were not rotated between the different sites, and the locations did not share staff and equipment. *See* 20 C.F.R. § 639.3(i)(3). No other "unusual circumstances" have been alleged that would support classifying the two plants as a "single site." *See* 20 C.F.R. § 639.3(i)(8); *Carpenters Dist. Counsel of New Orleans v. Dillard*, 15 F.3d 1275, 1290 (5th 1994). . . . The Bartlesville layoffs, accordingly, are irrelevant to the issue of whether the Houston employees were entitled to notice under WARN.

No mass layoff occurred at the single sites of employment where the original plaintiffs worked. Five of the plaintiffs worked at HCC's operations in three different locations in and around Houston. HCC laid off twenty-seven employees over a ten-month period. One of the named plaintiffs worked for PGHC in Houston; PGHC laid off eight employees who worked at that site. The layoffs at HCC and PGHC were not mass layoffs as defined by the Act, as the number of employees laid off did not meet the fifty-employee minimum. Thus, the Houston employees were not entitled to WARN notification. . . .

B

The district court also rendered summary judgment for Phillips because the plaintiffs had signed releases covering the allegations made in their complaint. . . . [2] Normally the release of federal claims is governed by federal law. *See, e.g., O'Hare v. Global Natural Resources, Inc.*, 898 F.2d 1015, 1017 (5th Cir. 1990) (Age Discrimination in Employment Act ("ADEA")); *Rogers v. General Elec. Co.*, 781 F.2d 452, 454 (5th Cir. 1986) (title VII of the Civil Rights Act of 1964). Public policy favors voluntary

---

2. Although this discussion is unnecessary to the issue of whether WARN was violated, given our holding in part III.A., *supra*, we include it as a further indication that this action is frivolous.

settlement of claims and enforcement of releases, *Rogers*, but a release of an employment or employment discrimination claim is valid only if it is "knowing" and "voluntary," *Alexander v. Gardner-Denver Co.*, 415 U.S. 36, 52 n.15 (1974). Once a party establishes that his opponent signed a release that addresses the claims at issue, received adequate consideration, and breached the release, the opponent has the burden of demonstrating that the release was invalid because of fraud, duress, material mistake, or some other defense. We examine the totality of circumstances to determine whether the releasor has established an appropriate defense. *O'Hare.*

1.

Each original plaintiff signed a release shortly after his or her termination of employment. The releases stated that signing the release was a condition to participation in the company's enhanced supplemental layoff pay plan, advised the employee to consult an attorney, gave ample time to consider the release, and specifically covered all claims relating to the individual's employment or layoff. The Bartlesville plaintiffs signed similar releases.

The requirements of WARN pertain to an individual's employment and termination, issues addressed in the releases. Phillips provided enhanced benefits for those employees who signed the releases. These benefits were in addition to the basic severance plan benefits that the employees would have received regardless of whether they had signed the releases. The original plaintiffs are making claims on matters addressed in their release, and the Bartlesville plaintiffs attempted to join the lawsuit that involved claims on matters addressed in their release. Thus, all elements of a valid release are present.

Williams has provided no credible evidence that the releases were obtained by fraud or duress. There is no genuine issue of material fact that the releases were valid.

Williams contends that the releases were invalid because they did not mention WARN. This argument is meritless. There is no obligation under WARN or the common law for the defendants to mention WARN for the releases to be valid. The releases stated that they included all claims relating to the "time of my employment or to my layoff. . . ." WARN applies to layoffs and the releases addressed all claims related to the plaintiffs' layoffs; thus, the releases barred WARN claims. *See Fair v. International Flavors & Fragrances, Inc.*, 905 F.2d 1114, 1117 (7th Cir. 1990) (holding that a release of claims relating to employment barred claim under Employee Retirement and Income Security Act of 1974 ("ERISA")).

Plaintiffs also argue that the waivers did not comply with the Older Workers Benefit Protection Act ("OWBPA"), 29 U.S.C. § 626(f). Plaintiffs have asserted no age discrimination claim, and their proffered analogy between WARN and the ADEA does not survive scrutiny. The OWBPA places specific requirements on waivers of age discrimination claims in order for them to be considered knowing and voluntary. This statute is a change from the common law, and there is no similar obligation imposed on employers under WARN.

Williams contends that the waivers are invalid under a totality of the circumstances test. She claims that the combination of five factors makes the waivers invalid, but she identifies no precedent suggesting that these factors are dispositive. Williams carried the burden to demonstrate that there was a genuine issue of material fact on a defense to the validity of the releases. She was obligated to produce some evidence of fraud, duress, or other basis for holding the release invalid. She has not done so, thus summary judgment was appropriate.

Even if we accept Williams's statement of the totality of circumstances test, she cannot prevail. She identifies several elements to consider: (1) a plaintiff's education and business experience; (2) the role of each plaintiff and class member in deciding the terms of the release; (3) the clarity of the agreement and all related documents referred to in the releases; (4) whether each plaintiff and class member was represented by or consulted with an attorney; and (5) the amount of time each plaintiff and class member had possession of or access to the release before signing it.

Concerning the plaintiffs' education and business experience, there [is] no evidence suggesting that they could not read or understand the releases. The cases relied upon by the plaintiffs are distinguishable by whether the individual who signed the release understood the claims released. There is nothing in the record establishing a genuine issue of material fact that the plaintiffs did not know what they were doing.

Plaintiffs argue that none of them negotiated the terms of the releases. There is no evidence that plaintiffs were denied an opportunity to negotiate, nor that they were given a "take it or leave it" offer. The releases informed each employee that he should consult a lawyer and allowed a reasonable period, in most instances up to forty-five days, to consider the releases. The plaintiffs signed the releases and never asserted in their declarations that Phillips had precluded them from negotiating. There is no evidence sufficient to create a genuine issue of material fact.

The releases were clear, simple, and easily understood. The release precluded all claims related to the plaintiffs' "employment" or "layoff." This is not technical jargon, and it covers the plaintiffs' WARN claims. The plaintiffs do not indicate what provisions could have been incomprehensible to them, as they were written in plain English. There is also no evidence of duress that could have forced them to sign involuntarily.

The plaintiffs also claim that the releases should be invalidated because the defendants presented no evidence that each plaintiff and class member actually consulted with an attorney. The releases signed by the plaintiffs stated:

> You should thoroughly review and understand the effect of the release before signing it. To the extent that you have any claims covered by this release, you will be waiving potentially valuable rights by signing. You are also advised to discuss this release with your lawyer.

Thus, defendants advised the plaintiffs to consult a lawyer. Plaintiffs suggest that Phillips should have offered to supply a lawyer, but they offer no authority imposing this duty. Even without signing the releases, plaintiffs were entitled to substantial layoff benefits that could have been used to finance a lawyer, either individually or jointly. It is not Phillips's fault that the plaintiffs chose not to consult a lawyer after being advised to do so. Plaintiffs do not contest the final element of the test, as they were given as much as forty-five days to consider the releases.

2.

Even if a release is tainted by misrepresentation or duress, it is ratified if the releasor retains the consideration after learning that the release is voidable. A person who signs a release, then sues his or her employer for matters covered under the release, is obligated to return the consideration. Offering to tender back the consideration after obtaining relief in the lawsuit would be insufficient to avoid a finding of ratification. *Grillet v. Sears, Roebuck & Co.*, 927 F.2d 217, 220-21 (5th Cir. 1991).

For signing the releases, the original plaintiffs as a group received $ 210,853.65 in consideration in an enhanced plan benefits and $56,632.38 in basic plan benefits. The original plaintiffs did not return the consideration to the defendants, even after making claims that the releases were voidable. Thus, the plaintiffs ratified the releases even if, *arguendo*, they were not knowingly and voluntarily signed. *Grillet.* . . .

NOTES

1. *A Tale of Several Regimes.* Understanding when a release agreement is effective depends on the applicable legal standard, which varies depending on the substantive claim being released. *Williams* deals with the standard for the validity of releases under WARN, a federal statute that does not deal explicitly with requirements for releasing claims. In upholding the plaintiffs' releases, the court applies a general "knowing and voluntary standard," which it drew from a Title VII case, *Alexander v. Gardner-Denver Co.*, 415 U.S. 36, 52, n.15 (1974). This test, elaborated in a variety of ways by the lower courts, applies to WARN, Title VII, the Americans with Disabilities Act ("ADA"), the Family and Medical Leave Act ("FMLA"), and ERISA.

In contrast, some statutes — most notably the ADEA — contain provisions directly governing release agreements or have been interpreted to impose special requirements. *Williams* alludes to, but declines to apply, the more demanding regime that exists under the Older Workers Benefit Protection Act. OWBPA is a 1991 amendment to the ADEA, which requires that a release be "knowing and voluntary" and that, "at a minimum," the employer comply with a variety of procedural requirements including:

(A) the waiver is part of an agreement between the individual and the employer that is written in a manner calculated to be understood by such individual, or by the average individual eligible to participate;

(B) the waiver specifically refers to rights or claims arising under this chapter;

(C) the individual does not waive rights or claims that may arise after the date the waiver is executed;

(D) the individual waives rights or claims only in exchange for consideration in addition to anything of value to which the individual already is entitled;

(E) the individual is advised in writing to consult with an attorney prior to executing the agreement;

(F) (i) the individual is given a period of at least 21 days within which to consider the agreement; or

(ii) if a waiver is requested in connection with an exit incentive or other employment termination program offered to a group or class of employees, the individual is given a period of at least 45 days within which to consider the agreement;

(G) the agreement provides that for a period of at least 7 days following the execution of such agreement, the individual may revoke the agreement, and the agreement shall not become effective or enforceable until the revocation period has expired. . . .

29 U.S.C. §626(f)(1). More specific disclosures are also required "if a waiver is requested in connection with an exit incentive or other employment termination program offered to a group or class of employees," *id.* at (H), and the statute has particular provisions governing settlement once an EEOC charge or suit has been filed. *Id.* at §626(f)(2). Even more protective of employees is the Fair Labor Standards Act, which generally deems waivers and settlement of claims unenforceable without Department of Labor supervision. *See* Evan Hudson-Plush, Note, *WARN's Place in the FLSA/Employment Discrimination Dichotomy: Why a Warning Cannot Be Waived*, 27 Cardozo L. Rev. 2929, 2945-48 (2006).

Finally, where the underlying claims involve only state law, a release is likely to be subjected to an even lower level of scrutiny than would be true under the general "knowing and voluntary" standard applied in *Williams* under WARN. Most likely, the validity of such releases would be determined as a matter of ordinary contract law, although state-to-state variations are possible depending in part on the state right at issue.

   2. *Comparing Standards: "Knowing and Voluntary" versus Common Law.* Invalidating a release agreement under basic contract principles can be quite difficult. The requisite consideration and assent are generally present and easy to establish: the employer provides severance or other benefits in exchange for the release, and both parties, or at least the employee, sign a written agreement. The only way for an employee to void the contract is to demonstrate a defense like fraud or duress. And, as the "tender back" discussion in *Williams* indicates, exercising a right to void a contract may require the return of the consideration received.

   While a few federal courts treat the enforceability of releases as a matter of normal contract principles, the vast majority apply some version of a "totality of the circumstances" test to all non-OWBPA claims to determine whether a waiver is knowing and voluntary where federal statutory rights are at stake. That test looks to a number of factors, as one commentator explains:

> To determine whether a person's consent is knowing and voluntary under the totality of the circumstances, courts apply a list of factors: the person's education and business experience, the person's role in determining the release's provisions, the release's clarity and specificity, the time the person had to review and consider the release, whether the person read the release and considered its terms before signing it, whether the person knew or should have known his or her rights upon executing the release, whether the person was represented by an attorney or had other independent advice, whether there was consideration for the release, and whether the person's consent was induced by improper conduct by the employer, including whether the employer encouraged or discouraged the person from consulting with an attorney. This list is not exhaustive, and the absence of any one factor is not dispositive. The factors are not to be treated as a checklist, and courts do not insist on rigid adherence to them.

Daniel P. O'Gorman, *A State of Disarray: The "Knowing and Voluntary" Standard for Releasing Claims Under Title VII of the Civil Rights Act of 1964*, 8 U. Pa. J. Lab. & Emp. L. 73, 85-88 (2005); *see also* Craig Robert Senn, *Knowing and Voluntary Waivers of Federal Employment Claims: Replacing the Totality of Circumstances Test with a "Waiver Certainty" Test*, 58 Fla. L. Rev. 305 (2006) (critiquing the uncertainty produced by multi-factor test, especially because of those factors not within "employer control."). Which standard does *Williams* apply? Contract? Totality of the circumstances? Something in between?

3. *Comparing Standards: "Knowing and Voluntary" versus OWBPA.* There is obviously a large overlap between the factors used in the knowing and voluntary standard and the requirements OWBPA prescribes, but OWBPA is harder-edged. For example, while one factor under the knowing and voluntary test is the time the employee had to consider the release, OWBPA requires a minimum of 21/45 days and also prescribes a week's "cooling off" period for revocation. Courts have tended to require strict compliance with OWBPA. *See Am. Airlines, Inc. v. Cardoza-Rodriguez,* 133 F.3d 111 (1st Cir. 1998) (invalidating release for failure to explicitly advise employees to consult an attorney).

From a positivist perspective, it is easy to explain why ADEA claims are subject to more stringent requirements than claims under most other federal statutes — Congress so provided. But what justifies OWBPA's imposition of these highly specialized criteria? In other words, what is so special about releases of age discrimination claims in general and releases of such claims following an RIF in particular? Should comparable requirements be placed on other types of waivers, such as those in *Williams,* or ordinary severance agreements? What about waivers of procedural rights, like the right to a jury trial or agreements to shorten applicable statutes of limitations? We will revisit this last question when we look at pre-dispute arbitration agreements in the next section.

4. *Back to the Common Law.* Despite the development of specialized standards, the common law is not entirely irrelevant to assessing a release either under the knowing and voluntary standard or under OWBPA. For example, both incorporate the requirement of "consideration," and all releases are subject to contractual defenses. Note that *Williams* considers and rejects the applicability of the defenses of fraud and duress. The presence of undue influence, *see Odorizzi v. Bloomfield School Dist.,* 54 Cal. Rptr. 533 (Ct. App. 1966), unconscionability, see discussion on page 949, or mistake could negate a release as well. These defenses may be relevant even in the ADEA context since OWBPA provides a floor, not a ceiling, and it is possible that an employer could comply with the letter of the statutory obligations but still mislead or over-persuade the employee in a way that triggers a common law contract defense. But, as the *Williams* court stresses, the common law places the burden of persuasion on the party challenging the release. Once the employer shows offer and acceptance and consideration, the contract is established, albeit subject to the employee proving some invalidating factor. In contrast, under the OWBPA, the burden is on the employer to demonstrate its compliance with the statutory requirements.

Contract is also an appropriate source of law for interpreting and applying a release agreement. Assuming the agreement is valid pursuant to the appropriate standard, contract principles will determine whether the release covers a particular claim, the terms of the employer's payment commitment, and other issues about scope and application of the agreement. *See, e.g., Riley v. American Family Mutual Ins.,* 881 F.2d 368, 373 (7th Cir. 1989) (finding it "unnecessary to create a distinct federal body of law" to interpret release agreement where "plain reading" indicated plaintiff had persevered only state administrative discrimination charge and waived right to *de novo* review by federal court). In cases of high-level employees, some of whom sign written agreements that cover issues of severance and layoff at the outset of employment, a release can raise contract interpretation questions similar to those explored in Chapter 3, such as whether termination was for cause or whether other contractual contingencies have been triggered. *See, e.g., Dell Computer Corp. v. Rodriguez,* 390 F.3d 377 (5th Cir. 2004) (parol evidence should be admitted to determine whether prior wrongdoing of CEO permitted employer to withhold stock under separation agreement).

5. *What About Bargaining Power?* In *Williams*, the plaintiffs, unable to prove fraud or duress, urged that their releases should be void in light of their lack of sophistication, limited education, and inability to negotiate vis-à-vis the employer. Why do you think the Fifth Circuit rejects this line of argument? Is the court rejecting the contention that the "totality of the circumstances" test applies to waivers of WARN rights? Or is it concluding that the plaintiffs failed to make their case under that standard? At one point, the court disparages the contention that the release agreement was a "take it or leave it offer," finding no evidence to support this claim. Is the court suggesting that the employees had more power to bargain than they realized? It seems unlikely that Phillips would have negotiated different terms with different employees, but that is not impossible. Is the court implicitly stating that the ability to dicker over terms is important to the validity of a contract? Or is the court simply unsympathetic to the plaintiffs given that they stood to gain $2 million in additional compensation and benefits under the release? Could an argument like the one advanced by the plaintiffs work in the OWBPA context, assuming the technical requirements of the statute have been satisfied?

6. *The Two-way Release.* While the main benefit for workers of signing a release is severance pay, there are sometimes other advantages, as where the release is reciprocal (waiving claims by the employer against the employee) or where it supersedes past agreements imposing duties on the employee. In *Avery Dennison Corp., v. Naimo*, 25 IER Cases 690 (N.D. Ill. 2006), the parties entered into an agreement terminating their employment relationship; the writing contained a merger clause stating that it superseded all prior agreements, including the employee's written employment agreement, which contained a 12-month noncompete. On the basis of that clause, a court dismissed the employer's subsequent attempt to enforce the noncompete against the employee, who began contacting former customers post-termination. The lesson for employers, as always, is to carefully read all the relevant documents. The employer in *Avery* most likely sought to merge the prior employment contract into the separation agreement in order to avoid any future employee claims to salary or benefits it owed during employment; in the process it failed to consider the prior contract's noncompetition clause. *Avery* also offers a reminder to employees. Getting laid off is difficult enough without a noncompete hampering one's prospects of re-employment. The presentation of a termination agreement is a good time to try to secure other benefits besides severance, such as a release from such commitments.

7. *"Good" Releases Crowding out "Bad" Ones.* Although *Williams* holds that OWBPA does not control outside the ADEA, risk-averse employers are well advised to satisfy the more demanding standards of OWBPA whenever they seek releases. Most releases, therefore, are structured along OWBPA lines. As a practical matter, this allows the employer to develop a single standardized release agreement and set of procedures that human resources personnel can use in all cases, without having to make individual judgments about whether a particular termination might implicate the ADEA. In addition, abiding by the OWBPA requirements provides enhanced certainty that the release will hold up if challenged since any release that satisfies OWBPA is almost certain to satisfy other tests. For employees, this means that those offered a release will have the opportunity to review, consider, and even revoke their agreement, effectively

reaping the benefits of the OWBPA irrespective of whether they raise ADEA claims or are even protected by the statute. *See, e.g., Neely v. Good Samaritan Hosp.*, 345 F. App'x 39 (6th Cir. 2009) (release that granted worker time to consider the agreement consistent with OWBPA was properly revoked by race discrimination plaintiff notwithstanding fact that she never raised age discrimination claim).

8. *Ratification and Tendering Back.* *Williams* states that even if a release is subject to a valid contract defense, the employee will "ratify" the agreement if she retains the benefits of the agreement (the severance pay) despite learning the release is voidable. In short, a plaintiff who seeks to challenge a release must tender back the consideration received where only the knowing and voluntary standard governs. In contrast, ratification is not possible under OWBPA if the release is inadequate; there is therefore no need to tender back the consideration received in order to file an ADEA suit. *See Oubre v. Entergy Operations*, 522 U.S. 422, 427 (1998) (rejecting any requirement of ratification and requiring return of consideration: any such rule "would frustrate the statute's practical operation as well as its formal command" since discharged employees will often have spent the money received and therefore be unable to tender back).

9. *Waivers of Administrative Rights.* Although employees can release their rights to sue under the federal discrimination laws, including the ADEA where the OWBPA waiver requirements are met, employees may not release their rights to file administrative charges with the EEOC. *See* 29 U.S.C. §629(f)(4); *EEOC v. Cosmair, Inc.*, 821 F.2d 1085 (5th 1987) (waiver of right to file administrative charges, if covered by employee's release, would be void against public policy). Why are releases of administrative claims so objectionable, particularly if the waiver complies with the stringent requirements of the OWBPA? What public policies are at stake with such releases that are not implicated by the employee's promise not to sue?

For employers, the distinction between waivers of legal and administrative rights is an important one. To the extent a release provision purports to waive administrative rights, that clause is generally considered void, and the employer may not treat the filing of an administrative charge as a breach of the agreement. The effect of such a provision on the rest of the release, however, is unclear. *Compare Wastak v. Lehigh Valley Health Network*, 342 F.3d 281, 292 (3d Cir. 2003) (finding administrative rights waiver severable and employee's promise not to sue enforceable notwithstanding the invalid clause) *with Bogacz v. MTP Prods., Inc.*, 694 F. Supp. 2d 400, 406 (W.D. Pa. 2010) (suggesting that release containing such a waiver of administrative rights could be misleading and therefore not knowing and voluntary under OWBPA regulations).

10. *Will Uncle Sam Foot Part of the Bill?* From an employee's perspective, a question that often arises is whether a settlement can be structured to reduce the tax consequences, especially where large amounts are paid out in a given year. Other than stretching payouts over several years to avoid pushing the employee into a higher income bracket, the answer is usually no. Severance pay, like the wages it replaces, is taxable. Indeed, the Internal Revenue Code, 26 U.S.C §104(a)(2), generally excludes from gross income only "the amount of any damages received (whether by suit or agreement) on account of personal injuries or sickness. As a result, not only severance but most employment-related recoveries—back pay, front pay, recoveries for emotional harm, etc.—became taxable. Only in a few instances, for example, physical assault or physical sexual harassment, may it be possible to characterize some or all of the settlement in such a way as to exclude it from taxable income. Further, the employee's attorney should alert her client that if proceeds of a settlement are taxable, the employer may legally withhold taxes on any payment made. *Rivera v. Baker West, Inc.*, 430 F.3d 1253 (9th Cir. 2005).

Taxation issues also loom large where attorney's fees are involved. Until recently, these were taxable to the employee as income, *Comm'r of Internal Revenue v. Banks*, 543 U.S. 426 (2005); although such fees were usually deductible, limitations on deductions and the Alternative Minimum Tax often meant that employees paid taxes on the fees they recovered after litigation or upon settlement and on the fees paid to their attorney. Adam Liptak, *Tax Bill Exceeds Award to Officer in Sex Bias Suit*, N.Y. TIMES, Aug. 11, 2002, §1, p. 18. Congress responded to this problem in the American Jobs Creation Act of 2004, which amended 26 U.S.C. §62 (19) to allow deduction of fees and costs, whether received in litigation or settlement, free of the restrictions that earlier applied.

PROBLEM

13-5. Harold Brown was a 59-year-old district sales manager for AMF Bowling Products Group. After 26 years of service, he was offered early retirement. Harold requested and was given the opportunity to take the offer to an attorney. After consultation, he accepted the offer by executing the following "Severance Agreement":

I. Resignation

I, HAROLD BROWN do voluntarily submit my resignation from AMF Bowling Products effective August 1.

II. Severance Payout

Based on 1.5 weeks of pay per completed year of service, severance pay will total $30,581. (37.5 weeks). . . .

III. Waiver

I, HAROLD BROWN, accept the severance entitlement outlined above and understand that this represents the entire severance entitlement and no other provisions are express or implied. I accept the terms and conditions of this entitlement and release AMF from any outstanding obligations or litigation in this matter.

Harold has come to believe that he was pushed to resign because of his age and would like to pursue litigation. How would you advise him on the question whether the above agreement precludes suit? Besides possible procedural defects under the OWBPA, do you see any contract-based arguments for challenging the agreement?

Note on Employer Obligations and Exceptions
Under WARN

As *Williams* makes clear, an employer contemplating a RIF must take a number of specific procedural steps in planning and executing a layoff. While an effective release will cover a multitude of legal mistakes, employers must first attempt to comply with the governing statutory requirements. With respect to WARN, the first question is whether a proposed action requires notice. Determining whether WARN's notice provisions are triggered often turns on a number of technical questions. Generally speaking, WARN requires employers with 100 or more employees to provide 60 days' notice to affected employees in the event of a mass layoff or plant closing. As *Williams* demonstrates, whether an RIF constitutes a "mass layoff" at "a single site" may result in litigation. While Phillips Petroleum engaged in a "mass layoff" at its Oklahoma location, its layoffs in Houston did not meet the statutory minimum.

Another common area of WARN litigation is the various exceptions to its notice requirement. There are two principal exceptions. In the case of a plant closing, an employer is excused from the 60-day requirement where providing notice would impede its ability to obtain capital or business that would enable the employer to avoid the closing. In the case of both plant closings and layoffs, an employer is excused where the closing or layoff is due to business circumstances that were not reasonably foreseeable.

A high-profile example of a layoff implicating the latter exception is *Roquet v. Arthur Andersen*, 398 F.3d 585 (7th Cir 2005). Workers who lost their jobs following the Department of Justice's ("DOJ") indictment of Arthur Andersen in connection with the 2001 collapse of Enron brought suit against the accounting firm alleging violations of WARN in failing to provide them with advance notice of their layoffs. Arthur Andersen defended by arguing that the DOJ indictment and subsequent demise of the firm were not reasonably foreseeable. The plaintiffs countered that, once the DOJ began investigating Arthur Andersen in the wake of the Enron scandal, the firm should have known that it would lose business and need to massively reduce staff. In a divided decision, the Seventh Circuit found for the defendant:

> [T]he Department of Labor has provided some guidance regarding when the "unforeseen business circumstances" exception applies. . . . A business circumstance may be reasonably unforeseeable if it was caused by some sudden, dramatic, and unexpected action, or by conditions outside the employer's control. 20 C.F.R. § 639.9(b)(1). When determining whether a mass layoff was caused by unforeseeable business circumstances, courts evaluate whether a similarly situated employer exercising reasonable judgment could have foreseen the circumstances that caused the layoff. *Id.* § 639.9(b)(2). Thus, a company will not be liable if, when confronted with potentially devastating occurrences, it reacts the same way that other reasonable employers within its own market would react.
>
> The parties dispute whether Andersen established either element of the exception — causation and foreseeability. The district court concluded that the need for mass layoffs was caused by the public announcement of the indictment on March 14. We agree. Up until then, Andersen suffered no marked loss of business despite a spate of negative publicity. It is clear that economic hemorrhaging really did not begin until word of the indictment got out. The plaintiffs contend that Andersen's felonious misconduct caused the layoffs, not the indictment. But, while it is true that the illegal acts of some Andersen

employees were the root cause of the firm's ultimate downfall, not until the indictment became public did it feel the pain. . . .

In determining whether a crippling business circumstance is foreseeable, we must bear in mind that "it is the 'probability of occurrence that makes a business circumstance "reasonably foreseeable," ' rather than the 'mere possibility of such a circumstance.' " The layoffs began on April 23, which means that Andersen was required to notify employees 60 days earlier, or February 22. The plaintiffs argue that the indictment was reasonably foreseeable on that date because "the DOJ disclosed to Andersen that an indictment was highly probable." But the record does not support this position. . . . Indeed, as of February 22 it was not a foregone conclusion that Andersen would be indicted as a company—in the past, the government typically went after culpable individuals, not companies as a whole. By all accounts, this was an unusual move by the DOJ. There is evidence in the record suggesting that Andersen could have reasonably foreseen the indictment by March 1—the date it was told by the DOJ that it was being indicted. But hope still remained that the dreaded act could be stalled if not avoided.

Id. at 588-89. The court also noted that requiring notice under such circumstances could lead fragile companies to lay off workers prematurely rather than fighting to stay afloat. *Id.* at 589-90.

The dissent disagreed on the court's view of the facts and the law. It concluded that, while the firm could not have foreseen layoffs on February 22, it should have known that an RIF was coming when the DOJ informed it on March 1 of the likelihood of an indictment. The dissent found that Arthur Andersen should have at least been obligated to give notice as of that date and accused the majority of "tak[ing] an all-or-nothing approach—if 60 days' notice is impossible, then no notice at all is required," inconsistent with the statute. *Id.* at 591.

Remedies under WARN are limited. The goal of the statute is not job protection as such; it seeks merely to provide employees with a window of time to plan for the disruption of a layoff, begin searching for new employment, and if necessary, obtain new skills. Consequently, an employee can receive only the wages and benefits to which he or she would otherwise have been entitled for each day of the violation (up to 60 days). This may not amount to much for the individual worker, but for the employer who might have to pay this amount to each worker in a mass layoff, the stakes are high. In addition, employers who violate WARN may, in some instances, be assessed a daily statutory penalty. 29 U.S.C. §2104.

Note on Managing the Risk of Systemic Discrimination Claims in Planning a RIF

One of the most significant concerns of employers conducting a reduction in force is the risk of liability under discrimination laws. Particularly in large-scale layoffs, systemic claims may potentially be brought by class action. The stakes have heightened since 2004 when the Supreme Court determined that disparate impact liability is available under the ADEA, albeit under a standard more deferential to employers than under Title VII. *See Smith v. City of Jackson*, 544 U.S. 228 (2005), discussed in Chapter 9.

For these reasons, employers are well advised to carefully review the criteria they use in selecting employees for layoff and how those criteria apply. The employer must ensure not only that its managers do not intentionally base layoff decisions on protected status, but also that neutral criteria do not disparately impact workers with protected status, or, if they do, that the disparity can be legitimately explained by other business considerations. One group of practitioners offers the following checklist:

... II. Create and Document the Layoff Plan

A. Articulate and document economic and other business justifications for the layoff. If an employee files a wrongful layoff case, this documentation will lay the foundation for the employer's case. . . .

C. Articulate and document the basis for determining the number of positions the employer will cut in each work unit.

1. Determine the positions and skills within each work unit which the employer must retain to achieve its articulated business goals. This assessment should precede, and should not take into account, an assessment of the skills of the individual incumbents.

2. Establish criteria for determining which positions an employer will eliminate within a work unit to achieve articulated business goals.

D. Standardize the methodology and criteria for selecting individuals for layoff.

1. Use objective criteria to the extent possible. . . .

3. Define the method by which the employer will determine the relative ranking of employees for layoff purposes. [I]t is inadvisable to rely solely on past performance evaluations because these are likely to be written in highly complimentary terms and are not designed for comparing employees on the skills, knowledge and abilities required for post-RIF jobs. Rather, it is more sensible to prepare special assessment ratings in connection with layoff selection which assess relative skills, knowledge, abilities and other qualifications. . . .

a. Use a "cutback" evaluation form, perhaps developed under the supervision of a professional. . . . Performance-based selection criteria should relate to functions that will remain after the RIF. These evaluations should not include a final "score" because layoffs which deviate from score order are difficult to justify. . . .

b. Give explicit written guidelines, comprehensible later to a judge and jury, for supervisors who are completing the evaluation forms. The employer should review these guidelines in the supervisory briefings which precede the evaluation process and distribute them to each evaluator to demonstrate that the company did not rely on unguided opinions or arbitrary judgments. These guidelines should instruct supervisors to examine an employee's performance reviews, disciplinary record and other specific documents before filling out the evaluation forms.

c. Where possible, arrange for multiple raters having personal knowledge of the employee's performance (e.g., two levels of supervision) to evaluate the employee. Each evaluator should rate the employee independently — without knowledge of the ratings given by other evaluators.

d. Create a review committee which includes minorities, women and older workers to review tentative layoff decisions to ensure the employer has followed the guidelines.

e. Have the human resources department review ratings for thoroughness, apparent consistency within the organization and consistency with the individual's past evaluations and disciplinary records as reflected in the personnel file. . . .

5. Accurately document the legitimate business factors that justify the particular layoff decision, e.g., comparative seniority, experience, performance evaluations and elimination of tasks performed by incumbent. . . .

V.   Review the Tentative Layoff

A. Conduct an adverse impact analysis of the tentative layoff list by race, sex and appropriate age bands under the attorney-client privilege. . . .

C. Review the impending layoff in light of the following questions:

1. Are WARN Act notices necessary?

2. Will the layoff breach employment contracts (express contracts or promises implied from oral assurances, length of service, commendations or salary increases), the covenant of good faith and fair dealing, employee handbooks, labor contracts, layoff policies or past practices?

3. Will the layoff impact whistleblowers, complainers or persons about to vest in pension or retiree health benefits or violate other public policies?

4. Will the reduction in force affect workers on pregnancy leave, family leave or medical leave?

5. Is collective bargaining necessary?

Ethan Lipsig et al., *Planning and Implementing Reductions in Force*, C922 ALI-ABA 1165, 1231-36 (1994). As a practical matter, an employer that plans to obtain OWBPA releases will necessarily have to take some of these steps in order to provide the requisite disclosures to employees. In addition to its procedural requirements, OWBPA provides that where "an exit incentive or other employment termination program [is] offered to a group or class of employees," the employer must provide each employee with information about all employees eligible for the incentive or program, including their ages and job titles. The purpose of this provision is to give employees adequate information on which to determine whether it is in their interest to waive potential substantive claims. In effect, OWBPA thus ensures a kind of pre-suit discovery to would-be plaintiffs. Although employers may dislike the provision for this reason, compliance can be useful from a risk management perspective. As the excerpt suggests, culling this information may alert the employer in advance to possible liability risks raised by the statistical composition of its selected class of workers.

Employers who run into trouble in conducting a layoff tend to be those who fail to employ objective criteria, fail to apply such criteria consistently, or fail to document their layoff procedure. Consider the court's description of the RIF selection process in *Oberg v. Allied Van Lines, Inc.*, 1996 U.S. Dist. LEXIS 4717 (N.D. Ill. April 11, 1996):

> In advance [of the RIF Allied's parent company] sent two of its top ranking personnel managers to interview every manager at Allied. After doing so, these two officials developed a blueprint for the reductions which was carried out by Allied management.
>
> Allied thereafter launched a selection procedure in connection with its reduction which was unclear, undocumented and ripe for problems, including claims for discrimination. No written guidelines for termination were prepared. No documents were

prepared to explain why certain employees were terminated compared to others and it appears that in some instances employees' evaluations were ignored.

Naturally, different supervisors interpreted the criteria in different ways and applied them based upon the circumstances attendant to their own business units rather than in some rigid, mathematical manner. As Allied's senior management considered the changes, the names of individuals whose employment status would be affected by the changes were forwarded on to Allied's RIF committee. The committee consisted of Allied Human Resources and Legal Department personnel.

Among the evidence plaintiffs sought to rely on was the following statement from a report authored by executives of Allied's parent company to assist in the RIF:

Despite the recent incidence of high turnover there are still many managers in the organization with very long service. No doubt this has encouraged the atmosphere of insular bureaucracy that still pervades part of the business.

Id. Do you see how the way the RIF was conducted could have encouraged, or at least enabled, age discrimination? As the lawyer for Allied, what would you have recommended the company do differently in planning major layoffs? Incidentally, the employer in *Oberg* had obtained releases from the terminated employees; however they were found invalid for failure to comply with all of the OWBPA disclosure requirements. *See Oberg v. Allied Van Lines, Inc.,* 11 F.3d 679 (7th Cir. 1993).

PROBLEM

13-6. Union Mortgage & Lending ("UML"), located in Boston, has acquired Connecticut Family Credit ("CFC"), located in Hartford, and plans to consolidate operations in Boston. CFC employed three accountants, of which UML must select two for layoff. Herk is a 61-year-old white male with 12 years of seniority. He currently earns $75,000 per year. His performance evaluations are consistently good but not outstanding. Joeline is a 42-year-old white woman with six years of seniority. She currently earns $68,000 per year. Her performance evaluations are similar to Herk's. She has strong ties to her previous employer of eight years, a large Connecticut-based bank with whom CFC did significant business. Miguel is a 29-year-old Hispanic male who arrived at CFC eight months ago from a big New York accounting firm. He earns $62,000 per year. His paper credentials exceed those of Herk and Joeline, and he has excellent interpersonal skills. Miguel's performance has not yet been formally evaluated; however, the general manager at CFC believes he is a "rising star." UML consults you about which accountant to retain. How would you advise your client to go about this decision? What risks are associated with laying off each of these three employees? What additional information might you seek from CFC before deciding? Are there any special precautions UML should take once it makes its decision? Once you have made your selections, draft a separation letter which UML will send to the affected employees apprising them of the decision.

C. MANAGING UNFAVORABLE FORA AND ADVERSE LAW

The previous sections of this chapter explored methods employers may use for preventing employment disputes or at least resolving them internally. Inevitably, some disputes escalate to the point that an aggrieved worker wishes to pursue legal action. The traditional step in such situations is for the employee to file a complaint in court provided he or she has taken the requisite administrative steps in the case of claims arising under federal discrimination law. One way that employers plan for the risks associated with this possibility is to contractually alter the default principle that disputes are litigated in the court the plaintiff chooses, complete with that forum's choice-of-law principles. A common method of doing this is to require all workers, as a condition of initial or continued employment, to arbitrate any dispute that may arise during the course of the employment relationship. Some employers go further and try to structure the arbitration terms, either procedurally or substantively, to minimize the risk of the employee prevailing or, at least, to reduce the amount of exposure in such situations. These issues are taken up in the first subsection. In addition, where law is uncertain or harm is difficult to prove, employers sometimes attempt to contractually define the financial consequences of a dispute, often through the use of a stipulated damages clause. This is covered in subsection 2.

1. Pre-dispute Arbitration Agreements

Arbitration is an alternative to traditional court litigation through which parties employ a third-party, nonjudicial decision maker to adjudicate their dispute in a private proceeding. From the perspective of the employer, the purpose of a pre-dispute arbitration agreement is to avoid protracted and expensive litigation and steer potential disputes to fora that the employer considers more cost-efficient, predictable, and, perhaps, friendlier to its interests. Because it is private, the arbitration process varies depending on the particular forum and rules the parties select. In many instances, parties opt for an established arbitration service, such as the American Arbitration Association, which has an extensive set of rules and procedures for resolving employment disputes and a cadre of trained arbitrators. *See AAA National Rules for the Resolution of Employment Disputes* (2005) *available at* http://www.adr.org/sp.asp ?id=22075. But parties might also choose a less formal venue or develop their own set of rules and procedures. For these reasons, arbitrations vary significantly in terms of the expertise and background of the arbitrators; whether lawyers or other advocates participate; the formality with which testimony is presented; and the degree of attention to evidentiary and other procedural rules.

In theory, opting for arbitration does not reduce the risk of being on the losing end of a dispute but merely reduces the costs of resolving it by substituting a cheaper and speedier alternative mechanism. Such features could make arbitration a more accessible, and hence more effective, form of dispute resolution for employees who lack the time, financial resources, and access to counsel necessary to pursue litigation in court. *See* Samuel Estreicher, *Saturns for Rickshaws: The Stakes in the Debate over*

Predispute Employment Arbitration Agreements, 16 OHIO ST. J. ON DISP. RESOL. 559 (2001).

However, arbitration is quicker and less costly precisely because certain procedures and safeguards associated with court litigation are abandoned. Further, since employers generally select the particular forum and its procedures, it is possible that arbitration will favor employers in both substantive outcomes and generosity of remedies. Even in an objectively neutral forum, the "repeat player" effect may lead arbitrators to favor those who are most likely to want to use their services in the future—employers. *See* Sarah Rudolph Cole, *Incentives and Arbitration: The Case Against Enforcement of Executory Arbitration Agreements Between Employers and Employees*, 64 UMKC L. REV. 449, 472-79 (1996); Cynthia Estlund, *Rebuilding the Law of the Workplace in an Era of Self-Regulation*, 105 COLUM. L. REV. 319, 397-98 (2005).

Such concerns are heightened by the common employer practice of requiring employees to sign contracts to arbitrate upon applying for or commencing a job that is well before a dispute actually arises. In contrast to the decision to arbitrate an existing dispute, an employee faced with a pre-dispute arbitration agreement is less likely to either appreciate the importance of choice of forum or consult counsel. *See* Matthew T. Bodie, *Questions About the Efficiency of Employment Arbitration Agreements*, 39 GA. L. REV. 1, 41 (2004) (comparing post-dispute agreements to pre-dispute arbitration agreements and determining that the latter "are more likely to be based on primitive guesswork, or less, on the part of the employee" and that employers are likely to have significant informational advantages that they may use "to construct inefficient agreements that employees would not agree to if they had perfect information"). Moreover, such agreements are generally boilerplate documents which individual employees are rarely in a position to refuse. If employees are not able to negotiate the terms or arbitration agreements, or even rationally weigh the trade-offs involved in agreeing to the employer's chosen forum and procedures, such agreements could effectively serve as waivers of substantive employment rights. *See* David S. Schwartz, *Mandatory Arbitration and Fairness.* 84 NOTRE DAME L. REV. 1247 (2009); Katherine V.W. Stone, *Mandatory Arbitration of Individual Employment Rights: The Yellow Dog Contract of the 1990s*, 73 DENV. U. L. REV. 1017 (1996).

Yet another set of objections to arbitration stems from the fact that, as a private dispute resolution mechanism, arbitration may not serve the wider goals of the law, particularly the antidiscrimination statutes, even if it achieves justice in individual cases. Chief among the concerns are the confidentiality of the process, which arguably inhibits public education about discrimination and limits the development of the law by removing a large source of potential precedent cases. *See* Geraldine Szott Moohr, *Arbitration and the Goals of Employment Discrimination Law*, 56 WASH. & LEE L. REV. 395, 426-39 (1999).

Debates about the relative merits and limitations of arbitration as an alternative dispute resolution mechanism underlie an evolving body of doctrine on the legal enforceability of pre-dispute employment arbitration agreements. The starting point for that analysis is the 1925 Federal Arbitration Act ("FAA"), which provides that a written arbitration clause in any "contract evidencing a transaction involving commerce . . . shall be valid, irrevocable, and enforceable, save upon such grounds as exist at law or in equity for the revocation of any contract." 9 U.S.C. §2. If a party who has signed an arbitration agreement files suit in court, the FAA commands the judge to stay the proceedings on motion of the opposing party; this remits the plaintiff only to the designated arbitral forum if she still seeks relief. However, there are several limitations on the statute's scope. The FAA applies only to maritime transactions and "transactions involving commerce." In addition, Section 1 of the Act excludes "contracts of employment of seamen, railroad employees, or any other class of workers engaged in foreign or interstate commerce." 9 U.S.C. § 1. Are ordinary employment contracts within this exclusion? Are they even covered by the statute at all (i.e., are they "transactions involving commerce")?

In addition to these questions of statutory interpretation, another important set of issues concerns the relationship between private arbitration and employee statutory rights. Employment arbitration agreements typically apply to any workplace dispute, but they are most often invoked by employers defending against federal statutory claims, such as discrimination claims. The employee's right to be free from discrimination includes the statutory right to have her claims heard in a court of law before a jury. One of the foundational questions of private ordering in employment law is whether an employer can change that by private contract.

The question of enforceability of an arbitration agreement in the individual employment setting of a statutory employment claim was first addressed by the Supreme Court in *Gilmer v. Interstate/Johnson Lane Corp.*, 500 U.S. 20 (1995), an age discrimination suit. The plaintiff had signed an arbitration agreement in order to register as a securities representative with the New York Stock Exchange; that agreement, although not entered into with his employer, required Gilmer to arbitrate any dispute arising with other registered members of the exchange, including his employer. The Supreme Court held the agreement enforceable. It found nothing in the text or underlying policy of the ADEA that precluded the submission of age discrimination claims to private arbitration. *Id.*; *see generally* Charles A. Sullivan, *The Story of* Gilmer v. Interstate/Johnson Lane Corp: *Gilmering Antidiscrimination Law*, Employment Discrimination Stories (Friedman ed., 2006).

Because *Gilmer* involved an arbitration clause in the plaintiff's securities license application, the Court did not consider whether the FAA would compel arbitration of an agreement directly between an employer and employee. It declined to address the question whether employment agreements are within the scope of the FAA or its exclusion for certain "contracts of employment." These questions subsequently came before the Court in *Circuit City v. Adams*, 532 U.S. 105 (2001), involving an employment application containing an arbitration clause. The Court held that employment agreements are "transactions involving commerce" within the meaning of the FAA and that the Section 2 exclusion of railroad employees, seamen, and "other workers engaged in . . . commerce" embraced only transportation workers and did not reach ordinary employment contracts. Therefore, according to the Court, employment arbitration agreements are subject to enforcement under the FAA, provided that they constitute or form part of a valid contract and "involv[e] commerce."

In sum, federal law requires enforcement of an arbitration clause in any employment contract that counts as "a transaction involving commerce" — provided only that such a clause is enforceable as a matter of state contract law. Further, the FAA preempts state law to the extent that it would treat arbitration agreements differently than other contracts. *See Doctor's Assocs. v. Casarotto*, 517 U.S. 681 (1996) (striking down state law prescribing special procedural requirements for arbitration agreements). This interpretation of the FAA and its preemptive scope has been criticized by some. *See, e.g.*, David S. Schwartz, *Correcting Federalism Mistakes in*

Statutory Interpretation: The Supreme Court and the Federal Arbitration Act, 67 L. & CONTEMP. PROBS. 5 (2004) (arguing that FAA preemption is inconsistent with congressional intent and contrary to Court's conservative majority's purported support for federalism). However, given the Supreme Court's rulings, currently the primary legal avenue for defeating an employment arbitration agreement is to prove a defense to contract under state law. The cases that follow explore such efforts.

Circuit City Stores, Inc. v. Adams
279 F.3d 889 (9th Cir. 2002)

NELSON, C.J.

The Supreme Court granted certiorari, reversed this court's prior decision, and remanded for proceedings in accordance with its opinion in *Circuit City Stores, Inc. v. Adams*, 532 U.S. 105 (2001). Now that the Federal Arbitration Act ("FAA"), 9 U.S.C. § 1 et seq., applies to the arbitration agreement in this case, we must decide whether the district court erred in exercising its authority under the Act to compel arbitration.

I. Factual and Procedural Background

On October 23, 1995, Saint Clair Adams completed an application to work as a sales person at Circuit City. As part of the application, Adams signed the "Circuit City Dispute Resolution Agreement" ("DRA"). The DRA requires employees to submit all claims and disputes to binding arbitration.[1] Incorporated into the DRA are a set of "Dispute Resolution Rules and Procedures" . . . that define the claims subject to arbitration, discovery rules, allocation of fees, and available remedies. Under these rules, the amount of damages is restricted: back pay is limited to one year, front pay to two years, and punitive damages to the greater of the amount of front and back pay awarded or $5000. In addition, the employee is required to split the costs of the arbitration, including the daily fees of the arbitrator, the cost of a reporter to transcribe the proceedings, and the expense of renting the room in which the arbitration is held, unless the employee prevails and the arbitrator decides to order Circuit City to pay the employee's share of the costs. Notably, Circuit City is not required under the agreement to arbitrate any claims against the employee.

An employee cannot work at Circuit City without signing the DRA. If an applicant refuses to sign the DRA (or withdraws consent within three days), Circuit City will not even consider his application.

[Adams filed a state court lawsuit against Circuit City and three co-workers alleging sexual harassment. Circuit City responded by filing a petition in federal district court to stay the state court proceedings and compel arbitration. The Supreme Court

---

1. The DRA specifies that job applicants agree to settle "all previously unasserted claims, disputes or controversies arising out of or relating to my application or candidacy for employment, employment and/or cessation of employment with Circuit City, *exclusively* by final and binding *arbitration* before a neutral Arbitrator. By way of example only, such claims include claims under federal, state, and local statutory or common law, such as Age Discrimination in Employment Act, Title VII of the Civil Rights Act of 1964, as amended, including the amendments to the Civil Rights Act of 1991, the Americans with Disabilities Act, the law of contract and law of tort." (emphasis in original).

held that the FAA applied to the contract between Adams and Circuit City and remanded for an assessment of the legality of the arbitration agreement under California law.]

II. Discussion

Circuit City has devised an arbitration agreement that functions as a thumb on Circuit City's side of the scale should an employment dispute ever arise between the company and one of its employees. We conclude that such an arrangement is unconscionable under California law.

A. Applicable Law

The FAA was enacted to overcome courts' reluctance to enforce arbitration agreements. The Act not only placed arbitration agreements on equal footing with other contracts, but established a federal policy in favor of arbitration, and a federal common law of arbitrability which preempts state law disfavoring arbitration.

Section 2 of the FAA provides that arbitration agreements "shall be valid, irrevocable, and enforceable, save upon such grounds that exist at law or in equity for the revocation of any contract." 9 U.S.C. §2 (emphasis added). Thus, although "courts may not invalidate arbitration agreements under state laws applicable only to arbitration provisions," general contract defenses such as fraud, duress, or unconscionability, grounded in state contract law, may operate to invalidate arbitration agreements. *Doctor's Assocs., Inc. v. Casarotto*, 517 U.S. 681, 687 (1996).

Adams argues that the DRA is an unconscionable contract of adhesion. Because Adams was employed in California, we look to California contract law to determine whether the agreement is valid.

Under California law, a contract is unenforceable if it is both procedurally and substantively unconscionable. *Armendariz v. Found. Health Psychcare Svcs., Inc.*, 6 P.3d 669, 690 (2000). When assessing procedural unconscionability, we consider the equilibrium of bargaining power between the parties and the extent to which the contract clearly discloses its terms. A determination of substantive unconscionability, on the other hand, involves whether the terms of the contract are unduly harsh or oppressive.

B. The DRA and Unconscionability

The DRA is procedurally unconscionable because it is a contract of adhesion: a standard-form contract, drafted by the party with superior bargaining power, which relegates to the other party the option of either adhering to its terms without modification or rejecting the contract entirely. Circuit City, which possesses considerably more bargaining power than nearly all of its employees or applicants, drafted the contract and uses it as its standard arbitration agreement for all of its new employees. The agreement is a prerequisite to employment, and job applicants are not permitted to modify the agreement's terms—they must take the contract or leave it.

See Armendariz (noting that few applicants are in a position to refuse a job because of an arbitration agreement).

The California Supreme Court's recent decision in *Armendariz* counsels in favor of finding that the Circuit City arbitration agreement is substantively unconscionable as well. In *Armendariz*, the California court reversed an order compelling arbitration of a FEHA discrimination claim because the arbitration agreement at issue required arbitration only of employees' claims and excluded damages that would otherwise be available under the FEHA. The agreement in *Armendariz* required employees, as a condition of employment, to submit all claims relating to termination of that employment — including any claim that the termination violated the employee's rights — to binding arbitration. The employer, however, was free to bring suit in court or arbitrate any dispute with its employees. In analyzing this asymmetrical arrangement, the court concluded that in order for a mandatory arbitration agreement to be valid, some "modicum of bilaterality" is required. Since the employer was not bound to arbitrate its claims and there was no apparent justification for the lack of mutual obligations, the court reasoned that arbitration appeared to be functioning "less as a forum for neutral dispute resolution and more as a means of maximizing employer advantage."

The substantive one-sidedness of the *Armendariz* agreement was compounded by the fact that it did not allow full recovery of damages for which the employees would be eligible under the FEHA. The exclusive remedy was back pay from the date of discharge until the date of the arbitration award, whereas plaintiffs in FEHA suits would be entitled to punitive damages, injunctive relief, front pay, emotional distress damages, and attorneys' fees.

We find the arbitration agreement at issue here virtually indistinguishable from the agreement the California Supreme Court found unconscionable in *Armendariz*. Like the agreement in *Armendariz*, the DRA unilaterally forces employees to arbitrate claims against the employer. The claims subject to arbitration under the DRA include "any and all employment-related legal disputes, controversies or claims *of an Associate* arising out of, or relating to, an Associate's application or candidacy for employment, employment or cessation of employment with Circuit City." (emphasis added). The provision does not require Circuit City to arbitrate its claims against employees. Circuit City has offered no justification for this asymmetry, nor is there any indication that "business realities" warrant the one-sided obligation. This unjustified one-sidedness deprives the DRA of the "modicum of bilaterality" that the California Supreme Court requires for contracts to be enforceable under California law.

And again as in *Armendariz*, the asymmetry is compounded by the fact that the agreement limits the relief available to employees. Under the DRA, the remedies are limited to injunctive relief, up to one year of back pay and up to two years of front pay, compensatory damages, and punitive damages in an amount up to the greater of the amount of back pay and front pay awarded or $5,000. By contrast, a plaintiff in a civil suit for sexual harassment under the FEHA is eligible for all forms of relief that are generally available to civil litigants — including appropriate punitive damages and damages for emotional distress. The DRA also requires the employee to split the arbitrator's fees with Circuit City. This fee allocation scheme alone would render an arbitration agreement unenforceable. But the DRA goes even further: it also imposes a strict one year statute of limitations on arbitrating claims that would deprive Adams of the benefit of the continuing violation doctrine available in FEHA suits. In short, and just like the agreement invalidated by the California Supreme Court in *Armendariz*, the DRA forces Adams to arbitrate his statutory claims without affording him the benefit of the full range of statutory remedies. . . .

≡ **Martindale v. Sandvik, Inc.**
≡ *800 A.2d 872 (N.J. 2002)*

LaVecchia, Justice.

This appeal addresses the enforceability of an arbitration agreement contained in an application for employment. The courts below concluded that the agreement to arbitrate executed by the parties was valid and enforceable. . . . We agree and affirm the judgment of the Appellate Division.

I.

Plaintiff Maureen Martindale applied and was hired for the position of Benefits Administrator with defendant Sandvik, Inc. in 1994. When she applied, plaintiff had to complete and sign an "Application for Employment" that included an arbitration agreement that appeared on page four of the application. The arbitration agreement stated:

> As a condition of my employment, I agree to waive my right to a jury trial in any action or proceeding related to my employment with Sandvik.
> I understand that I am waiving my right to a jury trial voluntarily and knowingly, and free from duress or coercion.
> I understand that I have a right to consult with a person of my choosing, including an attorney, before signing this document.
> I agree that all disputes relating to my employment with Sandvik or termination thereof shall be decided by an arbitrator through the labor relations section of the American Arbitration Association.

Plaintiff also submitted a resume that set forth her educational background and extensive experience in the field of benefits administration.

It is undisputed that defendant provided her with the opportunity to ask questions about the application and the arbitration agreement and to consult a third party, including an attorney, before signing the documents. Although plaintiff asked questions about the position, she did not ask any questions about the application. According to plaintiff, defendant informed her that she was required to sign page four of the application; nonetheless, there is no claim that plaintiff was coerced into signing the arbitration agreement. . . .

[In 1996, plaintiff experienced medical problems related to pregnancy and took disability leave. She obtained authorization for a post-delivery family and medical leave, but prior to its commencement was notified that her position had been eliminated in a reorganization. Plaintiff brought suit alleging violations of the New Jersey Family Leave Act and the New Jersey Law Against Discrimination ("LAD"). Defendant moved to stay the proceedings and compel arbitration.]

II. . . .

C. . . .

Basic contract principles render a promise enforceable against the promisor if the promisee gave some consideration for the promise. We have explained the well-established rule of consideration as follows:

> The essential requirement of consideration is a bargained-for exchange of promises or performance that may consist of an act, a forbearance, or the creation, modification, or destruction of a legal relation. *See* RESTATEMENT (SECOND) OF CONTRACTS § 71 (1981). If the consideration requirement is met, there is no additional requirement of gain or benefit to the promisor, loss or detriment to the promisee, equivalence in the values exchanged, or mutuality of obligation. *See* RESTATEMENT (SECOND) OF CONTRACTS § 79 (1979).

Put another way, "[a] very slight advantage to one party, or a trifling inconvenience to the other, is a sufficient consideration to support a contract when made by a person of good capacity, who is not at the time under the influence of any fraud, imposition or mistake."

In all jurisdictions that have considered the question, courts have held that the creation of an employment relationship, which is achieved when the employer agrees to consider and/or agrees to hire the applicant for employment, is sufficient consideration to uphold an arbitration agreement contained in an employment application. . . .

Similarly, in New Jersey, continued employment has been found to constitute sufficient consideration to support certain employment-related agreements. *See, e.g., Hogan v. Bergen Brunswig Corp.*, 378 A.2d 1164 (App. Div. 1977) (holding that continuation of plaintiff's employment for approximately three years after plaintiff signed letter acknowledging restrictive covenant against post-employment competition constituted sufficient consideration to enforce agreement).

The arbitration agreement contained in the Application for Employment signed by plaintiff was supported by consideration in the form of defendant's willingness to consider employment of plaintiff. The agreement provided that plaintiff would agree to waive her right to a jury trial and submit all disputes relating to her employment, including termination, to arbitration "as a condition of employment" with defendant. Although defendant was under no obligation to actually hire plaintiff, defendant's consideration of plaintiff's application, its extension of an offer and the commencement of employment, and thereafter the provision of compensation and on-going employment constituted sufficient consideration to support the parties' agreement to arbitrate their disputes. That agreement is binding, as would be any other contractual term not contrary to public policy contained in a signed employment application that led, as here, to employment.

D.

Plaintiff contends in the alternative that the agreement to arbitrate her statutory claims against her employer constituted a contract of adhesion and that therefore it is not enforceable. A contract of adhesion, simply put, is a contract "presented on a take-it-or-leave-it basis, commonly in a standardized printed form, without opportunity of the 'adhering' party to negotiate except perhaps on a few particulars." *Rudbart v. North Jersey Dist. Water Supply Comm'n*, 127 N.J. 344, 353, 605 (1992).

Even if the Application for Employment in this case, including the arbitration provision, was found to constitute a contract of adhesion, that does not render the contract automatically void. The observation that a contract falls within the definition of a contract of adhesion is not dispositive of the issue of enforceability. Such a finding "is the beginning, not the end, of the inquiry." In determining whether to enforce the terms of a contract of adhesion, courts must look not only to the standardized nature of the contract, "but also to the subject matter of the contract, the parties' relative bargaining positions, the degree of economic compulsion motivating the 'adhering' party, and the public interests affected by the contract." Similar to a consideration of contract formation, the decision whether an arbitration agreement constitutes an unenforceable contract of adhesion is fact-sensitive, and therefore must be determined on a case-by-case basis.

The United States Supreme Court in *Gilmer* declared that "[m]ere inequality in bargaining power . . . is not a sufficient reason to hold that arbitration agreements are never enforceable in the employment context." As the Appellate Division explained in *Young v. Prudential Insurance Company of America, Incorporated*, 688 A.2d 1069 (1997), "the Supreme Court [in *Gilmer*] obviously contemplated avoidance of the arbitration clause only upon circumstances more egregious than the ordinary economic pressure faced by every employee who needs the job." Virtually every court that has considered the adhesive effect of arbitration provisions in employment applications or employment agreements has upheld the arbitration provision contained therein despite potentially unequal bargaining power between employer and employee.

Turning to the arbitration agreement contained in plaintiff's Application for Employment, we do not find determinative the fact that plaintiff was required to sign an employment application containing an arbitration agreement in order to be considered for employment. The employment application was not offered on a take-it-or-leave-it basis. Defendant gave plaintiff an opportunity to ask questions about the application and to take it with her for further quiet review or, perhaps, consultation with family, friends, or a professional such as an attorney. Plaintiff herself was an educated person who was experienced in the field of human resources. Nothing in the record indicates that plaintiff asked to alter any terms of the application or that Sandvik would have refused to consider her for the position if she did not assent to the arbitration provision as presented. Accordingly, we are not persuaded that plaintiff was forced to sign an inflexible contract of adhesion in the circumstances of her completion of the Application for Employment.

Nonetheless, even if the arbitration agreement could be so characterized, the agreement's subject matter and the public interests affected lead to the conclusion that it should not be invalidated. Plaintiff has failed to demonstrate how the terms of the arbitration agreement were oppressive or unconscionable. . . .

III. . . .

Finally, plaintiff claims that she did not knowingly and voluntarily waive her right to pursue her statutory claims in a judicial forum. Although plaintiff's level of sophistication is not central to our inquiry, we note nonetheless that plaintiff read and understood the Application for Employment before she signed it. . . . [S]he did not ask any questions about the application form . . . and she declined the offer to take the application home or to consult with another party. . . . We agree with the courts below that concluded that plaintiff knowingly and voluntarily agreed to arbitrate her statutory causes of action against her employer.

STEIN, J., dissenting. . . .

The narrow question for the Court is whether we should allow employers to extract concessions in a job application form, such as a waiver of the right to a jury trial, from prospective employees. Contrary to the majority's conclusion, I would hold that the standardized arbitration agreement that job applicants were required to sign as a prerequisite to consideration for employment with defendant is unenforceable as a matter of public policy.

. . . Irrespective of plaintiff's alleged sophistication, that defendant possessed considerably more bargaining power than did plaintiff as a prospective employee is obvious. Our common experience informs us that individuals faced with a need to find employment would be unlikely to refuse to sign a pre-printed employment application containing a mandatory arbitration clause if signing the form was a precondition to further consideration for the job. Moreover, as was the case in *Circuit City Stores,* because the arbitration clause in defendant's application form lacked mutuality, plaintiff's employer "was free to bring suit in court or arbitrate any dispute with its employees." The lack of mutuality in the agreement exacerbates its inequity.

On prior occasions we have determined that public policy demands invalidation of agreements resulting from inequitable bargaining positions. [The dissent cited state precedents that invalidated an exculpatory clause in a lease agreement and a provision in a migrant worker's employment contract permitting immediate eviction upon discharge.]

. . . [T]o hold that a mandatory arbitration agreement in an employment application violates public policy does not disfavor arbitration, but rather recognizes "the inherent inequity" in requiring an individual to sign an agreement that substantially alters his or her rights at such a particularly vulnerable time when they are under pressure to find employment.

In my view, public policy requires this Court to invalidate a mandatory arbitration agreement, or any analogous agreement of consequence, that a prospective employee is forced to sign as a condition of being considered for a job. "Grossly unfair contractual obligations resulting from the use of such expertise or control by the one possessing it, which result in assumption by the other contracting party of a burden which is at odds with the common understanding of the ordinary and untrained member of the public, are considered unconscionable and therefore unenforceable." Although the issue is not before us, I would assume that after an employee is hired an employer would be free to enter into an employment agreement that provides for arbitration of disputes, provided no disabling unfairness is implicated in the negotiation or terms of the agreement. We should not countenance a practice by which employers take unfair advantage of prospective employees by requiring their consent to arbitration agreements contained in printed employment application forms as a precondition to being considered for a job.

NOTES

1. *Just Plain Contracts.* Having mastered the various tests for releases of substantive rights, were you surprised by the absence of a heightened "knowing and voluntary" standard for agreements to arbitrate? Or that such agreements need not comply with OWBPA where ADEA claims are concerned? Since the federal discrimination laws afford plaintiffs the right to a jury, one could argue that a waiver or release of that right should be subject to the same tests that apply to the release of substantive claims. Some legal scholars have suggested that a more rigorous standard of voluntariness should apply in assessing employees' assent to arbitration. *See, e.g.,* Eileen Silverstein, *From Statute to Contract: The Law of the Employment Relationship Reconsidered,* 18 HOFSTRA LAB. & EMP. L. J. 479 (2001). Although a few courts appear to closely scrutinize employee assent to arbitration agreements, *see, e.g., Alonso v. Huron Valley Ambulance,* 357 F. App'x 487 (6th Cir. 2010) (finding agreement unenforceable where employees were given only general information about employer's alternative dispute process which was provided one month after they began employment), efforts to apply the OWPBA requirements or Title VII's knowing and voluntary standard to arbitration agreements have generally been rejected. *See, e.g., Rosenberg v. Merrill Lynch, Pierce, Fenner & Smith, Inc.,* 170 F.3d 1 (1st Cir. 1999). Thus, where arbitration is concerned, the Supreme Court has established what appears to be a simple rule: arbitration agreements are subject to normal state contract-law analysis. Why should there be a distinction between waivers of procedural rights and releases of substantive claims? Is there a stronger case for heightened judicial examination of employee consent in the latter situation? Or should freedom of contract prevail in enforcing arbitration agreements and perhaps also where release agreements are concerned?

2. *Contract Formation.* If "plain vanilla" contract law applies to arbitration, employers seeking to enforce an arbitration agreement must establish offer, acceptance, and consideration. The employers in both *Circuit City* and *Sandvik* seem to have covered these bases by requiring applicants to sign and return written documents (manifesting their assent) in return for being considered for employment (consideration). Not all employers have planned as well. For example, some have attempted to impose arbitration on existing workers merely by unilaterally amending an employee handbook or providing an e-mail notification. The results in these situations have been mixed. *Compare Campbell v. Gen. Dynamics Gov't Sys. Corp.,* 407 F.3d 546, 556-58 (1st Cir. 2005) (no enforceable arbitration agreement where policy distributed via hyperlink in e-mail notification and employee did not reply to message) *and Salazar v. Citadel Communs. Corp.,* 90 P.3d 466, 469-70 (N.M. 2004) (no enforceable arbitration agreement where policy was annexed to employee manual permitting employer to modify manual at will) *with May v. Higbee Co.,* 372 F.3d 757, 764 (5th Cir. 2004) (assent to arbitration manifested by conduct where employee signed acknowledgment that she received copy of rules and unambiguously notified employees that they "are deemed to have agreed . . . by virtue of . . . continuing employment" to arbitrate any dispute between employer and employee). Should the manner in which the employer establishes and communicates its arbitration policy matter in assessing contract enforceability? If most employees simply sign whatever documents the employer places before them in the application process, why is it any more objectionable to bind them to a handbook or e-mail arbitration policy?

3. *Invalidating Doctrines.* If assent and consideration are established, an employee's only means of defeating an arbitration agreement is to invoke one of the traditional defenses to contract explored in Section B, such as fraud, duress, mistake, or unconscionability. *Circuit City* primarily explores unconscionability, which, you may recall from your first-year Contracts class, is often defined as a lack of meaningful choice coupled with terms unreasonably favorable to one side. *See e.g., Williams v. Walker-Thomas*, 350 F.2d 445 (D.C. Cir. 1965). This description embraces the idea of "procedural" and "substantive" unconscionability, the former concept dealing with the manner in which agreement is reached and the latter concept referring to the fairness of the terms themselves. In which respect is the *Circuit City* arbitration agreement unconscionable? Why isn't unconscionability a problem for the court in *Martindale*?

There are a surprising number of decisions striking arbitration clauses as unconscionable. *See e.g., Hall v. Treasure bay Virgin Isle. Corp.*, 371 F. App'x 311 (3d Cir. 2010) (arbitration agreement imposing 30-day statute of limitations and requiring nonprevailing party to pay costs was substantively unconscionable); *Murray v. United Food & Commercial Workers Intl. Union*, 289 F.3d 297, 302-04 (4th Cir. 2002) (arbitration agreement giving employer discretion in naming possible arbitrators and constraining arbitrators' ability to rule on authority of employer's president was unconscionable and unenforceable); *Saylor v. Ryan's Family Steak Houses*, 613 S.E.2d 914, 922 (W. Va. 2005) (arbitration agreement was an unenforceable contract of adhesion where plaintiff had a tenth-grade education, was applying for low-skill server position, and employer was a multi-state restaurant chain). *But see Circuit City v. Ahmed*, 283 F.3d 1198 (9th Cir. 2002) (arbitration agreement not unconscionable where employee given opportunity to opt out within 30 days of receiving written materials and video presentation of terms); *In re Odyssey Healthcare*, 310 S.W.3d 419 (Tex. 2010) (finding evidence that employee would incur substantial expense in complying with arbitration agreement insufficient to show unconscionability). Indeed, arbitration may be the only area of American law where unconscionability doctrine seems alive and well. *See generally* Jeffrey W. Stempel, *Arbitration, Unconscionability, and Equilibrium: The Return of Unconscionability Analysis as a Counterweight to Arbitration Formalism*, 19 OHIO ST. J. DISP. RESOL. 757, 766-67 (2004). Does this mean that courts are applying greater scrutiny to arbitration agreements than other types of contracts in determining whether their terms are unconscionable? That would seem to violate the FAA's prohibition against state laws discriminating against arbitration. The issue is currently before the Supreme Court. *Laster v. AT&T Mobility LLC*, 584 F.3d 849 (9th Cir. Cal. 2009), *cert. granted sub nom., AT&T Mobility LLC v. Concepcion*, 130 S. Ct. 3322 (2010).

Along these lines, consider the dissent in *Martindale*, which urges that an arbitration agreement, or any "analogous" agreement signed as a condition of being considered for a job, should be invalid as a matter of public policy. This is a strong statement. Taken literally, it would invalidate a salary agreed to as a condition of employment and allow the employee to sue in restitution for the value of her services. It seems unlikely that Justice Stein would carry the point this far. Rather, the dissent appears to focus on the issues peculiar to arbitration, like the "waiver of the right to a jury trial." If so, his approach disfavors agreements to arbitrate in comparison to other contractual terms of employment. Recall that the Supreme Court has held that only "general" state contract law applies: the states are not permitted to establish different rules for arbitration. *E.g., Doctor's Assocs. v. Casarotto*, 517 U.S. 681 (1996) (striking down state law prescribing special procedural requirements for arbitration agreements). Do Justice Stein's opinion and decisions that rigorously apply the unconscionability doctrine lean too much on the unique character of arbitration agreements? Doesn't this run afoul of the FAA preemption doctrine? Or is there some explanation — besides "discrimination" against arbitration agreements — for the seemingly anomalous preponderance of unconscionability findings and other invalidating doctrines in the arbitration context? Again, the Supreme Court may soon shed some light on this question in the *Concepcion* decision.

4. *Class Action Waivers.* The issue of judicial "discrimination" against arbitration agreements has been front and center in a series of California cases involving arbitration agreements that preclude class-based proceedings. In *Gentry v. Superior Court*, 165 P.3d 556 (Cal. 2007), the California Supreme Court invalidated such an agreement in a case involving violation of FLSA overtime requirements. Extending its holding in a nonemployment case involving a class action waiver in a consumer credit card agreement, the court held that at least some waivers of class rights in overtime cases are unconscionable:

> [W]hen it is alleged that an employer has systematically denied proper overtime pay to a class of employees and a class action is requested notwithstanding an arbitration agreement that contains a class arbitration waiver, the trial court must consider . . . the modest size of the potential individual recovery, the potential for retaliation against members of the class, the fact that absent members of the class may be ill informed about their rights, and other real world obstacles to the vindication of class members' right to overtime pay through individual arbitration. If it concludes, based on these factors, that a class arbitration is likely to be a significantly more effective practical means of vindicating the rights of the affected employees than individual litigation or arbitration, and finds that the disallowance of the class action will likely lead to a less comprehensive enforcement of overtime laws for the employees alleged to be affected by the employer's violations, it must invalidate the class arbitration waiver to ensure that these employees can "vindicate [their] unwaivable rights in an arbitration forum."

Id. at 463. The court specifically rejected the employer's argument that its holding violated the FAA prohibition on discrimination against arbitration agreements, asserting that its ruling would apply to "class action waivers in arbitration provisions and nonarbitration provisions alike." *Id.* at 465. In spring 2010, the Supreme Court granted certiorari on this issue in a Ninth Circuit case rejecting the same argument and reaching the same result in a case involving the enforceability of a class action waiver in the arbitration provision of a wireless service agreement. *See Laster v. AT&T Mobility LLC*, 584 F.3d 899 (9th Cir. 2009), *cert. granted, AT & T Mobility LLC v. Concepcion*, 130 S. Ct. 3322 (2010). Much of the existing state law jurisprudence on the enforcement of employment arbitration may hinge on the result. If the Court reverses the Ninth Circuit, consistent with its past pro-arbitration rulings, the result will likely call into question not only decisions like *Gentry* that involve class action waivers, but the full line of employment cases that have liberally applied the unconscionability doctrine to void a variety of harsh provisions in arbitration agreements.

5. *Who Decides?* A related question is who decides issues of unconscionabily and other contractual defenses to arbitration clauses — a court or the arbitrator? As the cases you have read so far would suggest, issues of the validity of the arbitration agreement, including unconscionability, are generally decided by a court, under the theory that parties may not be compelled to use the arbitral forum absent an enforceable agreement. The Supreme Court recently reaffirmed that this is the general rule. *Granite Rock Co. v. International Brotherhood of Teamsters*, 130 S. Ct. 2847 (2010). On the other hand, issues as to the scope of the arbitration clause, such as whether a particular type of dispute falls within the jurisdiction of the arbitrator, are generally decided by the arbitrator. The Supreme Court has made clear that this includes disputes over whether the agreement permits parties to bring class-based arbitration proceedings. *See Green Tree Financial Corp. v. Bazzle*, 539 U.S. 444 (2003). However, a recent Supreme Court arbitration case involving arbitration of an age discrimination claim blurs the distinction. In *Rent-A-Center West, Inc. v. Jackson*, 130 S. Ct. 2772 (2010), the employer's arbitration contract provided not only for arbitration of all employment disputes, but also that "[t]he Arbitrator, and not any federal, state, or local court or agency, shall have exclusive authority to resolve any dispute relating to . . . enforceability or formation of this Agreement, including . . . any claim that any part of this Agreement is void or voidable." The majority held that this committed any question as to unconscionability of the contract to the arbitrator. In light of *Rent-A-Center*, one would expect such delegation clauses to become increasingly common in employer-drafted contracts.

6. *Bifurcating the Agreement?* One way to think about the result in *Circuit City* is to recognize that the agreement did far more than merely substitute an arbitral tribunal for a judicial forum. It also limited the employees' substantive rights by providing for far smaller remedies than would be available in a court suit. Should this part of the agreement (as opposed merely to the agreement to arbitrate) be subject to some sort of more rigorous test? Compare that to *Martindale*, in which the employer did not seek to alter substantive rights. To understand the distinction, suppose that, instead of requiring employees to agree to arbitrate, Circuit City had required as a condition of employment that all applicants waive their rights to more than one year of back pay under Title VII. Such an agreement would not be within the FAA. If viewed as a prospective waiver of substantive rights, it would likely be invalid as such waivers are generally considered void. If viewed as a release, it would at least be subject to the knowing and voluntary test and probably void to the extent it was prospective. Why should the employer escape the more searching standards associated with waivers and releases merely because it places the offending clause in an arbitration agreement?

While courts have not generally framed the issue in terms of bifurcation, they sometimes "sever" bad clauses, striking down only the objectionable provisions while still enforcing the agreement to arbitrate. *See, e.g., Morrison v. Circuit City Stores, Inc.*, 317 F.3d 646, 675 (6th Cir. 2003); *Gannon v. Circuit City Stores, Inc.*, 262 F.3d 677, 682-83 (8th Cir. 2001); *see also Hadnot v. Bay, Ltd.*, 344 F.3d 474, 478 (5th Cir. 2003). Is this a good response to unconscionable arbitration agreements? Note that the practice is similar to the "blue pencil" approach some courts have applied in enforcing overbroad noncompete agreements, as discussed in Chapter 8, and it raises similar questions. Might severance, or "bifurcation," encourage overreaching by assuring employers that they will get arbitration no matter how outrageously they draft their agreements? Some courts have responded to this concern by refusing to sever agreements that reflect employer overreaching. *See, e.g., Parilla v. IAP Worldwide Services, VI, Inc.*, 368 F.3d 269, 289 (3d Cir. 2004) ("[A] multitude of unconscionable provisions in an agreement to arbitrate will preclude severance and enforcement of arbitration if they evidence a deliberate attempt by an employer to impose an arbitration scheme designed to discourage an employee's resort to arbitration or to produce results biased in the employer's favor."). What are the ethics of attorney participation in such drafting? *See* Martin H. Malin, *Ethical Concerns in Drafting Employment Arbitration Agreements After* Circuit City *and* Green Tree, 41 BRANDEIS L. J. 779 (2003).

7. *A "Modicum of Bilaterality."* In refusing to compel arbitration, *Circuit City* points out that the agreement does not subject *employer* claims to arbitration. Why is "bilaterality" important? In *Armendariz v. Foundation Health*, 6 P.3d 669 (Cal. 2000), relied on by *Circuit City*, the California Supreme Court analogized the absence of bilaterality in an employment arbitration agreement to a physician/patient agreement that provided for judicial review only in the event the plaintiff won an award in excess of $25,000. In the physician/patient context, the court said that such a provision would be impermissible as tantamount to making arbitration binding if the plaintiff lost, but nonbinding if the plaintiff won a substantial award. Do you agree with this analogy?

If a bilateral commitment is an important factor in courts' unconscionability analysis, employers could easily address that issue in the drafting and planning stage. Why, then, would Circuit City exclude its claims against its workers from its arbitration clause? Employer suits against their employees are relatively rare: the employee is typically judgment-proof, and juries tend not be sympathetic to employers as plaintiffs. At first blush, it would seem that employers have little to lose and perhaps much to gain by committing themselves to the same dispute resolution procedure that they impose on their employees. On the other hand, consider some of the employer claims that you studied in Chapter 8 concerning workplace property and related rights. Can you think of reasons why an employer might be very reluctant to allow those claims to be addressed through arbitration? A few decisions have held that courts have the authority to issue a preliminary injunction in unlawful competition actions irrespective of the existence of a bilateral arbitration agreement in order to preserve the status quo pending the arbitration proceeding. *See, e.g., Spinks v. Automation Personnel Serv Inc.*, 2010 WL 1424024 (Ala. April 9, 2010). Employer-drafted arbitration agreements typically provide for the right of an employer to seek such preliminary relief in court even if disputes are otherwise subject to arbitration. From the employer's perspective, the desirability of such a clause should be apparent: Competitive harm might be done during the arbitration proceedings, and a court might hesitate to issue an injunction when the noncompetition period has expired.

8. *"Mutuality" and Consideration.* What the *Circuit City* court refers to as "bilaterality" is often confused with "mutuality of obligation." A few courts have held that an arbitration agreement is "illusory" and consequently lacking consideration where the agreement does not treat employer and employee claims equally or where the employer retains significant discretion over the arbitration policy. *See e.g., Gibson v. Neighborhood Health Clinics*, 121 F.3d 1126 (7th Cir. 1997); *Cheek v. United Healthcare of Mid-Atlantic, Inc.*, 835 A.2d 656, 661 (Md. 2003) (refusing to enforce arbitration clause in employment manual which reserved to employer permission to alter agreement "at its sole and absolute discretion . . . with or without notice").

Most courts, however, have rejected this argument, pointing out that contract law does not require equivalency of obligation with respect to specific terms but merely that "the contract as a whole is otherwise supported by consideration on both sides." *Walters v. AAA Waterproofing*, 85 P.3d 389, 392 (Wash. Ct. App. 2004); *see also Oblix v. Winiecki*, 374 F.3d 488, 491 (7th Cir. 2004) (that the employer "did not promise to arbitrate all of its potential claims is neither here nor there. [Plaintiff] does not deny that the arbitration clause is supported by consideration — her salary."). *But see Saylor v. Ryan's Family Steak Houses*, 613 S.E.2d 914, 924 (W. Va. 2005) ("meager" promise to review employment application insufficient consideration to support applicant's promise to submit all disputes to arbitration).

9. *Pre-hire vs. Post-hire Agreements.* Is there a distinction between pre- and post-hire arbitration agreements? In his *Martindale* dissent, Justice Stein notes that an employer would be free to insist on an arbitration contract after hire. Why? Are employees who are already employed more or less likely than applicants to be able to refuse a required arbitration agreement? *See* Rachel Arnow-Richman, *Cubewrap Contracts: The Rise of Delayed Term, Standard Form Employment Agreements*, 49 ARIZ. L. REV. 637, 655 (2007) (arguing that employers who insist on post-hire arbitration and other boilerplate provisions "capitalize on preexisting [power] imbalances" between the parties by delaying "deal-breaking terms" of employment until the point where the worker already has a sunk investment in his or her new job and is unable to refuse).

What is the contractual consideration in the post-hire situation? Recall the concept of "continued employment" to support contractual enforcement of personnel manuals and subsequent revisions in Chapter 2. That doctrine is also invoked where employers seek to enforce noncompete agreements signed during the employment relationship. Courts disagree as to whether it is applicable in the arbitration context. *Compare May v. Higbee Co.*, 372 F.3d 757 (5th Cir. 2004) (continued employment demonstrates assent to mid-term agreement to arbitrate) *with Gibson v. Neighborhood Health Clinics*, 121 F.3d 1126 (7th Cir. 1997) (continued employment not consideration).

10. *Employee-friendly Arbitration?* Can arbitration be fair to employees or does the fact that employers choose arbitration mean that any system they adopt will necessarily trammel employee rights? In *Armendariz*, the California Supreme Court held employment arbitration agreements enforceable under state law provided they do not amount to a waiver of statutory rights. It adopted five minimum requirements for lawful arbitration of discrimination claims: The arbitration agreement must (1) provide for neutral arbitrators, (2) provide for more than minimal discovery, (3) require a written award, (4) provide for all types of relief that would be available in court, and (5) not require employees to pay either unreasonable costs or any arbitrators' fees as a condition of access to the arbitration forum. *See* 6 P.3d at 682 (citing *Cole v. Burns Intern. Security Serv.*, 105 F.3d 1465 (D.C. Cir. 1997)). Would an employer be likely to adopt an arbitration agreement that met these criteria? Or does it defeat the advantages the employer is seeking by choosing the alternative forum? *See generally* Michael Z. Green, *Debunking the Myth of Employer Advantage from Using Mandatory Arbitration for Discrimination Claims*, 31 RUTGERS L. J. 399, 421-31 (2000).

11. *Comparing Costs, Comparing Access.* In *Circuit City*, the court notes that the fee allocation scheme alone would render an arbitration agreement unenforceable. How should arbitration be financed? Unlike judges, arbitrators are private individuals rather than civil servants; the parties must pay for their services, which can easily cost more than a thousand dollars per day for each arbitrator. In contrast, a party need only pay a one-time filing fee to initiate a suit in federal court, and this may be waived on a demonstration of indigency.

Before you conclude that courts are more financially accessible than arbitration, however, consider the time and money that attorneys invest in preparing cases for trial.

Many plaintiffs in employment cases do not pay out-of-pocket for legal representation, but as a consequence lawyers are extremely cautious about the cases they will pursue on contingency. It has been suggested that lawyers in private practice will not take on cases without a minimum of $75,000 in provable economic damages. Think about what types of employees are likely to have claims with this much money at stake. Would it surprise you to learn that an estimated 95 percent of employees who seek legal help are turned away? Does this change how you feel about arbitration? Of course, if arbitration is such a good idea, the employer and employee can always agree to arbitrate after a dispute has arisen — there is no need for an arbitration agreement as a condition of employment.

Even if aspects of arbitration are beneficial to some employees, that doesn't answer the question about who pays for it. If shifting part of the cost to the employee is prohibited, that must mean that the employer pays the full freight. Is that such a good idea? Won't arbitrators tend to be influenced by who is paying their fees?

12. *Third-party Suits.* Although the Supreme Court has supported private arbitration, it has drawn an important limit on the reach of its holdings as concerns public agencies. In *EEOC v. Waffle House*, 534 U.S. 279 (2002), the Court held that government agencies are not bound by a private agreement to arbitrate between an employer and employee. As a result of this decision, the EEOC (and presumably analog state agencies) can take up a victim's cause by pursuing its own claim against the offending employer in court on behalf of the victim, even where that individual would be precluded from doing so on his or her own behalf. Indeed, the Court held that in so doing the EEOC could seek victim-specific relief including full monetary damages. *Id.* at 295-96 ("The agency may be seeking to vindicate a public interest, not simply provide make-whole relief for the employee, even when it pursues entirely victim-specific relief."). Even if Adams had been forced to arbitrate her sexual harassment claim, the EEOC could have sued on her behalf. But before you conclude that this is a gaping loophole in the protection arbitration agreements afford employers, note that the EEOC prosecutes only a tiny fraction of discrimination charges lodged with it. From an employer's risk management perspective, enforceable arbitration agreements still make good sense. And, of course, antidiscrimination claims are only a subset of potential employee suits.

13. *Arbitration in the Unionized Workplace.* Notwithstanding the debate over employers' use of pre-dispute arbitration agreements with individual employees, courts and scholars alike have long supported arbitration in the unionized workplace. What accounts for this difference? Katherine Stone has argued that arbitration is appropriate when adopted by members of a "shared normative community," such as a unionized trade or industry. In that situation, community members are able "to participate in framing the shared institutions, values, and rules that grow out of that common experience." *See* Katherine V.W. Stone, *Rustic Justice: Community and Coercion Under the Federal Arbitration Act*, 77 N.C. L. Rev. 931, 1029 (1999). On the other hand, arbitration processes adopted in the individual employment context generally are selected unilaterally by the employer. A less subtle distinction is that union arbitration generally involves two repeat players — both the employer and the union representing the aggrieved worker frequently appear in the selected forum — and the union may be better able to bring expertise to bear on the dispute in every phase of the proceeding.

However, some take the view that what's good for the goose is good for the gander. As Judge Easterbrook of the Seventh Circuit put it in upholding a standardized agreement to arbitrate in *Oblix v. Winiecki*, 374 F.3d 488, 491 (7th Cir. 2004): "How could one call it unconscionable when an employer treats unrepresented workers . . . the same as it treats its organized labor force?"

Yet another theory in support of arbitration in the non-union environment is that increased reliance on arbitration in the non-union workplace could lead to the establishment of minimum standards of conduct that may operate much like a union contract, ultimately creating more legal protection for non-unionized workers. As Professor Sid Moller explains:

> [The trend toward non-union arbitration] will lead both to the emergence of contract obligations or their functional equivalent and to the relatively informal practices of the past being supplanted by a more formal, law-centered system of governance. The material with which to build a contractual model is already present in the non-union employment relationship [in the form of non-legal relational norms]. Although not as formalistic as litigation before courts or administrative agencies, arbitration is an adjudicatory function and has much in common with such processes. The requirements of procedural fairness and a decision-making methodology designed to weigh competing claims will inevitably lead to the articulation of rights and duties. . . .
>
> Once employers and their attorneys fully appreciate the ramifications of these developments, prudence will dictate a conservative course of action, which translates to a set of "minimum standards" with regard to both procedural and substantive matters. Otherwise, the risk that an arbitrator will impose such standards when the employer feels it can least afford them remains.

Sid L. Moller, *Birth of Contract: Arbitration in the Non-Union Workplace*, 50 S.C. L. REV. 183, 232-33 (1998). Are you convinced?

14. *A Statutory Solution?* If one concludes that as a policy matter pre-dispute arbitration agreements of the kind at issue in *Circuit City* and *Martindale* are not desirable, the simplest way to eliminate the problem is statutory amendment. Congress could amend the FAA to more broadly and explicitly exempt employment agreements, thereby superseding the Supreme Court's *Circuit City* decision. Alternatively, Congress could amend the various federal antidiscrimination and minimum labor standards laws to preclude arbitration of claims arising under those statutes. Congress took this approach in the Dodd-Frank financial reform bill, which amended whistleblower protections under Sarbanes-Oxley. *See* 18 U.S.C.A. §1514A(e). Dodd-Frank also barred mandatory pre-dispute arbitration for the new whistleblower protections it created. See Chapter 5. Pre-dispute agreements are also invalid under the federal Employee Polygraph Protection Act. *See* 29 U.S.C.A. §2005(d) ("The rights and procedures provided by this chapter may not be waived by contract or otherwise.").

PROBLEM

13-7.   You are in-house employment counsel for Cobalt Light Fixtures, a national company with employees all over the United States. The CEO would like to consider adopting an arbitration program as a means of reducing liability for employment disputes. She has asked you to make a recommendation and draft a sample contract. What would you counsel her about relative advantages and disadvantages to using arbitration? What features should your arbitration program have? Can you draft an agreement that would be enforceable in all states, including California? How would you recommend introducing it to the workforce?

---

2. Liquidated Damages Clauses

≣ ***Smelkinson SYSCO v. Harrell***
≣ *875 A.2d 188 (Md. 2002)*

THIEME, J.

Appellant Smelkinson SYSCO, Inc. (SYSCO), asks us to enforce the stipulated damages provision of a Settlement Agreement and General Release that the company entered into with former employee James E. Harrell, appellee. The parties agreed, *inter alia*, that, if Harrell breached the agreement, SYSCO's damages would include the $185,000 the company paid to settle pending and future disputes with Harrell. [The trial court ruled that the clause was an unenforceable as a penalty.]

Harrell, a SYSCO truck driver for 13 years, filed race discrimination, labor complaints, and workers' compensation claims against the company. After consulting with counsel, Harrell and SYSCO settled those claims in a confidential "global" settlement covering all pending and potential claims involving Harrell and SYSCO. The parties executed a Settlement Agreement and General Release (the Settlement Agreement) dated July 2, 2001, and submitted it to the Workers' Compensation Commission for approval. The terms of that agreement became effective upon the Commission's August 31, 2001 approval of it as an "Agreement of Final Compromise and Settlement."

Under the Settlement Agreement, Harrell resigned his employment and promised never to seek re-employment with SYSCO. In addition, he covenanted that he would not "disparage" SYSCO and that he would "neither voluntarily aid nor voluntarily assist in any way third party claims made or pursued against the Company." SYSCO, in turn, agreed not to challenge Harrell's unemployment compensation appeal and to pay Harrell a total of $185,000.[3]

At issue in this appeal is the parties' agreement regarding damages. With independent counsel advising him, Harrell agreed to the following stipulated damages provision in Paragraph 7 of the Settlement Agreement:

> Mr. Harrell agrees not to disparage the Company and the Company agrees not to disparage Mr. Harrell. . . . It is expressly understood that this paragraph is a *substantial and material provision* of the Agreement and *a breach of this paragraph will support a cause of action* for breach of contract and will entitle the aggrieved parties *to recover damages flowing from such breach specifically, including, but not limited to, the recovery of any payments made pursuant to paragraph numbers 1 and 2 above as well as payments made pursuant to the Agreement of Final Compromise and Settlement pending before the Maryland Workers' Compensation Commission.* It is expressly agreed that *the non-exclusive damages set forth in this paragraph in the event of a breach are not a penalty but are*

---

3. Of that payment, $149,999 was allocated to the workers' compensation claims and the remaining $35,001 was allocated to Harrell's federal labor and discrimination claims.

fair and reasonable in light of the difficulty of proving prejudice to the Company in the event of such a breach. . . .

(Emphasis added.)

Shortly after executing the Settlement Agreement and accepting full payment under it, Harrell breached his promises not to disparage SYSCO and not to assist third-party claimants. In a letter dated December 11, 2001, Harrell wrote to Mike Cutchember, a SYSCO shop steward, on behalf of John Womack, a SYSCO employee with whom Harrell worked. In its entirety, the letter states:

> John Womack called me on 12/14/01, about a problem with [J.B.] a white female supervisor at Sysco. He had said to me weeks before I left Sysco: she tried to get him fired, by blaming him for an accident, that happened two months earlier by someone else. We've talked off and on and he often said, that she has been harassing him at work. John Womack is one of the drivers I daily talked with for years while working at Sysco. I would make several drivers know what was going on in my affairs for my protection, and witness. I had also told him about [J.B.] hugging me and I didn't know if it was a plan they had against me.
>
> [J.B.] hugged me twice while in the warehouse at the docks; after she and [A.A.] came to a stop trying to get something on me. I told [P.M.] a shopsteward about [J.B.] hugging me; he said, that is sexual harassment. And I should file a complaint on her about that, but I didn't. This was a time when Sysco was doing everything they could to frame me for anything so they could fire me; but [there] was no legal reason, but the charges I filed against them concerning racial discrimination.
>
> A District Sales Manager rode with me on a route one day, and he was harassing the customers about me, and asking them "do I do my work". He also watched everything I did, how fast I drove, and came into the back room when I was talking to a customer and wrote notes as we talked. One salesperson tried to get a customer to write a bad letter against me to get me fired, but they refused. Three of the employees at that stop told me about this, this is the same place where [J.B.] and [A.A.] came harassing me and the customer for over an hour. If I can be of any more help let me know.

The next day, on December 12, 2002, Womack initiated race discrimination charges against SYSCO at the Maryland Commission on Human Relations. Like Harrell, Womack complained that he was the victim of racial discrimination by J.B., a white female safety supervisor.

[This letter came to SYSCO's attention as part of Womack's suit. SYSCO then filed suit against Harrell for breach of contract and ultimately moved for summary judgment. The trial court found Harrell in breach of the nondisparagement clause and of another prohibiting him for "aiding and assisting third-party claims" against SYSCO. He was prospectively ordered to "perform each and every obligation" imposed upon him by the Settlement Agreement, but the court held the liquidated damages clause applied only to disparagement, and held it unenforceable because it "smacks directly of a penalty." The court found it "hard to see how a simple disparagement . . . could in any reasonable way be equated to a damage amount of $185,000." The case proceeded to trial, after which the court entered judgment for SYSCO, granting nominal damages only.]

I. Stipulated Damages

SYSCO challenges the trial court's decision not to enforce the parties' agreement that SYSCO could recover the $ 185,000 it paid to Harrell if Harrell breached his non-disparagement covenant. We find merit in SYSCO's challenge, even though for the reasons set forth below, we do not view the clause in question as a liquidated damages agreement.

A. Liquidated Damages[4]

The term "liquidated damages" means a "specific sum of money . . . expressly stipulated by the parties to a . . . contract as the amount of damages to be recovered by either party for a breach of the agreement by the other." *Traylor v. Grafton*, 332 A.2d 651 (Md. 1975). As a general rule, "a liquidated damage clause is within the substantive law of contracts, and — if not a 'penalty' — is an enforceable provision as a sum agreed upon by the parties to be paid in the event of a breach, enforceable as any other provision or valid promise in the contract."

. . . The burden of proving that a particular damage stipulation is not enforceable is "on the party seeking to invalidate" it. Maryland courts generally consider the following three factors as the defining characteristics of an enforceable liquidated damages clause:

(1) clear and unambiguous language providing for "a certain sum";
(2) stipulated damages that represent reasonable compensation for the damages anticipated from the breach, measured prospectively at the time of the contract rather than in hindsight at the time of the breach; and
(3) a "mandatory binding agreement[ ] before the fact which may not be altered to correspond to actual damages determined after the fact."

See Holloway v. Faw, Casson & Co., 572 A.2d 510 (Md. 1990). . . .

By including an agreed damages provision in the contract, contracting parties reduce the cost of contract breakdown by eliminating the expense of calculating damages and by reducing the likelihood of litigation. Either or both parties to a contract, therefore, commonly enjoy the right to terminate at some cost. . . .

The trial court, Harrell, and SYSCO premised their debate over the enforcement of Paragraph 7 on the conclusion that this is a liquidated damages provision. As a threshold matter, we point out that this characterization is not dictated by the parties' use of the label "liquidated damages." Although courts certainly consider "the nomenclature used by the parties," we are not bound by it when other language and circumstances support a different conclusion. For example, the parties' description of their damage agreement as liquidated damages "is not determinative in passing upon whether or not the payment of the designated sum is in fact a penalty." Instead, "the decisive element is the intention of the parties," which "is to be gleaned from

---

4. The Law of Liquidated Damages is one of the most ancient concepts in the law. For example, one of the relics of Hammurabi's reign (1795-1750 BC) is the code, which provides: "If a man has knocked out the eye of a patrician, his eye shall be knocked out." Jewish law provided some interesting remedies with societal as well as private law consequences. *Exodus* 22:1 provides: "If a man shall steal an ox, or a sheep, and kill it, or sell it; he shall restore five oxen for an ox, and four sheep for a sheep."

After quite literally centuries of veneration of these concepts, like the camel's nose under the tent, once the concept of "penalty" crept into this area, the law of liquidated damages became *sui generis* within the law of contracts by overtly insulting the freedom of parties to structure their own agreement which is universally acknowledged to be at the heart of the law of contracts. Why should such clauses be treated differently than other contract provisions that may be equally unfair or one-sided?

the subject matter, the language of the contract and the circumstances surrounding its execution[,]" taken as a whole. We follow the same approach in determining whether a stipulated damages remedy is a liquidated damages clause.

Although the trial court focused on the second feature of a valid liquidated damage agreement, we shall set aside, for the moment, the question of whether the amount of stipulated damages in Paragraph 7 is reasonable. This is because we conclude that the agreement lacks both the first and third characteristics of a liquidated damages clause, in that it does not clearly identify a "certain sum" and does not create a "binding agreement before the fact that may not be altered to correspond to actual damages." By agreeing that the non-breaching party is "entitled . . . to recover *damages flowing from* such breach" (emphasis added), Harrell and SYSCO selected the same type of *post hoc* yardstick that traditionally has been used to measure actual or "unliquidated" damages. Instead of agreeing to either a pre-determined amount of damages, or to a formula for damage, in the event of a breach, the parties more broadly agreed that the recoverable damages "flowing from such breach" would include the settlement payments. Significantly, they also agreed that SYSCO's damages would . . . be "not limited to" that amount if the company also could show other actual damages from Harrell's breach. The parties' understanding that this agreement was not a mandatory and binding stipulation fixing the amount of damages at the $185,000 paid to Harrell is underscored by their explicit agreement that the stipulated "damages set forth in this paragraph in the event of a breach" are "*non-exclusive.*" (Emphasis added.) Because Paragraph 7 does not contain a pre-determined "ceiling" on the amount of "damages flowing from" Harrell's breach of the *non-disparagement* covenant, we conclude that it is an unliquidated damage stipulation rather than a liquidated damages clause. . . .

B. *Enforcement of Paragraph 7 Damages*

It is debatable whether a stipulated damages clause such as the one before us is subject to the "reasonableness" or "penalty" standard that applies to a liquidated damages clause, or, instead, whether it is measured against a more deferent standard, such as unconscionability, that applies to other contractual terms. That question need not be answered to resolve this appeal, however. Assuming *arguendo* that this provision may not be enforced unless it is reasonable, we nevertheless conclude that it satisfies that test.

Determining whether a stipulated remedy is unreasonable "can be hard for the same reason the parties [find] it hard to calculate actual damages in the first place: what's the benchmark against which the stipulated damages will be compared to determine whether they are" reasonable? *Scavenger Sale Investors v. Bryant*, 288 F.3d 309, 311 (7th Cir. 2002). Moreover, as Judge Easterbrook observed in upholding the damages clause of a settlement agreement, "everything depends on which end of the telescope one looks through." *Id*.

Here, the language and circumstances surrounding the Settlement Agreement conclusively establish that both Harrell and SYSCO considered this stipulated damage remedy to be reasonable. They reasonably conceded that SYSCO would suffer harm to its reputation and/or additional labor and litigation expenses if Harrell continued to disparage the company for allegedly creating a hostile work environment in which long-term African-American union employees such as his co-worker Womack and himself were harassed, unfairly disciplined, not compensated for injuries, and retaliated against. In addition, Harrell reasonably acknowledged the difficulty SYSCO would have in proving a specific dollar figure for the "prejudice" "flowing from" his breach of the *non-disparagement* covenant. Thus, the record shows that Harrell understood that this settlement rested squarely on his assurances to SYSCO that this proof problem would not leave SYSCO out-of-pocket $185,000 with only a toothless remedy in the event he continued to disparage the company.

What SYSCO bought through the negotiated settlement, then, was immediate and long-term "peace" with Harrell, with the attendant right to expect that it would no longer have to expend money, effort, or goodwill in responding to his disparaging allegations. Indeed, the language in Paragraph 7 and the circumstances surrounding the execution of the Settlement Agreement leave no doubt that SYSCO and Harrell struck a bargain that was designed to prevent precisely what happened here — that SYSCO would pay Harrell $185,000 to drop all his allegations, claims, and agitations against the company, only to have Harrell later resume them. Without Harrell's assurance that he would not do so, SYSCO would not have agreed to pay Harrell $185,000 to settle his claims. Thus, Harrell's agreement that it is "fair and reasonable" for the "damages flowing from such breach" to include that settlement money was a negotiated cornerstone of this Settlement Agreement.

In this respect, Paragraph 7 fairly may be viewed as both a disincentive to Harrell *and* an assurance of performance to SYSCO. To the extent that it might arguably be characterized as exacting a "penalty for breach," we see nothing unreasonable about such a clearly understood and expressed *quid pro quo*. To the contrary, there are important reasons to enforce this remedy. . . .

In refusing to enforce Harrell's agreement regarding damages, the trial court effectively immunized Harrell from the consequences of deliberately breaching his obligations under the Settlement Agreement. We agree with SYSCO that, as a matter of policy and practice, if an employee is permitted to disregard the covenants upon which he settled, and then avoid the damage remedy that he agreed to, then "no employer should consider a settlement in these types of cases because it will likely be left without adequate redress in the event of a breach." . . .

As alternative grounds for this appeal, SYSCO complains that the trial court erred in refusing to let the jury decide the amount of its actual damages. . . . At trial and before this Court, however, SYSCO conceded that it did not offer any evidence that its pecuniary loss exceeded the $185,000 it paid in "peace money." To the contrary, counsel for SYSCO acknowledged the company's inability to prove such damages, observing that "this type of harm, which is reputational in nature, is hard, if not impossible, to quantify in dollar terms." Given this record, SYSCO is not entitled to a new jury trial on actual damages. . . .

NOTES

1. *Settlement versus Initial Contract.* SYSCO involves a nondisparagement clause and a stipulated damages clause in a settlement agreement. But both clauses, particularly stipulated damages clauses, can be used in basic employment contracts. As we saw in Chapter 3, contracts for fixed-term or other secure employment arrangements, particularly with high-level employees, are often structured to allow parties to "breach" upon payment, either by providing severance to an employee terminated without cause or requiring forfeiture of deferred compensation to the employee who voluntarily terminates prematurely. Nondisparagement contracts entered into upon hire have generally not been as common, but in an era of Internet-enhanced communications and proliferating blogs, there may be reason for employers to consider adopting them more frequently. As you consider the questions below, ask whether and when you might use either kind of clause in drafting the initial employment contract or in settling a matter after an employment dispute has arisen, or in both contexts.

2. *Nondisparagement versus Defamation.* One way of thinking about nondisparagement clauses is as a form of private ordering responding to the limits of tort law. Where an employee makes statements adverse to an employer's interests, an employer could pursue a defamation claim irrespective of whether the parties agreed to a nondisparagement clause. But, as we saw in the discussion of employee defamation claims in Chapter 5, the key to liability in this tort is the falsehood of the statement. Nondisparagement by virtue of a contract provision prevents the employee from saying or writing damaging things about the employer, even if they are true. Further, a valid nondisparagement clause will also avoid complicated questions such as whether a statement is privileged or represents an opinion rather than a fact that would likely arise if the same statement were to be challenged in tort. *See Eichelkraut v. Camp*, 513 S.E.2d 267 (Ga. Ct. App. 1999) (defamation law not relevant to contract claim for disparagement).

3. *Nondisparagement of Employees.* Employers are not the only ones who seek nondisparagement protection, and it is common for settlement agreements to have mutual covenants providing that neither side will disparage the other. This provides employees with the same advantages as employers in avoiding the proof hurdles associated with a defamation claim. A similar way of protecting the interests of the employee is for parties to agree to the content of any reference the employer will supply if contacted by prospective employers. They may decide that an employer can supply only a "neutral" reference — dates of employment, titles held, and the like — or they may draft an actual reference letter and include it as part of the settlement agreement. *See, e.g., Giannecchini v. Hospital of St. Raphael*, 780 A.2d 1006, 1008 (Conn. Super. Ct. 2002). While obviously useful for employees, this practice can also be beneficial to the employer. As you saw in Chapter 5 references are a common source of defamation claims by employees. By obtaining the employee's approval of the reference in conjunction with a settlement of all claims, the employer can avoid the risk that future tort claims will arise.

4. *The Public's Right to Know?* Since nondisparagement clauses prevent individuals from speaking the truth, there is an obvious tension between such clauses and the public's general interest in learning more about individuals and entities with whom they might deal. Such agreements have been criticized as private gag orders through with parties can hide criminal or other misconduct from the public eye. At the same time, they can result in backlash where such behavior ultimately comes to light. The recent Catholic Church priest pedophilia scandals demonstrate that concealing serious wrongdoing can have devastating public relations effects as well as provide more ammunition to those injured by the employee wrongdoers.

Nondisparagement law is still in its infancy, but as of yet, courts have not been inclined to strike down nondisparagement clauses on public policy grounds, even in situations where such an argument was especially plausible. For example, *Patlovich v. Rudd*, 949 F. Supp. 585 (N. D. Ill. 1996), rejected such an argument in enforcing a nondisparagement clause against a former employee physician who alleged that another doctor in the employer's practice had made a medical error and tried to conceal it from the patient. The court recognized a policy in favor of open communication between doctor and patients, but it held that it did not reach the former employee's alleged disclosure of the error and cover-up via hundreds of anonymous letters. Perhaps more pointedly, the court in *Giannecchini v. Hospital of St. Raphael*, 780 A.2d 1006 (Conn. Super. Ct. 2002), held a hospital in breach of the terms of a settlement agreement that promised a neutral reference to a former nurse who had been discharged for making serious medication errors. It did so despite recognizing that the settlement agreement, while benefiting both contracting parties, was "affirmatively disadvantageous" to future patients. *Id.* at 1010; *see also Cooper Tire & Rubber Co. v. Farese, Farese & Farese Prof. Ass'n*, 423 F.3d 446, 457 (5th Cir. 2005) (finding nondisclosure agreement not violative of public policy, despite fact that it could be used to hide illegal activity, where employer sought to enforce agreement against former employee who supplied affidavit and testimony concerning employer's alleged spoliation of evidence); *Katz v. S. Burlington Sch. Dist.*, 970 A.2d 1226, 1229 (Vt. 2009) ("Plaintiff's claim here is premised upon a vague allegation that the nondisparagement clause may prevent Durckel from 'blow[ing] the whistle on the district's corruption.' This is plainly insufficient to void the clause on public policy grounds."); *cf. Henley v. Cuyahoga County Bd. of Mental Retardation & Developmental Disabilities*, 141 F. App'x 437 (6th Cir. 2005) (rejecting First Amendment challenge to nondisparagement clause in agreement with public agency).

   5.   *Limiting Nondisparagement Clauses to Comply with Public Policy.* Most nondisparagement clauses are framed in terms of prohibiting employees from "voluntarily" disparaging the employer. The notion here is that employees are free to speak when they are subpoenaed or otherwise under legal compulsion. Further, employees may have a nonwaivable right to report what they believe to be law violations to the authorities. Some nondisparagement clauses make this distinction clear, perhaps to avoid criticism that they are overbroad and therefore invalid. In some cases, there is a more concrete public policy than a generalized public right to know. We saw in Chapter 9 that the antidiscrimination laws protect employees from retaliation for, inter alia, participating in proceedings raising discrimination claims, and the Supreme Court has made clear recently that retaliation against employees but outside the employment context is also barred. *See Burlington Northern & Santa Fe Ry. v. White*, reproduced at page 654. Might a nondisparagement clause violate this provision by barring an employee from reporting a violation to the EEOC? *See EEOC v. Severn Trent Servs.*, 358 F.3d 438 (7th Cir. 2004) (finding "inadequately reasoned" a district court opinion enjoining the employer from enforcing a nondisparagement clause to prevent a witness from participating in an EEOC investigation). Should an employer's suit for breach of a nondisparagement clause be barred by the antiretaliation provisions (or more generally, the public policy tort) where the employee voluntarily discloses discrimination or other violations of public policy to an enforcement agency?

   6.   *Enforcing Unenforceable Clauses.* The pairing of a stipulated damages clause with a nondisparagement clause in the *SYSCO* settlement agreement likely reflects some careful planning on the employer's part. While many firms want a nondisparagement commitment and such clauses are increasingly standard in settling employment (and other disputes), they are very difficult to enforce by way of damages. This is because harm is often hard to prove and even harder to quantify. In *SYSCO* itself, the agreement allowed the employer to obtain damages in addition to the amount it paid Harrell, but the employer essentially conceded its inability to prove any pecuniary loss suffered as a result of disparagement. Could SYSCO have claimed the costs of defending Womack's suit as damages? Maybe not, because Womack might have gone forward without Harrell's supporting letter, or because Harrell could have been subpoenaed by Womack in any event.

In this regard, nondisparagement clauses are similar to noncompetition clauses, which also pose proof of loss problems. It can be difficult for an employer to show, for instance, that a loss of business or profits resulted from the competitive behavior of a particular employee. Also, in both contexts, the cat is typically out of the bag once the disparagement or competition takes place. For this reason, both clauses are typically enforced by injunctions, often sought in advance of a breach. Once a breach occurs, however, a stipulated damages clause might be the only way for an employer to obtain any monetary relief in such cases.

On the other hand, stipulated damages clauses create their own enforceability problems — the employee is frequently judgment proof. While the employer prevails in *SYSCO*, it is by no means clear that it will be able to enforce any judgment it gets against Harrell. But if enforcement is even a possibility, it may influence employee conduct. This may be true even if the clause is invalid as a penalty. Some employers think the *in terrorem* effect of a possible large judgment hanging over the head of the employee is the best insurance of compliance, even if the validity of the clause is dubious. Is it appropriate for a lawyer to draft a clause she knows to be unenforceable?

7. *Liquidated Damages versus Penalties.* This is the second time you have encountered a case in which an employee defends against an employer's claim on grounds that the contract provision in question was an unenforceable liquidated damages clause. In *American Consulting Environmental Safety Services, Inc. v. Schuck*, reproduced at page 496 in Chapter 8, the court held that the defendant-employee was not required to reimburse her employer for training costs, concluding that the repayment amount stipulated in the parties' contract was disproportionate to the employer's actual loss. The rule limiting the enforceability of stipulated damages clause to those that are reasonable has been subject to criticism. Footnote 4 of *SYSCO* argues that freedom of contract is antithetical with court-imposed limitations on stipulated damages and seems to suggest that freedom of contract should prevail. The footnote is inartful, however, in its reference to the Code of Hammurabi, which is comparable to a statute that prescribes penalties for particular forms of misconduct. A closer analogy is *The Merchant of Venice*, where the parties agreed that damages for failure to repay a loan will be, literally, a pound of flesh. Is Judge Thieme really arguing that parties should be able to set whatever they wish (perhaps short of dismemberment) as stipulated damages? Perhaps it depends on who the parties are and the nature of the contract. Note that stipulated damages clauses are especially common in heavily lawyered commercial agreements between sophisticated parties. There is a lively academic literature on the merits of judicial policing of such clauses, focusing in particular on the economic case for and against intervention. *See, e.g., Lake River Corp. v. Carborundum Co.*, 769 F.2d 1284, 1288-89 (7th Cir. 1985); Alan Schwartz, *The Myth That Promisees Prefer Supracompensatory Remedies: An Analysis of Contracting for Damage Measures*, 100 Yale L. J. 369 (1990).

8. *Judge Thieme's Fancy Footwork.* Whatever the commentators contend, the law has historically viewed liquidated damages clauses, unlike most other contractual

terms, as subject to judicial policing. The RESTATEMENT (SECOND) OF CONTRACTS sets forth the conventional view in § 356(1):

> Damages for breach by either party may be liquidated in the agreement but only at an amount that is reasonable in the light of the anticipated or actual loss caused by the breach and the difficulties of proof of loss. A term fixing unreasonably large liquidated damages is unenforceable on grounds of public policy as a penalty.

Is the law in Maryland significantly different? Are you persuaded by the court's analysis that the clause in question is *not* a liquidated damages clause? The court seems to view it as a minimum damages clause, but isn't that a variety of liquidated damages? Since Judge Thieme goes on to conclude that the clause is not a penalty, the issue is not important in this case — but note that he has cleverly set up the possibility that such clauses in the future are not reviewable for "reasonableness" but only for unconscionability, a much more difficult basis for challenge.

Judge Thieme's discussion of reasonableness is itself a paragon of confusion. He focuses heavily on what Harrell understood and agreed to, but why should consent matter if the whole point of the reasonableness doctrine is that parties are not permitted to agree to penalties? He speaks of SYSCO losing the benefit of its bargain, but the company might have had used more reasonable means of protecting itself, for instance by drafting the agreement to permit it to rescind upon a breach the nondisparagement clause. Of course, true rescission would mean that, while the employer would recover the compensation paid, the employee would similarly regain the rights to assert the claims the settlement agreement was designed to extinguish. Perhaps that is precisely why the clause ought to be deemed unreasonable — it allows the employer to have its cake and eat it too. Finally, Judge Thieme appears concerned that if the clause is not enforced, SYSCO will receive no damages from Harrell's breach. But that is simply a consequence of the fact that SYSCO cannot prove any loss; contract law does not permit damages unless actual harm is suffered.

9. *Private Ordering in Response to Judicial Limits on Private Ordering.* Notice that the stipulated damages clause in *SYSCO* not only provides for a minimum recovery but affirmatively asserts that the amount is "fair and reasonable" and not a "penalty." What is going on here? Can parties really "agree" *ex ante* on how a principle of public law will apply to their contract? In other words, can they stipulate as to a conclusion of law? Whether or not they can, they often try. In the noncompete context, for instance, it is increasingly common for agreements to contain language attesting to the reasonableness of the scope of the restraint or the right of the court to reduce the agreement if overbroad. Perhaps to his credit, Judge Thieme does not rely on the "fair and reasonableness" language in assessing whether the stipulated amount runs afoul of the liquidated damages rule. Might it have been appropriate, however, to rely on it as evidence that the clause was in fact a liquidated damages clause? After all, it is quite certainly an invocation of the legal standard applicable to those types of clauses.

10. *Representing Harrell.* Nondisparagement clauses are so routine that attorneys sometimes treat them as simply more boilerplate. *SYSCO* makes clear that attorneys representing employees must at least drive home to their clients the seriousness of the clause and the resultant consequences of breach, particularly when the agreement includes a damages stipulation. In hindsight, maybe Harrell should have been advised not to sign the settlement in the first place. Or perhaps his lawyer should have made more of an effort to strike or limit the nondisparagement clause. If you were that lawyer, how would you have proceeded? Would you have tried to renegotiate, or would you have been concerned that doing so would jeopardize the deal? In other words, do you think the employer, if otherwise satisfied with the terms of settlement, would have been willing to go forward without the nondisparagement clause?

11. *Alternative Methods of Enforcing Settlement.* If the employer is worried about the possibility of breach and the dubious validity of a liquidated damage clause (or perhaps the uncollectability of any resultant judgment), are there any other planning techniques available? Another possibility for an employer worried about disparagement is to structure the payout not as a lump sum but as a stream of payments whose continuance depends on the employee not breaching the nondisparagement clause (or other clause in the contract).

PROBLEM

13-8. You are representing management in negotiating a settlement with the attorney for a former employee, an individual who is well liked by current employees and still socializes with them. He was employed in the Human Resources department for many years before his termination and had access to all relevant policies and their application by the corporation over that period of time. His lawyer indicated early in the negotiations that "there was a lot of dirty laundry" that would be relevant to the employee's age discrimination and state whistleblower claims. You are comfortable with all the terms of the proposed settlement, but are very concerned about the ex-employee stirring up trouble and/or leaking sensitive information. Try drafting language to include in the final agreement that will address these concerns. Do you think your draft will be acceptable to the employee's attorney?

D. EMPLOYMENT PRACTICES LIABILITY INSURANCE

Individuals and businesses often transfer risk for financial losses they may incur by paying premiums to insurance carriers. In the employment context, employers have been required for about a century to carry workers' compensation insurance, but until relatively recently there was little market (and therefore little availability) for insurance for other employment-related liabilities. This was largely because the law posed few risks for employers, other than contractual claims by very highly placed employees, which were not the kind of loss normally contemplated by insurance in any event.

As statutory and decisional employment law began providing more meaningful remedies, some employers sought to recover both the costs of defending suits by workers and liabilities incurred when such suits were successful by making claims under traditional business coverage, General Liability ("GL") policies, or Director and Officer ("D&O") policies. These efforts were often a stretch. For example, the typical GL policy obligates the insurer to pay damages arising from property damage or personal injury caused by a covered occurrence. *See* Francis J. Mootz III, *Insurance Coverage of Employment Discrimination Claims*, 52 U. MIAMI L. REV. 1, 10-11 (1997). In most cases, the policy would seem not to cover an employee's suit, and GL polices often reinforced this with an explicit "employee exclusion" typically providing that the policy does not cover "bodily injury" to any "employee of the insured arising out of and in the course of employment by the insured." *See Am. Motorists Ins. Co. v. L-C-A Sales Co.*, 713 A.2d 1007 (N.J. 1998) (policy exclusion precluded coverage for employee's age discrimination claim). *But cf. Griffin v. Cameron Coll.*, No. 96-0951 1997 U.S. Dist. LEXIS 14218, *5 (E.D. La. 1997) (mental anguish suffered by student as a result of alleged ADA violations by university constituted "bodily injury" under general liability policy). While GL policies have been found to reach a few employment-related claims, such as defamation, *see Meadowbrook v. Tower Insurance Co.*, 559 N.W.2d 411, 413 n.1 (Minn. 1997), they provided, at best, very spotty coverage for employment-related risks.

As the threat of substantial liability increased, insurance carriers had two responses. The first was to strengthen the exclusions to lessen the risk of being held liable under traditional policies; and the second was to develop a new product — Employment Practices Liability Insurance ("EPLI") policies, which are specifically geared to employment-related practices. These policies typically cover liability arising out of the insured's employment-related offenses against its employees, including the costs of defending claims. They may also cover liability by agents of the employer (personal liability is a risk for some aspects of employment law but not for others). A typical Web site offering such policies states that the following risks are covered:

- Sexual Harassment
- Discrimination
- Statute Violation
- Negligent Hiring
- Negligent Supervision
- Negligent Promotion
- Negligent Retention
- Disabilities
- Breach of Contract
- Wrongful Termination
- Loss of Consortium
- Emotional Distress
- Invasion of Privacy
- Drug Testing
- Mental Anguish
- Libel
- Slander
- Wage and Hour Disputes

See http://www.epli.com/ (last visited August 9, 2010). This range of coverage, however, may be somewhat deceptive. Insurance companies are in the business of managing their own risks, and some policies are subject to significant exclusions. For example, EPLI policies usually exclude punitive damages from coverage. Further, policies may have significant deductibles to reduce the "moral hazard" that insurance creates.

There is an ongoing debate as to whether coverage of risks such as punitive damages and, indeed, insurance for any intentional employer conduct is against public policy. The argument to this effect is that shifting the loss to insurers blunts the employer incentives to comply with the law. *See generally* Richard A. Bales & Julie McGhghy, *Insuring Title VII Violations*, 27 S. ILL. U. L. J. 71 (2002). The contrary argument is that insurance actually increases compliance. Insurance companies seek to limit their risk not only through exclusions from coverage, but also by taking steps to require that the firms they cover are well positioned from a liability perspective. Thus, they deny coverage, or at least charge higher premiums, to higher risks, that is, firms that do not have policies and procedures in place to reduce potential liability. As Professor Mootz puts it, "the regular and rational adjustment of premiums in response to proactive measures designed jointly by the insurer and the employer has the potential to have a profound impact in the workplace." Mootz, *supra*, at 78.

There is an evolving literature on how insurers attempt to reduce risk for their insureds. *See, e.g.*, Brian T. McMillan, *Managing the Risk of Employment-Related Practices Liabilities by Influencing the Behavior of Employee Claimants*, 21 W. NEW ENG. L. REV. 427 (1999); Jack S. McCalmon, *Effective Loss Control Techniques for Employment Practices Liabilities: An Assessment of How EPLI Carriers Should Seek to Transform the American Workplace*, 21 W. NEW ENG. L. REV. 447 (1999). Needless to say, a prime focus of such efforts is creation of "bullet-proof" prevent-and-correct policies in order to trigger the affirmative defense for sexual harassment claims. But procedures for dealing with employee complaints can also address other potential risks, and either avoid them or reduce the employer's exposure by creating the opportunity to resolve difficulties early. Even more basic management tools may be part of an insurer's checklist for a good risk. For example, such things as whether the potential insured has an employee handbook, requires employees to execute an acknowledgement of at-will status, or uses a formal employee evaluation policy may all be part of the insurer's decision to sell coverage and at what price. Similarly, the increasing requirement of arbitration of employment disputes may stem in part from demands by insurers in an effort to reduce both potential adverse judgments and the cost of defending claims.

PROBLEM

13-9. You are outside counsel for new law firm, High Tech, which expects to open its doors within the next week. The firm is comprised largely of former attorneys of a much larger firm, Hanover & Windsor. It has three partners, all of whom were partners at Hanover, and five associates, most of whom were Hanover associates. It also has about eight support staff, mostly paralegals and assistants. While the attorneys are all highly specialized in their field of expertise — patent law — they rely very heavily on you for advice on the business-oriented aspects of setting up a new business. And, because the firm's client base is still somewhat uncertain, it is determined to keep its expenses as low as possible for the first year.

You just received a phone call from Hi High, managing partner. He was meeting with an insurance agent about liability and malpractice insurance, and the agent pitched something called "EPLI," insurance against employment-related suits. The premium would be about $10,000 a year. High feels confident about his ability to assess risks for what he calls "normal" insurance, but is "out of my league" with this stuff.

He wants to know whether this is a good idea and what questions he should ask the agent before going forward. Advise him.

E. BANKRUPTCY AS RISK MANAGEMENT

While bankruptcy is a specialized field of study that can be, at most, mentioned here, it is a last-gasp risk management technique that some firms, particularly those in the airline industry, have successfully used to deal with financial problems caused in large part by collective bargaining agreements that impose higher costs on them than on their competitors. *See* Micheline Maynard, *Airlines' Woes May Be Worse in Coming Year*, N.Y. TIMES, Dec. 27, 2004, at A1. A recent example outside the airline setting is the automobile bankruptcies of GM and Chrysler. *See generally* Ralph Brubaker & Charles Jordan Tabb, *Bankruptcy Reorganizations and the Troubling Legacy of Chrysler and GM*, 2010 U. ILL. L. REV. 1375.

Outside the unionized setting, bankruptcy is less likely to be a tactic used by employers but it nevertheless poses a threat to individual employment contracts. This reality means that the attorney representing employees negotiating such arrangements needs to worry not only about paper rights but also about the solvency of the company. This is an increasing concern as the length of the contract stretches into the future. Similarly, bankruptcy can also jeopardize pending employment claims. *See generally* Joanne Gelfand, *The Treatment of Employment Discrimination Claims in Bankruptcy: Priority Status, Stay Relief, Dischargeability, and Exemptions*, 56 MIAMI L. Q. 601 (2002). Finally, the financial health of the company can influence an employee's preference for lump-sum payments over more structured arrangements.

Table of Cases

Principal cases are in *bold italics*.

Table of Secondary Authorities

Index